ASIA

IN THE MAKING OF EUROPE

IN THE MAKING OF EUROPE

DONALD F. LACH and EDWIN J. VAN KLEY

VOLUME

III

A
Century of
Advance

BOOK ONE: TRADE, MISSIONS, LITERATURE

THE UNIVERSITY OF CHICAGO PRESS

CHICAGO AND LONDON

THE UNIVERSITY OF CHICAGO PRESS, CHICAGO 60637
The University of Chicago Press, Ltd., London

Library of Congress Cataloging-in-Publication Data
(Revised for volume 3)

Lach, Donald F. (Donald Frederick), 1917–
  Asia in the making of Europe.

  Vol. 3 –by Donald F. Lach and Edwin J. Van Kley.
  Includes bibliographies and indexes.
    Contents: v. 1. The century of discovery. 2.v.—
  v. 2. A century of wonder. Book 1. The visual arts.
  Book 2. The literary arts. Book 3. The scholarly dis-
  ciplines. 3. v.—v. 3. A century of advance. Book 1.
  Trade, missions, literature. Book 2. South Asia.
  Book 3. Southeast Asia. Book 4. East Asia. 4 v.
    1. Europe—Civilization—Oriental influences.
  2. Asia—History.   3. Asia—Discovery and exploration.
  I. Van Kley, Edwin J.   II. Title.
  CB203.L32   303.48'2405'0903   64-19848

  ISBN 0-226-46765-1 (v. 3. bk. 1)
  ISBN 0-226-46767-8 (v. 3. bk. 2)
  ISBN 0-226-46768-6 (v. 3. bk. 3)
  ISBN 0-226-46769-4 (v. 3. bk. 4)

This publication has been supported by a grant
from the National Endowment for the Humanities,
an independent federal agency.

To
ALMA LACH
and
ELAINE VAN KLEY

Contents

PART I

The Continuing Expansion in the East

Contents

PART II

The Printed Word

Contents

BOOK TWO

PART III

The European Images of Asia

Contents

BOOK THREE

(PART III CONTINUED)

[x]

Contents

Contents

Abbreviations

AHSI	*Archivum Historicum Societatis Iesu*
Annales. E.S.C.	*Annales: Economies, sociétés, civilisations; revue trimestrielle*
Asia	Earlier volumes of this work: D. Lach, *Asia in the Making of Europe,* Vols. I and II (Chicago, 1965–77)
BR	Blair, Emma H., and Robertson, James A. (eds.), *The Philippine Islands, 1493–1898* (55 vols., Cleveland, 1903–9)
BTLV	*Bijdragen tot de taal-, land- en volkenkunde van Nederlandsch-Indië*
BV	[Commelin, Isaac (ed.)], *Begin ende voortgangh van de Vereenighde Nederlantsche Geoctroyeerde Oost-Indische Compagnie . . .* ([Amsterdam], 1646). (First edition published 1645. Facsimile edition published in Amsterdam, 1969. The facsimile edition has volumes numbered I, II, III, and IV, corresponding to vols. Ia, Ib, IIa, and IIb of the 1646 edition.)
CV	[Churchill, Awnsham and John (eds.)], *A Collection of Voyages and Travels, Some Now First Printed from Original Manuscripts . . .* (4 vols.; London, 1704)
"HS"	"Works Issued by the Hakluyt Society"
JRAS	*Journal of the Royal Asiatic Society*

Abbreviations

NR — L'Honoré Naber, Samuel Pierre (ed.), *Reisebeschreibungen von deutschen Beamten und Kriegsleuten im Dienst der Niederländischen West- und Ost-Indischen Kompagnien, 1602–1797* (13 vols.; The Hague, 1930–32)

NZM — *Neue Zeitschrift für Missionswissenschaft*

PP — Purchas, Samuel, *Hakluytus Posthumus, or Purchas His Pilgrimes:* . . . (20 vols.; Glasgow, 1905–7. Originally published 1625.)

SCPFMR — *Sacrae Congregationis de Propaganda Fide Memoria Rerum* (Freiburg, 1971)

Streit — R. Streit, *Bibliotheca Missionum* (30 vols.; Münster and Aachen, 1916–75)

Ternaux-Compans — H. Ternaux-Compans, *Bibliothèque asiatique et africaine* (Amsterdam, 1968; reprint of Paris, 1841–42 ed.)

TR — Thévenot, Melchisédech, *Relations de divers voyages curieux qui n'ont point esté publiées, ou qui ont esté traduites d'Hacluyt, de Purchas & d'autres voyageurs anglois, hollandois, portugais, allemands, espagnols; et de quelques Persans, Arabes, et autres auteurs orientaux* (4 vols.; Paris, 1663–96)

"WLV" — "Werken uitgegeven door de Linschoten Vereeniging"

ZMR — *Zeitschrift für Missionswissenschaft und Religionswissenschaft*

A Note to the Illustrations

Study of the illustrations of Asia published in seventeenth-century Europe shows that the artists and illustrators tried in most cases to depict reality when they had the sources, such as sketches from the men in the field or the portable objects brought to Europe—plants, animals, costumes, paintings, porcelains, and so on. Many of the engravings based on sketches and paintings are convincing in their reality, such as the depiction of the Potala palace in Lhasa (pl. 384), the portrait of the "Old Viceroy" of Kwangtung (pl. 323), and the drawings of Siamese and Chinese boats. A number of Asian objects—Chinese scroll paintings, a Buddhist prayer wheel, and small animals—appeared in European engravings and paintings for the first time. Asians, like the Siamese emissaries to France, were sketched from life in Europe and their portraits engraved.

When sources were lacking, the illustrators and artists filled in the gaps in their knowledge by following literary texts, or by producing imaginary depictions, including maps. The illustrations of Japan, for example, are far more fantastic than those depicting other places, perhaps because Japan so stringently limited intercourse over much of the century. Printing-house engravers frequently "borrowed" illustrations from earlier editions and often "improved" upon them by adding their own touches which had the effect of Europeanizing them.

Illustrations were "translated" along with texts in various ways. If the publisher of a translation had close relations with the original publisher or printer he might borrow the original copperplate engravings or have the original publisher pull prints from the original plates to be bound with the translated pages. Engraved captions could be rubbed out of the plate and redone in the new language, although many printers did not bother to do so. Lacking the cooperation of the original printers, new engravings could still be made from a print. The simplest method was to place the print face down on the varnished and waxed copper plate to be engraved and then to rub the back of the print causing the ink from the print to adhere to the waxed surface of the plate. The resulting image was then used to engrave, or etch with nitric acid, the new plate, and being reversed it would print exactly as the original version printed. If the engraver wanted to avoid damaging the print, however, which he might well need to finish the engraving, he would use a thin sheet of paper dusted with black lead or black chalk to transfer the image from the print to the new copper plate. He might further protect the print by putting oiled paper on top of it while he traced the picture. This procedure worked whether the print was face down or face up against the plate. In fact it was easier to trace the picture if the print were face up, in which case the new plate would be etched in reverse of the original plate. For a seventeenth-century description of the ways in which new plates could be etched from prints see William Faithorne, *The Art of Graveing and Etching* (New York, 1970), pp. 41–44 (first edition, London, 1662). See also Coolie Verner, "Copperplate Printing," in David Woodward (ed.), *Five Centuries of Map Printing* (Chicago, 1975), p. 53. We have included a number of illustrations that were "borrowed" by one printer from another: see, for example, plates 113 and 114; 117, 118, and 121; 174; 312 and 313; 412 and 413; 419–21.

Most of the following illustrations were taken from seventeenth-century books held in the Department of Special Collections in the Regenstein Library at the University of Chicago. Others have been obtained from libraries and archives in Europe and the United States, which have kindly granted us permission to reproduce them. Wherever possible, efforts are made in the captions to analyze the illustrations and to provide relevant collateral information whenever such was available.

Almost all of the four hundred or so illustrations were reproduced from the photographs taken (or retaken) by Alma Lach, an inveterate photographer and cookbook author. We were also aided and abetted by the personnel of the Special Collections department—especially the late Robert Rosenthal, Daniel Meyer, and Kim Coventry—in locating the illustrations and in preparing them for photography. Father Harrie A. Vanderstappen, professor emeritus of Far Eastern art at the University of Chicago and a man endowed with marvelous sight and insight, helped us to analyze the illustrations relating to East Asia. C. M. Naim of the Department of South Asian Languages at the University of Chicago likewise contributed generously of his skills, particularly with reference to the Mughul seals (pls. 117, 118, and 121 here depicted. The China illustrations have benefited from the contributions of Ma Tai-loi and Tai Wen-pai of the East Asian Collection of the Regenstein Library and of Zhijia Shen who generously gave freely of her time and knowledge. The captions for the Japan illustrations have been improved by the gracious efforts of Yoko Kuki of the East Asian Collection of the Regenstein Library. Tetsuo Najita of Chicago's History Department lent a hand in the preparation of the caption for pl. 432. Ann Adams and Francis Dowley of Chicago's Art Department helped us to analyze some of the engravings, especially those prepared by Dutch illustrators.

To all of these generous scholars we express our sincere gratitude for their contributions to the illustration program.

Illustrations

[xix]

BOOK THREE

FOLLOWING PAGE 1380

BOOK FOUR

FOLLOWING PAGE 1730

Illustrations

Illustrations

Maps

Preface

Almost fifteen years have slipped by since the final books were published of Volume II of *Asia in the Making of Europe*. Aware as I then was of the immensity of the task that lay ahead in carrying forward this project, I invited Edwin J. Van Kley, a former student and now professor of history at Calvin College, to become my collaborator on volumes III and IV. This choice I made with great deliberation for I knew that I required a co-author with extensive linguistic skills, broad historic understanding of both Europe and Asia, lucid literary style, good health, and considerable patience. Fortunately, Van Kley accepted my invitation and began immediately and continued steadily to labor at this back-breaking task. The authorities of the University of Chicago Press agreed with their customary affability to this co-authorship as Van Kley and I had arranged it.

We are indebted, as I was in the earlier volumes and books, to a host of institutions, foundations, and individuals. First and foremost we are deeply obligated to the University of Chicago and Calvin College for their patient forbearance, unswerving research support, and allocations of free time. Our colleagues in history regularly took up the slack for us in everyday academic affairs, listened patiently as we tried out our ideas on them, and freely offered us information and advice from their specialities—or just in general! None contributed more to Van Kley than the late M. Howard Rienstra and none more to Lach than T. Bentley Duncan. Our students, it should also be noted, patiently listened in class and out to our research stories and sometimes stimulated us by their questions.

Our research has taken us to many different sites in recent years. Van Kley spent much of 1977 at Mansfield College, Oxford, while consulting the rare books in the Bodleian and other libraries. He also worked for extended periods in the libraries of Holland and other parts of western Europe. I profited from leading a round-the-world tour (1973) sponsored by the Asia Society of New York which visited the Asian footholds once held by the Portuguese from Bahrain in the Persian Gulf, to Goa, to Flores in the Lesser Sundas, and eventually to Macao. We have both visited the Far East in recent years to participate in conferences held at Taipei and Manila. From these meetings we went on to mainland China, Japan, Hong Kong, and other places which held meaning for our work on this project.

At my home base in the Regenstein Library I was supported by grants from the Social Science Division of the University of Chicago and by a one-year fellowship from the Guggenheim Foundation (1983–84). Van Kley received financial aid from the Shell Foundation (1971, 1974), the Newberry Library (1972–73), the American Council of Learned Societies (1975–76), the Calvin Alumni Society (1977), and the Midwest Faculty Seminar of the University of Chicago (1979–80, 1982–83). Two Calvin Research Fellowships (1982–83, 1986–87) and three sabbatical leaves for Van Kley appreciably exceeded in generosity what is usually expected of a "church related college in the Midwest."

Our requests for special materials received careful attention and a sympathetic ear from the late Robert Rosenthal, longtime curator of Special Collections of the Regenstein Library, and from Conrad Bult, assistant director of the Calvin College Library. We have also depended heavily on the general resources of both our institutions and upon their Inter-Library Loan officers, especially upon Lynne Hopkins of Calvin College. We are also heavily in debt for day-to-day consultation on specific questions falling within the provenance of the following librarians: on South Asia, Maureen Patterson, Bill Alspaugh, and James Nye; on East Asia, Ma Tai-loi, Tai Wen-pai, Zhijia Shen, Barbara Chapman Banks, and Yoko Kuki. As is apparent from the illustrations, our debt to the Regenstein's Special Collections and its staff is enormous.

From the funds available to us, we were able to hire a number of research assistants. In Chicago I worked with the help of both graduates and undergraduates. Theodore N. Foss, now at Stanford University, helped to complete Volume II and got us launched on Volume III. In these early stages I was also aided by Katy O'Brien, lecturer at the University of Chicago, and by Tamara Vincelette, now a lawyer practicing in Denver. Daniel Goffman, presently an Ottoman specialist at Ball State University, helped to bring the Muslim dimension into clearer focus for us by the special bibliographic studies he made. Roy Vice and Richard Yntema helped to put together and to improve the first two chapters. Robert Deitel, now a Ph.D. candidate in history at Yale, worked on the book as a Chicago undergraduate. Stuart and Sondra Feldstein were married to each other as undergraduates and the wife succeeded the husband as my assistant. James Cunningham spent several years helping with the completion of this volume, particularly lending his expertise in economics to chapter i and the appendix on spice prices. He also compiled the list of Jesuit letters and put them into chronological order. Meanwhile in Grand Rapids Van Kley employed several undergraduates. He extends special thanks to Michael Abma and to Raymond Kapteyn; Ray almost single-handedly compiled the first draft of the Sources Bibliography. For typing the seemingly endless first drafts and revisions we particularly thank Sondra Ostenson, Cindy Boender, Dianne Vander Pol, and Jane Haney. To all we offer our sincere gratitude for their devotion.

A number of the chapters which follow have been read critically, commented on, and corrected, by specialists. The last section of chapter i, "Empire and Trade," was read before, and commented upon by, participants of the United Nations University Conference held at Cambridge under the sponsorship of Professor Joseph Needham. A summary of chapter ii, "The Christian Mission," was presented in Taipei at a conference on Matteo Ricci and was published in its proceedings.[1] It has also been at the heart of a seminar which I offered for five years at the University of Chicago, mainly to divinity students. The section on Protestant missions has been read critically by Amy Gordon of Denison University and by Richard De Ridder and Robert Recker of the Calvin Theological Seminary.

Certain of the chapters depicting the European images have been examined by Asian specialists. The chapters on Mughul India have benefitted from the comments and corrections of Kali Charan Bahl and C. M. Naim of the University of Chicago. Chapter xi on southwest India was carefully scrutinized by Father Cyriac Pullapilly, a priest of the Malabar Church and professor of history at St. Mary's of Notre Dame; he also added a few pithy comments which have been incorporated into the text and footnotes. Rani Fedson, a Tamil specialist, saved us from making many errors by her careful survey of chapter xiii in which we deal with the Coromandel Coast. Paul Wheatley, the eminent geographer, graciously read and corrected chapter xiv on the lesser states of continental Southeast Asia. Our materials on Siam in chapter xv were examined by Frank Reynolds of the University of Chicago's Divinity School. Anthony Reid of the Australian National University's Research School of Pacific Studies in Canberra read chapters xvii and xviii on Insulindia and made helpful suggestions. Chapter xix on the Philippines and the Marianas was checked by the late Fred Eggan and by Violetta Lopez-Gonzaga of La Salle College, Bacolod City, Philippines. Chapters xx, xxi, and xxii on China and its periphery were corrected and added to by Ho Ping-ti, emeritus professor of the University of Chicago. Chen Min-sun, professor of history at Lakehead University in Ontario, like Professor Ho a Ming-Ch'ing specialist, carefully read and corrected chapters xx and xxi on China. Chapter xxii on China's periphery benefitted greatly from the

---

[1] *International Symposium on Chinese-Western Cultural Interchange in Commemoration of the 400th Anniversary of the Arrival of Matteo Ricci, S.J., in China* (Taipei, 1983), pp. 297–310.

careful corrections and advice of Matthew Kapstein of Columbia University and James Bosson of the Department of Oriental Languages, University of California, Berkeley. Joanne Cho read and corrected the materials on Korea. Harry Harootunian of Chicago and Derek Massarella of the Faculty of Economics at Chuo University, Tokyo, each read and made many worthwhile suggestions for the improvement of chapter xxiii on Japan. The same chapter was also carefully scrutinized and corrected by Michael Huissen, who teaches at Bunkyo University in Tokyo. The maps were prepared with the aid of the geographers at the University of Chicago.

The staff of the University of Chicago Press has coped ably and cheerfully with the intricacies of this massive work. Penelope Kaiserlian, Associate Director, presided over this entire enterprise with understanding, forbearance, restraint, and quiet wisdom. Without the watchful eye and persistent questions of Kathryn Krug, our manuscript editor, we would have enshrined in print many more than we have of outright mistakes and misleading statements. John Spottiswood, Joe Claude, and Joseph Alderfer produced and designed these books with great competency and imagination. The layout of the illustration program was done by Cameron Poulter, the designer of the earlier volumes in this series. As always, many others at the press cheerfully contributed to various aspects of this lengthy undertaking. We can only hope that it has been worth their time and efforts.

An attempt has been made, though somewhat sporadically and haphazardly, to provide a degree of uniformity with respect to the spellings and romanizations of Asian names and terms. To prevent confusion from compounding we have for the most part followed in this volume the spellings used in the preceding volumes of the series. For Chinese we have continued to use the Wade-Giles transliterations and for place-names those spellings which most commonly appear on maps in English. Terms from Thai, except for place-names, have been given whenever possible in the romanizations preferred by the Royal Institute, Bangkok (1954). Vietnamese terms usually appear in the modern alphabet of the Annamese language. For the other Asian languages we have generally used spellings that seemed to us to be intelligible to readers of English. In the case of India with its plethora of languages it seemed most practical to adopt no common norm. We have tried to give Persian or other equivalents for the terms recorded by the Europeans in their descriptions of Mughul India. South Indian terms, when they are not clear in common English, are given Malayalam, Tamil, and Telugu equivalents. The same procedure has been followed in dealing with Maldive, Sinhalese, Indonesian, Chamorro, and Filipino names and terms. The complexities involved in these transliterations are not of our making alone. In our European sources Asian names and terms appear in romanizations propounded by seventeenth-century Iberians, Dutchmen, Germans, Italians, Englishmen, and Frenchmen, who had no precedents to follow and who could not have anticipated the maze they were creating. Modern Western scholars, beginning with Father Rhodes, the "Apostle of Vietnam," have tried without notable success to make things better for the European reader by creating "standard methods" of transliteration. But to this day there exist genuine and profound scholarly differences on how best to provide romanizations for both the calligraphic and the alphabetical languages of Asia. It is therefore out of dire necessity rather than perversity that we preserve the disorder that is our inheritance.

Finally we wish to accept responsibility for what we have elaborated and concluded in this volume. Errors and omissions, as well as imbalance, are endemic to massive works. While regretting these faults, we remain happy that we made the effort. It is our hope that these books, and the volumes that precede them, will provide a solid ground on which to base systematic comparative studies of the early modern period in world history.

Our deepest debt is owed to our wives, Alma Lach and Elaine Van Kley. Their lives were frequently disrupted by the demands of their researching and writing husbands. Still they contributed unstintingly to the project by generously giving time, energy, and encouragement to this volume. Alma Lach, as she has before, freely contributed her photographic talents to provide this volume with a host of illustrations. Without our wives this would be a different volume and we would be different men! As a small expression of our gratitude we therefore dedicate this volume to them.

DONALD F. LACH

Introduction

For a survey of the general objectives of *Asia in the Making of Europe* see the introduction to Volume I. Volume III, the present work, entitled *A Century of Advance,* is a continuation and analogue of Volume I, called *The Century of Discovery.* It deals with the seventeenth century in much the same way that Volume I covers the sixteenth century. The significance of 1600 as a transitional date is discussed in the Introduction to Volume I.

For the present volume the terminal date of 1700 is at best approximate. In both northern Europe and Asia the great nations and empires were then at the apogee of their power and influence. The Dutch and English East India Companies had come to dominate the trade between Asia and Europe at the expense of Portugal. Independent Portugal, like its neighbor Spain, had begun by 1700 to concentrate upon its relations with the Americas rather than with Asia. France, the newest actor on the Asian stage, made a late but spectacular entry which was quickly followed by a series of military and political setbacks. The other European powers, including the Holy Roman Empire, were still forced to watch from afar in 1700 while the Atlantic nations dominated the sea-lanes and the trade between Europe and Asia.

Most notable in the seventeenth century was the advance of European merchants and missionaries into the continental states and archipelagoes of Asia. From coastal footholds won in the previous century, they penetrated the interiors of the Asian states and even the courts of Mughul India, Siam, Arakan, Mataram, China, and Japan. This deeper penetration, while it produced more and better information, did not lead to European political or territorial aggrandizement in the great continental states. Empire-building was generally limited to the archipelagoes (Insulindia and the Philippines), to isolated islands (Formosa, Guam, and perhaps Ceylon), and to separated city-states (Cochin, Malacca, and Makassar). When the French attempted to suborn the kingdom of Siam, they were summarily ejected in 1688 by native action. The Europeans were most successful in working with one another and with cooperative natives in building new, or expanding old, coastal commercial cities: Manila, Nagasaki, Macao, Batavia, Colombo, Madras, Bombay, and Calcutta. From these strategically located entrepôts they became increasingly more effective in controlling inter-Asian trade and in supplying European markets.

Northern Europe dominated the trade except for that which traversed the Pacific. Catholic missionaries, increasingly drawn from all over Europe, continued to enjoy a virtual monopoly of evangelizing in areas not ruled by the Dutch or by the Muslims. The Jesuits, once the predominant mission order, were forced more and more to share the mission fields with the other orders and with secular priests sent out by the *Propaganda fide* in Rome and the Society of Foreign Missions in Paris. Debates over ecclesiastical jurisdictions and mission policies produced bitter controversies within the Catholic Church and between it and the nation-states. The Dutch Reformed pastors confined their missionary work to places dominated by their compatriots, especially in Insulindia and Formosa. Without the support of religious orders, the Dutch pastors in the East concentrated upon ministering to the spiritual needs of those of their faith. Both the Catholic priests and the Protestant pastors added cultural and intellectual dimensions to the European perception of the East.

Beginning around 1600, Russians had begun to penetrate eastern Siberia as part of an unofficial drive toward the Pacific by merchants and adventurers. Shortly after the triumph of the Manchus in China in 1644, some of these pioneering Russians began to push southward toward the Amur River. When clashes between Russians and Chinese resulted, it became evident to both powers that an understanding over a frontier would have to be concluded. With the aid of the Jesuits, the Treaty of Nerchinsk (1689) was worked out and the boundary set at a mountain range just to the north of the Amur. Tsar Peter I thereafter tried unsuccessfully to work out trade arrangements with Peking. So at century's end the Russian Eurasiatic state existed more as a hope than as a reality. Its Asiatic portion remained unimportant to western Russia except as a source of revenue; Peter and his advisers continued to be more interested in Western technology than in the development of eastern Siberia. Nothing was published *in Russian* before the 1700's about the eastern part of the empire or about Russian experiences with Asians. What contemporaries knew about Russia's eastward advance came from western European publications. As a consequence, in this volume as in the preceding ones, we have no Russian publications to include in our construction of the Western images of Asia.

The public of western Europe, on the other hand, learned in detail of the European progress in Asia from the reports of merchants, missionaries, and adventurers, as well as from the products of the East which poured into Europe in a never-ending stream. Most of the seventeenth-century printed reports came off the presses of northern Europe—more from Dutch presses than from all the rest. Spain and Portugal continued to publish notices of victories in the East, though these were becoming rarer by the latter half of the century. Engravers and cartographers in the Low Countries and France continually sought to improve their depictions by consulting the printed reports as they came out. The Jesuit letters and letterbooks, as well as other mission reports, emanated from the presses of Rome and other Catholic publishing centers. Most of the important merchant and missionary reports were reprinted and some were revised before being reissued. Many were translated for wider distribution and some were republished in the great travel collections of De Bry, Purchas, Commelin, and Thévenot. Even the newly established learned societies of France and England got into the act by publishing articles on Asia of scholarly interest as well as reviews of some of the most important reports dealing with the botany, zoology, and medicine of the East.

From these numerous published materials the "curious reader" of the seventeenth century certainly had no problem learning about Asia and its various parts. The images relayed of the great continental states like China and India were much sharper, deeper, and more comprehensive than those of the previous century. The seventeenth-century Europeans had the advantage of using the works of their predecessors and of having better access to the society or culture under review. Through their understanding of many of the native languages, the Europeans, particularly the missionaries, were now better able than previously to penetrate the high cultures of India, China, and Japan. In particular, they learned much more than their predecessors about the content of Hinduism, Buddhism, and Confucianism and of the hold these doctrines had upon their devotees. In the insular regions of Asia, and in smaller states where the Europeans were seen as a mounting threat to the existing order, setbacks as well as victories had to be recorded. All the Europeans except the Dutch were expelled from Japan by 1640; twenty years later the Dutch themselves were forced out of Formosa by the Chinese cohorts of Koxinga. In the Philippines, in Indonesia, and in some parts of India, the Muslims periodically checked the advances of the Christians and threatened their converts. In the religiously tolerant Buddhist states of Arakan and Siam, even the most zealous Christian missionaries were frustrated by what they saw as the religious indifference of the population. In Vietnam, with its mixed cultural and religious traditions, the Catholics were more successful in making conversions than they were anywhere else except for the Philippines and the Marianas.

From the diverse images of the various parts of Asia it became manifestly clear that the Europeans in the field were engaged in a commercial and religious struggle. While progress was recorded for most places, it could readily be seen that the Europeans were not universally successful in imposing their will upon abject Asians. Many of the victories recorded by the Dutch and English were at the expense of the Iberians, as in India, Ceylon, Insulindia, and Japan. The new Asian places being revealed had been penetrated by individual missionaries, merchants, and adventurers, as in Central Asia, Tibet, Korea, Laos, Australia, and a few Pacific islands. As the circle of knowledge was thus widened, previously unknown places were related to those with which most Europeans were already familiar. By 1700 it was only the fringes of continental Asia north of India and China, the interior of Australia (and information on the size and shape of Australia), and the insular reaches of the South Seas such as New Zealand which remained unknown to the Europeans.

In what follows, as in Volume I, an effort is made to check the seventeenth-century sources against the best of recent scholarship. Most troubling to modern scholars is the seventeenth-century authors' practice of borrowing from their predecessors or contemporaries without attribution. We have tried, though not always with success, to indicate in the text or footnotes whenever such unacknowledged appropriations have taken place. An attempt is also made to determine whether the various authors are reporting personal experiences or merely relating hearsay or bazaar gossip. Seventeenth-century travelers were usually far less insulated from local populations than are most travelers today. They traveled more slowly, had much more contact with local people, and generally stayed in one place longer. What they report, therefore, frequently reflects not only their own observations and preconceptions, but also the impressions they received from talking and living with natives. We have sought to indicate the length and depth of the recorded personal experiences of the individual authors and whenever possible to point out their biases. In the process we learned that their biases were sometimes more apparent than real. For example, a Dutch pastor wrote with rare objectivity about Hinduism, an English adventurer described without serious prejudice the everyday life of Kandy in Ceylon, and some sincere Jesuits recorded without malice or rose-colored spectacles the Manchu takeover in China. We also discovered that modern scholars have sometimes used these seventeenth-century sources without sufficiently analyzing the individual texts or their authors. Such omissions are particularly troubling when the seventeenth-century European text is the only source available or when it is contradicted by others of equal veracity, whether native or European. It should be noted that where indigenous sources and learned information existed, some of the Europeans endeavored to use them. For the reconstruction of the past in many places, the Europeans are the only authorities or the only ones to provide specific dates or statistics. Because they usually picked up what was different from Europe, the European sources are also rich in mundane information about most

Asian places and aspects of native life which native writers ignore or take for granted.

No effort is undertaken in this volume to assess the impact of this information on the arts, sciences, ideas, institutions, economy, and practices of the Europeans. This topic of audience response is reserved for Volume IV, the next projected work in this series.

The Continuing Expansion in the East

Introduction

Europe's commercial and religious involvements in Asia underwent momentous changes during the seventeenth century. During its first half, Portugal's Estado da India withered and Lisbon's eastern trade declined. Spain's Pacific empire based on the Philippines was meanwhile extended into the Moluccas in 1606, while the Spaniards abandoned their earlier efforts to penetrate Cambodia. In 1662 they withdrew from the Moluccas and concentrated their attention upon securing their hold on the Philippines, the Marianas, and the galleon trade between Acapulco and Manila. Throughout the century they were challenged by the Dutch, who were building their commercial empire in Java and on other islands in Indonesia. The English, after a few frustrating attempts to establish themselves in the Spiceries, centered their efforts upon trade with the Mughul empire through its western port of Surat. By 1641 the Dutch had captured from the Portuguese the strategic port of Malacca and had established themselves in Formosa (Taiwan). In the meanwhile, the Tokugawas excluded from Japan all Europeans except the Dutch. Shortly after mid-century, the Dutch drove the Portuguese out of Ceylon and took control of their Malabar factories and trade. By the time Portugal won back its independence from the Habsburgs in 1668, the Estado da India was limited to Goa and a few footholds to the north of it, to Macao on China's southeastern coast, and to Timor and a few islands in the Lesser Sundas. At this juncture, the France of Louis XIV dramatically burst onto the scene in an effort to catch up in the race for Asian trade and national glory. French fleets and embassies appeared in Asia during the last two decades of the century, as Louis XIV sought an alliance with Siam and a check on Dutch power in eastern India. The expulsion of the French from Siam in 1688 left the exploitation of Asia for the remainder

[3]

of the century in the hands of the well-entrenched Dutch, the expanding English, and the languishing Iberians. While the powers of western Europe invaded Asia by sea, the Russians in the latter half of the century were opening eastern Siberia and extending their influence overland to the frontiers of China.

The Christian missions administered by the Spanish and Portuguese patronages declined along with the Iberian secular power, but not so precipitously or completely. Leadership in the mission field was maintained by the Jesuits in India, China, and the Philippines, aided, and sometimes hampered, by the mendicant orders, the secular clergy, and the state. In Japan, Christianity and Christians came under violent attack from 1614 until the expulsion in 1640 of all Europeans except the Dutch Protestants. Refugee missionaries and their converts found sanctuary in Macao and Manila. From these two centers, the Jesuits thereafter carried the work of evangelizing to Vietnam, Siam, and even Laos. In continental Southeast Asia they soon came into conflict with the secular priests sent out, beginning in the 1660's, by the *Propaganda fide* in Rome and by the *Missions étrangères* in Paris. In Europe, national and fratricidal disputes over control of the Catholic missions became more numerous and divisive in the last few decades of the century. The French Jesuits as servants of both the French king and the pope became ever more prominent in the China mission, while control of the mission in Vietnam was assumed by the French secular clerics of the Paris Society of Foreign Missions. In India, the French Jesuits based in Pondicherry began to evangelize at the end of the century in the Carnatic (Karnatak). The Madura mission founded by Roberto de Nobili at the beginning of the century continued to grow and flourish until its end. In general, the Catholic mission was most successful in Vietnam, the Philippines, south India, and Ceylon. The Jesuit accommodationist mission failed in Japan and had only a limited success in China.

While the Dutch and English built up their control of maritime trade, their Protestant ministers concentrated their efforts on the Europeans at their commercial stations. The Dutch Calvinists enjoyed only a few successes in the conversion of natives on Amboina in Indonesia and on the island of Formosa. In Ceylon and Malabar they made but slight progress in converting heathens or in making Protestants out of the local Catholics. Culturally the Portuguese Catholic world in Asia did far better in resisting Dutch power than did the Estado da India.

Islam remained a menace to the Christians in the East, as it continued to expand in India, Southeast Asia, and the Philippines. By century's end, a few Orthodox priests from Russia appeared at Peking, thus bringing into Asia representatives of all the world's great religions not native to the East.

CHAPTER I

Empire and Trade

The Spanish had been fascinated since Magellan's time by the immensity of the Pacific (*Mar del Sur*) and by the possibility that islands on its western side, especially the Moluccas and the Philippines, could be added to their conquests through voyages dispatched from Mexico and Peru. Such hopes went long unrealized because the early navigators were unable to negotiate the return trip successfully. Andrés de Urdaneta's discovery in 1565 of a return route from the Philippines to New Spain was followed two years later by the first of the voyages sent out from Peru to discover the *terra australis,* the unknown "fifth continent" whose existence had been postulated by European geographers since classical times.[1] Cartographers of the sixteenth century, especially Oronce Finé and Gerhard Mercator, had placed the *terra australis* on world maps and charts even though no firm knowledge of a vast southern continent was at hand. In an effort to obtain more accurate information about the East, Philip II sent his Neapolitan cosmographer Juan Bautista Gesio to Lisbon in 1569 to participate in renewed discussions about the placement of the papal demarcation line in Asia.[2] Gesio returned to Madrid in 1573 with a collection of maps, relations, *roteiros* (rutters, navigational manuals), and descriptions relating to the Moluccas.[3] Events in Asia

[1] For a summary discussion see Donald Brand, "Geographical Exploration by the Spanish," in H. R. Friis (ed.), *The Pacific Basin: A History of Its Exploration* (New York, 1967), pp. 109–44.

[2] One of the outstanding issues between the Spanish and Portuguese related to the exact location of the Moluccas and to their rightful ownership. On the 1519–29 Spanish-Portuguese controversy over the Moluccas see *Asia,* I, 114–19. (All references to earlier volumes of *Asia in the Making of Europe* will appear in this form.)

[3] This collection, along with some Chinese books donated to the king by the Portuguese clergy, was eventually added to the holdings of the Escorial library. See G. Andres, "Juan Bautista Gesio, cosmografo de Felipe II . . . ," *Boletín de la Real Sociedad Geografica* (Madrid), CIII (1967), 365–67.

had also contributed to the difficulty in resolving the issue of who ruled the Moluccas. In 1574 the Portuguese had lost the fortress of Ternate to a confederation of local Muslim rulers,[4] and their center in the Spiceries hereafter was moved to the nearby island of Tidore. Five years later Sir Francis Drake entered the harbor of Ternate to lay the foundation for an English claim to the trade of the Spiceries.[5]

The Iberian controversy over the Moluccas was officially resolved when the Portuguese crown was taken over in 1580 by Philip II and his cohorts. Portuguese navigators and cosmographers were soon brought to Madrid to work jointly on projects relating to navigation, exploration, and colonization with members of the Academy of Mathematics founded by the king in 1582.[6] Earlier Portuguese and Spanish explorers had reported on the northern coast of New Guinea in their accounts of voyages which had touched on its shores between 1526 and 1545; it was generally believed for long thereafter that they had been to the northern coast of the legendary austral continent and on the point of discovering a new "Peru" or "India" between America and New Guinea. Indeed, the viceroy of Peru, who was charged with the administration of the Pacific region, had sent out two ships in 1567 under Alvaro de Mendaña y Neyra (1541–95) to find the "fifth continent" and to begin its colonization. Mendaña got no further than the southern coast of the Solomon Islands.[7] Francisco Gali in 1582–83 voyaged from Acapulco to the Philippines, from there to Macao, noticing Formosa en route, and then returned to Acapulco. His report prepared in 1585 was published in Jan Huyghen van Linschoten's 1598 edition of the *Itinerario* and in its contemporary English translation (Bk. III, chap. liv) by J. Wolfe.[8] Other Spanish voyagers meanwhile sighted or were wrecked upon the islands of the Marianas chain from the Maug island to Guam.[9]

In Madrid the armchair navigators and cosmographers of Philip II concluded that Mendaña had actually touched upon the northern shore of the great southern continent and that another voyage should be sent out to verify this conclusion. Four ships were dispatched from Callao in 1595 under Mendaña's leadership with the Portuguese navigator Pedro Fernandez de Quiros (d. 1615) as pilot-major. Although they failed to find the austral con-

[4] See *Asia*, I, 621–22.
[5] See *ibid.*, p. 623.
[6] See Andres, *loc. cit.* (n. 3), p. 366.
[7] See G. Schilder, *Australia Unveiled* (Amsterdam, 1976), p. 28; and D. H. K. Spate, *The Spanish Lake* (Minneapolis, 1979), pp. 119–21. The name "Solomon" was attached to imaginary islands in the Pacific before Mendaña made his discovery. It was evidently part of the vocabulary of those who sought the biblical land of Ophir. See C. Jack-Hinton, *The Search for the Islands of Solomon, 1567–1838* (Oxford, 1969), p. 31.
[8] For a summary of the voyage see J. Burney, *A Chronological History of the Discoveries in the South Sea or Pacific Ocean* (5 vols., London, 1803–17), II, 58–61. The first separate printing of Gali's report was published as *Viaje y descubrimientos y observaciones desde Acapulco a Filipinas, desde Filipinas a Macao, y desde Macao a Acapulco* (Amsterdam, 1638).
[9] See A. Sharp, *The Discovery of the Pacific Islands* (Oxford, 1960), pp. 86–87.

tinent, or even to regain the Solomons, Mendaña and Quiros discovered four islands of the Marquesas de Mendoza group in the mid-summer of 1595.[10] Mendaña died shortly thereafter; so Quiros, accompanied by Mendaña's wife, led the survivors over a tortuous route to the Philippines. In Manila, Quiros made the acquaintance of Dr. Antonio de Morga, a new arrival from Mexico and the lieutenant to the governor of the Philippines. Convinced that a continent lay near the Marquesas, Quiros let Morga know in secret his belief that the Marquesas were also of vital strategic importance for control of the route between New Spain and the Philippines. Quiros prophesied that the king himself would finally have to decide how best to exploit this dramatic discovery.[11]

Quiros returned shortly to New Spain, arriving at Lima on June 5, 1597, to tell the story of the maritime tragedy and to assess his scientific findings. When he urged the viceroy to sponsor a new Pacific expedition, Quiros was told to return to Spain and lay his proposal before the king. While en route to Europe, Quiros learned that Philip II had died and that 1600 would be celebrated in Rome as a Holy Year. He determined to undertake a pilgrimage to Rome, where, on August 28, 1601, he was received in audience by Pope Clement VIII (r. 1592–1605), to whom he related the story of his discoveries in the South Seas and from whom he received encouragement to carry forward his enterprise of bringing Christianity to its insular peoples. He also informed Cristoforo Clavius (1538–1612) and other scientists in Rome of the existence of a great tract of mainland near the Marquesas from which its "comely inhabitants" had once emigrated.[12]

Armed with letters of support from the pontiff and the Spanish ambassador to the Holy See, Quiros returned to Spain in 1602. King Philip III (r. 1598–1621) was much more impressed by the religious than by the scientific thrust behind Quiros' plan. Quite unenterprising himself, the king was most concerned about his personal salvation and believed that it might best be assured by bringing Christianity to the pagan world. Quiros had no trouble convincing the king by his memorials that the discovery of a new continent with its millions of souls waiting to be saved would advance significantly the king's hope for salvation and a spiritual conquest of the world.[13] Spain, it was then commonly alleged, was the only one of the expanding European states to possess such a "civilizing mission."[14]

[10] See Jack-Hinton, *op. cit.* (n. 7), chap. iv.

[11] See Celsus Kelly (trans. and ed.), *La Austrialia del Espiritu Santo,* "Works Issued by the Hakluyt Society" (hereafter "HS"), 2d ser., CXXVI–VII (2 vols., Cambridge, 1966), I, 12–13.

[12] See the letter (Feb. 2, 1602) of the duke of Sesa, Spain's representative to Rome, to Philip III as translated in *ibid.*, II, 302.

[13] See R. Ferrando Perez, "Felipe III y la politica española en el Mar del Sur," *Revista de Indias,* XIII, No. 54 (1953), 543–44.

[14] See A. Rodríguez-Moñino, "Bibliografía hispano-oriental," *Boletín de la Real Academia de la Historia,* XCVIII (1931), 418–19.

Though some of the ministers and advisers of the king opposed Quiros' proposal for the dispatch of a new Pacific expedition, Philip III himself acceded to the request. A fleet of three ships finally sailed from Callao late in 1605 to look for the austral continent. After sighting many atolls and previously uncharted islands, Quiros anchored his ships on May 3, 1606, in "Big Bay" of Espiritu Santo Island in the New Hebrides. Though he tried for thirty-six days to continue exploration of what he called "La Austrialia del Espiritu Santo," his efforts were thwarted by adverse winds and currents as well as by difficulties with his men. Leaving two of his ships to fend for themselves, Quiros decided to return to Mexico by the northern route, without seriously exploring "La Austrialia."[15] Luis Vaez de Torres, one of Quiros' captains, proceeded to Manila and in 1607 surveyed the coast of New Guinea, determined that it was an island and not part of the austral continent, and finally sailed to the Spice Islands. He was the first European to navigate successfully the dangerous strait now named for him.

Upon his return, Quiros' reception was lukewarm in Mexico and Madrid. From 1607 to 1614 he addressed about seventy memorials to the king requesting support for a colonizing and Christianizing expedition to "La Austrialia." His navigational acumen and his qualities of leadership being in question, the opponents of his project successfully thwarted his best efforts until 1614, when he received permission to return to Peru. Quiros died at Panama in 1615, but his influence continued to be strong in Spain and elsewhere.

While the Spanish explored in the Pacific, the Portuguese in Asia struggled to retain the maritime footholds they had won in the sixteenth century. At the dawn of the seventeenth century, the Asian sector of Portugal's "tridimensional empire" (Asia, Africa, and Brazil) remained *territorially* just about what it had been during the entire latter half of the sixteenth century. The Estado da India, with its capital at Goa, still stood firmly on cornerstones that were strategically located to protect and command the sea lanes from Mozambique to Japan. Within this extended maritime empire, Portugal's urban colonies continued to function and flourish as trading posts under the command of royal officials. The Portuguese themselves did not settle in large numbers at these outposts. In 1590 there were probably no more than fourteen thousand European-born Portuguese scattered throughout the Estado; much more numerous were the Luso-Asians who performed a mediating role between natives and Portuguese.[16] In Goa and Cochin and their dependencies, as well as in Malacca and Macao, the Portuguese dominated life, and European practices prevailed. Elsewhere in

[15] For details of the voyage and his discoveries see Kelly (ed.), *op. cit.* (n. 11), I, 38–50.
[16] Estimate in T. B. Duncan, "Navigation between Portugal and Asia in the Sixteenth and Seventeenth Centuries," in C. K. Pullapilly and E. J. Van Kley (eds.), *Asia and the West* (Notre Dame, 1986), pp. 10–11.

Asia, at the lesser outposts, the Portuguese came and went like trading ped-
dlers, only occasionally making a show of force. After their fortress on Ternate in the Moluccas had fallen in 1574, the Portuguese returned to the clove
islands and built a new fortress on neighboring Tidore. In this same decade
the Portuguese abandoned Chale on the Malabar coast and the small island
of Tunata. From the annexation of Damão in 1559 to the end of the sixteenth century no other territorial changes occurred.[17] Nor would Portugal's
territorial outposts be added to over the course of the seventeenth century;
rather, many would be lost to its Spanish and Dutch competitors.[18]

The Iberian union, legally completed in 1580–81 by King Philip II of Spain
(Philip I of Portugal), was effectively in operation by 1600, both in Europe
and overseas. According to the agreement signed by the king at Tomar in
April, 1581, Portugal was left with substantial control over its own administration and its overseas empire.[19] Gradually the Iberian union became an
economic, cultural, and political merger that produced new opportunities
for the Iberians at home and overseas. While continuing to govern their own
empire, the Portuguese were permitted to travel within the Spanish empire
and to trade freely in Spain itself. The Portuguese were not to trade or settle
in the Spanish empire; an identical prohibition applied to the Spanish with
respect to the Portuguese empire. Economically the two empires comple-
mented each other, since the bullion from Spanish America was essential to
the traffic with India. Soon a Portuguese merchant community sprang up in
Seville, some members of which became subjects of Spain in order to participate legally in Seville's trade with America.[20] In East Asia the Spanish Philippines became part of a new commercial and military triangle with Manila,
Malacca, and Macao at its vertices and with the Spice Islands at its center.
The Pacific itself and the trade between Manila and Acapulco was held to be
a Spanish monopoly closed to all comers.

Unfortunately for the Portuguese, the Iberian union also involved them
in the foreign policy and wars of Philip II and his successors. Participation in
the Armada sent against England in 1588 had cost the Portuguese serious
losses of ships and men. The death of Philip II a decade later was followed
by erosion of the agreement he had signed at Tomar. King Philip III entrusted the government to the duke of Lerma (in power from 1598 to 1618),

---

[17] For a contemporary description of Portugal's Asian empire, probably prepared in 1580 or
1581 for the instruction of Philip II and his advisers, see the *Livro das cidades, e fortalezas que a
coroa de Portugal tem nas partes da India, e das capitanias, e mais cargos que nelas ha, e da importancia
delles,* as reproduced by F. P. Mendes da Luz in *Studia* (Lisbon), VI (1960).

[18] For a fresh and realistic appraisal of the extent and character of the Portuguese position in
Asia see T. B. Duncan, "The Portuguese Enterprise in Asia, 1500–1750" (unpublished typescript), chap. i.

[19] For a good summary of the twenty-five stipulations signed by the king see A. H. de
Oliveira-Marques, *History of Portugal* (2d ed., New York, 1976), p. 315.

[20] J. Boyajian, *Portuguese Bankers at the Court of Spain, 1626–1650* (New Brunswick, 1983),
pp. 58–60.

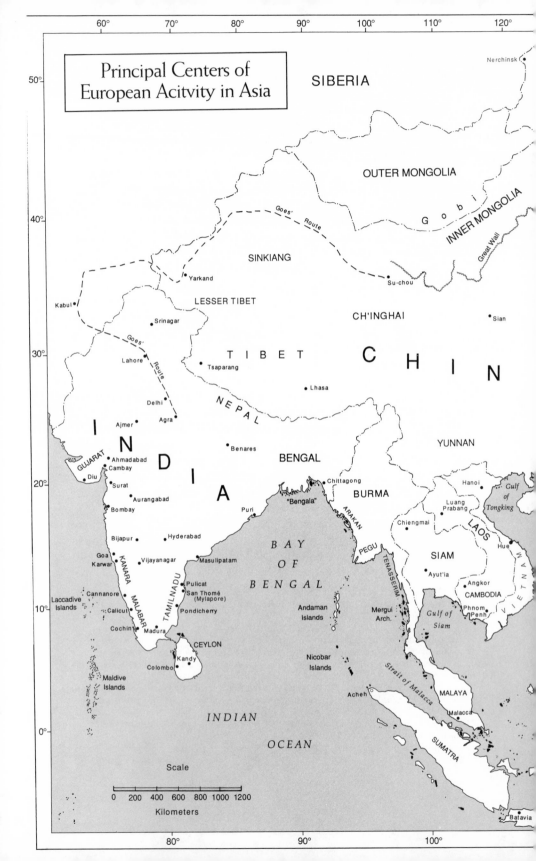

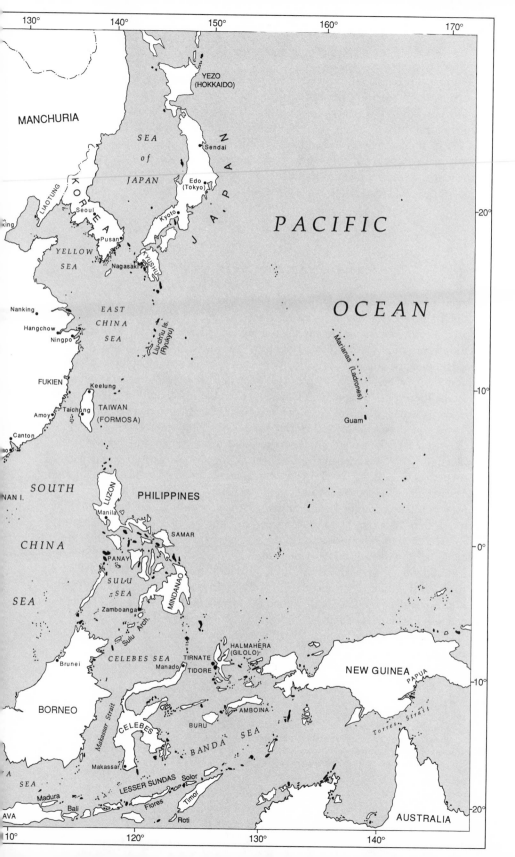

Francisco de Sandoval, who began to centralize authority in Madrid; he was frequently charged by the Portuguese with violating the guarantees undertaken by Philip II. In 1600, for example, the crown sent to Portugal a three-man committee to take over the supervision of local finance, including the Casa da India.[21] These, and similar arbitrary acts by Madrid, made Philip III personally unpopular in Portugal and increased resistance to Habsburg rule. In East Asia the Spanish in Manila were suspected of plotting to gain control of Macao, Malacca, and the Spiceries was well as a foothold in Japan.

I

THE IBERIAN MARITIME EMPIRE OF THE EAST

Intensification of the inter-Iberian rivalry came at a time when the Dutch and English first arrived in Eastern Seas to challenge the Iberian monopoly.[22] From Goa to Macao the Portuguese immediately assumed a cautious and defensive posture, for by 1600 they and the Spanish had learned to respect the naval prowess of the northern European powers. The Dutch "heretics," also "rebels" in the eyes of the Spanish crown, were initially regarded by the Iberians as pirates who had to be driven quickly and decisively from Eastern waters. Beginning in the 1590's large elements of the Portuguese forces had been committed to the conquest of Ceylon and Mozambique. Consequently they were unable to respond immediately and firmly to the Dutch threat elsewhere in the East. From 1603 to 1609 the Iberians vainly tried to sweep the seas clean of Dutch intruders. The conclusion of the Twelve Years' Truce in 1609 between King Philip III and the United Provinces officially brought an end to this action by granting the Dutch the right to trade in the East. The Dutch agreed to carry on no business in the ports controlled by the Spanish and Portuguese; elsewhere, it was stipulated, they could trade with "all other" rulers and peoples. Although the Dutch began to build their imperial base in Java, they did not ignore India and Persia completely; the English directed their main drive towards India and Persia, the heartland of the Estado da India. The appearance of Portugal's European enemies in the East had also the effect of encouraging Asian rulers and merchants to resist more vigorously the control and impositions the Portuguese tried to maintain on trade and navigation.

In the Habsburg period (1580–1640), Goa was the capital of an Asian em-

---

[21] The councils created by Philip II, especially the Council of State, continued in general to rule Spain and its empire in the seventeenth century. See C. H. Carter, "The Nature of Spanish Government after Philip II," *The Historian*, XXVI (1963), 5–7.

[22] In what follows, we have based our organization of the Iberian empire in Asia to the date 1615 upon the uncompleted doctoral dissertation of Thomas E. White tentatively entitled "Seventeenth-Century Spanish Sources on East Asia," chaps. i–iii.

pire which included almost fifty official settlements. Around 1610 these settlements boasted a peak population of approximately forty thousand natives and Europeans; these numbers declined to roughly thirty thousand souls by 1635.[23] A treaty of 1576 between Goa and Bijapur had secured Goa from land attack; Bijapur, constantly fearful of the Mughuls, was simply not about to oust the Portuguese. Goa's regional trade with Ceylon, Malabar, Gujarat, and the Persian Gulf cities was then far more valuable than its direct commerce with Lisbon. All communications and trade with Lisbon were supposed in normal circumstances to funnel through Goa. *Cafilas,* or annual convoys, were sent out from Goa to protect the Eastern seaways, to check on unlicensed trading vessels, and to bring relief to beleaguered Portuguese outposts.[24] While rich in trade, Goa was poor in food and short of soldiers. Still, in the early years of the seventeenth century, neither the Dutch nor the English dared attack Goa directly. Rather they defied openly the authority of Goa to license their vessels, harassed Portuguese shipping, and occasionally blockaded its harbor. They also sought alliances and trade compacts with the Indian princes and commercial towns hostile to the Portuguese. In their turn, the Portuguese in India, since they never could expect to receive adequate direct military support from Europe, began on their own to enlist the help of Indian princes, including Muslim rulers, to aid in the protection of Goa against the rising threat of Mughul power on land and of the Dutch and English at sea. By 1617 the Portuguese had organized an alliance of Deccan sultans against the Mughuls, English, and Dutch.[25] The government in Goa also relied increasingly on cooperative Brahmans and Parsis to negotiate for them with the Mughuls and other Indian rulers.[26] But the full story of Portugal's relations with the states of India cannot be told until scholars exploit the records still available at Goa and elsewhere in India.[27]

[23] Based on a review of the available figures prepared for us by T. Bentley Duncan. Some previous estimates for the early seventeenth century place Goa's population at a peak of 225,000, and make it the size of contemporary London. Much of the confusion over Goa's population has arisen from the overestimates of D. L. Cottineau de Kloguen (in *An Historical Sketch of Goa* [Madras, 1831]) calculated from a register of confessions. Other figures usually cited are loosely based on parish records and on the assertions of travelers and missionaries who aver that "Goa may be about as big as Tours" (Jean Mocquet in 1609), or that "Goa is about the same size as Pisa" (Francesco Ramponi in 1698). A recent unsatisfactory effort to estimate Goa's population is contained in M. Hugo-Brunt, "The Portuguese Settlement at Goa in India," *Plan* (Toronto), IX (1968), 72–86, 108–22. For later figures see below, pp. 853–54; by century's end Goa's population had declined to 20,000.

[24] Duncan, *op. cit.* (n. 18), pp. 507–12, gives the history of the Goa *Cafilas.*

[25] See B. G. Tamaskar, "Malik Ambar and the Portuguese," *Journal of the Bihar Research Society,* XXXIII (1947), 25–44.

[26] See P. S. S. Pissurlencar, *Agentes da diplomacia portuguesa na India (Hindus, muçulmanos, judeus, e parses)* (Goa, 1952), pp. liii–lv.

[27] For a recent summary account of the relevant materials see D. G. Kesivani, "Western Commercial Enterprises in the East. Some Oriental Archival Sources," in M. Mollat (ed.), *Sociétés et compagnies de commerce en Orient et dans l'Océan Indien* (Paris, 1970), pp. 546–48. Also see H. Heras, "The Portuguese Alliance with the Muhammadan Kingdoms of the Deccan," *Journal of the Royal Asiatic Society* (hereafter *JRAS*) (Bombay Branch), n.s., I (1925), 122–25; P. M. Joshi,

Many of the Portuguese commercial ventures in Eastern waters were supported financially by Japanese and Gujarati investors. But with the steady decline of Portuguese fortunes, the Asians like their European counterparts became increasingly wary about entrusting their capital to the Iberians and shifted it to Dutch and English enterprises.[28]

On Ceylon, the Portuguese had established their earliest relations with the Sinhalese state of Kotte, located on the island's western coastal plain. Operating as armed merchants, the Portuguese had sought after 1505 to participate in trade from the fortress and base they had erected at Colombo and to support in Kotte native rulers friendly to their interests. Almost to the end of the sixteenth century, their position in Ceylon had remained insecure. They finally conquered the Jaffna peninsula in 1591, and three years later an expeditionary force was sent from India to undertake the pacification of Kotte and the inland kingdom of Kandy. After some serious initial setbacks the Portuguese consolidated their rule over Kotte between 1594 and 1601. Thereafter their major objective was to annex the mountainous and Buddhist state of Kandy in order to complete the territorial conquest of Ceylon. From 1602 to 1612 the Portuguese sent expeditions twice annually into Kandy before the Dutch could come to its aid. In the process Kandy was ravaged, but remained independent.[29]

Malacca was a thriving entrepôt in the early seventeenth century, strategically located between the Indian and Pacific trading zones and between the monsoons and the trade winds. As a fortress city it had to import most of its food. Its Portuguese garrison and naval units were used to protect the city from local enemies in the nearby Malayan and Sumatran kingdoms, to keep the strait open to the trade so vital to its existence, and to control the local population when natural disasters or trade stoppages occurred. Malacca was located on the way to the spice-producing areas coveted by the Dutch and English and in a good position to thwart their enterprises in insular Southeast Asia. An initial Dutch foray into the Spiceries was repelled in 1601–2 by a fleet sent out from Malacca. The Dutch nonetheless persisted stubbornly in their effort to neutralize Malacca, particularly after the founding of their East India Company in 1602. In 1606 they concluded a trade agreement and alliance with the sultan of Johore, the great Malay enemy of Por-

---

"Muhammad Adil Shah (1627–1656) and the Portuguese," *Journal of Indian History*, XXXIII (1955), 1–10; A. Sen, "Murshid Quli Khan's Relations with the European Merchants," *Indian Historical Quarterly*, XXXV (1959), 16–42.

[28] See K. N. Chaudhuri, "The English East India Company in the Seventeenth and Eighteenth Centuries: A Pre-modern Multinational Organization," in Leonard Blussé and Femme Gaastra (eds.), *Companies and Trade* (The Hague, 1981), p. 46; Femme Gaastra, "The Shifting Balance of Trade of the Dutch East India Company," in *ibid.*, p. 64; and Eiichi Kato, "Unification and Adaptation: The Early Shogunate and Dutch Trade Policies," in *ibid.*, p. 228.

[29] Based on T. Abeyasinghe, *Portuguese Rule in Ceylon, 1594–1612* (Colombo, 1966), chaps. i–iii; and G. D. Winius, *The Fatal History of Portuguese Ceylon: Transition to Dutch Rule* (Cambridge, Mass., 1971), chap. i.

tuguese Malacca, and simultaneously bombarded the city. The Dutch were driven off by a fleet dispatched from Goa. Although the city remained in Portuguese hands, the Dutch gradually succeeded in undermining its trade by patrolling the seas of Indonesia and forcing the traders to go to Java instead. The Dutch also allied themselves with Iskandar Muda (d. 1636), the young sultan of Acheh who had won his throne in 1607. Acheh's rise was linked to the revival of the spice trade via the Red Sea and Egypt; it was the center for Islamic merchants driven from Malacca and other Portuguese-held ports.[30] The Dutch and the Achinese sent an invasion fleet to take Malacca in the summer of 1615; after a few initial successes this serious threat to Malacca was beaten off by a Spanish fleet from Manila.

Macao, the Portuguese outpost on the south China coast since the mid-1550's, remained an unfortified trading center of about ten thousand souls at the turn of the sixteenth century.[31] The quiet of the Portuguese in Macao was disturbed in 1599 by efforts undertaken by the Castilians based in Manila to bypass Macao and to establish direct trade with Canton.[32] Two years later the Dutch appeared and began to harass Portuguese shipping between Macao and Japan. Later Dutch efforts, such as that of Cornelis Matelief in 1607, to negotiate directly with the Chinese were uniformly unsuccessful. The Chinese, who had learned to tolerate and work with the Portuguese, were unwilling to extend similar privileges to the unknown northern Europeans. The Twelve Years' Truce (1609–21) ended for a time the Dutch efforts to break the monopoly of the China trade enjoyed by the Portuguese and Macao.[33]

The Moluccas, situated at the center of the East Asian triangle dominated by the Iberians, was the major objective of the Dutch drive eastward. The Muslim ruler of Ternate in the Moluccas, eager to see the Portuguese eliminated, sent envoys in 1600 to England and the United Provinces to negotiate treaties of commerce and aid. The ruler of Tidore, Ternate's Muslim neighbor and enemy, sent his representative to Manila in 1601 to enlist the aid of the Spanish.[34] From 1601 to 1603, Portuguese forces from Malacca and

---

[30] See K. N. Chaudhuri, *Trade and Civilisation in the Indian Ocean* (Cambridge, 1985), pp. 74–75, 104, 108–14; Denis Lombard, "Questions on the Contact between European Companies and Asian Societies," in Blussé and Gaastra (eds.), *op. cit.* (n. 28), pp. 184–85; M. C. Ricklefs, *A History of Modern Indonesia* (Bloomington, Ind., 1981), pp. 29–33.

[31] R. Ptak, "The Demography of Old Macao, 1555–1640," *Ming Studies*, XV (1982), 27–35. Ptak estimates six hundred Indo-Portuguese families in 1600, with a total population of about ten thousand (p. 28).

[32] See T. T. Chang, *Sino-Portuguese Trade from 1514 to 1644* (Leyden, 1934), pp. 109–10.

[33] For the later history of the Macao trade see C. R. Boxer, *Fidalgos in the Far East, 1550–1770* (The Hague, 1948), chap. vii; for a review of the archival sources for the period after 1630 see G. B. Souza, "Portuguese Trade and Society in the South China Seas," *Itinerario*, III (1979), 64–73. On the early Dutch efforts to trade in China see E. J. Van Kley, "China in the Eyes of the Dutch, 1592–1685" (Ph.D. diss., Dept. of History, University of Chicago, 1964), pp. 1–17.

[34] For details on these missions and on contemporary happenings in the Moluccas see B. de Leonardo y Argensola, *Conquista de las islas Malucas* (Madrid, 1609), pp. 254–64.

Spanish units from Manila tried without success to retake Ternate. A Dutch naval expedition of 1605 forced the Portuguese to retreat from the Moluccas and Amboina. In response to these losses, the Spanish in the Philippines on royal orders from Madrid raised an armada of thirty-six vessels and a force of about two thousand sailors and soldiers.[35] By April, 1606, Ternate capitulated to Governor Pedro Bravo de Acuña. "The Conquest of the Moluccas," as the Spanish referred to this victory, was celebrated by fiestas in Manila and Spain. But the conquest was actually not complete, for the Dutch remained entrenched on Banda and Amboina and within easy reach of the clove islands. Part of Ternate itself soon fell to the Dutch. As for the Portuguese, they remained in the Moluccas as subjects of Philip III, while the administration of the Moluccas was placed under Manila. Although the Portuguese officially retained general control over the clove traffic, a measure of it was diverted from the old market of Malacca to the new market of Manila.

The spiritual and temporal conquest of the islands of Solor and Timor in the Lesser Sundas had been initially undertaken in 1566 by Portuguese Dominican fathers. Rich in white sandalwood, these islands had long attracted the attention of merchants and voyagers from China, the Philippines, and the Moluccas, as well as from Malacca, seventeen hundred miles to the northwest and at the opposite end of the Indonesian archipelago.[36] Before the end of the sixteenth century the Portuguese had built a fortress on Solor and had established a small garrison there to protect the native Christians and their own trade. The Dutch, shortly after their appearance in the Moluccas, began attacking Solor, and they captured its fortress in 1613. The refugees from Solor fled to Larantuka on the eastern tip of nearby Flores where they established a settlement that effectively resisted all seventeenth-century Dutch attempts to capture it.[37] Since the Dutch chose not to settle at Solor permanently, the Portuguese were able after 1620 to continue their trading and Christianizing there. The outposts on Solor and Flores soon became intermediaries in the rich Timor-Macao-Makassar trade. Once Portugal lost Malacca to the Dutch in 1641, the Portuguese continued to expand their activities from Solor to the surrounding islands of Timor, Flores, Roti, Savu, and Sumba, and to carry on trade with all friendly merchants. Over these islands they managed to hold a superficial suzerainty even though their footholds were repeatedly attacked by the Dutch. Officially hostilities ended in the Lesser Sundas in 1661 with the conclusion of a Luso-Dutch peace treaty.[38]

[35] On the Spanish expedition see *ibid.*, pp. 351–89; the author gives the figure of three thousand personnel. Here we prefer the authority of Antonio de Morga, *Sucesos de las islas Filipinas*, trans. and ed. J. S. Cummins, "HS," 2d ser., CXL (Cambridge, 1971), 232.

[36] See *Asia*, I, 599, 601, 617n.

[37] See Boxer, *op. cit.* (n. 33), p. 176.

[38] Based on Humberto Leitão, *Os portuguesas em Solor e Timor de 1515 a 1702* (Lisbon, 1948), *passim*. Also see below, pp. 139–40.

Dutch attacks on the Philippines began in 1600 and were followed by efforts to establish direct commercial contacts with China and Japan. In Manila the local Chinese (*Sangleys*), then numbering around twenty thousand, revolted in 1603. After the outnumbered Spanish managed with Filipino help to crush the uprising, Manila began to fear an attack from China.[39] Since their early forays against the Spanish were generally unsuccessful, the Dutch in 1609, while the truce was being worked out in Europe, planned a major offensive against Manila in the hope of breaking the Iberian hold on the Moluccas and of diverting the China trade from Manila to Bantam. Early in 1610 a Dutch fleet tried to enter Manila Bay, but it was defeated and its admiral killed at the first battle of Playa Honda (April 25). Knowing that the Dutch had allied themselves with the Moros, the Spanish responded by campaigning against the Moros in Mindanao and Sulu and by building forts in the Moluccas. Even though this was technically a period of truce with the Dutch, Governor Juan de Silva of Manila nonetheless began in 1611 to assemble a large fleet and enlisted the cooperation of Goa to help in launching a general Iberian offensive to drive the Dutch from the Indonesian archipelago. While the Manila fleet relieved the siege of Malacca in 1615, the Portuguese squadron from Goa was intercepted and turned back by the Dutch. When this setback was accompanied by the death of De Silva at Malacca, the Spanish returned to Manila and the Dutch were hereafter permitted to continue their trading and naval activities in relative peace. With the failure of De Silva's offensive, the Portuguese, who were almost as fearful of Spanish ambitions as they were of the Dutch, had no wish to launch further joint enterprises. The Spanish, both in Madrid and Manila, began to urge defense and consolidation rather than a new military offensive against the Dutch in Asia.[40]

At Nagasaki in 1600 the Portuguese were the only Europeans trading on a regular basis with Japan. The Jesuits, who were by then missionizing in Kyoto and in several other cities of Kyushu and Honshu, claimed around three hundred thousand Japanese converts. In 1600 both the Jesuits and the Portuguese merchants feared the possible threats to their monopolies from the Spanish in the Philippines and from the Dutch and the English. The arrival of the "Liefde" at Beppu in April, 1600, brought to Japan a Dutch captain, Jacob Quaeckernaeck, and his English pilot, Will Adams, who had survived a terrible voyage through the Straits of Magellan and across the Pacific. Still the Dutch and English pioneers did not represent as immediate a threat to the Portuguese in Japan as that posed by Manila. The northern Europeans possessed neither nearby bases nor experience in Eastern warfare or trade. This deepening hostility between the Spanish and Portuguese in East Asia had repercussions in Madrid. Pedro de Baeza, a veteran of trade in

---

[39] See H. de la Costa, *The Jesuits in the Philippines, 1581–1768* (Cambridge, Mass., 1967), pp. 205–7.

[40] *Cf.* below, pp. 312–13.

the East, published around 1609 a memorial to the crown in which he called for mutual assistance rather than competition among Philip III's subjects in Asia.[41] On their side, the Japanese, who were well aware of the difference dividing the Europeans, generally treated the foreigners impartially and tolerated their alien practices until 1614. Indeed, Philip III addressed a letter to the emperor of Japan in 1613 thanking him for the kind and generous treatment accorded the Iberian merchants and missionaries.[42]

While Portuguese officials and merchants sought simply to maintain control of their maritime empire from Colombo to Nagasaki, certain of their countrymen undertook some surprisingly successful freebooting enterprises in continental Southeast Asia. The Spanish conquistadorial spirit, so evident in the contemporary suggestions for attacks on China and Cambodia from the Philippines, seems to have rubbed off on a few Portuguese adventurers of the early seventeenth century. The end of the Spanish intervention in Cambodia around 1600 was followed by Portuguese forays into Burma and Siam.[43] In Burma a band of Portuguese mercenary soldiers fought and schemed their way into positions of power during the first fifteen years of the century. Led by Salvador Ribeyro de Souza and Felipe de Brito e Nicote, the *feringhi* (Frankish, or European) mercenaries in the armies of Toungoo, Arakan, and Siam took advantage of the sack of Pegu in 1599 to occupy Syriam, Pegu's western port, with limited aid from the king of Arakan. De Brito, becoming constantly more independent and daring in his actions, journeyed to Goa in 1603. Because the Portuguese in Goa needed the timber of Pegu, he received a warm reception there. He obtained the hand in marriage of the niece of Viceroy Ayres de Saldanhada, official recognition of his title as "Captain-General" of Pegu, and military reinforcements. Supported by the Mon chieftains of Pegu, De Brito gradually became master of Lower Burma and the commerce that entered it from Bengal, Martaban, and Malaya. By 1605 the Jesuits began to appear in Lower Burma as they sought to establish a permanent mission there. While De Brito consolidated his position in Pegu, the king of Ava was undertaking the reunification of central Burma. Ava invaded Pegu in 1613 and captured Syriam along with its Portuguese "king." De Brito and his closest associates were executed, and the other Portuguese captives carried off as slaves. Some of the Portuguese ultimately made their way to Ayut'ia where they helped the Siamese in 1614 to fend off the Ava forces trying to recover Tenasserim. As a reward for their

---

[41] See the excerpt in English translation in C. R. Boxer, *The Christian Century in Japan, 1549–1650* (Berkeley, 1951), pp. 425–26.

[42] For general discussions see L. Norton, *Os portugueses no Japão, 1543–1640* (Lisbon, 1952); and M. Teague, "The Portuguese in Japan," *Geographica*, I (1965), 80–94.

[43] See L. P. Briggs, "Spanish Interventions in Cambodia, 1593–1603," *T'oung-pao*, XXXIX (1949), 132–60; C. R. Boxer, "Portuguese and Spanish Projects for the Conquest of Southeast Asia, 1580–1600" *Journal of Asian History*, III (1969), 118–36; and in the same author's "Spaniards in Cambodia," *History Today*, XXI (1971), 280–87. Also see *Asia*, I, 570–71.

services, the Portuguese were granted diplomatic and commercial concessions in Tenasserim.[44] Portuguese and Eurasian mercenaries and pirates continued in the 1620's and 1630's to be very active in Arakan and Lower Burma. They were not finally expelled from the Ganges delta until Chittagong was conquered in 1666 by the Mughuls.

While a few freebooters sought to expand the empire, the Habsburg official policy in the East was cautious and defensive, except in Ceylon, the Moluccas, and the Pacific. In the other insular areas the Portuguese were susceptible to challenge by the rising maritime power of the Dutch and English. However, to 1615 the Portuguese, sometimes with the aid of the Spanish, showed themselves capable at Malacca and elsewhere of holding their own against the northern Europeans. In insular Southeast Asia, Macao, and Japan, the inter-Iberian rivalry, while potentially dangerous to the Portuguese, was partially counterbalanced by the growth of an Anglo-Dutch rivalry in the Moluccas and Java. Many of the native rulers and merchants, who had at first welcomed the Dutch and English as counterweights to the Portuguese, soon learned by hard experience that the northern Europeans were equally difficult to deal with in commerce and quite as rapacious as the Portuguese. The conclusion in Europe of the Twelve Years' Truce (1609) provided after 1615 a brief but uncertain respite to the Portuguese defenders of the Estado da India and to Manila. The official and unofficial trade of the Portuguese continued to flourish as commerce retained its priority over conquest. Portuguese military and naval efforts undertaken in Ceylon, the Lesser Sundas, the Moluccas, and Lower Burma were designed to protect and expand trade. While the Portuguese spice monopoly in Europe was certainly broken by the early years of the seventeenth century, the maritime empire in Asia remained intact and continued to function to 1615, though the pressure upon it mounted and its cost of maintenance rose sharply. In the Pacific, the Spanish explorations of the insular regions were still carried on to help protect the galleons and to open a new world of missions.[45]

In Europe, as well as in Asia, the Portuguese were becoming increasingly restive under Habsburg rule. Persons close to the spice trade began to protest, particularly after the Dutch blockade of Lisbon in 1606, that the Spanish connection had produced economic chaos everywhere. The Twelve Years' Truce, strongly opposed in Portugal, was generally held to be ineffective in the East. The naval conflicts of 1611 and 1614 with the English off Surat increased Portugal's fears about its future in the Indian Ocean. Inflation and other serious and chronic economic and social problems at home were not alleviated by the truce or by the duke of Lerma's measures to cope with them. The internal wars with the Moriscos from 1609 to 1614 also helped to strain the Iberian union and to raise agonizing questions about its

---

[44] *Cf.* the cordial treatment of the Danes in 1621. See below, pp. 90–91.
[45] See below, pp. 218–19.

viability. The Portuguese became increasingly worried by the men and resources being diverted by the crown to the maintenance of the empire in
America and West Africa. But the most dramatic and shaking event of all
was the change that took place in Japan from 1614 to 1616 with its government's decision to expel all Catholic missionaries and to place restrictions
upon the trade with Macao and Manila.[46]

In Spain itself, the reformers (*arbitristas*) had long been warning that the
country was on the verge of economic and moral collapse. Memorialists
from the Philippines began to complain in 1617 about the distressing conditions in the islands and about the need to protect and conserve their resources.[47] But most of these warnings fell on deaf ears, since the government
of Philip III was distracted by more pressing problems in Europe. The outbreak of the Thirty Years' War in Bohemia in 1618 was followed by the reinforcement of the Spanish armies in the Low Countries. At Madrid a
consulata of 1619 took note of Castile's internal problems and of the imperative necessity to reform government and to manage the colonies more effectively. But it was not until after Philip III's death in 1621 that his successor
began to heed the memorials of Fernando de los Rios Coronel and Duarte
Gomes Solis on the worsening conditions in the Philippines and India.[48]
Now, however, it was too late, for the war with the Dutch was resumed in
1621 and colonial reform shelved "for the duration."

While the Spanish memorialists warned about what might happen in
Asia, things there were indeed going from bad to worse. In Japan the death
of Tokugawa Ieyasu in 1616 was followed by a new assault upon Christianity and by a stricter enforcement of the laws limiting foreign entry, trade,
and the rights of Japanese to go abroad. By 1624 the Japanese had cut off all
connections with the Philippines: however, they still permitted the "Great
Ship" of the Portuguese to come annually from Macao. From time to time a
few daimyos of southern Japan made overtures to Manila for the restoration
of trade. Other more militant daimyos pressed for an invasion of Macao and
the Philippines, even though trade with Macao was still a highly profitable
enterprise for both the Portuguese and their Japanese associates. In fact during the 1630's the Macao trade had some of its most profitable years.[49] The
Japanese Christians meanwhile continued to be subjected to a systematic
persecution by the government and its agents. Finally the Shimabara rebellion broke out in Kyushu during 1637–38. Because the Portuguese of
Macao were suspected of having helped to foment the rebellion, the Japanese in 1639 decreed the immediate and permanent cessation of the Macao-

---

[46] On Manila's trading relations with Japan see below, pp. 35–36.
[47] See below, p. 336.
[48] See below, pp. 336–38.
[49] On the gradual decline of Spanish-Japanese relations after 1615 see W. L. Schurz, *The Manila Galleon* (New York, 1959), pp. 111–14; on the Macao trade see C. R. Boxer, *The Great
Ship from Amacon* (Lisbon, 1959), pp. 86–154. On the Japanese trade with Indochina see below,
pp. 236–37.

Nagasaki trade, a commerce that had endured for ninety-five years. The Dutch, who had consolidated their trade at Hirado after 1609 and who had regularly menaced the Philippines, Macao, and shipping on the high seas, were generally accused by the Iberians of having conspired with the pagan Japanese authorities to bring down the Catholics and the Iberian relationship with Japan.[50]

Although the Dutch were not entirely responsible for the Iberian debacle in Japan, they were certainly the main agents seeking to drive the Iberians from insular Southeast Asia and the China seas. Beginning in 1619, two years before the expiration of the truce in Europe, the Dutch undertook a general maritime offensive against their opponents in the East Indies, both Asians and Europeans. After driving the English out of the central and eastern islands of the Indonesian archipelago, the Dutch attacked Macao in 1622 and Manila two years later. Although neither city fell, the Dutch were successful for a time in bringing the trade of both Iberian outposts to a virtual halt through blockades, harassment of the shipping lanes, and the establishment in 1624 of a permanent factory and fortress on the strategically located island of Formosa. While Macao fortified itself in response to the Dutch threat, the Spanish countered the Dutch move into Formosa (Fort Zeelandia at Tainan) by establishing in 1626 a base of their own in northern Formosa at Keelung. Like Manila and Macao, the Portuguese outpost of Malacca survived the Dutch attacks on its commerce as well as the offensive launched in 1629 by Acheh, the Sumatran ally of the Dutch. Over the following two decades, the Iberians enjoyed a respite from Dutch pressure, a period in which a degree of economic prosperity and military security returned to the Iberian trading centers.

The revival of Macao's prosperity was aided by a traffic in arms with the Ming rulers of China who were engaged with the Manchus in a civil war which began around 1620 and went on to 1644. Macao also continued to profit from the established Japanese and Indochinese trade and from a clandestine exchange with Manila that developed in the 1630's. In Manila the trans-Pacific trade also revived, as the Chinese silk junks came back to the city after the lifting of the Dutch blockades. Once Manila experienced a mild economic and building boom, its governors launched a military attack against the Moros of Mindanao and the Muslim outposts in the Sulu Sea. By 1635 the Spanish had captured Zamboanga, a Moro center at the extreme western tip of Mindanao. But the Spanish were not then successful in dominating by their offensive the threat posed by the Moros to the central and northern Philippines. Using Zamboanga as a base, the Spanish subsequently launched campaigns against the Camucones of eastern Borneo, who pillaged and took slaves in the Bisayan Islands from time to time.

[50] See L. Pérez, O.F.M., "Las relaciónes diplomáticas entre España y el Japon," *Archivo Ibero-Americano*, XXXI (1929), 79–114; and J. O. Ronall, "Spain and Japan—Early Diplomatic Relations," *Eastern World*, XI, No. 12 (1957), 38–39; XII, No. 1 (1958), 24–25.

These mid-century forays were the last of the Spanish expansionist moves in insular Southeast Asia.

In India, the Portuguese held their own against the Dutch and English to the end of the Habsburg period (1640). Along its west coast, the main Portuguese outposts north and south of Goa continued to function much as they had at the end of the sixteenth century. The coastal towns of Kanara, which had been developed as Portuguese stations in the last generation of the sixteenth century, still supplied pepper, rice, textiles, and saltpeter.[51] The main threat to Onor, the modern Honavar and then the principal port of export for Kanara pepper, came from the emergence of the inland state of Ikkeri between 1602 and 1629. Eager to placate the expansionist ruler of Ikkeri, the Portuguese authorities in Goa bowed to his demand that he should set the terms for the pepper trade of Kanara. In Malabar the Portuguese faced no similar threat from the landward side. Cochin, the Portuguese center in India next in importance to Goa, continued to supply the Portuguese with teak and other timbers used for building ships in India. It was abandoned, however, in 1611 as a port of lading for Lisbon-bound carracks. Still coastal shipping and private trade continued to prosper at most of Malabar's cities, and the Portuguese became ever more involved in these local enterprises. An uncertain peace was worked out with Calicut, Portugal's oldest enemy in Malabar, and a factor was maintained there to issue licenses to vessels sailing the seas of the East where the Portuguese still had power enough to control maritime activity. In the coastal waters from Goa south to Quilon, the Portuguese held the upper hand throughout the Habsburg period.[52]

Goa's regional trade with the Persian Gulf was handed an abrupt setback by the fall of Ormuz in 1622 to allied Anglo-Dutch-Persian forces, the first of the Portuguese strongholds to be taken. Although the Portuguese crown had sought in the sixteenth century to control the overland trade from Ormuz, this policy had never enjoyed more than a limited success.[53] The fall of Ormuz itself did not halt completely the commerce between Goa and the ports of the Persian Gulf at the end of the overland route. The Portuguese obtained Persian silks and carpets, Arabian horses, and the pearls of Bahrein at nearby places on the Gulf—at Muscat, Jask, Kung, and elsewhere. Although Muscat fell to the Osmani Arabs in 1650, the Portuguese were still trading in the Gulf cities at the end of the seventeenth century.[54] The over-

[51] Saltpeter (potassium nitrate) was the chief constituent in gunpowder. It is also used as medicine and as a food preservative.

[52] Based on A. R. Disney, *Twilight of the Pepper Empire* (Cambridge, Mass., 1978), chap. i.

[53] For the sixteenth-century history of the Gulf and Red Sea trade with Europe see Duncan, *op. cit.* (n. 18), pp. 95–101.

[54] For discussion of the fall of Ormuz as an episode in the "structural crisis" of European-Asian trade see N. Steensgaard, *The Asian Trade Revolution of the Seventeenth Century* (Chicago, 1974). For a critical review see T. B. Duncan, "Niels Steensgaard and the Europe-Asia Trade of the Early Seventeenth Century," *Journal of Modern History*, XLVII (1975), 512–18.

land messenger service and caravan trade continued under Ottoman polic-
ing to operate effectively throughout the century.[55]

The Portuguese position in Ceylon worsened markedly in the last decade
of the Habsburg period. From 1612 to 1630 the Portuguese forces in Ceylon, most of the time under the command of Dom Constantino de Sá, had
never been able to overcome the king of Kandy; at the same time the Portuguese in Colombo were not seriously threatened by Kandy. The stalemate
in Ceylon ended when Dom Miguel de Noronha, third count of Linhares,
became viceroy of India in 1629. Impatient with Sá's inactivity, Linhares accused Sá of neglecting his duty and of seeking private gain from his post.
Stung by his superior's rebukes, Sá undertook in 1630 a campaign against
Kandy with only the scanty forces at his command. Disaster followed and
Sá and a number of the leading Portuguese *fidalgos* were killed. This defeat
was followed by Kandy's unsuccessful siege of Colombo and by the inauguration of a new era of stalemate. Around 1635 Raja Sinha proclaimed himself King of Kandy and Emperor of Ceylon. Shortly thereafter he made
contact with the Dutch on the Coromandel coast of India and offered to
negotiate with them. In 1638 Raja Sinha signed a treaty that the Dutch had
designed to make the Kandyans pay for the protection provided and to give
the Dutch exclusive access to the cinnamon at prices lower than those paid
by the Portuguese.[56] The Dutch, despite Raja Sinha's protests, immediately
sought to oust the Portuguese from Ceylon. Galle, south of Colombo, was
captured and the Dutch became lords of the southern tip of Ceylon. Events
taking place elsewhere saved the Portuguese from being forced out completely at this time. They continued to trade at Colombo until 1658.

In the final years of the Habsburg period, the Portuguese were on the defensive everywhere in Asia, especially on the high seas. Beginning in 1637
the Dutch blockaded Goa annually, making the normal carrack trade with
Lisbon virtually impossible. During the entire decade of 1631 to 1640 only
fifteen vessels arrived in Lisbon from Asia, a smaller number than in any
previous decade.[57] The Portuguese outposts, all vulnerable to attack from
the sea, had become by 1635 the main military objectives of the Dutch; to
that date only Ormuz had been wrested from the Portuguese. While the
Dutch molested Portuguese trade everywhere possible, they concentrated in
the 1630's on bringing down Malacca and on controlling the shipping in its
strait. By 1631 the Dutch began to enjoy good relations with Siam, the
major power of continential Southeast Asia and traditional suzerain of Malaya. Beginning in 1635, a regular patrol of fast boats was kept in the strait
to prey upon Portuguese shipping, and in effect to blockade the port. The
sultan of Johore in 1637 again allied himself with the Dutch. A Dutch fleet

[55] See H. Furber, *Rival Empires of Trade in the Orient, 1600–1800* (Minneapolis, 1976), p. 9.
[56] For a summary of this treaty see Winius, *op. cit.* (n. 29), pp. 38–39.
[57] See Duncan, *loc. cit.* (n. 16), Table I.

stationed in the Indian Ocean prevented reinforcements from being sent to the relief of Malacca. While still shaken by the news of Japan's closure in 1639, the small Portuguese colony of Macao heard in 1641 that their lifeline to Goa had been severed with the surrender of Malacca to the Dutch and that, as a result of events in Europe, further trade with Manila was forbidden.

In Lisbon it had become clear to Portuguese nationalists that no part of the empire was safe and that the fiscal and human exactions of the crown for the war in Europe were bound to weigh more heavily on Portugal each passing year. A convention concluded with England in 1635 had reduced the overseas enemy to the Dutch and their allies in Asia, much to the relief of the Portuguese in India. Long hostile to the Iberian union, the non-Castilians were eager by 1640 to revolt against the heavy-handed, centralizing regime of Olivares and Philip IV. In June Catalonia revolted and by November a conspiracy of independence-minded Portuguese aristocrats had gained the support of the duke of Bragança. Before the end of the year, the secession of Portugal from the Spanish crown had been proclaimed and at Lisbon the Bragança duke was crowned King John IV. Throughout Portugal's Asian empire the news was received with joy and relief. No one was able to anticipate that to make the secession effective would require twenty-eight years of war with Spain and the loss of most of the Estado da India.

To 1640 the decline of the Portuguese empire in Asia had been blamed upon the Spanish crown; the responsibility for the series of vital losses in Portugal's Restoration era (1640–68) may be traced to the continuing war of defense at home and to the inability of the Portuguese crown to protect its Asian outposts from the depredations of the Dutch. In 1641 all further intercourse between the Portuguese and Spaniards in Asia was banned by both Lisbon and Madrid. A ten-year (1641–51) Luso-Dutch truce was officially concluded that gave, but only after 1645, a temporary respite to the beleaguered Portuguese East. In an attempt to salvage whatever they could in Indonesia after the fall of Malacca, the Portuguese took advantage of the truce to shift the center of their East Indian trade to Makassar in the Celebes and to their surviving outposts in the Lesser Sundas. Macao, after losing its profitable trade with Japan and Manila, had to rely for its very existence upon commerce with Canton, Makassar, Flores, and Timor. After the end of the war with Spain in 1668, the Portuguese sent two trade missions to Peking in 1670 and 1678. Very few results came from these overtures, as the Portuguese continued to be restricted to Macao.[58]

The Spanish in Manila likewise suffered drastic financial losses by the cur-

---

[58] See Fu Lo-shu, "The Two Portuguese Embassies to China during the K'ang-hsi Period," *T'oung pao*, XLIII (1955), 75–94; L. Petech, "Some Remarks on the Portuguese Embassies to China in the K'ang-hsi Period," *ibid.*, XLIV (1956), 227–41; and J. E. Wills, Jr., *Embassies and Illusions: Dutch and Portuguese Envoys to K'ang-hsi, 1666–1687* (Cambridge, Mass., 1984), pp. 82–144.

tailment of the trans-Pacific trade brought on in 1637 by the disruption of the junk traffic from China, the naval activities of the Dutch, and new rebellions by the Chinese of Luzon. In 1642 the Dutch launched a third major offensive against the Moluccas, the southern Philippines, and the Spanish foothold on Formosa. The Spanish were driven from Formosa but managed to hold on in the Moluccas. As if this were not enough, Manila suffered a terrible earthquake in 1645, in which more than one-half of the city was destroyed and six hundred of its inhabitants killed. Before Manila could recover from the earthquake, the Dutch tried unsuccessfully in 1646, and again in 1647, to capture the Spanish headquarters in the East. The Philippines were probably saved from further Dutch onslaughts by the conclusion in Europe of the Treaty of Münster (1648) between the United Provinces and Spain. While this treaty brought an end to the Eighty Years' War of Dutch Independence, it also brought with it a general recognition that the Dutch presence in the East was permanent and that the Spanish hope of further Asian conquests was effectively checked.

The Peace of Westphalia (1648) rang the curtain down on the Habsburg bid for an Austro-Spanish hegemony in Europe. Deserted by their Austrian ally, the Spanish continued to war alone against France and Portugal. The expiration of the Portuguese truce with the United Provinces in 1651 inaugurated a three-sided colonial war, centered mainly in the Atlantic, in which the English and Dutch fought each other (the Anglo-Dutch war of 1652–54) as well as the Portuguese. A treaty of 1654 with England formally granted the British the right to trade directly with Portugal's Asian outposts except Macao. But the continuing War of Independence in Iberia still prevented the Portuguese from sending reinforcements to Asia. The Lisbon government finally concluded that the Portuguese were unable to resist everywhere effectively, especially after France concluded peace with Spain in 1659. Obviously the homeland and independence had to be given the priority. Portugal's Asian footholds, being the most distant and the least defensible of its holdings, were left to languish or to survive on their own as the Portuguese reinforced their positions in Africa and Brazil. Excluded from Brazil and Angola, the Dutch resumed the war against Portugal, blockaded Lisbon, and in 1661 exacted a treaty by which they received a heavy indemnity in cash as well as the same trading rights in Asia granted the English seven years before.

For twenty-five years, from 1640 to 1665, the Portuguese suffered one disaster after the other in the Estado da India. Colombo was lost in 1656; the rest of Ceylon two years later. Goa had fallen into decline, particularly after the Portuguese were driven out of the Arabian peninsula and the Persian Gulf region in the 1650's. Goa had steadily shrunk in size and importance, and its economy had come to be dominated by indigenous merchants.[59]

---

[59] See M. N. Pearson, "Indigenous Dominance in a Colonial Economy: The Goa Rendas,

While the peace treaty between Portugal and the United Provinces was being worked out in Europe, the Dutch indemnified themselves for their losses in Brazil by taking over the Malabar coast; between 1661 and 1663 the Dutch invested Quilon (1661), Cranganore (1662), Cochin (1663), and Cannanore (1663). To cement their friendship with England, the Portuguese presented Bombay in 1661 to Charles II as part of a dowry for Catherine of Bragança. All that remained of the Portuguese East were Goa, Damão, Diu, Bassein, the Lesser Sundas, and Macao. Of these remnants, Macao was undoubtedly the most thriving center with its growing population.[60] The end of the war with Spain in 1668 provided the Portuguese with a generation and more of peace (to 1704) in which to recover from their losses, to concentrate upon internal development, and to forge closer links to Brazil and the outposts in Africa.[61]

The Spanish empire of the East had evaporated as a grandiose dream of the past by the time Madrid recognized the independence of Portugal. The cessation of trade between Manila and Macao after 1640 had left the Philippines without a European trading partner in Asia. Within Manila, the Chinese community remained a source of continuing anxiety to the Spanish authorities. What were always tense relations became a dangerous internal division in 1662, when the famous Ming leader of China, Koxinga (Cheng Ch'eng-kung), took over Formosa, demanded tribute from Manila, and threatened invasion of the Philippines. The Chinese of the Philippines, feared by the Spanish as a "Trojan Horse" ally of Koxinga, once again began to defy their less numerous overlords. It was under these conditions that Manila withdrew its garrison from Ternate, the last Spanish foothold in the Moluccas. While the cloves of the Moluccas had been legally reserved to the Portuguese until 1640, the Spanish on Ternate thereafter had sent the cloves to Manila. Even so, it remained the opinion of many in Manila in 1662 that the cost of defending and maintaining Ternate was greater than the returns from the clove trade. Dismay over the withdrawal from Ternate was overshadowed by relief in Manila when news of Koxinga's death arrived there.[62]

With the abandonment of Ternate, the city of Manila—once thought to be the future imperial city of Iberia in the East—was reduced to the Spanish administrative, religious, and trade center of Luzon and the Visayas in the Philippines and the entrepôt in the galleon trade between China and Mexico. Thwarted in Japan, the Moluccas, and Indonesia, the intrepid Jesuits turned eastward in 1668 from the Philippines to Guam in the Mariana Is-

---

1600–1700," in J. Aubin (ed.), *Mare Luso-Indicum* (2 vols., Paris, 1972), II, 61–73. Also see above, p. 11, n. 27.

[60] Duncan estimates Macao's population at over 10,000 in 1635, and as including 850 Portuguese households (*op. cit.* [n. 18], p. 406). R. Ptak (*loc. cit.* [n. 31], p. 28) estimates the population of Macao to be 40,000 in 1640.

[61] See C. R. Boxer, *The Portuguese Seaborne Empire, 1415–1825* (London, 1969), chap. vi.

[62] See Schurz, *op. cit.* (n. 49), pp. 138–42. Also see below, p. 37.

lands. While many of the galleons and fleets of the past had touched upon Guam on the way to the Philippines, it was not until 1668 that the crown ordered the Acapulco galleons to put in there to take on provisions and supplies. By 1681 Guam had a mission, a fort, a garrison, and a governor.[63] By the end of the seventeenth century, Spanish explorers and missionaries had learned that there were many islands in the vicinity of Guam; to two of the insular chains uncovered they gave the names Marianas and Carolines.[64] As a result of this change in direction, the Spanish empire in the East had definitively become a Pacific rather than an Asian empire by the end of the seventeenth century.

2

IBERIA'S SHRINKING TRADE

Philip II had sought to unify Iberia's fiscal administration through the creation of a Council of Finance in 1591. In Portugal some of the offices created by Dom Manuel in the early sixteenth century were abolished and the Casa da India and the spice trade placed under the jurisdiction of this new council. The Cardinal Archduke Albert, the governor of Portugal, was recalled to Madrid in 1593 and replaced by a regency council that ruled at Lisbon until 1600. Despite these centralizing reforms in government, the Portuguese generally remained cooperative so long as Philip II lived, for he continued to abide by the promise of Tomar to assign Portuguese offices only to Portuguese.[65] Philip III threatened this delicate balance and in 1602 appointed Castilian ministers to the Council of Portugal. From 1604 to 1614 a Council of India created by the crown was supposed to administer overseas affairs, but its influence was limited because the Council of Finance continued to control economic matters. Luis Mendez de Vasconcelos expressed in 1608 his concern about the effects of the discoveries upon the economy of Portugal in the *Dialogos do sitio de Lisboa:*

> The price of the brilliant discoveries, the bravery and endurance, was that as we went forward in the discovery of the world, the cultivation of Portugal grew worse and the rural population diminished.[66]

While the accuracy of this statement may be questioned, it was opinions like these that contributed to the growing discontent in Portugal with Habsburg

[63] Schurz, *op. cit.* (n. 49), pp. 247–48. Also see W. J. Barrett, *Mission in the Marianas, 1669–70* (Minneapolis, 1975). Also see below, p. 37.

[64] See Sharp, *op. cit.* (n. 9), pp. 87–88.

[65] On the general government of the colonies during the Iberian union see F. Mauro, *Le Portugal et l'Atlantique au XVIIe siècle, 1570–1670* (Paris, 1960), pp. 433–35.

[66] As translated and quoted in J. B. Trend, *Portugal* (London, 1957), p. 146.

rule. Sebastianism, an almost pathological belief that the young King Sebastian had not really died at the battle of Alcacer Kebir (1578) and would soon return to the throne of Portugal, mounted swiftly in popularity as part of the protest against the centralizing economic and overseas policies of the Habsburgs.[67]

The spice trade, still potentially one of the crown's major assets, had suffered a serious decline as a result of the wars, especially when the Dutch and English began to blockade ports and harass shipping in the Atlantic as well as in Eastern seas. The failure of private contractors to meet their spice quotas had forced the crown, back in 1591, to reassume reluctantly the administration of trade and to reorganize the Casa da India. Early in Philip III's reign, reports reached Madrid that the Casa da India and the Armazem da India (dockyards and warehouses) were malfunctioning. Between 1598 and 1602 a special appointee of the king examined the records and questioned officials; these investigations brought to light a number of irregularities on the part of the functionaries. Two years later a reform was undertaken and a number of officials summarily discharged.[68] However, the organizations themselves apparently underwent little change in basic structure, for in 1628, when their administration was conveyed to the Portuguese India Company, the offices and functions of these two separately administered agencies remained very much what they always had been.[69] The Casa da India collected duty and tolls on all merchandise from overseas and sold the pepper on the king's account; its officials supervised the loading and unloading of the ships, inspected them for contraband, and paid the crews. The Armazem built, repaired, and provisioned the vessels, obtained the crews, and provided navigational materials.[70] To 1628 they both remained under the supervision of the Council of Finance, the overall authority in matters relating to the royal treasury.

The Carreira da India ("India run" or "passage to India"), the voyage covering the vast distance between Lisbon and Goa, had been one of the greatest achievements of sixteenth-century naval technology. The India fleets, though there were shipwrecks and losses of life from disease and malnutrition, generally had made the voyage out and back regularly and efficiently. Between 1497 and 1590, a full 87 percent of the ships sailing from Lisbon had arrived at their destinations; 88 percent of the return trips had been made successfully. The entrance of the Dutch and English upon the scene changed this happy condition drastically. In 1591, for the first time in the sixteenth century, no ship returned to Lisbon; in 1598–99, when a pow-

---

[67] See *Asia*, I, 135, 139; Oliveira-Marques, *op. cit.* (n. 19), pp. 317–18; and F. P. Mendes da Luz, *O consehlo da India* (Lisbon, 1952), pp. 81–82.

[68] Mendes da Luz, *op. cit.* (n. 67), pp. 47–52; and J. L. Azevedo, *Épocas de Portugal económico* (Lisbon, 1947), pp. 152–54.

[69] See Disney, *op. cit.* (n. 52), p. 87.

[70] See Mendes da Luz, *op. cit.* (n. 67), pp. 59–67.

erful English fleet blockaded Lisbon, no ships left or returned to the Tagus. Naval attacks and the fear of attacks also forced the Portuguese to take new risks that greatly increased the number of shipwrecks. Shortages of funds in Lisbon and Goa brought about a decline in shipbuilding and maintenance standards as well as in seamanship and pilotage. Still the Carreira made a comeback. From 1591 to 1630, the average annual tonnage dispatched to India to meet the Dutch threat increased by 38 percent over the figure for the period from 1521 to 1590. Indeed, the first decade of the seventeenth century was one of the busiest times, particularly in carrying troops, weapons, and ammunition to India. Losses of ships, lives, and merchandise nonetheless mounted in the forty years from 1590 to 1630. Spread too thin in the East, the Portuguese navy, outgunned and outrun by the smaller Dutch vessels, became increasingly unable to protect the outposts and convoy the merchant vessels safely. Losses to the Dutch finally forced the Portuguese to concentrate upon the Atlantic and to leave the Estado da India to its own devices. From 1631 to 1670 only one or two Indiamen a year arrived at the port of Lisbon, usually with less than an average of nine hundred tons of cargo. With the coming of peace in 1668, the condition of the Carreira failed to improve. Portugal had by then decided to expend its major overseas efforts upon the protection and development of Brazil.[71] Even at its zenith, the trade with Asia by the Carreira amounted to no more than 2 percent of the total trade carried on in the Indian Ocean.[72]

In the East, from the time when Portuguese first appeared in its ports, four distinctly separate trading areas existed: the countries around the Red Sea and the Persian Gulf, South Asia, the Southeast Asian insular and mainland states, and the Far East (China, Japan, Taiwan, Korea, and the Philippines). India, with its central location, openness to penetration, and diverse and adaptable economic organizations, was the most accessible and versatile of these trading regions. Around 1600 it was certainly the world's greatest producer of cotton textiles; India cloth exports dominated overseas markets from east Africa to the Philippines.[73] For their part, the Portuguese had left the Asian coastal trading network relatively undisturbed; they quietly adapted themselves to it and their private traders participated in it.[74] During the first decades of the seventeenth century, the Portuguese concentrated upon purchasing Indian pepper in Kanara and Malabar rather than the cloths of Gujarat, Coromandel, and Bengal. No matter what they imported from India directly, the Portuguese had to pay for most of it in precious metals,

[71] Based on Duncan, *loc. cit.* (n. 16), pp. 20–21.
[72] See Duncan, *op. cit.* (n. 18), p. 187.
[73] For an illuminating study of another aspect of this inter-Asian trade see Sucheta Mazumdar, "A History of the Sugar Industry in China: The Political Economy of a Cash Crop in Guangdong, 1644–1834" (Ph.D. diss., Dept. of History, University of California, Los Angeles, 1984).
[74] Lombard, *loc. cit.* (n. 30), pp. 179–87.

the only commodity that found ready market there. But this was not a total disaster, because the purchasing power of silver increased by 50 percent in being moved from one ocean to the other.[75] In the Malay-Indonesian area, the Portuguese traded Indian cloths for food, spices, sandalwood, and China goods. To 1641 the trade between Goa and Malacca was maintained on an intermittent basis by using small vessels that could evade the Dutch patrols.

In India, the Portuguese had moved into Kanara after the defeat of Vijayanagar at Talikota (1565) to take advantage of the political and economic divisions produced by the impending collapse of the old Hindu empire. Here they had seized three coastal towns and had quickly established fortresses and factories. Onor became the principal port of export for Kanara pepper, a product of higher quality than the pepper of Malabar or Indonesia. At other ports of Kanara, the Portuguese obtained rice to feed Goa and other Asian outposts, especially during years of drought and famine. From 1602 to 1629, Venkatapa, the nayak (governor) of Ikkeri, waged a series of expansionist wars in Kanara. Successful in conquering the pepper lands by 1623, the ruler of Ikkeri forced the Portuguese to buy Kanara pepper from him at higher prices than they had previously paid. The Portuguese met Venkatapa's terms and held on for a period to their three footholds in Kanara.

The Kanara outposts were important to the Portuguese as alternatives to Malabar, whose coastal towns had long been the major suppliers of export pepper. Cannanore, Calicut, Cochin, Quilon, and Travancore were established Malabar kingdoms with their own mercantile facilities and were not subject to one another or to any distant imperial ruler. The Portuguese trade in these towns was governed by contracts or agreements which fixed the delivery price of pepper. The Malabar princes entered into these arrangements to protect themselves against a fall in prices. The conduct of business in Malabar was in the hands of the Moplahs (the Indianized descendants of Muslims), the Jews, and the Gujaratis.[76] Calicut, still the most important state of Malabar and the long-time enemy of the Portuguese, experienced an economic revival in the early years of the seventeenth century, possibly because of the decline of Portuguese power. The Portuguese factor at Calicut at this time issued *cartazes* (licenses) for a fee to vessels engaged in regional trade and did little else. Most of Portugal's commercial activity in Malabar was centered in Cochin, whose rulers had first begun to trade with the Portuguese in 1501. Aside from pepper, the Portuguese obtained teak and other woods at Cochin for shipbuilding. Cochin was also the leading entrepôt in

---

[75] On the constant flow of silver to India see F. Braudel, *Civilization and Capitalism, 15th–18th Centuries,* trans. Sian Reynolds (3 vols., New York, 1981–84), II, 198–99; III, 490–91; on the flow of silver through the Red Sea to Surat, II, 126–27; III, 478–79.

[76] On the importance of native merchants and brokers to the Europeans' ability to do business in Asia see *ibid.*, III, 489–90.

south India for the interregional trade in which Portuguese private trad-ers were prominent participants. Beginning in 1611, the pepper of Malabar was no longer shipped directly from Cochin to Lisbon; it was sent in swift coastal vessels to Goa for transshipment to Europe.[77]

The Portuguese seaborne pepper trade, created as a royal monopoly, had supplied most of Europe's pepper from 1503 to 1540. Thereafter pepper de-liveries at Lisbon had declined relatively as supplies by the overland route increased. With the breakdown of the Cape-route monopoly in the 1590's, Portuguese imports were limited to about one-fourth of the pepper con-sumed in Europe. Throughout the sixteenth century the Portuguese had tried to manage their pepper imports to maintain the price level at thirty-five to thirty-eight ducats per quintal, the price attained in the century's sec-ond decade. In the last years of the century, when imports by the Cape route became more limited and uncertain, the Portuguese could not raise the price of pepper without losing many of their European customers to the import-ers of pepper by the Levantine route.[78] In spite of persistent efforts to in-crease imports from 1610 to 1635, the Portuguese share in the European pepper market declined as the Dutch and English imports increased and as prices became lower at Amsterdam than at Lisbon. All hope of recovery ended with the outbreak of the war with Spain in 1640 and the consequent loss of the Spanish markets in Europe and overseas. By 1670, Portuguese pepper imports met only 1 percent of the European demand.[79]

Until 1618 the "Great Ship" to Japan left annually from Goa to Malacca, Macao, and Nagasaki. Thereafter, and until the cessation of trade with Japan in 1638, smaller and swifter vessels were used on the run to Macao to avoid the Dutch and their Asian allies. At Macao the Portuguese acted as middlemen in the trade between China and Japan by exchanging Japanese silver for Chinese silk. Although the Chinese were officially forbidden to trade with Japan, a clandestine direct trade was carried on despite all regu-lations and the protests of the Portuguese at Macao. Japanese junks also competed with the Portuguese for China's trade by making government-authorized sailings to the markets of Indochina and insular Southeast Asia in what were known as "August Red-Seal ships."[80] While the Dutch inter-fered in the Japan-China trade, their early successes were confined to mo-nopolizing the trade of Indonesia and to harassing Macao's commerce with

---

[77] Based on Disney, *op. cit.* (n. 52), chap. i.

[78] See C. H. H. Wake, "The Changing Pattern of Europe's Pepper and Spices Imports, *ca.* 1400–1700," *Journal of European Economic History,* VIII (1979), 387–88.

[79] Based on the analyses and tables in Duncan, *op. cit.* (n. 18), pp. 118–29. In 1670 the esti-mated European average annual consumption amounted to about thirty-five hundred tons (seven million pounds), or about three times what it had been in 1500 (see *ibid.*, p. 712, n. 3). By 1688 the total European market, according to the Dutch, amounted to 8.6 million pounds. See Wake, *loc. cit.* (n. 78), p. 391.

[80] So called from the special "red-seal licenses" granted to oceangoing merchant ships. See below, pp. 236–37.

the Moluccas, Malacca, and Goa. Despite such competition, the Portuguese merchants of Macao, and their Jesuit collaborators, enjoyed good profits from their role as middlemen. Their associates in Japan apparently had a similar experience, for some of them amassed personal fortunes and all of them fought as long as possible to keep the Japanese government from banning the trade or taxing it to death. The two cities concerned—Macao and Nagasaki—likewise profited from the trade and both experienced a substantial growth in size during the first generation of the seventeenth century.[81]

The prosperity of the Estado da India depended heavily upon Portugal's ability to maintain command over the Eastern seas and to tax the interregional trade. The revenues obtained from the sale of licenses and from the customs paid at Ormuz, Goa, Diu, Cochin, and Malacca were enough at the beginning of the seventeenth century to sustain Portugal's Asian enterprise.[82] To extract the greatest returns from trade, the representatives of the crown in Goa sold protection to the Asian traders, and they had to have enough military strength to deliver it. Phrased differently, since the Europeans had little beyond precious metals to exchange for Asian products, they sold their services and their commercial and shipping skills to the princes and merchants involved in the inter-Asian trade. Since no Asian state, or confederation, possessed enough naval power to challenge their maritime supremacy, the Portuguese maintained their hold upon the sealanes of India until around 1630, even though Asian traders were sometimes also required to purchase safe conducts from the Dutch and English.[83] The rulers of India were not concerned that their merchants paid extra taxes to the Portuguese for the right to sail the seas and carry on commercial activities.[84] In fact, they sometimes hired the Portuguese themselves to convoy pilgrim ships to Mecca or purchased permits for other voyages. The Portuguese, followed by the Dutch and English, paid for their concessions in Asia by facilitating a peaceful interregional trade.

Portuguese trade in Asia, despite the strenuous efforts made by the crown to protect it, declined steadily during the first four decades of the seventeenth century. The revenues of the viceregal government in Goa decreased sharply, primarily because of reduced returns from customs.[85] By 1635, Goa's revenue from the sales of licenses had declined over a single generation by 90 percent.[86] In northern India by 1634 only Bassein, Chaul, and Damão were producing revenues greater than costs. Diu's importance as a trading center declined as Surat's grew, and by 1642 Diu's revenues had de-

---

[81] Based on the introduction to Boxer, *op. cit.* (n. 49).

[82] See Steensgaard, *op. cit.* (n. 54), pp. 88–89.

[83] On the naval question in the Indian Ocean see M. A. P. Meilinck-Roelofsz, *Asian Trade and European Influence in the Indonesian Archipelago between 1500 and About 1630* (The Hague, 1962), p. 122. See also Chaudhuri, *op. cit.* (n. 30), pp. 77–79.

[84] See M. N. Pearson, *Merchants and Rulers in Gujarat* (Berkeley, 1976), pp. 131–32.

[85] See table showing Goa customs returns from 1600 to 1634 in Disney, *op. cit.* (n. 52), p. 51.

[86] See Duncan, *op. cit.* (n. 18), p. 557.

clined by two-thirds. The loss of Ormuz in 1622 cut off the substantial revenues enjoyed by the crown from the duties levied on its rich trade and
reduced substantially the trading activities of the Portuguese in northwestern India and the Persian Gulf region. By 1635, Goa's trade with Gujarat had
fallen off sharply.

The exports of pepper to Portugal through Goa likewise declined abruptly.
In the first decade of the century 10 percent of southwest India's annual production was dispatched to Lisbon.[87] By the late 1620's the exports of pepper
amounted to less than one-half the average level attained in the sixteenth
century.[88] The rising prices of pepper in Malabar and Kanara produced friction between the pepper-traders and local suppliers and authorities. To obtain pepper more cheaply, the Portuguese resorted frequently to force and
to dishonest practices.[89] The consequent decrease in returns from the commerce in pepper was accentuated by Dutch competition in Europe and by a
decline in the selling price at Lisbon in the 1620's.[90] High prices in Asia and
low prices in Europe accentuated the decrease in both the quantities imported and the profits realized. By 1635, Goa's Asian trade amounted in
value to seven times Lisbon's Carreira trade.[91]

While the Estado da India managed to survive the Habsburg era, its decline could readily be observed in the chronic and growing shortages of
warships, cash, manpower, and experienced leaders. The Habsburgs, faced
by similar problems in Europe and America, had only reluctantly reassumed at the end of the sixteenth century the overseas trade and shipping
monopolies. The successes of the Dutch and English chartered companies
were not lost upon the Iberian political and economic memorialists and reformers. Duarte Gomes Solis, a New Christian merchant, repeatedly proposed to the crown between 1612 and 1621 the formation of a joint-stock
company to take over Portugal's trade with Asia.[92] When the crown was
about ready to respond positively to Solis' proposals, the political climate
darkened in 1621 with the death of the king and the expiration of the Twelve
Years' truce. This was followed in 1622 by the fall of Ormuz, a sharp temporary decline in silver imports from America, and a depression in the textile
industry. Finally, it was in connection with Olivares' "Great Project" of 1624
to create a series of interlocking companies to reinvigorate the international
trade of Spain and to check the expansion of the Dutch, that the Portuguese
India Company proposal was revived and carried to completion.[93]

Dom Jorge Mascarenhas, who was appointed president of the Lisbon *Ca-*

---

[87] Disney, *op. cit.* (n. 52), p. 36.
[88] *Ibid.*, pp. 61–62.
[89] *Ibid.*, p. 35.
[90] See below, pp. 112, 121–23.
[91] Duncan, *op. cit.* (n. 18), pp. 510–11.
[92] Converts from Judaism or Islam were called New Christians. On Duarte Gomes Solis' life
and experience with Asian trade see Boyajian, *op. cit.* (n. 20), pp. 25–26.
[93] See Disney, *op. cit.* (n. 52), pp. 72–74.

mara in 1624, took the initiative in funding and organizing the Company. He tried to raise capital in Lisbon by loans and by the issue of new bonds to municipalities. The crown itself sought to obtain similar investments from other municipalities—all without great success.[94] The capital garnered in this manner amounted to less than one-third of what the crown finally had to find. Still, of all of Olivares' "projects," only the scheme for the Portuguese India Company survived by 1628. Since private entrepreneurs were averse to becoming involved in the India trade by subscribing to the Company, the crown itself became its major fiscal sponsor in the hope of attracting private capital once it began functioning. In an inaugural decree of 1628 the crown promised to provide a substantial sum to be paid in three annual installments; included in these payments were five oceangoing vessels, fully supplied, as well as naval stores, pepper, and cash. The Company commenced operations in 1628 with a bit more than one-half the capital its sponsors had sought to raise.[95]

By the terms of its charter, the Portuguese India Company was to be governed in Lisbon by a seven-man board of directors responsible to the Board of Trade (*Conselho do Comercio*) in Madrid. Dom Jorge Mascarenhas was appointed its president, and the other six directors selected were rich New Christian merchants of Lisbon.[96] Public response to the new Company was negative. The Portuguese believed that the project was economically unsound and part of a Spanish scheme to circumvent the promises of Tomar by putting control of the India trade into the hands of New Christian merchants who were but nominally Portuguese and who were themselves unwilling to invest in the Company of which they were the directors. And at Goa, when Viceroy Linhares arrived there in 1629 with instructions to set up the administration of the Company in India, he found the local Portuguese merchants reluctant to cooperate in a new enterprise that might infringe upon their private commercial activities and that could not be sustained by the waning Portuguese naval power in the Indian Ocean.[97]

The Company received by its royal charter the monopolies of pepper, coral, ebony, and cowries, as well as the right to collect charges and duties on private goods shipped in its vessels. Bullion and specie, known as "pepper money," were shipped to Goa. Pepper shipments constituted 81 percent of the tonnage of the company's exports to Portugal in 1630 and 96 percent in the following year. But for the years between 1629 and 1633, only five-eighths of the average quantity loaded at Goa actually arrived in Lisbon. The financial losses experienced en route from shipwrecks and delays were exacerbated by the higher price of pepper in India and by its declining price

[94] See T. A. de Carvalho, *As companhias portuguesas de colonização* (Lisbon, 1902), pp. 24–25.
[95] Disney, *op. cit.* (n. 52), pp. 79–86.
[96] On the New Christian merchants of Lisbon see Boyajian, *op. cit.* (n. 20), pp. 26–36.
[97] Disney, *op. cit.* (n. 52), pp. 87–97.

in Europe. In fact, the price of pepper at Lisbon had been declining ever since the late sixteenth century, when the established price at the Casa da India was thirty-two cruzados per quintal. Little wonder that the crown complained in 1634 that pepper prices were "so high" in Cochin and "so much reduced" in Lisbon.[98] At the time of that remark, the crown had already liquidated the Portuguese India Company (by a declaration of April 12, 1633) and returned control of the India trade to the Council of Finance. The Portuguese hereafter were barely able to maintain annual communication by sea between Lisbon and Goa, even though by 1637 only Ormuz had fallen to competitors.[99] The Casa da India, after its restoration to Portuguese control in 1640, continued to function much as it had ever since the issuance of its original *Regimento* in 1509.[100] At Lisbon an Overseas Council was created in 1643 to replace the Council of Finance as the supreme administration for Portugal's overseas activities.[101]

The failure of the India Company and the virtual cessation of the Carreira trade led in India to a truce and an alliance between Portugal and England. The Anglo-Spanish peace of 1630 was applied to India in 1635 as the Portuguese reluctantly accepted the principle that other European nations had a legal right to trade in the Indian Ocean. The extension of the treaty to India was initiated by the Portuguese and English at Goa and Surat out of their common and growing concern over Dutch activities in the Indian Ocean, southern India, and Ceylon. The cinnamon of Ceylon, officially declared a royal monopoly in 1614, had become by 1631 the cherished spice, for it made up to some extent for the Portuguese losses in the trade of fine spices from the Moluccas.[102] Indeed, Ceylon was the last of the insular spice producers wrested from the Portuguese. While losing control of their outposts, the Portuguese in Asia increasingly employed large fleets of small coasters made in India, as well as native craft, to avoid the northern European fleets and to remain active in the inter-Asian trade.[103] In the latter half of the century an informal empire of Portuguese traders replaced the formal Estado da India.[104]

The Portuguese revolt of 1640 against the Habsburgs brought in its wake new political, military, and commercial alignments in Europe. In 1641 King John IV, the Bragança ruler of Portugal, concluded an agreement with the Dutch, who were also fighting for independence from Madrid. In Asia,

[98] As quoted in *ibid.*, p. 111. Also see Disney's Table 6 on p. 112 for the prices of pepper at Lisbon. For comparative European prices see below, pp. 121–23.

[99] See Duncan, *loc. cit.* (n. 16), p. 20.

[100] For the text of King Manuel's administrative order see D. Peres (ed.), *Regimento das Cazas das Indias e Mina* (Coimbra, 1947); for a listing of the decrees and letters patent issued to clarify and modify the original document see pp. xii and xiii of Peres' introduction.

[101] See Duncan, *op. cit.* (n. 18), p. 207.

[102] *Ibid.*, p. 567.

[103] Meilinck-Roelofsz, *op. cit.* (n. 83), pp. 185–86.

[104] Duncan, *op. cit.* (n. 18), pp. 631–32.

however, the officers of the Dutch East India Company ignored the treaty until 1645 and continued to attack Portuguese shipping and strongholds. By 1658 the Dutch had completed their conquest of Ceylon and by 1663 the trade of Malabar had fallen to them. In the meantime, the Portuguese tightened their ties with England by the Anglo-Portuguese treaties of 1642, 1654, and 1661. Peace between the Dutch and Portuguese in Asia came only in 1663—and after the Portuguese had lost all their pepper establishments in India.[105] To make their ties with England more binding, the Portuguese reluctantly ceded Bombay in 1661 as part of the dowry of Catherine of Bragança. The formal Portuguese trading empire in Asia was thus reduced to the Lesser Sundas, Macao, and Goa and three other stations in India.

From 1668, with Portugal at peace, only one or two ships sailed annually in each direction, the great carracks became fewer, and yearly tonnage coming into Lisbon declined. Spice imports became minuscule as Portuguese merchants concentrated upon buying more precious commodities of small bulk. Profit in Europe was maintained in the last years of the century by imports of pearls, gems, diamonds, and textiles from India, and textiles, porcelains, and furniture from China; rich imports from Brazil helped to make this an "age of gold and diamonds" for Portugal. Some merchants wanted direct trade between Macao and Lisbon, to avoid taxes and controls at Goa. In Asia, the Portuguese outposts maintained themselves as an informal empire by their participation in the interregion trade. In the latter half of the century, the Carreira da India became a branch of the Portugal-Brazil commerce.[106] The European traffic in Asian spices was left in large measure for the Dutch and English to enjoy. Increasingly, the Portuguese became intermediaries in the trade of the Atlantic and Mediterranean regions dominated by the northern Europeans.[107]

From the foundation of Manila in 1571, the Spanish began to investigate the resources and trading potential of the Philippine archipelago. To their disappointment they did not find cloves or other local products of great commercial value. They learned that Mindanao grew its own variety of cinnamon (*Cinnamomum mindanaense*) and that small quantities of gold were found in the islands. Soon it became clear that the natural and human resources of the islands alone were not rich or developed enough to sustain a lucrative trade across the Pacific. Manila, with its enclosed bay, could never be more than the Spanish entrepôt at which the spices, drugs, and textiles of the East were exchanged for the precious metals of America.[108] While the Portuguese retained a limited and direct trade to Europe, the Castilians had

---

[105] *Ibid.*, pp. 154–55.

[106] See Oliveira-Marques, *op. cit.* (n. 19), pp. 344–46; Duncan, *loc. cit.* (n. 16), p. 22.

[107] See J. G. da Silva, "Portugal and Overseas Expansion from the Fifteenth to Eighteenth Centuries," *Journal of European Economic History*, VIII (1979), 685.

[108] See W. L. Schurz, *op. cit.* (n. 49), pp. 27–28.

to rely ever more heavily upon what turned out to be the China-America trade carried on by the Correra de Filipinas.

The government in Manila was charged by the crown to aid the Portuguese in the maintenance of their Asian empire. But the Portuguese generally viewed with suspicion the motives and objectives of the Castilians. In their turn, the Manileños were reluctant to provide men, money, and arms for the Portuguese as long as the Portuguese tried to exclude them from the Chinese and Japanese trade and to maintain their own position as middlemen. Spanish efforts to negotiate with the Chinese for direct trade were in contravention of the law of 1593 forbidding Castilians access to Macao, and were regularly spiked by the Portuguese. Beginning in 1608, the Manila government was granted permission by the crown to send one vessel annually to Macao to purchase supplies. The Portuguese, who were legally permitted to travel to Manila, extended this privilege to the point of sending their ships to Manila laden with "China goods," particularly after 1619, when the regular Chinese junks began coming in fewer numbers. As the civil war progressed in China after 1620, Manila became increasingly dependent upon Macao to supply the annual galleons with their cargos for Mexico. Macao, in its turn, came increasingly to rely upon Manila for its trade once the Dutch began to menace the shipping lanes between Malacca and Macao. The Portuguese merchants took advantage of their middleman position to exact higher prices from the Spanish than the Chinese had customarily charged. Wearying of the Portuguese exactions, the Manileños repeatedly petitioned the crown to take action to prevent the impoverishment of their city. Finally, in 1636 the connection between Macao and Manila was officially severed by royal decree; nonetheless, a clandestine trade continued until 1640, when Macao regained its independence and began to war with Manila. [109] Portuguese ships from Macao did not return to Manila again until 1670, or until after the civil wars had ended both in China and in Iberia. At this same time, the Portuguese sent a mission to Peking in the hope of working out better trading conditions in China. Although the mission failed, the Portuguese continued nonetheless to bring "China goods" to Manila. But they were not again to enjoy a monopoly position, for now they were in constant competition with a growing number of Chinese junks.

Tokugawa Ieyasu, upon coming to power in Japan in 1598, began to resent Macao's intermediary role in Japan's foreign trade and let the Manileños know that he wanted to trade directly with them. Two years later, ten Japa-

---

[109] See *ibid.*, pp. 132–33. *Cf.* William S. Atwell, "International Bullion Flows and the Chinese Economy circa 1530–1650," *Past and Present*, XCV (1982), 68–90. Atwell sees the Chinese economy as being almost entirely dependent on foreign silver. The break in trade with Japan and the cessation of the Manila-Macao trade were decisive factors in the monetary crisis that led to the fall of the Ming dynasty. Atwell's argument is questionable, however, since Dutch exports of silver from Japan were at their peak in 1640. See Kato, *loc. cit.* (n. 28), p. 224.

nese trading junks appeared at Manila carrying a letter from Ieyasu requesting direct trade between Japan and New Spain. While this proposition was being considered, a direct trade between Nagasaki and Manila developed, much to the consternation of Macao. Beginning in 1608, annual ships went from Manila to Uraga, but the Spanish did nothing officially to promote a direct trade between Japan and Mexico. In 1610, a Japanese vessel built by Will Adams sailed directly to Mexico on the pretext of returning ex-governor Don Rodrigo de Vivero, whose ship had been wrecked off Japan in 1609.[110] Another Japanese vessel arrived in Mexico during 1612 with Friar Luis Sotelo aboard and the Japanese embassy destined for Europe.[111] The embassy's failure to persuade the Spanish to give up their monopoly of the trans-Pacific trade was a factor in bringing about the closure of Japan to the Spanish in 1624. Over the period from 1603 to 1617, a total of 126 voyages had been made between Japan and the Spanish colonies, 5 of which were trans-Pacific voyages. About two thousand Japanese resided in Manila when the trade ceased. The commerce between Manila and Nagasaki had consisted mainly of supplies and Japanese art objects for Manila, and raw silk and other Chinese products for Japan. The Japanese, who were exporters of silver and copper, were naturally not interested in importing precious metals.[112]

Like Macao and Japan, the Moluccas constituted a source of friction between the Spanish and Portuguese as well as a battleground between the Iberians and the northern Europeans. Shortly after the union of the two crowns, the Spanish had begun helping the Portuguese to pacify the Moluccas, for the government in Manila hoped to make the spice trade a profitable adjunct to the China trade. The appearance of the English and Dutch also forced the Spanish and Portuguese to cooperate in holding and exploiting the Spice Islands. The reconquest of the islands in 1606 by an allied expeditionary force from Manila was followed by a new political and commercial dispensation in the Moluccas. In 1612, the government of the Moluccas and the responsibility for its military protection were placed under the jurisdiction of Manila. The Portuguese, who required the resources of the Moluccas to maintain their Asian empire, continued to enjoy officially a monopoly of the spice trade. Don Gerónimo da Silva, an experienced soldier, was named governor of the Moluccas with his headquarters on the island of Ter-

[110] J. L. Alvarez, "Don Rodrigo de Vivero et la destruction de la Nao Madre de Deus, 1609," *Monumenta Nipponica*, II (1939), 479–511.

[111] See below, pp. 210–12.

[112] See Boxer, *op. cit.* (n. 41), pp. 301–2; on the Japanese background see N. Murakami, "Japan's Early Attempts to Establish Commercial Relations with Mexico," in H. M. Stephens and H. E. Bolton (eds.) *The Pacific Ocean in History* (New York, 1917), pp. 467–80; for the figures on the voyages see E. Sola, "Notas sobre el comercio Hispano-Japonés en los siglos XVI y XVII," *Hispania*, XXXIII (1973), 274–77. For documents relating to the trade and the embassy to Europe see A. N. Ortega, "Noticia entre Mexico y el Japon, durante el siglo XVII," *Archivo histórico diplomático Mexicano*, No. 2 (1923).

nate. In one of his first reports to Philip III, Silva observed that an abundance of cloves existed in the islands and suggested that they be sold in Manila to offset the cost of maintaining the ships and the garrison in the islands.[113] This was but the first of many complaints to the king about the injustice of requiring Manila to maintain and defend the Moluccas while the Portuguese were permitted to reap the economic benefits of the clove trade. By 1640 the Moluccas cost Manila almost all the subsidy the Philippine government received annually from New Spain.[114] Defense of the Moluccas also tied down ships and soldiers that might have been used for Manila's attacks upon the Moros.

Manila was prohibited by a decree of 1607 to export cloves directly to America. But the city acted as an entrepôt in the clove trade of Asia; Portuguese and Asians frequently came there from Macao, Malacca, and Goa to purchase fine spices. The galleon carried illicit cloves to New Spain from time to time, but most of the spices sold in Mexico came via Europe until the dissolution of the union in 1640. Thereafter the Spanish competed with the Dutch for the spice trade but without much success. They collected cloves at Ternate and marketed them at Manila, mostly to Asian customers, it appears. Although the Spanish stubbornly fought the Dutch in the Moluccas, they finally abandoned Ternate in 1662 as part of their preparations to defend Manila from the expected onslaught of Koxinga, which never came.[115] Hereafter the Spanish, like others, bought most of their fine spices from the Dutch.

The galleon commerce between Manila and Acapulco which went on with remarkable regularity from 1565 to 1815 was always more of a silk than a spice trade.[116] From 1604 to 1620, the Portuguese and the Chinese supplied Manila with constantly increasing amounts of silk fabrics. In these years of its prosperity the "*náo de China*," as the galleon was called, was a ship of about one thousand tons constructed of Philippine hardwood (*molave*). Most of them were built at Cavite by Filipino laborers. The cargo, mostly of Chinese silks, was restricted to what could be bought at Manila for no more than a total of 250,000 Mexican or Peruvian pesos; in Acapulco

---

[113] Letter of April 13, 1612, published in *Correspondencia de Don Geronimo de Silva, 1612–17* in *Colección de documentos ineditos para la historia de España* (113 vols., Madrid, 1842–1912), III, 5–15. Many of the letters in this collection relate to the Moluccas; they have not been generally used as sources so far as we have been able to determine.

[114] See Schurz, *op. cit.* (n. 49), pp. 140–41.

[115] The best Spanish sources for the commerce of the Philippines are the two memorials of 1637 and 1640 by Juan Grau y Montfalcon. The first is translated into English in E. H. Blair and J. A. Robertson (eds.), *The Philippine Islands* (55 vols., Cleveland, 1905–9), XXVII, 55–212.

[116] See P. Chaunu, "Le Galion de Manile, grandeur et décadence d'une route de la soie," *Annales*. E. S. C., VI (1951), 447–62; and C. R. Boxer, "Manila Galleon 1565–1815," *History Today*, VIII (1958), 538–47; on Spanish shipping in general see A. P. Usher, "Spanish Ships and Shipping in the Sixteenth and Seventeenth Centuries," in *Facts and Factors in Economic History* (Cambridge, Mass., 1932), pp. 189–213.

this cargo had a sales value of double that amount. Many of the galleons carried to Mexico much more than they were legally permitted. The cargo space, divided theoretically into four thousand packages, was alloted annually by a committee to the citizens and religious orders of Manila. The ships leaving Acapulco normally had an easy three months' voyage if they sailed in the period from March to June; ordinarily they left Manila in June or July for an arduous return voyage of no fewer than six months.

In Spain, the crown was under severe and regular pressure by the mercantilist communities of Seville and Lisbon to limit the galleon trade. The bullionists of both cities deplored the large amounts of American treasure which were being diverted from Europe to Asia, sometimes as much as two to four million pesos annually, to maintain the Philippines, the missions, and the silk trade.[117] The silk producers of Spain and Mexico feared the competition of Chinese materials; indeed, the Mexican industry of silk raising was eventually killed by the Chinese competition. The crown had but two choices: withdraw from the Philippines or limit the amount of treasure committed to the colony and its trade. The religious orders in Europe and throughout the empire opposed vigorously and successfully the abandonment of the Philippines. Badgered from all sides, the crown tried from 1590 onward to limit the trade by restricting the numbers, tonnage, and cargoes of the galleons. To halt the flow of treasure from Peru to pay for Chinese goods, the crown in 1631 prohibited all trade between Mexico and Peru.[118] These measures failed so miserably that in 1635 Pedro de Quiroga was sent to Acapulco to oversee the enforcement of the many restrictions on the trade. In Manila the merchants responded by refusing to provide cargoes for the next three annual voyages. This crisis was followed in 1640 by the Portuguese revolt and the severing of commercial ties between Macao and Manila, an event which enabled the Dutch and English to participate more fully in the silk trade. Portuguese secession also brought an end to the close commercial relations between the Portuguese and Seville, where the Portuguese had maintained a prosperous colony of two thousand merchants.[119]

Both Manila and its galleons weathered these storms, and so the silk trade over the Pacific continued throughout the remainder of the century. The exchange of products from China for precious metals from America continued to dominate commercial activity at Manila. Indeed, the economy of the entire trading region (Philippines, Japan, Taiwan, Macao, and the Moluccas) continued to react sensitively to events in China. A record level of imports from China entered Manila in 1611–12; a nadir was reached in 1671–75.

---

[117] See C. R. Boxer, "*Plata es Sangre:* Sidelights on the Drain of Spanish-American Silver in the Far East, 1550–1700," *Philippine Studies,* XVIII, No. 3 (July, 1970); see also Atwell, *loc. cit.* (n. 109), pp. 72–74 for the size of the silver shipments from Acapulco.

[118] W. Borah, *Early Colonial Trade and Navigation between Mexico and Peru,* No. 38 of *Ibero-Americana* (Berkeley, 1954), p. 127.

[119] See Juan Regla, "Spain and Her Empire," in *The New Cambridge Modern History* (Cambridge, 1961), V, 375.

The decline of China imports after 1650 reflects in part the appearance at Manila of merchants who brought competitive textiles from India into the galleon trade. The Manila-Madras trade was carried on by Armenian, Indo-Portuguese, English, and Spanish merchants and consisted of an exchange of piece-goods and saltpeter for Spanish silver.[120] Manila was the only East Asian mart which brought together the goods of Spanish America, Ch'ing China, and Mughul India. For Spain, the maintenance of the galleon trade involved heavy outlays of silver and gold throughout the seventeenth century, primarily for the expenses of the military and naval forces needed to protect the Philippines. These expenditures, when added to the precious metals shipped to the East by the Cape route, possibly cost Spain more than one-third of the total contemporary American production of precious metals.[121] Throughout the East, except for a few places in south India, the Spanish silver real remained the major medium of exchange and unit of account in international trade over the entire seventeenth century. In Spain itself, the precious metals were driven out of circulation after 1625 by vellon, a cumbersome and unstable medium of exchange of copper, or of copper and silver.[122] This debasement of Spain's coinage contributed to a monetary disorder that helped produce the economic chaos that characterized Spain in its years of decline.

Though there were those in Spain who proposed after 1640 the establishment of direct trade between Cadiz and Manila via the Cape route, nothing came of these suggestions, and the Philippines were increasingly left to fend for themselves. Shipments of silk from Mexico to Spain ceased altogether. In 1658, Magino Sola, a Jesuit, was sent to Madrid as procurator for the Philippines with instructions to inform the king of the sorry state of Manila's economy.[123] In his memorial of 1660, Sola claimed that the galleon trade, which had suffered interruptions since 1635, had to be revived if Manila were to endure and that troops, colonists and professional men needed to be sent to its succor. Opposed by the textile manufacturers at home, these and other pleas from Manila were ignored. In the latter years of the century, the galleon trade was reduced to an intercolonial trade between Manila and Acapulco dominated by a small body of professional merchants on both sides of the Pacific. The armed forces were neglected and the few replacements sent were inexperienced soldiers and sailors from Mexico. Still the galleon trade, reduced as it was to what Mexico could absorb, remained sufficiently profitable to keep Manila prosperous and strong enough to be

[120] See S. D. Quiason, *English "Country Trade" with the Philippines* (Quezon City, 1966), chaps. i–iii. For a list of the twenty-five voyages made from 1674 to 1706 see pp. 43–44.

[121] Based on P. Chaunu, *Les Philippines et le Pacifique des Ibériques (XVIe, XVIIe, XVIIIe siècles)* (Paris, 1960), pp. 252–53, 266–69.

[122] See E. J. Hamilton, *War and Prices in Spain, 1651–1800* (Cambridge, Mass., 1947), p. 10. On the Spanish government's short-sighted policy of minting grossly overvalued copper vellon, see Boyajian, *op. cit.* (n. 20), pp. 40, 170.

[123] See H. de la Costa, *op. cit.* (n. 39), pp. 414–16.

commercially active and politically free for the remainder of the seventeenth century.

3

THE DUTCH EMPIRE

For the Dutch, the seventeenth century was a golden age of economic prosperity at home and of expanding influence throughout the world. Amsterdam had replaced Antwerp by 1600 as the commercial and cultural capital of the Netherlands. The Eighty Years' War (1568–1648) with Spain was the great catalyst in which the transformation took place. It disrupted existing institutions and trading patterns and forced the Dutch to political, commercial, and maritime innovation. The seven northern provinces, or the United Provinces, led the resistance to Spain and profited most from the victories. Once they had seceded from Spain, the Dutch created their own kind of oligarchic republic. Holland and Zeeland, the two provinces most involved in maritime activity, dominated the evolution of the Dutch nation. Their mariners and merchants were active participants in commerce and fishing in the Atlantic and the Baltic before the Eighty Years' War began. Once continuous war broke out in 1572, the mariners and merchants led the fight and gradually assumed political and economic power within the independent provinces and the town councils; staunchly they opposed Catholicism as much as they did Spain and militantly promoted Calvinism in the republic. Although the Calvinists never became the majority, they did begin rapidly to dominate government and trade. Municipal and other governmental offices were reserved to those professing orthodox Calvinism. These officials soon formed a self-perpetuating oligarchy which excluded all others from participating in government and left control of the republic in the hands of some two thousand upper-middle-class Calvinists. The States General, the only national administrative body, was an assembly of delegates from the seven sovereign provinces that met at The Hague. The delegates were closely bound by the instructions of their provincial assemblies. Leadership in the States General was assumed intermittently by the representatives of Holland, the wealthiest province, and by the House of Orange, whose prince commanded the armed forces. Amsterdam through its highest official, the Pensionary, dominated both the province of Holland and the States General. Serious confrontations usually occurred when the princes of Orange rallied the other provinces to challenge the predominance of Amsterdam and Holland.[124]

---

[124] Based on C. R. Boxer, *The Dutch Seaborne Empire, 1600–1800* (London, 1965), pp. 4–19. On the gradual and incomplete domination of government and trade by Orthodox Calvinists,

Amsterdam's ascendancy within the republic was based on its rapid growth as an international trade center second to none in Europe. Its population which numbered less than forty thousand in 1514 had more than doubled by 1600; over the course of the seventeenth century it doubled again to reach about two hundred thousand.[125] The metropolitan region of Amsterdam, one of Europe's most densely populated centers, included within a radius of twenty-one miles eight major cities: Amsterdam, Leyden, Haarlem, Utrecht, Gouda, Delft, Rotterdam, and The Hague; by the 1620's a full 60 percent of the United Provinces' population lived in towns.[126] The banks, mints, and marine insurance chambers of the major towns provided the capital and the financial facilities required for the expansion of trade. The port of Amsterdam was modified and enlarged, and a pattern for the city's development, a plan for three rings of additional canals, was announced in 1607 to encourage internal growth away from its busy harbor.[127]

Dutch seaborne traffic profited in the 1590's from the invention of the fly-boat (*fluit*), a cargo vessel that could be built cheaply in large numbers and manned by relatively few sailors.[128] Since the fly-boats ordinarily mounted no guns, they had to move under convoy of naval vessels. The Dutch navy, which had not existed in 1568, had become a menacing threat by 1600 to the Spanish and Portuguese fleets in the Atlantic and in Eastern seas. In European waters, the Dutch merchant marine swiftly began to usurp the carrying trade from the Baltic to the Mediterranean. Dutch bottoms carried the grain and timber of the north, English woolens, and salt of the south to exchange ports on the Atlantic seaboard. Despite wartime prohibitions and financial risk, direct trade with Iberia became constantly greater after 1580. In cooperation with Germans and with Portuguese New Christians, the Dutch also began to trade directly with Brazil shortly after the turn of the century.[129] The precious metals of the New World, imported directly or purchased in Europe, provided them with their coinage and added substantially to their ability to trade in Asia at a profit.

---

many of whom were wealthy southern immigrants, see C. Bangs, "Dutch Theology, Trade, and War, 1590–1610," *Church History,* XXXIX (1970), 470–82.

[125] For a comparison of Amsterdam's population to that of other European cities see the table in R. Mols, S.J., "Population in Europe, 1500–1700," in E. M. Cippola (ed.), *The Sixteenth and Seventeenth Centuries,* Vol. II of *The Fontana Economic History of Europe* (London, 1977), pp. 42–43. Also see J. de Vries, *European Urbanization, 1500–1800* (Cambridge, Mass., 1984), pp. 140–41, 271.

[126] See P. Clark (ed.), *The Early Modern Town, A Reader* (London, 1976), p. 2.

[127] See J. W. Konvitz, *Cities and the Sea. Port City Planning in Early Modern Europe* (Baltimore, 1978), pp. 34–36. On Amsterdam as the financial capital of Europe see Braudel, *op. cit.* (n. 75), III, 236–45.

[128] See Braudel, *op. cit.* (n. 75). III, 190–93 on the lower costs to build and maintain ships and on the lower costs for labor in the Netherlands.

[129] On the Portuguese New Christian merchants and bankers at Amsterdam, their "New Jerusalem," see A. Castillo, "Dans la monarchie espagnole du XVIIe siècle; les banquiers portugais et le circuit d'Amsterdam," *Annales. E. S. C.,* XIX (1964), 311–16.

Once they had successfully turned back the land forces of Spain and had witnessed the defeat of Philip's Armada in 1588, the Dutch rapidly expanded their trade in the South Atlantic, the Mediterranean, and the Levant. Since the spice and bullion markets of Atlantic Europe were controlled by Spain, the Dutch had access to them only by trading in contraband, a precarious activity at best and one which could always be halted by a well-enforced embargo. The uncertainty about getting spices through Iberia led the Dutch to examine the possibility of sailing directly to the East in their own vessels. In 1592 Cornelis de Houtman was sent to Lisbon to investigate the conduct of the spice trade and returned two years later urging the dispatch of direct voyages to the East.[130] Information on conditions in the Portuguese East, relayed to the Dutch mercantile community by Jan Huyghen van Linschoten on his return to Enkhuizen in 1592, also helped to inspire the creation in 1594 of the "Company of Distant Lands," an organization founded by nine merchants to dispatch two voyages directly to the East in defiance of the Portuguese monopoly. Contemporaneously a special map of the Moluccas, based on the Portuguese charts of Bartolomeu Lasso, was published at Amsterdam by Petrus Plancius (1552–1622), an eminent Dutch theologian and geographer.[131] While the Dutch merchants were outfitting their fleets, Linschoten published in 1595 his *Reysgheschrift,* a set of detailed sailing instructions for the Cape route to Asia culled from Portuguese rutters.

The fleet of Cornelis de Houtman which sailed from Amsterdam in April, 1595, was guided to the East by a manuscript copy of the *Reysgheschrift.*[132] In his *Itinerario* (1596) Linschoten advised the Dutch, as he must have done orally before this work was printed, that the Portuguese empire in the East was a decaying structure and that the Portuguese were powerless to stop the Dutch from voyaging to the East. He counseled them to avoid the west coast of India, Malacca, and the other centers of Portuguese power and to sail directly to Java where the Portuguese possessed very little strength. De Houtman heeded this advice and cruised about in the seas of the Malay-Indonesian region for eight months without being discovered by the Portuguese. De Houtman's fleet returned in August, 1597, with a small cargo of pepper purchased at Bantam. Its success, though slight in financial returns, was heralded in the published descriptions of the voyage which quickly appeared.[133] Most impressive to contemporaries was the simple fact that this

---

[130] See G. Masselman, *The Cradle of Colonialism* (New Haven, 1963), p. 86.

[131] See J. Keuning, "Sixteenth-Century Cartography in the Netherlands," *Imago Mundi,* IX (1952), 59–60.

[132] For a comprehensive list of all Dutch ships that sailed for Asia from 1595 to 1794 see, J. R. Bruijn, F. S. Gaastra, and I. Schöffer (eds.), *Dutch-Asiatic Shipping in the Seventeenth and Eighteenth Centuries,* Vol. II: *Out-bound Voyages from the Netherlands to Asia and the Cape,* and Vol. III: *Homeward-bound Voyages from Asia and the Cape to the Netherlands* (Rijks Geschiedkundige Publicatien 166, 167; The Hague, 1979).

[133] For a detailed bibliographical rundown see below, pp. 437–39.

pioneer voyage proved that the Dutch might safely breach the Portuguese monopoly and establish a direct commerce with the East Indies.

New trading conglomerates and companies popped up like mushrooms in the United Provinces. In 1598 five different companies dispatched no fewer than twenty-two ships to the East. One of the fleets, commanded by Olivier van Noort of Rotterdam, took the route around South America across the Pacific and around the Cape, to make the first Dutch circumnavigation of the world. The fleet of Jacob van Neck, which followed the Cape route both going and coming back, returned in July, 1599, with a rich cargo of spices that netted the investors a neat 300 percent return on their money.[134] Stimulated by this financial windfall, Dutch investors plunged heavily into this new enterprise. In 1601 fourteen fleets or a total of sixty-five ships sailed for the East Indies. But none of these voyages realized the great financial success of Van Neck's first venture. The pre-companies competed with one another as well as with the Portuguese in Europe and Asia. Their competition in the marts of Java helped to raise the purchase price and to deplete the available stocks of pepper. Individually the pre-companies were not powerful enough to protect themselves for long against the Iberian response to their invasion of the East. Clearly it had come to be in the interest of the pioneer companies, their investors, and the Dutch state to halt the cutthroat competition by molding the contending companies into a single corporation. The English, it was known, had successfully organized a single chartered Company in 1600 to trade in the Indies.

From the fifteen fleets sent to the East between 1598 and 1602, the date of the formation of the United East India Company, the Dutch had learned much more about the East and its sea routes than could be found in Linschoten's *Itinerario*.[135] The pre-Company voyages had left factors behind in Bantam, in the Malay peninsula, and in the Moluccas, to collect cargoes for the fleets. Permanent trading factories were necessary to collect cargoes ahead of time, for when the ships arrived from Europe the local stocks were quickly depleted and the prices painfully high.

The early Dutch voyagers had occupied Mauritius Island as a launching point in the Indian Ocean on their way from Madagascar to the Sunda Strait, a southerly route which avoided the Portuguese strongholds but which had many hardships and dangers of its own.[136] They had violated

---

[134] For the financial results of this most successful of the pre-Company voyages, as well as the fourteen other less fortunate ones, see Hans den Haan, *Moedernegotie en grote vaart, een studie over de expansie van het Hollandse handelskapitaal in de 16- en 17- eeuw* (Amsterdam, 1977), p. 112.

[135] For a neat table of the voyages see R. Bonaparte, "Les premiers voyages des Neerlandais dans l'Insulinde, 1595–1602," *Revue de géographie*, XIV, Pt. 2 (1884), 55. See below, pp. 437–44 for a review of the contemporary materials published on these early voyages.

[136] See G. Schilder, *op. cit.* (n. 7), p. 54. The Dutch discovery of the westerly winds blowing across the southern edge of the Indian Ocean was an enduring contribution to world sea routes. J. R. Bruijn, "Between Batavia and the Cape: Shipping Patterns of the Dutch East India Company," *Journal of Southeast Asian Studies*, XI (1980), 251–65.

Spain's monopoly of the Pacific and by this route one ship, the "Liefde," had reached Japan in 1600; others from the West soon appeared at the entrance to Manila Bay and at Brunei in Borneo. Joris van Spilbergen's fleet of three ships had left Zeeland in 1601, and by the following year he had negotiated a treaty with the king of Kandy in Ceylon. From there he had sailed to Acheh on the northern tip of Sumatra to negotiate with its ruler and to cruise around Malacca in search of Portuguese ships. In short, the pre-Company voyagers had reconnoitered the Iberian empire at its southern and eastern extremities and had begun to poke at its soft underbelly from Mozambique to the Philippines. By concentrating on the southern route and by basing themselves in Java, the Dutch soon acquired a strong strategic position, not dependent on the monsoons, from which they could function effectively at all times of the year.[137]

Even before the Dutch fleets left for the East in 1598, the leaders of the States General had urged the competing merchants to avoid conflicts in the Indies and to cooperate with one another to realize the common aspiration of defeating the Iberians, of establishing direct trade with the Indies, and of reaping rich financial rewards. In 1600 Jan van Oldenbarneveldt, Advocate or Grand Pensionary of Holland, persuaded the Estates of Holland to take the lead in bringing the companies together to form a national monopoly. A commission was formed in Holland which prepared a report in 1601 advocating the creation of a new Company which should include all the existing ones. Bitter resistance came from the merchants of Zeeland to Holland's proposal. Nevertheless, formal discussions on uniting the various East India companies into one began in the States General in 1601. After a series of acrimonious debates, Maurice of Nassau, the prince of Orange, joined forces with Oldenbarneveldt to end the contention and to consolidate the country. The States General on March 20, 1602, passed a resolution to amalgamate the existing companies into a single monopolistic corporation called the United Netherlands Chartered East India Company (abbreviated VOC, for *Vereenigde Oostindische Compagnie,* and known less formally, in English, as Jan Company).[138]

Granted for twenty-one years, the charter endowed the VOC with a monopoly of Dutch trade and traffic east of the Cape of Good Hope and west of the Straits of Magellan, or in that portion of the world's surface claimed by the Iberians as their monopoly. Within this demarcation the Company,

[137] See Meilinck-Roelofsz, *op. cit.* (n. 83), p. 182.
[138] The standard account of the pre-companies and of the founding of the VOC is in F. W. Stapel (ed.), *Geschidenis van Nederlandsch Indië* (5 vols., Amsterdam, 1938–40), II, 275–475; III, 5–44. Stapel had earlier edited and annotated the basic history of the VOC prepared by Pieter van Dam, the advocate of the VOC from 1652 to 1706. Based on the Company's secret papers and archives, Van Dam's *Beschryvinge van De Oost-indische Compagnie* remained unpublished until the Commission for National Historical Publications entrusted to Stapel its preparation for the press. It finally appeared in four volumes at Amsterdam in 1927 and 1929. For a more detailed bibliographical discussion see W. Ph. Coolhaas, *A Critical Survey of Studies on Dutch Colonial History* (The Hague, 1960), pp. 21, 25–26.

being confronted by the certain opposition of Spain and Portugal, was granted authority to wage defensive war, negotiate treaties of peace and alliance in the name of the States General, and build fortresses. Civilian, naval, and military personnel could also be enlisted by the Company. At home the Company was established as a union of six chambers—Amsterdam, Zeeland, Rotterdam, Delft, Hoorn, and Enkhuizen—governed by seventeen directors (*de Heeren XVII*) who sat alternately at Amsterdam for four years and at Middelburg for two years. Eight of the directors were to be from Amsterdam, four from Zeeland, and five from the four other chambers. The chambers endowed the VOC with an initial capital of about 6.5 million guilders, more than half of which Amsterdam provided.[139] Investment was open to all, and subscriptions came into the chambers from all over the Netherlands and even from abroad, some very small and others huge; enthusiasm for the new venture ran high because of the substantial profits won by certain of the pre-Company voyages. Constituted virtually as a state within the state, the VOC quickly became a powerful economic and political force in the Netherlands. Like other Dutch oligarchies of the seventeenth century, its governing board (the Seventeen) progressively came to be dominated by the wealthiest merchants of Amsterdam, its most important stockholders.[140]

Since the VOC was empowered to extend the war against the Iberians into Asia, maritime war became part of trading.[141] Although the government was supposed to keep out of Company matters, it generally supported the VOC in conflicts with foreigners. A minority of Netherlanders continued, even after the formation of the Company, to oppose a policy which linked trade to war. As part of the transition from private enterprise to the assumption of the monopoly by the VOC, Admiral Wybrand van Warwijck in 1602 headed a joint expedition of fourteen vessels prepared by the pre-companies on their own initiative and for their own profit. Van Warwijck was ordered by the VOC to seek out the most reliable spice marts and to find a good place for a permanent headquarters in the East. In addition to laying the foundations for Dutch power in the East, Van Warwijck brought his investors a profit of 165 percent on their capital, half of which came from the spoils of war.[142] Profits of this size helped to ease the pangs of conscience experienced by those investors who opposed linking trade to war.

The fleets sent out immediately after 1602 followed the lines laid down by

[139] For the original subscription figures see Stapel (ed.), *op. cit.* (n. 138), III, 28. On the advantages and liabilities of the decentralized structure of the VOC see F. Gaastra, *loc. cit.* (n. 28), pp. 51–52.

[140] On the investments of the Amsterdam elite in the VOC see P. Burke, *Venice and Amsterdam: A Study of Seventeenth-Century Elites* (London, 1974), p. 58.

[141] For a contemporary description of a sea fight of 1602 between the Dutch and the Portuguese in the East Indies see *A True and Perfect Relation* . . . (London, 1603) as reprinted in B. Penrose, *Sea Fights in the East Indies in the Years 1602–1639* (Cambridge, Mass., 1931), pp. 43–51.

[142] For details on this extraordinary expedition see Stapel (ed.), *op. cit.* (n. 138), III, 30–41.

the pre-Company voyages. Their commanders sought allies in Ceylon and Sumatra, loaded cargoes of pepper at Bantam, and explored the possibilities of direct trade with China and the Moluccas. They quickly learned that prospects were poor for immediate direct trading relations with Ceylon and China. The VOC's first fleet sailed for the East in December, 1603, and included thirteen heavily armed vessels that carried about twelve hundred men. Its commander, Steven van der Hagen, was under orders to intensify action against the enemy, show the flag before Goa, attack Portuguese shipping, conclude agreements with the coastal states of India, endeavor to take Malacca, and uproot the Spanish in the Moluccas. Within less than two years (December, 1604–July, 1606) Van der Hagen reconnoitered the west coast of India as far north as Gujarat and concluded a friendship treaty with Calicut. He defeated the Portuguese at Amboina (1605), placed the island under Dutch administration, and worked out an agreement with its ruler to sell cloves only to the VOC. He also punished the Spanish at Tidore while making a treaty with Banda. In short, he laid the groundwork on which his successors would erect the Dutch edifice of trade by forced agreements and treaties. From the Spice Islands, Van der Hagen returned to Bantam, where he took on a substantial cargo for Holland. He also brought home valuable information on the interregional trade of Asia, particularly on the importance of Indian textiles to the commerce with Malaya and Indonesia.[143]

The Portuguese, after having established a margin of naval superiority in the East, had become accustomed by the late sixteenth century to trade in peace and mostly with unarmed ships. The first Dutch forays in the East therefore benefited from an element of surprise as well as from superior naval equipment and tactics and larger numbers of better-trained sailors and soldiers.[144] The relatively small Dutch ships were fast and maneuverable and adapted well to coastal sailing and fighting. They were provided with heavy artillery superior both in number and caliber to those carried on the Iberian vessels. Their commanders preferred to fight long-range artillery duels with the Portuguese ships and fortresses and to avoid boarding tactics and frontal attacks on fortified emplacements. From the outset it became clear that the heavier armament, superior organization, and better seamanship of the Dutch gave them a decisive edge in naval warfare and in controlling the sea-lanes of the East.

Still the fleet of eleven ships commanded by Cornelis Matelief that left Europe in May, 1605, met stubborn resistance at the Portuguese outposts. It besieged Malacca unsuccessfully in 1606 and failed to dislodge the Iberians from the Moluccas.[145] From the Spiceries it sailed to the China coast, but

---

[143] Based on Masselman, *op. cit.* (n. 130), pp. 163–66.

[144] The Dutch sent an estimated five thousand men a year to Asia, which gave them a much larger active population in Asia. See Braudel, *op. cit.* (n. 75), III, 224–25.

[145] For the Dutch siege of Malacca see *An Historical and True Discourse . . .* (London, 1608) as reprinted in Penrose, *op. cit.* (n. 141), pp. 55–85.

Matelief failed to establish there the trade relations Amsterdam was demanding. On returning to Bantam, Matelief learned that the English had begun activities in the Spiceries. Despite his disappointing performance and the bad news he brought back, Matelief was publicly thanked by Oldenbarneveldt and Prince Maurice when he returned home in September, 1608.

For the United Provinces the VOC had meanwhile become a powerful economic and political force and a new weapon in the Dutch war against Spain. While Matelief besieged Malacca, the States General in 1606, under pressure from the VOC and other mercantile interests, launched an attack against the Iberian vessels in European waters, especially the silver fleets from America. When the Dutch audaciously attacked and defeated a larger Spanish fleet near Gibraltar in 1607, the government in Madrid made peace overtures. Secret negotiations were carried on for the next two years that led to the conclusion of the Twelve Years' Truce of 1609. Although Prince Maurice, the VOC and other merchants, and influential Orthodox Calvinists opposed the truce, the peace party of Oldenbarneveldt won the day because of the threatening conditions in Europe and the East. Dutch armies were bogged down in Flanders, pepper prices were falling sharply, no dividends were being paid, the Spanish had beaten the Dutch in the Philippines and the Moluccas, and King Henry IV of France was trying with the aid of Dutch and Flemish renegades to form his own East India Company. A respite was needed, in Oldenbarneveldt's view, to resolve the growing internal conflicts over religion, politics, and trade and to reinforce the international position of the United Provinces.

By the time the truce was concluded, the Dutch had won some important victories in their attacks upon the Portuguese centers in Asia, but had had less success in their forays against the Spanish. Dutch traders had obtained a foothold at Patani on the east coast of the Malay Peninsula in 1601, and from there they soon penetrated Siam. Both of these were exchange areas for Japanese and Chinese goods; Patani was a dependency of Siam, and Siam a vassal of China. Two ambassadors were dispatched to Europe from Ayut'ia, Siam's capital; after many delays they finally arrived in Holland during September, 1608. Although they were well received and remained until January 30, 1610, the Siamese emissaries apparently accomplished little. At any rate, the Dutch failed to obtain the direct connection with the China trade that they had hoped to work out through Siam. A bilateral exchange with Siam, involving as it did a trade in European produce for hides and pepper, was certainly not as attractive to the VOC as a brisk commerce in Chinese products would have been.[146]

---

[146] See P. Pelliot, "Les relations du Siam et de la Hollande en 1608," *T'oung Pao,* 2d ser., XXXII (1936), 223–29; and J. J. L. Duyvendak, "The First Siamese Embassy to Holland," *ibid.,* 286–92. Braudel, *op. cit.* (n. 75), III, 219–20 mentions the Dutch having an exclusive privilege of producing pewter which they sold as far away as Europe. Deer pelts were sold in Japan.

The lure of the China trade magnetized the Dutch from the beginning. Upon their first arrival in the East they had contacts with Chinese merchants at Bantam, Patani, and many other Eastern marts. Here they also met merchants from Japan, some of whom were Christian converts of the Jesuits. At Ayut'ia the Japanese had a settlement of their own between 1605 and 1610.[147] Mostly the overseas Japanese and Chinese were hostile to the Dutch. In their eagerness to win direct trade with the East Asian countries, the Dutch made forays in all directions, particularly against the Iberian footholds. They explored the coasts of continental Southeast Asia, attacked Macao and Manila, and they were the ones to actually discover Australia in 1605, when Quiros was just setting out from Peru. Increasingly they sought battles with their opponents as they abandoned their earlier policy of avoiding the Iberian routes and outposts.

Because they needed the cloth of Coromandel to barter in Indonesia, the Dutch established factories in the ports of the Indian state of Golconda in 1605.[148] By 1606 a Dutch post was also established in northwestern India at Surat in Gujarat to purchase cotton cloths and indigo.[149] In 1608 the VOC sent a yacht to the East to announce the imminence of the truce with Spain and to urge the immediate conclusion of treaties with the rulers of the East who did not yet have official relations with the VOC. Again failing to crack the Portuguese barrier of Macao, the Dutch proceeded to Japan and in July, 1609, worked out an arrangement for a Dutch factory at Hirado. In the next month a treaty was signed with Banda in the Moluccas, and the nearby island of Banda-Neira was annexed. So, by the time the truce was concluded in Europe in April, 1609, the Dutch had won or were winning footholds in most of the Eastern trading regions. Their spectacular successes in inflicting losses on Portuguese shipping and naval power were counterbalanced, however, by their failure to conquer the Iberian strongholds of Goa, Malacca, Manila, Ternate, and Macao.

Naval successes in Asia provided great satisfaction to the States General. More dubious from the stockholders' viewpoint were the economic results of the VOC's activities. From 1606 to 1609 profits fell from 75 percent to 25 percent.[150] To remedy this situation and to strengthen the VOC's position in the East the Seventeen, in consultation with the States General, decided in 1609 to overhaul the VOC's administration. The practice of having the last arriving admiral take over immediately from his predecessor was blamed

---

[147] See E. W. Hutchinson, *Adventurers in Siam in the Seventeenth Century* (London, 1940), p. 27.

[148] Golconda's port was Masulipatam. Until the Dutch came there its foreign trade was controlled by Persian merchants. See Shah Manzoar Alam, "Masulipatam, a Metropolitan Port in the Seventeenth Century, A.D.," *The Indian Geographical Journal*, XXXIV (1959), 33–42.

[149] For the history of Dutch activities at Surat see B. G. Gokhale, *Surat in the Seventeenth Century* (London, 1978), pp. 162–68, and O. P. Singh, *Surat and Its Trade in the Second Half of the Seventeenth Century* (Delhi, 1977), chap. iv.

[150] Cf. below, pp. 66–67.

for the Company's increasingly poor record in the marketplace. This arrangement, like the similar scheme followed by the Portuguese, had produced divisions of authority, mismanagement, and neglect abroad. It had failed to provide continuity and had limited administrative planning both in Europe and Asia. To make administration more rational and efficient, the Seventeen decided to appoint a governor-general of the Indies and a council of five members to command in the East. The stress in policy was changed from unrelenting warfare against the Iberians everywhere to the consolidation of government and trade at Java. While the truce of 1609 was only intermittently respected in the East, it provided the Iberians and the Dutch with an uncertain respite and an opportunity to secure more firmly their tenable footholds.[151]

Governor-General Pieter Both, a southern Netherlander who had previously served in the East, arrived at Bantam in December, 1610, accompanied by a group of colonists. The first item on his agenda was to find a new site for the colony, a headquarters that would be more secure and that had a better climate than Bantam. In 1611 he concluded an agreement with the local ruler which allowed the Dutch to establish an unfortified factory at Jakatra, a town at the mouth of the Jiliwong River whose harbor is protected by several islands. Thereafter he concentrated upon securing the Dutch outposts at the eastern end of the Indonesian archipelago. The Portuguese fortress at Solor was captured in 1613 and new contracts for spice deliveries were imposed upon a number of Moluccan rulers. Increasing English activities in Java and the Moluccas still posed an ominous threat to Dutch monopolistic efforts when Both retired from office in 1614.

Perhaps Both's signal achievement was his willingness to bring Jan Pieterszoon Coen (*ca.* 1587–1629) into his administration. As a youngster Coen had been sent to Italy in 1600 to serve a lengthy apprenticeship at Rome in bookkeeping and merchandising. He returned to his native city of Hoorn in 1607 and departed in that same year for India with the fleet of Pieter Verhoeff, the fifth sent out by the VOC. Upon arrival at Bantam in early 1609, he quickly became enmeshed in the problems of the Company. In 1610 he returned to Holland, where he submitted a report to the VOC on conditions in the East. Appointed a chief merchant, the twenty-six-year-old Coen returned to the East in 1613 and was soon elevated to the headship of the Bantam office and to the post of bookkeeper-general of the entire Dutch enterprise in Asia.[152]

In this new capacity Coen was responsible for preparing a comprehensive report on all the financial activities of the VOC in the East. But he and Governor-General Both were not content merely to report on profits and losses. They sent off to Holland in January, 1614, a *Discourse to the Honorable Directors*

---

[151] See Masselman, *op. cit.* (n. 130), p. 296; and Furber, *op. cit.* (n. 55), pp. 34–35.
[152] See Masselman, *op. cit.* (n. 130), pp. 296–306.

Touching the Netherlands Indies State which was in essence a recommendation for basic policy changes and a blueprint for empire-building. Submitted in full to the States General, the *Discourse* proposed that the Dutch in the East should move from the defensive to the offensive; the main objective of this new policy was to acquire a monopoly of the inter-Asian trade that Coen deemed potentially more profitable than the direct trade with Europe. Ruthless enforcement of the monopoly of the commerce in the fine spices would require Dutch settlers and slaves, where necessary, to make certain that the spices were produced and that the harvest was sold to Dutch merchants exclusively. A group within the Seventeen immediately supported this aggressive policy, and Coen was elevated to the Council of the Indies and appointed as second in command to Gerald Reynst, the successor to Pieter Both as governor-general.

Not everyone in Holland favored a resumption of expansion in the East. The States General, unlike the more aggressive members of the VOC, feared that conflict with the English in Asia might work to the detriment of the United Provinces in Europe. As early as 1610, the Dutch had proposed a union with the English East India Company that was turned down by the English because they feared cooperation with a richer and better-armed partner. The continuation of Anglo-Dutch conflicts in the East occasioned several colonial conferences (1613, 1615, 1618–19) at which the Dutch maintained that prior occupation and the validity of their contracts with the native rulers entitled them to exclude others. The English argued that no single nation might legally prevent any other nation from sailing the seas or participating in international trade. Finally, because their truce with Spain was to end in 1621, the Dutch agreed to an accord with the English in 1619. By its terms they conceded to the English one-third of the spice trade of the Moluccas and one-half of the pepper trade of Java. The navies of the two cooperating states were to form a "defense fleet" to protect their common interests in Asia and to harass the Iberians.[153]

While peace was being worked out on paper in Europe, hostilities continued in the East. In 1615 Coen, with Reynst's concurrence, had initiated a program designed to halt all non-Dutch trade in the waters of the Indies. A decree of the Council of the Indies in Jakatra required that all unlicensed native Asian trade should cease or run the risk of being confiscated. The English, who had many fewer ships in Asian waters than the Dutch, defied the edict of Jakatra and continued their trading in the Indonesian archipelago. The Dutch in the Moluccas, despite the truce with Spain, warred from bases on the islands of Banda and Amboina against the entrenched Spanish and Portuguese. They negotiated more monopoly contracts with the native

---

[153] See Part II (Leyden, 1951) of G. N. Clark and W. J. M. van Eysinga, *The Colonial Conferences between England and the Netherlands;* also on the London conference of 1613 see C. H. Alexandrowicz, *An Introduction to the History of the Law of Nations in the East Indies (Sixteenth, Seventeenth, and Eighteenth Centuries)* (Oxford, 1967), pp. 57–60.

rulers of the other Spice Islands. To Coen's chagrin and frustration, the Moluccan rulers often failed to abide by these extorted contracts and defiantly sold the spices to all comers after the Dutch war vessels went elsewhere. While the Accord of 1619 was being announced in Europe, open war raged in Indonesia between the Dutch and English. With its promulgation in the East, Coen, in his first term (1619–23) as governor-general, raged against the accord in his letters to Holland and tried his best to sabotage it. The only successful Anglo-Dutch venture, except for harassment of the Iberian trade, was a joint naval action of 1621 which destroyed a Portuguese fleet in the Indian Ocean.[154]

Coen and the Dutch in Asia continued after 1619 the earlier policy of conquest and monopoly, while charging the English with failure to cooperate in their program. Long frustrated by what he thought of as the perfidy of the Moluccan rulers, Coen undertook in the 1620's a series of conquests designed to assure complete Dutch control of Amboina and the Bandas. Resistance in the Bandas was crushed ruthlessly and lands were confiscated and redistributed; Dutch overseers thereafter worked them with slave labor. Recalcitrant Moluccans were carried off to Java as slaves and their chiefs were tortured and executed. The chiefs allowed to remain behind were forced to swear that they would faithfully fulfill their contracts. Repression of the local population was followed by further attacks upon the English in the islands. As incidents multiplied, the English became convinced that they would have to withdraw. Before a retreat could be effected, the Dutch governor of the Moluccas ordered the infamous "Massacre of Amboina" in March, 1623; ten Englishmen and ten Japanese mercenaries were beheaded on charges of conspiring to overthrow Dutch authority.[155]

The Dutch challenged the English in western India as well. Late in 1620, Pieter van den Broecke arrived at Surat to assume the post of "Director for Arabia, Persia, and India." Over the next eight years he strengthened the Dutch factories at Broach, Cambay, Ahmadabad, Agra, and Burhanpur in India and nurtured the burgeoning Dutch outposts in Persia. The Dutch movement into the Persian Gulf region particularly outraged the English, who were just then beginning to establish good relations with the shah. The Persians, tired of Portuguese domination of Ormuz and the Gulf, had turned to the English for naval support and for new trade outlets.[156] But the English were not destined to replace the Portuguese as monopolists of the Gulf trade. In 1623 the Dutch secured a treaty with the shah that allowed them to establish factories at Gambroon and Ispahan, to trade freely in articles not expressly forbidden, and to be exempted from tolls. The Dutch were so fa-

[154] See Furber, *op. cit.* (n. 55), p. 44.

[155] On the Dutch repressive measures see L. Kiers, *Coen op Banda, de conqueste getoest aan het recht van den tijd* (Utrecht, 1943), and D. K. Bassett, "The 'Amboina Massacre' of 1623," *Journal of Southeast Asia History*, Vol. I, No. 2 (1960), pp. 1–19.

[156] See below, pp. 76–77.

vored by the shah because they alone could supply in large quantities the fine spices wanted in exchange for Persian silks.

Coen was also determined to participate directly in the China trade and to tighten commercial ties between Japan and Batavia (the Dutch name for Ja-katra adopted in 1619). To this end the Dutch attacked and blockaded Manila, sometimes with the aid of English vessels. While successful in interrupting the trade between Manila and Macao, these efforts did not provide the Dutch with a steady supply of China goods. A direct attack upon Macao under-taken in 1622 was repelled by its Sino-Portuguese defenders and the Dutch thereafter retreated to the Pescadores Islands where they set up a base.[157] Over the following two years, Dutch vessels preyed from the Pescadores upon the coast of Fukien and successfully interrupted the Macao-Nagasaki commerce. The Chinese ordered the Dutch to evacuate the Pescadores and sent war junks and landing forces to enforce this command. Since Ming au-thority was then on the wane, especially in Fukien, the Chinese finally agreed to a compromise with the Dutch. This understanding provided that the Dutch should withdraw from the Pescadores to Taiwan and, in return, Chinese merchants should be permitted to travel to Taiwan, not then con-sidered to be an integral part of the Chinese empire, to trade with the Dutch. Even had they attempted it, the Ming authorities were probably powerless at this point to prevent the merchant-corsairs of Fukien from carrying on business with Taiwan.[158]

The appearance of the Dutch on strategically located Taiwan threatened not only Macao's trade with Japan but also Spanish and Japanese commercial security. The founding of the Dutch Castle Zeelandia on the southwestern coast of Taiwan (modern Tainan) in 1624 provoked the Spanish to establish a settlement at Keelung on the northern tip of Taiwan in 1626. Since this was just two years after their expulsion from Japan, the Spanish hoped to com-pete with the Dutch and the Portuguese for the commerce of both China and Japan from this Taiwan outpost. The Japanese, who claimed sovereignty over Taiwan, became indignant about the invasions of the Dutch and Span-ish, and particularly resentful of the treatment meted out by the Dutch to the Japanese adventurers and merchants who had been trading and settling in Taiwan for a full generation.[159] To force the Dutch to recognize its sover-eignty in Taiwan, the Japanese government in 1628 placed an embargo on trade and had the Dutch governor kidnapped. For two years thereafter the embargo remained in force. By 1634, as Japan's "closed country" policy evolved, the Japanese were forbidden to go to Taiwan, and thereafter the Dutch were left to their own devices at Castle Zeelandia.[160]

[157] For an account of this famous battle see Boxer, *op. cit.* (n. 49), pp. 105–6.

[158] See J. E. Wills, Jr., *Pepper, Guns and Parleys. The Dutch East India Company and China, 1622–81* (Cambridge, Mass., 1974), pp. 21–23.

[159] See Meilinck-Roelofsz, *op. cit.* (n. 83), p. 358, n. 37.

[160] Based on Boxer, *op. cit.* (n. 49), pp. 110–41; also see the same author's *The Christian Cen-*

The forward policy of the Dutch in the East had been planned originally by Coen. After his return home in February, 1623, it was carried on by his trusted friend Pieter de Carpentier, who served as governor-general at Batavia from 1623 to 1627. While in Holland, Coen sought to convince the Seventeen that trade could not be pursued successfully without war and that Dutch colonies should be set up in the East to harness the profitable inter-Asian trade. While his critics assailed his policies for their failure to produce higher profits, the directors acquiesced to his brutal plan for establishing and conserving a spice monopoly in the Moluccas. While the shareholders complained about the expenses of Coen's military activities, the directors urged the use of force to maintain the spice monopoly. The directors refused to countenance the use of force elsewhere in Asia to acquire trading privileges or to extend the VOC's territorial rule. When Coen returned to Batavia in September, 1627, to begin his second term as governor-general, he was immediately confronted by hostilities with the Javanese, who threatened the position of the Dutch at Batavia. Coen himself died in 1629 defending Batavia from the onslaughts of the central Javan kingdom of Mataram. The success of the Dutch in holding Batavia under these adverse circumstances demonstrated to the local rulers the superiority of European sea power and the effectiveness in Asian warfare of mercenaries organized and trained by Europeans.[161]

The successors of Coen were no longer confronted by effective local resistance in Java or the Moluccas. They were free to concentrate upon building a Dutch seaborne empire of trade based on Batavia. The only continuing challenges to the Dutch in maritime Asia came from their European competitors. Anthony van Diemen, during his term of office (1636–45), concentrated upon conquering the Portuguese outposts in the maritime regions from Goa to Malacca—the so-called Western Quarter of the Dutch empire. Van Diemen also hoped to broaden the VOC's field of commercial exploration in the southern and eastern latitudes, especially in Australia. To this end, Abel Janszoon Tasman was sent out on two expeditions (1642–43 and 1644) which unveiled New Zealand and charted the north coast of Australia and put it on the world map.[162] But because the explorations were costly and yielded no immediate profits, the directors ordered them discontinued.

Dutch attacks on the Portuguese outposts, a resumption of the VOC's earlier strategy, had begun in 1636 at Ceylon in the hope of obtaining control of the cinnamon trade. Although the Portuguese had been weakened by the attacks of Kandy, the Dutch were unable to oust them from Colombo

---

tury (n. 41), chap. viii, especially pp. 371–73. On the diplomatic efforts by Jacob Specx to prevent a break in Japanese-Dutch trade over events in Taiwan, see Kato, *loc. cit.* (n. 28), pp. 222–27.

[161] See Furber, *op. cit.* (n. 55), pp. 49–50. On the unsuccessful siege of Batavia by Sultan Agung of Mataram, see Ricklefs, *op. cit.* (n. 30), pp. 40–44.

[162] On Tasman's discoveries see Schilder, *op. cit.* (n. 7), chaps. xiv–xv.

until 1656. In the meantime, the Dutch obtained in 1635 the right to trade in Bengal, where the Portuguese had been operating since 1580. While they traded precariously at Hugli and Pipli in Bengal, the Dutch also obtained access in 1638 to inland and upriver Patna, the main producer of saltpeter. As part of a grandiose effort to replace the Portuguese in the Bay of Bengal, they had also set up factories in 1635 at Syriam in Pegu and at Ava, an upriver town near Mandalay. The efforts undertaken in 1637 to establish Dutch outposts in Malabar were unsuccessful, as were the nearly contemporary endeavors to maintain profitable factories in Indochina. Still Dutch traders appeared from time to time at most of the commercial centers of Asia and took an increasingly prominent and assertive role in the inter-Asian trade.

The final collapse of the formal Portuguese empire in Asia was brought about mainly by Dutch naval power.[163] Van Diemen inaugurated, in 1636, a program of regular patrols of strategic water routes and of annual blockades of the main Portuguese ports. The trading vessels of all countries were forced to obtain Dutch passes when sailing the seas between Cambay and Macao. The English, who opposed the Dutch policy in the Indian Ocean as much as the Portuguese did, were warned not to interfere with the Dutch blockade of Goa or to provide aid to Portuguese shipping. Van Diemen also insisted, contrary to the advice of the directors in Holland, that the Company's trade in Asia could not be sustained without further territorial conquests. In 1640 he seized the cinnamon ports of Negombo and Galle in Ceylon. Malacca finally fell to the Dutch in January, 1641, just about eleven months before the Dutch-Portuguese truce was ratified in Europe. Thereafter the Dutch drove the Spanish out of Taiwan in 1642 and the VOC consolidated further its position in the Moluccas. Goa, Malabar, Colombo, Flores, Timor, and Macao were the only important places remaining under Portuguese control when Van Diemen died in 1646.

Batavia, officially recognized by the Seventeen as the capital of the Dutch Indies on March 4, 1621, was built according to Coen's plans. After the immolation of the old city of Jakatra in 1619, Coen had ordered constructed on its site a large fortress and a small Dutch town with canals and bridges reminiscent of Amsterdam. Officially the VOC claimed sovereignty over Batavia and its environs "by right of conquest."[164] The Javan princes of Bantam and Mataram fought the Dutch, as well as each other, for control of Batavia until 1639. Thereafter Van Diemen completed the construction of Batavia and brought to fruition the earlier policy of encouraging the development of its sizable Chinese community. The Chinese were granted special trading and residential privileges. The Statutes of Batavia, drawn up between 1636 and

[163] *Cf.* above, pp. 21–24.
[164] See B. H. M. Vlekke, *Nusantara. A History of the East Indian Archipelago* (Cambridge, Mass., 1945), p. 126, n. 37.

1642, put into formal legal order the customs and practices which made life possible in this ethnically and religiously mixed community. By the end of Van Diemen's tenure in 1646, Batavia was firmly established as the headquarters of a Dutch maritime empire that stretched from the Persian Gulf to Japan. All the Dutch factories reported to Batavia and every effort was expended to funnel through Batavia both the trade to Europe and the inter-Asian commerce. Malacca was thus superseded by Batavia as the nexus of Eastern commerce.[165]

In 1650 the directors in Holland issued a set of General Instructions for the guidance of the Batavia government which replaced the earlier ones and became the fundamental law of the Dutch in the Indies for the remainder of the Company's history. It also provided contemporaries, as well as later historians, with a systematic review of the Dutch position in the East at midcentury. The directors described the three types of trade prevailing in Asia. First, there was the commerce carried on in regions where the Dutch possessed territorial jurisdiction by treaty or by conquest: Batavia, Malacca, Pulicat (in India), Zeelandia (Formosa), and a few Moluccan islands. Second, there were exclusive trading privileges for the VOC in those places where agreements had been concluded (often under duress) with native princes and the shogun of Japan. Finally, there was the trade with such Asian nations as Siam and India in which the Dutch were required to compete with other foreign merchants and to negotiate with the local rulers on a basis of equality.[166]

The enterprise of the Dutch in Asia continued after 1650 to undergo expansion through diplomacy, pressure, duress, and conquest. From their base at Malacca, the Dutch sponsored the resurgence of the sultanate of Johore, the traditional Malay enemy of the Portuguese who had aided the Dutch conquest of Malacca. Through their treaty and commercial relations with Johore, the Dutch were able to extend their control over the principal import and export products of the Malay peninsula and its archipelago, to exclude competitors, such as the English, from this trade, and to monitor the traffic in the vital Straits of Malacca.[167]

From Batavia the Dutch gradually undermined the state of Mataram, whose sultans claimed jurisdiction over all of Java except for the tiny sultanate of Bantam. To 1677 the Dutch acknowledged the independence of Mataram by sending embassies periodically to its court with costly gifts. The gradual disintegration of the loosely knit empire of Mataram gave the Dutch the opportunity in 1677 and thereafter to act as "protector" of its sultan in his struggles with vassals and various pretenders to the throne. As part of its policy of supporting Mataram, Batavia intervened in the affairs of

---

[165] See *ibid.*, pp. 130–33. On the development of Batavia see below, pp. 106–7, 1313–22.
[166] See Boxer, *op. cit.* (n. 124), pp. 92–94.
[167] See L. Y. Andaya, *The Kingdom of Johor, 1641–1728* (Kuala Lumpur, 1975), chap. i.

Bantam, occupied it in 1682, and brought it under the supervision of the Company two years later.[168] Batavia, despite the reluctance of the directors at home to engage in costly military enterprises, thus came to control all of Java's trade and was in a position to exclude from its marts the merchants of the VOC's European competitors.[169]

The remainder of the Indonesian archipelago, except for Borneo, had meanwhile come more firmly under Dutch supervision. Control over the Moluccas was tightened after 1640 and efforts were made to convert the pagan, Catholic, and Muslim peoples there to Calvinism in the hope of rendering them less rebellious. In response to this program, the sultan of Makassar in Celebes, long an enemy of the Dutch, prepared for war. His fears were heightened after 1663 when the Spanish retired from Ternate and the Dutch began to move in. As the leading representative of Islam in the region, the ruler of Makassar was especially hostile to the Dutch missionary drive. He was also determined to protect Makassar's position as an international mart of the spice trade open to all comers. With the support of the Portuguese, English, and Danes, he had long resisted the efforts of Batavia to monopolize the fine spices. In his determination to defy the Dutch, the sultan of Makassar fortified his city and began to build a navy with the help of his European supporters. Alarmed by this development, Batavia in 1666 sent an expedition against Makassar led by Cornelis Speelman. After a difficult war of two years' duration, Speelman forced the sultan in 1669 to conclude a treaty by which the Dutch obtained a monopoly of Makassar's trade and the right to establish a fortress there. Refugees from Makassar, even its young princes, fled to places not subject to the Dutch. Gradually the whole of Celebes and some adjacent islands came under the overlordship of Batavia.[170]

Nor was Sumatra spared in the Dutch drive to control the trade of the Malay-Indonesian region. The tin of the Malay Peninsula, much in demand in Europe and India, was controlled in part by the sultanate of Acheh, the Sumatran kingdom at the entrance to the Straits of Malacca and overlord of its west coast.[171] Supported by Johore, the old enemy of Acheh on the Malay Peninsula, the Dutch began after 1650 to foment rebellion in Acheh's vassal territories and periodically blockaded the ports of western Sumatra. By 1663 the Dutch had secured treaties with three of Acheh's vassals by which the VOC guaranteed their independence of Acheh in return for a mo-

---

[168] The Sultan of Bantam sent an embassy in England in 1681–83 to ask for help against the Dutch. See W. Fruin-Mees, "Een Bantamsch gezantschap naar Engeland in 1682," *Tijdschrift voor Indische taal-, land- en volkenkunde,* LXIV (1924), 207–26.

[169] See Vlekke, *op. cit.* (n. 164), pp. 158–61.

[170] *Ibid.,* pp. 147–52. On the Dutch allies in the conquest of Makassar, Arung Palakka, and the Bugis, see L. Y. Andaya, *The Heritage of Arung Palakka: A History of South Sulawesi (Celebes) in the Seventeenth Century* (The Hague, 1981), pp. 73–155.

[171] See G. W. Irwin, "The Dutch and the Tin Trade of Malaya in the Seventeenth Century," in Jerome Ch'en and N. Terling (eds.), *Studies in the Social History of China and South-East Asia* (Cambridge, Mass., 1970), pp. 267–87.

nopoly of their trade. Other sultanates soon followed suit as most of Sumatra came under the supervision of Batavia. All other Europeans, except for the English who built a fortress on Sumatra's west coast near Benkulen in 1684, were excluded from trading in Sumatra.[172]

The disintegration of most of the Indonesian states between 1650 and 1685 enabled the VOC, despite a definite reluctance on its part to assume far-ranging territorial and administrative responsibilities, to create a formal maritime empire of commerce in Southeast Asia. Batavia acted as sovereign over nothing except its own territory; it performed rather as a suzerain or protector of a vast number of small client or semi-client states nominally ruled by native lords. Except in Batavia itself, the Dutch made only a few efforts, as in Amboina and Formosa, to convert the natives to Calvinism or to impose European ways. To them the Malay-Indonesian region was a vastly complicated trading network with Batavia at its center. The desire for monopoly and control of trading conditions prompted the Dutch to undertake military expeditions to make and break rulers. Cooperation of the native kings with the Dutch, as in the cases of Johore and Ternate, sometimes produced commercial and political benefits for the native state. The Dutch were remarkably successful in controlling the myriad sea-lanes of the region, though piracy remained endemic to many coastal areas. Whatever promoted trade and profits was cultivated; whatever was without profit, such as exploration or evangelizing, was either discouraged or abandoned quickly.

As the Dutch eliminated European competition in the Malay-Indonesian region, they contemporaneously fought fiercely with both natives and Europeans in South Asia. The termination of the uneasy Dutch-Portuguese truce in 1652, followed two years later by the end of the war with England, permitted the Dutch to prepare for their final assault in Ceylon. Beginning in 1638 the Dutch had actively worked with Raja Sinha of Kandy in efforts to evict the Portuguese and to monopolize the cinnamon of Ceylon. From their first arrival the Dutch had also shown signs of being territorially ambitious. They had expanded into the interior from their coastal footholds in an effort to control the lands which produced the cinnamon. A Dutch expedition sent to Ceylon from Batavia was aided by Raja Sinha in besieging and capturing Colombo in 1656. Over the next two years the Dutch forces isolated and overran the remaining Portuguese strongholds and conquered Jaffna. Although the VOC claimed possession in 1658 of all the holdings previously in the hands of the Portuguese, their control of the cinnamon lands was never so extensive or complete, for Raja Sinha had profited from the expulsion of the Portuguese to extend Kandy's jurisdiction over territories and ports on both coasts. Consequently the Dutch were never able to

---

[172] See Vlekke, *op. cit.* (n. 164), pp. 152–54.

monopolize cinnamon production and commerce and were forced to deal with Raja Sinha and his successors. Indeed, the VOC maintained the legal fiction that they were in Ceylon to protect the king's lands.[173]

From Ceylon it is a short step to the pepper ports of Malabar, and the Dutch were quick to take it. Individual Dutch merchants and several fleets had appeared at these ports during the first half of the seventeenth century, and efforts had been made on a number of occasions to set up factories, particularly at Calicut. Several of the Malabar princes, like Raja Sinha of Kandy, had originally been eager for alliances with the Dutch. But as time wore on, most Malabar rulers became increasingly wary about the monopolistic nature of Dutch trading policies and practices, particularly once it became obvious that Portuguese power was declining. By the time Colombo fell in 1656, the danger to the Portuguese strongholds in Malabar had become imminent.

The Dutch campaign of 1657 was directed against the remaining Portuguese outposts in Ceylon and the port of Quilon in Malabar. It was commanded by Rijcklof van Goens, an old India hand and an important member of the Batavia Council who had his headquarters at Colombo. In December, 1658, the Dutch took the Portuguese fortress of Quilon and in the next month concluded a treaty with its queen. By its terms the Portuguese were banished and their possessions transferred to the VOC. The queen also agreed to sell pepper to the Dutch exclusively, to protect Dutch merchants, and to admit no vessels to the port without a Dutch pass. By this treaty it became patently obvious that the Dutch were as rapacious and greedy as the Portuguese and were more capable of enforcing their demands. The Dutch garrison left behind by Van Goens finally had to be withdrawn in 1658 because of local and Portuguese resistance. This initial reverse, followed by several other minor setbacks, convinced the authorities at Batavia that different tactics would be required for the conquest of Malabar.[174]

The Dutch turned in 1661, as they had in the past, to Calicut. With the aid of its Zamorin and his allies, the Dutch recaptured Quilon in December of that year and in 1662 concluded agreements with its ruler and the king of Travancore reinstating the treaty of 1659. In the meantime, Dutch forces commanded by Van Goens captured the town of Cranganore in January, 1662, and imposed a similar treaty upon it. In association with the Zamorin, the Dutch then proceeded to the conquest of Cochin; it required two expeditions before Cochin finally capitulated on January 7, 1663. By the terms of the treaty concluded three months later, the king of Cochin acknowledged the "Honorable Company" as his protector, promised to deliver pepper and wild cinnamon exclusively to its agents, and agreed to govern Cochin's

[173] See J. Arasaratnam, *Dutch Power in Ceylon, 1658–1687* (Amsterdam, 1958), chap. i.
[174] See T. I. Poonen, *A Survey of the Rise of Dutch Power in Malabar* (Trichinopoly, 1943), pp. 68–72.

overland and overseas trade according to the dictates of the Company.[175] Cannanore, deprived of all hope of help from Cochin or Goa, quickly fell to the Dutch in February, 1663. Between this date and 1678 the Dutch consolidated their hold upon these important Malabar cities and their dependencies and subjected them to a commander directly responsible to Batavia.[176] Over the remainder of the century the Dutch occupied themselves with solidifying their positions in India and Ceylon and with controlling as much as possible of the inter-Asian trade.

On the Coromandel Coast, where they regularly purchased the cloth sold in further Asia, the Dutch had secured a firm foothold by the 1630's. From here they had expanded their activities into Burma and Bengal. The factories in Burma remained under Coromandel's jurisdiction until they were abandoned in 1680; Bengal was created as an independent directorate in 1655, for Dutch trade prospered there.[177] In Ceylon, meanwhile, Van Goens, who was its governor from 1622 to 1675, dreamed of making Colombo the successor to Batavia as the base of Dutch power in the East. His ambition was to undermine the independence of Kandy and establish simultaneously a Dutch monopoly over the trade of India's Malabar and Coromandel coasts. Van Goen's expansionist activities, although opposed by Batavia, achieved a degree of success because of the support he received from the Seventeen. However, the mounting expenses of Van Goen's program shortly brought the directors around to Batavia's viewpoint and resulted in the governor's recall. Thereafter, the Dutch followed a policy of conciliating Kandy and of relaxing their hold on Ceylon's inter-Asian trade.

The command over the Coromandel market which the Dutch possessed at mid-century was gradually eroded by English, Danish, French, and Indian competition for its cloths, saltpeter, foodstuffs, and slaves. Burdened with rising military and administrative costs, and periodically embroiled in India's internecine wars, the Dutch became increasingly less able to operate with as small a margin of gross profit as their competitors and fought a losing battle over the last generation of the century to maintain their Coromandel trade as a paying proposition. By the end of the century it was only in Bengal and Malabar that the Dutch retained a strong position on the Indian subcontinent, though they still possessed factories at Surat and other sites in western India as well as in Persia.[178]

Only in Java, Formosa, Ceylon, and the Moluccas had the VOC become a territorial power exercising direct rule. Outside the perimeters of Indone-

---

[175] For its full terms see *ibid.*, pp. 115–18.

[176] *Ibid.*, pp. 200–202.

[177] For a study of the impact of the trading companies on the composition, direction, and extent of Bengal's part in the interregional trade and on the role of the Bengali merchants see O. Prakash, "The European Trading Companies and the Merchants of Bengal, 1650–1725," *Indian Economic and Social History Review*, Vol. I, No. 3 (1964), pp. 37–63.

[178] See Furber, *op. cit.* (n. 55), pp. 80–83; T. Raychaudhuri, *Jan Company in Coromandel,*

sian waters the Dutch had not been able to monopolize seaborne trade or establish strong bases. Even in Sumatra the English had successfully defied the best efforts of the Dutch to keep Indonesia as their own preserve. The spice monopolies in Ceylon and the Moluccas required constant surveillance to prevent them from slipping away from Dutch control. The trade with Siam, Japan, and China was generally carried on under terms prescribed by these Asian nations. As the only Westerners permitted to trade in Japan after 1640, the Dutch possessed, from a European viewpoint, a monopoly of access to Japan and its commerce. The Philippines and Flores remained closed to the Dutch at century's end.

The story of the VOC's efforts to establish direct relations with China is long and complex. Frustrated in their efforts to follow the Portuguese into Macao, the Dutch were well satisfied for a time with their trading station on Taiwan. From their early reversals the Dutch learned that force would not be successful in opening China, and so they turned to negotiation. But it was difficult to negotiate with a government caught in the grip of civil war from 1620 to 1644. The Ch'ing (Manchu) conquest of coastal China set immigrants scurrying to Taiwan, and sea robbers interfered seriously with the VOC's maritime connections to Taiwan and Japan. The Dutch sent an embassy to the Ch'ing court in 1655–56, but China's new Manchu rulers remained aloof. Thereafter, the government in Batavia decided to reinforce Taiwan and to defend it against the expected invasion of Cheng Ch'engkung (known as "Koxinga" in the European records) a native of Fukien, a Ming loyalist, and the commander of a huge fleet of war junks.

In 1661–62 Koxinga drove the Dutch from Taiwan, and they lost their main channel of trade with China. To Batavia and Holland the loss of Castle Zeelandia came as an upsetting surprise, for it was the most serious setback so far experienced by the VOC in Asia, a possible indication that their empire was militarily overextended. The Dutch naval forces, in alliance with Ch'ing land armies, sought revenge in 1662–64 by attacking Cheng's coastal strongholds in Fukien. In return for their cooperation in helping to pacify Fukien, the Dutch expected trading concessions from Peking. But the Chinese had other plans. They wanted Dutch naval aid for an attack upon Taiwan, since the Ch'ing navy was then no match for Cheng's forces.

Over these differences, as well as over mutual suspicions of the other's motives, Sino-Dutch relations steadily deteriorated from 1664 to 1669. The VOC mission sent to Peking in 1666–67 under Pieter van Hoorn obtained no trading concessions from the K'ang-hsi emperor and indeed led in 1668 to a formal revocation of all special Dutch trading privileges. Thereafter, a considerable amount of unofficial private trading went on between Dutch and Chinese, especially at Foochow. It was on the initiative of Peking that

---

1605–90 . . . (The Hague, 1962), pp. 209–11; Arasaratnam, *op. cit.* (n. 173), chaps. ii and iii.

official negotiations were resumed in 1679 when the Ch'ing court sent a low-level embassy to Batavia bearing an imperial rescript asking for naval aid. But the Dutch, involved in military activities elsewhere, had neither the vessels nor the inclination to dispatch a fleet to China.

After the unaided Ch'ing successfully conquered Taiwan in 1683, the Chinese no longer asked Dutch assistance. The Dutch, on their side, made a final attempt to improve trading conditions by sending the embassy of Vincent Paets to Peking in 1685–87. This embassy failed; three years later the Dutch stopped sending trading ships to China because they ordinarily yielded little profit. The Chinese, on their side, had in 1684–85 decided to modify their maritime policies; they permitted Chinese merchants to engage in maritime trade, allowed all foreigners to trade in China, and established a system of tolls on all Chinese and foreign ships involved in trade. By this act it became more profitable for the Dutch to buy Chinese goods in Batavia from Portuguese and Chinese merchants than to send trading fleets to China. The failure of the Dutch to establish direct trade with China was a major factor in the VOC's subsequent decline in the eighteenth century.[179]

The Dutch at no time occupied a special position in China as they did in Japan and elsewhere. Their superiority in sea power, so decisive in Indonesia, Ceylon, and southern India, posed no serious threat to the great continental states: the Mughul empire, Siam, and China. It was, however, their edge in sea power and military efficiency which enabled the Dutch to expel the Portuguese from their vital outposts and to limit the activities of the Spanish and English in Asia. From Coen's time to the end of the century, the men in the field advocated the use of force whenever they met resistance. Negotiation was ordinarily resorted to, as in the case of China, only when the opposition was too strong to intimidate. On these occasions the Dutch in Japan and in the embassies sent to China were sometimes as obsequious as the Orientals were reputed to be. Under pressure from the Seventeen in Holland to stimulate and maintain trade at all costs, the men in the field were required to improvise and to be innovative in the methods adopted and the goals pursued. Almost any strategy or tactic would be accepted by the Seventeen if they felt certain that a profitable trade would be maintained, even to the point of tolerating the private trading enterprises of their servants. War and territorial commitments, both officially frowned upon by the Seventeen, were generally justified by declaring them to be essential to the protection or extension of trade. But the costs of war and administration, as they mounted over the century, contributed to a growing determination in Holland to abandon all enterprises, such as sending trading fleets to China, which could not possibly show a substantial profit.

---

[179] Based on Wills, *op. cit.* (n. 158), *passim;* also Braudel, *op. cit.* (n. 75), III, pp. 222, 228. On the Paets' embassy see J. Vixeboxse, *Een Hollandsch gezantschap naar China, 1685–87* (Leyden, 1946).

4

JAN COMPANY'S TRADE

The trade with Asia was but one face of the multifaceted Dutch international commerce. From 1580 onward the ships and merchants of Holland and Zeeland had come to dominate the herring and grain traffic of the Baltic, and by 1600 they had extended their trading activities to Archangel in Russia. Much of the grain purchased in the Baltic region was sold in the Iberian Peninsula for salt, silver, and spices. From Lisbon and Seville the Dutch merchants traveled to Livorno, the free port of Tuscany, and to Genoa and Venice. In 1612 they negotiated a commercial treaty with the Turks, to whom they soon began to sell Asian products carried around the Cape and transshipped from Amsterdam to the marts of the Levant. This development occurred at a time (1590 to 1630) when the overland traffic between the Levant and the Persian Gulf was at one of its lowest points. In general, the effects of the East India trade upon Dutch international commerce became apparent by 1620; by 1635 the spices exported from Amsterdam to the Baltic exceeded the herring trade in value.[180]

The elevation of the United Provinces to the level of the most important shipping and trading center of Europe was led by Holland and Zeeland, the two provinces most involved in maritime trade and industry. The shipbuilding industry centered in these two provinces had been firmly established by the fourteenth century and went through its greatest period of innovation in the late sixteenth. Dutch shipbuilders concentrated from the beginning upon constructing fishing and merchant vessels, generally from Baltic timber. To the time of the Spanish Armada (1588) the Dutch vessels sent on convoy duty were converted merchantmen. To meet the Spanish challenge the Dutch organized admiralties which began the construction of warships. Private shipbuilders, left to their own devices, continued to turn out commercial vessels in constantly mounting numbers and of standard designs that were readily adaptable to particular requirements. Finally, in the late sixteenth century they developed and perfected the *fluit,* a long-distance cargo vessel of three to five hundred tons that provided the Dutch with a cheap means of transportation, enabling them to take the lead in northern Europe's carrying trade.[181]

Wherever the Dutch went in Asia they carried shipwrights with them to build small cargo vessels to reduce the need to carry goods of inter-Asian trade in European vessels. The warships and larger cargo vessels were gen-

[180] See D. W. Davies, *A Primer of Dutch Seventeenth-Century Overseas Trade* (The Hague, 1961), pp. 11–14.

[181] See R. W. Unger, "Dutch Ship Design in the Fifteenth and Sixteenth Centuries," *Viator,* IV (1973), 403–11.

erally built in Holland.[182] Since the *fluit* was not armed, it could not function under the dangerous maritime conditions prevailing in the Indian Ocean trade. To satisfy their needs in Asia the Dutch built pinnaces, larger and more heavily timbered vessels that had a deeper draft and were in fact the warship version of the *fluit*. They were sturdier and more heavily armed than the native craft, and faster and more maneuverable than most of the other armed merchantmen. The pinnace gave the Dutch a marked advantage in inter-Asian trading over the native vessels and the larger armed merchantmen of their European rivals.[183]

The Dutch East Indiamen (*retourschepen*), built by the VOC on its own docks in Holland, were specially designed for the voyage to Asia. They possibly evolved from the pinnaces and ranged from around four to five hundred tons at the beginning of the century to around twelve hundred by its end. Ordinarily they carried more cargo than a warship and were more defensible than lightly armed cargo vessels.[184] A special committee of the VOC was responsible for outfitting and equipping the India fleets in conjunction with the directors of the participating chambers. Each chamber had its own master who outfitted, equipped, repaired, and supervised the building of the East Indiamen belonging to it. The chambers were not permitted to build or buy ships without the consent of the Seventeen.

Only ten to twelve Indiamen ordinarily sailed in the VOC's fleets. The duration of the sea passage between the Low Countries and Batavia was normally nine months. Ships left in November or December and arrived at Batavia in the following August or September after a voyage of about 3,400 miles. The returning ships sailed from Batavia in October or November, from Ceylon in November or December, and docked for unloading during the following summer at the Texel, a small island at the entrance to the Zuider Zee.[185] When the United Provinces was at war, the returning ships had to avoid the channel, sail around Scotland, and dock after August 15. Lighters carried the imported goods over the network of Dutch waterways to coastal and interior towns. The fine spices and the more costly textiles were stored at Amsterdam within the *Oost-Indische Huys,* the headquarters of the Company after 1605. The bulkier and heavier goods—pepper, saltpeter, and copper—were used as ballast on the ships and stored in other warehouses in Amsterdam and neighboring towns.[186]

---

[182]For example, see Furber, *op. cit.* (n. 55), p. 45.

[183]See J. H. Parry, "Transport and Trade Routes," in E. E. Rich and C. H. Wilson (eds.), *The Cambridge Economic History of Europe,* IV (Cambridge, 1967), 213.

[184]For a detailed description of the *retourschip* see R. W. Unger, *Dutch Shipbuilding before 1800* (Assen, 1978), pp. 47–48.

[185]On the organization of these fleets see Bruijn, *loc. cit.* (n. 136), 252–55.

[186]See K. Glamann, *Dutch-Asiatic Trade, 1620–1740* (Copenhagen, 1955), pp. 25–28. Based on Van Dam (see above, n. 138) and Dutch archival materials, this is the best general account available. For a more general survey of patterns of trade in the seventeenth century see

The Charter of 1602, renewed in 1623, 1647, 1672, and 1696, gave to the Company a monopoly of the trade east of the Cape of Good Hope. In the Low Countries the monopoly of the Asiatic imports was generally effective; in Asia the Company was never able, except in the case of certain of the fine spices, to render its monopoly complete. The Dutch, in contrast to the English, were successful in controlling interloping and smuggling. They were less successful than the Portuguese in preventing their nationals from working for other European countries. They were far more efficient than any of their contemporaries in maintaining a regular schedule of voyages, in funneling Asian products into their own Eastern emporiums, and in marketing their imports profitably in Europe. The VOC established and maintained a system of reports, record keeping, and rational decision-making that was more efficient and resourceful than most contemporary state bureaucracies. Its weakest feature was the heterogeneous accounting system, based on factories and chambers, which made virtually impossible an accurate reckoning of the profit and loss of the general operations.[187] Still it is possible to assert that the VOC in Asia delivered solid profits for much of the seventeenth century, especially so in the years from 1631 to 1653 and from 1664 to 1684. Thereafter the inter-Asian trade declined, and the VOC relied ever more heavily on sending Asian goods to Europe.[188] In the homeland, meanwhile, most of the contemporary complaints by stockholders related to the bookkeeping practices of the Company and to dividend payments.[189]

Over the course of the century, the VOC issued regulations to govern all aspects of its activities: the hiring of personnel in Europe and Asia, the techniques of loading and unloading ships, and the duties of its servants from governor-general, to cartographer, to cooper. It was this emphasis upon *control* and *monopoly* which characterized the VOC's policies at all levels. The Seventeen were determined to buy the fine spices at fixed prices, exclude all others from the commerce, and manage the supplies put on the market in Europe in the hope of selling them at constant prices. Merchants from all over Europe consigned goods to Amsterdam and invested the proceeds from their sales in wares for resale in the homeland. Price lists were printed weekly to which the interested could subscribe. Many of Europe's

---

Glamann's essay in E. E. Rich and C. H. Wilson (eds.), *The Cambridge Economic History of Europe*, V (Cambridge, 1977), chap. iv.

[187] The most authoritative study of the financial records of the VOC is W. M. F. Mansvelt, *Rechtsform en geldelijk beheer bij de Oost-Indische Compagnie* (Amsterdam, 1922). His view that anarchy in record-keeping was created by the multiplicity of chambers which kept their own records is challenged by M. Morineau, in P. Léon (ed.), *Histoire économique et sociale du monde* (6 vols., Paris, 1978), II, 164–68.

[188] F. Gaastra, *loc. cit.* (n. 28), pp. 58–65.

[189] Van Dam, *op. cit.* (n. 138), Bk. I, Pt. 1, pp. 285–95; for a list of the dividends paid to stockholders from 1620 to 1702 see pp. 433–36.

rulers kept temporary or permanent agents in Amsterdam to purchase salt-peter, copper, ships, and other necessities of war. Dutch and foreigners alike invested sums, both large and small, in its industrial, trading, and financial establishments, particularly after the conclusion of the Truce of 1609. Wealthy Dutch merchants also invested heavily in international trade and in foreign concerns, notably in the Swedish copper industry. In short, Amsterdam as an entrepôt enjoyed a practical monopoly of western European foreign trade that was based on a superior shipping technology, fine storage facilities, credit arrangements, insurance systems, and excellent business information.[190]

While the goods from the East were being unloaded at Amsterdam, the arrangements for their marketing began. Bulletins were sent out to correspondents throughout northern Europe notifying them of market conditions, the expected offerings, and the date of auction. Little is known about the suppliers and purchasers of the goods in the spice trade. It is clear that syndicates were formed, early in the century, sometimes including the directors themselves, as efforts were made to obtain a corner on one commodity or the other. In 1620 and 1622 syndicates bought by contract all of the Company's pepper at prearranged prices and with the condition attached that the Company would not put pepper on the market again for a specified period of time.[191] Sales by contract remained more common than public auctions in the first half of the century. Most purchases were paid for in "pieces of eight," or Spanish silver reals. To 1648, the year when the war with Spain ended, the Dutch obtained most of their Spanish coins through Hamburg. The export of gold and silver bullion was strictly prohibited by the United Provinces until the second half of the century.[192] Trading monies were generally more abundant in Amsterdam than in any other European market.[193]

By 1690 when the public auction system was well established and predominant, the conditions for the sale of merchandise had become detailed and explicit. Sales were made to the highest bidder, were payable in cash at Amsterdam, and were to be delivered within two weeks to the purchaser. An elaborate schedule of rebates for prompt payment and penalties for failure to abide by the Company's rules were part of the prescribed conditions. The VOC sold goods directly from the warehouse to receive quick returns on their investments. All questions arising over bidding, payments, and de-

[190] Based on V. Barbour, *Capitalism in Amsterdam in the Seventeenth Century* (Ann Arbor reprint, 1966), chap. i. Also see Braudel, *op. cit.* (n. 75), III, 236–45.

[191] This departure may have been influenced by the trade depression of 1619 to 1622 outside the United Provinces; see R. Romano, "Encore la crise de 1619–22," *Annales, E. S. C.,* XIX (1964), 31–37. A longer version of his argument appeared first in R. Romano, "Una crisi economica, 1619–1622," *Rivista storica italiana,* LXXIV (1962), no. 3.

[192] Glamann, *op. cit.* (n. 186), pp. 29–33, 51–52.

[193] M. Morineau, "Quelques remarques sur l'abondance monétaire aux Provinces-Unies," *Annales. E. S. C.,* XXIX (1974), 767–76.

liveries were to be settled by the decisions of the Company. Finally, the purchaser was to donate to charity one guilder for each thousand spent.[194]

To maintain an adequate and constant supply of pepper and spices on the Amsterdam market was constantly a trouble to the Company. Gluts were feared as much as scarcities. A sound knowledge of the commodities and the market was required to buy the correct quantities and qualities. The first estimates of the annual consumption of pepper in Europe, made in England in 1621 and in Holland in 1622, put it at around 7 million pounds; an estimate of 1688 by the Seventeen raised it only slightly.[195] The percentages of pepper actually put up for sale in Europe by the Dutch and English companies were clearly larger in the second half of the century than they had been in the first half when the Portuguese brought in almost 1.5 million pounds annually. Whatever the European demand for pepper, the production of India and the Malay-Indonesian archipelago could normally supply it easily. The Dutch, of course, obtained most of their pepper from Java, Sumatra, Malaya, and Borneo. Pepper from the various regions were of different qualities and brought different prices. The Dutch at Batavia, beginning around 1622, mixed the various types together and marketed the pepper in Europe under one name, black or brown, and at one price. White pepper was first offered at the Amsterdam auctions in 1655–56.[196]

Black (or brown) pepper was the only commodity regularly imported in substantial quantities throughout the seventeenth century. The absolute quantities carried to Amsterdam were greater in the second half than in the first; relatively, however, the proportion of pepper in the total Dutch imports from Asia decreased in the second half of the century as textiles became more important. Like the Antwerp merchants of the sixteenth century, the directors of the VOC tried to conceal the quantities of pepper available in the hope of keeping the market stable. During the first two decades (to 1619), or as long as supplies remained short, the prices of pepper at Amsterdam rose steadily and with but few downturns.[197] Profits on this trade could have then been considerable, because in 1618 pepper sold in Amsterdam brought about five times its purchase price in Java.[198] In evaluating this and all other statistics, it should be recalled that the expenses of the Company in establishing the trade and in Eastern warfare were probably mounting swiftly at the same time.

The financial condition of the VOC was extremely weak in its early years. From 1602 to 1612 it lost more than three hundred disillusioned investors of the more than eight hundred original shareholders. No dividends were paid

[194] See Van Dam, *op. cit.* (n. 138), Bk. I, Pt. 2, pp. 269, 295–98.
[195] *Cf.* the estimate in Duncan, *op. cit.* (n. 18), p. 66, of seven million pounds in 1670, or about three times what it had been in 1500.
[196] Glamann, *op. cit.* (n. 186), pp. 17, 73–75.
[197] See the appendix to this chapter, on prices and quantities in the spice trade.
[198] Glamann, *op. cit.* (n. 186), p. 76.

until 1610, and then in spices and cash; another decade elapsed before the next dividend was paid, partly in cash and partly in commodities. Under pressure from the investors it was decided in 1623 to pay an annual dividend of 10 percent, but only after all the outstanding debts had been paid. After 1631 an annual dividend was paid regularly.[199] Hereafter the loudest protests ended, but the shareholders complained constantly that dividends should be greater.[200]

The quantities of pepper imported began falling in the period when a co-operative purchasing program with the English was initiated (1619 to 1623). With the breakdown of these arrangements after the Amboina massacre, free competition again became the order of the day. The resumption of the war with Spain in 1621 was followed by a general downward trend in Amsterdam pepper prices, but with sharp upturns in 1637–38. The disruption of the Lisbon market by the Revolution of 1640 and the fall of Malacca in 1641 brought about a temporary decline in Portuguese imports that might help to explain the price fluctuations at Amsterdam from 1638 to 1648 and the sharp rise there of pepper imports. The end of the war with Spain in 1648 was followed by a decline in prices until 1643–54 when a sharp rise again occurred, possibly related to interruptions produced by the first Anglo-Dutch war (1652–54). Thereafter pepper prices at Amsterdam fell steadily, but with occasional jumps, until 1688–89. At that date they again rose sharply, possibly because of dislocations in the London market occasioned by the Glorious Revolution.[201] Over the century as a whole, pepper prices ranged from a high of 85 guilders per pound in 1638 to a low of 35 in 1683, an event possibly related to the Dutch conquest in the 1680's of Bantam and its production.[202] Apparently the market became glutted in the 1680's, for the imports of pepper in Holland were far lower in that decade than in the previous four.[203] At this time the Dutch also began selling the abundant Indonesian pepper in India, even as they had been supplying pepper to Persian and Chinese merchants since the 1630's. Chinese and English competition for the inter-Asian pepper trade stiffened in the last years of the century. And because of the high prices being demanded at the century's end in Amsterdam, the European competitors of the VOC began to buy pepper from the Dutch in Asia to supply their national markets.[204]

Pepper dominated Asian imports until mid-century, with fine spices and

[199] See Haan, *op. cit.* (n. 134), pp. 114–15, 122.

[200] For Braudel's discussion of profits of the VOC see *op. cit.* (n. 75), III, 225–27. On the taxes that the VOC paid to the state see *ibid.*, II, 445–47.

[201] On the relationship between pepper imports, prices, and European events see Haan, *op. cit.* (n. 134), pp. 82–83.

[202] See spice appendix. For a critical analysis of the quantities and prices of pepper at the Amsterdam market see Glamann, *op. cit.* (n. 186), Appendix E.

[203] See the profile of pepper returns in P. Léon (ed.), *op. cit.* (n. 187), II, 174.

[204] See Glamann, *op. cit.* (n. 186), pp. 83–86.

textiles taking the second and third places, respectively. But this is by no means a fair reflection of what the Dutch East Indiamen carried to Amsterdam. A ship's manifest of 1648 depicts more accurately the diversity of goods delivered there. Aside from large quantities of pepper, spices, and diverse textiles, it includes powdered sugar of China and Bengal, saltpeter, sampanwood, ginger, cowries from the Maldives, benzoin, lacquer gum, wax, 4,321 diamonds, 590 pieces of porcelain, indigo, cotton thread of Surat, ebony, bezoar stones, and lacquerwares of Japan.[205] Over 380,000 pounds (*livres*) of cinnamon is also listed, eight years before the Dutch had actually taken Colombo. Although it does not appear on this list, tea from China and Japan began for the first time to be sold at the auctions of 1651–52 in Amsterdam.[206] On the manifest for a Dutch fleet of 1688, Chinese tea figures prominently in the listings along with large quantities of Chinese "tin" (an alloy of copper, zinc, and nickel) and saltpeter. Most of these commodities, other than pepper and spices, were not subject to the monopoly given the VOC by its charter.[207]

The fine spices were the only products tightly controlled by the Company, and three decades had to pass before it cornered the trade in nutmegs and cloves. Met by Iberian, English, and local Asian resistance, the Dutch painfully and slowly enforced an effective control over the Banda Islands, Amboina, Ceram, and the Moluccas. The Bandas, completely conquered by the Dutch in 1621, had long supplied nutmeg and mace in exchange for foodstuffs and textiles.[208] Once they were taken over by the Dutch colonists the Company possessed complete control over nutmeg and mace production. In the meantime the Company sought to concentrate clove production by limiting it to the villages of Amboina and by destroying the trees on the nearby and much larger island of Ceram. This decision was based on the conviction that Amboina could produce enough by itself to meet the combined demand of Europe and Asia, and that by limiting cultivation to Amboina the Company could easily monopolize the trade and set the purchase and sale prices of the cloves. The policy of extirpating the clove trees was not successful even on Ceram. Cloves still eluded the Dutch as they poured forth from Ceram and the Moluccas into the central market of Makassar to be purchased by all comers until its conquest by the Dutch in 1669. The advance of the Dutch against the Portuguese in Ceylon meanwhile raised hopes that the Company would be able to monopolize its cinnamon production. This objective was never realized fully because of Kandy's determination to pursue an independent course. The Company was able, however, to organize the collection and delivery of cinnamon in Ceylon by

[205] See Léon (ed.), *op. cit.* (n. 203), II, 18.

[206] Glamann, *op. cit.* (n. 186), p. 18.

[207] *Ibid.*, pp. 11–12. For the cargo of 1688 see George Meister, *Der orientalisch-indianische Kunst- und Lustgärtner . . .* (Dresden, 1710), pp. 259–63.

[208] On the trade of the Bandas see Meilinck-Roelofsz, *op. cit.* (n. 83), pp. 93–96, 219.

gradually extending its control of the traditional system. After 1660 the Dutch exercised a practical monopoly over the export of cinnamon to Europe.[209] The gross annual profit realized on nutmeg sales after 1685 was often over 1,000 percent of the purchase price.[210]

The Company's monopoly of cloves and cinnamon came later and was never as complete as the monopoly of nutmegs and mace. The failure of the Company to monopolize clove cultivation meant that it had to maintain a rigorous check upon the trading lanes and marts of Asia. Since cloves were cultivated on many islands, it was not possible to control "smuggling," as the Dutch called it, over the innumerable sea-lanes traversed by Asian shipping; even the Europeans could not be shut out of the cheap clove markets until the fall of Makassar. At Amsterdam clove prices declined steadily from 1630 to 1656; obviously the monopoly was not then fully in control of the trade.[211]

The price of cinnamon in Europe rose sharply after the Dutch completed their conquest of Ceylon in 1656–58. At New Castile, a place for which we have good series, the price rose sharply in 1659 and continued to increase until 1666, presumably because of shortages. In Asia meanwhile cinnamon prices rose also, but not as fast as in Europe. In 1660, when the price in Asia peaked, the Seventeen fixed the price in the Indies to make it unprofitable for others to trade in cinnamon or to carry it to Europe. Sales dropped thereafter as many Asian and European merchants turned to the wild cinnamon (*cassia ligna*) of Malabar as a cheap substitute for true cinnamon. Once the Dutch began their domination of Malabar in 1663 they demanded that the local rulers with whom they had treaties should cooperate in halting the commerce in Malabar cinnamon.[212] By 1665 the Dutch monopoly of cinnamon, both in Asia and Europe, had become a reality. Cinnamon prices on the Amsterdam market remained relatively constant, but not as constant as clove prices, from 1664 to 1694. Cinnamon prices at London fluctuated much more.[213]

The monopoly of the fine spices was achieved by the Company only in the last generation of the century. Control of nutmeg and mace, beginning in 1621 with the conquest of Banda, was not actually completed until after the capture of Makassar. The Company regularly sought to limit clove production, even on Amboina, to maintain prices. Cinnamon from 1664 onward existed as a practical monopoly of the Company. Throughout most of the century the Dutch sold the fine spices in Asia at artificially elevated prices; even with this self-imposed handicap they managed to sell one-third of their stock through their factories in Asia. Generally, the Asiatic facto-

[209] See Arasaratnam, *op. cit.* (n. 173), chap. viii.
[210] For nutmeg prices see Glamann, *op. cit.* (n. 186), pp. 92–93.
[211] See spice appendix, and Glamann, *op. cit.* (n. 186), pp. 96–98.
[212] For the treaty arrangements see above, pp. 58–59.
[213] For price series see spice appendix; also see Arasaratnam, *op. cit.* (n. 173), pp. 188–92.

ries, such as Batavia, were given a certain latitude in raising prices when scarcities appeared. In Holland, where they disposed of the remainder of the fine spices, the directors sold them mostly at auction from around 1650 to the date when they could maintain a fixed price. Thereafter they sold them by contract.[214]

The fine spices were the only Asian commodities over which the Dutch East India Company exercised a practical monopoly. But from a European viewpoint it also exercised a monopoly over the direct trade with Japan after 1640. Under the capable leadership of Jacob Specx, the Dutch successfully adapted to the changing political climate in Japan. After initially using Hirado largely as a base for privateering, the VOC directors recognized Japan's potential as a trading partner by 1621. Except for the years 1627 to 1632, when Dutch-Japanese relations were strained over events in Taiwan, the VOC exchanged Chinese silk for Japanese silver in steadily increasing amounts.[215]

Copper, gold, and silver from Japan, tin from Malacca, and small amounts of gold from Sumatra and Malacca were purchased whenever possible by the Dutch for resale in Asian markets. Copper from Japan first appeared in the Amsterdam market in 1628, where it apparently helped to drive down the price of Swedish copper. From 1638 to 1645 Japanese copper, used as ballast on the ships, was brought to Europe sporadically, often in large quantities after 1655. Still the main Dutch trade in Japanese copper remained in Asia, particularly for resale in India, Ceylon, and Persia where the prices for it were higher than in Europe until the very last years of the century. The Dutch, it should be noted, were never able to monopolize the trade in Japanese copper, since most of it was exchanged directly with the Chinese. In effect, the Dutch and the Chinese competed with each other for Japan's copper exports.[216]

The Company's exports of silver from Japan flowed out in a steady stream from 1640 to 1668, in some years exceeding the silver exports from Amsterdam to Batavia. Silver, like copper, generally purchased more in Asia than in Europe; consequently the Dutch resold it in Asia for other commodities. When the Japanese government forebade the export of silver in 1668, the Dutch began buying gold from Japan. During the 1660's, substantial discoveries of gold had been made in Japan, and by 1670 the Dutch began purchasing it in large quantities. During the second half of the seventeenth century Japan's extraction of precious metals possibly equaled in quantity the production of American mines. In maritime Asia, Japan's production helped to

---

[214]See Glamann, *op. cit.* (n. 186), pp. 102–9.
[215]See Kato, *loc. cit.* (n. 28), 207–29; Seiichi Iwao, "Japanese Foreign Trade in the Sixteenth and Seventeenth Centuries," *Acta Asiatica*, XXX (1976), 1–18; E. Kato, "The Japan-Dutch Trade in the Formative Period of the Seclusion Policy—Particularly on the Raw Silk Trade by the Dutch Factory at Hirado, 1620–1640," *Acta Asiatica*, XXX (1976), 34–84.
[216]Glamann, *op. cit.* (n. 186), chap. ix.

offset trade imbalances experienced by the Dutch in individual regions; to Europe it meant that lesser quantities of precious metals had to be exported to the East. The decline in exports of precious metals from Japan in the 1680's hurt the Dutch inter-Asian trade and probably contributed to the VOC's declining profits in the East.[217]

In the second half of the century Jan Company became heavily involved in the business of importing Asian textiles. The capture of a Portuguese carrack off Johore in 1603 provided the VOC with its first cargo of Chinese raw silk. Pleased with its reception on the Amsterdam market, the Seventeen in 1608 ordered their representatives in Asia to establish trading relations with China, either directly or indirectly, and in the meantime to buy Chinese silk at Patani. Among unspun raw silks the Chinese variety was preferred to the Persian and Italian products, though they all sold well on the Amsterdam market. The supplies of Chinese silk for Europe were usually irregular because they were also much in demand in Japan, and the VOC gave the Japanese market priority in all varieties of Chinese silk. The Company began in 1623, as part of its temporary policy of cooperation with the English, to import Persian silks. Hereafter more Persian than Chinese silk was bought for the Amsterdam market; both types had to compete in Europe with silks from Italy, France, and the Levant. When Persian silk prices rose steeply in 1636–37, the Dutch returned to Chinese silks and also began to import Bengali silks.[218] From 1640 to the end of the century the Dutch maintained factories at Tongking to purchase Chinese silks. While the Japanese refused to buy the Persian silks, they were willing to buy Bengali silks when Chinese silks were scarce and expensive. In Europe the Bengali silks could be sold more cheaply than any of the other Asian silks and so gradually came to dominate silk imports from the East. In Bengal the Dutch in 1655 set up a headquarters at Hugli and a special silk bureau at Kasimbazar. The VOC was followed into Bengal by the English, and soon keen competition developed over Bengali silks, from threads to fancy woven materials. Over the course of the seventeenth century the English were not able to catch up to the Dutch in total annual textile imports.[219]

After 1670 the number and variety of Indian cotton imports substantially increased. Unpainted fabrics and batiks from Coromandel, regularly exchanged in Indonesia by the Dutch and others for pepper and fine spices, began to become more common in Europe. A modest number of Coromandel and Gujarati coarse piece goods (Gunnees especially) were brought to Europe for reexport to the West Indies and Africa. After 1665 the Dutch, as well as the English, began to import larger quantities of the finer Indian

[217] See *ibid.*, pp. 54–63; and Gaastra, *loc. cit.* (n. 28), 64–65.
[218] Braudel claims that the Dutch did not buy Persian silks because they wanted to export silver for trade in the Indian Ocean. Braudel, *op. cit.* (n. 75), III, 217–18.
[219] Glamann, *op. cit.* (n. 186), pp. 112–31.

cottons, particularly calicoes. The better-quality Indian cotton cloths began to be used in Europe for tablecloths, towels, hangings, rugs, and upholstery, as well as clothes. The "Indian craze" of the 1680's and 1690's was based on the ready availability and relatively cheap prices of Bengali silks and cottons. By 1697 one-third of the total value of the VOC's imports was in Bengali textiles.[220]

The profits realized from the Company's trade in Asia and Europe are impossible to determine accurately. Its "country trade" in Asia is usually estimated as having been more profitable, from the 1640's onward, than its Asia-Europe trade. In the interregional trade, spices, copper, silver, and gold moved from west to east. Wealthy native merchants in Indonesia, India, and elsewhere were partners and associates of the Dutch and provided goods, services, and often capital for their enterprises.[221] To 1660 the Dutch had seven East Indiamen in operation to every three English vessels; in contrast to their rivals, the Dutch were primarily concerned about the East India trade and less inclined to be attracted by Africa, the Americas, and colonization.[222] The Company's direct trade between Batavia and Amsterdam showed a steady increase over the second half of the century, thanks to the rising demand for fine textiles and saltpeter in Europe. Still, the annual returns from the trade always fluctuated, and most of the time the directors had to borrow money to pay for the next outgoing fleet and its cargo. Before 1654 the net profit to the shareholders on a business totalling 25 million guilders amounted to an estimated 9.7 million guilders or about 38 percent. Over the twenty years from 1674 to 1693, during the India craze, the volume and the percentage of profit went even higher.[223]

The financial successes of the VOC in the seventeenth century were not primarily dependent upon its spice monopoly. It had to compete in Europe and Asia for most products, especially for the textiles which brought its prosperity to a peak. Its spice monopoly and the expansion of the "country trade" after 1640 provided the Dutch enterprise with a control system in the East (centered at Batavia) which none of its rivals possessed. The VOC itself was a business enterprise that initiated a change of scale in international commerce by its stability, efficiency, and far-flung activities. Still, the profits of the East India Company, large as they became, were modest when compared to the returns garnered by the Dutch from shipping and commerce in Europe.[224] At no time was the VOC's trade with Asia more than a small percentage of the Republic's total commerce. Jan Company doubtless

---

[220] *Ibid.*, pp. 132–45. For the importance of textiles in the preindustrial economy see Braudel, *op. cit.* (n. 75), II, 312–13.

[221] For example, see J. J. Brennig, "Chief Merchants and the European Enclaves of Seventeenth-Century Coromandel," *Modern Asian Studies*, XI (1977), 321–40.

[222] Furber, *op. cit.* (n. 55), p. 78.

[223] Based on Glamann, *op. cit.* (n. 186), pp. 86–87.

[224] *Ibid.*, p. 11; and Davies, *op. cit.* (n. 180), pp. 53–54.

stimulated the trade and industry of the Republic and was especially important for the direct and indirect employment it provided and the business innovations it inaugurated.[225] But the market for Asian goods was limited, and the risks involved in Asian trade were greater than those of European commerce. To investors the European trade was more attractive than the Asian enterprise, for it took them much longer to turn over their capital when they bought shares in the VOC. It is not possible at this time to calculate accurately the impact of the Asian trade on the Dutch economy.[226] It should be emphasized, however, that many contemporaries continued to believe in 1700 that the trade with Asia was highly valuable and with great potential for further development.

5

THE ENGLISH EAST INDIA COMPANY

England's entry into the race for the seaborne commerce of the East was inspired by the news of the rich cargoes brought back in 1599 by four ships from the Dutch fleet of Van Neck. Prior to this time London merchants had worked to gain direct access to the spice marts of Asia by routes north and south of the sphere of Iberian control. Unsuccessful in these efforts, they formed the Levant Company in 1581 to exchange at Mediterranean ports the cloths, tin, and arms of England for the Asian products selling there. At first their only major competitor in this commerce was Venice. But then the Dutch erupted into the Mediterranean in the 1590's with the Baltic grain to sell in markets where grain shortages were common. The slowdown after 1590 of traffic on the overland route from India to the Mediterranean raised spice prices there to levels that only the Dutch could afford to pay. This Dutch conquest of Mediterranean trade came at the same time as their pre-Company voyages to the East, which the merchants of the English Levant Company closely watched. Some of the London merchants, like Richard Hakluyt the geographer, promoted the idea of emulating the Dutch by sending out English ships to the East via the Cape Route. After the Dutch had proved to English satisfaction that such voyages could be made safely and profitably in spite of the Iberian monopoly, the London promoters began petitioning Queen Elizabeth for permission to send a fleet to the East.

---

[225] Various efforts have been undertaken to calculate the proportion of the East India trade to the whole of Dutch trade. I. J. Brugmans estimates that for the period 1660 to 1698 the VOC accounted for something more than 9 percent of the Republic's overseas trade. See his "De Oost-Indische Compagnie en de welvaart in de Republiek," in *Welvaart en Historie. Tien Studien* (The Hague, 1950), pp. 28–37. Others consider this estimate to be low. See Boxer, *op. cit.* (n. 124), pp. 278–81, and Haan, *op. cit.* (n. 134), pp. 183–84.

[226] On the profits of long-distance trade compared to short commercial runs see Braudel, *op. cit.* (n. 75), II, pp. 368, 403, 408, 430–32, 453–57.

Once it had become clear that the war then going on with Spain was drawing to a close, the reluctant queen in 1600 finally acceded to their entreaties.[227]

In 1600 the population of Elizabeth's England (not including Scotland and Wales) numbered over 4 million, or more than three times that of the United Provinces; by the beginning of the eighteenth century it had mounted to 5.8 million, while the Dutch figure only increased from 1.5 million in 1620 to 1.9 million in 1690. London, the fourth in size among Europe's cities in the early seventeenth century, had become by its end the largest, with a population of over four hundred thousand. Most of England's international commerce went through London and the coastal towns of the south, and during the latter half of the century it became ever more concentrated in London. The crown, normally debt-ridden before the Revolution of 1688, relied heavily for its income upon customs receipts. Taxation in the home counties became frightfully burdensome over the century, as capital concentrated at London and came more firmly under the control of rich merchants, joint-stock companies, and banks. Still, to 1660, England remained basically an agrarian economy, as were those on the continent, perhaps with the sole exception of the United Provinces.[228]

The English East India Company, chartered on the last day of the year 1600, was granted a monopoly of Eastern trade for a period of fifteen years; with it went the opportunity to compete in a worldwide multilateral trading system.[229] Many of the merchant-adventurers who formed the new Company were also prominent in the Levant Company. From their perspective the creation of the East India Company was not an independent commercial venture but an effort to separate the spice trade from the rest of the Levantine trade. The connection between the Levantine and Asian enterprises was maintained throughout the first half of the century; indeed, the English, like the Dutch, were quick to begin reexporting spices to the Levant. The English, again like their European competitors, had difficulty in defining a comprehensive policy for Eastern trade. The tin and cloths exported to the Levant were not salable in further Asia; and the silver required for Eastern trade was not as plentiful in London as in Amsterdam. A bit of the despair felt by the Company's servants in the East was succinctly expressed by Thomas Aldworth in a letter of 1614 from Surat: "English cloth [woolens] will not sell; it was only bought at first by great men to cover their elephants

[227] See W. Foster, *England's Quest of Eastern Trade* (London, 1933), chap. xiv. For the texts of two of the petitions see J. N. Das Gupta, *India in the Seventeenth Century as Depicted by European Travellers* (Calcutta, 1916), pp. 242–51.

[228] Based on Mols, *loc. cit.* (n. 125), pp. 38–44; and the article on "The British Isles" by Charles Wilson in C. Wilson and G. Parker (eds.), *An Introduction to the Sources of European Economic History* (Ithaca, N.Y., 1977), pp. 115–54.

[229] The leading authority on the history of the East India Company and its role in world trade is K. N. Chaudhuri. See his works on *The English East India Company. The Study of an Early Joint-Stock Company, 1600–1640* (London, 1965), and his *The Trading World of Asia and the English East India Company, 1660–1760* (Cambridge, 1978).

and make saddles for their horses. But for garments they use none in these parts." [230]

A chief asset of the English East India Company was the simple organization provided by its charter. The Court of Committees composed of twenty-four directors was elected annually by the General Court of shareholders. Under a governor and his deputy, the Court of Committees was the executive organ and responsible only to the shareholders; it initiated policy and managed operations. Its twenty-four members were generally assigned to subcommittees charged with preparing the voyages, cargoes, loadings, and sales. A staff of paid officials performed routine business. From the outset a group of wealthy London merchants, most of whom were also involved in other foreign trading ventures, assumed control of the administration. The original 217 shareholders of the General Court included a broad range of individuals, from members of the aristocracy to widows and orphans as well as a number of foreign investors. The London merchants welcomed aristocratic investors, because they realized from the beginning that the Company would need interested spokesmen at the royal court. Most of the foreign investors were Dutch; they were received willingly in the hope that they would act as sources of intelligence on the activities of the VOC. [231]

During its first decade of operations, the Company tested trade routes and experimented with commodities and business methods at home and in Asia. Until 1614 separate voyages were sent out, often with different groups of shareholders investing in each venture. Separate annual voyages were replaced in 1614 with joint-stock ventures of several years' duration. Until 1608 the Company waited for the return of one fleet before dispatching another. Annual fleets were sent thereafter. The fleets of 1601 and 1604, respectively commanded by James Lancaster and Henry Middleton, went to the East Indies to set up a factory at Bantam, to buy pepper, and to seek out the cloves and nutmegs at their source in Banda and Amboina. Factories were necessary to collect cargoes ahead of time, for when the ships arrived from Europe local prices skyrocketed. From the experience gained through these early voyages, the English learned that Indian textiles were essential to barter in Indonesia for pepper and spices.

To aid them in breaking into the "country trade," the English in 1610 employed two Dutchmen, Pieter Floris and Lucas Antheunis. Previously four fleets commanded by the Englishmen had tried unsuccessfully to set up permanent trading posts at Surat and on the Coromandel Coast. On behalf of the English Company the Dutchmen traded successfully on the Coromandel Coast and at Siam, and their ship returned in 1615 with a rich cargo.

[230] As quoted in F. J. Fisher, "London's Export Trade in the Early Seventeenth Century," *Economic History Review*, 2d ser., III, No. 2 (1950), 159.

[231] For a social analysis of the trading companies formed in the years from 1575 to 1630 see T. K. Rabb, *Enterprise and Empire: Merchant and Gentry Investment in the Expansion of England* (Cambridge, Mass., 1967), pp. 27, 39, 149–50.

Thomas Best, the commander of the voyage of 1612, finally obtained permission from the Mughuls for the English to trade on a regular and permanent basis at Surat. Once a trading station was set up at Surat in 1613 the Company's commerce in Asia assumed the basic pattern that would characterize it for the remainder of its history: silver from Europe was used to purchase in India the textiles bartered in Indonesia for pepper and spices to export to England.

Between 1610 and 1620 developments took place rapidly in Europe and Asia. The difficulties with the Dutch over the Moluccas were temporarily set aside, in Europe at least, by the Accord of 1619.[232] From Surat the English meanwhile became involved in the trade with Persia. Both at Surat and at Ormuz they were confronted by hostile Portuguese. In Southeast Asia the English factory organization was gradually extended from Bantam to Acheh and other ports of Sumatra where the cloths of Surat were more in demand. In 1613 factories were also established at Makassar and in western Borneo for procurement of spices. Sir Thomas Roe, England's emissary to the Mughul court from 1615 to 1618, worked out the conditions for English trade in the Mughul empire. Agents from Surat opened subordinate India factories at Agra, Ahmadabad, Burhanpur, and Broach, as well as at Masulipatam on the Coromandel Coast, to purchase indigo, textiles, and saltpeter. Further to the east, factories were founded at Hirado in Japan, at Ayut'ia in Siam, and at Patani on the eastern coast of the Malay peninsula.

The factory at Hirado suffered throughout its brief history (1613–23) from its isolation and a lack of regular and sustained communication with Bantam.[233] Its factor, Richard Cocks, in cooperation with his colleagues at Ayut'ia and Patani, nonetheless had managed by 1618 to establish a small but profitable trade with Cochin-China and Cambodia. By 1620 the president of the Surat factory exercised control over the Indian and Persian trade, and the president of the Bantam factory over the rest of the English outposts. Expansion halted around 1623 as the Company began to concentrate upon the consolidation of its trading organization.[234]

From 1620 to 1640 the Company faced Asian crises and trading problems that made profitable commerce extremely difficult. The proliferation of new factories slowed to a halt. Despite Cock's protests, in 1623 the Company withdrew its personnel from East Asia. Internal conditions in Japan, Siam, and Indochina made profitable and regular trade impossible to maintain. Because of poor market conditions the Dutch, in some cases even before the English withdrawals, likewise abandoned their factories in East Asia with the notable exception of Japan. While English competitors (the Courteens) tried in 1637 to open direct trade with China, the directors of the

[232] See above, p. 50.

[233] For its history in brief scope see D. H. Willson, *A Royal Request for Trade. A Letter of King James I to the Emperor of Japan Placed in Its Historical Setting* (Minneapolis, 1965), pp. 17–21.

[234] See Furber, *op. cit.* (n. 55), pp. 40–42.

English East India Company did not seriously consider resuming direct trade with East Asia until 1657.[235]

In cooperation with the Persians and the Dutch, the English captured the Portuguese fortress at Ormuz in 1622. In return for their help the English received half the spoils, half the customs, and were declared to be forever free from paying duties at Ormuz. But they in no way enjoyed a monopoly of the Gulf trade, for the shah in 1623 concluded a treaty with the Dutch much to the disadvantage of the English. The Dutch were more readily able than the English to furnish the silver and fine spices the Persians wanted in return for their textiles.[236] Wars had meanwhile broken out in Europe, bringing with them trade dislocations and currency debasements. The English trade in woolens suffered a particularly severe depression. Agitation began in London against the export of silver for Asian products.[237] It was in this climate that Thomas Mun (1571–1641), sometimes called the Father of Mercantilism, wrote in 1621 his defense of the Company in response to those who charged that "the gold, silver, and coyne of Christendom, and particularly of this King-dome, is exhausted, to buy unnecessarie wares."[238] The smaller shareholders of the Company clamored loudly, as they had before, for quicker and larger profits, and expressed impatience with the directors' response that profit-taking would have to be delayed until the trade could be placed on a firmer footing.

The Dutch-English Accord of 1619 was strained seriously by the news which arrived in London of the "Massacre of Amboina" of 1623.[239] It should not be assumed, however, that the English withdrawal in 1623 from the Spiceries, Japan, and Siam resulted from the "Massacre"; it was rather the Company's earlier disillusionment with the unwillingness of the Dutch to abide by the Accord in the Indonesian region that prompted the directors in London to order the abandonment of factories unable to operate at a profit.[240] The withdrawal was followed by a renewed concentration on the India trade. Off the coasts of western India and in the Indian Ocean the Dutch still

---

[235] Competition with the Dutch is usually advanced to account for the English withdrawal. While this was the case in insular Southeast Asia, it was the poor market conditions on the continent and in Japan which led to the English decision. See D. K. Bassett, "The Trade of the English East India Company in the Far East, 1623–1684," *JRAS*, 1960, pp. 32–47, 145–57. Also see the same author's "The Trade of the English East India Company with Cambodia," *JRAS*, 1962, pp. 35–61. The short-lived Cambodian enterprise of 1651–57 was established without official sanction. Also see J. B. Eames, *The English in China* (London, 1909), chap. i.

[236] See above, pp. 51–52.

[237] See J. D. Gould, "The Trade Depression of the Early 1620's," *Economic History Review*, 2d ser., VII (1954), 81–90.

[238] *A Discourse of Trade* (London), p. 5. He argues that export of specie is necessary for the balance of trade.

[239] See above, p. 51.

[240] The only connection between the decision to withdraw and the "Massacre" is the coincidence of dates. London's policy of abandonment was adopted well before the "Massacre" occurred and before news of it reached England. See D. K. Bassett, "Trade . . . in the Far East, 1623–84," (n. 235), pp. 34–35.

cooperated with the English in attacking Portuguese and local shipping. When the Mughul emperor threatened to close Surat in reprisal, a compromise agreement of 1624 granted the English almost complete freedom of trade throughout his empire in return for ceasing their attacks on local shipping.[241] Trade in Gujarat was almost halted by the severe famine that began in 1630 and persisted long thereafter. Scarcities of commodities at Surat led the Company to direct its efforts to the development of new trade on the Coromandel coast, in Persia, and in Bengal. Finally, since the Portuguese had become less of a threat than the Dutch to the British position in India, a truce was concluded in 1635 with the Portuguese.

In England the anxious Company thereafter found its monopoly being seriously challenged. King Charles in 1637 granted a patent to the Courteen Association, a group of discontented servants and business rivals of the Company, to trade in those parts of the Indies where the Company had no factories. In 1637 Courteen sent the first English expedition to China: four ships and two pinnaces under Captain John Weddell. This fleet sailed by way of Goa to Macao where it was badly received both by the Portuguese and the Chinese. Clearly the Anglo-Portuguese truce, as the Portuguese understood it, was not meant to open Macao to the English.[242] The Courteen Association thereafter turned its attention to other parts of Asia; in England it continued to challenge the Company. The Courteen Association was dissolved in 1646 under pressure of fiscal losses and civil war. Private trade by such groups, as well as by the Company's own servants, was never completely suppressed in the seventeenth century.

During the first phase of its history, down to the outbreak of civil war in 1642, the East India Company figured prominently in the business affairs of England and Europe. In London it became a major builder and lessor of ships. The English East Indiamen, like those of the Dutch, were usually of three hundred tons or more. Smaller ships were built to compete in the port-to-port trade of the East and were employed as dispatch ships to carry messages between England and the factories in Asia. At their Blackwell Yard on the Thames, the Company built naval repair docks, foundries, a spinning house for manufacturing ropes, and numerous storehouses for timber, canvas, and provisions. After 1626 the Company began to manufacture its own gunpowder, an industry previously monopolized by the Evelyn family.[243]

A total of seventy-six ships were either built or purchased by the Company between 1600 and 1640. A few great ships were built in the earlier years weighing nine hundred to one thousand tons, but after 1628 none exceeding six hundred tons burden. Provisions and bullion ballasted the ships

[241] Furber, *op. cit.* (n. 55), p. 47.
[242] See Eames, *op. cit.* (n. 235), pp. 11–12.
[243] For more details on the Company's activities in London see Chaudhuri, *The English East India Company* (n. 229), pp. 89–103. On p. 91 he gives sailing lists for 1601–40.

on the outward voyage, enough provisions for twenty-four months on the Bantam fleet and for eighteen on the Surat fleet. The round trip ordinarily took at least sixteen months. The ships left London at the beginning of March, arrived at the Cape in June or July, and then proceeded either to Bantam or Surat. Having learned from the sailing experience of the Portuguese and Dutch, the English suffered very few shipwrecks because of navigational or nautical errors. Even when the English became heavily engaged in the "country trade," they built very few ships in Asia.

The Company's imports from the Indies were financed by the export of precious metals and a few goods from Europe, the profits from the "country trade," and short-term borrowing from local merchants in the Indies. The drain of precious metals, a source of constant complaint by the critics of the Company, was tolerated primarily because their real value was much higher in Asia than in Europe.[244] From the very beginning of the trade the English merchants realized that ready money was the key to success. The Spanish real, always in short supply in England, was purchased in the markets of Holland and France. When the government prohibited the general export of silver and gold from England in 1615, the Company was treated as a special case and allowed to continue its exports. The precious metals were paid for by the reexport of pepper, spices, and textiles to the continent and the Levant.

By 1640 London had become a market for Eastern wares comparable to Lisbon. Since very few Oriental commodities were in demand in England (pepper excepted), the Company had to resell most of its Asian imports to the continent. Pepper exceeded in volume and value all the Company's other imports; the profits from its sale were also far greater than those realized from other Asian imports. The early voyages came back laden with pepper, so the Company was soon able to meet England's limited demand. The demand for pepper was inelastic, and a glut was quickly produced. The Company thereupon sought alternative imports and markets. In the East they tried to buy the fine spices at the source, and added indigo, textiles, and saltpeter to their purchases. Once pepper became a dead commodity in England, the Company turned to continental markets to dispose of its surpluses.

Consumption of pepper in England fluctuated between two and three hundred thousand pounds annually; the Company's imports of pepper never dropped below five hundred thousand pounds and usually went much higher. The agents of the Company in Asia seem to have bought whatever amount was needed to ballast the ships. The peak of pepper imports came between 1617 and 1630. To sell their surpluses to European consumers the Dutch and English engaged in price wars. Although the Dutch were successful in monopolizing the fine spices, they failed to drive the English out

---

[244] For a table listing the exports in money and goods from 1601 to 1640 see *ibid.*, pp. 114–15.

of the pepper business. Until the middle of the century it remained at the heart of the English enterprise. Cloves purchased at Makassar were the only fine spices imported directly to England from the East; the others were brought in from the Netherlands.

To protect the home market, the king in 1609 forbade his subjects to buy pepper from any source other than the East India Company. The fixed price of pepper was proclaimed to be 2s-6d per hundredweight. Prices nonetheless rose from 1615 to 1617, possibly because of an increasing demand on the continent. When the Thirty Years' War broke out in 1618, the Company learned that the markets of western Europe were full of pepper.

The Company's trade in cloves peaked in 1635 and prices declined thereafter.[245] Study of the pepper and spice trade from the English viewpoint highlights the inelasticity of demand, the slow rate of its growth, and the effects of the tightening Dutch monopoly of the spices.

Between 1600 and 1640 the direct trade with India became increasingly more important to the English Company than the spice trade. Indigo, calicoes, saltpeter, and sugar offered brighter commercial prospects in both Asia and Europe. At this period the Dutch were not the main competitors in the indigo trade; the Company's rivals were the Portuguese and Levantine indigo purveyors. As the prime import from Surat, indigo was sold as dye to the English cloth industry. The depression of the 1620's, most severe in the woolens trade, brought about a decline in the demand for indigo. Later, as cotton and silk textiles came into the English market in quantities, the demand for indigo rose again. The first imports of saltpeter reached England in 1626 and showed regular expansion thereafter, particularly during the civil war. A boom in cotton textile imports occurred in the same decade, and many of the calicoes were reexported to the continent, North Africa, and the Levant. Persian silk first reached England in 1619, and the Company thereafter tried without great success to expand its importation. After experimenting with Chinese silk purchases in 1614–15, the Company forbade its servants to buy them.

During the first forty years of its existence the English East India Company might be thought of as the poor man's version of the VOC.[246] It suffered from a chronic shortage of finance capital, a limited home market, and an unfavorable situation for reexport to the continent. According to estimates made at a later date, the first joint-stock venture (1613–21) made a profit of 87.5 percent, the second (1617–32) made only 12.5 percent, and the third (1631–42) did somewhat better, in that it paid a dividend of 35 percent spread out over ten years.[247] The Company's most difficult period lay in the late 1620's when it suffered most from the hostilities with the Dutch. Its

[245] See spice appendix.
[246] See Braudel, *op. cit.* (n. 75), II, 450 on the different shareholding patterns of the VOC and the English East India Company.
[247] See Furber, *op. cit.* (n. 55), p. 65.

coffers were drained by the heavy outlays required for protection of the trade, by an unusual loss of ships, and by the interest on monies borrowed to pay the shareholders their dividends. After a brief revival in the 1630's, the financial fortunes of the Company steadily declined. The onset of the civil war between 1640 and 1642 increased the angle of decline until virtual collapse came in the 1650's.

Although faced with serious financial setbacks, famine, and a suffocating trade depression, the Company's servants in the East managed somehow to survive the debacle that overtook the Company in Europe. The truce with Portugal (1635) was followed by the Anglo-Portuguese treaty of 1642 terminating hostilities in India and on the high seas, both countries then suffering from deep civil divisions at home. The Surat factory began to buy small "country ships" built in the nearby Portuguese ports of Bassein and Damão. English merchants took advantage of the truce and peace to extend their commercial footholds on the Coromandel coast. In 1640 they founded a settlement at Madraspatam, just north of the Portuguese outpost of San Thomé (in Mylapore, part of modern Madras; the name Madras gradually began to be adopted for this area in general during the last two generations of the seventeenth century). The following year, 1641, with the permission of the local ruler, they started to build Fort St. George. This had hardly been undertaken when war broke out in south India as Golconda and Bijapur, both Muslim states, partitioned the remnants of the old Hindu kingdom of Vijayanagar. These wars of the mid-1640's produced famine in south India and seriously disrupted its textile production for about three years. With the restoration of order, the Europeans were permitted to retain their factories in south India because of the financial benefits they brought to the region. Madras in 1651 was elevated to replace Bantam as the Company's southern headquarters. In the following year Cromwell obtained a treaty with Portugal which permitted English merchants to trade freely in all of Portugal's eastern possessions except Macao.[248]

The Company in London had become moribund by mid-century, and its directors and others involved in foreign trade sought new courses to pursue. The great success of the rival VOC, some urged, could be attributed to its closer relationship to the state, to the extraordinary powers granted to its representatives in the East, to the centralization of its trade at Batavia, and to the greater efficiency of Amsterdam's distributive system. In the past the crown had supported the East India Company's monopoly and other privileges only because of its dependency on revenues received from customs and loans; King Charles I had even encouraged "interloping." The English, unlike the Dutch, had no settlement in the East over which they exercised dominion, from which they commanded adjacent markets, and to which they could send colonists. In India, where the English trade had become

[248] *Ibid.*, pp. 66–73.

concentrated, the representatives of the Company had to deal with local officials and possessed no power, except naval attacks or cessation of trade, to enforce their demands or to maintain privileges already won. While little could be done to change conditions in the East, something could be achieved at home by developing a better distributive system.

From the outset the distribution of Asian imports had been left to individual members of the Company or to wholesalers. In the 1650's the director, then hard pressed for ready money, began to hold regular auctions. Quarterly auctions were held in London which gradually began to be attended by dealers from continental markets. These specialists, who came from as far away as eastern Europe, were well schooled in the actual conditions of trade in their home markets: the stocks already in hand, the prices of substitute goods, the best times and routes for shipping, and the regional tastes. From the Company's viewpoint the quarterly auctions provided information about the state of the market as well as indicators of possible trends in demand. The auctions, because they were held at one location and on specified dates, made it easier for buyers and sellers to get together to exchange goods and news. Before the auctions opened, printed lists were circulated on which appeared the type, quantity, quality, and opening prices of the goods to be sold. In the course of the auction the final sale price was determined by free bidding among the dealers present. Rings or syndicates of buyers bent on depressing prices were apparently not numerous enough to elicit complaints from the Company.[249]

During England's republican years the Company retained a legal monopoly of the East India trade by virtue of a resolution of the House of Commons in 1650 reaffirming it. Private ventures were, however, pursued successfully and with impunity; in fact, the trade was officially thrown open to all comers from 1654 to 1657. Internecine competition, coming in addition to the international competition with the Dutch, brought temporary ruin to the trade. Even the Company's critics attributed the failures to its inability to control interloping and to the unlimited competition prevailing in England and Asia. In 1657 a new charter was granted to the Company providing for a single and permanent joint-stock system to replace the existing successive joint-stock structures terminable at brief intervals. With the Restoration of the Stuarts, King Charles II in 1661 granted a new charter which likewise provided for a permanent joint-stock system. He assigned additional powers to the Company to deal with interlopers, to make war and conclude peace with non-Christian princes, and to maintain civil and criminal jurisdiction in the Asian outposts.[250]

This new legitimacy and permanency added greatly to the strength of the

---

[249] Based on Chaudhuri, *The Trading World* (n. 229), pp. 131–35. For the Dutch auctions *cf.* above, pp. 65–66.

[250] Furber, *op. cit.* (n. 55), pp. 75–76.

Company and to the role of its merchants in England's foreign relations. The crown began to act as spokesman and advocate of the Company in its relations with the Dutch and other foreign powers.[251] With the crown's support, its imports from Asia underwent an enormous growth to 1684. Pepper and fine spices continued to be imported, and a shift in consumer taste developed into a craze for Asian textiles, tea, and coffee.

The first task confronting the revivified Company was to establish its pepper trade on a firm footing in Asia. The Dutch blockade and embargo of Bantam from 1651 to 1659 had reduced its importance and had correspondingly stimulated the growth of the lesser factories on Sumatra. Once Bantam was reopened it reassumed the position of prime supplier until the Dutch took it over in 1682. Thereafter the Company shifted its pepper purchases to Benkulen in Sumatra where a factory was set up in 1685.[252]

In 1661 Surat remained the center of the Company's northern trade in India. To cut overhead costs Surat was forced to reduce the number of outlying factories subordinate to it. The cession in 1661 of Bombay to the English crown, as part of the dowry of Charles' Portuguese queen, opened new vistas in northwestern India. Formally occupied by the English in 1665, Bombay was leased to the Company three years later. The harbor and island were soon fortified, but the Company's hope of developing it as a replacement for Surat was long deferred. The convenience of Bombay's deep harbor and its separation from the turmoil of the mainland were counterbalanced by its reputedly unhealthy climate and its lack of direct connection to the caravan routes which traversed the rich and fertile plains of Gujarat and linked Surat to the marts of northern India.[253] Although Bombay in 1687 became the administrative headquarters of the Company in western India, Surat continued to function for long thereafter as its chief trading center.

On India's east coast, Madras had become the Company's principal trading post by 1661. From here the English, like the Dutch before them, had followed the traditional trade tracks from the Coromandel coast across the Bay of Bengal to the ports and bazaars of the Ganges delta. To the Europeans Bengal was well known as a major source of high-quality muslins, raw silk, and saltpeter. The unfavorable navigational conditions for large ships generally prevailing in the delta forced the Europeans to limit their Bengal trade to the towns along the Hugli river. Consequently the English factories in Bengal remained unfortified and functioned as dependencies of Madras. From 1661 to 1680 Madras gradually overtook Surat as the Company's major trading port in the whole of India. When a serious rebellion against the Mughuls erupted during 1696 in Bengal, the governor allowed European factories to fortify themselves to protect the trade. By the end of

[251] S. A. Khan, *The East India Trade in the Seventeenth Century* (New Delhi, 1975), pp. 98–99.
[252] See Chaudhuri, *The Trading World* (n. 229), pp. 53–54.
[253] For a map of the main caravan routes, as of *ca.* 1650, see *ibid.*, p. 48.

the seventeenth century the Company possessed three fortified outposts—Bombay, Madras, and Calcutta—at the vertices of a triangle of trade. Internally these places were connected to one another and to the great inland marts of India by caravan and river routes. But with their growing naval power, the English expanded their Asian commerce mainly along the sea routes.[254]

From Bantam the English sent ships and merchants in the 1670's and 1680's to open trading stations in Taiwan, Tongking, and Amoy. The Dutch, as much as they might have wanted to, were unable at this time to prevent the English from competing with them for the China trade. Between 1670 and 1673 the English tried seriously to enter the Japan trade through the factories set up at Tongking and Taiwan. The directors of the Company, under pressure at home to export woolens instead of precious metals, were willingly convinced by their agents at Bantam and elsewhere in Asia that they might crack the Dutch monopoly in Japan by sailing there directly to sell woolens. After their ships were turned away from Nagasaki in 1673, the English concentrated on breaking into the coastal trade of China, especially at Amoy and Fukien.[255] The conquest of Taiwan in 1683 by the Ch'ing rulers of China ended English activities there; the following year the Company closed its Siam factory as well. Four years after the opening of Canton in 1685 the English began sending trade missions there; the Tongking factory also continued to supply China goods until it was closed in 1697.[256]

Any type of comparison between the Dutch and the English as naval powers in the East will show that the Dutch fleets held a decided edge during the first half of the century.[257] In the Atlantic the Anglo-Dutch war of 1652–54 was but the first of three (second, 1665–67; third, 1672–74) by which the English established naval superiority over the Dutch in European waters.[258] The East India Company, which had built its own Indiamen in the first half of the century, began to charter its ships in 1658 from private shipowners who bore all the risks. During the thirty trading seasons between 1658 and 1687, the vessels hired by the Company made 404 voyages between London and the East, or an average of 13 per season. Most of the time twenty East Indiamen were at sea. To keep up with this brisk trade the Company concentrated most seriously on the efficient utilization of its shipping, particularly with regard to the cargo allocations made for the direct voyages or for the interregional trade. The ships destined for the return trip to Europe had to be loaded carefully to maintain a balance between high-

---

[254] Based on *ibid.*, pp. 51–53.
[255] For Dutch activities off the China coast during this hectic period see above pp. 60–61.
[256] See Bassett, "Trade . . . in the Far East, 1623–84" (n. 235), pp. 40–42, 153, 156. The Dutch maintained their factories at Tongking without serious interruption from 1640 to 1700.
[257] See Meilinck-Roelofsz, *op. cit.* (n. 83), pp. 194–95.
[258] See C. R. Boxer, *The Anglo-Dutch Wars of the Seventeenth Century, 1652–1674* (London, 1974).

value and low-value goods, and to carry enough merchandise to pay for the voyage without endangering the ship from overloading. Over the century the financial losses suffered by the Company from shipwreck were rarely very serious.[259]

A full quantitative picture of the Company's major trading activities has been made possible by the survival of its account books from 1664 onward, the date of the establishment of the Company's permanent capital. While building up its working capital the Company was slow to declare dividends, for they were generally paid out solely from earned profits. Over the first seven years following its new charter in 1657, the Company declared a total dividend of 60 percent paid in three installments of 20 percent each. Three annual dividends followed which ranged from 40 percent to 50 percent. By 1670 the receipts from the Company's London sales began regularly to exceed £1 million annually, and dividends began to be paid yearly thereafter until 1690, the peak coming in 1682. The receipts, steadily on the rise from 1662 to 1682, generally exceeded payments, but often only by a small margin. Even with all the records and data available, it still is not possible to calculate the Company's profits accurately. The directors considered that they and their enterprise were financially successful—and so did the Dutch and the rest of the world.[260]

The prosperity of the Company during the Restoration was based on its expanding trade in cotton piece goods, calicoes, and muslins. Textiles were different from the other Asian imports in that they enjoyed a more elastic demand. Imports of calicoes, a generic name used in the records for most of the cheaper cottons, rose from 240,000 pieces in 1663–69 to 861,000 in 1699–1701; in the later years of the century two-thirds of these were re-exported.[261] In the imports of 1664–78 the share of pepper varied between 15 percent and 30 percent of the total. For the same period cotton and silk piece goods accounted for almost one-half; thereafter they amounted on the average to between 60 percent and 70 percent of the whole. Indigo and saltpeter fluctuated between 2 percent and 5 percent. Tea, imported from Bantam, did not exceed 1 percent of the imports until 1690, and coffee amounted to roughly the same. Until 1700 Surat and Madras supplied between 60 percent and 80 percent of the total imports, the popular Bengal textiles being funneled through Madras.[262] By 1688 one-half of the India goods reexported from London were cotton piece goods.[263]

In India the administrative and military costs of the Company mounted

[259] Furber, *op. cit.* (n. 55), p. 91; and Chaudhuri, *Trading World* (n. 229), pp. 71–74.
[260] See Chaudhuri, *Trading World* (n. 229), pp. 415–25.
[261] See R. Davis, "English Foreign Trade, 1660–1700" in W. E. Minchinton (ed.), *The Growth of English Overseas Trade in the Seventeenth and Eighteenth Centuries* (London, 1969), p. 82.
[262] *Ibid.*, pp. 96–98.
[263] Furber, *op. cit.* (n. 55), p. 92.

steadily. The development of Bombay, chiefly under President Gerald Aungier (r. 1669–77), as its seat of naval and military power placed new and burdensome fiscal responsibilities upon the Company. The rise of the Mahrattas on the continent involved the Company, indirectly and then directly, in warfare. Sivaji's (1627–80) defiance of the emperor Aurangzib (r. 1659–1707) in 1674 precipitated a series of Mahratti wars centered in the Western Deccan which continued well beyond the end of the century. These wars signaled the beginning of a great Hindu revival that eventually brought about the collapse of the Mughul Empire in the eighteenth century. Reverberations were felt throughout the Mughul Empire and by the English. Sir John Child, commander of the Company's forces in India, was faced by the overwhelming task of protecting shipping and factories from the side effects of these wars, particularly once Sivaji began to build up a Mahratta navy. In the 1680's the Company was forced to shut down its inland factories in Gujarat and speed up building its fortifications at Bombay and Madras. Soon a state of general war developed between the English and Aurangzib which ended in 1690 with the defeat of the Europeans everywhere. But Aurangzib, well aware of the financial benefits of European trade, had no desire to expel the English after their defeat.

These temporary setbacks in India were contemporaneous with the Revolution of 1688 and its aftermath in England.[264] To the end of the century and thereafter the profits of the East India Company went into a decline. Between 1692 and 1697 the Company's stock fluctuated wildly in price, declining from a high of £200 per share to a low of 37. The accession of William of Orange in 1688 provided the enemies of the Company with new hope. Working primarily through the Parliament, the interlopers endeavored to put together a political alliance to break the Company's monopoly. The Company was charged with disrupting the nation's economy by its vast exports of bullion, by its failure to export English goods, and by its disregard for the infant cotton textile industry. The defeat in India in 1690 served further to validate the attacks of its enemies. The main object of the interlopers was to convince the government to open the trade to private English merchants or to enlarge the membership of the Company. A struggle between the "Old Company" and a "New Company" of interlopers, chartered in 1698, went on over the next decade. The effect of these years of turmoil was to transfer to Parliament the right of controlling grants of privilege to the Company in return for regular and substantial loans to the state.[265]

Chaotic trading conditions in India were exacerbated in Europe for the Company by a rising tide of hostile public opinion to textile imports, by new competition from France, and by the War of the League of Augsburg (1688–97). Measures to protect the domestic textile industry were inaugu-

[264] *Ibid.*, pp. 92–98.
[265] *Ibid.*, pp. 98–102.

rated in 1685 when Parliament placed an additional duty of 10 percent *ad valorem* on imported cotton piece goods.[266] Scarcities of the whole range of East Indian goods, including pepper, characterized the entire decade of the nineties, and their prices generally increased; textile supplies did not recover from the disruptions produced by the Mughul wars until 1699.[267] Violent weaver riots broke out in London in 1697 during which the India House, the headquarters of the Company, was attacked. Three years later Parliament, confronted by an alliance of the weavers and the gentry, passed an act prohibiting the import, use, or wearing of "all wrought silks, Bengalls, and stuffs mixed with silk, or herba, of the manufacture of Persia, China, or East India, and all calicos [cotton fabrics], painted, dyed, printed or stained. . . ."[268] This decree helped to bolster the English domestic printing and finishing industry but did not check the Indian imports of the Company or foster domestic manufacture of cotton cloths. The Company remained in a bad financial condition at century's end; dividends had not been declared since 1690, and the directors repeatedly had difficulty raising working capital.[269] An additional duty of 15 percent was imposed in 1700 on the gross sales of Indian textiles at the Company's auctions.[270] Buyers were apparently limited to dealers who intended to reexport their purchases.[271] England's continental market was also shrinking, since regulations had been put into effect in France, previously one of the Company's best customers, to curtail or exclude textile imports.[272]

During the Stuart period, the Company, like its Dutch competitor, possessed a legal monopoly of the home market, fought its own wars in the East, and functioned as a state within a state. As a rule it could rely on the support of the crown in maintaining the monopoly and in using diplomacy to reinforce its interests abroad. In India the president of Bombay frequently acted as if he were the king's own minister in the relations carried on with the Mughuls and other princes. Like the Dutch, the English possessed only limited territorial ambitions in Asia, though there were those who advocated dominion and argued that the greater Dutch commercial successes had resulted from the political strategy which they had continuously followed. Both companies sought by their purchasing and selling practices, in Asia as well as in Europe, to command the markets and to impose upon them a

---

[266] Chaudhuri, *Trading World* (n. 229), p. 294; also see R. Davis, "The Rise of Protectionism in England, 1689–1786," *Economic History Review,* 2d ser., XIX (1966), 306–17.

[267] Chaudhuri, *Trading World* (n. 229), pp. 324, 345.

[268] As quoted in *ibid.,* p. 295.

[269] *Ibid.,* p. 460.

[270] Braudel considers this tariff as decisive in the later development of the Industrial Revolution. Only by the introduction of machines could the English cotton industry compete with India; see *op. cit.* (n. 75), III, 567, 571–74.

[271] Chaudhuri, *Trading World* (n. 229), p. 295.

[272] See below, p. 102. On the extreme measures proposed to stop the import of cotton cloth from India, see Braudel, *op. cit.* (n. 75), II, 178–80.

centralized and bureaucratic system of exchange and distribution. In Asia the Dutch were far more successful than the English in controlling the "country trade," though both made steady profits from the sale of maritime passes. In Europe they commanded the market through their contract sales and auctions of Asian imports; both generally managed by their control of supplies to prevent sudden gluts, shortages, and price fluctuations. The English Company was much slower and far less successful than its Dutch counterpart in attracting trading capital, in establishing a strong political base in the East, and in controlling private trade and interloping. The relative backwardness of the English Company reflected the general under-development of England in financial matters; for example, the Bank of Amsterdam founded in 1609 antedated the establishment of the Bank of England by eighty-five years. However, by the end of the seventeenth century the English East India Company, then England's largest single corporate body owned privately, had maneuvered itself into an economic position that would soon permit it to overtake and outstrip its Dutch rival in marketing Asian commodities.[273]

6

THE LESSER COMPANIES

The earliest of the minor companies to challenge the Dutch and English enterprises was established in Denmark in 1616.[274] Founded by King Christian IV (1588–1648), the Danish East India Company endured through several reorganizations until 1800. At the dawn of the seventeenth century the elected king of Denmark ruled over a maritime empire of wide extent between the Baltic and the North Sea. The waters of The Sound, commanded by Copenhagen and Malmo, formed its center. To the east of The Sound lay Scania on the coast of southern Sweden, as well as the Danish islands of Gotland, Bornholm, and Oesel, which gave Denmark its preponderance in the Baltic; to the west lay Danish Zealand, Fyn (Funen), and Jutland. Norway, a dependency of Denmark since 1526, constituted its northern hinterland. In its foreign relations Denmark stood with its back to Sweden and faced outward to Germany and the United Provinces. Determined to crush

---

[273] *Ibid.*, pp. 20, 109, 115–17, 131–34, 208, 411.

[274] For the Company's history see Gunnar Olsen, *Dansk Ostindien, 1616–1732* (Copenhagen, 1952); K. Glamann, "The Danish East India Company," in M. Mollat (ed.), *op. cit.* (n. 27), pp. 471–77; Jacques Macau, *L'Inde danoise: la première compagnie (1616–1670)* (Aix-en-Provence, 1972); and Furber, *op. cit.* (n. 55), pp. 211–13. For the Danes in India see Kay Larsen, *De Dansk-Ostindische koloniers historie I–II* (Copenhagen, 1907–8). The first part is on Tranquebar; the second on Bengal and the Nicobars. See also Ole Feldbaek, "The Organization and Structure of the Danish East India, West India and Guinea Companies in the Seventeenth and Eighteenth Centuries," in Blussé and Gaastra (eds.), *op. cit.* (n. 28), pp. 135–58.

Sweden, Christian IV initiated the War of Kalmar (1611–14), which brought an uneasy peace between Sweden and Denmark for the following thirty years. From this war the Danes learned the value of the royal fleet as an instrument for securing the country and maintaining control over the surrounding seas. The king, whose main revenues came from the transit dues imposed upon ships and merchandise passing through The Sound, took advantage of more than a decade of peace from 1614 to 1625 to enlarge the port facilities of Copenhagen, to rebuild the navy, and to launch ambitious commercial projects.[275]

It was in this atmosphere of expansiveness that the king decided to begin competing for the trade of the East. Jan de Willum and Herman Rosenkranz, two Dutch merchants engaged in business in Denmark, proposed to Christian IV in 1615 the creation of a Danish East India Company. By a patent of March 17, 1616, the king authorized the establishment of a Company at Copenhagen to trade with the countries of the east and the Pacific region, and to set up factories wherever the princes of Asia would sanction it. The Company's first counselor was Roland Grappe, a veteran of seven voyages to the East with the VOC. While Grappe advised sending the Company's first voyage to the Coromandel Coast, another Dutchman, Marcel de Boshouwer, convinced the king to send it to Ceylon. Boshouwer, who had served the VOC in Ceylon, had returned to Holland to work out an alliance for the king of Kandy with the Dutch Company. Once the Dutch decided they were not in a position to aid Kandy in warring against the Portuguese, Boshouwer turned to Christian IV and represented himself as the plenipotentiary of the king of Kandy. In this capacity he worked out terms for a treaty of alliance and commerce (March 30, 1618) between Denmark and Kandy which was to be effective for seven years. By its terms Denmark was to send military aid to Kandy and was to receive in return a monopoly of European commerce with Ceylon. The officers of the Company's first voyage were instructed to carry the treaty to Kandy for ratification, to provide immediate military and naval support to its king, to collect payment from Kandy for the aid rendered, and to establish Danish forts and factories in Ceylon and on the Coromandel Coast.[276]

The Danish Company headquartered in Copenhagen, then a city of no more than fifteen thousand inhabitants, received its initial capital of 188,000 rixdales from the king and three hundred shareholders. The king, a fancier of Asian exotica, was the most enthusiastic and largest investor.[277] While most of the original investors were Copenhagen merchants, the largest pri-

---

[275] For his Copenhagen project see Konvitz, *op. cit.* (n. 127), pp. 38–45.

[276] For a reproduction of this "treaty" see Olsen, *op. cit.* (n. 274), p. 39.

[277] Prince Christian of Anhalt visited Copenhagen in 1623. In his diary he describes the royal collection, tells of two ships being outfitted for trade to the East Indies, and reports on a visit to the king's "silk house." See G. Krause (ed.), *Tagebuch Christian des Jüngeren, Fürst zu Anhalt* (Leipzig, 1858), pp. 94–96.

vate shareholders were Jan de Willum and his brother David. Some of the smaller Danish cities, Norway, and Hamburg also invested. In addition to the initial and subsequent subscriptions of the crown, the king provided the armed ships necessary for the expeditions. When the Company required additional funds, particularly in the 1630's and 1640's after most of the foreign investors withdrew, the king placed heavy pressure upon Danish merchants, nobles, and professional people to invest in the Company. Throughout the seventeenth century the crown worked hard to keep the Company independent of foreign control, even though overtures had to be made at times of great stress to sell out to the Dutch and English companies. When the Company was reorganized in 1670—the end of its first period—the crown, through its newly founded Board of Trade, continued its efforts to limit foreign financial participation.

The Company's first voyage, commanded by Ove Gjedde and manned by Dutch officers and sailors, left Copenhagen in November, 1618. The two great ships outfitted by the Company were accompanied by a pinnace and escorted by two of the king's warships. After an arduous voyage the Danish fleet finally arrived at the Bay of Trincomalee in eastern Ceylon in May, 1620. The king of Kandy refused to accept Boshouwer's treaty or to pay for Danish aid; rather he concluded a new treaty with Gjedde in August, 1620, ceding Trincomalee to the Danish along with the obligation to fortify it. While these negotiations went on, two Danish vessels sailed on to Tanjore in south India; Gjedde himself followed in the autumn of 1620 and concluded on November 19 an agreement with the nayak of Tanjore. A Danish agent crossed the Bay of Bengal in 1621, probably in a native craft, and established relations with the Siamese governor of Tenasserim. On the return voyage to Europe Gjedde stopped at Trincomalee to inspect the progress made in building a fort and in gathering a cargo of cinnamon. Little had been done by the Danes left behind, and so Gjedde left in disgust. By 1622 the Portuguese took over at Trincomalee.[278]

The remnants of the Danish fleet returned to Copenhagen during 1622–23. The two returning ships carried mostly pepper and exotic woods purchased in India. In the East, Gjedde's accomplishments were much more substantial. While the Kandy agreement failed, his most enduring achievement took place on the Coromandel Coast. Here he obtained a *farman* (written grant) from the nayak of Tanjore which permitted the Danes to build a factory and a fortress at Tranquebar, and to trade duty-free in the nayak's domain. Other Europeans, except for the Portuguese already at Negapatam, were excluded from Tanjore. The Dutch and English, then heavily involved in conflict with each other over Indonesia, were in no position to prevent the establishment of the Danesborg settlement in Tranquebar. Trade relations initiated with Tenasserim also seemed to be off to a good start. The

[278] See Olsen, *op. cit.* (n. 274), pp. 42–79.

appearance of the Danes in the Siamese provinces on the Bay of Bengal was welcomed by King Song Tham (r. 1610–28). He had long been disturbed by the growing power and demands of the Dutch traders and wanted other European connections. His governor at Tenasserim issued letters in the Danes' favor in 1621 giving them preferential treatment with respect to the payment of port duties and fees.[279]

Before leaving India, Gjedde named Roland Grappe factor of Tranquebar and Trincomalee. In 1623 the "Pearl," a vessel of five hundred tons, left Denmark for Tranquebar; two years later it returned with a good cargo and with Jon Olaffson aboard. An Icelander and a gunner at Danesborg, Olaffson left for posterity a memoir written between 1661 and 1679 of his earlier observations in India.[280] By 1626 the Danes had factories at Masulipatam, at Pondicherry, and at Pipli in Bengal.[281] East of India they quickly set up factories at Bantam, Makassar, and Sukadana in western Borneo. But it was the beginning of disaster for the Company when, in 1625, Christian IV took his country into the Thirty Years' War in Germany.

The Company's early voyages probably lost money. No dividends were paid in the 1620's or early 1630's; instead the king and the other stockholders were forced to pour more capital into the enterprise just to keep it afloat.[282] In 1628–29 a shortage of capital forced the Danes in India to sell their stocks of indigo and saltpeter to the Dutch and to put Danesborg up for sale or lease. They could expect little help from home once disaster confronted Christian IV on the battlefields of Germany. Still the Danes in India continued in these dark years to profit enough from the "country trade" to keep the Company alive.

To the Dutch and English in the East the Danes were interlopers who operated under the protection of their fleets without bearing a share of the costs. They could not crush the Danish trade because of foreign policy considerations related to their countries' involvements in the European wars. In India the Danes were often able to offer lower prices and spoil the market for their more tight-fisted competitors. In this game they allied themselves with the Portuguese and carried Portuguese cargo and refugees on their ships. Their main trade gradually centered at Makassar where they exchanged spices for Coromandel cloth. They regularly circumvented the Dutch spice monopoly, and probably enjoyed profits from a few of their voyages. The "Christianshaven" returned to Copenhagen in 1635 with 83,940 pounds of pepper, 28,142 of saltpeter, and smaller quantities of cottons, woods, sugar,

---

[279] For the Siamese texts and their translations see His Highness Prince Dhani Nivat and Major Erik Seidenfaden, "Early Trade Relations between Denmark and Siam," *Selected Articles from The Siam Society Journal*, VIII (1959), 271–88. The original texts were discovered in the archives at Copenhagen early in the twentieth century.

[280] See the English translation by Dame Bertha Phillpotts, *The Life of the Icelander Jon Olaffson, Traveller to India*, Vol. II (London, 1932), in "HS," 2d ser., LXVIII.

[281] See Raychaudhuri, *op. cit.* (n. 178), p. 112.

[282] Macau, *op. cit.* (n. 274), pp. 52–62.

indigo, ginger, porcelain, and diamonds. These wares were purchased in the East for 58,000 rixdales and were estimated to be worth 145,000 in Copenhagen. The "Saint-Anna" in 1637 unloaded a cargo of cloves which had cost 76,000 rixdales and would sell for 200,000.[283] On the Coromandel coast the Dutch were required more than once to cut spice prices to retain their hold on the market.

After Grappe returned to Copenhagen in 1637, Danesborg declined swiftly. Its European personnel, including two Lutheran pastors, lived by piracy and pillage. By the 1640's, the Danes were forced again to try to sell Danesborg to the Dutch. A sale was not effected; the relations between the Danes and the Dutch on the Coromandel Coast were worsened when the Dutch and Swedes declared war on Denmark in 1643. The disastrous Peace of Brömsebro forced on Christian IV in 1645 brought an end to all hope of help from Europe. Only seventy-two men were known to be working in all of the Company's factories.[284] Thereafter the remnants of the Danish holdings fell increasingly under Dutch control. The Dutch even employed soldiers in the 1650's to protect the Danish fort. Gradually the VOC reduced the Danish factories to minor satellites. The Dutch conquest of Makassar in 1667–68 ended swiftly and sharply all independent Danish activity in the spice trade.[285]

In an effort to regain its independence both in Europe and in Asia, the Danish Company was reorganized in 1670 by King Fredrick III (r. 1648–70) and his advisers. Most of the new capital came from the crown, Copenhagen merchants, prominent officials, and members of the nobility. Although an effort was made to exclude foreign investors, two Dutch brothers were again key figures in the Company. The factory at Bantam, under English protection, became at first the main focus of the new Danish activity in the East. From here the Danes began to send out voyages eastward, sometimes in the company of renegade Dutch merchantmen. In 1676 the "Fortuna," which had sailed from Copenhagen two years earlier, arrived at Foochow in China. The first Danish ship ever to reach China, the "Fortuna" apparently did not enjoy commercial success.[286] Once they had been exposed to the difficulties of direct trading with China, the Danes concentrated on becoming intermediaries in the trade between Manila, Indonesia, and India.[287] After the Dutch drove their European competitors from Bantam in 1682, the Danes operated as neutral traders between Tranquebar, Celebes, Borneo, and the Philippines. While Dutch and English trade suffered during the War of the League of Augsburg, the Danes profited. Tranquebar enjoyed a period of modest prosperity from 1687 to 1704, and the Lutherans laid the

---

[283] See *ibid.*, pp. 51–52.
[284] *Ibid.*, pp. 85–94.
[285] See Raychaudhuri, *op. cit.* (n. 178), pp. 114–15.
[286] On the "Fortuna" voyage see Wills, *op. cit.* (n. 158), pp. 160–61.
[287] On the Manila trade of this period see above, pp. 38–39.

foundations for their Tranquebar mission in this period of rising expectations. Hopes were still high for the future when the Company's charter was renewed in 1698. However, this proved to be the climax for the Company founded in 1670. In the early eighteenth century it experienced serious setbacks, was dissolved in 1729, and replaced three years later by the Danish Asiatic Company.[288]

While Denmark, one of the least populous countries of Europe, pursued Asian trade with modest success, France, the most populous of Europe's nations, was slow to form a permanent Company and to establish direct and continuous trade with the East. This delay can be explained in part by the geopolitical and economic characteristics of the country. Compared to the United Provinces and England, France was much larger in area and far less centralized. The diversity and separation of its many regional markets, as well as the strong particularism of its coastal provinces, discouraged national enterprises. Except for Bordeaux, La Rochelle, and Nantes, its Atlantic ports were isolated coastal enclaves. Internal customs and tolls inhibited overland, riverine, and maritime trade. Paris, located at a long distance from the sea on the winding and tortuous Seine, lacked the easy access to maritime trade enjoyed by Amsterdam and London. The regional ports at the mouth and on the course of the Seine were only loosely tied to Paris, whose economic life depended primarily upon internal trade relations. To develop the French navy and overseas trade Louis XIV felt compelled in the 1660's to embark on a program of building new port cities on the Atlantic coast.[289]

This is not to say, however, that the French had no interest in maritime enterprises and trade with Asia. In the early seventeenth century, the merchants and navigators of Normandy and Dieppe had sent ships to the East and had formed local mercantile societies to finance the voyages and to market imports. In 1600 the merchants of Saint-Malo, Laval, and Vitré had formed a society with a capital of 80,000 ecus to trade with the Moluccas and Japan. Six months later, in May, 1601, two vessels were sent around the Cape whose French navigators had earlier been employed by the Dutch. One of the vessels wrecked in the Maldive Islands and one of its passengers, François Pyrard of Laval, began at this point the extraordinary peregrinations which brought him safely back home in 1611.[290] The other vessel reached Ceylon and went on to trade at Acheh in Sumatra, but was captured by the Dutch off Cape Finisterre on the return voyage. Thereafter a group of Dieppe merchants, supported by southern Netherlanders (Flemish) anxious to participate in the Asiatic trade, received letters patent on June 1, 1604, from King Henry IV awarding them the exclusive right for fifteen

---

[288] See Furber, *op. cit.* (n. 55), p. 213.
[289] See Konvitz, *op. cit.* (n. 127), p. 83. On France's backwardness and subservience to Holland in terms of commercial capitalism, see Braudel, *op. cit.* (n. 75), III, 256–60.
[290] For his account of his odyssey see below, pp. 396–97.

years of the navigation to the Indies. Opposition from the Normans, the Dutch, and the Duke de Sully, Henry's minister, prevented this group from sending out even a single ship before the king's assassination in 1610.[291]

After the king's death, the charter of the Dieppe Company was renewed in 1611, eight years before its expiration date, for a period of twelve years. But during the hectic years (1610–24) of Marie de Médicis' regency, little was accomplished by this group. Its inactivity encouraged merchants of Rouen and elsewhere to seek a transfer of the royal privilege to them. The queen, who shared her deceased husband's desire for a French enterprise, fused the contending merchant groups into a new Company of the Moluccas to which she awarded in 1615 the royal privilege for eighteen years. The Normans, with aid from Dutch deserters and malcontents, sent two small expeditions to the East in 1616: from Honfleur three vessels were dispatched to India and two to Bantam. Two of these vessels were lost in the East and one returned from Bantam in 1617 with a modest cargo and with letters from the Dutch in Bantam asserting that in the future the Dutch would exclude all French vessels from the East Indies, Japan, and the Philippines.[292]

The merchants of Saint-Malo and their Antwerp allies were meanwhile not inactive. In 1616 this group sent two vessels to Java. On the way they stopped at Pondicherry on the Coromandel Coast where its nayak gave the French permission to build a fortress and a factory. At Bantam the Dutch confiscated one of the French ships, for which their government later paid a small indemnity. The other vessel returned to Saint-Malo with a rich cargo of pepper, indigo, diamonds, semi-precious stones of Ceylon, several Chinese chests, and textiles. In the hope of gaining revenge for their losses at the hands of the Dutch, the two French companies agreed to combine their resources and to send an armed expedition to Java. In 1619 three vessels carrying a crew of 275 and 106 cannons sailed from Honfleur. They were met by a Dutch fleet off Sumatra and one of the French vessels and its cargo was captured. A second French ship was left in the East to try its fortunes in the "country trade." The third vessel finally returned to Le Havre in 1622. The French court, under pressure from the Estates of Brittany and Normandy, protested to the Dutch government about this interference with trade. Finally the Dutch agreed, in a condition attached by Richelieu to the Treaty of Compiègne signed in 1624 and directed against the Habsburgs, that they would not only cease interfering with French trade but would also provide assistance to French merchants trafficking in the East and West Indies. Two

---

[291] See J. Barassin, "Compagnies de navigation et expéditions françaises dans l'Océan Indien au XVIIe siècle," *Studia* (Lisbon), No. 11 (Jan. 11, 1963), pp. 375–76; the southern Netherlanders were officially forbidden to invest in Dutch firms; but many of them did so in contravention of the law. Others sought investments, as here, in French maritime enterprises. See E. Stols, "The Southern Netherlands and the Foundation of the Dutch East and the West India Companies," *Acta Historiae Neerlandicae, Studies on the History of the Netherlands,* IX (1976), 41–42.

[292] See Barassin, *loc. cit.* (n. 291), pp. 377–78.

years later, when Richelieu became superintendent-general of navigation and commerce, the French possessed nothing more than promises of a port in the Persian Gulf and at Pondicherry, a substantial fund of information on Eastern navigation and trade, an offer of alliance from Acheh, a Malouin factor at Bantam, and an abortive Company of Morbihan that wanted to establish at Nantes the foundation for direct trade with China.[293]

Under Richelieu's administration the merchants of northwestern France continued to take the initiative in organizing overseas ventures, those of Dieppe taking the lead. In the decade 1630–40 a number of local societies were organized and voyages undertaken. Gilles de Regimont of Dieppe explored the markets of India and the Persian Gulf in 1630–32; several years later, on behalf of his fellow citizens he reconnoitered the Bay of Bengal. Further expeditions were sent into the Indian Ocean by the Dieppe group in 1635 and 1637 that attracted attention to Madagascar and adjacent islands. These activities soon sparked the interest of Richelieu and King Louis XIII (r. 1624–43), who encouraged the Dieppoise to establish trading stations and colonies in the Madagascar region. On February 15, 1643, the king signed letters patent transforming the Dieppe society into the Company of the Orient. Regimont and his associates meanwhile established a colony on Madagascar called Fort-Dauphin and renamed the island Dauphiné. From 1643 to 1664—a period when France was involved in international war, in the civil strife of the Fronde, and in the charge of Mazarin—little was done to develop Madagascar or to expand Eastern trade. When Louis XIV personally took over the reins of government in 1661, France was still in the pre-Company stage of its history and was known to the Dutch and English as their single best market for spices and textiles.[294]

In the eyes of Louis XIV and Jean Baptiste Colbert, the royal superintendent of finance, the French were in economic vassalage to their neighbors and were being forced to pay tribute in the form of high prices for imports. In their view the earlier French endeavors to establish trade with the East had foundered for lack of unity, national direction, capital, and naval support; the Dutch Company, Colbert's *bête noire* as well as his model, was esteemed to be prosperous because it was a united mercantile monopoly that enjoyed the support and protection of the state and the confidence of the country's leading merchants. It was Colbert's opinion that the Madagascar colony of the French Company of the Orient, though temporarily in trouble, should be rescued so that it might become a French base of eastern trade comparable to Batavia. In France itself the greater merchants of Paris, as well as the lesser merchants of the port cities, should be recruited to invest in and work for a chartered Company to deprive France's neighbors of the profits they enjoyed from commanding the French market.

[293] *Ibid.*, pp. 378–82.
[294] *Ibid.*, pp. 382–85.

To sell this program to a skeptical merchant community, Colbert sent out agents to the northwest provinces and to Antwerp. The French provincial merchants pleaded poverty; the Antwerp merchants had no desire to have their capital controlled by the French king. To convince the merchants of Paris, previously not interested in Eastern trade, he had propaganda pamphlets prepared by the academician François Charpentier outlining the royal program. He held meetings to put pressure upon the merchants to cooperate; the merchants' enthusiasm was barely lukewarm because they feared the crown's control. With the staunch support of the king he resolutely went ahead to create what historians have repeatedly called "Colbert's Company."[295]

In the spring of 1664 the chief merchants of Paris elected under pressure twelve of their own number as syndics and charged them with organizing a privileged Company capitalized at fifteen million livres. Even though they resorted to making what amounted to forced loans from the nobility, the financiers, and the cities, the syndics were able to raise subscriptions of only a little more than eight million livres, including three million from the king, before the formal establishment of the Company. The *Compagnie des Indes Orientales* charter, dated September 1, 1664, was granted for fifty years. It entitled the Company to a monopoly of the trade east of the Cape, transferred to it the ownership of Madagascar and adjacent islands with the obligation to propagate Christianity there, and endowed it with broad powers in the East to conduct diplomacy and to make war and peace. To encourage the Company further, the crown granted it an interest-free loan of three million livres, exempted it from ship-building taxes, volunteered to provide its fleets with naval escorts, and granted it special subsidies on imports and exports. Like many other royal institutions, it was awarded a distinctive coat of arms.[296]

The Company at once began to prepare its first fleet. The syndics had in hand 2.5 million livres of the total subscription, in addition to the king's contribution. As demanded by the king and Colbert, the syndics first prepared for the rehabilitation and peopling of Madagascar as a way station on the route to India. A purchasing commission visited the ports of France and Holland to acquire ships and naval stores. Colonists were recruited and employees engaged to run day-to-day operations. Twenty-two Dutch sailors, thirteen pilots, and eight merchants were naturalized and taken into the business; all but two were Protestants. Three agents—Beber, Mariage et Du Pont, and La Boullaye Le Gouz—were dispatched overland to obtain *farmans* in favor of the Company from the shah of Persia and the Mughul emperor. The Company's first fleet sailed from Brest on March 7, 1665; it included

---

[295] See Paul Kaeppelin, *La compagnie des Indes orientales et François Martin* (Paris, 1908; reprinted at New York in 1967), pp. 3–4.

[296] *Ibid.*, pp. 5–7.

five vessels manned by 212 men, carrying 279 merchants, clerks, and colonists, and with a cargo of silver and merchandise valued at 115,500 livres.[297]

The dispatch of the fleet was followed by the organization of the Company along the lines laid down by the terms of its charter. An assembly of the shareholders was convened at the Louvre on March 20, 1665, in the king's presence and with Colbert presiding. Here they went through the form of electing directors, most of whom were the former syndics nominated by the crown. The directors were then divided into three commissions charged respectively with administration in France, the purchase and equipping of ships and armaments, and the organization of exports and imports. The decision was made to establish factories in Bengal, on the Coromandel Coast, and in China. Finally, it was decided to outfit a great expedition to sail in 1666. Most of the determinations about the location of factories were made by Colbert in consultation with François Caron (1600–73), a naturalized Dutchman with great experience in the East and the designated director-general of the French factories-to-be. In the spring and summer of 1665 the maritime centers of the Company were established at Le Havre and Port-Louis on the Atlantic and its wharves and warehouses were built there.[298] For six years some of the Company's ships were outfitted and repaired at Le Havre. It was soon decided, however, that the ships sailing from this port were too exposed to enemy action in the Channel.[299] The Company abandoned the Seine region around 1670 and began to concentrate its activities on the south coast of Brittany. Opposite Port-Louis on a south Breton estuary, the Company was given the land of Lorient in 1665 as a place to construct its ships. But because the Company's situation was so precarious, only one ship a year, on the average, was built between 1668 and 1684. Lorient, as the Company's future center, only began to develop when it was taken over by the French navy at the outset of the War of the League of Augsburg in 1688.[300]

The initial capital of the Company and the patience of its shareholders were exhausted within eighteen months. Much of the money went to the outfitting of the first three fleets and to the colonization efforts. The directors and the shareholders, unlike the king and Colbert, were eager to forget about Madagascar and to inaugurate direct trade with the East. Royal patents were awarded to certain of the directors who were also manufacturers to encourage them to produce glass and textile products for sale in the East. To mollify the shareholders and to show his confidence in the Madagascar enterprise, the king promised to advance another two million livres to the Company. Thanks to the king's bequest, the Company was quickly able to

[297] *Ibid.*, pp. 8–10.
[298] *Ibid.*, p. 11. On Caron see Furber, *op. cit.* (n. 55), p. 106.
[299] On Company activities at Le Havre based on its account books see Charles Leroy, *La Compagnie royale des Indes orientales au Havre de 1664 à 1670* (Rouen, 1936).
[300] See Konvitz, *op. cit.* (n. 127), p. 93.

outfit its great expedition of eleven vessels carrying 1,688 persons, of whom 1,055 were merchants and colonists. The objective of this expedition, which sailed from La Rochelle on March 14, 1666, was to establish the colony firmly and to launch commercial operations in India. Caron sailed with this fleet and carried instructions on how to proceed with the establishment of French factories in India and China.[301]

In 1667 Caron languished in Madagascar; in France the Company's financial condition continued to go downhill. To keep the enterprise afloat the king promised to subscribe an additional two million livres to its support; many of the other investors continued to delay paying their pledges. The Paris merchants and directors of the Company regularly urged the abandonment of the expensive and debilitating Madagascar project and demanded that Colbert get on with the establishment of direct trade.[302] Early in 1668 Caron finally arrived at Surat with two vessels. He learned at once that La Boullaye le Gouz had successfully obtained a factory site and a *farman* from Aurangzib giving the French the same trading rights as the Dutch and English. Caron hastily obtained cargo enough for one vessel and dispatched it before he "lost" the monsoon of 1668. He also sent overland a report of his arrival in which he apologized for the poor quality of the merchandise he had hastily purchased and sketched out an elaborate plan to cooperate militarily with native rulers throughout Asia.[303]

News of Caron's arrival in India was announced in Paris by the directors in a circular letter of September 15, 1668; optimistic forecasts about the Company's future also began to appear in print. An assembly of the shareholders was held at the Tuileries on December 15 presided over by the king himself. Colbert read a report on the Company's condition and the king expressed his satisfaction with the enterprise, made additional promises of financial support, and displayed open irritation with those shareholders who were not paying up their subscriptions. At the end of January, 1669, Caron's vessel from Surat arrived at Port-Louis. Although the merchandise it carried was only a sample of what Caron intended to send in the future, the king was overjoyed. Colbert decided to sell its cargo in Paris. The directors, encouraged by this success, more than ever pleaded for the abandonment of Madagascar and for greater concentration on the establishment of factories in the East. Caron also wrote from India urging a quick end to the hapless Madagascar colony. Finally in the second half of 1669 the king unceremoniously transferred Madagascar to the royal domain and eventually relieved the Company of all responsibility for it.[304] Thereafter the Company directed its total effort to Eastern commerce.

From the beginning of his personal rule, Louis XIV was unrelenting in

---

[301] For a list of the French voyages see Kaeppelin, *op. cit.* (n. 295), pp. 653–61.
[302] *Ibid.*, pp. 15–21.
[303] See Furber, *op. cit.* (n. 55), pp. 106–7.
[304] See Kaeppelin, *op. cit.* (n. 295), pp. 20–25.

his determination to break the Dutch command of maritime trade. In this he had the support of Charles II's England. During 1669 Colbert decided to carry France's commercial war against the Dutch to the East. Jacob Blanquet de La Haye was appointed commander of a great naval expedition which was to defeat the Dutch in the East and establish new forts and factories in Ceylon and at Bangka off Sumatra. The royal fleet, called the "Persian squadron" to conceal its true destination, sailed from Rochefort on March 29, 1670. It included five ships, one frigate, three pinnaces, 238 cannons, and 2,100 men; the Company sent three merchant vessels along to benefit from its protection. In short, it was the most powerful fleet ever dispatched from Europe into the Indian Ocean. After a lengthy and incident-filled voyage, the French fleet arrived at Surat in September, 1671. By this time the Dutch were well aware of De La Haye's true objectives and had taken measures to defend their factories and ships.[305]

When De La Haye arrived at Surat, the French factory was torn by dissension, and Caron, its designated leader, was off in Bantam. The French agents at Surat, who resented Caron both because he was a foreigner and because of his imperious personality, saw their enterprise in India as resting on shaky foundations. On Caron's return to Surat in November, 1671, the royal squadron prepared to challenge the Dutch. On January 6, 1672, with Caron aboard, it sailed southward for Ceylon where the Dutch bottled it up in the harbor of Trincomalee. Running short of provisions, the fleet escaped to the Coromandel Coast and seized San Thomé near Madras. In the process De La Haye alienated the king of Golconda, who had earlier permitted the French to build a factory at Masulipatam. In Europe meanwhile war had again broken out between the Dutch and the Anglo-French allies; on hearing this, Caron sailed for Europe and perished in a shipwreck off Lisbon. Caught between the land forces of Golconda and the Dutch fleet, the French at San Thomé lost what little support they had earlier received from the English at Madras. After withstanding two sieges, De La Haye and the remnants of the "Persian squadron" returned to France in early March, 1675, almost five years after they had left. Just one positive achievement survived this debacle. François Martin, who was to become the Van Diemen of France's India enterprise, had received permission during the first siege of San Thomé from Sher Khan Lodi, the enemy of Golconda, to set up a new French factory at Pondicherry, sixty miles south of Madras. This site was later to become the headquarters of the French in India.[306]

Except for the year 1673, the Company successfully sent annual fleets to Surat during the five years of De La Haye's absence in the East; in every one of these years one to three ships returned to France with merchandise. As a rule the sales were held at Le Havre or La Rochelle. The returns, despite

[305] *Ibid.*, pp. 28–30.
[306] Based on Furber, *op. cit.* (n. 55), pp. 110–12.

adverse conditions in both Europe and Asia, were far better than in any previous period and were finally enough to defray the Company's expenses. De La Haye's failure, though admittedly serious for the crown and the Company, was counterbalanced for the shareholders by what seemed to be the beginnings of profitable trade. The directors encouraged these optimistic hopes by an adroit financial manipulation which enabled them to overvalue the Company's assets and to declare an unearned dividend. But the Company remained financially weak, its leadership divided, and its sailings irregular. The most reliable link connecting Surat to Paris remained the overland messenger service.[307]

Over the next decade the Company remained the creature of Colbert and was no more of an independent association of profit-seeking merchants than it ever had been. The crown, confronted in 1675 by a coalition of continental powers who had come to the support of the Dutch, had little time or money to put into Eastern commerce. Still, with the conclusion of the Peace of Nijmegen (1678) the directors again tried to outfit ships. In 1680 they sold off their old vessels, those thought to be no longer seaworthy enough to weather the voyage to India, to raise enough capital to outfit and load two ships. In India the Company was deeply in debt and so its exports of 1681 were used mainly to satisfy creditors there. Driven to desperation by the Company's failure to revive, Colbert forced its directors in 1682 to open the trade to individual merchants, even foreigners, on the condition that they use the Company's ships and pay freight and other charges. At the suggestion of François Martin the Company began to focus its attention upon Pondicherry and the Coromandel coast where textiles were estimated to be 30 percent cheaper than at Surat. With these changes in policy the Company had just begun to make a profit when Colbert died on September 6, 1683.[308]

The Marquis de Seignelay (1651–90), Colbert's son, was immediately appointed by the king to be Secretary of State for the Navy and director of all maritime commerce, including that of the East India Company. For the moment nothing changed in the affairs of the Company, but a new outbreak of war with Spain and the United Provinces forced a postponement in developing Pondicherry, an outpost very much at the mercy of Batavia's naval power. Once the ships of 1684 departed, Seignelay called a meeting of officials to reorganize the Company. On this occasion the provost of the merchants reported that since 1675 the Company had sent fourteen vessels to India with 3,400,000 livres of silver and merchandise; eight had returned with cargoes purchased in India for 1,870,000 livres. In the six sales held in France the Indian products had brought 4,370,000 livres, or more than double the purchase price. The Company had made significant economies

---

[307] On the fictitious dividend see the discussion of the stockholders' meeting of 1675 in Kaeppelin, *op. cit.* (n. 295), pp. 127–29.

[308] *Ibid.*, pp. 129–39.

by concentrating its activities at Port-Louis in France and at Surat and Pondicherry in India. Its losses were attributed to the Madagascar enterprise, inexperience, and war. The conclusion was reached that the trade in itself was good. The provost had almost nothing to say about the part played in Company operations by the private capitalists who had invested in the voyages of 1682, 1683, and 1684, and who probably made their dispatch economically possible.[309]

With this summary accounting before him, Seignelay began to liquidate the Company founded by his father. The reorganized Company, formed officially on March 3, 1685, took over what remained of the former Company's assets, almost one million livres. Some of the private merchants of a few years before now became shareholders in the Company. Little pretense was maintained that the new Company was an association of merchants, for in fact it was more completely and immediately under royal control than its predecessor. Its twelve directors were chosen by the king from among those who invested twenty thousand livres or more. The directors, as intermediaries between the shareholders and the king, were divided into three administrative groups: general management, accounting, and conduct of commerce. With its new administration in place the French Company in 1685 began the most active phase of its history.[310]

The reorganized Company began to do business in a country at peace and excited by new and entrancing possibilities in the East. Two emissaries from Siam, accompanied by a Catholic priest, had arrived on an English vessel in October, 1684. They were received eagerly by Seignelay and the king, both of whom were well aware of Siam's importance in Asia's interregional trade. A French national Catholic mission, dependent upon the largesse of the country and court rather than the papacy, had been functioning at Ayut'ia since 1662.[311] The missionaries at this distant outpost had to depend upon the vessels of other nations to carry them back and forth, and so they had for a long time been petitioning the court to take an interest in Siam. For his part, Phra Narai, the king of Siam, had apparently become increasingly concerned about the growing Dutch predominance over Eastern trade and was in search of countervailing forces. An envoy was sent to France in 1680, but he was lost at sea; letters from Louis XIV were meanwhile delivered to Ayut'ia by the priests as well as by itinerant French traders. The envoys of 1684 were sent to France to obtain an alliance in exchange for trade concessions in Siam, a prospect that appealed to both the missionaries and the traders of France.[312] Seignelay was especially eager to open a factory at a

---

[309] *Ibid.*, pp. 140–44.

[310] *Ibid.*, pp. 193–97.

[311] For its history see below, pp. 241–56, 420–22.

[312] Khun Walit and Khun P'ichit were the names of the two emissaries. See E. W. Hutchinson, "Four French State Manuscripts Relating to Embassies between France and Siam in the Seventeenth Century," *Selected Articles from The Siam Society Journal*, VIII (1959), pp. 95–96.

mart which was a distribution center for the merchandise of China and Bengal. Two royal vessels left Brest on March 3, 1685, to carry the emissaries as well as the French mission to Siam.

While waiting hopefully for good news from Siam, the directors of the new Company concentrated upon developing the direct trade with India. Vessels now began to be sent to Pondicherry as well as Surat on a more regular schedule and with fewer mishaps. Still the French fleets too often were delayed or missed the monsoon. From Pondicherry, François Martin urgently advised the new directors to extend operations to Bengal, the greatest textile producing region of India. The directors, for their part, concentrated upon putting the Company on a firmer financial basis in France and at Surat. Too often they had to borrow money to outfit their fleets and to repay such loans from the proceeds of the next sale. From Surat, the agents of the Company regularly complained that shortages of ready money prevented them from making purchases when prices were lowest. Throughout the remainder of its history the Company in all of its branches continued to borrow in anticipation of future sales—a practice that helped to bring about ruin in 1707.

Trouble came to the Company from another direction in this era of great expectations. The French textile industry, badly shaken in 1685 by the forced emigration of its Huguenot workers with the Revocation of the Edict of Nantes, had also begun to suffer from the mounting competition of cheap Indian imports. Louvois, the minister of manufactures and internal commerce, complained that the export of vast amounts of treasure to pay for textile imports would eventually prove ruinous. Memorials from industrial centers, such as Dieppe, charged that the East India Company had not seriously tried to sell French commodities at Surat, to limit the import of Indian textiles, or to establish a base, comparable to Batavia, where spices could be obtained cheaply. The directors responded that the general European market for French textiles had shrunk because of the vast imports of rival companies, but this assertion made no impression on critics. In 1686 the government began placing heavy duties on cotton cloth imports. Painted calicoes and cloths for painting were banned and the Company was required to sell painted cloths outside of France. The decree of 1686 banning all Indian cloths was amended in 1687 to permit the entry and sale of white cotton piece goods needed by the French dying and painting industry. The Company was also authorized to import annually a given quantity of silken materials with the condition that it sell abroad a given amount of French merchandise.[313]

Seignelay and the directors responded creatively to these protectionist decrees. They ceased purchasing painted cloths at Surat and limited their imports to white cottons, drugs, and pepper. More ships began to be sent

[313] Kaeppelin, *op. cit.* (n. 295), pp. 203–5.

annually to the Coromandel Coast. The French seriously started to develop trade with Bengal, where textiles could be purchased that were not on the prohibited list. By 1691 the Company, thanks to Martin's activities, began to build its own factory at Chandernagore in Bengal.[314] In Paris meanwhile eight new directorships were created and sold, as serious efforts were made to restore the Company's credit in France and India. In 1684 ships from the East Indies began to arrive at Saint-Malo.[315] The returns from sales of white cottons, as well as other items, netted good profits in 1687–88. In Siam, according to reports, the future looked rosy for the development of French trade and political influence. In a memoir to the king of 1688 Seignelay predicted that in four years' time the French would be firmly entrenched in the "country trade" of the East and would be carrying on "a trade infinitely more profitable than that of the English and at least equal to that of the Dutch."[316]

The outbreak of a general European war in November, 1689, brought an end to optimistic trade forecasts. At that time, too, both the king and Seignelay received a rude shock on hearing that a revolution had occurred in Siam during 1688 that brought with it a sharp setback to the French garrison there.[317] In 1690 the crown extended the war to the East. A mixed fleet of six royal and Company ships was dispatched under Admiral Abraham Duquesne-Guiton to pick up the survivors of the Siam fiasco, to take prizes en route, and to return with the goods stored in India on the Company's account. Until the conclusion of the Peace of Ryswick in 1697 the crown assumed a constantly increasing amount of direct authority over the Company and its assets. Faced by a maritime struggle with both the Dutch and English, the French navy had great difficulty protecting merchant shipping. Mixed fleets of merchant and naval vessels returned with cargoes from the East in 1691, 1694, and 1697. Duquesne-Guiton's squadron returned in 1691 with a valuable cargo of saltpeter and piece goods; the returns from the two other mixed fleets were poor. The Company nonetheless struggled on by borrowing wherever and whatever it could. From 1699 to 1701 the returns from the peacetime voyages of the Company again raised hopes. But these were dashed in 1701 with the outbreak of the War of the Spanish Succession and resumption of maritime blockades and prize-taking.[318]

During the hectic last years of the century the Company's monopoly of France's Eastern trade was definitively broken. According to its charter the Company was supposed to develop trade with all of Asia, including the Pa-

---

[314] See Indrani Ray, "The French Company and the Merchants of Bengal (1680–1730)," *Indian Economic and Social History Review*, VIII (1971), 41–42.

[315] See J. Delumeau *et al.*, *Le mouvement du port de Saint-Malo (1681–1720)* (Paris, 1966), p. 270. Other arrivals here followed in 1685 and 1687.

[316] As quoted in Kaeppelin, *op. cit.* (n. 295), p. 216.

[317] See E. W. Hutchinson, "The Retirement of the French Garrison from Bangkok in the Year 1688," *Selected Articles from The Siam Society Journal*, VIII (1959), 159–99.

[318] See Furber, *op. cit.* (n. 55), pp. 118–20.

cific region. Once the French had been driven from Siam, the Company's possibilities for establishing trade east of India all but vanished. Impatient with the inactivity of the Company, French missionaries, navigators, and private entrepreneurs petitioned the crown to license *new* organizations to establish trading relations with China and the South Seas. Colbert's Company had made a few tentative attempts to work out trading relations with Indochina and China; it had never come close to exploiting the privileges granted it in the Pacific. The Jesuit missionaries, especially Father Joachim Bouvet (1656–1730) who was then in France, announced that China now permitted trade at Canton to all comers and that France should begin sending vessels there. Others stressed the fact that Spanish control over the route around the Strait of Magellan and across the Pacific was weakening, even as Spain itself was. With the coming of peace in 1697, it was no longer possible for the government to ignore the pleas of those who pressed for the right to organize ventures designed to open China and the Pacific to French enterprise.

Jerome de Pontchartrain, who succeeded Seignelay in 1690, agreed to permit private voyages to China on condition that the Company should receive as compensation five percent of the proceeds. The first to take advantage of this concession were Jean Jourdan de Grovel, a wealthy shipowner, and his partners. In March, 1698, their frigate called "Amphitrite" sailed from La Rochelle for Canton under the command of Chevalier de la Rocque. At the sale of 1700 the cargo of the "Amphitrite" netted a profit, but the Company received, in spite of its protests, only a 2.5 percent dividend. Thereafter Jourdan and his partners organized the *Compagnie de la Chine,* the first of a series of competing China companies formed between 1700 and 1719.[319]

Early in 1698, while preparing his venture, Jourdan met at Paris with Noel Dancycan, one of the chief merchants of Saint-Malo. Impressed by the growing weakness of Spain, Dancycan apparently convinced Jourdan that they should cooperate in carrying the French flag to the coast of Chile and into the Pacific. After some hesitation, in September, 1698, the crown sanctioned the creation of the *Compagnie Royale de la mer Pacifique* with a privilege of thirty years to conduct trade and to establish factories and colonies on islands and coasts of the Pacific region not already held by other European powers. Although Pontchartrain was appointed president of the new Company, Jourdan and his partners in Paris actually managed it. The first expedition left La Rochelle in December, 1698, under the command of De Beauchesne. For the next three years its two ships, the first French vessels to sail in the Pacific, explored the tip and the west coast of South America as well as the adjacent islands. From the economic side the De Beauchesne ex-

---

[319] For a genealogical chart of the French commercial companies of this period see E. W. Dahlgren, *Les relations commerciales et maritimes entre la France et les côtes de l'océan Pacifique* (Paris, 1909), p. 122; for the history of the voyage and trade see C. Madrolle, *Les premiers voyages français à la Chine. La compagnie de la Chine, 1698–1719* (Paris, 1901).

pedition raised hopes that a market had been found in Peru where French goods could be exchanged favorably for silver and the products of China.[320] From 1701 to 1720 the Company sent out regular voyages from Saint-Malo to South America and into the Pacific Ocean.[321]

The French East India Company, more than any of the other chartered companies, remained under the direct control of the state throughout its history. France's leading merchants, like foreign capitalists, were timid about investing in a Company over which they had only limited authority.[322] Indeed, as time passed, Colbert and the king acted more and more independently and regularly ignored the wishes and petitions of the shareholders, as, for instance, in their determination to pacify and colonize Madagascar. The unwillingness of the merchants to subscribe to this and other of the Company's riskier enterprises led to regular capital shortages and deficit financing. The interests of the Company were regularly sacrificed to the needs of the state, particularly during Louis XIV's numerous wars. In the East the trading activities of the Company were hampered by its inability to dispatch regular annual voyages, to maintain stocks of capital and merchandise at the factories, and to participate more fully in the "country trade." The French, as latecomers in the East, were always on the defensive; even when the king sent naval expeditions beyond the Cape—the "Persian squadron" of 1670 and the Siamese expedition of 1685—they ended in disaster. The French relied heavily on textile and saltpeter imports and relatively little on pepper. Limited to trading in India after the Dutch took over Bantam in 1682, the French dependence on textiles became even greater. With the protectionist decrees of 1686–87 the Company was forced to limit its imports to those legally marketable in France. Unlike those of the Dutch and English companies, the French sales were not regular or attractive enough to be of great international interest. The failure of the Company to win footholds east of India led to the final breakdown of its monopoly in 1698. The French craze for Indian textiles was ended by 1700 and replaced by the exotic dream of *Chinoiseries*.

7

EUROPEAN-ASIAN ECONOMIC RELATIONS AT CENTURY'S END

By 1700 trade by the Cape route was a complex enterprise that involved the Portuguese government, four chartered companies, and an uncertain number of avowed and clandestine "interlopers." The Atlantic voyage itself, despite

---

[320] See Dahlgren, *op. cit.* (n. 319), chap. ii.

[321] For a list of arrivals and departures see Delumeau *et al., op. cit.* (n. 315), pp. 286–87.

[322] Braudel, *op. cit.* (n. 75), II, 540–41, states that French capitalists invested in tax farming rather than in commerce.

two centuries of navigational experience, continued to be more dangerous than the galleon passages across the Pacific from Mexico to Manila. Piracy was endemic to the Indian Ocean and in most Eastern waters where shipping was valuable. The Asian states were generally too short of naval power or not sufficiently interested in maritime trade to control piracy. The ruling princes of India and Southeast Asia expected the Europeans to keep peace on the seas in return for trading privileges. To carry on trade in these infested waters, the Portuguese had originally armed some of their ships and factories as they accommodated themselves to uncertain commercial conditions. The appearance of the Dutch and English in the East brought with it the European type of sea warfare: armed merchantmen, convoys, blockades, sieges, and naval encounters. Over the course of the century the three European naval powers sold maritime passes to vessels traversing the Asian sealanes under their control and realized profits from this traffic. By the latter years of the century the Dutch and English companies maintained small private navies to patrol coastal waters and to track down corsairs. The maintenance of armed fleets, factory guards, and fortresses became a constantly mounting charge against the proceeds of trade.

The Europeans in Asia generally had only a limited interest in territorial acquisition and hegemony. The Iberians had acquired Goa, Malacca, Diu, Manila, Timor, Flores, and the Moluccas by conquest, and Macao by a tacit understanding with the Chinese. In India, besides Goa, the Portuguese retained footholds at century's end along the sixty-mile coastal stretch from Bassein to Damão; in addition, they held the fortress of Diu and had economic control of its Gujarati hinterland. The "Province of the North," as the Portuguese called these sites on the Bay of Cambay, was commercially prosperous but regularly under pressure or attack from land and sea. A few miles south of Bassein the English held sovereignty over Bombay, a gift of the Portuguese crown and the English Company's only territorial possession in western India. By treaty the Dutch controlled the pepper trade of Malabar and the cinnamon production of Ceylon. By *farmans* of the local nayaks on the Coromandel Coast the English had a factory at Fort St. George (Madras), the French at Pondicherry, and the Danes at Tranquebar. Other Indian ports, such as Surat, Calcutta, and Masulipatam, were places where all law-abiding merchants and companies were permitted to build factories and to become part of local business.

To the east of India, by 1700 the Dutch controlled all the major trading centers except Macao, Manila, and Benkulen in Sumatra. From Batavia the Dutch managed and taxed the international trade of the Malay-Indonesian archipelago because they commanded the sea-lanes and the region's major marts. The Dutch suffered less than their rivals from direct interloping by virtue of their greater military strength and their ruthless use of it. They also rigorously regulated the production of the fine spices in the Bandas, Amboina, and the Moluccas through agents and colonists. In this monopoly system, the native population was kept in bondage, the production of spices was restricted to what the Company expected to sell, and compulsory delivery at prices fixed by the Company was enforced. The VOC, despite occasional objections from its chiefs in Holland, had put into place by 1700 a system of commercial vassalage that extended geographically from Malabar to the Spice Islands and was based on treaties and contracts negotiated with or forced upon local Asian rulers. Even so, the Dutch were never able to keep their European rivals from buying pepper in Malabar and Sumatra.

In eastern Asia the Europeans possessed no such special position of control. The Dutch held their privilege of trade in Japan by accepting terms prescribed by the shogun's government. Political conditions in Indochina militated against the establishment of permanent factories there; even so, Dutch, English, and Asian merchants became fixtures at Tongking during the latter half of the century. Although it was itself unprofitable, the Dutch factory at Tongking supplied until 1700 the Chinese silks and other goods needed for the lucrative Japan trade. From 1685 to 1697 the English purchased most of their China goods through their factories at Tongking. The opening of Canton to international trade in 1685 and the subsequent overseas activities of Chinese merchants made the Indochinese factories completely unnecessary and unprofitable. Instead of sending vessels to China's ports the Dutch became content to purchase Chinese goods at Batavia from Chinese and Portuguese merchants. The English and French undertook direct commercial voyages to China beginning in 1697–98. While the Dutch Company ordinarily operated effectively from its Asian headquarters of Batavia, renegades and privateers still evaded the VOC's control and participated in the inter-Asian trade from Korea to Madagascar.

The VOC itself had become a vital cog in the machinery of the "country trade" over the course of the seventeenth century. During the previous century the Iberians had left the inter-Asian trade almost entirely in private hands, the crown consequently garnering few profits from it. From the middle of the seventeenth century onward the VOC dominated the movement in southeastern Asia of the spices and metals which circulated from east to west and of the textiles and metals that traveled from west to east. The VOC's major role in the export of Japan's copper, silver, and gold quickly made Batavia into the major financial center of maritime Asia. Profits from the "country trade" increasingly helped the VOC to sustain its European trade and to decrease its reliance on silver exports from Europe. By contrast, the Portuguese, English, French, and Danish profits from the "country trade" were minuscule. As a consequence of Dutch commercial dominance in Asia east of India, the English were forced to rely increasingly on the textile commerce, both in Asia and Europe. The Dutch, as they gradually cut down on their commitments in the Americas, concentrated their abundant resources, acumen, and industry upon the preservation and development of the Asian side of their worldwide trading empire.[323]

The overland route from India through Persia and the Ottoman Empire remained open at most times throughout the century. The Portuguese continued to send dispatches and special envoys over the land route between Lisbon and Goa, as they had in the past. At the beginning of the seventeenth century the land voyages between India and Portugal had become so numerous that the crown in 1613 forbade departures from Lisbon via the overland route without royal authorization.[324] With respect to the caravan trade the most serious blockage occurred between 1590 and 1630, or during the period when the English, Dutch, and Danish East India companies were inaugurating their enterprises and when the principal shipping lanes shifted definitively away from the Red Sea and the Persian Gulf to the Cape route. The land routes were thereafter used primarily by messengers and envoys and for gold shipments. French merchants and travelers used the overland route more frequently than others, in part because of a longstanding relationship to the Ottoman Empire and in part because they lacked a permanent national maritime connection until the 1660's. The hinterland states of Europe, in their efforts to establish trading companies free from Atlantic dominance, also tried to establish relations overland with the Ottoman Empire and Persia. By the end of the century the caravan trade, or whatever remained of it, was dominated on its European side by Armenian, Persian, and Jewish merchants.

Many of the princes and peoples of the Asian states profited from the worldwide commerce opened to them by the Europeans. Japan, China, and the Philippines, a traditional triangle of trade, were pulled into new commercial directions by the advent of the Europeans. The Japanese and Chinese, as well as the European merchants of Macao and the Philippines, profited from the commercial order imposed on the inter-Asian trade by the Dutch and on the Pacific commerce by the Spanish. The Mughul emperor, as well as other Indian princes, valued the European trading companies enough to grant them *farman*s, to receive their emissaries with the fanfare usually reserved for ambassadors, and to permit them to continue trading, as in the case of the English at Bombay, even after defeating them in battle. In the rest of Asia, and even in those places where the Europeans exercised territorial control or suzerainty, many princes, nobles, and merchants accepted the Europeans as new trading partners. The number of trade agreements entered into voluntarily probably exceeded those concluded under duress, except in the Malay-Indonesian archipelago. Asian rulers occasion-

[323] Furber, *op. cit.* (n. 55), pp. 87–88.

[324] For the discussion of this subject and for summaries of three of the seventeenth-century Portuguese relations of land voyages to India see Virginia Rau, "Les portugais et la route terrestre des Indes à la Méditerranée aux XVIe et XVIIe siècles," in M. Cortelazzo (ed.), *Mediterraneo e Oceano Indiano* (Florence, 1970), pp. 91–98.

ally sent emissaries to Europe to work out better trading conditions or to seek military support. Siam alone, because of its king's refusal to submit to Dutch, English, or French coercion, became a backwater of the maritime commerce; its neighbors, by contrast, were able to expand their international trade substantially. Without question the Europeans helped to integrate Asia's scattered and parochial economic regions, to establish *new* trading marts at Macao, Manila, Batavia, Madras, Bombay, and Calcutta, and in the process to redefine trading patterns and to modify commercial practices. The great influx of silver from America, Europe, and Japan flooded constantly into China and India where it helped to raise commodity prices in both countries.[325] The intensified demand for India's textiles certainly produced changes in that industry's organization. Thus by 1700 Asia had become part of the international economic community and had begun to change, to profit, and to suffer from this tightening relationship.[326]

Europe's economy similarly changed and developed as a consequence of the commerce with Asia. As it became centered at Amsterdam and London, the Asian trade helped northwestern Europe to obtain the commercial and industrial supremacy it has enjoyed ever since. Economically speaking the seventeenth was a black century for Spain, Italy, and Germany, a golden (silver) century in the Netherlands and England, and a varicolored century in France. The ascendancy of the north brought about the eclipse of the Antwerp-Lisbon trade connection and reduced the two ports to secondary roles as distribution markets. Shifting trade patterns also contributed to the decline of Venice and other centers of the Adriatic and eastern Mediterranean regions, and to the rise of the free port of Leghorn (Livorno) as a new entrepôt in Italy from which the East India companies obtained their supplies of coral for dispatch to the East. On the Atlantic coast many ports, especially Amsterdam and Copenhagen, were modified and enlarged, partly to accommodate the growing Asian trade. In France the crown created the city of Lorient for the benefit of the French East India Company.

While the Asian trade was independently organized by the various nations boasting chartered companies, all of Europe became progressively enmeshed in it. The Portuguese crown monopoly, never entirely free of foreign participants, was succeeded by chartered companies dominated by a

[325] See A. Hazan, "The Silver Currency Output of the Mughal Empire and Prices in India during the Sixteenth and Seventeenth Centuries," *The Indian Economic and Social History Review,* VI (1969), pp. 85–116. Glamann, in "The Changing Patterns of Trade," in Rich and Wilson (eds.), *The Cambridge Economic History of Europe,* V (Cambridge, 1978), writes (p. 213): "The great influx of silver and gold from the Americas extended to Asia from Europe, and the price revolution accompanied it." Also see Atwell, *loc. cit.* (n. 109), pp. 68–90; Braudel, *op. cit.* (n. 75), III, 217, 490–91.

[326] I. Wallerstein specifically excludes Africa and Asia from the capitalist world-economy of his Phase B (1600–1750) of the modern world system. What he understands by the "capitalist world-economy" is not clear, or is perhaps too constricted. *The Modern World-System II. Mercantilism and the Consolidation of the European World-Economy, 1600–1750* (New York, 1980), pp. 7–9.

broad range of independent businessmen, navigators, and bureaucrats. Germans, English, and others regularly served the VOC, and Dutch entrepreneurs and capital participated in the development of trading companies in Denmark, Sweden, France, and England. By 1650 the commercial ties between the Channel ports, Scandinavia, Germany, and Poland became tighter as merchants from these places went to Amsterdam and London to buy Eastern wares. France and the Holy Roman Empire continued throughout the century to be avid consumers of Asian products: spices, saltpeter, textiles, and exotica. Such expanding business activities of the East India companies contributed significantly to trade imbalances, capital transfers, and monetary fluctuations as well as to the extension of Europe's multilateral payment system.

Like the Portuguese before them, the Dutch and English companies put into touch two different economic and political systems. In the process they themselves were transformed from commercial enterprises into Asian territorial powers and from concessionaires into proprietors. Nor were the private companies willing to share their concessions and acquisitions with the sponsoring state. In 1664 the Dutch East India Company brusquely declared:

The places and fortresses which have been taken in the East Indies ought not to be regarded as national conquests, but as the property of the individual merchants who have the right to sell them to whomever they wish, be it to the King of Spain or to another enemy of the United Provinces.[327]

But this process was a physiological metamorphosis rather than a deliberate transformation. Determined to maintain their sources of profit, the Companies resorted to war and extended their dominion only when trade was threatened or when monopoly of supply was their object. In contrast to the other European chartered companies (of which there were many in the seventeenth century), the Dutch and English East India companies were distinguished for their longevity, the wide extent of their field of action, their great financial means, their appeal to wealthy investors, their bureaucratic structure, their centralization and command of their European markets, their financial records, and their political and economic influence both at home and abroad.[328]

If imitation be true flattery, the Dutch and English East India companies were certainly the object of it. Efforts of the Portuguese and French to organize companies of their own had failed in the first half of the century for want of capital and general merchant interest and support. In the Portuguese case, the crown, rather than the mercantile community of Lisbon, had initiated action and at an unpropitious time when discontent with Habsburg rule was on the rise in Portugal; its India Company lasted for five years be-

---

[327]L. Dermigny, "L'organisation et le rôle des compagnies," in Mollat (ed.), *op. cit.* (n. 27), p. 451.

[328]*Ibid.*, pp. 444–46.

fore being dissolved. In the French case the early initiatives were taken by local merchant groups of the northwest who had been unable, even with the crown's encouragement, support, and guidance, to unify their efforts and agree on a proper plan to follow. It was only after Colbert and Louis XIV took charge in 1661 that the great resources of the crown forced a relatively successful French Company into existence in 1664. Although Colbert hoped to create a mercantile monopoly with the support of the Paris merchants, his Company never rivaled the Dutch Company in strength and failed to drive it out of business. On the contrary, the era of Louis XIV's greatest influence in the 1670's and 1680's was precisely the period when the Dutch and English companies enjoyed their greatest prosperity. The Danish Company, founded in 1616 and reorganized in 1670 by King Frederick III, likewise had its most successful time during the last generation of the century.

The successes of the companies along the Atlantic seaboard were watched closely throughout the century by jealous merchants and petty princes of the hinterland, from Scotland to the little Dalmatian republic of Ragusa (Dubrovnik), a commercial link between Europe and the East whose economy was closely tied to Venice.[329] Like the Englishman Charles Davenant, these rulers of Europe's interior were convinced that "if the East-India Trade carry out the Gold and Silver from this side of the World, 'tis truly . . . at the Cost, and Expense of France, Germany, Spain and the Northern Kingdoms, who have little, or no Opportunities of Trading thither."[330] To rectify their adverse trade balances, merchants and rulers of the other European states made numerous unsuccessful or only briefly successful efforts throughout the century to free themselves from dependence on the established companies by organizing their own enterprises: Genoa (1647), Brandenburg (1658–60; 1684–88), Habsburgs (1660–62), Sweden (1626; 1668–1674), Scotland (1693–1707). In many of these efforts, including the one in Scotland, the prime movers were disenchanted former employees of the great companies or independent mercantile groups, particularly Armenians. By the late seventeenth century, influential Armenian merchants were prominent at most of Europe's marts and were viewed by the great companies as real or potential infringers.

Spice prices (see appendix) further illustrate the European-wide involvement in Asian commerce. European pepper consumption increased over the seventeenth century as competition intensified and prices fell.[331] Pepper is one of the few Asian commodities for which several continuous price runs

---

[329] Until an earthquake destroyed their city in 1667, the Ragusans played a minor role both in the overland and maritime spice trade. See N. Mirkovich, "Ragusa and the Portuguese Spice Trade," *The Slavonic and East European Review*, XX (1942–43), pp. 174–87; also see V. Vinaver, "Mercanti e bastimenti di Ragusa in India, una leggenda," in Cortelazzo (ed.), *op. cit.* (n. 324), pp. 177–90, for a corrective to many of the claims about Ragusan activities in India.

[330] *An Essay on the East-India Trade* (London, 1696), p. 15.

[331] Consumption declined during the Thirty Years' War, but increased dramatically in the latter half of the century. Wake, *loc. cit.* (n. 78), pp. 390–91.

exist; and pepper was the only one of the spices not monopolized by the Dutch. Incomplete runs of pepper prices are extant from seventeen marts of western and southern Europe. Thirteen of these series are included in the appendix; the others (Würzburg, Munich, and two for London) were omitted because they reported opening prices at auctions and not transacted market prices. In addition to the price runs for Amsterdam, the most continuous series come from the secondary northern European markets of Augsburg and Bruges. The price runs for the Spanish marts are virtually continuous. A series for Lisbon exists only for the period 1627–32, the dates of the Portuguese India Company. While, in general, these lists are crude and incomplete, import prices are about the best barometers available for measuring the global trade cycle at that time.

Much of the interest in chartered companies was inspired by a growing demand throughout Europe for cheap Asian products. After the Portuguese virtually ceased importing pepper at mid-century, the northern companies increased their imports and gradually came to command the market. The Portuguese confined their imports in the latter half of the century to items of small bulk and great value, such as fine spices, textiles, China goods, and diamonds. Indian cotton textiles, which began to be imported in volume only during the latter half of the century, were new products to most of Europe. Their immediate popularity, as well as factors internal to the European industry, played havoc with Europe's established textile trade. English woolens, French and Italian silks, and German linens lost out at home and in foreign markets to Indian calicoes. The Dutch textile industry, with the exception of the Leyden woolen and the Haarlem linen industries, remained relatively prosperous and undisturbed. Strange as it may seem, the consumers of northern Europe living in a cold climate were quicker to take to cottons than southern Europeans.

The cotton textile imports, unlike the silks, had no serious competition from European products.[332] Silk, in contrast to cotton, was widely cultivated in Europe. By the early seventeenth century several European nations had their own silk industries and others were later to set them up. The craft of silk manufacture was less difficult to learn because the twisting of the fibers reeled from a cocoon required less human ingenuity and dexterity than preparing yarn from raw cotton. When a European cotton textile industry finally developed, it consequently concentrated at first upon finishing and printing the unfinished or semi-finished Indian fabrics. The calicoes im-

---

[332] Certain European textiles, such as the fustians, included cotton imported from Egypt and Turkey. The fustians were a mixture of cotton and linen produced by rural workers in Spain, Lombardy, the Lake Constance region, and in several French provinces. This crude cloth was never able to compete with the finer and cheaper cottons of India. See Jan de Vries, *The Economy of Europe in an Age of Crisis, 1600–1750* (Cambridge, 1976), p. 104. For a good discussion of the calicoes and their impact on the British textile industry, see Chandra Mukerji, *From Graven Images: Patterns of Modern Materialism* (New York, 1983), pp. 166–209.

ported before mid-century, both finished and unfinished, were generally used in the home and were not worn on the person. Once it became clear that cotton cloths were cheap, washable, and relatively fast in color they began to be worn as underclothes and outer garments by all classes. For the well-to-do, the finer fabrics were made into summer apparel or worn as accessories to ornament the garments of both men and women. Premiums were paid by the elegant for chintz and silks in new and original designs not seen in Europe before. No wonder the weavers of London complained (1719) that "Ev'ry jilt of the town gets a calico gown."[333]

The introduction of coffee and tea produced a concommitant craze for exotic beverages. Coffee from the southern Yemen and Ethopia was known as a beverage in the Levant by the fifteenth century and in Italy by the sixteenth century. When the Dutch got to the East, they experimented with its cultivation in Java and Ceylon; they did not produce a significant coffee harvest in Java until about 1708. Around mid-century coffee beans from Mocha, used as ballast as peppercorns were, began to be regularly imported into Europe via the Cape route. In the early years of the Restoration the English East India Company began to import coffee in substantial quantities. By the 1690's it was dispensed regularly in England and on the continent in smoke-filled coffee houses.[334] Tea was somewhat slower to catch on in England, but by 1704 it was regarded as a commodity in general use. It had become a significant Dutch import by mid-century and exercised thereafter an appreciable influence on Dutch social life. Enormous imports of cheap chinaware, as well as smaller imports of elegant porcelain tea and coffee services, helped to promote the fad for exotic beverages.[335]

The popularity of Asian wares inspired new developments in established European industries and commercial practices. From Seville to London, merchants and industrialists regularly warned that the trade of Asia was draining Europe of its silver and undermining some of its basic industries. The trade could not be balanced by exports since, aside from bullion, the only European commodities salable in Asia were weapons, ammunition, and a few mechanical instruments and gadgets such as scissors and needles. The Spanish galleon trade, like the trade via the Cape route, had become primarily a textile commerce confined to bringing Chinese silks and Indian cottons to Spain's American colonies. In Mexico an infant silk industry disappeared under an avalanche of imported Asian textiles. Spanish textile

[333]Chaudhuri, *Trading World* (n. 229), pp. 15, 227, 281–83, 343–48. On the popularity of cotton textiles in Restoration England see P. J. Thomas, *Mercantilism and the East India Trade* (London, 1926), chap. ii.

[334]Chaudhuri, *Trading World* (n. 229), pp. 359–61; also see Glamann, *op. cit.* (n. 186), chap. x.

[335]Chaudhuri, *Trading World* (n. 229), pp. 387, 406–7. Also see E. Van Kley, "The Effect of the Discoveries on Seventeenth-Century Dutch Popular Culture," *Terrae Incognitae*, VIII (1976), 36–39.

manufacturers called for a cessation of imports and even for the abandonment of Manila. Dislocation and unemployment hit the entire European textile industry in the 1680's. The threat to the Portuguese, French, and English industries was met by new protectionist legislation and ultimately by prohibitions. To these measures the companies responded by shifting their imports to wares from China (porcelains, lacquers, and tea), cotton yarn, and other noncompetitive products; they also tried to increase their re-exports to southern and eastern Europe, Africa, the Levant, and America. Interloping merchants, according to the records of the companies, continued to trade in the prohibited textiles; the companies warned that the more the state sought to control trade the more the contraband trade would grow.

If the first thought of the European manufacturers had been protectionism and prohibition, the second was imitation. In the dyeing and printing of textiles they began to use Asian colors and to copy Asian patterns. Efforts were made to learn and master the Indian techniques employed in weaving, dyeing, and printing. For example, a three-hundred-page account of piece-goods production in western India was written in 1678–80 by a French factor at Surat.[336] Knowledge of textile techniques was also transmitted to Europe by Armenian merchants.[337] Other industrialists, especially the makers of ceramics, sought to imitate the Chinese products in order to compete. The shipbuilding industries in England, France, and the Netherlands, where most of the East Indiamen were built, were forced to innovation in ship design by demands of the Asian trade; the Dutch industry exhibited modern characteristics in its ability to maintain consistent quality by developing standardized and repetitive methods of production.[338] A rising import of diamonds fostered the growth at Lisbon and Amsterdam of the diamond-cutting craft and industry.

The Asian trade also stimulated the adoption of new forms of business organization and commercial methods. It was the economic demands of trade at a long distance, necessarily costly and speculative, which transformed the chartered companies into corporate monopolies. As business organizations devoted to international trade, the East India companies sought to centralize and impose controls and management on markets that were traditionally decentralized and that functioned by individual efforts. The two greatest companies were private in origin and dominated by the merchant capitalists of London and Amsterdam. Their rivals were state-inspired and much less successful. All the companies operated over vast distances, in

[336] His manuscript was discovered in the Bibliothèque Nationale (Paris) in 1966. See Furber, *op. cit.* (n. 55), p. 242.

[337] P. Leuilliot, "Influence du commerce oriental sur l'économie occidentale," in Mollat (ed.), *op. cit.* (n. 27), p. 617. *Cf.* H. E. van Gelder, "Oud-Nederlandsch Aardewerk," *De Gids,* LXXXVIII (1924), 1–18.

[338] On shipbuilding as a basic industry of the United Provinces see Charles Wilson, "Transport as a Factor in the History of Economic Development," *Journal of European Economic History,* II (1973), 331.

complex markets, and required heavy capital outlays as well as state cooperation. As semi-public bodies they enjoyed special rights of sovereignty in the East, freedom to export bullion from the homeland, and exemption from or reduction of customs dues. The companies had to learn how to administer a market dependent upon the vagaries connected with the arrivals and departures of fleets. Investors and credit had to be found, crews and cargoes rounded up, ships built and maintained, imports marketed, and records kept. To order the trade in spices and textiles they elaborated the auction system into regular meetings of merchants governed by the rules they laid down. They determined the quantities to be sold, established minimum prices, and published regular price-currents. By controlling the market, they eliminated many risks—scarcities and glut—inherent to the spice trade, and put themselves into a position to diversify commercially with their saltpeter, indigo, and textile imports.

From the outset both the Dutch and English companies possessed clear legal personalities. After a brief passage of time the Dutch Company possessed its own large fixed assets not dependent upon shifting groups of investors; the English Company evolved into a permanent corporation only during the last generation of the century. The corporate structure of the companies gave them a collective strength and unity of purpose not available to smaller merchant organizations. The corporate monopoly was not a popular device; the English Company in particular had to advance "loans" to the state to preserve its charter and its monopoly. In the United Provinces the merchants governing the VOC often sat on and dominated the councils of state, particularly those concerned with trade and foreign policy. During the latter half of the century both companies possessed wide influence in business and politics at home and abroad as they sought to harness political power and privilege to commercial ends. Although they complained bitterly about political interference with their activities, the governors of the companies tended to blame most of their setbacks on price changes in Asia or on interruptions of trade in Europe. While economic theorists had long tried to link price levels to the volume of currency in circulation, leaders of business and government remained content to explain price changes in traditional terms: bad harvests, wars, or unexpected disasters.[339] The companies controlled supplies according to their calculations of what their rivals planned to import, the cost of storing inventories, the elasticity of demand, and current price levels. Their system of bookkeeping did not permit them to reckon long-term profits or to measure the performance of particular segments of the enterprise with a view to future planning.

The English East India Company, in particular, was generally under fire for exporting vast quantities of bullion in return for luxury goods and for

---

[339]Chaudhuri, *Trading World* (n. 229), p. 99. See Braudel's comments on the importance of precious metals for preindustrial economies, *op. cit.* (n. 75), II, 546–49.

failing to nurture the export of England's woolens and tin. When its charter was renewed in 1698, it stipulated that one-tenth of the Company's total exports should be in English wares.[340] This requirement, along with the Company's economic need to reexport spices and its legal obligation to keep Asian textiles off the English market, made the Company utterly dependent on the reexport trade. By 1700 reexports represented about 30 percent of England's total exports.[341] The growth of textile protectionism in France and Spain further complicated matters for the English. In an effort to diversify their imports and to escape a growing number of restrictions, the English, like the French, began in the end years of the century to pursue the China trade in dead earnest.

The prolonged and general economic depression of the seventeenth century, when compared to the prosperity enjoyed by sixteenth-century Europe, was probably brought on in the main by a decline of the amount of money in circulation. By 1651–60 the supply of bullion coming in from America was one-sixth of what it had been in the last decade of the sixteenth century and it kept declining throughout the remainder of the century. Consequently, the large and regular purchases of bullion by the European East India companies increasingly disturbed the mechanisms of European commerce, finance, and business activity.[342] General prices fell constantly beginning in 1650, particularly wheat prices, and the Amsterdam price of wheat increasingly became the standard for all of Europe.[343] Population decline in Spain, Italy, and Germany, and slowed-down growth elsewhere, reduced consumption and production in the fringe economic regions of Europe. Wars, famine, disease, and internal migrations from time to time disrupted the markets and trade patterns of most countries. Within this bleak design of depression and disruption the markets of Amsterdam and London, with their vast and regular import and reexport trades in overseas products, stand out brightly as spots of relative prosperity, activity, and steady growth in population.[344] In these cities the merchant, rather than the

---

[340] Chaudhuri, *Trading World* (n. 229), p. 219.

[341] C. Wilson, *England's Apprenticeship* (New York, 1965), p. 161.

[342] K. N. Chaudhuri, "Treasure and Trade Balances: The East India Company's Export Trade, 1660–1720," *The Economic History Review*, 2d ser., XXI (1968), 480–81; on Europe's monetary stock and the decline of silver imports from 1620 onward see G. Parker, "The Emergence of Modern Finance in Europe, 1500–1730," in C. Cipolla (ed.), *The Fontana Economic History of Europe* (New York, 1977), II, 527–30.

[343] On wheat prices as the best and surest guide in this period to major economic fluctuations see F. Braudel and F. Spooner, "Prices in Europe from 1450 to 1750," in Rich and Wilson (eds.), *The Cambridge Economic History of Europe*, IV (Cambridge, 1967), pp. 392–93 and graph on p. 464.

[344] "France continued to suffer serious setbacks [in population growth] periodically throughout the second half of the seventeenth century. . . . The evidence from England suggests a less volatile pattern of development with moderate growth continuing throughout the later sixteenth and seventeenth centuries. . . . Only Holland seems to have displayed trends seriously counter to the broad European pattern of some slowing down or stagnation for a substantial part of the seventeenth century: there, growth continued vigorously throughout most of the

industrialist, was the mover of the economy, for investments in commerce were far larger than in industry. Europe's credit facilities came to be concentrated in these two cities. Capital formation from trade bolstered the companies' political powers: for example, the hiring of troops and the attraction of allies through subsidies.[345]

For England and the United Provinces, the Asian trade was never in first place in tonnage or value since it was at first exceeded by the European and Levant and then later by the Atlantic and European trade. By 1698 the East India trade of the VOC amounted in value to around 10 percent of all Dutch trade.[346] It was, however, pivotal to the economy of Europe through the extent and variety of the companies' activity in the reexport trade to the continent, Africa, the Levant, and America; it was also an "engine" stimulating the economic and financial expansion of the late seventeenth century.[347] By this time the accumulated capital of these two channel states, derived in part from their extensive overseas imports, and, especially after 1670, from their imports and reexports of spices, textiles, saltpeter, indigo, and other small wares of great value, contributed substantially to their political and economic endurance. Was it not possible therefore that the trade with Asia, more than any other single external or internal factor making for change, gave these two relatively small maritime nations the edge of economic and military security they enjoyed in the age of Louis XIV?[348]

---

seventeenth century until about 1680 when the signs are that it ceased, and a decline began that ran on until at least the middle of the eighteenth century." This is the conclusion of S. Flinn, *The European Demographic System, 1500–1820* (Baltimore, 1981), p. 79.

[345] "In the seventeenth century the *strongest* states were those which dominated *economically* and the United Provinces were in first place." From I. Wallerstein, *op. cit.* (n. 326), p. 33. On p. 113 he makes a more qualified and somewhat contradictory assertion: "At the beginning of our period, in 1651, the United Provinces was the 'strong' state. By the end, in 1689, England and France were both 'stronger' than the United Provinces and about equal to each other."

[346] See I. J. Brugmans, "De Oost-Indische Compagnie en de welvaart in de Republick," *Tijdschrift voor Geschiedenis*, LXI (1948), 230. This is an approximate figure which has been estimated by others to be too low. See above, pp. 72–73.

[347] See D. Rothermund, *Europa und Asien im Zeitalter des Merkantilismus* (Darmstadt, 1978), p. 76. *Cf.* the theory of "leading" sectors propounded in W. Rostow's *The Stages of Economic Growth* (Cambridge, 1960). Also see Braudel, *op. cit.* (n. 75), II, 408, 600–601.

[348] Based in part on J. G. Van Dillen, "Economic Fluctuations and Trade in the Netherlands, 1650–1750," in E. Earle (ed.), *Essays in European Economic History, 1500–1800* (Oxford, 1974), pp. 199–211. Also see F. J. Fisher, "London as an 'Engine' of Economic Growth," in Bromley and Kossmann (eds.) *Britain and the Netherlands* (The Hague, 1971), pp. 3–16; and H. Klein, "De zeventiende eeuw, 1585–1700," in W. Van Stuijvenberg (ed.), *De economishche geschiedenis van Nederland* (Groningen, 1977), pp. 106–15.

Spice Prices and Quantities in the Seventeenth Century

This appendix contains price and quantity data on pepper, cinnamon, and cloves for the seventeenth century.[1] It does not include data from source materials which quote opening ask prices—the price asked from bidders by the spice supplier to open the auction—since such prices remain unchanged over long periods, even in years when the transacted prices fluctuate greatly as a result of changes in supply.

Examination of the data shows certain trends in prices over the century. The Dutch East India Company's inability to establish a monopoly of the supply and distribution of pepper meant that price stability was not achieved in Europe. Pepper prices declined in the first decade of the seventeenth century, and fluctuated over the next twenty years. At Andalusia pepper fell in price from 340 in 1601 to 249.3 in 1611, and at Augsburg from 280 in 1600 to 154 in 1611. Pepper fluctuated in price, ranging from 203.8 to 308, between 1615 and 1630 in Andalusia. By 1640 a general upward trend had caused pepper to peak at 694.2 in Andalusia and at 294 at Augsburg. The 1640's saw a downward trend as pepper's price fell to 245.6 at Andalusia in 1649 and to 115 at Augsburg, both prices less than half the 1640 peaks. Augsburg's prices continued to fluctuate around 100 until 1665, with short-lived peaks of 224 in 1666 and 186 in 1667. After 1668 the price fell into single digits through 1688. The remainder of the century saw pepper prices at Augsburg in the low 100's.

Cinnamon prices followed a similar pattern in the early 1600's, with prices falling at Andalusia from 437.8 in 1601 to 283.2 in 1611. The next two decades were years of flux, as cinnamon prices ranged at New Castile from 246.5 to 578. The 1630's were a period of recovery for cinnamon, as its price surged from 348.5 at Andalusia in 1631 to 580.9 in 1640. The 1640's were a time of high cinnamon prices, with peaks at Andalusia of 1,235.3 in 1642 and of 1,121.4 at New Castile in 1644. Prices retreated in the 1650's, followed by another surge in the 1660's and 1670's with prices topping 2,000 at New Castile. The final two decades of the century saw cinnamon fluctuate in the 900–1,300 range at New Castile.

[1] For price data for the sixteenth century, see *Asia,* I, 143–47.

Cloves followed an upward trend for the first decade, rising at Andalusia from 391 in 1601 to 710 in 1611. The next fifteen years saw prices fluctuate between 493 and 965.6. In 1626 prices began fluctuating at higher levels, never dropping below 900 and sometimes reaching 2,000 at Andalusia. The series at New Castile shows cloves rose in the latter 1600's from 1,207.1 in 1651 to a peak of 3,477.6 in 1677, with prices subsiding for the rest of the century to the 1,200–1,500 range.

In general, then, we see patterns in all three spices. Pepper and cinnamon fell in the first decade, while cloves rose. All three spices were in flux in the next two decades, and in flux at higher levels from 1630 to 1650; there began a rise in the third quarter of the century, and an ebb in the final quarter of the seventeenth century.

KEY TO TABLES

TABLE 1: PEPPER PRICES

Amsterdam (1): guilders per pound, from N. Posthumus (ed.), *Nederlandsche Prijsgeschiedenis* (2 vols., Leyden, 1943), Vol. I, pp. 174–75.

Amsterdam (2): "grooten Vlaems" or "halve stuivers" per pound, from W. A. Horst, "De Peperhandel van de Vereenigde Oost-Indische Compagnie," in *Bijdragen voor Vaderlandsche Geschiedenis en Oudheidkunde,* Ser. 5, Vol. III (1941), pp. 100–101.

Andalusia: maravedis per pound, from Earl J. Hamilton, *American Treasure and the Price Revolution in Spain, 1501–1650* (Harvard Economic Studies, Vol. XLIII, Cambridge, Mass., 1934), pp. 358–69.

Antwerp: stuivers per pound, from Charles Verlinden, *Dokumenten voor de geschiedenis van prijzen en lonen in Vlaanderen en Brabant* (Bruges, 1959), Vol. I, p. 114.

Augsburg: deniers per pound, from M. J. Elsas, *Umriss einer Geschichte der Preise und Löhne in Deutschland* (Leyden, 1936–49), Vol. I, p. 623.

Bruges: livres per pound, from Verlinden, *op. cit.,* p. 114.

Leipzig: deniers per pound, from Elsas, *op. cit.,* Vol. II, p. 533.

Leyden: guilders per pound, from Posthumus, *op. cit.,* Vol. I, pp. 660–61.

Lisbon: cruzados per heavy quintal, from A. R. Disney, *Twilight of the Pepper Empire, Portuguese Trade in Southwest India in the Early Seventeenth Century* (Cambridge, Mass., 1978), p. 112.

New Castile: maravedis per ounce, from Hamilton, *op. cit.,* pp. 370–75 for 1600–1650; maravedis per pound, from Hamilton, *War and Prices in Spain 1651–1800* (New York, 1969), pp. 238–41 for 1651–1700.

Old Castile/Leon: maravedis per pound, from *ibid.,* pp. 376–83.

Stift Klosterneuburg: kroners per pound, from Alfred Francis Pribam, *Materialen zur Geschichte der Preise und Löhne in Österreich* (Vienna, 1938), p. 460.

Valencia: deniers per ounce, from Hamilton, *American Treasure,* pp. 384–89.

Vienna: kroners per pound, from Pribam, *op. cit.,* pp. 281–82.

TABLE 2: CINNAMON PRICES

Amsterdam: guilders per pound, from Posthumus, *op. cit.,* Vol. II, p. 149.

Andalusia: maravedis per pound, from Hamilton, *American Treasure,* pp. 358–69.

Munich: deniers per pound, from Elsas, *op. cit.,* Vol. IIa, p. 574.

New Castile: maravedis per pound, from Hamilton, *American Treasure*, pp. 370–75.
Old Castile/Leon: maravedis per pound, *ibid.*, pp. 376–83.
Stift Klosterneuburg: kroners per pound, from Pribam, *op. cit.*, p. 460.

TABLE 3: CLOVE PRICES

Amsterdam: guilders per pound, from Posthumus, *op. cit.*, Vol. II, pp. 154–55.
Andalusia: maravedis per pound, from Hamilton, *American Treasure*, pp. 358–61.
Antwerp: stuivers per pound, from Verlinden, *op. cit.*, Vol. I, p. 114.
Leyden: guilders per pound, from Posthumus, *op. cit.*, Vol. I, pp. 660–61.
New Castile: maravedis per pound, from Hamilton, *American Treasure*, pp. 370–75.
Old Castile/Leon: maravedis per pound, *ibid.*, pp. 375–78.
Stift Klosterneuburg: kroners per pound, from Pribam, *op. cit.*, p. 460.

TABLE 4: SPICE QUANTITIES

Amsterdam: pepper quantities from Horst, *loc. cit.*, pp. 100–101; clove quantities
from K. Glamann, *Dutch Asiatic Trade, 1620–1740* (Copenhagen, 1958).
Lisbon: from Disney, *op. cit.*, p. 162.
London: from K. N. Chaudhuri, *The English East India Company* (London, 1965),
p. 148, for 1603–40, and from Chaudhuri, *The Trading World of Asia and the English East India Company, 1660–1760* (Cambridge, 1979), p. 524, for 1664–1700.

TABLE 1: SEVENTEENTH-CENTURY PEPPER PRICES

Year	Amsterdam (1)	Amsterdam (2)	Andalusia	Antwerp	Augsburg	Bruges	Leipzig	Leyden	Lisbon	New Castile	Old Castile/Leon	Stift Klosterneuburg	Valencia	Vienna
1600	…	…	…	…	280	…	302	…	…	…	…	…	…	112.5
01	…	…	340	…	280	…	257	…	…	24.5	…	…	…	75
02	…	…	309.6	…	224	72	173	…	…	22.3	…	81.2	…	70
03	…	…	251.8	…	168	56	123	…	…	16.7	…	…	7.6	52.5
04	…	…	232.7	…	157	58	120	…	…	10.7	…	55.6	…	45
05	…	…	241.2	…	157	48	128	…	…	…	…	53.8	…	…
06	…	…	294.7	…	154	…	153	…	…	…	…	52.5	…	…
07	…	…	272	…	164	52	135	…	…	21.4	…	60	…	…
08	…	…	274.8	…	168	…	144	…	…	16.1	…	48	…	…
09	.80	…	272	…	168	36	123	…	…	…	…	48.8	…	…
1610	…	…	…	…	168	22	124	…	…	…	…	…	8.0	…
11	…	…	249.3	…	154	40	120	…	…	21.4	…	…	7.5	…
12	…	…	…	…	162	46	…	…	…	…	…	…	7.0	…
13	…	…	…	…	168	…	144	…	…	…	…	…	…	64
14	…	…	254.9	…	168	38	150	…	…	22.1	…	…	…	…
15	…	…	203.8	…	182	…	216	…	31.5–34	…	…	…	…	…
16	…	…	237.8	…	210	52	…	…	…	17	…	…	7.0	…
17	…	…	272	…	196	…	…	…	42.5–45	21.4	…	…	…	…
18	…	…	276.3	…	196	44	…	…	…	21.4	…	…	…	…
19	…	…	204	…	189	…	…	…	…	…	…	…	13.0	…
1620	…	…	257.8	…	203	…	306	…	…	21.4	…	…	…	…
21	…	…	…	…	420	…	108	…	…	22.7	…	…	7.5	…
22	…	2,000	266.6	…	560	42	108	…	…	21.4	…	…	7.5	…
23	…	…	272	24	140	…	…	…	…	17	…	…	7.7	…
24	.80	…	238	14	157	40	…	…	…	21.4	…	…	8.0	…
25	.79	2,000	204	…	157	40	…	…	…	20.1	…	…	…	…
26	.67	…	305.3	…	157	…	…	…	…	…	306	…	…	…
27	…	…	246	…	168	…	…	…	17–19.5	24	340	…	…	…
28	.58	…	272	…	154	…	108	…	19–22.5	23.8	340	…	7.0	…
29	…	…	…	…	140	33	96	…	22	24	328.7	…	…	…

(continued)

TABLE 1: SEVENTEENTH-CENTURY PEPPER PRICES (Continued)

Year	Amsterdam (1)	Amsterdam (2)	Andalusia	Antwerp	Augsburg	Bruges	Leipzig	Leyden	Lisbon	New Castile	Old Castile/Leon	Stift Klosterneuburg	Valencia	Vienna
1630	.58	...	308	...	140	29	...	...	25	20	306	52	5.2	...
31	.53	...	...	...	126	28	...	...	24	...	204	...	5.5	...
32	.60	...	271.9	...	168	33	...	...	24	20	255	...	...	55.2
33	.66	...	238	...	168	...	...	...	...	20.8	...	...	5.5	...
34	.70	...	204	...	196	36	...	...	...	26.8	160	...	6.5	...
35	.54	...	310	...	175	36	...	...	...	20	170	...	8.6	...
36	.61	...	255	...	168	36	...	...	...	20	161.5	...	7.8	...
37	.75	...	433.1	...	203	36	...	...	...	26	204	...	10.0	...
38	.85	...	340	...	196	36	...	...	...	26.8	346	...	9.9	...
39	...	...	408	...	294	84	...	...	...	31	408	...	8.9	...
1640	...	6,000	694.2	...	280	...	...	1.2	...	46.5	612	...	17.0	...
41	.66	10,000	613	...	162	75	...	.75	...	48	340	...	13.1	...
42	.70	6,000	538	...	168	38	...	...	...	...	476	...	...	...
43	.70	...	578	...	126	...	...	...	...	48	476	...	7.3	...
44	...	...	433.1	...	140	...	...	.75	...	36	408	...	7.0	...
45	.67	...	328.7	...	140	40	...	...	...	...	340	...	6.9	...
46	.60	...	...	...	158	...	...	...	...	28	...	...	...	...
47	...	...	316.6	...	140	...	...	...	...	22.7	408	...	6.7	...
48	.57	...	238	...	126	...	...	...	...	...	340	...	...	...
49	.51	...	245.6	...	115	...	...	.55	...	21.4	289	...	6.0	...
1650	.51	...	297.5	...	108	...	...	.51	...	...	204	...	5.1	...
51	.43	...	...	...	105	36	...	.48	...	...	221	36	...	...
52	.43	...	...	...	91	33	...	...	...	...	263.5	36	...	...
53	.61	...	...	...	119	36	...	...	...	...	272	...	...	...
54	.64	8,000	...	...	119	36	...	.68	...	...	314.5	...	...	...
55	...	8,000	...	...	105	38	...	...	...	...	272	...	...	...
56	...	6,905	...	...	84	31	...	...	...	...	221.4	...	...	...
57	...	...	...	...	105	32	...	...	...	...	197.8	...	...	...
58	...	...	...	...	...	32	...	.48	...	...	209.7	...	...	...
59	...	...	...	...	90	34	...	.59	...	...	204	...	...	...
1660	...	...	...	...	98	28	...	...	...	...	209.7	...	...	...
61	...	...	...	...	98	32	...	...	...	...	204	...	...	...
62	...	...	...	...	98	32	...	...	...	...	229.5	...	...	...

Year								
63				100			255	
64	.61			98	33		246.5	
65	.61			112	34		306	
66				224	52	1.35	408	
67		10,000		186	54		442	
68		14,800		131	44		425	
69	.59	7,974		98	30		408	
1670		6,000		84	30		340	
71	.43	10,000		84	26		294.7	
72	.50	3,000	12	86	24		323	
73		11,500	10		26		334.3	
74	.43	11,500	10	91	28		340	
75	.35	19,000	10	70	26		311.7	
76	.34			74	24		265.6	
77		7,500	8	63	24		255	21
78	.29	6,000	7	63	22		255	22
79		6,000	11	80	22		272	23
1680	.34	9,000	9	84	22		204	
81		15,000	9	84	22		157.3	
82	.28	7,600	8	84	22		131.8	
83	.35	8,800	8	77	22		116.9	
84		5,800	10	77	22		123.9	
85		6,500	9	84	22		133.9	
86	.36	7,200	8	77	24		136	
87		8,900	9	84	24		166.8	
88	.55	8,360	12	94	28		170	
89	.68	8,000	13	126	36		263.5	
1690		5,300	14	129	36		312.4	
91		9,000	15	135	36		263.5	
92	.61		17	135	36		257.1	47.1
93			16.33	135			250.8	
94	.42	10,000	13.4	119	36		218.9	46
95		2,700		105	24		210.4	
96		7,800		105			215.3	
97		10,000		133	26		212.5	
98	.25	12,000		129	24		217.8	
99				128	24		212.5	
1700					27		187	

TABLE 2: SEVENTEENTH-CENTURY CINNAMON PRICES

Year	Amsterdam	Andalusia	Munich	New Castile	Old Castile/Leon	Stift Kloster-neuburg
1600	. .	. .	. .	. .	. .	. .
01	. .	437.8	. .	288.6	374	. .
02	. .	349.9	. .	255	208.7	. .
03	. .	361.3	. .	. .	289	192
04	. .	308.1	. .	180.4	170	60
05	. .	306.4	. .	270.6	267.8	84.8
06	. .	331.5	. .	289	289	90
07	. .	379.7	. .	. .	272	. .
08	. .	369.8	. .	246.5	289	. .
09	. .	335.8	. .	. .	384.3	74.4
1610	. .	. .	. .	. .	442	. .
11	. .	283.2	. .	255	284	. .
12	. .	289	. .	238	238	. .
13	. .	284.8	. .	246.5	272	. .
14	. .	260.7	. .	255	272	. .
15	. .	382.5	. .	246.5	272	. .
16	. .	340	. .	263.5	272	. .
17	. .	246.5	. .	. .	285.1	. .
18	. .	216.8	. .	238	258.5	. .
19	. .	201.9	. .	238	208.7	. .
1620	. .	206.1	. .	. .	204	. .
21	. .	. .	. .	. .	178	. .
22	. .	184.9	. .	238	. .	. .
23	. .	191.5	. .	272	187	. .
24	. .	212.5	. .	238	272	. .
25	. .	306	. .	292.5	408	. .
26	. .	306	. . .	345	374	. .
27	. .	555.3	. .	578	550.1	. .
28	. .	561	. .	476	. .	. .
29	. .	476	. .	487.3	544	. .
1630	. .	408	. .	442	544	72.9
31	. .	348.5	. .	340	540.3	. .
32	. .	507.2	. .	510	464	. .
33	. .	620.5	. .	544	629	. .
34	. .	752	. .	603.8	680	. .
35	. .	555.3	. .	510	544	. .
36	. .	485.2	. .	476	. .	. .
37	. .	564.8	. .	612	. .	. .
38	. .	577.3	. .	546.3	544	. .
39	. .	580.9	. .	652.7	634.7	. .
1640	. .	566.7	. .	690.1	657.3	. .
41	. .	1,130.5	. .	1,107	1,088	. .
42	. .	1,235.3	. .	930.2	1,768	. .
43	. .	901	. .	862.6	1,350.7	. .
44	. .	991	. .	1,121.4	884	. .
45	. .	981.8	. .	977.6	1,020	. .
46	. .	929.3	. .	977.6	748	. .
47	. .	753.7	. .	. .	782	. .
48	. .	722.5	. .	970.4	884	. .
49	. .	566.7	. .	714	1,088	. .

Year	Amsterdam	Andalusia	Munich	New Castile	Old Castile/Leon	Stift Kloster-neuburg
1650	. .	850	. .	. .	. .	120
51	. .	. .	. .	589.3	. .	120
52	. .	. .	. .	697	. .	. .
53	. .	. .	. .	748	. .	. .
54	. .	. .	. .	725.3	. .	. .
55	. .	. .	. .	657.3	. .	. .
56	. .	. .	. .	641.8	. .	. .
57	. .	. .	. .	748	. .	. .
58	. .	. .	. .	986	. .	. .
59	. .	. .	. .	1,139	. .	. .
1660	. .	. .	. .	1,292	. .	. .
61	. .	. .	631	1,360	. .	. .
62	. .	. .	656	1,411	. .	. .
63	. .	. .	590	1,504.5	. .	. .
64	3.6	. .	525	1,768	. .	. .
65	3.28	. .	. .	1,768	. .	. .
66	. .	. .	. .	1,904	. .	. .
67	. .	. .	. .	1,861.5	. .	. .
68	. .	. .	. .	1,683	. .	. .
69	3.08	. .	. .	1,541.3	. .	. .
1670	. .	. .	. .	1,586.7	. .	216
71	3.15	. .	. .	1,700	. .	. .
72	3.5	. .	. .	1,847.3	. .	. .
73	. .	. .	. .	2,040	. .	. .
74	3.06	. .	. .	2,187.3	. .	. .
75	4.9	. .	. .	2,040	. .	216
76	3.25	. .	. .	1,989	. .	. .
77	3.16	. .	. .	1,926.7	. .	165
78	. .	. .	. .	1,904	. .	180
79	3.28	. .	784	2,006	. .	180
1680	. .	. .	784	1,496	. .	. .
81	. .	. .	877	1,360	. .	202.5
82	3.13	. .	840	1,088	. .	. .
83	3.13	. .	840	1,076.7	. .	. .
84	. .	. .	840	1,110.7	. .	. .
85	. .	. .	812	1,003	. .	. .
86	2.75	. .	784	918	. .	. .
87	. .	. .	1,344	1,088	. .	. .
88	3.00	. .	. .	1,139	. .	. .
89	2.99	. .	728	1,088	. .	. .
1690	. .	. .	. .	1,258	. .	. .
91	3.00	. .	784	1,088	. .	. .
92	3.00	. .	728	1,088	. .	288
93	3.00	. .	784	1,088	. .	. .
94	3.00	. .	. .	1,088	. .	256
95	. .	. .	. .	1,122	. .	288
96	. .	. .	. .	1,088	. .	. .
97	. .	. .	. .	1,224	. .	. .
98	. .	. .	1,008	1,122	. .	. .
99	. .	. .	. .	1,292	. .	. .
1700	. .	. .	784	1,088	. .	. .

TABLE 3: Seventeenth-Century Clove Prices

Year	Amsterdam	Andalusia	Antwerp	Leyden	New Castile	Old Castile/ Leon	Stift Kloster- neuburg
1600	. .	. .	. .	. .	. .	. .	. .
01	. .	391	. .	. .	. .	30.1	. .
02	. .	385.3	. .	. .	. .	17	. .
03	. .	384.6	. .	. .	. .	22.9	192
04	. .	333.2	. .	. .	. .	26.9	157
05	. .	534.8	. .	. .	. .	37.7	198
06	. .	630.9	. .	. .	. .	43.9	. .
07	. .	778.2	. .	. .	. .	59.2	192
08	. .	773.8	. .	. .	. .	65.9	. .
09	6.9	725.3	. .	. .	. .	68	143
1610	. .	. .	. .	. .	. .	65.9	. .
11	. .	710	. .	. .	. .	. .	. .
12	. .	612	. .	. .	. .	65.9	. .
13	. .	714	. .	. .	. .	. .	. .
14	. .	493	. .	. .	. .	. .	. .
15	. .	710	. .	. .	. .	42	. .
16	. .	612	. .	. .	. .	. .	. .
17	. .	566.7	. .	. .	. .	. .	. .
18	. .	586.5	. .	. .	. .	54	. .
19	3.3	510	. .	. .	. .	. .	. .
1620	. .	578	. .	. .	. .	82.5	. .
21	. .	. .	. .	. .	. .	. .	. .
22	. .	680	. .	. .	. .	. .	. .
23	. .	680	96	. .	. .	56.5	. .
24	2.71	544	96	. .	. .	61.9	. .
25	2.82	. .	. .	. .	. .	51	. .
26	4.23	965.6	. .	. .	. .	96.3	. .
27	4.65	1,931.2	. .	. .	. .	187	. .
28	. .	2,896.8	. .	. .	. .	. .	. .
29	. .	1,576.2	. .	. .	. .	136	. .
1630	5.40	1,448.4	. .	. .	. .	119	384
31	5.40	1,448.4	. .	. .	. .	. .	. .
32	5.40	2,051.9	. .	. .	. .	170	. .
33	5.40	1,408.6	. .	. .	. .	. .	. .
34	5.40	1,388.1	. .	. .	. .	. .	. .
35	3.28	1,247.2	. .	. .	. .	136	. .
36	2.68	1,271.6	. .	. .	. .	129.2	. .
37	2.83	1,040.9	. .	. .	. .	. .	. .
38	2.55	1,086.3	. .	. .	. .	136	. .
39	. .	964.2	. .	. .	. .	85	. .
1640	2.69	1,058.6	. .	. .	. .	76	. .
41	2.51	1,088	. .	. .	. .	93.5	. .
42	2.42	1,327.7	. .	. .	. .	119	. .
43	2.46	965.6	. .	. .	. .	102	. .
44	. .	933.7	. .	. .	. .	68	. .
45	2.49	986	. .	. .	. .	85	. .
46	2.66	1,207	. .	. .	. .	102	. .
47	. .	1,277.3	. .	. .	. .	102	. .
48	3.90	1,904	. .	. .	. .	119	. .
49	3.75	1,314.7	. .	. .	. .	129.2	. .

Year	Amsterdam	Andalusia	Antwerp	Leyden	New Castile	Old Castile/ Leon	Stift Kloster- neuburg
1650	3.47	1,428	. .	. .	. .	. .	210
51	3.50	. .	. .	3.50	1,207.1	. .	210
52	3.50	. .	˙. .	. .	1,477.3	. .	. .
53	3.50	. .	. .	. .	1,790.1	. .	. .
54	3.50	. .	. .	3.50	1,567.4	. .	. .
55	. .	. .	. .	. .	1,362	. .	. .
56	. .	. .	. .	. .	1,704.4	. .	. .
57	. .	. .	. .	. .	1,292	. .	. .
58	. .	. .	. .	. .	1,208.7	. .	. .
59	. .	. .	. .	. .	1,276.6	. .	. .
1660	. .	. .	. .	. .	1,410.9	. .	. .
61	. .	. .	. .	. .	1,343	. .	. .
62	. .	. .	. .	. .	1,589.5	. .	. .
63	. .	. .	. .	. .	1,679.5	. .	. .
64	6.28	. .	. .	. .	1,797.3	. .	. .
65	5.43	. .	. .	. .	2,373.2	. .	. .
66	5.89	. .	. .	. .	3,044.7	. .	. .
67	7.25	. .	. .	. .	3,156.8	. .	. .
68	. .	. .	. .	. .	2,864.5	. .	. .
69	6.78	. .	. .	. .	3,044.7	. .	. .
1670	. .	. .	. .	. .	3,670.3	. .	336
71	5.42	. .	. .	. .	2,988.8	. .	. .
72	5.38	. .	. .	. .	3,054.1	. .	. .
73	. .	. .	120	. .	3,088.9	. .	. .
74	4.39	. .	. .	. .	3,088.9	. .	. .
75	4.21	. .	. .	. .	3,556.4	. .	. .
76	. .	. .	. .	. .	2,760	. .	. .
77	. .	. .	. .	. .	3,477.6	. .	210
78	. .	. .	. .	. .	2,686	. .	210
79	. .	. .	. .	. .	2,417.4	. .	210
1680	. .	. .	. .	. .	2,283.1	. .	. .
81	. .	. .	. .	. .	1,477.3	. .	225
82	. .	. .	. .	. .	1,410.9	. .	. .
83	. .	. .	. .	. .	1,208.7	. .	. .
84	. .	. .	. .	. .	1,208.7	. .	. .
85	. .	. .	. .	. .	1,298.8	. .	. .
86	. .	. .	. .	. .	1,033.6	. .	. .
87	. .	. .	. .	. .	1,292	. .	. .
88	. .	. .	. .	. .	1,292	. .	. .
89	. .	. .	. .	. .	1,292	. .	. .
1690	. .	. .	. .	. .	1,895	. .	. .
91	. .	. .	. .	. .	1,208.1	. .	. .
92	. .	. .	. .	. .	1,433.1	. .	320
93	. .	. .	. .	. .	1,410.9	. .	. .
94	. .	. .	. .	. .	1,769	. .	320
95	. .	. .	. .	. .	1,564	. .	320
96	. .	. .	. .	. .	1,145.5	. .	. .
97	. .	. .	. .	. .	1,343	. .	. .
98	. .	. .	. .	. .	1,394	. .	. .
99	. .	. .	. .	. .	1,360	. .	. .
1700	. .	. .	. .	. .	1,394	. .	. .

TABLE 4: SEVENTEENTH-CENTURY SPICE QUANTITIES

Year	Pepper			Cloves
	Amsterdam (thousands of pounds)	Lisbon (quintals)	London (thousands of pounds)	Cloves Amsterdam (millions of pounds)
1600	. .	. .	. .	. .
01	. .	. .	. .	. .
02	. .	. .	. .	. .
03	1,675.5	. .	. .	. .
04	. .	. .	. .	. .
05	. .	. .	. .	. .
06	. .	. .	. .	. .
07	. .	. .	. .	. .
08	. .	. .	. .	. .
09	. .	. .	. .	. .
1610	458.983	. .	. .	. .
11	. .	. .	. .	. .
12	. .	9,509	. .	. .
13	. .	8,002	100	. .
14	. .	6,402	597	. .
15	. .	10,355	510	. .
16	. .	15,841	783	. .
17	. .	4,387	1,748	. .
18	. .	11,591	1,483	. .
19	. .	10,892	292	450–500
1620	. .	5,999	480	. .
21	. .	7,586	980	. .
22	. .	5,878	1,615	324–60
23	. .	9,158	1,057	. .
24	. .	. .	1,658	. .
25	. .	21,373	1,270	. .
26	. .	9,970	2,928	. .
27	. .	14,830	1,238	. .
28	. .	5,821	1,112	. .
29	. .	5,505	1,065	. .
1630	. .	10,884	790	. .
31	. .	9,061	455	. .
32	. .	565	1,072	. .
33	. .	9,686	1,750	. .
34	. .	9,045	480	. .
35	. .	. .	860	. .
36	. .	. .	974	. .
37	. .	. .	. .	. .
38	. .	. .	886	. .
39	. .	. .	. .	. .
1640	. .	. .	600	. .
41	. .	. .	. .	. .
42	. .	. .	. .	. .
43	. .	. .	. .	. .
44	. .	. .	. .	. .
45	. .	. .	. .	. .
46	. .	. .	. .	. .
47	. .	. .	. .	. .
48	. .	. .	. .	. .
49	. .	. .	. .	. .

	Pepper			Cloves
Year	Amsterdam (thousands of pounds)	Lisbon (quintals)	London (thousands of pounds)	Cloves Amsterdam (millions of pounds)
1650	. .	. .	. .	. .
51	. .	. .	. .	. .
52	. .	. .	. .	. .
53	. .	. .	. .	. .
54	. .	. .	. .	. .
55	. .	. .	. .	360
56	. .	. .	. .	600
57	. .	. .	. .	. .
58	. .	. .	. .	. .
59	. .	. .	. .	. .
1660	. .	. .	. .	. .
61	. .	. .	. .	. .
62	. .	. .	. .	. .
63	. .	. .	. .	. .
64	. .	. .	1,168	. .
65	. .	. .	2,025	. .
66	. .	. .	. .	. .
67	. .	. .	194	150
68	. .	. .	. .	150
69	. .	. .	3,042	200
1670	7,974	. .	4,296	170
71	6,000	. .	2,874	. .
72	10,000	. .	7,586	. .
73	20,000	. .	845	. .
74	50,000	. .	1,347	. .
75	60,000	. .	4,437	. .
76	60,000	. .	4,457	. .
77	. .	. .	8,127	. .
78	58,000	. .	4,377	. .
79	. .	. .	2,783	. .
1680	2,000	. .	3,031	. .
81	. .	. .	5,109	. .
82	. .	. .	2,302	. .
83	. .	. .	1,280	. .
84	45,000	. .	1,318	. .
85	47,500	. .	1,837	. .
86	10,000	. .	454	. .
87	21,000	. .	1,423	. .
88	. .	. .	1,821	. .
89	32,000	. .	386	. .
1690	. .	. .	3,537	. .
91	. .	. .	1,264	. .
92	45,000	. .	461	. .
93	4,394,600	. .	329	. .
94	3,870,000	. .	. .	. .
95	4,300,000	. .	. .	. .
96	100,000	. .	1,318	. .
97	. .	. .	938	. .
98	100,000	. .	2,051	. .
99	70,000	. .	1,403	. .
1700	70,000	. .	1,862	. .

CHAPTER II

The Christian Mission

Immediately after Pope Leo X granted the *Jus patronatus* (1514) to the Portuguese crown, the superstructure of its Eastern ecclesiastical establishment had begun to be raised. Goa was consecrated in 1558 as the metropolitan see, and thereafter the *padroado* (patronage) functioned effectively as the Portuguese religious agency in Asia.[1] At the beginning of the seventeenth century Goa exercised ecclesiastical jurisdiction in the Portuguese East through the bishoprics of Malacca (1557), Cochin (1558), Macao (1575), Funai (1588), Cranganore (1601; elevated to an archbishopric in 1605), and Mylapore (1606). Its dependence upon the crown for finances, protection, and support placed the archdiocese of Goa more directly under national supervision than the church in Portugal itself. Five synods held in Goa from 1567 to 1606 had reorganized the bishoprics of the *padroado* in line with the decrees pronounced at the Council of Trent and had set down principles for dealing with problems relating to conversions, the elimination of heathen customs and practices, and the expulsion of the Muslims from the Portuguese centers. The St. Thomas Christians of southwestern India (the Serra) had meanwhile been formally subjected to the Latin rite and placed under the protection of the Portuguese crown by the edicts of the Synod of Diamper (June 20–26, 1599).

---

[1] For the history of the *padroado* in the sixteenth century see *Asia*, I, 230–45; for an overview see A. da Silva Rego's article on the *padroado* in *New Catholic Encyclopedia* (Washington, 1967), X, 1114–16. Also see C. R. Boxer, "The Portuguese Padroado in East Asia and the Problem of the Chinese Rites 1576–1773," *Instituto portugues de Hong-kong*, Boletim No. 1 (July, 1948), pp. 199–226; and C. K. Pullapilly, "Religious Impact of the Discovery of the Sea Route to India," in C. K. Pullapilly and E. J. Van Kley (eds.), *Asia and the West* (Notre Dame, 1986), pp. 173–94.

Negotiations with the civil authorities of Asia had won significant formal concessions for the spread of the Christian message to areas not subject to Portuguese control. A treaty of 1598 with Calicut granted to the Zamorin's subjects the right to become Christians. A Jesuit delegation to the court of Vijayanagar obtained in 1599 the right to send missionaries into that Hindu empire. Other Jesuits at Lahore and Agra received in 1601 Akbar's written permission to evangelize in the Mughul realm. In the Far East, the Jesuit Matteo Ricci, who had first entered China in 1582, was permitted to proceed to Peking in 1601. Contemporaneously the Jesuit mission in Japan claimed three hundred thousand converts and seemed to have made peace with the government.

It also appeared in 1600 to the Portuguese Jesuits in eastern Asia that the threat to their monopoly from the Spanish missionaries based in the Philippines had been checked by actions taken both in Europe and in Japan. The Jesuits had secretly obtained from Pope Gregory XIII (r. 1572–85) a brief (January 28, 1585) which forbade all secular priests (those under the direct jurisdiction of their bishop) and regulars (those living under the rule, or *regula,* of a religious order; technically, this does not include the Jesuits) from entering China or Japan to carry on the work of evangelizing; this decree was reaffirmed in 1597. Once Philip III (r. 1598–1621), the Spanish-Portuguese king, learned that the papacy had granted the Jesuits a monopoly of the Japan-China mission without consulting Spain, he undertook negotiations with Rome which produced a compromise. Pope Clement VIII (r. 1592–1605) opened China and Japan to all comers in 1600. He mollified the Jesuits by granting to Portugal in the bull *Onerosa Pastoralis* (December 12, 1600) the right to require all missionaries destined for Africa and the East to sail from Lisbon. Japan was formally opened to the Mendicants provided they went there by way of Lisbon-Goa and in Portuguese ships. Excommunication was prescribed for all missionaries who attempted to enter Japan, China, or India by way of America and the Philippines. Such a harsh decree seemed to be required by the troubles experienced by the mission in Japan which had culminated in 1597 with the crucifixion at Nagasaki of six interloping Spanish Franciscans and twenty of their converts. The Jesuits, possibly because of their connection with the lucrative Macao trade, temporarily escaped the wrath of the Japanese. At the dawn of the seventeenth century it therefore appeared that the Portuguese-Jesuit monopoly of the Christian enterprise in eastern Asia was to remain intact and to enjoy new triumphs.

This bright horizon was gradually beclouded by the subsequent decline of the Portuguese empire in the East. Tensions between the secular and religious authorities at Goa, particularly over the failure of the state to provide the prescribed stipends for the clergy, led to recriminations which reechoed in Lisbon, Madrid, and Rome. The successes won by the Protestant Dutch and English in the East forced a reevaluation of the Catholic enterprise. King Philip III, who had evangelizing ambitions for Spain in the Pacific and the East, was no friend of the Portuguese-Jesuit monopoly even though he officially recognized it. At his suggestion Pope Paul V (r. 1605–21) by a bull of 1608 exempted the mendicant orders from the *Onerosa*.[2] The Spanish Franciscans, in particular, continually inveighed against the Jesuit monopoly in Japan, tried repeatedly to enter China and Japan, and sought diligently to establish missions in the Moluccas—all in what the Portuguese claimed as part of the *padroado*. Rome itself handed the *padroado* its most severe setback when Pope Gregory XV (r. 1621–23) by a bull of January 6, 1622, created the Congregation for the Propagation of the Faith (*De Propaganda Fide*), a central agency empowered to supervise the missions, to appoint priests for the missions, and to maintain surveillance over Catholic teachings in foreign fields.[3]

The archbishops of Goa[4] continued, as they had in the latter half of the sixteenth century, to rule religion and to wield a degree of political power over the Portuguese fortresses, settlements, and mission stations throughout the East. Their vast archdiocese had gradually been divided into suffragan dioceses which became increasingly independent of the authority of the metropolitan. The see of Ankamali (Cranganore) was separated in 1600 from the bishopric of Cochin to give the St. Thomas Christians a jurisdiction of their own.[5] Six years later the bishopric of Mylapore was separated from Cochin as a new jurisdiction for the lengthy Coromandel coast and Bengal. Both bulls of foundation recognized the rights of the Portuguese king as patron even though his temporal influence in these regions was restricted to a few coastal settlements and fortresses. Those parts of India not subject to suffragan dioceses remained theoretically under the direct authority of the archbishop of Goa, even though the crown's temporal authority was limited to Goa and a few other coastal places and islands along India's west coast.[6] From the crown's viewpoint the whole of India and the rest of the East belonged to the *padroado:* China was under Macao, Japan under Funai, and Indonesia under Malacca.

Over the course of the sixteenth century the *padroado* had increasingly become hostage to the temporal power. No priest, regular or secular, could legally be dispatched to the East without royal permission. The clerics destined for Asia were required to assemble at Lisbon and to take an oath of loyalty to the king before their departure. The crown provided free transportation on its ships and paid small stipends to the missionaries. Once they arrived at Goa the newcomers were subjected to close control by the secular authority and to a rigorous examination by the Inquisition with respect to their religious convictions and their loyalty to the royal patron. Foreign mis-

---

[2] See D. Ferroli, S.J., *The Jesuits in Malabar* (2 vols., Bangalore, 1951), II, 170.
[3] On its history see below, pp. 222–26.
[4] See appendix, Archbishops of Goa in the Seventeenth Century, at the end of this chapter.
[5] On the St. Thomas Christians see *Asia,* I, 266–69.
[6] See below, p. 135.

sionaries were taught the Portuguese language, a tool indispensable to their work; even their names were "Lusitanized." The prelates of the *padroado,* as well as the simple priests, were not officially permitted to correspond directly with Rome, although many of them did so anyway.

During the years of the Spanish-Portuguese union (1580–1640) its Habsburg rulers tightened the royal control as they sought to become the Eastern vicars of the Roman pontiff. A professor of Salamanca, Juan Soloranzo Pereira (1575–1653), published at royal expense a justification for extending the king's authority over the ecclesiastical establishment. His *De Indiarum Iure* (Madrid, 1629) advocated almost total royal control over ecclesiastical activities in the East and was adopted by the Madrid government as its official position paper on civil-ecclesiastical relations in the overseas world. In 1642 the portion of this work relating to ecclesiastical government was placed on the *Index of Forbidden Books.*[7]

Dependent upon the state for funds, transportation, and protection, the fortunes of the *padroado* declined during the seventeenth century along with the Carreira and the Portuguese fortress-settlements in the East. To 1640 the government of the church in Goa continued to function effectively despite the progressively active interference of Rome and the Propaganda. Pope Urban VIII (r. 1623–44) in 1627, five years after the formal establishment of the Propaganda, ordered the missionaries to observe under pain of censure the decisions of the Propaganda with respect to Japan. Six years later, in 1633, the same pope decreed an end to the policy that missionaries must travel to Asia exclusively through Portugal, as provided by the bull *Onerosa,* and promised excommunication to any who tried to impede their travel by other routes.[8] Lisbon and Goa reacted belligerently to this papal decree and made life in the East extremely difficult for the missionaries who avoided the Portuguese monopoly by sailing in Spanish, Dutch, or English vessels or by traversing the overland routes. Conflicts between the Goa authorities and the missionaries sent to the East by the Propaganda became increasingly numerous and vindictive as the secular authorities in Lisbon continued to insist that the Holy See by administrative acts was guilty of unilaterally abrogating the *padroado*. The impasse between Lisbon and Rome produced a dilemma for the Portuguese prelates in the East, most of whom staunchly maintained their allegiance to the crown.

While relations between the Propaganda and the *padroado* were deteriorating, the independence movement in Portugal was becoming more vociferous in its attacks upon the Habsburg government. The elevation of King John IV in 1640 as the king of independent Portugal went unrecognized by the Holy See. Under pressure from the Spanish Habsburgs, the papacy

[7] See F. Coutinho, *Le régime paroissial des diocèses de rite latin de l'Inde des origines (XVIe siècle) à nos jours* (Louvain and Paris, 1958), pp. 9–12.

[8] See E. R. Hull, S.J., *Bombay Mission-History with a Special Study of the Padroado Question* (2 vols., Bombay, 1927–30), I, 45.

refused to negotiate with the Portuguese crown until Spain recognized its independence in 1668. For twenty-eight years the Portuguese church, both in Europe and overseas, functioned as a national Catholic church without formal ties to Rome. Shortly after coming to power John IV forbade the authorities in Goa to receive missionaries sent by the Propaganda unless they had come via Lisbon and with royal license. Bishoprics, including the archbishopric of Goa, were left vacant for long periods, and the missions, except for the flourishing Jesuit mission at Madura, were left on their own. Royal decrees continued to be issued against the foreign missionaries sent to the East by the Propaganda; some were tried and imprisoned by the Inquisition of Goa and others were sent back to Europe. The St. Thomas Christians, caught in the struggle between the *padroado* and the Propaganda for control of the archbishopric of Cranganore, began again in these years to reassert their independence of the Latin authorities.

Nor did the struggle cease with the restoration in 1668 of formal relations between Madrid and Lisbon, and Rome and Lisbon. For their part, the Spaniards in the East refused to recognize the authority of either the *padroado* or the vicars apostolic of the Propaganda. In 1672 the Portuguese crown ordered the viceroy of Goa to seize any bishop or missionary sent by the Propaganda without Lisbon's approval and to deport him to Portugal. Pope Clement X (r. 1670–76) issued a series of bulls in 1673 which officially stripped the *padroado* of certain of its privileges. He continued to demand recognition of the rights of the Propaganda to send missionaries to the East by any route whatsoever, to establish freely its vicars apostolic throughout the East, and to receive the obedience of the Portuguese bishops and clerics in Asia. This pope also issued a brief in 1673 prohibiting the publication of books or writings by members of the mission orders until they had been examined and approved by the Propaganda. In 1674 the Jesuit general formally required the Jesuits in the field to obey the vicars apostolic. In 1682 missionaries were officially forbidden by Rome from taking the oath of allegiance to the *padroado* demanded by the crown. The Jesuits, even those residing in Goa and Macao, refused to follow the crown's orders. This jurisdictional feud was exacerbated by heated controversies between the Jesuits, the secular hierarchy, and the orders of friars over missionizing methods.

Throughout the latter half of the century the debate became ever more intense over the "accommodation" issue, or the degree to which Christianity could and should compromise with local customs and practices in advancing the faith. The related questions of the Malabar rites and the Chinese rites jeopardized the missionary endeavor in Asia and divided the Church in Europe. In 1690 Pope Alexander VIII (r. 1689–91), despite the opposition of the Propaganda and the French missionaries, divided the diocese of Macao into three sees with bishops at Macao, Nanking, and Peking. Once their areas of jurisdiction were delineated in 1695, the new bishoprics were formally recognized as suffragans of the archbishopric of Goa and as being under the jurisdiction of the *padroado*. The pope also stipulated, perhaps somewhat late in the day for Portugal, that no alterations could be introduced into the *padroado,* even by the papacy itself, without the consent of the Portuguese king.[9] The century ended before the issues between Rome and Lisbon and the debates over "rites" received permanent resolutions.[10]

I

THE FRIARS OF THE "PADROADO"

In India the archbishopric of Goa theoretically exercised direct authority over Christian affairs from Tibet to Kashmir and southward along the west coast of India to the archbishopric of Cranganore. Aleixo de Meneses, Goa's Augustinian archbishop from 1595 to 1610, was a power in the political life of Goa, where he acted as governor from 1607 to 1609.[11] A report sent to Rome in 1621 by his successor, Cristovão de Sá, indicates that there were then twenty-seven parish churches in the Goa area: nine in the city itself, and eighteen in the neighboring villages. At Bardez there were ten parishes and more than twenty at Salsette. A similar report of 1640 informed the Holy See of the existence of seventy-nine parish churches in the Portuguese terrritory of Goa. Secular priests were never as numerous in India as the regulars, for they were usually dispatched to India for a three-year period and then returned to Portugal. The three great orders of Portugal—Franciscans, Jesuits, and Dominicans—had been entrusted by the king with the evangelization of the Goa region and with the care of its Christians. In 1555 Bardez had been assigned to the Franciscans, the peninsula of Salsette to the Jesuits, and the Islands near Goa into two equal jurisdictions of the Jesuits and the Dominicans. A 1645 report to Rome indicated that no natives had been admitted to the Christian orders. In the second half of the century a native secular clergy gradually replaced the Europeans in the parishes of the Islands, but Bardez and Salsette remained in the hands of the Franciscans and Jesuits. The Franciscans, in particular, remained difficult for the archbishops to control, as they sought to govern Bardez through their own *Collegio dos Reis Magos.*[12]

[9] See Boxer, *loc. cit.* (n. 1), pp. 208–9. Also see below, p. 266.
[10] For a listing of the papal and royal decrees and acts see Hull, *op. cit.* (n. 8), pp. 46–48; for a discussion of the "rites controversy" see below, pp. 260–69.
[11] Meneses returned to Portugal in 1611 to become archbishop of Braga and president of the Royal Council of Portugal in Madrid. He died in 1617. See M. Müllbauer, *Geschichte der katholischen Missionen in Ostindien von der Zeit Vasco da Gamas bis zur Mitte des 18. Jahrhunderts* (Freiburg im Breisgau, 1852), p. 363.
[12] See Coutinho, *op. cit.* (n. 7), pp. 47–49; 66–70. For the history of the Jesuit mission of Salsette to 1660 see the previously unpublished history of Inacio Arcamone, S.J., as reproduced and edited in Lagrange Romeo Fernandes, "Uma descripção e relação 'Di Sasatana Peninsula'

The Portuguese Franciscans, organizationally at first under the Observant Province of Portugal, were the earliest and most numerous of the friars to work in Asia.[13] By 1619, when the Franciscans in the *padroado* numbered around four hundred, the papacy recognized the growth and importance of their Asian enterprise by creating the independent Province of St. Thomas.[14] A fractricidal struggle between the Observant Franciscans and the Reformed Observants of the Piedade province had been transplanted from Portugal to India during the sixteenth century, and it continued to rage in the seventeenth century. In 1629, over the strenuous objections of the Observant Province of Portugal and India, Rome permitted the Reformed Observants to organize in India the independent Province of Madre de Deus. Most of the Portuguese Franciscans, irrespective of their affiliation within the complex organization of their order, concentrated their activities in the Portuguese outposts, where they maintained convents and churches and ministered to the Portuguese, their wives, and their children.

Throughout the seventeenth century the Franciscans continued to be the largest in number of the Portuguese friars in Asia. At the dawn of the century their most successful missions were in Goa, Malabar, and Ceylon. Small missions struggled for survival on the Coromandel Coast at Mylapore, Negapatam, and Tranquebar; on the Fishery Coast at Tuticorin; and in the northern India outposts of the Portuguese.[15] East of India, the Portuguese Franciscans had convents at Malacca and Macao from which they periodically sent out friars on missions to Pegu, Cambodia, Java, and the Moluccas.[16] After the Dutch capture of Malacca in 1641, most of its Catholic clergy fled to Makassar, including the Franciscans and their hospital.[17] The victories of the Dutch at Makassar, Ceylon, Coromandel, and Malabar in the 1660's forced the Portuguese Franciscans to seek refuge in Goa and northeastern India where the Portuguese retained footholds. In Goa, where most of them congregated, they became a mounting drain on the royal purse. In Burma, a small but permanent mission was established at Ava and Pegu around 1660. At Acheh in Sumatra a few Franciscans ministered to the needs of the Portuguese, and others appeared at Timor in the late seventeenth century to aid the Dominicans on that Portuguese-controlled is-

---

(1664) do Padre Inacio Arcamone," *Archivum Historicum Societatis Iesu* (hereafter *AHSI*), L (1981), 76–120.

[13] On their early sixteenth-century activities see *Asia*, I, 234–35; 262.

[14] Between 1590 and 1630 the numbers of Franciscans doubled, going from two hundred to four hundred. These data are given in T. B. Duncan, *The Portuguese Enterprise in Asia* (unpublished typescript), Table 24.

[15] See A. Meersman, *The Franciscans in Tamilnad* in Supplementa XVII of the *Neue Zeitschrift für Missionswissenschaft* (hereafter *NZM*)(Fribourg, 1962), pp. 50, 57–60, 96–99, 121.

[16] See M. Teixeira, *The Portuguese Missions in Malacca and Singapore, 1511–1958* (3 vols., Lisbon, 1961–63), II, 133–35, 145–48. On the Spanish Franciscans at Malacca see below, p. 215.

[17] See A. Meersman (ed.), *Historia missionum ordinis Fratrum Minorum*, Vol. I. *Asia centro-orientalis et oceania* (Rome, 1967), p. 266.

land.[18] Other Franciscans continued to minister secretly and openly to native converts in the Dutch-controlled regions of the East. The worsening Franciscan position in the *padroado,* when coupled with an official desire of the crown to cut down on the number of religious in the East, served to discourage young Portuguese from entering the order. With the waning of enthusiasm for the mission the number of Portuguese Franciscans in the East dropped by 1700 to 280 friars, most of whom were stationed in India.[19]

The Dominicans, like the Franciscans, were well established in India and Ceylon before the end of the sixteenth century.[20] Individual Dominicans had made forays east of India especially after the founding of the Goa convent and the formal establishment of the Dominican enterprise in 1548. Diego Bermudez, the first vicar-general of the Dominican Congregation of the Holy Cross of the East Indies, had arrived at Goa in that year accompanied by a group of twelve friars. One of these friars, Gaspar da Cruz, had soon left India for Malacca and other points east.[21] In 1554 he founded the Dominican convent of Malacca, and then went on to Cambodia to establish a mission there. Unsuccessful in Cambodia, he went on to China and visited at Canton in 1556 just before the founding of Macao. Although Cruz had to return to Portugal in 1568, the Dominicans continued to prosper at Malacca, the first bishop being Friar Jorge de St. Luzia of Aveiro. From Malacca the Dominicans irregularly sent out small groups of missionaries to Siam, Cambodia, and the Lesser Sundas. A few friars traveled extensively in the East.[22] Like their Franciscan confreres, the Portuguese Dominicans respected the mission monopoly enjoyed by the Jesuits in China and Japan; the Dominicans possessed a convent at Macao until 1640, where the friars lived who ministered to the Portuguese and the Christian converts.[23]

In 1610 the Dominicans reached their peak in numbers and influence. Three hundred and ten Portuguese Dominicans lived in Asia, most in convents at nine Portuguese centers (Goa, Cochin, Chaul, Damão, Bassein, Diu, Colombo, Malacca, and Macao). They were involved in the affairs of the Goa Inquisition and were the only one of the orders to supply it with inquisitors.[24] Only a few lived at mission stations where the work was mainly

[18] *Ibid.,* pp. 275–78; also see Teixeira, *op. cit.* (n. 16), II, 132.

[19] See Duncan, *op. cit.* (n. 14), Table 24.

[20] For the Portuguese Dominicans in the East to 1706 see L. de Cácegas, *História de São Domingos, particular de reyno, e conquistas de Portugal* (4 vols., Lisbon, 1623–1767), especially III, 393–433, and IV, 649–703. Also B. Biermann, "Die Mission der portugiesischen Dominikaner in Hinterindien," *Zeitschrift für Missionswissenschaft und Religionswissenschaft* (hereafter ZMR), XXI (1931), 305–27.

[21] For his biography see *Asia,* I, 748–49.

[22] For the contemporary account of Dominican activities in Cambodia, see Gabriel Quiroga de San Antonio, *Breve y verdadera relacion de los succesors del reino de Camboxa* (Valladolid, 1604). Reprinted in 1914 and edited by A. Cabaton. Also see below, p. 309, for San Antonio's peregrinations.

[23] See R. P. F. Andre-Marie, O.P., *Missions Dominicaines dans l'Extreme Orient* (Paris, 1865), I, 123–24.

[24] See Duncan, *op. cit.* (n. 14), pp. 287, 302.

with natives. At Negapatam, for example, the Dominicans, beginning in 1604, ministered primarily to the Portuguese and their families. A short-lived (1604–13) mission to Burma during De Brito's ascendancy there was typical of the Dominican enterprises undertaken outside of the major Portuguese centers. Martyrdoms of the strong-willed Dominicans were common in places not enjoying the protection of the secular arm.[25]

The only permanent mission stations maintained by the order were isolated at the extremities of the *padroado* in Mozambique and the Lesser Sundas.[26] Beginning in 1561 the Dominicans had begun work in the Lesser Sundas on the small island of Solor off the eastern coast of the larger island of Flores.[27] Five years later the friars built a stone fortress on Solor to protect the native Christians and the Portuguese families from attacks by the Islamic rulers of the neighboring islands. Around 1600 the Dominicans (often called "white friars" in Indonesia) claimed one hundred thousand converts in twenty-seven *kampongs* (Malay for village or the special quarter in a town) of Solor, Flores, and Ende.[28] The Solor-Flores-Timor complex was an important trading region at which the sandalwood and slaves of Timor, as well as pepper and fine spices from the Moluccas and other islands, were exchanged with merchants from Makassar, Manila, and Macao. The Dutch, in a short-lived effort to control the rich trade of this region, captured and destroyed the Dominican fortress on Solor in 1613. The defeated Portuguese and Dominicans found refuge at Larantuka on the eastern tip of Flores where the Dominicans had earlier made converts. In 1616 the Dutch abandoned Solor but stayed at Ende until 1618 when they decided that its trade was not rich enough to fight for.[29] The Dominicans on Flores meanwhile received reinforcements at the end of 1614 of five friars headed by Miguel Rangel (d. 1645), the visitor and vicar-general of the Dominicans in the East Indies.[30] Once the Dutch withdrew, the Christians of Larantuka, supported by the raja of Sika, returned to Ende and Solor. Three years later the visitor João das Chagas arrived at Larantuka in the company of Friar Luis de An-

---

[25] For numerous examples see Andre-Marie, *op. cit.* (n. 23), chap. ii. On De Brito in south Burma see below, pp. 234–35.

[26] For the Mozambique mission see Duncan, *op. cit.* (n. 14), pp. 296–97.

[27] For a map of Flores-Solor-Timor see *ibid.*, map 3. In Portuguese contemporary accounts "Solor" is frequently used to mean any or all of the seven Portuguese settlements of this region as well as Solor itself.

[28] The Dutch later estimated the number of Catholic converts in this region at 12,250. See C. R. Boxer, *Fidalgos in the Far East 1550–1770* (The Hague, 1948), pp. 175–76. By 1606 around sixty-four Dominicans had worked in this region and had converted an estimated 50,000 natives according to P. K. Piskaty, *Die katholische Missionsschule in Nusa Tenggara* (*Südost-Indonesien . . .*) (Steyr, 1964), p. 47. Almost all recent scholars are convinced that the contemporary estimates of conversions are inflated substantially. The friars, desirous of impressing their superiors with numbers, counted baptisms, sometimes purely symbolic mass affairs, in their conversion figures. See Duncan, *op. cit.* (n. 14), pp. 251–52.

[29] J. Bot, "Mission History Sketch of the Lesser Sunda Islands," *Mission Bulletin* (Hong Kong, 1955), p. 575.

[30] For his biography see Cácegas, *op. cit.* (n. 20), IV, 696–700.

drada and three other priests. There they joined the six missionaries already at work in the Solor region under the supervision of Vicar Francisco Barradas. Andrada remained in the Lesser Sundas for the following nine years, during which time he claimed to have built two churches and to have baptized more than three thousand natives. The Jesuits made a brief foray (1624–26) to the nearby island of Savu, but were ordered out by the viceroy when Andrada protested to the secular authorities that this island was part of the Dominicans' preserve.[31]

From the beginning of their venture in the Lesser Sundas, the Dominicans had been embroiled in the civil wars which pitted powerful local families against one another. Nearby Islamic rulers, especially the sultan of Makassar, like the Portuguese and Spanish, supported one or the other of these feuding families. Around 1630 the Dominicans were driven out of Ende and thereafter both trade and conversions were concentrated at Solor and Larantuka; Timor, which was without satisfactory harbors for trading vessels, was regularly visited by the Dominicans and Portuguese merchants, but no settlement existed there at this time. Miguel Rangel, who had returned to India from Europe in 1625, again visited Solor during 1629–30 with reinforcements for its mission and aid from Goa and Malacca that put the mission on a firmer and more permanent footing.[32] He himself sailed on to China from Flores to carry on trade and to inspect the Dominican convent at Macao. On his return to India he was appointed bishop of Cochin in 1631. Later he wrote a glowing account of Solor's role as an intermediate point in the Timor-Macao trade that was open to all comers and free of Dutch control.[33]

The loss of Malacca to the Dutch in 1641 served to strengthen the Portuguese position in the Lesser Sundas. Many of the Catholic Eurasians of Malacca at first sought refuge at Makassar. The bishop of Malacca, Paulo da Costa, tried to establish a residence at Larantuka, but eventually had to flee to Timor and then to Macao, leaving Solor-Flores without a bishop. The conclusion of a truce in 1642 between the Dutch and the newly independent Portuguese regime provided for the drawing of a demarcation line in eastern Indonesia. Bali and Lombok were hereafter to be Dutch preserves; Sumbawa and Timor were to be open to both parties; only Flores and the Do-

---

[31] See B. Biermann, "Frei Luis de Andrada und die Solor-mission," *ZMR*, XLIII (1959), 176–87. Andrada returned to Goa in 1627 and thereafter memorialized the Propaganda in Rome, vainly it would seem, to separate the Dominican province of India from the mother province in Portugal. He pointed out that the Franciscans had won such a separation (*cf.* above, p. 135), and that they had only 90 (?) religious in the East while the Dominicans there numbered 320 in 71 convents.

[32] See Teixeira, *op. cit.* (n. 16), II, 96.

[33] Two reports by Rangel were published at Lisbon: one in 1624 and the other in 1635. See R. Streit, *Bibliotheca Missionum* (30 vols., Münster and Aachen, 1916–75; hereafter cited as Streit), V, 100. The first was a memorial to the king and the second a *relação* of Christian triumphs in Solor during his second visit there.

minican settlements of Larantuka and Sika were to remain under Portuguese administration. In northern Timor (now called Timor Dili) an uneasy alliance became a firm friendship between the dominant De Hornay family and the Portuguese.[34] Both the Dutch and the Portuguese in these years of precarious truce cut sandalwood on Timor, and the Dominicans held a contract to furnish it to the Hollanders.[35]

An attack on Makassar by the Dutch in 1660 forced a new dispersion of its Catholic community of around three thousand persons: 110 Portuguese went to Siam and Batavia, 530 to Macao, and 120 to Timor.[36] Antonio Macedo, appointed Dominican superior and commissioner of Solor in 1660, took to Larantuka the belongings of the Dominican church of Makassar. In February, 1661, a Luso-Dutch treaty was signed which brought an official end to fifty years of hostilities in the Sundas. The Luso-Asian traders who hereafter remained on Timor and Flores paid little more than lip-service to the authority of Goa, Macao, or the Dominicans, and acted independently in their own self-interest. At the end of 1679 only sixteen Dominicans remained in the Sundas. During the last generation of the century the real rulers of Portuguese Timor were the descendants of Jan de Hornay, a renegade Netherlander, and the Luso-Asians called "Black Portuguese" by the Dutch.[37] An intermittent civil war continued to rage between the De Hornay and the Da Costa families for control of Larantuka and its lucrative trade. The Dominicans, as well as the secular clergy, likewise looked to the trade for their sustenance. By the end of the century only about 130 Dominicans remained active at Goa, at a few Portuguese settlements on India's west coast, and in the Lesser Sundas.[38] Around 1700 Larantuka was left to the Da Costa family as the Portuguese centered their activities at Lifao on Timor. The inhabitants of modern Flores in independent Indonesia still remember fondly the years of Luso-Asian preeminence.[39]

The Hermit Friars of St. Augustine were the last of the Portuguese orders to enter the eastern mission field. A contingent of ten Augustinians had first arrived at Goa on September 3, 1572. At the request of the Portuguese crown, two of the original twelve sent out from Lisbon went directly from Mozambique to Ormuz. The Persian Gulf mission, abandoned earlier by both the Jesuits and the Dominicans, became the prime target of Augustin-

---

[34] See Piskaty, *op. cit.* (n. 28), pp. 47–48; and Bot, *loc. cit.* (n. 29), p. 576.

[35] See Boxer, *op. cit.* (n. 28), p. 179.

[36] Figures from Teixeira, *op. cit.* (n. 16), II, 24, 100.

[37] See Duncan, *op. cit.* (n. 14), p. 295.

[38] *Ibid.*, Table 24.

[39] When Lach visited Flores in 1973, its governor had Portuguese-style dances and plays presented and proudly displayed whatever remained of the "Portuguese days." For further detail on the vestiges of the Portuguese presence in these islands see the richly illustrated work of Antonio Pinto da Franca, former consul of Portugal in Indonesia, who traveled for five years to compile his *Portuguese Influence in Indonesia* (Djakarta, 1970). Especially valuable are his lists of Indonesian words derived from Portuguese.

ian endeavor to 1622. From the Gulf the persistent friars penetrated the Persian empire and by 1602 had a convent at Ispahan.

Manpower from Europe meanwhile had continued to flow into Goa during the last generation of the sixteenth century. By 1580 an Augustinian church and monastery had been built at Malacca. The appointment in 1596 of the Augustinian Aleixo de Meneses (1559–1617) as archbishop of Goa inaugurated a period (1596–1610) of most rapid expansion for the Augustinian enterprise. In numbers the friars in the East increased from 99 in 1600 to 155 in 1610; in terms of space they began in these same years to establish convents outside of Goa along the west coast of India, in Ceylon, on the Coromandel Coast, and in distant Bengal.[40]

Goa was the nerve center of this quickened Augustinian activity. Construction of their convent of *Nossa Senhora da Graça* began in 1597. A college was opened at Goa in 1602.[41] Mother Filipa da Trindade, with the encouragement of Meneses, founded in 1606 the nunnery of St. Monica which followed the Augustinian rule.[42] From the outset the Augustinians, like the Dominicans and Franciscans, recruited many of their numbers in Asia. Between 1600 and 1649, the peak years of their activity in the East, the Augustinians enrolled 89 percent of their personnel in Asia. Most of the novices were young men who had been recruited or impressed in Portugal for service in India. Upon arriving in Goa these youths, most of whom came from the Lisbon area, often preferred a novitiate to the other forms of employment available for untrained and inexperienced Portuguese. Such a career ordinarily was far less dangerous and more secure than soldiering, since most of the Augustinians ministered to the Portuguese and their families in the well-established urban enclaves of India's west coast: Goa, Damão, Bassein, Thana, Chaul, and Cochin.[43] Most of the time about one-third of the Augustinians lived in the enormous convent at Goa.[44] But not all of the Augustinians were raw youths from Lisbon. A few were regularly sent to Goa from Portugal to administer the order and to keep its records. Notable is the case of Father Felix de Jesus (d. 1640), who was sent to Goa in 1605 to write the history of the missionary Congregation of India. He spent the last thirty-five years of his life in Goa's convent keeping track of the Augustinian activities in the East.[45]

[40] For the numbers of friars see Duncan, *op. cit.* (n. 14), Table 24.
[41] For a nice description of the Augustinian establishment at Goa see M. Collis, *The Land of the Great Image* . . . (New York, 1943), p. 61.
[42] For its subsequent history see Duncan, *op. cit.* (n. 14), pp. 310–12.
[43] See T. A. Lopez, O.S.A., *La Orden de San Agustin en la India (1572–1622)* (Valladolid, 1977), p. 122, for this list of places.
[44] See Duncan, *op. cit.* (n. 14), pp. 316–19.
[45] He wrote a manuscript history of Augustinian beginnings, dated Goa, January 15, 1606, which is preserved in the Public Library of Evora (Codex CXV 1–8). It has been edited and published by A. Hartmann, O.S.A., in "The Augustinians in Golden Goa . . . ," *Analecta Augustiniana*, XXX (1967), 5–147. He supposedly carried his history down to 1637, but this part of his work has never been found.

A flurry of missionary activity outside Goa marked the early years of the seventeenth century. It was probably at the demand of Archbishop Mene- ses, the hero of Felix's history, that Friar Leonardo da Graça and three com- panions were sent to Bengal in 1599. By 1601 an Augustinian mission was established at Hugli, a center of Portuguese commercial enterprise in the Ganges delta which functioned independently and without direction from Goa. From an ecclesiastical viewpoint Bengal was then under the jurisdic- tion of the Cochin diocese, and Friar Leonardo was delegated by its bishop to be vicar-general and dean as well as being the Augustinian provincial of Bengal. The Augustinians resisted fiercely the efforts of the other orders to work in Bengal. From their convent at Hugli they soon fanned out to work in the scattered Bengali towns where the Portuguese conducted business. Leonardo himself was recalled to Goa in 1602 and sent to open a mission in Ceylon.[46]

The Augustinians were tolerated by the Mughul governors of Bengal, in order to encourage the Portuguese merchants to come there rather than to the rival kingdom of Arakan across the bay.[47] By 1614, after much striking about in the merchant towns of Bengal, the Augustinians determined to de- velop Hugli as their permanent center and to erect dependent mission sta- tions at Dacca and Pipli. In contemporary reports the Augustinians claimed numerous converts among the Bengalis. Some credence must have been ac- corded these claims, for the Jesuits tried around 1620 to establish a mission at Hugli. The Augustinians immediately protested against this invasion of their territory and claimed that exclusive parish rights in all Bengal had been accorded them by the bishop of Mylapore. While the missionaries attacked each other, the Mughul authorities and their Muslim cohorts began around 1625 to attack them both. When Shah Jahan, a strict Muslim, became Mughul emperor in 1628, the situation of the Europeans in Bengal worsened ab- ruptly. Hugli itself was sacked in 1632 by strong Mughul forces intent upon halting the slaving activities of the Portuguese based in Arakan. The Augus- tinian establishments were burned and a few of the missionaries were carried off in captivity to Agra.[48]

Portuguese renegades and adventurers had begun working for Arakan during the last years of the sixteenth century. Felipe de Brito, the so-called king of Pegu, was but the most successful and independent of the Por- tuguese mercenaries employed by Arakan.[49] Eurasian Portuguese as well as native Portuguese were organized into military companies to protect Chit-

---

[46] Based on A. Hartmann, "The Augustinian Mission of Bengal (1599–1834)," *Analecta Au- gustiniana*, XLI (1978), 166–69. Leonardo was replaced in Bengal by Friar Gaspar dos Reis.

[47] For a map showing the early Portuguese settlements at the mouths of the Ganges and on the Bay of Bengal see C. E. Luard and H. Hosten (trans. and eds.), *Travels of Fray Sebastien Manrique, 1629–1643*, "HS," 2d ser., LIX and LXI (Oxford, 1926–27), Vol. I, p. xxiv.

[48] See Hartmann, *loc. cit.* (n. 46), pp. 182–84. Also see below, p. 234.

[49] On his rise and fall see above, p. 16.

tagong and other Arakanese-held places from the expansionist activities of the Mughuls in Bengal. To keep the Mughuls off balance the Portuguese mercenaries based at Dianga periodically pillaged the coastal places of Bengal and carried off captives. These attacks embarrassed the viceroys of Goa who were doing their best to maintain friendly relations with the Mughuls. The Augustinians, who began working in Arakan around 1621, thereafter formed a link between Goa and the Portuguese adventurers at Chittagong, Dianga, and Mrauk-u, the royal capital of Arakan. The Portuguese Augustinians participated in the Arakan enterprise by baptizing the captives brought from Bengal. The Augustinians were also successful in converting members of Arakan's royal family, two of whom they sent to Goa for further instruction at the motherhouse. With the sack of Hugli in 1632 many Portuguese from Bengal fled to Arakan for refuge.[50]

Shah Jahan, possibly because he wanted to avoid forcing the Portuguese into the hands of Arakan and to keep the commerce of Bengal from declining, quickly permitted the Portuguese to return after the sack of Hugli. Little by little the Augustinian presence was reestablished. All efforts by the other orders to wrest control of the Bengal mission from the Augustinians were thwarted when Viceroy Pedro da Silva (r. 1635–39) granted their demands for a privileged position in Bengal.[51] With the fall of Malacca in 1641, many displaced Portuguese fled to Bengal. The Dutch occupation of Ceylon in 1658, and the English and Dutch expansion into the Coromandel cities, also drove many more Portuguese and Luso-Asians to Bengal. Here they began to work in the European factories, including the swiftly expanding Dutch and English outposts. Many Bengalis, particularly those who worked with or under the Europeans, became converts to Catholicism under the tutelage of the intrepid Augustinians. The French physician, François Bernier, reported that in 1666 Hugli boasted eight to nine thousand Christians and the rest of Bengal more than twenty-five thousand. In their endeavors the Augustinians were aided by important Bengali converts. Still the Augustinians continued to be bothered by Jesuit efforts to "help out" with the Christian mission to Bengal. They finally lost their monopoly: the French opened a factory at Chandernagore in 1688, the French Jesuits, unlike the earlier Jesuits, were permitted to work in Bengal in 1690, and the Propaganda began to send its own fathers to Hugli and elsewhere in the 1690's. By the end of the century the back of the *padroado* had been broken in Bengal. The Augustinian mission declined hereafter, but it remained one of the most important of the Portuguese missions in India and it was only finally extinguished in 1834.[52]

[50] For further detail see Collis, *op. cit.* (n. 41), chap. vii. Also Hartmann, *loc. cit.* (n. 46), pp. 179–84.

[51] For the seventeen privileges granted the Augustinians, including freedom from the political control of Goa, see *O Chronista de Tissuary* (Nova Goa, 1867), I, 60.

[52] See Hartmann, *loc. cit.* (n. 46), pp. 184–91.

In 1700, there were 143 Portuguese Augustinians working throughout the East, or just somewhat more than one-half of the number who evangelized there in 1630, the peak year. They possessed eight convents (Goa, Thana, Chaul, Bassein, Damão, Macao, Hugli, and Ispahan) the most important of which, outside of Goa, was the convent of Hugli.[53] Outside of western India, it should be noted, the Augustinians worked in places where the Muslims were firmly entrenched. In Bengal, as elsewhere, most of their converts were non-Muslims.

The friars of the *padroado,* for all their zeal at the beginning of the seventeenth century, fought a losing battle in Asia. With the decline of Portugal's secular domain, the friars generally abandoned their missionizing activities and assumed a defensive posture. They left areas where the crown was unable to support them and congregated at their convents in Goa and at the Portuguese fortress-factories on India's west coast.[54] A few Franciscans worked clandestinely or openly in Dutch-dominated territories. In the Lesser Sundas the Dominicans held on by cooperating with the local magnates of trade and the political rulers. The authorities in Goa and Lisbon, weary of supporting large numbers of friars in the beleaguered enclaves, discouraged their enterprises. Very few Indians were permitted to join the orders.[55] In Goa and elsewhere a native secular clergy gradually began to replace the friars as priests to the faithful. Under these conditions it is not surprising that some of the friars began to lead far from exemplary lives or to abandon their vocations. By 1700 there were approximately 750 Portuguese friars (Franciscans, Dominicans, and Augustinians) working in Asia, or about the same number as at the beginning of the century; this was a decline from the high point of 1630 when they numbered almost 1,100.[56] Along with the decline in numbers after 1630 went an increase in disobedience, particularly during the period 1640–68 when Portugal and Rome were at odds. Even after the restoration of relations with the Vatican, the friars of the *padroado* vegetated at Goa and at the other Portuguese enclaves. Their fervor for conversions gone, the friars in Asia held on until 1833–34 while their numbers and influence steadily dwindled.[57]

---

[53] See Duncan, *op. cit.* (n. 14), Table 24, and p. 317; in a report sent to the crown in 1682 on the history of the Augustinians in India to 1669, Simao da Graça, O.S.A., gives the greatest space and attention to the mission in Bengal. See Hartmann, *loc. cit.* (n. 46), p. 163.

[54] For a summary account of Portuguese missions in India as of *ca.* 1660 see M. Godinho, *Relação do novo caminho que fez por terra e mar, vindo da India para Portugal no ano de 1663 . . .* (Lisbon, 1665), pp. 11–12, 53, 216–22.

[55] To 1661 no more than six or seven Indians had been admitted to the Franciscan order, and several of those who were ordained were permitted entry in Rome rather than in India. See C. R. Boxer, "The Problem of the Native Clergy in Portuguese India 1518–1787," *History Today,* XVII (1967), 774.

[56] Duncan, *op. cit.* (n. 14), Table 24.

[57] Based on *ibid.,* pp. 329–31.

2

THE "PADROADO" JESUITS IN SOUTH ASIA

The Jesuits of the *padroado* had a happier experience than the friars. Under the guidance of Valignano, superior of the mission in the East from 1574 until his death at Macao in 1606, the Jesuits had grown rapidly in numbers and had taken over leadership of the Christian mission from Goa to Naga-saki.[58] By 1605 the original huge Jesuit province of India had been divided into three subdivisions: North India (Goa), South India (Cochin), and China and Japan. Directly subject to the Goa province were the Portuguese com-mercial enclaves of northern India, Mysore, the Mughul Empire, Cathay, and Persia; Cochin administered Jesuit activities in the rest of India, Ceylon, Malacca, the Moluccas, and Pegu. Macao was headquarters for all of the Portuguese Jesuits working in East Asia. Within these provinces the Jesuits ran more than one hundred establishments: colleges, rectories, and resi-dences. Almost six hundred Jesuits worked in the East during the first de-cade of the seventeenth century, a number far larger than could be boasted by any one of the orders of friars. Since the total membership of the Society in 1600 was ten thousand, the Jesuits of the *padroado* constituted 6 percent of the total.[59]

Between 1600 and 1700 around 930 Jesuits, counting both brothers and fathers, arrived in the East via Lisbon and the Cape route.[60] Substantially more than one-half of this number were of Portuguese birth. Jesuits of Spanish nationality, who had constituted more than 20 percent of the Jesuits working in the *padroado* during the sixteenth century, almost vanish from the lists in the seventeenth century—presumably because of their greater preoccupation with American missions and because of the growing rupture between the Portuguese nation and the Spanish Habsburgs. Around one-third of the Jesuits who went east during the seventeenth century were non-Portuguese, with the Italians succeeding the Spanish as the largest "foreign" contingent. Over the course of the century the number of Italians declined sharply, particularly during and after the period (1640–68) of the break be-tween Rome and Lisbon. As relations between the *padroado,* the Propaganda, and later the French, became more strained, increasing numbers of northern Europeans appeared in the East: Germans, Austrians, Swiss, Flemish, Dutch, and French. Neither Rome nor the Jesuit general was willing to see the So-

---

[58] For the history of the Society's activities during the sixteenth century see *Asia,* I, 245–314.

[59] See A. Viegas (ed.), *Relação anual das coisas que fizeram os padres da Companhia de Jesus nas suas missioes . . . nos anos de 1600 a 1609 . . . pelo Padre Fernão Guerreiro . . .* (3 vols., Coimbra, 1930), I, 1–5. On Guerreiro's work see below, pp. 316–18. Also see Duncan, *op. cit.* (n. 14), Table 24 and p. 359.

[60] See Duncan, *op. cit.* (n. 14), Table 25.

ciety created by Loyola as the strong right hand of the papacy fall as fully under the control of the Portuguese crown as the friars had. The Jesuit mission in the East remained broadly European in every sense of the word, particularly since the Jesuits only slowly admitted a few East Asians to their ranks.[61]

In India the Jesuits, following the instructions of Valignano, concentrated on conversions and generally tried to leave pastoral care to the secular priests and the friars. Every superior in the Society from the general down to the vice-provincials watched closely and in detail the progress of Christianity in Goa and elsewhere in India. In his letters to the India provincials, General Claudio Acquaviva commented on everything from conversion policy to feet-washing.[62] Francisco Cabral (1528–1609), the provincial in Goa from 1592 to 1597 and former vice-provincial (1582–84) of Japan, wrote in 1596 in great prolixity about the efforts being made by the Moors and Gentiles to discredit the Jesuits before the Portuguese secular authorities by charging them unjustly with carrying out conversions by force.[63] Evidently the Jesuits of Goa continued for long thereafter to be charged with being more forceful in their methods than the friars of nearby Salsette and Bardez.[64] Goa was totally Catholic at the beginning of the seventeenth century and by 1619 the entire native population (eighty thousand) of the peninsula of Salsette had been converted.

Nicolas Pimenta (1546–1613), the Jesuit visitor to the East Indies from 1596 to the end of Nuño Rodrigues' tenure (1597–1602) as provincial, enjoyed, even among the Portuguese and the Jesuits themselves, a reputation for extreme severity and aggressiveness. Pimenta took advantage of the Portuguese-Calicut treaty of 1598, by which the Zamorin's territories were legally opened for the first time to the missionaries, to send a few Jesuits there. The Italian Jesuit Giacomo Fenicio (*ca.* 1558–1632) studied Indian languages there and after 1600 prepared his history and description of the "Indian sects" called *Livro da seita dos Indios Orientais.*[65] But this effort was short lived for the Zamorin soon returned to his anti-Portuguese policy when Dutch vessels began to appear off his coast. Visitor Pimenta was evidently satisfied with the progress being recorded by the Jesuits in the northern stations at the city of Bassein, the island of Salsette (Tana), and the fortress of Chaul. He set up a house at Diu around 1600 from which the Jesuits were thereafter sent out to Ethiopia, Agra, and Lahore.[66]

---

[61] Based on *ibid.*, Table 26.

[62] See J. Wicki, "Auszüge aus den Briefen der Jesuitengenerale an die Obern in Indien (1549–1613)," *AHSI*, XXII (1953), 152.

[63] See A. Rebello (comp.), *Compendio de algumas cartas que este anno de 97 vierao dos Padres da Companhia de Jesu* (Lisbon, 1598), pp. 17–18.

[64] See H. Heras, S.J., *The Conversion Policy of the Jesuits in India* (Bombay, 1933), p. 47.

[65] On Fenicio see below, pp. 874–76. See L. Ambruzzi, "Il contributo dei missionari cattolici alla conoscenza delle religioni . . . dell' India," in C. Costantini *et al., Le missioni cattoliche e la cultura dell' Oriente* (Rome, 1943), pp. 274–76, for the book's history.

[66] See Müllbauer, *op. cit.* (n. 11), pp. 106–7.

The Jesuit connection to Akbar, the Mughul ruler (r. 1556–1605), dated back to 1580 but with several periods of interruption.[67] Father Jerome Xavier (d. 1617), a grandnephew of the Apostle of the Indies, was at Akbar's side from 1595 to the "Great Mogul's" death in 1605. Through their command of Persian, Xavier and his associate were able to communicate directly with Akbar and his court. In 1601 Akbar finally gave permission in writing for his subjects to embrace Christianity. Two years later Brother Bento (Benedict) de Goes (1562–1607), a Portuguese who had worked with Xavier at Akbar's court, departed from Agra with Akbar's encouragement and blessing for an overland journey to China. Disguised as an Armenian merchant, Goes set out in March, 1603, to journey across "the roof of the world" to find Father Matteo Ricci in Peking and to determine whether or not Cathay and northern China were one and the same place. By his arduous voyage he established, to the satisfaction of the Jesuits at least, the identity of Cathay and northern China. Unhappily he died at Su-chou in western China in 1607 before reaching Peking and Ricci.[68]

Among the Jesuits at the Mughul court, Cathay was sometimes confused with Tibet where, it was rumored, large numbers of Christians had lived. Goes' expedition was supposed to clarify these matters. Although it demonstrated that Cathay was China rather than Tibet, the belief that Tibet had once been home to many Christians persisted, bolstered by occasional descriptions of Tibetan rituals which seemed to resemble those of the Christian church. In 1624 Father Antonio de Andrade was sent to investigate and hopefully to make contact with Tibetan Christians. Andrade journeyed across the Himalayas at Mana Pass to Tsaparang on the upper Sutlej in western Tibet. He found no Christians but was favorably received by the local king, who gave him permission to establish a mission. Back in Agra in late 1624, he returned to Tsaparang with two other Jesuits during the following year. The mission established by Andrade endured until 1635; Andrade himself left Tsaparang in 1630. After 1635 missionaries continued to visit Tsaparang until 1650 when the kingdom of Guge, including Tsaparang, was annexed by Ladakh. Altogether, twenty-six missionaries visited western Tibet between 1625 and 1650.

At the time of Akbar's death in 1605, Xavier and Father Antonio Machado resided at Agra while Fathers Manuel Pinheiro and Francisco Corsi worked at Lahore. In both cities the Jesuits had a numerically small, but staunch, group of converts. While the Jesuits had not succeeded in winning Akbar to Christianity, they had high hopes for the conversion of Prince Salim, who became Emperor Jahangir (r. 1605–27) when he succeeded his fa-

---

[67] For the history of Akbar and the Jesuits to 1600 see *Asia,* I, 275–77.

[68] For a summary in English of the contemporary letters and notices in Guerreiro's *Relação* (see n. 59) and the *Histoire* of Pierre du Jarric, a work heavily based on Guerreiro's, see C. H. Payne (trans. and ed.), *Jahangir and the Jesuits* (New York, 1930), pp. 119–82. Maps of the journey are included.

ther in office. But the Jesuits were much too sanguine about the prospects for Jahangir's conversion. From the beginning of his reign Jahangir played off the mullahs and the Jesuits against each other, and listened to their disputations as a display put on for his pleasure. Increasingly he began to use the Jesuits as emissaries to Goa and as courtiers who could supply him with information and exotica of the Christian world.[69]

The appearance of William Hawkins and other Englishmen at Surat and Agra in 1608 posed new problems for the Jesuits. Jahangir greeted the newcomers cordially, granted their request to trade at Surat, quizzed them on Christian doctrine, and asked for their estimates of the military capabilities of the Portuguese at Diu and Goa. The viceroy in Goa responded to this new threat by breaking off relations with Jahangir. Even though Jahangir then revoked his grant of permission to the English to maintain his trade with the Portuguese, neither the Jesuits nor the Portuguese merchants were able to recover the monopolistic position that they once enjoyed in the Mughul court. The growing prominence of the Protestant English and Dutch along India's west coast also gradually extinguished the dream of Jahangir's conversion to Catholicism. In 1615 Xavier and Pinheiro returned to Goa. Although they were replaced by younger men, the Jesuits' mission to the Mughuls continued to suffer from the indifference of Jahangir to their religious message and from the growing strength of the English in northwestern India.

While being forced gradually on the defensive in the north, the Jesuits took the offensive in south India and Ceylon. In 1597–98 Visitor Pimenta toured south India to inspect the missions there and to launch a new initiative. What he hoped to do, in contrast to what had gone on before, was to penetrate areas that were outside the Portuguese enclaves and subject to native jurisdiction. The objective of the south India mission was, like those of the Mughul Empire, China, and Japan, to focus on the establishment of contact with the ruling elites, to learn local languages and customs, and to concentrate on converting the upper rather than the lower castes. With the conclusion of the Synod of Diamper in 1599, the Jesuits based in Cochin began to push into the interior, to the east coast, and even to remote Bengal. Around twenty-five Jesuits supervised the thirty-five stations situated from Cochin south to Coulam (Kottakulam) and ministered to their fourteen thousand Christians.[70] The mission on the Fishery Coast, established by Xavier himself, suffered an irreparable loss in 1600 when the virtuous and persistent Henrique Henriques died.[71] Here Henriques and his associates had

---

[69] See *ibid.*, pp. 3–115; also E. Maclagan, *The Jesuits and the Great Mogul* (London, 1932), chap. v, and pp. 342–58. Also see G. M. Toscano, *La prima missione cattolica nel Tibet* (Parma, 1951).

[70] Müllbauer, *op. cit.* (n. 11), p. 117.

[71] On his career see *Asia*, I, 270–71, 433–34.

founded and preserved with little outside aide a mission that in 1601 numbered about twenty Jesuits who served seven residences: Tuticorin, Punical, Manapore, Bempara, Trichandur, Manaar, and Periapatam.[72] By order of the viceroy the Franciscans in 1600 were required to turn over to the Jesuits the missions they had pioneered at Travancore, the Fishery Coast, and the northern sector of Ceylon. Contemporaneously, from his headquarters at Mylapore, Pimenta went into the interior and arranged with the nayaks (viceroys) of Gingee, Tanjore, and Madura, three southeastern dependencies of the ailing empire of Vijayanagar, to permit Christian mission work in their territories. The Jesuits also received permission from the imperial government itself to carry on Christianizing activities at Chandragiri, then the capital of Vijayanagar. Several Jesuits, who had been sent by sea from Mylapore to Bengal and Pegu in 1598–99, soon withdrew from that unfriendly region where the Augustinians claimed a monopoly.[73] Jesuit prospects in Vijayanagar likewise dimmed quickly because of the interminable wars sweeping the declining Hindu empire. While a small Christian community at Madura continued to endure, it was not until Roberto de Nobili (1577–1656) arrived there in 1606 that it was placed on a firm footing.

The gifted scion of an aristocratic Tuscan family, Nobili determined at age seventeen to join the Society; he was ordained priest in 1603. Near the end of that year he left for Lisbon to study Portuguese and to be otherwise prepared for a mission to the East. After a turbulent voyage the young Jesuit landed at Goa on May 20, 1605. For the next five months Nobili remained in Goa at the Jesuit college as he became acclimatized and completed his theological studies. Early in 1606 he voyaged to Cochin to join its college whose new provincial was his fellow Italian, Alberto Laerzio (1557–1630).[74] Nobili soon moved on to Tuticorin to join the Jesuits already working on the Fishery Coast. Here he studied Tamil for seven months until he was dispatched to Madura, the leading center of south Indian Hinduism.

The viceregal state of Madura was created around 1540 as a tribute-paying dependency of the Hindu empire of Vijayanagar. Its nayaks ruled over a territory approximately the size of Portugal in area, which extended from Urrattur and Valikandapuram in the north to Cape Comorin in the south, from Combinatore, Erode, and Dharapuram in the west to Ramesvaram and the sea in the east.[75] Its coastal places, including Tuticorin on the Fishery Coast, were well known by 1600 to the Portuguese and the Jesuits. At the

---

[72] Müllbauer, *op. cit.* (n. 11), pp. 123–24.
[73] For details on the Jesuits see *ibid.*, pp. 130–33; on the Augustinians see above, p. 142.
[74] See V. Cronin, *A Pearl to India. The Life of Roberto de Nobili* (London, 1959), chaps. i–ii; and P. R. Bachmann, *Roberto Nobili, 1577–1656. Ein missionsgeschichtlicher Beitrag zum Christlichen Dialog mit Hinduismus* (Rome, 1972), chaps. i–ii. Both books owe a heavy debt to the unpublished biography and translations of the late Father Agustin Saulière, S.J., a lifelong missionary in Madura.
[75] See H. Heras, *The Aravidu Dynasty of Vijayanagar* (2 vols., Madras, 1927), I, 131–32.

center of Madura on the Vagai River lay Madura City where the nayak held court. For eleven years before Nobili's arrival, a small band of Portuguese and Paravan Christians living on the city's outskirts had been ministered to by Gonçalo Fernandes (1539–1621), a Portuguese Jesuit. Although Fernandes had not made a single high-caste convert during his initial tenure in Madura, he was permitted to build a church, a school, and a small hospital where everything was dispensed freely to Hindus and Christians alike. Laerzio, who was troubled by the stagnation of the Madura mission, met at Tuticorin in November, 1606 with Fernandes and Nobili to plan its future. Here they decided that Nobili should go to Madura as Fernandes' assistant.[76]

Nobili, shortly after his arrival in Madura, wrote to his cousin in Rome: "I am now in a famous city of this country, . . . crowded with wicked idols, as was formerly the famous city of Rome."[77] Clearly, if success in missionizing Madura were to be expected, a new tack would have to be taken. To win over the Hindus without the support of Portuguese arms would require an accommodation to local practices and customs. Fernandes had followed in Madura the established conversion and ministering techniques prevailing in the seaports. Like any other ethnocentric European he thought the Hindus should acknowledge the superiority of Christian and Portuguese beliefs and practices, even as they recognized the ascendancy of Europe's navies and arms. He took pride in the designation "Parangi," the name given to the Portuguese by the south Indians. This word, taken over from the Muslims, is probably the Tamil and Telugu version of the common Asian designation (*farangiha* and related words) of Europeans as "Franks." To the south Indians the word "Parangi" certainly referred to the culture, religion, and customs of the Portuguese, but it also meant foreigners who observed no caste rules and belonged therefore to the untouchables and the other polluting castes. For a Hindu to become a Parangi meant a complete loss of caste; the higher the caste he belonged to the greater was his loss in status on becoming a Christian![78] As a traitor to his caste, the native Parangi was completely compromised and had to take refuge with the Portuguese. Nobili quickly let the Hindus know that he was not a Parangi but an Italian from a Roman family of high caste who taught the true religion and not the religion of the Parangis. From the Sudra teacher at Fernandes' school, Nobili learned much more about the Hinduism and castes of Madura. He was informed that those who followed a way of life resembling that of a Christian priest were called *sannyasis*, holy men who renounced all worldly things including caste. Since the status of *sannyasi* was open both to Brahmans and non-Brahmans, Nobili decided to adopt the dress, diet, and austere way of life of the *sannyasis* as his method of penetrating Hindu culture.

Nobili's plan, though it was revolutionary, was quickly sanctioned by

[76] Bachmann, *op. cit.* (n. 74), pp. 37–40.
[77] As quoted in Heras, *op. cit.* (n. 75), I, 367.
[78] See Cronin, *op. cit.* (n. 74), pp. 42–43.

Provincial Laerzio and Archbishop Francisco Ros (1557–1624), the episcopal ruler of Cranganore, within whose jurisdiction Madura lay. Ros, who
was also guardian of the St. Thomas Christians, had long before learned
from his work among them that compromises could and should be made
with local usages. Fernandes, who was technically Nobili's superior, was
fundamentally disturbed by this experiment in acculturation and reproached
his assistant for arrogance. He was particularly outraged by Nobili's decision to dissociate himself from the Portuguese to avoid the stigma of the
Parangis. Determined nonetheless to pursue his new course Nobili in 1607
withdrew to his own hut, hired Brahmans to prepare and serve his scant
meals of rice and herbs, and claimed to be of the Raja caste. Since members
of this caste were required to have royal blood in their veins, he based his
claim upon the descent of his family from Emperor Otto III (r. 996–1002).[79]
When Laerzio transferred Fernandes to the coast, Nobili was left free to pursue his experiment in living like a Raja of Madura.

Between 1607 and 1609 the "*sannyasi* from Rome" began to cultivate the
young Brahman intellectuals who attended the Hindu university of Madura.
All their conversations were carried on in the elegant Court (High) Tamil
which Nobili had mastered and within the confines of his mud and straw
hut. Nobili baptized five of the young men and gave them Christian-
European surnames. By 1609 he had sixty converts, and in another two
years they numbered one hundred and fifty.[80] In the wake of these successes
came new troubles. Late in 1608 or early in 1609 the nayak Muttu Krish-
nappa (r. 1601–8 or –9) died and was succeeded by his son Muttu Virappa
(1609–23).[81] To Nobili the new nayak was an unknown quantity and possibly open to suggestions from the enemies of the Jesuit missionary. Nobili
had also begun to study Telugu, the language of the nayaks, and Sanskrit,
the language of the Brahmans, to give himself two more avenues into the
life and religions of south India. He first learned to speak Sanskrit and to
read Grantha, the angular Tamil script of Sanskrit. From Sivadarma, his
Sanskrit teacher and would-be guru, he surreptitiously received the texts
of the Vedas, the secret books of the Brahman caste and the most sacred of
Hindu writings. Nobili's penetration of the Vedas and his conversion of
Sivadarma raised questions of great moment for both Hindus and Christians. Theologians of both religions began to question his probity when he
sought by becoming "the guru of the lost [fourth] Veda" to reconcile Hindu
and Christian teachings. Salvation, he claimed, was not possible merely by

---

[79] See *ibid.*, pp. 50–58; Bachmann, *op. cit.* (n. 74), pp. 48–53.
[80] See W. V. Bangert, S.J., *A History of the Society of Jesus* (St. Louis, 1972), p. 153.
[81] The occasion of the nayak's death gave Nobili the opportunity to observe the practice of
suttee (*satī*, widow-burning). Unlike most European observers he did not react with horror or
condemn this ceremony as an example of Hindu barbarity. In his reports he stressed what he
regarded as its positive aspects: the loyalty and devotion of the wives to their ideals. See Bachmann, *op. cit.* (n. 74), p. 61.

following the other three Vedas, the laws of Vishnu, Brahman, and Siva, and by performing good "works." Nobili insisted on the primacy of faith.[82]

While some of the Hindu philosophers denounced Nobili's view, others came to believe that he was advocating "the way of knowledge," a favorite tenet of the orthodox Madura school of Hinduism.[83] The critics among Nobili's European brothers were not so readily satisfied. A first important conflict came in 1609–10 when Nobili and his little flock of sixty built a new church architecturally in the style of a Hindu temple which they reserved exclusively to the use of his high-caste converts. The Portuguese and lower-caste Christians were not permitted to enter this new church. To the Christians of Fernandes' congregation their exclusion constituted another intolerable example of Nobili's arrogance. Fernandes, long frustrated by the failure of his complaints to move Laerzio and Ros against Nobili, decided to appeal to a higher court. For him it was a propitious time, for Pimenta had just been appointed for a second tour (1609–13) as visitor to the Jesuit provinces of Goa and Malabar. Pimenta and the theologians of Goa, long concerned that the Madura mission had gone astray, were quick to respond to Fernandes' grievances and at once launched an investigation of Nobili's methods.

In his complaint to Pimenta, Fernandes alleged that Nobili, for whom he was confessor, denied being a Parangi, dressed himself as a guru, refused to sit at table for meals, took meals by himself that were served by his own Brahmans, built his own house and chapel from which all Portuguese were excluded (including Fernandes himself), gave to his converts new Brahman threads with a small cross attached inscribed with the Latin name of Jesus, purified himself by bathing before mass, changed words in the Tamil liturgy, forbade his converts to attend Fernandes' church, taught his converts that he came from a country other than Portugal, claimed royal descent, and thought that all teachers of the gospel should be of noble lineage.[84] In response to these allegations Pimenta ordered Laerzio and his colleagues at Cochin to determine whether the Madura mission should be reformed or dissolved. The provincial addressed fifteen searching questions, based on Fernandes' allegations, to ten of the new converts.[85] On the basis of this special inquiry Laerzio declared that the allegations of Fernandes were without foundation or exaggerated.[86]

Pimenta, through his personal secretary Luis Cardoso (evidently not a

---

[82] Over the long-debated question of whether or not Nobili falsified this fourth Veda see Bachmann, *op. cit.* (n. 74), pp. 76–82. On his debates with the Brahmans see below, pp. 1014–17.

[83] See Cronin, *op. cit.* (n. 74), chap. vii; and Bachmann, *op. cit.* (n. 74), pp. 96–98.

[84] See Bachmann, *op. cit.* (n. 74), p. 118. The sacred Brahman thread is worn by the highest castes; it is composed of three cords, ordinarily worn diagonally across the body, over the left shoulder.

[85] For their responses see Cronin, *op. cit.* (n. 74), pp. 151–52.

[86] For Laerzio's subsequent career see J. Dehergne, S.J., *Répertoire des Jésuites de Chine de 1552 à 1800* (Rome, 1973), p. 140.

Jesuit), meanwhile began to gather additional allegations against Nobili. After examining the financial records of the Society, Cardoso concluded that the Madura mission was an extravagant and unnecessary luxury.[87] In Goa Pimenta presented Nobili's case to five theologians for their consideration. After determining that the thread worn by the Christian Brahmans might be tolerated, the theologians condemned the baths as being superstitious, the changes in the liturgy as being dangerous, and the separation from Fernandes as being schismatical. Pimenta sent a summary of this opinion to Nobili along with a copy of Fernandes' letter and his own condemnation of Nobili's methods. Since Pimenta was not empowered by the general to suppress the mission, Nobili, Laerzio, and Archbishop Ros quickly sent off letters to Rome defending their positions. Since two years had to elapse before Rome could be expected to respond, Nobili continued with his work and by 1611 his converts numbered 150.[88]

While the battle with Pimenta raged, Laerzio in 1610 decided to send Antonio Vico (1565–1640) to work with Nobili. In Rome, Vico and Nobili had first become friends; in India, Vico had taught theology at Cochin while he watched with admiration Nobili's successes at Madura. Vico was unqualifiedly opposed to Pimenta's censure of Nobili's methods. Shortly after his arrival at Madura, Vico composed a tract for dispatch to Rome refuting the allegations of Fernandes and the Goa theologians. Clearly the issue was becoming national as well as theological, since the Italian Jesuits stood staunchly behind Nobili despite the fact that they were all working within the *padroado* and being supported financially and militarily by the Portuguese crown.

Provincial Laerzio was replaced in 1611 by Pedro Francisco (1568–1623), a Portuguese Jesuit with over two decades of experience in India. He was appointed by Pimenta to reverse Laerzio's policies, to block Nobili's plan to extend his mission to the hinterland of Madura, and to galvanize Fernandes into action. He began by urging Fernandes to adopt a few of the ascetic customs followed by Nobili, to become more involved in Indian life, and to work with the higher castes. By modifying his methods in this way, Fernandes might show Nobili the correct path leading to accommodation with native ways and make unnecessary his separate parish. Pedro Francisco wrote to Nobili on August 11, 1613, ordering him to renounce many of the pagan ceremonies and customs he had adopted, to combine forces with Fernandes' congregation, and to perform no baptisms until these terms were met. Nobili claimed that the very existence of his mission would be compromised by obeying the provincial's order and that this was precisely what the general wanted most to avoid. The general had actually proposed in his letters of December, 1612 to Ros, Francisco, and Nobili that they hold a

[87] See Bachmann, *op. cit.* (n. 74), p. 120.
[88] See Cronin, *op. cit.* (n. 74), pp. 156, 161.

conference and work out together precisely what could be altered at Madura without endangering in any way whatsoever the existence of the mission.[89] Pedro Francisco evidently decided to make this decision himself and expected Nobili to obey his orders without further question.

If he expected blind obedience, Francisco was disappointed. Nobili, accompanied by Ros, went to Cochin in 1613 to discuss the Madura mission as the general had suggested. Provincial Francisco refused to speak to them, but ordered Nobili to put in writing for dispatch to Rome his interpretation of the general's letter.[90] Ros agreed completely with Nobili's understanding of it, questioned the recommendations of the Goa theologians, and condemned Fernandes' behavior in his response to the Jesuit general.[91] General Acquaviva never had the opportunity to react to Ros' complaints about the Jesuit superiors in India, for he died at Rome on January 31, 1615.

The new provincial of Cochin, Gaspar Fernandes, summoned Nobili to Cochin in 1615 to discuss his mission. Archbishop Ros and some of his Jesuit friends felt freer to rally to Nobili's side, for the new provincial was at least neutral in the matter of the Madura mission. Both in Cochin and in Rome, where Nobili's problems were beginning to be better understood, everything seemed in 1616 to be moving in favor of his program. But at this point a new and more powerful enemy appeared in the person of Dom Frei Cristovão de Sá e Lisboa (d. 1662), the successor to Meneses as archbishop of Goa and primate of India. Everywhere on the defensive in India the Portuguese, and especially the archbishop of Goa, began to fear an alliance between the Protestants and their Indian enemies.[92] Archbishop de Sá suspected that concessions to the Madura mission would antagonize the ruler of Madura and would encourage the Christian Brahmans of Goa and elsewhere to return to their former practices previously interdicted by the Portuguese.[93] In combination with Portugal's European enemies, the Brahmans of the seaports might even evict the Portuguese from their Indian footholds. Nor was this viewpoint without foundation; in southern India the Danes were at Tranquebar and the Dutch operated at several bases. Nobili thus came to be seen as a political as well as a religious danger to Portuguese primacy.

In Rome the question of missionary methods in Asia had meanwhile become a matter for discussion and decision. The China missionaries, who had long been following a policy of adaptation, had appealed to the papacy for permission to translate the Bible and other religious writings into Chi-

---

[89] See Bachmann, *op. cit.* (n. 74), pp. 166–67.
[90] For the text of Nobili's letter see Cronin, *op. cit.* (n. 74), pp. 191–97.
[91] See Bachmann, *op. cit.* (n. 74), pp. 172–75.
[92] Cf. above, pp. 10–11.
[93] The Goa councils of 1567, 1575, and 1585 had ordained that converts had to stop wearing their caste threads, and the Portuguese secular arm enforced this prohibition. See Bachmann, *op. cit.* (n. 74), p. 188.

nese and to use the native spoken language in the liturgy and in the administration of sacraments.[94] With the acceptance of this request in 1615, debate
began in Rome over the conflict in India between Nobili and the archbishop
of Goa. Pope Paul V in 1616 ordered archbishops de Sá and Ros to study the
much-disputed matter of the Brahman's thread, sandalpaste (forehead mark-
ing), baths, and other practices to determine whether or not converts should
be allowed to retain them.

Since two years would pass before the papal brief could arrive at Goa,
Nobili and Vico with Ros' permission resumed their ministry in Madura.
Again they performed baptisms, but only to Hindus of the Sudra caste.
They continued to bombard General Mutio Vitelleschi (r. 1615–1645) and
their friends and relatives in Rome with letters about funds, caste, and other
Hindu practices. When the pope's brief finally arrived at Goa in December,
1617, Sá rejected its suggestion for a conference and insisted that Nobili be
judged by the Inquisition, a Portuguese institution. In response to the archbishop's appeal, the Chief Inquisitor in Lisbon, a friend of the Jesuits, ruled
that the papal decision superseded the earlier pronouncements of the Goa
Inquisition and ordered it to be observed. A second brief from the papacy
ordained the convocation of a conference at Goa and insisted that Nobili
himself should participate in its discussions and decisions and write a report
of the affair.

In December, 1618, Nobili and the ailing Archbishop Ros set sail for Goa.
The conference was scheduled to begin on February 4, 1619, in the archbishop's palace. Before it was convened Ros and Nobili circulated a position
paper setting forth their views on the civil character of the thread, tufts (in
the Brahman tonsure, a small tuft of hair was left longer than the rest), and
baths. Primate Sá, after learning that these treatises had received a favorable
reception by some of the designated participants, packed the conference by
inviting a number of friars and secular priests to participate in it as voting
members. The primate himself set the tone of the meeting by declaring at
the outset:

In my opinion the thread and tuft ought not to be tolerated. Even if they are caste
signs and have no religious significance, to tolerate them will cause scandal in the
diocese of Goa.[95]

The Jesuit position was presented by Andrea Palmeiro (1569–1645), a Portuguese theologian of high reputation who had succeeded Pimenta in 1618
as visitor of the Malabar Province. By his own admission Palmeiro had intended to end the Madura mission until he read Nobili's memorandum.
After weighing the missionary's arguments, he reversed his former position
and agreed that "the emblems signify not religion but caste and social rank."

---

[94] On this issue see below, pp. 178–79.
[95] As translated in Cronin, *op. cit.* (n. 74), p. 212.

Similar to Palmeiro's was the experience of Dom João Fernandino de Almeida, a Portuguese secular priest, canon lawyer, and Second Inquisitor of Goa. Originally hostile to Nobili's methods, he had come to agree with Palmeiro on the civil character of the emblems.[96] The venerable Archbishop Ros, who had consistently supported Nobili, stressed that there was nothing in the methods followed at Madura which had not been borrowed from apostolic times. The church, he asserted, had a duty in the interest of saving souls to permit its Indian converts to retain whatever Hindu rites and ceremonies were strictly social.[97] Archbishop de Sá and his claque responded, according to Nobili's report, with sarcasm and innuendo. "A Father of the Society of Jesus," screamed the primate of India, "has passed to paganism and he asks us to connive in his apostasy!"[98] After Nobili had spoken in his own defense, the primate called for a vote. The First Inquisitor condemned Nobili; the Second voted in his favor. Of the remaining twenty theologians and priests, just four voted for Nobili. On the following Sunday, Archbishop de Sá jubilantly delivered a homily in his cathedral in which he publicly accused Nobili of favoring idolatry and diabolical practices.

Although Nobili lost the skirmish in Goa, he won the war in Europe. After the conclusion of the conference both parties immediately dispatched letters to Rome to make their cases known there. Others in high places in Europe, including confidantes of the Habsburg king and the Inquisitor of Portugal, received letters from Ros. The irate archbishop denied the veracity of the account sent to Europe by his primate and included in his own dispatches supporting letters from Diogo Valente Correia, the Jesuit bishop of Japan, the Second Inquisitor, and the ruler of Cochin, Vira Kerala Varma (r. 1605–35).[99] In Lisbon the Supreme Inquisitor Dom Martins de Mascarhenas rejected Archbishop de Sá's appeal to condemn Nobili and forwarded in 1621 his own opinion to Rome supporting the Jesuit. Pope Gregory XV (r. 1621–23) appointed a commission to examine the accumulated documentation and to render an opinion. Headed by Peter Lombard, an eminent Irish theologian, the commission studied Nobili's methods and the opinions of his adversaries and at the end of 1622 issued a verdict in favor of permitting the caste signs. On January 31, 1623, Pope Gregory issued the apostolic constitution *Romanae Sedis Antistites* officially allowing caste emblems and ablutions on condition that all idolatrous significance be detached from them in the mind and practices of the convert.[100] In December, 1624 the constitution arrived in Goa inaugurating a new phase in the mission history of India.

During the years of controversy the condition of the mission in Madura

[96] *Ibid.*, p. 215.
[97] See Bachmann, *op. cit.* (n. 74), p. 196.
[98] Cronin, *op. cit.* (n. 74), p. 219.
[99] See Bachmann, *op. cit.* (n. 74), pp. 198–99.
[100] Cronin, *op. cit.* (n. 74), pp. 225–30.

had deteriorated. Nobili was often absent and most of the time forbidden to perform baptisms. The periodic wars between Vijayanagar and Madura had heated up in 1614 when the emperor died. In the wars of succession which followed, the nayak was forced to move his residence from Madura northward to Tiruchirapalli, a natural rock fortress. Nobili and many of his converts, some of whom were soldiers or courtiers, followed the nayak to this northern base. War and famine impoverished both the people of Madura and the mission. Because of the dispersal of the mission, the Jesuit general in 1619 ordered Gaspar Fernandes, provincial of Malabar, to dispatch at least two Jesuits to Madura to help out Nobili and Vico. The provincial, supported by Visitor Palmeiro, who had spoken on behalf of Nobili at Goa, refused to send either men or money into the interior. In 1620 Palmeiro himself appeared in Madura. He visited both the "Old Residence" of Fernandes and the "New Residence" of Nobili. In his report Palmeiro asserted that the Madura mission would have to be reformed in all aspects were it to survive. He concluded his gloomy prospectus by pointing to its meager numbers; in fact Nobili's congregation in 1623 included about three hundred Christians. Palmeiro's change of heart about Nobili and Madura, it should be recalled, occurred before the arrival in India of the papal constitution.[101]

A new nayak, Tirumala (r. 1623–59), came to power in Madura at this juncture. Immediately he moved his court back to Madura and launched a program of expansion which had as its ultimate objective Madura's complete independence of Vijayanagar. Nobili, advised by his friends in Rome that the papal decision would be in his favor, inaugurated in 1623 an expansion program of his own. Working out from his base in Tiruchirapalli, he set out as a wandering *sannyasi,* accompanied by several Brahman disciples, to spread the faith to other places. With the arrival of Gregory's constitution he began again to baptize high-caste Hindus. On Christmas Day, 1625, he baptized Tirumangalam Nayak, now *de facto* ruler of northern Madura, along with his entire household of eleven persons. After he was joined by Emanuel Martinz as second assistant, Nobili traveled extensively in south India founding new missions. His task was made lighter when the friendly Laerzio returned to Cochin in 1627 for his second tour of duty as Provincial. By the time of Laerzio's death in 1630 the mission comprised three major centers, each with a number of dependencies. The crowning glory for the mission was the official permission Nobili obtained for himself in 1630 to preach freely and to build churches in all parts of Madura.[102]

Events external to Madura endangered the mission just when it appeared to be prospering. In 1630 the viceroy in Goa withdrew state financial assistance from the church. Disputes in 1631 over the bad treatment of the pearl fishers by the Portuguese commander at Tuticorin led to a break between

---

[101] See Bachmann, *op. cit.* (n. 74), pp. 203–7.
[102] Cronin, *op. cit.* (n. 74), pp. 231–43.

Madura and the Portuguese. The nayak, always on the lookout for allies, began to make overtures to the Dutch at Pulicat. Outraged by the defection of the independent Tirumala, the Portuguese concluded an agreement with Vijayanagar to conduct warfare jointly against Pulicat and Madura. The missionaries, who were caught between these two fires, tried to maintain a posture of neutrality. Both the viceroy and the nayak were outraged by their disloyalty. Although peace was concluded in 1639, the enemies of the mission in Madura succeeded in having Nobili and Martinz imprisoned by Tirumala in 1640.

Tirumala released the missionaries near the end of 1641. To recover from his losses, and to enlarge his staff, Nobili decided to adopt a new tactic. To teach Christianity to all castes without running the danger of pollution, he needed religious teachers who could associate freely with both the high and the polluting castes. From his study of Hindu practices he had learned that within the Vellalas (one of the best known of the Sudra subcastes) there functioned a group called *pandarams* who enjoyed the respect of the high castes even though they had many low-caste disciples. Nobili decided to create a corresponding group within his mission whom he called *pandara-swamis* or religious teachers. They were to observe the prohibition against meat-eating, were not to hire Brahmans, and were to work in harmony with Indian lay catechists. Balthasar da Costa, a Portuguese and Nobili's first *pandaraswami,* was an instant success after his appointment in 1640. Working from the higher to the lower castes, he and the lay catechists baptized many low-caste adults. Great successes soon won new enemies for the mission. To check their attacks Nobili turned again to Tirumala. His goal was to win for his brethren the same privilege he personally possessed, of propagating the gospel freely in Madura. The nayak was won over to this proposition in 1644 by the gift of a small organ sent from Cochin. Hereafter the mission prospered even though Nobili, his eyesight impaired, was forced to leave Madura in 1654. He spent the last days of his life in the small hut outside Mylapore where he died in 1656.

When Nobili first arrived, there were few Christians in the hinterland of southern India. When his mission reached its zenith in 1644, the Christians there numbered 4,183. The rest of the Malabar Province, limited to seaport towns, had at that date a total of 190,268; Cochin, 2,700; Cranganore, 450; Quilon, 14,700; Mannar, 5,450; Colombo, 11,150; Jaffna, 33,300; Mylapore, 1,700; Pegu-Ava-Bengal, 2,000; Moluccas, 12,600.[103] After Nobili's departure a small group of his followers continued his system of ministering to the widely scattered Christian communities of Madura, Marava, Tanjore, Gingee, and Satyamangalam.[104] Incessant local wars, famines, epidemics,

---

[103] See Ferroli, *op. cit.* (n. 2), II, 415–16.
[104] On the value of Nobili's work see S. Neill, *A History of Christianity in India. The Beginnings to A.D. 1707* (Cambridge, 1984), pp. 300–309, 552–54.

and migrations impeded their progress and dispersed their communities. Even so they continued to baptize large numbers.[105] The fortress town of Tiruchirapalli, where Emanuel Martinz acted as superior until his death in 1656, became again the center of the entire mission. Leadership of the faltering mission was taken over in 1659 by Anton de Proenza, and over the following three years the mission took a new lease on life. Under his successors the mission languished, until Balthasar da Costa went to Europe as procurator and in 1673 sent to India seventeen recruits for the Malabar mission.[106]

The new Jesuit contingent for India was led by Father João de Britto (1647–93), the son of one of Portugal's leading families.[107] Only eight of the Jesuits destined for Malabar survived the turbulent trip to Goa. There they docked on September 4, 1673; Britto and his companions, after a respite at Goa, sailed southward in 1674. They disembarked at a small landing spot between Dutch-held Cranganore and Cochin, and trekked overland eastward to the College of Ambalakat, which the Jesuits had founded in 1662 to escape the reach of the Dutch. After studying Tamil for several months, Britto and a veteran missionary, André Freire, journeyed across the Indian peninsula from Ambalakat to Kolei in the Gingee country. On their way they passed through Madura where they were welcomed by its Christian communities. In Gingee the Christians faced the hostility of the Muslim sultan of Bijapur who had captured Gingee in 1652 and had overthrown its nayak. Seven years later Tanjore likewise had fallen to Bijapur and its ally, the sultanate of Golconda. When the two Jesuits arrived at Kolei on July 30, 1674, the Dutch had just driven the French out of San Thomé and were rampaging along India's southeastern coast.[108] In sum, political conditions were hardly auspicious for the new Jesuits of the *padroado*.

Kolei was a little mission station on the southern border of Gingee and close to the Tanjore frontier. Freire, who had started his mission at Tanjore in 1661, had personally done much to build up the Kolei outpost. Britto spent one year at Kolei for his apprenticeship, then undertook his first independent assignment at Tattuvanchari in Tanjore. Wars, floods, and pestilence vitiated his labors there. In 1678 he was transferred to Kuttur in Gingee to establish a new mission in the jungle. By following Nobili's methods, Britto

---

[105] For specific figures for the period from 1656 to 1687 see Müllbauer, *op. cit.* (n. 11), pp. 211–12, n. 1.

[106] Cronin, *op. cit.* (n. 74), pp. 216–17. A second group of eight destined for China and led by Intorcetta departed from Lisbon on March 25, 1673, in the same fleet. Of this contingent, only Intorcetta survived the voyage.

[107] For his early life see A. Saulière, S.J., *Red Sand. A Life of St. John de Britto, S.J., Martyr of the Madura Mission* (Madura: de Nobili Press, 1947), chaps. i–iii. This book "meant for young people," in the words of its author, is worthy of scholarly attention, for its author was probably the leading authority on the Madura mission of the seventeenth century. For an "adult version" based on Saulière's work see Albert M. Nevett, S.J., *John de Britto and His Times* (Anand, 1980).

[108] See above, p. 99.

had access both to the Brahmans and the lower castes; unlike Nobili, Britto concentrated from the beginning on the lowest castes of southeast India. His insistence that all the priests of the Madura mission should follow the ascetic model of Nobili produced difficulties for him with the Propaganda and Provincial Gaspar Affonso, a Portuguese and an opponent of the Nobili method of adaptation. Like his predecessor, Britto was charged in 1682 by his superiors with arrogance, recklessness, and stubbornness.[109]

The Annual Letter for 1683 was penned at Madura by Britto in April–May, 1684.[110] In it he relates the worsening conditions experienced by the Christians of Tanjore and Gingee as he saw them during his unceasing travels around the Madura mission. In 1685 he was appointed superior of the mission, which now included a new center in Tinnevelly set up in the previous year under the supervision of Father Maria Xavier Borghese, a son of the great Roman family. The new superior was confronted by a systematic persecution of the Christians of Tanjore and by a rapid diminution in the number of active missionaries in an "abandoned field, which has only eight of us left to cultivate it."[111]

Once a semblance of quiet had returned to Tanjore, Britto entered the Marava country, from which all missionaries had been expelled in 1679. Located between Madura and the Palk Strait, Marava was a parched and poor region dominated by headmen called poligars who were little more than robber barons. The dominant poligar, Raghunatha Setupati (r. 1674–1710), had his headquarters at Ramnad from whence he guarded the causeway to the famous temple of Rama on the island of Pamban.[112] Britto had long cherished the idea of reopening the mission in Marava despite the prohibition laid down by Setupati. During the summer of 1686, Britto baptized over two thousand persons before he and his companion were arrested, imprisoned, and tortured.[113] His superiors in India had practically given up hoping for his release and had let Lisbon know that he would probably not survive. Finally in October the poligar cross-questioned Britto, freed him, and forbade him to return to Marava.

After his ordeal in Marava, Britto's superiors sent him to Europe as procurator of the Malabar mission. He arrived at Lisbon in September, 1687, where he was given an almost royal reception. After all, had he not almost been the first Portuguese missionary to suffer blessed martyrdom in India? Was he not also the former page of Dom Pedro, who had become King Pedro II in 1683? The Portuguese nobleman, now clad as a *sannyasi*, excited interest and astonishment throughout his travels in Portugal by his

[109] See Saulière, *op. cit.* (n. 107), pp. 241–42.
[110] Summarized and with many direct quotations, in *ibid.*, chap. xiv.
[111] As quoted in *ibid.*, p. 308.
[112] For the history of the Setupatis' rule from Ramnad in the Marava country see Heras, *op. cit.* (n. 75), I, 354–62.
[113] See Ferroli, *op. cit.* (n. 2), II, 82.

Hinduized life style. He never made the expected trip to Rome, because of the hostilities still dividing the Portuguese from the Vatican. Although the king wanted him to remain at his side in Lisbon, the persistent Britto finally won royal permission to return to India.[114]

Britto arrived at Goa on November 2, 1690, and was greeted effusively by Emmanuel Rodrigues, his old superior and now the provincial of Goa. While in Goa, he was appointed visitor of the Malabar province. On February 24, 1691, he and his companions arrived at Ambalakat, and four days later went to Topo (Talai) to report to Freire, now provincial of Cochin, on his mission to Europe. Britto went on to Pondicherry, the French outpost, to thank Governor François Martin for the service he had rendered to the Malabar mission and to straighten out a jurisdictional conflict that had arisen between the Portuguese and the French Jesuits.[115] On his way to Pondicherry he visited Madura and many of the other mission stations. After leaving Pondicherry in August, 1691, he completed his visitation by passing on to San Thomé and then to the small Christian communities in northern Gingee. Now he was prepared to return to Marava to reclaim his converts and to carry on the work he was earlier forced to abandon.

War was raging in the north of Marava that involved the forces of Marava, Tanjore, and Madura. So for eight months (September, 1691, to May, 1692) Britto established himself in a forest on the border of Madura and Marava where he baptized thousands. On May 27, 1692, the feast day of St. John, Pope and Martyr, he entered Marava to suffer what Jesuit writers like to call his "second martyrdom."

Once inside Marava, Britto stationed himself in the forest of Muni, where a poligar ruled who, it was thought, was indifferent to religion and would therefore tolerate Christian activities. But when thousands of Christians began to enter this region from other parts of Marava, the poligar gradually began to evince concern about this abnormally popular *sannyasi*. Even some of the ruler's relations became converts, particularly once they heard that Britto was curing diseases and exorcising devils. Tadiya Teva, a prince of the royal house and the poligar of Siruvalli, became a Christian in January, 1693, after he had miraculously recovered from a lingering illness. Before receiving baptism, the poligar repudiated all his wives except the first. The youngest of his wives and niece of the Great Poligar refused to take her dismissal calmly and complained bitterly to her uncle that her husband had been bewitched by the Christian sorcerer. Britto and his companions were taken in custody to Ramnad on January 11. Fearing an uprising by his

---

[114] See Saulière, *op. cit.* (n. 107), chap. xix, for an excellent description of his reception and stay in Portugal (September, 1687, to March, 1689).

[115] Father Guy Tachard and other French Jesuits based at Pondicherry were then in the process of setting up the Carnatic mission to the north of the Madura mission. For further detail see below, pp. 258–59.

numerous Christian subjects, the poligar delayed the execution until February 4, 1693.[116] One hundred sixty years later the martyred Father João de Britto was beatified in 1853 by Pius IX; he was canonized by Pope Pius XII on June 21, 1947. The efforts of these early Jesuits in the interior of India still continue to bear fruit. In 1962 the Archdiocese of Madura, a metropolitan see since 1953, could count 227,000 Catholics in a population of seven million.

Elsewhere in south India the cause of the Jesuits declined as Portuguese power waned. Especially disastrous was the rebellion of the St. Thomas Christians of the Serra against the Latin rite.[117] By the terms of the Synod of Diamper (June 20–26, 1599), the Malabar Christians of St. Thomas had been required to recognize the pope as universal pastor, to be under the protection and authority of the Portuguese crown, to be subject to the Inquisition of Goa, and to abide by the decrees of the Council of Trent. (They were, however, allowed to continue using their Syriac liturgy.) The administration of the Serra was thereafter entrusted to the Jesuits, who had been running a seminary and school at Vaipocota near Cochin since 1581. Father Francisco Ros, professor of Syriac at the seminary and a Catalan subject of King Philip II (III in Spain) of Portugal, was named bishop of the Diocese of Ankamali and suffragan of Goa, with concurrence of the crown. The consecration of the new bishop at Goa on January 25, 1601, stimulated a negative reaction among the St. Thomas Christians. They felt that their traditions of independence had been violated by both church and state. Politically they were required after Diamper to be subject to the Portuguese government based in distant Goa. Religiously their metropolitan see had been lowered to the rank of an ordinary diocese subject to Goa. The new bishop, for all of his sensitivity to their beliefs, needs, and customs, had the temerity to establish his permanent residence at Cranganore where a Portuguese garrison was located. The bishop of Cochin, within whose diocese Cranganore was located, protested Ros' decision to reside in his see. Pope Paul V (1605–21) responded to these protests by restoring to Ankamali its archepiscopal control. Two years later he divided the bishopric of Cochin and placed Cranganore within the archbishopric of Ankamali.[118]

While calm was temporarily restored by these measures, many of the St. Thomas Christians, especially the native clergy, continued to resent the Latinizing of their church and the direction of its hierarchy by Europeans. The Jesuit metropolitan, unlike their patriarchs of old, supervised the archdio-

---

[116] Based on Saulière, *op. cit.* (n. 107), chaps. xx–xxiv. For a description of the modern annual festival of St. John de Britto on February 4 see Nevett, *op. cit.* (n. 107), pp. 1–2.

[117] For the history of the St. Thomas Christians to the Synod of Diamper see *Asia*, I, 231, 266–269, and Pullapilly and Van Kley (eds.), *op. cit.* (n. 1), pp. 187–89.

[118] See E. Tisserant, *Eastern Christianity in India* (Bombay, [1957]), pp. 71–75.

cese himself and thus reduced in status the local archdeacons who had previously occupied positions of weighty responsibility. Archdeacon George de Cruce, whose orthodoxy Ros questioned, particularly resented being forced into the background. When Ros decided to accompany Nobili to Goa in 1618, the archbishop appointed as his temporary replacement the superior of the seminary at Vaipocota rather than George. While this event produced a rupture between the Jesuits and the local clerics, the old archbishop managed to heal the wound before his death in 1624.

Archdeacon George welcomed Estaban de Brito when he became the new archbishop of Ankamali and for a time peace reigned. To cajole the archdeacon and his followers, Brito gave them a greater share of administrative responsibility, especially with respect to clerical nominations. But conflict was renewed in 1638 when Francesco Donati, a Roman Dominican and apostolic emissary of the Propaganda, arrived in Malabar to start a school for the training of the native clergy in Syriac. Archbishop Brito, unlike his distinguished predecessor, had no knowledge of Syriac, the liturgical language of the Syro-Malabar church. When the archbishop opposed Donati's intrusion, George and other discontented Malabars accused him and his fellow Jesuits of being out of touch and with trying to maintain the archbishopric as their monopoly. In his letters to the king and the pope, the archdeacon praised Donati and condemned the Jesuits. While the king continued to insist that Jesuits should control the affairs of Ankamali, the Propaganda in 1636 forbade under pain of excommunication the exclusion of non-Jesuits from the see.

George died in 1637 and was soon succeeded as archdeacon by his nephew, Thomas de Campos. Archbishop Francisco Garcia (1580–1659), who had succeeded Brito around 1641, refused to honor the concessions made by his predecessor to the new archdeacon. Unable to resolve his differences with the Jesuits, Campos appealed for help to the raja of Cochin and to other opponents of the Jesuits. Finally he wrote directly to the patriarchs at Cairo, Antioch, and Babylon, asking each of them to send an archbishop to the Serra.

Much of the hostility toward the Jesuits stemmed from the failure of the royal government to pay the promised stipends to the native clergy and parishes.[119] Archbishop Garcia, who had himself been impoverished by the crown's inability to pay its obligation, appealed for monetary help to Lisbon. The crown, free of Habsburg control after 1640 and at odds with the Vatican, urged Viceroy Linhares to pay the tithes. The viceroy, while claiming that the available monies could not meet all the demands levied upon them, informed the king in 1648 that the Jesuits in the Serra were few and that they were losing control. The St. Thomas Christians, led by Archdeacon Cam-

[119] See Ferroli, *op. cit.* (n. 2), II, 27–29.

pos, demanded that the Serra be opened to all orders, for they had the unqualified support of the pope and the Propaganda in their opposition to the
Portuguese-Jesuit monopoly.[120]

The revolt of the Serra reached its climax in 1652–53. In the spring of
1652 a certain Atallah arrived at Surat and then proceeded overland to Mylapore where he was interned in the Jesuit college. From here he secretly
penned a letter in Syriac to Archdeacon Campos announcing his arrival. He
also told the archdeacon that he had been appointed by the pope as patriarch
of the Syro-Malabar church and requested the dispatch of an armed force to
escort him into the Serra.[121] In fact, he signed the letter as "Ignatius, Patriarch of India and China." Knowing the St. Thomas Christians would
welcome him, the Portuguese authorities had Atallah covertly carried off to
Goa. Once they learned of this precipitous action, the archdeacon and his
followers declared that they would no longer obey Archbishop Garcia. In
May, 1653, the schismatics proclaimed Campos metropolitan, and he assumed the title of Mar Thomas I. The secession of the St. Thomas Christians became complete, except for four hundred loyalists, when it was
rumored that Atallah had been burned at the stake in 1654 as a heretic.[122]

Rome received news of the St. Thomas schism in 1655 from Father Hya-
cinth de Magistris, an Italian Jesuit and the emissary of Archbishop Garcia.
The remnant of loyalists in the Serra meanwhile requested the Carmelites of
India to keep Rome informed of their plight. The Propaganda quickly sent
to the Carmelites an apostolic commissary in the person of the Italian Father
Hyacinth of St. Vincent, O.C.D. He was accompanied by two other Italian
fathers, Giuseppe di Santa Maria Sebastiani and Matthew of St. Joseph.
Hyacinth and Matthew went by sea via Lisbon; Sebastiani took the quicker
overland route accompanied by two German Carmelites. Despite the opposition of the Portuguese and the Jesuits, Sebastiani went immediately to
Edapally, the residence of Mar Thomas, where he arrived in 1657. Because
of their growing fear of Dutch activities off the coast of Malabar, the Portuguese authorities and Bishop Garcia gradually came to accept the peace-
making activities of the Carmelites.

While Father Sebastiani received a hearing from a number of communities and priests, Mar Thomas refused to step down, and most of the St.
Thomas Christians sternly refused to respect the authority of Archbishop
Garcia. In the meantime the apostolic commissary had arrived at Goa late in
1657; he died there in 1661 without healing the breach. Sebastiani was
meanwhile sent back to Rome via the overland route and arrived there early
in 1659 with his report. On learning of conditions in Malabar, Pope Alexan-

---

[120] See Linhares' letter of January 15, 1648, to the king as quoted in *ibid.*, p. 31.

[121] For a Latin translation of this letter see Tisserant, *op. cit.* (n. 118), pp. 78–79n.

[122] Atallah (1590–1654) was probably not burned at the stake. For his career see J. Thekedathu, S.D.B., *The Troubled Days of Francis Garcia, S.J., Archbishop of Cranganore (1641–59)*
(Rome, 1972), pp. 73–82; also Neill, *op. cit.* (n. 105), pp. 316–31.

der VII (r. 1655–67) secretly consecrated Sebastiani in Rome as titular bishop of Hierapolis (December 15, 1659) with the title of Vicar Apostolic and Administrator of the Archbishopric of Cranganore. The new appointee was given unusually broad powers, for his major charge was to bring an end to the schism by any means whatsoever.[123]

Accompanied by two Maronite Christians who knew Syriac, Sebastiani again took to the road on February 7, 1660. At Aleppo he heard that Garcia had died and that the Dutch were seriously threatening the Portuguese position in Malabar. Arrived at Cochin in May, 1660, he announced for the first time that he had been consecrated as a titular bishop and was about to take over the administration of his see. Many of the Christian communities quickly rallied behind Mar Thomas, and he escaped all attempts of the Portuguese authorities to capture him. From a refuge in the hilly hinterland he continued to wield a considerable authority. When Cochin fell to the Dutch (January 6, 1661), Sebastiani was ordered out of Malabar. Before leaving, he was permitted by the Dutch commandant to convene a synod for the purpose of selecting a new bishop for the St. Thomas Christians still in union with Rome. The unanimous choice of the synod was Alexander de Campos (Parampil Chandy), a cousin of Mar Thomas. The schism was not resolved by this act, for Thomas de Campos continued to war against his cousin and the European missionaries.[124] The Dutch governors of Cochin, who were more interested in pepper than souls, made no efforts to convert Malabar to Calvinism. Moreover, a number of Dutch Catholics lived and worked in its port cities and were inclined to support their coreligionists so long as they remained politically cooperative. The Dutch were, however, rigorous in eliminating the ecclesiastical as well as the political influence of Goa. It was by their hands that the declining power of the *padroado* in south India was given its death blow.

Individual Jesuits had worked in Ceylon during the sixteenth century when it was a Franciscan preserve. Usually they were drawn from among those stationed on the Fishery Coast or at Mannar. In 1594 the Franciscans had been granted by the crown the exclusive right to evangelize in Ceylon. A shortage of friars hampered the development of the mission as a Franciscan monopoly, and the Portuguese secular authorities, who were involved in expanding their hold into northern Ceylon at the turn of the century, wanted the more aggressive Jesuits to start a mission in Ceylon.[125] In 1600 the viceroy in Goa ordered the Franciscans to turn over to the Jesuits the

[123] Based on Thekedathu, *op. cit.* (n. 122), pp. 78–84.

[124] See Neill, *op. cit.* (n. 105), pp. 321–32, on the efforts to heal the split. On the continuing problems of the Propaganda missionaries in Malabar see the 1689 report of Pietro Paulo di S. Francesco, O.C.D., as summarized in J. Metzler, "Die Kongregation in der zweiten Hälfte des 17. Jahrhunderts," *Sacrae Congregationis de Propaganda Fide Memoria Rerum* (hereafter *SCPFMR*) Vol. I/1 (Freiburg, 1971), pp. 302–3.

[125] On the Portuguese military expansion see above, pp. 10–12.

administration of their churches in the northern half of Ceylon. In April, 1602, Father Diego da Cunha, a Jesuit missionary of Manaar, was appointed superior and dispatched to Ceylon with three companions. Although the Franciscans opposed the establishment of the Jesuit mission, the issue was resolved by the authorities of church and state by dividing the island into northern (Jesuit) and southern (Franciscan) jurisdictions. The Jesuits, who knew Tamil from their Fishery Coast experiences, concentrated at first in Colombo and other west-coast towns where Tamil was the leading language. In 1605 they set up a college at Colombo where they trained the sons of the indigenous nobility and princes. Four years later they built a new church in Colombo with monies granted by the government in Goa. Certain of the Jesuits began to learn Sinhalese to enable themselves to evangelize more effectively in the interior and in the south. Others acted as military chaplains to the Portuguese troops who were bent upon capturing Kandy and other unpacified towns and regions.[126]

In 1616 two of the Jesuits were "martyred" by soldiers from Kandy in revenge for the death of certain Buddhist priests at the hands of the Portuguese.[127] These acts were connected with the revolt in 1616–17 of Nicapety Bandar, a former collaborator and a Christian, who had struck up an alliance with the king of Kandy directed against the Portuguese occupying forces.[128] Owing to these circumstances, the fifteen Jesuits on the island were recalled from the interior to the college of Colombo. Around 1620 disputes with the Franciscans and the secular authorities over monies and grants-in-aid endangered the position of the Jesuits in Colombo for a period. Once the financial base of the mission was restored the Jesuits continued their educational and missionary activities in Colombo, in the newly conquered kingdom of Jaffna, and at Mannar and Galle. But the unending wars with Kandy periodically brought abrupt halts to Jesuit activities. Even more ominous for the Catholics were the efforts being made in the 1620's by the Protestant Dutch and Danish to establish relations with Kandy and to set up outposts of their own on Ceylon's east coast.[129]

The mission of Jaffna, pioneered by the Franciscans in the sixteenth century, became after 1622 the most prosperous of the Jesuit enterprises in Ceylon. By 1629 they boasted sixteen residences in Jaffna and some fifty thousand converts. Good progress in the Tamil language enabled the missionaries at Jaffna to carry on a robust educational program for native youths of the higher classes. The pressure from the Dutch mounted and on June 22,

[126] See S. G. Perera, S.J., "The Jesuits in Ceylon in the XVI and XVII Centuries," *The Ceylon Antiquarian and Literary Register*, II (1916–17), 1–11.

[127] *Ibid.*, pp. 75–79.

[128] For a description of this revolt see the summary of Antonio Bocarro's *Decada 13 da Historia da India* as translated in P. E. Pieris (ed. and trans.), *Ribeiro's History of Ceilão* (Colombo, 1909), pp. 195–96.

[129] See Perera, *loc. cit.* (n. 126), II (1916–17), 224–35; III (1917–18), 19–35.

1658, the fortress of Jaffna fell to them. On November 28, 1658, Father Francisco Baretto wrote:

The Colleges of Colombo, Jafnapatam, and Negapatam, with all the Residences in which innumerable Christians were looked after, are all captured. We have also lost the mission and whole of the Fishery Coast. . . . I am afraid all the missions of the east will be ruined completely.[130]

This pessimistic forecast was not borne out by events. A small number of Dominicans and Augustinians had begun to work in Ceylon after 1606. The Franciscans, building on their sixteenth-century missions in the kingdom of Kotte, had made steady progress during the first half of the seventeenth century. By 1628 they claimed fifty-four churches in Kotte, twenty-four in Jaffna, and five in Mantotta, under the supervision of twenty-four missionaries.[131] Despite their hostility to the Jesuits, the Franciscans invited the missionaries of the Society to establish a college at Galle in their territory. The imprint of Catholicism remained profound in Colombo, Galle, Negombo, and Jaffna, as the Dutch conquered Ceylon between 1638 and 1658. The Dutch, as they gradually took over the island, drove out the Catholic missionaries, began persecution of their converts, and sought to introduce Reformed Christianity by duress. Despite Dutch efforts to extirpate "Portuguese Catholicism," most of the converts remained faithful and sheltered the priests who visited them surreptitiously. Carmelites and Theatines from Malabar made occasional forays into Ceylon to perform baptisms and provide the other sacraments. The dark period (1658–87) ended in Ceylon with the advent in 1687 of Father Joseph Vaz (1651–1711), a native of Goa and a member of the Oratory. Under his tutelage the Catholic church of Ceylon was revitalized despite the open hostility of the Dutch governors.[132] So the Catholics of Ceylon managed to preserve a remnant which became a flourishing community under British rule during the nineteenth century.

Much had been achieved by the Jesuits in south India and Ceylon for both the church and scholarship during the years of the *padroado*. While the prescriptions of Diamper had failed to bring the totality of the St. Thomas Christians permanently within the Latin rite, a sizable remnant remained, on which the Carmelites and the seculars would build. Around 1700 the Madura mission included an estimated eighty thousand Christians. From Madura, the first of the inland missions, the successors of Nobili established Christian communities throughout southern India and gave one of their own to martyrdom and sainthood. The Jesuits of Mysore, administratively

[130] *Ibid.*, VI (1920–21), 38.
[131] Data from Paulo de Trindade's, *Conquista espiritual do Oriente* . . . as summarized in R. Boudens, O.M.I., *The Catholic Church in Ceylon under Dutch Rule* (Rome, 1957), pp. 34–40.
[132] See Boudens, *op. cit.* (n. 131), pp. 88–115.

within the Goa Province, adopted the approach of Nobili after mid-century. Great progress in penetrating the languages and literatures of south India and Ceylon was also recorded by the Jesuits from the time of Henriques to Father Constanzo Giuseppe Beschi (1680–1747), who entered the Tanjore mission in 1711.[133] The Jesuits brought European books, printing, medicine, and education into south India and Ceylon. Through their colleges and hospitals they performed social services as part of the propagation of the gospel.[134] After the capture of Malabar by the Dutch, most of the Jesuits admitted to the region were non-Portuguese, especially Italians and Germans, who continued the adaptation policies of Nobili and concentrated upon the cultural mission. In 1697 only forty-six Jesuits were attached to the Malabar province, twelve of whom were stationed at Goa. Within the province itself five worked at Cochin, four at Cranganore, seven at Quilon, six on the Fishery Coast, five at San Thomé (Madras), seven in Madura, four in Pegu, and four in Bengal. The Jesuits of the *padroado* were completely eliminated by the century's end from Colombo, Jaffna, Malacca, and the Moluccas.[135]

3

THE "PADROADO" JESUITS IN EAST ASIA

Long a favorite stamping ground of the Jesuits, in the seventeenth century East Asia was the scene of the greatest defeats and victories experienced by the Society. Macao, base for the evangelization of Japan, China, and Indochina, was a *padroado* diocese suffragan to Goa, with jurisdiction over China, the Moluccas, and other territories in East and Southeast Asia. Beginning in 1588, Japan was technically subject to its own see of Funai, but the first of its bishops reached there only in 1596. On the Jesuit chart of organization, Japan and China were classified as a single province in 1605, but each was in fact administered at the beginning of the seventeenth century by vice-provincials who reported to Visitor Valignano, the superior of these missions from 1575 to 1606.[136] In 1608 the vice-province of Japan was elevated in Rome to the status of a province, but the change did not take effect in Japan until 1611. China continued to be administered by superiors and vice-

---

[133] For a list of Nobili's Tamil writings see Cronin, *op. cit.* (n. 74), pp. 269–70; on Beschi's works see Ferroli, *op. cit.* (n. 2), II, 302–3.

[134] See K. A. Nilakanta Sastri, *A History of South India from Prehistoric Times to the Fall of Vijayanagar* (3d ed., Madras, 1966), p. 321.

[135] See Ferroli, *op. cit.* (n. 2), II, 280. The last Jesuit left the Moluccas in 1677. See Cornelius Wessels, S.J., "Catalogus patrum et fratrum e Societate Iesu qui in missione Moluccana ab a. 1546 ad a. 1677 adlaboraverunt," *AHSI*, I (1932), 237–53.

[136] For a list of the superiors of the Jesuit mission in Japan see C. R. Boxer, *The Christian Century in Japan* (Berkeley, 1951), p. 445; for the superiors of the Jesuit mission in China see Dehergne, *op. cit.* (n. 86), pp. 317–18.

provincials throughout the seventeenth century. After Valignano's death in 1606, the succession of Jesuit visitors charged with overseeing the missions in both China and Japan rarely stayed in East Asia for more than a few years at a time.[137] Macao, the religious and commercial entrepôt of East Asia, probably had a population of six to seven thousand at the beginning of the century, a majority of whom were Luso-Asians.[138] Around thirty Jesuits lived permanently in Macao, but many others stopped there, sometimes for extended periods, on their way to and from the missions in Japan, China, and Indochina. The Jesuits owned a modest residence in the city that had been constructed in 1565. The college of Madre de Deus (popularly called St. Paul's), inaugurated by Valignano in 1594, provided advanced training for clerics destined for the missions. Next to the college, on an elevation, stood the Church of Saint Paul. When the original Jesuit church burned in 1601, it was replaced by 1603 with a new and more elaborate church whose facade still stands.

The Jesuit establishment in Macao was maintained in large part by the profits garnered from the Society's investments in the trade between Macao and Japan. The terms for this participation had been set in a 1578 contract concluded between Valignano and the mercantile community of Macao. Raw silks and piece goods, purchased at the biannual Canton fairs by the Macaoese, were sent annually on the "Great Ship" from Macao to Nagasaki, where the silks were exchanged for silver and copper. The captain-major of the "Great Ship," who was usually in Macao for a one-year stopover on the way from Goa to Nagasaki, served as interim governor of Macao while his ship was being readied. Because of disputes between the captains-major and the municipal council of Macao, the king, beginning in 1623, appointed captains-general to act as regular governors of the city. Thereafter the authority of the captain-major was limited to the governance of his ship and the Portuguese trading community at Nagasaki. The Jesuits were vital to the conduct of this trade, particularly in Japan, where they acted as interpreters and sometimes as commercial agents for themselves as well as for Portuguese and Japanese investors.[139]

The intermediary role of the Jesuits at this period is graphically illustrated by the career of the Portuguese Jesuit João Rodrigues (1561–1633), who was known to his contemporaries as "Tcuzzu" (Japanese, *tsuji*) or "the interpreter." Apart from a brief visit to Macao in 1596, Rodrigues spent

[137] For a list of the visitors of Japan and China see Dehergne, *op. cit.* (n. 86), pp. 321–22.

[138] For the history of Macao in the sixteenth century see *Asia,* I, 295–97; this population estimate is based on C. R. Boxer, "Macao as a Religious and Commercial Entrepôt in the Sixteenth and Seventeenth Centuries," *Acta Asiatica,* XXVI (1974), 65–66. Also see R. Ptak, "The Demography of Old Macao, 1555–1640," *Ming Studies,* XIV (1982), 28.

[139] On the organization of the trade at Macao see C. R. Boxer, *The Great Ship from Amacon. Annals of Macao and the Old Japan Trade, 1555–1640* (Lisbon, 1959), pp. 7–12. As an example of the direct Jesuit stake in the trade see the "list of the goods sent by the Jesuits from Macao to Japan in 1618" as reproduced in *ibid.,* pp. 185–89.

thirty-three consecutive years in Japan between 1577 and 1610. Although he traveled extensively in Japan, his base of operations was at Nagasaki, the commercial city on the island of Kyushu which owed its swift growth and its prosperity, as Macao did, to international trade. Active during the years of Valignano's command of the Japan mission (1579–1606), Rodrigues rose rapidly in power and influence because of his obviously superior command of Japan's language and customs. As a Portuguese, and one of the very few Portuguese then working in the Jesuit mission of Japan, Rodrigues occupied a unique position as "interpreter." Increasingly he was called upon to act as a personal intermediary between the Nagasaki Jesuits and the political authorities of Japan.

The Spanish and Italian Jesuits, who had dominated the Japan mission from its founding to 1600, were much less committed than either Valignano or Rodrigues to the maintenance of the Portuguese monopoly and to the encouragement of the Macao trade. In brief, the Spanish Jesuits in Japan suffered from a conflict of loyalties. For them the question of admitting Spanish friars from the Philippines became an issue of loyalty to Society or to country.[140] The Portuguese Bishop Pedro Martins, S.J. (d. 1598), who arrived in Japan in 1596, bluntly declared that "Japan belongs to the Portuguese crown."[141] When this pronouncement was followed by the "martyrdoms of the twenty-six" in February, 1597, the Spanish friars became more than ever convinced that the Portuguese Jesuits, including the new bishop, had turned Hideyoshi against them. In the review of mission policy which followed the "martyrdoms," the Jesuits concluded that Bishop Martins should return to Macao to appease the friars and hopefully to turn away Hideyoshi's wrath.[142] Even though Hideyoshi had ordered their expulsion in March, 1597, the Jesuits there in 1598 included forty-six priests, seventy-nine brothers, and a sizable number of Japanese *dojuku,* or lay catechists. Rodrigues and a few others had been specifically exempted from Hideyoshi's order since the Japanese considered them vital to the trade. Most of the other Jesuits were confined to Nagasaki to await deportation, but only a token eleven of them were actually sent back to Macao at this time. In fact, reinforcements for the mission arrived in August, 1598, including Valignano and Luis Cerqueira, the new bishop of Funai. The arrival of the well-known visitor and the uninvited bishop produced no great excitement among the Japanese. Hideyoshi was dying and the succession struggle was about to break out which would result in a seizure of the supreme authority by Tokugawa Ieyasu, the most powerful of the diamyos.

The Jesuits, who had always felt threatened by the unpredictable and im-

[140] Too often it has been assumed by both ecclesiastical and secular historians that the Jesuits of Japan were united in their opposition to the admission of the Spanish friars. For an analysis of this question see M. Cooper, S.J., *Rodrigues the Interpreter* (New York, 1974), pp. 122–25.

[141] As quoted in *ibid.,* p. 132.

[142] *Ibid.,* pp. 140–41.

petuous Hideyoshi, hoped to fare better under whatever new political order emerged. In 1598 Rodrigues was appointed procurator, or treasurer, of the mission, and was sent on a round of visits to powerful lords to apprise them of Valignano's return and to test the political waters. Ieyasu, he was quick to learn, was expanding his authority and plotting to depose the six-year-old Toyotomi Hideyori. The issue was joined in the summer of 1600 between the Tokugawas and the daimyos supporting Hideyori. By October Ieyasu had routed the troops of his enemies at the decisive battle fought at Sekigahara. Many of the Christian daimyos fought with Ieyasu or came over to his side after Sekigahara, and were handsomely rewarded with grants of fiefs. Rodrigues was immediately sent to visit the victor and to speak on behalf of the Jesuits of Nagasaki. Although Ieyasu was a fervent Buddhist, he reversed his predecessor's policy by regularizing the status of the Jesuits and by officially confirming their right to maintain residences at Miyako, Osaka, and Nagasaki. The Jesuits took this concession as tantamount to condoning their activities everywhere in Japan; but they were soon to learn that Ieyasu could be quite as capricious as his predecessor.

Ieyasu, even more so than Hideyoshi, thought of the Jesuits primarily as cogs necessary to the smooth functioning of the machine of trade. In 1601 he appointed Rodrigues as his personal commercial agent at Nagasaki and ordered the Portuguese merchants to conduct their business through him.[143] At first the Jesuits welcomed this appointment as an opportunity to extend their influence. Initially Ieyasu was likewise quite satisfied with this arrangement and even partially compensated the mission for what it lost when the Dutch captured the carrack of 1603. For a time the mission quietly grew and by 1603 it had around seventy priests in Japan. In 1602 two Japanese Jesuits were ordained and began to work at catechizing and as disputants. Even Bishop Cerqueira felt safe enough to come out of hiding to celebrate mass publicly and to take over the administration of his diocese. When Valignano left Japan for the last time in January, 1603, the future of the Catholic mission looked bright.

Had it not been for their European rivals and would-be rivals in religion and commerce, the Japan mission and the Macao trade might have enjoyed a much longer period of prosperity. Always hostile to the friars from the Philippines, the Jesuit bishop wrote in 1604 to his archbishop in Goa that the Spanish friars "aspire . . . to subordinate the spiritual [jurisdiction] of Japan to the archbishop of Manila, and to make this commerce common to both Spaniards and Portuguese."[144] The Protestants, at this period, were more of a commercial than a religious threat, although Will Adams, a native of Kent and an unrepentant Protestant, who had been in Japan since 1600, began

---

[143] *Ibid.*, pp. 199–200.
[144] As quoted in C. R. Boxer, *op. cit.* (n. 136), p. 171. For the Spanish view of the Japanese mission see below, pp. 208–14.

around 1605 to compete with Rodrigues for Ieyasu's favor. An imbroglio with the Christian family of Omura in 1604–5 over the governance of Nagasaki led to the only serious setback suffered by the Jesuits in these years. In anger Omura Yoshiaki and some of his relatives and retainers abjured Christianity and embraced the Nichiren sect of Buddhism. The Jesuits were excluded from Omura's territories where they had sought refuge in the past at times of persecution. Still Christian relations with Ieyasu continued to be outwardly cordial. In 1606 Bishop Cerqueira was graciously received at court as the official head of the church in Japan, and in the following year Vice-Provincial Francesco Pasio (r. 1600 to 1611) was similarly honored by both Ieyasu and his son Hidetada, who was then but newly installed as shogun in Edo.[145] Nor was the work of conversion being forgotten during the Tokugawa rise to power. In the first six years of the seventeenth century, the number of Christians reportedly more than doubled, rising from 300,000 in 1600 to 750,000 in 1606. All of the new converts were of the non-noble classes, for no ruling daimyo accepted baptism after 1600.[146]

Prosperity had its price. The Spanish friars continued to protest to the authorities of church and state in Europe about the monopolistic character of the Jesuit enterprise and to inveigh against the Society's involvement in the conduct of trade. The mission itself, despite its commercial activities, was chronically in debt to the merchants of Nagasaki and Macao. The rapid growth in the number of unmonied converts continually increased the financial drain on the mission.[147] Dutch attacks on the Macao-Nagasaki trade were becoming constantly more threatening and costly, adding to the financial and psychological insecurity of the mission. Ieyasu, even while receiving the Jesuits cordially, warned the Christians in 1606 to confine their conversions strictly to the lower classes, and he issued a decree officially forbidding nobles to accept Christianity. He also meanwhile reversed Hideyoshi's policy of Buddhist persecution and encouraged its revival.

When the annual ship failed to appear in 1608, the atmosphere began to darken swiftly. The following year the Dutch and Spanish both sent delegations to Japan offering new commercial possibilities to Ieyasu. Conditions rapidly worsened for the Portuguese as the Japanese merchants turned against Rodrigues and the Jesuits. Threats were made that persecutions of the Christians might begin again if Rodrigues continued to function as trade intermediary. The bonzes, who had become the religious advisers of the Tokugawas, warned that the foreign creed was a threat to Japan's new unity.

[145] For details of these receptions see Cooper, *op. cit.* (n. 140), pp. 211–16.
[146] See Boxer, *op. cit.* (n. 136), p. 187. These figures may be somewhat inflated, for Jesuit sources of 1614 claim slightly fewer than three hundred thousand converts. See *ibid.*, pp. 320–21. Cf. the view of J. Laures, S.J., in *The Catholic Church in Japan. A Short History* (Rutland, Vt., 1954), pp. 140–43, of this as a period of "mediocre progress" in contrast to the successes of the sixteenth century.
[147] For a detailed discussion of the mission's indebtedness see Cooper, *op. cit.* (n. 140), chap. xii.

In an effort to appease hostile elements at court and in the Japanese mercantile community, Cerqueira and Pasio urged Rodrigues to wind up his complicated business affairs and prepare to leave Japan. In March, 1610 Rodrigues left for Macao and spent the remaining twenty-three years of his life in China. He was replaced unofficially as trade negotiator and interpreter by Will Adams.[148]

It was shortly after Rodrigues' departure that systematic persecution of the Christians began. Ieyasu, like his predecessors, had tolerated the Christian missionaries out of fear of arousing the Christian daimyos and of endangering the Macao trade. He was constantly fearful, during the years of his rise to power, of a possible military alliance between the Christian daimyos and the Iberians. The deaths and apostacies of the Kyushu Christian daimyos between 1600 and 1612, and the prohibitions against other lords accepting baptism, left the Christian community without significant political protection or military support. The appearance of the Dutch and Spanish as possible trading partners lessened the dependency of the Japanese upon the Macao trade. Japanese ships were also beginning to compete successfully in the silk trade. The monopoly of the Jesuits as intermediaries could now also be broken as Portuguese and Japanese merchants came to know enough of each others' language to carry on business negotiations without benefit of interpreters. Talk of a possible Spanish invasion from the Philippines and evidence of Christian collaboration with the internal enemies of the Tokugawas finally convinced Ieyasu to act positively against the Christians.

The "Great Persecution," as the Jesuits refer to the actions of the Tokugawa regime against the Christians, commenced in 1613–14. Memorials addressed to the government denounced the Christians for espousing a doctrine that taught its believers to place a spiritual power over the temporal authority of the daimyos and the *bakufu* (shogun's government in Edo), to follow codes of conduct inimical to the traditional social and moral order, and to disdain the native religions of Buddhism, Confucianism, and Shinto. Repressions, which had occurred sporadically before, now became more systematic as the daimyos emulated the Tokugawas in prohibiting the public and secret practice of Christianity and in punishing those who were now seen as threats to the stability of the country. Churches were closed and recalcitrants forced into exile or condemned to death. On January 27, 1614, the famous edict was issued which ordered the expulsion of the Christian missionaries and commanded the Japanese Christians to return to the religions of their ancestors.

The edict was delivered to the Jesuits in Kyoto on February 14 along with orders to prepare a list of their members and institutions. They were also commanded to proceed to Nagasaki for deportation. Several of the more visible and active Japanese Christians received similar orders from their

[148] See *ibid.*, chap. xiii.

daimyos. While a few of the Europeans were able to go into hiding, the vast majority obeyed the order to assemble at Nagasaki. The Jesuit colleges and residences in the regions of Nagasaki, Arima, Hakata, Bungo, and the Kwanto were closed. Over five hundred persons, including Japanese auxiliaries, then belonged to the working organization of the Jesuits; fourteen Franciscans, nine Dominicans, and four Augustinians ministered to flocks far smaller in number than the approximately three hundred thousand Christians claimed by the Jesuits. After months of delay in Nagasaki, the missionaries and a number of prominent Japanese Christians were put aboard the "Great Ship" and several junks on November 7 and 8. Sixty-two Jesuits, including Provincial Valentim Carvalho (1559–1630), and fifty *dojuku* wound up in Macao; twenty-three Jesuits, seven friars, and the leading Japanese Christians were disembarked in Manila. A remnant which included at least twenty-eight Jesuits, fourteen friars, and five Japanese priests remained behind in hiding to minister to the Japanese Christians. Technically the Jesuit Province of Japan continued to be administered by a provincial stationed in Macao until the eighteenth century. It had under its jurisdiction many other territories such as Korea, Indochina, and Siam. European missionaries endeavored from time to time to join those left behind, and many, like Rodrigues in Macao, vainly petitioned the Society and the secular authorities to support their individual efforts to return to Japan.[149]

While the missionaries awaited deportation, old half-quenched fires flamed up anew in Japan. The forces of Hideyori and the house of Toyotomi, supported by a number of Christian warriors, were overwhelmed at Osaka castle in June, 1615, thus bringing to an end the threat from that quarter to the supremacy of the Tokugawas. Hidetada, who had been grooming himself at Edo to take over from his father, became full shogunal master of Japan on Ieyasu's death in July, 1616. The *bakufu* tightened its grip hereafter on the daimyos and on the foreign merchants. The Europeans (Portuguese, English, and Dutch), and by 1636 the Chinese as well, were confined to the ports of Nagasaki and Hirado and were permitted to make just one pilgrimage annually to Edo to present New Year's gifts to the shogun. In a decree of October 1, 1616, Hidetada strengthened Ieyasu's anti-Christian measures, and for the first time the foreign missionaries, once discovered, began to die for their faith.

In Kyushu, where most of them resided, the persecution of the Christians

---

[149] See Boxer, *op. cit.* (n. 136), pp. 320–27; and Laures, *op. cit.* (n. 146), pp. 164–66. Notice the disparities in their figures. We have generally followed Laures, the "official" historian of the Catholic Church in Japan. We have adjusted his figures in Boxer's direction whenever we thought the latter's statistics were more reliable or whenever we were convinced by his analysis and arguments. For another set of figures see Cooper, *op. cit.* (n. 140), p. 268. None of the disparities is great enough to alter significantly our general understanding of the expulsion. The sharpest conflict in the sources relates to the number of Japanese Christians in 1614—from 250,000 to 750,000! Also see Duncan, *op. cit.* (n. 14), p. 425.

was particularly harsh, culminating in 1622 with the "great martyrdom" of Nagasaki. On this occasion twenty-three Christians, including a number of missionaries, were burned at the stake, and twenty-two of their collaborators beheaded. Iemitsu, who succeeded as shogun upon Hidetada's retirement in 1623, continued the persecution policy and extended it to the northeastern provinces where many of the Kyushu and southwestern Christians had sought refuge. A few Christians had even fled to far northern Yezo, where they were followed by several of the Jesuits who were in hiding.[150] While sporadic executions of the recalcitrants continued, the government hereafter sought to make apostates rather than martyrs. Ingenious tortures were devised to force the Christians to renounce their faith and to collaborate with their inquisitors in rooting out crypto-Christians.

Foreign trade continued on a restricted basis. The Japanese red-seal (officially licensed) ships were gradually phased out of existence between 1633 and 1636, as Iemitsu moved towards the completion of his "closed-country" (Sakoku) policy. In 1634 Japanese were officially forbidden to go abroad. Morbidly fearful of a collaboration between the Iberians and the Japanese enemies of the Tokugawas, the bakufu increased internal taxation heavily to create as much self-sufficiency as possible. The daimyos in Arima and other southwestern regions, where the Christians and crypto-Christians had been most numerous and stubborn, made intolerable demands upon the farmers who were already suffering from a series of crop failures. This policy of localized fiscal exploitation, coupled with the anti-Christian program of the central government, helped to produce the Shimabara revolt of 1637–38 in Kyushu. After a lengthy struggle in which thirty-seven thousand were reportedly killed, Japan was closed to all Europeans except the Dutch. If one excepts those killed in the Shimabara rebellion, five thousand to six thousand persons were martyred between 1614 and 1640 for their faith, a number probably never exceeded in the history of the Catholic Church in a single country.[151] After the closure of Japan, the persecution was continued over the remainder of the seventeenth century. Crypto-Christians when discovered continued to be tortured, killed, or driven into exile until 1875.

The China mission was the most distinctive and renowned of all the Jesuit enterprises of the seventeenth century. One of the Society's founders, Francis Xavier, had died while endeavoring to gain entrance into China. His immediate successors, once the Portuguese had established a trading center at

---

[150] According to the Jesuit letters, one of their number was at Matsumae on Yezo in 1613. Another appeared there in 1618, and a third in 1620. Girolamo de Angelis, a Sicilian Jesuit who went there in 1618 and again in 1621, wrote a letter of 1621 to Europe which included a small map of the island. See P. D. Schilling, "Il contributo dei missionari cattolici nei secoli XVI e XVII alla conoscenza dell' Isola di Ezo e degli Ainu," in C. Costanini et al., op. cit. (n. 65), pp. 152–56.

[151] Boxer, op. cit. (n. 136), pp. 360–61; and Laures, op. cit. (n. 146), pp. 178–79.

Macao, resorted to every conceivable device to penetrate the "Middle Kingdom." The appearance of Valignano at Macao in 1577–78 had led quickly to the adoption of the missionizing method of accommodation or adaptation, and to preferments for cultured Italian Jesuits who were not involved personally in the rivalries of the Iberians. Michele Ruggieri of Naples and Matteo Ricci of Macerata led the way into China, traveling from Macao to Kwangtung. Ruggiero soon returned to Rome, while from 1582 to 1600 Ricci "sinicized" himself to bridge the cultural gulf which separates an educated European from a cultivated Chinese. Meanwhile he had made progress northward, with occasional setbacks, until he arrived in the imperial city of Peking on January 24, 1601. Here he lived out the remainder of his years, dying there on May 11, 1610.[152]

"The Wise Man from the West," as Ricci was denominated by one of his more recent biographers, spent the last decade of his life, as he had the previous eighteen years, in working out a method for insinuating Christianity into the high civilization of China. Unlike India and Japan, China under the Ming dynasty was politically integrated. Its culture, when compared to other great societies of the time, was remarkably cohesive and self-assured. The Chinese possessed a common written language of great antiquity and a literature comparable in sophistication to that of Europe. Its philosophical, scientific, and religious traditions likewise vied with those of seventeenth-century Europe. In the arts and crafts the Chinese enjoyed a rich heritage which owed relatively little to other cultures. Ricci had quickly learned after entering China that he would have to adopt the dress and manners of a Chinese gentleman, master the language, study sympathetically and seriously the Confucian classics, and develop friendships with the literati. To pique their curiosity about himself and Christianity, Ricci wrote books in Chinese about European ideas on "memory" and "friendship," prepared a world map, and presented gifts of clocks, paintings, and other European productions. He found that he could weld closer ties with the scholarly officials of the provinces and the capital by friendly discussion rather than by debating or preaching. As a consequence of this policy Ricci and the Jesuits came to be associated with the literary and philosophical societies, especially the Tung-lin Academy, in which political factions critical of the regime were forming.[153]

[152] On the Jesuit penetration of China see *Asia*, I, 795–802.

[153] The Ricci bibliography is extensive and constantly becoming richer. Indispensable to any study of Ricci is P. d'Elia, S.J. (ed.), *Fonti Ricciane* (3 vols., Rome, 1942–49). For a fascinating biography in English, based heavily on the *Fonti*, see the work of Vincent Cronin (also the able biographer of Nobili), called *The Wise Man from the West* (New York, 1955). For an analysis of Ricci's contribution to the development of the accommodation policy in China see the comprehensive but somewhat contentious study by G. H. Dunne, S.J., *Generation of Giants. The Story of the Jesuits in China in the Last Decades of the Ming Dynasty* (Notre Dame, Ind., 1962), chaps. i–v. For a recent and interesting interpretation see J. Spence, *The Memory Palace of Matteo Ricci* (New York, 1984).

Ricci's preference for courteous understanding and friendly discussion did not produce large numbers of converts. When he became superior of the mission in 1597, there were no more than one hundred Christians in China, excluding Macao. Tiny by comparison to the contemporary mission of Japan, the China mission, "formed" in its character by Ricci, never engaged in mass conversions. This was not entirely a result of Ricci's policy, for the China mission never enjoyed direct Portuguese military and political support as did the India mission. But neither did it suffer at the beginning from nationalistic divisions. It operated legally within the *padroado,* although it attained independence of the rector of Macao in 1604, since it was an exclusively Jesuit mission. Within the Jesuit organization it remained under the vice-province and province of Japan until it was itself elevated in 1618 to the status of vice-province and in 1623 declared independent of the Japan province. These organizational concessions were granted in simple recognition of the fact that the residences in China were too remote from the secular and ecclesiastical authorities of the *padroado* to be controlled as other missions were. The Jesuits in China nonetheless were indirectly subject to Portuguese control, for they traveled on Portuguese ships, entered and exited through Macao, were furnished with funds and supplies by the Portuguese, received money from the Jesuit investments in the "Great Ship," and used Portuguese as the official spoken language in the mission.[154] But the "portugalizing" practiced effectively in Portuguese-controlled ports was never attempted by the Jesuits in their efforts to convert the Chinese of the mainland.

After Ricci's arrival in Peking, the missionary effort began to make better progress. The Spanish Jesuit Diego de Pantoja (1571–1618), who had entered Peking with Ricci, concentrated on conversions in the capital and its environs and was aided by the Portuguese Gaspar Ferreira (1571–1649) who arrived in 1604. By 1605 the Jesuits had their own residence in Peking and over 100 converts from all levels of society.[155] Despite growing financial stringencies Valignano sent eight more missionaries into China in 1604–5. The Neapolitan astronomer, Sabatino de Ursis (1575–1620), joined Ricci at Peking in 1607. When Ricci died in 1610 there were five Jesuit residences (Chaoch'ing [1583], Shaochou [1589], Nanch'ang [1595], Nanking [1599], Peking [1606]) in China with an estimated 2,500 converts living in their environs.

Of the more than one dozen Jesuits who worked in China during the first decade of the century, the most important to the history of the mission, after Ricci himself, were the Italian Niccolò Longobardo (1565–1655), who had been at Shaochou since 1597, and the Portuguese Manuel Dias the Elder (1559–1639), who was superior of the southern residences (1603–09) and liaison with Macao. Notable also was the activity of the Cantonese brother,

[154] Dehergne, *op. cit.* (n. 86), pp. 325–27.
[155] See Dunne, *op. cit.* (n. 153), p. 101.

Sebastian Fernandes Tchong (*ca.* 1562–1621), one of the first Chinese to be admitted to membership in the Society. Originally sponsored by Ricci, Fernandes Tchong worked as a missionary at Peking from 1604 to 1608 and traveled extensively on behalf of the Society before and after those dates.[156] According to a directive of 1606, Chinese converts were not to be ordained to the priesthood because they were too immature in the faith. The most distinguished and influential of the early converts were Hsü Kuang-ch'i (1562–1633) and Li Chih-tsao (1565–1630), two scholar-officials who also contributed substantially to the successes won by the Jesuits at Peking and elsewhere.[157]

After Ricci's death Longobardo was appointed superior of the China mission, a post he held from 1610 to 1622. Although he was the choice of Ricci, Longobardo was generally much less cautious and specifically much more determined than his predecessor to establish new residences and to win official freedom to propagate the gospel. He also endeavored to expand upon the intellectual apostolate pioneered by Ricci. No sooner had Nicolas Trigault (1577–1628), a Flemish Jesuit, arrived in Peking during 1611 than Longobardo sent him to Europe as procurator of the mission. Trigault, who had spent about two years in China, was instructed to obtain policy directives from Rome on a series of thorny administrative questions and was especially to obtain a new status for the China mission of independence from the beleaguered Japan Province. He was delegated to obtain permission from the Holy See to translate the liturgy into Chinese and to permit the ordination of Chinese to the priesthood. He was directed to seek additional financial aid and personnel for the mission and to collect as many Western books on science and religion as possible. With his instructions in hand, as well as the *Commentaries* of Ricci, the Annual Letter for China (1610–11), and the abridged Annual Letter of Japan (1609–12), Trigault sailed from Macao for Goa in February, 1613. From Goa he traveled overland via Ormuz, Persia, and Egypt to Rome, where he arrived on October 11, 1614.

Trigault spent almost all of the next four years in Europe. In response to Longobardo's requests for concessions specific to the China mission, the Holy See reacted swiftly. Spurred by Cardinal Robert Bellarmine, the teacher and advocate of both Nobili and Ricci, the Holy Office in the presence of Pope Paul V granted permission on January 15, 1615, for the priests in China to wear a head-covering while celebrating mass, to translate the Bible into literary Chinese, and to ordain Chinese as priests. The Chinese converts, like their non-Christian countrymen, were offended by the appear-

---

[156] For a discussion of Ricci and his colleagues see C. W. Allan, *Jesuits at the Court of Peking* (Shanghai, 1935), pp. 57–60. For their biographies see Dehergne, *op. cit.* (n. 86). Also see Min-sun Chen, "Hsü Kuang-ch'i (1562–1633) and His Image of the West," in Pullapilly and Van Kley (eds.), *op. cit.* (n. 1), pp. 27–44.

[157] For their biographies see Arthur W. Hummel (ed.), *Eminent Chinese of the Ch'ing Period (1644–1912)* (Washington, 1943).

ance of an uncovered head on solemn public occasions. They also saw no reason why a religious ceremony should be celebrated in a language they could not understand. Even though a papal brief of June 27, 1615, formally authorized these concessions, Chinese converts were *not* hereafter ordained and the Chinese language was *not* adopted as the liturgical language, probably because of the debate over "terms." The only concession acknowledged by practice was the head-covering worn by the priest while celebrating mass.

It was probably the Jesuits themselves, rather than any other agency of the Church, who blocked the formation in China of a native clergy and the adoption of the Chinese liturgy. The Japan Jesuits in Macao who had strongly opposed the Longobardo program of independence for the Chinese mission, were equally hostile to the special concessions Trigault obtained in Rome. Based on their own experiences in Japan they opposed the idea of a native clergy, since they believed that converts new to the faith were culturally unprepared for the disciplined and celibate life followed by Christian priests. The Japan Jesuits also saw Longobardo's initiative as part of a more general effort to free the China mission from the control of the *padroado,* to bypass the Japan provincial, and to seek direct support for the China mission from the papacy and the non-Iberian Catholic powers of Europe.[158]

The Iberians and the Japan missionaries were not entirely mistaken in their estimate of the objectives behind Trigault's mission. While in Rome he completed the translation into Latin of his version of Ricci's memoirs and wrote up his own glowing account of the state of the mission.[159] While these books were being published he set out on a propaganda tour of western Europe that first took him to southern Italy and Spain. Public attention in Iberia and Italy was then being drawn to Japan by the Date mission, an enterprise of the Spanish Franciscan friars that detracted from Trigault's activities in Europe on behalf of the China mission.[160] Trigault returned to Rome and by special permission attended the General Congregation of the Society (November 5, 1615–January 26, 1616). Here he told the assembled provincials the needs of the China mission and Longobardo's hopes for obtaining from the emperor a declaration giving freedom to Christianity. With the support of General Mutio Vitelleschi, he proposed the continuation and expansion of Valignano's program of cultural adaptation. In the course of these discussions he indicated that messages and reports could be sent more expeditiously via Manila than by the Portuguese route. In May, 1616, he left Rome for a final tour that took him to the major cities of northern Italy,

---

[158] See Dunne, *op. cit.* (n. 153), pp. 162–70. For further detail on the question of the liturgy see F. Bontinck, *La lutte autour de la liturgie chinoise aux XVIIe et XVIIIe siècles* (Louvain, 1962), pp. 21–55. Both authors cited here absolve Trigault from the charge, first leveled by Daniello Bartoli, S.J. (1608–85), that he had gone beyond Longobardo's orders in requesting the native clergy and the Chinese liturgy.

[159] See below, pp. 512–13.

[160] On the Date mission led by Luis Sotelo, O.F.M., see below, pp. 210–12, 331–32.

Lyons, the south German cities, and his hometown of Douai. Several months later he journeyed southward through France and Madrid.

Because Trigault addressed himself freely to the princes and prelates of Catholic Europe and received aid and encouragement from most of them, the Spanish and Portuguese missionaries claimed to be fearful that their king might close the field of foreign missions to other nationals. Philip III, in fact, raised his annual subsidy to the China mission; it was the Portuguese clerics of the *padroado,* especially Gabriel de Matos, the procurator of the Japan mission, who objected most seriously to Trigault's efforts to bring a sizable number of non-Iberians into the China mission. Finally, after receiving official permission, Trigault sailed from Lisbon on April 16, 1618, with the money, the books, and twenty-two of the recruits he had won for the mission during his stay in Europe. Of the twenty-two, only ten were Portuguese Jesuits.[161]

While Trigault in Europe was reporting glowingly in print and in person on the prospects for Christianity in China, storm clouds began to darken the bright horizons of the Jesuits working there. Trigault had been in Hangchow (Chekiang) when the Italian Lazzaro Cattaneo (1560–1640) founded a mission in 1611 in that city of beauty and art. Aided by Christians from Shanghai, and especially by Hsü Kuang-ch'i and Li Chih-tsao, this new enterprise got off to a flying start. One of the leading local lights and a well-known critic of the eunuchs who dominated the court, the scholar-official Yang T'ing-yun (1557–1627) was baptized in 1613. He at once became an ardent advocate of Christianity and Western learning. In Peking, De Ursis and Pantoja had meanwhile begun to work with the Board of Rites to reform the Chinese calendar. De Ursis also constructed hydraulic machines that became the talk of the capital and wrote treatises in Chinese on the general subject of hydraulics. The nationwide publicity given these Jesuit activities soon made for them many powerful enemies, particularly among those Chinese who had "lost face" to the Westerners. The court eunuchs were similarly disturbed by the growing influence of the Jesuits, particularly since they were so closely associated with the eunuchs' political enemies in the secret societies.[162]

Nanking, once the capital of China, was during the early seventeenth century the seat of what the Jesuits saw as one of their most promising missions. As a city, Nanking was more impressive than Peking, more centrally located, and a center of national government second only to Peking. All the agencies of imperial government existing in Peking had their duplicates in Nanking; the city swarmed with officials eager to advance themselves to the bureaucracy of the capital. Ricci himself had founded its mission in 1599,

---

[161] See E. Lamalle, S.J., "La propaganda du P. Nicolas Trigault en faveur des missions de Chine, 1616," *AHSI,* IX (1940), 49–120. Also see C. Dehaisnes, *Vie du Pere Nicolas Trigault de la Compagnie de Jesus* (Tournai, 1861), chaps. iv and v; and Dunne, *op. cit.* (n. 153), p. 178.

[162] See Dunne, *op. cit.* (n. 153), pp. 112–17.

and in 1609 Alfonso Vagnone (1568[69?]–1640), an able Italian Jesuit, became its superior. Alvarez Semedo (1585[86?]–1658), a Portuguese Jesuit, joined the mission in 1613; Semedo was one of five Portuguese fathers then in China out of a total of fifteen Jesuits. At Nanking the Jesuits owned a spacious residence in the city and a house with an orchard outside the walls. From these places they ministered to a Christian congregation that was then probably the largest and most active in China.

The success of the China mission, based as it was on cultural affiliation, aroused open hostility in 1615–16 both in Macao and Nanking. Valentim Carvalho, the provincial of Japan who had taken refuge in Macao in 1614, proscribed a year later the methods being followed by the successors of Ricci and ordered them to concentrate upon preaching the gospel.[163] Since Carvalho himself had no personal acquaintance with China proper, it is likely that his blast was inspired by Rodrigues the Interpreter. Between 1613 and 1615 Rodrigues traveled in China and spent eighteen months with Vagnone in Nanking. From these experiences Rodrigues concluded that the Middle Kingdom was a fertile mission field that was not being properly cultivated by its Italian superiors. He was vehement in his denunciation of the accommodation policy, particularly as it related to the question of the Chinese terms for "God," "soul," and other Christian ideas.[164]

The mission also came under attack in 1615 from Shen Ch'ueh, the vice-director of the Nanking Board of Rites. Between May, 1616, and February, 1617, Shen memorialized the throne several times to take immediate action against the foreign priests and their subversive religion. By their teachings, he alleged, the Jesuits undermine the public's belief in the religions native to China and lead the people morally astray. They consort with the Portuguese at Macao, obtain funds from unknown sources, and are of the same nation as those who have occupied Luzon and maltreated the Chinese residents in Manila. They insinuate themselves into court circles and attract the attention of the literati by their allegedly superior knowledge of astronomy. In Nanking they possess a strategically located residence from which they organize regular meetings at which they practice magical rites. Their secret society, which is similar to the feared White Lotus sect, keeps careful records of its members. Persons privy to this conspiratorial sect recognize one another by secret gestures and identifying marks. Whatever Shen's motives were for making these allegations, it seems clear enough that such an interpretation could be placed upon the activities of the Jesuits by those who had no knowledge of or interest in Christianity and who were genuinely alarmed by the resistance to the crown being fomented by the secret societies.[165]

[163] *Ibid.*, p. 123.

[164] See Cooper, *op. cit.* (n. 140), pp. 279–89.

[165] For this summary of Shen's anti-Christian arguments see E. Zürcher, "The First Anti-Christian Movement in China. Nanking, 1616–21," in P. W. Pestman (ed.), *Acta Orientalia Neerlandica* (Leyden, 1971), p. 191. On the Chinese response to the Christian mission, see also

When Shen's initial memorial won support from the Peking head of the Board of Rites, Hsü Kuang-ch'i countermemorialized on behalf of the Jesuits.[166] In August, 1616, the Board of Rites, while still awaiting the emperor's reply, began to proceed against the missionaries. Vagnone and Semedo were imprisoned and the Jesuits elsewhere began to seek refuge with their influential converts. The emperor finally responded on February 14, 1617, by signing an edict ordering the deportation of Vagnone, Pantoja, and their companions. The suppression was effective only in Nanking; it was but partially enforced in Peking where Longobardo and Sambiasi remained quietly in the residence of Hsü Kuang-ch'i. Only Pantoja, De Ursis, Vagnone, and Semedo were actually expelled; by 1624 both Semedo and Vagnone had returned. The Jesuits who remained behind quietly continued their work under the protection of their converts. In 1617 they founded a new residence at Chiench'ang in Kiangsi and in 1621 new missions at Chiating (Kiating) near Shanghai and at Yangchou. As for Shen, he was promoted around 1620 to head the Peking Department of Rites, a post in which he lasted for only a short time. This suppression of the Jesuits, half-hearted as it was, is best seen as part of the growing political struggle between the eunuch party of the court and its political enemies of the academies. When all private academies were prohibited in 1625, the Jesuits weathered the storm and continued to expand their activities, even during the worst years (1621–27) of eunuch domination.[167]

Several of the eight European priests who remained in China during the persecution assembled at Hangchow to improve their command of Chinese language and literature. Yang T'ing-yun, the Christian scholar-official, acted as their teacher. His favorite student was Giulio Aleni (1582–1649), the Italian Jesuit who founded in 1620 the missions in Shansi and Shensi, provinces far to the west of the earlier Jesuit establishments. In this project he was aided by the Chinese scholar-official Ma San-chih who studied Western mathematics with Aleni and who accepted baptism himself in 1621. Aleni was followed into northwestern China by Trigault, who had returned to Macao from his European tour in 1619. In 1623 Trigault went to K'aifeng in Honan province, a city that had attracted Longobardo because of his interest in the ancient Jewish community there. Both Ricci and Longobardo had heard from Jewish informants that traces could be found in northwestern China of earlier Christian activities. In 1625 Trigault was joined by Vagnone who really put the mission in Chiangchou (Shansi) on sound foundations. Trigault then moved into the neighboring province of Shensi where the

---

J. Gernet, *China and the Christian Impact: A Conflict of Cultures,* trans. J. Lloyd (Cambridge and Paris, 1985); J. D. Young, *Confucianism and Christianity: The First Encounter* (Hong Kong, 1983).
    [166] See Dunne, *op. cit.* (n. 153), pp. 132–133.
    [167] See Zürcher, *loc. cit.* (n. 165), pp. 192–93; for a theological interpretation of the basic conflict between Chinese civilization and Christianity see D. Lancashire, "Anti-Christian Polemics in Seventeenth-Century China," *Church History,* XXXVIII (1969), 218–41.

Nestorian Monument had been discovered in 1623 near the old capital city of Sian.[168]

The Jesuits, including Ricci, had long been puzzled that no mention appeared in Chinese annals and histories about earlier Christian activity in China. They knew that the friars had worked in China during the Mongol (Yüan) dynasty, and expected to find evidence of this evangelizing in the Chinese records. The western provinces, being the gateway to China by the overland route, were the most likely places to discover traces of earlier relations with Christianity. For evangelizing, it was important to the missionaries to find Christian antecedents in China, for one of the most common Chinese objections to Christianity was its newness. In a society where age and tradition are revered, novelties, while interesting, are suspect and likely not to be regarded seriously. This is why the superiors of the early mission made every effort to track down all possible leads to earlier Sino-Western contacts and to identify the "Cathay" of Marco Polo as the northern China that they knew.[169]

The Chinese themselves, who saw Shensi as their first great historical center and as the place from which their earliest emperors came, were constantly searching for antiquities in Sian and its vicinity. Whether the Nestorian Monument with its parallel inscriptions, in Chinese of the T'ang epoch and in Syriac, was first discovered in 1623 or 1625 has been a subject of considerable debate. The Jesuits first learned of it through the report prepared by Trigault in 1625. Decipherment of the inscription revealed, much to the delight of the Jesuits, that the Christian faith in its Nestorian form had been practiced in the T'ang period, particularly during the seventh and eighth centuries. To the Chinese of the Ming dynasty this discovery established Christianity as a religion which had been permitted and honored by the emperors of the glorious T'ang and so lent to the teaching of the Jesuits a new credibility. The first publication in 1631 of the monument's text in Europe produced a controversy over the authenticity of the stone that went on for the next two centuries and more.[170]

The discovery of the ancient text on the monument, with its references in Chinese to Christian concepts, sharpened the debate over the "term question" that had divided the Jesuits ever since the death of Ricci. A mission conference called by Valignano at Macao in 1600 had approved Ricci's terms for "God" (either *T'ien-chu*, "Lord of Heaven" or *Shang-ti*, "highest Lord"; a simple *T'ien* would also suffice). For "spirit" he advocated *T'ien-cheng* and

---

[168] For further detail see F. Margiotti, O.F.M., *Il cattolicismo nello Shansi dalle origini al 1738* (Rome, 1958), pp. 82–91.
[169] See below, pp. 338, 1575–76, for the Jesuit overland travels.
[170] For the history of the discovery and the ensuing debate see Henri Havret, S.J., *La stèle chrétienne de Si-ngan-fou* (Shanghai, 1895); for a scholarly treatment of the stone and supporting discoveries since made in western China see P. Y. Saeki, *The Nestorian Documents and Relics in China* (2d ed., Tokyo, 1951), and Margiotti, *op. cit.* (n. 168), pp. 52–54. Also see below, pp. 485–86.

for "soul" *Ling-hien*. Ricci himself did not attend this conference or the following meetings of 1603 and 1605, at which Valignano also presided. Longobardo, who was also working in China and therefore not present at these conferences, was less satisfied than others with the terms employed by Ricci. He was particularly dubious about the words for "God" and thought that misinterpretation could be avoided by "sinicizing" the Latin *Deus* just as the missionaries in Japan had "nipponicized" it. Soon after he succeeded Ricci as superior, Longobardo received a communication from the new Visitor Francesco Pasio (1554–1612), informing him that the whole matter would again be reviewed. After consulting all the missionaries and a few Chinese scholars it was decided in 1612 to prohibit the use of *Shang-ti* in spite of objections raised by stalwart followers of Ricci.[171]

The descent of the Japan Jesuits upon Macao in 1614 deepened the division. Like Rodrigues many of the Japan Jesuits were startled to learn how far accommodation had been carried in the China mission. Questions arose both over the terms employed in China and the practices and customs which the converts were permitted to follow. The "rites question," as this second issue came to be called, gradually emerged as another source of bitter controversy. In 1603 Ricci had issued his directive on the rites and it was approved by Valignano. The founder of the mission declared that two customary rituals were to be permitted: traditional honors to Confucius and essential ancestral ceremonies. Ricci held that these rites were morally admissible to Christians because they were outside of religious philosophy and isolated from the superstitions associated with Buddhism, Taoism, and Sung neo-Confucianism. He argued that Confucianism had originated, according to his informants and to his reading of the classical texts, as social observances. In its primitive form Confucianism was a simple monotheism that had over time acquired illicit accretions that should be stripped away by re-educating the Chinese to an understanding of original Confucianism as a primitive stage on the journey toward Christ. He believed that the retention of the universally practiced rites honoring Confucius and the ancestors was indispensable to the success of the apostolate. Such rites, he declared, were "certainly not idolatrous, and perhaps not even superstitious."[172]

Although the Jesuits generally followed the Ricci program in the mission field, the controversy widened throughout the seventeenth century. By 1665 issues relating to the accommodation policy had been discussed at no fewer than seventy-four mission conferences.[173] Longobardo, who dis-

[171] See J. Metzler, *Die Synoden in China, Japan und Korea, 1570–1931* (Paderborn, 1980), pp. 11–14.

[172] Based on the official Catholic version of the "Chinese Rites Controversy" written by F. A. Rouleau, S.J., for the *New Catholic Encyclopedia* (Washington, D.C., 1967), III, 612; and on the critique of J. S. Cummins, "Two Missionary Methods in China: Mendicants and Jesuits," in V. Sanchez and C. Fuertes (eds.), *España en Extremo Oriente* (Madrid, 1979), pp. 46–47.

[173] See Metzler, *op. cit.* (n. 171), p. 12.

agreed with Ricci on "terms," was thoroughly in agreement with his position on the "rites" as civil ceremonies. [174] Rodrigues, who was as delighted as the other Jesuits were with the discovery of the Nestorian stone, claimed that its Chinese text, in which the word "God" appears in a "sinicization" of the Syriac "Allaa," supported his contention that an established Chinese term should not be used to designate the Christian deity. In a polemic sent to Europe in 1626 Rodrigues declared that his position on the "term question" was supported by Provincial Manuel Dias the Younger (in office 1623–35), Longobardo, Pedro Ribeiro (1570–1640), Gaspar Ferreira, and brother Pascoal Mendes (1584–1640), a Chinese preacher "who knows the most about the language and literature of China." Rodrigues claimed that the opposition was headed by Manuel Dias the Elder and included many uninformed newcomers to the mission. [175] Late in 1627 and early in 1628 nine Jesuits assembled at the Chiating mission near Shanghai. The major issue debated at this assembly revolved around the "term" question. Longobardo, who had never been reconciled to Ricci's use of *T'ien-chu* for "God," continued until his death in 1655 to be worried over this vexing question. Many of the controversial memoranda prepared in the early years of this internal dispute were destroyed as the Jesuits sought to keep their divisions from disedifying their converts. Longobardo's treatise was one of the few of the anti-Ricci writings to escape suppression. [176] For the rest of the missionaries the "term" issue was gradually forced into the background, as more immediate problems and dilemmas began to threaten the very existence of the mission. To this day Chinese Catholics still use *T'ien-chu* as their name for the Christian God. [177]

The controversy increasingly became a general conflict over missionizing methods and, in particular, over the rites. The Jesuits in the Philippines, for example, had little or no understanding of the adaptation being practiced in China; they even denounced the friars in Manila for accepting too passively the syncretism of their Chinese converts. From the beginning the method of Europeanizing the converts followed in the rest of the world seemed to them equally suitable for eastern Asia. They could also point to the failure of the Valignano program in Japan as an example of what might happen when compromise with native practices went too far. When the first Franciscans and Dominicans came to China in the 1630's, new elements entered the conflict. The first friars brought with them doubts about the Jesuit method being followed in China and a determination to preach and teach as they had elsewhere. Since the Jesuits thought the friars had no right to be in China, they ignored the Spanish mendicants or rebuked them for their ignorance of China. The meeting in China of the missionaries of the *padroado*

[174] See Dunne, *op. cit.* (n. 153), p. 295.
[175] See Cooper, *op. cit.* (n. 140), p. 327.
[176] See Cummins, *loc. cit.* (n. 172), pp. 59–60.
[177] See Dunne, *op. cit.* (n. 153), chap. xvi.

and the *patronato* at a time when the political division of the Iberian peninsula was becoming a chasm, also brought the mission into a national conflict
that continued for long thereafter to exacerbate its difficulties in both Europe and Asia.[178]

In Peking, far removed from Macao and the machinations of other Europeans, the Jesuits faced a separate set of problems. The Ming dynasty of the
Wan-li era (1573–1620) had exhibited a growing weakness at the center. Increasingly torn by factionalism, the court and the government came to be
dominated by palace eunuchs. The reign of the T'ien-ch'i emperor (1620–
29) was thoroughly controlled by Wei Chung-hsien, leader of the eunuch
party and violent enemy of the reform-minded academies, clubs, and secret
societies. Imperial decline in China was paralleled by the rise of Manchu
power in eastern Tartary beyond the Great Wall. Nurhaci (1529–1626) had
managed during the course of his life to mold the disunited tribes of eastern
Tartary into an effective fighting force. In 1609 he ceased paying tribute to
Peking and seven years later proclaimed himself emperor. In 1618 Nurhaci
began to attack intramural China in an effort to destroy the Ming and to
establish his own dynasty in Peking. In their attack upon the Ming the Manchus were aided periodically by Chinese.[179] A civil war followed which
lasted until 1644, paralleling in time the Thirty Years' War (1618–48) in
Europe.

The Jesuits in Peking were at first not involved in the civil war. Because
the edict of expulsion had not been revoked, they were left in an ambiguous
position and remained extremely cautious and prudent. Longobardo, who
officially became superior of the Peking group when Manuel Dias the
Younger was appointed in 1623 as the first vice-provincial of the China mission, returned in this year to the imperial capital where he was soon joined
by Johann Terrenz Schreck (Terrentius) (1576–1630), a German Jesuit recruited by Trigault. A brilliant mathematician and a student of Galileo,
Schreck was sent to China in response to the repeated pleadings of the
Jesuits for missionary-astronomers to work on the reform of the Chinese
calendar. News of the discovery of the telescope and of its revelations had
been announced by the Jesuits in a Chinese publication of 1615. Despite the
1616 injunction of the Holy Office prohibiting Galileo from publicizing the
Copernican doctrine on the motion of the earth, the Jesuits in China continued to work with the telescope and to transmit his discoveries. They retained, with reluctance on the part of some of them, the geocentric theory of
Ptolemy rather than adopting the new heliocentric theory of Copernicus.[180]
Before leaving Europe, Schreck had spent several years collecting materials

---

[178] On the successful Portuguese revolt of 1640–68 against the Habsburgs see above, p. 22. For
its effect on the missions see H. Bernard, S.J., *Les îles Philippines du grand archipel de la Chine,
1571–1641* (Tientsin, 1936), pp. 205–22.

[179] See F. Michael, *The Origins of Manchu Rule in China* (Baltimore, 1942), pp. 2–3.

[180] Joseph Needham consequently refers to the Jesuit astronomy in China as "the imperfect
transmission." See *Science and Civilization in China* (Cambridge, 1970), III, 437–47.

and scientific instruments for the Peking enterprise. When Galileo refused to respond to Schreck's questions, the Jesuits managed to obtain assistance for him from Johannes Kepler. In Peking he also had help from the Cologne Jesuit, Johann Adam Schall von Bell (1592–1666), who had started out with him on the long trek from Europe to Peking.[181]

While the Jesuit-scientists at first spent most of their time studying the Chinese language, their colleagues and converts in Peking worked to rehabilitate Christianity's reputation with the Chinese. At Macao, Schall and other Jesuits had participated during 1622 in the defense of the city against the Dutch. The repulse of the powerful Dutch fleet by a small garrison in an unfortified city stirred the admiration of the Chinese. It was thought that the Portuguese victory was made possible by their effective use of cannon fire.[182] The authorities of Kwangtung thereafter permitted the Portuguese to fortify the city. In the process the Macaoese began the manufacture of cannons. In the north, the Manchus had meanwhile administered a crushing defeat to the Chinese forces in Liaotung during March, 1622. Hsü Kuang-ch'i and others of the Christian converts had long been urging the government to import "foreign cannon" and experts in their use to meet the attacks of the Manchus. When the party of reform temporarily came back to power in 1622 they took control of defense. Gradually with the aid of the "foreign guns" they pushed the Manchus northward over the next several years. To acquire weaponry, the Chinese had used the reluctant Jesuits in the role of intermediaries and as military advisers. As a reward for their services the Jesuits were granted tacit permission by the Board of War to reside in Peking. Implicitly they were also granted the right to resume their public ministry.[183]

The presence in government of officials friendly to them contributed to a growing feeling of confidence among the Peking Jesuits. Schall in particular began to make important friends. He presented to the imperial court a list of the mathematical and astronomical works the Jesuits had brought from Europe and he put on display their collection of scientific instruments.[184] With

---

[181] See Pasquale M. D'Elia, S.J., *Galileo in China. Relations through the Roman College between Galileo and the Jesuit Scientist-Missionaries* (Cambridge, Mass., 1960), pp. vi–vii. On the heated issue of "Did the Jesuits Hide the Heliocentric System from the Chinese?" (pp. 51–56), D'Elia expounds the view that the heliocentric theory was not accepted by a majority of the European scientists until the eighteenth century. The Jesuit scientists in China, some of whom were convinced Copernicans, were not engaged in a conspiracy or following blindly the ecclesiastical injunctions against the heliocentric theory but were, like secular scientists, simply divided in their opinion. It might be added that under the circumstances prevailing in Peking it would hardly have been prudent to stress the controversies existing within Western astronomy while seeking to convince the Chinese of its superiority.

[182] On this battle see Boxer, *op. cit.* (n. 28), pp. 72–93.

[183] See Dunne, *op. cit.* (n. 153), pp. 183–87. Also C. R. Boxer, "Portuguese Military Expeditions in Aid of the Mings against the Manchus, 1621–1647," *T'ien Hsia Monthly*, VII (1938), 24–36.

[184] See A. Väth, *Johann Adam Schall von Bell, S.J.* (Cologne, 1933), p. 68. J. Duhr's French biography (1936) is an adaptation of Väth's work and the English biography by Rachel Att-

the aid of these instruments he predicted accurately the lunar eclipse of October 8, 1623. Shortly thereafter Schreck arrived in Peking and both he and Schall began again to concentrate on language study. The work of conversion progressed slowly in the capital from 1624 to 1627 as the new missionaries dedicated themselves to learning about China and its people. In 1626 Schall published a small book in Chinese describing the telescope and its construction.[185]

Improving conditions in Peking were reflected in the provincial missions. Aleni pioneered a Christian community at Ch'angshu in Kiangsi in 1623 and converted Ch'ü Shih-ssŭ (1590–1651), an eminent scholar-official who later became a leading Ming loyalist. From Kiangsi, Aleni moved south to Fukien in 1625 and shortly succeeded in setting up a mission in Foochow. With the support of several of the local gentry he began to discuss Christianity with intellectuals in a number of Fukien's cities. Conversion of gentlemen who enjoyed enough wealth to have more than one wife was difficult in Fukien as elsewhere in China. While attracted to the Christian message, very few of the scholar-officials were inhuman enough to turn their extra wives and concubines out of their homes in order to abide by the precepts of a foreign faith and its proscription of polygamy.[186]

Schall, who had shown his mettle in Peking, was sent in the autumn of 1627 to Sian, the most historic of China's living cities. The way had been paved in Shensi, beginning in 1620, by the enterprise of Aleni, Vagnone, Trigault, and others. Schall was joined by Semedo at Sian early in 1628. The newcomers, though they had the support of two of the Chinese scholars who had aided Trigault, were treated roughly by the Chinese. Semedo, who considered that life in a Nanking prison was more tolerable than the situation in Sian, was transferred in 1629 to Nanch'ang in Kiangsi province. Left alone in Sian the intrepid Schall expanded the mission as he gradually won a few more converts. He continued with his Chinese studies, observed the lunar eclipse of January 21, 1628, and sought to determine the exact latitude of Sian. From the caravan leaders who periodically arrived in Sian he gathered information on the routes and the geography of inner Asia. From a Muslim caravan leader he learned in detail about the various routes, stations, distances, and articles of trade. On the basis of this information he dispatched to Rome in 1629 his own conclusion confirming Ricci's assertion, that "Cathay" was indeed northern China and that Marco Polo's "Khanbaligh" was Peking.[187]

While Schall labored in Sian, the Jesuit scientists in Peking had become

---

water (1963) is an adaptation of Duhr's work. Hence, there is but one original biography, that of Väth.

[185] See D'Elia, *op. cit.* (n. 181), pp. 33–38.
[186] See Dunne, *op. cit.* (n. 153), pp. 187–92.
[187] See Väth, *op. cit.* (n. 184), pp. 74–81.

more deeply involved in court affairs. The unexpected death of the emperor in 1627 brought an end to the dominance of Wei Chung-hsien and the eunuch party, much to the relief of the Jesuits and their friends. In 1629 Hsü Kuang-ch'i returned to government as senior vice-president of the Board of Rites by appointment of the Ch'ung-chen emperor (r. 1627–44). Many other friends of the Jesuits also came back to Peking under the new dispensation. Hsü in his new post was in a strategic position to reopen the question of calendar reform and to pit the astronomy of the West against the Muslim and Chinese systems. In consultation with Schreck, Hsü planned a showdown for June 21, 1629. On this date an eclipse of the sun was to occur. The exponents of the three rival systems were required to put in writing their predictions of the time of its occurrence and the duration. The Jesuit prediction was precisely accurate and the other two were not. Hsü thereupon declared that the traditional systems of astronomical reckoning were unreliable and that the only remedy lay in following the European method. An imperial edict of September 1 entrusted the calendar reform to the missionaries and their pupils.

Longobardo and Schreck were appointed as paid officials of the new Calendrical Bureau and furnished with a workshop in which to make instruments. Schreck proposed a vast translation project of Western scientific texts and urged the speedy construction of telescopes and other scientific equipment. Around 1628 Schreck composed a treatise in Chinese entitled *Abridged Theory on Measures of the Sky* in which he discussed the use of the telescope and described sunspots.[188] Before he could write more on this subject, Schreck died in May, 1630, slightly less than one year after the astronomical competition had been won. Hsü immediately appointed Schall and Giacomo Rho (1592–1617), an Italian Jesuit then working in Shansi, to replace Shreck at the Calendrical Bureau.[189]

The scientific victories of the Jesuits in Peking were published in the *Imperial Gazette* that was read throughout the empire. In the provinces, as in the capital, the missionaries began in 1630 to carry on their work more publicly. Conversions increased as the Chinese populace came to realize that the missionaries continued to negotiate with Macao on behalf of the government for supplies of artillery and firearms. Five new missionaries entered the field in 1630 to work in the provincial stations. The star of Hsü Kuang-ch'i continued to rise in Peking and the mission basked in its brilliance. Schall and Rho were busily translating Western technical treatises into Chinese for the instruction and use of their assistants. Knowledge of the Galilean discoveries were transmitted to Korea in 1631 and to Japan several years later. The greatest loss of these years came with the death on November 8, 1633, of

---

[188] Evidently he was unaware of the fact that sunspots had previously been described many times over in the Chinese records. See Needham, *op. cit.* (n. 180), III, 435.

[189] See D'Elia, *op. cit.* (n. 181), pp. 40–41; and Dunne, *op. cit.* (n. 153), pp. 208–14.

Hsü Kuang-ch'i, "the first man in China after the emperor himself" according to the Jesuits.[190] This evaluation is more than a pious Jesuit exaggeration, for Hsü was posthumously awarded the honorary title of Junior Guardian (changed in 1643 to Grand Guardian) of the Heir Apparent and was canonized, or officially awarded the perpetual admiration of his countrymen.[191]

Most remarkable to any fair observer were the successes won by a handful of Jesuits in the short space of little more than a single generation. There were an estimated five thousand Chinese Christian converts by 1615, thirteen thousand by 1627, and thirty-eight thousand by 1636.[192] By 1634 the Jesuits had twelve permanent residences located in seven of China's fifteen provinces. These stations were ministered to by twenty-three European priests and four Chinese lay brothers.[193] Especially prosperous were Vagnone's mission in Shansi and, until 1637, Aleni's community in Fukien. The Christian converts came from all social classes of Peking and the provinces. By 1636 the Jesuits had penetrated the most tightly closed and highest classes of Chinese society. Of the 38,000 converts claimed in 1636 about 300 were men of letters, more than 140 were relatives of the imperial family, more than 40 were palace eunuchs, and several were palace women who formed in 1637 a Christian group called "Ladies of the Imperial Palace."[194] In the provinces the Jesuits were protected and financed by the local gentry and minor officials as well as by hundreds of enthusiastic converts with no special educational qualifications or governmental ties.

While Hsü lay on his deathbed, a new series of events unfolded which spelt future trouble for the prospering China mission. In 1633 Rome ordained, over the objections of Portugal, that the missionaries might travel to East Asia by any route they chose and not necessarily by way of Lisbon as they had previously been required to do. Although no papal restrictions had been imposed on missionary travel to Asia since 1608, the crown's wishes in this matter were regularly followed.[195] The Spanish Dominicans and Franciscans were not bound after 1608 by ecclesiastical restrictions on travel to China and Japan, but the Spanish Jesuits were confined to the *patronato* by the policy of the Society. The friars from the Philippines, after suffering set-

---

[190] Väth, *op. cit.* (n. 184), p. 103; quoted approvingly in Dunne, *op. cit.* (n. 153), p. 220.

[191] See his biography by Y. C. Yang in Hummel, *op. cit.* (n. 157), p. 318.

[192] See Duncan, *op. cit.* (n. 14), p. 414; and Dehergne, *op. cit.* (n. 86), p. 330.

[193] See Dunne, *op. cit.* (n. 153), pp. 303–4.

[194] See Dehergne, *op. cit.* (n. 86), p. 330. Zürcher, *loc. cit.* (n. 165), pp. 189–90, avers that the Jesuits writers have overrepresented the eminence and reputation of their converts.

[195] It should be recalled (see above, p. 132) that the papacy had granted in 1608 to the mendicant orders the right to follow the route of their own choice to the Far East. But all of the mendicants in the *padroado* were Portuguese by background and subject to the royal monopoly. The Jesuits in Portuguese Asia, although drawn from several nationalities, were dependent upon the crown for transportation and for access to Macao. Consequently the Jesuits of the *padroado* were not inclined to follow other routes, even though they increasingly became interested in the possibility of the overland route as the Dutch harassment of sea travel became more costly in lives, time, and money.

backs in their initial efforts to penetrate the Jesuit's monopoly of Japan and China, had made no endeavors to enter China until after the Spanish set up an outpost on Formosa in 1626. Then, early in 1632, two Dominicans, dispatched by the Spanish governor of Formosa to obtain trading relations with Fukien, managed after severe hardships to make their way to Foochow. Although the Dominicans were officially ordered to leave China, the Italian Father Angelo Cocchi (d. 1633) found a hiding place in the village of Fuan to the north of Foochow. Here he was joined in 1633 by Juan Bautista de Morales, another Dominican, and by two Franciscans. The Franciscans in 1634 set up their own mission in the village of Tingtow. For the Jesuits in China, the appearance of Spanish friars in Fukien heralded the onset of new disputes over missionizing methods and the outbreak in 1637–38 of troubles with the secular authorities of Fukien.[196]

Except for the difficulties experienced by the Jesuits in Fukien the mission continued to expand and prosper during the final years of the Ming dynasty. At Vagnone's death in 1640 his Shansi mission boasted more than 8,000 Christians and 102 Christian communities. In Shensi, where Etienne Faber (1597–1657), a French Jesuit, worked from 1635 until his death, the mission expanded rapidly throughout the tortuous last years of the dynasty and thereafter. The aged Longobardo in 1636 took time off from supervising the mission in Peking to carry the faith into Shantung. New missions were opened in Hukwang (1637) and in Szechwan (1640), two far western provinces. The greatest successes of these years were scored in the Shanghai region, where the Italian Francesco Brancati (1607–71) and Candida Hsü (1607–80), granddaughter of Hsü Kuang-ch'i, worked after 1637. General Vitelleschi in 1640 recognized the rapid extension of the mission and the changing political conditions in China by naming Aleni superior of the north and Francisco Furtado (1589–1653), a Portuguese Jesuit, superior of the south. By 1650 around 150,000 Chinese had come to profess Christianity, out of a total population of 150,000,000.[197]

In Peking, Schall and Rho with their Chinese collaborators and assistants of the Calendrical Bureau continued to study the divergences between European and Chinese astronomy. They concentrated on the development of instruments and in 1634 presented a telescope of European maufacture to the emperor. Included in the explanation of its use were the following sentences: "With such an instrument one can observe not only the sky but also objects several *li* distant. . . . It is very useful for watching the enemy in cannon's range."[198] Information on the history of European astronomy appeared in Chinese early in 1635, and five years later Schall, who worked at

---

[196] See B. M. Biermann, *Die Anfänge der neueren Dominikanermission in China* (Münster, 1927), chap. ii, and Dunne, *op. cit.* (n. 153), pp. 235–66.

[197] See Dunne, *op. cit.* (n. 153), pp. 303–9; and see Dehergne, *op. cit.* (n. 86), *passim* and his map of the Christian residences in China at the end of the Ming in 1644, facing p. 352.

[198] As translated and quoted in D'Elia, *op. cit.* (n. 181), p. 49.

the Calendrical Bureau without European associates after Rho's death in 1638, published a short *History of Occidental Astronomers,* in which Galileo's name is written phonetically as "Chialileo." While proposals were made for official adoption of calendar reform, Schall was faced by the continuing opposition of those who rejected the "foreign astronomy." Even though Longobardo and Schall had ready access to the court and made converts of both palace eunuchs and ladies, the darkening political situation prevented the last of the Ming emperors from putting their new calendar officially into use.

The return of Schall to Peking in 1630 coincided with the beginning of the end for the Ming dynasty. Shensi and Shansi suffered severely at this time from prolonged famine, increasing banditry, and seething popular discontent. The spread of famine and its attendant problems into other western provinces brought an organized resistance into being that was led by Li Tzuch'eng (1605?–45), a rebellious and ambitious Shensi freebooter.[199] The government, under pressure from the Manchus in the north, responded to Li's insurrection weakly and ineptly. In 1642 Schall was called away from his calendrical studies and in desperation the emperor ordered him to manufacture cannon. In the provinces many of the other European priests as well as their converts clung steadfastly to the weakened government, for they were appalled by the prospect of "barbaric" Manchus and corrupt insurrectionists overrunning the country and putting out the light of Chinese civilization as they knew it. Li, aided by some of his associates within the city, entered Peking on April 25, 1644, without meeting serious resistance. The betrayed emperor ordered his three sons to hide and then hanged himself on "Coal Hill" to the north of the imperial palace. Once the dynasty collapsed, the Ming army of the north under Wu San-kuei (1612–78) combined with the Manchus to defeat Li and his revolutionary forces. The imperial city, subject to terror throughout the spring of 1644, welcomed the Manchus as deliverers.[200]

Schall was the only Jesuit eyewitness to these momentous events. On October 30, 1644, he was there when the Manchus proclaimed the Ch'ing dynasty and the Shun-chih emperor. Several months later the new emperor adopted the Western calendar officially.[201] The proclamation of a new dynasty in Peking did not end the resistance of the Chinese in the provinces. Success in extending Manchu rule was confined in the first year of its existence to the four northern provinces of Chihli, Shantung, Shansi, and Shensi. Mastery and pacification of the rest of China required almost twenty years; the last of the Ming pretenders was not driven from the empire until 1659. The Jesuits and many of their converts were confronted by the inescapable and painful necessity of taking sides. Schall, like most of the other

[199] See the article on him by Tu Lien-che in Hummel, *op. cit.* (n. 157), I, 491–93.
[200] See Dunne, *op. cit.* (n. 153), pp. 316–22.
[201] For the relevant documents see Fu Lo-shu (trans. and ed.), *A Documentary Chronicle of Sino-Western Relations (1644–1820)* (2 vols., Tucson, Ariz., 1966), I, 3–5.

witnesses to the disaster which swept Peking, quickly began to cooperate with the new order and came to enjoy the favor of its leaders. He was shortly appointed director of the new Imperial Board of Astronomy, the successor to the defunct Calendrical Bureau. While a few of the Jesuits approved of Schall's collaboration, those in the south continued to work with the Ming loyalists and other enemies of the Manchus.[202]

The Ch'ing conquest was not a victory for the Manchus alone. After 1644 Chinese collaborators of every social level worked with them. From the time of the Manchu occupation of Liaotung in 1621, the local Chinese had allied themselves militarily with the Manchus and had helped to teach them about life and culture south of the Great Wall. Wu San-kuei and other Chinese military leaders from Liaotung put the remnants of the northern Ming army at the disposal of the Ch'ing. Wu fought on the side of the Manchus for the next thirty years and was accorded high honors by them. Other Liaotung military collaborators were rewarded with feudatories in the south and their children were permitted to intermarry with members of the imperial clan. While they suffered severely from massacres, land confiscations, and fiscal exactions, the Chinese were most outraged by the order to grow queues and to shave their heads in the Manchu manner. The offense felt with respect to this requirement was mitigated somewhat for the proud Chinese by the easing of the tax burden and by the economic recovery of the country's most productive areas after 1650.[203] The most stubborn regional resistance to the Ch'ing pacification program came from the Cheng family that had dominated the Fukien coast since the 1620's.[204]

Throughout these tumultuous years the Christian missionaries increasingly fought among themselves both in China and Europe. The story of the Portuguese Jesuit, Gabriel de Magalhães (1610–77), epitomizes some of the issues that began to divide the Jesuits. While the Manchus were approaching Peking, he and Lodovico Buglio (1606–82), a Sicilian Jesuit, were in distant Szechwan where they were taken prisoner and forced to work for Chang Hsien-chung (1605–47), a local rebel and aspirant to imperial power. The two missionaries were rescued in 1647 by the arrival in Szechwan of an advance guard from the Manchu army. Its commander, on learning the priests were colleagues of Schall, carried them off to Peking in 1648. There they were branded as collaborators of Chang and confined to prison. Although Schall tried to help them, he was warned by friends and the minister in charge to refrain from interfering with the legal process.

After two years of imprisonment the Jesuits were released into the custody of a Manchu official and given the status of slaves. While their master

---

[202] Dunne, *op. cit.* (n. 153), pp. 322–25. The Board of Astronomy is also sometimes referred to in English as the Bureau of Mathematics.

[203] Based on the summary in J. E. Wills, Jr., *Pepper, Guns, and Parleys* (Cambridge, Mass., 1974), pp. 11–12.

[204] *Ibid.*, pp. 15–17.

allowed them practical freedom, Magalhães complained, as he had before, that Schall was responsible for their plight. He soon won others over to his view, and in 1649 was joined by Furtado, Longobardo, Buglio, and Ferreira in framing a petition urging the provincial to dismiss Schall from the Society. Schall, who was a blunt and outspoken person, had probably offended his less prominent, and possibly jealous, colleagues. As an official of the empire, he had readily adopted the mandarin life-style. He was reputedly on friendly terms personally with the Shun-chih emperor and had adopted a Chinese child as his grandson. Charges of disrespect to superiors, of holding an office not appropriate to a priest, and of leading an unchaste life were leveled against Schall by his detractors. Eventually he was saved from expulsion by an investigating committee of three consultators who exonerated him completely in 1653. Echos of this internecine imbroglio continued to be heard in Europe long thereafter.[205]

A less personal vendetta went on contemporaneously between the Jesuits who supported the Ming pretenders and those who had made their peace with the Manchus. Hope for a Ming restoration had reached a high point in 1648 when all of the southern provinces, except Fukien, were temporarily freed of Ch'ing authority. In this same year most members of the pretender's family were converted to Christianity, thus giving the Jesuits a greater stake than ever in the restoration of the Ming dynasty. This short-lived Ming resurgence was followed by swift retaliation from the north and by the final capitulation of Canton on November 24, 1650. Driven westward by the Ch'ing armies, the last pretender set up court at Anlung in Kweichou province. Andreas Köffler (1612–52), an Austrian Jesuit, was stationed at the court as spiritual adviser to its Christians and was joined there for a short period in 1650 by Michael Boym (1612–59), a Polish priest. Boym was sent to Rome in 1651 accompanied by André Cheng, a Chinese convert. The Polish Father was charged with delivering letters from the Christian empress dowager Helena to Pope Innocent X and the Jesuit general in which she asked their prayers for the Ming cause and requested the dispatch of more missionaries to China.

After taking the overland route from Goa to the Mediterranean, the two Christian messengers arrived at Venice in December, 1652. Because he posed as a legate of the Ming in his interview before the Doge, Boym was reprimanded by Jesuit General Goswin Nickel. The two envoys received a cold reception in Rome where they waited for three years without receiving a papal interview. The enemies of the China Jesuits, and they were numerous in Europe by this time, accused Boym of being a fraud who had never even been to China. Finally, in 1655, Pope Alexander VII (r. 1655–67) and the Jesuit general penned replies to the letters they brought. Boym and

---

[205] For a lengthy *apologia* on Schall's behalf see Dunne, *op. cit.* (n. 153), pp. 325–38.

Cheng left Lisbon in 1656, but the replies never reached China, for Boym died in 1659 before reaching there. The Ming cause died the same year.[206]

Boym's experience in Europe illustrates how intense and bitter the conflict over the Asian missions had become. The papacy, which did not then recognize the independence of Portugal, had supported unswervingly the losing cause of Spain. While the war with Portugal went on, Spain was forced in 1648 to recognize the independence of the Dutch Republic and in 1659 to make peace with France. The China Jesuits, still dependent upon the goodwill of the Portuguese, were caught in this crossfire and several others. The Dominicans, Franciscans, as well as certain fathers of the Propaganda, were unrelenting in their condemnation of the Jesuit position on the Chinese rites. J. B. de Morales, the Dominican who had been stationed in Fukien, appeared at Rome to present the position of the friars on the rites question. By a decree of 1645 the Congregation of the Propaganda ordained that certain of the Confucian rites might not be performed by Chinese converts.[207]

In response to this action the Jesuits sent Martino Martini (1614–61) to Europe in 1650 to present their case. Political conditions being very chaotic in southern China, Martini left from Fukien rather than Macao and eventually was taken to Batavia as a prisoner of the Dutch. Finally he made it by sea to Bergen, Norway, and then overland to Rome. Arrived there in 1654, Martini argued ably that the import of the rites had been misrepresented by mendicants whose experience of China had been limited and superficial. He then explained in detail Ricci's characterization of the rites as civil ceremonies without religious content. A decree of 1656 from the Congregation of the Inquisition permitted the rites on condition that they were indeed civil in nature as the Jesuits claimed. The earlier condemnatory decree continued in force if the rites were indeed religious as the friars alleged they were. The lines were thus drawn in Europe for each side to prove its case to the satisfaction of the Christian community at large.[208]

Things went well in Peking for a number of years after Schall was cleared in 1653 of the charges leveled against him by his fellow Jesuits. His friendship with the emperor and his position as director of the Board of Astronomy, while being discussed adversely in Europe as a role unsuited to a priest and missionary, guaranteed security to the missionaries in Peking and elsewhere where Manchu authority prevailed. When a Dutch embassy visited Peking in 1656–57, its members were astonished to see how highly the emperor esteemed the Jesuit. Schall was swiftly advanced in grade until he reached the pinnacle of the bureaucratic hierarchy on February 2, 1658; he

---

[206] *Ibid.*, pp. 340–46.

[207] For details see A. S. Rosso, O.F.M., *Apostolic Legations to China of the Eighteenth Century* (South Pasadena, Cal., 1948), pp. 110–13. On J. B. de Morales before the Propaganda see *SCPFMR*, Vol. I/I, pp. 192–93.

[208] *SCPFMR*, Vol. I/I, pp. 296–99.

was named Imperial Chamberlain and a mandarin of the first class, first division. In his conversations with the young emperor, Schall broached the subject of Christianity. Like many other intellectuals of China, the emperor listened attentively and respectfully to the priest's explanations of Christian teachings. And, like many before him, he became intellectually interested but remained personally unwilling to embrace the faith. Schall proclaimed that monogamy was the stumbling-block for "he could not overcome the lust of the flesh." [209] During the last few years of his life, the young emperor turned away from Schall and established closer ties with the Buddhist-eunuch party at the court.

The Jesuits had lost personnel and property during the civil wars. In these years many of their great pioneers died natural deaths; the venerable Longobardo passed to his reward in 1655 at the age of ninety-five. The Christian communities of Fukien, including those founded by the friars, suffered most, for they were victimized along with the entire population of the province's coastal region by the drastic measures taken by the Ch'ing to defeat the rebellious Cheng Ch'eng-kung (Koxinga). [210] Elsewhere, however, the established missions made rapid gains in the work of conversion. The Ch'ing government generally assumed a benign attitude toward all Christian activity. The Spanish Dominicans opened a new mission in Chekiang in 1655 and another in Shantung five years later. Even Buglio and Magalhães, previously Schall's personal enemies, worked quietly in the capital as they enjoyed the calm brought on by his influence. Schall himself received a reinforcement in 1660 when Ferdinand Verbiest (1623–88), a Belgian astronomer, arrived in Peking to assist him.

The death of the Shun-chih emperor in February, 1661, brought an end to these halcyon days. Resentment of the Jesuits, long smoldering, flared into the open. Both Chinese and Manchus had watched critically and closely during the period of dynastic transition the diverse roles taken by the Jesuits in serving the Ch'ing victors, the Ming loyalists, and local rebels. They also suspected that the Jesuits with their connections to Macao and the Portuguese were politically more ambitious than they pretended. Manchu officials in the capital had disliked the close relationship of Schall and the emperor, and saw it as alien and unhealthy. The four Manchu regents for the seven-year-old K'ang-hsi emperor shared the bureaucratic and military hostility to Schall and his fellow Jesuits. The so-called Oboi regency (1661–69), which ruled collectively for the first five years of its existence, was quick to order the imperial commissioners in the provinces to investigate Jesuit activities and to report back to Peking. [211]

A new antimissionary movement was spearheaded by Yang Kuang-hsien

---

[209] As quoted in Dunne, *op. cit.* (n. 153), p. 351.
[210] See above, p. 60.
[211] See R. B. Oxnam, *Ruling from Horseback. Manchu Politics in the Oboi Regency, 1661–69* (Chicago, 1975), p. 148.

(1597–1669), a firebrand and a self-appointed campaigner against Christianity in China.[212] In documents submitted to the Board of Rites he charged Schall with making errors in his astronomical calculations, an accusation reported by disgruntled Muslim proponents of traditional astronomy. He claimed that the missionaries were teaching false and subversive ideas to the people and plotting the overthrow of the new dynasty. Like earlier detractors, he accused the missionaries of practicing magic and of plotting revolt in their conventicles. Open persecution of the Christians began in 1661 and went on to 1664 in Szechwan, Hukwang, Kiangsi, and Shantung. In these provinces churches were destroyed, missionaries arrested, and converts imprisoned and even executed.[213] In the capital the charges against Schall and his cohorts were ignored until the regent Oboi began personally taking over the direction of government. A staunch Manchu soldier, Oboi distrusted the Chinese bureaucracy and determined to eliminate all vestiges of the Ming era still remaining, including the missionaries.

Yang Kuang-hsien, supported now by Oboi, published in 1664 a powerful attack on the Jesuits. He condemned Schall as a "posthumous follower of Jesus, who had been the ringleader of the treacherous bandits of the kingdom of Judea."[214] He alleged the Christians falsely taught that the Chinese were descended from the Hebrews, an alien tribal people. The regents, alarmed that the Christians were fomenting rebellion as Yang claimed, arrested Schall, the other Jesuits in Peking, and certain of their Chinese associates. A spectacular trial nine months in length was conducted during 1664–65. On April 30, 1665, the regents announced their verdict: Schall and seven Chinese were condemned to death. Verbiest, Buglio, and Magalhães were to be flogged and deported. The Jesuits and two of the Chinese won a reprieve when an earthquake that rocked Peking on May 1 was interpreted as a sign of heavenly displeasure with the outcome of the trial. The four Jesuits were permitted to remain in Peking, but their cohorts in the provinces were officially exiled. Twenty-five Jesuits, four Dominicans, and one Franciscan were kept in detention at Canton until 1671; three Dominicans remained in hiding in Fukien.[215] All churches in the empire were closed, and the Chinese converts were placed under heavy surveillance. It was not until the K'ang-hsi emperor took over personal command of the empire in 1669 that the Christian movement regained a substantial freedom.

[212] For his biography see the article by Fang Chao-ying in Hummel, *op. cit.* (n. 157).

[213] See Oxnam, *op. cit.* (n. 211), p. 149.

[214] As quoted in *ibid.*

[215] See Dunne, *op. cit.* (n. 153), p. 363. The single Spanish Franciscan imprisoned at Canton was Antonio Caballero de Santa Maria (1602–69), the best known of the Franciscans to work in China during the seventeenth century. He was a friend of Schall and was understanding of the Jesuit position in the rites controversy. See A. Väth, "P. F. Antonio Caballero de Santa Maria über die Mission der Jesuiten und anderen Orden in China," *AHSI*, I (1932), 291–92. For his portrait see Cummins, *loc. cit.* (n. 172), facing p. 108.

In China, as elsewhere in the East, the *padroado* and the Portuguese secular authority were on the defensive by the 1660's. From the beginning of the century the Spanish missionaries had violated the jurisdictions and challenged the authority of the *padroado* in Asia. King Philip III generally supported the Spanish missionaries and interceded with the papacy on their behalf from time to time.[216] Beginning with the expulsion of the missionaries from Japan in 1614, Rome itself began to take a more direct interest in supervising the mission in the East. Members of the curia, such as Cardinal Robert Bellarmine, supported the accommodation policies followed by Ricci and Nobili despite the strictures of the Portuguese clergy against them. The founding of the Congregation for the Propagation of the Faith in 1622 brought into being a central agency that increasingly threatened Portugal's authority over the missions. In a reaction to Rome's new initiative, the Habsburg rulers of Spain and Portugal tightened royal control over mission activities in the East, and unseemly conflicts occurred between the Goa authorities and the agents of the Propaganda. The pope's decision of 1633 to end the restriction that required missionaries to travel exclusively through Lisbon coincided with the demise of the Portuguese India Company. This was followed by growing unrest in Portugal with the Habsburg rule. When Japan cut off all trade with Macao in 1638, the financial base of the Portuguese mission in East Asia was shattered. Macao and the mission received further shocks when trade with Manila ended in 1640 and when Malacca fell to the Dutch in 1641.

The Portuguese war of independence brought with it a cessation of formal relations between the *padroado* and the papacy from 1640 to 1668. Clashes over ecclesiastical authority in the East became more numerous and vindictive. Portuguese bishops died off and their sees were left vacant. The military decline of Portugal in the East forced many of the friars at endangered or conquered outposts to leave their stations and congregate at Goa. Propaganda missionaries, and vicars apostolic after 1658, began to assume authority over decadent *padroado* dioceses, especially in continental Southeast Asia.[217] In south India the St. Thomas Christians revolted against the *padroado* bishops in 1652–53. The losses of Ceylon and the Malabar cities to the Dutch reduced Goa's authority in south India to a shadowy jurisdiction by the 1660's. Those Catholic missionaries who were thereafter permitted to work in Dutch-controlled areas were non-Portuguese.

The serious decline of *padroado* authority was closely related to missionizing policies. In the settlements directly under Portuguese control the policy of Europeanization of the converts was heavily dependent upon the state. When Portugal's secular control weakened or vanished, the Christian enterprises likewise lost out. In the stations outside of Portuguese control, the

[216] See above, p. 134, and below, pp. 266–267.
[217] For discussion of the missions in continental Southeast Asia see below, pp. 232–50.

missions languished for want of financial support, and in Bengal, south India, and China they had to depend on the continuing support of their loyal native converts. Nowhere in the mission field, not even in "accommodationist" China, had the Europeans encouraged the growth of a native clergy. Of the 184 Jesuits who worked in China between 1600 and 1649, 14 were Chinese, 2 Japanese, 1 Korean, and 1 Chinese-Korean; they were all classified as brothers, for the Society refused to consider Chinese mature enough in the faith for ordination.[218] In India a native secular clergy began to be numerous only as the friars became fewer and less devoted to the ministry. A remnant survived in Ceylon during the Dutch period of moderate control. In Japan, where a substantial number of natives had been trained as lay catechists, the Christian community endured despite official persecution. Christianity likewise survived in the interior of south India after the death of Nobili with the aid of native *pandaraswamis* (religious workers) and lay catechists recruited for mission work and despite political turbulence.

The Jesuits were especially responsible for introducing non-Portuguese missionaries into the *padroado*. The friars and the secular hierarchy were solidly Portuguese in background, many from Lisbon and its environs, or Luso-Asians and Europeans recruited in the East. In the first six decades of the seventeenth century, Jesuits of Italian background became particularly prominent: Valignano, Ricci, Nobili, Longobardo, Vagnone, Aleni, and Martini. The Italians were also the leading proponents of the adaptation policy, and they had powerful friends in Rome who supported their innovations in the field. Before 1660 they were joined by Lowlanders (Trigault and Verbiest), Germans (Schreck and Schall), Austrians (Köffler), and Poles (Boym) who assumed leading roles in the mission. João de Britto, the martyred Jesuit and saint, was the only prominent Portuguese to follow the policy of adaptation during the years of his apostolate in south India.

The Portuguese crown, always anxious about its primacy, sought to limit the number of foreigners admitted to the mission; the Portuguese were especially suspicious of the Spanish and successfully excluded them from direct participation in the *padroado* after 1600. The China mission, in particular, was international in character and became even more so during the K'ang-hsi period (1661–1723). Although the Portuguese had never enjoyed a perfect monopoly in the *padroado,* they constantly struggled after 1665 to maintain even a modicum of authority. While Lisbon won a technical victory in the 1690's in reasserting its authority over the China mission, the claims of the *padroado* continued to be hotly contested both in Europe and Asia. On the initiative of the Propaganda, the bishoprics of Nanking and Peking were created in 1690, thus removing most of China from the ecclesiastical jurisdiction of Macao. The new bishoprics were, however, to remain subject to the metropolitan see of Goa in a bow to Portuguese sensi-

---

[218] See Duncan, *op. cit.* (n. 14), p. 366.

tivity on the subject of the *padroado*. Gradually even this concession eroded as the vicars apostolic continued to maintain control over a part of the China mission.[219] On paper at least, the *padroado* continued to function in India until October 25, 1953.[220]

4

THE SPANISH "PATRONATO" OF THE EAST

Like the Portuguese *padroado*, the Spanish *patronato real* represented the elevation of medieval systems of noble and royal church patronage to the national level. Through a series of bulls issued in 1493, and again in 1508, the papacy had charged the Spanish crown with the spiritual conquest of the New World. In its turn the crown entrusted the mission to the regular clergy. The geographical extent of the *patronato* was left vague, and the conditions for its operation were defined empirically over time. The king was obligated to provide financial support and protection to the church in its overseas possessions, so the missionaries were carried aboard royal ships to America, the Philippines, and the Moluccas. Once they were engaged in mission work, the crown through its colonial agents provided stipends for the maintenance of the missionaries and allowances for their missions, churches, schools, orphanages, and hospitals. As the crown's power became more centralized in Iberia itself, royal control over ecclesiastical activities in the colonies tightened correspondingly.

The *patronato*, originally a specific apostolic concession by the papacy to the crown, had evolved by the seventeenth century into a royal vicariate. Spanish political theorists alleged that the *patronato*, once granted, was irrevocable and was invested solely and exclusively in the crown. While the papacy rejected the royal claims to total authority over the colonial church and placed on the *Index* the books of the royal political theorists, there was little that it could do in practice to limit the crown's control. In the Philippines, especially, the crown ruled the ecclesiastical establishment by decree. Treated as an agency of the crown, the church in the Philippines took advantage of its political position to exert a profound influence upon the formation of government policies and their enforcement.[221]

---

[219] See the table of the various nationalities in the China mission in Dehergne, *op. cit.* (n. 86), pp. 398–401. On the vicars apostolic in China see below, pp. 262–69.

[220] See F. de Almeida, *História da igreja em Portugal* (4 vols., new ed., Barcelos, 1968), II, 41–42.

[221] For a general discussion of the status of the religious orders in the *patronato* see W. E. Shield, S.J., *King and Church. The Rise and Fall of the Patronato Real* (Chicago, 1961), chap. xiii. Also see the article on the Philippines by H. de la Costa, S.J., in the *New Catholic Encyclopedia* (Washington, 1967), XI, 280–84.

Spanish Augustinians inaugurated Christian work in the Bisayan Philippines during 1565. After the establishment of Manila in 1571 as the Spanish headquarters in Asia, Franciscans (1577), Jesuits (1581), and Dominicans (1581) began working in the Philippines. In 1578 Manila was raised to the status of an episcopal see suffragan to Mexico; two years earlier Macao had received its elevation to a bishopric dependent on Goa. Rivalry and jurisdictional disputes between the two new bishoprics grew steadily, despite the fact that both the *padroado* and the *patronato* were after 1580 the overseas ecclesiastical agencies of the same Spanish Habsburgs. The Portuguese and Spanish each claimed that the other was guilty of trespass in the insular East. Philip II, who was bound by the provisions of the Union of Tomar to administer the two empires separately, regularly turned down the appeals from Manila for royal sanction to send missionaries, and even military expeditions, to the Jesuit preserves of Japan and China within the *padroado*.[222]

The Dominican Domingo de Salazar (r. 1581–1592) was appointed first bishop of Manila. Between 1582 and 1586 he summoned into session a synod of representatives from the orders to meet with the Dean of the Cathedral in an effort to resolve many of the problems which the church encountered in the conquest, settlement, and administration of the Philippines. Questions had been raised in both Europe and Asia about the propriety of the church's part in the military conquest of the islands and their peoples. The synod concluded that the Spaniards and the missionaries had acted correctly in subjecting the inhabitants to a just, temporal rule for the purpose of bringing them to Christianity.[223] With respect to mission methods, the synod made no fundamental decisions except to ordain that natives were to be instructed on the catechism in their own languages and not in Spanish.[224] Otherwise the Spanish missionaries employed the techniques of evangelizing followed in Mexico and the West Indies: that is, Hispanization of indigenous institutions, mores, social practices, and religious beliefs.[225]

The Christianizing of the Philippines proved to be a long and arduous task. To bring better governance to the growing church, Manila was erected in 1595 into an archdiocese with suffragan dioceses at Nueva Segovia (Cagayan), Nueva Caceres (Camarines), and Santisimo Nombre de Jesus (Cebu). The crown, in order to minimize friction and duplication of effort, decreed in 1594 that no two orders might work within the same province and that each missionary group should have its own region to evangelize.[226] Royal commands also prohibited missionaries from evangelizing without a knowl-

---

[222] For the founding years of the mission see *Asia*, I, 296–301, 306–9.

[223] See H. de la Costa, S.J., *The Jesuits in the Philippines, 1581–1768* (2d ed., Cambridge, Mass., 1967), pp. 23–28.

[224] *Ibid.*, p. 35.

[225] See J. L. Phelan, *The Hispanization of the Philippines* (Madison, Wis., 1959), especially chap. iii.

[226] See K. S. Latourette, *A History of the Expansion of Christianity* (New York, 1939), III, 310.

edge of the language or languages native to their region of activity. Progress was swift in the lowlands and in non-Muslim areas. Converts from the scattered clan villages were enticed or coerced to leave their rice fields and to resettle into larger communities to make supervision easier. Mission schools, chapels, and medical centers were built in the new Christian communities. Before 1600 Manila had three hospitals: one each for Spaniards, Chinese, and natives.

By 1595 more than 450 regular clerics had embarked for the islands,[227] and a large percentage of them got there; still, priests were universally in short supply, even in the Manila area. Many of the missionaries persisted in hoping that they might be sent to Japan or continental Southeast Asia to break new ground for the faith in less primitive countries. Those regulars who worked gladly in the Philippines constantly chafed against the bishops' claims of authority to supervise them in their roles as parish priests. Theoretically, once a mission had become a smoothly running parish, the regulars were expected to turn it over to secular priests for pastoral care. But the shortage of parish priests and their lack of training in the native languages made the Spanish regulars irreplaceable. In their capacity as parish priests, the regulars feared that willing acceptance of episcopal visitations and discipline would endanger their corporate unity and possibly subject them to conflicting orders from bishop and provincial. It was primarily in the Manila region, where Christianity had put down its roots most firmly, that the issue between the regular and secular hierarchies was most impassioned. The episcopacy and the seculars recognized tacitly that in most of the islands the regular missionary-priest remained essential to the preservation of the gains already registered in the flatlands. In the mountains the people remained pagan, and in the southernmost islands the natives were pagans or Muslims barely touched by the Europeans. In 1606 the regular clergy received reinforcements from the Augustinian Recollects, a Spanish contemplative order.

Missionary statistics on numbers of converts are usually suspect and often at great variance with one another. This is particularly true of figures from the Philippines. From the approximations available it appears that at first converts (or pacified natives) were few, and mainly children. With the arrival of larger numbers of regulars, progress became more rapid, the first decisive period of success coming between 1576 and 1586. By 1594 there were 267 regulars in the Philippines and the number of baptized natives was claimed to be 286,000.[228] In 1598, according to Governor Tello's report to the king, there were 395 regulars working in the Philippines: 299 priests,

---

[227] See the list in F. J. Montalbán, S.J., *Das spanische Patronat und die Eroberung der Philippinen* (Freiburg im Breisgau, 1930), p. 108.

[228] See Phelan, *op. cit.* (n. 225), p. 56. In 1597 the Franciscans claimed 243,568 souls. See A. Abad, "Los Franciscanos en Filipinas, 1578–1898," *Revista de Indias*, XXIV, nos. 97–98 (1964), 416.

and 96 lay brothers.[229] By 1600, there were 15 Jesuit priests and their lay brothers ministering to 12,696 Christians in ten different mission stations.[230] By the end of the sixteenth century about one-half of the inhabitants in the conquered territories had been baptized.[231]

The Spanish Jesuits of the Philippines never enjoyed a monopoly of the mission, for it was a state enterprise designed to pacify the islands. The Augustinian and Franciscan pioneers worked primarily in the Tagalog country of Luzon (in Ilocos, Pampanga, and the Camarines), in the Bicol-speaking region south of Manila, and in Cebu and Panay. The Dominicans built most of their parishes in the provinces of Cagayan, Ilocos, and Pangasinan in northern Luzon and replaced the Augustinians as ministers to the Chinese of Manila. The Jesuits, who had mainly performed mission tours until 1590, began thereafter to build permanent stations, first in Manila and its vicinity and after 1593 in the eastern Visayan islands of Cebu, Negros, Leyte, Bohol, and Samar. The Augustinian Recollects ministered to communities scattered throughout the archipelago.

All the orders had religious establishments and missions in Manila, a city of about six thousand inhabitants at the beginning of the century. Antonio de Morga, an administrator and layman, describes the religious establishments of the city as they were before his departure in 1607: the cathedral, the Augustinian friary, the Dominican priory, the friary of St. Francis, and the Jesuit College of San José.[232] In their compound the Jesuits opened around 1595 a grammar school for Spanish boys.[233] It was not until 1611 that the Dominican University of Santo Tomas began to function, an institution which still exists in Manila.

While the missionaries were partners to the conquest, they were generally critical of the harsh treatment meted out by the Spanish soldiers and officials to the *indios* (pure-blooded Filipinos; also Christian Filipinos as opposed to Muslim Filipinos or Moros). The ordinary soldiers often preyed upon the helpless, for they received no salary or rations when not actively on a campaign. The clergy accepted without demur the proposition that the *indios* should be taxed to pay for the "saving faith" being brought to them. The priests complained, however, that the tax rates were exorbitant and reported to Europe that the land and the people were too poor to pay the burdensome levies laid upon them. Bishop Salazar was ardent in championing native rights in his reports to the king, and he excoriated the harsh methods followed in collecting tribute and in the recruitment of natives for forced labor

---

[229] See Luz Ausejo, "The Philippines in the Sixteenth Century," (Ph.D. diss., Dept. of History, Univ. of Chicago, 1972), p. 478.

[230] See De la Costa, *op. cit.* (n. 223), p. 187, and the maps on pp. 108, 147.

[231] See Ausejo, *op. cit.* (n. 229), p. 502.

[232] See J. S. Cummins (ed. and trans.), *Antonio de Morga. Sucesos de las Islas Filipinas* (Cambridge, 1971), in "HS," 2d ser., CXL, 284.

[233] For a map of the Jesuit compound in the old walled city see De la Costa, *op. cit.* (n. 223), p. 193.

and military services. He successfully inveighed against the enslavement of the *indios*.[234] The governors and royal officials denied the accusations of the clerics, and Morga, in a report of 1598 to the king, charged the missionaries with immorality, illicit trading, deliberate misinterpretation of royal orders, and bad treatment of the *indios* in their charge. The Augustinians were singled out by others as particularly poor representatives of the faith.[235]

The missionaries were at first not clear as to the king's plans for the Philippines, and for a long time they remained hopeful that Luzon might be used primarily as a launching pad for missions to Japan, China, and Southeast Asia. The physical features of the archipelago, the dispersion of its peoples, and the scarcity of priests deterred the extension of the missions to the southern islands. In 1586 the only Spanish settlements ouside of Luzon with resident priests were those of Cebu and Arevalo. From the beginning the missionaries sought no mass conversions and insisted that the Filipinos be instructed in basic Christian tenets before being baptized.[236] Both the Dominicans and Franciscans impressed the *indios* by their patience, charity, and poverty. All the orders won the hearts of the *indios* by their willingness to learn and their ability to teach in the language of the people with whom they worked. By royal decree, Castilian was used as an auxiliary language in the mission stations and was required for natives interested in becoming brothers and priests. Key Christian concepts, such as God, Trinity, and the names of the sacraments were retained in their Spanish form to avoid confusion arising over Christian and pagan terms. In the Philippines, as in Japan, the "term question" never provoked the controversy that surrounded it in China.[237]

While the mission expanded constantly among the people of the conquered territories, problems related to the pagan past plagued the fathers. Too often the converts saw Christianity mainly as a new form of magic to effect miraculous cures or to exorcise demons. The *indios* frequently identified the missionaries as a better brand of *baglons* and *katalonans*, the traditional medicine men. The Spanish demanded from their converts a complete severance from the idols, spirit-houses, rites, and superstitions of the past. To preserve their position the medicine men threatened the converts and went into hiding to escape the retaliation of the Spaniards. The requirement of monogamy, here as elsewhere, was regularly a stumbling block in the way of the conversion of chieftains and men of substance. The male convert was required to give up all but his first wife, and with the dismissal of the other wives went the loss of the dowries they had brought with them. The priests

---

[234] See Ausejo, *op. cit.* (n. 229), pp. 444–59.
[235] See Cummins (ed. and trans.), *op. cit.* (n. 232), p. 289, n. 1.
[236] See J. L. Phelan, "Pre-Baptismal Instructions and the Administration of Baptism in the Philippines during the Sixteenth Century," *The Americas,* XII (1955–56), 5.
[237] Based on Ausejo, *op. cit.* (n. 229), pp. 479–91.

inveighed against what they saw as the "immoralities" of the natives. Unchaste women were denounced and unusual sexual devices prohibited; women who protected their virginity against native or Spaniard were praised openly. The Spanish, who were not permitted by law to hold slaves themselves, tried vainly to deprive the *indios* of their slaves and to prevent the continuation of the practice.

To reach the active adult population the fathers concentrated on teaching the children and older men. Most of the villagers willingly sent their children to mission schools to learn reading, writing, and music as well as the catechism. The most apt pupils and the sons of chieftains acted as assistants in the Christian services and were groomed to teach others the fundamentals of the new faith. The Jesuits, in particular, sought the conversion of the chieftains and other social leaders as the base for an elite lay group that would act as a moral and religious catalyst to the society at large, a technique followed everywhere by the Jesuit apostolate. Confraternities and sodalities were organized to perform special devotions, to undertake charitable works, and to support the social reforms, such as monogamy, advocated by the missionaries.[238] The rituals, sacraments, and celebrations of the church were attuned to native interests and inclinations. Since confession was enthusiastically accepted by the *indios,* the priests prescribed those penances, such as scourgings, which seemed to be preferred. On feast days grand processions, banquets, and choral programs in the native language greatly attracted people who enjoyed few other forms of innocent amusement.[239]

As the century progressed, the Spanish Jesuits took the initiative away from the other orders in opening new mission stations. Organizationally the Philippines were initially a vice-province of the Society under the Province of Mexico. The Jesuits in the Philippines, as they began in the 1590's to erect permanent establishments, argued that a mission so far from Mexico and Europe could be properly administered only by a superior with the powers of a provincial. In 1602 Pedro Chirino (1558–1635) was sent to Rome as procurator of the vice-province with instructions to inform General Acquaviva about the great progress and resources of the mission and of its desire for independence from Mexico. Chirino's report of 1604 on the future of the mission was so rosy that Acquaviva ordered him to write it up for publication.[240] The general, convinced by Chirino's account that the mission was viable and promising, agreed in 1605 to its elevation to the status of full-fledged province.[241] Perhaps this decision reveals something about the preferences of Philip III and his influence in Rome, for the flourishing Japa-

---

[238] See De la Costa, *op. cit.* (n. 223), p. 201.
[239] Based on Ausejo, *op. cit.* (n. 229), pp. 493–503.
[240] On Chirino's book published in 1604 by the press of Estaban Paulino at Rome see below, p. 372.
[241] See De la Costa, *op. cit.* (n. 223), pp. 221–22.

nese mission of the Portuguese Jesuits did not receive full recognition as a separate province until three years later.[242]

The Jesuits were always short of trained men to carry on the necessary works of education and proselytizing. The province sent procurators to Europe every six years or so to seek reinforcements for the mission. Infusions of new blood were injected into the mission in 1615, 1622, 1626, 1632, 1636, and 1643. Most impressive in terms of the numbers of recruits was the last of these transfusions: forty-two missionaries from twelve of the European provinces of the Society. Previously almost all the missionaries had come from the Spanish and Italian provinces, with the Spaniards being far more numerous. By the late 1630's the widespread demand upon Spain for missionaries had drained its provinces of men and money. With the Portuguese, Catalan, and Neapolitan revolts of the 1640's, increasing pressure from the Dutch both in Europe and Asia, and a plague that ravaged Andalusia, the Jesuits were forced to recruit more missionaries in Belgium, Germany, Austria, and Italy. In 1656, fifty years after its establishment, a grand total of 272 Jesuits had entered the Philippine province from abroad: 151 priests, 98 scholastics, and 23 lay brothers.[243] No record exists of any *indio* or mestizo member of the Society, either lay brother or priest, before the expulsion of the Jesuits from the Philippines in 1768.[244] Europeans, including creoles born in the Philippines, were the only local persons accepted for admission to the Society.

In the first half of the century, as the province grew in numbers, its responsibilities and activities likewise increased. In the peak year of 1643, the 133 Jesuits of the province ministered to five colleges and eleven residences. Thereafter the number of missionaries began to decline and the available personnel had to be spread more and more thinly over the stations. Meanwhile enthusiasm for the mission had begun to wane, dissension had grown more open between European and creole Jesuits and between Jesuit and Dominican educators, and expulsions from the Society had become more numerous. Controversy brought to the surface the differing practices being followed by the Jesuits at their Tagalog and Bisayan stations. Jesuit financial investments in the Manila area had prospered along with the galleon and expanding entrepôt trade of the city. Although the Dutch made many efforts to cripple the trade and destroy the city, Manila's affluence grew until it was stricken by the disasters of the 1640's: severance of the Macao trade, frequent interruptions of the galleon trade, and the earthquake of 1645. In the Bisayas the resentment of the *indios* mounted as new exactions of forced labor were decreed in 1649. During the following years the Spanish had to put down a series of revolts that swept the Bisayan missions.

[242] See above, p. 168.
[243] Based on De la Costa, *op. cit.* (n. 223), pp. 223–26.
[244] *Ibid.*, p. 234.

Spanish and Christian pacification of the maritime sectors of Luzon and the Bisayan islands was virtually completed by mid-century. A few Christian footholds then existed also along the northern coast of Mindanao. In the Bisayas, where Moro attacks were an omnipresent danger, the Christian settlements were often located a short distance inland for protection against the seaborne invasions of slave-hunting Muslims. By 1655 the Jesuits ministered to fifty-nine parishes, most of them in the bishopric of Cebu, with three others on Mindanao. The Franciscans then possessed fifty-three parishes mainly in central Luzon and the Camarines. The Dominicans continued to maintain their parishes, eighteen in number, in northern Luzon and at Manila; they increasingly centered their activity in Manila and its charitable institutions. The Augustinians, whose early ascendancy in the mission deteriorated from internal malaise and a curious lack of interest in the Philippines, managed fifty-six parishes running south from the Ilocos to Panay and Cebu. The Augustinian Recollects supported eleven missions, four of which were on Mindanao, with others widely scattered in isolated and sometimes hostile regions.[245]

The European crisis experienced by Spain from 1640 to 1668 was reflected in the abrupt decline of Manila's prosperity.[246] Magino Solá (1695–1664), a young Jesuit, was dispatched to Madrid in 1658 to memorialize the throne on the losses being suffered in the Philippines with the slowdown and interruption of the galleon trade. His suggestions for expanding the trade set off a great debate in Spain between the Christian orders and the textile interests on the feasibility and desirability of maintaining the Philippines. Contemporaneously the issue, long smoldering, between the seculars and regulars in the Philippines again broke into flame. While the crown was generally disposed to support the seculars, the clergy in the Philippines remained predominately regular and still irreplaceable. The seculars continued to be too few and insufficiently trained to take over the missions.

The regulars had to make a few concessions in their battles with the crown, the secular clergy, and the textile interests, but they did not retreat from their well-entrenched positions in the Philippines and in the Manila trade. The Jesuits in 1664 even won the concurrence of King Philip IV to recruit one-fourth of their missionaries outside of Spain "provided that they are my vassals [from Spanish-held regions such as Naples], or belong to the hereditary realms of the House of Austria."[247] The Philippine missions, like the other Jesuit missions in the East, thus began to be more international in character, particularly after 1675, when the crown permitted as many as one-third of the missionaries to come from outside Spain.[248] But the thorny

---

[245] Based on the appendix and accompanying charts and maps in Phelan, *op. cit.* (n. 225), pp. 167–76.
[246] See above, pp. 24–25.
[247] As quoted in De la Costa, *op. cit.* (n. 223), p. 437.
[248] *Ibid.*, p. 439.

question of episcopal jurisdiction, and the persistent rivalries of Dominicans and Jesuits in Manila, continued to bedevil the mission and to exasperate the superiors in Madrid and Rome down to the end of the century.

The Philippine mission was handicapped from the outset by the determination of the friars to use it as a staging ground for the extension of the Christian enterprise to other places. The Franciscans, who had first entered Japan in 1584 in the company of a Macao merchant, were most determined to break the Portuguese-Jesuit monopoly.[249] The martyrs of 1597, canonized as the "Twenty-six Holy Martyrs" in 1862, quickened the desire of all four religious orders of the Philippines for duty in Japan. The Franciscan Jeronimo de Jesus (d. 1601) reconnoitered Japan in 1598 and received a friendly welcome from Ieyasu. Custos Francisco de Mantilla then wrote to the pope that the Franciscans, unlike the Jesuits, had received a general permission to live, evangelize, and celebrate the mass openly throughout Japan.[250] Indeed, the Franciscans were allowed in 1599 to build a church in Edo, a concession they interpreted as a welcoming gesture. They held that their method of working with all social classes and their teaching by word and example had won favor in contrast to the Jesuit method of concentrating on conversion of the daimyos and of pressuring the people of the fiefdoms to accept the new religion of their rulers.

The other mendicant orders had long cast covetous eyes upon the prospering Japan mission. Augustinians and Franciscans began shortly to write letters to the king about the state of Christianity in Japan. From their priory established at Macao in 1587, the Augustinians reported on the activities of the "Theatines" (Jesuits) in the Macao-Nagasaki trade.[251] The Augustinians, unlike the Franciscans, halted their efforts to enter Japan once the papal bull had been published at Manila in 1596 authorizing the Portuguese-Jesuit monopoly of Japan. Four Augustinians, as passengers aboard the ill-fated "San Felipe," were shipwrecked off Tosa on the Japanese coast in 1597 and were in Nagasaki to witness the martyrdoms of that year. Through these early observers the Augustinians in Manila kept track of events in Japan and assessed its future prospects as a rich mission field.[252]

[249] On the Franciscans in Japan to 1597 see *Asia*, I, 305–9; also B. Willeke, "Die Ankunft der ersten Franziskaner in Japan," *ZMR*, XLIII (1959), 166–76; and J. L. A. Taladriz, "Notas para la historia de la entrada en Japon de los Franciscanos," in V. Sanchez and C. S. Fuertes (eds.), *España en Extremo Oriente . . . Presencia Franciscana* (Madrid, 1979), pp. 3–32.

[250] See L. Lemmens, *Geschichte der Franziskanermissionen* (Münster, 1929), p. 158.

[251] The older orders resented the name given to the Society and often referred to the Jesuits as "Theatines"; after all, they were all dedicated to Jesus and not the Jesuits alone. The order of Theatines was founded in 1524 as a Congregation of Regular Clerics dedicated to reform of Catholic life and liturgy. In the seventeenth century they evangelized in India under the aegis of the Propaganda. See below, p. 363.

[252] Based on A. Hartmann, O.S.A., *The Augustinians in Seventeenth-Century Japan* (Marylake, Ontario, 1965), chap. i.

The 1598 arrangement of the Franciscans with Ieyasu revived hopes in Manila for better religious and commercial relations with Japan. The Spanish received Ieyasu's permission to evangelize with the attached condition that trading relations with Manila would be forthcoming. A Japanese emissary was sent to Manila in 1602 to Pedro Bravo de Acuña (d. 1608), newly arrived governor of the Philippines, asking for shipbuilders and for regular trade at the port of Uraga. Although he refused to send shipbuilders, Acuña acceded to the request for trade. He also responded affirmatively to the demands of the friars that they be permitted to send missionaries to Japan. The Dominican prior at Manila, B. P. Francisco de Morales (1567–1622), had meanwhile begun negotiation on his own with Japanese Christians from Satsuma about the possibility of opening a mission in that fief. Shimazu Yoshihiro, the ruling daimyo of Satsuma, agreed in 1602 to receive a Dominican mission, probably because he himself wanted trade relations with Manila. Although there were mixed feelings in Manila about reopening missionary and commercial relations with Japan, official permission was granted in 1602 for the missionaries of all orders to go to Japan.[253] The Jesuits in the Philippines, unlike the mendicants, were slow to invade the monopoly of their fellow-Jesuits of the *padroado*.

The Manila mendicants were assigned to specific mission territories in Japan: the Franciscans first centered their attention on Miyako and northeastern Honshu, the Dominicans on Satsuma, and the Augustinians on Bungo. In 1603 Luis Sotelo (1574–1624) led a contingent of four Franciscans to Miyako where he was introduced to Ieyasu by his colleague Jeronimo de Jesus. Through the Christian daimyo Goto Joao, he became acquainted with Date Masamune (1566–1646), the lord of Sendai in northeastern Japan. Morales contemporaneously headed a party of five Dominican friars to Satsuma, whose Shimazu ruling family permitted them to build a church and to evangelize. Two Augustinians arrived at Hirado in August, 1602. Diego de Guevara (d. 1621), the Augustinian vicar provincial, went on to Miyako where he was given hospitality by the Franciscans and introduced to Ieyasu. After two interviews with the shogun, Guevara obtained official sanction to evangelize in Bungo.[254] Alarmed by these intrusions, and armed with the papal brief of 1603 forbidding the friars to enter Japan by way of Manila, the Jesuit Bishop Cerqueira in 1604 notified the friars that they had to leave Japan at once. The friars ignored the order and argued that Rome had misunderstood the situation. In their decision to await further developments, the friars were vindicated when Pope Paul V in 1608 opened Japan to the mendicant orders of Manila.[255]

[253] *Ibid.*, p. 39; and C. R. Boxer and J. S. Cummins, "The Dominican Mission in Japan (1602–22) and Lope de Vega," *Archivum fratrum praedicatorum*, XXXIII (1963), 7–8.

[254] See Hartmann, *op. cit.* (n. 252), p. 41.

[255] See Boxer, *op. cit.* (n. 136), pp. 240–41.

[209]

While developments in Europe favored the friars, their situation in Japan generally worsened from 1608 to 1614. The Dominicans, who had never made many converts in Satsuma, began in 1608 to lose the support of its Shimazu family. Strongly opposed by the local Buddhists, the Dominicans in their eagerness for a notable success illegally baptized a local samurai who was promptly executed for having accepted Christianity in defiance of the shogun's prohibition against doing so. This untoward event, when coupled with the failure of trade to develop, brought about the expulsion of the Dominicans from Satsuma in May, 1609. Morales and two others went to Nagasaki where they established the Dominican Church of the Rosary. Other Dominicans founded churches in Hizen, hereafter their principal mission field, and at Kyoto and Osaka. Never more than ten in number at any one time, the Dominicans had to limit their activities to a few centers and to be content with occasional visits to other places.[256] The Augustinians, who were even fewer in number than the Dominicans, made an uncertain progress at Usuki in Bungo and in some neighboring towns. In 1611–12 the Augustinians moved their enterprise to the more protected confines of Nagasaki. The Catholic center of Japan, Nagasaki then boasted more than twenty thousand Christians out of a population of forty thousand, four parishes staffed by native clerics, and houses and churches of all four of the orders.[257]

Of the Spanish mendicant orders, the Franciscans held the greatest stake in Japan and tried to extract the most from it. They were also the main critics of the Jesuits both in Japan and Europe. While the Jesuits railed against the rashness of the *"frailes idiotas,"* the Franciscans scoffed at the sterility and weakness of the method of cultural compromise, scorned the dubious morality of Jesuit direct involvement in trade, and derided their obsequiousness in cultivating the upper classes. Still the friars evidently learned something from the Jesuits. They held out the bait of trade with Manila, their leaders stayed as close as possible to the court, and they occasionally presented gifts to Ieyasu. In 1608 they were officially permitted to built a church at Uraga in the Kwanto where the trading ships from Manila landed. While a few worked in Nagasaki and western Honshu, Sotelo and several associates opened a new mission field in northern Honshu. In 1611 they received official permission from Date Masamune to propagate the gospel freely in Oshu (Mutsu). They built a church in Sendai, Masamune's headquarters city, from which they extended their activities into the hinterland.

The association of Sotelo and Date belongs to the annals of both religion

---

[256] See Boxer and Cummins, *loc. cit.* (n. 253), pp. 9–11. For a list of European Dominicans who worked in Japan from 1602 to 1622, and a map showing the locations of their churches see *ibid.*, pp. 71–73.

[257] Hartmann, *op. cit.* (n. 252), pp. 50–51. For a list of the twenty-eight Augustinians who worked in Japan beginning in 1584 see *ibid.*, p. 157.

and trade. Ieyasu and a number of the daimyos had been progressively disappointed by the limited character of the trade with Manila.[258] Increasingly
the Japanese began to talk of bypassing Manila and of establishing direct
commercial and political relations with Mexico and Europe. In 1610 the
Franciscan Alonso Muñoz was sent to Mexico and Spain as the representative of the "emperor" of Japan.[259] In response to the Muñoz mission,
Sebastian Viscaino was sent from Acapulco to Japan by the viceroy of Mexico. Ieyasu received him cordially and gave Viscaino a formal permission to
survey the east coast of Japan to make Spanish shipping safer. While completing his survey, Viscaino lost his ships in a storm. On a vessel supplied
by Masamune he returned to Mexico in the company of a new embassy
headed by Masamune's retainer, Hasekura Rokuemon, and by the Franciscan Sotelo, now out of favor with Ieyasu.[260] Viscaino carried gifts from
Ieyasu of *byobu* (pictorial screens) and armor. This delegation of 150 Japanese merchants and emissaries arrived at Mexico City early in 1614, where
70 of the Japanese were baptized and their leaders interviewed by the viceroy
of Mexico.

While most of the Japanese stayed behind in Mexico, twenty members of
the embassy continued on to Spain and finally arrived at Seville in October,
1614. Hasekura was baptized shortly after arriving in Europe. The purpose
of the mission is revealed by the letters addressed to the city of Seville,
Philip III, and the pope, by the observations of the Venetian ambassador to
Rome, and by the Jesuit letters. The Jesuits, who watched this Franciscan
mission with jaundiced eyes, systematically reported on Sotelo's activities
and aspirations. Jeronymo de Angelis, a Sicilian Jesuit who had worked in
Masamune's territory before the departure of Sotelo, informed the Jesuit
general that the Franciscan planned to be the primate of Japan. Date's letters
asked Seville to send shipbuilders and pilots to Japan. They requested perpetual agreements of friendship with the king and the pope as well as more
Franciscan missionaries for northern Japan. They promised a hospitable reception for Spanish ships and a readiness to turn back the Dutch and English. They asked reciprocity for Japanese ships arriving in Spanish and
colonial ports. In the appeal to the pope, Date asked for a great prelate to
head the church in northern Japan and implied that he was about to supplant

[258] On the nature of the trade see above, pp. 35–36.
[259] See A. Abad, "El P. Alonso Muñoz," *Archivo Ibero-Americano* (Madrid), XIX (1959),
126–31. Muñoz never returned to Japan.
[260] The best and most recent review of the Western sources on the embassy is in J. Schütte,
S.J., "Die Wirksamkeit der Päpste für Japan im ersten Jahrhundert der japanischen Kirchenge-
schichte (1549–1650)," *Archivum historiae pontificiae*, V (1967), 222–45. The most comprehensive collection of sources is *Dai Nippon Shiryo (Japanese Historical Materials)* (Tokyo, 1909),
Vol. XII, Pt. 12. It also contains a map tracing the routes taken by the embassy. For another
collection of sources see C. Meriwether, "A Sketch of the Life of Date Masamune and an Account of His Embassy to Rome," *Transactions of the Asiatic Society of Japan*, XXI (1894), 66–91.
Also see below, pp. 331–32.

the Tokugawas in ruling Japan. Pope Paul V responded to this plea by provisionally appointing Sotelo archbishop of Japan, subject to the approval of the Spanish king. Philip III and the Council of the Indies, who had reacted to the initial overtures of the emissaries in a cold and noncommittal manner, immediately took umbrage at Sotelo's appointment as a violation of the *patronato*. In 1618 Sotelo and Hasekura returned to the Philippines; the Japanese envoy went home in 1620 while Sotelo stayed on in Manila. Sotelo's effort to establish a mission in Japan independent of the Franciscan Province of San Gregorio in the Philippines was declared to be an act of insubordination to both the crown and his own superiors. The Spanish merchants at Seville and in the Philippines accused Sotelo of trying to establish direct trade between Japan and Mexico in violation of the galleon system which required that all Pacific voyages should ply, without exception, only between Acapulco and Manila. Finally Sotelo returned to Japan, where he was martyred in 1624.

Whatever motives lay behind the dispatch of the Date-Sotelo embassy, clearly nothing was accomplished for the mission in Japan. Even before Sotelo left for Europe, his superiors had recalled him to Manila for estranging Ieyasu by disobeying his commands. Ignoring the orders of Manila, Sotelo collaborated with Date in an effort to establish direct commercial relations with Mexico in return for Date's support of his personal desire to lead the Christian enterprise in Japan. If Date actually planned to overturn the Tokugawas, possibly in collaboration with Toyotomi Hideyori's retainers, all hope for this enterprise was lost in 1615 with the fall of the Osaka fortress and the death of Hideyori. If Sotelo genuinely hoped to lead a new Christian movement in Japan with the support of the papacy and Date, his chances for the realization of this dream vanished with the Tokugawa anti-Christian decrees of 1613–14 and the opposition of the Spanish secular authorities, including the crown, to his unauthorized project. To some contemporaries, as well as to some historians of the mission, Sotelo had produced "a sad and disgraceful comedy" that detracted from the exemplary fortitude then being displayed by the Christian missionaries and converts in Japan.[261]

While Sotelo traveled in Europe (1614–18), the plight of the Christians in Japan steadily worsened. Nagasaki itself was in a confused state as missionaries and converts from other places congregated there in obedience to the government's order. The death of Bishop Cerqueira in 1614 was followed by an internal division of the beleaguered community, a succession crisis known as the "Nagasaki schism." After the Jesuit superior Valentim Carvalho (1560–1631) was elected vicar of the diocese, the Franciscan superior Diego de Chinchon (d. 1617) persuaded the Japanese clergy that the succession was invalid. The opposition so formed declared Carvalho's election

---

[261] For evaluations of the mission see Meriwether, *loc. cit.* (n. 260), pp. 58–60.

null and void and turned the office over to Francisco de Morales, the Dominican superior. Both the clergy and laity took sides in the ensuing controversy, dividing thereby the Christian community at a time when unity was most essential to survival.[262]

Backbiting and squabbling among the Christians seemed to confirm the government's view of them as troublemakers, lawbreakers, and smugglers. The cooperation of certain Christians with Hideyori in the defense of Osaka castle reinforced the Tokugawas' conviction that the Christians, especially those from Manila, were intent upon political meddling and were possibly an advance force of conquistadors. Christian attacks upon the Buddhists and Shintoists, including the destruction of their temples and gods in Christian-dominated areas, had stirred a broad public animosity against the Christians.[263] Of the twenty-six Franciscans in Japan, six continued to work there secretly. Following Sotelo's lead, they concentrated their efforts in eastern Japan at a fairly safe distance from the authorities.[264] Seven of the nine ordained Dominicans contrived to escape expulsion, the highest proportion managed by any of the orders. Of the three Augustinians then in Japan only one, Hernando Ayala, remained behind. This lone Augustinian sought refuge with the Dominicans and worked in the underground with them.[265] The Dominicans for several years enjoyed the protection of Toan Murayama, the deputy governor of Nagasaki and a member of the Dominican Confraternity of the Rosary. When Murayama died in 1619, the authorities began to root out the Dominicans and their allies systematically.[266]

The martyrdoms, while they gradually forced the Christians into the underground, into apostasy, or into the next world, seemed to inspire members of all the orders to perpetuate the mission and to give succor to the Japanese Christians. Five Franciscans continued to work in Japan after the "Great Martyrdom" of 1622 and the formal severance of trade relations with Manila.[267] Diego Collado (d. 1638) the imperious, energetic, and indefatigable Dominican, was one of two of his order to survive the "Great Martyrdom." At the end of 1622 he left Japan to seek reinforcements in Ma-

---

[262] Ultimately Carvalho's election was upheld by the archbishops of Goa and Manila. On this disedifying episode see D. Pacheco, S.J., "The Europeans in Japan, 1543–1640," in M. Cooper (ed.), *The Southern Barbarians. The First Europeans in Japan* (Tokyo, 1971), pp. 79–80.

[263] For a summary of the principal reasons for the persecution see the article by J. F. Schütte, S.J., on "Japan, Martyrs of," in the *New Catholic Encyclopedia*, VII, 835–45.

[264] See Lemmens, *op. cit.* (n. 250), pp. 170–72. The sources differ on the number of Franciscans working in Japan in 1614. The figure given here is from the article on "Japan" by A. Schwade in the *New Catholic Encyclopedia*, VII, 828–35. Duncan, *op. cit.* (n. 14), pp. 419–20, whose figures come from the Jesuit *Monumenta historica Japoniae*, gives "around fifteen" as the number. Boxer and Cummins, *loc. cit.* (n. 253), p. 13, assert that out of ten Franciscans only six remained secretly in Japan. They all agree that six stayed on in hiding.

[265] See Hartmann, *op. cit.* (n. 252), p. 59.

[266] Murayama had been converted originally by the Jesuits but went over to the Dominicans in 1611. The Jesuit Rodrigues in 1618 described him as "a leading Judas." See Boxer and Cummins, *loc. cit.* (n. 253), pp. 16–17.

[267] See Lemmens, *op. cit.* (n. 250), p. 171; also see above, pp. 174–75.

nila. Discouraged by the lack of response there, he left for an extended stay in Europe. There he kept alive an interest in Japan through his negotiations with the Propaganda and by his publications.[268] His efforts reinforced the Propaganda's negative attitude towards the Jesuits. In 1635 he reappeared in Manila with a contingent of twenty-three religious and the pope's permission to establish a new congregation, independent of the Philippine Province of the Rosary, dedicated to the evangelizing of China and Japan. In the Philippines his project was vetoed by the local Dominicans and by the archbishop on the grounds that the pope had violated the *patronato* in granting Collado permission to divide the Philippines province of his order into two parts without first obtaining royal approval.[269]

The Jesuits in the Philippines, who had, for the most part, passively observed the frantic efforts of the Franciscans and the Dominicans to recoup their losses in Japan, were at first inclined to limit their role to the provision of aid and sanctuary for the Christian refugees from Japan. After 1624, at the request of certain Nagasaki Christians, the Jesuits in Manila were authorized by the archbishop to erect and maintain a college for training Japanese priests to minister in their homeland. This project failed for lack of recruits.[270] The most dramatic Jesuit effort to reopen Japan from the Philippines occurred in connection with the personal mission of Father Marcello Mastrilli (1603–37), a Neapolitan Jesuit who had promised to carry the gospel to Japan after having been saved from death by the intercession of Xavier.[271] After briefly accompanying the Spanish expedition of 1637 into Mindanao, Mastrilli in company with several other priests went off to Japan. His martyrdom in the pit during October, 1637, inspired a plethora of stories praising his miraculous life and exemplary death. Other Jesuits under Antonio Rubino (1578–1643) sailed to Japan in 1642 and in 1643, even after it had become clear that the Office of Investigation at Edo, created in 1640, had made quite impossible the clandestine entries of Europeans into Japan. The first Rubino group was martyred at Nagasaki; some members of the group apostatized and were thereafter kept in a prison for Christians.

When the "Great Persecution" first began, the Dominicans and Augustinians had deliberately sought martyrdom in hopes of keeping their converts strong in the faith.[272] While a few Jesuits later apostatized, the friars all went to their deaths without denying the faith.[273] Whether or not it was these examples of Christian courage that inspired the Japanese Christians, thousands of them certainly gave their lives for their beliefs. By 1640, when the mis-

---

[268] On his publications see below, p. 342. On his tireless efforts on behalf of the mendicants of Japan see below, p. 226.

[269] See Boxer and Cummins, *loc. cit.* (n. 253), pp. 23–26; on the reaction in the Philippines see De la Costa, *op. cit.* (n. 223), pp. 377–79.

[270] See De la Costa, *op. cit.* (n. 223), pp. 370–72.

[271] On this visionary and his renown in Europe see below, pp. 345–46.

[272] See Boxer, *op. cit.* (n. 136), pp. 332–33.

[273] For a list of the Apostate Fathers (1633–43) see *ibid.*, p. 447.

sion effectively ended, 1,600 Europeans and Japanese were recorded by name as having died for the faith.[274] Of those who died in the Great Persecution of 1614 to 1640 Pope Pius IX in 1867 beatified a group now known as the 205 Blessed Martyrs.

While the Philippine missionaries fought a losing battle in Japan, some of their colleagues tried desperately to reestablish permanent mission stations in the Spiceries.[275] Reconnoitered by Xavier himself, the Christian mission in the Spiceries had remained a Jesuit monopoly until the Portuguese fortress on Ternate was captured in 1574 by a confederation of Muslim rulers. A few Jesuit refugees managed to escape to neighboring Amboina, and by 1578 the Portuguese had built a new fortress on Tidore, the rival of Ternate in the Moluccas.[276] The Spanish Franciscans, often called the "migratory birds" of the missions, had first arrived at Manila in 1577. Their custos, Pedro de Alfaro, was convinced that the pope had never intended them to remain on station in the Philippines and immediately began to plan the extension of the mission. In 1578 a group of Franciscans landed in Borneo in the vanguard of a Spanish invading force sent to punish the sultan of Brunei.[277] Alfaro and three other friars secretly left Manila in 1579 for China where they established a friary at Macao. Other Spanish Franciscans founded a convent at Malacca in 1581, three years before the Portuguese Franciscans arrived there. Franciscan General Francisco Gonzaga decided in Rome that the Malacca convent should be run by the Portuguese friars since political control of the city belonged to Portugal. By 1590 the friary of Macao was also taken over by Portuguese Franciscans.[278] In 1593 a number of Spanish Franciscans appeared at Amboina, then considered to be a Jesuit preserve. All of the Catholic missionaries were driven from Amboina when the Dutch captured that island in 1605.[279] These were but the earliest of the long-continuing Portuguese-Spanish religious confrontations in this much-disputed arena.

The initiative in missionizing the Spiceries was grasped in 1606 by Spanish religious from Manila. Representatives of the four orders working in the Philippines accompanied the naval expedition of De Acuña which established a long-term (1606–62) Spanish military and political presence in the

---

[274] According to the catalog (1646) of Antonio Cardim (1596–1659) as cited by J. F. Schütte, *loc. cit.* (n. 260), p. 245.

[275] For the definition of the Spiceries used here see *Asia,* I, 592–93.

[276] *Ibid.,* pp. 289–90.

[277] See S. Stokman, O.F.M., "De eerste Missionarissen van Borneo," *Historisch Tijdschrift,* VII (1928), 351–56; and R. Nicholl (ed.), *European Sources for the History of the Sultanate of Brunei* (Brunei, 1975), pp. 35–58.

[278] See Meersman *op. cit.* (n. 17), pp. 263–64; and Manuel Teixeira, "Os Franciscanos em Macau," in Sanchez and Fuertes (eds.), *op. cit.* (n. 249), pp. 309–39.

[279] See C. Wessels, *Histoire de la mission d'Amboine depuis sa fondation . . . à 1605* (Louvain, 1934).

Spiceries.[280] Sultan Sahid Bardat of Ternate, his sons and principal nobles, were carried off to Manila by the victorious Spaniards. The other rulers in the Moluccas, including the sultan of Bachan, quickly recognized that the center of political gravity had shifted to Manila and offered their vassalage to Spain. Five of the princes (*Cachiles*) of Ternate were baptized in 1608 by Franciscans in Manila. On Ternate itself the Augustinians set up a cloister, and the Franciscans converted its chief mosque into their church. From Ternate the Spanish missionaries soon made tours into the neighboring islands and to more distant places, such as Gilolo (Halmahera) and Bohol in northern Celebes, where the Jesuits of the *padroado* had earlier founded Christian communities and where the Spanish had forts.[281] The Portuguese Jesuits were left generally to their own devices and received little aid from the Spanish governors and religious orders.[282]

The resumption of Dutch attacks in 1607 forced a Spanish retreat from the Makian and Bachan islands in the Molucca group. The Dutch built a fortress on Ternate itself which was separated from the Spanish outpost by nothing but a hill. Here, as elsewhere in Indonesia, the Dutch employed Japanese mercenaries to help hold their fortress. In 1612 the Dutch built a fortress on Tidore. Subsequent Dutch campaigns in the Spiceries, particularly those of 1616–18, limited even further the Catholic evangelizing activities. The Franciscans from Manila avoided the mushrooming Dutch fortresses in the Moluccas and went on to Manado and Makassar in Celebes where the Jesuits had worked earlier.[283] The Spanish Augustinians, who kept a few friars in their convent of Ternate whenever possible, finally retreated from the Molucca mission in 1625 in deference to the insistence of the bishop of Malacca and the Portuguese Augustinians. The Spanish governors of the Moluccas and the Franciscans cooperated thereafter in retaining both political control and religious enterprise in the Spiceries from Ternate to Makassar. The friars were used as political emissaries by the governor from time to time, and often as sailors or soldiers. The Spanish Dominicans and Jesuits were less inclined than the Franciscans to violate the claims of the *padroado,* since the Portuguese Dominicans were well established in the Lesser Sundas and since the Jesuits of Macao were so heavily involved in the trade of the region.[284]

Originally the Spanish had become active in the Spiceries to support the

[280] On the "reconquest" of the Spiceries see above, p. 14.

[281] See C. Wessels, "De katholieke missie in het Sultanaat Batjan (Molukken), 1557–1609," *Historisch Tijdschrift,* VIII (1929), 145; C. Wessels, "De Augustijen in de Molukken, 1544–46, 1601–25," *Historisch Tijdschrift,* XIII (1934), 54–59; L. Perez, "Historia de las misiones de los Franciscanos en las islas Malucas y Celebes," *Archivum Franciscanum Historicum,* VII (1914), 203.

[282] Between 1546 and 1677 the Jesuits sent a total of eighty-one missionaries into the Moluccas, of whom forty-three were Portuguese. See C. Wessels, *loc. cit.* (n. 135), p. 253.

[283] On the Jesuit tours there see *Asia,* I, 618–19, 621.

[284] See above, pp. 138–39.

Portuguese against the Dutch. Concommitantly, however, their descent upon the Spiceries in 1606, and their later activities there, became part and parcel of their broad-scale anti-Moro or anti-Muslim program. Muslim raiders from Mindanao, the Sulu archipelago, and more distant Borneo seemed able to mount hit-and-run attacks at will upon the Philippines, especially the Bisayan islands. Captives from these Bisayan raids, including many Christians, were sold in the slave markets of the Malay archipelago. The Dutch, frustrated by their failures to conquer Manila, encouraged the Muslim raiders and combined with them from time to time to attack the Catholic installations. In 1616, when Governor Juan de Silva sent out his huge fleet to drive the Dutch from the Spiceries, the Sulus in combination with the Dutch and fellow Muslims from Palawan and Brunei attacked Manila itself.[285] While the Spanish survived these attacks, they were not able to mount new drives against the Muslim strongholds for a decade. The Dutch in the Spiceries, though few in number, were able to harass the Spanish supply lines to Ternate and to destroy the isolated Catholic communities of the Spiceries by periodic naval forays. The Dutch increasingly won support from Muslim rulers throughout the archipelago, from Mindanao to Sumatra, and in 1621 from their English rivals, in their determined effort to drive out the Spanish and Portuguese. In the Philippines, and in Spain itself, complaints began to be heard about the cost of maintaining the Spanish position in the Spiceries and about the diversion of effort away from the consolidation of Spanish control over the Philippines. In 1628 the Spaniards from the Philippines were involved in hostilities at four widely separated places: on Formosa, in the Moluccas, in Bisayan waters with the Moros, and in northern Luzon where a revolt had broken out.[286]

After enjoying a decade of comparative peace, the government of Manila launched a campaign in 1637 to conquer Mindanao and Jolo in the Sulu archipelago. While these operations had succeeded by 1646, the Spanish in Manila were meanwhile confronted in 1639–40 by a new and bloody Chinese uprising. The Dutch in 1641 captured Malacca and in the following year drove the Spanish out of Formosa. The Portuguese revolt against the Habsburgs, beginning in 1640, led to the cessation of the Manila-Macao trade and to new Dutch attacks upon the reeling Philippines. In the Moluccas the scattered Christian communities, both Portuguese and Spanish, were alleged to include 12,600 Christians as of 1644.[287] In 1653 the Spanish Jesuits formally took over the Society's obligations in the Moluccas, and priests were sent irregularly from Manila to Ternate until the Spanish garrison at Ternate withdrew in 1662.[288]

---

[285] See De la Costa, *op. cit.* (n. 223), pp. 320–21.

[286] See *ibid.*, p. 342.

[287] This figure taken from the estimate of the Christians falling within the jurisdiction of the Jesuit Province of Malabar in Ferroli, *op. cit.* (n. 2), II, 416.

[288] See De la Costa, *op. cit.* (n. 223), p. 454.

The Franciscans were the most aggressive of the orders from Manila during the last two decades of Spain's control of Ternate. A new mission was opened in 1641 under their auspices on Sangihe, the northernmost island in the Sangihe group lying north of Celebes, which formed a bridge between the Philippines and their station reestablished at Manado. King Buntuan, overlord of the Sangihe kingdom of Kalanga, became a convert to win Christian aid against his rival, the Muslim ruler of Tabukan on the same island. At Manado the Franciscans were in conflict during these years with the Portuguese Jesuits. In 1655 three Jesuits began evangelizing on Siau Island in the Sangihe group. By 1656 Jesuits from Zamboanga in Mindanao had made around seven hundred converts among the Camucones of Borneo.[289] These missions continued to function weakly until the Spanish withdrawal from Mindanao and Ternate in 1662–63. Over the next four years the Dutch drove the remaining Spanish missionaries from the Spiceries. Two Jesuits continued on at Siau until the Dutch reconquered that tiny island in 1677. Seven Franciscans joined the Dominicans on Timor, and a few other Franciscans worked surreptitiously on islands loosely held by the Dutch.[290] In 1687 Antonio Ventimiglia, an aristocratic Sicilian Theatine, went alone into the Biadju upcountry in Borneo where he evangelized for eight years before being murdered in 1695. In Rome where he was called the Apostle of Borneo, the Propaganda in 1692 created the Vicariate Apostolic of Borneo, named Ventimiglia as its first incumbent, and entrusted its development to the Theatines.[291] The Catholic missions in Indonesia were effectively defunct by the end of the seventeenth century, except for the Portuguese-Dominican enterprise in the Lesser Sundas.[292]

More permanent than the missions in the Spiceries were the few Christian successes registered by the Spanish missionaries in Oceania. The early Pacific voyagers, especially Quiros, had sought for new souls as well as new lands in the Pacific. Quiros conducted the expedition of 1605 as if it were a religious crusade. Franciscan and Augustinian priests and lay brothers worked closely with the crews of the early voyages to preserve order aboard ship and to enforce religious observances. They planted crosses on the islands and captured native children to be brought up in the faith in the Philippines or in New Spain.[293] In the austral lands there were no Muslims or Protestants to block the Christianizing of the heathens or to challenge the

[289] See Stokman, *loc. cit.* (n. 277), pp. 349–50.

[290] See Meersman, *op. cit.* (n. 17), pp. 226–78; and Perez, *loc. cit.* (n. 281), pp. 635–52; and De la Costa, *op. cit.* (n. 223), pp. 454–55.

[291] See Teixeira, *op. cit.* (n. 16), II, 180–81; also Stokman, *loc. cit.* (n. 277), p. 350–51.

[292] *Cf.* above, pp. 138–40.

[293] See A. Gschaedler, "Religious Aspects of the Spanish Voyages in the Pacific," *The Americas,* IV (1948), 303–14.

authority of the Spanish crown. The Pacific was a "Spanish lake" whose wealth was deemed to be fabulous and whose savage and numerous peoples were thought to be ready for civilizing and Christianizing.[294]

Six Franciscans accompanied the Quiros expedition of 1605, and one of their number, Martin de Munilla (d. 1606), chronicled the voyage and prepared a detailed description of the islands discovered, especially of their inhabitants. When Quiros returned to Spain in 1607, he began immediately to promote his plan for the colonizing and evangelizing of the austral lands. In his memorials (1607–14) to the crown requesting authorization of his enterprise, Quiros was supported by the powerful Franciscans of Spain. After the death of Quiros in 1615, his project was transformed by Friar Juan de Silva into a Franciscan missionary plan.

King Philip III was personally inclined to favor the proposals of Quiros and Silva; the Council of the Indies opposed their plans as too ambitious, uncertain, and expensive. Silva, a veteran of military and missionary enterprises in America, had convinced the superiors of his order, including Juan de Torquemada, the provincial in Mexico, that the austral lands of Quiros should be made into one vast Franciscan mission. His first three memorials were studied by the king and the Council of the Indies in 1619. To test the reactions of a broader public, these basic documents were printed at Seville in 1621 by order of the Council.[295] Silva, who was then confessor to the royal household, had reason to hope for eventual state support of his project. He had stressed in his memorials the commitment of his order and the willingness of his confreres, including superiors, to volunteer for the mission. He countered the problem of expense by arguing that this conquest would not meet a concerted resistance. It would be an entirely spiritual effort and therefore minor in cost. His hopes for state support were ended when the king died in 1621, shortly before the publication of the memorials.

Disappointed by the state's lack of positive response, Silva petitioned Pope Urban VIII and the Propaganda in 1623 to sponsor the Franciscan project and sent copies of his book to Rome. He enlisted the aid of leading churchmen and seculars in the colonies to win over the papacy and the new government in Spain. Dr. Sebastian Clementi, chaplain of the royal chapel at Lima, even proposed to Rome the creation of a new military order to lead the enterprise in the mid-Pacific. Rome, like the Spanish crown, took these proposals under advisement and did little else. In his memorials to Philip IV, Silva reminded the crown repeatedly that Spanish rights under the *patronato* could be justified only by continuing the spiritual conquest of the heathen world. But still no positive response was forthcoming, and one could hardly

---

[294] On the early voyages see above, pp. 5–8.

[295] Entitled *Advertencias importantes, acerca del buen Govierno, y Administracion de las Indias, assi en lo espiritual, como en la temporal.*

have been expected from a government engaged in war with the Dutch in Europe and in the East and West Indies.[296]

The lure of the South Pacific and the unexplored austral continent continued to inspire men's minds after the failure of the Franciscan project. Stimulated by the news of the rich discoveries reported on by Quiros and others, the Dutch and English sent voyages of exploration into the southwest Pacific from 1616 to 1643.[297] Their intrusions into the "Spanish lake" were carried out for plunder and prospective trade rather than for discovery, settlement, or evangelizing. The Spanish Franciscans meanwhile had directed their energies towards the maintenance of their missions in the Spiceries and to the opening of missions in China and Indochina. The Spanish merchants on both sides of the Pacific lost whatever interest they had in Oceania as it became increasingly apparent that there was little of a material nature to gain by developing the poor islands used as stopovers on the galleon routes. With the withdrawal of Spain from the Moluccas in 1662, a new and more successful attempt was undertaken to bring the faith to the islands of Oceania.

The Spanish Jesuits, whose activities were now concentrated almost exclusively in the Philippines, assumed leadership of this new enterprise. One of their number, Diego Luis de Sanvitores (1627–72), single-handedly and in spite of opposition from the secular and ecclesiastical authorities, founded a mission in the Ladrones islands (Marianas). While on a tour of duty (1662–67) in the Philippines, he received official permission from Marie Anne of Austria, the queen-regent of Spain, to pursue his pet project. When his tour was over, two years after he had been given the permission, he returned to Mexico to raise money and to find volunteers. Accompanied by four priests, one student for the priesthood, and thirty lay catechists, he landed at Guam in July, 1668. While on shipboard he studied Chamorro, the language of the islands he renamed the Marianas in honor of his queen-sponsor. Five years later he suffered martyrdom at the hands of an apostate father who had opposed the baptism of his child. The "martyrdom" of Sanvitores inspired among Christians everywhere an interest in the Marianas which helped the mission to endure.[298]

Sanvitores had established his base at Agana on the island of Guam, the

---

[296] Based on C. Kelly, O.F.M., "The Franciscan Missionary Plan for the Conversion to Christianity of the Natives of the Austral Lands as Proposed in the Memorials of Fray Juan de Silva, O.F.M.," *The Americas*, XVII (1961), 277–91; and the same author's introduction to *La Austrialia del Espiritu Santo. The Journal of Fray Martin de Munilla, O.F.M., and Other Documents Relating to the Voyage of Pedro Fernandez de Quiros to the South Sea (1605–06) and the Franciscan Missionary Plan (1617–27)*, "HS," 2d ser., CXXVI–VII.

[297] See C. Jack-Hinton, *The Search for the Islands of Solomon, 1567–1838* (Oxford, 1969), chap. vi.

[298] For his biography see the introduction to W. Barrett (trans.), *Mission in the Marianas, An Account of Father Diego Luis de Sanvitores and His Companions, 1669–70* (Minneapolis, 1975).

largest and most populous of the thirteen islands in the Marianas chain.[299] The Marianas enterprise was under the jurisdiction of the Jesuits' Philippine province. A small garrison of Filipino and Spanish soldiers was stationed in the islands to protect the missionaries from the hostile natives. Reports from Sanvitores and his companions were edited and summarized for publication in Europe by Andres de Ledsma (1610–84), the procurator of the Philippine province. In Spain and Mexico hopes began to rise that the pacified Marianas might become the stepping-stone on the way to the austral continent and the rich Solomon Islands.[300] But pacification did not come easily. Bloody insurrections swept the islands in 1674–76 and 1684–85, in which ten missionaries died. The Jesuits persisted and were reinforced after 1674 by the Franciscans and Dominicans eager to expand their fields of activity and to advance the cause of empire.

The Jesuit letters published in Europe, as well as the martyrdom of Sanvitores, stimulated an interest in the Marianas far out of proportion to the Christian successes won there. The growing inability of the crown to finance new and remote missions had led the Jesuits to seek private financing from noble patrons. Once their monopoly was broken, the Spanish Jesuits, having lost their zeal for dangerous missions, began increasingly to recruit non-Iberian missionaries, especially in Italy and Germany. Among the most generous contributors to the missions of the Spanish Jesuits was the duchess of Aveiro, Maria Guadalupe de Lencastre (1630–1715). The Mother of the Missions, as she came to be called, transformed her palace at Madrid into a center of information. She was dismayed by the lack of enthusiasm shown by the crown and the Spanish Jesuits for the South Seas mission and personally encouraged the missionaries to rescue the heathens of the East by bringing to them the security of the faith. Eusebio Francisco Kino (1645–1711), the famous Jesuit pioneer of the Pacific Coast missions in America, was but one of several missionaries whom she patronized. In 1680 he wrote consolingly to her: "In Germany our Company esteem very greatly the missions of the Marianas Islands, with no less desire to be sent to convert those people."[301] But, despite his zeal, Kino was never permitted to try his hand in evangelizing the Marianas. Karl von Boranga, an Austrian priest, and Augustin Strobach, a Moravian priest, were sent to the Marianas in 1681, and three years later both were killed in a martyrdom of the kind Kino had envisaged for himself. A few Jesuits from central Europe continued to appear in the Marianas over the remainder of the century.[302]

---

[299] For a list of the native and Christian names for the islands see De la Costa, *op. cit.* (n. 223), p. 456.

[300] See Jack-Hinton, *op. cit.* (n. 297), pp. 172–75.

[301] As quoted in H. E. Bolton, *Rim of Christendom. A Biography of Eusebio Francisco Kino, Pacific Coast Pioneer* (New York, 1936), pp. 58–59. For a biography of the Duchess see E. J. Burrus, *Father Kino Writes to the Duchess* (Rome, 1965).

[302] See De la Costa, *op. cit.* (n. 223), Appendix C.

The Marianas was one of the least desirable and most dangerous of the Jesuit missions. The missionaries, especially Luis de Morales (1647–1716), nonetheless continued to explore and map the islands. The Spanish government, which needed access to the islands for the galleon trade, doggedly worked for their pacification. To keep their peoples under better surveillance, the Spanish military in 1685 began transplanting the peoples of the smaller islands to Guam and Rota. Closer administration of the islands brought the frequent revolts to an end and forced the islanders to accept the Spanish way of life. By the middle of the eighteenth century paganism had all but vanished in these islands.

The enduring successes of the missionaries of the *patronato* were limited to the Philippines and the Marianas. The Spanish missionaries experienced a partial success in China, where they began to work in 1632 within the Portuguese-Jesuit monopoly. During the last generation of the seventeenth century they made an effort to take over the leadership of the China mission from the Portuguese and the French.[303] For a period the Spanish missionaries from the Philippines challenged the Jesuits in Japan. The Christian failure in Japan, while not completely the responsibility of the Spanish friars, produced charges from the Jesuits blaming them for the "Great Persecution" of the Tokugawas. While the friars denounced the Jesuits for their commercial activities, some of their own members likewise involved themselves in trade and in political chicanery. In the Moluccas the Christian enterprise depended entirely upon the support of the secular authority for its existence. Here, and in the Philippines, the missionaries encouraged the state to undertake military crusades against the Dutch and the Muslims. Wherever the state maintained its power, the *patronato* prospered. By the latter half of the century, the Asian empire of Spain was limited to the Christianized Philippines and to a few islands in the mid-Pacific.

5

"PROPAGANDA FIDE" (1622), "MISSIONS ETRANGÈRES" (1664),
AND THE JESUITS

Like many of the other Counter-Reformation agencies created by Rome, the Sacred Congregation for the Propagation of the Faith (*Propaganda fide*) was founded to regain the souls lost to Protestantism in Europe and to take the gospel to heathen lands. To the church of the post-Tridentine era, converting pagans and reconverting heretics were but two sides of the same coin, as the history of the Jesuits vividly illustrates. Organizations specializ-

---

[303] See below, pp. 262–63.

ing in the conversion of Jews and Muslims (1543) and pagans and heretics (1568) had prepared the way for the Asian mission initiatives of Pope Gregory XIII, the pontiff who died in 1585 shortly after receiving the legates from Japan.[304] Efforts to centralize the administration of foreign missions were undertaken in 1599 during the pontificate of Clement VIII (r. 1592–1605). At this time the moving spirit in advocating papal control of the missions was Cardinal Giulio Antonio Santori (1532–1602); with his death this original initiative languished, but his proposals lived on in the minds and hearts of others. He wanted the establishment of a permanent congregation of cardinals for the propagation of the faith, the creation of an organization to raise money for the missions, the erection of a publishing house to print Christian literature for distribution in the missions, and a college for the training of missionaries.[305]

The Carmelite Tommas a Jesu, friend and associate of Santori, published in 1613 his *De procuranda salute omnium gentium* (Antwerp), a program for centralizing control of the missions in Rome. Other Carmelites, and a number of Capuchins, continued to advocate the creation of a new congregation on the model of the one proposed earlier by Santori. These efforts did not bear fruit until the brief pontificate (February 9, 1621, to July 8, 1623) of Gregory XV. This pope and his nephew, the Papal Secretary of State Ludovico Ludovisi (d. 1632), had both been educated in Jesuit schools and shared the Society's enthusiasm for Catholic resurgence; together they inaugurated the canonization process for both Loyola and Xavier. On January 6, 1622, Gregory officially created the *Propaganda fide,* the last of the important congregations established by the Counter-Reformation papacy. This was a political as well as a religious act, since it let the Iberians know that Rome was now determined to pursue an independent course with respect to overseas missions. It was also a signal to Catholic Europe that the papacy, which had begun under Clement VIII to lean upon France rather than Spain, intended to persist in its program of limiting the Iberian patronages and of sponsoring the rejuvenation of the French church.

[304] See *Asia,* I, 688–705.

[305] The idea that a central agency should promote and direct mission efforts goes back at least to Ramón Lull (1232–1316). Shortly after the Council of Trent, Pope Pius V, despite the expressed fears of King Philip II, created in 1568 two congregations of cardinals, one to promote the Counter-Reformation in Germany and the other to oversee missions. The cardinals then attempted to reassure Philip II that their commission was only concerned with the spiritual side of the missions and that the overseas church "*in materialibus*" would not be interfered with. When Gregory XIII sought to revitalize Pius' congregation on overseas missions, Philip II "vetoed" this act. The congregation of 1599 was created in the year after Philip's death. See especially J. Metzler, "Wegbereiter und Vorläufer der Kongregation," *SCPFMR,* Vol. 1/1, pp. 38–69. Also see K. Hoffmann, "Das erste päpstliche Missionsinstitut," *Zeitschrift für Missionswissenschaft,* XII (1922), 76–82; J. Schmidlin, "Die Gründung der Propaganda Kongregation," *Zeitschrift für Missionswissenschaft,* XII (1922), 1–2; A. Mulders, *Missionsgeschichte. Die Ausbreitung des katholischen Glaubens* (trans. from Dutch into German by J. Madey; Regensburg, 1960), pp. 259–87; and the article on "Propagation of the Faith, Congregation for the," by R. Hoffman in *New Catholic Encyclopedia,* XI, 840–44.

Fortunately for the proponents of the Propaganda, Gregory's successor as pope, Urban VIII (r. 1623–44), was equally dedicated to the missions and continued the new approach to their supervision. Born as Maffeo Barberini, the new pope had been educated by the Jesuits of his native city of Florence. On his election day (August 5, 1623) he completed the work of his predecessors and issued the bulls of canonization for Loyola, Xavier, and Neri. He authorized in 1632 the establishment of the "Lazarist fathers," or congregation of Priests of the Mission, founded by Vincent de Paul (and thus also known as Vincentians). He opened China and Japan in 1633 to all missionaries and forthrightly informed the Iberian powers that the papacy was no longer willing to accept quietly their terms for missionizing the East.

The Congregation of the Propaganda, as originally constituted, consisted of thirteen cardinals, two prelates, and a secretary, who were to meet monthly.[306] One of the two original prelates was Ludovico Ludovisi, the Papal Secretary of State who dominated its activities over the next decade. The other was Juan Bautista Vives (1545–1632), a Spanish promoter of missionary education and of the same family as Juan Luis Vives, the famous humanist of the early sixteenth century. J. B. Vives donated the Palazzo Ferrantini in the Piazza di Spagna and most of his fortune as a foundation for the Urban College (also called the College of the Propaganda).[307] It was opened in 1627 as an international training center for secular priests destined for the missions; its building, redesigned by Gian Lorenzo Bernini, functions to the present day as a meeting place for the Propaganda and is dedicated to the Three Wise Men, the first of Jesus' converts from the pagan world. Bulls of 1637 and 1639 established a school within the college for the training in religion of about one dozen youths, of whom six should be Indian Brahmans when available.[308]

Of all the founders the most influential in putting the Propaganda on a firm footing was Francesco Ingoli (1578–1649), the secretary of the congregation and its operational chief during the first twenty-seven years of its existence.[309] In its early years the congregation systematically assembled materials on the status of the missions and studied the means being used to propagate the faith. The fee of five hundred gold ducats paid by each newly named cardinal was assigned to the support of the Propaganda.[310] Legacies

---

[306] For their names see J. Metzler, "Foundation of the Congregation 'de Propaganda Fide' by Gregory XV," *SCPFMR*, Vol. 1/1, p. 87.

[307] On the origins of the Urban College see *ibid.*, pp. 53–54, 76–77.

[308] See L. von Pastor, *The History of the Popes from the Close of the Middle Ages* (40 vols., trans. into English by Dom Ernest Graf, O.S.B.; London, 1938), XXIX, 212–15.

[309] For a list of the secretaries of the Propaganda to 1842 see Gaetano Maroni, *Dizionario di erudizione storica-ecclesiastica* (102 vols., Venice, 1840–61), XVI, 257–60. On Ingoli see J. Metzler, "Francesco Ingoli, der erste Sekretär der Kongregation," *SCPFMR*, Vol. 1/1, pp. 197–243.

[310] On this fee see Metzler, *loc. cit.* (n. 306), pp. 98–100.

from cardinals and other churchmen as well as considerable sums collected by the Carmelites and Theatines soon swelled its coffers. Catholic princes were asked to help in financing its activities; Protestant princes were reassured that its missionizing would be conducted peacefully. The first reports received by the Propaganda from the great missionary orders (Jesuits, Dominicans, Franciscans, and Augustinians) made overly optimistic estimates of great future success if only more money and men could be supplied.[311] The papal nuncios, who were slower to report than the orders, were more guarded in their evaluation of mission prospects in their assigned provinces.

Antonio Albergati (1566–1634), papal representative (*colletore*) in Portugal from 1621 to 1624, wrote in 1623 a frankly pessimistic report on the *padroado*. As he saw it, Christian affairs in the Portuguese empire were in a sorry state with little prospect for improvement. He attributed this condition to cruel treatment of the natives, the far-from-exemplary lives being led by Portuguese laymen and religious in the overseas world, the enmity of the regulars toward the secular hierarchy, rivalry and conflict between the orders, and the subordination of spiritual to national interests. The missionaries themselves, almost all Portuguese in nationality, he deemed to be interested only in mundane affairs and bent upon personal and family enrichment. Albergati recommended that more zealous and valiant missionaries, as well as those of other nationalities, should be sent into the *padroado*. The Portuguese king ought to be urged, he wrote, not to appoint members of the orders to Asian sees, because such bishops too often discriminated against the seculars and against the regulars of other orders. The Propaganda must do its utmost to end fraticidal disputes between the orders. Missionaries should travel to Asia over the land route to evade the control of the Iberians over the number and nationality of the missionaries being dispatched to the East. Finally, drawing upon his experience as papal nuncio in Germany, Albergati advised increasing the number of bishoprics in Asia to improve supervision of the missions.[312]

The Propaganda, in its efforts to promote unity and uniformity, decreed that every missionary in the field should file an annual report with the congregation. From the dearth of such individual reports in the archives it appears that the requirement was observed mainly in the breach. Still, information continued to funnel into Rome in the form of general reports from the orders, the nuncios, and laymen. In reacting to the information received, Ingoli became increasingly critical of the missions for their failure to admit natives to Holy Orders. He observed that an indigenous clergy, such as they had founded in Japan, would help the faith to deepen its roots, uphold the

---

[311] For details on these reports from the superiors of the orders working in Asia see Mulders, *op. cit.* (n. 305), pp. 266–67.

[312] See Laurentz Kilger, "Die ersten Jahre Propaganda—eine Wendezeit der Missionsgeschichte," *Zeitschrift für Missionswissenschaft*, XII (1922), 18–20.

rights of natives, and keep the converts loyal to the church at times of stress. He criticized the mighty Jesuits, seemingly without avail, for their unwillingness to ordain as priests well-qualified Indians and Chinese.[313]

To lend substance to their oft-expressed desire for native priests, the Propaganda trained the wealthy Brahman of Diwar known as Matteo de Castro Mahalo and had him ordained in Rome in 1631. Charged by the pope himself to concentrate on the converson of Brahmans, Castro Mahalo returned to Goa in 1633. The Goa curia denied the validity of his credentials and the Portuguese did all in their power to prevent him from carrying out his mission. After a stormy career in India and a minimum number of successes, he returned to Europe for the last time in 1658 and died at Rome in 1677.[314] In this encounter with the *padroado,* as in many subsequent ones, the Propaganda came off second best.

During the first decade of its existence the Propaganda spent much effort trying to mediate the heated debate between the mendicants and Jesuits of Japan. On the eve of the congregation's foundation the "Great Martyrdom" of Nagasaki had occurred, and each group of religious vehemently blamed the other for the increased violence of the persecution in Japan. Diego Collado, the Dominican vicar-provincial of Japan, had come to Rome in 1622 as procurator and advocate of the mendicant orders. In 1625 the Propaganda began formal consideration of the issues he raised and, in conjunction with the royal councils of Spain and Portugal, tried to effect a compromise. The parties concerned gradually came to agree over the next several years that all the orders should have free access to Japan by the most convenient route. But it was only after a bitter battle had been waged that the pope (1633) and the crown (1634) decreed that Japan should be open to all comers and that the missionaries were free to go there via the Philippines as well as by way of India. Pope Urban VIII further decreed excommunication for any who tried to impede them. By this brief the papacy and the Propaganda clearly took the side of Spain and the mendicant orders.[315]

Ingoli and the congregation also met with a modicum of success in their efforts to denationalize the missions and to encourage cultural adaptation.[316] Missionaries were urged not to act as the political, diplomatic, or commercial agents of their homelands or to collaborate in overthrowing Asian gov-

---

[313] See G. de Vaumas, *L'éveil missionaire de la France* (Lyon, 1942), p. 257; and for Ingoli's memorandum (1644) to the successor of Urban VIII see J. Grisar, "Francesco Ingoli über die Aufgaben des kommenden Päpstes nach dem Tode Urbans VIII (1644)," *Archivum Historiae Pontificiae,* V (1967), 290–91.

[314] For Matteo's career see Ferroli, *op. cit.* (n. 2), II, 174–83; C. R. Boxer, *Race Relations in the Portuguese Colonial Empire, 1415–1825* (Oxford, 1963); and Th. Gesquiére, *Mathieu de Castro, premier Vicaire Apostolique aux Indes. Une création de la Propagande à ses débuts* (Bruges, 1937).

[315] For a detailed account of this lengthy and disedifying controversy in Europe see L. M. Pedot, O.S.M., *La S. C. de Propaganda Fide e le missioni del Giappone (1622–1838)* (Vicenza, 1946), pp. 65–230.

[316] For Ingoli's memorandum of 1638 or 1639 summarizing his objections to the patronages see Metzler, *loc. cit.* (n. 309), p. 222.

ernments. In 1633 Urban VIII threatened to excommunicate missionaries who became involved in commerce for personal or family enrichment. To promote Christianity as a universally valid religion not subject to any single nation or culture, the Propaganda obtained papal decrees ordering the missionaries to be zealous in learning the local languages and to be free in permitting the converts to retain rites, manners, and customs not contrary to religion and morality. It approved of and supported the accommodation policies followed by the Jesuits in Peking and by Nobili in Madura. To supply the missions with Christian books and other literary materials, in 1626 the Propaganda set up its own printing press, the *tipografia poliglotta* (now *vaticana*).[317] Catechisms, Bibles, grammars, and dictionaries were hereafter printed in most of the major Asian languages at this press as they became available. Ingoli contemporaneously began to collect a mission library including "history books from all peoples," because missionaries need to know the local customs, morals, and political tendencies to carry on their work successfully.[318] To help the cardinals of the congregation understand better the problems of the mission fields, the practice soon developed of providing each of them with a small reference library.[319] The Propaganda also tried to arbitrate the disputes between the missionary orders and the feuding European nationalities. Where national pride and self-interest were involved, as in the cases of the Portuguese and Spanish missions, the Propaganda could only slowly burrow its roots into the cracks and crevices of the rocky crag of empire.

The reorganization of the missionary hierarchy in the East was one of the first items on Ingoli's agenda. Since there were not enough bishoprics to supervise Christian activities adequately, Propaganda proposed the creation of new sees directly under the papacy and independent of Portugal. Since priests were always in short supply, Propaganda urged the training and ordination of a native clergy. The bishops and missionaries dispatched by Rome, too often unevenly distributed, were to work in areas of the East where the Portuguese and Spanish possessed no political claims, especially in the hinterlands. The barefoot Carmelites and the Capuchins, both relatively young mission orders with no long-standing privileges or commitments, were favored by the Propaganda. Beginning in the 1630's the Propaganda launched its program of erecting independent bishoprics. The Japanese bishopric of Funai, which had become vacant, was declared in 1632 to be an archbishopric directly dependent on Rome. To circumvent the legal right of the Portuguese king to appoint a new bishop of Japan, Propaganda used the medieval office of titular bishop, a superior appointed by Rome who should rule without

[317] On the polyglot press see Willi Henkel, "The Polyglot Printing-office of the Congregation," *SCPFMR,* Vol. 1/1, pp. 335–49, especially the list of works published, pp. 346–48.
[318] This collection was apparently incorporated in the 1660's into the library of the Urban College. See J. Metzler, *loc. cit.* (n. 124), pp. 299–300.
[319] *Ibid.,* p. 256.

territorial jurisdiction until improved conditions would permit the naming of a resident bishop by the king. In Asia the titular bishops of the Propaganda were called vicars apostolic; they possessed the power and dignity of a residential bishop *in partibus infidelium* and reported directly to the pope.[320]

The first titular bishops of the East were appointed in 1638. Franciscus Antonio de Santo Felici was named titular archbishop of Myra (in Lycia, modern southern Turkey). He was charged with the administration of the Japan mission, but was prevented by conditions from getting to his see. Matteo de Castro Mahalo, the converted Brahman educated at the Urban College, was named bishop of Chrysopolis and administrator of "Idalcan" (a part of the bishopric of Goa in western India), Pegu, and Golconda. While Castro Mahalo languished in Rome, he was succeeded by Custodius de Pinho (r. 1669–97), a Discalced Carmelite and a Brahman from the environs of Goa, who was designated vicar apostolic of Bijapur and Golconda. Pinho made peace with the Portuguese and worked with the Propaganda for the erection in 1671 of the see of Kanara. Thomas de Castro, an Indian Theatine, arrived at Mangalore in 1677 to administer this new and short-lived diocese. Until 1928 Catholic jurisdiction in western India remained divided between Goa and the Vicariate of the Great Mogul, the name later given to the diocese which Pinho had labored mightily to place upon firm foundations.[321]

In Rome the Propaganda also forged ahead with its plans. In 1648 the Congregation completed a catalog of the places outside Portuguese India where new bishoprics should be erected: Bengal, Solor, Makassar, Siam, and Ceylon. For personnel the Propaganda encouraged the Carmelites and Theatines, two of the Counter-Reformation orders which had participated in the founding of the Propaganda, to recruit and train missionaries for the apostolic vicariates being contemplated. In 1659, as Portuguese power waned in Malabar, the Propaganda founded the vicariate of Verapoly (Malabar), assigned it to the Carmelites, and named Giuseppe de Santa Maria as its first bishop. After the Dutch captured the Malabar cities, the Franciscans were permitted to remain at their posts. In practice, the Dutch allowed only Italian, Belgian, and German Catholic missionaries access to Malabar after 1663.

For political and economic support of its new enterprises in the East, the Propaganda reluctantly turned to France for aid. The French had long been watching with an interest bordering on envy the religious and commercial triumphs claimed by the Portuguese and Jesuits in the East. When King Henry IV readmitted the Jesuits to Paris in 1603, he justified his action in part by pointing to the Society's spectacular achievements in China.[322] Dur-

---

[320] See Mulders, *op. cit.* (n. 305), pp. 274–78; for the term "vicar apostolic" see F. J. Winslow's article in *New Catholic Encyclopedia*, XIV, 638–39.

[321] See Ferroli, *op. cit.* (n. 2), II, 174; and the article on "India" by J. Wicki in the *New Catholic Encyclopedia*, VII, 435–44.

[322] See Pastor, *op. cit.* (n. 308), XXIII, 179.

ing the reign of Louis XIII (1610–42) France experienced a grassroots revival of piety and a reform in clerical training that produced what some historians have called a seventeenth-century Catholic Renaissance. The *Compagnie du Saint-Sacrement* founded in 1630 by clerics and laymen was dedicated to internal missions and later to evangelizing in Canada. Between 1642 and 1660, while the war with Spain ground to a close, seminaries were founded in unprecedented numbers throughout the country.[323] Central to this renewal was Vincent de Paul (1581–1660) and his Congregation of Priests of the Mission, an order which undertook the religious instruction of the poor and lowly in France and soon extended its activities overseas.[324] This rising concern with religion and missions was transformed into a national evangelizing effort when the *Société des missions étrangères* was established at Paris in 1664, the year of the founding of the French East India Company.[325]

The individual who tied the apostolic aspirations of the Propaganda to the French flag was Alexandre de Rhodes (1591–1660), a Jesuit of Avignon, later known as the Apostle of Vietnam. He had left France in 1618 and arrived at Macao in May, 1623. From 1624 to 1626 he was in Cochin-China and from 1627 to 1630 in Tongking, then two separate states of Indochina (Vietnam). For the next ten years he ministered to the Chinese Christians of Macao in the capacity of "Father of the Christians," an office then common in the Portuguese missions. He returned to Cochin-China in 1640 as superior of its Jesuit mission and was exiled in 1645.[326] From Macao he sailed in 1645 for Europe accompanied by a Chinese convert. Upon his arrival at Rome in 1649 he urged the Propaganda to send bishops to Indochina to create an indigenous clergy to minister there to the needs of what he hoped would become flourishing and enduring Christian communities. The Propaganda, since it had experienced a number of failures in its efforts to obtain volunteers for its projects, assigned Rhodes the task of finding suitable candidates. Like the congregation itself, Rhodes soon learned that recruitment was difficult so long as the Propaganda possessed no means of protecting its bishops from the reprisals of the Portuguese. Rhodes returned to France in 1652 to start forging the link between the Propaganda and the French church that bound them together for the remainder of the century.[327]

Rhodes, like other Frenchmen of his day, resented "the way our good French folk allow foreigners to grow rich off the East Indian trade." He was also convinced, despite the disillusionment of the Propaganda with· French

---

[323] See R. Mousnier, *The Institutions of France under the Absolute Monarchy* (trans. by Brian Pearce; Chicago, 1979), pp. 340–42.
[324] On the early missions of the Vincentians see Vaumas, *op. cit.* (n. 313), chap. iii.
[325] For its history see above, pp. 95–105.
[326] On Rhodes' missionary activities, see below, pp. 236–40.
[327] For a brief summary of Rhodes' career see Dehergne, *op. cit.* (n. 86), pp. 215–16.

missionaries, that "the piety of France's bishops is capable of carrying the Gospel to both one place and the other."[328] The Propaganda, on the other hand, had under Ingoli's leadership wanted to end the national patronage system and develop in Asia native churches directly dependent on Rome. But the efforts to attain these objectives in Japan and India had foundered on the rock of Portuguese resistance. Clearly it had become imperative by the time Ingoli died in 1649 to avoid confrontations with the Iberian powers and to concentrate on those parts of Asia where they had little or no control. France, the only great Catholic and Atlantic power which did not possess economic or religious stakes in Asia, might provide the Propaganda with the personnel, finances, and protection it needed to carry out its missionary program. The Propaganda hesitated for a number of years to cement this alliance until it could obtain safeguards thought to be strong enough to prevent its enterprise from becoming a French patronage.

The problem of personnel was the first to be attacked. Rhodes had suggested in 1650 that several bishops should be sent to Indochina to build up an indigenous clergy. Volunteers for such posts were few because of the omnipresent danger presented by the Portuguese, Dutch, and English. French Capuchins sent to India by the Propaganda via the land route had been treated as intruders or worse by the Portuguese secular and religious authorities.[329] Four Discalced Carmelites of the Propaganda tried vainly to restore Rome's authority in Malabar from 1657 until the Dutch captured Cranganore in 1662.[330] According to the Portuguese the papal decree of 1633 permitting the regulars to take any route whatsoever to Asia did not apply to the secular priests recruited by the Propaganda.[331] Ingoli and his successor, Dionisio Massari (in office 1649–1657), had sponsored several unsuccessful missionary efforts of the Vincentians in Africa and America. The failure of these enterprises led Rome to jump to the unwarranted conclusion that the French clerics were not firm or persevering enough in their missionary vocation.

The Vincentians, on their side, were inclined to blame the Propaganda for their failures. In 1653 Vincent de Paul wrote that many pious and zealous Frenchmen hoped that the pope would provide an adequate organization to carry on missions in the Far East.[332] While in Paris in 1653, Rhodes met Louis Bagot, a fellow-Jesuit and the spiritual director of a group of diocesan priests who styled themselves *Les bons amis*. Immediately members of this

[328] From the translation of his travel account in Solange Hertz, *Rhodes of Viet Nam* (Westminster, Md., 1966), pp. 31, 238.

[329] For the setbacks suffered by the French Capuchins sent out by the Propaganda before 1660 see Vaumas, *op. cit.* (n. 313), pp. 356–59.

[330] On the St. Thomas schism see above, pp. 162–65.

[331] Mulders, *op. cit.* (n. 305), p. 285.

[332] See R. Chalumeau, C.M., "Saint Vincent de Paul et le Saint-Siège," *Archivum Historiae Pontificiae*, V (1967), 265.

group volunteered for the mission to Asia. But the Propaganda still remained hesitant about letting its enterprise fall under the control of the French church. To reassure Rome on this score the Assembly of the French Clergy in 1655 voted the funds necessary to maintain the three who volunteered to be bishops. The French bishops were to be based at Avignon, then a papal protectorate.[333]

François Pallu (1625–84) and several others of the bons amis journeyed to Rome in 1657 to present their case to Pope Alexander VII (r. 1655–67). After submitting their proposal to a commission of four cardinals, the pope decided in their favor. He divided the Far East into three vicariates apostolic (Tongking, Cochin-China, China) and directed that they be responsible to the Propaganda. In 1658 Pallu was named titular bishop of Heliopolis (Baalbek) with jurisdiction over Tongking, Laos, and five provinces of southwestern China. Pierre Lambert de La Motte (1624–79) was named bishop of Berytus (Beirut) with jurisdiction over Cochin-China, four provinces of southeastern China, and the island of Hainan. In 1660 Ignace Cotolendi (1630–62) was appointed bishop of Metellopolis (Medele) with jurisdiction over three provinces of northeastern China, Tartary, and Korea. All were to be aided by seculars in training indigenous Christians as catechists and priests. With the cautious consent of the Propaganda, the new bishops in partibus infidelium were granted the right to found a seminary in Paris for training secular priests as missionaries and for promoting missions generally. After a series of false starts, La société des missions étrangères (The Society of Foreign Missions) came into being with the sanction and support of both king (1663) and pope (1664).[334]

The Paris society was not constituted as a religious order. It was founded as an organization of secular priests and lay persons dedicated to the propagation of the gospel in foreign lands. Its Paris seminary on the Rue du Bac, where it still stands, became the center for the recruitment and training of missionaries. It had no single superior but was ruled by the French bishops, the vicars apostolic, and the directors of its seminary. Recruits had to be less than thirty-five years of age to be admitted to the seminary. On entering the society the individual had to vow to spend his days in missionary work. The society, in its turn, agreed to meet the temporal needs of the missionary from funds contributed by the Propaganda, the crown, and charity-minded institutions and persons. The explicit object of the society's missions was to work, as the Propaganda insisted, for the formation of indigenous clergy and churches. Between 1660 and 1700 it sent one hundred missionaries to Asia.[335]

[333] See H. Chappoulie, Rome et les missions d'Indochine au XVIIe siècle (2 vols., Paris, 1943), I, 115.

[334] J. Guennou, Les Missions Etrangères (Paris, 1963), pp. 79–90.

[335] See the article "Paris Foreign Mission Society" in The New Catholic Encyclopedia, X, 1016–17.

While the Paris society was being formed, the French bishops prepared to depart for their sees. In its instructions of 1659 the Propaganda ordered the vicars apostolic to leave secretly, to travel overland to India, to avoid all areas controlled by the Portuguese, and to remain silent about their destination and mission. Once at their posts in China and Indochina they should recruit, educate, and ordain qualified young native men and notify the Propaganda of any who seemed worthy of the episcopate. They should adapt themselves to local customs and communicate regularly to the Propaganda their problems, successes, and failures. In the spirit of Ingoli they should always have before their eyes the fostering of a native clergy.

The newly appointed vicars apostolic, despite the admonition of secrecy, began to publicize their mission even before its departure from France. In cooperation with the *Compagnie du Saint-Sacrement,* the bishops published pamphlets to arouse public interest and involvement in the new missionary effort of secular priests and laymen that they were heading.[336] Funds and recruits were called for to assure the success of what was promoted as a patriotic challenge. The Propaganda, the Portuguese, the Dutch, and the Jesuits immediately reacted against what they saw as a French national effort to break into the commerce and apostolate of Asia. Their suspicions were given substance when in 1659 the *Saint-Sacrement* began to organize a *Compagnie de Chine* modeled on the Dutch East India Company. The failure of this commercial enterprise was followed in 1660 by the interdiction of the *Saint-Sacrement* by Cardinal Mazarin, then the effective ruler of France.

While these untoward events were going on, the king, the Assembly of the French Clergy, the *Saint-Sacrement,* and a number of private donors advanced the funds necessary to defray the costs of the first expedition. After being rebuked by the Propaganda for their part in promoting public fanfare, the French missionaries left quietly from Marseilles for the Levant in three separate groups, each of which was headed by a vicar apostolic. Lambert de La Motte and two companions left on November 27, 1660; Cotolendi and three missionaries on September 3, 1661; Pallu and nine associates on January 3, 1662. Once they arrived in the Levant the French missionaries traveled by caravan and under cover of night to the Persian Gulf. On this long and fatiguing trip a few died and several deserted. From the Persian Gulf the remaining missionaries went by sea to Surat. To avoid the Portuguese, who were under orders to capture and send them to Lisbon, Lambert and his two companions proceeded overland to Masulipatam, India's international port on the east coast. Here they obtained passage on a Moorish vessel which took them to Tenasserim. From this Siamese-controlled port they proceeded by riverboats and barges to Ayut'ia. Of the seventeen who departed, just nine finally arrived in Siam between 1662 and 1664, after more than two

---

[336] The most important of these was the brochure entitled *Etat sommaire des missions de la Chine* (Paris, 1659).

years en route. Cotolendi himself died at Masulipatam while awaiting passage to Siam.[337]

From Ayut'ia, established sea routes connected Siam to India, Indochina, and China. But Lambert and Pallu were not able to proceed to Indochina because of the continuing persecution of the Christians there. Nor were they able to proceed to Macao and China, for the Jesuits warned them that the Christians were then being attacked by the Oboi regime of Peking.[338] In Ayut'ia the French missionaries found a Christian community estimated at two thousand souls who were being ministered to by four Jesuits, two Dominicans, two Franciscans, and some secular priests. The superior of the Jesuits was Tomaso Valguarnera (1608–77), a Sicilian who had been sent by Macao to serve the Japanese Christians in Siam. When Pallu arrived in 1664 with four more priests and a layman, the French missionaries at Ayut'ia became nine in number. Although they were soon under attack from the Portuguese, the French decided to remain at Ayut'ia and to establish there a staging ground for the penetration of the lands east and west of Siam. Since the Siamese clearly tolerated Christian activity, the French missionaries decided to establish at once a training school for young boys. In 1665 King Narai (r. 1657–88) sanctioned the school and gave his permission for the enrollment of ten Siamese students. Shortly thereafter the Jesuits followed suit and organized a school of their own. All the Christian missionaries were granted the privilege to travel freely about the country and to preach wherever they wished. These early successes encouraged the French missionaries, inexperienced as they were, to believe that the king himself might become a convert and that his subjects would follow him in adopting Christianity.[339]

The French at Ayut'ia decided to send Pallu back to Rome to explain their decisions to remain in Siam and to report on their conflict with the Portuguese. He left Siam in 1665 and by April 20, 1667, was back in Rome. After several years of negotiation, Clement IX in 1673 finally decreed the erection of Siam as an apostolic see that should be assigned to the successor of Cotolendi. The pope again forbade both the regular and secular priests from engaging in Asian commerce even though the men in the field were desperate for funds. He also ordered the regulars in the East Indies mission to recognize the authority of the vicars apostolic and to work with them harmoniously. The Jesuits, the mendicants, and the Portuguese secular hierarchy would long claim exemption from this papal order.[340]

---

[337] See Guennou, *op. cit.* (n. 334), chap. vii. For the route followed by Lambert de la Motte see Chappoulie, *op. cit.* (n. 333), I, 131–33; and E. W. Hutchinson, "Journal of Mgr. Lambert, Bishop of Beritus, from Tenasserim to Siam in 1662," *Selected Articles from the Siam Society Journal*, Vol. VIII. *Relationship with France, England, and Denmark* (Bangkok, 1959), pp. 91–94.

[338] See above, pp. 196–97.

[339] See E. W. Hutchinson, "The French Foreign Mission in Siam during the XVIIth Century," *Selected Articles from the Siam Society Journal*. Vol. VIII. *Relationship with France, England, and Denmark* (Bangkok, 1959), pp. 26–36.

[340] For a summary of the ensuing jurisdictional struggle see Mulders, *op. cit.* (n. 305), pp. 285–88.

Before the arrival of the vicars apostolic in Siam, Christian penetration of continental Southeast Asia had been sporadic and unsystematic. European and Asian merchants had regularly traded in the marts of the region stretching from the Bay of Bengal to the western ports of Indochina where Portuguese political control was nonexistent. The Propaganda believed that this was a region in which its missionaries might work without serious opposition from the Portuguese or the Jesuits. Its first project for the erection of a bishopric in Asia centered on Bengal, where the Augustinians dominated missionary activity. In 1624 the Augustinian vicar-general had proposed to Ingoli the creation of an independent bishopric at Hugli, a city where the friars claimed to have fourteen thousand Christian converts. This proposal had been soberly considered even though Bengal was technically subject to Goa and Mylapore and was beginning to be penetrated by the Portuguese Jesuits.[341] Although this initial project was scuttled, the Augustinians continued their efforts to free their Bengal mission from the control of the *padroado*.[342] Until the last decade of the century, when Propaganda missionaries entered Bengal in force, the Augustinian mission centered at Hugli continued to dominate Christian activity in the delta of the Ganges without further serious interference from Goa or the Jesuits.[343]

A few friars from Malacca and the Philippines had worked in Siam and Burma intermittently during the last years of the sixteenth century. Caught up in the whirlwind of wars the missionaries at Ayut'ia and Pegu had left in despair for safer places.[344] The Jesuits, who had paid almost no attention to Burma and Siam during the sixteenth century, became active at Pegu during De Brito's brief period (1604–13) of glory there.[345] In 1613 the Jesuits Diogo Nunes and Manuel da Fonseca were captured by the king of Ava after De Brito's defeat. Along with the Portuguese and Luso-Asian supporters of De Brito, they were enslaved and carried off to Upper Burma. Here the Christians were given lands to cultivate and Fonseca ministered to them until his death in 1652. These Christian communities of *bayingyi* (a Burman form of *feringhi* or Franks) existed into the twentieth century.[346] Beginning around 1640 the Propaganda sought to revive the mission in Pegu. Portuguese men-

[341] See C. Alonso, O.S.A., "Primer projecto de Propaganda Fide para la creación de un obispado en Bengala (1624–25)," *Augustinianum*, VI (1966), 77–90.

[342] For lists of the personnel in the Augustinian vice-province of India as of 1638 and 1642, especially prepared for the Propaganda, see C. Alonso, O.S.A., "Agustinos en la India. Relaciónes y listas de religiosos inéditas (1624–42)," *Analecta Augustiniana*, XXXVII (1974), 283–96.

[343] See above, p. 142.

[344] See *Asia*, I, 285–86.

[345] For Guerreiro's account in the *Relations* see C. H. Payne (trans.), *Jahangir and the Jesuits* (New York, 1930), pp. 185–276.

[346] See L. Besse, S.J., and H. Hosten, S.J., "Father Manoel da Fonseca, S.J., in Ava (Burma), 1613–52," *Journal of the Asiatic Society of Bengal*, n.s., XXI (1925), 27–48; and Maung Kaung, "The Beginnings of Christian Missionary Education in Burma 1600–1824," *Journal of the Burma Research Society*, XX (1930), 62–63.

dicant and Jesuit missionaries were joined in this enterprise by Italian Theatines and French Capuchins.[347] In 1665 Burma was entrusted to the Paris Society of Foreign Missions as an extension of the Siam mission. By 1667 a small but permanent mission was shakily maintained in Pegu with the aid and cooperation of the Portuguese. It endured until 1817.[348]

Luso-Siamese relations began to improve in 1605–6 with the death of King Naresuan (r. 1590–1605) and the arrival of the Dutch in Siam. The new royal regime assiduously cultivated relations with Goa and invited Portuguese merchants and missionaries to come to Ayut'ia. The outbreak of war between Ava and Siam in 1613 increased Ayut'ia's interest in closer relations with the Portuguese. The inauguration of the "Great Persecution" in Japan brought both European and Japanese Christian refugees to Siam. A Dominican was sent from Goa in 1616 to convince the Siamese to restore relations with Malacca and to resist Dutch and English efforts to break into the trade. In 1621 the king of Siam gave the Catholic Christians freedom to preach, convert, and build a church in Ayut'ia. Dominicans and Franciscans were immediately sent from Malacca to establish a mission, and they were soon followed by Jesuits from the Japan province. It was the presence in Siam of increasingly large numbers of Japanese Christians that stimulated the new Jesuit interest in Siam.[349] By 1626 around four hundred Japanese Christians were living there. Some of the Jesuits were employed in engineering works then being undertaken to control the Menam river. All this cordiality ended abruptly with the downfall of the Piren dynasty in 1629. When Prasat Thong (r. 1630–56) came to the throne, he succumbed to Dutch pressure and forced the Catholic missionaries to leave Ayut'ia in 1633. Very few Portuguese missionaries worked openly over the next decade in Siam, Pegu, or Arakan.[350]

The Siamese, as they sought to play the Europeans off against one another, cultivated the Dutch from 1631 to the fall of Malacca in 1641. Fearful of the growing Dutch preponderance, Siam thereafter turned to the Portuguese again. Dominicans were shortly sent from Macao and Makassar to revive the mission in Ayut'ia. Occasionally Jesuits from the Japan province visited Siam to aid the Dominicans and to minister to the Japanese-in-exile. The missionaries, who often served as chaplains to the Portuguese in the royal army, were periodically granted concessions by the king. They were given a Buddhist temple to convert into a church. Christians who had been

---

[347] See Pastor, *op. cit.* (n. 308), XXIX, 246.

[348] See Duncan, *op. cit.* (n. 14), p. 280; and Guennou, *op. cit.* (n. 334), p. 188.

[349] See J. Burnay, "Notes chronologiques sur les missions Jésuites du Siam au XVIIe siècle," *AHSI*, XXII (1953), 171.

[350] Based on B. Biermann, "Die Mission der portugiesischen Dominikaner in Hinterindien," *ZMR*, XXI (1931), 323–25; J. J. Gonçalves, "Os portugueses na Siao," *Boletim da sociedade de geografia de Lisboa*, LXXV (1957), 444; and L. Besse and H. Hosten, "List of Portuguese Jesuit Missionaries in Bengal and Burma (1576–1642)," *Journal of the Asiatic Society of Bengal*, n.s., VII (1911), 15–23.

enslaved by the Dutch and Siamese were allowed from time to time to purchase their freedom. The mission endured and even expanded before the arrival of the first missionaries from France in 1662.[351] But converts were few in the best of times, for natives could not become Christians under Siamese law without royal approval. The king and his nobles could not readily be converted since they were dedicated to Buddhism and polygamy. The missionaries therefore had no choice but to minister to the Portuguese and Japanese Christians while currying the king's favor.[352]

The Christian enterprise in Indochina (Tongking, Cochin-China, and Cambodia) during the first half of the century likewise experienced both setbacks and successes. Adventurers, merchants, and friars from Malacca and Manila had become involved on the Cambodian side of the war being waged with Siam after 1593. The Siamese victory of 1603 had brought an end to the Spanish influence in Cambodia, even though hotbloods lobbied in Madrid for long thereafter asking for a major military effort. They hoped to obtain control of the Mekong Delta as a first step to the commercial and religious penetration of Indochina and eventually China. Siam, it was estimated, could be overwhelmed and occupied by a force of one thousand from the Philippines.[353]

It was from Macao rather than Manila that serious Christian penetration of the Indochinese peninsula was initiated. Long-established commercial relations between Macao and the ports of Indochina had informed the Jesuits about the Annamite kingdoms of Tongking and Cochin-China that stretched southward from China's Yunnan province to Champa. These two kingdoms, technically in vassalage to China, were known to be constantly at war with each other. They were reputed to be wealthy and regularly in need of the weapons that only the Europeans could supply. As a consequence, the Portuguese from Macao usually had free access to the ports of Hanoi and Hue (founded 1626), the rival capital cities of Tongking and Cochin-China respectively. The arrival of the Dutch in 1601 off the coasts of Indochina gave the rulers of Tongking and Cochin-China a possible alternative to the Portuguese and Macaoese traders.

Japanese red-seal ships, many of which carried political refugees fleeing from the Tokugawa rule, appeared regularly in the ports of Indochina beginning in 1604. Over the next twelve years at least 179 red-seal ships departed from Japan. Of this number 80 went to Indochina, 37 to Siam, and 34 to the Philippines.[354] The Japanese emigres were much better received and more comfortable in Annam (Tongking and Cochin-China) than elsewhere

---

[351] For the establishment and history of the permanent Jesuit mission founded after 1660 see Burnay, *loc. cit.* (n. 349), pp. 185–202.

[352] See Biermann, *loc. cit.* (n. 20), pp. 324–25.

[353] See *Asia*, I, 309–12.

[354] See N. Peri, "Essai sur les relations du Japon et de l'Indochine aux XVIe et XVIIe siècles," *Bulletin de l'École Française d'Extreme-orient*, XXIII (1923), 30–31.

because of the cultural affinities of language, social practices, and mores stemming from the common Chinese background of both the Annamese and Japanese civilizations. In nearby Cambodia, where an Indianized culture dominated, the Japanese alienated the natives by their foreign and unruly behavior.[355] When Japanese Christians in sizable numbers began to appear in Annam after 1614, they were soon followed by Jesuit priests.

Jesuit evangelization of the Annamite kingdoms was pioneered by Francesco Buzomi (1576–1639), a Neapolitan, and several Portuguese Jesuits of Macao. By Easter, 1615, they were celebrating mass at the port of Tourane in Cochin-China. Since Japan remained closed, missionaries continued to leave Macao regularly for the new field opening in Cochin-China. One of these was Cristoforo Borri (1583–1632), a Milanese who was in Cochin-China from 1618 to 1621; on his return to Europe he published in Italian during 1631 the first European account of Cochin-China and the establishment of the Jesuit mission there.[356] In December, 1624, six Jesuits under the leadership of Gabriel de Matos (1572–1633), the visitor to the mission, joined Buzomi's group. One of their number was Alexandre de Rhodes, the "Apostle of Vietnam." An avid student of language, Rhodes quickly learned to preach in the Vietnamese then spoken in Tongking, Cochin-China, and Champa.[357] Christian communities of neophytes were shortly organized at Fai-fo, an ancient commercial center vital to the seaborne trade with China, and at Tourane and Hue. Sai-voung (r. 1613–35) of Cochin-China tolerated the Jesuits and their evangelizing only so long as the ships from Macao came to Fai-fo. When they failed to appear in 1625, the king immediately ordained an end to Christian activities in Cochin-China; similar edicts were issued several times more down to the end of Buzomi's tenure as superior in 1639. Here, as in China, the Jesuits quickly learned to seek refuge among the converts or to take brief excursions to Macao until the storms had passed.[358]

Even though the Jesuit position in Cochin-China was still precarious, the superiors in Macao decided in 1626 to open a mission in the northern kingdom of Tongking. Rhodes, because of his command of the Vietnamese language, was chosen to head the new enterprise. In March, 1627, he arrived in Tongking aboard a Portuguese merchant ship in the company of a Luso-Japanese priest assigned to minister to the Japanese Christians. Trịnh Tráng

---

[355] Complaints about Japanese behavior were not limited to Cambodia. Their unruliness also elicited rebukes from the authorities in Manila, Cochin-China, and Siam. See Boxer, *op. cit.* (n. 136), p. 295.

[356] For his biography and a bibliographical rundown of his book and its numerous translations during the seventeenth century, see C. B. Maybon, "Notice sur Cristoforo Borri et sur les éditions de sa 'Relation,'" *Bulletin des amis du Vieux Hué*, XXXVIII (1931), 270–75. The 1633 partial English translation by Robert Ashley was republished in 1970 by *Theatrum Orbis Terrarum*. An annotated edition of the French version (1631) was published in 1931 by Lieutenant-Colonel Bonifacy of the University of Hanoi. Also see below, p. 377.

[357] See Hertz (trans.), *op. cit.* (n. 328), pp. 49–50. Previously only Father Francisco de Pina was able to preach without an interpreter.

[358] Based on Chappoulie, *op. cit.* (n. 333), I, 22–26.

(r. 1623–57), who was then at war with Sai-voung of Cochin-China, was intrigued by the gifts Rhodes gave him and invited the Jesuit to stay at the royal capital of Hanoi. The king ordered a spacious house built for the Jesuit that was soon converted into a church. Since he enjoyed the royal patronage, Rhodes quickly had a series of successes. In the first year he baptized the king's sister, 17 close relatives of the king, and 1,200 adults. According to his own testimony he baptized 5,500 more, including 200 native priests.[359] The converted priests he trained as catechists to aid him in preparing the neophytes for baptism. The first troubles occurred, as they did in many other Asian countries, over the Christian condemnation of polygamy. The king himself came under fire from the palace women, who feared for their own futures should he decide to accept Christianity. Under pressure from his wives, their families, and their eunuchs, the king turned against Rhodes. In 1630 the Jesuit was banished and disconsolately returned to Macao, never to visit Tongking again.

While Rhodes worked in Macao for the next decade, the mission in Tongking continued to function fitfully. Working quietly, two or three Jesuits ministered to the faithful and carried on the work of conversion. By 1640 the Jesuits claimed ninety-four thousand converts and more than one hundred large churches. Official persecution began in 1643 with charges that the Christians were destroying the images and holy places of the non-Christians. In Cochin-China the four or five Jesuits who at this time were working there under Buzomi were likewise always uncertain about the king's mood and their safety. On Buzomi's death in 1639 the Cochin-China mission claimed at least thirty thousand Christians. It also suffered from a renewal of royal persecution. The Jesuits were charged with having prevented the rains from coming by their magical incantations.[360]

In 1640 the Jesuit position in East Asia was everywhere in danger. Antonio Rubino, the ill-starred visitor to China and Japan, dispatched Giovanni Francesco Ferrari (1608–71) to Tongking and Rhodes to Cochin-China to restore the missions "laid waste by the banishment of all the Fathers."[361] For the next five years the Jesuits went secretly to their assigned posts, where they were protected by the converts. So long as the Macao merchants were conducting business, the Jesuits were tolerated. When the merchants returned to Macao, the Jesuits were regularly forced to leave, too. They sought to beguile the king with gifts of clocks and books of mathematics and natural science. While these overtures won some short respites, the enemies of the Jesuits at court intensified their attacks upon the Christians, and there were martyrdoms in 1645. In both Annamite kingdoms the rulers began to look to Manila as an alternative trading partner. When Spanish vessels

[359]Hertz (trans.), *op. cit.* (n. 328), pp. 64–65.
[360]Based on Chappoulie, *op. cit.* (n. 333), I, 24–26; and Pastor, *op. cit.* (n. 308), XXIX, 247.
[361]Rhodes in Hertz (trans.), *op. cit.* (n. 328), p. 80.

landed on these shores, they were warmly welcomed. Back in Macao his superiors decided to send Rhodes to Europe to ask for help in forwarding the missions of Indochina. After an arduous journey through the Dutch blockade to Surat, he went overland to the Mediterranean. Rhodes arrived in Rome on June 27, 1649, claiming to be "as strong and fresh for any task as when I left Rome for India thirty-one years before." [362]

While Rhodes was on his way home, the political-military situation in Annam changed dramatically in favor of Cochin-China. Hiền-Vương (Nguyễn Phúc-Tần), its new ruler (r. 1648–87), extended his authority by 1653 over Champa all the way south to Cape Varella. Over the next few years he conquered a large part of Cambodia and in 1658 sacked its capital of Udong. The Jesuits in Macao meanwhile decided that they could not abandon the Christians of Cochin-China completely. The Sicilian Metello Saccano (1612–62) and several other Jesuits were sent to Hanoi with gifts for the king and promises that Macao would supply cannons for his armies. In 1655 Pedro Marques (1613–70), a Luso-Japanese born at Nagasaki, and François Rivas relieved Saccano who then went to Rome on behalf of the Japan province. Carlo della Rocca (1613–70), an Italian father, followed the armies of Hiền-Vương into Cambodia in an effort to inaugurate a mission there. The years 1656–57 were a relatively peaceful time for the missionaries. Troubles came again in 1658 when the expected artillery from Macao failed to arrive. Once the cannons finally appeared in 1659, the Jesuits were left in peace at Fai-fo, Tourane, and Hue.

A military defeat administered by Trịnh Tạc (r. 1657–82), the new ruler of Tongking, turned the Cochin-Chinese against the Jesuits once more in the 1660's. It was at this point that a letter arrived from Lambert de La Motte in Siam announcing that he was coming to Cochin-China. The Jesuits advised the vicar apostolic of the deteriorated conditions prevailing there and warned him that his appearance might well do more harm than good to the Christian cause. In response to this warning Lambert decided to remain in Siam and to send in his place Louis Chevreuil, a French secular priest (1627–93), who had just arrived at Ayut'ia with Pallu. [363]

Father Chevreuil, who had arrived in Siam during January, 1664, left for Cochin-China just five months later. Armed with the title of vicar-general, he arrived at Fai-fo on July 26 with a Japanese interpreter as his sole companion. He traveled secretly to Hue, where he lodged in the house of Jean de la Croix, a Christian manufacturer of artillery for the royal armies. From here he moved on to Tourane, where Marques tended a small church. Chevreuil, accompanied by Marques, returned to Fai-fo, where he rented a house. Once established, he presented his credentials as vicar-general to the Jesuits and asked for their formal submission to his authority. Fearing the

---

[362] From *ibid.*, p. 236. For his subsequent career in Europe see above, pp. 229–30.
[363] Based on Chappoulie, *op. cit.* (n. 333), Vol. I, chap. x.

reaction of their superiors in Macao, the four Jesuits of the *padroado* in Cochin-China equivocated in their responses. While divergences subsequently developed between the Jesuits and the representatives of the vicar apostolic, the court resumed its attacks upon the Christians. Many of the new converts quickly renounced the faith, but forty-three of the faithful were martyred in 1665. Three of the Jesuits were expelled and a few months later Chevreuil was also obliged to leave.

Chevreuil was succeeded in Cochin-China by Antoine Hainques (d. 1670), a young and brilliant French secular priest. He entered the kingdom of Hiền Vưởng in Japanese dress and proceeded to Fai-fo late in 1665. In the following spring two Jesuits from Macao disembarked at Fai-fo but stayed there for just three months. Hainques thereafter was the only missionary in the kingdom until 1668 when Domenico Fuciti, one of the Jesuits expelled three years earlier, appeared bearing letters from Macao authorizing him to act as vicar-general. Jean de la Croix and other local Christians sided with the Jesuits in the ensuing contest; however, Fuciti shortly returned to Macao. Despite such jurisdictional problems Hainques continued his evangelizing work. Shortly before he died in 1670, Hainques reported to the Propaganda that during his five-year stay he had baptized 2,440 natives while the catechists had brought 3,920 to the faith. For the nonce, the Christians of Cochin-China were left to survive on their own.

While Hainques carried on in Cochin-China, Louis Chevreuil was sent to Cambodia to join Paulo d'Acosta, a Portuguese priestly refugee from Makassar who had been ministering to the Portuguese families at Phnom Penh. At Udong the Jesuit Carlo della Rocca, formerly active in Cochin-China, now ministered to five or six hundred Christian refugees from Cochin-China. A Piedmontese, Della Rocca was inclined personally to take a sympathetic attitude towards the French missionary. From Della Rocca, Chevreuil learned that the Buddhist Cambodians were even more difficult to convert than the Siamese. Scandalized by the commercial activities of the Macao Jesuits in the Mekong Delta, Chevreuil began to write accusatory letters to his superiors. Early in 1670 he was kidnapped by the Portuguese, taken by boat to Macao, and was there charged with heresy. Like other French priests before him, he was sent to Goa. He finally wound up at Surat, where he met Pallu.[364]

After the departure of Rhodes from Cochin-China in 1645, the Jesuits enjoyed a relatively lengthy respite from regular persecution. In Tongking news of the Christian successes in China was conveyed to Hanoi by emissaries sent to Peking with tribute. In Peking they had observed that the Jesuits were held in high esteem by the ruling circles, and they let it be known in Hanoi that the fathers had even contributed to the learning of China's celebrated mandarins. In 1645 João Cabral (1598–1669), vice-provincial of the Japan province, and four other Jesuits joined Girolamo Majorica (1591–1656)

---

[364] Based on *ibid.*, Vol. I, chap. xii.

and the little group of missionaries at Hanoi who had escaped banishment. Progress in Christianizing went steadily ahead for the next decade and more under the generally benevolent reign of Trịnh Tráng. Occasional attacks on Christian churches and residences occurred, but these incidents were not serious enough to halt the gradual organization of the church in Tongking. Since the Jesuits were never more than seven or eight in number, they traveled from place to place to visit the Christian communities. The catechists, seventy in number by 1656, were the true bulwark of the expanding church. The Jesuits aided them by providing books of piety in Annamese versions prepared by Rhodes and Majorica.[365] Once a week the superior in Hanoi attended a general audience to present gifts to the king and to test the political waters at the court. Native Christians employed by the crown, as well as court women, also kept the Jesuits informed.

The death of Trịnh Tráng in 1657 brought his son Trịnh Tạc (r. 1657–82) into power in Tongking. At first the new ruler's attitude towards the Christians followed that adopted by his father. Gradually, however, he began to listen to those among his advisers who saw the Christian missionaries as a foreign, new, and divisive influence. They taught a creed which conflicted with traditional beliefs and threatened to undermine the king's authority. The officials attributed the military defeats suffered in the last years of the previous reign to the internal disunity of Tongking and to the support given the ruler at Hue by the Portuguese of Macao. The king himself soon became convinced that his Christian subjects had too many loyalties other than the allegiance owed to him. In June, 1658, the Swiss superior Onuphre Borges (Burgi) was ordered to recall to Hanoi all the Jesuit missionaries then traveling in the provinces. In the following month all of the Jesuits, except Borges and Joseph Tissanier (1618–88) were embarked for Macao. While the king threatened to prohibit Christianity entirely, he continued to tolerate the Jesuits and their converts to prevent commercial relations with Macao from being suspended altogether. The Jesuits also had rich and powerful friends in Hanoi, especially Japanese Christian merchants, who supported their cause at the court. At the end of 1660 Trịnh Tạc began extensive military preparations to resume the war against Cochin-China and to ward off a possible attack from the Manchu armies then consolidating their hold on south China. To reinforce his own rule, Trịnh Tạc outlawed in 1662 all false doctrines, including Taoism, Buddhism, and the "new law" of the Christians. The Manchu blockade (1662–67) of Macao completely cut off its trade with Tongking and led in 1663 to the banishment of all the Jesuits.[366]

When François Pallu arrived at Siam early in 1664 he learned that Christianity was proscribed in his vicariate of Tongking. Taking his lead from

---

[365] See Hoang Xuân-hãn, "Girolamo Maiorica, ses oeuvres en langue Vietnamienne conservées à la Bibliothèque Nationale de Paris," *AHSI*, XXII (1953), 203–14.

[366] Based on Chappoulie, *op. cit.* (n. 333), Vol. I, chap. xiii.

Lambert de La Motte, who had earlier decided against traveling to Cochin-China himself, Pallu decided to remain in Siam. When he departed for Europe one year later, he left to Lambert the decision as to when to send priests into Tongking. He also left instructions for his missionaries to distinguish their vocation from that of the Jesuits, since the latter had been rendered suspect by the conquests and commercial ambitions of their compatriots. The representatives of the *Missions étrangères,* while always remaining outwardly cooperative with the Jesuits, should present themselves to the Tonkinese as Frenchmen whose king claimed not a single inch of land in the East. In the spring of 1666, after hearing favorable news from a catechist of Hanoi, Lambert dispatched François Deydier (1634–93) to Tongking with the powers of vicar-general. Deydier, dressed as a poor sailor, arrived at Hanoi early in August, 1666. Here he lived in secret with Raphael Rhodes, a rich Christian Cochin-Chinese merchant. Although he was rebuffed by the Japanese Christians ministered to by the Jesuits, Deydier quickly won the support of the native catechists. With fifteen of them as his students, Deydier conducted classes aboard a boat that was constantly on the move. Two of the students were sent to Siam early in 1668 where Lambert ordained them; they shortly returned to Hanoi to work as priests under Deydier's guidance. By 1669 Deydier estimated that ten thousand had been baptized, including one of the wives of the king.[367]

At this juncture Fuciti and two other Jesuits from Macao arrived in Tongking, the first members of the Society to appear there since the banishment of 1663. Trịnh Tạc reacted angrily to the reappearance of the Jesuits and renewed his attack on the Christians. On July 13, 1669, he ordained that no foreign vessels should be permitted to proceed up the Red River to Hanoi. All foreign vessels were to dock at Hien (today Nhon-duc), the center of foreign trade; all foreign nationals staying on in Tongking would thereafter be obliged to reside there. Deydier, who blamed the Jesuits for this turn of events, wrote from his place of "exile" in Hien that he was cheered in this same eventful summer by the arrival of a vessel of the newly formed *Compagnie des Indes Orientales.* The French ship had on board Lambert de La Motte and two of his secular priests, Jacques de Bourges (1630–1714) and Gabriel Bouchard.

Trịnh Tạc welcomed the French merchants as competitors to the Dutch and other Europeans doing business in Tongking. He permitted them to construct a factory at Hien in the hope that he would receive more artillery made in Europe. But he did not relax his repression of the Christian movement, for the Dutch and Portuguese warned him that the French were determined to aid the Christians. And on this matter the king was not misinformed. With new support behind him Deydier read his credentials as vicar-general to the Jesuits and demanded their obedience to him as the head of the church

[367] *Ibid.,* chap. xiv.

in Tongking. Fuciti rejected the order, citing the decision of General Piccolomini of 1650 to the effect that the Jesuits were exempt in the areas where they were already working from the authority of the priests of the Propaganda.

Since Lambert de La Motte sagely remained aboard the French ship, he did not personally confront Fuciti. The bishop did ordain as priests seven natives recommended by Deydier. On February 14, 1670, in the company of three French missionaries and the nine indigenous priests, he convoked a synod to organize the fledgling church of Tongking. Parishes were assigned to the priests and specific tasks were given to the catechists. The temporal and financial administration was delegated to two laymen of each parish or community. The bulls which had been read to Fuciti were to be proclaimed in the church with as much dispatch as possible. Nobody was to exercise the functions of priest or catechist without patents from either the bishop or the vicar-general. For those Christian women who wished to devote their lives to religion, Lambert created the *Amantes de la Croix de Jesus-Christ* (Lovers of the Cross of Jesus Christ). The bishop then returned in mid-April, 1670, to Siam accompanied by Gabriel Bouchard. Left behind at Hien with Deydier, Jacques de Bourges wrote to his brother: "We live here as French merchants with no wares other than the holy evangel." [368]

Before his arrival in Tongking, Jacques de Bourges had been entrusted by Lambert with a delicate diplomatic mission. The French bishops in Siam had become convinced by the time they arrived at Ayut'ia that Rome could not be made to understand by letters alone how much help was needed in Asia and Europe to protect the Propaganda'a mission from the machinations of the Portuguese and the Jesuits. Conveyed to Europe aboard an English ship, Bourges arrived at Rome on October 9, 1664. Since 1661 the Portuguese, who did not yet have official relations with Rome because of the war still being fought against Spain, had been protesting both to France and the papacy against the dispatch of the three French bishops to the East. After reading the reports of the French bishops and hearing Bourges' memorial, a special commission of cardinals quickly published a series of decrees in January, 1665, extending and consolidating the jurisdiction of the vicars apostolic. Cambodia and Champa were added to the diocese of Cochin-China, and all placed under the authority of Lambert de La Motte. A papal decree followed in February by which the two bishops in Siam were authorized to appoint a successor to Cotolendi. Rome refused at this juncture to extend the jurisdiction of the vicars apostolic to Siam and Pegu, suggesting that the bishops might find their situation too comfortable in Siam and not push ahead to claim their sees further to the East. In a memorial of 1666, Manfroni, secretary of the congregation, attributed the difficulties being experienced in China, Tongking, and Cochin-China to the intransigence of the regular missionaries (read Jesuits) in supporting the jurisdictional claims

---

[368] *Ibid.*, chap. xv; quotation on p. 237.

of the *padroado*. While the French bishops were still urged to insist upon the submission of the regulars, Manfroni warned that the cooperation of the orders was still needed in the recruitment of missionaries and in the financing of the Christian enterprise.[369]

Pallu and Lambert de La Motte meanwhile had developed plans of their own in Siam. Unable to proceed to their sees in Indochina, they decided to establish a school in Siam and to create an "apostolic congregation" designed to transform their small group of secular priests into a regular order. To win papal approval of their plans, Pallu himself set out for Rome on January 17, 1665. Taking the land route, he arrived at Rome in April, 1667, when Alexander VII was on his deathbed. The atmosphere in Rome was also darkening for Pallu as members of the Propaganda began to fear that the French East India Company and the Gallicans of Paris were taking more than a religious interest in the mission. The official resumption of normal relations in 1668 between Portugal and Rome also obliged the Propaganda to respond more positively to Lisbon's protests. In its turn Spain began at this time to feel menaced in its control of the *patronato* by the arrival in the East of the Propaganda's agents. Madrid notified Rome in 1669 that the French bishops would not be permitted to extend their jurisdiction over regions subject to the Spanish crown.[370]

While Pallu awaited Rome's response to his suggestions he went to France where he was received at Saint-Germain by Louis XIV on January 28, 1668. The king and Colbert promised on this occasion to give their unqualified support to the mission. After a long delay, Pope Clement IX on July 4, 1669, issued a brief which extended the jurisdiction of the vicars apostolic to Siam and placed it under the jurisdiction of the bishop of Nanking who was yet to be appointed. By a brief of the following September the pope commanded the regular missionaries in the East to present their credentials to the vicars apostolic and to request of them permission to carry on their missionary activities. Catechists were required to take an oath of obedience to the vicars and any other vows previously taken were declared null and void. The regulars were again forbidden to trade for their own enrichment. Pallu had lost only one round in his bout with the ecclesiastics of Europe: both the *Missions étrangères* and the Propaganda refused to authorize the project of the "apostolic congregation." The directors of the Paris seminary were openly critical of the aggressive stubborness of their bishops, particularly of Lambert de La Motte. Pallu left France on April 11, 1670, on a vessel of the East India Company and in the company of six priests recruited for the mission. He also carried letters and gifts from the pope and Louis XIV to Narai.[371]

---

[369] *Ibid.*, chap. xvi.
[370] See O. Maas, "Zum Konflikt der spanischen Missionäre mit den französischen Bischöfen in der chinesischen Mission des 17. Jahrhunderts," in H. Finke *et al.*, *Gesammelte Aufsätze zur Kulturgeschichte Spaniens* (Münster, 1930), II, 189–90.
[371] Based on Chappoulie, *op. cit.* (n. 333), Vol. I, chap. xvii.

Pallu spent more than three years on his return trip to Siam, during the course of which his earlier attitude of moderation and prudence toward his religious foes was transformed into one of impatience and hostility. Arrived at Surat in October, 1671, he learned through letters awaiting him there of Lambert's denunciation of the Macao Jesuits, of the unauthorized synod held in Tongking, and of the harsh treatment of Chevreuil by the Portuguese. While he temporarily suspended personal judgment, he knew from his recent experiences in Europe that these events would produce repercussions there, especially in Paris. To explain these matters more fully he sent Charles Sevin, one of the priests who had left France with him, back to Paris and Rome. Sevin was instructed to obtain from Rome a condemnation of the Goa Inquisition for its treatment of Chevreuil and formal sanction for the synod held in Tongking by Lambert without prior consultation of the Propaganda. From the king, Sevin was to request protection against the depredations of the Portuguese. Sevin carried to Europe a report written by Chevreuil, who had arrived in Surat shortly before the emissary's departure, detailing for the cardinals of the Propaganda how their agents in the East were maltreated by the Portuguese and the Jesuits. He also carried several letters directed to Colbert in which Pallu urged the Company to take a more active interest in the East and to support the French mission with the king's naval power. This appeal for temporal help ran directly contrary to the wishes of the Propaganda to eliminate national competition in the mission field.

Sevin arrived in France during August, 1672. In Paris the directors of the seminary were appalled to learn of what was transpiring in the East. At a meeting held in November at the residence of Cardinal de Bouillon, Grand Almoner of France, Sevin presented his complaints formally to the directors of the seminary, the Jesuit provincial of Paris, and Guillaume de Lamoignon, first president of the Parlement of Paris. The provincial agreed to forward Sevin's accusations to the Jesuit general in Rome, while warning that friends of the Jesuits everywhere were outraged by the charges of corruption and immorality being leveled against the Society. Lamoignon supported the vicars apostolic, even though he was revered by the Jesuits as one of their staunchest proponents. The cardinal himself, at the request of *Missions étrangères*, forwarded to the king Pallu's request for protection. This was not, however, the most propitious moment, for Louis XIV was then at war with the United Provinces and desired the friendship and cooperation of Portugal.

Sevin arrived in Rome at the beginning of 1673 to find the Propaganda still unswerving in its support of the vicars apostolic. The Jesuits' responses to Sevin's charges were largely ignored by the cardinals of the commission. On their recommendation a series of briefs was issued by Pope Clement X in 1673–74 defining the boundaries of the *padroado* and the sees of the vicars apostolic. The commission decreed that the briefs of the sovereign pontiff had the force of law throughout the Indies and did not require the approbation of Lisbon. In all parts of the Indies not directly subject to the temporal dominion of the king of Portugal the vicars apostolic were declared exempt from the jurisdiction of the Inquisition of Goa; its jurisdiction was limited strictly to territories actually subject to Goa and Lisbon. To make perfectly clear his decision to end the Portuguese claim of a spiritual monopoly in the East Indies, Innocent X (r. 1644–55) completed the work of his predecessors by declaring that the secular priests and their lay associates might go to Asia by any route whatsoever and were not obliged to obtain a visa at Lisbon. Any person, lay or religious, who contravened these decrees would be punished by excommunication. Another brief approved the synod convened by Lambert de La Motte in Tongking during February, 1670. The bull *Decet Romanum* (December 23, 1673) repeated earlier papal pronouncements placing the regulars under the vicars apostolic in areas not directly under Portugal's authority. One month later the Jesuit general agreed in writing and under oath to require members of the Society to observe all the papal decrees with respect to the vicars apostolic.[372]

While Rome was getting its house in order, the French began to attack the Dutch in the East. The "Persian squadron" commanded by Blanquet de La Haye appeared off the east coast of India in 1672.[373] Pallu learned this happy news when he arrived in Bengal during August on his return trip to Siam. He wrote to Blanquet de La Haye at Mylapore expressing the hope that a French victory in India would have the effect of transferring the right of patronage from the king of Portugal to Louis XIV and of replacing Goa with Mylapore as the Metropolitan see. He also wrote Colbert urging an attack upon Bantam and the erection there of a factory that would take away from Batavia its command of eastern trade. Pallu's hopes for a French empire of the east were dashed when Blanquet de La Haye's forces were defeated at Mylapore in September, 1674, by the arms of Golconda and the Dutch.

Pallu, accompanied by Chevreuil, returned to Siam on May 27, 1673, about eight years after his departure. In rejoining Lambert de La Motte he quickly learned that the difficulties with the regular missionaries in Siam had not abated. The Jesuit superiors in Siam remained adamant in their loyalty to the *padroado*. The general seminary of the French, founded in 1668, was prospering under the direction of Louis Laneau (1637–96) and Pierre Langlois (1640–1700), both of whom were serious students of the languages of Cochin-China and Siam. At the end of September, 1673, the reunited vicars apostolic named Laneau successor to Cotolendi as vicar apostolic of Nanking with jurisdiction over the kingdom of Siam. He was formally installed on Easter day, 1674, and took the title of Bishop of Metellopolis previously assumed by Cotolendi. The letters and gifts from Europe had won

[372] See *ibid.*, pp. 271–98.
[373] See above, p. 99.

for the French missionaries a gracious reception from King Narai. The appearance of the French fleet and its occupation of Mylapore had not escaped the notice of the Siamese. In his conversations with the missionaries, Narai offered a port in his kingdom to France and let them know that he intended to send an embassy to Europe in response to the overtures of Louis XIV and the pope.

With matters now seemingly in order in Siam, Pallu left in August, 1674, for Tongking. Forced by storms to take refuge at Cavite, he was arrested by the Spanish authorities for violating the *patronato* and was sent back to Rome via Mexico and Madrid![374] Lambert de La Motte, who was invited at this time by Hien-vuong to take up his post in Cochin-China, was delayed in his departure by King Narai, who wanted him to remain in Siam to expedite relations with the French. Gabriel Bouchard and Jean Courtaulin were sent in his stead to relieve the missionaries already there. Finally, Lambert received permission to leave and on July 23, 1675, he embarked to take up his see in Cochin-China after officially spending twelve years in Siam. Laneau was left behind to deal with the thorny problem of imposing his episcopal authority on the unwilling Jesuits and Dominicans.[375]

In Cochin-China the Christians had been left without a permanent European missionary in 1670 when Antoine Hainques and Pierre Brindeau died. Lambert, accompanied by Benigne Vachet and Guillaume Mahot, had gone off secretly from Siam to Cochin-China in the summer of 1671 to proclaim the papal bulls which gave supreme authority to the vicar apostolic and to organize the church. At Fai-fo, the center of Christianity in Cochin-China, Lambert convened a synod in January, 1672, attended by the French priests and their catechists; the Jesuits and their catechists boycotted the meeting. In April, 1672, Lambert and Vachet had returned to Siam with a dozen Cochin-Chinese children for training in the seminary. Already present in the school were pupils from Tongking, the enemies of the Cochin-Chinese.

A new war had broken out in the summer of 1672 launched by Tongking against Cochin-China. The attack had been repelled, and by the spring of 1673 the Tonkinese army had retreated northward. During the war years the persecution of the Christians had been intensified, but the European missionaries, both French and Jesuit, had continued their proselytizing in secret. Once Hièn-Vûong had secured his territory, the persecution had gradually been relaxed. In the autumn of 1673 Lambert had sent gifts to Hièn-Vûong that were presented to him by Mahot. Advised by his Minister of Foreign Affairs that the French missionaries represented a powerful European nation then establishing cordial relations with Siam, the ruler had received the gifts graciously and had suggested to Mahot that he invite Lambert to return.

[374] See De la Costa, *op. cit.* (n. 223), I, 448, and Maas, *loc. cit.* (n. 370), pp. 190–91; also below, p. 249.
[375] Based on Chappoulie, *op. cit.* (n. 333), I, 298–324.

While Lambert negotiated with the king of Siam to authorize his departure, his priests in Cochin-China had continued their efforts to bring the Jesuits to submission. Hien-vuong, constantly becoming more anxious to have Lambert at his court, had continued to issue invitations to the vicar apostolic in Siam. Finally, Lambert left Siam in a Cochin-China vessel sent by Hien-vuong.

Once he arrived in Cochin-China in the summer of 1675, Lambert went immediately to Hue. Here he was told that he might establish a permanent residence at Fai-fo, and that he would be permitted from time to time to visit the royal city. He was free to evangelize, but was prohibited from holding great assemblages. While he was received cordially by the officials in Hue, the Jesuits continued to resist him openly. Lambert finally excommunicated Joseph Candone, the Jesuit superior; in turn he was excommunicated by Candone. After touring the country, Lambert obtained permission from Hien-vuong to return to Siam to carry on necessary activities there. Before leaving Cochin-China, Lambert established permanent jurisdictions for the three French priests left behind. Courtaulin was to remain in the center of the country where Mahot would later join him. Vachet would have the north, including Hue, as his territory. Bouchard would remain in the south. Lambert himself arrived back in Siam during the middle of May, 1676, rejoicing that the French missionaries in Cochin-China had been granted written permission to travel about freely and had obtained the right to send new missionaries into the country whenever they became available.[376]

While the clouds were being dispersed in Cochin-China, the threat of new storms in Tongking remained. Deydier and Bourges, who lived as French merchants at Hien, secretly worked with the seven Tonkinese priests ordained by Lambert before his departure in 1670. The governor of the province in which Hien was located was a forthright enemy of the Christians; he kept Deydier in prison from 1670 to 1672. The lone Jesuit then working in Tongking, Domenico Fuciti, still remained in hiding at Hanoi. Here he was joined in 1671 by Giovanni Filippo Marini (1608–82), the provincial of the Japan Province and author of a book on his earlier experiences in Tongking published at Rome in 1663.[377] One of the leading critics of the vicars apostolic in Europe and a favorite of the king of Portugal, Marini brought his personal vendetta to Tongking. He declared the indigenous priests ordained by Lambert unfit to perform baptisms and other pastoral functions; in their turn, the Tonkinese priests wrote to the Propaganda to denounce Marini and the Jesuits of Macao. Trịnh Tạc, outraged by the failure of his military attack upon Cochin-China, turned his wrath against the Jesuits and expelled Marini in the spring of 1673. Several other Jesuits remained in hiding in the country. Both Christian groups, despite their fratri-

[376] Based on *ibid.*, chap. xxii.
[377] See below, pp. 382–83.

cidal hostilities, continued to baptize the natives in substantial numbers. In 1676 two Spanish Dominicans from the Philippines arrived in Tongking, much to the consternation of both the French missionaries and the Jesuits. The French priest-merchants, who had heard of the activities of the Persian squadron, waited vainly at Hien for French ships to come. By 1677 it had become clear that the Tongking mission, whose bishop had never arrived, needed prompt help simply to survive.[378]

Succor came for Tongking and the other French missions in the guise of a Cistercian priest. Antonio Brandão (d. 1678), the new archbishop of Goa, arrived at his metropolitan see on September 24, 1675, determined to end the schism in the East by accepting and enforcing the briefs of Pope Clement X. General Paulo Oliva was equally committed and notified the Jesuits in writing in 1673 and 1674 that they should submit themselves promptly to the orders of the vicars apostolic. After a brief period of hesitation the Jesuits under the jurisdiction of Macao obeyed their superior. During 1677 most of the Jesuits working in Indochina and Siam accepted the authority of the French vicars. Despite their victory the French were not entirely happy with the Jesuit capitulation. In Indochina, particularly, they wanted nothing less than the complete withdrawal of the Jesuits.

The French, now well installed in Siam and enjoying Narai's favor, were in a position to take over leadership from Macao. Religious from Manila likewise began to gravitate to Siam. Lambert de La Motte, who had struggled for eighteen years to put the new missionary enterprises on firm foundations, saw the Seminary of St. Joseph in Siam as the training center for an indigenous clergy that would spread the Christian message to the masses of continental Asia from India to China. On June 15, 1679, he died in Siam, the scene of his greatest triumphs.[379]

Pallu, who had been taken prisoner by the Spanish in the Philippines in 1674, finally arrived in Spain during November, 1676. The Madrid government, which had received strong protests from the papacy about Pallu's arbitrary arrest and deportation, received him cordially. Soon he was permitted to take the overland route through southern France to Rome. He arrived in the Eternal City on June 5, 1677, in the midst of the celebrations attending the elevation of Innocent XI (r. 1676–89) to the papacy. The new pope gave Pallu several audiences, during which he related his complicated personal experiences in the East and discussed the state of the mission enterprise in continental southeast Asia. Despite the pope's benevolence towards him and the mission, Pallu became embroiled in controversies that kept him in Rome for the next three years.[380]

---

[378] Based on Chappoulie, *op. cit.* (n. 333), Vol. I, chap. xxiv.
[379] Based on *ibid.*, chap. xxiv.
[380] See *ibid.*, II, 1–5. On the missions and Innocent XI see R. J. Maras, *Innocent XI, Pope of Christian Unity* (Notre Dame, 1984), pp. 225–28.

Dom Pedro, the regent of Portugal, had mounted an offensive at Rome to recover legal control of the *padroado*. To this end he had dispatched Luis de Sousa (1637–90), archbishop of Braga and a canon lawyer, to the papal court as advocate of the Portuguese case. In several memoirs to the pope and the Propaganda, the Portuguese called upon Rome to reaffirm the rights of patronage, to live up to the contracts concluded over a long period of time with Lisbon, and to recall to Europe the French vicars. The French response framed by the Paris seminary and Pallu alleged that the popes had never intended to give the kings of Portugal a full and irrevocable grant of all of the East Indies or a permanent religious monopoly in Asia. Whatever the legal status of the *padroado* might be, the French charged in 1677 that the Portuguese were too weak and ineffectual in the East to implement their responsibilities, to carry the faith to the pagans, or to check the progress of the Dutch heretics. Rome itself adopted a pragmatic rather than a legal approach to these issues, since it wanted neither to recall the French bishops nor to estrange the Portuguese. The pope wrote Dom Pedro in 1680 to the effect that the privileges accorded by the Holy See to the vicars apostolic did not compromise the spiritual prerogatives of the Portuguese crown in their established stations in the Indies. At odds with France over the *régale*[381] and other national demands of the Gallicans, Innocent XI had no desire to wage war with Portugal over the *padroado,* particularly since Lisbon exercised political authority in Brazil and other overseas territories important to overseas missions.[382]

The Jesuits still retained close relations with Lisbon despite the fact they had been required in 1674 and thereafter to submit themselves formally to the vicars apostolic in the East. Pallu, who was personally hostile to the Jesuits for the part they had played in his detention by the Spanish, arrived in Rome ready to do battle with the Society. Many members of the curia and the pope himself were hostile to the Jesuits. Innocent XI was strongly antipathetic to Father François de La Chaise (1624–1709), the Jesuit confessor of Louis XIV, who supported the crown on the question of the *régale* and related issues. The Commission of the East Indies formed by the Propaganda was seriously disturbed by the failure of the Jesuits to acquiese immediately to the papal order of submission and began to urge the recall of the recalcitrant Jesuits from the East. The commission also proposed that all missionaries in the East, secular and regular alike, should be required to take an oath of obedience to the French vicars under pain of excommunication. Innocent XI,

---

[381] The papacy and Louis XIV, supported by the French clergy, fought from 1673 to 1682 over the *régale,* the king's right to dispose of the revenues and benefices of vacant bishoprics. In 1682 the French clergy issued a Declaration of the Rights of the French Church which remained the cornerstone of the Gallican movement throughout the old regime. The tensions between France and Rome over this issue abated gradually after the death of Innocent XI in 1689. See Maras, *op. cit.* (n. 380), pp. 109–29.

[382] Based on Chappoulie, *op. cit.* (n. 333), Vol. II, chaps. i–iii.

once it became known in Rome that the Jesuits in the field were finally obeying their general's order to submit, introduced a more moderate tone into these discussions. As in the *padroado* issue, the pope, warned repeatedly by the Jesuits, began to fear that severe treatment of the missionaries might lead to a complete interdiction by Lisbon of the sea route to the East.

A renewal of hostilities between the Jesuits and the French missionaries in Indochina forced the Propaganda to take definitive action. Spurred on by its new secretary, Edoardo Cibo (1630–1705; in office, 1680–95), the East Indies Commission of the Propaganda issued a series of decisions in 1680 which received quick papal approval. General Oliva was ordered to recall Ferreira, Fuciti, Acosta, and Candone and to command all the Jesuits remaining in Asia, including those in China, to take a vow of obedience to the appropriate vicar apostolic. By a series of decrees of the same year the Propaganda divided the missions of the Far East into six great vicariates: north China (six provinces) was assigned to Gregorio Lopez (d. 1690), a Chinese Dominican; south China (nine provinces) to Pallu himself; Tongking to Deydier and Bourges, both being elevated to the episcopacy; Lambert de La Motte was to retain Cochin-China, and Laneau was to remain in charge of Siam. Pallu and Lambert were to coordinate the whole Eastern enterprise as General Administrators, or as metropolitans of the East in fact if not in name.[383]

Bearing his new title of vicar apostolic of Fukien, Pallu left Rome in the spring of 1680 for France. Flushed with his great successes in Rome, Pallu was not entirely prepared for the difficulties facing him on arrival in his homeland. He had learned on his earlier visit to Paris that the directors of the seminary in the Rue du Bac were not pleased with the anti-Jesuit campaign fostered first by Lambert, and then by Pallu. To fight the Jesuits in France in 1680 was to be stigmatized as a Jansenist and to run the risk of provoking the ire of De La Chaise and the king. While in Rome, Pallu had sought to win the support of the court by writing to Colbert of the opportunities for glory and commercial expansion that awaited France in the East. Shortly after his arrival in Paris, Pallu learned that the king felt that the oath prescribed for the missionaries was absolutely incompatible with the liberties of the Gallican church and an infringement of his royal prerogative. The king was also angered by the attacks on the Jesuits and refused to see Pallu. It was the Jesuit General Oliva who finally produced a formula satisfactory both to Rome and Paris: the French missionaries were to take the oath prescribed by Rome "with the permission" of the king of France! This compromise effected, Pallu was received by the king, granted minor honors, and assured that France would support the mission.[384] Near the end of March, 1681, Pallu once again went to sea, this time on a vessel of the French East India Company that sailed from Port-Louis. He was accompanied by ten

[383] *Ibid.*, chaps. iv–v.
[384] *Ibid.*, chap. vi.

new missionaries and carried letters and gifts from Louis XIV to the rulers of Siam and Tongking. After a lengthy stay at Surat, he arrived at Siam in July, 1682, more than three years after the death of Lambert de La Motte. He was greeted by Laneau, the successor to Lambert and Pallu's co-head of the missions. Laneau's elevation displeased Pallu, because he thought the bishop of Siam had been weak and overly conciliatory in his dealings with the Dominicans in Tongking and the Jesuits in Siam. Pallu ordered the regulars to take the oath prescribed by the Propaganda; the viceroy of Goa demanded that they should swear to uphold the *padroado*. Resistance to the Propaganda's oath, inspired by fear of recriminations from the Portuguese, soon spread to other mission stations.

In Goa a commission was set up to reform the administration of the missions and to check the growing authority of the French vicars. The regular missionaries, particularly those who continued to depend upon Portugal and Spain, were caught between two fires. Counsels of moderation continued to emanate from the directors of the seminary in Paris as they endeavored to throw water on the flames of this potential new schism. In Siam, Antoine Thomas (1644–1709), a Belgian Jesuit, and at Peking Ferdinand Verbiest, another Fleming, also played conciliating roles. Both took the oath and urged their colleagues to do so. Pallu left Siam in June, 1683, to take up his post in Fukien. On his arrival there on January 24, 1684, he immediately began to demand oaths of submission from the missionaries of south China. The China Jesuits, under orders from their general to take the oath, constituted no problem for Pallu. The Spanish missionaries, like the Portuguese in Siam, refused to take the oath until they should receive orders from their king. Pallu died at Mo-yang in Fukien on October 29, 1684, regretting his failure to bring the missionaries of China into strict compliance with the orders of Rome.[385]

The mission in Siam became the focus of France's activities in the East during the 1680's. Ayut'ia, King Narai's capital, became a "French Macao" for missionaries and merchants departing for and returning from the stations further to the East. The vicars apostolic had long hoped to establish closer ties between Narai and Louis XIV. A mission sent from Siam was lost at sea in 1681 in the vicinity of Madagascar. When Pallu returned to Siam in 1682 he learned that a new figure of importance had emerged at the court of Ayut'ia. A Greek merchant and adventurer, Constantine Phaulkon (1647–88) had arrived at Ayut'ia in 1678 with Richard Burnaby, the new factor of the English East India Company. Within two years Phaulkon had successfully insinuated himself into Narai's service. He was converted to Roman Catholicism by the Jesuit Antoine Thomas in 1682 and married a Japanese Christian of Ayut'ia. Phaulkon and the French swiftly became allies, a relationship encouraged by Narai, who remained eager for French support against the Dutch. Phaulkon by 1683 was known to the Europeans as "Barcalon" and to Siamese as the acting *Phrakhlang,* or Minister of Finance and Foreign Affairs.[386]

On January 25, 1684, two Siamese legates and the missionary Benigne Vachet left for France. They arrived at Calais in November and excited a lively curiosity in northern France on their way to Paris. In the discussions which ensued at the French court Vachet managed to convince the royal ministers that Narai and his subjects could be converted if the missionaries received increased political and financial support as well as reinforcements in personnel. He reassured the French that they could count on Phaulkon's collaboration.

The Chevalier de Chaumont was selected as Louis XIV's ambassador, and he was assisted by the Abbé de Choisy, a strange and enigmatic figure who kept a journal of the voyage.[387] These two official French emissaries were accompanied by Vachet, the two Siamese envoys, four missionaries recruited by the Paris seminary, and six Jesuits. Colbert and other courtiers had long nurtured the desire to send mathematicians and astronomers to the East. They had heard reports, especially from the Flemish Jesuit Philippe Couplet (1622–93) who was at court in 1684, about the way in which Schall and Verbiest had opened the way for Christianity in China by brilliant displays in Peking of Western scientific learning. On hearing of this enterprise the Propaganda insisted that the French Jesuit scientists be required to take the oath of obedience to the vicars apostolic. The French Jesuits, led by De La Chaise and supported by the court, insisted that the Jesuits were being sent as scientific observers and not as missionaries. Therefore they were, according to the French, subject only to the king of France and the Jesuit general. Despite the opposition of Rome, the six Jesuits destined for China left France without taking the oath and sailed with Chaumont from Brest on March 3, 1685.

The introduction into the mission of French Jesuit scientists who enjoyed the wholehearted support of Louis XIV took the entire Christian enterprise into new directions. Even the Dutch, who were not then at war with France, received them cordially at the Cape and at Batavia. The Jesuits of the *padroado* welcomed them as newcomers and brothers who would appreciate their difficulties in dealing with the vicars apostolic. Jean de Fontaney (1643–1710), the superior of the French Jesuits, was surprised by the friendly reception accorded the scientists by Laneau and the secular priests in Siam. Shown the king's orders to the effect that the Jesuits were not required to

---

[386] On Phaulkon's career see Luang Sitsayamkan, *The Greek Favourite of the King of Siam* (Singapore, 1967), and E. W. Hutchinson (trans. and ed.), *1688. Revolution in Siam. The Memoir of Father de Bèze, S.J.* (Hongkong, 1968). Also see below, pp. 1193–96.

[387] See R. W. Gibbin, "The Abbe de Choisy," in *Selected Articles from the Siam Society Journal,* Vol. VIII, *Relationship with France, England, and Denmark* (Bangkok, 1959), pp. 1–16. For further details on his book see below, pp. 420–21.

take the oath, Laneau readily acquiesced. King Narai, while still disdaining conversion to Christianity for himself, was utterly bewitched by the European scientific instruments, just as the Jesuits thought he would be.[388]

Chaumont himself, somewhat naively, was disappointed that Narai and Phaulkon seemed to show little interest in Christianity. He and others had been led by Vachet to believe that the Siamese king was on the point of accepting baptism. The king was only beguiled by Western science and his minister only intrigued by the possibility of a political and military alliance with France that would help to bolster his waning personal authority at the court. In this ambition Phaulkon was seconded by Guy Tachard (1648–1712), a Jesuit with missionary experience in South America and a confidante of De La Chaise. In 1686 Tachard returned to France with Chaumont and a new Siamese embassy. This second Siamese delegation was given a public welcome in France with an enthusiasm that exceeded by far that accorded the first Siamese embassy.[389]

Tachard pushed the representative of the Paris seminary into the background, and negotiated singlehandedly with the royal ministers. Acting under a secret arrangement with Phaulkon, he set the stage for a military alliance and won the dispatch to Siam of a French expeditionary force. Tachard also let it be known that a new tactic would have to be employed to Christianize Siam once it had become clear that Narai was not about to accept conversion. It would be wiser to insinuate French laymen and Jesuits into positions of importance and through them bring Siam to Christianity. To this end the king designated twelve Jesuit mathematicians to work specifically in the mission and began to enroll laymen for service in Siam.[390]

At the Rue du Bac and in Rome these decisions were met by protests, since France certainly appeared to be converting the Propaganda's international mission into a national enterprise. Despite the protests of the Sorbonne's Gallican theologians, the Propaganda insisted that this second group of Jesuits must take the oath required of all missionaries embarking for the East. Through the mediation of De La Chaise, the king finally agreed that the Jesuits should take the oath. Although they followed the king's order, Tachard and his companions prepared a long protest at Brest in 1687 which reiterated their contention that their first loyalty and obligation was to the king and to the Society.[391]

The vessels of the crown sailed from Brest in March, 1687, under the royal plenipotentiary Simon de La Loubère (1642–1729), diplomat, poet, and scholar. He was accompanied by Claude Ceberet Du Boullay, one of the directors of the French East India Company who carried full powers to conclude a commercial agreement. The military complement of over six hun-

[388] Based on Chappoulie, *op. cit.* (n. 333), Vol. II, chap. viii.
[389] For details see below, p. 425.
[390] See Hutchinson, *loc. cit.* (n. 339), p. 45.
[391] Based on Chappoulie, *op. cit.* (n. 333), Vol. II, chap. x.

dred men under the command of Marshall Desfarges was hopefully to be stationed at Bangkok and Mergui. Also aboard were the Abbé de Lionne of the Paris seminary, the priest who had administered the oath to the reluctant fourteen Jesuit mathematicians and Tachard, and who technically supervised them both at sea and in the East. From the beginning of the voyage Tachard and La Loubère disagreed as to the objectives of the mission and the tactics to follow.

This second French embassy arrived in Siam on September 27, 1687. Only 492 of the 636 soldiers survived the voyage of almost seven months. La Loubère, following his instructions from the king, sought first of all to have published the agreement of 1685 allegedly worked out by Chaumont with Phaulkon which set down in detail the conditions under which the missionaries might evangelize and teach in Siam. Tachard, who had long worked hand-in-glove with Phaulkon, urged the French diplomat to be patient and not to force an issue which might weaken Phaulkon at court. Tachard sarcastically noted also that it was important to make converts before publishing privileges! Laneau and the Abbé de Lionne did not share Tachard's views and pressed for publication. Their tenacity on this matter forced out into the open the hostility Phaulkon felt towards the French bishops for questioning his policies; he charged that if Narai had not adopted the Christian faith the fault lay with Laneau who, after twenty-seven years in Siam, spoke the language so badly that the king could not understand him. He also charged that the Christians of Tongking loyal to the Jesuits had been left in a condition of spiritual distress with the recall of Fuciti and Ferreira and alleged that Laneau, who contended that he was powerless to do so, would not permit the recently arrived Jesuits to go to their rescue. Although Laneau had permitted the French Jesuits to carry on their mission freely in Siam, Tachard remained angry with the French bishops. Despite the internal divisions of the French and the growth of an anti-French party at the court, a commercial treaty was concluded with Narai in December 1687. Urged on by Phaulkon, Tachard returned to Europe in 1688 with two Tonkinese catechists—Denir Ly Thanh and Michel Phoung—who were instructed to relate their distress story to the pope.

Tachard arrived in France to find that De La Chaise was urging a reconciliation of the Jesuits and the court with both the Paris seminary and the Propaganda. After being received at Versailles, Tachard left Paris for Italy on November 5, 1688. Acting in his capacity as ambassador of the king of Siam, Tachard carried gifts and a letter from Narai to Innocent XI. He was accompanied by Siamese mandarins and the two catechists from Tongking. Since this was billed as a diplomatic mission, Tachard, despite his long-standing feud with the priests of the Propaganda, was graciously received in Rome. Nobody in Europe knew at this juncture that Narai had died and that Phaulkon had been decapitated by his political enemies in Siam's revolution of 1688.

On December 23, 1688, the mission from Siam was officially received by the pope at a splendid public ceremony. Of the eight cardinals who attended the pope on that occasion five were members of the Propaganda's Commission for the East Indies.[392] The conciliatory spirit that Tachard had first experienced in France he also found in Rome. The Propaganda, encouraged by the pope, now began to realize that the oath it had required from the missionaries had produced more division than unity. Designed to deter nationalism, it had provoked negative, hostile responses from the rulers of Portugal, Spain, and France. Not wishing to become embroiled with Spain, the Holy See on November 23, 1688, had abolished the oath for the Augustinians, Dominicans, and Franciscans of the *patronato*. After meeting with Tachard, the Commission for the East Indies repealed the requirement that the missionaries of Siam, Cochin-China, Tongking, and China should take an oath of obedience to the vicars apostolic. The Jesuit general was invited to dispatch four members of the Society to Tongking and Cochin-China to replace those who had been recalled. In France the breach was healed by a convention of sixteen articles concluded between representatives of the Jesuits and the Paris seminary on March 13, 1689. The Jesuits agreed to recognize the authority of the vicars apostolic in Indochina and to work with them to end the schism dividing the Christians in Tongking and Cochin-China. By these acts the papacy won recognition of the supreme authority of its bishops; the French clergy, officially at least, was now united in its evangelizing efforts in the East. Portugal, in its determination to maintain the *padroado,* remained at odds with the papacy and the French priests.[393]

The revolution of 1688 in Siam brought an end to the French-Siamese alliance. The garrison left behind by La Loubère and Ceberet was confined to the fortress of Bangkok by Siamese forces. Bishop Laneau was taken hostage by the Siamese to guarantee the withdrawal of the French forces. Desfarges, his troops, and the French Jesuits departed in November, 1688, much to the relief of the embittered Siamese.[394] The small contingent of Europeans left behind were treated roughly by the Siamese. Most of the French secular priests and laymen of the mission were imprisoned until the spring of 1691; the Portuguese Jesuits and Dominicans were not molested by the Siamese. Authoritative reports of these events were not circulated in France until 1691. By that time Louis XIV was involved in a general European war which prevented him from sending further missions to Siam.[395]

The French Christians received solace and aid during these terrible years

[392] For the documents exchanged in Rome see P. Carretto, "Vatican Papers of the XVIIth Century," in *Selected Articles from the Siam Society Journal,* Vol. VII, *Relationship with Portugal, Holland, and the Vatican* (Bangkok, 1957), pp. 177–94.

[393] Based on Chappoulie, *op. cit.* (n. 333), Vol. II, chap. xi.

[394] See E. W. Hutchinson, "The Retirement of the French Garrison from Bangkok in the Year 1688," *Selected Articles from the Siam Society Journal,* Vol. VIII, *Relationship with France, England, and Denmark* (Bangkok, 1959), pp. 159–99.

[395] See above, pp. 103–4.

from Jean-Baptiste Maldonado (1634–99), a Flemish Jesuit of long experience in Siam. When Maldonado had first arrived at Siam in 1673, he strongly opposed the French vicars apostolic. A member of the Jesuit Province of Japan, he had looked to Macao and Goa for direction. But after Laneau was named bishop of Siam, Maldonado and his colleagues cooperated with the French mission and ignored orders sent to them by Goa. It would appear that Maldonado's relations with Tachard and the French Jesuits were only proper rather than friendly. The Portuguese who remained in Siam after the retirement of the French garrison quickly began to work for Maldonado's removal. In 1691 Aleixo Coelho (1626–post 1690) was appointed Jesuit visitor to Siam, Cambodia, and Cochin-China. He commanded Maldonado to leave Siam for Macao and then quickly embarked for Cambodia himself. Laneau, who was still in prison, saw Coelho's action as an infringement of his authority. In this opinion he was evidently supported by Maldonado, who agreed to carry letters to Rome from Laneau protesting Coelho's activities. Instead of returning immediately to Macao, Maldonado went to Pondicherry, the French station on India's east coast. He remained in India for two years in a vain effort to find transportation to Europe. Finally he went to Macao in 1694, where he stayed for the next eighteen months. During this time of retreat he composed his *Illustre certamen,* the story of the martyrdom (February 4, 1693) of João de Britto in India.[396] Maldonado was then sent to the Cambodian mission, where he died in 1699.[397]

In India the first French missionaries had been Capuchins from the missions founded in the Levant in 1626 with the approval of the Propaganda. Two members of the Custody of Aleppo, Ephrem de Nevers and Zeno de Bauge, had gone overland to Surat and there built a church and a house between 1636 and 1639. In nearby Bombay, as well as at Surat, the Portuguese Franciscans had been active as ministers and missionaries for more than a century before the arrival of the two French Capuchins.[398] On orders of his superiors Ephrem left Surat in 1640 with the assignment of establishing a mission in Pegu; Zeno remained behind in Surat. Ephrem journeyed overland to Vijayanagar, then occupied by Golconda, where he was warmly received by the sultan. From there he proceeded in 1642 to Madras, then under Golconda's jurisdiction, and to the Portuguese-controlled diocese of Mylapore. The English, who had just completed building Fort St. George in the previous year, welcomed the French priest with open arms. The British personnel of the fort included a number of English and Irish Catholics who were being ministered to by Portuguese priests. Concerned by this close association of their Catholics with the Portuguese, the British officials

---

[396] See above, pp. 161–62.
[397] See Burnay, *loc. cit.* (n. 349), pp. 193–96.
[398] See Hull, *op. cit.* (n. 8), pp. 15–20. The Portuguese Jesuits owned properties in the Bombay islands, but were not active there.

invited Ephrem to stay at Madras. With the permission of his superiors, Ephrem established a parish and mission at Madras under British protection. In 1649 Ephrem was captured by the Portuguese, taken to Goa, and imprisoned there for almost two years. Under threats of reprisals from the papacy, the French and English governments, and the sultan of Golconda, the Goa authorities released Ephrem and permitted him to return to Madras in 1651. The Madras apostolate, supported by the British, grew steadily thereafter and endured in peace until the late eighteenth century.[399]

From Madras the Capuchins pushed northward in 1677 into the Tamil region where the city of Pondicherry was founded in 1683 by François Martin of the French East India Company. In 1686 French Jesuits appeared in Pondicherry and were joined three years later by others who had been expelled from Siam. François Martin, who had close relations with João de Britto and the other Madura missionaries, encouraged the French Jesuits to work in harmony with the Capuchins and the Madura fathers.[400] The priests of the Paris Foreign Mission Society expelled from Siam likewise began to work at Pondicherry in 1689. Tachard, the Jesuit, only slowly gave up his hope of reviving the Siam mission. Urged on by De Britto, he finally decided in 1692 to concentrate on a French mission to the interior of India which would take off where the Madura mission ended and expand northward into the Telugu country.

Little progress in this new enterprise was made before the Dutch captured Pondicherry in 1693. Tachard was imprisoned, and the other Frenchmen were prohibited for the following year or so from carrying on their regular activities. Once the war ended, Pondicherry was returned to the French in 1694 and Tachard released. He was then named superior of the French Jesuits in the East Indies and China. To carry the French Jesuit mission to the hinterland of Pondicherry, Tachard enlisted the aid of two Jesuit missionaries from the Madura mission who were well acquainted with the customs and languages of south India. Fathers Pierre Mauduit (1664–1711) and Jean Bouchet (1655–1732), two French Jesuits of the *padroado,* inaugurated after 1695 the Carnatic (Karnatak) missions in the Telugu country, the vast region north of Madura and the Tamil country that extended as far north as the Mughul empire. In 1699 the Jesuits received permission from the bishop of Mylapore, who claimed jurisdiction of the Carnatic, to minister to the Telugu peoples providing that they followed the methods of Britto and worked in collaboration with the Madura mission. In 1700 the French mission became independent of the Jesuit Province of Madura, but their superior, Charles de La Breuille, could not assume the title of provincial for fear

[399] See A. P. Jann, O.M.C., *Die katholischen Missionen in Indien, China, und Japan* (Paderborn, 1915), pp. 194–205; and N. Kowalsky, "Die Errichtung des Apostolischen Vikariates Madras . . . ," *NZM,* VIII (1952), 36.
[400] On the Madura mission see above, pp. 149–58.

of estranging the Portuguese, since Lisbon forbade the office of provincial or visitor to non-Portuguese Jesuits. By 1702 Bouchet, superior of the Carnatic, worked with Jean Baptiste de La Fontaine (d. 1718) and another Madura priest as *sannyasis* (sometimes called "Roman monks" by the natives) in the Telugu country. Encouraged by Rama Ragio, a ruler in this region, they laid the foundations for what was to become during the eighteenth century one of the most flourishing missionary enterprises of the French Jesuits.[401]

Other French expellees from Siam went to Bengal, Indochina, and China. Led into Bengal by the astronomer Jacques Duchatz (1652–93), the French Jesuits ministered to the French and to other non-Portuguese merchants of the delta. In 1690 one group of Jesuits established a residence at Chandernagore, where the French had founded a factory in 1688. After Louis XIV officially authorized in 1695 the establishment of missions at all the French stations in India, the Jesuits were followed into Bengal by secular priests and laymen employed by the Propaganda and the Paris Society of Foreign Missions. The Augustinians, who had previously monopolized the Bengal mission, were not able to resist the French intrusion, for their numbers and their parishes had declined along with the withdrawal of the Portuguese from the delta. Tachard himself died in 1712 while visiting the Bengal mission. Until 1778, when the last Jesuits withdrew from Bengal, tensions were constant between the Augustinians of Hugli and the Jesuits at Chandernagore.[402]

After the expulsion of the French from Siam, the missions in Indochina came more directly under the control of the Propaganda and the Paris Society. This process had begun earlier with the recall of the Jesuits and the proclamation (1678) in Rome of the primacy in Tongking and Cochin-China of the French priests. In 1682 Bourges was made bishop of west Tongking, Deydier of east Tongking, and Mahot of Cochin-China. At the invitation of the French a number of Spanish Dominicans from Manila began to collaborate in 1676 with the French priests working in Tongking. On the death of Deydier in 1693 the Spanish Dominicans assumed responsibility for the vicariate of east Tongking. In 1687 the papacy entrusted the vicariate of Cochin-China to Francisco Peres, a Luso-Asian prelate with no great love of the French. After Tachard's successful trip to Rome with the Tongking catechists, the French Jesuits in 1692 were permitted to send two new missionaries to Tongking. Ferreira and Candone were later permitted to return to their posts in Annam. Finally the missions in Indochina were definitively detached from the jurisdiction of Macao by a decree of October 23, 1696.

---

[401] See [Antonius Kroot], *History of the Telugu Christians by a Father of the Mill Hill St. Joseph's Society* (Trichinopoly, 1910), pp. 1–14; Ferroli, *op. cit.* (n. 2), II, 572; and Müllbauer, *op. cit.* (n. 11), pp. 247–48.

[402] On the Augustinian mission see above, pp. 142–43. Also see Hartmann, *loc. cit.* (n. 46), pp. 190–91.

A drama was played out in Cochin-China during the last decade of the century which illustrates once again how dependent the mission was on the whims of the ruler. Nguyễn Phúc Chu (r. 1691–1725) was not unaware of the role the French had played in Siam and reacted accordingly. He was decidedly cool in his attitude towards the missionaries and listened willingly to the accusations leveled against them by the Buddhist priests at his court. To palliate the suspicious ruler, the Spanish Jesuit and mathematician Juan Antonio Arnedo (1660–1715) was sent from China to Cochin-China in 1695. Although Phúc Chu was pleased to have Arnedo at his court, he nonetheless turned against the missionaries. In 1698 he threw them all into jail, including Arnedo. The Spanish Jesuit was soon released but the other missionaries were left to languish. The French priest Langlois and the Jesuits Candone and Belmonte died in prison. Arnedo, once restored to favor, worked on the ruler to relax the harsh restrictions he had imposed upon the missionaries and their converts. By 1704 the mission was allowed to reopen. Arnedo personally became the king's confidante and was entrusted with a diplomatic mission to Macao. Here, as in China, the Christians were tolerated for their usefulness to the ruler.[403] In Tongking, where they were likewise on the defensive, the missionaries were tolerated in the hope that a commerce might be established through them with the French East India Company. From Rome's viewpoint, control of the missions in Annam was firmly in the hands of the Propaganda, and their personnel was not restricted to nationals of any single European country or religious order. The church in Indochina, where Buddhism was less strong than in Burma and Siam, continued to progress during the eighteenth century.

The issues dividing the Catholic mission came sharply into focus in China during the last generation of the century. The K'ang-hsi emperor wrested personal control of the government from the overbearing regent Oboi in 1669 and reversed many of the policies the regent laid down. He ended the anti-Christian program of 1665, gave their churches back to the missionaries, permitted the Chinese converts to retain their faith, and posthumously restored Schall's titles that had been stripped away by the Regency. He did not officially reverse the decree against Chinese and Manchus converting to Christianity; he ordered that the ban should remain in force,[404] but in practice he permitted the missionizing to proceed so long as the Christians remained cooperative and tractable. He reinstated Verbiest to his post at the Board of Astronomy, and the young ruler studied Western mathematics under the Jesuit's guidance. He rapidly grew to admire Verbiest and his Jesuit colleagues at Peking for their medical, artistic, mechanical, and schol-

---

[403] Based on M. Pachtler, *Das Christenthum in Tonkin und Cochinchina* (Paderborn, 1861), pp. 192–97.
[404] For a translation of the appropriate part of the decree of September 5, 1669, see Rosso, *op. cit.* (n. 207), p. 123.

arly skills and employed their talents in a number of projects. He accorded them favors and expected nothing but cooperation and obedience in return.[405] At the outset of K'ang-hsi's reign there were in China an estimated two hundred thousand Christians. A Portuguese embassy was received at the court in the summer of 1670. Beginning in 1671 the twenty-five missionaries imprisoned at Canton were freed and began the return to their stations. Claudio Filippo Grimaldi (1638–1712), a Jesuit engineer and mathematician, left Canton for the imperial capital. Despite the opposition of the Jesuit visitor at Macao, a new group of Spanish Franciscans entered China in 1672. In January, 1673, Tome Pereira (1645–1708), a Portuguese musician, joined the other Jesuits in Peking and was soon teaching the curious emperor to play Christian hymns on the spinet. In 1673 the "War of the Three Feudatories" broke out, a civil war that wracked China for eight years and almost cost K'ang-hsi his throne. The Jesuits, as had happened earlier, were pressed into service as makers of munitions. To express his gratitude for their services, in 1675 the emperor visited their church and workshops and with his own hand wrote the inscription "Honor God" in beautiful Chinese characters. Copies of this imperial inscription were thereafter painted on the front of the other Jesuit churches in China.

Matters were meanwhile not going so well for the Jesuits in Europe. In 1669 Pope Clement IX had reaffirmed the two earlier decrees with respect to the rites question. The Dominican Domingo Fernández Navarrete, who had escaped from Canton in 1669, arrived at Rome in January, 1673, to present the views of the friars on rites and methods in the China mission. After receiving little or no satisfaction from the Propaganda, he retreated to Madrid to begin writing his *Tratados*.[406] Later in the same year Pope Clement X forbade the publication of books on the missions without the approbation of the Propaganda and then ordered the missionaries in China to obey the vicars apostolic.[407] In 1676 at Madrid Navarrete published the first volume of his widely circulated work which brought the controversy over the Chinese rites to the general public of Europe. His second volume was suppressed by the Spanish Inquisition.[408] The Peking Jesuits were meanwhile being roundly criticized in Europe for their role as munition makers to the Chinese emperor.

The Portuguese in 1677 proposed to Rome an arrangement by which the missionaries of the *padroado* would acknowledge the authority of the vicars

---

[405] See J. Spence, *Emperor of China. Self-Portrait of K'ang-hsi* (New York, 1974), p. xviii.
[406] See above, p. 197, and below, pp. 358–60.
[407] For the Constitution of 1673 see above, p. 134. The Jesuit letterbooks were published at irregular intervals after the closure of Japan to the Society in 1614. For a brief period (1650–54) a new series of Annual Letters appeared, but most publications about the missions were published by private enterprise. The Society resumed official publication in 1702 when the *Lettres édifiantes* began to be issued. See J. Correia-Afonso, S.J., *Jesuit Letters and Indian History* (Bombay, 1955), p. 38. Also see list of Jesuit letterbooks, below, beginning on p. 1983.
[408] See Rosso, *op. cit.* (n. 207), pp. 124–25.

The Christian Mission

apostolic providing the appointees were not French in nationality. Rome's response was swift. In 1678 Pope Innocent XI, on the insistence of Pallu and the Paris Society, issued his brief requiring all the missionaries to take a solemn oath to submit themselves to the vicars apostolic. In China where the Jesuits were actually not very numerous, trouble developed between the Peking and the Iberian missionaries. King Charles II of Spain in 1678 agreed to maintain ten missionaries in China drawn from the Spanish orders working in Manila. For a time the Spanish Jesuits hoped to assume leadership over the mission in China. Alarmed by this turn of events, Verbiest wrote to the Propaganda asking for the dispatch of French missionaries to China.[409]

The papacy responded in 1680 by rearranging the old vicariates and by demanding that the missionaries then being dispatched to China should all take the oath to submit to the authority of the vicars apostolic. The Spanish Augustinians set up their first convent in Kwangtung in 1680 without taking the oath, without consulting the Propaganda, and without acknowledging the appropriate vicar apostolic.[410] The Propaganda in 1680 named Bernardino della Chiesa, scion of a noble Venetian family, vicar apostolic and sent him along with four other Italian Franciscans to China.[411] Della Chiesa and Pallu arrived in China during 1684. Shortly after his arrival, Pallu named Charles Maigrot (1652–1730) of the Paris Society as his successor. When Della Chiesa arrived at Canton he found twenty-three Spanish missionaries (twelve Franciscans, seven Dominicans, and four Augustinians) congregated there. They were on their way to Manila, on orders of Pallu, because they refused to take the oath.

Pallu and Maigrot, both being secular priests and ardent Frenchmen, objected to the appointment of Della Chiesa, a Franciscan and an Italian, to the vicariate in China. They also objected to his view, once he arrived at Canton, that the Spanish priests should not be forced to take the oath over the wishes of their king. The forced retreat of the Spanish priests, in Della Chiesa's eyes, would endanger the entire Christian enterprise in south China. The Propaganda, as it received conflicting reports from China, made vain efforts to reconcile the differences between its emissaries. Under pressure from the Spanish orders, supported by the crown, the Propaganda decided in November, 1688, to suspend the oath for the Spanish religious who entered China from Manila.[412] After Pallu's death, Della Chiesa, who had been named by Rome as Pallu's successor, raised the interdict and the Spanish mis-

---

[409] See Dehergne, op. cit. (n. 86), pp. 333–34.
[410] Alvaro de Benavente (1646–1709) and two companions opened this new mission. See M. Merino, O.S.A., Misioneros Agustinos en el Extremo Oriente, 1565–1780 (Madrid, 1954), p. 41.
[411] For the Propaganda's relations with Della Chiesa see F. Margiotti, "La Cina, ginépraio di questioni secolari," SCPFMR, Vol. 1/2, pp. 615, 617–18.
[412] For details of this controversy see A. van den Wyngaert, O.F.M., "Mgr. Fr. Pallu and Mgr. Bernardin Della Chiesa," Archivum Franciscanum Historicum, XXI (1938), 17–47.

sionaries returned to their stations. A jurisdictional struggle then developed between Maigrot and Della Chiesa over the leadership of the vicariate.[413]

In the struggle to establish its authority over the Iberian patronages the Propaganda had worked with the Paris Society and until 1680 had enjoyed the support of the French government. But Louis XIV, who resented the oath demanded of the French missionaries as an infringement of his prerogative, began to favor the French Jesuits over the other French missionaries. Spurred on by his confessor, the Father de La Chaise, and by Colbert until his death in 1683, the French king had gradually determined to chart an independent course.

From Peking, Verbiest had written to Rome requesting the dispatch to China of French Jesuits trained in Western science. One of the first Jesuits to make an individual response to this appeal was Antoine Thomas, a native of Namur in Belgium. In 1677 Thomas, on his way to Lisbon, stopped at Paris, where he made a courtesy call at the Paris Mission Society. There he made the acquaintance of Jean de Fontaney, a fellow Jesuit-mathematician and, later, superior of the China mission. In Spain he met and received encouragement and support from the Duchess Marie d'Alveiro. Thomas left Lisbon in April, 1680, converted Phaulkon in Siam in 1682, and went on to Macao in that same year. On K'ang-hsi's invitation he went to Peking late in 1685 where he joined the elderly Verbiest on the Board of Astronomy.[414]

While Thomas was on his way to Peking, the project of sending French Jesuit scientists to Peking was maturing in Paris. Philippe Couplet, a Belgian as were Verbiest and Thomas, had worked in the Chinese provinces since 1661 before being sent to Europe in 1681 as procurator of the China vice-province of the Society. Late in 1684 he visited the French court to request the dispatch of learned Jesuits to Peking. It was probably on this occasion that the decision was finally taken to send five French priests to China under the leadership of Fontaney. On December 9, 1684, De La Chaise wrote ecstatically to the Jesuit general in Rome that the Jesuit mission would be sent. In his letter sent to Verbiest with the missionaries, De La Chaise refers to K'ang-hsi and Louis XIV as the two most powerful sovereigns in the world and the two greatest patrons of the sciences. Officially the Jesuit mathematicians were sent as scientific observers and were not required to take the oath to the vicars apostolic.[415]

On March 3, 1685, the six French Jesuits set sail at Brest for Siam on "l'Oyseau." Fontaney, already well known for his astronomical observations, was accompanied by Tachard and four Jesuit-mathematicians destined for the China mission: Jean-François Gerbillon (1654–1707), Louis-Daniel

---

[413] See Dehergne, op. cit. (n. 86), pp. 334–35.

[414] See Yves de Thomaz de Bossierre, Un belge mandarin à la cour de Chine aux XVIIe et XVIIIe siècles. Antoine Thomas, 1644–1709 (Paris, 1977), pp. 7, 14–20, 35–6.

[415] See V. Pinot, La Chine et la formation de l'esprit philosophique en France, 1640–1740 (Paris, 1932), pp. 44–48. Also see above, pp. 251–52.

The Christian Mission

Le Comte (1655–1728), Claude de Visdelou (1673–1737), and Joachim Bouvet (1656–1730). To avoid the Portuguese center of Macao the French Jesuits were landed at Ningpo on July 23, 1687. The local officials, unaccustomed to unexpected visitors from Europe, opposed sending them on to Peking. Finally, through the good offices of Verbiest, they were summoned to the court.

The French Jesuits arrived in Peking on February 7, 1688, just in time for Verbiest's funeral. Three of their number were permitted to go to the provinces: Fontaney to Shanghai and Visdelou and Le Comte to Chiangchou in Shansi. Gerbillon and Bouvet remained at the court and in the service of the emperor despite the objections of Pereira and the other Portuguese to their intrusion. Nonetheless the two French Jesuits carried on the activities of Verbiest in conjunction with Pereira, even though their personal relations were far from cordial. Despite internecine strife the Peking Jesuits served K'ang-hsi well and won his favor by the part Gerbillon and Pereira played in the conclusion of the Sino-Russian treaty of Nerchinsk (August 28, 1689).

Beginning in 1676 Verbiest had become interested in the struggle going on between the Chinese and the Russians for control of the Amur River valley. The Jesuits, who had long been looking for an overland route between China and Europe that would be safer than the sea voyage, had earlier sought for a passage through Persia. In 1673 Pope Clement X, in an effort to keep open the direct lines of communication with the Asian missions, had issued a brief permitting the missionaries to bypass Lisbon and to use the land routes to India and the Far East. Three years later a Russian mission led by N. G. Spathar had arrived in Peking, and Verbiest established cordial relations with him in the hope of getting the Russian government to accord the Jesuits free passage across Siberia. Until his death Verbiest continued to correspond with the Russians and to perform services for them in Peking. When negotiations were inaugurated at Nerchinsk, Gerbillon and Pereira accompanied the Manchu-Chinese delegation as advisers and interpreters. The treaty, which brought a halt to Russia's southeastward expansion, was negotiated in 1689 with the aid of the two Jesuits. They used Latin in their discussions with the Russians, and the official copy of this peace treaty was prepared in the Latin language under their direction.[416]

While Pereira and Gerbillon worked together at Nerchinsk, their temporary collaboration did not bring an end to the French-Portuguese conflict in Peking. Pereira, who had earned the gratitude of the Russians as well as the Chinese at Nerchinsk, obtusely neglected, as a Portuguese and as an opponent of the land route, to press the Russians for permission to traverse Sibe-

[416] Based on J. Sebes, S.J., *The Jesuits and the Sino-Russian Treaty of Nerchinsk (1689). The Diary of Thomas Pereira, S.J.* (Rome, 1961), chaps. iv and v. For a summary background of the meeting of the Manchu and Russian empires see E. Widmer, *The Russian Ecclesiastical Mission in Peking during the Eighteenth Century* (Cambridge, Mass., 1976), pp. 1–25.

ria freely even though other Jesuits in Europe were contemporaneously striving to win such a concession from the tsar.[417] By 1688 the need for the land route had become particularly imperative once the French had suffered defeat in Siam and once the Portuguese crown required missionaries embarking from Lisbon to take an oath to subject themselves to the *padroado*. This revival of the *padroado*, accompanied as it was by the demands of Spain, finally forced Rome to abolish the oath on January 6, 1689.

But K'ang-hsi knew little about these European rivalries. He was indebted to the missionaries, met with them informally, and acquiesced unofficially to their Christianizing activities. Technically, however, the missionaries were still in violation of the law, and he watched their religious activities closely. When he toured Shantung and the Yangtze provinces, the missionaries were careful to follow the lead of the local officials in receiving him. Since there was no established institutional means for dealing with the missionaries, the local Chinese officials tolerated their activities so long as they were no threat to public order. Difficulties developed in Chekiang in 1690–91 which led to a repression of the missions there by officials who were clearly acting within their legal rights. To clarify the status of the missions and to discourage repression, the missionaries sought a more formal recognition from the emperor. Pereira, as the superior of the Peking mission, memorialized the emperor in 1692 asking for official toleration of Christianity in China. After heated deliberations at the court the emperor issued the desired edict on March 22, 1692. By its terms, existing churches throughout China were given protection, and Christians were permitted freedom of worship. The edict accorded Christianity a definite, legal status, comparable to that enjoyed by the Lama temples, and recognized that the new faith presented no danger to public tranquility or to imperial authority.[418]

The years following the edict were marked by a steady growth in the number and influence of the Christians and the missionaries in China. In 1693 K'ang-hsi, after being cured of an illness by the Jesuits, gave the foreign savants their own residence near the imperial palace, as well as additional land, money, and the permission to build a church within the precincts of the sacred *huang ch'eng* (imperial city). He sent Bouvet to Europe as his emissary to Louis XIV. Here, as in the case of the Nerchinsk negotiations, the Jesuits were acting as the emperor's emissaries in contacts with the outside world. During the last years of the century, Grimaldi served as director of the Board of Mathematics, Pereira worked on mechanical contrivances, Gerbillon and Bouvet tutored the emperor in geometry and philosophy, and

---

[417] See Sebes, *op. cit.* (n. 416), pp. 139–41.
[418] For an English translation of the edict's text as given in Charles le Gobien, S.J., *Histoire de l'édit de l'empereur de la Chine . . .* (Paris, 1698), pp. 83–84, see A. H. Rowbotham, *Missionary and Mandarin. The Jesuits at the Court of China* (Berkeley, 1942), p. 110. Also see J. Spence, *Ts'ao Yin and the K'ang-hsi Emperor, Bondservant and Master* (New Haven, 1966), pp. 134–36; and Rosso, *op. cit.* (n. 207), pp. 128–29.

Brother Gio Gherardini, an Italian architect, began to teach Western painting at the court.

In all the provinces, except Kansu in the far west, native converts practiced the Christian faith where the missionaries had residences.[419] In total the Chinese converts numbered around 300,000 by 1700. The missionaries included an estimated 117 in 1701: 59 Jesuits, 29 Franciscans, 8 Dominicans, 15 secular priests (mostly from the Paris Society), and 6 Augustinians. In terms of nationality the missionaries remained divided into Spanish Franciscans, Augustinians, and Dominicans; French seculars and Jesuits; Portuguese friars, Jesuits, and seculars; and a colony of Italian Franciscans and Jesuits. At the very end of the century the German Jesuits in the mission sought to organize their own national group at Peking.[420]

While the evangelizing prospered in China, the Europeans continued to battle one another over national issues and the rites question. Pope Alexander VIII (r. 1689–91) completely reversed the policies of his predecessor, and returned direction of the China mission to the *padroado* despite the protests of the Propaganda and the *Missions étrangères*. By the bull *Romani Pontifices* (April 10, 1690) he acquiesced to the Portuguese suggestions for the erection of the two new sees of Nanking and Peking.[421] These two new dioceses, like Macao, were to be dependencies of Goa, and the old stipulations were reaffirmed by which the Portuguese crown would support the mission. Any changes desired by the papacy in Lisbon's right of patronage now required the consent of the crown. The areas of jurisdiction of the new dioceses were determined in 1695 according to a plan proposed by the Portuguese. The jurisdiction of the diocese of Macao was limited to the peninsula, nearby islands, and the neighboring provinces of Kwangtung and Kwangsi. Nanking was assigned the seven central provinces and the islands off the coast of Chekiang and Fukien. Peking was to hold sway over the seven northern provinces, their offshore islands, Korea, and Tartary. The China mission was thus removed from the Propaganda's control.

While such dispositions were readily decided upon in Europe, their implementation in China required time and adaptation to existing conditions. Although the Portuguese missionaries disputed Maigrot's authority, he continued to claim jurisdiction over Fukien and Chekiang. Gregory Lopes (Lo), the Chinese Dominican who had been awaiting his consecration since 1674, was finally elevated officially to his see in 1685 by Della Chiesa. Here he ruled until his death in 1690. Della Chiesa himself, whose position long remained ambiguous, was finally recognized in 1690 as bishop of Peking, and in 1699 he took over as his cathedral the Jesuit Church of the Holy Virgin. Macao was entrusted to the Portuguese João de Casal (d. 1735), who ar-

---

[419] For a map of the residences as of 1701 see Dehergne, *op. cit.* (n. 86), p. 352b.

[420] See *ibid.*, p. 336.

[421] Rome did not remember in 1690 that Peking had been erected as an archdiocese in the fourteenth century. See Pinot, *op. cit.* (n. 415), p. 17.

rived at his see in 1692. Conflicts arose between Goa and Macao when Casal tried to take control over the entire China mission through his Portuguese appointees.[422]

While these matters were tortuously being worked out in China, the papacy again shifted course. Possibly this change in direction was motivated by the hope that toleration would make the mission flower and would increase substantially the demand for missionaries and priests. In 1696, despite the opposition of the Portuguese, Innocent XII (r. 1691–1700) created eight vicariates in China, located, except for Fukien, in those parts of the country previously not well cultivated. French Lazarists arrived in China during 1697 to take advantage of this new dispensation, which limited the jurisdiction of the *padroado* bishops to two Chinese provinces each.[423] With Indochina detached definitively from Macao, the missionaries of the Paris Society were entrusted with Szechwan and Yunnan in the southwest, regional neighbors to the French missions in Annam.[424] In addition to this, the French won another skirmish in 1700 when the French Jesuits were freed from Portuguese control and placed under the jurisdiction of their own superiors. Still, the best established Christian communities remained under the sees of the *padroado,* even though the jurisdictions of Nanking and Peking were later limited to the two cities and their immediate environs. The division of the China mission along these lines produced a feeling of uneasiness and fear among the Spanish and Italian friars that they were in danger of being expelled from the field.[425]

In Europe an uneasy peace had been concluded in 1689 between the papacy and the leading Catholic rulers by the abolition of the oath and by the revival of cooperation between Rome and Lisbon. In the same year, the French Jesuits and representatives of the Paris Society (March 13, 1689) signed a peace treaty in sixteen articles, approved by the archbishop of Paris and the king, which ended their jurisdictional rivalries. With these institutional matters settled, the conflict over the Chinese rites took stage center.

Throughout the 1680's France had been torn by religio-political issues: the Gallican articles, the *régale,* the Revocation of the Edict of Nantes, the Jansenist-Jesuit controversy, Quietism, and the issue of the Chinese rites. The papacy, which had straddled the rites issue by its previous declarations, came under increasingly heavy pressure to provide the contending parties with an unequivocal decision.[426] The promulgation of the Edict of Toleration (1692) for Christianity in China lent a new urgency to the case for an

---

[422] For details of this imbroglio of 1690 to 1700 in China see A. van den Wyngaert, O.F.M., "Le patronat portugais et Mgr Bernardin Della Chiesa," *Archivum Franciscanum Historicum,* XXXV (1942), 3–34.

[423] See Metzler, *loc. cit.* (n. 124), pp. 249–50.

[424] See Guennou, *op. cit.* (n. 334), p. 187.

[425] In 1698 twenty Franciscans remained in China in locations from Kwangtung to Shantung. See K. S. Latourette, *A History of Christian Missions in China* (New York, 1929), pp. 110, 118.

[426] On the decrees of 1645, 1656, and 1669 see above, pp. 195, 261.

official resolution of the rites question. Pope Innocent XII assigned Maigrot, since 1687 vicar apostolic of Fukien, the unenviable task of inquiring into the associated problems of terms and rites. Maigrot was no friend of the orders and was under pressure from the Portuguese after 1690 to vacate his office. Fearful of what toleration and the revival of the *padroado* would do to the China mission, Maigrot declared quickly against the Jesuit position. Immoderate accommodation, in his estimation, might lead to an erosion of Christianity's identity in China and to its classification as one of China's religions, with Christ being merely the fourth god in the national pantheon. In 1693 he forbade to the Christians of his see the use of *T'ien* and *Shang-ti* as terms for God and directed the missionaries to interdict the Confucian and ancestral rites to their converts. The Portuguese vicar-general of Fukien, Jose Monteiro, S.J., refused to abide by Maigrot's ruling and declared himself exempt from his jurisdiction. At this time, Maigrot wrote a mandate which he sent to Europe with Nicolas Charmot, M.E.P., for presentation to the *Missions étrangères*. Charmot arrived in Paris with Maigrot's report and supporting documents in 1694. Two years later these materials were presented by the Paris Society to Innocent XII with a request for a definitive ruling.

The Jesuits, both in China and Europe, responded quickly and indignantly to Maigrot's initiative. In China, the Jesuits and their Franciscan and Augustinian sympathizers, as well as the Portuguese, declared that Maigrot and the other French superiors who supported him had lost their jurisdictions in 1690 by the erection of the three bishoprics of China. In Europe, Louis Le Comte responded to Maigrot's charges and to those of the Dominicans by publishing in 1696 his *Nouveaux mémoires sur la Chine* on behalf of the French Jesuits. In this work he also claims that the French Jesuits should be credited with winning the Edict of Toleration and predicts that K'ang-hsi himself will be converted by the Jesuits at his court. When this was followed in 1697 by the publication of Charles Le Gobien's *Histoire de l'édit de l'empereur de la Chine,* the Paris Society entered the fray in dead earnest. In Rome the Holy Office of the Inquisition began in 1697, on instructions from the pope, to examine the arguments and the supporting documents submitted by both sides. To influence the decision of that illustrious group, the proponents entered into a pamphleteering war that produced a public reaction with repercussions throughout all of Europe. Leibniz in Protestant Germany, fearing that contacts between Europe and China might be severed, sprang to the side of the Jesuits in his *Novissima Sinica* (1697; reissued in 1699).[427]

While the cardinals in Rome debated, the *Missions étrangères* launched a new attack in Paris that was designed to influence these deliberations. Its

---

[427]For a listing of some of the pamphlet titles see below, p. 430, n. 241.

leaders enlisted the aid of the archbishop of Paris Louis Antoine de Noailles (1651–1729), Bishop Bossuet, and Madame de Maintenon. Supported by this powerful triumvirate, the Paris Society submitted six propositions derived from the writings of Le Comte and Le Gobien to the theological faculty of the Sorbonne for condemnation. By a decree of October 18, 1700, five of the six propositions were condemned outright and the remaining one was condemned with qualifications. The Jesuits' position was condemned primarily for its acceptance of Chinese ethics as a system adequate to human needs and as valid as the Christian revelation because of its antiquity. In essence, the theological faculty charged the Jesuits with breaking that bond which ties morality indissolubly to revealed religion.

While Paris sought to influence by these means the discussion going on in Rome, the Jesuits prepared a coup of their own. At Le Comte's suggestion the Jesuits in Peking (Grimaldi, Pereira, Thomas, and Gerbillon) memorialized the emperor on November 30, 1699, asking his opinion of their understanding of the Confucian rites. In a rescript issued one year later the emperor responded:

These things written herein [on the civil character of the rites] are excellent and in harmony with the Great Way. To revere Heaven, to serve ruler and parents, to reverence teachers and elders, is the custom common to the whole world. There is nothing here to be emended.[428]

Several days later the Peking Jesuits sent their memorial and K'ang-hsi's rescript to Rome along with an explanatory letter. But even before the issuance of the emperor's rescript, Innocent XII had died on September 27, 1700. While the pope's death produced a temporary lull in the official proceedings and in the public debate, the controversy over the Chinese rites continued well into the eighteenth century to plague the church, even though an official decision unfavorable to the Jesuits was taken as early as September, 1701, by the Propaganda and the Inquisition. In the eyes of Rome the Chinese emperor, despite his learning and eminence, had no competence or authority to rule on Christian issues.[429]

6

THE PROTESTANT MISSIONS

During the sixteenth century the Protestants had no missions in the East. In their teachings neither Luther nor Calvin had emphasized the missionary

---

[428] As translated in Rosso, *op. cit.* (n. 207), p. 145.
[429] See *ibid.*, p. 146.

obligation recognized by the Catholics and Anabaptists as a command of Christ to spread the gospel throughout the world (Matt. 28:19).[430] The Lutheran and Calvinist movements had concentrated on establishing their churches and in winning recognition of their right to exist. While the Lutherans had won legal status in the Holy Roman Empire by the Peace of Augsburg in 1555, the Calvinists were not accorded a similar recognition until 1648. As they focused on self-preservation, the Protestants had neither the will nor the opportunity to develop agencies overseas to carry out missions. Endless divisions promoted by doctrinal, regional, and national differences plagued the Protestants throughout the sixteenth century. The Catholics, who retained a monopoly of the heathen world, regularly reproached and chided the Protestant heretics for "perverting Christians" while ignoring the conversion of Jews, Turks, and heathens.

A few lonely voices had called for the Lutherans to compete with the Jesuits and to carry the "true Gospel" into Asia.[431] But the Protestants had no religious orders to take mission initiatives even if they had been inclined theologically to accept the Catholic challenge. Imagine how effective the Catholic missions would have been had evangelizing been left exclusively in the hands of the secular clergy! The Lutherans, in particular, taught that the apostles, to whom Christ's admonition had been directed, had offered the Christian message to the entire world. The pagans had ignored the opportunity so presented. Contemporary human efforts, Catholic or Protestant, were consequently of no avail in bringing the faith to those who persisted in living in ignorance; the mission was and remained exclusively the work of God and not of man. Later Lutheran commentators and orthodox theologians continued to maintain this viewpoint as they concentrated upon making converts in the European states and shoring up the foundations of their new churches.[432]

The national church of England and the Reformed church of the United Provinces were forced to focus some of their attention upon Asia with the formation of the English East India (1600) and the Dutch East India (1602) companies. Neither company was obligated by its original charter to pro-

---

[430] Calvin's view of the heathen world was based mainly upon his doctrine of grace being common to all. Much better informed about the heathen world than Luther, Calvin actually participated in the planning of the abortive Huguenot expedition to Brazil of 1558. See S. M. Zwemer, "Calvinism and the Missionary Enterprise," *Theology Today*, VII (1950), 209–11; A. G. Gordon, "The First Protestant Missionary Effort: Why Did It Fail?" *International Bulletin of Missionary Research*, VIII, No. 1 (Jan., 1984), 12–18.

[431] For an example of 1585 see *Asia*, I, 702.

[432] For the attitudes of the reformers and their followers towards missions there exists an extensive literature. Especially see G. Warneck, *Outline of a History of Protestant Missions* (trans. from the 7th German ed. by George Robson; Chicago, 1901), chaps. i–ii; Latourette, *op. cit.* (n. 226), III, 25–28; W. R. Hogg, "The Rise of Protestant Missionary Concern, 1517–1914," in G. H. Anderson (ed.), *The Theology of the Christian Mission* (New York, 1961), pp. 95–111; F. H. Littell, "The Free Church View of Missions," in *ibid.*, pp. 112–21; and S. Neill, *Christian Missions* (Harmonsworth, 1964), pp. 220–27.

vide for the maintenance of Protestant clergy in the East or to support missions.[433] Like the Catholics, the Protestants considered that the state and its agencies were responsible for Christianity and the missions in the overseas territories. In other words they exported to Asia the Augsburg formula of *cuius regio, eius religio* (whose state, his religion; that is, in X's territory, X's religion is official), and eventually left its enactment to the companies.

Roman Catholics, who were still numerous in the United Provinces, were not employed by the Calvinist-dominated VOC, and their clergy was not legally permitted to work either as ministers or missionaries in its stations; the Catholics were believed to be dangerous potential allies of the Portuguese or Spanish.[434] In 1598 the Church of Amsterdam had begun sending lay preachers or "comforters of the sick" on the pre-Company voyages to the East.[435] Once the VOC began to function in 1603, theological students and preachers were recruited, usually for brief terms, to minister to the Dutch in the East and to perform missionary services. Very few of the early preachers remained after the expiration of their contracts, and shortages of pastors quickly developed. This is not surprising, since pastors were in short supply at home.

Beginning in 1609 the governors in the East Indies were instructed to care for the pastors and lay teachers under their jurisdiction. The *classis* (a governing group consisting of the pastors and elders of the churches in a given district, organizationally subject to the synods) of Delft and Delftland issued a call in 1614 to preserve the Christian religion in the Indies, to form a college for the preparation of pastors destined for service in the East, and to establish schools where pastors might in the course of time instruct selected natives in the faith. Other ecclesiastical groups of Holland deplored the disorganized condition of Christianity under the VOC and called for the translation of religious writings into Malay. The great Synod of Dort in 1619 called upon the States General to advance the cause of Christianity in the East but without indicating by what specific means.[436]

In 1617, on the eve of the convocation of the Synod of Dort, the directors of the VOC drew up instructions for the guidance of the governors in Java in dealing with matters of religion. They were formally empowered to regulate the propagation of Christianity in the East and to build schools. They

---

[433] Warneck, *op. cit.* (n. 432), p. 43, incorrectly asserts that the VOC "was distinctly bound by its state charter to care for the planting of the church and the conversion of the heathen in the newly won possessions." The most authoritative study of the VOC and its relation to religious activities is C. W. Th. Baron van Boetzelaer van Asperen en Dubbeldam (ed.), *Pieter van Dam, Beschryvinge van de Oostindische Compagnie. Vierde Boek* (The Hague, 1954); the only work in English to exploit it is that of C. R. Boxer, *The Dutch Seaborne Empire 1600–1800* (New York, 1965), pp. 132–149.

[434] See W. Ph. Coolhaas, *A Critical Survey of Studies on Dutch Colonial History* (The Hague, 1960), p. 37.

[435] On the pre-Company voyages see above, pp. 42–44.

[436] See A. M. Brouwer, "De Zending onder de Oost-Indische Compagnie," in H. D. J. Boissevain (ed.), *De Zending in Oost en West* (2 vols., The Hague, 1934), I, 29, 34–37.

were also urged to cooperate in a spirit of good will with the pastors and "comforters of the sick" sent out as Company servants to guide and aid the religious program of the VOC.[437] In the Company's "renewed charter" of 1622–23 a specific provision was included charging it with "the preservation of the common faith."

Under pressure from the pastors at home, who were watching the Catholics organizing the Propaganda, the VOC sponsored a *Seminarium Indicum* administered by the theological faculty of the University of Leyden. Under the personal direction of Anton Walaeus (1573–1634?), a professor of theology and a noted Counter-Remonstrant, the *Seminarium* met from 1622 to 1633 in his house. Twelve pastors were prepared in this period for work in the East. The *Seminarium* was discontinued because of its cost, because the pastors it prepared were more interested in missionizing than in carrying out the colonial program of the VOC, and possibly because of Walaeus' involvement in religious controversy.[438]

With the encouragement of the secular authorities who were eager to find support for the VOC's expansion into the "Great East," religious activities were inaugurated in 1605 at Ternate and Amboina as the Portuguese were being expelled from those islands. Here the Dutch confronted a native population among whom the Jesuits had converted around sixteen thousand to Catholicism; the remainder of the people were animists or Muslims.[439] Most anxious to retain the good will of the sultan of Ternate, the VOC concluded a contract which provided that Dutch converts to Islam should be extradited and that native converts to Christianity should be turned over to the sultan's justice. In Amboina, where the Dutch hold was not so shaky, the youths of the island began shortly after 1605 to be trained by Dutch laymen in reading, writing, reckoning, and praying. Matthias van den Broecke, the first Reformed preacher in the Indies, began to work at Amboina in 1612. He and Caspar Wilten, who arrived two years later, inaugurated preaching in Malay. They were followed by Sebastiaen Danckaerts (in Amboina from 1617 to 1619) whose Malay sermons were repeated by others long after his departure. In 1620 four Amboina youths were sent to Holland to study religion.[440] Adriaan Jacobszoon Hulsebos, a noted pastor, and two lay preachers traveled to Banda and Amboina in 1622 to establish church organizations in those islands. He and his companions were drowned on a voyage from Banda to Amboina. Hereafter Amboina continued to attract a number of

---

[437] For the text see Boetzelaer (ed.), *op. cit.* (n. 433), pp. 67–72.
[438] See Warneck, *op. cit.* (n. 432), pp. 43–44; C. W. Th. Baron van Boetzelaer van Asperen en Dubbeldam, *De protestantsche Kerk in Nederlandsch-Indië*, . . . *1620–1939* (The Hague, 1947), pp. 17–19; H. W. Gensichen, *Missionsgeschichte der neueren Zeit* (Göttingen, 1976), p. T11; and J. D. de Lind van Wijngaarden, *Antonius Walaeus* (Leiden, 1891), pp. 189–221. For Walaeus' dispute with G. J. Vossius see D. Nobbs, *Theocracy and Toleration* (Cambridge, 1938), pp. 52–55.
[439] On the Catholic missions in the Moluccas see above, pp. 215–18.
[440] See Brouwer, *loc. cit.* (n. 436), I, 29–33.

good pastors, the most renowned of whom was François Valentijn who worked there from 1684 to 1694 and again from 1705 to 1713.[441]

Danckaerts, who had returned to Holland in 1620, was a serious student of the Malay language. He had written a book on the condition of Christianity in Amboina that was published on his return home.[442] He was also the translator of the Malay catechism and the compiler of a Malay vocabulary generally used by Dutch pastors in the Indies for a long time thereafter. These works were published while he conferred with the synods about a formula for the realignment of the Indies church to the decisions of the Synod of Dort. In Jakatra just before it became Batavia in 1621, Hulsebos had begun to organize a formal church. After hearing of Hulsebos' death in the East, Danckaerts hastily returned to Batavia in July, 1624, in the company of Justus Heurnius (1587–1652) and J. Du Praet. This group was shortly joined by George Candidius, later to be founder of the Formosa mission.

On their arrival at Batavia, the clerics found the church in total disarray. To bring order out of chaos, they called for the convocation of a general church assembly. From August 6 to October 20, 1624, the clerics met three times weekly with representatives of the VOC under the general chairmanship of Danckaerts. This "great assembly" produced what is known as the ecclesiastical ordinance (*Kerkorde*) of 1624, the constitution in forty-six articles of the Reformed church in the Indies as officially authorized by Governor-General Pieter de Carpentier. By its terms the administration of the church was centered at Batavia and left mainly in the hands of Danckaerts and Heurnius. Candidius left for the Moluccas even before the assembly convened. It was decided that Heurnius and Antonius Dirckszoon were to work in Batavia and Du Praet in Amboina. All the pastors were to be under the direction of the governor-general and to seek to establish a religious order in the Indies which would conform as much as possible to the organizational structure of the homeland Reformed church. In Batavia the preachers and lay teachers were to extend their ministry beyond the Dutch community to the natives, the Malays, Japanese, and Chinese. They were to root out the practices of the Muslims, heathens, and "other blinded nations." Preaching and teaching was to be in a language understandable to the people.[443] Heurnius, who worked in Batavia until 1633, inveighed against the iron control exercised over religious affairs by the civil authorities. Ten years after Heurnius' departure, Governor Van Diemen drew up a new ecclesiastical ordinance without consulting the church at home. The original constitution, which could not incorporate the entire gamut of doctrinal decisions taken at

[441] Boetzelaer, *op. cit.* (n. 438), pp. 24–27.

[442] *Historisch en grondich verhael van en standt des Christendoms int quartier van Amboina* (1621). Reprinted in abridged form in *BTLV*, n.s., II, 105ff. Also see below, pp. 448–49.

[443] Heurnius concentrated at the beginning of his tenure upon the Chinese population of Batavia, and prepared a Chinese-Dutch dictionary as well as translations into Chinese of Christian writings and Reformed doctrine. See Brouwer, *loc. cit.* (n. 436), I, 42.

Dort or anticipate the changes that would later take place within the empire, was thereby modified in 1643 by a new and more detailed ecclesiastical ordinance that limited even more strictly the independence of the church. A special ordinance was promulgated for the church of Amboina in 1673.[444]

The Dutch church in the East was more closely supervised by the civil authorities than were the Spanish and Portuguese religious establishments. The secular rulers in the Indies assigned the pastors to their posts, paid their salaries, decided where they should open schools, determined what language they should use in the various territories, and censored their letters to the church authorities at home.[445] While the Reformed preachers ministered mainly to the Europeans, they were encouraged by the VOC to convert the natives, particularly in places where Dutch control was shaky and the local populace restless. The pastors sometimes received a sum per head (*discipelgeld*) for making converts in places far distant from Batavia, in the Moluccas or Ceylon.[446] Such an inducement was necessary since the pastors often preferred to congregate at Batavia under the protection of Dutch guns. Mass baptisms were facilitated by the presentation of "gifts" or by a grant of special privileges to the converts. Punishments were sometimes meted out to those who refused conversion or failed to bring their children to the pastors for baptism. Conversion in Indonesia became tantamont to naturalization and led to the enjoyment of privileges usually reserved to Europeans. Those natives who were received into the church without lengthy instruction and inward preparation were often recognized as being but nominal Christians and were generally excluded from the Lord's Supper until their devotion had been tested. Since not more than one in ten were admitted to Communion, this practice later produced a controversy over "separation of the sacraments" which became intense both in Holland and in Asia.[447]

While control over the church in the Indies remained firmly in the hands of the VOC, the church in Holland pursued an independent course in its relations to the missions. Several of the *classes* concerned themselves with the Eastern missions, recruited and examined the persons sent, and corresponded with them. No effort was undertaken, however, to raise money for the missions or to found missionary societies. The *classis* of Amsterdam, whose members dominated the VOC, soon became the leader in sending out pastors. Through the intellectuals of the "Second Reformation," a continued interest in the Eastern mission was maintained. It was first reflected in the *De legatione evangelica Indos capessenda admonitio* (1618) of Justus Heurnius.[448] Young Heurnius, writing at the time of the Synod of Dort and when

---

[444] See Boetzelaer, *op. cit.* (n. 438), chap. ii.
[445] Boxer, *op. cit.* (n. 433), p. 134.
[446] Boetzelaer, *op. cit.* (n. 438), p. 132.
[447] See Gensichen, *op. cit.* (n. 438), p. T11.
[448] For a summary of the contents of this rare book see J. R. Callenbach, *Justus Heurnius, eene bijdrage tot de geschiedenis des Christendoms in Nederlandsch Oost-Indië* (Nijkerk, 1897), pp. 52–53.

the truce with Spain was running out, urged the VOC to promote the faith by building schools for indigenous children and by sponsoring the translation of the Bible and other important Christian writings into the local languages. He was, however, no advocate of the policy of accommodation, and castigated the Jesuits for their use of it in China. Like the Catholic friars, he thought the missionary should simply preach Christ and his cross. The Orthodox Calvinists, who had won the day over the Arminians at the Synod of Dort, proved to have almost no taste for foreign missions.

Heurnius' work was followed by other missionary tracts and by Hugo Grotius' *De veritate religionis Christianae* (1627), an outline "of the Truth of the Christian Religion" prepared for his countrymen "not only to their own profit, but also to the propagating of the Christian religion."[449] Grotius was especially concerned that the simple seamen working in Eastern ports might be victimized religiously by Jews and Muslims. But the church as a whole failed to respond to the champions of the missionary movement or to the scathing attacks of the Roman Catholics. Still at war with Spain until 1648, the Dutch church generally rejected the idea that it should emulate the Catholics in the organization and advancement of missionary work.

The most successful of the early Dutch missions was founded in remote Taiwan. Determined to participate directly in the China trade and to carry its war against the Iberians into East Asia, the VOC concluded a tacit agreement with the Ming authorities that permitted them to establish a trading post on Taiwan to which Chinese merchants might freely come.[450] In 1624 the Dutch built a fort and trading depot (which they called Castel Zeelandia) off southwestern Formosa on the small island of "Tayouan" (Taiwan) which commanded the entrance to the natural harbor of modern Tainan City.[451] The Spanish from the Philippines responded in kind by establishing a fort and trading post at Keelung on the northern tip of Formosa in the following year. Here they acted as a counterweight to the spread of Dutch control over Formosa and the trade of the region until they were driven off the island in 1642.[452]

From Fort Zeelandia the Dutch advanced onto the mainland of Formosa and bought land at a place then called Sakam from the Sirayas, the dominant tribe of the region. It was with the primitive Sirayas that the Dutch had their initial experiences with native life and society. The Sirayas, who practiced an animistic religion headed by priestesses (*Inibs*), were organized into vil-

---

[449] Quoted from J. Clarke (trans), *The Truth of the Christian Religion by Hugo Grotius . . .* (Cambridge, 1860), p. 2. This work was later translated into Malay and Arabic. On the "Second Reformation" and on the "renewal of the face of the earth" see J. van den Berg, *Constrained by Jesus' Love . . .* (Kampen, 1956), pp. 18–20.

[450] See above, p. 52.

[451] This small island, through silting, has since been joined to the mainland of Formosa and has been incorporated into Tainan City. Its name, Tayouan (also spelled Taoun and Taiwan in contemporary European materials), has since replaced Formosa as the name for the whole island.

[452] Cf. above, pp. 52, 54.

lages run by a council. The villages fought constantly with one another, for they apparently respected no single tribal authority. Since the Sirayas were but one of several headhunting tribes of Formosa, the Europeans were not faced by an organized native resistance as they were elsewhere in the East. Taiwan moreover had not previously been touched by Islam, Buddhism, or Catholicism, religious rivals that the Dutch met with elsewhere in their commercial empire. Their most serious competitors were the Chinese and Japanese merchants and pirates who used the ports of western Formosa as outposts.[453]

"Comforters of the sick" or lay preachers had landed at Formosa in 1624 with the earliest Dutch contingents. In August, 1627, the first Dutch minister arrived at Fort Zeelandia in the person of George Candidius (1597–1647). He had been accepted as a minister-missionary by the *classis* of Amsterdam and sent out to the East in 1624. Shortly after his arrival in Formosa, Candidius settled down in a Siraya village to study their language and customs as a prelude to winning their confidence. In the process he came to realize that the Sirayans were faster to learn than the Moluccans, with whom he had previously worked, that there was no central authority to oppose his religious activities, and that the native religion had no firm hold on the population. Moral pressure supported by the secular authorities should be enough, he believed, to persuade the Sirayans to abandon their pagan beliefs and immoral practices. By Christmas, 1628, he claimed that over one hundred natives "could repeat the prayers, and could answer with facility the principal questions which man must know for his salvation."[454] Three years later he baptized his first converts, a group of about fifty natives, and then left for a furlough in Batavia.

Candidius had been joined in Formosa in the middle of 1629 by the Reverend Robertus Junius (1606–55), a product of Walaeus' *Seminarium* of Leyden. While serving the Dutch residents at Fort Zeelandia, Junius studied the Siraya language. Candidius returned to Formosa in 1633 determined to prepare native youths for the clergy. The two missionaries were aided in their educational efforts by the lay teachers and catechists, many of whom were Dutch exservicemen who knew little more than how to read and write. The VOC authorities, mainly interested in trade and profits, were inclined to leave the administration of the Siraya villages to the ministers and teachers and to expect the mission to survive on the donations, fines, and taxes collected from the natives and the Chinese living among them. Burdened by the onerous responsibility of collecting taxes and administering secular justice, the missionaries aroused the ire of the Sirayas. Those

---

[453] See J. J. A. M. Kuepers, *The Dutch Reformed Church in Formosa, 1627–1662. Mission in a Colonial Context,* Vol. XXVII in *Schriftenreihe der Neuen Zeitschrift für Missionswissenschaft* (Immensee, 1978), pp. 7–10. Kueper's work is heavily based on W. M. Campbell, *Formosa under the Dutch, Described from Contemporary Records . . .* (London, 1903; reprinted Taipei, 1967).

[454] As quoted in Kuepers, *op. cit.* (n. 453), p. 14.

who opposed Dutch rule found support from neighboring tribes outside the jurisdiction of the fort and skirmishes occurred. To protect their converts and the investments of the Company, the secular authorities and the missionaries implored Batavia to send a military expedition to Formosa.

The first troops arrived in August, 1635, to inaugurate the pacification of the island. The villages of the hostile tribes were ravaged, threatened with punishments, and forced to conclude peace agreements. The terms included recognition of Dutch sovereignty, promises not to molest the Dutch or the Chinese residents, and guarantees to support the Dutch in further actions against the unpacified tribes if such were deemed necessary. Within a year the villages of the western plain from Zeelandia to the southern tip of the island had acquiesced to the terms imposed by the Dutch. The extension of Dutch domination northward along the western coast began in 1636 and was completed by the forced withdrawal in 1642 of the Spanish from Fort Santo Domingo at Tamsui.[455]

Day-to-day administration of the pacified villages, except for those in the immediate environs of Zeelandia, remained in the hands of the native leaders and the European teachers and ministers. Junius and Candidius explained the peace arrangements to the villagers, opened schools for the young, and instructed the adults in Christianity. After the final departure of Candidius in 1637, Junius shouldered the burden of the mission by himself. Lacking European preachers and teachers, Junius started to prepare native youths for the ministry and the classroom. While he did not force baptisms or accept converts indiscriminately, Junius and the Dutch civil authorities insisted that the converts accept Dutch religion and customs as essential steps on their way to civilization. Before Junius left in 1643 over five thousand natives had been baptized, around fifty native teachers had been trained, and a Dutch Consistory had been formed to govern the native church of Formosa.[456]

Junius' successors, released for a brief period from the political duties he had found so onerous, were closely supervised by the Consistory. Anxious to spread Dutch influence more widely, the Consistory neglected the native church and sent the few available teachers and preachers into areas where the gospel was unknown. Simon van Breen, who worked in Formosa from 1643 to 1647, convinced the Consistory that the native Christians were inadequately trained and required more instruction in the faith and in civilized modes of life. He expanded on the catechism introduced by Junius, but this new version proved to be too lengthy and not sufficiently adapted to local practices and customs. The policy of accommodation followed by the pioneers was gradually eroded after 1643 as the authorities of church and state

---

[455] See *ibid.*, pp. 17–19; and on the Spanish expulsion by the Dutch naval forces see the translation from Juan Ferrando's *Historia de los PP. Dominicos en las Islas Philipinas y en sus Misiones del Japon, China, Tung-kin y Formosa* in Campbell, *op. cit.* (n. 453), Appendix A, pp. 495–98.
[456] *Ibid.*, pp. 19–24.

insisted upon a more thorough grounding of the natives in the ways and beliefs of their Dutch overlords.

The first reports to Europe of Junius' successes painted a rosy prospect for the future growth of Reformed Christianity in Formosa. The churches of Holland celebrated what they considered to be miraculous achievements in Formosa by publishing in 1646 a Latin tract prepared by Caspar Sibellius.[457] Junius, who had meanwhile returned to Holland to take up a pastorate at Delft, stimulated further interest in the mission by instructing prospective missionaries in the Siraya language and customs. News reached Holland in 1647 that the great expectations for the Formosa mission were not being fulfilled. Outraged by the neglect of the mission, Junius criticized his successors and accused the *classis* of Amsterdam of failing to support the mission adequately. The acrimonious and unseemly controversy that followed, involving the Consistory of Formosa, the *classis* of Amsterdam, the VOC, and Junius, reflected the disappointment of all parties at the deterioration of the mission.[458]

Under a new team of missionaries, a revitalization of the Formosa church began in 1647. Daniel Gravius (1616–78), after two successful years at the mission in Batavia, set the stage for the new endeavor in Formosa during his stay between 1647 and 1651. With the aid of native catechists he revised the Formulary of Christianity to conform more strictly to the Dutch catechism. It was used for the remainder of the mission's history as the basic text for instruction of the Sirayas.[459] Translations into Siraya of Dutch prayers and the Gospels of Matthew and John were also prepared by the ministers and their catechists.[460] While these firm foundations for the native church were being laid, the ministers clashed repeatedly with the civil authorities in Zeelandia, especially with Governor Nicolas Verburg who ruled Formosa from 1650 to 1653. It was also during his tenure that the Chinese population, constantly on the increase since the Dutch occupation, became restive.

On his return to Batavia, Verburg wrote a report on Formosa, dated March 10, 1654, in which he comments on the lamentable condition of the mission there. He asserts:

The young natives—although they have been baptized—learn some doctrines by heart like parrots, but do not really understand what they repeat, or the truth of the things they learn by rote.

---

[457] Translated into English as *Of the Conversion of five thousand nine hundred East Indians In the Isle Formosa neere China* . . . (London, 1650). Reprinted in William Campbell, *An Account of Missionary Success in the Island of Formosa* . . . (London, 1889), I, 28–43.

[458] See Kuepers, *op. cit.* (n. 453), pp. 26–33.

[459] Published in Amsterdam in Latin letters as *Patar ki Tna'-'ming an ki Christang. Formos et Belge.* (1661). Reprinted in *Memoirs of the Faculty of Literature and Politics, Taihoku Imperial University* (Taipei), Vol. IV, no. 1 (1939).

[460] Published in Holland under the direction of Gravius in 1661–62.

In his recommendations for releasing the Formosans from "their Egyptian bondage," Verburg urged closer supervision by Batavia, limitation of the field of operations to central Formosa, diminution of the fines imposed upon those natives not attending church or school, an increase in the number of clergymen sent, and the extension of missionary contracts to a term of ten successive years.[461]

The last decade (1653–62) of the Dutch mission's existence in Taiwan was plagued by controversies with Batavia over personnel and money, by famines and epidemics, and by the mounting threat from Koxinga and his Chinese supporters on Formosa. Despite these depressing conditions, the church of Formosa was kept alive by Antonius Hambroek (1606–61) and a number of younger ministers, at least three of whom had been prepared in Holland by Junius. The new missionaries, discouraged by the many native languages prevailing on this relatively small island, proposed that religious instructions should be imparted in Dutch, a language known to the younger Formosans and many of the Chinese traders. The Consistory wrangled with Batavia over mission methods, and the news of Koxinga's impending invasion produced disagreements between the Dutch authorities in Batavia and Formosa.

Fort Zeelandia held out against the far superior forces of the Ming loyalist for almost a year, but finally surrendered to Koxinga on February 1, 1662; the Dutch surrender brought an abrupt end to the mission. Frederick Coyett, the governor of Formosa from 1656 to 1662, was released, and he returned to Holland. His book *Verwaerdloose Formosa* (Abandoned Formosa), first published anonymously at Amsterdam in 1675, relayed to Europe in gruesome detail the story of the Dutch defeat. The martyrdom of Reverend Hambroek, first described by Coyett, was later immortalized in Dutch patriotic poetry and drama.[462] The Formosan Christians, officially the allies of the Dutch, slowly gave up the foreign faith in the absence of the missionaries and other servants of the VOC. These native Christians were left without teachers or religious works printed in their own language; the books published in the Netherlands were never delivered to Formosa since they were not available in Asia until after the loss of the island. Still, as late as 1715, the French Jesuit Joseph de Mailla (1669–1748) met several Formosans who could understand Dutch and write their own language in Latin letters. Use of the romanized forms of the vernacular endured until the latter half of the nineteenth century.[463] In present-day Tainan it is still possible to view the remains of Fort Zeelandia.

---

[461] See Campbell, *op. cit.* (n. 453), pp. 292–97.

[462] See R. C. Croizier, *Koxinga and Chinese Nationalism. History, Myth, and the Hero* (Cambridge, Mass., 1977), p. 29. A recent edition of Coyett's book in Pierre Lamback's English translation of 1923 has been issued by Inez de Beauclair and is called *Neglected Formosa* (San Francisco, 1975).

[463] See Kuepers, *op. cit.* (n. 453), p. 43; and Boxer, *op. cit.* (n. 433), p. 145.

The loss of Formosa shocked the VOC and alarmed the Dutch public about the future of the maritime empire and the missions in the East. To a national sentiment warmed by the contemporary victories in Ceylon (1658) and western India (1662), the Dutch diplomatic and military defeats in eastern Asia were felt as a dash of cold water.[464] The VOC, after the Formosa defeat, cooperated with the Chinese for a period in several unproductive campaigns against Koxinga's forces in Fukien and on the high seas. In Holland a more positive approach to the missions in Asia was advocated by Gijsbert Voetius (1593–1680), a prominent theologian and one of the intellectual founders of Dutch Pietism. In his writings Voetius advocated more careful education and selection of pastors for the mission field and the adoption of the Jesuit program of cultural affiliation with the leading elements in Chinese, Japanese, and Cochin-Chinese society. His close friend and disciple Johann Hoornbeck (1617–66) wrote a systematic treatise on mission theology called *De conversione Indorum et Gentilium* (Amsterdam, 1669). In this work he surveys the history of heathen and pagan peoples and urges the Reformed Christians to emulate the Jesuit conversion methods, to institute a Congregation for the Propagation of Faith, to establish a seminary devoted solely to the training of missionaries, and to initiate the Jesuit system of reporting on missions by letter-writing.

Very few of these hopes for a new approach to missions were being realized in Asia at that time. The Dutch capture of Ceylon in 1658 brought with it a new opportunity to establish the "true Christian Reformed faith" in territories dominated politically and economically by the VOC.[465] Two Dutch clergymen had arrived at Galle in 1642, sixteen years before the completion of the conquest, to attend to the needs of that city's small band of Calvinists. The military defeat of the Portuguese was followed by a systematic effort to destroy Catholicism in Ceylon along with all other vestiges of Portuguese control. In essence, the Reformation was carried to Ceylon by Dutch preachers with the aid and support of the VOC as part of the general policy of destroying the Lusitanian heritage in the East.[466]

The Dutch Protestants, who had learned about the vitality and staying power of the Catholics from their experiences at home, were nonetheless initially hopeful of eliminating the Catholics in Ceylon. In contrast to its situation in Europe, the Catholic church in Ceylon was new, scattered, and surrounded by pagans and Muslims. The Dutch soon came to realize, how-

---

[464] The Dutch embassy of 1655–57 had been politely received by the new Ch'ing government in Peking, but few positive results ensued from it. See below, pp. 483–84.

[465] See above, p. 167. Also see E. Van Kley, "Some Seventeenth-Century European Protestant Responses to Matteo Ricci and His Mission in China," in Pullapilly and Van Kley, *op. cit.* (n. 1), pp. 199–201.

[466] On the Dutch religious enterprise in Ceylon see Latourette, *op. cit.* (n. 226), III, 289–91; Boudens, *op. cit.* (n. 131), *passim;* S. Arasaratnam, *Dutch Power in Ceylon, 1658–1687* (2 vols., Amsterdam, 1958), Vol. II, chap. x; and Boxer, *op. cit.* (n. 433), pp. 146–49.

ever, that Catholicism, like the Portuguese language, had penetrated deeply into the lives of the estimated 250,000 Sinhalese and Tamil Catholics in Ceylon. But obviously there were many among the converts who were Christian in name only, and who would without "Christian help" revert to heathen beliefs and practices. The task for the Dutch, as they saw it, called for the expulsion of the Catholic clergy and the destruction of whatever Catholic buildings could not be adapted to their own needs. In short, the Reformation should be introduced into Ceylon as expeditiously and completely as possible to make secure the political and economic ascendancy of the VOC in the face of possible Portuguese counterattacks.

The spiritual advance into Ceylon was led by the Reverend Philippus Baldaeus (1632–72) and four other pastors from Batavia. Baldaeus assigned himself and one other pastor to Jaffna, the Tamil area of north Ceylon where the Christians were most numerous. Two other pastors were sent to Galle, and a lone preacher to Colombo. Aided by lay teachers these pastors began the takeover of the churches and schools. To transform the faith of the Roman Catholics to the "true Reformed faith," Baldaeus adapted the teaching methods inherited from the Catholic priests to the needs of the Dutch Reformation. As Junius had earlier done in Formosa, he prepared a formulary of Christian tenets in question and answer form. It was adopted in 1659 as the official method of teaching the fundamentals of Protestantism. The pastors, like the priests before them, herded the children of Jaffna, Mannar, Colombo, and Galle into the schools and taught them the new Christian formulas. Once they had been sufficiently instructed, the children were baptized and received into church. The adults were generally disregarded since many were too attached to heathen and/or Catholic practices to be reformed easily.

Language was a particularly stubborn issue to resolve. All efforts failed to teach in Dutch and to force the people to learn it. Portuguese, the only European language widely known in the island, had to be used for a long time as the medium for teaching and preaching the Dutch faith. Baldaeus learned Tamil himself and urged the other preachers to study the native language and to prepare instructional materials in them. With the aid of native Christians, Baldaeus translated into Tamil the Ten Commandments, the Lord's Prayer, and the Articles of Faith.[467] After he left Ceylon in 1665 Baldaeus

---

[467] On the language question and for a listing of some of the devotional works translated into Malay, Formosan, Tamil, and Sinhalese see C. A. L. van Troostenburg de Bruijn, *De Hervormde Kerk in Nederlandsch Oost-Indië onder de Oost-Indische Compagnie, 1602–1795* (Arnhem, 1884), pp. 398–503. On p. 398 the author writes, based on his own experiences in Batavia: "Our language is extremely difficult for foreigners to learn." The same conclusion had been arrived at much earlier by a long line of Dutch preachers, merchants, and administrators who were frustrated by their failures to teach their language to the natives, particularly when they observed how Portuguese and English progressed in the East. On the Portuguese language in the Dutch mission see *ibid.*, pp. 453–54.

wrote a book relating his impressions of the southern coasts of India and Ceylon that was published at Amsterdam in 1672.[468]

From the works of Baldaeus and others, as well as the records of the VOC, there emerges a shadowy picture of the Dutch mission program in Ceylon. The Company expelled the priests from the island and proclaimed in 1658 the death sentence for anyone harboring Catholic clergymen. Preferments in employment and other inducements were granted to cooperative native Christians. Severe restrictions were placed upon the Muslims, who were competitors for both the trade and the souls of the Sinhalese. As in the United Netherlands, the Dutch exercised a modicum of practical moderation in the enforcement of their religious decrees to preserve political stability. Outward conformity to the policies of the Company and the church was taken to be a sufficient acknowledgment of Dutch authority. Catholic practices were tolerated so long as they were not public. In the villages no serious efforts were undertaken to stamp out the religious observances of the Hindus and Buddhists. The missionaries stressed elementary education, and significant numbers of pupils attended school in the cities where Dutch power was concentrated. The VOC remunerated the pastors, but the lay teachers and the maintenance of the schools had to be paid from the fines exacted from defaulters, both Dutch and native. As elsewhere in Asia, the Dutch church in Ceylon was closely supervised by the civil servants of the VOC. Baldaeus, who had been bold enough to challenge the authority of Governor Van Goens, was summarily shipped off to Europe in 1665. Under his successors the Dutch mission languished until the last decade of the century.[469]

The severe repression enacted in the early years of Dutch control forced Catholicism underground in Ceylon, and a number of the exiled Portuguese priests took refuge in the interior kingdom of Kandy. Occasionally efforts were made by the Propaganda to smuggle priests into Ceylon from Goa. Since these attempts were unsuccessful, the Ceylon Catholics remained without priests from 1658 to 1687.[470] Careful surveillance of Ceylon's coast by the ships of the VOC made it next to impossible to carry on illicit trading or mission activities. Still the VOC, despite the protests of some pastors, progressively pursued a policy of noninterference and aloofness in religious matters. The natives themselves, attracted to the amulets, statues, and colorful ceremonies of Catholicism, found Calvinism too austere and foreign for their taste. While openly submitting their children to Protestant instruction and baptism, some natives secretly had them taught and baptized in the Catholic faith as well. Father Joseph Vas (1651–1711), a native of north India and a member of the Oratory of Goa, learned Tamil in Malabar as

---

[468] See below, pp. 493–95.

[469] Based on Arasaratnam, *op. cit.* (n. 466), II, pp. 220–27.

[470] See R. Boudens, "Attempts of Catholic Missionaries to Enter Ceylon in 1681–83," *JRAS* (Ceylon Branch), n.s. IV (1955), 35–44.

preparation for his secret ministry to the Catholics of Ceylon undertaken in 1689. Other clergy from Goa joined him from time to time to help preserve Roman Catholicism on the island.[471]

That Catholicism was well rooted and sometimes practiced openly in strongly Catholic regions was no secret kept from the Dutch. Both pastors and the Company were acutely aware of the failure of the Reformation in Ceylon. Even in Jaffna, where the Dutch had claimed sixty-five thousand converts in 1663, the Protestant cause was in severe decline, according to the report of 1689 prepared by Hendrik Adriaan van Rheede tot Drakestein.[472] He observed that the Dutch had produced but a small harvest of nominal Christians because the preachers ordinarily did not know the native languages and were usually on the island for only short periods of time. Of the ninety-seven Dutch clergymen who worked in Ceylon from 1642 to 1725 only eight were fluent in a native tongue. A new tack was taken by establishing two seminaries for the training of a local clergy. The first was founded in 1690 near Jaffnapatam to train pastors and lay preachers for the Tamil-speaking regions. The second, founded six years later at Colombo, prepared natives for the ministry to the Sinhalese-speaking areas. The seminaries were supported by funds obtained from the sale of elephants, the taxes on fishing, and fines. The Tamil seminary functioned until 1723; the Sinhalese until 1796.[473]

In Indonesia itself the Calvinist ministers concentrated upon the conversion of the native Catholics and made only sporadic efforts to spread the faith to non-Christians. Efforts were undertaken to reach the non-Muslims by preaching and teaching in Portuguese or Malay. To this end, the Dutch translated Christian writings into these languages, but still the vast majority on Java and the other large islands quite correctly perceived the pastors to be agents of the despised VOC. Elsewhere Muslims were placed under very strict surveillance in Dutch-controlled territories, and eventually they banded together for self-protection under the leadership of the sultan of Makassar. After the Dutch captured Makassar in 1667, the anti-Muslim laws were gradually relaxed at Batavia and elsewhere in the islands to preserve peace in the interests of business. In 1722 it was estimated that close to one hundred thousand Christians of various nationalities and races lived in Batavia and its environs.[474]

In the smaller islands at the eastern end of the archipelago, the Dutch pastors established an enduring church only at Amboina. Like the Portuguese and Spanish before them, the Dutch were able to impose their will upon

[471] On the Catholic mission in Ceylon see above, pp. 165–69.

[472] See Arasaratnam, *op. cit.* (n. 466), II, p. 148.

[473] See Boudens, *op. cit.* (n. 131), p. 209; and Boxer, *op. cit.* (n. 433), p. 209.

[474] See J. Richter, *Die evangelische Mission in Niederlandische-Indien, Fern- und Südost-Asien, Australia, America,* Vol. V of his *Allgemeine evangelische Missionsgeschichte* (Gütersloh, 1931), p. 9.

these scattered, rich, and relatively isolated islands. Their control of the seas helped to prevent the Roman Catholic missionaries or the teachers of Islam from returning to minister to their converts. Candidius, Heurnius, Valentijn, and other able pastors visited the eastern islands from time to time and encouraged other pastors to help fill the ranks that were always being depleted in these remote outposts. Huernius, who labored in these islands from 1633 to 1638, was the father of the Reformed faith of Amboina.[475] The civil authorities stimulated the interest of the pastors by providing prospective converts and by paying a specified sum for each person baptized. Failures to send children to school or to attend church were punished by fines. Under these conditions the Dutch were able to claim at the end of the seventeenth century a congregation of almost forty thousand Christians on Amboina alone. While many were certainly Christians in name only, the Reformed faith, staunchly supported by the Company, put down deeper roots in Amboina than elsewhere in the East. To this day, close cultural and religious ties are maintained between the Dutch and the Amboinese, a conclusion that is best supported by reference to the flight of large numbers of anti-Javanese Amboinese to the Netherlands when Indonesia became independent of Dutch rule in 1963.[476]

William Carr, English consul at Amsterdam and traveler on the continent, wrote admiringly in 1691 of the Dutch East India House at Amsterdam and of the directors who "as good Christians have been at great charge in planting the gospel in many parts" of the East.[477] Certainly by comparison to the English, the Dutch had won enough missionary successes in the seventeenth century to stir the envy and admiration of those across the channel who were then just beginning to think seriously about foreign missions. The English East India Company, always primarily concerned about the encouragement of commerce, generally followed a policy of noninterference in local affairs in the East until the last two decades of the century. The Company feared, not without reason, that religious propaganda, if systematically carried out, would arouse the hostility of the inhabitants and the rulers of the ports of India where they conducted their business affairs on sufferance.[478] Unlike the Dutch in Java, Formosa, Amboina, and Ceylon, the English held no control over territories where they could use the secular arm to support religious activity. In India the English at Surat and Madras were confronted by great native states whose rulers were powerful enough to expel them and to cut off trade should the occasion arise. It was only with

---

[475] In ill health Heurnius returned to the Netherlands in 1638, where he spent the last thirteen years of his life revising, preparing, and publishing Christian materials in the Malay language.

[476] See Latourette, *op. cit.* (n. 226), III, 304–6; Boxer, *op. cit.* (n. 433), p. 146; Boetzelaer, *op. cit.* (n. 438), pp. 126–31.

[477] From *An Accurate Description of the United Netherlands* (London), p. 34, as quoted in Boxer, *op. cit.* (n. 433), p. 133, n. 6.

[478] *Cf.* Neill, *op. cit.* (n. 432), p. 232.

the acquisition of territorial control over Bombay in 1665 that plans were launched in India and England to undertake a more active religious program.

While the Company was under no official obligation to meet the religious needs of its servants, it began in 1607 to provide ships' chaplains. Once the English were permitted in 1614 to build a factory at Surat, the Company regularly recruited chaplains; certain of the recruits were well enough instructed to compete with the Jesuits already ensconsced at Surat. Patrick Copeland, a chaplain with mission interests, returned to England in 1614 with "a young man, an Indian . . . who is very apt to learn." After receiving further instruction from Copeland, this son of the "Bay of Bengala" was baptized in London on December 22, 1616, at the church of St. Dionis Backchurch before an assemblage which included members of the Privy Council, the Lord Mayor and Aldermen, and members of the East India and Virginia Companies. "Peter" (the baptismal name was selected for the young Indian by King James himself) was the first Indian to become an Anglican. Several weeks later Copeland and Peter returned to India.[479]

In these early years English ships still contested with the Dutch and Portuguese for the trade of south India and the Indonesian archipelago. Factories were established at Masulipatam on the Coromandel Coast (after 1610) and at Bantam in Java (1612). Chaplains, who had signed up in England for the duration of a particular ship's voyage, visited these outposts occasionally. Even though the Dutch in the East were far from friendly to the English, they did permit several Anglican pastors during the period of alliance (1619–23) to minister to their countrymen in Java. Certain of the pastors disappointed the English Company by engaging in private trade, by leading debauched lives, or by proving to be too frail or otherwise unfit for life as a Company servant; others, like Edward Terry, Sir Thomas Roe's chaplain at the Mughul court from 1617 to 1619, performed their pastoral functions ably and faithfully. In 1655 Terry published a memoir of his experiences.[480]

The English in southeastern India relied until 1640 upon the willingness of the local rulers and the Dutch to tolerate their trading activities. The pastors here chafed at the restrictions under which they had to work. Francis Day and other English merchants of the Coromandel Coast initiated negotiations on their own with Golconda to obtain the right to trade and to build a fort at Madras, a site where a Portuguese settlement already existed at Mylapore. The directors in London discouraged this enterprise, for they believed that the possession of sites and forts meant disputes with the native rulers and additional commitments potentially injurious to trade and profit.

---

[479] The Book of Common Prayer contained no service at that time for adult baptism; it was added in 1662. See *ibid.*, p. 232, n. 1. For details on religious activities see F. Penny, *The Church in Madras . . . in the Seventeenth and Eighteenth Centuries* (3 vols., London, 1904), Vol. I, chap. i; E. Chatterton, *A History of the Church of England in India* (London, 1924), chaps. i–iii. For a summary account see M. E. Gibbs, *The Anglican Church in India* (New Delhi, 1972), pp. 3–8.

[480] See below, pp. 566–67.

Fort St. George nonetheless began to be built in 1640, and many of the Portuguese in the area were attracted to work there as builders, traders, and soldiers. Along with the Portuguese came their families and their priests, both sources of future difficulties for the English at Madras.

The Portuguese priests ministered to their own flock and to the English and Irish Catholic soldiers at the fort. They were joined in 1642 by Ephrem of Nevers, a French Capuchin.[481] The factors urged the newcomer to stay on as priest to the non-Portuguese Catholics at Madras, for they wished to curtail the growing influence of the Portuguese at the fort. The Protestants were without a chaplain until the arrival in 1647 of William Isaacson from Surat, the factory to which Fort St. George had become subordinate two years earlier. While Isaacson was still resident chaplain at the fort, Father Ephrem was kidnapped in 1649 by Portuguese agents and carried off to Goa. Isaacson was succeeded at the fort by Robert Winchester in 1650, but he left in the following year and its Protestants were again without a chaplain. In the meanwhile Ephrem returned to Madras in 1651 and was soon joined by another French priest.

The return of Isaacson in 1654 with several chaplains brought an end to the ecumenical atmosphere at the fort. English soldiers, most of whom were Protestants, had contracted alliances with Luso-Asian women who were often Catholics. The right to baptize the offspring of these religiously mixed unions became a subject of dispute between the priests and the chaplains. When Isaacson called for the expulsion of the French priests, the factors protected the Catholics and worked out a compromise on the issue of baptism. The secular authorities also mediated disputes between the High Churchmen and the Puritan chaplains, who would not conform to The Book of Common Prayer. Around 1670 the Company ordered an end to the persecution of Catholics, Muslims, and Indians and told the chaplains to instruct the black slaves in Christianity and to free them after a specified period of service as Christians. The carrot, it was thought, was more effective than the stick. By 1676 all the chaplains were in regular Anglican orders and most other divisive issues resolved.

Streynsham Master, governor of Madras from 1677 to 1682, projected the building of a church within the walls of Fort St. George and was supported in this enterprise by the factors and merchants. The Protestants, tired of worshipping in makeshift chapels in the fort, wanted a proper church. St. Mary's church, a small stone and brick edifice with a rounded roof, was built between 1678 and 1680. Richard Portman, the first licensed chaplain to work in India, consecrated St. Mary's in 1680, with the approval of the bishop of London. The church, as rebuilt in 1759, still stands and is today recognized by the Archaeological Department of India as a building of historical interest.

---

[481] On his career see above, pp. 257–58.

Surat, the main British commercial and administrative center in western India until 1672, was not the site of significant religious development. Its strategic location in the trading world of the Indian Ocean made Surat, in Sir Thomas Roe's words, "the fountain and life of all the East India trade." The English establishment at Surat, though large in size, was monastic in character, since only the president was permitted to have his wife with him. The factory boasted a small chapel where a minister was usually in attendance, but proposals to build a church were left unrealized. The minister's main task was to offer daily prayers, conduct Sunday services, visit the subordinate factories, teach the children, and set a moral example. A few of the ministers indulged in private trade and made a good income on the side from fees charged for performing religious rites. Others lapsed in their personal behavior and morals, and a few were sent home for neglecting their duties.[482]

The English Company had long looked with covetous eyes upon Bombay as "the best place on the West Indian coast." Projects for conquering or purchasing Bombay from the Portuguese had been advanced by both the Company and its agents in the field. Ceded finally to the British king by the Portuguese crown in 1661 as part of the marriage dowry of Catherine of Bragança, Bombay was leased to the Company in 1668. According to the terms of the treaty of 1661, the Roman Catholic inhabitants of Bombay, as subjects of the king of England, "were to enjoy the free exercise of . . . [their] religion as they do now." When the Company took over the administration, the inhabitants of Bombay, like those of Madras, enjoyed complete toleration in religion—a fact which probably helps to explain the city's rapid development.[483]

When Gerald Aungier took over in 1672 as governor of Bombay, its three hundred English inhabitants were housed in the fort and worshiped in one of its upper rooms. The new governor anticipated a rapid growth for the city as Hindu and Portuguese merchants and refugees flocked there to seek safety and trade at a place remote from the wars and disruptions of the continent. Optimism about the city's future probably accounts for Aungier's decision to undertake the construction of a church large enough to hold one thousand people. Once the foundation walls of the church were raised, the construction had to be indefinitely postponed, since Bombay suffered for the remainder of the century from war and its effects and from the Company's declining prestige at home. Bombay cathedral was not completed until 1718. Trouble developed at Bombay, as at Madras, between Roman Catholics and Anglicans over the baptism of children of religiously mixed unions. Aungier and his successors took a hard line against Catholic bap-

---

[482] See Penny, *op. cit.* (n. 479), p. 75, and Chatterton, *op. cit.* (n. 479), pp. 13–15.
[483] See Hull, *op. cit.* (n. 8), p. 20; and W. Ashley-Brown, *On the Bombay Coast and Deccan. The Origins and History of the Bombay Diocese* (London, 1937), p. 78.

tisms, the Jesuit properties, and proselytizing priests. Friction between the Portuguese and the English at Bombay ultimately led to the expulsion of the Portuguese clerics in 1720.[484] In both Bombay and the newly founded city of Calcutta progress in religious activity had to await the beginning years of the eighteenth century.[485]

In England churchmen, disappointed servants of the Company, and intellectuals began to question early in the century why the blessings of the Anglican gospel and English civilization were making no progress in the East.[486] But it was not until the Restoration of 1660 that a missionary awakening began to take place. Richard Baxter, a well-known nonconformist, suggested in 1660 in a letter to the Company that Grotius' book in the Arabic translation (Oxford, 1660) of Edward Pococke should be sent to the Company's servants for distribution in the East.[487] Why he believed, as others in England did, that a work in Arabic could be widely read in India is a mystery. Perhaps it merely indicates the inadequacy of the information on India then available in England, or Baxter's personal failure to understand what had been written about the languages current in the East. Ten years later Baxter wrote to John Eliot, the Anglican missionary and founder of Harvard College: "The industry of the Jesuits and friars and their successors in Congo, China, and Japan shame us all, save you."[488]

Leadership in bestirring the East India Company was assumed in 1677 by Robert Boyle (1627–91), the renowned chemist who was then a director of the Company. Supported by the eminent bishops John Fell (1625–86) of Oxford and Gilbert Burnet (1643–1715) of Salisbury, Boyle proposed a plan for the propagation of the gospel in the Indies. Citing the example of the Dutch in Batavia, Boyle urged the Company to propagate the gospel "among the natives, in whose countries we have flourishing factories." He sponsored Thomas Hyde's Malay translation of the Four Gospels and Acts of the Apostles that was published at Oxford in 1677.[489] He also suggested the publication of "a confutation of the authentic books wherein the Bramins religion is contained," a project that apparently went unrealized.[490] Discouraged, Fell wrote to the archbishop of Canterbury in 1681 bemoaning "the shame that lay upon us, who had so great opportunities by our commerce in the East, that we had attempted nothing towards the conversion of the Na-

---

[484] See Hull, *op. cit.* (n. 8), pp. 25–27.
[485] On Calcutta's early religious history see Chatterton, *op. cit.* (n. 479), chap. iv.
[486] See Van den Berg, *op. cit.* (n. 449), pp. 22–24.
[487] Robert Boyle underwrote the translation and in 1673 sent three dozen copies to a merchant in the Levant for distribution there. See T. T. Birch (ed.), *Robert Boyle, The Works* (Hildesheim, 1965; photographic reproduction of the London edition of 1772), I, ci.
[488] As quoted in Van den Berg, *op. cit.* (n. 449), p. 26.
[489] Entitled *Jang Ampot Evangelia derri tuan Kitu Jesu Christi duan Beorboutam derri jang Apostoli Borsacti Bersalin dallam Bassa Malayo*. In the Newberry Library, Chicago.
[490] See Birch (ed.), *op. cit.* (n. 487), I, cix–cx.

tives, when not only the papists, but even the Hollanders, had laboured herein."[491] At the same time Boyle and several of his associates on the Company's board established a fund in 1681–82 "towards the encouragement of such as should learn the Malasian language, and fit themselves for the service of God in the East."[492] After special training the Company's chaplains were to engage in missionizing in the East. Little came of this plan, for Fell died in 1686, the Company's charter lapsed in 1693 to be renewed for five years only, and wars and piracy endangered the British position in western India. From this experience the English learned, as the Dutch were learning at the same time in Ceylon and elsewhere, that Portuguese and the native languages were more important than either Arabic or Malay in advancing the cause of Protestantism in India.

The enemies of the Company, as well as its more enlightened friends and directors, were responsible for pointing up its failures in planting the Anglican religion in the East. In 1695 when the Company was in dire straits, Humphrey Prideaux, dean of Norwich and a staunch advocate of missionary work, produced a report on the state of the factories in the East. At his suggestion, when the Company's charter was renewed in 1698, a clause was included obliging the Company to maintain a minister at every fort and major factory in the East; each appointee had to be approved by the ecclesiastical authorities in England. The chaplains were to know Portuguese and "to apply themselves to learn the native language of the country where they shall reside."[493] The Company was to provide schoolmasters for the Christian instruction of Europeans and natives in its service. While this program was not quickly implemented, the Company was forced to recognize, eighty-six years after establishing its factory at Surat, that it had a religious and moral duty to those who served it and lived under its protection. Contemporaneously the Society for Promoting Christian Knowledge (S.P.C.K.) was founded to be followed three years later by the incorporation under royal charter of the Society for Propagation of the Gospel in Foreign Parts (S.P.G.).[494]

While these newly founded missionary societies concerned themselves mainly with missions in America, they also took more than a passing interest in the Danish mission at Tranquebar on India's east coast. Active at Danesborg (Tranquebar) and other Eastern ports since 1620, the Danish Company generally sent Lutheran chaplains and pastors to the East.[495]

---

[491] As quoted in Penny, *op. cit.* (n. 479), p. 96.
[492] As quoted in *ibid.*
[493] As quoted in *ibid.*, p. 123.
[494] For the general conditions surrounding the founding of these mission societies see W. O. B. Allen and E. McClure, *Two Hundred Years. The History of the Society for Promoting Christian Knowledge, 1698–1898* (London, 1898), chaps. i–ii.
[495] For the history of the Danish East India companies see above, pp. 89–93.

The Christian Mission

There they ministered to the Danes and Germans and occasionally baptized slaves. When the Company was reorganized in 1670, its charter included a clause (paragraph 5):

As it is to be hoped that many of the Indians, when they shall be properly instructed will be turned from their heathen errors, there shall always be priests in the ships and in the territory belonging to the Company, and the King [Frederick III] promises to promote such Priests as have been in the service of the Company.[496]

But the king's interest in converting the heathen produced no significant missionary activity in the seventeenth century. The sole exception to this rule was Jacob Worm, a somewhat irascible pastor who was literally banished to Tranquebar in 1680. Called the Danish Apostle of India, Worm reputedly made translations into Tamil and preached to the natives in the streets. Although the New Danish Company enjoyed a degree of prosperity during Worm's stay (1681–91) in India, no proper Danish mission functioned at Tranquebar before 1706.

The German Lutherans, a few of whom had served with the Dutch and Danish companies in the East, were by and large without concern for missions. In the seventeenth century no German state had territorial outposts or traded on its own behalf in the East. A few sporadic efforts were made in the latter half of the century, especially by Brandenburg, to organize a chartered Company for trade to the East.[497] Religiously the German territorial states, whether Lutheran or Calvinist, operated under the principle of *cuius regio, eius religio*, with no obligation or authority to carry religious teachings beyond their political boundaries. In 1651, the theological faculty of the University of Wittenberg reaffirmed the orthodox Lutheran view that the Great Commission (Matt. 28:19) had expired with the original apostles, that the heathens had been offered the true faith and had rejected it, and that Protestant princes were only obligated to propagate the gospel in their own lands.

A few Lutheran religious leaders, like Baxter in England, and the men of the "Second Reformation" in the Low Countries, rejected the orthodox view, watched with fascination the Catholic achievements in overseas missions, and called for a Lutheran apostolate. At the University of Kiel, where Danish influence was strong, two professors advanced a proposal for a seminar in Oriental languages and missions, an unrealized idea which may have stimulated the proposals of Baron Justinian von Welz (1621–68).[498] Welz, who had spent several of his student years at Leyden (1641–43), was the first Lutheran to call openly and clearly for missionary activity. He published six tracts in 1663–64 to express his concern over the spiritual coldness and lax morality of Lutheran society and proposed the organization of a Jesus-

---

[496] As quoted in J. F. Fenger, *History of the Tranquebar Mission* (Second Bicentenary edition, Madras, 1906), p. 10.
[497] See above, p. 111.
[498] See Genischen, *op. cit.* (n. 438), p. T12.

loving Society to promote spiritual piety and to recruit student volunteers for missions. In 1664 he presented these ideas to a meeting, held in Regensburg, of the major Lutheran princes. He received a cold reception on this occasion, and his proposals were attacked and satirized by Johann H. Ursinus, the influential General Superintendent at Regensburg. In his "Admonition to Justinian" Ursinus exhibits a broad knowledge of activities and events in the overseas world, thus revealing that his opposition to Lutheran missions was based upon secular concerns as well as theological grounds. Ursinus tauntingly wrote in 1664:

> Tell us once, where you will begin . . . ? In a place where there are already Christians? or where there are none? Where there are Christians you come too late. . . . The English, Dutch, Portuguese, and Spanish control a good part of the farthest seacoast. To which place? Thirty years ago the Japanese fiercely rooted out their Christian congregations. . . . Will you go there? In China only recently the Tartars mercilessly murdered the Christians and their preachers [a reference to the Oboi regency in all probability]. Will you go there? Where then, you honest Germans?[499]

Bitterly disappointed, Welz renounced his title of nobility and went off to Surinam as a missionary. He died there in 1668.

Unlike his fellow German Protestants, Leibniz saw the Jesuits and their policy of cultural affiliation as a model for Protestants to follow. The great philosopher and mathematician watched carefully the progress of the Catholic missions and sought through his correspondence to keep informed of their progress, particularly in China. Leibniz urged the Calvinist rulers of Brandenburg-Prussia to take the lead in organizing a Protestant missionary endeavor as part of his program of church reunion. For a time he hoped to win the cooperation of Tsar Peter of Russia in opening an overland route to China via Siberia. In his mind scientific interchange with the Chinese would advance human civilization and contribute to the greater glory of God. His ideas on missions stimulated the growing interest of August Hermann Francke, one of the leading professors at the newly founded Pietist University of Halle. And it was through Francke that the Danes obtained the services of Batholomäus Ziegenbalg and Heinrich Plutschau, the two young Pietist preachers who pioneered the Lutheran mission in Tranquebar after 1706.[500]

At the beginning of the seventeenth century the Catholic missionaries worked at the fringes of Asia from the Persian Gulf region to the Philippine Islands. A few Jesuits meanwhile began to penetrate the Mughul Empire,

---

[499] Excerpted from the translation in J. A. Scherer (trans. and ed.), *Justinian Welz. Essays by an Early Prophet of Missions* (Grand Rapids, Mich., 1969), pp. 101–2.

[500] On Leibniz, Francke, and the Danish mission see F. R. Merkel, "The Missionary Attitude of the Philosopher G. W. von Leibniz," *International Review of Missions,* IX (1920), 399–410; and D. F. Lach, *The Preface to Leibniz' Novissima Sinica* (Honolulu, 1957).

south India, and China. The earlier Jesuits, who had worked their way into Japan, had begun by the dawn of the century to have their monopoly threatened by the Spanish friars from the Philippines. As the missions grew apace, they were torn asunder internally by national and fratricidal rivalries and jealousies which originated both in Europe and in the field. In an effort to bring the missions under Rome's control and supervision, the Congregation for the Propagation of the Faith (*Propaganda fide*) was created in 1622. Its early efforts to denationalize the missions and to unite the orders behind Rome were met by resistance from the Iberian states and others with vested interests in the Portuguese (*padroado*) and the Spanish (*patronato*) patronages. Around mid-century the Propaganda reluctantly began to look to the French church for financial and political support. The foundation in Paris of the *Missions étrangères* in 1664 injected new disruptive elements into what was already a maze of contending religious forces. French vicars apostolic and secular priests were sent to the East to establish bishoprics and mission stations in Asian areas not already co-opted by the Iberian missionaries. Faced by the hostility of the *padroado* and by native resistance in Vietnam, the French built up a mission base at Ayut'ia in the 1660's. Both the secular priests and the French Jesuits increasingly relied thereafter on the support of the French state and its East India Company. Despite the protests of Rome the French mission was nationalized, so that by century's end the Propaganda had to be content to play one national enterprise off against the other to maintain a modicum of authority over the Asian missions.

Everywhere in the East, the *padroado* and the Portuguese secular authority had been forced on the defensive by the 1660's. From the beginning of the century onward the Spanish missionaries had violated its sphere and had challenged its authority. King Philip III generally supported the Spanish missionaries and interceded with the papacy on their behalf from time to time. Beginning with the expulsion of missionaries from Japan in 1614, Rome itself began to take a more direct interest in supervising the mission in the East. Members of the curia, such as Cardinal Robert Bellarmine, supported the accommodation policies followed by Ricci and Nobili despite the strictures of the Portuguese clergy against them. The founding of the Propaganda brought into being a central agency that increasingly threatened Portugal's authority over the missions. In a reaction to Rome's new initiative, the Habsburg rulers of Spain and Portugal tightened royal control over mission activities in the East, and unseemly conflicts occurred between the Goa authorities and the agents of the Propaganda. The pope's decision of 1633 to end the restriction requiring mission travel exclusively through Lisbon coincided with the demise of the Portuguese India Company. This was followed by growing unrest in Portugal with Habsburg rule. When Japan cut off all trade with Macao in 1638, the financial base of the Portuguese mission in East Asia was shattered. Macao and the mission received new shocks when trade with Manila ended in 1640 and when Malacca fell to the Dutch the following year.

The Portuguese war of independence brought with it a cessation of formal relations between the *padroado* and the papacy from 1640 to 1668. Clashes over ecclesiastical authority in the East became more frequent and vindictive in this period. Portuguese bishops died off and their sees were left vacant. The military decline of Portugal in the East forced many of the friars at endangered or conquered outposts to leave their stations and congregate at Goa. Propaganda missionaries, and vicars apostolic after 1648, began to assume authority over decadent *padroado* dioceses, especially in continental Southeast Asia. In south India the St. Thomas Christians revolted against the *padroado* bishops in 1652–53. The losses of Ceylon and the Malabar cities to the Dutch reduced Goa's authority in south India to a shadowy jurisdiction by the 1660's. Those Catholic missionaries who were thereafter permitted to work in Dutch-controlled areas were ordinarily non-Portuguese.

The serious decline of *padroado* authority was closely related to missionizing policies. In the settlements directly under Portuguese control, the policy of Europeanization of the converts was heavily dependent upon the state. When Portugal's secular control weakened or vanished, the Christian enterprises likewise lost out. In the stations outside of Portuguese control, the missions languished for want of financial support and in Bengal, south India, and China they had to depend on the continuing support of their loyal native converts. In the first half of the century nowhere in the mission field, not even in "accommodationist" China, had the Europeans encouraged the growth of a native clergy. Of the 184 Jesuits who worked in China between 1600 and 1649, 14 were Chinese, 2 Japanese, 1 Korean, and 1 Chinese-Korean; they were all classified as brothers, for the Society refused to consider Chinese mature enough in the faith for ordination.[501] In India a native secular clergy began to be numerous only as the friars became fewer and less devoted to the ministry. A remnant of Catholics survived in Ceylon during the Dutch period of moderate control. In Japan, where a substantial number of natives had been trained as lay catechists, the Christian community endured despite official persecution. Christianity likewise survived in the interior of south India after the death of Nobili with the aid of native *pandara-swamis* (religious workers) and lay catechists recruited for the mission work.

The Jesuits especially were responsible for introducing non-Portuguese missionaries into the *padroado*. The friars and the secular hierarchy were solidly Portuguese in background, many from Lisbon and its environs, or Luso-Asians and Europeans recruited in the East. In the first six decades of the seventeenth century Jesuits of Italian background became particularly

---

[501] See Duncan, *op. cit.* (n. 14), p. 366. The first Chinese to become a priest was ordained at Coimbra in 1665. See Dehergne, *op. cit.* (n. 86), p. 332.

prominent: Valignano, Ricci, Nobili, Longobardo, Vagnone, Aleni, and Martini. The Italians were also the leading proponents of the adaptation policy, and they had powerful friends in Rome who supported their innovations in the field. Before 1660 they were joined by Lowlanders (Trigault and Verbiest), Germans (Schreck and Schall), Austrians (Köffler), and Poles (Boym) who assumed leading roles in the mission. João de Britto, the martyred Jesuit and saint, was the only prominent Portuguese to follow the policy of adaptation during the years of his apostolate in south India.

The Portuguese crown, always anxious about its primacy, sought to limit the number of foreigners admitted to the mission; the Portuguese were especially suspicious of the Spanish and successfully excluded them from direct participation in the *padroado* after 1600. The China mission, in particular, was international in character and became even more so during the K'ang-hsi period (1661–1723). Although the Portuguese had never enjoyed a perfect monopoly in the *padroado,* they constantly struggled after 1665 to maintain a modicum of authority. While Lisbon won a technical victory in the 1690's in reasserting its authority over the China mission, the claims of the *padroado* continued to be hotly contested both in Europe and Asia. On the initiative of the Propaganda the bishoprics of Nanking and Peking were created in 1690, thus removing most of China from the ecclesiastical jurisdiction of Macao. The new bishoprics were, however, to remain subject to the metropolitan see of Goa in a bow to Portuguese sensitivity on the subject of the *padroado.* Gradually even this concession eroded as the vicars apostolic continued to maintain control over a part of the China mission.[502] By 1700 the French Jesuits in China were released from Goa's grasp and reported only to their own superiors. On paper at least, the *padroado* continued to function in India until October 25, 1953.[503]

The enduring successes of the missionaries of the *patronato* were limited to the Philippines and the Marianas. For a period the missionaries from the Philippines challenged the Jesuits in Japan. The Christian failure in Japan, while not completely the responsibility of the Spanish friars, produced charges from the Jesuits blaming them for the "Great Persecution" of the Tokugawas. The Spanish friars experienced a partial success in China, where they began to work in 1632 within the Portuguese-Jesuit monopoly. During the last generation of the seventeenth century the Spanish missionaries made a belated and unsuccessful effort to take over the leadership of the China missions from the Portuguese and the French. While the friars denounced the Jesuits for their commercial activities, some of their own members likewise involved themselves in trade and in political chicanery. In the Moluccas the Christian enterprise depended entirely upon the support of the secular authority for its existence. Here, and in the Philippines, the missionaries en-

---

[502] See the table of the various nationalities in Dehergne, *op. cit.* (n. 86), pp. 398–401.

[503] See F. de Almeida, *História da igreja em Portugal* (new ed., 4 vols., Barcelos, 1968), II, 41–42.

couraged the state to undertake military crusades against the Dutch and the Muslims. Wherever the state maintained its power, the *patronato* prospered. But by the latter half of the century, the Asian empire of Spain was limited to the Christianized Philippines and to a few islands in the mid-Pacific. The Catholic missions in Indonesia, except for those of the Portuguese Dominicans in the Lesser Sundas, were defunct by 1700.

The China mission founded by Ricci, like the south India mission created by Nobili, was dominated by the Jesuits throughout the century. While dependent upon the Portuguese for transportation overseas, the Jesuits made every effort not to "Portugalize" their converts. Without protection from the secular arm, the Jesuits in China and Madura disdained the evangelizing methods of the friars and accommodated themselves, as they had earlier in Japan, to the dominant native cultures. The Jesuits studied local languages and traditions, cultivated friendships with members of the educated and official classes, and gradually penetrated from the major centers into interior regions. They creatively evolved methods of adapting themselves and the Christian message to local conditions. Cut off from the European enclaves, they necessarily lived like natives. They studied closely the religious and social practices of the Hindus and Chinese in order to insinuate Christian ideas and beliefs with a minumum of friction. Native converts were used as lay catechists and admitted to the Society as brothers, but they were generally thought to be too immature in the faith to be ordained as priests. The Jesuits in both missions depended upon their converts for financial aid and political guidance.

In China the Jesuits had the advantage of working within a unified culture and a single state. As in Europe, they were able to use their superior training in the arts and sciences to mingle comfortably with elites and to be introduced at court. They translated Western astronomical works into Chinese, proved by their accurate predictions the superiority of European astronomy and mathematics, and obtained appointments for themselves in the prestigious Calendrical Bureau of the empire. They made themselves indispensable by acquiring or making artillery for the imperial army. Although they were caught up in the civil wars accompanying the fall of the Ming dynasty, they quickly "accommodated" to the Manchus and became even more influential at court in the K'ang-hsi period. They recruited scientists from all over western Europe, and especially from France in the waning years of the century, in the vain hope of converting the emperor himself through Western learning to Christianity. They won a partial and dubious victory when they obtained an Edict of Toleration in 1692 which made Christianity one of the four faiths that could be freely practiced in China. By 1700 the China mission boasted an estimated three hundred thousand converts or exactly the number claimed for Japan one century earlier.[504]

---

[504] The victory of atheistic Communism in China since 1949 raised many questions among

In the Asian mission fields as reorganized by the Propaganda and the *Missions étrangères* the greatest progress was made in Vietnam. Jesuits from Macao, especially Alexandre de Rhodes, had been tolerated in Cochin-China and Tongking so long as the Portuguese traders came with arms. But conversions came slowly and uncertainly for the Jesuits, possibly because of the temporary character of their mission and because they paid more attention to the Japanese Christian refugees than to proselytizing the Vietnamese. The arrival of the French vicars apostolic and the secular priests produced mission rivalries in continental Southeast Asia with the Jesuits of the *padroado* that did not benefit the mission. Once the Europeans ceased fighting among themselves, Christianity made great strides in Vietnam. The Propaganda and the French clerics cooperated in the training of large numbers of lay catechists, many of whom became priests. The flourishing Vietnamese mission, unlike the China mission, remained at century's end firmly in the hands of the Propaganda and retained no relationship to the *padroado*.

The Protestant missions, especially those sponsored by the Dutch, were much more closely controlled than the Catholic missions by the European states and the chartered trading companies. Without the aid of orders dedicated to missions, the Protestant pastors mainly worked with the European Christians in Asia. From their base in Batavia the Dutch pastors concentrated their missionary efforts on the islands which the VOC wanted to control. In the Spiceries they centered their attention on Amboina where they taught and preached to the natives in the Malay language. Converts in the islands were given special privileges by the VOC. Everywhere in Indonesia the pastors were confronted by the hostile Muslims and better-established Catholic missions supported by the Portuguese and Spanish based in Macao and Manila. The Reformed ministers made their most sustained and successful effort in Taiwan, where they confronted no Muslims or other established religions. There the pastors worked among the Sirayas, native tribal groups who possessed no unified political or religious organization. With the support of Dutch arms and ships the pastors and native aides carried out a civilizing mission for about two decades (1642–62) to make converts to Dutch ways and religion. After the Dutch defeat in Taiwan, some Calvinists back home began to urge the adoption of an accommodation policy of the Jesuit type. The only effect of these suggestions was a mild response in India and Ceylon, where the austere Reformed faith had failed to destroy the

---

churchmen and others as to the reasons for the failure of Christianity in China after such auspicious beginnings. For example, see Malcom Hay, *Failure in the Far East. Why and How the Breach between the Western World and China First Began* (Wettoren, Belgium, 1956). While Hay traces the breach to the machinations of the Jansenists and their sympathizers and to the general incompetence of the Roman curia, others have raised questions about the efficacy of the Jesuit policy of accommodation and compromise with Chinese culture and religion. Certainly, some would argue, the foreign faith of Marxism succeeded by overwhelming rather than by compromising with China's traditional culture. Contemporary Jesuits nonetheless hope to return to China.

well-entrenched Catholic missions and the Portuguese heritage. The English Protestants in Bombay and Madras meanwhile sought to maintain and establish the Anglican faith surrounded by non-Christians and Portuguese Catholics. The Danes had irregularly sent Lutheran chaplains to Tranquebar on the Coromandel Coast; they finally established a permanent Lutheran mission only in 1706.

The Catholic missionaries and the European agencies of the church provided Europe with a splendid documentation on the missions in the letter-books. The Franciscans sent a delegation from Japan to Iberia and Rome (1614–18) which produced more results for Europe than for Japan. The Propaganda in Rome set up its own college for the training of native clerics and a printing press for the publication of religious books in Asian languages and of mission reports in European languages. In Paris a seminary was established for the training of French secular clerics for the missions. The Jesuits studied native languages and even Romanized the Annamese language. They translated Hindu and Chinese classics, or parts of them, for publications in European languages. Missionaries of various orders, as well as Jesuits and secular priests, collected information on Asia's geography, flora, fauna, and products. The controversy in Europe over rites had as a by-product a polemical literature in which many of the religious and social ideas of India and China were conveyed, albeit in distorted form, to a European-wide audience. The Protestants, who never followed the Jesuits in their admiration for Hindu and Chinese civilization, nonetheless enriched Europe's culture by their studies of the Malay and Siraya languages. Their original descriptions of the beliefs and practices of Hinduism as well as their scholarly cooperative works on the flora of Malabar enlarged substantially Europe's understanding of the subcontinent.

Certainly Europe learned more about Asia from the missions than the Asians generally learned about either Europe or Christianity. Nonetheless, by the end of the seventeenth century, Christianity had triumphed in the Philippines, the Marianas, and Amboina, had made notable progress in establishing itself in Vietnam, Ceylon, and south India, and continued to maintain bridgeheads in the Mughul and Chinese empires.

The Archbishops of Goa in the Seventeenth Century

Name	Affiliation	Dates of Tenure
Aleixo de Meneses (de Jesus)	Augustinian	1595–1610; Governor, 1607–9
Cristóvão de Sá (de Lisboa)	Hieronymite	1611–22
Sebastião de São Pedro (Bishop of Cochin)*	Augustinian	Suffragan, 1622–25; Metropolitan, 1625–29
Miguel Rangel (Bishop of Cochin)*	Dominican	Suffragan, 1629–33; Metropolitan, 1631–33
Francisco dos Martires	Franciscan	1635–52
See left officially vacant	Papacy did not recognize independent Portugal	1652–74
Antonio Brandão	Cistercian	1674–78
Interregnum		
Manuel de Sousa Meneses	Secular	1681–84
Alberto da Silva	Augustinian	1685–88
Pedro da Silva (Bishop of Cochin)*	Affiliation unknown	Suffragan, 1689–91
Agostinho da Anunciação	Order of Christ	1691–1713

NOTE.—Names, affiliations, and dates of the archbishops of Goa extracted from Fortunato de Almeida and Damião Peres, *História da igreja em Portugal. Nova edição* (Porto and Lisbon, 1968), Vol. II, pp. 701–2.

*Pope Gregory XIII, in a brief of December 13, 1572, had ordained that the bishop of Cochin should administer the archbishopric of Goa during periods of vacancy.

The Printed Word

Introduction

The history of printing in the seventeenth century, like that of Europe's overseas activities, relates mainly to the extension and consolidation of the revolutionary and heroic advances made in the previous century.[1] In the seventeenth century the production of books became occupationally differentiated, with the publisher rather than the printer acting as the control figure and organizer of the trade. More interested in profits than in quality, the publishers turned out books that were inferior to the typographical masterpieces of the sixteenth century.[2] With the spread of literacy to people other than churchmen, academics, and selected gentry, the publishers and authors catered increasingly to new needs and tastes by printing cheaper books in handier sizes. Editions continued to be limited to around one thousand copies or less, but reprints and the translated editions of popular books such as Pinto's *Travels* became more common.[3] While many books continued to be published in Latin, the production of works in the national languages steadily grew. A brisk export trade in books throughout western Europe encouraged translations from one vernacular to the other.

During the Thirty Years' War the center of gravity in book production moved with finality out of the disrupted German cities to the Netherlands. The Plantin-Moretus press in Catholic Antwerp continued throughout the seventeenth century to publish a variety of religious and scientific books in Latin and in the vernaculars for distribution to an international audience

[1] On the printed word in the sixteenth century see *Asia*, I, 148–51. For a survey of Renaissance geographical literature to the 1620's see B. Penrose, *Travel and Discovery in the Renaissance, 1420–1620* (Cambridge, Mass., 1955), chap. xvii.
[2] See C. Clair, *A History of European Printing* (London, 1976), pp. 272–73.
[3] See below, p. 324.

interested in the acquisition of splendid books. In the economically prosperous north, the Dutch of the Golden Age were furnished with many
of their university textbooks and editions of classical authors by the acquisitive house of Elsevier.[4] The Amsterdam firms founded by Joost de
Hondt (Hondius) and Willem Blaeu early in the century specialized in the
engraving of maps and the compilation of atlases, which they published in
Latin, Dutch, German, French, and Spanish editions. More books, pamphlets, and newsletters were probably printed in the Netherlands than in all
of the rest of Europe, as Amsterdam became the continent's greatest book
market before the end of the century.[5] In France, printing and publishing
went into state service with the establishment in 1618 of a Royal Chamber of
Booksellers, Printers, and Binders of Paris, an agency which came to monopolize and regulate the whole book trade. In 1640 the *Imprimerie Royale*
was set up in the Louvre with Sebastien Cramoisy as its directing head.[6] In
the latter half of the century Paris printing houses eclipsed those of the
French provinces but not those of the Spanish Netherlands and Holland.
The printers of Antwerp and Amsterdam published low-cost books in
French. Some of these could not be printed in France itself because of their
seditious, libelous, or heretical character.[7] English printing, under the supervision of the Stationers' Company until 1695, got on its feet financially
by publishing the writings of popular authors from Shakespeare to John
Bunyan. The English bibliography is simpler because no Jesuit letterbooks
were produced in that Protestant and anti-papist country. In the early years
of the century the English East India Company encouraged the publication
of a series of journals which announced the successes of the voyages to the
East. In Holland, much more so than in England, pamphlets and chapbooks
were issued telling about the fleets, their discoveries, and their cargoes, as
part of the commercial information supplied by the VOC to its investors
and customers.[8]

Most historians of printing have generally treated cavalierly the book production of southern Europe during the seventeenth century. They rightly
emphasize the new prominence assumed by the Dutch and French, while
asserting that book production in Italy and Iberia remained in a state of "re-
spectable mediocrity."[9] It is assumed, with some justice, that the baneful

[4] See D. W. Davies, *The World of the Elseviers, 1580–1712* (The Hague, 1954).
[5] See K. H. D. Haley, *The Dutch in the Seventeenth Century* (London, 1972), pp. 123–24.
[6] See D. T. Pottinger, *The French Book Trade in the Ancien Régime, 1500–1791* (Cambridge, Mass., 1958), pp. 122–31; 143–44.
[7] See H.-J. Martin, *Livre pouvoirs et société à Paris au XVIIᵉ siècle (1598–1701)* (2 vols.; Geneva, 1960, 1969), II, 732–40.
[8] See S. H. Steinberg, *Five Hundred Years of Printing* (3d ed., Harmondsworth, 1974), chap. ii. On the early English tracts see J. Parker, *Books to Build an Empire* (Amsterdam, 1965), chap. x.
[9] The judgment of James P. R. Lyell in R. A. Peddie (ed.), *Printing, A Short History of the Art* (London, 1927), p. 164. Elizabeth Eisenstein (*The Printing Press as an Agent of Change* [2 vols.; Cambridge, 1979], I, xiv, n. 8) admittedly draws most of her examples from England and France.

influence of the church, the Inquisition, and the censorship of both church and state stultified innovation in printing techniques and limited subject matter to noncontroversial topics. But these assumptions are justified only in part; there continued to be a flourishing and productive printing industry in Iberia. As in the north, its reading public was fed a steady diet of classical, religious, and scientific works supplemented by popular dramas, romances, travel books, and maritime tragedies. Even in Habsburg-dominated Portugal, the public continued to call for and to read works about the overseas empire in Asia, an empire that was not perceived to be in decline before the capture of Ormuz in 1622.[10] Biographies of famous Asian administrators and Jesuit missionaries kept alive an interest in the great feats of past and present. Separate bibliographies appeared in both Portugal and Spain listing the books on the Iberian expansion into the East.[11] Portuguese chroniclers and historians made efforts to buoy national pride during the "Babylonian Captivity" of the nation by compiling a general history of the Lusitanian monarchy and celebrating its overseas conquests.[12]

After 1600 "so many books about the New World came out that it is difficult to keep our bearings."[13] The northern printers, like the Venetian compilers of Ramusio's collection in the mid-sixteenth century, quickly realized that the interest of the reading public in the overseas world was constantly growing. In England, Samuel Purchas continued Hakluyt's project of publishing English versions of reports from the overseas world by authors of many nationalities. The De Bry family of Frankfurt and the Amsterdam printers produced huge collections of illustrated voyages that were frequently translated and reprinted over the course of the century. Melchisédech Thévenot, royal bibliographer of King Louis XIV of France, had published at Paris beginning in 1663 his *Relations de divers voyages curieux,* a collection, mainly of Oriental travels, translated from the compilations of Hakluyt, Purchas, and a number of later authors.

Habsburg ascendancy in Portugal brought a definite end to Lisbon's control of information on the routes, ports, and products of Asia.[14] At the beginning of the seventeenth century the Portuguese began to publish their rutters (*roteiros,* navigational guides) and to reissue in translation and in new editions many of the relevant writings of the past. The public, and therefore the publishers, could still be thrilled by circumnavigations or by factual reports of previously unknown lands such as Tibet or Australia. Increasingly, compendia were issued which dealt in greater depth than formerly with

[10] See A. J. Saraiva, *História da cultura em Portugal* (3 vols.; Lisbon, 1950–62), II, 138–40.
[11] Especially see F. M. Rogers (ed.), *Europe Informed: An Exhibition of Early Books Which Acquainted Europe with the East* (Cambridge, Mass., and New York, 1966), pp. 3–8.
[12] See H. M. A. Kömmering-Fitzler, "Fünf Jahrhunderte portugesische Kolonialgeschichtsschreibung," *Die Welt als Geschichte* (Pt. 2), VIII (1942), 104–17.
[13] The words of L. Febvre and H.-J. Martin, *The Coming of the Book. The Impact of Printing, 1450–1800* (London, 1979), p. 280.
[14] On the Portuguese "policy of secrecy" see *Asia,* I, 151–54.

China, parts of India, or Siam. Contemporary events in Asia were given wide publicity by writers who were themselves involved in these changes: the Manchu defeat of the Ming in China or the "Revolution of 1688" in Siam. Hinduism, Buddhism, and animism were examined and commented upon by European authors who made extended investigations of Asian religions. Itineraries in travel books were more frequently based on memoirs or diaries meticulously kept by the travelers themselves while in the field. Sketch maps were prepared to provide European cartographers with more accurate materials on the coasts and interiors of the Asian lands. Botanical specimens were collected and sketched by both Europeans and natives for the compilers of herbals in Europe. The appearance in Europe of Orientals—Moluccans, Filipinos, Japanese, Malays, Burmese, Siamese, and Chinese—inspired the publication of newsletters and periodical articles about their homelands and customs.

In Asia, the European printing press had a checkered career during the seventeenth century. In the beginning years it continued to be used in India and the Philippines to provide the missionaries and their converts with Christian materials in the native languages, Portuguese, and Spanish. In China and Japan the European press functioned only until 1640, as a return was gradually made to xylographic printing. At Goa and Rachol in India the Jesuit press ceased to function around 1674.[15] The Dutch East India Company set up a press with movable type at Batavia which began to print books in 1668.[16] Two Dutch commercial agents who were pious Calvinists translated the Four Gospels, the Psalms, and the Acts into Malay during the middle years of the century to bring the Word of God directly to the people in a language familiar to them.[17] Dictionaries and word lists were published in Europe of a number of Asian languages.

Jesuit letters and letterbooks from the East continued to be issued throughout the century.[18] In Europe they were edited and often included in relations such as those produced by Fernão Guerreiro in Lisbon or Pierre Du Jarric in Bordeaux. The Jesuits and the other missionizing orders sent "living letters," or practicing missionaries, to Europe to report on events in the field and often to write up their experiences for publication. For modern historians of China and Southeast Asia much material lies hidden about their areas in the letterbooks produced by the Jesuit Province of Japan. With

---

[15] See C. R. Boxer, *Exotic Printing and the Expansion of Europe* (Bloomington, Ind., 1972), pp. 8–10.

[16] See the forthcoming series by Katherine S. Diehl, *Printers and Printing in the East Indies* (projected in seven volumes). For a rapid survey of printing in East Asia see the contribution of H. Bernard-Maitre in Febvre and Martin, *op. cit.* (n. 13), pp. 212–15.

[17] See Eric Fenn, "The Bible and the Missionary," in S. L. Greenslade (ed.), *The Cambridge History of the Bible* (Cambridge, 1963), p. 385.

[18] On the sixteenth-century Jesuit letters and the histories based on them see *Asia*, I, 314–31, 427–67, 794–815.

their expulsion from Japan in 1613–14, the refugee Jesuits established their provincial headquarters in Macao. From here they left for the missions in China, Vietnam, Cambodia, and Laos over the remainder of the century. Their reports on these places to superiors and colleagues were often published in the so-called Japan letters. The Dominicans, Franciscans, and Augustinians also became more prolific in the seventeenth century in recording their deeds and activities in the East. With the creation of the Congregation of the Propaganda (1622) and the Paris Mission Society (1664) a spate of new reports began to be published, particularly at Rome and Paris. These Catholic mission accounts, especially when utilized in conjunction with merchant reports, enlarged significantly the territory opened to European readers. Tibet, Laos, Korea, and the Marianas appeared for the first time in sharp focus. The missionary writings sparked controversies over methods of conversion, and in 1673 the pope required the missionaries to submit their proposed publications to the Propaganda for review and approbation.

In the chapters of Part II which follow, the European published materials are organized by the nation in which they were first published and in chronological order, or approximately so. The Jesuit writings published all over western Europe are listed chronologically in a tentative checklist at the end of the bibliography, below, beginning on page 1983 (in Book 4).

CHAPTER III

The Iberian Literature

Spanish and Portuguese publications are here treated jointly because of the union of the two crowns (1580–1640), the disruptions and entanglements produced by the prolonged war of independence (1640–68), and the growing tendency of the Portuguese to write in Spanish in hopes of attracting a wider European audience. In Habsburg Iberia the secular reading public was broadened as formal secondary education became more widespread under the leadership of the Jesuits.[1] By 1600 the Society, with the help of local patrons, had established colleges in most major cities and towns. The students attracted to these colleges would go on to become recruits for the professions and the bureaucracy. Instruction in the Jesuit colleges followed the *Ratio Studiorum,* a curriculum which emphasized rigorous training in grammar, philosophy, theology, and morality, supplemented by substantial courses in mathematics, history, geography, and astronomy. As earlier at Toulouse and Clermont in France, the Iberian students of the Jesuits were probably required to own and read the letterbooks of the missions.[2] Despite a general decline in Iberian university education, many non-Spanish students, including large contingents of Portuguese before 1640, matriculated at the prestigious university of Salamanca to study law in preparation for governmental careers in both Iberia and the colonies.[3] Books in Spanish were published increasingly at Madrid, instead of at Seville or Salamanca, as

---

[1] In Toledo literacy was slightly less than 50 percent at the end of the sixteenth century. In the early years of the seventeenth it was slightly more than one-half and by the second part of the century had risen to 55 percent. See H. J. Graff, *The Legacies of Literacy* (Bloomington, Ind., 1987), p. 191.

[2] On Jesuit education in sixteenth-century France, see *Asia,* II, Bk. 3, 480–81.

[3] See R. L. Kagan, *Students and Society in Early Modern Spain* (Baltimore, 1974), pp. 50–55, 203–4.

it became the administrative and artistic center of the monarchy. Many Spanish titles also came off the presses of Brussels and Antwerp in the Spanish Netherlands.[4] A number of books on Asian matters were published in Mexico, Manila, and western India in both the Iberian and the local languages.

The Spanish publications differ from those of other European nations inasmuch as they include a larger number of printed memorials about the East addressed to the crown and the royal councils. These were generally prepared by those who had returned from the East advocating greater national support for the Moluccas, the Philippines, and the galleon trade. The Portuguese rutters (navigational guides) on eastern voyaging were published and kept up to date. The *Décadas* of Barros on the Portuguese East were continued by Couto, Lavanha, and Faria y Sousa. Thorough coverage was given to history and prevailing conditions in the Philippines by a series of ground-breaking books that were published between 1609 and 1667. The conquest of the Moluccas in 1606 was celebrated in major and minor works of the early century; the abandonment of the Spiceries in 1662 was not given equal attention in the literature. In addition to Jesuit letters and letterbooks, numerous pamphlets and books appeared in Iberia celebrating the martyrdoms in Japan, the Japanese embassy of 1614, the canonization (1622) of Xavier, and the "discovery" (1625) of Tibet. Histories of the missions in Cambodia, Japan, and the Philippines were followed by celebrations of the religious progress made by the Portuguese on the west coast of India. Authentic and fictional travel books, both retrospective and contemporary, attracted a large reading public. Biographies of famous Asian administrators published in Portugal helped to stimulate national pride. Works on China, published mainly in Spanish, began to appear in 1642 and became more numerous once the Dominicans and Jesuits were embroiled in the rites controversy. The Iberian materials dealing with the Mughul Empire and southern India are slight, compared to those produced by the other European nations. As the Iberian role in Asia became restricted to the Pacific and the Philippines, and to a few Portuguese outposts in western India and off the south China coast, the appearance of books on the East declined abruptly in the last two decades of the century.[5]

I

EXPLORATION, CONQUEST, AND MISSION STATIONS

The Spanish explorations of the Pacific Ocean from 1567 to 1607 stimulated the missionizing zeal of both King Philip III (r. 1598–1621) and Pope

[4] See J. Peeters-Fontainas, *Bibliographie des impressions espagnoles des Pays-Bas* (Louvain and Antwerp, 1933).

[5] This generalization seems to apply also to the collection of manuscript materials. See the

The Iberian Literature

Clement VIII (r. 1592–1605). Pedro Fernandez de Quiros (d. 1615), a pilot who had explored the Pacific extensively from Callao in Peru, sought by writing memorials to inspire a continuing official enthusiasm in Spain for the discovery of the austral continent, or the unknown southland, and for the spiritual conquest of the natives of the insular world of the Pacific. To this end he addressed seventy memorials to the king between 1607 and 1614.

Quiros' eighth memorial was published in several Spanish editions by 1610[6] and shortly thereafter was translated into German (1611), Dutch (1612), Latin (1612), French (1617), and English (1617).[7] It includes brief summaries of his voyages of 1595–97 and 1605–6 as well as bits of information about the islands and peoples of the South Pacific. His maps and globes, as well as his memorials, helped to inspire contemporary navigators, such as Jacob Le Maire, and later explorers, such as Tasman, Bougainville, and Cook, to look for the austral lands. In 1615 Fray Juan de Torquemada, O.F.M., published a narrative of the Quiros expedition in his *Monarquia Indiana* (Seville)[8] which was to prompt a Franciscan plan of 1617–27 to missionize in the austral lands. Several manuscript maps and drawings are extant at Simancas which purport to show the lands and peoples Quiros discovered.[9]

While Quiros urged the exploration and conquest of the *terra australis,* other voices in Madrid were calling for a resumption of the Spanish intervention in Cambodia.[10] Urged on by Luís Peréz Dasmariñas, the Spanish

---

listing in A. R. Rodriguez Moñino, "Bibliografia Hispano-Oriental," *Boletín de la Academia de la Historia* (Madrid), XCVIII (1931), 429–70.

[6] *El Capitan Pedro Fernandes de Quiros con este son ocho los memoriales* (Seville?). Several printed and manuscript copies are in the British Library. The Princeton University Library possesses a photocopy of *Relaçion de un memorial que prestando a su Magestad el Capitan Pedro Fernandez de Quir, sobre la población y descubrimiento de la quarto parto del mundo, Australia incognita . . .* (Pamplona, 1610).

[7] A facsimile version of the first edition was issued as a separate by Carlos Sanz. The first English edition was translated from the French version. A different English translation was published by Samuel Purchas in 1625; see S. Purchas, *Hakluytus Posthumus, or Purchas His Pilgrimes* (20 vols; Glasgow, 1905–7), XVII, 218–31. Hereafter cited as *PP*. A Dutch translation also appeared in the *Begin ende voortgangh* (1645). For further bibliographical detail see C. Kelly (ed. and trans.), *La Austrialia del Espiritu Santo* (2 vols.; "HS," 2d ser., CXXVI–VII; Cambridge, 1966), II, Appendix 3.

[8] Reprinted at Madrid in 1723. For extracts from this rare work see C. De Brosses, *Histoire des navigations aux terres australes* (Paris, 1756), I, 309–33; A. Dalrymple, *An Historical Collection of the Several Voyages and Discoveries in the South Pacific Ocean* (2 vols.; London, 1770–71), pp. 108–43; and C. Markham (ed.), *The Voyages of Pedro Fernandez de Quiros, 1595–1606* (2 vols.; "HS," 2d ser., XIV–XV; London, 1904), II, 405–51.

[9] For some of the maps and all of the drawings see Kelly, *op. cit.* (n. 7), Pls. I, II, IV, V, VIII, X, XI, XII. Ethnographical and artistic commentary on the drawings may be found in R. Ferrando Perez, "Zeichnungen von Südsee—Eingeborenen . . . ," *Zeitschrift für Ethnologie,* LXXIX (1954), 75–81.

[10] On the sixteenth-century activities of the Spanish and Portuguese in Cambodia see *Asia,* I, 309–12; for a survey of these enterprises in a broader context see C. R. Boxer, "Portuguese and Spanish Projects for the Conquest of Southeast Asia, 1580–1600," *Journal of Asian History,* III (1969), 118–36.

governor of the Philippines, and by other hotheads at Manila, the conquistadors of Madrid memorialized King Philip III to redeem the good
name of Spain by using Manila as the base for a new series of military expeditions in Southeast Asia. In 1603 Pedro Sevil, a veteran of the first Cambodian expedition, published at Valladolid, in Spain, his proposal for the
conquest of Indochina and other countries of the East.[11] After the failure of
his effort to win the court's support, Sevil returned to Manila and in 1606
took part in the Spanish conquest of Ternate.

A far more sophisticated memorial advocating the conquest of Cambodia
appeared in print at Valladolid in 1604. The work of a Dominican friar,
Gabriel Quiroga de San Antonio (d. 1608), it is entitled *Breve y verdadera
relacion de los sucesos del Reyno de Camboxa.*[12] From the beginning of the
Spanish intervention in Cambodia, the Dominicans had taken the lead in
evangelizing there, sometimes with the aid of a few Franciscans. San Antonio himself undertook a mission of nine years' duration in the course of
which he circumnavigated the world. He left Seville in mid-summer of 1594
and returned to Lisbon in the spring of 1603. During that time he spent two
and one-half years at Manila (June, 1595, to February, 1598), about two
years in Malacca (1598–1600), and over two years in Ceylon and south India
(1600–1603).[13] On his return to Valladolid, San Antonio associated himself
with Sevil and the other captains and wrote his own informed memorial addressed to Philip III. Divided into three parts, this quarto volume of eighty-
three pages deals with the sixteenth-century expedition of Juan Juarez de
Gallinato to Cambodia, the heroic and picaresque exploits of Diego Belloso
(Veloso) and Blaz Ruiz de Hernan Gonzalez in Southeast Asia, and the story
of San Antonio's own travels and experiences on his voyage around the
world. His descriptions of Cambodia, including a special section on Angkor
Thom,[14] are particularly revealing even if they are secondhand; his other discussions are even less original and not as critical. San Antonio has many interesting things to say about the Philippines, Malacca, Ceylon, and south
India and about events there around the turn of the century.[15]

[11] *Conquista de Champan, Camboja, Siam, Cochinchina y otros paises de Oriente.* Translated by
Antoine Cabaton in "Le mémorial de Pedro Sevil [de Guarga] à Philippe III . . . (1603)" in
Bulletin de la commission archéologique de l'Indochine (Paris, 1914–16), 1–102. For this same year,
H. Ternaux-Compans in his *Bibliothèque asiatique et africaine* (Amsterdam, 1968; reprint of
Paris, 1841–42, ed.; hereafter cited as Ternaux-Compans), lists the following title: *Discurso en
que se justifica la jornada de Cambaja y Siam en las Indias orientales.* Since we have not seen this
latter work, it has not been possible to determine whether it is from Sevil's memorial or an
entirely independent tract, possibly by Christoval de Jacque de los Rios.
[12] Reprinted and translated into French in A. Cabaton (trans. and ed.), *Brève et véridique relation des événements du Cambodge* (Paris, 1914). For a detailed study of the background to and
consequences of the Cambodian projects see M. Teixeira, "Diogo Veloso e a gesta lusíada em
Cambodja," *Actas da Congresso internacionál de história dos descobrimentos* (Lisbon, 1961), Vol. V,
Pt. 1, pp. 339–77.
[13] For details of his voyage see Cabaton, *op. cit.* (n. 12), p. 207.
[14] For further discussion see B. P. Groslier and C. R. Boxer, *Angkor et le Cambodge au XVI*
siècle, d'après les sources portugaises et espagnoles (Paris, 1958), pp. 21–23, 61–62, 84–85.
[15] San Antonio's account undoubtedly depended also upon materials obtained from the sol-

Proposals for military and missionizing adventures in the central Pacific and in Indochina were shelved in Valladolid (which served as the Habsburg capital from 1600 to 1606), partly because they were of dubious practicality and mostly because of the government's greater interest in the conquest of the Moluccas. Very little was known in Europe about the fate of the Portuguese and the Christian communities in the Spiceries after the fall of Ternate in 1574 to the Muslim League. From reports current in northern Europe and from their own observers in the Netherlands, the Spanish learned about the appearance of English and Dutch vessels in the Spiceries and of their operations and observations there. Reports from the Philippines also filtered into Madrid relating to events in the Moluccas and other parts of insular Southeast Asia. An enemy of the Muslim League, the independence-minded king of Ternate sent a mission of obedience to Lisbon soon after Philip became king of Portugal. Other rulers of the Moluccas addressed their vows of obedience to the governor of Manila. Still the Muslim League remained active, as it sought to control the spice trade by playing off the Iberians against the newly arrived Dutch and English.

Ternate, in particular, managed to remain relatively independent, and its ruler openly sent embassies to London and Amsterdam around 1600 to negotiate for perpetual peace and commerce with the English and Dutch. In 1602 the Dutch concluded an agreement with Ternate by which they were granted the monopoly to purchase cloves. At this juncture the ruler of Tidore began to look to Manila as an ally against the growing power of Ternate. The English, represented in the Moluccas from 1604 to 1606 by Sir Henry Middleton, acted for a brief period as interested observers, intermediaries, and proponents of an antimonopolistic policy for the spice trade. The Iberians would accept no compromise and were especially determined to expel the Dutch from their foothold at Ternate. A rising fear in the Philippines about the prospect of a Chinese or Japanese intervention in the Moluccas also strengthened the Spanish in their resolve to send a naval expedition from Manila against Ternate and the Dutch fleet in the Spiceries. Unable to resist the Spanish expeditionary force of thirty-six vessels carrying about two thousand infantrymen, the Dutch fleet retired, and Ternate capitulated on April 10, 1606. Fiestas were held in Manila to celebrate the victory.

The architect of Spain's Moluccan policy was Pedro Ferríandez de Castro Andrade y Portugal (1560–1634), the count of Lemos and the president of the Council of the Indies from 1603 to 1610. This famous adviser to Philip

---

diers at Madrid and the reports of the Dominican friars who had lived in Cambodia and elsewhere in the East. See L. P. Briggs, "Spanish Intervention in Cambodia, 1593–1603," *T'oung pao*, XXXIX (1949), 160n. The soldier Christoval de Jacque's memorial is superior in detail and more objective in tone than San Antonio's; it was possibly published in 1606. It is available in French translation in H. Ternaux-Compans (ed.), *Archives des voyages* (2 vols. in 1; Paris, 1840–41), I, 241–350.

III and *"mecenas español"* celebrated the Spanish victory for himself and his country by sponsoring the writing and publication of the *Conquista de las islas Malucas* (Madrid, 1609) of Bartolomé Leonardo de Argensola (1562–1631).[16] Brother of the famous poet Lupercio, Bartolomé had been educated at the new University of Huesca. After taking Holy Orders he became in 1588 the curate and rector of Villahermosa in Valencia. Several years later, as chaplain to Empress María de Austria, he lived in Madrid, where he associated with many of its leading literary, artistic, and political lights. When the empress died in 1603, he became freer to pursue his secular interests. The count of Lemos, who knew of Argensola's literary talent and historical bent, quickly settled upon him as a person well qualified to write the history of Spain's involvement in and conquest of the Spice Islands. To this end he provided Argensola with papers, letters, and other materials from the archives of the Indies. The book that appeared in 1609 has been described as one whose prose style is among the "most palatable and pleasant in our language."[17]

Dedicated to the king, Argensola's *Conquista* is a handsome volume, almost four hundred pages in length, which summarizes the history of Europe's relations with the Moluccas from the beginnings to 1606. He divides the story into ten books, the first seven of which deal with background events of the sixteenth century and include descriptions of the geography, peoples, and products of the Moluccas and their neighbors. For these materials he drew, as he freely admits in the text, upon the chronicles of Barros and Couto, the descriptions of Gabriel Rebelo and António Galvão, the Jesuit letters (especially those from Father António Marta), and the mission history of Maffei. The materials on the events leading directly to the conquest itself he extracted from the letters, documents, and papers sent from Goa and Manila to the Council of the Indies. He reports that his information on Dutch activities in the Moluccas came from "las relaciónes de Hugo," that is, Jan Huyghen van Linschoten, although some of it appears to have come from the published reports of the second Dutch voyage under Cornelis van Neck and Wybrand van Warwijck.[18]

Strictly speaking, Argensola's account is a history in a world setting of Spain's gradual progress in winning control over the Moluccas. But it is also

[16] The following citations are to this original edition. It was reprinted in 1891 at Zaragoza as Vol. VI of the *Biblioteca de escritores aragoneses* with a long introduction and appreciation written by Miguel Mir. In 1706 a French translation appeared at Amsterdam in three volumes. Two years later John Stevens published an English translation to which a map and several engravings were added: *The Discovery and Conquest of the Molucca and Philippine Islands* (London, 1708). Around 1710 a German edition, probably translated from the French, appeared at Frankfurt. James A. Robertson has translated excerpts relating to the Philippines from the original edition into English in E. H. Blair and J. A. Robertson (trans. and eds.) *The Philippine Islands, 1493–1898* (55 vols.; Cleveland, 1904–9), XVI, 217–317. Hereafter cited as BR.

[17] See M. Mir, *op. cit.* (n. 16), p. ci. For a portrait of B. L. de Argensola see the engraving of S. A. Carmona reproduced with the article on him in *Enciclopedia universal ilustrado*.

[18] Argensola, *op. cit.* (n. 16), pp. 254. For a bibliography of the second Dutch voyage see below, pp. 439–41; for Argensola's use of these accounts see below, pp. 1399, 1427.

a tract for the times and a graceful piece of political and dynastic propaganda. Published at a time when the Spanish were becoming forthrightly pessimistic about the future of their empire in Europe and overseas, it proclaims that Spain still possessed the determination and strength to undertake conquests in distant places and to bring them off successfully. In his digressions on people and places, Argensola also adds significantly to the stockpile of information on Asia, especially on the Moluccas, Java, Sumatra, and Ceylon. His book also ties together neatly the affairs of Europe with struggles in the overseas areas, for he sees the spice trade in its worldwide ramifications and makes his reader acutely aware of its immediate and potential interest for Japan and China. Through his accounts of the embassies sent from the East Indies to Europe he shows that diplomatic relations, not just trade, conquest, and missionizing, could be carried on with insular Southeast Asia. And, here for the first time, the world had at hand an entire book centered directly on the Moluccas that could be read with profit and pleasure.[19]

The state of affairs in the Philippines, the heart of Spain's eastern empire, became increasingly a matter of concern to the government of Philip III. The new century had opened with the appearance in Manila Bay (October, 1600) of two Dutch warships under the command of Admiral Olivier van Noort as a forthright challenge to Spain's command of the Eastern seas. Letters were quickly dispatched to Madrid about Van Noort's bold foray, letters which warned also about the possibility of difficulties with China.[20] The insurrection of Manila's Chinese community in 1603 seemed to foreshadow a major disaster for the Spanish in the Philippines. Reports from administrators and missionaries predicted, though incorrectly, an attack from China in support of the "Sangleyes" (Chinese in the Philippines). Pamphlets by eyewitnesses were circulated in Spain reporting on the revolt and its suppression, the efforts being undertaken to placate the Chinese, and the preoccupation of the Chinese government with domestic disasters and with war in Korea—events that supposedly prevented China from being more aggressive in the South Seas.[21] From 1607 to 1609 a series of memorials was presented by Pedro de Baeza, a lawyer born in Mexico, urging the crown to take advantage of the conquest of the Moluccas and the stabilizing of its

---

[19] It was a major source for Matías de Novoa (d. 1652), Spanish diplomat, courtier, and historian, when he wrote an account of the Spanish stake and victory in the Moluccas into his annalistic *Memorias,* one of the fundamental manuscript histories of the reigns of Philip III and Philip IV. See Vol. LX of *Colección de documentos inéditos para la historia de España . . .* (Madrid, 1875), pp. 300–349, and the prologue by Antonio Cánovas del Castillo.

[20] See documents translated in BR, XII, 83–168; XIII, 221–315.

[21] For example, *Relación del levantamiento de los Sangleyes, nación Gentil, habitadores en las Islas Filipinas . . .* (Seville, 1606). This was written by a soldier in the Philippines and abridged and prepared for publication by Miguel Rodriguez Maldonado. For an English translation see BR, XIV, 119–39.

control over the Philippines, from Luzon to Mindanao, to become more directly involved in the spice trade.[22]

The Portuguese, who had so closely guarded their special knowledge of the sea routes to the East, began in the seventeenth century, probably under Spanish pressure, to share their information with others. From the time of Prince Henry onward, the Portuguese navigators had been required to prepare *roteiros* (rutters) of their voyages. Those delineating the routes to India and beyond were at first not printed, and the manuscript copies were closely kept. While other nations surreptitiously obtained copies of the manuscripts from time to time, the excellent pilot guides of João de Castro and others remained securely in the hands of the Portuguese until after Philip became king. The Portuguese were then required to share their knowledge with the Spanish, and gradually they came to share it with others as well. In Goa, Jan van Linschoten acquired copies of a number of *roteiros* which he then printed in his *Itinerario* (1596), a book which was subsequently translated into English, French, Latin, and German. A copy of Linschoten's work became around 1600 an essential part of the pilot's library when navigating the Eastern seas.[23]

Once Linschoten had brought the *roteiros* to public view, the Portuguese also began to publish them. The first printed collection was prepared by Manoel de Figueiredo (1568–1630), cosmographer-major of Portugal from 1607 to 1621. His *Hydrographia,* first printed in 1608, includes instructions for the pilot and *roteiros* for the voyages from Lisbon to the Portuguese outposts, including India. Most important was the *roteiro* of Vicente Rodrigues as published in an adaptation possibly prepared by the cosmographer and historian, João Baptista Lavanha (1555–1624).[24] Figueiredo's work was reprinted, with a few revisions and additions, in 1609, 1614,[25] 1625, and 1632, and it became a model for similar works that were contemporaneously and subsequently issued. The most important *roteiro* hereafter prepared was based on Rodrigues'; this was the work of Gaspar Ferreira Reimão, published separately at Lisbon in 1612.[26] Shortly thereafter Dom António de

---

[22] For example, see *Jesus Maria Pedro de Baez, vezino desto valla de Madrid. Dizo, q̃ por V. Excel me mâdar hazer este memorial . . . de los Indias Orientales . . . y demos partes de la mar del Sur* (1608?). This is the title of one of the five printed memorials listed as belonging to the Library of Congress.

[23] See C. R. Boxer, "Portuguese Roteiros, 1500–1700," *The Mariner's Mirror,* XX (1934), 177–78. Also see the collection of manuscripts included in Quirino de Fonseca, *Diários da navegação de Carreira da India nos annos de 1595, 1596, 1597, 1600, e 1603* (Lisbon, 1938).

[24] Rodrigues' *roteiro* had earlier been published by Linschoten. For a modern reprint see F. Pereira, *Roteiros portuguezes da viagem de Lisboa á India nos seculos XVI e XVII* (Lisbon, 1898), pp. 15–92. On Lavanha also see below, p. 328.

[25] Copies of the 1614 edition may be found in the Library of Congress and the New York Public Library. It includes a map and tables.

[26] *Roteiro de navagaçam e carreira da India . . .* For a modern reprint with an introduction by A. Fontura de Costa see the book issued in 1940 by the Agência geral das Colónias (Lisbon).

Atáide compiled a fine manuscript collection of *roteiros* which amplified Reimão's thorough work.[27] The collections compiled later in the seventeenth century added very little to the excellent summary *rotieros* of Rodrigues and Reimão.[28]

Along with the *roteiros* a spate of shipwreck narratives printed in pamphlet form began to appear at Lisbon early in the seventeenth century. Manuel Godinho Cardoso published in 1602 the story of the "Santiago," wrecked in 1585, along with the itinerary followed by its survivors.[29] A second "Santiago" was captured in 1602 in an action against the Dutch, and along with it the first manuscript of the historian Diogo do Couto's seventh *Década* was lost. Melchior Estacio do Amaral reports on this latest disaster as well as on the misfortunes of the "Chagas" in 1594, in related narratives of 1604, in which he also sets down the reasons for the loss of thirty-eight *náos* of India over a period of twenty years and proclaims Portugal's exclusive right to conquest and navigation in the East.[30] Here as elsewhere the Portuguese blamed their maritime losses on their involvement in wars, not of their own choosing, with Spain's enemies.

Even the eminent historian, Diogo do Couto (1542–1616) tried his hand at writing a maritime tragedy. In 1611 he set down the story of the "São Thomé" wreck of 1589 as part of one of his other works that remained in manuscript for many years after his death.[31] Indeed, a number of Couto's other works were not printed during his lifetime. Couto had lived in India, mostly at Goa, during his last fifty years, except for a brief return trip (1569–71) to Portugal. Beginning in 1595 he became Keeper of the Archives of Goa and official chronicler. At an even earlier date he had apparently re-

[27] See the three volumes published by the Agência geral do Ultramar with introduction and notes by Humberto Leitão and entitled *Viagens do reino para a India e da India para o reino (1608–1612). Diarios de navegação coligidos por D. António de Ataíde no século XVII* (Lisbon, 1957–58).

[28] See Boxer, *loc. cit.* (n. 23), 183–85.

[29] Entitled *Relaçam do naufragio da Náo Santiago e Itinererio da gente que delle se salvou.* (A *náo* was a large ship of six hundred to sixteen hundred tons, called a carrack or galleon by English sailors.) Ternaux-Compans (p. 93) lists under 1601 the *Naufragio de Jorge d'Albuquerque et prosopei a en su luvor* (Lisbon) by Pedro de Texeira. We have been unable to locate other references to Texeira's work.

[30] Ternaux-Compans (p. 97) gives the date of the first narrative as 1602, but this is not confirmed in other bibliographies. Both editions were printed by António Alvares; the second is entitled *Das Batalhas do Galaeom Sanctiago com Olandeses. E da náo Chagas que ardeo antre as Ilhas, com Ungleses. Das causas porque em 20. annos se perderão 38 náos da India. De como a conquista & navegação do Oriente não perténce a nação senão à Portuguese. . . .* For details see C. R. Boxer, "An Introduction to the História Trágico-Marítima," in the special volume *Miscelânea de estudos em honra do Prof. Hernâni Cidade,* published in the *Revista da Faculadada de Letras* (Lisbon), 3d ser., Vol. XXIII (1) (1957), 48–99; and F. M. Rogers (ed.), *Europe Informed: An Exhibition of Early Books Which Acquainted Europe with the East* (Cambridge, Mass., and New York, 1966), pp. 131–36; and pl. 3 for a reproduction of the title page given above.

[31] His *Relação do naufragio da Náo S. Thomé . . .* was first published in the eighteenth century in the collection of Gomes de Brito (II, 153–213). See *Asia,* II, Bk. I, 131–35. A modern English translation is in C. R. Boxer (trans.), *The Tragic History of the Sea, 1589–1622* in "HS," 2d ser., CXII (Cambridge, 1959), 53–104.

solved to continue the monumental *Décadas* of Barros. Although he was faced by open and subterranean opposition both in Portugal and India, Couto succeeded in completing eleven *Décadas* and the first five chapters of the twelfth. Only four of the *Décadas* were published during his lifetime: IV (1602); V (1612); VI (1614); and VII (1616); the others, including *Década X*, the first and the longest that he wrote, lay for a long time in manuscript until they were published by others in summaries and abridgments, or as a whole.[32] Those published before Couto's death cover the history of the Portuguese in India and the East from 1526 to 1564. Here he has much less to say than Barros about China and Japan; but his works are particularly valuable for their treatments of Ceylon, Malacca, and the Moluccas.[33] The fourth (the first published), and the tenth *Décadas* are the best extant examples of Couto's works and are the only ones that can be compared in quality to the *Décadas* of Barros.[34]

Missionary letters flowed into Europe at the beginning of the seventeenth century, where they were often published separately or as parts of larger compendia. The Portuguese Jesuits continued to dominate this channel of information. The Spanish Franciscans, Augustinians, and Dominicans, however, began to publish an increasing number of accounts of their activities in the East, especially about their problems in Japan and the Philippines.[35] In contrast, the Jesuit letters published in Iberia during the first decade of the seventeenth century concentrate on the stunning victories of the Society in India, China, and Southeast Asia rather than on the setbacks being experienced in Japan.[36]

In Europe the Jesuits celebrated their victories in Asia with the publication around the turn of the century of a whole series of volumes lauding the life of Xavier and his achievements in the East.[37] In Portugal the Jesuit Fernão

[32] For their publication history see C. R. Boxer, "Three Historians of Portuguese Asia (Barros, Couto and Bocarro)," *Instituto Português de Hongkong. Boletim*, No. 1 (July, 1948), pp. 26–28. For the use of Couto's material by Faria y Sousa, see below, pp. 354–55.

[33] Most of his materials on Ceylon have been translated into English by Donald Ferguson "The History of Ceylon from the Earliest Times to 1600 A.D., as Related by João de Barros and Diogo do Couto," in *JRAS, Ceylon Branch*, XX (1909), 61–109. His account of the Moluccas is based on the manuscript of his contemporary, Gabriel Rebelo, who had spent thirteen years in the Spiceries.

[34] Estimate of A. F. G. Bell, *Diogo do Couto* (Oxford, 1924), p. 37.

[35] For example, Francisco Tello de Guzmán, governor of the Philippines, wrote *Relación que embio de seys frayles españoles dela orden de San Francisco que crucificaron los del Iapon, este año próximo passado de 1597* (Seville, 1598); Juan de Santa Mariá, *Relación del martirio que seys padres descalços Franciscõs, tres hermanos de la compañia de Jesus, y decisiete Japones podecieron* (Madrid, 1601); Pedro de Santiago, *Relación de lo cue hicieron los religiosos augustinos en el transito a las Indias* (n.p., 1605); and Joam dos Santos, *Ethiopia oriental, e varia história de cousas notaveis do Oriente, e da christiandade que os religiosos da ordem de prègadores nelle fizerão* (Evora, 1609).

[36] For example, *Cartas que o padre N. Pimenta . . . escreveo a géral della [26 Nov., 1599] ao [1 Dec., 1600] nas quaes . . . relata o sucesso da . . . victoria que A. Furtado de Mendoça alcãcou do Cunhale* (Lisbon, 1601). For translations of Pimenta's letters see H. Hosten, S.J. (trans.), in *Journal of the Asiatic Society of Bengal*, n.s., XXIII (1927), 57–107.

[37] On the apotheosis of Xavier see *Asia*, I, 327–28. Add to the standard biographies of Tur-

The Iberian Literature

Guerreiro (1550–1617), superior of the House of the Professed in Lisbon, compiled a five-volume *Relaçam* based on letters received from the Jesuits in the overseas world, especially Asia. Published in 1603, 1605, 1607, 1609, and 1611, these volumes follow closely the Jesuit successes in India, China, Japan, and the East Indies. The first of Guerreiro's volumes was translated into Spanish by the Jesuit António Colaço (1568–1647) and published at Valladolid in 1604; its section on China was translated into German as *Historischer Bericht* . . . (Augsburg, 1611). The final volume was translated into Spanish by Dr. Christoval Suárez de Figueroa and published at Madrid in 1613 or 1614, and a partial translation from Portuguese into German was published as *Indianische newe Relation* (Augsburg) in 1614.[38] Both German translations were by Chrysostom Dabertzhofer.

In his "to the reader" Guerreiro indicates that he conceived of his *Relaçam* as a continuation of Luis de Guzman's two-volume *Historia de las missiones . . . en la India Oriental . . . China y Iapón*.[39] As a consequence he usually begins his accounts with 1600, the date when Guzman left off. In moving from area to area in the East, he ordinarily starts with a review of the number and location of Jesuit establishments, the persons working in them, and the activities with which they busied themselves. He indicates that by 1601 the Jesuits had divided the Orient administratively into three provinces: (1) North India, (2) South India, (3) China and Japan. He claims that in these provinces they had more than one hundred houses—including colleges, rectories, and residences—in which almost six hundred Jesuits worked.[40]

The Province of North India included, apart from the Portuguese coastal outposts from Goa northward, the missions of "Mogor" (Mughul Empire), Cathay, and Persia. Guerreiro's materials on Jesuit-Portuguese relations with Akbar became the basis for Part III of Pierre Du Jarric's influential *Histoire* of the missions to 1610.[41] In his discussion of the Province of South

---

sellinus (1596), Lucena (1600), and Pedro de Ribadeneira (1601), the popular book by Thomas de Villacastin, *Apostolica vida, virtudes y milagros del santo padre y maestro Francisco Xavier* (Valladolid, 1602). Also see below, pp. 333–34.

[38] A modern edition of Guerreiro's *Relaçam* was published in three volumes at Coimbra and Lisbon (1930–42) under the editorship of Artur Viegas, who also provided it with a good index and a preface. Vol. I of Viegas' edition includes the first two of the original volumes; Vol. II the next two; and Vol. III the final volume and the index. Our references are to the Viegas edition entitled *Relação Anual*. For a partial synopsis of the contents of the five original volumes see Streit, V, 16–17, 22–28, 39, 48, 60–61, 70.

[39] Published at Alcalá de Henares, 1601. For discussion of Guzman's *Historia* see *Asia*, I, 465–67.

[40] Viegas, *op. cit.* (n. 38), I, 1–5.

[41] On Du Jarric see below, p. 396. For a discussion of the relationship between his work, Guzman's *Historia*, and Guerreiro's *Relaçam* see C. H. Payne (ed. and trans.), *Akbar and the Jesuits. An Account of the Jesuit Missions at the Court of Akbar by Father Pierre du Jarric, S.J.* (London, 1926), pp. xxix–xxxiii, xxxviii. For modern translations relating to the early phase of the "Mogor" mission directly from the Portuguese see H. Heras, S.J., "The Siege and Conquest of the Fort of Asirgarh by the Emperor Akbar," in *Indian Antiquary*, LIII (1924), 33–41; and H. Hosten, S.J., "Fr. Fernão Guerreiro's Annual *Relation* of 1602–3 on the Mogor Mission," *The Examiner* (Bombay), Nov. 22, 1919 (pp. 469–70), and Nov. 29, 1919 (pp. 478–80).

[316]

India, including thereunder the rest of India as well as the mission stations in Malacca, the Moluccas, and Pegu, he is especially informative on conditions in Bengal and Pegu.[42] With respect to the Province of China and Japan, he concentrates initially on the fortunes of the Christians in Japan after the death of Hideyoshi (1598) to 1602 and notes the arrival of the Dutch.[43] In his section on China to 1602 he relates the story of the Jesuit penetration of the mainland, describes Nanking in detail, and comments on the good will exhibited by the mandarins.[44] This is followed by a summary of the wars being fought in the Moluccas and the hardships of the Christians at Amboina and elsewhere.[45]

The second volume of Guerreiro's original series is particularly valuable for its accounts of Pegu, of Goes' mission to Cathay, and of events taking place in Agra.[46] This is followed by a summary of conditions in south India and Ceylon with special attention being accorded to the court of Vijayanagar.[47]

The third volume of the original series begins with a review of conditions, both spiritual and temporal, in Japan during 1603–4, with special attention to martyrdoms and conversions.[48] This is followed, almost by way of contrast, with a discussion of the successes in China and with much more information on native life: trade, the civil service examination of 1604, and the Moors of China.[49] A brief section on the Moluccas precedes a review of events in Bengal, Pegu, and south India.[50]

Volume IV of Guerreiro's *Relaçam* (1609) begins with the pithy comment: "it is a rare thing to have peace in Japan. . . ."[51] It then goes on to provide details on the persecutions being suffered by the native Christians.[52] A letter of 1605 from Father Alfonso Vagnone (1568[69?]–1640) in Nanking provides the basis for another glowing account of the achievements of the

---

[42] Viegas, *op. cit.* (n. 38), I, 42–49. Most of this material is translated into English in C. H. Payne (trans. and ed.), *Jahangir and the Jesuits* (New York, 1930), Pt. III, chap. i.

[43] Viegas, *op. cit.* (n. 38), I, 54–234; Leon Pagés in his history of Christianity in Japan follows Guerreiro's "somewhat scrappy narrative," according to J. Murdoch and I. Yamagata, *A History of Japan during the Century of Early Foreign Intercourse 1542–1651* (2 vols.; Kobe, 1903), II, 427n.

[44] Viegas, *op. cit.* (n. 38), I, 235–66.

[45] *Ibid.*, I, 267–83.

[46] *Ibid.*, I, 285–314. For an English translation of the materials on Pegu see Payne, *op. cit.* (n. 42), Pt. III, chaps. ii–iii; for the Goes mission see *ibid.*, Pt. II, chap. ii; for the strife at Agra see the translation in E. Maclagan, *The Jesuits and the Great Mogul* (London, 1932), pp. 229–34.

[47] Viegas, *op. cit.* (n. 38), I, 315–413. For a systematic account of the Jesuits at the court of Venkata II that is heavily based on Guerreiro's compilation see H. Heras, S.J., *The Aravidu Dynasty of Vijayanagara* (Madras, 1927), chap. xxi. Also see Heras, "The Jesuit Influence in the Court of Vijayanagar," *The Quarterly Journal of the Mythic Society* (Bangalore), XIV (1923), 130–40.

[48] Viegas, *op. cit.* (n. 38), II, 5–87.

[49] *Ibid.*, II, 89–126.

[50] *Ibid.*, II, 133–63. The chapter on Pegu is translated in its entirety in Payne, *op. cit.* (n. 42), Pt. III, chap. iv.

[51] Viegas, *op. cit.* (n. 38), II, 217.

[52] *Ibid.*, pp. 217–89.

Jesuits in China.[53] This is followed by a summary of the struggle between the Iberians and the Dutch in the Moluccas, and by an account of Jesuit triumphs in Malacca, Pegu, and India around 1605.[54] In discussing the Jesuit Province of North India he tells of the death of Akbar (October 27, 1605) and of the succession struggle that followed.[55] Hereafter more follows on the mission to Cathay of Goes extracted from Matteo Ricci's letter (February 2, 1604) sent to Father Jerome Xavier and forwarded by him to Europe.[56]

Guerreiro's final volume, first published in 1611, discusses events of the years 1607 to 1609. It begins with a review of the Jesuit establishment at Goa, the nerve center of the Society's enterprise in the East. Most revealing are the efforts made by the Jesuits to convert Emperor Jahangir and to become useful to him.[57] Guerreiro next presents material he had recently received concerning the mission to Cathay.[58] With respect to south India he brings up to date the status of the missions there. A chapter follows on Jesuit activities in Pegu, Siam, Malacca, and the Moluccas,[59] and on Roberto de Nobili's enterprise in Madura.[60] The remainder of this volume relates to the state of Christianity in Japan and China. Aside from the usual descriptions of conversions and persecutions, the materials on Japan contain details on Mount Fuji, on the journey from Osaka to Nagasaki, and on some smaller places rarely mentioned in earlier writings.[61] In the section on China, reference is made to the fact that three of the four Jesuits in Nanking are devoting themselves to study of the Chinese language.[62]

Students of Indian history, in contrast to the specialists in Chinese and Japanese history, have depended heavily on Guerreiro's collection in reconstructing the history of the late sixteenth and early seventeenth centuries.[63]

The Iberian Jesuits and other ecclesiastics produced early in the seventeenth century a spate of separate memoirs and histories, as well as combinations of the two, on the individual missions and nations of Asia. One of

---

[53] *Ibid.*, pp. 290–302.

[54] *Ibid.*, pp. 303–45; the materials on Pegu appear in English translation in Payne, *op. cit.* (n. 42), Pt. III, chap. v.

[55] Viegas, *op. cit.* (n. 38), II, 347–81; for translations of these materials into English see Payne, *op. cit.* (n. 42), Pt. I, chaps. i–iv, and J. A. D'Silva, "On the Rebellion of Khusrū," *Journal of Indian History*, V (1926), 267–81.

[56] Viegas, *op. cit.* (n. 38), II, 381–90; part of this material is translated in Payne, *op. cit.* (n. 42), Pt. II, chap. iii.

[57] Viegas, *op. cit.* (n. 38), III, 1–25; most of this is translated into English in Payne, *op. cit.* (n. 42), Pt. I, chaps. v–ix.

[58] Viegas, *op. cit.* (n. 38), III, 25–30; translated in Payne, *op. cit.* (n. 42), Pt. II, chap. iv.

[59] Viegas, *op. cit.* (n. 38), III, 67–89; most of the materials on Pegu and Siam are translated in Payne, *op. cit.* (n. 42), Pt. III, chaps. vi–vii.

[60] Viegas, *op. cit.* (n. 38), III, 89–113.

[61] *Ibid.*, pp. 115–231.

[62] *Ibid.*, pp. 231–38.

[63] In addition to the references already cited, see H. Hosten, S.J., "The Annual Relation of Father Fernão Guerreiro, S.J. for 1607–08," *Journal of the Panjab Historical Society*, VII (1918), 50–73.

the best examples of this genre is the book by Pedro Chirino (1557–1635), a Spanish Jesuit, entitled *Relación de las islas Filipinas, i de lo que en ellas an trabaido los padres de la Compañia de Jesús* (Rome, 1604).[64] Sent to the Philippines in 1590, Chirino evangelized among the Tagalogs of Luzon and among the Pintados of the more southern islands, especially in the Bisayans. While at Manila he knew Morga and was evidently shown that part of his manuscript (Bk. VIII) devoted to a description of the Philippines.[65] In 1602 Chirino left the Philippines to return to Rome as procurator for the Eastern mission. At the royal and pontifical courts he succeeded in obtaining support in resources and men to carry on the work in the Philippines, recently made a separate province, a status which freed it from the control of Mexico. Indeed the Jesuit general Claudius Acquaviva was so impressed by Chirino's report on the Philippines that he asked him to prepare it for publication.[66] Shortly thereafter Chirino returned to Spain and shipped out for the Philippines again, where he continued to work for the rest of his life as a missionary, educator, and writer.

Chirino's is the earliest printed history devoted exclusively to the Philippines and to the beginning of the Jesuit mission there. He based his account on Morga's manuscript and on the Annual Letters of his confreres, in addition to his own experiences from 1590 to 1602. Much less concerned than Morga with secular matters, Chirino is particularly informative on the social and religious practices of the Bisayans.[67] He was himself a student of languages, especially Tagalog and Bisayan, and so comments at length on them and on their social implications.[68] And, as a natural result of his missionizing and teaching activities, he is especially good on native religious beliefs and related practices.[69] Most surprising is the amount of space he gives to the flora, agriculture, and trade of the numerous islands he visited. All subsequent historians of the Philippines—and until this century they have mostly been ecclesiastics—have relied heavily on Chirino for their accounts of the first years of Spain's serious penetration of the islands.[70]

One of the most widely circulated of the Jesuit letterbooks contained the account by Diego de Pantoja (1571–1618) written from Peking in 1602 to Luis de Guzman, historian of the Jesuit mission and provincial of Toledo.

[64]Reproduced in a Manila edition of 1890; a newer edition appeared at Manila in 1969 by the Historical Conservation Society. Fully translated into English in BR, XII, 173–321; XIII, 29–217. Our references are to this translation.

[65]On Morga see below, pp. 326–28.

[66]For details on Chirino's mission to Rome see H. de la Costa, *The Jesuits in the Philippines, 1581–1768* (Cambridge, Mass., 1961), pp. 222–23.

[67]BR, XII, see especially pp. 202–9; 220–21.

[68]*Ibid.*, pp. 235–44; XIII, 169–70.

[69]*Ibid.*, II, 263–71, 293–96, 302–8.

[70]Most recently acknowledged by De la Costa (*op. cit.* [n. 66], p. 223), a Jesuit, and by the late Luz Ausejo, a laywoman and a Bisayan, in "The Philippines in the Sixteenth Century," (Ph.D. diss., Dept. of History, University of Chicago, 1972), pp. 266–67.

Entitled *Relación de la entrada . . .* , Pantoja's long letter was first published as a separate book at Seville in 1605.[71] A native of Valdemora near Seville, Pantoja entered the novitiate in the Province of Toledo. After completing his studies, he left for Asia in 1596 with Father Niccolò Longobardo. Though he was originally assigned to the Japan mission, Valignano decided upon Pantoja's arrival at Macao in 1599 to send the newcomer to Nanking to join Father Matteo Ricci. He took with him from Macao many of the presents that Ricci and he carried to Peking in the following year.

From perusal of his *Relación* it seems clear that in Spain Pantoja had read Marco Polo and Mendoza on China, had consulted maps, and had spoken with others about the Middle Kingdom; indeed he had requested an assignment to Asia.[72] His letter is a gem; it provides some of the most interesting and accurate information about China that became available during the first half of the seventeenth century. With it he dispatched to Guzman samples of Chinese printing in the form of courtesy cards, books, and maps. He even provides brief instructions on how to read the Chinese maps.[73]

The greatest Christian victory of these early years was the submission of the St. Thomas Christians of the Malabar church to the authority of Rome. It was at the Synod of Diamper (June 20–26, 1599) that the Augustinian archbishop of Goa, Aleixo de Meneses (1559–1617) pressured the St. Thomas Christians into making public acknowledgment of the complete supremacy of the Roman pope and of their willingness to realign their creed and rites with those of the Latin church.[74] That the civil and religious authorities worked closely together in Portuguese India is best illustrated by the appointment in 1602 of Archbishop Meneses to the post of governor, an office which he held to 1609. Shortly after accepting this civic responsibility, Meneses in 1603, with the collaboration of António de Gouvea (1575–1628), a fellow Augustinian then resident in Goa, prepared for the press his version of how the St. Thomas Christians were forced to cut their traditional ties with the patriarch of Chaldea and to acknowledge the authority of the Portuguese *padroado* and the Latin hierarchy.[75]

This victory of the Portuguese and the Catholic Church in India was proclaimed in Europe by the publication at Coimbra in 1606 of Gouvea's edi-

---

[71] A large extract from this letter was earlier published in Guerreiro, *Relaçam* (Evora, 1603), and is reproduced in Viegas, *op. cit.* (n. 38), I, 239–66; almost the whole of this letter is included in the Spanish translation of Guerreiro's first volume by Colaço (Valladolid, 1604), pp. 539–682. It is probably the version in the Colaço edition to which reference is made in L. Pfister, *Notices biographiques et bibliographiques sur les Jésuites de l'ancienne mission de Chine (1552–1773)* (Shanghai, 1932), I, 73. Reprinted at Valencia in 1606, Colaço's version was translated into Italian (Rome), Latin (Mainz), and French (Lyons) in 1607. Aegidius Albertinus translated the Italian version into German (Munich) in 1608. *PP*, XII, 331–410 translated in 1625 the Latin version into English. Our references are to this English translation.

[72] *PP*, XII, 361, 363, 375, 384, 392, 402.

[73] *Ibid.*, p. 410.

[74] For further detail see *Asia*, I, 268–69.

[75] See Jonas Thaliath, *The Synod of Diamper* ("Orientalia Christiana analecta," No. 152; Rome, 1958), p. 200.

tion of the *Jornada do Arcebispo de Goa Dom Frey Aleixo de Menezes*.[76] In both the title and the text Gouvea perpetuates the erroneous idea that the St. Thomas Christians, after living apart from the Roman communion for one thousand years, had been brought back to the true faith by Meneses within the space of a few months. The *Jornada* is divided into three books with continuous pagination; included in the same work, though paged separately, are the Acts of the Synod of Diamper.[77] Almost immediately after its appearance, the *Jornada* was translated into Spanish and French; the Spanish translation of Francisco Muñoz evidently remained in manuscript, while the French version, translated from the Spanish by Jean de Glen, was published at Antwerp and Brussels in 1609. The Acts of the Synod were not translated into French with the *Jornada*. An English version of the Acts in the Gouvea text was translated by Michael Geddes (1650?–1713) and published in 1694; the original Latin text of the Acts did not appear in print until 1745.[78] What is most important about both the *Jornada* and the Acts are the insights they give into the prevailing customs and practices of the St. Thomas Christians and of the Malabar people in general.[79]

A number of books appeared at the turn of the century to tell the story of the martyrdoms in Japan in 1597.[80] The Franciscans, in particular, were outraged by the martyrdoms and by their own expulsion from Japan. One of those expelled was Marcelo de Ribadeneira (dates unknown), a friar who spent the next nine months at Macao. He was then dispatched to Manila, where he was ordered by his superiors to prepare a report on conditions in the East for the secular and religious authorities in Europe. Before leaving the Philippines he interviewed the Franciscans there about their Asian experiences as part of his preparation for writing and, presumably, for making a case against the Jesuits who were alleged to be responsible for the Franciscan debacle in Japan.

Ribadeneira's *Historia de las islas del archipiélago Filipino y reinos de la gran China, Tartaria, Cochin-China, Malaca, Siam, Cambodge y Japon* was pub-

---

[76] Complete title: *Iornada do Arcebispo de Goa Dom Frey Aleixo de Menezes primaz da India Oriental, religioso da ordem de S. Agostinho. Quando foy as Serras do Malavar, & lugares em que morão os antigos Christãos de S. Thome, & os tirou de muytos erros & heregias em que estavão, & reduzio à nossa Sancta Fè Catholica, & obediencia da Santa Igrega Romana, da qual passava de mil annos que estavão apartados.* For more documentation on Meneses during his reign as archbishop of Goa see C. Alonso, "Documentación inédita para una biografía de Fr. Alejo de Meneses, O.S.A., Arzobispo de Goa, 1595–1612," *Analecta Augustiniana*, XXVII (1964), 263–333.

[77] Entitled *Synodo diocesam da igreia e bispado de Angamale dos antigos Christaõs de San Thome* . . . it is divided into two parts and bound with the *Jornada*.

[78] For the full bibliographical story see Thaliath, *op. cit.* (n. 75), Appendix. The English version is part of a Protestant attack upon the missionary practices of the Catholics called *The History of the Church of Malabar* (London). See below, p. 587.

[79] Also see António de Gouvea, *Relaçam em que se tratem as guerras e grandes victorias que alcançou o grãde rey da Persia X'a Abbas do grão Turco Mahometto* (Lisbon, 1611) for other relevant materials on Portuguese activities in the Indian Ocean. This work was translated into French and published at Rouen in 1646.

[80] See *Asia*, I, 717–18. To those cited add Santa Mariá, *op. cit.* (n. 35).

lished at Barcelona in 1601,[81] the year when Guzman's history of the Jesuit missions appeared at Alcalá. In both works about one-half of the total deals with Christian activities and internecine difficulties in Japan. Indeed, Guzman was so much on the defensive that he added to his history a list of the objections to it along with his responses.[82] While neither author has much that is new to report about Japan itself, Ribadeneira's own eyewitness account as well as the reports he collected from other Franciscans provide a slightly different perspective on China and the Philippines, one that in some ways adds to that of the Augustinian Mendoza's book. His is also the first extended account of Japan by a non-Jesuit writer.[83]

The first two books of Ribadeneira's *Historia* concern the discovery and penetration of the Philippines, China, Siam, and Cochin-China, especially by the Franciscans and the Dominicans. Like his secular contemporaries, Ribadeneira was particularly interested in China and the Chinese of Manila. For the great sufferings of the Franciscans in China he depends upon Mendoza's account supplemented by the eyewitness testimony of Friar Francisco de Montilha and some Portuguese who had been prisoners in Tartary.[84] Of collateral interest is his account of the efforts undertaken by the Franciscans to establish a mission in Cochin-China as part of a program designed to open China to the evangel.[85] He also provides a brief review of Siam based on reports from the Franciscans who began trying in 1582 to establish a mission there.[86] The remainder of the first volume is devoted to biographies of the Friars Minor, Discalced, who had worked in the East, particularly in the Philippines.

Two years later (1603) another mission history appeared at Valladolid, the work of the Benedictine Antonio San Román de Ribadeneyra.[87] In contrast to the eyewitness "history" of Ribadeneira, San Román's book is a genuine history based on the best printed sources available in Europe.[88] Though it adds nothing substantively new to the story of the Portuguese and Christian expansion in Asia, it merits attention because it put the general history of overseas activities into the Spanish language and so brought the best of the

[81] Reissued in 1613 by the same publisher in a corrected and revised version. A modern version edited by Juan R. de Legísma was published at Madrid in 1947.

[82] Guzman, *op. cit.* (n. 39), II, 645–712.

[83] See the English translation by P. G. Fernandez of Ribadeneira's *Historia,* prepared and printed by the Historical Conservation Society (2 vols.; Manila, 1970). The entire text of Vol. II is devoted to the history of Christianity in Japan as Ribadeneira recounts "the glorious martyrdom of my illustrious brothers and companions in St. Francis" (II, 656). He acknowledges in the prologue (I, 8) that he has depended heavily for the story of the martyrdoms on the book by Juan de Santa Maria (see above, pp. 315,n.35).

[84] *Ibid.,* I, 383–87; 399–403. It is not clear what he means by Tartary, for he includes the kingdom and people of Pegu within it (see *ibid.,* pp. 420, 427).

[85] *Ibid.,* I, 417–20.

[86] *Ibid.,* I, 422–38.

[87] *Historia general de la Yndia Oriental . . . desde sus principios hast' el año de 1557.*

[88] For his list of authors consulted see Rogers (ed.), *op. cit.* (n. 30), pl. 5.

Portuguese chroniclers to a European audience. Another popular book which brought certain of the Spanish conquests in the East, especially in the Moluccas, to a broad public was the *Historia general de los hechos de los Castellanos* . . . (8 decades, Madrid, 1601–15) by Antonio de Herrera y Tordesillas (1559–1625), the official chronicler of the Indies. At the end of its eighth decade there appears a map of the East Indies and Oceania. Herrera's *Descripcion de las Indies Occidentales* . . . (Madrid, 1601), despite its title, contains some description of the Philippines, the China coast, the Liu-ch'iu Islands, and Japan.[89]

A number of the earlier authors were translated anew into Spanish after the turn of the century. Don Martin de Bolia y Castro issued at Saragossa in 1601 a new Spanish version of Marco Polo translated from Latin. The stories of the prodigies of Pierre Boaistuau appeared in Spanish in 1603; five years later the history of Barlaam and Josaphat from the version attributed to St. John Damascus appeared at Madrid. Botero's *Relazioni universali* (1591–92) was translated by Diego de Aguiar and published in Spanish in 1603 and in 1608 at Valladolid; Jaime Reballosa published at Barcelona in 1610 a survey based on Botero's *Relazioni* of the current state of Christianity throughout the world. Botero's little study on *The Greatness of Cities* (1588) was translated from Italian and published at Barcelos in 1605. So, besides all the new accounts by eyewitnesses, there appeared in fresh Iberian versions a number of authoritative accounts from the distant and the immediate past, as well as practical books for language study by the missionaries in Japan, the Philippines, and China.[90]

A number of travelogues, authentic and fictional as well as combinations of the two, were published in the Iberian languages during the second decade of the seventeenth century. Pedro Teixeira (1563–1645?), a Portuguese-Jewish merchant, made several trips to Asia in the years from 1586 to the date of his settlement at Antwerp in 1605. His *Relaciónes* . . . (Antwerp, 1610), mainly an authentic narrative, centers on his lengthy experiences in Persia and Ormuz. The story of his journeys of 1600–1601 and 1604–5 includes intelligent and careful descriptions of Malaya and Indonesia.[91] His last journey was made overland from India to Italy, primarily because of the predatory activities of the Dutch in the Indian Ocean.

A few years later a similar trek was undertaken by the Franciscan friar,

---

[89] Herrera's *Descripcion* was translated into French (Amsterdam, 1622), into Latin by De Bry, and into English by Purchas, for which see *PP,* XIV, 427–592.

[90] For example, João Rodriguez, *Arte de lingoa de Iapon* . . . (Nagasaki, 1604–8); T. Mayor, *Simbolo de la fe en langue y letra China* (Birondoc en Philippinos, 1607); C. Ximenez, *Doctrina cristiana en lengua Bisaya* (Manila, 1610).

[91] A French translation appeared in 1681; John Stevens translated it into English during the first decade of the eighteenth century. This original English translation was revised and annotated by W. F. Sinclair and D. Ferguson, in *The Travels of Pedro Teixeira with His "Kings of Hormuz," and Extracts from His "Kings of Persia,"* in "HS," 2d ser., IX (London, 1902); see especially pp. 1–23.

Gaspar de San Bernardino, who wrote down and printed his experiences at the request of Margaret of Austria, the Queen of Spain and Portugal. His *Itinerario da India por terra ate este reino de Portugal* . . . (Lisbon, 1611) reveals something about the unsafe conditions in the Indian Ocean and the close relations then existing between Goa and Ormuz.[92]

Hernando de Moraga, a Franciscan friar based in the Philippines, voyaged westward in 1617 to Malacca, Goa, and Ormuz. From here, like Teixeira and San Bernardino, he journeyed overland through Persia. At Baghdad he was received by the Spanish ambassador, D. Garcia de Silva y Figueroa, who presented him to the shah in 1618. Moraga returned overland and by way of the Mediterranean islands to Spain. Upon his arrival at Madrid in January, 1619, the king asked him to write a report of his travel experiences. His *Relación* . . . (Seville, 1619) itself adds little to the accounts of Asia prepared by his predecessors in traveling overland. However, he wrote many letters to contemporaries on the Philippines and reputedly published *De las cosas, y costumbres de los Chinos, Japones, Turcos y otras naciones del Asia* (Madrid, 1619) on orders from Philip III.[93]

Two partially fictional travel accounts were published at Lisbon and Madrid in 1614. The first was the *Peregrinaçao* of Fernão Mendes Pinto, one of the most widely circulated travelogues of the seventeenth century. Pinto, who had traveled in Asia from 1537 to 1558, served as an informant to Barros, the Jesuit historians, and other chroniclers before his death in 1583.[94] He also wrote, in his last years, the story of his Asian adventures, apparently for the edification of his children. Upon his death this manuscript was passed from one archivist to the other until finally it was deposited in the *Torre do Tombo*. Here it was revised, rearranged, and edited by Francisco de Andrade, the custodian and the chief historian of Portugal, and his associates. A Castilian translation, with a defense of Pinto, was prepared by Francisco de Herrera Maldonado, a cleric and minor literary figure, that was printed in two variant editions at Madrid in 1620.[95] It was Herrera Maldonado's version which was translated into other European languages. By 1700 Pinto's travels had appeared in nineteen separate editions in six languages; numerous excerpts and fragments from it were included in travel collections and other compendia. Certainly no other seventeenth-century Iberian work on

---

[92] Reprinted in 1854 at Lisbon. A short extract from the *Itinerario* is translated into English in Hugh Murray, *Historical Account of Discoveries and Travels in Asia from the Earliest Times to the Present* (Edinburgh, 1820), I, 382–84.

[93] His *Relación* was quickly translated into Italian and published at Milan in 1619. For his biography and his letters on the Philippines see L. Pérez, "De Filipinas a España. Naufragio de una armada en el siglo XVII," *Archivo Ibero-Americano*, IX (1922), 289–320. The reference to *De las cosas*, a book which we have not seen, is from Streit, V, 78, who obtained his information from José Mariano Beristain y Souza, *Biblioteca Hispano-Americana Septentrional* (4 vols.; Mexico City, 1883), II, 296. We have been unable to locate this title in the National Union Catalogue or in the British Library and Bibliothèque Nationale catalogs.

[94] Cf. *Asia*, I, 325, 327.

[95] Cf. below, pp. 334–35.

Asia enjoyed a comparable diffusion; and certainly Pinto may rightly be characterized as "the Mandeville" of his day.[96] Similar to Pinto's travelogue is the *Historia y viages del mundo* (Madrid, 1614) of Pedro Ordóñez y Cevallos (b. *ca.* 1550), sometimes known as "the grateful priest."[97] According to this book, Ordóñez spent about thirty years (1567–97) knocking about the world. Most students of his work believe that he was indeed in Spanish America, and perhaps in the Philippines. Much more scepticism exists over the authenticity of his professed travels in Asia. He claims in his prologue to have visited "all five parts of the world." But some of his materials on Asia he clearly gathered from the letters of the Jesuit Nicolas Pimenta (1546–1614), for he reproduces (fols. 166v, 252v) extracts from them.[98] Included in his itinerary are visits in 1590, one of the few precise dates given in the book, to Nagasaki, Canton, and Macao. From China he went to Cochin-China where he allegedly remained for four years—at a time when certain of the Spanish in Manila and Madrid were preparing for an intervention in Cambodia.[99] Ordóñez proceeded from Indochina back to Spain by way of Malacca, Goa, and the Cape of Good Hope. In 1597 he arrived at Jaen, the town of his birth in southern Spain.

In addition to the *Viages* there is attributed to Ordóñez a brief *Tratado de las relaciones verdaderas . . . de la China, Cochinchina, y Champas* (Jaen, 1628) compiled from a miscellany of sources.[100] Indeed this may have been based on the raw materials in the Asian sections of the *Viages,* for the background materials are factual while the story of his adventures with the royalty of Cochin-China appear to be fictional. Both of these books are written as autobiographies and references to the *Viages* appear occasionally in the *Tratado* whenever the author insists upon the veracity of his travels in the East. He concludes the *Tratado* with a note to the effect that he met in Madrid in 1617 with Ivan de la Piedad, bishop of Macao, from whom he received letters addressed to him from Cochin-China. While he mentions meeting Diogo

---

[96] A mountain of "Pintoalia" has risen over the past three and one-half centuries. Literary, religious, and historical scholars have debated at length the credibility and meaning of this book. For a listing of modern scholarly writings see C. R. Boxer, *The Christian Century in Japan: 1549–1650* (Berkeley and Los Angeles, 1951), pp. 453–54, n. 15. Also see G. Schurhammer, "Fernão Mendez Pinto und seine Peregrinaçam," *Gesammelte Studien,* II, 23–103. It was not until the twentieth century that new and complete versions of Pinto's travels appeared. A Japanese translation was published at Tokyo (1979–80) in three volumes. The first annotated critical version in English was edited and translated by Rebecca D. Catz, *The Travels of Mendes Pinto* (Chicago, 1989).

[97] Reissued at Madrid in 1691. There are three modern reprints: 1905 (Madrid), 1942 (Bogotá), and 1947 (Buenos Aires). The imprints issued in South America omit the Asian materials.

[98] See Groslier and Boxer, *op. cit.* (n. 14), p. 52, n. 2.

[99] He was purportedly in Southeast Asia from 1589 to 1593. For an analysis of his discussion of Southeast Asia see E. C. Knowlton, "South East Asia in the Travel Book by Pedro Ordóñez de Ceballos," *Proceedings of the Second International Symposium on Asian Studies* (Hong Kong, 1980), pp. 499–510.

[100] Finished by Bartolome Ximenes Paton and published posthumously. At least three copies of this rare work are in United States libraries.

Veloso and other historical figures in Cambodia, knowledge of their activities were current throughout the Spanish empire. Until more solid evidence is forthcoming, it must be concluded that Ordóñez' travels in Asia, except perhaps for the Philippines, were the product of his fertile imagination.[101] In the year following the printing of the *Tratado* the adventures of Ordóñez were put on the stage in the *Comedia* (1629) of Friar Alonso Remon.

2

A NERVOUS ERA OF PEACE, 1609–21

While earlier ecclesiastical and lay writers had commented extensively on the Philippines and on Spain's activities in the East, the first authoritative, synthetic presentation by a secular writer was Antonio de Morga's *Sucesos de las Islas Filipinas* (Mexico, 1609).[102] A lawyer by training, Morga (1559–1636) was appointed in 1593 by Philip II to take up a legal post in Manila as second in command to the governor. Upon arriving at Manila in June, 1595, Morga assumed his new duties with zeal. It was not long before he also began work on the *Sucesos,* for Gabriel Quiroga de San Antonio reports having seen in 1598 the text of his descriptive account (chap. viii) of the Philippine Islands.[103] Likewise the Jesuit Pedro Chirino, and possibly Argensola, saw Morga's manuscript, or parts thereof, before they wrote their own books.[104] In the meantime he displayed great energy in carrying out his administrative duties, in writing ordinances, in dispatching reports and letters to Spain, and in leading the naval attack upon Van Noort. Tired by the press of his constantly mounting duties, by the criticism heaped upon him for allowing Van Noort to escape, and by difficulties with his daughter and her lover, Morga petitioned for a transfer. He left Manila for New Spain in July, 1603, just eight years after his arrival there, never to return to the Philippines.

"The prince of the historians of the Philippines," as W. E. Retana calls him,[105] Morga was the first layman to write an account of the Spanish Philippines and the last before the nineteenth century. He is a detached observer who refers to himself in the third person. His knowledge of the inner work-

[101] See Groslier and Boxer, *op. cit.* (n. 14), p. 60, n. 3.

[102] Around twenty-five copies of this original edition are extant. The definitive scholarly edition with supporting documents was published in 1909 by W. E. Retana. English editions include H. E. J. Stanley's translation published in 1868 for the Hakluyt society; the 1904 translation in BR, Vols. XV and XVI; and the new Hakluyt edition translated and edited by J. S. Cummins in "HS," 2d ser., CXL (Cambridge, 1971). For a detailed discussion of the various editions see Cummins, pp. 29–37, and Ausejo, *op. cit.* (n. 70), pp. 268–69.

[103] See above, pp. 203–4.

[104] See Cummins, *op. cit.* (n. 102), p. 27. On Chirino see below, p. 372; on Argensola see above, pp. 311–12.

[105] "La literatura histórica de Filipinas de los siglos XVI y XVII," *Revue hispanique,* LX (1924), 315.

ings of the administration provided him with insights denied the ecclesiastics who wrote about the Philippines. He was also quite able to look objectively at the churchmen and their evangelizing activities. Judicious in temperament, he resisted the imprudent demands of those soldiers, bureaucrats, and ecclesiastics who advocated conquests in Japan, China, and Cambodia.[106]

The *Sucesos,* published in the year (1609) of Argensola's triumphant book, of the expulsion of the Moriscos from Spain, and of the conclusion of the Twelve Years' Truce with the Dutch in Europe, implicitly argues for a policy in the East that should focus upon the maintenance and strengthening of the Spanish position in the Philippines. Perhaps because of his personal experience with Van Noort, he warns particularly about the growing Dutch menace. Since they "make the voyage more quickly and surely" than the Spanish or Portuguese, the Dutch "will be difficult to drive from the East, where they have done such a great harm both spiritual and temporal."[107] The Chinese, too, constitute a potential threat to the security, trade, and morality of the Philippines. While he explicitly praises the Spanish for their worldwide conquests, he is, if anything, an advocate of consolidation rather than of continuing the conquest beyond the Philippines and the Moluccas.

When Morga arrived in the Philippines, his books were in his baggage; at his death in 1636 his library contained Mendoza's book on China, two volumes by Botero, Román's *Républicas* (1595), Argensola's *Conquest of the Moluccas,* and Pinto's travels in Spanish.[108] Although there is nothing bookish about the *Sucesos,* the reader can quickly detect that its author was a man of learning with a critical and analytical mind. In the first seven chapters especially, Morga exhibits a ready familiarity with the relevant books, charts, and rutters, as he reviews the history of Spain's activities in the Philippines and their environs from Magellan's time to 1607. For the years of his stay in Manila (1595–1603), he provides the texts of a number of letters and decrees as well as records of conversations. In the process he has provided his readers with sources that were otherwise unavailable. From the time of its publication the *Sucesos* was quoted, plagiarized, and acclaimed as the basic European work on the Philippines.

In his preface "To the Reader" Morga proclaims that the conquest of the Philippines

provides a spacious field in which historians may extend themselves, for such is their office. Indeed it is at once sufficiently serious and entertaining to merit their attention and it is in no wise beneath their professional dignity to treat of Indian wars and adventures, for only those who have not experienced them, are likely to underestimate them.[109]

---

[106] See Cummins, *op. cit.* (n. 102), p. 5.
[107] *Ibid.,* p. 244.

[108] *Ibid.,* pp. 15–16.
[109] *Ibid.,* p. 47.

In the final chapter he departs from his chronological renditions of Spanish activities to provide "a brief compendium and account of the characteristics of these regions, of their inhabitants, the method of governing and converting, together with other details." [110] Because his own experiences were largely limited to Manila and its environs, Morga's account centers on Luzon. "Also," he asserts, "much that is said of Luzon is true of, and applies in general terms to, the other islands." [111] Particularly valuable for later students was Morga's decision to give, wherever possible, the names of native places, institutions, offices, and social practices "in the form common and current in these parts." [112] His attention to indigenous products and to the importation and conscious experimentation in the Philippines with the plants and animals of China, Japan, Spain, and Mexico is one of the more fascinating and instructive features of this account. [113]

In the second decade of the seventeenth century, as Spain enjoyed a respite from the grueling war in the Netherlands, the government of Philip III kept in close touch with its representatives in the Moluccas and the Philippines. [114] Meanwhile the royal cosmographer João Baptista Lavanha revised and published the fourth *Década* of Barros (Madrid, 1615), which recounts the events for the years from 1526 to 1538, with additions from the works of Couto and other contemporaries of the editor. It was in the post-Magellanic era discussed here that Spain and Portugal had their first conflict over control of the Spiceries, a conflict concluded by the Saragossa agreement of 1529, under which Spain constantly writhed until it conquered the Moluccas from its base in the Philippines in 1606.

The Portuguese, now writhing themselves over the Spanish invasion of their Asian empire, published works claiming priority in the discovery of Australia and in the conquest of Pegu. In the service of the crown in India, Manuel Godinho de Heredia (also Eredia: 1563–*ca.* 1623), a cosmographer and cartographer born in Malacca, published at Goa in 1613 his *Declaracam de Malaca e India meridional com o Cathay.* In this work and in the accompanying maps he depicts the voyages of Mendaña (1595) and Quiros (1606) in the Pacific, claims that in 1601 the Portuguese discovered "India meridional" or Australia, and presents an essay on the comparative geography of Asia. [115]

In Europe, meanwhile, two Portuguese who wrote in Castilian to obtain

---

[110] *Ibid.*, p. 48.
[111] *Ibid.*, p. 246.
[112] *Ibid.*, p. 49.
[113] See especially *ibid.*, pp. 252–59.
[114] For example, see the correspondence of Governor Gerónimo da Silva with Philip III about conditions in the Moluccas, especially the battles with the Dutch in the years from 1612 to 1617, as reproduced in *Colección de documentos inéditos para la historia de España* (Madrid, 1868), Vol. LII. These letters are especially rich in materials on political and social conditions in the Moluccas. For the period 1617 to 1620 see the documents published in BR, Vol. XVIII, dealing with the Philippines, Spanish trade, and the ever-expanding Dutch menace.
[115] For commentary and a reproduction of his world map see G. Schilder, *Australia Unveiled* (Amsterdam, 1976), pp. 22–23. An English translation of Heredia's book by J. V. Mills was published in the *JRAS, Malay Branch,* VIII (1930), 1–288; in 1882 Léon Jansen translated into

a larger audience began to celebrate the deeds of Filipe de Brito e Nicote in Pegu after 1600. Brito, the nephew of Jean Nicot (the famous French ambassador and linguist),[116] was renowned in Portuguese Asia for his heroic acts at Syriam, the port of Pegu. A certain Juan Pérez in 1614 published at Cuenca a *Relación* which purported to tell the true story about De Brito's adventure.[117] Three years later Father Manuel de Abreu Mousinho, a native of Evora who had worked for a period in Goa, published a *Breve discurso* at Lisbon, which he dedicated to the king's favorite, the duke of Lerma.[118] In this account, the leading role in the conquest of Pegu is taken away from Brito and given to Salvador Ribeyro de Souza. Abreu Mousinho, who evidently wrote this book after his return to Portugal, seems convinced that the Portuguese pacified Pegu between the deposition of Nandabayin in 1599 and the accession of Anaukpetlun in 1605 and then peacefully withdrew. In the process of telling his story the author provides a vivid picture of Lower Burma and insights into the reasons for the Portuguese activities at Syriam. Stability in Pegu was essential to a trade in which the Portuguese brought much-needed salt and took in return valuable building materials for their shipyards in India.

Under pressure in India from the Mughuls, Dutch, and English, the Portuguese concluded a military alliance in 1617 with the sultans of the Deccan.[119] In Portugal itself, sentiment for the defense of India was stirred by the publication in 1616 and 1617 of a history of India under the viceroy Luis de Ataide, who ruled from 1568 to 1571, and again from 1578 to 1581, and who was one of the more independent and energetic military leaders of

---

French and published an autograph manuscript of this same work (as well as several maps) which he found in the Royal Library of Brussels, and entitled it *Malaca, L'Inde méridionale et le Cathay*. A self-portrait of Heredia is reproduced in the Portuguese encyclopedia. On his maps see A. Cortesão and A. Teixeira da Mota, *Portugaliae monumenta cartographica* (5 vols.; Lisbon, 1960), IV, 39–60.

[116] See *Asia*, II, 276–77, and below, pp. 1124–29.

[117] Entitled *Relación muy verdadera de un caso nuevamente sucedido en la India de Portugal, en que se cuenta como un cavallero Portugues llamado Felipe Brito, que es governador, y Capitan general en aquellas partes por su Magestad vencio a un Rey gentil del Pegú*. We have not been able to locate this book. Reference is from the *Boletim internationál de bibliografia Luso-Brasileira*.

[118] Entitled *Breve discurso en que se cuento la conquista del Reyno de Pegu . . hecha por los Portugueses desde el año de mil y seyscientos, hasta el de 1603. Siendo Capitan Salvador Ribera de Soza, natural de Guimaraés, a quien los naturales de Pegu eligieron por su Rey*. Translated in full, though somewhat inaccurately, by A. MacGregor in his "A Brief Account of the Kingdom of Pegu, Translated from the Portuguese," *Journal of the Burma Research Society*, XVI (1926), 99–138. MacGregor did not know that Abreu Mousinho was the author of this work; that fact was revealed by J. L. McCallum in *ibid.*, XXIII (1933), 130. The original Spanish edition, from which MacGregor did not work, was translated anonymously into Portuguese around 1711 when it was appended to publications of Pinto's *Peregrinação*. The first separate Portuguese edition known was published at Lisbon in 1829, the version apparently translated by MacGregor. The most recent Portuguese edition was published at Barcelos in 1936 with an introduction by M. Lopes d'Almeida.

[119] See B. G. Tamaskar, "Malik Ambar and the Portuguese," *Journal of the Bihar Research Society*, XXXIII (1947), 25–44.

Portuguese India.[120] At Lisbon, Manoel da Conceicam published in 1617 the sermon preached at the funeral of Aleixo de Meneses, the Augustinian archbishop and governor of Goa who was celebrated for his success in bringing the Malabar Christians firmly under the rule of Rome.[121] In the meantime the Jesuit pastor of Quilon, Diogo Gonçalves (1561–1640), prepared a *História do Malavar* (*ca.* 1615) as a handbook for missionaries being dispatched to Travancore, in which he describes the country, people, and strange customs prevailing on the southwest coast of India and comments on how accommodations to natural and human obstacles could be made in this inhospitable territory.[122]

That the Iberians were nervous about their future in the East is best attested by the publication of a Spanish translation at Madrid of the *Iournal* (Amsterdam, 1618), telling about the voyage around the world of Willem Corneliszoon Schouten and Jacob Le Maire in the very year in which it first appeared in Dutch.[123]

Contemporaneously the Iberians suffered another reversal when active persecution of the Christians in Japan was resumed in 1614. During the early period (1603–14) of Tokugawa Ieyasu's shogunate, the Christians in Japan were generally tolerated and left alone, except for a few unofficial and isolated attacks upon them. Ieyasu himself decided in 1610 to send an emissary to Madrid, but apparently very little came of this overture.[124] Hopes for the continuing prosperity of the Japan missions also encouraged the Dominicans and Franciscans to begin once again sending missionaries from the Philippines to Japan. A patent was issued at Rome on December 10, 1608, elevating Japan to the status of a Jesuit province, and several years later Valentim Carvalho (1560–1631) took office as its first provincial.[125] While the appearance of the Dutch and English in Japan clearly endangered the Iberian monopoly, the Protestants were few in number and had no nearby base, such as the Philippines or Macao, from which to approach Japan. So the Jesuits and the friars, while well aware of the threat from the northern Europeans and uncertain of Ieyasu's intentions, continued to fight each other both in Japan and Europe. Philip III wrote to the emperor of Japan in

---

[120] Written by Antonio Pinto Pereyra around 1575, this history was edited by Miguel da Cruz and published in two parts at Coimbra under the title *Historia da India no tempo en que a governovo visorey dom Luis de Ataide.*

[121] *Sermão funeral do arcebispo de Goa, D. Fr. Aleixo de Menezes,* Lisbon, 1617. For his role in the Synod of Diamper see above, pp. 320–21.

[122] This book was not published at the time, but probably circulated in India, Portugal, and Rome in manuscript copies. See Josef Wicki, S.J. (ed.), *Diogo Gonçalves S. I. Historia do Malavar (Hs. Goa 58 des Arch. Rom. S. I.)* (Münster, 1955), pp. ix–xv.

[123] See Ternaux-Compans, p. 134. For a bibliographical rundown of the *Iournal* see P. A. Tiele, *Mémoire bibliographique sur les journaux des navigateurs néerlandais . . .* (Amsterdam, 1867), pp. 41–56. Tiele does not list a Spanish translation. Also see below, pp. 445–48.

[124] See N. Murakami, "Japan's Early Attempts to Establish Commercial Relations with Mexico," in H. M. Stephens and H. E. Bolton (eds.), *The Pacific Ocean in History* (New York, 1917), p. 472.

[125] See J. F. Schütte, S.J., *El Archivo del Japon . . .* (Madrid, 1964), pp. 19–23.

1613 thanking him for his generous treatment of the Iberian merchants and missionaries.[126]

Nothing illustrates the precarious nature of the Iberian-Christian position in Japan as well as the story of the embassy sent to Europe in 1614–15.[127] It centers on the activities of Luis Sotelo (1574–1624), a Franciscan who had begun working in Japan in 1603 and who was designated in 1610 (before he fell ill) to lead Ieyasu's abortive mission to Europe.[128] Three years later Sotelo was thrown into prison in Edo in one of the unofficial outbursts of persecution. Sotelo was saved from martyrdom at this point in his career by the intervention of Date Masamune (1567–1636), the daimyo of Oshu in northeastern Japan and an ally of the Tokugawas.[129] Whether it was Date's or Sotelo's idea to send an embassy to Europe is not clear. Whatever the case may be, Sotelo sailed for Europe on October 21, 1613, with Hasekura Rokuemon (1571–1622), Date's retainer and titular chief of the embassy, and a large retinue of Japanese merchants and attendants. After brief halts at Manila and Acapulco, the embassy arrived at Mexico City in January, 1614. Many of the sixty-eight Japanese in Hasekura's suite ended their journey in Mexico; the remainder, a group of about thirty, took passage on a ship leaving Vera Cruz for Spain. They arrived at Seville in October, 1614.

Shortly after their arrival a brief *Relacion* was published which purported to summarize an edict by Date establishing the Christian faith in "all of his kingdom" and ordering the dispatch of his ambassador to Spain in the company of Sotelo, a native Sevillian.[130] The ambassadors presented a letter from Date to the city as well as token gifts of a sword and a poniard.[131] In the letter, Date indicated his desire to introduce Christianity to his realm and asked for shipbuilders and pilots to be sent him who might help establish an annual voyage between Seville and Sendai, his major port. Once the welcoming festivities ended, the embassy hurried on to Madrid and a reception by Philip III on December 20, 1614. From Date the king received a letter, similar in content to the letter addressed to Seville, five Japanese utensils as gifts, and proposed articles of agreement as the basis for a treaty.[132] Philip's reaction to the proposal for a treaty of perpetual friendship was a polite refusal

---

[126] Part of this letter of June 20 is reproduced in Rodríguez Moñino, *loc. cit.* (n. 5), pp. 433–34.

[127] Also see above, pp. 210–12.

[128] On his career see Lorenzo Pérez, *Apostolada y martirio del B. Louis Sotelo* (Madrid, 1924); also Streit, V, 397–98.

[129] See C. Meriwether, "A Sketch of the Life of Date Masamune and an Account of His Embassy to Rome," *Transactions of the Asiatic Society of Japan*, 1st ser., XXI (1893–94), 1–105.

[130] *Relacion breve, y sumaria del edito que mandó publicar en todo su Reyno del Bojō, uno de las mas poderosos del Iapon, el rey Idate Masamune, publicando la fé de Cristo, y del embaxador que embio a españa, en compañia del reverendo padre Fr. Luys Sotelo . . . que viene eo embaxada del Emperador del Iapon, hijo de Sevilla, y lo que en el viage le sucedio* (Seville, 1614). Reprinted in Pérez, *op. cit.* (n. 128), pp. 267–69; also see Streit, V, 399.

[131] For the text of the letter in English translation see Meriwether, *loc. cit.* (n. 129), pp. 70–72.

[132] Text in English in *ibid.*, pp. 72–74. The most interesting of the proposed articles are those which proffer a primitive form of consular jurisdiction as well as a promise of hostility to the English and Dutch.

to commit himself. While the embassy toured in Italy during 1615–16,[133] news began reaching Spain about the renewal in 1612–14 of the attacks upon the Christians in Japan.

When enthusiasm for the mission was at a peak, Christoval Suárez de Figueroa published in 1614 his translation of Guerreiro's Portuguese collection of materials on the status of the Jesuit mission in the East in 1607–8, possibly as a reminder to the public that the Jesuits rather than the Franciscans had spearheaded Christian evangelizing in Japan.[134] Two years later, in 1616, the Jesuit procurator of Japan, Pedro Morejon (1562–1634?), reported in a short *Relación*, first published in Mexico, on the persecutions reinaugurated in 1614.[135] Hereafter Morejon reported at frequent intervals on the continuing attacks upon the Christians. Gabriel de Matos (1572–1633), a Portuguese Jesuit resident in Japan, contemporaneously published a *Relaçam* (1616) of his own, in which he dated the resumption of the systematic persecutions back to May, 1612, or from before Sotelo had left for Europe.[136] In the meantime Sotelo himself was publishing pamphlets at Seville telling about the warm reception of his embassy by the pope and the bright prospects for the future of the mission in Japan.[137] He nonetheless delayed his return to Japan, probably in the hope that conditions for the Christians would again improve. His most famous convert, Hasekura, arrived back in Japan only in 1620, and was coldly received. Sotelo delayed his own return for another two years, and was burned alive there in 1624.[138]

Although the Dominicans in Japan and the Philippines had been ordered in 1609 to begin sending regular reports to Rome, no serious effort was made to comply until after the resumption of the anti-Christian attacks. The Dominicans had sent a contingent of five missionaries from the Philippines to Japan in 1601 at the request of the daimyo of Satsuma. A few others followed from 1606 to 1612, including Jacinto Orfanel (1578–1622), the most conscientious of the Dominican correspondents and writers in Japan. A copy of his letter of March 28, 1615, reporting on the persecutions, eventually found its way into the hands of Lope de Vega, who used it as a basic source in preparing his essay, *Triunfo de la fee en los reynos del Japon* (1617). In the process the great dramatist became a publicist of the Dominican cause, as his literary rival, Cristoval Suárez de Figueroa, had earlier championed the

---

[133] For a map of its travels in Europe and for most of the relevant documents in Western languages and in Japanese, see Imperial University of Tokyo, *Dai Nippon Shiryo (Japanese Historical Materials)* (Tokyo, 1909), Pt. XII, Vol. XII.

[134] For the exact title of Suárez de Figueroa's translation see Streit, V, 72; on Guerreiro's works see above, pp. 315–18.

[135] Full title in Streit, V, 408. Translated into English by W. W. and published in 1619.

[136] See Streit, V, 409. Also see the *Relación* (1617) of Luis Piñeyro on this period in *ibid.*, pp. 428–29. Also translated into French in 1617.

[137] *Ibid.*, p. 409. Reprinted in Pérez, *op. cit.* (n. 128), pp. 270–74.

[138] For a recent fictional account of the Hasekura embassy see Shusaku Endo, *The Samurai*, trans. Van C. Gessel (New York, 1982).

Jesuits.[139] Somewhat later, news reached Europe of the martyrdom suffered by the Dominican Alfonso de Navarrete, brother of Lope's friend, the canon Pedro de Navarrete.[140] Orfanel in Japan was meanwhile collecting the manuscripts that would eventually become the foundation for the standard history of the Dominicans in that country.[141]

In Europe the Jesuits were busily preparing for the beatification and canonization of Francis Xavier, their Apostle to the East. Shortly after his death in 1552, the Society had begun to collect materials, to prepare biographies, and to encourage at every turn those ecclesiastical and secular personages in Europe and the East who advocated sainthood for Xavier.[142] The Iberians, especially the Portuguese, had worked fervently for his beatification throughout the years before the final investigation began in 1610. The Jesuit history (1600) of Guzman, the Portuguese *Décadas* of Couto, and even the publication of Pinto's *Peregrinação* (1614) helped to remind the public of Xavier's stellar achievements in Asia during the mid-sixteenth century. Witnesses were interviewed after 1610 with respect to his teachings, conversions, and miracles in the places of Europe and Asia (from Rome to Malacca) where Xavier had worked. João de Lucena's Portuguese biography (1600) was translated into Spanish by Alonso de Sandoval and published at Seville in 1619; the Latin biography (1594) of Tursellinus was translated into Castilian by Pedro de Guzman and published at Pamplona in 1620. Pope Paul V beatified Xavier on October 25, 1619; in the following year a satire in verse on the beatification was printed at Barcelona.[143]

Xavier was canonized by Pope Gregory XV (r. 1621–23) on March 12, 1622, in the company of Philip Neri, Ignatius Loyola, Teresa of Jesus, and Isidore of Madrid. Throughout Spain and its empire the beatifications and canonizations were celebrated in special services, adulatory sermons, and public festivals of thanksgiving. These occasions themselves were commemorated by published accounts of the proceedings.[144] The celebrations were especially numerous and spectacular in Madrid because of the simultaneous canonization of St. Isidore, the twelfth-century agricultural laborer and the city's patron saint, with the Jesuit saints of Iberian origin.[145] Publica-

---

[139] See J. S. Cummins (ed.), *Lope Felix de Vega Carpio. Triunfo de la fee en los reynos del Japon* (London, 1965), pp. xxxv–vi, xl. On Suárez de Figueroa's work, see above, p. 316.

[140] See Domingo González, *Relación del martyrio de Fr. Alfonso de Navarrete. . . .* (Manila, 1618).

[141] See below, p. 342.

[142] See *Asia*, I, 326–28. Also for more detail see G. Schurhammer, "Historical Research into the Life of Francis Xavier in the Sixteenth Century," in L. Szilas (ed.), *Xaveriana* (Lisbon, 1964), pp. 90–114.

[143] *Satyra al beato Francisco Xavier de la Compañia de Jesus.*

[144] For example, Diego Marques de Salgueiro, *Relaçam das festas que a religiam da companhia de Jesu fez em . . . Lisboa, na beatificaçam do beato P. Francisco de Xavier* (Lisbon, 1621); Fernando de Monforte y Herrera, *Relación de las fiestas que has hecho el Colegio Imperial de la Compañia de Jesus de Madrid en la canonización de San Ignacio de Loyola, y S. Francisco Xavier* (Madrid, 1622).

[145] For example, Miguel de Leon, *Fiestas de Madrid, celebrados a XIX de Junio de 1622 años, en la canonizacion de San Isidro, S. Ignacio, S. Francisco Xavier . . .* (Madrid, 1622); *Breve relación de la*

tions describing the canonization festivities appeared also in 1622 at Barcelona, Lisbon, and Seville.

A renewal of interest in China developed in the 1620's, possibly inspired by the festivals honoring Xavier and by the resumption of persecutions in Japan. Following Ricci's death in 1610, the Jesuits in China had concentrated their activities at Nanking. While the official persecution of the Christians was going on in Japan, certain Chinese authorities suppressed Christian work at Nanking from 1616 to 1621, possibly because they feared that the Jesuits, in collaboration with their friends from the Chinese literati, were politically hostile and dangerous to the unstable Ming government.[146] In Europe, notice was taken of the attacks of the Manchus on the Ming when a pamphlet was published at Lisbon in 1620 which purported to be the translation of a memorial of 1618 sent by the provincial governors to the emperor of China telling of their wars against the "Tartars" (Manchus).[147] Jesuit refugees from Japan were meanwhile crowding into Macao or opening new mission outposts in Cochin-China (1614) and Cambodia (1615).[148] At Seville, Duarte Fernandez published in 1621 his Spanish translation of Nicolas Trigault's Latin book, originally published in 1615, based on Ricci's writings about the early Jesuit successes in China.[149]

Canon Francisco de Herrera Maldonado, the translator and apologist of Pinto, had defended the Portuguese traveler, confirming Pinto's assertions about Asia by comparing them to those of accredited authors.[150] From his numerous references to a variety of authors, it is clear that Herrera Maldonado had read widely about Asia before publishing his translation in 1620. Appended to his *Epitome historial del Reyno de la China,* published at Madrid later in the same year, there is a catalog of the authors cited and consulted, numbering seventy-six separate entries.[151] Many of the authors listed are Jesuit letter-writers or the compilers of letterbooks. While the bibliography is not organized alphabetically and does not seem to follow any system, it

---

estampa en que estava pintada su santidad con los Cardenales y demas personages que asistieron a las ceremonias de la canonización de los Santos Isidro de Madrid, Ignacio de Loyola, Francisco Xavier, Teresa de Jesús y Felipe Neri (Madrid, 1622).

[146] See E. Zürcher, "The First Anti-Christian Movement in China, Nanking (1616–21)" in P. W. Pestman (ed.), *Acta orientalia Neerlandica* (Leyden, 1971), pp. 188–95.

[147] *Memorial que os Mandarins ou Governadores do Reyno da China mandarão ao seu Rey, em que che davão côta das grandes guerras que tinhão com os Tartaros; et dos admiraveis sinaes qua apparecarão no mesmo Reyno o anno de 1618 etc* (4 pp.; Lisbon 1620). We have not seen this pamphlet; if authentic, it is probably the first Chinese memorial translated into a European language and printed. It must have been addressed to the Wan-li emperor (1573–1620) by governors from northeastern China where the Manchus were already penetrating successfully.

[148] See Schütte, *op. cit.* (n. 125), pp. 22–23.

[149] *Istoria de la China i cristiana empresa hecha en ella: por la compañia de Jesus* (Seville, 1621). See below, pp. 512–13, for bibliography.

[150] See Schütte, *op. cit.* (n. 125), pp. 22–23.

[151] His *Epitome* in some exemplars bears the date 1621 rather than 1620. For a reproduction of his bibliography, and for identifications of its entries, see Rogers, *op. cit.* (n. 30), pp. 21–35.

was nonetheless one of the most important bibliographical summaries of materials relating to China produced by 1620. It was used as a source by A. R. Leon Pinelo (d. 1660) in the preparation of his *Epitome de la biblioteca Oriental i Occidental, Náutica i Geografica* (Madrid, 1629), the first independent bibliography of books and authors relating to the overseas discoveries. The importance of these books for contemporaries is attested to by Lope de Vega, who wrote a sonnet praising China which is included in the preliminaries to Herrera Maldonado's work as well as in the permission to publish Leon Pinelo's bibliography.

In the twenty chapters of the *Epitome historial* itself, Herrera Maldonado provides an ethnohistory of China as well as news about recent events there. The first twelve chapters offer very little that is new about China and the Chinese. In chapters xiii through xvii he discusses the death, interment, and burial ceremonies that took place with the demise on March 30, 1617, of the empress dowager and mother of the reigning Wan-li emperor.[152] Chapters xviii and xix report on the miraculous appearance of the crucified Christ at Goa on February 23, 1619. The final chapter is a calculation of the annual income of the emperor of China extracted from Chinese treasury records by Father Michele Ruggiero (here "Miguel Rogerio," as in the official Jesuit catalog), the companion of Ricci who returned to Europe in 1590 with many such translations.[153]

Other Jesuit writers subsequently began to warn the Spanish that the Dutch had again become active off the China coast and were seeking to establish a trading outpost in Fukien.[154]

3

IMPERIAL BREAKDOWN IN EUROPE AND ASIA, 1621–41

The outbreak of war in Bohemia in 1618 was followed three years later by the resumption of the Spanish-Dutch wars in Europe. Philip IV, the new king of Spain, was thereafter forced like his predecessors to commit the manpower and wealth of Spain to the prosecution in northern Europe of a lengthy war that accelerated the economic, military, and political decline already in progress. The Portuguese, who had resented since 1580 their own involvement in Spain's wars, began in the 1620's to pursue a more indepen-

---

[152] Presumably he is referring here to Li-shih (1546–1614). The *Dictionary of Ming Biography*, ed. L. Carrington Goodrich (2 vols.; New York, 1976), I, 857–59) and Semedo in chapter vii of his *History of China* (1642) give the date of her death as March 18, 1614, or more than three years before the date given in the title of Herrera Maldonado's *Epitome*. We have been unable to account for this discrepancy in dates.

[153] On Ruggiero see *Asia*, II, Bk. 3, 528–29.

[154] See Streit, V, 761, for the title of a Jesuit letter published at Seville in 1629 on this subject.

dent course both in Europe and Asia. The economic and moral collapse of Spain about which the reformers (*arbitristas*) had long been warning was given official acknowledgment in a *consulta* (a written report to the king or a royal council) of 1619, a document which describes the assorted ills of Castile and prescribes remedies for their cure.[155]

Memorials from men who had been to the colonies specified the local illnesses and made proposals for reform that sometimes appeared in print. There is the example of Hernando de los Ríos Coronel (1559–1621) who was originally sent in 1588 as a soldier to the Philippines. After participating in the Cambodian expedition of 1595, he returned to Manila where he prepared two years later a map of Luzon, Formosa, and a part of the China coast—one of the earliest examples of Spanish cartography of the Far East. When he returned to Spain in 1605 he prepared a chart of the sea route from Manila to Acapulco; five years later on his return trip to the Philippines he wrote a rutter of the reverse passage.[156] In 1617 he was back in Spain as procurator-general of the Philippines to inform the king of the distressed condition of the islands and to propose reforms.[157]

Since Philip III had apparently failed to respond satisfactorily to his memorials, Coronel addressed a lengthy relation to his successor, Philip IV, which was published at Madrid in 1621. His *Memorial y relación* is a substantial volume divided into three parts. The first reviews the history of the Spanish in the Philippines to the first battle of Playa Honda with the Dutch in 1610. The second concentrates on the immediate needs, resources, and potential of the Philippines. The third details the progress of the faith in the Philippines, with a few asides on the losses in the Moluccas and on the need to conserve and protect the rich resources of these insular regions for Spain.[158] On the whole, this is an excellent report by an informed observer on the rapid decline of Spain's Asian empire in the first fifteen years of the seventeenth century.

In Portugal the sentiment had long been growing that the troubles of Spain could be attributed in part to poor management of the overseas empire. Neither Madrid nor Seville was properly located on the sea or as intimately involved and as well organized as Lisbon to command maritime

---

[155] See Michael Gordon, "Morality and Politics in Seventeenth-Century Spain: The Arbitrista Pedro Fernandez Navarrete" (Ph.D. diss., Dept. of History, University of Chicago, 1972), pp. 26–27.

[156] A previously unrecorded petition by Coronel of four folio pages on the navigation routes to the Philippines by the Cape of Good Hope is in the Lilly collection at Indiana University. It is dated Madrid, *ca.* 1620.

[157] For an English translation of his memorials of 1617 to 1620 see BR, XVIII, 289–342.

[158] Complete title is *Memorial y relación para su magestad, del Procurador General de la Filipinas, de lo que conviene remediar, y de la requeza que ay en relas, y en las Islas del Maluco* (Madrid, 1621). Translated into French in Melchisédech Thévenot (ed.), *Relations de divers voyages curieux* (4 vols.; Paris, 1663–96; hereafter cited as TR), Vol. I; a summary and partial translation in BR, XIX, 189–297.

commercial and naval operations. Already in 1608 Lúis Mendes de Vasconcelos, a captain in the armadas sent to the east, had published a book entitled *Do sitio de Lisboa,* in which he advocated, in a manner reminiscent of Botero, the removal of the king's capital to Lisbon, the natural center of Iberia.[159] After the publication of the *consulta* of reform in 1619 and the resumption of war in northern Europe, the economic planners again turned their attention to the mounting problems of maintaining the galleon trade and to more effectively controlling and administering overseas commerce.

The most important proposals for the reorganization of Eastern navigation and trade were prepared and published by Duarte Gomez Solis (1561[62?]– *ca.* 1630), a Portuguese New Christian who had made his fortune in the India trade. Resident in India from 1586 to 1601, Solis was for a time in charge of the pepper trade and acted as a counselor on financial affairs to Governor Manuel de Sousa Coutinho (r. 1588–91) at Goa. In Madrid he wrote his first *arbitrios* on questions of navigation and commerce in 1612 and addressed them to the king. Ten years later he published the *Discursos sobre los comercios de las dos Indias, donde se tratan materias importantes de estado, y guerra.*[160] In the dedication to the new king, Philip IV, and in the prologue to the reader, Solis makes clear that he is speaking from personal experience and that he had earlier found it difficult to impress Philip III's government with the gravity of the situation on the high seas and at the outposts in the East.

The *Discursos* starts with two letters which Solis had addressed in 1612 to the duke of Lerma, followed by a third of the same year to Juan de Cirizia, secretary to the Council of State. These memorials vigorously set forth some of the reasons for the maritime and commercial decadence of Spain and Portugal. In the text which follows the letters, he attributes Spain's decline to the intense rivalry displayed between the king's Portuguese and Spanish subjects in the East, to the stupendous and constantly growing losses in ships and manpower on the high seas,[161] to the expenditure in other countries of the silver from America, to excessive borrowing by the state, to the depopulation and impoverishment of the countryside, to the pitiful state of agriculture and industry, and to the squandering of Spain's resources and military power by a short-sighted government. He supports his arguments on these and other points with an abundance of statistical detail drawn from

---

[159] For a summary see J. C. de Magalhães, *História do pensamento economica em Portugal. Da idade-média ao mercantilisimo* (Coimbra, 1967), pp. 183–96. For Botero's work on cities see *Asia,* II, Bk. 2, 237–40.

[160] Reproduced, reorganized, and edited by M. B. Amzalak in a Lisbon publication of 1943. The original bore neither the place of publication nor the printer's name.

[161] *Cf.* João Pereira Cortereal, *Discursos sobre la navigation de las nãos de la India de Portugal* (Madrid, 1622). Discussed in D. Barbosa Machado, *Bibliotheca Lusitana* (4 vols.; Lisbon, 1741–59), II, 720. The author invented a locating instrument that was commented on by the cosmographer, Valentino de Sà. Also see Lourenço Brandão, *Discurso sobre et susteno de las navegacion de las armadas del reyno de Portugal . . .* (Madrid, 1622).

his own experiences and from the writings of others. Among other things he proposes the creation of a *junta* of commerce directed by practical businessmen to advise the government on commerce and finance.[162] In 1628 Solis went one step further by publishing a tract advocating the creation in Portugal of an East Indies Company to manage the "India trade."[163]

News from India meanwhile produced a minor sensation in Europe with the announcement that the "Great Cathay" had been discovered by a Jesuit father in the "kingdoms of Tibet." From 1580 onward the Jesuits at the court of Akbar, followed by Ricci in China, had urged the exploration of the land route between India and China. They hoped by this means to determine whether China and Cathay were the same place, whether the peoples of inner Asia were or were not Christians, and whether a land route between Lahore and Peking was feasible. Benedict (Bento) de Goes pioneered an arduous route northeastward from Agra via Lahore between 1603 and 1607 and died at Su-chou in western China before he could make it to Peking. Reports of his discoveries were published by Guerreiro in 1607–8, and thereafter the identification of Cathay with China began to be accepted in Europe. Some Jesuits in India, however, continued to believe that Tibet was the Cathay of Marco Polo.

The Portuguese Father Antonio de Andrade (1580–1634), superior of the Jesuit mission to Agra, with the moral support of Jahangir successfully completed in 1624 an exploratory visit to Tibet from which he returned safely to Agra.[164] This reconnaissance, however, was undertaken for mission work and not for geography.

Immediately Andrade dispatched a letter from Agra telling his superiors about his voyage and his observations in Tibet. The press of Matteo Pinheiro in Lisbon published it in 1626 under the pompous and misleading title *Novo descobrimento de Gram Cathayo ou Reinos de Tibet,* a claim never advanced by Andrade himself. Throughout Catholic Europe this "discovery" was hailed as a great victory for the faith and as possible aid in circumventing the dangers from the Protestant fleets on the lengthy sea route from India to China. The original Portuguese version of Andrade's account was translated into Castilian immediately (1626), followed the next year by versions in Italian (Rome and Naples), French (Paris and Ghent), and German (Augsburg).

---

[162] For a fuller summary see M. B. Amzalak, *Anciens économistes portugais* (Lisbon, 1940), pp. 13–17.

[163] Entitled *Alegación en favor de la Compañia de la India Oriental y comercios ultramarinos, que de nuevo se instituyó en el Reyno de Portugal,* this work was reissued and edited by M. B. Amzalak in *Anais do Instituto Superior de Ciencias Económicas e Financeiras,* Vol. XXIII (1955), Pts. I and II. For a full analysis of Solis' economic thought see Magalhães, *op. cit.* (n. 159), pp. 199–223. For the background to and history of the Portuguese India Company see A. R. Disney, *Twilight of the Pepper Empire . . .* (Cambridge, Mass., 1978), chaps. v–viii.

[164] For details on the Jesuit interest in Tibet and on Andrade's letters see G. M. Toscano, *La prima missione cattolica nel Tibet* (Parma, 1951), pp. 41–48. Also *Asia,* I, 278, 467.

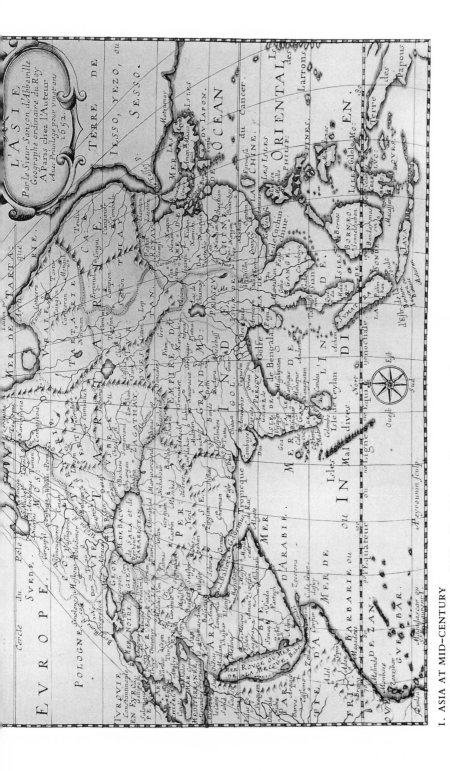

1. ASIA AT MID-CENTURY
Frontispiece to Nicolas Sanson d'Abbeville, *L'Asie en plusieurs cartes nouvelles* . . .
(Paris, 1652).
This is a hand-colored engraving. Pl. 5 is from the same book.

2. GENERAL MAP OF ASIA

From Johan Blaeu, *Atlas major,* Vol. X, Bk. 1 (Amsterdam, 1662), between pp. 1 and 2.

Johan Blaeu was the cartographer of the Dutch East India Company. This map
had been newly delineated by his father, Willem Blaeu, and first issued in or about
1620. For Blaeu's biography see I. C. Koeman, *Joan Blaeu and His Grand Atlas*
(Amsterdam, 1970), chap. i.

   Pls. 4, 9, and 11 are also from *Atlas major*.

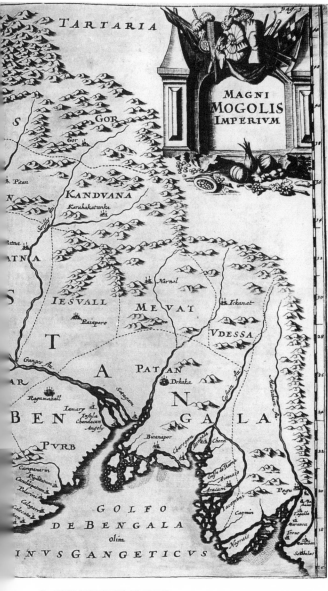

3. THE MUGHUL EMPIRE

From Dapper's *Asia* (Nuremberg, 1681), following the
preface.

Based almost completely on William Baffin's map
(1619) except for the decorations and the captions. (See
the introduction to maps of India, in illustrations to
Bk. 2, below.) Notice the tree-lined highway from
Agra to Lahore, a prominent feature of the Baffin
maps.

Pl. 68 is the frontispiece of *Asia*.

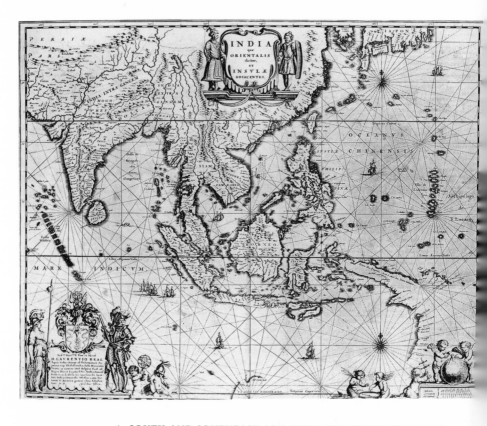

4. SOUTH AND SOUTHEAST ASIA FROM THE MALDIVES TO THE MARIANAS

From Blaeu, *op. cit.* (pl. 2), Vol. X, Bk. 1, between pp. 85 and 86.

Notice that Korea is an island. Also that Australia is seemingly a part of New Guinea.

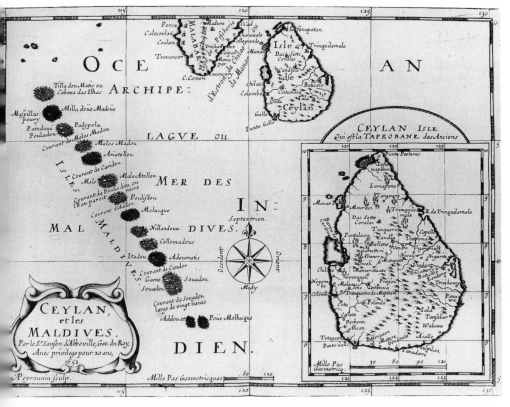

5. CEYLON AND THE MALDIVES

From Sanson d'Abbeville, *op. cit.* (pl. 1).

Mentions "Pirard de S. Malo" in text. Certainly the map is based on Pyrard as well as on Portuguese sources.

6. CONTINENTAL SOUTHEAST ASIA
From Robert Morden, *Geography Rectified* (2d ed.; London, 1688),
p. 411.
Text mentions no sources, but refers in general to "modern
relations."

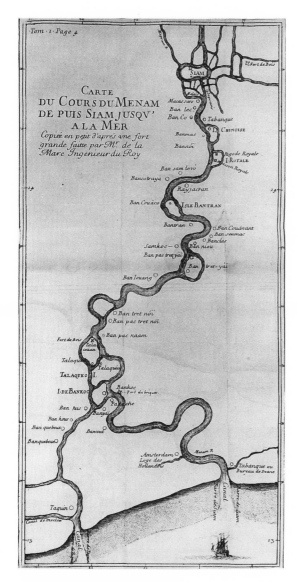

7. THE COURSE OF THE MENAM FROM AYU'TIA TO THE SEA

From Simon de La Loubère, *Du royaume de Siam* (2 vols.; Paris, 1691), I, between pp. 4 and 5. Pls. 35 and 84 are also from this book.

Copied for La Loubère from a larger version made by "M.ʳ de la Mare, Ingenieur du Roy."

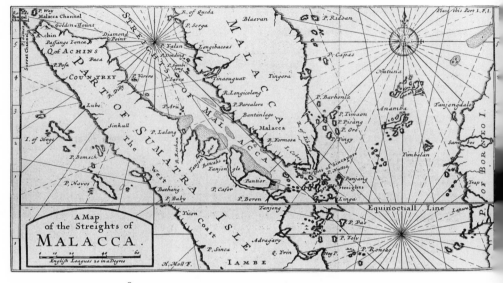

8. **MALACCA AND ITS ENVIRONS**
Map by H. Moll in William Dampier, *Voyages and Descriptions* (2d ed.; London, 1700), Vol. II, Pt. 1, p. 1.

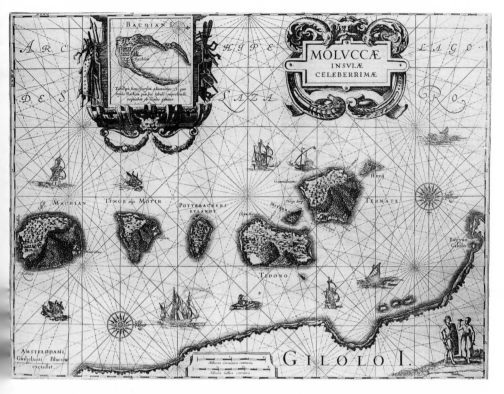

9. THE MOLUCCAS

From Blaeu, *op. cit.* (pl. 2), Vol. X, Bk. 1, between pp. 89 and 90.

Blaeu printed this map from plates acquired by his father, Willem Blaeu, from Joost de Hondt (Hondius) in 1629 for the *Theatrum orbis terrarum* (1635 to 1655). See I. C. Koeman, *op. cit.* (pl. 2), pp. 31, 83.

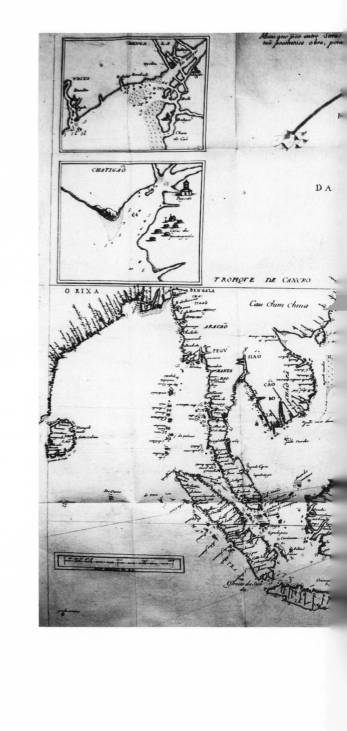

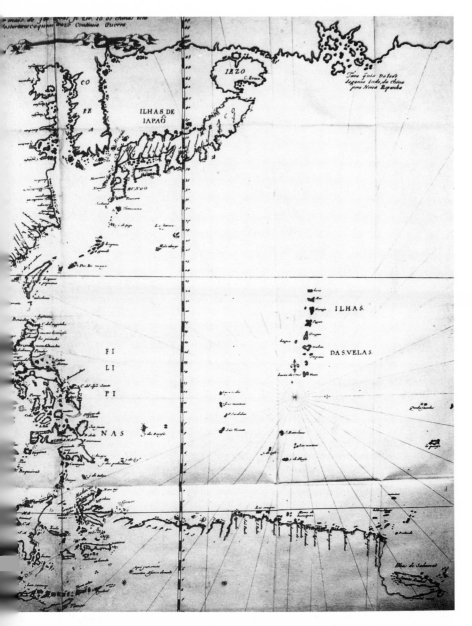

10. ASIA FROM THE BAY OF BENGAL TO THE MARIANAS

From Melchisédech Thévenot (comp.), *Relations de divers voyages curieux . . .* , II (Paris, 1666), following "Relation des isles Philippines faite par un religieux qui y a demeuré 18. ans." Pl. 23 is also from this book.

This relation was translated from a Spanish manuscript in the cabinet of Dom Carlo del Pezzo. Obviously the map too is of Spanish or Portuguese provenance. It shows the Marianas (Ladrones) as Ilhas das Velas (Islands of the Sails), Korea as a peninsula, and Yezo (Hokkaido) as an island.

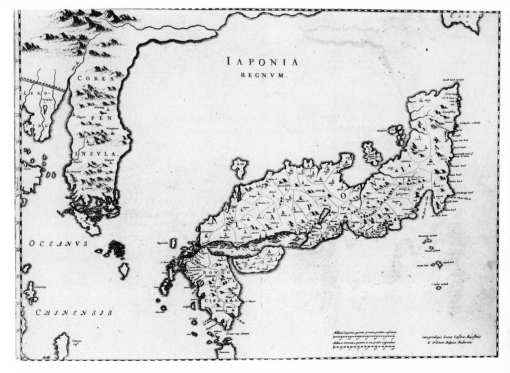

11. JAPAN AND KOREA

From Blaeu, *op. cit.* (pl. 2), Vol. X, Bk. 2, Martini collection, between pp. 168 and 169.

This is the Martino Martini map based on Jesuit sources which was drawn in 1649. It was the most accurate map of Japan produced in seventeenth-century Europe. A number of later maps, particularly those produced before the surveys of the late eighteenth century, relied heavily on Martini's map. See Hugh Cortazzi, *Isles of Gold. Antique Maps of Japan* (New York and Tokyo, 1983), pp. 43–44 and pl. 63.

Notice that Korea is correctly shown as a peninsula rather than an island, but that it is not clear from this map whether it is connected by land to Yezo. In preparing this map, Martini was apparently influenced by the Japanese portolan charts of East Asia. See H. Nakamura, "The Japanese Portolans of Portuguese Origin of the Sixteenth and Seventeenth Centuries," *Imago mundi,* XVIII (1964), 44.

12. (FACING PAGE, TOP) THE HARBOR OF SURAT

From Gabriel Dellon, *Nouvelle relation d'un voyage fait aux Indes Orientales* (Amsterdam, 1699), between pp. 48 and 49. Pl. 30 is also from this book.

The ship that seems to be burning in the harbor is possibly being careened. It is likely being cleaned, scraped, and recaulked. Furze or brushwood fires were used to burn off weeds and barnacles in a process called breaming. Occasionally ships being breamed caught fire and were destroyed. See Peter Kemp (ed.), *The Oxford Companion to Ships and the Sea* (London, New York, and Melbourne, 1976), p. 106.

The Indian ships in the foreground are of four different types, probably used in coastal sailing.

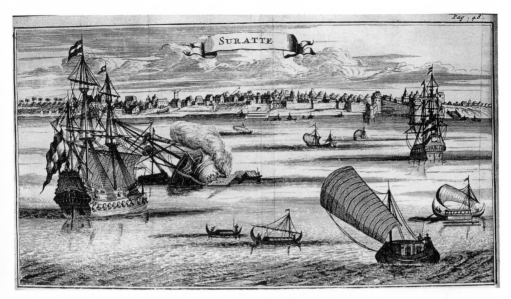

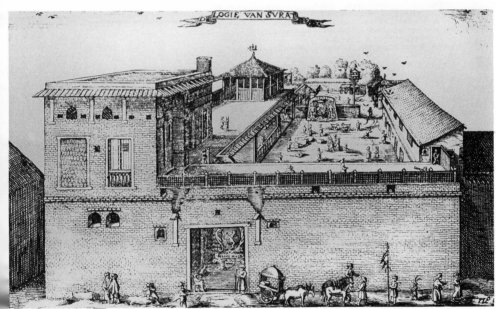

13. THE DUTCH FACTORY AT SURAT (*CA.* 1622?)

From *BV* (facsimile ed., Amsterdam, 1969), III, journal of Pieter van den Broecke, between pp. 106 and 107.

De foro Goæ frequentato, Leylon illis dicto, vbi variæ negociationes exercentur.

Era hac eſt repraeſentatio foriLeylon dicti , quod in Metropoli totius India Goa frequentatur; reſidet autem in vrbe Goa & vicerex & Archiepiſcopus: & frequentiſſima eſt ibidem negociatio quotidiana, qualis in hoc ſchemate patet. quæ vtſingula manifeſtius diſcernantur ſuis notis diſtinximus.

1. Sub hoc numero deſignantur Palankyn ſiue lectica, de quibus agitur in 35. Icone, in quibus deferuntur mulieres ita tectæ, vt à praetereuntibus minime conſpicantur, ipſæ vero obuios quoſque recte contueri poſſint.
2. Mangones equos phaleratos in foro domitantes, appenſis ſimul tintinnabulis, æquorum ſonitu & equi animentur, & emptores alliciantur.
3. Nutrices lactentes Luſitanorum infantes, ſiue Slauæ à Luſitanis impraegnatæ, quarum liberi editi manent in poteſtate dominorum.
4. Operarij, circumferentes aquam fontanam in vrceis per vrbem.
5. Proclamatores mercium, qui & mancipia, & quaſcunque alias res venales habent.
Atque hæc praecipue deſignanda fuerunt. cætera in Hiſtoria luculenter patent.

K 2

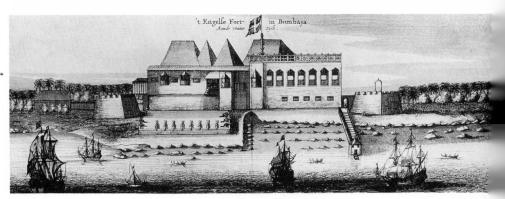

14. (TOP) THE DAILY MARKET AT GOA
From Johann Theodor de Bry and Johann Israel de Bry (comps.), *India orientalis*, II (Frankfurt, 1599), pl. 37. Pls. 18, 19, 20, 34, 36, and 70 are also from this book.
    Notice the Portuguese-type houses in the background.

15. (BOTTOM) THE ENGLISH FORT AT BOMBAY FROM THE WATER SIDE
From Philippus Baldaeus, *Naauwkeurige beschryvinge van Malabar en Choromandel* (Amsterdam, 1672), I, between pp. 70 and 71. Pl. 63 is also from this book.

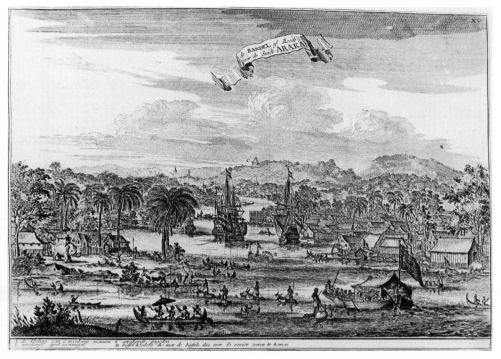

16. THE HARBOR AND WHARF OF ARAKAN

From Wouter Schouten, *Reistogt naar en door Oostindien*
(4th ed.; 2 vols.; Amsterdam, 1780), I, between pp. 106
and 107. Pl. 64 is also from this book.

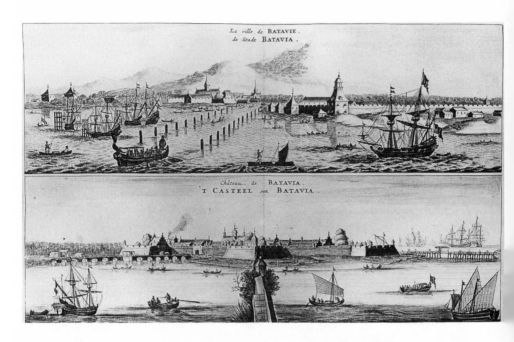

17. CITY AND FORTRESS OF BATAVIA (*CA.* 1655)
From Johann Nieuhof, *Die Gesandtschafft . . .* (Amsterdam, 1666), between pp. 36 and 37. Pls. 24, 25, 33, 65, and 69 are also from this book.

V.
INSVLAE AMBOYNAE SITVS
ET CONDITIO.

NSVLÆ *facies ex tabula patet. Ad quam cum Hollandi appuliſſent, de Amboyna Al-mirans Thalaſſicus, tribus nauibus, Karkollis dictis, probe armatis & inſtructis, in oc-curſum ipſis proceſſit, & qua gratia aduenirent, rogauit. Quod ab Hollandis cum re-ſciuiſſet, cum tormentorum fragore, quaſi ipſis gratularetur, iterum diſceſſit. Incolarum vero Amboynæ deſcriptio Alphabetica hæc eſt. A. Colonus loci eſt, cultrum latum ma-nu gerens, quo opera ſuas in ſyluis conficit. B. Ciuis eſt, haſtam vlnarum aliquot longi-tudine ferens, qua expeditiſſimus in iaculando eſt. C. Fæmina eſt, ad forum contendens, fructus venales manu ſurſum porrecta geſtans. D. Almirans eſt, miniſtris ſuis comitatus: quorum vnus Tireſol ſeu vm-braculum ei prætendit. Veſtitus eſt tunica lata manticulata, quam plerunque in humeros rciectat: & in-ſuper caligis ſericis, Luſitanica forma ſartis & paratis. E. Triremes ſunt, Karkolla dictæ, quibus curſum pernicem faciunt; contuitu mira & inſolentes.*

b 2

18. AMBOINA AND ITS INHABITANTS
From De Bry, *op. cit.* (pl. 14), V (1601), pl. 5.
    The boats marked by "E" are "Karkolla" (from Malay, *cora-cora*), or galley-type large merchant vessels. The Dutch later built vessels of this type to guard the coasts of their Indonesian outposts.

IX.
DOMVS, NEGOTIATIONI-
BVS AVT COMMERCIIS HOLLANDORVM
agitandis attributa.

*D o m o mercatoria Hollandis indulta, merces suas exposue-
runt, & lancem cum ponderibus à Sabandro acceperunt.
Pondus autem illud Bantani Kalti nominant, quod pon-
deris nostri libras quinque cum parte quarta continet. Hic
incolæ suas merces ponderabant, & cum aliis Hollandorum mercibus per-
mutabant. Appictus est hic quóque sclauus in Banda, quo is gestu aut
habitu cum fructibus & vino palmeo ex syluis veniat. Fœmina vero lite-
ra B. designata, operariaest, in forum ferendis pro mercede fructibus &
rebus aliis portandis destinata seu conducta.*

19. DUTCH FACTORY AT BANDA
From De Bry, *op. cit.* (pl. 14), V (1601), pl. 9.
  Notice the prominent role played by women (B) in
public trading.

21. (FACING PAGE, BOTTOM) RECEPTION OF THE DUTCH ENVOYS IN CAM-
BODIA (1659?)
From Arnoldus Montanus, *Ambassades memorables . . . vers les empereurs du Japon . . .*
(Amsterdam, 1680), p. 30. (See also plates 22, 26, 27, and 97.)
  This entire depiction is apparently based on the text. The two figures in the lower
right appear to be Japanese soldiers in the employment of the king of Cambodia as
palace guards.

20. TIDORE AND ITS FORT
WITH DUTCH AND ENGLISH SHIPS IN THE HARBOR
From De Bry, *op. cit.* (pl. 14), VIII (1607).

Tidore was captured by the Spanish in 1606. By 1612 it had two Spanish forts and a town of Portuguese *casados* (married people). See H. Jacobs, S. J. (ed.), *Documenta Malucensia* (3 vols.; Rome, 1974–84), III, 224–25.

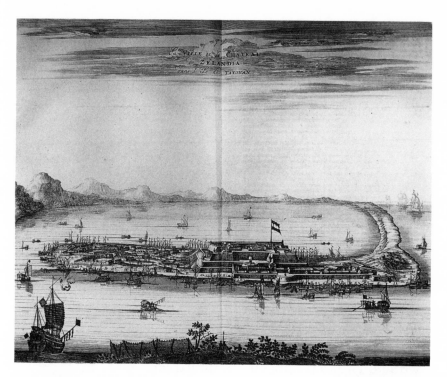

22. (TOP) THE TOWN AND CASTEEL (FORT) OF ZEELANDIA IN TAIWAN

From Montanus, *op. cit.* (pl. 21), between pp. 40 and 41.

Probably taken from Johann Nieuhof, *Het gezantschap der Neêrlandtsche Oost-Indische Compagnie aan den grooten tartarischen cham, den tegenwoordigen keizer van China* (Amsterdam, 1665), according to I. H. Van Eeghen, "Arnoldus Montanus's Book on Japan," *Quaerendo,* Vol. II, No. 4 (1972), p. 266.

Except for the caption at the top, this is identical with the plate in Olfert Dapper, *Gedenkwaerdig bedryf* (2 vols. in 1; Amsterdam, 1670), between pp. 40 and 41.

23. (BOTTOM) RECEPTION OF THE DUTCH AMBASSADORS IN PEKING (OCTOBER 2, 1656)

From Thévenot, *op. cit.* (pl. 10), III.

This looks like a close-up based on an engraving in Nieuhof, *Het gezantschap,* I, between pp. 172 and 173. Obviously the two are not from the same plates.

24. (TOP) MACAO

From Nieuhof, *op. cit.* (pl. 17), between pp. 42 and 43.

    Notice the fortress on the right and the gun emplacements on the top of the highest hill on the left. The smoke from the Dutch battleship in the foreground and from the hill on the left probably indicate that a battle is in progress, perhaps one of the Dutch attacks on Macao.

25. (BOTTOM) CANTON

From Nieuhof, *op. cit.* (pl. 17), between pp. 48 and 49.

    Notice differences in architecture between Macao and Canton.

Le Magazyn de la Compagnie, à FIRANDO.

26. THE DUTCH FACTORY AT FIRANDO (HIRADO)
From Montanus, *op. cit.* (pl. 21), p. 24. (Also on p. 24 of the German edition.)
　This is an authentic depiction of the Dutch lodge at Hirado, according to Professor Seiichi Iwao of the University of Tokyo. See Van Eeghen, *loc. cit.* (pl. 22), p. 257.
　The Dutch left Hirado for Deshima in 1640 on the orders of the Japanese.

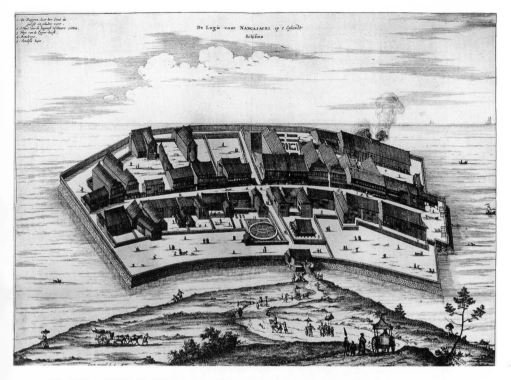

27. THE DUTCH FACTORY ON DESHIMA IN NAGASAKI HARBOR
From Montanus, *Denckwürdige Gesandtschafften* (Amsterdam, 1669), between pp. 48 and 49. Also in the French edition (Amsterdam, 1680), between pp. 50 and 51, where there are more identifications on it.

This is the earliest known depiction of this famous artificial island, according to Professor Seiichi Iwao of the University of Tokyo. See Van Eeghen, *loc. cit.* (pl. 22), p. 257.

Notice the narrow drawbridge which connects the island to the mainland in the foreground just forty feet away. The island is surrounded by a palisade. The store or factory is the first building and just across from the flower garden. The ships load and unload on the opposite side of the island. For further description see p. 49 in German edition.

Deshima, or "the island that juts out," was built in 1636 by Nagasaki merchants to isolate the Europeans. The numerous Chinese merchants in Nagasaki lived in the city proper until 1688 when they were confined to a "China town." For a Japanese depiction of this fan-like island see H. E. Plutschow, *Historical Nagasaki* (Tokyo, 1983), p. 52.

28. DIFFERENT TYPES OF PALANQUINS IN INDIA

From Giovanni Francesco Gemelli Careri, *Voyage du tour du monde* (Paris, 1727), III, between pp. 22 and 23. Pl. 103 is also from this book.

The word "palanquin" derives from Sanskrit, *palyanka,* meaning "bed." "Andor" or "Andora" is the Portuguese word for "litter." As shown here the litter is a covered or enclosed palanquin. Both types are shown carried by negroes. The "retz" is a net-like litter carried on a pole by Kanarese.

29. MERCHANTS OF BANTAM (*CA.* 1675)

From the diary of J. P. Cortemünde, a Danish sailor of the royal ship "Oldenborg" who traveled to the East between 1672 and 1675. Courtesy of Det Kongelige Bibliotek, Kort- og Billedafdelingen, Copenhagen.

On the left stands a Muslim merchant, in the center a Javanese, and on the right a Chinese with his fan and parasol. Also see G. Olsen, *Dansk Ostindien, 1616–1732* (Copenhagen, 1952), p. 125.

30. MAN AND WOMAN
OF GOA

From Dellon, *op. cit.* (pl.
12), facing p. 208.

Notice that the parasol
is held by a servant standing behind the woman.

Habitans de Goa

31. CHINESE (*SANG-
LEY*) MERCHANT
COUPLE OF MANILA

From a colored drawing
in a Manila manuscript of
ca. 1590. See Boxer (ed.),
*South China in the Six-
teenth Century* ("HS," 2d
ser., CVI; London, 1953).
For a discussion of the
origin of the word "Sang-
ley" see *ibid.*, p. 260, n. 2.

32. THE DUTCH FLEET BEFORE BANTAM IN JULY, 1596

From Willem Lodewyckszoon (G.M.A.W.L.), *Premier livre de l'histoire de la navigation aux Indes orientales* . . . (Amsterdam, 1609), p. 22v. Pl. 98 is also from this book.

Thee ou Cha.

33. THEE [TEA] OR CHA BUSH

From Nieuhof, *op. cit.* (pl. 17), p. 347.

The leaves and the size of the bush are compared in the text to the European wild ros Notice women picking the leaves and carrying them off in baskets on their heads.

I.

DELINEATIO CONVIVII A TERNATENSIVM REGE
Generali Neccio exhibiti.

 *Vm Hollandi ad Ternatem Insulam, quæ ad Molucas pertinet,
duabus nauibus appuliſſent, à Rege eius ſplendido admodum con-
uiuio ſunt excepti, qui ſuperiori tabulæ loco in lectulo regium in
morem gemmis & auro nitente holoſericoq; conſtrato conſidens, ad
vtrumq; menſæ latus aſſidentes ſibi Generalem Neccium & Con-
ſiliarios Subpræfectosq; eius habuit, & hucusq; quidem menſa illa
eleganti mappa & rotundis orbiculis inſtrata fuit, poſt illos autem ſedentes reliqui na-
uium miniſtri partem menſæ folijs & herbis virentibus conſtratam occuparunt. Menſa autem ipſa vna cum lectulo in theatro quodam nonnihil à terra eleuato conſtituta
fuit. Aſtabant ei Regis filij cum Nobilibus alijs menſæ miniſtrantes. Durante autem
prandio, Molucenſes incolæ palæſtram exercere & omnis generis ludos conuiuis exhi-
bere cogebantur.*

A 2   *II. DELI*

---

34. TERNATE BANQUET FOR THE DUTCH
From De Bry, *op. cit.* (pl. 14), VIII (1607), pl. 1.

This depicts a banquet given by the king of Ternate for Admiral Jacob Corneliszoon van Neck in June, 1601. While the Europeans banquet on an elevated
platform, the locals entertain by putting on duels of gladiators who look more European than Indonesian.

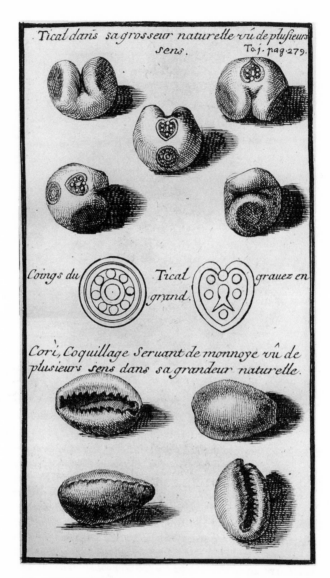

Tical dans sa grosseur naturelle vû de plusieurs sens.

To.j. pag.279.

Coings du ⊙ *Tical grand.* ♡ *grauez en*

Cori, Coquillage seruant de monnoye vû de plusieurs sens dans sa grandeur naturelle.

35. COINS OF SIAM: TICAL AND "CORI" (SEASHELLS)

From La Loubère, *op. cit.* (pl. 7), II, facing p. 279.

The tical of Siam was a short cylinder of silver bent double which carried the two stamps shown here in the middle of the illustration.

The "Cori" are the small white cowry shells used as currency throughout the East until the early nineteenth century.

DECLARATIO ET EXPLI-
CATIO VOCABVLORVM QVORVN-
DAM MALAYCORVM, QVAE LINGVA VNI-
uerfæ Indiæ Orientali vfitatior eft, non fecus ac apud nos Gallica. Quam qui
callent, vbiuis fere verfari commode queunt. Lufitanicæ quoque
linguæ peritia ibi valde commoda eft, cum interpretes
vbiuis Lufitanicam callentes re-
periantur.

A.

Alforees,	Terebra.	Beeff,	Adefine.
Addollaley,	Frater.	Buda,	Infans.
Arys,	Dies.	Bariing,	Ponere.
Aly;	Illic.	Bretoun,	Facere.
Ayam,	Gallina.	Bantel,	Puluinar.
Ada;	Habeo.	Banges,	Surgere.
Arynga,	Lumen.	Backelay,	Bellare.
Ambel,	Accipe.	Bras,	Oryza.
Addeparapas,	Soror.	Balacca,	Dorfum.
Apon;	Calceus.	Baon,	Humeri.
Anton,	Dentes.	Brat,	Grane.
Ampo,	Venenare.	Bantaren,	Mori.
Apy	Ignis.	Byte fecata,	A Egrotus fum.
Alys,	Palpebra.	Batu,	Lapis.
Abbacatta,	Quid dicitis.	Baccalayo,	Pugillare.
Affa,	Tamarindi.	Baccat,	Adurere.
Alia.	Zinziber.	Bctangia,	Interrogare.
B.		Banghe.	Multum.
Backeyen,	Brachium.	Beta babpa.	Pater meus.
Backy,	Pes.	Borron.	Auis.
Blouvvaer.	Foris.	Bange.	Multum.
Bevvangdarner,	Sanguinem mittere.	**C.**	
Bilby,	Emere.	Combaly,	Referte.
Benue,	Occidere.	Carboo.	Bubalus.
Balmarys daula,	Pridie.	Camby,	Hircus.
Bebc,	Anas.	Caruguanler,	Mifericors.
Bengo,	Macis.	Chyny,	Soluere.
Botonuum,	Inuentum.	Citghel,	Parum.
Balmary,	Heri.	Caiumains,	Cinnamomum.
Berny,	Dare.	Capyet,	Calx.
Batta,	Later collus.	Chynta,	Mæftus.
Bafaer,	Magnus.	Capelle,	Caput.
Bedyl,	Bombarda.	Cayo,	Pileus.
Bayck,	Bonum feu merx.	Catfion,	Puer.
Bacfart.	Magnus.	Calappen,	Nyces.
Barapa,	Quot. quàm multum.	Cadda,	Sacerdos.
Bygimana,	Quid agitur.	Cargha,	Elephantus.
Bauuin,	Cadere.	Calamp,	Penna.
Barappe itu,	Quanti hoc.	Cartas,	Papyrus.
Bacabaten,	Iam.	Chinfim,	Annulus.
		Cotni,	Sacci.

Caluc-

36. FIRST PAGE OF A
THREE-PAGE MALAY VOCABULARY
WITH LATIN EQUIVALENTS
From De Bry, op. cit. (pl. 14), V (1601),
p. 57.

INTERPRETATIONE

D' alcuni Vocaboli Orientali, ò non vfati nel puro
Italiano, contenuti nella Prima, e Seconda Speditione.

A Bbafis. Moneta di circa due giulij nella Perfia.
    Adregià. Principe de'Mori Malauari, ò loro Capo.
Agà. Capitano, ò Padrone.
Aldea. Villaggio.
Aleàs. Elefante femina.
Alfandica. Dogana.
Almadìa. Barca lunga, e ftretta;con molti remi nell' Indie
Amouco. Chi giura di morire per difefa, ò vendetta d'al-
    cuno, ò di fue robe.
Arecca. Frutto fimile alla Noce mofcata
Afphaino, *ò Spahino*. Caualiere del Turco, ò Soldato à
    Cauallo
Auanìa. Aggrauio ingiufto per Impoftura
Baniano. Gentile, Mercante, Medico, ò fimile, di Cafta, ò
    Tribù particolare.
Bareccumpazan. Fattione Boreale de'Chriftiani di San
    Thomè
Bafsià, ò Bafcià. Capo, ò V. Rè. Si dà pure a' Giannizzari
Bazzarro. Villaggio, doue fia Mercatone' Regni de Mala-
    uari
Beduini; ò Bedeuì Arabi del Deferto
Betli. Foglie fimili all' Hedera, buone per lo ftomaco
Borillo. Ferro fimile ad vn puntarolo grande
Brahamane. Sacerdote Gentile.
Cabaia. Toghetta, ò Giubba
Cadì. Giudice de'Mori
Cafar. Gabbella, Dogana, ò datio de'foli Chriftiani
                            Cafre

37. ORIENTAL WORDS
AND THEIR ITALIAN
EQUIVALENTS
From Giuseppe di Santa Maria Sebas-
tiani, Seconda speditione all' Indie orientali
(Rome, 1672), introductory material be-
fore chap. i. Pl. 78 is the title page of
this book.

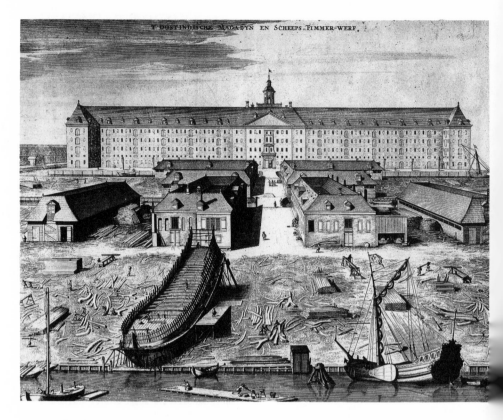

38. WAREHOUSE AND SHIPYARD OF THE DUTCH EAST INDIA COMPANY IN AMSTERDAM

From Caspar Commelin, *Beschrijvinge van Amsterdam* (2 vols.; Amsterdam, 1693–94), II, between pp. 734 and 735. Courtesy of the Department of Rare Books and Special Collections, the University of Michigan Library.

Built in 1661, this is located on Oostenburg, a man-made island in the old harbor on the north side of Amsterdam. The print dates from 1694. For further detail see J. R. Schiltmeijer (ed.), *Amsterdam in 17e eeuwse prent* (3d ed.; Amsterdam, 1968), pp. 101–2.

39. THE OLD EAST INDIA HOUSE IN LONDON

From a painting in the possession of Mr. Pulham of the India House, 12 × 8 inches. Reproduced by permission of the India Office Library (The British Library).

This was the headquarters in Leadenhall Street of the English East India Company from 1648 to 1726.

40. THE EAST INDIA HOUSE IN AMSTERDAM (POST 1606)

From Caspar Commelin, *op. cit.* (pl. 38), p. 733. Courtesy of the Department of Rare Books and Special Collections, the University of Michigan Library.

The original building on the left dates from the mid-sixteenth century and was rented to the VOC in 1603. Construction on the newer building to its right must have begun shortly thereafter. The entryway carries the date 1606. See Schiltmeijer (ed.), *op. cit.*, pp. 64–67 and pl. 40.

41. A COMPOSITE OF EAST INDIAN BIRDS
From A. Churchill's edition of Nieuhof's *Voyages*, (*CV*, 3d ed.; 6 vols.; London, 1744), II, facing p. 292.

HIMVS ET TOMAS CAPITE PRIMVM ENVERSO SVSPENSI
DEMVM OBTRVNCATVR.

MICHAEL ET LINVS EXVRVNTVR MAXENTIA TRVNCATVR.

42. JOACHIM AND THOMAS
SUSPENDED HEAD DOWN

From Nicolas Trigault, *De christianis
apud Iaponios triumphis* (Munich, 1623),
p. 240. Pls. 43, 44, 45, 47, 48, 49, and 56
are also from this book.

43. THE EXECUTION OF THREE
JAPANESE CONVERTS

From Trigault, *op. cit.,* p. 231.

**44. THE CRUCIFIXION
OF DOMINIC**
From Trigault, *op. cit.*,
(pl. 42), p. 464.

DOMINICVS CHRISTI CAVSSA IN CRVCEM ACTVS.

**45. PREPARATION
FOR A SUSPENSION
IN JAPAN**
From Trigault, *op. cit.*,
p. 362.
    Notice kneeling Christians with crosses on their
foreheads.

GERMANI GOROSVQVE ET ALIORVM SVPPLICIA
CHRISTI CAVSA EXANCLATA.

O CHRISTI VICTIMÆ VIVÆ CONCREMANTVR.

46. (ABOVE) THE PERSECUTION
AND TORTURE OF CHRISTIANS
IN JAPAN

From [Crasset], *Histoire de l'eglise du
Japon* (Paris, 1689), II, between pp. 50
and 51.

47. (LEFT) EIGHT CHRISTIANS
BEING BURNED ALIVE
IN JAPAN

From Trigault, *op. cit.* (pl. 42), p. 165.

**48. SUSPENSION OF A
JAPANESE CHRISTIAN
WITH A WEIGHT ON HIS BACK**
From Trigault, *op. cit.* (pl. 42), p. 323.

CHRISTIANI MANIBVS PEDIBVSQ IN TERGVM REVINCT
DORSOQ GRANDI SAXO IMPOSITO   SVSPENDVNTVR

**49. TORTURE OF CHRISTIANS
AT ARIMA**
From Trigault, *op. cit.*, p. 300.

ARIMÆ IN CHRISTIANOS ATROCITER SEVITV

50. JOHANN ADAM SCHALL, S.J., CLAD AS A CHINESE COURT MANDARIN
AND HEAD OF THE CALENDRICAL BUREAU

From Athanasius Kircher, *La Chine illustrée*, trans. by F. S. Dalquié (Amsterdam, 1670), between pp. 152 and 153. Pls. 51 and 52 are also from this book. (These illustrations are also in the 1667 Latin edition.) "Here I think it fitting to include drawings of Fr. Adam Schall, who is dressed as a mandarin of the Department of Astronomy. . . . So, in the drawing you see Fr. Adam Schall with the picture of a crane on the front of his gown which he wears in the royal court" (C. Van Tuyl [trans.], *China illustrata by Kircher, Translated . . . from the 1677* [*sic*] *Original Latin Edition* [Muskogee, Okla., 1987], pp. 100–101).

On February 2, 1658, Schall was made a civil mandarin first class, first division, and named Imperial Chamberlain to the Shun-chih emperor. As a sign of his rank, he wore a red button on his hat and a gold embroidered crane with wings outspread on a square patch of his tunic. For the embroidered patch of a civil official of the first rank *cf.* Zhou Xun *et al., Five Thousand Years of Chinese Costumes* (San Francisco, 1987), fig. 318.

51. THE MIRACULOUS CROSS OF THOMAS THE APOSTLE AT MYLAPORE IN INDIA

From Kircher, *op. cit.* (pl. 50), facing p. 74.

This depiction of the Thomas (or Mount) cross and its inscription is based in part on an illustration in João de Lucena's biography of Xavier (Lisbon, 1600).[1] The Netherlandish engraver added the persons, the altar and its accoutrements, the Jesuit insignia, and the background decorations. The letters of the inscription and the figure of the cross (similar to a Maltese cross) were probably copied by Lucena's engraver from a crude pen-sketch brought back to Europe.[2] The Amsterdam engraver, in turn, apparently introduced embellishments of his own to the cross as well as variations to the letters of the illegible inscription.[3]

In 1547 the Portuguese had unearthed a granite slab while digging at the alleged site of Thomas' martyrdom. On it were incised this strange cross framed by a mysterious inscription.[4] Assuming that the cross dated from the time of the apostle himself, the Portuguese and their Indian converts treated it with the greatest reverence.[5] Tradition had it that the cross was formed on the stone by Thomas' own blood. Kircher reports that annually on December 21 at a mass held for the Blessed Virgin "this cross changes to various colors and suddenly drips much sweat and blood."[6] The peacock suspended over the cross is, according to Kircher, the insignia of the emperor of Vijayanager.[7]

Today the church on the St. Thomas mount houses this remarkable relic behind its main altar located on the spot where tradition has it that St. Thomas was martyred. The inscription remained a mystery until its decipherment by modern scholars, and even they were in disagreement for about fifty years over its meaning. Paleographers are now agreed that the lettering is probably of the eighth century and in Pahlavi or middle Persian. In the latest translation it reads: My Lord Christ, have mercy upon Abias, son of Chaharbukht, the Syrian, who cut this.[8]

[1] See the facsimile edition, *Historia da vida do Padre Francisco de Xavier* (2 vols.; Lisbon, 1952), I, facing p. 168.

[2] *Cf.* the pen-sketch of the cross executed in 1579 by A. Monserrate, S. J., as reproduced in H. Hosten, S. J., "Saint Thomas and San Thomé, Mylapore," *Journal of the Asiatic Society of Bengal*, n.s., XIX (1923), facing p. 207. The form of the cross and the surrounding arch in Lucena's biography of Xavier are almost identical to Monserrate's but the inscription is entirely different. In fact, the inscriptions are different in all three of the examples we have examined.

[3] For a good reproduction of the cross and a legible inscription see E. P. T. Winckworth, "A New Interpretation of the Pahlavi Cross-Inscriptions of Southern India," *The Journal of Theological Studies*, XXX (1929), 241.

[4] Compare this to the discovery of the Nestorian Monument at Sian in China in 1623, as Kircher himself does. Modern scholars have also noticed the similarity in form between the eighth-century Nestorian cross on the Sian stele and the Thomas cross. See P. Y. Saeki, *The Nestorian Documents and Relics in China* (Tokyo, 1951), p. 26.

[5] See S. Neill, *A History of Christianity in India* (Cambridge, 1984), pp. 47–48.

[6] From Van Tuyl (trans.), *op. cit.* (pl. 50), p. 50. Kircher learned about this miracle and similar beliefs from his reading of Lucena and from an informant, P. P. Godigney, the Portuguese Jesuit rector of Cochin, who talked with him in Rome. The cross has not exuded "sweat" since 1704. See Herman D'Souza, *In the Steps of St. Thomas* (San Thomé, 1952), pp. 61–62.

[7] Mylapore is known as the peacock city and peacocks figure in several of the traditional stories about the death of St. Thomas. See Neill, *op. cit.*, pp. 33, 35.

[8] From Winckworth, *loc. cit.*, p. 243. "The Syrian" probably refers to Abias' Syrian or Nestorian faith.

Crux miraculosa S. Thomæ Apostoli
Meliaporæ in India.

G. Matthaus Riccius Macerat: è Soc. Jesu
prim: Chriāuæ Fidei in Regno Sinarum
propagator.

Lÿ Paulus Magnus Sinarum Colaus
Legis Christianæ propagator.

52. RICCI AND HIS CONVERT PAUL

From Kircher, *op. cit.* (pl. 50), facing p. 154.

Matteo Ricci and "Paul," the Christian name taken by Hsü Kuang-ch'i (1562–1633) after his conversion in 1603. Above Ricci's head is written his Chinese name, Li Ma-t'ou. Ricci is dressed in a Ming costume appropriate to scholars from the West; according to Kircher (p. 101), all the Jesuits wore similar garb before the Manchu Conquest. Paul is likewise dressed in a Ming costume, one especially designed for officials. On his head he wears the typical *fu tou* or black gauze cap with wings. The dress itself is that of an official of high rank. *Cf.* the Ming dynasty official depicted in Zhou Xun *et. al., op. cit.* (pl. 50), fig. 235, p. 153. In Ricci's time Hsü was associated with the Han-lin Academy and with the imperial agency entrusted with the education of the heir apparent. See Chen Min-sun, "Hsü Kuang-ch'i and His Image of the West," in E. J. Van Kley and C. K. Pullapilly (eds.), *Asia and the West: Encounters and Exchanges from the Age of Explorations* (Notre Dame, 1986), p. 31.

53. PORTRAIT OF NICHOLAS TRIGAULT, S.J.
Executed around 1630 by an artist of Van Dyck's circle. Printed with
permission of the Musée de la Chartreuse, Douai (Inv. 27).

Regiani sotto de
quali si comprende
la Missione
del Giappone

A. Tunkino B. Cocincina C. Cambodia D. Siam E. Lao F. Macassar G. Cantáom H. Giapp

I. Clowet sculp.

54. FRONTISPIECE TO GIAN FILIPPO DE MARINI'S *DELLE MIS-SIONI* (ROME, 1663)

Reproduced in *Historia et relatione del Tunchino e del Giappone . . . del P. Gio: Filippo de Marini* (Rome, 1665). Engraving by Clowet.

The Jesuits hoped to use the Chinese language in bringing the light of the gospel to the diverse peoples of the extensive Province of Japan. The characters on the book held by the priest read: "Sacrifice to the God of heaven and earth; the Ten Commandments of the Lord of Heaven."

The little ape shown here is possibly an emblem of the universality of Western arts and sciences. See H. W. Janson, *Apes and Ape Lore in the Middle Ages and the Renaissance* (London, 1952), p. 306.

55. TITLE PAGE OF NICOLAS TRIGAULT'S *DE CHRISTIANA EX-PEDITIONE* (1615).

Notice how the Jesuits associate Francis Xavier, shown on the left, with Matteo Ricci, shown on the right, as the founding fathers of the China mission. Xavier was canonized in 1622. Some Jesuits up to the present day have continued to press for sainthood for Ricci.

DE CHRISTIANIS APVD IAPONIOS
TRIVMPHIS
SIVE DE GRAVISSIMA IBIDEM CONTRA CHRISTI
FIDEM PERSECVTIONE EXORTA
ANNO M DC XII
VSQ. AD ANNVM M DC XX.
LIBRI QVINQ.
In annos totidem summa cum fide ex annuis Societatis
IESV litteris continuis historiæ serie distributi.
AD SERENISSIMOS PRINCIPES
GVLIELMVM PARENTEM,
FERDINANDVM ET MAXIMILIANVM,
S.R.I. SEPTEMVIROS ELECTORES, ALBERTVM.
COM. PAL. RHENI VTRIVSQ.
BAVAR. DVCES.
Auctore P. Nicolao Trigautio
eiusdem Societatis Sacerdote
Belga Duacensi.
Cum
Raderi
AVCTARIO ET ICONIBVS
SADELERIANIS
MONACHII
CIƆ IƆC XXIII.

Cum Priuilegio Summi Pontificis, et Sac. Cæsareæ Maiest. ad decennium

56.

HISTORIA
DE LAS MISSIONES
QVE HAN HECHO LOS
RELIGIOSOS DE LA COMPAÑIA
DE IESVS, PARA PREDICAR EL SANCTO
Euangelio en la India Oriental, y en los Reynos
de la China y Iapon.
ESCRITA POR EL PADRE LVIS
de Guzman, Religioso de la misma Compañia.
PRIMERA PARTE
EN LA QVAL SE CONTIENEN SEYS LIBROS
tres de la India Oriental, vno de la China, y dos de Iapon.
DIRIGIDA A DOÑA ANA FELIX DE GVZMAN,
Marquesa de Camarasa, Condesa de Ricla, Señora del
Adelantamiento de Caçorla.

Año   1601

CON PRIVILEGIO.
EN ALCALA, por la Biuda de Iuan Gracian.

57.

A
Short Account
OF THE
DECLARATION,
Given by the
CHINESE Emperour
Kam Hi,
In the Year 1700.

Nos autem predicamus Chriſtum Crucifixum.
But we do Preach Chriſt Crucify'd. 1 Cor. 23.

LONDON:
Printed in the Year MDCCIII.

1703

58.

EPISTOLA
PATRIS NICOLAI
PIMENTÆ
Viſitatoris Societatis IESV in
India Orientali.

Ad R. P. Claudium Aquauiuam
eiuſdem Societatis Præpoſitum
Generalem.
Goæ viij. Kal. Ianuarij 1599.

Indiæ
I.

ROMAE,
Apud Aloyſium Zannettum.
M DCI.
Superiorum permiſſu.
CF

59.

HISTORICA RELATIO
DE
ORTU ET
PROGRESSU FI-
DEI ORTHODOXÆ
In
Regno Chinenſi
Per
Miſsionarios SOCIETATIS JESU
Ab
Anno 1581. usque ad Annum 1669.
Noviſsimè collecta
Ex Literis eorundem Patrum Societatis JESU
Præcipuè
R. P. JOANNIS ADAMI SCHALL
Colonienſis
Ex eadem Societate.
Editio altera, & aucta, Geographicâ Regni
Chinenſis deſcriptione; Compendioſa Narra-
tione de StatuMiſsionisChinenſis; Prodi-
giis, quæ in ultima Perſecutione con-
tigerunt; & Indice.
Cum Facultate Superiorum
Sumptibus JOAN. CONRADI EMMRICH
Civis & Bibliopolæ
RATISBONÆ Typis AUGUSTI Hanckwiß/
ANNO M. DC. LXXII.

60.

VITA
GASPARIS
BARZÆI
BELGÆ
E SOCIETATE IESV
B. XAVERII
In India Socij.
AVCTORE
P. NIC. TRIGAVLT
Eiuſdem Societatis Sacerdote.

AVGETVR

ANTVERPIÆ
Ex Officina Ioach. Trognæſij.
Anno M. DC. X.

61.

In conſpectv gen-
tivm revelavit Iv-
ſtitiam ſvam.

pſl. 97

INNOCENTIA
VICTRIX
SIVE
Sententia ComitiorumImperij Sinici
PRO
INNOCENTIA
CHRISTIANÆ RELIGIONIS
Lata Juridicè per Annum 1669.
&.
Iuſſu R. P. Antonij de Govvea Soc.
IESV, ibidem V. Provincialis
Sinico-Latinè expoſita
In Quam chēu metropoli provinciæ Quam tum in Regno Sinarum
Anno Salvtis Hvmanæ MDCLXXI.

62. THE *INNOCENTIA VICTRIX* OF ANTONIO DE GOUVEA

This work includes the text of an ambiguous imperial rescript of toleration for
Christianity in Latin translation as well as related Chinese official documents in Latin
translation. It was compiled by a group of Jesuit missionaries at Canton in 1671
under the direction of Antonio de Gouvea (1592–1677), the Portuguese vice-provincial, and was published by the Jesuit xylographic press in China. See C. R. Boxer,
Exotic Printing and the Expansion of Europe, 1492–1840 (Lilly Library, Indiana University, 1972), p. 41.

Mr. WOUTER SCHOUTEN van HAERLE

63. PORTRAIT OF PHILIPPUS BAL-
DAEUS, THE DUTCH MINISTER AND
MISSIONARY
Frontispiece from Baldaeus, *op. cit.*
(pl. 15), Pt. I.

64. (TOP, RIGHT) PORTRAIT OF
WOUTER SCHOUTEN
OF HAARLEM
From Wouter Schouten, *op. cit.* (pl. 16),
I, facing p. xiv.

65. (BOTTOM, RIGHT) PORTRAIT OF
JOHANN NIEUHOF
From the frontal materials in Nieuhof,
op. cit. (pl. 17).

JOAN NIEUHOF.

The true Effigies of F. Alvarez Semedo
Procurator of y Prouinces of Iapan & China
Tho. Cros. fecit

66. PORTRAIT OF ALVAREZ SEMEDO, S.J.

Frontispiece to the English translation of Semedo, *The History of That Great and Renowned Monarchy of China* (London, 1655).

This engraving by Thomas Cross, an engraver for English book publishers, was copied from an anonymous engraving in the original Italian edition of Semedo's book (Rome, 1643). Clothed in his priestly garments Semedo seems to be writing Chinese in the book he holds. Even though Cross was well known for his skill in engraving scripts, the "Chinese" on the book is not legible and appears to be but a crude effort to imitate characters. On Thomas Cross see M. Corbett and M. Norton, *Engraving in England in the Sixteenth and Seventeenth Centuries* (Cambridge, 1964), pp. 277–78, 302.

67. PORTRAIT OF JEAN DE THÉVENOT
Frontispiece, Jean de Thévenot, *Travels* (London, 1687).
Engraved by William Faithorne.

68. FRONTISPIECE, OLFERT DAPPER'S *ASIA*

From *Asia, oder: Ausführliche Beschreibung des Reichs des Grossen Mogols und eines grossen Theils von Indien* . . . (Nuremberg, 1681).

69. FRONTISPIECE, NIEUHOF'S *GESANDTSCHAFFT*

From Nieuhof, *op. cit.* (pl. 17). Prepared by Johann Nieuhof himself, his brother Hendrick, or by someone in Van Meurs' workshop, this frontispiece serves as a visual introduction to the more than 150 engravings in the book taken from Johann Nieuhof's drawings. The central figure, presumably the emperor since his hand rests upon the globe, is actually Nieuhof's portrait of the "Old Viceroy" of Kwangtung (see pl. 323). Although Nieuhof actually saw the Shun-chih emperor when he was in Peking, he admits in his text that he and the Dutch ambassadors were too far away to see anything but a bit of the emperor's face. Here the "emperor" is sitting as a judge of the Han Chinese who were probably ac-cused of defying Manchu laws regarding the removal of all hair and beards except the queue. One of the accused has his head in a cangue, a square board or yoke that rested on the shoulders without chafing the neck.

In 1669 John Ogilby employed Wenceslas Hollar, the famous etcher, to copy this engraving as the title page for his English translation of Nieuhof's work. For a thorough discussion of Hollar's etching see M. Corbett, "The Dutch Mission to Peking in 1655," *Quaerendo,* Vol. XVI, No. 2 (Spring, 1986), pp. 131–36. Corbett fails to note that the Hollar etching reverses the original copper engraving.

Die Gesandtschafft
die Ost-Indischen Compagney
in den Vereinigten Niederländern.
an den
Grossen Tartarischen Cham
und nunmehr auch Sinischen Keyser.
Mit Röm. Käyf. Maj. Privilegio.

In Amsterdam,
Gedruckt und verlegt durch Jacob Mörs, Buch- und Kunst-händlern alda. 1666.

70. FRONTISPIECE TO DE BRY, *INDIA ORIENTALIS*, PT. V

From De Bry *op. cit.* (pl. 14), V (1601).

At the top is the "flying fox," the great bat that astounded European seafarers. Below is an outrigger of the kind used in the islands of Southeast Asia.

71. FRONTISPIECE TO JOHANN VON DER BEHR,
DIARIUM, ODER TAGEBUCH . . . (JENA, 1668)
Notice the Indian elephant and the one-horned rhinoceros as symbols of Asia.

Pl. 91 is the title page of this book.

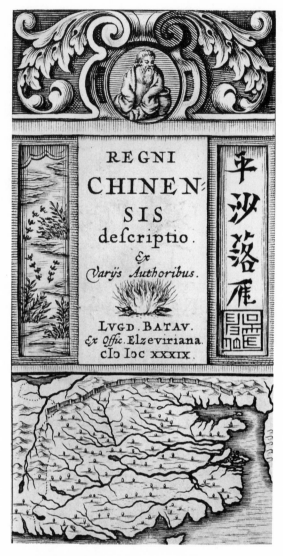

**72. A CHINESE PAINTING TITLE PAGE
(LEYDEN, 1639)**

The Chinese inscription reads *Ping-sha Luo-yen,* or
"Geese Descend to the Sand Flats." This is a common
theme in Chinese painting; it is one of the eight views of
the Hsiao and Hsiang rivers that illustrate the poems of
Sung Ti (twelfth century A.D.). This is certainly the earliest effort to imitate a Chinese landscape painting in a
European publication. *Cf.* pl. 316.

   The map at the bottom is a rough approximation of
China from Hainan to the Great Wall.

A Voyage to East-India.

Wherein

Some things are taken notice of in our paffage thither, but many more in our abode there, within that rich and moft fpacious Empire *Of the Great Mogol.*

Mix't with fome Parallel Obfervations and inferences upon the ftorie, to profit as well as delight the *Reader.*

Obferved by Edward Terry (*then Chaplain to the Right Honorable Sr.* Thomas Row *Knight*, *Lord Ambaffadour to the great Mogol*) *now Rettor of the Church at* Greenford, *in the County of* Middlefex.

In *journeying often, in perils of waters*, *in perils of Robbers*, *in perils by the Heathen*, *in perils in the Sea.* 1 Cor. 11, 26.

The Lord *on high is mightier than the noife of many waters ; yea, than the mighty waves of the Sea,* Pfal. 93. 4.

———— *Digitis à morte remotus Quatuor, aut* Septem.——Ju. Sat.12. *Qui nefcit orare*, *difcat navigare. Ubique Naufragium.*

London, Printed by *T. W.* for *J. Martin*, and *J. Allftrye*, at the Bell in *St. Pauls* Church-Yard, 1655.

73.

Generale Beſchrijbinge van

INDIEN.

Ende in 't beſonder

Kort verhael van de Regering, Ceremonien, Handel, Vruchten en Geleghentheydt van 't Koninckrijck van Guſuratten, ſtaende onder de beheerſchinghe van den Groot-Machtighen Kouinck CAJAHAN: anders genaemt den grooten

MOGOR.

Uyt Verſcheyden Autheuren ende eyghen onder-bindinge bergabert ende by een gheſtelt:

Door

JOHAN van TWIST, Geweſen Overhooft van de Nederlantſche Comtooren, *Amadabat*, *Cambaya*, *Brodera*, ende *Brotchia.*

Hier achter is by-geboeght de aenwijſinge ban meeſt alle Kuſten/ Drooghten ende Reden/ om boor gantſch Indien is ſeylen.

MYN GLAS LOOPT RAS

t'AMSTELREDAM,

Voor Jooſt Hartgerts, Boeck-berkooper in de Gaſthups-Steegh/ beijdén het Stadt-Hups / in de Boeck-winckel. 1648.

74. *GENERALE BESCHRIJVINGE VAN INDIEN . . . DOOR JOHAN VAN TWIST* (AMSTERDAM, 1648)
The inscription "My glass empties quickly" was possibly the trademark of the press of Joost Hartgers, the Amsterdam book dealer and publisher.

Folget

Ein Schreiben /

Des VolEdlen/Gestrengen vnd Vesten

Johan Albrecht von Man-

delslow /

So Er auß der Insel Madagascar an M. Adamum Olearium
gethan / in welchem Er seine Reise auß Persien nach
Ost-Indien durch den Oceanum Summarischer
Weise erzehlet.

Gedruckt zu Schleßwig /
Im Jahr / 1645.

75. TITLE PAGE, JOHAN ALBRECHT
VON MANDELSLO, *EIN SCHREIBEN
. . . SO ER AUSS DER INSEL
MADAGASCAR AN M. ADAMUM
OLEARIUM GETHAN, IN WELCHEM
ER SEINE REISE AUSS PERSIEN NACH
OST-INDIEN . . . ERZEHLT*
(SCHLESWIG, 1645)

Phil à Sta Trinitate

Orientalische
Räisebeschreibung.

Worinnen unterschiedliche Be-
gebenheiten seiner Räise / vielerley Orientalische Landschafften / das Gebürg / Meer
und Flüsse / die Zeit-Rechnung der Fürsten so darinnen geherrschet / ihre Einwohner so wol Christen
als Unglaubige /

ingleichem auch

Die Thiere / Bäume / Pflantzen und
Früchte so darinnen gefunden werden / end-
lich mancherley Geschichten so darinnen
sich haben zugetragen.

Franckfurt /

In Verlegung Joh. Georg Schiele.

M DC LXXI.

76, 77. (ABOVE AND FACING PAGE)
TITLE PAGE AND FRONTISPIECE,
PHILIPPE DE SAINTE-TRINITÉ,
*ORIENTALISCHE REISEBESCHREI-
BUNG* (FRANKFURT, 1671)

P. à S T,
ORIENTA
LISCHE
Reise
Beschrei
bung.

SECONDA SPEDITIONE

ALL' INDIE

ORIENTALI

DI MONSIGNOR

SEBASTIANI

FR. GIVSEPPE DI S. MARIA

DELL'ORDINE DE'CARMELITANI SCALZI

PRIMA
VESCOVO DI HIERAPOLI,

HOGGI DI BISIGNANO,

E BARONE DI SANTA SOFIA,

Ordinata da

ALESSANDRO VII,

DI GLORIOSA MEMORIA.

IN ROMA, Nella Stamperia di Filippo M. Mancini. 1672.

CON LICENZA DE' SVPERIORI.

78.

HISTORIA
ET RELATIONE
DEL TVNCHINO
E DEL GIAPPONE

Con la vera Relatione ancora d'altri Regni, e Prouincie
di quelle regioni, e del loro gouerno politico.

Con le Missioni fatteui dalli Padri della Compagnia di Giesù, &
Introduttione della fede Christiana, & Confutatione di
Diuerse Sette d'Idolatri di quelli habitatori,

DIVISA IN CINQVE LIBRI

OPERA DEL P. GIO: FILIPPO DE MARINI
Della medema Compagnia.

ALLA SANTITA' DI N. S.

ALESSANDRO
PAPA SETTIMO.

Francini
Cesarej

Roma

IN ROMA, Nella Stamperia di Vitale Mascardi, MDCLXV.
CON LICENZA DE'SVPERIORI.

79.

MEMOIRS
AND
OBSERVATIONS

Topographical,] [*Natural,*
Physical, | | *Civil,*
Mathematical, | | and
Mechanical,] [*Ecclesiastical.*

Made in a late

JOURNEY
Through the
EMPIRE of CHINA,
And Publifhed in feveral Letters.

Particularly upon the *Chinefe* Pottery and Varnifhing ; the Silk and other Manufactures ; the Pearl Fifhing ; the Hiftory of Plants and Animals. Defcription of their Cities and Publick Works ; Number of People, their Language, Manners and Commerce ; their Habits, Oeconomy, and Government. The Philofophy of *Confucius.* The State of Chriftianity, with many other Curious and Ufeful Remarks.

By *LOUIS LE COMPTE* Jefuit,
Confeffor to the Dutchefs of *Burgundy,* one of the Royal Mathematicians, and lately Miffionary into the Eaftern Countries.

Tranflated from the Paris *Edition, and illuftrated with Figures.*

London : Printed for *Benj. Tooke* at the Middle Temple Gate, and *Sam. Buckley* at the *Dolphin* over againft St. *Dunftans* Church in *Fleetftreet.* 1 6 9 7.

80.

AN
Hiftorical Relation
Of the Iſland
CEYLON,
IN THE
EAST-INDIES:
TOGETHER,

With an ACCOUNT of the Detaining in Captivity the AUTHOR and divers other *Englifhmen* now Living there ; and of the AUTHOR's Miraculous ESCAPE.

Illuftrated with Figures, and a Map of the ISLAND.

By *ROBERT KNOX*, a Captive there near Twenty Years.

LONDON,
Printed by *Richard Chiſwell*, Printer to the ROYAL SOCIETY, at the *Roſe* and *Crown* in St. *Paul's* Church-yard, 1 6 8 1.

81.

Offt begehrte Beschreibung
Der Newen ORIENTALischen
REISE/
So durch Gelegenheit einer Holsteinischen
Legation an den König in Persien geschehen.
Worinnen
Derer Orter vnd Länder/ durch welche die Reise
gangen/als fürnemblich Rußland/Tartarien vnd Persien/sampt
ihrer Einwohner Natur / Leben vnd Wesen fleissig beschrieben / vnd mit
vielen Kupfferstücken / so nach dem leben gestellet/ gezieret.
Item
Ein Schreiben des WolEdeln rc. Johan Albrecht
Von Mandelslo / worinnen dessen OstJndianische Reise ü-
ber denOceanum enthalten. Zusampt eines kurtzenBerichts von jetzigem
Zustand des eussersten Orientalischen KönigReiches Tzina.
Durch
M. ADAMUM OLEARIUM, Ascanium Saxonem,
Fürstl: Schleßwig-Holsteinischen Hoff-mathemat.

Mit Röm. Käys. Maj. vnd Churfl. Durchl. zu Sachsen
privilegijs auff 10 Jahr bey Verlust Tausend Thlr. nicht
nachzudrucken.

Schleßwig/ Bey Jacob zur Glocken.Jm Jahr 1647.

82. TITLE PAGE, ADAM OLEARIUS,
*OFFT BEGEHRTE BESCHREIBUNG DER
NEWEN ORIENTALISCHEN REISE . . .*
(SCHLESWIG, 1647)

BERNHARDI VARENI
Med. D.
DESCRIPTIO
Regni Japoniæ
ET
SIAM.
Item
De Japoniorum Religione & Siamensium.
De Diversis omnium Gentium Religionibus.
Quibus, præmissâ Dissertatione de variis Re-
rum publicarum generibus, adduntur quæ-
dam de Priscorum Afrorum fide excerpta
ex Leone Africano.

CANTABRIGIÆ,
Ex Officina *Joan. Hayes*, celeberrimæ Academiæ Ty-
pographi. 1673.
Impensis *Samuelis Simpson* Bibliopolæ *Cantab.*

83.

DU
ROYAUME
DE SIAM

Par Monſieur de LA LOUBERE
Envoyé extraordinaire du ROY
auprés du Roy de Siam en 1687. &
1688.

TOME PREMIER.

A PARIS,
La Veuve de JEAN BAPTISTE COIGNARD,
Imprimeur & Libraire ordinaire du Roy.
ET
ez JEAN BAPTISTE COIGNARD, Imprimeur &
Libraire ordinaire du Roy, ruë S. Iacques,
à la Bible d'Or.
M. DC. XCI.
AVEC PRIVILEGE DE SA MAJESTE.

84.

THE
HISTORY
OF THE
INQUISITION,

As it is Exerciſed at

G O A.

Written in *French*, by the Ingenious Monſieur *Dellon*, who laboured five years under thoſe ſeverities.

With an Account of his Deliverance.

Tranſlated into Engliſh.

LONDON,
Printed for *James Knapton,* at the *Queens-
Head* , in St. *Paul's* Church-yard.
M DC LXXXVIII.

85.

ATHANASII KIRCHERI
E SOC. JESU

CHINA
MONUMENTIS

QUA

Sacris *quà* Profanis,

Nec non variis

NATURÆ & ARTIS
SPECTACULIS,

Aliarumque rerum memorabilium
Argumentis

ILLUSTRATA,
AUSPICIIS
LEOPOLDI PRIMI

ROMAN. IMPER. SEMPER AUGUSTI
Munificentißimi Mecænatis.

A Solis Ortu   IHS   ufque ad Occafū

Laudabile   Nomen Dñi.

AMSTELODAMI,

Apud *Joannem Janßonium à Waesberge* & *Elizeum Weyerstraet,*
ANNO cIↄ Iↄc LXVII. *Cum Privilegiis.*

86. TITLE PAGE, ATHANASIUS KIRCHER, *CHINA ILLUSTRATA*
(AMSTERDAM, 1667)

87. PORTRAIT OF ATHANASIUS KIRCHER

From Kircher, *op. cit.*, facing fol. 1.

Depiction is of Kircher at age sixty-two in 1664, or three years before the *China illustrata* was first published.

Johann Jacob Saars/

Ost-Indianische
Funfzehen-Jährige
Kriegs-Dienste/

Und

Wahrhafftige Beschreibung/

Was sich Zeit solcher funfzehen Jahr/
von Anno Christi 1644. biß Anno Christi 1659.
zur See/ und zu Land/ in offentlichen Treffen/ in Belåge-
rungen/ in Stürmen/ in Eroberungen/ Portugåsen/ und Heydnischer/ Plåtze
und Stådte/ in Marchirn, in Quartirn, mit Jhm/ und andern Seinen
Camerades begeben habe/ am allermeinsten auf der grossen/
und herrlichen/ Jnsul

CEILON.

Zum andern mahl heraus gegeben/

Und mit vielen denckwürdigen Notis oder Anmerckungen/
wie auch Kupfferstücken/ vermehret/ und gezieret.

Psal. XXIV. vers. 1.

Die Erde ist des HErrn/ und was darinnen ist; der Erd-
boden/ und was darauf wohnet. Denn Er hat Jhn
an die Meer gegründet/ und an den Wassern bereitet.

Nürnberg/

Zu finden bey Johann Daniel Tauber/ Buchhåndlern/
Gedruckt bey Johann-Philipp Miltenberger/
Im Jahr Christi/ 1672.

88. TITLE PAGE, JOHANN JACOB SAAR, *OST-
INDIANISCHE FÜNFZEHEN-JÄHRIGE KRIEGS-
DIENSTE UND WAHRHAFFTIGE BESCHREIBUNG . . .*
(NUREMBERG, 1672)

VOYAGE
DES
INDES
ORIENTALES,

Mêlé de plusieurs Histoires
curieuses.

Par Mr CARRÉ.

TOME PREMIER.

' A PARIS,

Chez la Veuve de CLAUDE BARBIN, au
Palais , sur le second Perron de
la Sainte-Chapelle.

M. DC. XCIX.

Avec Privilege du Roy.

89.

THE
TRAVELS
OF
Sig. Pietro della Valle,
A Noble ROMAN,
INTO
EAST-INDIA
AND
Arabia Deserta.

In which, the several Countries, together with the
Customs , Manners , Traffique , and Rites both
Religious and Civil, of those Oriental Princes
and Nations, are faithfully Described :

In Familiar Letters to his Friend

Signior MARIO SCHIPANO.

Whereunto is Added

A Relation of Sir THOMAS ROE's Voyage
into the EAST-INDIES.

LONDON,

Printed by J. Macock, for Henry Herringman ; and are to be
sold at his Shop at the Blew-Anchor in the Lower-walk of
the New-Exchange. 1665.

90.

DIARIUM,
Oder
Tage-Buch/

über
Dasjenige/

So sich Zeit einer neun-jährigen

Reise zu Wasser und Lande/ meistentheils
in Dienst der vereinigten geoctroyrten Niederländischen Ost-Indianischen Compagnie, besonders in
denselbigen Ländern täglich begeben
und zugetragen.

Worbey
Der Innwohner Glauben/ Leben/ Sitten
und Kleidung/ so mit Augen gesehen/ fleißig auffgeschrie-
ben/ abgerissen/ und mit Kupffern gezieret/ zur
besserer Nachricht verzeichnet
worden

von

Johann von der Behr/ Not. Publ. Cæf.

JENA/
In Verlegung Urbani Spaltholtzens/
Buchhändlers in Breßlau/
Anno 1668.

91. TITLE PAGE, JOHANN VON DER
BEHR, *DIARIUM*
See also pl. 71.

L. 2

HISTORIA
INDIAE
ORIENTALIS,
EX VARIIS AVCTORI-
BVS COLLECTA, ET IVXTA
SERIEM TOPOGRAPHICAM REGNO-
rum, Prouinciarum & Insularum, per Africæ,
Asiæque littora, ad extremos vsque Ia-
ponios deducta,

*QVA REGIONVM ET INSVLARVM
situs & commoditas; Regum & populorum mores &
habitus; Religionum & superstitionum absurda varie-
tas; Lusitanorum item Hispanorum & Batauorum res
gestæ atque Commercia varia, cum rebus admira-
tione & memoratu dignißimis alijs, iucun-
da breuitate percensentur atq,
describuntur.*

AVTORE
M. GOTARDO ARTHVS
Dantiscano,

COLONIAE · AGRIPPINAE,
SVMPTIBVS VVILHELMI
Lutzenkirch.
ANNO M. DC. VIII.

92.

DICTIONARIVM
MALAICO-LATINVM
&
LATINO-MALAICVM.

CVM ALIIS QVAMPLVRIMIS
quæ quarta pagina edocebit.

Opera & ſtudio

D A V I D I S   H A E X.

R O M Æ,
ls & impenſis Sac. Congr. de Propag. Fide.
M D C X X X I.
SVPERIORVM PERMISSV.

93.

NOORD en OOST
TARTARYE,
Ofte
BONDIGH ONTWERP
Van
Eenige dier landen, en volken, zo als
voormaels bekent zyn geweeſt.

Beneffens

Verſcheide tot noch toe onbekende, en meeſt nóit
voorheen beſchreve Tarterſche en nabuerige geweſten,
lantſtreken, ſteden, rivieren, en plaetzen, in de

NOORDER en OOSTERLYKSTE
GEDEELTEN
Van

ASIA en EUROPA,

Zo buiten en binnen de rivieren *Tanais* en *Oby*, als omtrent de
Kaſpiſche, Indiſche-Ooſter, en Swarte Zee gelegen ; gelyk de lant-
ſchappen *Niuche, Dauria, Jeſſo, Moegolia, Kalmakkia, Tangut, Usbek,
Noorder Perſie, Georgia, Circaſſia, Crim, Altin,* enz. mitsgaders *Tingoe-
ſia, Siberia, Samojedia,* en andere aen Hare Z A E R Z E
MAJESTEITEN Kroon gehoorende heerſchappyen :

Met der zelver Lant-Kaerten :

Zedert nauwkeurigh onderzoek van veele jaren, en eigen ondervindinge
beſchreven, geteckent, en in 't licht gegeven,

Door

N I C O L A E S   W I T S E N.

t' Amſterdam, in 't jaer M D C X C I I.

94. WITSEN, TITLE PAGE
Photo from the James Ford Bell Library,
University of Minnesota; used with
permission.

SOME YEARES
TRAVELS

INTO
DIVERS PARTS OF
Asia and Afrique.

Defcribing efpecially the two famous Empires, the *Perfian*, and great *Mogull*: weaved with the Hiftory of thefe later Times

As alfo, many rich and fpatious Kingdomes in the Orientall India, and other parts of Asia; Together with the adjacent Iles.

Severally relating the Religion, Language, Qualities, Cuftomes, Habit, Defcent, Fafhions, and other Obfervations touching them.

With a revivall of the firft Difcoverer of America.

Revifed and Enlarged by the Author.

Segnius irritant Animos demiſſa per Aures
Quam quæ funt Oculis Subjecta fidelibus, & Quæ
Ipfe fibi præbet Spectator. Horat.

LONDON,
Printed by R. Bi^p. for *Iacob Blome* and *Richard Bifhop*. 1638.

95. TITLE PAGE, THOMAS HERBERT

A
COLLECTION

OF

Voyages and Travels,

SOME

Now firft Printed from *Original Manufcri*

OTHERS

Now firft Publifhed in English.

In SIX VOLUMES.

WITH A

General PREFACE, giving an Account of the grefs of NAVIGATION, from its firft Beginnin

Illuftrated with a great number of ufeful Maps and C Curioufly Engraven.

VOL. II.

The THIRD EDITION.

LONDON:

Printed by Affignment from Meff^{rs}. CHURCHILL,
For HENRY LINTOT; and JOHN OSBORN, at the *Golden-Ball* in *Pater-nofte*
MDCCXLIV.

96. TITLE PAGE OF CHURCHILL'S *VOYAGES*, 1744 EDITION.

97. FRONTISPIECE, MONTANUS, *DIE GESANTSCHAFTEN AN DIE KEISER VAN JAPAN* (1669)

From a separately bound version of the report on the emissaries at the imperial court of Japan, part of Montanus' *Denckwürdige Gesandtschafften* (see pl. 27).

The Japanese figures and paraphernalia on the left and in the center are set up to contrast with the European figures in the lower right.

PREMIER LIVRE
DE L'HISTOIRE DE LA
NAVIGATION AVX INDES
ORIENTALES, PAR LES HOLLANDOIS,
ET DES CHOSES A EVX ADVENVES: ENSEMBLE
les conditions, les meurs, & manieres de vivres des Nations, par eux abordees.
Plus les Monnoyes, Espices, Drogues, & Marchandises, & le pris d'icelles.

*Davantage les decouvremens & apparences, situations, & costes maritimes des contrees: avec
le vray pourtrait au vif des habitans : Le tout par plusieurs figures illustré : tres-
recreatif a lire a tous navigans & amateurs des navigations
lointaines, ez terres estrangeres.*

Par G. M. A. W. L.

Imprimé à Amsterdam, chez Cornille Nicolas, demeurant
sur l'Eauë, au Livre à escrire. L'an 1609.

98. TITLE PAGE, LODEWYCKSZOON,
PREMIER LIVRE
Notice the inset figures of East Indians at the top of the
map. Pl. 32 is also from this book.

MODI LOQVENDI

CAyin itou mattiacan góg itou . *Veſtes cum iſto valore compenſantur, ponderantur, æſtimantur.*

Saràtos maccan ſapoulo. *Centum reddit decem pro vſura , vel intereſſe.*

Orang pandjangàcan itou . *Narrantes factum extollunt.*

Dia djouwàl kita-orang . *Ipſe nos prodit.*

Topayan pounja pantat . *Pes hydriæ.*

Oubat itou catoudjou dengan penjakit ini. *Huic morbo medicamen congruit.*

Soucor-oucor. *Neque plus , neque minus.*

Baua-ilang . *Auferre , vt perdatur.*

Itou djatou ilang . *Id cadit perditum.*

Itou ſamma doſa lipat duacàli. *Eſt duplex peccatum.*

Balà-dua . *In duas partes findere.* Bagi dua. *dupliciter diuiditur.*

Dia jadi menberannac . *Eſt natus.*

Tahan pada maccan . *Ab edendo ſeipſum abſtinere.*

Iſſonja dua boulan . *Duobus poſt diem menſibus.*

Kirim catta . *Alicui denuntiare , vel certiorem aliquem facere.*

Beta poutous tuan pounja bac attahàn . *Salua tua ratiocinatione, vel ſermonē tuum interrūpo.*

Ambil artinja . *Opinionem , vel ſententiam percipere.*

Beta jadi berjadi . *Sum creatus.*

Salàmat datan . *Aduentus felix.*

Lalou tenga malam. *Mediam poſt noctem.*

Tondo hati . *Cor inclinare , vel dimittere.*

Pækei parampouan . *Mulierem cognoſcere.*

Hari domingo jang de alouwan, *vel de mouca. Dominica dies appropinquans.* jang de belaccan . *elapſa dies dominica.*

Dia britàcau . *Nuntium attulit, vel in lucem protulit.*

Dia palut cayinja ca-àtas . *Ipſa ſuccingit , vel ſubducit veſticulam.*

Appa ongco fadouli . *Tua quid refert.*

Outang itou dia tanghong . *Ad ipſum debitum ſpectat , vel ſolutio ipſi incumbit.*

Bouda itou boulom tanghong doſa . *infans peccati expers , vel nulli adhuc crimini obnoxius.*

Djicca

99. MODES OF DISCOURSE: PHRASES IN MALAY WITH LATIN TRANSLATION
From David Haex, *Dictionarium* (Rome, 1631). See also pls. 93 and 100.

tia . *Item obſtinatus, pertinax* .

Djahit . *Suere* .

Djahittan . *Opus conſutile* .

Djala . *Funda , vel rete iaɫile* . mendjàla . *Piſcari funda* .

Djalac , *vel* gongong . *Latratus canum* .

Djalàm mendjalàm . *Immergere ſe aquis* . *Item* djilam .

Djàlan . *Semita , via* . bedjalan *ire* .bedjalan-acan bouda.*vnà cum puero ambulatum ire*.djalanrayat . *via regia* .

Djaloudjor . *Faſciare* .

Diam , *vel* diem. *T aeere,quieſcere* .

Djam . *Hora* .

Djama . *Culex* .

Djaman . *Seneɫus, ſenex* .

Djaman-mouda . *Iuuenta* .

Djambàtang . *Pons* .

Djambing . *Lancea, vel haſta breuior* .

Djambol . *Criſta* .

Djamoc , *vel* djama . *Culex* .

Djamor . *Boletus , fungus* .

Djandji . *Promittere* . *Item concordare,contrahere*, djandjihan *vel* berdjandjihan *promiſſum* . *Item aſſenſio , contraɫus* .

Djanghot . *Barba* .

Djankit . *Dicitur quotieſcumque morbus, vel qualiſcumque defeɫus aliquem arripit* . *morbo tamen , non perſona coniungitur* .

v. g. demàm djankit pada radja, *febri rex detinetur* .

Djantan . *Maſcula beſtia* . babbi tida mau bedjantan ; *ſus verri non colludit* .

Djoumauwa . *Præſumere , & arrogantē eſſe,veluti ſeipſum alteri præponere,vel arripere locum ſibi non conuenientem* .

Djantong. *Cor* . *Dicitur etiam* diantong piſſang , *de flore Bonannes , vnde racemus prodit* .

Dingin . *Frigidus* . *Dicitur etiam*. dia hati dingin, *remiſit ab ardore animi*. dingin *præterea applicatur ſi quando potum refrigeraſſe,vel leniter frigefaɫū dicimus* .

Djari-manis . *Aniſum* .

Djari-tanghan . *Digitus* .

Djari-caki . *Digitus pedis* .

Djaring . *Neɫere* . *contexere veluti retia* .

Djarong. *Acus* .

Djatim . *Orphanus* .

Djatou . *Cadere* .

Djau . *Taurus* .

Dien . *Ceraſum* .

Djenis . *Qualitas, ſpecies , modus*. banja-djenis *multifarius* .

Djentan . *Vide* djantan .

Djerat . *Laqueus* .

Djerni . *Clarus , inſtar aquæ,vel ſpeculi* .

Diga-

100. SAMPLE PAGE FROM A MALAY-LATIN WORDLIST
From Haex, *op. cit.* (pl. 99).

Teutsch.	Maleysch.	Teutsch.	Maleysch.
Kastel	Gourett.	Mißfallen	Tita bischouk.
Küß / darauf zu sit-zen	Banthal.	Mitleyden	Ampon.
Kalch	Capon.	Mensch	Oran Itou.
Kram	Rede.	Meinung	Haman.
Köstlicher Stein.	Batou.	Meinen	Jamman.
Kompaß	Podomman.	Machen	Boat.
Krebs	Catan.	Merken	Canda.
Klein	Citgill.	Meinen	Tzinta oder Ingat.
Kokos	Nior.	Meistern	Pande brpekat.
Kiesen	Pilv.	Messen	Ducor.
Kinder	Anack.	Mangeln	Toucaer.
Knien	Batillo.	Wegen	Dollee.
Knüpfen	Dabondaen	Murmeln	Bassongot.
Kämmen	Eiser.	Wild	Lapan can.
Rennen	Bakanal.	Weich	Kita.
Kommen	Datan.	Mein	Ponga.
Kauen	Giget.	Mager	Conras.
Kiesen / Zanken	Backelay.	Morgen	Isso.
Kessel	Pario tampak.	?ehe	Lagy.
Kerze	Damaer.	Minder	Couran.
Kuchen	Dapor.	Menge	Bayntan.
Kaste oder Kiste	Potti.	Müd	Lala.
Kinder	Anack.	Messer	Pisou.
Kuhe	Sappy.	Messerschmied	Pande pisou.
Knebel	Dangobt.	Maurer	Pagera.
Korn	Gabon.	Münze	Harta.
Klein	Kitsie.	Münzmeister	Pande Harta.
Kriegführen	Mouso.	Merre / Thier	Canda Parampuan.
Krank	Sakyt.	Maus	Ticos.
Krankheit	Sakytan.	Milch	Sousou.
		Magd	Anadara.
		Mund	Molot.
Land	Darat.	Mann	Lacky.
Ans Land gehen	Piggy darat.	Monat	Boulan.
Leuchter	Damaran.	Maß	Ocuran.
Lampe	Lamaran.	Mitgesell	Sobott.
Lehren	Blavgeer.	Mauer	Cota.
Lauffen	Ballary.	Markt	Passaer.
Legen	Barenty.	Mahlzeit	Tampa maranan.
Laden	Sarat Carl.	Meister	Pande bellagaet.
Logiren	Saling.	Meel	Capon.
Leiten	Ongoucan.	Mensch	Oran.
Leyhen	Meyngam.	Milz	Colomary.
Lachen	Tetaua.	Mörder	Pande bounon.
einen Laut geben/Läuten	Pacol gantan.	Müd	Ticaer.
Leben	Idop.	Mond	Boulan.
Liefern	Barycan.	Müße	Toudong.
Lassen	Tingalcan.	Mast	Tiang.
Liecht	Ringan.	Muskatennüsse	Palla.
Leckerhafftig	Calaparan.	Mittag	Tingary.
Los	Tzerade.	Mutter	Maa.
Lang	Pangan.	Mostart	Sasaue.
Leiter mit Sprossen	Tanga.		
Lacken oder Tuch	Cayn.	Nacken	Moampeer.
Langer Pfeffer	Tabee.	Nehen	Maniayt.
Laus	Cotto.	Nageln	Pocol pocou.
Lippen	Debeer.	Nennen / einen Na-men geben	Namania.
Leichnamb / Leib	Baden.	Niesen	Batou.
Liebe	Casse.	Nötigen / Laden	Pangil macan.
Leuchten	Tarran.	Nehmen	Ambil.
Lunten	Sombo.	Nachmittag essen	Macan zoere.
Lügen	Dousta.	Neigen	Boat hambaer.
Liebhaben	Gyma.	Naß machen	Basso.

Nachstehe

101. SAMPLE PAGE FROM A GERMAN–MALAY WORDLIST

From Olfert Dapper, *Umbständliche und eigentliche Beschreibung von Asia . . .* (Nuremberg, 1681).

In EUROPE, AFRICK, ASIA have I gonne;
One journey more, and then my travel's done

102. PORTRAIT OF REVEREND EDWARD TERRY AT AGE SIXTY–FOUR

Frontispiece to Terry, *A Voyage to East-India* (see pl. 73).
Engraving by Robert Vaughn.

Li S. Iean Francois Gemelli Careri
Iurisconsulte âge de 48 ans en 1699.

103. PORTRAIT OF GIOVANNI FRANCESCO GEMELLI
CARERI AT AGE FORTY–EIGHT

From Careri, *op. cit.* (pl. 28), Vol. I.

This is an edition revised and augmented by Careri
himself. According to the preface, he also added new
illustrations.

104. PORTRAIT OF SIR THOMAS ROE
From Purchas, *Hakluytus Posthumus* (Glasgow, 1905), IV,
between pp. 320 and 321.

105. PORTRAIT OF JORIS VAN SPILBERGEN AT AGE
FIFTY-FOUR

Frontispiece, *De reis van Joris van Spilbergen naar Ceylon,
Atjeh en Bantam, 1601–1604,* "*WLV,*" XXXVIII (The
Hague, 1933).
   Probably engraved by Jac. de Gheyn.

Illustri Generoso Domino Oveno Gjedde Dno de
Tommerup, Equiti Aurato Regni Daniæ Thalassiarcho
Senatori, Ser: Reg: Maj: Præfecto Helsingburgensi:

Alb: cuwichters pin.   Alb: Haelwegh sculp et excu Cum priv R.D.

106. PORTRAIT OF OVE GJEDDE, ALSO OVA GEDDES
Courtesy of Det Kongelige Bibliotek, Kort- og Billedafdelingen,
Copenhagen.
  Admiral of the Danish fleet sent to Ceylon in 1620. Founder of the
fort at Tranquebar on the Coromandel Coast of India, he returned to
Denmark in 1622. An ode to his voyage was published shortly after
his return, the work of J. M. Gottorp.

Other editions were later issued in Polish (Cracow, 1628), Flemish (Ghent, 1631), Italian (Venice, 1646), and Latin (Rome, 1658).

Andrade and a Jesuit brother had joined a group of pilgrims at Delhi in 1624 who guided them on a long overland trek to Srinagar, the capital of Kashmir. From there they were guided through the Himalayas to Tsaparang, capital of the "kingdom of Guge" in Tibet, by a mountaineer and two young converts. Once on the roof of the world, Andrade was received at court and questioned about the outside world and about his interest in Tibet. After a considerable delay, the king granted him in writing what he had actually come for—a permission to establish a mission station in Tibet. The only condition attached was that he should return the next year. Andrade set up a mission at Tsaparang in 1625 that endured for the next twenty-five years. Reports from this mission by Andrade and others were sent to Europe at irregular intervals, and a few of them were appended to the later translations of Andrade's original letter and included in the Jesuit letter-books.[165] Through Andrade's book and his later letters and those of others, Europe learned more about Tibet's location, size, political divisions, religion, and customs. The dispute about Tibet as Cathay was muted, for Andrade himself decided that Cathay was a great city rather than a kingdom and was located in a territory bordering China on the north.[166]

While rejoicing in Andrade's success, the Iberians were more than disconsolate over the mounting losses to the Dutch on the high seas and over the continuing persecution of the Christian missionaries and their converts in Japan. Solis, as remarked above, had warned about the decline of Portugal's naval strength because of shortages of men, ships, materials, and money. He and others fondly recalled in their writings the great sixteenth-century victories of the Portuguese on land and sea as a form of mild protest against its weakened and tottering state in the 1620's.[167] Others rejoiced in the victories that were occasionally being won by the Portuguese in their engagements with the Dutch and English fleets in the East.[168] The Spanish, who were tied

[165] For example, Andrade's letter from Tibet of August 15, 1626, was published by Pinheiro, who also included an extract from it in Manoel da Veiga's *Relaçam Geral do Estado da Christandade de Ethiopia . . . e do que de nouo socedeo no descobrimento do Thybet, a que chamam gram Catayo* (Lisbon, 1628); it also came out in Castilian translation (Segovia, 1628). It appeared in *Lettere Annuae* (Rome, 1628), pp. 3–58, in *Histoire de ce qui s'est passé* (Paris, 1629). For a summary of this letter see Streit, V, 107–8. For translations of some of the Jesuit letters about Tibet not published in the seventeenth century see the appendices to C. Wessels, *Early Jesuit Travellers in Central Asia, 1603–1721* (The Hague, 1924) and H. Hosten, S.J. (ed.), "A Letter of Father Francisco Godhino, S.J., from Western Tibet (Tsaparang, August 16, 1626)," *The Journal of the Asiatic Society of Bengal*, XXI (1925), 49–73.

[166] See Toscano, *op. cit.* (n. 164), p. 105. Also see below, pp. 375–76.

[167] For example, see Luys Coelho de Barbuda, *Impresa militares de Lusitanos* (Lisbon, 1623). He ends the story at 1607; also see Luis de Sousa, *Historia de la religion de Santo Domingo, particularmente en los reynos y conquistas de la corona de Portugal* (s.l., 1623).

[168] *Relación cierta y verdadera de la feliz vitoria y prosperos sucessos que en la India Oriental han conseguido los Portugueses, contra armados muy ponderosas de Olanda y Persia este año de 1624 . . .*

down in northern Europe, had increasingly to leave the protection of the king's overseas empire to the Portuguese. As a result the Portuguese began to act with increasing independence both in Europe and in Asia.

Enthusiasm for the national history and its heroes was reawakened in Portugal with the rise of a new independence movement. On the occasion of Philip III's triumphal visit to Lisbon in August, 1619, the Jesuits pointedly presented before him in the patio of their College of San Antão a tragedy in five acts by Antonio de Sousa (1591–1652) called *Descobrimento e conquista da India por D. Manuel I.*[169] Fernando Ulvia de Castro followed with a book of aphorisms and *exempla* extracted from the first of Barros' *Décadas da Asia.*[170] Manuel Severim de Faria (1583–1655), priest and minor literary figure of Evora, published in 1624 his *Discursos varios politicos* (Evora) which included the first detailed biographies of Barros, Camoëns, and Couto to appear in print. This was followed in 1628 by the first reprinting in Portuguese of the initial three of Barros' *Décadas* and by a biography of Dom Luis de Ataide, the last viceroy of India before Portugal came under the sway of Philip.[171] In 1630 Father Lourenço de Mendonça, a native of Sesimbra in Portugal, addressed a supplication to the king requesting for the Portuguese the same rights in Spanish America that the Castilians enjoyed in Portuguese Asia.[172] An Augustinian friar, Antonio Freyre (1568–1634) published at Lisbon in 1630 an *Elogio do livro "primor e honra da vida soldatisca no estado da India."*

That the decade of the 1620's produced great concern in Iberia over the future of the Eastern empire is well illustrated by reference to the Latin work of Serafim de Freitas, a Portuguese professor of canon law at the University of Valladolid. His *De iusto imperio lusitanorum asiatico* (1625) was written as the official Spanish reply to the *Mare liberum* (1609) published anonymously by the young Hugo Grotius to justify the Dutch entrance into the East Indian trade.[173] In his justification of the Catholic-Iberian claim to

---

(Madrid, 1624); *Relación de la batalla, que Nuno Alvarez Botello . . . tuvo con los armadas de Olanda y Inglaterra en el estrecho de Ormuz* (Seville, 1626); and Francisco de Abreu (pseud. of Manuel Severim de Faria), *Relaçao universal do que sucedeu em Portugal e nas mais provincias do Ocidente e Oriente desde março de 625 até setembro de 625, desde março de 626 até agôsto de 627* (Evora, 1628).

[169] For its text see João Mimoso Sardinha (also Sardina), *Relación de la real tragicomédia con que los padres . . . recibieron . . . Felipe II de Portugal, y de su entrada en este Reino . . .* (Lisbon, 1620), pp. 125ff.

[170] Entitled *Aphorismos y exemplos politicos, y militares. Sacados de la priméira década de Juan de Barros* (Lisbon, 1621).

[171] Ternaux-Compans (p. 158) gives J. Pereyra de Macedo as the author and the date as 1629; this edition is not confirmed in other bibliographical aids. The catalog of the British Library lists an identical title, perhaps a reprint, as being published at Madrid in 1633.

[172] Published in Madrid.

[173] Grotius knew about Freitas' attack, but did not deign to reply to it. The first vernacular translation of Freitas' work appeared only in 1882, and then in French. It finally received a Spanish translation in 1925, three hundred years after it was first issued. For an analysis of the substance of the Grotius-Freitas controversy see C. H. Alexandrowicz, *An Introduction to the History of the Law of Nations in the East Indies (Sixteenth, Seventeenth, and Eighteenth Centuries)* (Oxford, 1967), chaps. iii and iv.

exclusive rights of empire in Asia, Freitas evinces both a great pride in Portugal's past achievements and a terrifying fear of imminent losses. His compatriots, both in Spain and Portugal, surely must have experienced similar feelings of despair as they read in pamphlets and books, or heard in sermons, about the numerous and continuing martyrdoms in Japan and the growing threat to the Philippines from the naval depredations of the Dutch.[174]

While the Japanese had officially severed all relations with Manila in 1624 and had ordered the deportation of all Spaniards, a few Spanish missionaries bravely continued to work in Japan. In 1626 the Jesuit Baltasar de Torres (b. 1563) of Granada and seven of his colleagues were executed at Nagasaki. News of this event was gathered from the Jesuit letters to Spain, probably by Antonio de Torres y Quesada, and published at Salamanca in 1630 and at Barcelona under a somewhat different title in the following year.[175] Torres, who had been in Japan since 1600, was burned along with the Portuguese provincial, Francesco Pacheco, who had outraged the shogun by coming into the country secretly with Portuguese merchants of Macao, whose business the Japanese still cultivated. At Madrid in 1633 the Jesuit Matias de Sousa (1596–1647) published a compendium of the successes won by Christianity in Japan followed by a report on the martyrdoms of 1629 and 1630.[176] Two years later the Japanese linguist and procurator of missions at Lisbon, Francisco Rodriguez, published in Madrid a catalog of the Jesuits martyred in Japan during 1632 and 1633 based on letters which arrived at Lisbon from Macao in 1635.[177] This relation was thereafter translated into Latin (Antwerp, 1636), Flemish (Antwerp, 1636), and Italian (Rome, 1636).[178]

Despite the martyrdoms and the prohibitions against entry, the missionaries persisted in their efforts to evangelize in Japan. In 1637 a group of Augustinians was executed; the account of their martyrdom was prepared and published at Manila in 1638 by Martin Claver (d. 1646), then prior of an Augustinian convent at Pasig in the Philippines.[179] Early in 1637 a group of Dominicans suffered martyrdom, their story being relayed to Europe in a tract prepared by Domingo Gonzáles (1574–1647), their provincial in the Philippines, which was published at Madrid in 1639.[180] The Neapolitan Jesuit, Marcello Francesco Mastrilli (1603–37) entered Japan illegally in 1635 and was executed two years later at Nagasaki.[181]

---

[174] For example, see the numerous Jesuit and Dominican letters that were published at presses in Spain, Mexico, Peru, and the Philippines about the valor displayed by the Christians in the martyrdoms of 1622. Or consult the work of Fernando da Silva, Spanish official in the Philippines, which treats of both threats: *Verissima relación en que se da quenta en el estado en que estan las guerras en las Filipinas, y reynos de el Japon, contra los Olandeses* . . . (Seville, 1626).

[175] *Relación de alguns de las cosas tocantes a la vida y glorioso martyrio que con su Provincial y otros siete Religiosos de la Compañio de Jesus, padecio el S. P. Baltasar de Torres; sacada de las cartas autenticas, que han venido del Japon* . . . (Salamanca, 1630). For the difference in titles see Streit, V, 528, 531.

[176] For the full title see Streit, V, 538.

[177] For the full title see *ibid.*, p. 543.

[178] See *ibid.*, p. 544.

[179] See *ibid.*, p. 548.

[180] See *ibid.*, pp. 435, 550.

[181] For his story see below, pp. 345–46.

Two months after Mastrilli's death, the Shimabara insurrection broke out in Japan. Whether the Christians and the Portuguese were responsible for the outbreak or not, the Tokugawa regime crushed the revolt in April, 1638, massacred thousands of Japanese converts, and forbade entry to all subjects of the king of Spain. The Portuguese, especially the merchants and missionaries at Macao, were determined not to accept the edict of closure and sought by various means to reopen negotiations with the Tokugawas. In Europe the Portuguese bitterly charged the Spanish with responsibility for their exclusion from Japan.

The Dominicans, who had suffered in Japan as much as any of the orders, were contemporaneously advancing their cause in the Philippines. The relationship between the two missions is best exemplified by the colorful career of Diego Collado (d. 1638), a Spanish Dominican. Collado had arrived in the Philippines in 1611 and eight years later went to Japan. There he met and worked with Jacinto Orfanel, the historian of the Dominican mission to Japan. Orfanel's historical compilation covering the years from 1602 to 1620 remained in manuscript when he was burned at the stake in 1622. Collado, who was delegated to return to Rome in 1622 as procurator of missions, took Orfanel's manuscript to Europe. During his years in Europe, Collado prepared Orfanel's book for publication and extended it to include the years to 1622. In 1630 he memorialized King Philip IV of Spain about the conditions and needs of the missions in Asia,[182] and in 1631–32 he published at Rome his works on the Japanese language.[183] At Madrid in 1633 Collado published Orfanel's augmented *Historia ecclesiastica de los sucessos de la christiandad en Japon, desde . . . 1602 . . . hasta . . . 1622*. The following year, before embarking once again for the Philippines, Collado addressed a memorial to the king in which he dwelt at length on the disputes between the Jesuits and the other orders in Asia.[184] Upon arriving at Manila, Collado sought to divide the Dominican province into two parts and to establish training centers in one of them for missionaries destined for China and Japan. Thwarted in this project, Collado was disciplined by his superiors. He left the Philippines in 1638 and died on the return trip in a shipwreck.

Collado was opposed and disciplined by Diego Aduarte (1569–1636), Dominican bishop of the province of Nueva Segovia on the island of Luzon. Aduarte first went to the Philippines in 1595; four years later he visited Macao, Cambodia, and Malacca, on a return trip to Europe. In 1607, after another brief period in the Philippines, he was named official procurator in

---

[182] Two of his printed memorials are in the British Library.

[183] *Modus confitendi et examinandi poenitentem Iaponensem, formula suamet lingua japonica* (Rome, 1631); *Ars grammaticae japonicae linguae* (Rome, 1632); *Dictionarium sive thesauri linguae japonicae compendium* (Rome, 1632). For a description of the *Ars grammaticae* see M. Cooper, S.J., *Rodrigues the Interpreter. An Early Jesuit in Japan and China* (New York, 1974), pp. 236–37.

[184] "Mémorial présenté à Philippe IV. . . ," in *Annales de la Société des soi-disans Jésuites . . .* III (1764).

Europe for the Philippine mission. He served his order thereafter in various capacities in Spain, Mexico, and France. Back in the Philippines in 1628, he wrote several relations of the martyrdoms and persecutions in Japan that were published in Manila (1629, 1631), Rome (1632), and Seville (1632).[185] Meanwhile, he was engaged in compiling the materials and writing the text of his pioneer history of the Dominican province of Santo Rosario in the Philippines. Since Aduarte died before completing the *Historia*, Domingo Gonzáles brought it down to 1636, added a biography of Aduarte, and had it published at Manila in 1640.[186]

In its published form, Aduarte's *Historia* chronicled the affairs of the missionary province from its founding in 1587 to 1636. From the outset the Province of Santo Rosario was designed to make the Philippines into the center of the Dominican enterprise in the East. From Manila the preaching friars could readily embark on missions to the Marianas, the Moluccas, Cambodia, China, and Japan, as well as to the southern Philippines. Aduarte's book is therefore a history of the entire East Asian and Pacific enterprises of the Dominicans to the death of Aduarte in 1636. The first volume deals with Dominican activities in the Philippines, China, and Cambodia before 1615. The second commences with an account of the persecutions of 1614–15 in Japan and carries that story to 1633. Interspersed among the chapters on Japan are accounts of the friars' activities on Formosa and in China and Cambodia. Of particular interest is the account of the permanent Dominican penetration of China between 1626 and 1635, when their fortunes were ebbing in Japan. It was to this waiting harvest that Collado, despite the objections of Aduarte and his sympathizers in the Philippines, wanted to send more friars as reapers of souls.[187]

The Dominicans in Europe likewise were watching the progress of their colleagues in Asia. Juan Garcia (also called Juan de la Cruz Garcias) wrote from the Philippines a report on the state of Christianity in the Philippines, China, and Japan that was published at Seville in 1633.[188] Five years later Garcia accompanied a group of Franciscans and Dominicans to Formosa and entered China's Fukien province from there.[189] At Lisbon in 1635 there was published a collection of three treatises by the Portuguese Dominicans António da Encarnação (d. *ca.* 1672), a teacher of theology in Goa, and

[185] At least two were published at Seville in 1632.

[186] Reissued in 1693 as the first part of a new history of the Philippine mission. The modern edition was prepared by Manuel Ferrero and published as Vol. XIV of the Biblioteca "Missionalia Hispanica" under the title: *Historia de la provincia del Santo Rosario de la orden de predicadores en Filipinas, Japon, y China* (2 vols.; Madrid, 1962–63).

[187] On Collado's brush with Aduarte, see De la Costa, *op. cit.* (n. 66), pp. 377–78.

[188] *Aviso que se ha embiado do . . . Manila, del estado que tiena la religion . . . en las Philipanas, Japon y . . . China.* Contemporaneously Juan Bautista de Morales (1597–1664), a Spanish Dominican, was preparing in China his *Linguae sinicae grammatica ars.*

[189] See Lorenzo Pérez, "Fr. Francisco de Jesús de Escalona y su Relación de China," *Extractum ex periodice Archivum Franciscanum historicum,* VIII (1915), 560.

Miguel Rangel (d. 1645), bishop of Cochin, sketching the activities of the Dominicans in the Indies.[190] Two of these treatises were devoted entirely to the mission on the island of Solor. Rangel's contains more information about Solor and its people than any other account published during the century.[191] Encarnação subsequently prepared other relations on missionary activities in the East, most of which were never published.[192]

During the 1630's the missionaries in the East actively studied the local languages and prepared vocabularies, grammars, and translations. A Spanish version of the Portuguese-Japanese dictionary of 1603 was issued at Manila in 1630 at the Dominican College of St. Thomas.[193] The Augustinian Pedro de Herrera (d. 1648), called by Father Gaspar de San Agustín "the Horace of Tagalog," published a confessional in that language at Manila in 1636.[194] Another Augustinian, Alonso de Mentrida (1559–1637), issued in the following year a dictionary of the Bisayan language and two of its dialects.[195] In India, meanwhile, the Jesuits translated several doctrinal tracts into Indian languages in an effort to show the stubborn Brahmans the error of their ways.[196]

Constantly on the defensive in India and on the high seas, the Iberians regularly bemoaned their losses and occasionally celebrated their victories. The names and deeds of those who had served the crown in the Indies appeared in print around 1630.[197] New or revised rutters for pilots and suggestions for altering the *padrón* (official map) likewise continued to appear.[198] Books honoring the soldiers and sailors fighting and dying in the East were occasionally published. Manoel Xavier (1602–61), a Jesuit educator of Goa, celebrated the efforts of Governor Nuno Alvarez Botelho to relieve the siege

---

[190] *Relaçoēs summarias de alguns serviços que fizerão a Deos, e a estes reynos, os religiosos Dominicos nas partes da India Oriental nestes annos proximos passados.* A modern edition is in Artur Basilio de Sá, *Documentação para a história das missões do padroado português do oriente. Insulindia* (5 vols.; Lisbon, 1958), Vol. V, pp. 227–347.

[191] Encarnação's treatise is entitled *Relaçam do principio da Christandade das ilhas de Solor, e da segunda restauração della, feita pellos religiosos da ordem dos prégadores;* Rangel's is *Relaçam das Christandades, e ihas de Solor, em particular, da fortaleza, que para emparo dellas foi feita.* . . .

[192] In 1665 another of his summaries was published at Lisbon. See Streit, V, 122, 161.

[193] Tomas Pinpin and J. Megaurha, *Vocabulario de Japón declarado primero en Portugues.* . . .

[194] *Confessionario en lengua Tagala.* Also see Streit, V, 344, A. de S. Gregorio published at Manila in 1645 a book in Tagalog explaining the mysteries of the Christian faith.

[195] *Diccionario de lingua Bisaya, Heligueyna y Harara de la isla de Panaē y Sugbu y para las demas islas* (Manila). Also see Streit, V, 271.

[196] Diego Ribeiro (trans.), *Declaraçam de doutrina christam collegida do cardinal Roberto Belarmino da Cōpanhia de Iesu e outros autores composta em lingoa Bramana vulgar* . . . (Rachol, 1632); Estêvão da Cruz, *Discursos sobre a vida do apostolo s. Pedro em que se refutão os principaes errores do oriente compostos em verso, em lengua bramana* . . . (2 vols.; Goa, 1634).

[197] Francisco García de Avila, *Para que se devan preferir todos los que huvieron servido en las Indias a su Majestad en conformidade de un decreto suyo* [Madrid].

[198] For example, *Memoria de lo que an de advertír los pilotos de la carrera de las Indias, a cerca de la reformación del padron de las cartas de marear, y los demas instrumentos de que usan, para saber las alturas y derrotas de sus viages.*

of Malacca in 1629–30. Published at Lisbon in 1633, after news of Botelho's death in battle became known, Xavier's book was dedicated to, and seen through the press by, Manuel Severim de Faria, the biographer of Barros. The Goa Jesuit apparently corresponded with and sent his manuscripts to Faria on a regular basis.[199] Pedro Barreto de Resende (d. 1651), who had acted in Goa as private secretary to Viceroy Dom Miguel de Noronha (r. 1629–35) returned to Lisbon in 1635 with plans and descriptions of India's cities and fortresses. None of these was published at the time, but they were later used by the historian Bocarro in preparing the *Livro das fortalezas da India,* finally published in 1936.[200] Others wrote accounts of maritime disasters, a genre of literature that had become popular in the sixteenth century.[201] Accounts of victories over the Dutch on land and sea continued to attract public attention.[202]

For Spain the protection and control of the Philippine Islands remained a matter of constant and mounting concern, particularly after France became actively involved in 1635 in the Thirty Years' War in Europe. The missionaries sent reports about the political situation in the Philippines to their superiors and associates in Spain that were then printed there to disseminate more widely the news they contained.[203] Of particular interest to Spanish readers were the events surrounding the life of Marcello Francesco Mastrilli (1603–37), the Neapolitan Jesuit. In 1633, while helping to dismantle an altar at the Jesuit College of Naples, Mastrilli was hit on the head by a hammer dropped by a carpenter. When the doctors despaired of saving his life, Mastrilli asked that a painting of St. Francis Xavier be placed beside his bed. Presumably cured by Xavier's intercession, the Italian Jesuit set out for Japan to fulfill a promise made to the saint, and his story became a part of miracle literature.[204] Mastrilli was driven by storms to the Philippines on his way to Japan, and his story attracted the attention of the public and the authorities

---

[199] Xavier's report is entitled *Victorias do governador da India Nuno Alvares Botelho* (Lisbon, 1633). See Streit, V, 120.

[200] Offprint from the *Arquivo português oriental.* This was an important book on the military condition of the Portuguese in India *ca.* 1630.

[201] Nuño da Conceiçam, *Relaçam, successo e viagem da capitaina N. senhora do Bom Despacho vindo da India* (Lisbon, 1631); José Cabreira, *Naufragio da náo Belem* (Lisbon, 1636). Both of these were reprinted in the eighteenth-century collection, *Historia tragico-maritima,* of Gomes de Brito. See *Asia,* II, Bk. 1, 131–35.

[202] See the little book in the Cleveland Public Library by Salvador do Coreto de Sampayo, *Relaçam dos successos victoriosos que na barra de Goa ouve dos Olandeses Antonio Tellez de Menezes, capitano geral do mar da India, nos annos de 1637 à 1638* (Coimbra, 1639); and *Relación de los successos de las armas españolas por mar y tierra en las islas Filippinas, y victorias contra Mindanao y con los Olandeses de Terrenate* (Madrid, 1639). This second tract is translated into English in BR, XXIX, 116–34.

[203] For example, the Augustinian father Diego de S. Juan Evangelista sent from Manila a letter to the prior of Zaragossa of the same order which was published at Madrid in 1636. See Streit, V, 541.

[204] *Relación de un prodigiosos milagro que San Francisco Xavier Apostel de la India ha hecho en la ciudad de Napoles este año de 1634* (Madrid, 1634). The story of Mastrilli's vision and martyrdom

of Manila.[205] Sebastián Hurtado de Corcuera, the governor and captain-general of the Philippines, invited the Neapolitan to act as chaplain to the expedition of 1637 against Magindanau in Mindanao. On June 2 of that year Mastrilli sent to the Jesuit provincial of the Philippines an account written at Taytay of the glorious Spanish victory over the Moros.[206] Shortly thereafter he departed for Japan, where he was beheaded at Nagasaki on October 17, 1637. In Europe brief relations of Mastrilli's martyrdom appeared shortly thereafter in Spanish and French.[207]

Mastrilli's report of the Magindanau campaign was included in the *Relación* of Diego de Bobadilla (1590–1648) published in 1638.[208] Bobadilla had spent twenty-two years in the Philippines before being sent in 1637 to Rome as procurator for the Jesuit mission. On his way to Europe he had his *Relación* published in Mexico. While in Europe he prepared a description, probably in 1640, of the Philippines, which remained in manuscript until it was translated into French and published in the 1696 edition of M. Thévenot's *Relations de divers voyages curieux.*[209]

Thévenot also included in his collection an account of affairs in the Philippines written by Admiral Don Geronymo de Bañuelos y Carrillo which had been published originally in Mexico in 1638.[210] At Madrid in 1639 an anonymous publication appeared describing Corcuera's campaign in Jolo in 1636–37.[211] These writings provided contemporaries with a fairly complete picture of Spanish successes against the Moros of the southern Philippines and are still the principal sources for Corcuera's campaigns.[212]

At Madrid, meanwhile, a debate raged at court over whether to abandon or hold the Philippines. In response to those who advocated abandonment, Juan Grau y Monfalcón, the state's procurator-general in Spain for Manila and the Philippines, addressed a lengthy informatory memorial to the crown that was published in 1637.[213] He stresses especially the importance of Ma-

---

was included by Juan Eusebio Nieremberg in his compilation (1645) recording the miracles of saints Ignatius of Loyola and Francis Xavier.

[205] See H. de la Costa, *op. cit.* (n. 66), pp. 383–84.

[206] Published at Madrid in 1645 (?). Translated ino English in BR, XXVIII, 253–305.

[207] For the titles see Streit, V, 547, 551.

[208] *Relación de las gloriosas victorias de D. Sebastian Hurtado de Corcuera . . . en mar y tierra, contra Cuchil Curralat.* Translated in BR, XXIX 86–101.

[209] Published in Paris. Bobadilla's work is in Vol. I, Pt. 2. For an English version see BR, XXIX, 277–311.

[210] *Del estado de las Philippinas y conveniencias de ellas.* Translated into English in BR, XXIX, 66–85.

[211] *Continuacion de los felices successos.* . . . H. de la Costa, *op. cit.* (n. 66), p. 663, n. 16 names Manila as the place of publication; the catalog of the British Library gives Madrid. For an English translation see BR, XXIX, 116–34.

[212] Corcuera himself wrote a memorial to the king on the ecclesiastical affairs of the Philippines that was published at Madrid around 1638. A copy is in the British Library. For other materials see BR, XXVII, 346–63.

[213] His *Memorial informatorio . . .* is in the Newberry Library (Chicago). For an English translation see BR, XXVII, 55–212.

nila and the islands to Eastern trade, to New Spain, and to the homeland itself. His memorial is particularly valuable for the specific detail it includes on products, routes, and revenues. Grau y Monfalcón followed the initial memorial with another of the next year which reinforces and explains further the points he had earlier made.[214] In 1640, while revolt against Madrid was in progress at Barcelona and Lisbon, Grau y Monfalcón again urged in print the retention of the Philippines for commercial reasons.[215] The last fourteen sections of this tract include the texts of four royal decrees on Philippine commerce and on the need for its continuation.

In the turbulent 1640's the friars in India kept Europe informed about religious and political changes at Goa and elsewhere on the subcontinent. The Augustinian Diogo de Santa Anna, in a Lisbon publication of 1640, reported on a miraculous crucifix kept in the choir of the chapel in the monastery of Monjos at Goa.[216] At Barcelona two works by the Franciscan Miguel de Purificação discussed Franciscan activities in the Indian province of St. Thomas and raised questions about elevating Indian-born Franciscans to positions of responsibility.[217] The Dominican vicar-general Manoel de Crus in 1641 delivered a discourse celebrating the installation of the count of Aveiras as viceroy of India, the last such official to be appointed by a Habsburg king. The text of this speech was printed at Goa in 1641 and republished at Lisbon in the following year.[218] Two years later Manoel Iacome de Misquita, a magistrate of Goa, published a summary of what happened in Portuguese India and Macao upon the acclamation of King John IV in those places.[219] At Lisbon in 1644 João Marques Moreira printed the *Relação da acclamação del Rey D. Joao IIII, na China.*[220]

---

[214] This tract includes eighty-one numbered paragraphs.

[215] *Justificación de la conservación, y comercio de las islas Filipinas* (Madrid, 1640 [?]). French translation in TR, Vol. I, No. 29.

[216] *Relaçam verdadeira do milagroso portento e portentoso milagre q aconteceo na India no santo crucifixo, q esta no coro do observantissimo mosteiro das Freiras de S. Monica da cidade de Goa, em oito de Feuereiro de 1636. & continuou por muitos dias . . .* A Spanish translation appeared in Madrid, also in 1640. See Streit, V, 127.

[217] *Relação defensiva dos filhos da India . . .* (1640); and *Vida evangelica de los frayles menores en Oriente* (1641).

[218] *Fala, que fes O. P. Manoel de Crus . . . no acto solemne, emque o conde, Ioam de Silva, Tello y Meneses, Visorey . . . da India.* For a reproduction of the title page and a bibliographical summary see C. R. Boxer, "A Tentative Check-List of Indo-Portuguese Imprints," *Arquivos do centro cultural português,* IX (1975), 583–85; for a modern reprinting see C. R. Boxer, *A Acclamação del Rei D. João IV em Goa e em Macau. Relaçõis contemporanes reeditas e annotadas* (Lisbon, 1932), pp. 49–66. The count was Viceroy from 1641 to 1646.

[219] *Relaçam do que socedeo nacidade de Goa, e em todas as mais cidades e fortalezas . . . da India* (Goa, 1643). For a reproduction of the title page and a bibliographical summary see Boxer, "Tentative Check-List" (n. 218), pp. 587–88; for a modern reprinting see Boxer, *op. cit.* (n. 218), pp. 11–47. For an annotated English translation of the portion relating to Macao see Boxer, *Macau na época da Retauração, Macau Three Hundred Years Ago* (Macao, 1942), pp. 123–32; also reprinted in the new edition published at Hongkong in 1984, pp. 175–76.

[220] Cited in Ternaux-Compans, p. 180.

4

THE RESTORATION ERA, 1641–1700

Antonio de Mariz Carneiro (d. 1666), cosmographer-major of newly independent Portugal, published in 1642 the first in a new series of rutters on the sea-lanes of the East.[221] The Indo-Portuguese Franciscan Gonçalo de S. José Velloso published at Goa in 1642 an account of an ill-fated embassy of 1638 that had been sent from Goa to the sultan of Acheh in Sumatra.[222] The Habsburgs of Spain confronted in 1640 by rebellion in Lisbon, Barcelona, and Naples, soon learned of new uprisings by the Chinese in the Philippines.[223] At Lisbon in 1643 Antonio Ficalho Ferreira (d. *ca.* 1646) published a brief account of a voyage made from Portugal to Macao.[224] Stories of shipwrecks on distant seas likewise continued to appear in Portugal while the war against Spain went on in Iberia.[225]

Nor was Japan forgotten about in Portugal. Bartholomeu Pereira (1588–1650), a Portuguese Jesuit, published at Coimbra in 1640 a Latin work celebrating the martyrdom of Francesco Pacheco at Nagasaki in 1626.[226] At Manila there appeared in print in 1641 the story of the martyrdom of D. A. de Almeida.[227] Antonio Francisco Cardim (1596–1659), a Portuguese Jesuit superior located in Macao, sent back to Lisbon a report that was printed in 1643 of the execution at Nagasaki in 1640 of four Portuguese emissaries sent to Japan from Macao.[228] Translations of this account quickly appeared in French, Italian, and Dutch. Contemporaneously a letter on the Shimabara

[221] *Regimento de pilotos e roteiro des navagçaoës et de India oriental* (Lisbon, 1642). Other compilations were published under his name in 1655 and 1666. For a critical discussion of Mariz Carneiro see Boxer, *loc. cit.* (n. 23), pp. 183–84.

[222] *Iornada que Francisco de Souza de Castro . . . fez ao Achem.* Reprinted with an introduction, notes, and facsimile of the text by C. R. Boxer, "Uma obra rarissima impressa em Goa no século XVII," *Boletim internacional de bibliografia Luso-Brasileira,* VIII (1967), No. 3, pp. 431–528. On Velloso's subsequent activities in the East see A. Meersman, *The Franciscans in the Indonesian Archipelago* (Louvain, 1967), pp. 168–72.

[223] *Relación verdadera del Levantamiento que les Sangleyes o Chinos hizieron en las Filipinas y de las vitorias que tuvo contra ellos el Governador Don Sebastian Hurtado de Corcuero, el año passado de 1640 y 1641* (Madrid, 1643). For an excerpt of this anonymous work in English translation see BR, XXIX, 257–58.

[224] *Relação do viagem a cidade de Macao* is an eleven-page memoir.

[225] *Naufragio, que fizeramos duas náos de India: O Sacramento, nosso Senhora da Atalya, no cabo de Boa Esperança* (Lisbon, 1648 [?]). Included also in the *Historia tragico-maritima* of Bernardo Gomes de Brito. Also see Francisco Manuel, *Ecco politico responde en Portugal la voz de Castilla sobre los interezes de la corona Lusitana y del Oceanico . . .* (Lisbon, 1645).

[226] *Paciecidos libri XII. Decantatur P. Franciscus Paciecus Lusitanus. . . . Japponiae provincialis. . . .*

[227] Alonso Mendez, *Relacion del martyrio de D. A. de Almeida.* Reference from Ternaux-Compans, p. 177.

[228] *Relação da gloriosa morte de quatro embaixadores Portuguezes da cidade de Macau . . .* (Lisbon). For later Portuguese efforts to penetrate Japan after this dramatic expression of uncompromising severity see C. R. Boxer, *A Portuguese Embassy to Japan (1644–47) Translated from an Unpublished Portuguese Ms., and Other Contemporary Sources, with Commentary and Appendices* (London, 1928).

revolt of 1637 written by a Portuguese sea captain, in prison at Omura when the uprising occurred, was published at Lisbon.[229]

A valuable account of conditions in China at the end the Ming dynasty was prepared by the Jesuit Alvarez Semedo (1585[86?]–1658). Semedo first worked as a missionary in China from 1613 to 1637. Over this period of twenty-four years he traveled widely in the interior. Like Trigault before him, Semedo was eventually sent back to Europe as procurator in Rome for the China mission. On the return voyage, he completed at Goa in 1638 his *Relação da propagação da fé no regno da China e outras adjacentes*. It was evidently this Portuguese original that came into the hands of Manuel de Faria y Sousa (1590–1649), the historian, who put it into historical form and order and had a Spanish translation printed in 1642.[230] In the meantime an Italian version was being prepared at Rome by Gianbattista Giattini under the watchful eye of the author. This text, which should probably be considered the preferred one, was soon translated into French (1645) and English (1655).[231] Excerpts from it were published in contemporary French, Latin, and German compilations.[232] In the seventeenth century and since, Semedo's *China* has been esteemed a reliable and comprehensive firsthand account by a keen foreign observer of the growing tumult that accompanied the last years of Ming rule.[233]

Substantial also was the *Itinerario* of Sebastião Manrique (d. 1669) first published in 1649. A native of Oporto, Manrique entered the order of the Augustinian Eremites at Goa in 1604. After a career as a missionary on India's west coast, Manrique went to Bengal in 1628 to join the Augustinian mission at Hugli that had been founded in 1599. From 1629 to 1636 he traveled and worked in Arakan. Back at Goa in 1637 he was dispatched by his superiors to "visit" the Augustinian missions in China and the Philippines. Three years later he returned to India for a brief period before setting out for Europe to become procurator for his order. He took the overland route and after an arduous three-year journey arrived at Rome in July, 1643. Here he set to work composing the story of his travels from 1629 to 1643. Written in

---

[229] Duarte Correa, *Relaçam do alevantamento de Ximabara* (1643). See Murdoch and Yamagata, *op. cit.* (n. 43), II, 649n., and Streit, V, 546.

[230] *Imperio de la China, i cultura evangelica en el por los religiosos de la Compania de Jesus* (Madrid) On Faria y Sousa see below, pp. 354–55.

[231] Following the discussion of E. M. Rivière in the *Supplément* (Vol. XII; 1968) to A. and A. de Backer and E. Sommervogel, *Bibliothèque de la Compagnie de Jésus* (Louvain, 1960), col. 806. This same bibliographer attributes to Semedo, on the basis of the title to its French translation (1643), the anonymous *Breve recompilação do principios, continuação, e estado da Christiandade de China* (Lisbon, 1642). Also see H. Cordier, *Bibliotheca sinica* (5 vols., Paris, 1904), col. 817; and Streit, V, 778.

[232] See Cordier, *op. cit.* (n. 231), cols. 25–26.

[233] We have used the English translation: *The History of that Great and Renowned Monarchy of China* (London, 1655). For an evaluation and a comparison of it to the Chinese sources on the Ming, see Chen Min-sun, "Three Contemporary Western Sources on the History of Late Ming and the Manchu Conquest of China" (Ph.D. diss., Dept. of History, University of Chicago, 1971), pp. 21–137.

an atrocious Castilian, the first edition of the *Itinerario de las missiones* appeared at Rome in 1649.[234] Four years later a new printing of the text of the first edition was issued at Rome by another printer and with a different title page. This second edition was reissued at Lisbon in 1946.[235] Manrique's travels are still valued as an excellent source for the study of seventeenth-century northern India and Arakan (Burma).[236]

In Portugal itself the exploits of leading figures of the past were celebrated to inspire and strengthen the independence and restoration efforts. The printer Paulo Craesbeck compiled and published at Lisbon the *Commentarios do Grande Capitão Ruy Freyre de Andrade* (1647) to "serve as a great incentive for Portuguese to perform similar and even greater martial exploits against the enemies of their natural King and of the Liberty of their country.[237] The heroic deeds of Freyre de Andrade were performed in the Persian Gulf and the Indian Ocean between 1619 and 1633; consequently the *Commentarios* informed the Portuguese public of the valiant though unsuccessful efforts of their countrymen to hold Ormuz and other strategic points against the Persians and the English, while receiving little or no support from Spain.

Craesbeck printed in 1651 a biography that was destined to become one of the most popular books ever to appear in the Portuguese language. The life of João de Castro, fourth viceroy of India (1547–48), written by the priest-patriot Jacinto Freire de Andrade (1597–1657), was reprinted dozens of times after its first appearance.[238] Sir Peter Wycke (1628–1699), geographer, diplomat, and fellow of the Royal Society, translated this biography into English and dedicated his work to Queen Catherine, the Portuguese consort of Charles II. Two folio editions of this English work appeared, the first in 1664 and the second in 1693.[239] The Jesuit Francisco Maria del Rosso translated Castro's biography into a Latin version that was published at Rome in 1727.

Freire de Andrade's work celebrates in an elegant and vivacious style the military and naval victories which the noble Castro won in the East, especially those in which he defeated Moorish forces. Castro's less spectacular achievements in science and his personal weaknesses are kept in the background. The texts of congratulatory letters from the king and his court to Castro are inserted to support the author's unqualified praise of his hero and

---

[234] It is this edition which was translated into English with introduction and notes by C. E. Luard assisted by H. Hosten, S.J., as *Travels of Fray Sebastian Manrique, 1629–1643* in "HS," 2d ser., LIX and LXI (Oxford, 1926–27).

[235] *Itinerário de Sebastião Manrique.* Edited with a preface by Luis Silveira.

[236] See especially Maurice Collis, *The Land of the Great Image, Being Experiences of Friar Manrique in Arakan* (New York, 1943).

[237] From the license to publish this work, written in 1643 by D. Frey Gaspar dos Reys, as translated in C. R. Boxer (trans. and ed.), *Commentaries of Ruy Freyre de Andrade . . .* (London, 1930), p. lv.

[238] *Vida de dom João de Castro, quarto visorey da India* was first reissued in 1671. Its popularity grew rapidly in the eighteenth and nineteenth centuries.

[239] *Life of Dom John de Castro, fourth viceroy of India* (London). Also see below, p. 574.

his celebration of the indomitable spirit of the Portuguese who fought by his side in India against numerous and powerful enemies. Equal valor, the author seems to say, is required of the Portuguese who must fight dauntlessly against overwhelming odds to retain the independence so recently won from Spain.[240]

In the East the religious orders meanwhile strove to get their houses in order to weather the disruptions produced by the war between Spain and Portugal and by the incursions of the Protestant fleets. At their printing presses at Goa and Manila they published the constitutions and regulations of the dioceses and orders.[241] The Jesuit Antonio de Saldanha (1598–1663), who had lived in India for forty years, published in 1655 the life of Saint Anthony of Padua in the spoken language of Goa.[242] Miguel de Almeida (1607–83), another Jesuit, had printed at Goa in 1658–59 a five-volume *Jardim dos Pastores* written in the Brahman dialect of Goa. In Manila, meanwhile, there appeared in print a tract commemorating a Filipino festival of the Virgin.[243]

At this time, too, startling news began to trickle out of China, where the Manchus were wiping up the pockets of Ming resistance that still remained in certain of the southern provinces. Matias de Maya (1616–*ca.* 1670), the procurator-general of the Jesuit province of Japan, who was working on the China coast, sent to Europe a letter telling of royal conversions in China. In 1650 Craesbeck at Lisbon printed this letter in a pamphlet of sixteen pages,[244] the first announcement to Europe of the royal conversions made in 1648 by the Jesuit Andreas X. Köffler (1612–52). Most of the immediate household of Chu Yu-lang (1623–62), grandson of the Wan-li emperor, were brought to Christianity by Köffler. The legal wife of Chu's father, the empress dowager, was baptized in 1648 under the Christian name Helena. Two years later she addressed letters to Pope Innocent X and the Jesuit General asking prayers for the Ming cause and for additional missionaries. These letters, entrusted to Father Michael Boym for delivery, did not arrive in Europe until 1652, the year after Helena's death and two years after the printing of Maya's Portuguese announcement of her conversion.[245] In the

---

[240] For a balanced appreciation of this model of Portuguese prose see J. B. Aquarone, *D. João de Castro. Gouvernour et Vice-Roi des Indes Orientales* (2 vols.; Paris, 1968), I, xix–xxii.

[241] For example: *Constituicoens do Arcebispado de Goa* (1649). For details see Boxer, "A Tentative Check-List" (n. 218), p. 591, and *Constitución de esta provincia de S. Gregorio de la ordens de Francisco* (Manila, 1655). Cited in Ternaux-Compans, p. 196.

[242] For bibliographical details see A. K. Priolkar, *The Printing Press in India* (Bombay, 1958), p. 21; also Boxer, "A Tentative Check-List" (n. 218), p. 593.

[243] *Relación festiva* . . . (1658).

[244] *Relação da conversão a nossa Sancta Fè da rainha e principe da China & de outras pessoas de casa real, que se baptizarão o anno de 1648.*

[245] For further details about this episode in China see A. W. Hummel (ed.), *Eminent Chinese of the Ch'ing Period* (Washington, D.C., 1943), I, 195. See Pfister, *op. cit.* (n. 71), pp. 284–85 for Maya's career. To place this episode in the context of late Ming resistance see Lynn A. Struve, *The Southern Ming, 1644–1662* (New Haven, 1984), pp. 139–66, especially n. 17, pp. 241–42.

meantime a Jesuit letterbook had appeared in Mexico (1650) and Madrid (1651) summarizing the progress being made in missionizing in China and the Philippines.[246]

In the mission field itself, the Dominicans pursued conversion policies far different from those followed by the Jesuits. Instead of concentrating on the court nobility and the high officials, the Dominicans prided themselves on working with the common and helpless people. A case in point is the story of Vittorio Ricci (1621–85), a relative of the great Jesuit Matteo Ricci. A native of Florence and a teacher in the Dominican college at Rome, Ricci followed J. B. de Morales, a fellow Dominican, to the East. Upon his arrival at Manila in 1648, Ricci ministered to its Chinese population for the next seven years. In 1655 he entered China with other Dominicans where he worked with orphans, abandoned children, and criminals, a veritable Saint Vincent de Paul of China.[247] Later he acted in diplomatic capacities as liaison officer for Koxinga with the Spanish authorities at Manila.[248] Morales, Ricci, and their fellow Dominicans in the East provided their colleagues in Europe with the ammunition they needed to attack at Rome the mission policies of the Jesuits in China.[249]

Spain's losses in Europe were reflected in the declining condition of its colonies. Economic rivalries between Mexico and the Philippines and between the colonies and the homeland brought serious interruptions, beginning in 1635, to the galleon trade between Manila and Acapulco.[250] To bring their sorry financial plight to the attention of the king, the colonists in the Philippines sent Magino Solá (1605–64), a Jesuit, to Madrid in 1658. Solá presented a memorial to the king in council in which he insisted that the galleon trade had to be maintained and expanded and that more and better troops, colonists, and professional persons had to be sent to the Philippines. Solá had this memorial printed at Mexico or Madrid in a pamphlet of twenty-seven numbered leaves.[251] The effects of Solá's memorial upon royal policy were apparently negligible. Indeed, the Council of the Indies may have responded negatively, for it shortly thereafter confiscated all copies of

[246] For the titles of the letters see Streit, V, 790, 792. Also see Diego Gomes Carneiro, *Historia da guerra dos Tartaros* (Lisbon, 1657).

[247] See R. P. F. Andre Marie, O.P., *Missions Dominicaines dans l'Extrême Orient* (2 vols.; Paris, 1865), I, 195–96.

[248] For his total career see J. M. González Sánchez, *Un misionero diplomatico. Vida del padre Victorio Ricci . . .* (Madrid, 1955); for his activities in Asia see J. E. Wills, Jr., "The Hazardous Missions of a Dominican: Victorio Riccio, O.P., in Amoy, Taiwan, and Manila," in *Actes du II³ colloque international de Sinologie* (Chantilly), IV (1980), 243–57.

[249] For Ricci's letters and the title of his manuscript history (1676) of the Dominican mission in China see Streit, V, 823.

[250] See W. L. Schurz, *The Manila Galleon* (2d ed., New York, 1959), p. 49.

[251] *Informe al Rey . . . Felipe quarto, en su real y supremo Consejo de las Indias, del estado eclesiástico y seglar de las islas Filipinas.* Usually cited as being printed in Mexico in 1658. The catalog of the British Library gives Madrid?, 1660?. For a summary of the printed memorial see De la Costa, *op. cit.* (n. 66), pp. 414–16. For the translation of a manuscript report by Solá of conditions in the Philippines during 1652 see BR, XXXVI, 49–52.

the Franciscan Bartolomé de Letona's description of the Philippines published at La Puebla in Mexico in 1662.[252]

During these years of strain, the Jesuits more than any other group informed Europe about the Philippines. The compilation of Francisco Colin (1592–1660) called *Labor evangélica* (Madrid, 1663) was prepared as a continuation of Chirino's unpublished *Historia*. Colin was in the Philippines for thirty-five years, during which time he acted as rector of the Manila College and as provincial (1639–44). Most of his massive work is devoted to the religious conquest of the islands, and it especially emphasizes the activities of the Jesuits. Colin, who knew well the writings of Barros, Maffei, Chirino, and Morga, conscientiously amplifies the accounts of his antecedents. His work brings Chirino's chronicle to 1632 and includes a synthesis of what was known around mid-century about the Philippines. He attempts to integrate his special knowledge of the geography and the natural world of the Philippines into the European scholarly traditions exemplified by Ptolemy and Clusius, the biologist. In brief, this is a work of scholarship as well as observation.[253] Three years after the publication of the *Labor evangélica* a lengthy Latin work by Colin was published at Madrid which endeavors to show how the overseas discoveries and the new knowledge of Asia garnered from them could help in the understanding and interpretation of the Old Testament stories.[254]

The Jesuits in the Philippines were meanwhile putting together the history of the Spanish and Jesuit activities in the southern islands. Francisco

---

[252] The original *Descripción de las islas Filippinas* exists in the United States in but one mutilated copy preserved in the Yale Library. A copy from a private library of Madrid is partially translated in BR, XXXVI, 189–217. This work is particularly valuable for its physical descriptions, especially of the damages in Manila when it was rocked by the earthquakes of 1654 and 1658.

[253] He completed the manuscript in the Philippines in 1656 and sent it off to Spain for publication. The *Labor evangélica* was translated into German and published in *Der neue Welt-Bott* (Vienna, 1748), Vol. IV, Pt. 26, pp. 1–116; Pt. 27, 1–36. It was edited and amplified with previously unpublished materials by Pablo Pastells (3 vols.; Barcelona, 1900–1902; covers dated 1904). This critical edition, now becoming increasingly rare itself, has been reissued on microcards by Inter-Documentation Company AG of Zug, Switzerland. Portions of the 1663 edition have been translated into English in BR, especially in Vol. XL, pp. 37–98. The Pastells edition includes many contemporary maps and a valuable index. Colin's work should be supplemented with Francisco Ignacio Alzina's (also Alcina) *Historia de las islas e indios de Bisayas*. The Jesuit Alzina (1610–74) was in the islands for more than thirty years before completing his *Historia* in 1668. This manuscript book is in the Biblioteca del Palacio (Madrid); the Philippine Study Group of the University of Chicago owns a positive microfilm. It is now being edited for publication by Professor Fred Eggan. An English translation of the partial Lenox text (N.Y. Public Lib., Rich Mss. 96) was made and published by Cantius Kobak O.F.M., in *Leyte-Samar Studies* (University of Tacloban), III, No. 1 (1969), 14–36. For the history of the Alzina manuscripts see E. D. Hester, "Alzina's Historia de Vizayas, a Bibliographical Note," *Philippine Studies*, X (1962), 331–65, and P. S. Lietz's additional comments in *ibid.*, pp. 366–78. Alzina's work is not treated here because it was not published in the seventeenth century.

[254] *India sacra, hoc est, suppetiae sacrae ex utraque India in Europam, pro interpretatione facili ac genuina quorundam locorum ex veteri Testamento qui adhuc Europaeos morantur interpretes; opus posthumum* (1666).

Combés (1620–65), a teacher of theology in Manila, wrote between 1662 and 1664 his *Historia de las islas de Mindanao, Iolo, y sus adyacentes*. Although the author died on the voyage to Acapulco in 1665, his manuscript got to Madrid where it was published in 1667.[255] Based on the author's experience of twelve years (1645–57) in Mindanao and neighboring islands, this is one of the most respected of the ethnohistories prepared in the seventeenth century. Domingo Ezquerra (1601–70), a native of Manila and a Jesuit missionary working at Carigara, published in 1663 a study of the Bisayan language of the island of Leyte.[256] In the Philippines, Spain's last firm foothold in Asia, the death of Philip IV in 1665 and the accession of his son, Charles II, were marked by the publication of a description of the ceremonies by a priest of Manila's Santiago parish.[257]

The Portuguese commentators of the Restoration era, in their bitterness over the decline of the earlier empire, tend to glorify the past unduly and to deprecate the present unqualifiedly. The case of Manuel Godinho (1632–1712), a Portuguese Jesuit who was in India from 1655 to 1663, illustrates this point. He returned overland and two years later published the journal of his travels on the route from Bassein to Ormuz and the Persian Gulf to Iraq, Syria, Egypt, and France, on his way back to Portugal.[258] He opens his relation with a description of conditions in India as of the date when he left it. He concludes by lamenting Portugal's past glories and its present decrepitude: "if it was a tree, it is now a trunk; if it was a building, it is now a ruin." In the first eight chapters he briefly describes conditions, especially of the Portuguese, in the ports of northwestern India. The remainder of the book concerns his trip overland and his experiences en route.

One of the most influential of the Restoration histories was the *Asia portuguesa* of Manuel de Faria y Sousa (1590–1649), knight of the Order of Christ. It was first published at Lisbon (1666–75) in three volumes put together by the author's son Pedro and the printer Henrique Valente de Oliveira. Faria y Sousa, an ardent admirer of Camoëns and Barros, had spent most of his adult life at Madrid in the service of the crown. A noted

[255] Reissued with introduction and notes by P. Pastells and W. E. Retana in 1887. For an English translation of the materials relating to the peoples of the southern islands see BR, XL, 99–182.

[256] *Arte de la lengua bisaya de la provincia de Leyte* (Manila). For the full title see Streit, V, 339. This work was reprinted at Manila in 1747.

[257] Francisco Deza, *Cenotaphia real . . .* (Manila, 1668).

[258] *Relação de novo caminho que fêz por terra e mar, vindo da India para Portugal, no año de 1663, o padre Manuel Godinho da Companhia de Jesus* (Lisbon, 1665). Second edition published in 1842. A reprint with an introduction by Augusta Reis Machado was published at Lisbon in 1944. For an evaluation and partial translation into English see E. Rehatsek, "Journal of Padre Manuel Godinho, S.J., from India to Portugal, in the Year 1663, by Way of Mesopotamia," *Calcutta Review*, XCIII, 63–97; and for a translation into English of chapters xix–xxiii see C. D. Ley, *Portuguese Voyages, 1498–1663* (London, 1948), pp. 333–60. Also see G. M. Moraes (trans.), "Surat in 1663 as Described by Manoel Godinho," *JRAS, Bombay Branch*, XXVI (1952), 121–33. On his experiences in India see below, pp. 741–43.

polygraph and correspondent, he collected materials of all kinds on the Portuguese enterprises overseas.[259] He initiated his career as a historian with his two-volume *Epitome de las historias portuguesas* (Madrid, 1628) in which he celebrated the *Décadas* of Barros and Couto and the peregrinations of Pinto.[260] He himself aspired to write the history of the Portuguese in a world setting, a project that Barros had contemplated but never realized.[261] To this end Faria y Sousa modeled his historical writing on the ancient authors, Barros, and Guicciardini. He wrote in Spanish, as did many Portuguese contemporaries, in an effort to ensure that his "historical poem" celebrating the Portuguese would reach a European-wide audience. The Spanish edition of *Asia portuguesa* was reissued several times during the seventeenth century and was translated into an English abridgment by Captain John Stevens and published at London in 1694–95 in three volumes.[262]

The revolt of Portugal in 1640 had brought a swift end to Faria y Sousa's personal publication plans. He and his family, like other patriotic Portuguese, were not permitted to leave Madrid or to publish works praising the Portuguese. Upon his death in 1649, his books, papers, and manuscripts were moved from Spain to Portugal in the custody of his son, Pedro. The son then prepared for publication the *Asia portuguesa*, a distillation of the father's manuscripts and papers. Volume I is substantively an epitome of Barros' work with each of its parts corresponding to one of the *Décadas*. Volumes II and III provide the documentary materials for the *Décadas* published by Couto and Bocarro. To the end of Volume III there is appended a list of the books and manuscripts used in the preparation of the *Asia portuguesa* with comments on their authority, credibility, and style.[263] Included in this bibliography are most of the books then in print which related to Asia, as well as manuscripts prepared by officials and missionaries in the field.[264] Especially useful for modern scholars of the Portuguese East are the materials concerning the period from 1620 to 1640 set forth in the final part of Volume III.

The miracles performed by Xavier in the East were celebrated once again by Diego Luis de Sanvitores (1627–72), a Jesuit superior in Mexico (and the founder of the mission in the Marianas) who wrote under the pseudonym Mathios de Peralta Calderón.[265] The work of the Jesuit Martino Martini (1614–61) on the Tartar (Manchu) conquest of China was first published in

[259] See above, p. 349, on his relations with Semedo.

[260] Reissued at Lisbon in 1663, at Brussels in 1677, and at Lisbon in 1730.

[261] For Barros' plan see *Asia*, Vol. II, Bk. 2, p. 140.

[262] *The Portugues Asia: Or, the History of the Discovery and Conquest of India by the Portugues; . . .*

[263] The favorites are Barros, Pinto, and Osorio.

[264] This discussion of *Asia portuguesa* is based on the introduction to the modern Portuguese edition (6 vols., Porto, 1945–47) written by Lopes d'Almeida.

[265] *El apostel de las Indias . . . san Francisco Xavier* was first printed in Mexico in 1661. It was reissued in 1665 at Pamplona. For full title see Streit, V, 157, 162.

Latin at Antwerp, and was issued at Madrid in Spanish translation in 1665.[266] In India, meanwhile, the Jesuit Ignacio Arcamone (1615–83) composed a book of sermons in the Konkani language that was published at Rachol in India in 1668.[267] The following year a study of the Tagalog language of the Philippines was published in Mexico by Augustín de la Magdalena (d. 1689).[268]

The second European work published on the Manchu conquest of China was prepared by Juan de Palafox y Mendoza (1600–1659), a Spanish bishop. Ordained a priest in 1629, Palafox was ten years later consecrated bishop of Puebla de los Angeles and appointed visitor-general to Mexico. In addition to his ecclesiastical and secular offices, Palafox was also in charge of the dispatch of vessels to the Philippines during his stay (1640–49) in Mexico. In this capacity, he collected "letters and memorials" on events in China that were forwarded to him through Macao and Manila. He apparently took this collection with him when he returned to Spain in 1649 to become bishop of Ossa. His *Historia de la conquista de la China por el Tartaro* was published at Paris in 1670.[269] A French version appeared in the same year, to be followed by an English version in the next year.[270]

Unlike Martini's eyewitness account, Palafox' *Historia* was based entirely on the reports of others. Though he may have read Martini's history, he does not acknowledge borrowing from it. Perhaps this was so because he wrote before reading Martini, or because of his open hostility to the Jesuits. He appears to rely almost completely on the materials gathered in Mexico, for he concludes his narration of what he calls the "revolution in China" with the events of 1647. His purpose in writing was avowedly "to take some measure of the present state of China under its new masters" and to point up a moral lesson to the princes of Europe about what happens to a state when internal decay and division are permitted to go unchecked. While he shows considerable skill in weaving together a coherent story from the tangled skeins of his sources, Palafox cannot always be relied upon for accuracy in dating or in depicting the roles of particular actors. The failure of the Ming

---

[266] *Tartaros en China Historia que escrivio en Latin . . . Martin Martinio . . . y en español traducida por el doctor D. Estevan de Aquilar y Zuniga.* For discussion of Martini and his writings see below, pp. 480–81, 525–27.

[267] *Ignacii Archamonis conciones per annum concannice composite,* from the listing in Ternaux-Compans, p. 218.

[268] *Arte de la Lengua Tagala.* Ternaux-Compans, p. 218, lists it under 1669; all other listings place it under 1679.

[269] Based on Chen Min-sun, *op. cit.* (n. 233), pp. 217–19. On the relationship of Palafox's work to other Western writings on the Manchu conquest see E. J. Van Kley, "News from China: Seventeenth-Century European Notices of the Manchu Conquest," *Journal of Modern History,* XLV (1973), 561–82.

[270] This English version and other English printings appearing in 1676 and 1679 were derived from the French version. The French translation itself was reissued in 1723, 1725, 1738. We have used the 1723 French edition: *Histoire de la conqueste de la Chine par les Tartares: . . .* (reissued, Amsterdam, 1732).

dynasty he attributes unreservedly to its contempt for and neglect of the military.[271]

The Jesuits in China, following Semedo's and Martini's leads, continued to report regularly on the effects of dynastic change. The Portuguese Jesuit Antonio de Gouvea (1592–1677), who joined the China mission in 1636, spent most of his time evangelizing in Fukien at the time of the Manchu takeover. During the middle years of the century he prepared a history of China based on Chinese and Portuguese sources and added an appendix on the Manchu regime.[272] In addition to collecting materials on the progress of the Jesuits in China, Gouvea published in 1671 at Canton a tract in Latin and Chinese proclaiming Jesuit innocence of the charges directed against them in 1664–66 by the Four Regents (the Oboi regency). Along with this tract he published the text of an imperial rescript of toleration of the Christian religion issued at Peking.[273]

In Madrid the young Jesuit writer Francisco García (1641–85) had to his credit an abundant literary production that included several works on the missions to the East. In a book printed at Alcalá de Henares in 1671 he reported, like Gouvea, on the persecutions suffered by the Christians in China from 1664 to 1668.[274] He derived this and his other books about the missions from the materials in the Jesuit letters. In 1673 he began to write about the expansion of Jesuit activities to the Mariana Islands (Ladrones) which had become a mission of the Jesuits' Philippine province in 1668. His first work on this subject was a brief tract on the life of Luis de Medina, a Jesuit pioneer killed in 1671 by the natives of Saipan.

In the following year, 1672, came the martyrdom of Diego Luis de Sanvitores, the founder of the Marianas mission and one of a handful of missionaries killed by the islanders in the last years of the seventeenth century.[275]

[271] For a fuller commentary see Chen Min-sun, "Philippine Sources of Palafox y Mendoza's History of the Conquest of China by the Tartars," *Annals of the Philippine-Chinese Historical Association*, V (1975), 51–62.

[272] This work in six books occupied Gouvea for about twenty years and ends with 1654. It has never been published, but was cited repeatedly by later Jesuit authors. See Pfister, *op. cit.* (n. 71), p. 223. A copy is in the Ajuda Library of Lisbon (mss. 49-V-1 and 2).

[273] *Innocentia victrix* . . . was printed in the Chinese manner with double leaves folded at the fore-edge and with a paper cover. A copy of this rare work is in the Lilly Library of Indiana University. For its title page see pl. 62.

[274] *Persecucion que movieron los Tartaros en el Imperio de la China contra la ley de Iesu Christo, y sus predicadores; y lo sucedido desde el año de 1664 hasta el fin del año de 1668.* Reprinted at Cadiz and Madrid in 1672.

[275] F. García, *Vida del venerable P. Louis de Medina, muerto por la fe en las islas Marianas* (Madrid, 1673); the Mexican Jesuit Francisco de Florencia (1619–95) published a martyrology (Seville, 1673) of Medina based on the letters of Sanvitores. Also see F. García, *Vida, y martirio de el venerable padre Diego Luis de Sanvitores . . . apostol de las islas marianas, y successos . . . desde . . . [1668] asta [1681]* (Madrid, 1683). Ternaux-Compans, p. 251, lists the following title: *Relacion de los successos de los missiones Marianas, desde el 25 de abril 1684 hasta el primero de mayo de 1685* (s.l., 1685); the British Library preserves a work by Gabriel de Aranda (d. 1709) entitled *Vida y gloriosa muerta del V. padre Sebastian de Monroy . . . que murió dilatando la fe alanceado de los barbaros en las islas Mariannas* (Seville, 1690).

A notice of his death written by one of his fellows was sent to Mexico and published at Seville in 1674.[276]

In China the rites controversy began to heat up anew after the cessation of official persecution in 1670. François de Rougemont (1624–76), a Netherlandish Jesuit who was in China from 1656 until his death twenty years later, was one of the most prolific correspondents and active proselytizers of his time.[277] He was also the author of a Latin history describing events in China from 1659 to 1666, a period of great trouble for the missionaries.[278] Upon its receipt in Europe, Sebastien de Magalhães (1634–1709) of Lisbon almost immediately translated Rougemont's Latin manuscript into Portuguese[279] and had it printed even before the publication of the original Latin version. The acquisitive printers of Lisbon thereafter reissued Couto's eighth *Década* (1673), the travels of Xavier (1674), and the relation, first published in 1617, of Jorge de Gouvea on the forty-five martyrs of Japan (1678).[280]

The most vehement and influential attack of the seventeenth century upon the activities of the Jesuits in China appeared in the writings of the Dominican friar, Domingo Fernández Navarrete (1618–86). At the age of twenty-seven he suddenly volunteered for missionary service in the Philippines after becoming acquainted with Bautista Morales, a leading figure in the Dominican mission to China. Morales, Navarrete, and other friars spent two years (1646–48) in Mexico where they witnessed the first round in the battle between Palafox y Mendoza and the Jesuits of his diocese, and where they read the materials collected by the bishop on China and the rites controversy.[281] Upon his arrival in the Philippines, Navarrete studied Tagalog and began missionizing and teaching. He left Manila in 1657 to return to Europe, but was stranded at Makassar. In June, 1658, he took a ship bound for Macao which had aboard the celebrated Jesuit Martino Martini and a number of recruits for the Society's China mission. Navarrete left Macao in 1659 to join the Dominicans working at Fu-an in Fukien province. Here he missionized happily until the onset of persecution in 1664. From 1666 to 1669 Navarrete, along with other friars and Jesuits, lived under house arrest in Canton.[282] Despite the protests of the Jesuits, Navarrete embarked at Macao in 1670 on a Portuguese ship bound for India. After a series of misadventures in India and on the Indian Ocean, he finally landed at Lisbon in

---

[276] *Relación escrita por uno de los padres de la mission, Mariana, remitada Mexico.* Sanvitores himself wrote letters to Europe before his death about his successes in the Marianas. A copy of a Jesuit report published around 1671 exists in the University of Minnesota Library. See Ward Barrett (trans. and ed.), *Mission in the Marianas. An Account of Father Diego Luis de Sanvitores, 1669–1670* (Minneapolis, 1975).

[277] See H. Bosmans (ed.), *Lettres inédites de François de Rougemont* (Louvain, 1913).

[278] *Historia Tartaro-Sinica nova* (Louvain, 1673).

[279] *Relaçam do estado politico e espiritual do imperio da China, pellos annos de 1659, até o de 1666* (Lisbon, 1672).

[280] On Gouvea's book see Streit, V, 418.

[281] On Palafox see above, p. 356.

[282] See above, p. 197.

March, 1672. Navarrete managed to get to Rome by January, 1673, where he reported to the pope on the religious situation in China. He was then dispatched to Madrid by his superiors where he began in 1674 to prepare for publication the tracts that were to become an arsenal for the enemies of the Jesuits.[283]

Navarrete began by setting down the debates with the Jesuits over the issue of the Chinese rites and related problems.[284] But he put this work aside for a time to prepare a background study that would make more comprehensible to European readers the problems being confronted by the missionaries in China. During the first half of 1675 he wrote the *Tratados historicos, politicos, ethicos y religiosos de la monarchia de China,* which was published at Madrid in 1676. The seven treatises in this substantial book are based on Navarrete's notes and diaries, official church documents, and translations of Chinese materials. Navarrete thus provides a rich background for the debate with the Jesuits that could also be used as instructional material for the new Dominican recruits to the Asian missions that he was in charge of procuring in Europe.[285]

The publication of the *Tratados* quickly produced responses from the Jesuits in Europe and China. In Spain the defense and counterattack were undertaken by the Society's Father Juan Cortés Osorio. He published two anonymous tracts attacking the *Tratados* and their author.[286] Cortés Osorio, who had never been to China himself, relied for his materials almost entirely on the Jesuit letters, and for his attack on Navarrete upon charges of dishonesty in reporting and interpretation. Like many of his contemporaries, Cortés Osorio also accused Navarrete of providing ammunition to the enemies of the Jesuits, especially the Jansenists and Protestants. He also sought to brand Navarrete as subversive of the interests of the state and addressed both of his tracts to the count of Villambrosa, president of the Supreme Council of Castile. Navarrete replied to these charges and others in two responses that were never printed. His manuscripts, however, were circulated to, and quoted by, a number of later critics of the Jesuits.[287]

Even though the *Tratados* was designed as an attack upon the Jesuits, it also became a popular source of information on China, India, and Makassar, the places Navarrete had visited. Indeed it seems to be the earliest Spanish relation describing seventeenth-century India. It is also one of the books which helped to spread the idea in Europe that China was a model state and far superior in many regards to the Christian countries of Europe. Voltaire

---

[283] Biography based on J. S. Cummins (ed.), *The Travels and Controversies of Friar Domingo Navarrete* (2 vols.; "HS," 2d ser., CXVIII, CXIX; Cambridge, 1962), I, xxi–xxvii.

[284] *Controversias de la mission de la gran China* was completed in 1677 but never published in full, allegedly because of the machinations of the Jesuits. See *ibid.*, pp. cv–cix.

[285] See *ibid.*, pp. lxxxiv–lxxxvi.

[286] Entitled *Memorial apologetico de los missioneros de la China al conde de Villa Hombrosa* (Madrid, 1676), and *Reparos historialis apologeticos . . .* (Pamplona, 1677).

[287] See Cummins, *op. cit.* (n. 283), pp. xciv–c.

and other Sinophiles of the Enlightenment quoted from its numerous translations. It was probably known more generally in England than elsewhere, after making its appearance in the first volume of Churchill's *Collection of Voyages* (1704). In Spain itself, Navarrete's work never enjoyed the popular response that greeted it in northern Europe, especially in those countries where the enemies of the Jesuits were powerful.[288]

A work that was popular in Spain, possibly because it antagonized nobody, was the relation first printed in 1680 of the round-the-world voyage of Sebastián Pedro Cubero (1640[45?]–1696), a native of Aragon.[289] Reputedly the first to make the overland voyage eastward from Spain to the East Indies, Cubero was on tour from 1672 to 1679. When in Rome during 1671, he had been appointed Apostolic Preacher to Asia and the East Indies by the Congregation of the Propaganda. In the travel account published on his return to Spain, Cubero comments on the west coast of India and especially on the decay of Goa. From there he sailed around the coast to Madras where he observed Hindu religious rites. Then he made his way to Malacca, where he was eventually thrown into prison by the Dutch rulers of the port. Banished from Malacca, he sailed to Manila and then to Mexico and Europe. The original version of his work was reprinted in 1682, 1684, and 1697; at Naples it appeared in Italian translation in 1682 and 1683.[290]

Five of the principal European works on Ceylon were completed in the 1680's. Three were by Portuguese, the fourth by the Dutch missionary Baldaeus, and the fifth by the English captain Robert Knox. The English and Dutch studies and the work in Spanish of João Rodriguez de Sá de Meneses (Spanish, de Sao y Menezes) were the only ones of these books on Ceylon to be printed in the seventeenth century.[291] Earlier there had been published at Lisbon a summary of the prodigious feats of arms performed in Ceylon in 1655 against the Dutch and Sinhalese.[292] The defeat of the Portuguese immediately thereafter appears to have halted the production of books on Ceylon until the 1680's.

The *Rebelion de Ceylan* (Lisbon, 1681) of Rodriguez de Sá de Meneses, written before 1640, was probably printed at this time because of its pa-

---

[288] See *ibid.*, pp. ci–civ.

[289] *Breve relacion, de la peregrinacion que ha hecho de la mayor parte del mundo . . . con el viage por tierra desde España, hasta las Indias orientales . . .* (Madrid).

[290] A summary in English may be found in Murray, *op. cit.* (n. 92), I, 334–44. A modern reprint of the original was published at Madrid in 1943. Bernou, the editor of Magalhães' work on China (see below, p. 362) claims that Cubero copied his materials on China from Mendoza and Pinto.

[291] Captain João Ribeiro's and Father Fernão de Queyroz's accounts of Portuguese defeats and conquests in Ceylon were not published until 1836 and 1916 respectively. Possibly they were too critical of Portugal's colonial policy in Asia. See C. R. Boxer, "An Introduction to João Ribeiro's 'Historical Tragedy of the Island of Ceylon,' 1685," *The Ceylon Historical Journal*, III (1953), 234.

[292] *Summaria relaçam dos prodigiosos feitos que as armas portuguesas obrasão na ilha Ceylão contra os Olandeses e Chingalas, no anno passado de 1655* (Lisbon, 1656).

triotic and retrospective character; it is a son's adulatory recounting of the military and administrative triumphs of the Portuguese national hero Constantino de Sá y Noronha (d. 1630) when governor of Ceylon between 1617 and 1622.[293] The Jesuit Fernão de Queyroz (1617–88) remarked in his *Conquest of Ceylon* completed in 1687 that the son's "affection was not so powerful as to get the better of truth" and that he "greatly esteems" this work as a historical source.[294] To others, like João Ribeiro, this book helped to keep alive "the life and courage and the wisdom of Constantino de Sá y Noronha."[295]

The Spanish also sought to keep alive an interest in Eastern affairs, though their hold in Asia was growing steadily weaker. José Martinez de la Puente, a writer about whom little is known, put together and published in 1681 a *Compendio de las historias de los descubrimientos, conquistas, y guerras de la India Oriental y sus islas* (Madrid). An anonymous Franciscan, one of the six on the island of Hainan in 1683, published a report on the greatness of China in Castilian without place or date. In Madrid a reissue appeared in 1682 of Lucena's biography of Xavier, followed in Mexico City by Baltasar de Medina's (d. 1697) life of San Felipe de Jesus (d. 1597), a Franciscan born in Mexico, who was the first of his order to be martyred in Japan.[296] In 1689 eight chronological tables on Spanish successes overseas, originally compiled by the Jesuit Claudius Clemens (*ca.* 1594–1642), were published at Valencia with additions to bring them up to date.[297]

Ecclesiastical problems in the Philippines produced a spate of controversial literature in Spain during the 1680's. Most of the issues revolved about the person of the Dominican archbishop of Manila, Felipe Fernández de Pardo (1610–89). The disputes began over payments to the parish priests for the administration of the sacraments and over the excessive punishments meted out to native believers for breaches of church law. Over these and other issues secular priests lashed out against the friars, Jesuits criticized Dominicans, and the civil authorities ended up in 1683 by banishing Archbishop Pardo from Luzon to one of the smaller islands. Naturally a controversy of such proportions in the Philippines produced reactions in Spain, Rome, and elsewhere in Europe.[298] Pardo's sentence was reviewed in Madrid; the king

---

[293] Translated into English by H. H. St. George in Vol. XI of the *JRAS, Ceylon Branch.*

[294] Fernão de Queyroz as translated by S. G. Perara in *The Temporal and Spiritual Conquest of Ceylon* (six books in three vols.; Colombo, 1930), Vol. II, Bk. 4, pp. 621–22.

[295] Quoted from P. E. Pieris (trans. and ed.), *Ribeiro's History of Ceilão* . . . (2d ed., Colombo, 1909), p. 229.

[296] *Vida, martyrio y beatification del proto-martyr del Japon San Felipe de Jesus* . . . (Mexico City, 1683).

[297] *Tablas chronologicos en que se contienan los sucessos eclesiasticos, y seculares de España, Africa, Indias Orientales, y Occidentales, desde . . . 1642, hasta . . . 1689 . . . por Vicente Joseph Miguel.*

[298] Based on the account in De la Costa, *op. cit.* (n. 66), pp. 475–502. The major publications in Spanish begin with *Copia de una carta, escrita al padre fray Alonso Sandin . . . Procurador general de . . . Santo Rosario de Philipinos* . . . (Madrid, 1683 [?]). Alonso Sandin (1630–1701) was then procurator of the Dominicans in Madrid. The case for the archbishop was championed by Friar

ruled in his favor and restored him to his office in 1687. After his return to Manila, the archbishop proceeded to root out his enemies mercilessly.

The Portuguese, who were in a bitter struggle with the papacy over control of the *padroado,* published almost nothing on the East in the 1680's. One of their compatriots, however, had his work posthumously published in French translation in 1688. Gabriel de Magalhães (1609–77), of the same family as the first circumnavigator of the world, worked as a Jesuit missionary in China from 1640 until his death. Beginning in 1650 he began composing an ethnohistory of China that he completed only in 1668. His manuscript, entitled *Doze excellencias da China,* was carried to Europe by Philippe Couplet in 1682. While in Rome, Couplet presented the manuscript to the French Cardinal Caesar d'Estrees (1628–1714), who read it avidly and then passed it on to D. Bernou, who prepared it for publication. The manuscript, when it arrived in Bernou's hands, was in a sorry condition. It had been half-burned by accident and its pages were totally out of order. Bernou reorganized the manuscript, translated it into French, and appended to it a biography of Magalhães written by Father Lodovico Buglio (1606–82), the constant companion of Magalhães in China. Bernou changed the title and published Magalhães' work as *Nouvelle relation de la Chine* (Paris, 1688). In his preface Bernou emphasized the originality of Magalhães' relation and its importance as a genuine contribution to the improvement of Europe's knowledge. Others must have recognized its quality, for it was almost immediately translated into English by John Ogilby and quickly reprinted in French.[299]

A challenge to Portuguese leadership of the mission to China came in 1685 with the advent of the French Jesuits.[300] Their new prominence in the mission helps to account for the Spanish translations of their writings published during the last decade of the seventeenth century. The controversial work of Michel Le Tellier (1643–1719), a Jesuit spokesman in the debate over the Chinese rites, was translated into Spanish and printed at Madrid in 1690.[301] It produced a storm within the Catholic world, particularly upsetting Antoine Arnauld and other Jansenists, and was placed on the *Index* in 1700. José López de Echaburu y Alcaraz, S.J., (1640–97) translated into Spanish the French original (1688) of the edifying story of Candida Hsü, a Chinese lady and convert.[302] At about the same time an anonymous trans-

Cristoval de Pedroche (1640–1715) in his *Breve, y compendiosa Relacion de la estrañez, y destierro de el señor Arcobispo . . .* (Seville, 1683). Translated into French as *Histoire de la persecution de deux saints évêques* (Paris, 1691), pp. 311–35. For additional publications see Streit, V, 303–14.

[299] *A New History of China* (London, 1688). See below, p. 424. The French reprints of the first edition appeared in 1689 and 1690.

[300] See above, pp. 263–64.

[301] The French edition first appeared in 1687 followed by reissues of 1688 and 1690. The title of the Spanish version is: *Defensa de los nuevos christinos, y missioneros de la China, Japon y Indias contra los libros* [by Jurien]. *Traducida de frances . . . por G. de Parraga.*

[302] The French original was translated by Philippe Couplet from an unpublished Latin manuscript of Pierre Joseph d'Orleans, S.J. The Spanish version is entitled: *Historia de una Gran*

lator published at Madrid a Spanish version of a circular letter in Latin written by Antoine Thomas (1644–1709), a Jesuit of Peking, telling of the death of Father Ferdinand Verbiest on January 28, 1688, at the Manchu-Chinese court.[303]

Friars and preachers of Iberian origin also kept on publishing their evangelizing achievements, past and present. Vicente Barbosa (1663–1721), a noted Theatine preacher, published in 1692 a progress report of the activities of his order in the East. The Theatines, who specialized in working with the common people, had first become active in India in 1639. By 1653 they had a church and an establishment of their own at Goa. Thereafter their missionaries concentrated upon carrying the evangel to those parts of south India not subject to Portuguese control or influence. Most notable was the effort they made to work in places where Dutch power was established or growing. In 1687 one of their number opened a mission in Borneo, but it lasted only until 1693.[304] It was this brave but futile effort which Father Barbosa celebrated in his Lisbon publication of 1692.[305]

News reached Europe in 1696 of K'ang-hsi's edict (March 22, 1692) of toleration for Christianity. It was announced by the publication at Lisbon of a Spanish account sent from Peking. The Jesuit Josephus Suarez (1656–1736), also called José Soarez, was its author. A native of Coimbra, Suarez left Portugal in 1680 before completing his novitiate. He arrived in south China in 1684 and was called to Peking four years later. There he was destined to spend the rest of his life. It was while acting as rector of the Jesuit college in Peking that he composed, originally in Latin, his book on the story of the mission's successful struggle to obtain toleration. His Latin text found its way into the hands of Leibniz who published it in the first edition of his *Novissima Sinica* (1697).[306] A Portuguese version, whether prepared by Suarez himself or a translator, arrived at Lisbon, where it was quickly translated into Spanish by Don Juan de Espinola.[307] This Spanish version went through three printings in 1696, two at Lisbon and one at Valencia. The work is divided into two parts: the first tells of the terrible obstacles previously faced by the missionaries, and the second relates the terms of the edict and its application after 1692.[308]

Señora Christiana de la China, llamada Doña Candida Hiu . . . Escrita por el R. P. Felipe Cuplet . . . (Madrid, 1691).

[303] For the title of this nineteen-page letter see Streit, V, 919.

[304] For the history of the Theatine mission see M. Müllbauer, *Geschichte der katholischen Missionen in Ostindien* (Freiburg im Breisgau, 1852), pp. 350–58.

[305] *Compêndio da relação, que veio da India o ano de 1691 a El-Rei Vosso Senhor D. Pedro II na nova missão dos clérigos regulares do Divina Providência na ilha de Borneu.*

[306] *Libertas evangelium Christi annunciandi et propagandi in imperio Sinarum . . .* This version may also have been published at Peking. See Streit, V, 933.

[307] *La libertad de la ley de Dios en el Imperio de la China. . . .* See Streit, V, 934–35.

[308] Ternaux-Compans, pp. 271–72 lists, though it does not appear elsewhere, a compilation of annual letters from China that he attributes to Suarez. It is entitled: *Cartas annuaes de la China*

José Sicardo (1643–1715), a Spanish Augustinian who had spent sixteen years as a missionary in Mexico, published in 1698 a summary history of the ill-fated Christian mission to Japan.[309] Dedicated to the Conde de Frigiliana y de Aguilar, who represented Aragon on the Council of State, this chronicle became broadly influential in Catholic circles and was especially esteemed by the Augustinians.[310] Since Sicardo himself had never traveled to the East, his comprehensive account of the Japanese mission was extracted from the writings of others. Book I begins with a general description of Japan and of the Augustinian advent there. Particularly useful are the discussions of the embassies exchanged between Japan and the Philippines. Books II and III present in chronological order to 1638 the martyrdoms of the Christians, both European and Japanese. The work ends with a catalog of the martyrs. Appearing as it did at a time when Catholic Europe had no direct relations with Japan, Sicardo's book served to keep alive a hope that the sacrifices of the earlier seventeenth century had not been made in vain and that Catholics might again return to Japan in the future.

Religious strife continued in the Philippines, but by 1694 the Augustinians and Jesuits had settled their jurisdictional differences amicably. The peace was again broken in 1697 when Don Diego Camacho y Avila (d. 1712), the new archbishop of Manila, began to make visitations to *all* the parishes of his see.[311] The parishes served by regulars resisted the episcopal visitations and a bitter controversy ensued. As part of his program, Camacho published a number of pamphlets at Manila. Members of the five religious orders active in the Philippines directed letters of complaint to Rome and Madrid denouncing Comacho's policies.[312] In 1700 King Charles II issued a decree approving the proceedings of his archbishop in disciplining the regular curates and promising his support in dealing with the orders. Five years later Rome followed suit by affirming the right of episcopal visitation to all parishes in the Philippines.

It was in the midst of the Camacho controversy that Gaspar de San Agustín (1650–1725) published at Madrid the first part of his *Conquista de las islas Philipinas*. A native of Madrid, San Agustín joined the Augustinians in 1667 and went to the Philippines in the following year. Designed as a

desde el año 1694 hasta el de 1697 (Valencia, 1698); also on this subject see the work of Juan de Irigoyen, a Jesuit, called *Relacion de las missiones de la Gran China, copiada de una carta, que escrivió de aquel reyno un ministro evangelico* (Cadiz, 1699). See Streit, V, 953–54.

[309] *Cristiandad del Japón, y dilatada persecución que padeció. Memorias sacras, de los martyres de las ilustres religiones de Santo Domingo, San Francisco, Compañia de Jesus; y crecido numero seglares: y con especialidad, de los religiosos del Orden de N. P. S. Augustin* (Madrid).

[310] See Manuel Merino, *Misioneros Agustinos en el extremo oriente, 1565–1780. Obra inédita que con el titulo "Osario Venerable," compuso el Agustino P. Agustin Maria de Castro, Año de 1780* (Madrid, 1954), pp. 210–11; for the eighteenth-century corrections of Sicardo's work by Maria de Castro see *ibid.*, pp. 499–512.

[311] See De la Costa, *op. cit.* (n. 66), pp. 525–26.

[312] For example, see the publications of 1697–98 preserved in the British Library under Camacho's name. For other materials see BR, XLII, 25–116.

backdrop for his account of the Augustinian mission to the Philippines, the first part of the *Conquista,* published in 1698, deals with the history of Spanish expansion from the discovery of the *mar del sur* to 1614. The second part, on the history of the mission from 1616 to 1698, was left in manuscript in the Philippines until it was finally published at Madrid in 1890.[313]

The Portuguese Jesuit Manoel Ferreira (d. 1699) was prominent in the mission to Cochin-China from 1658 until his death. Refugee missionaries from Japan had founded a mission in Cochin-China in 1615. They were followed by other Jesuits, from Macao and the Philippines. The advent of the French in Indochina brought about a conflict between the papacy and the Portuguese over what were deemed in Lisbon to be violations of the *padroado* by the French. In 1659 the Congregation of the Propaganda established Cochin-China, Tongking, and Nanking as an apostolic vicarate, and in 1673 declared Cochin-China to be independent of Nanking's control. Ferreira worked in Cochin-China during these years of jurisdictional conflict and lived to see the gradual decline of the mission based on Cochin-China. It is this story which he relates in his book published posthumously at Lisbon in 1700.[314]

The Iberian sources on Asia for the first quarter of the century are numerous, rich in detail, and sometimes optimistic about the future. Setbacks in Japan, Cambodia, Indonesia, the Malay Peninsula, and Ceylon after 1621 had the effect of removing, sometimes abruptly, these places from contemporary Iberian writings. The growing weakness of Spain and the restoration of independence to Portugal and its empire after 1640 helped to keep publications about Asia to a minimum—European events being more immediate and pressing. The dynastic change in China disturbed the missionaries there and turned their attention away from the understanding of Chinese civilization to matters pertaining to survival. The rites controversy, while it divided the Christians, helped to provide after 1670 a new and more informed look at Chinese government, history, learning, and customs. Japan, the shining hope of the sixteenth century and the early years of the seventeenth century, almost entirely vanished over the horizon for Catholics. Accounts of the martyrdoms experienced in Japan continued to be published, keeping alive a bitter memory of the successes of earlier times. A few new regions and peoples came within the purview of the Iberian reader, but only vaguely: hitherto unknown archipelagos of the south Pacific, Tibet, and the Manchus. Many places of India, Indonesia, and Malaya fell from view in Iberia after their capture by the Dutch. Some of the published reports actually deal more with the activities of the Dutch in Asia than with Asia's regions and peoples.

[313] For a complete bibliographical survey and for the contents of the second part see Streit, V, 319–24.
[314] *Noticias summarias das perseguições da missam de Cochinchina.* . . .

A few positive trends need also to be recalled. The literature of travel—real and fictitious—continued to attract publishers and readers. With the threat of the Dutch to sea travel becoming ever more potent, the accounts of travels overland increased in number: Goes (1608), Teixeira (1610), San Bernardino (1611), Moraga (1619), Andrade (1626), Manrique (1649), Godinho (1665), Cubero (1680). Circumnavigations in the tradition of Magellan—San Antonio (1604), Ordóñez y Cevallos (1614), and Cubero (1680)—continued to attract attention, even to the point of publishing in Spanish (1618) the Schouten-Le Maire account of the Dutch voyage around the world. Retrospective literature on the glories of the sixteenth-century empire was accompanied by serious historical studies; bibliographies on the overseas world were put together by Herrera Maldonado (1620), Leon Pinelo (1629), and Faria y Sousa (1675).

The mission histories continued to appear regularly, with additions to their number from Franciscans, Dominicans, and Augustinians. The editions of Guzman (1601), a Jesuit, and Ribadeneira (1601), a Franciscan, launched the competition in mission histories. The Dominican histories of Orfanel-Collado (1633) and Aduarte (1640) brought new dimensions to the genre and placed the Philippines at the center of all future evangelizing east of India. Colin's *Labor evangélica* (1663), published as a continuation of Chirino's manuscript history, provided data on the Jesuits in the Philippines to 1656. The Augustinians entered the field with the publication of Manrique's *Itinerario* (1649), followed by San Agustín's manuscript history (1699) of the mission in the Philippines. Finally, a number of important scholars and literati, including Clavius, Lope de Vega, and Leibniz in their number, watched the progress of the Iberian missionaries in Asia by studying the reports that filtered to them from men in the field.

CHAPTER IV

The Italian Literature

At the dawn of the seventeenth century the Spanish political and military presence in Italy remained unshaken. While suffering severe reversals in northern Europe, the Spanish were not openly attacked in Italy until the 1640's. Even then they were able to stifle the Neapolitan rebellion and to reassert their predominance. The losses suffered by the Spanish crown at mid-century in Iberia and northern Europe stimulated the Spanish governors of Italy thereafter to tighten their control. The papacy, which was likewise losing status and effectiveness in northern Europe, acted strongly in Italy to contain the growth of heresy and materialism. Italians, more than one dozen in number, meanwhile became increasingly prominent and powerful in the Asian mission of the Jesuits.[1] Indeed, the Portuguese complained bitterly about the violation of their *padroado* by the foreign Jesuits and by the papacy itself. While the Iberians were generally successful in keeping Italians out of direct participation in trade, they failed to hold inviolate their domination of the mission enterprise.

Most of the materials on Asia that funneled into Italy during the first decade of the seventeenth century were published in the form of Jesuit letterbooks. Addressed to the Jesuit general, the letters of Luis Fróis, long the Jesuits' leading reporter in Japan, had been translated from Portuguese into Italian at the end of the sixteenth century by Gasparo Spitilli (1561–1640), the Society's archivist and secretary to the general, and by Francesco Mercati (1541–1603), a Roman Jesuit. Their translations had been published

[1] For a general review of the place of the Italians in the Christian missions see G. B. Tragella, *L'impero di Cristo. Le missioni cattoliche nel mondo* (Florence, 1941), pp. 33–38.

usually at Rome, to begin with, and then in other Italian cities, especially Milan, Bologna, and Padua. For example, Fróis' accounts of the death of Hideyoshi and the "crucifixions of the twenty-six" had been quickly translated from Italian into Latin and German versions for more general distribution in Europe.[2] The Annual Letters, officially compiled and issued at Rome beginning in 1581, continued to appear on a semi-regular basis until at least 1619.[3]

Other publications excerpted or combined materials from the officially issued letterbooks.[4] These separate and unofficial publications were printed at Venice and other centers of commerce, apparently as profit ventures. The printing houses even issued translations of materials relating to the overseas enterprises of the Dutch.[5] The Venetians, in particular, remained diligent in keeping themselves abreast of developments in the spice trade. The *Herbario novo* of Castor Durante was issued at Venice in editions of 1602, 1617, 1636, and 1667,[6] and Garcia da Orta's work on the drugs of India in 1605 and 1616. The report of Cechino Martinello on the amomum and calamus plants he observed in Malacca was published as a separate pamphlet at Venice in 1604.[7]

I

THE JESUIT LETTERS TO MID-CENTURY

The Jesuits provided most of the information on the East that became available in print to readers of Italian during the first half of the seventeenth century. An administrative reorganization of the Society's hierarchy in the East had restricted Valignano's authority after 1595 to China and Japan. Nicolas Pimenta (1546–1613), a scholarly Portuguese Jesuit, had been sent to Goa in 1596 to act there as visitor with jurisdiction over the East Indies, or the provinces of Goa, Malabar, and their dependencies east of India. In the meantime Francesco Pasio (1551–1612), an Italian, had assumed practical charge of the mission in Japan about which he wrote regular reports to

[2] Fróis' letter of October, 1595, was issued in Italian translation at Rome in 1598 under the title *Raggualio delle morte di Quabacondo*. In the same year it was reissued at both Rome and Milan, and translated into Latin and German. Fróis' report on the crucifixions (*Relazione della gloriosa morte di 26 Christiani posti in croce per commandemento del re de Giappone*) was published in 1599 at Rome, Bologna, and Milan and shortly issued in Latin (1599), German (1599), and French (1600, 1604) versions. For more details on these publications see Streit, IV, 498, 506–7.

[3] See John Correia-Afonso, *Jesuit Letters and Indian History* (Bombay, 1955), p. 38; for a tentative list of Jesuit letterbooks, see below, beginning on p. 1983.

[4] For example, *Copia d'una breve relazione della Christianità del Giappone et della morte di Taicosama, signore de questo regno* (Venice, 1600).

[5] For example, *Tre navigationi fatte degli Olandesi e Zelandesi al Settentrione . . . verso il Catai e regno de' Sini . . .* (Venice, 1599).

[6] On Durante see *Asia*, II, Bk. 3, 438–39.

[7] *Ragionamenti . . . sopra l'amomo et calamo aromatico novamente, l'anno 1604, havuto di Malaca, città d'India*. A copy of this fifteen-page pamphlet may be found in the Bibliothèque Nationale.

Europe. After the death of Valignano in 1606 and of Ricci in 1610, Pasio was named visitor of China and Japan. On his way to visit the China stations he died at Macao in 1612. The reports to Rome and the Jesuit general from these Italian leaders of the Asian missions were widely circulated in Europe.

Pimenta's first published report on the mission stations of "the East Indies" was issued in 1601 at Mainz in Latin and at Rome in the Italian translation of Carlo Sassetti. Written in December, 1599, at Goa, Pimenta's *Lettera* includes reports especially prepared for him by the superiors of the Jesuit mission stations of eastern India, Pegu, and Malacca. The Roman version was reprinted the following year at Milan and Venice, while the original Latin compilation was quickly translated into French (Antwerp, 1601).[8] Pimenta's second report, prepared in 1600, was printed in Italian at Rome in 1602.[9] It includes additional reports on the mission stations as well as an account of Pimenta's travels in northern India. Rich in observations about conditions in India, this letter also includes bits of news about events in the Moluccas and China. Pimenta also reports on the withdrawal of the Jesuits from Cambodia in favor of the Dominicans and Franciscans.[10] A reprinting of this second report appeared at Venice in 1602; it was also translated into Latin (1602), German (1602), Portuguese (1602), and French (1603). An Augustinian relation of India written by Francisco Pereira (1585–1621) was published at Rome in 1606 and in French translations (Paris, 1606; Antwerp, 1607).[11] From these mission reports it was possible to follow in Italy the successes and reversals of Catholicism in India and southeastern Asia, and to learn, indirectly at least, something about the regions in which the missionaries were working.

The Jesuits of Italian origin—Valignano, Ricci, Longobardo, and Pasio—were especially active and important in the missions to China and Japan. Practically everything written by Pasio from 1597 to his death in 1612 deals with Christianity in Japan, where he was vice-provincial from 1601 until he became visitor in 1611. His letters of 1598 in which he tells of Hideyoshi's death were translated from Portuguese into Italian by Gasparo Spitilli and published at Rome in 1601.[12] This letterbook was reissued immediately in slightly shortened versions from presses in Venice and Brescia. Pasio's Annual Letter of 1601 written in Nagasaki reports in grim detail on the hardships suffered by the Christians of Japan in the civil wars that followed

---

[8] See Streit, V, 8–9.

[9] *Copia d'una del . . . Pimenta Visitore della Provincia d'India Orientale al molto Reverendo P. Claudio Acquaviva . . . del primo di Decembre, 1600.*

[10] Description of this report is based on the summary of the contents in Streit, V, 12–14.

[11] *Relatione autentica mandata . . .* For full title and bibliographical details see Streit, V, 36–37. For an account of the Augustinian mission in India see M. Müllbauer, *Geschichte der katholischen Missionen in Ostindien* (Freiburg im Breisgau, 1852), pp. 339–43. Also see S. Neill, *A History of Christianity in India . . . to A.D. 1707* (Cambridge, 1984), pp. 358–59.

[12] *Copia d'una breve relatione della Christianità di Giappone. . . .* This book also contains other letters (1598) written from China by Longobardo and from "Mogor" by Gerolamo Sciavier (Xavier).

Hideyoshi's death.[13] This Rome edition was reprinted in 1604 at Venice and Milan.[14] Because Pasio's Annual Letter for 1600 was lost in transit to Europe, a "supplement" to that document was prepared by Valentim Carvalho (1559–1631) that was published at Rome in 1603, the year when Pasio's letter of 1601 was also published there.[15] These publications were accompanied into print in 1603 by a letter of 1599 from Visitor Valignano also reporting on the changing political conditions in Japan.[16] From these accounts it became clear that the previously flourishing Jesuit mission in Japan was having serious difficulty surviving in the succession crisis of 1598 to 1601.

Two Annual Letters from Japan were prepared for 1603 by the Portuguese Jesuits Mateo de Couros (1568–1633) and Gabriel de Matos (1572–1633). Matos' letter, first published at Rome in 1605, tells of the return of peace to Japan under Tokugawa Ieyasu and of the resumption of missionizing.[17] Three years later Couros' Annual Letter appeared in a collection of three letters relayed to the Jesuit general by Pasio.[18] The others were written by the secretary to the Portuguese provincial of Japan, João Rodrigues Girão (1558–1629), on conditions at the mission stations in Japan from 1604 to 1606. Luis de Cerqueira (1552–1614), Jesuit bishop of Japan, meanwhile sent to Rome in 1604 a relation of the martyrdoms suffered by six Japanese Christians of noble station that was published there three years later.[19] At Venice a collection of materials selected from the published letters was put into print in 1608.[20]

The second decade of the seventeenth century began with the publication at Rome in 1610 of the Annual Letter on Japan for 1606, apparently written by the mission's procurator João Rodrigues "the Interpreter" (1561?–1633).[21] The Jesuit provincial meanwhile sent from Japan a relation of the martyrdoms of nine Japanese Christians in the "kingdom of Fingo" (Higo on Kyushu).[22] Very little more on Japan was published in Italy until 1615, the year in which the Hasekura mission was there (October, 1615, through January, 1616). The Jesuits then brought out the Annual Letter for 1609–10 written by Rodrigues Girão in which he touches upon the serious nature of

---

[13] *Lettera annua* . . . (Rome, 1603). For a summary of its contents see Streit, V, 367–72.

[14] Latin (1604) and French (1605) translations were also published in short order.

[15] *Sopplimento dell' annua del MDC.* . . . See Streit, V, 364–65.

[16] *Lettere* . . . *de' 10 d'ottobre del 1599* (Rome). Reissued in 1603 at Venice and Milan, and translated into German (1603), Latin (1603) and French (1604).

[17] For a summary of its contents see Streit, V, 31–33. This letterbook also includes reports of 1603 from the Moluccas and China. A second Italian edition appeared at Milan in 1606.

[18] *Tre lettere annue del Giappone* . . . (Rome, 1608). Reprinted at Bologna (1609) and Milan (1609) and translated into French (1609) and Latin (1610). See Streit, V, 385.

[19] *Relatione della gloriosa morte patita da sei Christiani Giaponesi.* . . . Reprinted in 1607 at Fermo and Bologna, and translated into French (Paris, 1607; Arras, 1608) and Flemish (1609).

[20] *Raccolta di relationi de' regni del Giappone* . . .

[21] *Lettera di Giappone dell' anno M.DC.VI del P. Giovanni Rodriguez.* A Latin edition was published at Antwerp, 1611. See Streit, V, 390.

[22] Author not known. For a summary of its contents see Streit, V, 391–92. In 1612 it was translated into Latin and French.

the Dutch attacks upon the sea-lanes from Macao to Nagasaki.[23] Directly related to the embassy itself was the publication in 1615 of Scipione Amati's *Historia del regno di Voxu del Giappone*. . . . Written by the interpreter and historian of the embassy, this little book in thirty-one chapters details the size of Oshu ("Voxu") and the holdings of its ruling family, recounts the achievements of the Franciscan Luis Sotelo, gives the itinerary taken by the embassy from Japan to Rome, and reproduces the documents brought by the envoys and the speeches made at their receptions.[24] After this gala visit, the official persecution of Christians in Japan became the main topic of the day; the letters published at Rome after 1615 mainly relate to the trials and martyrdoms of the Christians.

While the Japanese legates were being feted in Rome, Nicolas Trigault (1577–1628) was there to attend the General Congregation of the Society of Jesus that met from November 5, 1615, to January 26, 1616.[25] Trigault, who had just spent close to two years in China, had returned to Europe in December, 1614, to launch a propaganda campaign for the China mission. He and others of the Jesuits deplored the presence in Rome of the Franciscan-sponsored Japanese mission since it took attention away from their propaganda efforts. Niccolò Longobardo (1559–1654), who had succeeded Ricci in 1610 as superior-general of the China mission, had sent Trigault to Europe to obtain its independence from the authority of the Japan province, to procure recruits and funds, and to collect European books and precious gifts. In his baggage Trigault had brought to Europe the *Annuae* (Annual Letters) for China of 1610–11, the abridged *Annuae* of Japan for 1609–12, and a version of Ricci's commentaries.

Ricci had spent the first decade of the seventeenth century at Peking to establish the Jesuits in the imperial city and court. Most of the letters and letterbooks on China then being published in Europe were, however, not from his pen. The Sicilian Jesuit Longobardo had arrived in China during 1597 and was sent immediately to Shaochou. The following year he sent a letter to Europe that was published at Mantua in 1601.[26] In this book of thirty-two pages Longobardo tells of his initial experiences in making converts in this utterly strange land of northern Kwangtung and of his disputes

[23] For a summary of its contents see Streit, V, 402–5. It was translated into Latin and French during 1615. Rodrigues Girão (d. 1629) should not be confused with his namesake, Rodrigues the Interpreter.

[24] Materials on the origin and itinerary of the embassy reprinted in *Dai Nippon Shiryo* (*Japanese Historical Materials*), Pt. XII, Vol. XII (Tokyo, 1909), *passim*. In 1954 a facsimile reproduction of this rare work was issued at Tokyo by the Toyo Bunko (Oriental Library). A German translation of Amati's book was published at Ingolstadt in 1617. Also see V. Vigielmo, "The Preface and First Ten Chapters of Amati's *Historia del regno di Voxu* . . . Translated and Annotated," *Harvard Journal of Asiatic Studies*, XX (1957), 619–43.

[25] See Edmond Lamalle, "La propagande du P. Nicolas Trigault en faveur des missions de Chine, 1616," *AHSI*, IX (1940), 59–60.

[26] *Breve relatione del regno della Cina*. It was translated into French and published in 1602 at Paris. Also see Streit, V, 684–85.

with the Buddhists. The Annual Letter for 1601 was sent to Europe by Valentim Carvalho, rector of the Jesuit college at Macao, and was published at Rome in 1603. It deals with affairs at the college and with Jesuit activities in the interior of China.[27] A much more detailed report on the college and on the residences of China was prepared at Macao for the provincial of India by Diogo Antunes (1552–1611), a Portuguese father.[28]

Diego de Pantoja's celebrated letter from Peking of 1602 telling of the Jesuits' advent in China's capital was published at Rome in 1607.[29] Three years later there appeared Ricci's Annual Letter from China for 1606–7. In it Ricci reports on the condition of the mission stations in China and Japan and on the death of Bento de Goes. He includes a letter written in Peking by Gaspar Ferreira (1571–1649), the Portuguese Jesuit who carried to the imperial court in 1604 the polyglot Bible published by Plantin.[30] After arriving at Rome in 1614, Trigault arranged to have published in one substantial volume the Annual Letters from China of 1610 and 1611.[31] Written at Longobardo's command after the death of Ricci, these letters stress the importance of keeping Peking at the center of the missionary effort in China, the need to respect Chinese ways of dealing with foreigners, the contrast between the peace and order in China and the turbulence in Japan, and the desirability of making China into an independent province of the Society and of sending more missionaries to the waiting harvest.[32]

Materials on the Moluccas and the Philippines were sparse and rarely printed in Italian during the first years of the century.[33] It was only after Pedro Chirino's visit to Rome and the publication there in 1604 of his Spanish *Relación* that the Philippines began to receive greater attention.[34] In the following year the Annual Letter from the Philippines for 1602–3 written by Juan de Ribera appeared in Italian at Rome. It surveys the mission stations and stresses the importance of the Philippines as a staging ground for missionizing in China, Japan, and the Moluccas.[35] In 1611 the Annual Letter

[27] Reprinted at Venice and Milan in 1604, and translated and published in French at Liège (1604) and Paris (1605).

[28] First published in Matos, *Lettera annua di Giappone* (Rome, 1605), pp. 121–43. In this same collection is included (p. 140) an excerpt from a letter of 1602 by Ricci in Peking to Longobardo.

[29] Previously published in Iberia. See above, pp. 319–20. The Italian version was translated into German in 1608.

[30] Ricci's letter reissued at Milan (1610) and translated into German (1611) and Latin (1611).

[31] *Due lettere annue della Cina del 1610, e del 1611* (Rome, 1615). Reissued at Milan (1615) and translated into Latin editions of Augsburg (1615) and Antwerp (1615) and into Polish (Cracow, 1616).

[32] For a fuller summary of the contents see Streit, V, 705–15.

[33] One of the few works published was Francisco Vaez' Annual Letter of 1601 from the Philippines, which was included as a short appendix to a letterbook from Peru. See Streit, V, 243.

[34] On Chirino in Rome as procurator of the Vice-Province of the Philippines see H. de la Costa, *The Jesuits in the Philippines, 1581–1768* (Cambridge, Mass., 1967), pp. 200, 620. Also see above, p. 319, for bibliographical details.

[35] A second edition appeared at Venice in 1605; a French translation was published at Paris in the same year. For a summary of the contents see Streit, V, 247–49.

for 1608 was published at Rome. Its author, Provincial Gregorio López, reviews conditions in the mission outposts and refers especially to the difficulties with the Muslims being experienced in the "Pintados" (the Bisayan Islands) and in Mindanao.[36]

The missions of the Jesuits in South Asia and the Moluccas also received their share of attention in 1615 when a report of their activities as adjuncts of the provinces of Goa and Cochin was forthcoming at Rome.[37] It includes three letters written in 1611 by Jerome Xavier from Lahore about conditions in the Mughul empire. He comments that the sultan Salim (Jahangir) is well disposed towards the missionaries and well pleased with their gift to him of a history of the apostles in Persian. They hoped for his conversion, even though other members of his government were hostile towards the Christians and friendly to the Muslims. Xavier tells of Salim's decision to send embassies to Agra and Goa and of the part played in them by the Jesuits. He recounts dramatically the festivities that attended the conversion and baptism of some of Salim's family. The collection also contains a letter of 1612 on the mission at Madura and of Roberto de Nobili's language studies, disputes with the Brahmans, and personal accommodation to Indian ideas and practices.[38] Remarks appear in this same letter on the beginnings of Jesuit activity among the St. Thomas Christians. Its section on the Moluccas stresses how much the missionaries are harassed by the Dutch and English in insular Southeast Asia.

Even before the Japanese legates arrived at Rome in 1615, letters were being written by the Jesuits in Japan deploring the resumption of the general persecutions of Christians, the destruction of the mission stations, and the flight of some missionaries and converts to Macao, Cochin-China, and the Philippines. The Annual Letters from Japan for 1613 and 1614 were published separately at Rome in 1617. The letter for 1613, written by Sebastião Vieira (1574–1634) from Nagasaki, recounts the bravery of the Japanese martyrs and holds them up to Europeans as edifying examples. The letter for 1614, written by Gabriel de Matos, is much longer, gives in detail the losses suffered in the various mission stations, and concludes with a request for prayers for Japan.[39] These two books of 1617 appear to be the last of the published letterbooks devoted exclusively to events in Japan. Hereafter most

[36] Translated into German (1612) and French (1614). For a summary of its contents see Streit, V, 253–54.

[37] *Raguagli d'alcune missione fatte . . . nell' Indie Orientali. . . .* In 1614 a *Relazione breve del tesoro nuovamente acquistato nelle India orientali di Portugallo* was published at Milan, according to Ternaux-Compans, p. 127. We have located no other reference to this book.

[38] The censure in 1610 of Nobili, a Roman nobleman, for his adaptation to Indian customs produced rumors in Rome at this time that he was burning incense before idols, and caused some of his friends and supporters to write letters reviling him or pleading with him to return to the faith. See V. Cronin, *A Pearl to India. The Life of Roberto de Nobili* (New York, 1959), p. 189.

[39] For further detail see Streit, V, 419–29. Both Annual Letters were translated into French and published jointly at Lyons in 1618.

official Jesuit publications about Japan were restricted to brief selections from the Annual Letters or to separate edifying letters about the martyrdoms.

The Annual Letter for 1615–16 about Japan was written in Macao by the Dalmatian Jesuit Giovanni Vremans (1583–1620) and first published in a general collection issued at Naples in 1621.[40] A long letter, it reports in detail on the political and military strife in Japan, on the condition of Christianity in general and of the Jesuits in particular, and on the martyrdoms being suffered at the individual mission stations throughout the country.[41] It is followed by an Annual Letter from Goa written in 1619 by Gaspar Luís (1586–1648), a Portuguese Jesuit, in which note is taken of losses suffered from epidemics, typhoons, and earthquakes along the west coast of India.[42] The other letters in the Naples collection tell of a mission to the Mughul emperor, of the establishment of the mission in Cochin-China, and of Manchu advances towards Peking. In brief, this is a very informative volume on events in the East for the years from 1615 to 1619.[43]

For the years from 1619 to 1621 the Jesuits published at Rome in 1624 two separate volumes of selections from the letters written from Japan and China. In the compendium on Japan there is the expected discussion of persecution and martyrdoms.[44] The fourth letter is from Matsumae on the island of Yezo, written by Girolamo de Angelis (1567–1623), a Sicilian Jesuit. In 1618 De Angelis and other Jesuits went to Yezo to minister to Japanese converts who had fled there to escape persecution. Along with his letter of 1621 De Angelis included a small map of Yezo.[45]

The companion volume on China contains the Annual Letters for the years 1619, 1620, and 1621.[46] The first, written by Manuel Dias (1559–1639) from Macao, reports on the attacks against the Ming in Liaotung, the portents of disaster noticed by the Chinese, and the flight of the Jesuits in the north from the Manchu invaders.[47] The second letter, written from Macao by Wenceslaus Pantaleon Kirwitzer (1588–1626), a Bohemian Jesuit, tells of the return of Trigault and his recruits to Macao in 1620, the extension of the

---

[40] *Lettere annue del Giappone, China, Goa et Ethiopia*. Reprinted at Milan in the same year.

[41] For further details see Streit, V, 411–17.

[42] For further details see *ibid.*, pp. 78–79.

[43] Note should also be taken of a similar collection pertaining to 1622 published at Milan in 1623 and reissued at Bologna in the same year. Streit, V, 96, gives nothing but its title.

[44] See the first three letters in *Relatione di alcune cose cavate dalle lettere scritte ne gli anni 1619, 1620, e 1621, dal Giappone*. Reissued in 1624 at Milan and Naples. Translated into French (1625) and Latin (1625). Also see *Breve relazione del martyrio d'undeci religiosi dell' ordine di S. Domenico, sequato dell' Giappone nell' anno de 1618 e 1622* (Rome, 1624).

[45] Evidently he and his associate, the Portuguese Jesuit Diego Carvalho, also compiled an ethnohistory of Yezo. If so, it was not used by seventeenth-century writers and has not been found since. See D. Schilling, "Il contributo dei missionari cattolici nei secoli XVI e XVII alla conoscenza dell' Isola di Ezo e degli Ainu," in C. Costantini *et al.*, *Le missioni cattoliche e la cultura dell' oriente* (Rome, 1943), pp. 152–56. On Yezo in earlier cartography see *Asia*, II, Bk. 3, 484.

[46] *Relatione delle cose piu notabili scritti negli anni 1619, 1620, e 1621 dalla China* . . . (Rome, 1624). A second edition, at Milan, and a French translation were published in 1625.

[47] For a more detailed summary see Streit, V, 734–36.

Manchu invasion, and the heavy losses of the Chinese and Korean defenders.[48] The third letter, written by Trigault from north of Nanking, tells of the death of the Wan-li emperor in 1620, the succession crisis that followed, the military setbacks and losses being suffered on the northern frontier, and the Jesuit plan to extend their missionizing efforts to Korea.[49]

Three important Jesuit publications appeared at Rome in 1627. The general collection for the western half of the Asian mission contains several relevant letters.[50] From Goa, the Provincial Gironimo Maiorica (1589–1656), a Neapolitan, reported in 1620 on the state of the Jesuit colleges at Goa, Chaul, Tana, Bassein, Damão, Diu, Agra, and Salsette. In the following year he wrote a similar but briefer report in which he notices the printing of Marco Giorgeo's catechism in the Kanarese language of west India. In 1621 Giacinto Perreira (1598–1627), a native of Malacca, wrote from Cochin on conditions in Malabar, Bengal, Ceylon, and Malacca. João da Silva (1597–1624) wrote from Goa the report of 1623, the year prior to his death there, about the unhealthy climate of the city. Antonio de Andrade's brief notice of his first mission of 1624 to Tibet was also included in this general collection. And a letter by Sebastião Barretto (1567–1625) of 1624 summarizes events relating to Agra, including news of Andrade's progress through Kashmir on the way to Tibet.[51] A more complete account of the 1624 mission to Tibet written by Andrade himself after his return to Agra, was translated from Portuguese and published at Rome, also in 1627.[52]

Annual Letters from China and Japan for 1621 and 1622 were also printed in a compendium at Rome in 1627.[53] Its first two letters, written by the Jesuits Pietro Paolo Navarro and Gironimo Maiorica from Japan and Macao respectively, recount in gruesome detail the martyrdoms being suffered throughout the Christian community of Japan; everything else is omitted or briefly mentioned. The letter from Macao is a compendium of reports garnered from refugees and from a few letters carried by them from prisoners and those in hiding.[54] The letter of 1621 from China, written by Trigault from Hangchow, is full of material on the advance of the Manchus in northern China: the capture of Liaotung, the fear for the safety of Peking, and the outbreak of local rebellions against the young Ming emperor.[55] This is fol-

---

[48] For a more detailed summary see *ibid.*, pp. 738–40.

[49] For a more detailed summary see *ibid.*, pp. 744–49.

[50] *Lettere annue d'Etiopia, Malabar, Brasil, e Goa. Dall' Anno 1620. fin al 1624.* For contents see Streit, V, 111–12. A French translation was published in Paris in 1628.

[51] For detailed summaries of these letters see Streit, V, 85–86, 89–93, 97–105.

[52] On the Tibet mission and on publications about it in Iberia, see above, pp. 338–39. Entitled *Relatione del novo discoprimento del Gran Cataio ovvero Regno di Tibet* (Rome, 1627), this Italian version was translated into French and German versions published also in 1627. A modern Italian edition may be found in G. M. Toscano, *La prima missione cattolica nel Tibet* (Parma, 1951). For a modern Portuguese edition see F. M. E. Pereira (ed.) *O descobrimento do Tibet . . .* (Coimbra, 1921).

[53] For contents see Streit, V, 497–98. Another edition appeared at Milan in 1627.

[54] For more details see Streit, V, 466–74.

[55] For more details see *ibid.*, pp. 741–44.

lowed by a letter on the same subjects written by Alvarez Semedo from Nanch'ang, capital of Kiangsi province, in 1623 in which he reports that three million have died in these wars and that unrest is spreading throughout the country.[56]

Andrade's exploits in Tibet during 1626 was the leading subject in the *Lettere annue* published at Rome in 1628.[57] His second journey Andrade describes as being somewhat easier than the first, and he gives a description of the geographical situation and the political divisions of Tibet. He talks about the Lamaistic religion and of his need to learn the Tibetan language. Cathay, he asserts, is not an empire, but rather a large city and the capital of a province located very close to China.[58] The second of the two letters in this book is Kirwitzer's Annual Letter of 1624 for China that he wrote in Macao. Aside from reporting on the progress of the Jesuits, he comments on the weakness of the youthful Ming ruler, who has no interest in recovering Liaotung from the Manchus since it had produced no literati of consequence during the three hundred years of its rule by China.[59]

From his exile in Macao, João Rodrigues Girão wrote in 1625 the Annual Letter for Japan of 1624. It was published at Rome in 1628 in a separate book of 150 pages. Here he reviews the trials and tribulations of the Japanese Christians both for the year 1624 and for many previous years.[60] Immediately it was reissued at Naples, Milan, and Bologna, and translated into Latin (Mainz and Dillingen), French, Flemish, and German. The Latin version of Mainz is entitled *Historia Japonensis anni MDCXXIV.*

The newsletters from China published at Rome in 1629, along with a report from Ethiopia, announced the "discovery" of Tongking in Indochina.[61] Giuliano Baldinotti (1591–1631), a Tuscan Jesuit, was sent from Macao early in 1626 in the company of a Japanese convert to determine how Tongking might fit into the mission program. The city in the delta of the Red River had long before been "discovered" by the Portuguese; indeed Baldinotti was carried there aboard a Portuguese merchant vessel. To Europe at large, however, Baldinotti's reconnoitering report from Macao (November 12, 1626) was newsworthy as the first eyewitness description of Tongking to be printed.[62] The other letter from China in this collection is from Manuel

[56] For more details see *ibid.*, pp. 752–55. On Semedo see above, p. 349.
[57] For contents see Streit, V, 117.
[58] For a more detailed summary see *ibid.*, pp. 107–8.
[59] For a more detailed summary see *ibid.*, pp. 756–59.
[60] For a detailed summary see *ibid.*, pp. 515–21.
[61] *Lettere dell' Etiopia dell' anno 1626 . . . e della Cina dell' anno 1625, . . . Con una breve relatione del viaggio al regno de Tunguim, nuovamente scoperto* (Rome, 1629). Reprinted at Milan (1629) and translated into French (1629) and Polish (1629).
[62] This brief letter of ten pages was lost sight of almost at once, because it was quickly superseded by lengthier descriptions. It was translated into French from the copy of the *Lettere* in the National Library at Florence and published in the *Bulletin de l'École Française d'Extrême-Orient* (Hanoi), III (1903), 71–78. For an analysis of its contents see the inaugural dissertation (Würzburg) by Gustav Hermann Degel, "Die Erforschung des Festlandes von Hinterindien durch die Jesuiten am Eingang und Ausgang des 17. Jahrhunderts" (1905), pp. 17–29.

Dias the younger (1574–1659); written from Chiating near Shanghai, it describes conditions in central China for the year 1625.[63]

With China and Japan becoming too chaotic or dangerous for evangelizing, the Jesuits and the other orders began to concentrate on Southeast Asia.[64] In Rome, David Haex (b. *ca.* 1595), a native of Antwerp in the service of Pope Urban VIII (r. 1623–44), published in 1631 a Malay-Latin dictionary originally prepared in Ternate.[65] Published by and for the Sacred Congregation for the Propagation of the Faith and dedicated to Francesco Cardinal Barberini, this seventy-five page dictionary was designed to introduce the missionaries to the commercial Malay of Southeast Asia.

The Jesuits, following Baldinotti's foray into Tongking, published at Rome in 1631 Cristoforo Borri's (1583–1632) informative relation of Cochin-China.[66] Borri, a Milanese astronomer, had spent about four years in Cochin-China and had learned enough of the local language to hear confessions. His work, based on his own experiences in Indochina from 1617 to 1622 and on the Jesuit letters, is divided into two parts: the first on the country and the second on the mission. For a missionary account it is remarkably full on products, trade, agriculture, fauna, and customs. It is a fundamental source that was reissued in translation five times in the seventeenth century, four times in the eighteenth century, once in the nineteenth century, and at least twice in the twentieth century.[67]

For the decade 1632–41 the only relevant books published in Italy relate to the martyrdoms in Japan. This was, of course, the period when the door to Japan was being firmly and finally shut to the Catholic missionaries and their Iberian associates. It was also the time when the war in northern Europe was turning against Spain and when revolt against the crown of Castile was heating up and boiling over in Naples and Portugal. In China the Ming rulers were on their last legs and the Jesuits and other missionaries were becoming increasingly desperate about the future of the Christian mission there. In the Philippines, the Spice Islands, and Indonesia, the advances of the Dutch and English were watched fearfully as voices were raised through-

[63] Also published in *Sonus evangelii* . . . (Dillingen, 1630), pp. 44–81.

[64] The University of Minnesota library, for example, possesses what may possibly be a unique example of Augustiniana, Provincia de India Oriental: *Lettera del padre vicareo provinciale dell' ordine di Santo Agostino dell' India Orientale* (Rome, 1629).

[65] *Dictionarium Malaico-Latinum et Latino-Malaicum cum aliis quamplurimus quae quarta pagina edocebit. Opera et studio Davidis Haex*. Reprinted in 1632. See pls. 93, 99.

[66] *Relatione della nuova missione* . . . *al regno della Cocincina*, . . . (Rome, 1631). Translated into French (1631), Flemish (1632), English (1633), German (1633), and Latin (1633). The English and French editions include only the first part on the temporal conditions in Cochin-China. A French edition of 1931 has critical notes by Bonnifacy. An English translation may be found in A. and J. Churchill's *A Collection of Voyages and Travels* (4 vols.; London, 1704; hereafter cited as *CV*) and in John Pinkerton, *A General Collection of the Best and Most Interesting Voyages and Travels in All Parts of the World* (17 vols.; London, 1808–14), IX, 772–828. A reprint of this English version was published in 1970 in the *Theatrum orbis terrarum*.

[67] For Borri's life and significant contributions to learning and science see L. Petech's excellent article in the *Dizionario biografico degli italiani*.

out the Spanish world advocating a retreat from Asia. Indeed it appeared around 1640 as if the entire Catholic enterprise in Asia might suffer martyrdom along with the Christians of Japan.

At Rome in 1632 a letterbook was published detailing the sufferings of the Christians, native and foreign, in Japan in the years from 1625–27.[68] This was accompanied by an Italian translation of Diego Aduarte's report of the persecution of 1626–28 first published in Spanish at Manila in 1629.[69] These two publications were followed by a letterbook of 1635 written by Christovão Ferreira (1580–*ca.* 1652) from Japan telling of the persecutions for the years 1628 to 1630.[70] This was followed in 1636 by an Italian translation of Rodrigues the Interpreter's catalog of the Jesuits martyred in Japan during 1632 and 1633.[71] The commemoration of the centennial of Xavier's arrival in Japan was inaugurated by the publication at Naples in 1641 of the *Saverio orientale* of Bernardino Ginnaro (1577–1644).[72] Divided into four parts, this is a vast compendium of materials drawn from the Jesuit letters and other works on Japan itself and on the advance of Christianity there. The first part, over three hundred pages in length, describes the geography and natural history of Japan, and its native religions, history, and rulers. Included in this part (p. 26) is a new map of undetermined authorship that became a prototype for other maps of Japan prepared in Europe during the seventeenth century.[73]

One of those who used Ginnaro's map, or one common to both, was António Francesco Cardim (1596–1659), a Portuguese Jesuit who returned from eastern Asia to Rome *ca.* 1640 to represent the Province of Japan. In 1645 he published at Rome his *Relatione* of Japan in which he also deals at length with the missions in Macao, Tongking, Cochin-China, Hainan, Cambodia, and Siam, places within the Jesuit Province of Japan where he had worked from 1623 to 1638.[74] In 1646 he published in Latin at Rome a book containing eighty-five biographies of European missionaries and of native Christians who had been leaders in the Japan mission since the time of Xavier.[75] On page 12 he includes a map of Japan that is similar to, but not

---

[68] For contents see Streit, V, 533. Reprinted at Milan in 1632, and translated into Flemish (Antwerp, 1632).

[69] See Streit, V, 526, 532.

[70] See *ibid.*, p. 542. Reissued at Milan (1635) and translated in the same year into Latin and French.

[71] Streit, V, 544.

[72] *Saverio orientale ò vero Istorie de' Cristiani illustri dell' Oriente* . . . Originally planned to be a work in two volumes, the second was never published. See Streit, V, 554. At Bologna in 1648 Giacomo Certani published a new biography of Xavier as part of the centennial celebration.

[73] For a discussion of the Ginnaro map of Japan and its relationship to other maps see J. F. Schütte, "Japanese Cartography at the Court of Florence; Robert Dudley's Maps of Japan, 1606–1636," *Imago Mundi*, XXIII (1969), 46–50.

[74] See Streit, V, 558. Reprinted at Milan and translated into French in 1645–46.

[75] *Fasciculus e Iapponicis floribus, suo adhuc madentibus sanguine.* Translated into Portuguese *ca.* 1650. See Streit, V, 560–61. In 1646 at Rome another Latin catalog appeared which seems to be an extract from the *Fasciculus.*

exactly like, the Ginnaro map of 1641.[76] He also published at Rome in 1646 a
Latin translation of the Portuguese original that had been printed at Lisbon
in 1643 describing the execution during 1640 at Nagasaki of the four Portuguese envoys.[77] Cardim remained in Rome until 1655; then he returned to
Macao, to die there four years later.

2

NEW HORIZONS AND OLD POLEMICS

While the churchmen fretted about the loss of a splendid mission field, a few
of the Italian cities—Venice, Florence, Genoa—tried to break directly into
the spice trade. Ferdinando de' Medici, Grand Duke of Tuscany (r. 1587–
1609), hoped at the beginning of the seventeenth century to create an international port at Livorno (Leghorn) specializing in trade with the East. When
Francesco Carletti (*ca.* 1573–1636) returned to Florence in 1606 after circumnavigating the world, the grand duke interviewed him at length on the
East.[78] In 1623 some Genoese merchants, along with some Persians and Armenians, petitioned the Senate of Genoa to authorize a *Compagnia di Com-
mercio colle Indie Orientale*. A favorable response was not forthcoming until
1647, when the Company was authorized and formed. In the next year a
prospectus was published called *Capitoli della navigatione all' Indie orientale
della Compagnia di Genova*.[79] Others who feared the dangers of the water
route to the East advocated dispatching traders overland. In 1646–47, Robert
Dudley, an Englishman in the service of Florence, published at Florence six
books on navigation and mapping, which he dedicated to the grand duke.[80]
At any rate, by mid-century hopes were rising in some quarters that Italian
traders and navigators might go on their own directly to the spice marts
of Asia.

Like the Italian merchants, the Jesuits and the religious of other orders
began once again to shift their attention to India, after Portugal had asserted
its independence from the crown of Castile in 1640 and had reassumed control over its footholds in the East. The Portuguese Jesuit Francesco Barreto
(1599–1663), after twenty years' service (1624–44) in India, returned as
procurator to Rome, where he published in 1645 an important relation of

[76] See Schütte, *loc. cit.* (n. 73), pp. 46–50.
[77] Streit, V, 556, 561–62. His manuscript *Batalhas de Companhia de Jesus na sua gloriosa provincia do Japão* was not published until 1894.
[78] On Carletti's published work see below, p. 388.
[79] L. T. Belgrano (ed.), "Opuscoli di Benedetto Scotto gentiluomo genevese, circa un pro-
getto di navigazione pel settentrione alla Cina ed alle Indie Orientali editi nel principio del
secolo XVII," *Atti della Società Ligure di Storia Patria* (Genoa), V, 297–99n.
[80] *Dell' Arcano del Mare*. For an analysis see Schütte, *loc. cit.* (n. 73), pp. 30–32.

Malabar.[81] It begins with a brief but informative discussion of conditions in
Malabar, followed by a review of affairs in the missions to the St. Thomas
Christians and to Cochin, Ceylon, Jaffna, Madura, Mannar, the Coromandel coast, and Bengal. This was followed three years later by a very short
survey of conditions in the more eastward missions of Pegu, Arakan, and
Burma, as well as in the "Mogor" mission, prepared by Sebastião Manrique
(d. 1669), an Augustinian Eremite of Portuguese origin.[82] Manrique, after
traveling about in India for thirteen years (1628–41), also published at Rome
in 1649 his *Itinerario* written in Spanish.[83]

One of the most popular and influential travel books of the seventeenth
century was the *Viaggi* (1650) of Pietro della Valle (1586–1652), the "pilgrim." The scion of a noble Roman family, Della Valle left on his eastward
pilgrimage in 1614. After visiting Constantinople and Cairo he arrived in
Jerusalem in 1615 just in time to celebrate Easter there. Then he took the
land route eastward via Aleppo and arrived in Persia early in 1617. After
three years at Ispahan and elsewhere in Persia, he made his way to India,
where he landed at Surat in February, 1623. After traveling in the interior of
west and south India, he arrived in Goa. From Goa he went homeward
again by the overland route, arriving at Rome in March, 1624. In the course
of his travels Della Valle wrote letters to his friend, Mario Schipano in Naples, and in 1650 these letters were published in Rome in a book divided into
three parts: Turkey, Persia, and India. Included also are maps and plans of
the regions and cities he visited. In India he was particularly interested in
Hinduism, social practices, and ceremonies.[84]

Alexandre de Rhodes (1591–1660), a Jesuit born in Avignon, arrived at
Rome in 1645 after working for about twenty years (1623–43) as a missionary in East Asia. During this time he evangelized at Macao and went on
special missions to Cochin-China (1624–26) and to Tongking (1627–30).
Upon his return to Europe he published his *Relazione . . . di Tunchino*.[85] Part
I of Rhodes' relation provides a valuable ethnohistory of Tongking; Part II
relates the history of the Jesuit mission there. Rhodes also published an An-

[81] *Relatione delle missioni e Christianità che apartengono alla provincia di Malavar. . . .* See Streit,
V, 135; a French translation appeared in the same year at Tournai.
[82] See Streit, V, 137.
[83] For full title see *ibid.*, p. 138. It was reprinted at Rome in 1653. For fuller treatment see
above, pp. 349–50.
[84] Translated in the seventeenth century into English (1665), Dutch (1666), and German (1674).
Also reissued at Rome in 1658–63 with the biography of the author added. Four other Italian
editions appeared before 1700. A modern edition in English, *The Travels of Pietro Della Valle in
India* was published for the Hakluyt Society in 1892 with a critical apparatus by E. Grey. For
recent analyses of his life and work see Wilfrid Blunt, *Pietro's Pilgrimage* (London, 1953), especially Pt. III; Peter G. Bietenholz, *Pietro della Valle (1596–1652). Studien zur Geschichte der Orient-
kenntnis und des Orientbildes im Abendlande* (Basel and Stuttgart, 1962), pp. 105–9, 152–53,
171–81, 197–98; and M. Guglielminetti, *Viaggiatori del Seicento* (Turin, 1967), pp. 329–30.
[85] (Rome, 1650). Second printing at Milan in 1651. Translated into French (1651) and Latin
(1652). Excerpted in Degli Anzi, *Il Genio Vagante* (Parma, 1691), II, 263–301. Also see below,
pp. 408–9.

namite-Latin-Portuguese dictionary, presumably for the use of his successors in Vietnam, and a Latin-Annamite catechism for the converts. He himself was later sent to Persia, where he lived out his remaining years. His published works were to become foundation stones for the mission edifice of Indochina erected during the latter half of the seventeenth century.[86] Throughout his stay in Rome, Rhodes sought to impress his superiors with the need to dispatch bishops to Indochina to build the mission with the aid of a faithful native clergy.[87]

The sufferings of the missionaries in the East, especially in Japan, helped to produce a spate of retrospective publications around mid-century on the Eastern missions. The martyrdom of the two Carmelites who had accompanied the viceroy of India to Acheh in Sumatra during 1638 was brought to general attention only in 1652.[88] Michele Angelo Lualdi (d. 1673), a Roman theologian, reviewed in a publication of 1653 the rise and fall of the Eastern missions from 1498 to around 1638.[89] The first history in Italian of the Jesuits in the East was prepared and published (1653–63) by Daniello Bartoli (1608–85) as part of his unfinished project of writing the complete history of the Jesuit mission endeavor. Its first section, entitled *L'Asia* (Rome, 1653), recounts on the basis of the Jesuit letters and histories the activities of the Society in the East from Xavier's time to the 1580's.[90] The *Giappone* (1660), his second section, reviews the mission history of Japan from 1570 to its demise around 1640.[91] *La Cina* (1663) contains more on general background and secular history than Bartoli's previous volumes; it treats also the vagaries of the China mission from Ricci's entrance in 1583 to 1640.[92] The definitive Varese edition (Rome, 1667) differs from the original edition only in that it also contains Bartoli's version of the sixteenth-century expedition of Ridolpho Acquaviva to the Mughul court.[93]

Fresh news of China was brought to Europe in the 1650's by Martino Martini (1614–61), a Jesuit born at Trent in the Italian Tyrol. He had re-

[86] For the complete titles of his works see Streit, V, 593, 595. Also see below, pp. 408–9.

[87] To this end he published the *Relatione della morte di Andrea Catechista che primo de Christiani nel regno di Cocincina è stato ucciso da gl'infedeli in odio della fede, alli 26, di Luglio, 1644* (Rome, 1652). Translated into French in 1653. He was apparently responsible also for having the story published at Rome (1652) of the martyrdom at Nagasaki of Antonio Rubino (1579–1643), the Jesuit Visitor to China and Japan. See Streit, V, 564.

[88] F. Agostino, *Breve racconto del viaggio di due religiosi Carmelitani scalzi al regno di Achien, nell'isola di Sumatra* (Rome, 1652). See Streit, V, 144.

[89] *L'India orientale suggettata al vangelo.* This four-hundred-page history is dedicated to Pope Innocent X.

[90] This is described as *Parte Prima Dell' historia della Compagnia di Giesu.* Reissued at Genoa (1656) and Rome (1667) in the seventeenth century and in many more editions thereafter. Translated into Latin and printed at Lyons in 1666–67.

[91] The *Parte seconda* was not separately reprinted or translated in the seventeenth century.

[92] The *Terza parte* was translated into Latin and published at Lyons in 1670. Its sections on Chinese life were reprinted most recently at Milan in 1975 with an introduction and notes by Bice Garavelli Mortare.

[93] For a general appreciation of Bartoli's works see J. J. Renaldo, *Daniello Bartoli: A Letterato of the Seicento* (Naples, 1979), chap. iii.

turned aboard a Dutch ship that was forced off course by channel storms and finally landed in Norway. Martini made his way southward through Germany to Amsterdam. Here he had his *Atlas* printed and his Latin account of the Manchu takeover in China. In 1654, the year of his arrival at Rome, an Italian version of his "Tartar war" was published at Milan.[94] At Rome meanwhile, Martini, as procurator and vice-provincial of the China mission, published a brief Latin book listing the names and nationalities of the Jesuits in China, the numbers of Chinese converts, and the books published by the Jesuits in China.[95] Michael Boym (1612–1659), the Polish Jesuit and Ming supporter, meanwhile appeared at Venice in December, 1652, with a Chinese convert and emissary.[96]

For the remainder of the 1650's nothing of consequence on the East was published in Italy.[97] Giacinto (Hyacinth) de Magistris (1605–68), an Italian Jesuit of the Province of Malabar, wrote an account of the state of Christianity in Madura that was published at Rome in 1661.[98] He had returned to Rome himself to report to the papacy on the revolt of the St. Thomas Christians of the Serra. In his baggage he brought a book of translations into Portuguese and Latin from Indian books which he presented to Bartoli, the historian of the mission.[99] His report on Madura, while lengthy, is not generally informative except for its commentary on the "superstitions" and legends of the region.[100]

Giovanni Filippo de Marini (1608–82), an Italian Jesuit who had spent fourteen years missionizing in Tongking, returned to Rome after 1660 to report on the Province of Japan. The Society's Japan province had its headquarters at this time in Tongking: consequently his relation of 1663 deals with Indochina and China rather than Japan.[101] Aside from providing a lengthy summary of the Christian enterprise in Indochina, south China,

---

[94] *Breve historia delle guerre seguite in questi ultimi anni tra Tartari e Cinesi.* A second printing was issued at Milan in 1655, and an excerpt was published in Degli Anzi, *op. cit.* (n. 85), III, 417–65. Also see below, pp. 480–81.

[95] For the title and a complete summary of its contents see Streit, V, 800. Reprinted in 1655. Translated and published in German in 1654.

[96] See Guglielmo Berchet, "Un ambasciatore della Cina a Venezia nel 1652," *Archivio veneto,* n.s., Vol. XXIX, Pt. 1 (1885), pp. 367–80. He reproduces here five previously unpublished documents on the Boym visit (*cf.* above, pp. 194–95).

[97] Philippe Alegambe, a Jesuit bibliographer, published a number of letters from Jesuits who had been martyred in the East in his *Mortes illustres et gesta eorum de Societate Iesu* . . . (Rome, 1657); Girolamo Brusoni (b. 1614), a writer of romances and histories, amplified Botero's *Relazione* with materials gathered from the accounts of the East in the writings of voyagers and missionaries. See his *Varie osservazioni sopra le Relazioni Universali di G. Botero* (Venice, 1659).

[98] *Relatione della Christianità di Maduré.* A French translation appeared in 1663. See Streit, V, 156, 159.

[99] See D. Ferroli, *The Jesuits in Malabar* (Bangalore, 1951), II, 405.

[100] In 1661, the year of Magistris' report, a book on the "wars at Calicut" was published at Venice. The *Raguaglio delle guerre de Calecut* of Basapopi [?] is mentioned only in Ternaux-Compans, p. 310.

[101] *Delle missioni de' Padri della Compagnia di Giesu nella Provincia del Giappone, e particolarmente di quella di Tumkinó libri cinque* (Rome, 1663). Two years later new printings appeared at Rome

Siam, and Makassar, this work includes a description of Laos and of the visit of Giovanni Maria Leria, the first Jesuit to reside in that kingdom.[102] This is followed by a series of letters dated 1650 and 1655 between the Ming survivors (Achilles P'ang and the Empress Helena), the Jesuits, and Pope Alexander VII. Marini was also responsible for translating into Italian from Portuguese Antonio Rubino's report on Jesuit conversion methods in China, which inspired so much controversy that it was placed on the *Index* in 1680.[103]

In India the Jesuits were also plagued by troubles: the rebellion of the St. Thomas Christians of the Serra and the Dutch incursions in Malabar. Disturbed by this turn of events, Pope Alexander VII asked the Propaganda and the Carmelites to rescue the mission. In February, 1656, Giuseppe di Santa Maria Sebastiani (1623–89) and Vincenzo Maria di Santa Caterina da Siena (d. 1679) left for India with others. After vainly trying to work out a compromise and reunion of the contending factions in Malabar, the two friars returned to Rome in February, 1659, for further instruction. On December 15 of that same year, Sebastiani was appointed Apostolic Commissary of the Serra with powers to choose the Malabar bishop. He arrived back in India in 1660 and was there to witness the fall of Cochin (1661) and Cranganore (1663) to the Dutch. He returned to Rome in 1665 to write down the story of his frustrating experiences in India.

Sebastiani's *Prima speditione . . .* (Rome, 1666) recounts at length the reasons for his dispatch to India, the journey to Malabar, the efforts he made to heal the schism, and the return trip to Rome. In the account of his efforts at reconciliation, he digresses periodically on the customs of Malabar as sources of conflict.[104] At Rome, also in 1666, there appeared an Italian translation of the earlier journey to India of Philippe de Sainte-Trinité (1603–71), now general of the Carmelites, that had been published first in Latin during 1649.[105] The *Seconda speditione* (Rome) of Sebastiani did not appear until 1672. It is much more useful than the earlier volume; it reflects the fact that its author spent more time in preparing it. It begins with a table of Italianized Oriental words and their definitions. Then Sebastiani gives the reasons for his second voyage and recounts his activities at Cochin and Goa.[106] Even more reliable

---

and Venice under a new title: *Historia et relatione del Tunchino e del Giappone* (see pls. 54, 79). The texts of the new editions are identical with the *Delle missioni*. Marini's report was translated into French and published in 1666 and 1683. The Rome edition of 1665, dedicated to Pope Alexander VII, includes engravings of a royal guard (facing p. 63) and a mandarin (facing p. 271) of Tongking.

[102] See C. B. Maybon, "Notice biographique et bibliographique sur G. F. de Marini, auteur d'une relation du royaume de Lao," *Revue indochinoise,* July, 1910, pp. 15–25; August, 1910, pp. 152–82; Sept. 1910, pp. 257–71; Oct., 1910, pp. 358–65. On Leria, see below, pp. 1157–59.

[103] *Metodo della dottrina che i padri . . . insegnano a neofiti nelle missioni della Cina . . .* (Lyons, 1665).

[104] Reprinted at Rome in 1668.

[105] See Streit, V, 140, 165. This Italian translation was reprinted at Venice in 1667, 1676, and 1683 and at Rome in 1672. See below, p. 407.

[106] Reprinted at Venice in 1683 and at Rome in 1687. See pl. 78.

is the *Viaggio* (1672) of Sebastiani's companion on his first expedition to India, the Carmelite procurator Vincenzo Maria di Santa Caterina da Siena. Although he was in India for only a short period, Vincenzo's work is especially good on Hinduism and natural history, on south India's plants and animals particularly.[107]

For the missionaries destined to work in India and continental Southeast Asia, the Benedictine abbot Clemente Tosi published a handbook at Rome in 1669. His *Dell' India Orientale descrittione geografica et historica* is a huge work in two volumes. It was designed to provide missionaries with background and arguments enough to confute the idolatry, superstitions, and errors of the Gentiles. The first volume treats India proper and is based on the Jesuit letterbooks and on Manrique's work. The second volume deals with the continental countries from India eastward to south China, and its discussions of Arakan, Pegu, and Burma depend heavily on Manrique.[108] His materials on China and Indochina were amplified by the publication at Rome, also in 1669, of an Italian translation of the account of the voyages made to eastern Asia in the early 1660's by the three French bishops sent there by Pope Alexander VII as vicars apostolic.[109] In 1670 a letter of 1664 by Carlo della Rocca (1613–70), an Italian Jesuit in Cambodia, was published at Mantua.[110]

The Congregation of the Propaganda was responsible in the eyes of the Jesuits for helping to undermine their exclusive control over the Eastern missions. The Jesuit missionary endeavor, especially after the dramatic loss of Japan, was increasingly attacked by the other orders in their reports to the Congregation. The setbacks in India and China were attributed by the Jesuits' enemies to their methods of accommodation and to their concentration upon the conversion of the upper classes and the secular rulers. In 1671 the Sicilian Jesuit, Prospero Intorcetta (1626–96), who had first gone to China with Martini in 1657, was sent by the China mission to Rome as procurator. He was to report to the general and the Congregation on the impoverished condition of the mission and its pressing need for more money and men. To support his case he addressed to the Congregation a history of the mission from 1581 to 1669.[111] In it he stresses the large numbers of converts made by the Jesuits—many more than those baptized by the Dominicans and Franciscans. At the end he appended a translation of a letter from the court at Peking reassuring the Jesuits that the persecutions would cease.

---

[107] *Il viaggio all' Indie Orientali . . .* (Rome, 1672). Reprinted at Venice in 1693.

[108] Reissued in 1676 at Rome under a new title, *L'India orientale. . . .* For Tosi's dependence on Manrique see L. Ambruzzi, "Le missioni cattoliche e l'India," in Costantini *et al., op. cit.* (n. 45), p. 290.

[109] Written in French by François Pallu and first published at Paris in 1668. Pallu was in Europe from 1667 to 1670 and was possibly in Rome when the Italian translation was prepared. See Streit, V, 616, 618.

[110] See Streit, V, 620–21.

[111] *Compendiosa narratione dello stato della missione Cinese, cominciâdo dall' anno 1581, fino al 1669* (Rome, 1672). Translated into Latin 1672. See Streit, V, 849.

One of the main problems faced by the China mission was that of finding a safe passage from Europe to Peking and back again.[112] In 1661 the Jesuits Johann Grueber (1623–80) and Albert d'Orville (d. 1662) were dispatched from Peking to explore the land route westward from Sian through Tibet and the Himalayas to Agra. D'Orville died at Agra and Grueber was accompanied to Rome by Heinrich Roth (1620–68). Once in Italy, Grueber was quizzed in 1664 at Rome and Florence about his discoveries and observations. The great Jesuit savant, Athanasius Kircher, included summaries of some of his answers in the first edition (1667) of his *China illustrata* and summaries of others appeared in the French translation of 1670. Melchisédech Thévenot (1620–92), the renowned collector of travel literature, published Grueber's account in Italian, accompanied by a French translation, in the final part (1672) of his *Relations divers voyages curieux.* . . . [113] The French physician, François Bernier (1620–88), who was at the Mughul court from 1659 to 1667, derived much information from Roth and the other Jesuits at Agra for his history which appeared in an Italian version in 1675.[114] An Italian translation of the book prepared by the French bishops on their mission of 1666 to 1671 to Siam and Indochina was printed at Rome in 1677.[115]

During the remainder of the seventeenth century very little original material seems to have been published in Italian. This dearth certainly relates to the ascendancy of the French Jesuits in the missions of China, Indochina, and Siam, and to the Dutch takeover in Ceylon and Malabar. Only a few relevant works were translated into Italian between 1677 and 1697. One of these was Ambrosio Ortiz' (1638–1718) translation from Spanish of Francisco García's life of Sanvitores, one of the first missionaries and martyrs of the Mariana Islands.[116] The history of the Spanish penetration of the Marianas in Ortiz' version ends in April, 1684.[117]

The intense feelings generated within the church over its losses in the mission field, the hostility between Rome and Portugal, and the controversies among the orders over the "rites question" probably all bore a share of responsibility for the virtual cessation of mission publications in Rome. Indeed, the popes of the latter half of the century, particularly Innocent XI (r.

---

[112] This may account for the new edition of Marco Polo published at Trivigi in 1672 and the publication at Naples in 1673 of an Italian translation of Cubero's voyage around the world. On Cubero see above, p. 360.

[113] Entitled *Viaggio del P. Giovanni Grueber, tornando per terra da China in Europa.* It was later bound into the *Confucius Sinarum philosophus* . . . (Paris, 1687). It was also reproduced in Lorenzo Magalotti, *Notizie varie dell' imperio della Cina* (Florence, 1687). *Cf.* below, pp. 485–86, 528.

[114] *Istoria dell' ultima revoluzione delli stati del Gran Mogor* (Milan). First published in French, 1670; see below, p. 414. For discussion see E. Maclagan, *The Jesuits and the Great Mogul* (London, 1932), pp. 5, 110.

[115] The original French version, written by Luc Fermanel de Favery, appeared at Paris in 1674. See Streit, V, 630, 634.

[116] On García's work see above, p. 357.

[117] *Istoria della conversione . . . dell' Isole Mariane . . .* (Naples, 1686). Epitomized by Francesco Tinelli in his *Compendio della . . . Sanvitores* (Brescia, 1695).

1676–89), made serious efforts to reassert control over the missions and the publishing activities of the orders. A brief relation of the China mission by Philippe Couplet (1622–93) was published in Italian in 1687 while he was acting as procurator (1680–92) in Europe.[118] In 1695 Marcel Leblanc's (1653–93) account of the revolution of 1688 in Siam was translated into Italian.[119] At Florence in 1697 Count Lorenzo Magalotti (1637–1712) published a compendium of materials on China, including Grueber's report and some of his Latin letters. The remainder of this book was extracted from the *Confucius Sinarum philosophus* (Paris, 1687).[120]

It was not until the very last years of the century that the most important of the polemical writings of the rites controversy began to appear in Italian versions. The French Jesuits Le Comte and Le Gobien, in their tracts published at Paris in 1696 and 1698 respectively, asserted that the Dominicans, like the Jesuits, permitted their converts to continue practicing the Confucian rites. Since this aspect of the Jesuit policy of accommodation had been condemned by Charles Maigrot, the vicar apostolic of Fukien, the Dominicans responded bitterly and quickly to these charges. The Dominican general, Antonio Cloche, requested Noel Alexandre, a French Dominican, to prepare a rebuttal. Alexandre, a well-known professor and church historian of Paris, was provided with all the necessary ammunition from Rome. In 1699 the Dominicans published his *Apologia* in French and Italian at Cologne followed by a letter of Maigrot from Foochow to the director of the Seminary of Foreign Missions in Paris.[121] At Turin in 1699 there appeared an Italian translation of Le Gobien's history of K'ang-hsi's edict of toleration for Christianity, which he celebrated as a great victory for Jesuit methods. This was followed in 1700 by a Jesuit response to Alexandre's *Apologia,* also in Italian. In an anonymously issued series of seven letters, Alexandre responded to the Jesuits and followed this with a little book in which he equated the Chinese rites to those of the Greeks and Romans—that is, to idolatry and superstition.[122] Through these publications the issues behind the rites controversy, along with accompanying detail on Chinese beliefs and customs, were relayed to readers of Italian.

For this same public, the century ended with the publication at Naples of the *Giro del Mondo* of Giovanni Francesco Gemelli Careri (1651–1725).[123] A

[118] *Breve ragguaglio delle cose più notabili spettanti al grand' imperio della Cina* (Rome).

[119] *Istoria della rivoluzione del regno di Siam, accaduta l'anno 1688. E dello stato presente dell' India* (Milan). The French original was published at Lyons in 1692.

[120] *Notizie varie dell'imperio della China, e di qualche altro paese adiacente; con la vita di Confucio . . . e un saggio della sua morale.*

[121] Maigrot's letter of 1699 was published without a date of publication.

[122] *Lettere d'un dottore dell' Università di Parigi, dell' Ordine dei Predicatori, intorno alle idolatrie e superstizione della Cina* (Cologne, 1700). N. Alexandre, *Conformità delle cerimonie chinesi colla idolatria greca e romana, in conferma dell' Apologia de Domenicani missionari della China . . .* (Cologne, 1700). For the place of Noel Alexandre in this controversy see Anton Hängü, *Der Kirchenhistoriker Natalis Alexander (1639–1724),* (Freiburg, 1955), pp. 222–24.

[123] Six volumes (1699–1700). At least seven Italian editions were published between 1699 and 1708. Revised and augmented Italian editions were printed at Venice in 1719 and 1728. The

judicial functionary of the Habsburg rulers of Naples, Careri became tired and frustrated with his lot in Europe and decided to become a traveler to distant places. Entirely on his own and without support from state, church, or commercial company, he left Naples in 1693 for the Near East. A man of cultivation who spoke Italian, Spanish, and French, he was somehow able to gain entrance to countries where unattached Europeans were usually unwelcome. In India he was received at the military camp of Aurangzib; at Goa the Portuguese viceroy spoke with him, gave him a letter of introduction to the captain-general of Macao, and provided him with free passage to Macao. He arrived at Macao on August 4, 1695, and spent the next eight months in China. The European missionaries in China, who were awaiting fearfully a visitation from a papal emissary, suspected Careri of being a secret agent of the papacy. Consequently they, like the Portuguese officials of Macao, went out of their way to help him enter China proper and to make the arduous journey to Peking. Careri entered the imperial capital on horseback in November, 1695, and met with the Italian Jesuit Claudio Filippo Grimaldi (1638–1712), who arranged for him to have an audience with the K'ang-hsi emperor. After two months in Peking, Careri made his way back to Macao, where he embarked for the Philippines on April 8, 1696. After touring in the vicinity of Manila, Careri left on a galleon for Mexico, again as a guest! Finally he returned to Naples on December 3, 1698, thus completing his personal five-and-one-half-year tour of the world.

For five months after his return, Careri worked feverishly writing his *Giro*. The first two volumes, on Turkey and Persia, appeared late in 1699; the volumes on India, China, the Philippines, and Mexico were published in the following year. The journal of his travels, presumably kept while on tour, comprises just less than one-half of the text. The other half is drawn from his reminiscences and from previously published accounts.[124] Careri often acknowledges his indebtedness to earlier authors; at times, however, he, like many of his contemporaries, uses the work of others without attribution. At first his story was generally accepted at face value, even though some critics questioned the veracity of certain of his descriptions. His work came into disrepute in 1722 and thereafter, when Jesuits writing from Peking denied that he had ever been received by the Chinese emperor. While Churchill and the Abbé Prevost admitted his travels to their eighteenth-century collections, the Jesuits' accusations were accepted by a large number of skeptical critics of the eighteenth and nineteenth centuries. It was not until the present century that Careri's reputation was rehabilitated by specialists.[125]

French translations of 1719 and 1727 are not always trustworthy. Translated into English in 1704 in *CV*; it is found in Vol. IV of the third edition (1745).

[124] For a critical analysis of his text for the purpose of discovering his literary sources see Alberto Magnaghi, *Il viaggiatore Gemelli Careri (secolo XVII) e il suo Giro del Mondo* (Bergamo, 1900).

[125] *Ibid.*, but more especially Surindranath Sen (ed.), *The Indian Travels of Thevenot and Careri*

Possibly it was the popularity of Careri's *Giro* that impelled the Florentine publisher, Giuseppe Manni, to print the *Ragionamenti* (Chronicle) of Francesco Carletti (*ca.* 1573–1636) in 1701.[126] The printer Manni, who had published in 1697 Magalotti's *Notizie* of China,[127] collaborated with Jacopo Carlieri, one of Magalotti's associates, in putting Carletti's century-old account into print. A Florentine merchant, Carletti went from Florence back to Florence in circumnavigating the world between 1594 and 1606. On his return he reported to Grand Duke Ferdinando de' Medici on international trading prospects. The grand duke, who was eager to develop Leghorn (Livorno) into a center for trade with Brazil and the East Indies, had listened attentively to Carletti's oral reports, which were then written down as *Ragionamenti*. The original manuscript is no longer extant, but various texts derived from it seem to have been circulated in the seventeenth century. The edition published in 1701 was polished for printing, probably by the Florentine group that had become interested in East Asia during the final years of the century. Carletti's is a merchant's account and particularly valuable for its discussion of sixteenth-century trading practices and problems. It is also an important nonclerical source on conditions in Japan during the critical years of 1597–98.[128]

Most of the seventeenth-century Italian materials on Asia appeared in the letterbooks and other writings of the Jesuits. The letterbooks in Italian, particularly at the beginning of the century, were frequently translations of Portuguese and Spanish letterbooks; in the last generation of the century they were often translations of French writings. Because the Italian language was more current in Catholic Europe than any of the other vernaculars, the letterbooks in Italian were more often than not the means through which news from Asia was transmitted from Iberia to northern Europe or vice versa. Once the letterbooks were compiled, edited, and translated in Eu-

---

(New Delhi: National Archives of India, 1949); Philippe de Vargas, "Le 'Giro del Mondo' de Gemelli Careri, en particulier le récit du séjour en Chine, Roman ou Vérité?" *Schweizerische Zeitschrift für Geschichte,* V (1955), 417–51. For his Philippine experiences see BR, I, 51, 52, 65. For his comments on the sea journey from Manila to Acapulco see De la Costa, *op. cit.* (n. 34), pp. 229–31.

[126] *Ragionamenti di Francesco Carletti Fiorentino sopra le cose da lui vedute ne' suoi viaggi si dell' Indie Occidentali, e Orientali, come d'altri paesi. . . .* The modern critical edition was edited by Gianfranco Silvestro for the Crusca Academy and published at Milan in 1958; it is a printing of the manuscript in the Biblioteca Angelica at Rome, a document that is considered to be closer to Carletti's original version than the edition of 1701. Herbert Weinstock has translated the Angelica version into English as *My Voyage around the World by Francesco Carletti, a Sixteenth Century Florentine Merchant* (New York, 1964).

[127] See above, p. 386.

[128] See M. N. Trollope (trans.), "The Carletti Discourse; A Contemporary Italian Account of a Visit to Japan in 1597–98," *Transactions of the Asiatic Society of Japan,* 2d ser., IX (1932), 1–35; also see M. Cooper (ed.), *They Came to Japan, An Anthology of European Reports on Japan, 1543–1640* (London, 1965), pp. 64–65.

rope, the news they relayed was usually two to three years old by the date of publication.

The news was even older in the publications of the commercial printers who cannibalized the letterbooks for their own profit. The separates published by the printers of Venice, Milan, and Genoa generally tended to be less edifying and more curious than the official and semi-official publications of the Jesuits. The commercial printers were likewise freer to publish non-Jesuit, sometimes even Dutch and English, materials on the spice trade and on the struggle for control of its entrepôts and production centers. Still, the Italian commercial cities, despite the sporadic efforts of their printers, merchants, and political leaders, were never able to compete effectively in the seaborne spice trade.

The Jesuit letterbooks and travel accounts predominate among the materials on Asia published in Italian. Jesuits of Italian descent were prominent in the Asian missions, especially those of eastern Asia, throughout most of the seventeenth century. In the China mission the pioneers, Valignano, Ricci, and Ruggiero, were succeeded by Pasio, Longobardo, Grimaldi, Martini, and Intorcetta. Only during the last two decades of the century did the French supplant the Italians in the Jesuit's China mission. All of these provided information about the Middle Kingdom published in Italian. Borri, Rhodes, and Marini, among others, relayed to Europe reliable and important information about Indochina and the missions there. The letters of Nobili and Magistris opened Madura in south India to European readers.

From the Italian materials alone a strangely different view of Asia emerges. The Italians, unlike the Iberians, have almost nothing to report on the Spiceries, the Philippines, or the islands of the Indonesian archipelago. References to commercial centers like Malacca and Colombo appear only coincidentally in the Jesuit letterbooks. Carletti and Careri, the world travelers, are the only two to remark seriously on the trade of the East. Even though the Genoese formed a trading company around mid-century, the Italian published materials which appeared prior to its organization are virtually silent on overseas trade. The Italian sources, probably because of Rome's predominance, are heavy with mission history and slight on almost everything else. Nonetheless they are valuable as auxiliaries to the more complete and better-balanced Iberian, Dutch, French, and English sources.

CHAPTER V

The French Literature

Throughout the sixteenth century the French had watched from a distance the progress of overseas expansion and the contest for control of the Spiceries and the sea-lanes of the East. Because they were not directly involved in the trade and missions of Asia, the French were able to begin assessing, more seriously and fully than their neighbors, the meaning of the revelation of Asia for European civilization. In France itself serious rents, religious and political particularly, had begun around 1550 to appear in the fabric of life. The civil wars of 1562 to 1598 had exposed the weakness and tautness of its threads. Weary of watching the country tear itself apart, the *politiques* and others began to call imperiously for compromise, cessation of strife, and a reweaving of society's tissues. To King Henry IV (r. 1589–1610) was left the task of repair and restoration that helped France to regain its unity and to become again a positive force in international affairs.

For the king, the restoration of internal and external peace and order did not come easily. Shortly after his entry into Paris in 1594, its Parlement began to cause him trouble. Under pressure from the university and the Huguenots, the Parlement of Paris decreed in 1595 the expulsion of the Jesuits from France. The king, who needed the cooperation of the French clergy and the papacy to effect his program of religious compromise, steadfastly refused to issue an edict endorsing the exile of the Jesuits. The Jesuits themselves, meanwhile, left or were driven from the jurisdiction of the Parlement of Paris, some of them just to other parts of France. Henry began at the same time to urge a compromise between the Jesuits and their enemies. He refused to force the Parlements of the south to follow the lead, as was customary, of the Parlement of Paris. After proclaiming the Edict of Nantes (1598), granting limited toleration to the Huguenots, Henry undertook negotiations in 1601 to work out terms for the recall of the Jesuits. In 1604 he issued the Edict of Rouen, reestablishing the Jesuits throughout France, and pressured the Parlement of Paris into registering it.[1] By these two edicts the king established a legal base for bringing both the Huguenots and the Jesuits back into the mainstream of French society and effected an uneasy truce in religious hostilities.

The agony of France's prolonged war with Spain was ended in 1598 with the conclusion of the Peace of Vervins. Philip II of Spain, nearing the end of his life, had decided to negotiate with Henry, once the Bourbon had abjured Protestantism. Both countries needed peace badly at the end of the sixteenth century, in order to attend to other international commitments and to pressing domestic concerns. The winding down of the war in the Netherlands between Spain and the United Provinces also contributed to a growing understanding of the fact that Spain was on the defensive in northern Europe and that France might gradually replace Spain as the arbiter of its affairs. Henry IV began in the first decade of the seventeenth century to reestablish France as a leading power in Europe's international affairs and as a potential competitor in the new race for trade and influence in the East.

I

THE JESUIT LETTERS AND THE PRE-COMPANY VOYAGES

The establishment of the Protestant English (1600) and Dutch (1602) East India Companies raised hopes among the other maritime countries of northern Europe that they too might bypass the Iberian monopolists, send out national voyages directly to the East, and stake out claims of their own in Asia. The French, particularly the merchants of the seaport towns of Normandy and Brittany, were quick to react to these changing conditions. About seventy years after Jean Ango of Dieppe sent ships directly to the East, the merchants of northeastern France again became active.[2] In 1600 the merchants of Saint-Malo, Vitré, and Laval, with the aid of some disgruntled Dutch and Flemish merchants, organized a company to establish direct trade to the Moluccas and Japan. Two vessels were sent to the East in 1601, but neither returned; one was wrecked on the way out and the other off the coast of Spain in 1603 on its return from Sumatra. Meanwhile some merchants of Dieppe, after being assured the cooperation of certain Flemish and French merchants, obtained royal letters patent in 1604 giving them an exclusive privilege for fifteen years of sending voyages into the Indian Ocean.

---

[1] This account is derived from the Jesuit version set forth in H. Fouqueray, *Histoire de la Compagnie de Jésus en France* (5 vols.; Paris, 1910–25), II, 379–690. See also R. Mousnier, *The Assassination of Henry IV* (New York, 1973), Appendix 6.
[2] On the Ango expedition of 1529–30 see *Asia*, I, 177–78.

Because of strenuous opposition from the Dutch and the Bretons as well as from the Duc de Sully, this group was unable to dispatch a single vessel before the king's death in 1610.[3]

In connection with these first enterprises there appeared in French a spate of literature on Eastern voyages. In 1598, the year of the Edict of Nantes and the Peace of Vervins, French editions of several Dutch voyages were published in the United Provinces and quickly reissued in France.[4] These were followed shortly after 1600 by editions of Barent Langenes' *Thresor des chartes* (1602), first published in Dutch in 1598; the account of Van Neck and Van Warwijck's fleet, *Le second livre* (1601); and Van Noort's world voyage (1602).[5] A relation of the Philippines by Francisco Tello de Guzman (governor, 1596–1602) was translated from Spanish into French and published at Lyons (1599) and Paris (1599). Translations of retrospective materials from pertinent Italian, Spanish, and Latin works were likewise numerous in these years.[6]

During the years (1595–1604) of the Jesuits' official exile from Paris letterbooks were not numerous and were published generally in Rouen, Antwerp, Louvain, and Lyons.[7] Those published to 1602 dealt mainly with the persecutions and martyrdoms of 1597 in Japan, perhaps to suggest to the Parlement of Paris that the Japanese and the French had something in common in their mistreatment of the Jesuits. News of China written by Nicolas Lombard (Niccolò Longobardo) was published at Agen and Paris in 1602.[8] Nicolas Pimenta's letter of 1600 from Goa on Jesuit activities in India was published in French translation at Paris in 1603. The French Jesuits, it is clear, tried to keep the public informed of their Society's activities in the East. But those items which they managed to publish while still officially excluded from Paris comprise but a small fraction of the materials that were

---

[3] See C. de la Roncière, *Histoire de la marine française* (Paris, 1910), IV, 261–67; and J. Barassin, "Compagnies de navigation et expéditions françaises dans l'Océan Indien au XVIIᵉ siècle," *Studia* (Lisbon), No. 11 (1963), 375–77.

[4] Gerrit de Veer, *Vraye description de trois voyages de mer* . . . (Amsterdam, 1598, 1600, 1604, 1609; Paris 1599; translated into English in 1609); Willem Lodewyckszoon, *Premier livre*. . . . (Amsterdam, 1598, 1601, 1609); and the account of Cornelis de Houtman's voyage, *Iournal.* . . . (Middelburg, 1598; Paris, 1598).

[5] For discussion of these books see below, pp. 439–43.

[6] *Advis moderne du grand royaume de Mogor* . . . (Paris, 1598) is an excerpt translated from Peruschi's *Informatione* (Rome, 1597). On Peruschi see *Asia,* I, 452–53. Acosta's *Histoire naturelle et moralle des Indes,* translated from Spanish into French, appeared at Paris in 1598, 1600, 1606. On José de Acosta see *Asia,* I, 709, 806–8. Mendoza's Spanish history of China appeared in French in 1600, 1606, 1609, the last being a new translation from the Latin. Anthoine Colin's *Histoire des drogues* . . . (Lyons, 1602) was translated from Clusius' *Epitome* of the works of Garcia da Orta, Cristobal de Acosta, and Nicolas Monardes. A Latin edition (1602) of the older works of Góis and Teive was published in France. And Maffei's history of the Jesuits in the East in the French translation of François Arnault de la Borie, canon of Perigueux, appeared at Paris in 1605.

[7] On Jesuit printing in the first half of the century see H.-J. Martin, *Livre pouvoirs et société à Paris au XVIIᵉ siècle, 1598–1701,* (2 vols.; Geneva, 1969), I, 138–43.

[8] For titles see Streit, V, 9, 12, 321, 363, 685.

contemporaneously appearing in the Iberian and Italian letterbooks. Furthermore, the French Jesuits were not participants, at this time, in the eastern missions of the Society.

Materials written originally in French did not begin to appear in print until 1604. François Martin, a native of Vitré who had sailed to Sumatra and back on the "Croissant" from 1601 to 1603, was the first Frenchman to prepare a travel account of the eastward voyage. He was asked by Henry IV on his return to France to dictate the record of his experiences.[9] He was probably the ship's surgeon; his account contains many observations on the animals, plants, and drugs of the Indies as well as a treatise on scurvy. A revised and expanded edition of Martin's work appeared in Paris in 1609 to which a small dictionary of Malay was added.[10] The additions may have been the work of Martin's townsman, Pierre Olivier Malherbe of Vitré, who returned to France in 1609 after a world tour that had lasted for twenty-seven years. This intrepid traveler was received in audience several times by the king. Malherbe told the king about the gold and silver mines of the East Indies, outlined several routes which might be taken to them, and volunteered to conduct an expedition himself. This first French circumnavigator (if we may assume the truth of his story) also visited China, and in India he was received in audience by Akbar.[11] Both editions of Martin's book were dedicated to Henry IV.

The king, who was assassinated in 1610, by the allegedly Jesuit-influenced Ravaillac, went to his grave without realizing his overseas ambitions. His enthusiasm, shared by his queen, had the effect, however, of stimulating the publication, beginning in 1604, of a wide range of materials on the East. Judging from their publications, the French appear to have watched most closely the progress of the Dutch. The work of the Flemish geographer Cornelius Wytfliet (b. 1550), originally issued in Latin in 1598, was translated into French and published at Douai in 1605. Revised editions appeared in 1607 and 1611. Book II of his *Histoire universelle des Indes Orientales et Occidentales* deals with the East Indies and was derived by Wytfliet from the writings of Giovanni Antonio Magini (1555–1617), the Italian geographer, and other authors.[12] The edition of 1611 begins with a chronicle of the Portuguese voyages to 1608, followed by brief topical discussions of the various geographical areas of the Portuguese East and a survey of the progress there

[9] *Description du premier voyage faict aux Indes Orientales par les François en l'an 1603* . . . (Paris, 1604). For a complete bibliographical survey see Geoffrey Atkinson, *La littérature géographique française de la Renaissance. Répertoire bibliographique* (Paris, 1927), pp. 351–52.

[10] See Atkinson, *op. cit.* (n. 9), p. 407. For an analysis of his botanical observations, as well as those of other seventeenth-century French travelers, see E. and C. Flaumenhaft, "Asian Medicinal Plants in Seventeenth Century French Literature," *Economic Botany,* Vol. XXXVI (1982), Pt. 2, pp. 147–62.

[11] See Z. Bamboat, *Les voyageurs français aux Indes aux XVIIᵉ et XVIIIᵉ siècles* (Paris, 1933), pp. 34–39; also Barassin, *loc. cit.* (n. 3), pp. 376–77.

[12] For full bibliographical information see Atkinson, *op. cit.* (n. 9), pp. 363–64. On the edition of 1609 see *ibid.,* pp. 385–86.

of the Jesuit mission. In essence this popular book provided the reader of French with a simplified but informed description of the East. While Wytfliet included maps in his first book, on America, the second book, on the East, was not so favored.

Certain aspects of contemporary Dutch activities in the East could also be followed by readers of French. In two pamphlets of 1607 and 1608, notice is taken of the Dutch determination to continue their advance in the East Indies despite the setbacks they were then experiencing there at the hands of the Spanish.[13] The appearance of the Siamese mission of 1608 at the court of Count Maurice of Nassau, later Prince of Orange, was noted by an anonymous publication at Lyons of the same year.[14] The French were also kept up to date by the four editions which appeared between 1605 and 1609 of Pierre Victor Palma Cayet's popular chronology of events taking place after the conclusion of peace between Spain and France in 1598.[15] In 1610 the first French edition of Linschoten's famous book appeared, probably printed at Frankfurt.[16] At Amsterdam in the same year there came from the press of Cornelis Claeszoon a French collection of Dutch voyages.[17]

The Jesuits, after their return to grace in 1604, increased their efforts to translate into French the most important of their letterbooks. A substantial letterbook on the condition of the missions in China, Japan, and India was translated from Italian and published at Paris in 1604.[18] François Solier (1558–1628), a Jesuit biographer and martyrologist, provided, also in 1604, a French translation of two long letters from Japan relating what had happened there to the Christians after the death of Hideyoshi.[19] Father Pasio's Annual Letter from Japan for 1600–1601, which was published in Italian in 1603, appeared at Paris in 1605[20] along with Carvalho's letter of 1601 from China.[21] The Annual Letter from the Philippines for 1602 and 1603 appeared at both Rome and Paris in 1605.[22] Thus, within the first two years of their return to Paris, the Jesuits had made available in French the latest reports from their major missionary outposts in the East.

---

[13] Iudocus van Kerkhove, *Nouvelles des choses qui se passent en diverses et loingtaines parties du monde* . . . (Paris, 1607); and the anonymous *Sommaire recueil des raisons plus importantes, qui doyvent mouvoir Messieurs des Estats des Provinces Unies du Pays-bas, de ne quitter point les Indes. Traduit de Flamand en François,* La Rochelle, 1608. For full bibliographical information see Atkinson, *op. cit.* (n. 9), pp. 380, 391–92. On the Spanish conquest of the Moluccas see above, pp. 215–16.

[14] *Les ambassades, et presents du Roy de Siam envoyez à l'excellence du prince Maurice.* On the embassy see John Anderson, *English Intercourse with Siam in the Seventeenth Century* (London, 1890), p. 38.

[15] *Chronologie septenaire de l'histoire de la paix entre les roys de France et d'Espagne . . . avec le succez de plusieur navigations faicts aux Indes Orientales . . .* (Paris, 1605). Followed by updated editions of 1606, 1607, 1609. See Atkinson, *op. cit.* (n. 9), pp. 361–62.

[16] According to P. A. Tiele, *Mémoire bibliographique sur les journaux des navigateurs néerlandais* (reprint of 1869 ed.; Amsterdam, 1960), pp. 94–95.

[17] For details see *ibid.,* pp. 5–6.

[18] See Streit, V, 21.

[19] Published at Arras. See *ibid.,* p. 377.

[20] *Ibid.,* p. 380.

[21] *Ibid.,* p. 692.

[22] *Ibid.,* pp. 247–49.

On India, missionary materials by non-Jesuits began to be published in France. Francisco Pereira (d. 1621), an Augustinian superior, wrote a brief report to Spain on the work of the Augustinians in Bengal, Goa, and Ormuz, which was published in French translation in 1606.[23] The letter of Nicolas Trigault, the Flemish Jesuit, directed to the provincial of the Low Countries, was given wide circulation in France during 1608–9. Written from Goa on Christmas eve of 1607, it reviews at some length the state of the Jesuit missions throughout the East and comments on the threat posed by the Dutch fleet to Malacca and Amboina.[24] Jean Baptiste de Glen, an Augustinian theologian, published in 1609, in French, António de Gouvea's account of the Jesuit-Portuguese success in aligning the St. Thomas Christians of Malabar with the Latin Church.[25]

The Jesuits of France, like their colleagues elsewhere at this time, watched anxiously the course of events in Japan. In 1606 Gabriel de Matos' Annual Letter from Japan for 1603 was printed in French at Douai.[26] The story of the martyrdoms suffered by six Japanese Christian nobles sent by Luis Cerqueira, bishop of Japan, was printed in several French editions of 1607–8.[27] This was followed in 1608–9 by two editions of the Annual Letters from Japan of 1603, 1604, and 1605 printed at Douai and Lyons, respectively, again translated from the Italian.[28]

The entry of the Jesuits into China, as told in Pantoja's letter of 1602 from Peking to Luis de Guzman, was announced in France by its publication in 1607.[29] Guzman, the Spanish historian of the mission, was evidently instrumental in having Pantoja's letter widely circulated in all the Catholic coun-

---

[23] *Relation authentique envoyée par les Prélats, Viceroys, Grand Chancellier, et Secrétaire d' l'Estat des Indes à S. M. Catholique* [Philip II of Spain] . . . (Paris). This was translated from the Italian version published at Rome in 1606. Among other matters this letter recounts what happened to the Muslims converted by the Augustinians in 1602. It was possibly this account which led certain French printers to publish at Paris, Lyons, and Rouen in 1608 a letter falsely attributed to Diego de Magalhães. *La conversion de trois grands rois infidèles de la secte de Mahomet* is in fact a reprinting, probably pirated for profit, of a Jesuit letter originally published in 1571. See Streit, V, 44–45.

[24] First published at Bordeaux in 1608, according to Ternaux-Compans, p. 111. Other editions appeared in 1609 at Paris, Lyons, and Antwerp. See Atkinson, *op. cit.* (n. 9), pp. 409–11, and Streit, V, 49–50.

[25] On the original Portuguese account of 1606 see above, pp. 320–21. Glen's two-part translation of the Spanish version was published at Antwerp and Brussels. A copy of *La messe des anciens Chrestiens dicts de S. Thomas,* the second part of this work, is in the Regenstein Library, the University of Chicago. C. Th. A. I. [*i.e.,* M. Eudes], *Tradition catholiq. ou traicté de la croyance des Chrestians d'Asie . . . ez dogmes . . . controversez en ce têps* (n.p., 1609) may be based upon or excerpted from the Glen translation.

[26] From the Italian version of 1605. For its contents see Atkinson, *op. cit.* (n. 9), p. 371.

[27] The Portuguese original was published in 1604, but the French version was translated from the Italian edition of 1607. The French versions appeared at Paris (1607), Lyons (1607), and Arras (1608). See Streit, V, 383–84.

[28] For full bibliographical information see Streit, V, 387–88.

[29] Pantoja's *Advis* was published in French at Lyons (1607, 1608), Rennes (1607), Arras (1607), and Rouen (1608).

tries of Europe. His history, which covered the Eastern mission of the Jesuits to 1600, was also the inspiration for a massive compilation of Jesuit materials for the entire period of the Jesuit mission in the East down to 1610 put together by Pierre Du Jarric (1566–1617), a Jesuit and a professor of philosophy and moral theology at Bordeaux. Du Jarric's three-volume *Histoire des choses plus memorables advenues tant ez Indes Orientales . . .* (Bordeaux 1608, 1610, 1614) was assembled from the available Jesuit letters, letterbooks, and histories, as well as from the contemporary Portuguese compilation by Fernão Guerreiro.[30] Indeed, Guerreiro sent letters of advice, books, and memoirs to Du Jarric for his guidance and use. While relying heavily on the texts themselves, Du Jarric wove them together skillfully with a continuous narrative that is strongly reminiscent of Guerreiro's work. And like the Portuguese collection, it is a veritable mine of information, old and new, on the progress of the Jesuits in the East and on all of the countries in which they were active before 1610.[31]

The assassination of Henry IV in 1610 was followed by political changes favorable to the budding aspirations of the colonialists. The Duc de Sully, an opponent of overseas activities, was replaced in 1611 as *surintendant des finances* by Pierre Jeannin (1540–1622), president of the Parlement of Dijon, who sought to encourage the formation of commercial companies. When François Pyrard (d. 1621) of Laval returned to France in 1611, it was Jeannin, probably with the support of the queen regent, who encouraged the immediate publication of his *Discours* (1611). Pyrard had embarked aboard the "Corbin," one of two French vessels that left Saint-Malo in 1601. When the ship was wrecked in the Maldive Islands, Pyrard made his way ashore and spent the next four years at Male and its environs. He studied the Maldive language and was well treated by the sultan and his aides. In 1607 Pyrard was captured by a Bengali expedition and taken to Bengal. From there he made his way back to the west coast of India, where he was pressed into service by the Portuguese. For the next two years and more, he worked with the Portuguese and traveled to Ceylon and the Moluccas. He finally returned to Laval in 1611 and shortly went on to Paris.

Pyrard's *Discours du voyage des françois aux Indes Orientales . . .* (Paris, 1611) was first published in one volume dedicated to the queen regent. It is mainly a report of his adventures, to which he added a treatise on the plants and animals of the East based on his personal observations. Over the next several years, probably with the prodding of Jeannin and others, he rewrote

---

[30] On Guerreiro's *Relaçam . . .* see above, pp. 316–18.
[31] Part II was reissued at Arras and Valenciennes in 1611. A Latin translation called *Thesaurus* was published in 1615 at Cologne. In 1628 the Arras edition was also reprinted there. For an analysis of Du Jarric's sources see the introduction to C. H. Payne (ed. and trans.), *Akbar and the Jesuits. An Account of the Jesuit Missions to the Court of Akbar by Father Pierre du Jarric, S.J.* (London, 1926).

and expanded the original version, and in 1615 he published his two-volume *Voyage de François Pyrard*. It was after the publication of this revised version that Pierre Bergeron, an editor and collector of travel literature, began to work with Pyrard on preparing a newly revised edition of his unique account.[32] In 1619, just two years before the presumed date of Pyrard's death, the final version of the *Voyage* appeared at Paris. To it was added a Maldive vocabulary, the first to be published in Europe.[33] The sections on India and the East were also expanded in this edition, probably with materials extracted from one of the French editions (1610, 1614) of Linschoten's work. In the text, probably at Bergeron's urging, the author argues the need for France to participate more actively in overseas exploration and trade.[34]

Efforts to send out fleets from Brittany and Normandy met with no success during the years of the regency (1610–14) and the Estates-General (1614–15). In 1615 two merchants of Rouen combined with the merchants of Dieppe to form the "Compagnie des Moluques." This combine was granted letters patent giving them a monopoly of Eastern trade for eighteen years. Two ships were sent out from Honfleur in 1616. One was captured in Java by the Dutch; the other returned safely with a rich cargo. The Norman sailors held prisoners at Bantam sent letters in 1617 advising the French that they should not again try to penetrate the Moluccas, the Philippines, or Japan—territories then closed to them by the Dutch.[35]

The French, despite such warnings, continued to plan new expeditions.[36] Perhaps they were encouraged in their endeavors by the return to Honfleur of one of their vessels and by the publication in 1617 of the *Voyages* of Jean Mocquet (b. 1575).[37] A native of Vienne, Mocquet had been an apothecary at the court of Henry IV. In 1601 he was authorized by the king to travel abroad to collect specimens and rarities for the royal *cabinet des singularitez* at the Tuileries. Between 1601 and 1612 he made five voyages, the fourth taking him to Goa. In Goa around 1610 he met Pyrard who told him about the Maldives. In the *Voyages*, Mocquet describes the commerce of the Portuguese and condemns them roundly for their depravity and greed. A few

---

[32] See R. O. Lindsay, "Pierre Bergeron: A Forgotten Editor of French Travel Literature," *Terrae incognitae*, VII (1976), 33.

[33] On Pyrard's contributions see M. A. H. Fitzler, "Die Maldiven im 16. und 17. Jahrhundert," *Zeitschrift für Indologie und Iranistik*, X (1935–36), 215–56. See Flaumenhaft and Flaumenhaft, *loc. cit.* (n. 10), pp. 148–49, on his botanical observations.

[34] For an English translation of, and an introduction to, the 1619 edition see Albert Gray (trans. and ed.), *The Voyage of François Pyrard of Laval to the East Indies, the Maldives, the Moluccas, and Brazil* in "HS," o.s., LXXVI, LXXVII, LXXX (London, 1887, 1888, 1890). A French edition was published in 1679 in one volume and without the vocabulary. Abridged versions were translated in the seventeenth century into German and English: *PP*, IX, 563–70.

[35] See Barassin, *loc. cit.* (n. 3), pp. 377–79.

[36] At La Rochelle in 1615 there appeared in French the famous navigational manual of Pedro de Medina. On Medina see *Asia*, II, Bk. 3, 420–21.

[37] *Voyages en Afrique, Asie, Indes orientales et occidentales* . . . (Paris). Reprinted at Rouen in 1645 and 1665. Translated into Dutch (1656), German (1688), and English (1696).

years later Agustin Hiriart, a jeweler of Bordeaux who worked at the court of the "Great Mogor," was sending letters to his friends in France describing in glowing terms the wealth of India.[38]

The Molucca Company underwent a reorganization in 1617 and united its activities with those of the merchants of Saint-Malo. This syndicate sponsored the preparation and the dispatch of three vessels from Honfleur in 1619, the so-called Fleet of Montmorency. In 1620 the French vessels arrived at Sumatra; two were captured by the Dutch and one returned to Le Havre in 1622. Its pilot, Jean Le Tellier, finally published at Dieppe in 1631 his *Voyage fait aux Indes orientales*. Its commander, General Augustin de Beaulieu, also wrote a detailed account of Sumatra, but it was not published until Thévenot included it in his *Relations de divers voyages* (1663).[39]

The French publishers, stimulated by the growing enthusiasm for overseas exploits, contributed their share by printing retrospective and contemporary accounts of voyages and histories. A French translation of the earliest of Drake's voyages appeared at Paris in 1613.[40] Samuel de Champlain's (1567–1635) effort of 1612 to find a northwest passage to China was recorded in his *Voyages* published at Paris in 1613. This included a bit of sensational exotica, previously published in Spain and Italy, now translated into French; it told about the Indian, aged 380 years, who had been married eight times and who had grown a second set of teeth.[41] In 1614 a Latin reprint of Maffei's Jesuit mission history was issued at Caen, and at Rouen there appeared the eighth edition of L. de La Porte's translation of Mendoza's book on China as well as Jean Du-Bec-Crespin's *Histoire du Grand Tamerlane*.[42] The Normans, while undertaking Asian exploits of their own, appear also to have had a taste for the earlier achievements of others.

At Paris, also in 1614, there appeared the huge compendium by Pierre d'Avity (1573–1635), a geographer and one of the literati.[43] More than one hundred pages (chaps. xxiv through xxx) of this one-thousand-page volume deal with Tartary, China, Japan, Pegu, the Mughul Empire, Calicut, and Vijayanagar. Avity based his account on the older sources but updated it, using more recent materials. By 1659 this popular geography had gone through six reprintings in French and had been fully translated into English (1615) and German (1628).

News of contemporary activities hereafter began to appear more quickly in books written in French. A Paris printer issued late in 1615 the story of the reception accorded the Japanese emissaries on their entry into Rome on

---

[38] See Bamboat, *op. cit.* (n. 11), pp. 38–40.

[39] See Barassin, *loc. cit.* (n. 3), pp. 380–81. See below, pp. 410–11.

[40] *Le voyage de l'illustre . . . Chevalier François drach.*

[41] Paris, 1613. For the complete title see Ternaux-Compans, p. 125.

[42] At Lyons in 1615 appeared a Latin edition of Quintus Curtius Rufus' history of Alexander the Great's exploits in Asia.

[43] *Les estats, empires, et principautez du monde . . .* (Paris, 1614).

November 2, 1615.[44] At Amsterdam a report in French was published almost immediately after the return of the fleet of 1616 with its cargo from the East Indies.[45] The journal of Willem Corneliszoon Schouten's voyage (1615–17) to India by a new route, was printed with maps at Paris in a French version of 1618.[46] While the French printers kept apace of newsworthy developments, they also continued to print pertinent materials from the past. A book appeared at Paris in 1617 relating Quiros' discovery of the austral land, or the fifth part of the world, which stressed its untapped riches.[47] At Lyons a second edition of Colin's *Histoire des drogues,* translated from Clusius' *Epitome,* appeared in 1619 in a richly illustrated four-volume set. At Yverdon in 1619 a second edition was published of Claude Duret's *Thresor* of languages with its excellent depiction of Japanese characters.[48]

Even though the Society of Jesus lived under a cloud of accusation and hostility because of its alleged role in the assassination of Henry IV (1610), its French members diligently continued bringing out publications on the activities of the Jesuits in Asia. Michel Coyssard (1547–1623), a leading Jesuit educator, translated pertinent materials from Italian and Latin, sometimes openly, sometimes anonymously, and sometimes with his name in anagram form.[49] In these years most of his translations were published at Lyons, where he was vice-provincial of the Society until his death in 1623. In 1611–12 he had published there his translation of Tursellinus' Latin biography of Xavier. But about the contemporary Eastern exploits of their brothers, the French Jesuits published nothing between 1610 and 1614, a hiatus which is probably attributable to the domestic troubles confronting them after the assassination of the king. In 1615, in connection with the General Congregation of the Society held at Rome, an *Advis* appeared in French on reforming the Society that was presented originally in Portuguese by Fernando de Mendoça (1575–1648).[50]

---

[44] This was a translation from the *Acta Audientiae Publicae* (Rome, 1615). For details see Streit, V, 406–7.

[45] *Récit de ce qui s'est passé entre les Portugois et les Hollandois au delà de la ligne équinoxiale, avec la copie de la cargaison de trois navires chargés aux Indes pour venir en Hollande, et en Zélande, en 1616.* Listed in Ternaux-Compans, p. 132.

[46] For details see below, pp. 446–48, and Tiele, *op. cit.* (n. 16), pp. 41–47.

[47] *Copie de la requête présentée au roi d'Espagne par le capitaine Ferdinand de Quir, sur la descouverte de la cinquième partie du monde. . . .* Listed in Ternaux-Compans, p. 133. On Quiros see above, pp. 308–9.

[48] On Duret see *Asia,* II, Bk. 3, 522–23.

[49] While a teacher of rhetoric at the college of Clermont in Paris, Coyssard began as early as 1571 to translate the Jesuit letterbooks on the East into French. He left Paris around 1592, when the Jesuits at Clermont were coming under heavier pressure, to become vice-provincial at Lyons. Throughout the exile (1595–1604) Coyssard was one of the leaders of the Jesuit resistance in the south. During those years and in the years after the assassination of the king, he kept his identity secret by publishing the letterbooks anonymously or with his name in anagrams. For the anagrams he used and for the most complete bibliography of his translations available see Ernest M. Rivière, *Supplément* (Vol. xii; 1968) to A. and A. de Backer and E. Sommervogel *Bibliothèque de la Compagnie de Jésus* (Louvain, 1960), pp. 150–82.

[50] See Streit, V, 74.

The arrival in Italy in 1615 of the Japanese legates and of Nicolas Trigault, the Flemish Jesuit missionary, helped to revive interest in the overseas missions. At Douai, Trigault's native city and a center of Catholic learning, a translation into Latin was published in 1612 of the Italian version of the Japan letters for 1609–10.[51] At Lille two letters were published in 1614, the one from Gregory Lopes in the Philippines and the other from Matteo Ricci in China.[52] The letters from China brought back to Europe by Trigault were published in Latin at Augsburg (1615), Antwerp (1615), and Lyons (1616).[53] Similarly, the *De christiana expeditione . . .* based on Ricci's commentaries of China appeared at Augsburg (1615) and Lyons (1616). At Lyons a French version translated by D. F. de Riquebourg-Trigault, nephew of Nicolas and physician to the count of Nassau, also appeared in 1616. The Ricci-Trigault book was to remain the major authoritative work on China for the next fifty years.[54]

Japan began to reemerge on the French horizon with the publication at Paris in 1615–16 of the reception accorded the Japanese legates brought to Rome by the Franciscans.[55] Coyssard translated from Italian the letters from Japan of 1613 and 1614 and had them published at Lyons in two printings of 1618 and 1619.[56] *Annuae litterae* were published at Douai (1618) and at Lyons (1619) which include summaries of Jesuit activities in the Philippines during 1604–5 and 1613–14. At Paris meanwhile there appeared in French (1618) the history of the persecution of the Christians in Japan originally composed in Spanish by Luis Pigneyra.[57] And at Rouen in 1618 a French translation was issued of Amati's Italian history of "Voxu" originally published in 1615.[58]

Notice of the persecutions in Japan was followed by announcements of other attacks upon the Christians in the East. From the letters of Semedo and Kirwitzer a book was put together about the attack on the Jesuits in China, which was published in 1620 at Paris and Bordeaux.[59] At Valenciennes in the same year there appeared a two-volume *Histoire du massacre* of missionaries in the West and East Indies. Volume II includes three letters from the East on the disturbing conditions developing there.[60] Clearly, fears were mounting in France, as they were elsewhere in Europe, about the uncertain future of the entire Christian enterprise in the East.

In question also was France's ability to follow up the reconnaissance voyages to the East first undertaken by the merchant entrepreneurs of the Atlantic coast. The hostility of the Dutch East India Company to the probings

[51] See *ibid.*, pp. 391–92.
[52] *Ibid.*, p. 258.   [53] *Ibid.*, p. 716.
[54] The French version was reprinted at Lille (1617) and Paris (1618). See Streit, V, 717.
[55] See *ibid.*, p. 410.
[56] *Ibid.*, p. 437.
[57] *Ibid.*, p. 436. On Pigneyra's original work published in 1617 see above, p. 332.
[58] Streit, V, 417–18; also see above, p. 371.
[59] *Ibid.*, pp. 736–37.   [60] *Ibid.*, pp. 82–83.

[400]

of the French in Indonesia was a subject taken up in the negotiations between the governments of France and the United Provinces that began with the outbreak (1618) of the Thirty Years' War and the resumption (1621) of the Dutch-Spanish war. When the Dutch proposed an alliance with France directed against the Habsburgs, Richelieu demanded that the Dutch should not only cease their attacks upon the French fleets but also lend them all possible assistance and cooperation on the high seas and in the East and West Indies. Once these terms and others were agreed upon, the Treaty of Compiègne was signed in 1624. Two years later Richelieu was named by the king to be Grand Master of the navigation and commerce of France, thus bringing the French government itself into the competition for overseas trade and colonies. The initiatives of the private merchants in the Indian Ocean had provided the government with a few shaky footholds or promises of cooperation at Pondicherry on India's east coast, at Bantam, and in Sumatra. But Richelieu, who was absorbed with France's internal problems during the 1620's, made no immediate efforts to capitalize on these earlier probings of the East.[61]

The French were kept informed, however, of the steady progress being made by the Dutch and others in Eastern exploration and trade. A Provençal, Captain Marque d'Or, who had participated in a sea battle before Malacca, probably in 1606, between the Dutch and Portuguese, published in 1621 the story of this encounter in which he stresses the contributions of the four Frenchmen who fought in it.[62] At Amsterdam there appeared French translations of Joris van Spilbergen's *Miroir oost & west-indical* (1621), Jacob Le Maire's *Iournal* (1622), and a *Relation* (1622) of the expedition sent out by the Spanish in 1618 to discover Le Maire's strait.[63] At Paris in 1628 a book was published reporting on the return to Amsterdam in June, 1628, of eight ships from the fleet of Cornelis Matelief.[64] Interest in Eastern travel was also maintained by the publication in French for the first time of Pinto's *Voyages* (1628),[65] of Adam Olearius' *Relation* (1629) of his travels overland to Tartary and Persia, and of the round-trip journey from Paris to China made earlier in the century by Henri de Feynes, a courtier.[66]

The advocates of French overseas enterprise meanwhile provided tech-

---

[61] See Barassin, *loc. cit.* (n. 3), pp. 381–82. Religious wars again swept France from 1621 to 1629.

[62] *Furieuse et sanglante bataille donnée entre les Portugois et les Hollandois (auprès de Malacca)* . . . (Paris). Listed only in Ternaux-Compans, p. 141.

[63] *Relation de deux caravelles envoyées en 1618* . . . *sous la conduite de D. Juan de More, pour découvrir le détroit de Lemaire*.

[64] *Relation véritable de huict navires, venus des Indes orientales et occidentales.* . . .

[65] The atmospheric and faithful French translation was by Bernard Figuier. It was reprinted in 1645.

[66] *Voyage faict par terre depuis Paris iusques à la Chine.* . . . *Avec son retour par mer* (Paris, 1630). Feyne's journey probably took place between 1612–14. An English account, translated from the unlearned traveler's notes and manuscripts, appeared in 1615 entitled *An Exact and Curious Survey of the East Indies* . . . *by Monsieur de Montfart* [Feyne's title was Montferron].

nical tools for future use. Pierre Bergeron, the editor and collector, in his *Traicté de la navigation* . . . (Paris, 1629) describes the part of Frenchmen in overseas discoveries of the past and urges the France of his day to assume a leading role in commerce and missionary work.[67] This was followed by the publication at Amsterdam in 1630 of Mercator's *Atlas Minor* as revised by Hondius and translated into French by La Popelinière (d. 1608), one of the earliest advocates of French expansion.[68]

The Jesuits, who still suffered in France from the charge of being regicides, concentrated in their publications of the 1620's upon the brilliance of their successes in China. I. Bellefleur Percheron translated in 1622 a large compendium of materials from Spanish. His *Nouvelle histoire de la Chine* . . . (Paris) includes a French version of the *Epitome historial* . . . (Madrid, 1620) of Francisco de Herrera Maldonado as well as excerpts from the Iberian letterbooks relating to the progress being made by the Jesuits in China.[69] Another work on China, attributed to a certain "Louis Legrand" by Ternaux-Compans, has never been located by other bibliographers.[70] The case is quite otherwise for the popular *Histoire de la cour du roy de la Chine* (Paris, 1624) by Michel Baudier (1589–1645), court historiographer and bibliophile.[71] Baudier, according to his own testimony, was present at the Louvre in 1616 when a Flemish Jesuit, certainly Nicolas Trigault, recounted to the young king, Louis XIII, the marvels of the city of Peking and its court.[72] It was evidently on this occasion that Marie de'Medici presented the Jesuit with a rich tapestry to give to the Chinese emperor.[73] While a part of Baudier's description of the Chinese court is based upon what he had heard from Trigault, most of his book is clearly derived from Mendoza's popular history.

Trigault was back in China by 1620 and wrote the Annual Letter for that year from Nanking. Dated August 21, 1621, this long letter was published at Antwerp in Latin in 1625.[74] In the same year there appeared in French three other Jesuit letters from China from the years 1619 and 1620 as well as Trigault's relation for 1621. The *Histoire de ce qui s'est passé à la Chine*, the

[67] For a discussion of the *Traicté* see Lindsay, *loc. cit.* (n. 32), p. 35.

[68] On La Popelinière see *Asia*, II, Bk. 2, 314–16.

[69] For the full title of Bellefleur Percheron's translation see H. Cordier, *Biblioteca Sinica* (5 vols.; Paris, 1904–24), Vol. I, col. 20. On Herrera Maldonado's book see above, pp. 334–35.

[70] Ternaux-Compans, p. 126; entitled *Nouveaux mémoires de l'état de la Chine* (Paris, 1623), this is possibly an error for Louis Le Comte's work of the same title published in 1696. See Cordier, *op. cit.* (n. 69), cols. 20–21.

[71] Reprinted at Paris in 1626, 1631, 1642, 1668, and 1699 and at Rouen in two editions of 1638 and another of 1642. It was translated into English in 1634 and into German in 1679. Comparison of the texts of the 1631 and 1668 editions shows them to be identical except for the dedications and publishers.

[72] Baudier, *Histoire de la cour du roy de la Chine* (Paris, 1668), p. 13.

[73] *Ibid.*, p. 16. The tapestry apparently never reached its destination. See E. Lamalle, "La propagande du P. Nicolas Trigault en faveur des missions de Chine, 1616," *AHSI*, IX (1940), 63.

[74] *Rerum memorabilium in regno sinae gestarum.* . . .

first of a series under this general title, was translated from the Italian compilation (1624) by Pierre Marin (1562–1625) of the Jesuit college in Paris, a biographer of Loyola as well as a translator of other letterbooks.[75] Jacques de Machault, another Jesuit, translated and published a relation bearing a similar title in 1627.[76] It includes a number of lengthy and informed letters dated 1622 and 1623, especially those by Trigault and Semedo. At Paris in 1629 another in this series of French translations was published. It contains a lengthy letter by Kirwitzer from Macao relating what happened in China during 1624.[77] These French letterbooks, like those from which they were translated, are important sources for the period just prior to and immediately following the death of the Wan-li emperor in 1620.

Trigault, most famous as an intermediary between China and Europe, also acted as an informant on Japan. In 1623 there was published at Munich in Latin the account he prepared for the duke of Bavaria of the persecutions which took place in Japan from 1612 to 1620.[78] At Paris it was published in 1624 in a French translation by Marin.[79] At the same time there appeared a French version of the Spanish *Relación admirable . . .* (Seville, 1624) compiled from letters written in Manila telling of the martyrdoms of 1622 suffered in Japan.[80] In this charged atmosphere François Solier published his two-volume ecclesiastical history of Japan from the beginnings to 1624.[81] Nor did this bring to an end the Jesuit enthusiasm for martyrdoms. In 1628 a book was published at Bordeaux which recalled the first martyrdoms suffered in 1597 by three Japanese Jesuits.[82] And at Paris P. G. Vireau published a translation from the Italian of Rodrigues Girão's review of the persecutions in Japan written at Macao in 1625.[83]

News from other Asian regions was much better. While conditions in China and Japan worsened, the Jesuits claimed in a pamphlet of 1621 to have converted the "greatest king" in the East Indies along with six thousand of his subjects.[84] A summary of the most memorable Jesuit accomplishments for the years from 1621 to 1626 was issued at Pont-à-Mousson in 1628.[85] It contains letters recounting the successes won in India and Tibet, one of which was written from Tibet by the French Jesuit François Godin (1583–1633). Another collection of 1628, which also includes Godin's letter, as-

---

[75] See Streit, V, 755.

[76] *Histoire de ce qui s'est passé en Royaume du Iapon, et de la Chine* (Paris).

[77] See Streit, V, 761.   [79] See *ibid.*, p. 475.

[78] For the title see *ibid.*, pp. 463–64.   [80] *Ibid.*, p. 476.

[81] *Histoire ecclésiastique des isles et royaumes du Iapon* (2 vols.; Paris, 1627–29).

[82] See Streit, V, 521.

[83] *Histoire de ce qui s'est passé au royaume du Japon l'année 1624* (Paris, 1628).

[84] *La conversion du plus grand roy des Indes orientales à present regnât a la foy catholique, avec six milles habitans de son royaume . . .* (Bordeaux and Paris, 1621). See Streit, V, 88. It is reproduced in H. Ternaux-Compans, *Archives des voyages* (3 vols.; Paris, 1852), I, 173–79. Despite its title, this tract appears to refer to Africa rather than to the East Indies.

[85] See Streit, V, 116.

sures its readers that it contains certain news of the discovery of Cathay in what is a misrepresentation of Andrade's venture into Tibet.[86] It also contains the further startling but accurate announcement of the discovery of the Nestorian monument in China *ca.* 1625. Progress reports in 1628 on Jesuit activities in Malabar and the East Indies were translated from Italian and published at Paris.[87] In the following year the story of Tibet's penetration was set straight in another letterbook translated from Italian.[88] To judge from these translations the French reading public at this time ordinarily learned of the Jesuit successes just about two years after they were announced in the Iberian and Italian letterbooks.

Under Richelieu, France began to become increasingly involved around 1630 in the international conflicts and wars of Europe. The victories of the Spanish and Austrian Habsburgs in northern Europe were viewed in France with growing apprehension, since it seemed impossible to check their domination without going to war. Once the program of subsidizing the Dutch, the Danes, and the Swedes had failed, Richelieu began to prepare for open intervention. In 1635 France entered the war against the Habsburgs on land and sea. The French were at first on the defensive; it was not until 1640 that their forces were able to take the initiative away from the Spanish and imperial forces. Because of these serious involvements Richelieu was again forced to put aside his program of overseas expansion and trade.

While the royal government remained unable to undertake or to sponsor exploration and trade overseas, merchants of France's Atlantic towns continued to take some initiatives in the Indian Ocean. In these years such activity seemingly centered at Dieppe. But very little specific data is available on it because the Dieppe archives were burned in 1694.[89] Still, evidence for it exists in the book of Jean Le Tellier, a pilot in the fleet of 1620, that was finally published at Dieppe in 1631.[90] His *Voyage faict aux Indes Orientales . . . ,* in three parts, contains a folio of tables for navigation to the East. These tables were possibly in the possession of Gilles de Régimont, who voyaged to India and the Persian Gulf in 1630 and returned in 1632 with a rich cargo. Barred from the Moluccas by the Dutch, the ships of Dieppe tried to establish trading relations in Malabar, Coromandel, Bengal, the Persian Gulf, and Madagascar. In 1633 a company was formed at Dieppe by Régimont and his townsmen which thereafter sent voyages annually into the Indian Ocean. Once France gained an ascendancy in the European wars,

---

[86] See *ibid. Cf.* the Portuguese work which makes a similar claim, above, p. 338.

[87] See *ibid.*, pp. 116–17. This is one of the first references published in Europe to the Nestorian monument.

[88] See *ibid.*, p. 118.

[89] Most of what is known comes from the archives of towns in the vicinity and was put together in J. A. S. Desmarquets, *Mémoires chronologiques pour servir à l'histoire de Dieppe, et à celle de la navigation française* (2 vols.; Paris, 1785), I, 355–70.

[90] See above, p. 398. Reprinted at Dieppe in 1649.

Louis XIII in 1643 signed letters patent which transformed the Dieppe Company into the national *Compagnie de l'Orient.*[91]

Evidently nothing was published at the time on the Dieppe voyages. Throughout the 1630s the French were still treated to the martyrdoms suffered in Japan but to little else on the East. At Paris in 1633 the Annual Letters from Japan for 1625, 1626, and 1627 were translated from Italian and published.[92] The following year, also at Paris, there appeared a "true relation" of the martyrdoms suffered by the Discalced Augustinians.[93] In 1635, the year when the French intervention in the Thirty Years' War began, three more letterbooks on the persecutions in Japan were issued in French.[94] Finally the edifying story of Mastrilli's miraculous cure, vocation, mission, and martyrdom was translated into French and printed several times in 1639 and 1640, possibly for the celebration of the Xavier centennial.[95]

Except for the martyrologies, the French of the 1630's published very little that was new about the East. Borri's relation of Cochin-China was published in French translation at Rennes and Lille in 1631.[96] At Paris an English translation of Tursellinus' life of Xavier was issued in 1632 by the English College Press of Saint Omer. In the meantime Pierre Bergeron planned a collection of French travel accounts similar to those produced for England by Hakluyt and Purchas. In 1634 he brought out his *Relations des voyages en Tartarie,* a collection of medieval travel narratives to which the editor freely added his own comments on the places discussed by the authors.[97] While improving on William of Rubruquis, John of Plano-Carpini, and others, Bergeron also publicized the achievements of the French travelers of the past and urged contemporaries to follow their example. Though they were then unable to follow this advice, the French continued in this hectic period to amuse themselves with exotica relating to the overseas world.[98]

Following the creation of the *Compagnie de l'Orient* in 1643, the voyages sent out over the next decade from Dieppe concentrated upon establishing a French outpost at Madagascar.[99] Information on the past activities of the other maritime powers meanwhile continued to appear in French. Drake's

[91] See Barassin, *loc. cit.* (n. 3), p. 383. Also H. Froidereaux (ed.), *Documents inédits relatifs à la constitution de la Compagnie des Indes Orientales de 1642* (Paris, n.d.).

[92] See Streit, V, 539.

[93] Cited only in Ternaux-Compans, p. 168.

[94] For their titles, contents, and bibliographic information see Streit, V, 542–43.

[95] For the Spanish original of 1638 and for translations in other languages of this popular book see above, pp. 345–46. Another French edition appeared at Paris in 1696.

[96] On the original Italian edition see above, p. 377.

[97] See Lindsay, *loc. cit.* (n. 32), p. 37.

[98] For example, see Jean Puget de La Serre, *Balet des princes, indiens* . . . (Brussels, 1634); R. M. Du Rocher, *L'indienne amoureus, ou l'heureux naufrage: Tragi-comedie* (Paris, 1636); and *L'histoire de la vie et de la mort du Grand Mogor* (Paris?, 1640?), a satire in verse on the Abbé Pierre de Montmaur.

[99] See Barassin, *loc. cit.* (n. 3), pp. 383–84.

round-the-world voyage appeared in French at Paris in 1641.[100] Pierre Dan (d. 1649), a specialist on the Barbary pirates and North Africa, published in 1642 a catalog of the "marvels" housed in the royal chateau of Fontainebleau.[101] A review of Portugal's history under the House of Habsburg (1580–1640) was written by François Grenaille (1616–80) and published at Paris in 1643.[102] Ternaux-Compans lists what appears to be a French translation of Isaac Commelin's *Begin ende voortgangh,* published in the same year (1646) in which Commelin's original collection appeared. We have found no other evidence for its existence.[103] Louis Coulon (1605–64), a French geographer, translated Semedo's history of China from Italian and published it at Paris in 1645.[104] The only original piece on the eastward voyages was that by a "French gentleman" published at Paris around 1645. He claims to have voyaged all the way to China and back. To this work a hydrography is appended.[105]

Missionary reports were similarly few in number and often retrospective in content. The martyrdom in Japan of Guillaume Courlet, a Dominican of the Languedoc, and of other preaching friars was announced in a pamphlet published at Toulouse in 1641.[106] The French Jesuits quickly translated and published in 1643 and 1645 the relations of Cardim, originally published in Portuguese.[107] A letterbook of 1646 prepared by Jacques de Machault includes Cardim's relation as well as Barretto's report on the Jesuit Province of Malabar.[108] Evidently since they had so little good news to report, the missionaries concentrated on martyrdoms to convince the public in Europe of the firmness of their faith and the steadfastness of their converts.

The most celebrated travel book to appear in the 1640's was one allegedly based on the memoirs of Vincent Le Blanc (1554–*ca.* 1640), a native of Marseilles. During the last quarter of the sixteenth century, Le Blanc had traveled widely in Asia, Africa, and America. Through the good offices of Nicolas-Claude de Fabri, seigneur of Peiresc and a respected scholar, the manuscripts of Le Blanc were brought to the attention of Bergeron, the editor of travel materials. After acquiring some of Le Blanc's manuscripts, Bergeron realized that they were confused and jumbled. Before his death in 1637, Bergeron succeeded in bringing into order the whole of Part I and substantial portions of Part II. The work of editing the remainder of Part II

---

[100] See below, pp. 547–49.
[101] *Le tresor des merveilles de la maison royale de Fontainebleau* (Paris).
[102] *Le mercure Portugais.* . . .
[103] *Histoire du commencement et des progrès de la Compagnie des Indes, des Provinces-Unies des Pays-Bas, contenant les principaux voyages.* . . . (Amsterdam). Listed only in Ternaux-Compans, p. 183.
[104] It was reprinted at Lyons in 1667.
[105] *Relation d'un voyage aux Indes Orientales. Par un gentilhomme françois arrivé depuis trois ans. Avec une hydrographie* . . .
[106] Listed only in Ternaux-Compans, p. 177.
[107] See Streit, V, 557–59. See above, pp. 378–79.
[108] *Ibid.,* p. 136.

and all of Part III was continued by Louis Coulon.[109] *Les voyages fameux* was published at Paris in 1648 and reprinted in 1649 and 1658.[110] Though it is still cited frequently, *Les voyages fameux* remains suspect as a factual source. But it was important at the time in giving impetus to the French effort in the overseas world. A series of exotic works likewise helped to keep alive during these trying years an interest in the world beyond Europe.[111]

2

The Paris Society of Foreign Missions and the French East India Company

France's war with Spain continued after the conclusion of the general European Peace of Westphalia in 1648; internally France also experienced new and divisive conflicts in the tensions and wars of the Fronde (1648–53). Nonetheless, when the charter of the *Compagnie de l'Orient* expired in 1652, it was immediately renewed for twenty years.[112] While the Spanish kept the French fleets from voyaging to the East, information on Asia continued to be printed in France. The Discalced Carmelite Philippe de Sainte-Trinité (1603–71) had published at Lyons in 1649 a Latin version (*Itinerarium orientale*) of his *Voyage d'orient* that was published there in French in 1652.[113] Divided into ten books, this work is rich in descriptions of the physical features of India and in the history of Carmelite activities in the East. The Jesuits of Paris, while the Fronde was raging, published in 1651 a letterbook which surveys conditions in all the Jesuit mission stations of the East as of 1649.[114] On the basis of material drawn from the letterbooks and the works of Mendoza, Purchas, and Le Blanc, an atlas of colored maps and explanatory texts was published in 1652 by Nicolas Sanson d'Abbeville (1600–67), a royal geographer.[115]

The French began in these years to take a more serious interest in Indochina. Borri's relation of Cochin-China was again translated into French and

---

[109] The above discussion is based on Lindsay, *loc. cit.* (n. 32), pp. 36–37.

[110] It was translated into Dutch (1654) and English: *The World Surveyed; or the Famous Voyages* . . . (London, 1660).

[111] For example, Jean de Magnon, *Josaphat tragicomedie* [in verse] (Paris, 1647); and the same author's *Le Grand Tamerlane et Baiazet, tragedie* [in verse] (Paris, 1648). Also see the charming book by Salomon de Priezac, seigneur de Saugues, entitled *Histoire des éléphants* (Paris, 1650).

[112] See Barassin, *loc. cit.* (n. 3), p. 384.

[113] For its contents see Streit, V, 140. It was later translated into Italian (1666) and German (1671).

[114] *Relation de ce qui s'est passé dans les Indes Orientales en ses trois provinces de Goa, de Malabar, du Iapon, de la Chine, et autres pais nouvellement descouverts . . . Par le P. Iean Maracci Procureur de la Province de Goa, au mois d'Avril, 1649.* For a summary of its contents see Streit, V, 142–43.

[115] *L'Asie en plusieurs cartes nouvelles et en plusieurs traités* (Paris). Reprinted in 1662. See pls. 1, 5.

published at Paris in 1652.[116] A new stimulus was added by the writings of Alexandre de Rhodes (1591–1660) whose survey of the Jesuit mission in Tongking appeared in Italian at Rome in 1650 and was shortly translated into French by Henry Albi.[117] Rhodes' call for a more active pursuit of the mission in Indochina was evidently heard more clearly in Paris than in Rome. Perhaps this was true because there was no mission field in the East in which the French Jesuits were supreme.

Rhodes, who was anxious to find a capable bishop for Annam, was sent to Paris in 1652 by Pope Innocent X.[118] Here he found enthusiasm and financial support for a new mission under French leadership in court circles, in the Assembly of the Clergy of France, and among the French Jesuits. While recruiting personnel for the missions to Asia, he published at Paris in 1653 several books relating his own experiences in the East. The most important of these was his *Divers voyages et missions,* in which he provides his personal history as well as an excellent description of Indochina.[119] Though he insists in the preface that his interests are exclusively religious, Rhodes sheds a strong light on the important outposts of Eastern trade, on the Dutch and English in Java, on the overland route from Surat to Rome, and on the temporal conditions prevailing in the kingdoms of Indochina. While he spent as much time in south China as in Indochina, he clearly sees the future of the mission as being located in Indochina. To support his case for the piety of the Asian converts, he also had published in separate French editions a few examples of their martyrdoms.[120] Rhodes' student in the Annamite language, the Italian Jesuit Metello Saccano (d. 1662), wrote a survey of the progress of the faith in Cochin-China during 1646 and 1647 that was published in French (Paris) in 1653.[121]

The young Louis XIV, once the Fronde ended, became interested in the travels of his subjects overseas. He had looked favorably upon Rhodes' activities and had requested from François de La Boullaye Le Gouz (*ca.* 1610–*ca.* 1669) a recital of his travel experiences. Le Gouz, a native of Anjou, had left Paris in 1643 to begin his Eurasiatic journeys. On his way overland to India he met Rhodes in 1648 near Shiraz in Persia. The Jesuit, who at first

---

[116] For discussion of the Italian original see above, p. 377. Previously published in French at Rennes in 1631. See above, p. 405.

[117] For its title see Streit, V, 595. A Latin translation was published at Lyons in 1652. On Rhodes and his Italian works see above, p. 380–81.

[118] On his activities in France see H. Chappoulie, *Aux origines d'une église. Rome et les missions d'indochine au XVIIe siècle* (2 vols.; Paris, 1943), I, 107–10.

[119] This full account was preceded by a *Somaire* published earlier in 1653. A second printing of the *Divers voyages* was issued in 1666. There is also a modern English translation by Solange Hertz, *Rhodes of Viet Nam* (Westminster, Md., 1966).

[120] *La glorieuse mort d'André, premier catéchiste de la Cochinchine* . . . (Paris, 1653) was translated from the Italian original of 1652. Also see his *Relation de ce qui s'est passé en l'année 1649 dans les royaumes* . . . *du Iapon* (Paris, 1655). A Dutch version of this Japan relation was published in 1657.

[121] A Flemish translation was published at Antwerp in 1654.

took Le Gouz for a Persian lord because of his dress, arrived in Paris in 1652 at about the same time Le Gouz returned there from his journey. It was perhaps at Rhodes' suggestion that the king asked Le Gouz to appear before him dressed as a Persian to tell the story of his adventures. In 1653, just a few months before the publication of Rhodes' *Divers voyages,* there was printed at Paris the *Voyages et observations* of Le Gouz, a work notable for its section devoted to the worshippers of Rama.[122] Of the eastern regions he visited, Le Gouz is most informative on north India and its relations to Persia. He was sent back to Persia and India as France's envoy, but died at Ispahan before he could return to India.

Rhodes, who had spent twelve years working in China and who had brought to Europe a Chinese convert of Macao, gives only brief and impressionistic observations of China. While he was in Paris, however, his fellow Jesuits translated into French Boym's relation (1653) of the conversions of the Ming courtiers and Martini's history of the Tartar conquest of China.[123] In 1656 a new French translation appeared of Olearius' journey of 1633 to 1639 to Moscow, Tartary, and Persia, thus adding to the available documentation on the overland route. For navigational information the Jesuit Georges Fournier (1595–1652) published in 1656 at Paris his *Asiae nova descriptio.*[124] The Jesuits also produced in a Paris letterbook a survey of the state of their Asian missions from 1655 to 1659 which includes descriptions of the "curiosities" of those countries.[125] At this juncture France's long war with Spain was ended by the Treaty of the Pyrenees of 1659, Mazarin died in 1661, and the twenty-two-year-old monarch assumed power in his own right. For the remainder of the seventeenth century, France went on the aggressive both in Europe and in the overseas world.

The Age of Louis XIV also saw the appearance of more French materials on the contemporary East, both translated and original. Pietro della Valle's pilgrimage was translated into French and issued at Paris in printings of 1661, 1662, 1663–65, and 1670. Martini's history of China appeared in French at Paris (1662) and at Lyons (1667). Baudier's history of the court of China was reprinted at Paris in 1662, 1668, and 1669. The Englishman Thomas Herbert's voyage to Persia and the East Indies was translated into

---

[122] An augmented edition dedicated to Cardinal Capponi, the Vatican librarian, was published at Troyes in 1657. A Dutch translation appeared at Amsterdam in 1666. Le Gouz' work includes the story of the epic Ramayana and European illustrations based on popular Indian religious paintings. See P. Mitter, *Much Maligned Monsters* (Oxford, 1977), pp. 55, 60; for four pictorial reproductions from Le Gouz of episodes from the Ramayana, see *ibid.,* pl. 24. The 1657 edition contains four full-page plates and fifteen woodcuts of Indian gods, including Vishnu, Rama, Krishna, and Brahma himself. See Ernst Schierlitz, "Die bildlichen Darstellungen der indischen Göttertrinität in der alten ethnographischen Literatur" (Ph.D. diss., University of Munich, 1927), pp. 37–38.

[123] For its title see Streit, V, 796–97, 799.

[124] Also see Pierre Petit's versebook entitled *Gallorum indica navigatio auspiciis Ludovici regis* (Paris?, 1660?).

[125] See Streit, V, 153.

French by Wicquefort and published at Paris in 1663. Magistris' relation of Madura and south India likewise appeared in a French translation in 1663.

Melchisédech Thévenot (*ca.* 1620–92) began publishing at Paris in 1663 his *Relations de divers voyages curieux,* a collection of French translations from the compendia of Hakluyt and Purchas, from a number of separately issued accounts, and from a few which existed only in manuscript. Between 1663 and 1696, the *Relations,* the first important travel collection in French, was issued in many augmented editions so that the arrangement and collation of the copies vary enough to produce a bibliographical puzzlement. As custodian of the Royal Library from 1684 to his death, Thévenot was in a particularly advantageous position to review the latest travel literature, and to have it translated and published by the royal printers. The *Relations* is rich in illustrations and maps reproduced or adapted from the Dutch, Latin, English, and Iberian originals. It also includes translations from a few Persian, Arabic, and other Oriental sources preserved in the libraries of Leyden and the Vatican and in private collections.[126]

A majority of Thévenot's relations pertain to the countries, peoples, and natural world of Asia, for he aimed quite openly to provide the French with the latest and best materials on navigation, trade, and life in the East. In addition to voyages previously published elsewhere, the *Relations* includes in Volume I an extract from a journal prepared in connection with the Dutch embassy to China in 1655–57, an account of the Dutch loss of Formosa in 1663, and a part of Aleixo da Motta's rutter of the East Indies translated from a Portuguese manuscript. Of particular importance for Sumatra is the memoir of General Augustin de Beaulieu on his East Indian voyage of 1620–22, contained in Volume II.[127] This is followed by a series of accounts and maps relating to the Philippines and other islands such as Yezo (Hokkaido), as well as a map of the Indian Ocean prepared in 1649 by João Teixeira, the royal cosmographer at Lisbon. Thévenot translated materials on China and its flora by the Jesuit Michael Boym, which appear at the end of Volume II.[128] Volume III begins with Johann Nieuhof's account of the Dutch embassy of 1655 to China; it includes a number of spectacular engravings and a map of the route followed by the Dutch from Canton to Peking. Small

[126] The best bibliographical analysis is in the *Bibliotheca Lindesiana,* Vol. IV (1910), cols. 8830–41. It lists the contents of five volumes: three from the press of Jacques Langlois (1663) and one each from Sebastien Mabre-Cramoisy (1666) and Thomas Moette (1696). See the Library of Congress and the National Union catalogs for other editions. See also A. G. Camus, *Mémoire sur la collection des grands et petits voyages, et sur la collection des voyages de Melchisédec Thevenot* (Paris, 1802). We consulted the three-volume edition printed in 1663 by Sebastien Mabre-Cramoisy.

[127] "Relation de l'estat present du commerce des Hollandais et des Portugais dans les Indes Orientales: memoires du voyage aux Indes Orientales du General de Beaulieu." For a somewhat abridged modern edition of Beaulieu's journal see Eugene Guenin (ed.), *Agustin de Beaulieu, sa navigation aux Indes orientales, 1619–1622* (Paris, 1905).

[128] On Thévenot's translated selections from Boym's *Flora sinensis* (Vienna, 1656), see Flaumenhaft and Flaumenhaft, *loc. cit.* (n. 10), pp. 149, 152–53.

amounts of fresh information on China's neighbors appear in Volume III, especially on the Mongol language. Volume II of the later editions includes what may well be the *Decas secunda* of Martino Martini's synopsis of China's dynastic history to the year A.D. 1666 as well as a Manchu vocabulary and a small Chinese grammar.[129] Thévenot's parallel work, called *Recueil de voyages* (Paris, 1681; reprinted in 1682 and 1689), contains little of relevance except for a relation of the Baikov embassy sent overland from Russia to China in 1653.[130]

The growing interest of the king and Colbert in exploration and trade in the East was stimulated also by more recent reminders and materials. After Etienne de Flacourt (1607–60), the director-general of the *Compagnie de l'Orient,* died at sea, the elegy read at his funeral was published in 1661.[131] Since Flacourt had reestablished from 1648 to 1655 the French garrison at Fort Dauphin in Madagascar on the route to India, he was hereafter remembered as one of the founders of the French empire in the East. The wealth of Asia in precious stones and pearls was contemporaneously celebrated by Robert de Berquen in *Les merveilles des Indes Orientales* (Paris, 1661).[132] The French Jesuit Jacques Le Favre (1612–76), a scientist recruited by Rhodes, addressed a letter from Shanghai in 1657 announcing his arrival in China and commenting on conditions there, which was published separately at Paris in 1662.[133] News of developments in Tongking for the years from 1658 to 1660 was relayed to Europe by Joseph F. Tissanier (1618–88), another French Jesuit missionary.[134] At Paris from 1664 to 1684 there was published the lengthy account of the travels of Jean de Thévenot (1633–67), the nephew of Melchisédech. Among these accounts is the story of his trip overland from 1664 to 1667 during which he spent about one year touring in India.[135]

The French classicist and litterateur François Charpentier (1620–1702)

---

[129] The *Decas prima* of Martini's *Sinicae historiae* had been published at Amsterdam by Johan Blaeu in 1659. See below, pp. 526–27; and on the *Decas secunda* see below, pp. 1682–83.

[130] This is a French version of the Russian text which Thévenot received from Nicolaas Witsen. An earlier, very corrupt Latin version of the Baikov embassy appeared in some copies of Thévenot's *Relations de divers voyages curieux,* Vol. V. A German edition was published in 1689. A Dutch translation is included in Witsen's *Noord en Oost Tartarye* (Amsterdam, 1692), and an English is found in A. and J. Churchill (eds.), *A Collection of Voyages and Travels* (London, 1704). For details see John F. Baddeley, *Russia, Mongolia, China* (2 vols.; London, 1919), II, 130–31.

[131] Listed by Ternaux-Compans, p. 203.

[132] Reprinted in 1669.

[133] *Lettre du R. P. Jacques Le Favre . . . sur son arrivée a la Chine et l'estat present de ce royaume.* See Streit, V, 821.

[134] *Relation du voyage du P. J. Tissanier. Depuis la France jusqu'au royaume de Tungkin. Avec ce qui s'est passé . . . dans cette mission, depuis les années 1658–1660* (Paris, 1663). See Streit, V, 607. This is a substantial volume.

[135] *Relation d'un voyage fait au Levant. . . .* (three parts; Paris, 1664–84). Pt. 3 is on the East Indies, especially on India. It was reprinted at Rouen (1665–84) and at Paris (1689). It was translated into English (1687). The modern critical edition of the part on India is in S. Sen (ed.), *The Indian Travels of Thevenot and Careri* (New Delhi, 1949).

was charged by Colbert with writing a proposal for a *Compagnie des Indes Orientales* for submission to the king and thereafter to compose the relation of its founding.[136] The government itself got into the act by publishing a brochure on the conditions for trading under the company's auspices.[137] Johann Nieuhof's (1618–72) rendition of the Dutch embassy of Pieter de Goyer and Jakob de Keyser to the court of Peking appeared in several French versions from 1664 to 1666.[138] The French kept abreast of the contest between the Dutch and English in the East by publishing translations of diverse Dutch materials.[139] For an indication of the kinds of rare merchandise being sold at Montpelier in 1665, before Colbert's company became active, there is a catalog by Jean Fargeon.[140] The state of French scientific knowledge about India for the same date can be checked in the travel *Journal* of Bathasar de Monconys (1611–65),[141] a scientist of Lyons.

The French missionaries were meanwhile establishing more firmly their stake in the East. Pierre Lambert de La Motte (1624–79), the associate of François Pallu (1626–84) in founding the Mission Society of Paris, was named in 1658 the Bishop of Berytus (Beirut), the vicar apostolic of Cochin-China, and the ecclesiastical administrator of the Province of Southeastern China. At Ayut'ia in Siam the two French priests met again, and in 1664, the date of the French East India Company's charter, they founded at the Siamese capital the first seminary for native priests. The Jesuits, who watched with misgiving these activities of the French clergy, published a brief summary in 1665 of the sorry condition of the missions in China[142] and had Maffei's Latin history of their mission published in a French version at Paris.[143] This was followed in 1666 by a French translation of Marini's Italian description of Tongking and Laos.[144] Jacques de Bourges (*ca.* 1630–1714), a Parisian priest who had returned to Rome in 1663 to report on the mission in Siam, published at Paris in 1666 a relation of the overland voyage of Lambert to Siam in 1660–62.[145] The Jesuits then published at Lyons in 1667 in

---

[136] *Discours d'un fidèle sujet du Roy touchant l'établissement d'une compagnie . . . pour le commerce des Indes Orientales* (Paris, 1664). Reprinted in 1665. English translations appeared in 1664, 1676, and 1695. The *Relation de l'establissement . . .* was first published at Paris in 1665 and reprinted in 1666.

[137] *Articles et conditions . . .* (Paris, 1664).

[138] The Hague (1664), Leyden (1665), Paris (1666).

[139] For example, *Diverse pièces servant de réponse aux discours publiés par les Hollandais sur ce qui s'est passé entre l'Angleterre et la Hollande* (1665). Several of these discourses relate to Amboina. See Ternaux-Compans, p. 210.

[140] *Catalogue des marchandises rares, curieuses, et particulieres qui se font et debitent à Montpelier . . .* (Pezenas).

[141] Three vols.; Lyons, 1665–66.

[142] See Streit, V, 609.

[143] For a review of this translation see *Journal des Sçavants* (1666), pp. 108–10.

[144] It was printed twice in 1666. See Streit, V, 613. Also see above, pp. 382–83.

[145] *Relation du voyage . . .* (Paris, 1666). A second edition was published at Paris in 1668. Dutch editions appeared at Amsterdam in 1669 and 1683; a German edition was published at Leipzig in 1671. See Streit, V, 617.

one volume Martini's history of China and his description of the Tartar conquest.[146] In that same year Pallu's *Mémoire* on the state of the missions under the French vicars apostolic was put into print.[147] Thus, by the time the K'ang-hsi emperor took over the reins of China's government in 1669, it had become clear that the French were going to stay in the East and that they had received the support of their government in Siam and Indochina.[148]

The first voyage sent out in 1665 by the newly formed East India Company went only as far as Madagascar.[149] That this was but the beginning of a growing French interest in the East Indies is indicated by the publication in 1667 of substantial books on the riches of Asia.[150] Translations also continued to appear of English and Dutch materials on India and the East Indies.[151] At Paris there was printed for the first time in 1670 the Spanish original and the French translation of Palafox y Mendoza's history of the Tartar conquest of China.[152] In the same year there appeared in French, probably at Amsterdam, a summary account of the war conducted by the Dutch in Makassar from 1666 to 1669.[153] A French translation of Hendrik Hamel's account of his shipwreck and his description of Korea appeared in 1670.[154] In the same year the French version of Dapper's survey of Dutch activities in China appeared at Amsterdam.[155]

The relations of the missionaries for the years from 1668 to 1670 center on China and Southeast Asia. In Peking during these years the Jesuits were gradually being restored to a position of power at the court: in Siam and Indochina the French bishops were seemingly successful. François Pallu, the Bishop of Heliopolis, prepared during his stay in France from 1667 to 1670 an abridged account of the travels and experiences of the French bishops.[156] A Jesuit letterbook of 1668 includes selections of curiosa from the reports sent back to Paris by the French missionaries in the East: for example,

[146] See below, pp. 525–27.

[147] See Streit, V, 614.

[148] Louis XIV himself gave 1,000 livres per annum to support the mission. See E. W. Hutchinson, *Adventurers in Siam in the Seventeenth Century* (London, 1940), p. 44.

[149] See Urbain Souchu de Rennefort, *Relation du premier voyage de la Compagnie des Indes Orientales en l'île de Madagascar ou Dauphin, en l'an 1665* (Paris, 1669). Also included in his *Histoire des Indes orientales* (Paris, 1688). See below p. 422.

[150] See C., *Histoire des ioyaux, et des . . . richesses de l'Orient* (Geneva, 1667). Also Pierre de Rosnel, a professional silversmith, wrote on the gold and precious stones in his popular *Le mercure indien ou le tresor des Indes . . .* (Paris, 1667). A revised and augmented version was published in 1672.

[151] Briot (trans.), *Histoire de la religion des Banians . . . traduit de l'anglais* (Paris, 1667); *L'Evangile, traduit en malais par Brouwer* (Amsterdam, 1668); A. Roger, *Théâtre de l'idolatrie et la vraie représentation de la vie et des moeurs des bramines* (Amsterdam, 1670).

[152] See above, pp. 356–57. English translations appeared in 1671, 1676, and 1679.

[153] See below, pp. 498–99, 1447–48.

[154] *Relation du naufrage d'un vaiseau hollandais sur la coste de l'isle de Quelpaerts: avec la description du royaume de Coree* (Paris). On the original Flemish version see below, pp. 486–88.

[155] For details see below, pp. 490–91.

[156] *Relation . . . des missions . . .* (Paris, 1668). Translated into Italian in 1669 and reprinted in French in 1682. For bibliographical detail see Streit, V, 616.

Jacques Le Favre's letter of November, 1654, from Goa.[157] A separate collection on China includes three of Le Favre's letters of 1664 from China.[158] Two years later, in 1670, another assemblage of materials on China appeared, which also includes news of the problems being faced by the French missionaries in Indochina.[159] At Amsterdam, F. S. Dalquié published in 1670 his French translation of Kircher's *China illustrata* (1667) to which he appended the questions on China addressed to Johann Grueber by the grand duke of Tuscany as well as a Franco-Chinese dictionary.[160]

While Kircher had prepared one of the most widely circulated and most generally quoted books on China to appear in the seventeenth century, it was François Bernier (1620–88) who published what was probably the most original and popular account of India. Bernier, a native of Angers and a physician, was known in Paris as "le joli philosophe." After studying with Pierre Gassendi, the philosopher, he spent almost thirteen years (1656–68) traveling in the Mughul Empire. For eight of those years he acted as physician to Aurangzib, the Mughul emperor. When he returned to France in 1669, Bernier completed and saw through the press his four-volume *Histoire de la dernière révolution des états du Gran Mogul* (Paris, 1670–71).[161] Celebrated both for this work and for his philosophical tracts, Bernier enjoyed during his later years the friendship and confidence of Racine and Boileau. Aside from his literary and philosophical writings, he also published essays on various aspects of Asian civilization.[162]

Adrien Greslon (1618–95), a native of Perigueux and a Jesuit missionary, was in China from 1656 to his death, a period of forty years. His early years in China were spent under the trying conditions which the Jesuits suffered under the early Manchu rulers. Greslon, who was shunted from place to place in south China, kept a record of his experiences and those of his fellow Jesuits. With K'ang-hsi's assumption of power in 1667, the Jesuits gradually regained standing, and Greslon obtained enough leisure to write his history of life in China from 1651 to 1669. This work, evidently carried to France by others, was published at Paris in 1671.[163] Divided into three books,

---

[157] P. Chaigon (ed.), *Lettres des pays estrangères, où il y a plusieurs choses curieuses d'édification. Envoyées des missions de ces pays-là* (Paris).

[158] P. Chaigon (ed.), *Les dernières nouvelles de la Chrestienté de la China* (Paris, 1668).

[159] *L'état présent de la Chine, et des autres roiaumes voisins* (Paris).

[160] A. Kircher, *La Chine illustrée de plusieurs monuments sacrés que profanes, et de quantité de recherches de la nature et de l'art. . . .* See our pls. 296 and 353; also 86–87.

[161] Published in English in 1671 and 1675. There is a Dutch edition of 1672 and many subsequent editions in French and in translation. Irving Brock's English translation exists in a revised critical edition: Archibald Constable (ed.), *Travels in the Mogul Empire, A.D. 1656–1668* (Delhi, 1968).

[162] For example, he wrote a memoir on the "Quietism" of the Indies for the *Histoire des Savants* (1688) and an instruction manual for the reading of the Confucian Classics. For his complete bibliography see C. A. Walckenaer, *Vies de plusieurs personnages célèbres des temps anciens et modernes* (2 vols.; Laon, 1830), II, 74–77.

[163] *Histoire de la Chine sous la domination des Tartares. . . .* The copy in the Regenstein Library,

Greslon's history begins with an "Avertissement," evidently by another hand, which is designed to help the reader understand what Greslon is talking about, including therein the rules for pronouncing French transliterations of Chinese names. The first book recounts events of the Shun-chih period (1651–61), especially the emperor's relations with Adam Schall, his reception of the Dutch embassy, and his defection to the Buddhists. The second book deals with the early years of the K'ang-hsi emperor's minority, especially with the hostility of the Oboi Regency to the Jesuits, their trial in 1664–65, and the arrival of Le Favre as superior of the French missionaries. The third book continues with the persecutions and depicts clearly the downfall of the regents as the K'ang-hsi emperor moved toward the attainment of his majority and the Jesuits toward reinstatement in Peking.[164]

The first of several publications on Chinese medicine, all apparently taken from Father Michael Boym's manuscript "Medicus sinicus," appeared anonymously at Grenoble in 1671.[165]

Contemporaneously there appeared a number of other discrete books and parts of books on Asian subjects, both retrospective and new. At Lyons, Jean de Bussière (1607–78) published in 1670 a new life of Xavier. The description of South Asia and Ceylon by Philippus Baldaeus (1632–72) was translated from Dutch into a French version in 1672.[166] Louis Moreri (1643–80), the compiler of *Le grand dictionnaire historique* (Lyons, 1674), used the notes and papers of Gabriel de Chinon, a missionary in Persia, to prepare a relation of the Levant which traces the influence of the Persian religion and customs in India.[167] A small but influential work on the use of coffee, tea, and chocolate was likewise published in French in 1671; this is often attributed to Jacob Spon, also known as Philippe Dufour (1647–85).[168] Intorcetta's translations from the Confucian classics were published at Paris in a French version during 1673.[169] Three years later Jean Jovet published a

---

University of Chicago, includes the map of China, which has disappeared from many of the other extant copies. There was an Italian translation (Milan, 1676). An extract from Greslon's book is included in Aurelio degli Anzi (pseudonym of Conte Valerio Zani), *Il genio vagante* (Parma, 1693), pp. 139–44. Greslon's book was evidently not translated into other languages.

[164] Greslon is cited as a source for this hectic period by R. B. Oxnam, *Ruling from Horseback* (Chicago, 1968), pp. 148–49.

[165] *Les secrets de la médecine des Chinois, consistant en la parfaite connoissance du pouls, envoyez de la Chine par un François, homme de grand mérite. . . .* Attributed to Hervieu by some bibliographers, this work also exists in Italian (Milan, 1676). On Boym's authorship of *Les secrets* and other works see Edward Kajdański, "Michael Boym's *Medicus Sinicus*," *T'oung Pao*, LXXIII (1987), 162–89. For Boym's other publications see below, pp. 526, 538–39.

[166] See below, pp. 493–95. Also translated into English and German.

[167] *Relations nouvelles du Levant, ou traités de la religion . . . et des coûtumes des Perses . . . et des Gaures* (Lyons, 1671).

[168] Founded on the discourse by A. F. Naironi, it is entitled *De l'usage du caphé, du thé, et du chocalate.* Pierre Petit of Paris published around 1680 a Latin discussion of tea.

[169] Translated from the Italian version of 1672, it is entitled *La science des Chinois ou le livre de Cum fu-çu. . . .*

lengthy history of the religions in all known countries, including those of the East.[170]

The missionaries continued to dwell in their publications on the martyrdoms and victories of the past and on their hopes for the future in Southeast Asia. At Naumur in 1673 there was printed a commemorative biography and the letters of Richard de St. Anne (1585–1622), a Franciscan of Belgian origin martyred in Japan.[171] The French bishops in the East meanwhile kept the public informed about their activities in China, Indochina, and Siam through a series of published relations.[172] From these works it became clear that the French mission was becoming increasingly dominant in East and Southeast Asia despite the protests of the Portuguese and other national groups. It also had become evident that the French bishops were strongly supported by the crown and the papacy.

Jean Baptiste Tavernier (1605–89), son of a Parisian geographer and a Protestant layman of reputation, was one of the most celebrated travelers of the seventeenth century and one of its greatest authorities on the routes of Eastern travel and on the diamond mines of India. Between 1631 and 1668 he undertook six overland voyages to Turkey, Persia, and India. Soon after his final return to France, he was invited to an interview with Louis XIV, who conferred upon him in 1669 a title of nobility, Baron d'Aubonne. It was in his chateau near Geneva, with its orientalized decorations, that Tavernier prepared his notes for publication with the aid of Samuel Chappuzeau, a Protestant historian and playwright. In 1676–77 at Paris, Tavernier published in two volumes *Les six voyages,* one of the most popular books of the seventeenth century. The first volume is centered on Turkey and Persia; the second on India, Ceylon, and the East Indies. By 1712 this work was reprinted at least six times in French, three times in English, and one time each in German, Dutch, and Italian.[173]

Tavernier first arrived in India in 1640 on his second voyage. Over the next three years he visited Surat, Agra, Goa, and the diamond mines of Golconda. After returning to Paris with diamonds, he was again back in In-

[170] *L'histoire des religions de tous les royaumes* (3 vols.; Paris, 1676).

[171] For his biography see J. Masson, *Missionaires belges sous l'ancien régime (1500–1800)* (Brussels, 1947), I, 69–83. For the titles of these publications of 1673 see Streit, V, 570–71.

[172] *Relation des missions des evesques françois aux royaumes de Siam, de la Cochinchina, de Cambodge, et du Tonkin* (Paris, 1674) was written by Luc Fermanel de Favery. A second edition was printed in 1684 and an Italian translation at Rome in 1677. Pallu wrote a *Mémoire sur l'état présent des missions et des evesques français vicaires apostoliques dans la Chine et dans les royaumes de l'Orient* (n.p., 1677). In 1680 two continuations of this series appeared: *Relation des missions et voyages des evesques, vicaires apostoliques, et leurs écclesiastiques ès années 1672, 1673, 1674, et 1675* (Paris) and *Relation des missions et des voyages des evesques . . . ès années 1676 et 1677* (Paris).

[173] The best biography of Tavernier is by Charles Joret published at Paris in 1886; the most complete bibliography of his editions is in V. Ball (ed.), *Travels in India by Jean Baptiste Tavernier* (2 vols.; London, 1889), I, xl–xlvi, and in the second edition of Ball's translation, edited by W. Crooke (2 vols.; London, 1925), I, lx–lxvi.

dia at the beginning of 1645 investigating more extensively the diamond mines and revisiting Goa, from whence he sailed off to Ceylon and Indonesia. At Batavia he sold his diamonds and became involved in a financial dispute that embittered him toward the Dutch. Nonetheless he sailed to Europe in a Dutch vessel and arrived back in Paris in the spring of 1649. After selling off his precious stones again, Tavernier once more set out for the East in June, 1651. He finally made his way, despite many difficulties, to Masulipatam on the east coast of India by July, 1652. For the next two years he bought and sold diamonds and precious stones in India, finally returning to Paris in the autumn of 1655. Eighteen months later he started out again but did not arrive in Surat until May, 1659. From here he traveled via the Deccan back to the mines of Golconda. He returned to Paris in 1662 with a fortune in precious stones and a wife, the daughter of a French jeweler. In 1663 he left Paris for his last trip to India, where he arrived two years later after an extended stay in Persia. On this occasion he was received in 1665 by Aurangzib at Shahjahanabad (Delhi). Here he also met Bernier, who accompanied him to Benares and Patna. He went on alone to Dacca, and then returned across northern India to Surat. Tavernier arrived back in Paris late in 1668 to conclude his long series of Eastern adventures. His *Voyages,* as is obvious from the itinerary alone, are rich in materials on routes, traveling conditions, trading practices, the mines of Golconda, and the Dutch and English activities in the East. While Tavernier's contemporaries debated the authenticity of the *Voyages,* modern scholars agree that they constitute a valuable source for Indian history during the years from 1640 to 1667, or for almost a generation.[174]

Tavernier's activities did not cease with the publication of his *magnum opus.* In 1679 he had printed at Paris a collection of five treatises which had not been incorporated into *Les six voyages.*[175] He was aided in the preparation of these materials for the press by a M. de La Chapelle, secretary to M. de Lamoignon. The first book, dealing with Japan, a land not visited by Tavernier, seeks to show why the Christians were persecuted there, and it includes an interesting map of the islands. The second relation summarizes the negotiations undertaken by the French emissaries to Persia and India in the years following the establishment of Colbert's East India Company. The third book brings together Tavernier's own general observations, made during his voyages of the functioning of commerce in the East Indies. The fourth book relates what the author learned of Tongking through his brother Daniel

---

[174] His reports may be checked in part by consulting *The Travels of the Abbé Carré in India and the Near East, 1672 to 1674.* This work, only part of which was published in the seventeenth century, exists in a modern critical edition translated and edited by Lady Fawcett and Sir Charles Fawcett in "HS," 2d ser., XCV–XCVII (London, 1947–48).

[175] *Recueil de plusieurs relations et traitez singuliers et curieux . . . qui n'ont point esté mise dans ses six premiers voyages, devisé en cinq parties.* It contains two fine portraits of Tavernier and dedicatory verses by Boileau. Translated into English in 1680.

(d. 1648), who had actually worked there and who had prepared the map included in this treatise. Much of the information on Tongking is faulty. The final and longest relation is a book in itself which summarizes Tavernier's own hostile view of the ways in which the Dutch merchants and rulers conducted themselves in Asia. To these five books is appended a reprint of Tavernier's description of the interior of the seraglio, first published in 1675. This collection, like its predecessor, stirred controversies and polemics among contemporaries that were continued well into the eighteenth century.

But not all his contemporaries were suspicious of Tavernier's veracity and accuracy. To many, the aged traveler and merchant was a legend in his own day. Frederick William, the elector of Brandenburg, invited Tavernier to Berlin in 1684 to advise him on his projects of overseas trade and colonization. Both the elector and Tavernier were interested, along with certain Dutchmen, in promoting German Protestant commercial and mission programs in Asia. Tavernier hoped to become Brandenburg's emissary to the court of the "Great Mogul," even though he was then almost eighty years old. When the Brandenburg project failed, Tavernier began, after the Revocation of the Edict of Nantes (1685), to seek Protestant sponsors in Scandinavia. Possibly because these efforts also failed, he journeyed to Russia, evidently in the hope of winning the support of the tsar. Around 1689 he died and was buried in a Protestant cemetery near Moscow.[176]

In the course of his travels Tavernier had met numerous Frenchmen in India who were working there as merchants, jewelers, or physicians. Preparations in France itself for a more direct national participation in the commerce of Asia was meanwhile going ahead. F. Dassié, a shipbuilder for the royal navy and a student of hydrography, published in 1677 a practical guide for the construction of ocean-going vessels as well as navigational tables and *routiers* useful for sailing in Eastern waters.[177] In the same year François L'Estra (1650–97), a young servant of the French East India Company, published the journal of his voyage of 1671–75.[178] He had landed at Surat in 1671, was soon captured by the Dutch near Tranquebar, was kept in captivity at Batavia in 1673–74, and returned to France in 1675. Despite its concise and incomplete character, L'Estra's diary-like journal contains interesting and informative remarks on the European establishments in India and Indonesia. The French public was soon treated also to visual representations of the establishments and peoples of the East in a book of engravings published by Romein de Hooge (*ca.* 1650–1720), a Dutch artist who spent many of his

[176] See Charles Joret, "Le voyage de Tavernier (1670–89) . . . ," *Revue de géographie*, XII (1889), 161–74; 267–75; 328–41. Also see Ball (ed.), *op. cit.* (n. 173), pp. xxxiii–xxxvii.

[177] *L'architecture navale, avec le routier des Indes orientales et occidentales* (Paris).

[178] *Relation ou journal d'un voyage fait aux Indes Orientales. Contenant l'état des affaires du païs et les établissements de plusieurs nations que s'y sont faits depuis quelques années* (Paris, 1677). Reissued in 1698.

most productive years in Paris.[179] Equally stimulating was the publication in 1680 of Arnoldus Montanus' summary account of the Dutch embassies sent to the court of Japan,[180] for news of Japan in French had become very rare after the closure of Japan in 1640.

Southeast Asia meanwhile became ever more prominent in French publications. At Amsterdam in 1681 there appeared in French the *Voyages* in three volumes of Jan Janszoon Struys (1630–94), one of the Dutchmen who had served in the fleet of 1649–51 sponsored by the Genoese syndicate.[181] Appended to the final volume is a lengthy relation of the wreck of the "ter Schelling" off the coast of Bengal. In the same year, also at Amsterdam, the French version was published of Willem Ysbrantszoon Bontekoe's voyage to the East Indies. The Protestant historical writer Louis Dumay (d. 1681) contemporaneously issued at Geneva *Le prudent voyageur*, a description in three volumes of the political organization of all known nations.[182] Portugal and its dependencies were the subjects of a separate book published in French at Turin in 1682.[183] In 1684 a French version of Robert Knox' voyage to Ceylon appeared from a press in Lyons. In the same city Jacob Spon published in 1685 new treatises on coffee, tea, and chocolate.[184]

The writings of Ferdinand Verbiest (1623–88), a Belgian Jesuit who first went to China in 1659, now began to appear in French. His letter of 1678 from Peking on the progress of the mission was translated from Latin into French and published at Paris in 1681.[185] Verbiest's letters on his two trips into Tartary with the K'ang-hsi emperor were compiled to make a French book that appeared at Paris in 1685.[186] The European Jesuits were meanwhile compiling and translating Xavier's letters, probably in connection with the new biography of the Saint that appeared also in 1682.[187]

---

[179] *Les Indes Orientales et Occidentales, et autres lieux; representée en très belles figures* (Leyden, 1680[?]).

[180] *Ambassades mémorables de la Compagnie des Indes Orientales des Provinces Unis vers les empereurs du Japon* (Amsterdam). See below, pp. 488–89.

[181] This was his first voyage, the story of which is recounted in Vol. I of *Les voyages de Jean Struys* (2 vols.; The Hague, 1758–59). The edition of 1684 (Lyons) contains many maps and illustrations. On the Genoese company see above, p. 379.

[182] For Dumay's writings see P. Marchand (ed.), *Dictionnaire historique et critique par M. Pierre Bayle* . . . (rev. ed., 4 vols.; 1730), II, 36–38.

[183] P. Grognard, *La couronne du Portugal, ou la parfaite connoissance de ses royaumes.*

[184] *Traitez nouveaux et curieux du café, du thé, et du chocolate.* Reprinted in 1688 (Lyons) and 1693 (The Hague). On the earlier treatise see above, p. 415.

[185] Extracts from the French translation were included in *Le mercure galant*, September, 1681, pp. 194–214; April, 1682, pp. 135–38.

[186] Translated by D. D. from Verbiest's letters, this book is entitled *Voyages de l'empereur de la Chine dans la Tartarie. . . .* Verbiest's letters are also found in Pierre Joseph d'Orléans, *Histoire des deux conquerans Tartares qui ont subjugué la Chine* . . . (Paris, 1688). A Dutch translation is included in Nicolaas Witsen, *Noord en Oost Tartarye* (Amsterdam, 1692); an English translation appeared in *Philosophical Transactions*, XVI (1686–87), 35–62.

[187] Letters collected and published by A. Tulle. The new biography, written by Dominique Bouhours, was entitled *La vie de Saint François Xavier* (Paris).

3

SIAM AND CHINA

Interest in Siam mounted steadily in France throughout the first generation of Louis XIV's rule. The French bishops, who had begun building a mission at Ayut'ia in 1661–62 as the center of their enterprise in Southeast Asia, steadily assumed more leadership over the church's activities in continental Southeast Asia. In Paris, Colbert saw Ayut'ia as a trading center for the French East India Company, which along with Pondicherry and a port in Bengal, might give France an opportunity to dominate commerce in the Bay of Bengal. Narai, the king of Siam, had long looked with favor upon the French as potential allies in his struggle against the Dutch. To carry out his plan, Narai dispatched an embassy to France in 1680. The "Soleil d'Orient," on which the embassy sailed, disappeared at sea in 1681, and so it was not until several years later that a Siamese embassy actually arrived in France.

Letters from Siam and Bantam had led the French to think that the Siamese emissaries would arrive at Paris sometime in 1682 with their rich gifts for the king. In anticipation of this visit Claude de L'Isle, a geographer, compiled from the materials available to him a *Relation historique du royaume de Siam* (Paris, 1684). De L'Isle, who admits to having no specialized knowledge of the East, commences his book with a catalog of the authors he used in preparing it. This list includes almost every author who visited, or claimed to have visited, Siam, from Varthema in the early sixteenth century to the French bishops of the 1660's and 1670's. De L'Isle has no qualms about using Pinto as a source, for he asserts that belief in Pinto's reliability and accuracy had steadily increased as greater numbers of Frenchmen actually traveled in the East and saw its wonders for themselves.

A series of relevant publications appeared in rapid succession from 1685 to 1687, mainly as a result of the embassy that Louis XIV sent to Siam in 1685. The chief of mission was the Chevalier Alexandre de Chaumont (b. *ca.* 1640), a recent convert from Calvinism; his associate was François Timoleon (1644–1724), the Abbé de Choisy and one of the literary and social lights of Paris. Six Jesuit astronomers and mathematicians, as well as the ambassador's retinue, accompanied them. King Narai received the embassy near Ayut'ia on October 18, 1685, with full honors. Working through Constantine Phaulkon, the Greek-Venetian adventurer and confidante of the Siamese king, Chaumont sought the conversion of Narai to Christianity in return for an alliance with France. The king apparently showed little interest in becoming a Christian; though he showered the ambassador and his associates with favors and gifts, he made very few concessions of value to the traders.[188] He did, however, return Louis XIV's favor by sending an em-

---

[188] For details on the Franco-Siamese negotiations see Hutchinson, *op. cit.* (n. 148), pp. 92–111.

bassy of his own to France. The whole party disembarked at Brest in June, 1686; for the next nine months and more the Siamese were feted in France.[189]

Almost immediately on his return Ambassador de Chaumont published a report of his experiences in Siam.[190] To it there is appended a list of the presents sent by Narai to Louis XIV, his family members, and his advisers. Included in the list are many gifts of Chinese and Japanese origin. The Abbé de Choisy, who was disappointed by Narai's unreadiness to profess Christianity, returned to France to publish his account of the expedition in a charming book presented in the form of letters to a lady. Each evening, according to his plan, the Abbé sat down to record the events of the day. He was therefore able to publish what is in effect a diary of the entire voyage (March 3, 1685–June 18, 1686) that is remarkably detailed and accurate as well as pleasant and urbane.[191] Choisy's journal is valuable for its supplementary and occasionally critical observations on the conduct of Chaumont in the negotiations. Guy Tachard (1648–1712), the Jesuit mathematician and interpreter, likewise provides an oblique look at the French mission in his appraisal of the scientific and political results of the French enterprise in Siam and China.[192] Contemporaneously *Le mercure galant* published materials on Siam in its issues of 1684–88.

The renewed fascination with the East led publishers in France to print other materials, not directly related to the embassy.[193] An account of the earlier travels and experiences of Charles (or Gabriel) Dellon (b. 1649), a servant of the French East India Company in India, was published in 1685.[194] A physician by training, Dellon had served the Company in India from 1668 to 1673, where he made acute observations of the flora and fauna of Malabar. He left the employment of the Company to take up private practice in Damão, the Portuguese colony. After less than six months on his own, Dellon was arrested by the Inquisition and taken to Goa early in 1674. After being held prisoner for more than two years, he was taken to Lisbon,

[189] For a contemporary account of their reception see Jean Donneau de Visé, *Voyage des ambassadeurs de Siam en France* (2 vols.; Paris, 1686–87).

[190] *Relation de l'ambassade de Mr. . . . de Chaumont à la cour du roi de Siam* (Paris, 1686). Reprinted at Amsterdam in 1686 and at Paris in 1687. English and Dutch translations were published at London and Amsterdam respectively in 1687.

[191] *Journal du voyage de Siam fait en 1685 et 1686* (Paris, 1687). Reprinted at Paris in 1687 and at Amsterdam in 1688. There is also a reprint of 1930 (Paris) with a preface by Maurice Garçon.

[192] *Voyage de Siam des Pères Jesuites, envoyéz par le roy aux Indes et à la Chine. Avec leurs observations astronomiques, et leurs remarques de physique, de géographie, d'hydrographie, et d'histoire* (Paris, 1686). Reprinted at Amsterdam in 1687. Translations in Dutch (Utrecht) and English (London) appeared in 1687, 1688, and 1689. All of the editions are richly illustrated.

[193] The first part of the *The Travels of Sir John Chardin into Persia and the East Indies*, published at London in 1686, contains nothing on the lands east of Persia. Jean Chardin (1643–1713), a jeweler and a French Protestant, was actually in India as early as 1665, but he deliberately eschewed writing about it, according to his preface, since he "understood only the Vulgar languages . . . without the knowledge of that of the Brachmans. . . ." It was only in 1711 that his complete journal was published in French at Amsterdam in three volumes.

[194] *Relation d'un voyage fait aux Indes Orientales* (2 vols.; Paris). Reprinted at Paris in 1689 and in an augmented version at Amsterdam in 1699. An English translation appeared in 1698.

where he was released in 1677 on condition that he return to France immediately. Back in Paris he published his exposé of the Inquisition in Goa with the permission of Louis XIV.[195] He also specialized in tropical diseases and wrote a treatise on them which was appended to the 1699 edition of his *Relation d'un voyage*.

Dellon's materials on the French Company in India were supplemented by Urbain Souchu de Rennefort (*ca.* 1630–*post* 1689) in his *Mémoires pour servir à l'histoire des Indes orientales* (Paris, 1688).[196] Part I is a republication of Rennefort's relation of the first French enterprise in Madagascar which he had originally published in 1669.[197] No longer in the service of the Company thereafter, Rennefort watched critically the developments in the East under his successors. Part II reviews the ventures of François Caron (the Dutch adviser on the East) and others in India, and bemoans the desertion of Madagascar. It ends with a plea to the king for the reestablishment of Madagascar as France's base in Asia. Part II also includes discourses on the places and products of India and Ceylon drawn from the reports and writings of others.

Nicolas Gervaise (*ca.* 1662–1729), a young French secular priest who later became Bishop Nicolas of Tours, spent the years from 1681 to 1685 in Siam as a missionary. He returned to France in the company of two "princes of Makassar." The orphaned sons of "Daën Ma-Allé," a refugee prince of Makassar who had died in Siam, the boys were taken to France as wards of Louis XIV and educated at the Jesuit College in Paris. The royal youths were presented at court before they commenced their educational program. Gervaise, who acted as their tutor, was also called upon to employ his skill in the Siamese language while showing the emissaries from Siam around France in 1686–87. The following year he published at Paris the first separate book to appear in Europe on Makassar, a part of the great island of Celebes.[198] Gervaise, who dedicated this work to Father de La Chaise, Louis XIV's Jesuit confessor, hoped to stimulate French missionary and commercial activity in Celebes.

At Paris in 1688 Gervaise published his four-part history of Siam, which he dedicated to the king himself.[199] In this work he excludes from his consid-

---

[195] *Relation de l'Inquisition de Goa* (Leyden, 1687; Paris, 1688). It was immediately published in English and Dutch, and in 1689 in German. Modern scholars have often dismissed Dellon's account of the Inquisition as a forgery or fabrication. His reputation has, however, been rehabilitated in recent years, especially by A. K. Priolkar, *The Goa Inquisition* (Bombay, 1961), chap. iv.

[196] Reprinted at Paris and Leyden, also in 1688, under the title *Histoire des Indes orientales*. Jodocus Crull translated an extract from Rennefort's *Histoire* into English that was published as a supplement to the English version of Dellon's *Voyage* (London, 1698). The French version was reissued at Paris in 1702 under the auspices of the Company.

[197] See above, n. 149.

[198] *Description historique du royaume de Macaçar* (1688). Reprinted in an augmented edition of 1700 that was quickly translated into English: *An Historical Description of the Kingdom of Macassar in the East Indies* (London, 1701).

[199] *Histoire naturelle et politique du royaume de Siam.* . . . It was reprinted at Paris in 1689. There

erations those materials on the voyage and missions to Siam which could readily be found in other contemporary publications. He prepared his work as background for the French diplomats, traders, and missionaries who were planning at this time on going to Siam. His acquaintance with the Siamese language enabled him to provide his readers with materials, especially on history, customs, and religion, that were not otherwise available in France, and to rectify the misunderstandings perpetrated by Tavernier and other less sophisticated commentators. During his four years of residence in Ayut'ia, he had also acquired an understanding of Siam's unique position in the international political system of Southeast Asia and of the proper ceremonies to follow in the conduct of international relations with the court. In fact, there is hardly any aspect of politics or war that he does not touch upon in his remarkably authoritative survey of Siam in the 1680s.[200]

The clash over missionizing methods and the increasing predominance of the French in the Catholic hierarchy of Asia became matters of public debate in Europe during the 1680's. The publication in 1683 of the second volume of *La morale pratique des Jésuites* by Sébastian J. du Cambut de Pontchateau, a Jansenist and a collaborator of Antoine Arnauld, included a severe denunciation of the Jesuits in the East based on their own publications and on Navarrete's *Tratados*.[201] In the diatribe which followed, the Jesuits produced a number of notable publications especially designed to validate their position in the Chinese rites controversy. Michel Le Tellier (1643–1719), a renowned spokesman for the Jesuits and a leading controversialist, first responded on behalf of the China missionaries. Early in his career Le Tellier had edited Quintus Curtius' life of Alexander the Great, to which he added notes on India derived from his study of the sixteenth-century commentators on the East.[202] In 1687 he issued his *Defense des nouveaux chrestiens et des missionaires de la Chine, du Japon, et des Indes* (Paris) in response to the attacks on them in *La morale pratique* and in *L'Esprit* of Antoine Arnauld. The *Defense* remained at the heart of the bitter debate within the church until it was placed on the *Index* in 1700.[203]

Other Jesuit authors were quick to join the defence. Father Philippe Couplet (1622–93) of the China mission, who was forced by the controversy between Rome and Portugal to remain in Europe from 1682 to 1692,

---

is a modern English translation by H. S. O'Neill, *The Natural and Political History of the Kingdom of Siam, A.D. 1688* (Bangkok, 1928).

[200] This should be used in conjunction with the memoir of Father Claude de Bèze, first published at Tokyo in 1947. It was translated into English by E. W. Hutchinson in his work entitled *1688. Revolution in Siam* (Hongkong, 1968).

[201] See above, pp. 358–60.

[202] Q. *Curtii Rufi de rebus gestis Alexandri. . . . Interpretatione et notis illustravit Michael le Tellier . . .* (Paris, 1678), especially pp. 330–31.

[203] Reprinted in 1688 and 1690. Translated into Spanish and published at Madrid in 1690. See also Le Tellier's *Lettre à monsieur XX docteur, de Sorbonne, au sujet de la révocation faite par m. l'abbé de Brisocier de son approbation donnée en 1687 au livre intitulé Defense . . .* (1700).

made good use of his involuntary stay to publicize the achievements of the Jesuits in Peking. In 1686 he published in a Latin translation Verbiest's catalog of the Jesuits who had worked in China over the century from 1581 to 1681.[204] At Paris in the following year there appeared under Couplet's auspices and with his collaboration the famous *Confucius Sinarum philosophus*.[205] Dedicated by Couplet to Louis XIV, this work includes an introduction dealing with the Confucian classics and their Chinese commentators and with the theism of traditional China. These discussions are followed by a life of Confucius, probably by Intorcetta, a series of translations from the *Four Books,* and materials added by Couplet on the Chinese calendar and on the genealogies of the Chinese emperors.[206] To provide an example of the piety and fidelity of the Chinese converts, Couplet composed in Latin the story of Candida Hsü, which appeared in 1688 in the French version made by Father d'Orléans.[207]

The year 1688 saw the appearance in French of three other books on China. D'Orléans' history of the two Manchu conquerors, based on the writings of Martini and Schall, treats sympathetically the new regime in China.[208] The description of China, composed in Portuguese in 1668 by Gabriel de Magalhães (1611–77) and carried back to Europe by Couplet in 1682, was translated into French by Claude Bernou and finally published in 1688.[209] It is perhaps the most comprehensive and perceptive general description of China published during the second half of the century. At Amsterdam meanwhile there appeared a French work on the moral principles of Confucius which is usually attributed to Jean de La Brune, a Huguenot minister who had taken refuge in Holland. This small book, which is based on the introduction and Latin translations in *Confucius Sinarum philosophus,* was frequently reprinted hereafter and was translated into English in 1691.[210] Its tone, like that of the Jesuit informants, is adulatory of the rationality, urbanity, and humanity in the thought of the Chinese sage.

The French Jesuits who were sent to China in 1685 traveled via Siam on the way to their destination. While in Siam they wrote to their colleagues of the Academy of Sciences in Paris of the physical and mathematical observa-

---

[204] *Catalogus patrem Societatis Jesu qui ad anno 1581 usque ad 1681 in Sina . . . fidem propagarunt* (Paris). See Louis Pfister, *Notices biographiques et bibliographiques sur les Jesuites de l'ancienne mission de Chine, 1552–1773* (Shanghai, 1932), pp. xxi–xxii.

[205] On its group authorship and its content see David E. Mungello, *Curious Land: Jesuit Accommodation and the Origins of Sinology* (Stuttgart, 1985), pp. 247–99.

[206] In 1686 Couplet had published a part of these chronological materials in a separate book called *Tabula chronologica monarchiae Sinicae . . . ad annum post Christum 1683* (Paris).

[207] *Histoire d'une dame chrêtienne de la Chine* (Paris). It was translated into Spanish (Madrid, 1691) and Flemish (Antwerp, 1694).

[208] *Op. cit.* (n. 186). Reprinted in 1689 and 1690. An English translation was published in 1854 in "HS," o.s., XVII.

[209] *Nouvelle relation de la Chine* (Paris) See above, p. 362. Reissued at Paris in 1689 and 1690. It was translated into English by John Ogilby as *A New History of China . . .* (London, 1688). See Mungello, *op. cit.* (n. 205), pp. 91–96.

[210] *Lâ morale dê Confucius* (1688).

tions they had made in the course of their voyage and during their layover in Siam. In 1688 a Jesuit of Paris, Thomas Gouge (or Goüye) (1650–1725), published a book based on their observations to which he added the reflections of the members of the Academy and his own notes.[211] It includes, among other matters, descriptions of the animals of Siam, some based on dissections, as well as careful observations of typhoons and eclipses.

The Jesuit mathematicians had been accompanied to Siam in 1685 by Guy Tachard, the Jesuit intermediary between Phaulkon and the interested members of Louis XIV's court, especially Father de La Chaise. Tachard returned to France in 1686 to help prepare for the return of the Siamese embassy to Ayut'ia and for the dispatch to Siam in 1687 of two new French plenipotentiaries and the troops which were to man the French garrison in Bangkok. Tachard himself returned to Siam in 1687, and three months later left for France in the company of Simon de La Loubère, one of the French plenipotentiaries. Shortly after their departure, Phaulkon was overthrown in May, 1688, an event that was followed in November by the expulsion of the French garrison from Siam and by the conclusion of a treaty of friendship between Siam and the Dutch. In France, Louis XIV began demanding answers of the persons involved in the Siamese debacle.

Tachard, by the express order of the king, published at Paris in 1689 the story of his second voyage to Siam.[212] The fall of Phaulkon apparently left Tachard unmoved, for his hopes remain high in this book about the future of the French in Siam.[213] Indeed, he even tried, unsuccessfully, to return to Siam in 1690 and finally ended up in Pondicherry. The reports coming directly from Siam were far less hopeful. A letter from Louis Laneau (1637–96), the vicar apostolic who had been in Siam since 1661, was written in November, 1689, from a Siamese prison and published at Paris in 1690.[214] The publicist of the Jesuits, Pierre Joseph d'Orléans, prepared on the basis of Tachard's materials, as well as other Jesuit letters, a history of Phaulkon's career as first minister to the king of Siam and of his execution in 1688.[215]

Certain officers of the French expeditionary force, including Captain Pierre Desfarges, its leader, wrote upon their return to Europe their own versions of the disaster which overtook the French in Siam. An officer named Beauchamp, who was probably a prisoner of the Dutch, had his

[211] *Observations physiques et mathématiques à l'histoire naturelle et à la perfection de l'astronomie et de la géographie: Envoyées de Siam à l'Académie Royale des Sciences à Paris par les Pères Jésuites François qui vont à la Chine en qualité de Mathématiciens du Roy.* . . .

[212] *Second voyage au royaume de Siam.* It was reprinted at Amsterdam and Middelburg, also in 1689. It is often bound with Tachard's earlier book.

[213] Notices were published of this account in Berlin's *Acta eruditorum* (1689), pp. 479–85, and Paris' *Journal des Sçavans* (1689), pp. 272–76.

[214] A fifteen-page pamphlet entitled *Lettre de M. L'evesque de Metellopolis, Vicaire Apostolique de Siam au Supérieur et aux Directeurs du Séminaire des Missions-Etrangères étably à Paris.* . . .

[215] *Histoire de M. Constance, premier ministre du roy de Siam et de la dernière révolution de cet état, dédiée à N. S. P. le Pape Alexandre VIII* (Paris, 1690). Reprinted in 1962.

account printed at Middelburg in 1689.[216] In the following year De St. Vandrille, another officer, published his version at Paris, in which he lays blame for the debacle on Desfarges.[217] Vollant des Verquains, another of the disgruntled officers, published at Lille in 1691 a similar attack upon his superior and also upon the Dutch.[218] Captain Desfarges had his own view published anonymously in Paris and Amsterdam in 1691; notice was taken of his book in the *Journal des sçavants* for November 26 of that year.[219] At about the same time, a pamphlet was published in London which was based on several letters of 1688 and 1689 from Siam and Coromandel, and which purported to give "A full and true relation of the great and wonderful revolution that happened in the East Indies."[220]

The greatest contribution to Europe's knowledge of Siam came through the two volumes published by Simon de La Loubère (1642–1729), Louis XIV's envoy, who had spent four months in Siam during 1687 and 1688. His *Du royaume de Siam* (2 vols.; Paris, 1691) is "the best book yet published concerning the people of Siam and their customs in the seventeenth century."[221] La Loubère, who was a distinguished man of letters and mathematician as well as a student of public law and a career diplomat, went to Siam with his mind and his eyes open. He has almost nothing to say about the French project or about the political conditions at the Siamese court which preoccupied his countrymen. His is a lucid description of the physical environment and the practices, ceremonies, beliefs, and ideas of the Siamese, based upon his own careful observations and upon a judicious use of the writings of others, which he had studied before arriving in Siam. As a mathematician he became interested in the astronomy of the Siamese and presents in his book an excellent account of their computation methods. In many instances he includes translations, especially in Volume II, of materials from Thai and Pali texts. The engraved illustrations and maps included are in some instances as informative as the text. The tone of the book is intelligent, reasonable, and remarkably unbiased and penetrating. Two years after its publication La Loubère was honored by election to the French Academy.

The Jesuit Marcel Le Blanc (1653–93) was one of the fourteen mathematicians sent to Siam in 1687. He, like La Loubère, spent just four months at Ayut'ia. With the downfall of Phaulkon in 1688, he was sent back to France to relate the news. But he was captured by the Dutch at the Cape of Good

---

[216] *Relation du Sr. de Beauchamp.*

[217] *Relation des révolutions arrivées dans le Royaume de Siam.*

[218] *Histoire de la révolution de Siam, arrivée en l'année 1688.*

[219] Pierre Brunel, the Amsterdam publisher, reveals the author's identity in his preface to the *Relation des révolutions arrivées à Siam dans l'année 1688.*

[220] Reprinted in Thomas Osborne, *A Collection of Voyages and Travels* (2 vols.; London, 1745). From internal evidence it appears that the original was probably printed in 1693.

[221] The opinion of Hutchinson, *op. cit.* (n. 148), p. 156. There is another Paris edition of 1693, and Amsterdam reprints of 1691, 1700, and 1713–14. The English translation of 1693 was reprinted in 1969 by the Oxford University Press with an introduction by David K. Wyatt: *A New Historical Relation of the Kingdom of Siam* (Kuala Lumpur, 1969).

Hope and was held in prison at Middelburg until March, 1690. From here he wrote a short letter to Dijon, his native city, telling of the revolution in Siam; it was published in 1690.[222] After his release Le Blanc taught mathematics at Dijon for a year or so before setting off for China with Couplet. At Lyons in 1692 there was published his two-volume work on the "revolution" in Siam and on conditions in Southeast Asia generally.[223] His is a comprehensive and lengthy survey heavily based on the writings of others. His observations and remarks on the sea voyage apparently made his book valuable to navigators. It is not, however, often cited in the bibliographies and secondary works on Siam or Southeast Asia.

While the Jesuits were certainly not responsible for the French failure in Siam, their enemies in Europe gave them no rest about their losses elsewhere in Asia. The Jesuit Jean Crasset (1618–92) published at Paris in 1689 a two-volume history of the church in Japan which again tried to explain how the Christians lost out there.[224] His account of the earlier years, from Xavier to 1624, is based on Solier's *Histoire ecclésiastique* (1627); the most original and useful part of the book is that which covers the years from 1624 to 1658, a lengthy era of martyrdoms which he holds up as proof of the soundness of Jesuit conversion practices. This apologetic history did not silence the enemies of the Jesuits. In 1691 an anonymous publication appeared which charged the Jesuits with persecuting the Christian bishops of Paraguay and the Philippines.[225] The following year the Jesuits published a heavily documented history of their differences with the Dominicans and Franciscans in the mission fields, especially in China, down to 1674.[226] This was amplified by the publication of a French version of Martini's history and the life of Ricci by D'Orléans, the Jesuit publicist.[227] In 1696 a veritable explosion occurred with the publication at Paris of Louis Le Comte's (1655–1728) *Nouveaux mémoires sur l'état présent de la Chine,* a panegyric of Chinese civilization by a Jesuit who had been there from 1687 to 1692.[228] On his return

[222] See Streit, V, 669.

[223] *Histoire de la révolution du royaume de Siam. Arrivée en l'année 1688, et de l'état présent des Indes* (Lyons, 1692). Reprinted at Paris in 1697. Translated into Italian and published at Milan in 1695. His remarks on the civil war in Cambodia are reproduced in A. Brébion, *Bibliographie des voyages dans l'Indochine française du IXe au XIXe siècle* (Paris, 1910), p. 118–19. Le Blanc's volumes require further investigation. Strangely, they are not cited by J. C. Gatty in his introduction to the *Voiage de Siam du Père Bouvet,* first published at Leyden in 1963.

[224] *Histoire de l'eglise du Japon.* Reprinted in 1691 and 1715. Translated into Italian (1722), German (1738), and Spanish (1749). The first edition is well illustrated.

[225] *Histoire de la persécution de deux saints évêques, par les Jésuites, l'un D. Bernardim de Cardinas, l'autre D. Philippe Pardo, archévêque de Manille.*

[226] *Histoire des differens entre les missionnaires Jésuites d'une part et ceux des Ordres de St. Dominique et de St. Francois [sic] de l'autre. Touchant les cultes que les Chinois rendent à leur Maître Confucius, à leurs ancestres, et à l'Idole Chin-Hoan* (n.p., 1692). For a summary of its contents see Streit, V, 919–20.

[227] Printed respectively in 1692 and 1693. The translation of Martini's history of China was by the Abbé Lepelletier.

[228] Three volumes, Paris, 1696–98. Reprinted in 1701, even after its censure in 1700. It was immediately translated into English (1697), Dutch (1697), and German (1699). English editions

to France Le Comte became the confessor of the duchess of Burgundy and a prominent spokesman for the Jesuits in the heated controversy over the Chinese rites.

Other Jesuits were meanwhile engaged in more substantial activities. Philippe Avril (1654–98) published at Paris in 1692 the story of the efforts he and his companions had made between 1685 and 1690 to obtain permission to traverse Russia and establish a land route between Paris and Peking.[229] His book includes a description of Tartary and its peoples; it was perhaps the interest that Avril aroused in Tartary which inspired the republication in 1695 of Verbiest's relation of his two trips into Tartary in the company of the Chinese emperor.

In these years the K'ang-hsi emperor was becoming a living reality to the French, the "Louis XIV of China." Joachim Bouvet (1656–1730), a native of Mans and a Jesuit mathematician, had arrived at Peking in 1688. He and Father Jean-François Gerbillon, who had been in China since 1687, were accorded the unusual honor of acting as tutors and advisers to the emperor himself. They were also responsible, in part at least, for obtaining K'ang-hsi's edict of 1692 officially tolerating Christianity; the Jesuits were also optimistic in these years of bringing about K'ang-hsi's personal conversion. In 1693 the emperor charged Bouvet with the task of returning to France as his emissary and as a procurer of additional scholarly Jesuits. On his arrival at Paris in 1697 Bouvet published as a present for Louis XIV his *Portrait historique de l'Empereur de la Chine,* a depiction in which the two leading monarchs of the world are placed in juxtaposition.[230] This was followed by a magnificent book of forty-three engravings by Pierre Giffart, the Paris engraver, based upon the Chinese illustrated books and the paintings which Bouvet carried as gifts to the French king. Particularly striking are the portraits of K'ang-hsi and his mandarins in ceremonial and official dress.[231] Bouvet, during his stay of two years (1697–99) in France, recruited missionaries and corresponded or conversed with a wide range of European public figures and intellectuals. At this juncture he apparently avoided becoming directly involved in the furious debate over the Chinese rites.

The Jesuits based in Paris and Rome were not equally taciturn. The rites controversy in Europe was not limited to finding solutions to the old term

---

also appeared in 1698, 1738, and 1739. We used the London, 1738, edition, entitled *Memoirs and Remarks . . . Made in Above Ten Years Travels through the Empire of China. . . .*

[229] *Voyage en divers états d'Europe et d'Asie, entrepris pour découvrir un nouveau chemin à la Chine.* In 1693 it was reprinted at Paris and published at London in English translation.

[230] Translated into Latin, Dutch, and English in 1699.

[231] *L'estat présent de la Chine en figures* (Paris, 1697). This is now an exceedingly rare book. We consulted the copy preserved in the Bibliothèque Nationale (Rés. O² N. 31). The frontispiece in color is of Louis de France, the duke of Burgundy and heir apparent, to whom the book is dedicated. The engravings in the book itself are in black and white on the left and hand-colored on the facing right-hand page. Its brief text on the "idea of government in China" was apparently written by Bouvet.

question and to the issue of the civil or religious character of the Confucian ceremonies. In France, particularly, it became part of the Jesuit-Jansenist controversy and of the efforts of Louis XIV to dominate the China mission through the Paris Society of Foreign Missions and the Sorbonne's Faculty of Theology. In Rome, where the Society for the Propagation of the Faith had long sought to supervise the Asian mission through its vicars apostolic, there existed a persistent hostility towards the Jesuits because of their deter-mination to resist such control, particularly since the Propaganda was gen-erally under the influence of the other orders. It was indeed Charles Maigrot (1652–1730), the vicar apostolic of Fukien, who launched in 1693 the indict-ment of the traditional Jesuit position on the rites which had been endorsed officially in 1656 by Pope Alexander VII.[232] But it was the stir caused by the publication of the first volume of Le Comte's *Nouveaux mémoires* in 1696 which forced the papacy to set up a special commission of cardinals that worked for seven years (1697–1704) to resolve the issue and bring peace back to the church.

The polemics in France reached an almost hysterical pitch from 1697 to the death of Pope Innocent XII in 1700. Charles Le Gobien (1653–1708), the procurator in Paris for the China mission, allied himself with Le Comte in maintaining and explaining the Jesuit position. In 1697 he published a col-lection of materials on the China mission including an extract from the pref-ace to Leibniz' *Novissima sinica* (1697).[233] By this extract, and those from other non-Catholic and non-French authors, Le Gobien seems to be trying to show how general was the approval of the Jesuits and of their part in win-ning K'ang-hsi's declaration of toleration for Christianity. Indeed in his book of 1698, the Jesuit published a history of the edict; to this he added a clarification, addressed to the duke of Mainz, of the honors rendered by the Chinese to Confucius and their ancestors; and this is followed by letters and reports of actions relevant to the rites controversy.[234] It appeared in the same year as Volume III of Le Comte's *Nouveaux mémoires,* both of which stimu-lated the polemical tirade which followed.

The eminent Dominican theologian of the Sorbonne, Noel Alexandre (1639–1724), led the attack in France on the Jesuits' attitude towards the Chinese rites. A polemicist of renown, Alexandre had earlier engaged the Jesuit Gabriel Daniel (1649–1728) on the theological issues of probabilism, laxism, and Molinism. At Cologne in 1699 he published his lengthy state-

---

[232] For a discussion, perhaps somewhat overly critical of the Jesuit position, see A. S. Rosso, O.F.M., *Apostolic Legations to China of the Eighteenth Century* (South Pasadena, Cal., 1948), pp. 130–36.

[233] *Lettre sur les progrez de la religion à la Chine.* We have consulted the copy of this exceedingly rare book preserved in the Bibliothèque Nationale (O²N 371). For its contents in summary see Streit, V, 940. Some commentators follow H. Cordier, *op. cit.* (n. 69), cols. 835–36, in denying Le Gobien's association with this publication. On Leibniz' work see D. F. Lach, *The Preface to Leibniz' "Novissima Sinica"* (Honolulu, 1957).

[234] *Histoire de l'edit de l'empereur de la Chine en faveur de la religion chrestienne . . .* (Paris, 1698). For its contents in summary see Streit, V, 945.

ment of the history of the Dominicans in China and of their growing disillusionment there with the political activities and conversion practices of the Jesuits.[235] To document his case he reproduces in whole or in part many of the Dominican letters from China written in the period from 1631 to the 1690's. Appended to the French book there is a Latin selection of relevant documents.[236] The following year Alexandre published an attack upon the Jesuit position in which he endeavors to show the similarities between the Chinese ceremonies and the idolatrous rites of the Greeks and Romans.[237] At Paris he published in 1700 seven letters addressed to Le Comte on the problem of the Chinese ceremonies,[238] and at Cologne a collection of materials on the honors rendered to Confucius written by Dominicans and by members of the *Missions étrangères*.[239]

Alexandre and Nicolas Charmot of the *Missions étrangères* were responsible for bringing the case against the Jesuits to the theological faculty of the Sorbonne in 1700.[240] Under pressure from these French sources and the Holy Office in Rome, the faculty examined for censure certain passages and propositions in the *Nouveaux mémoires* of Le Comte and *L'Edit* of Le Gobien. While the examination was in progress the Jesuits and their enemies waged a war of pamphlets and polemical books.[241] A formal censure was published on October 18 and 19, 1700, after thirty sessions of the faculty. The death of Pope Innocent XII in September, 1700, brought a lull in the public dispute for a brief period.

The Jesuits, who had earlier helped to open Siam to the commercial and military forces of France, sought in the 1690's to revive the interest of the

[235] *Apologie des Dominicans missionnaires de la Chine ou Réponse au livre du Père Le Tellier Jesuite, intitulé, Défense des Nouveaux Chrétiens; Et à l'éclaircissement du P. Le Gobien de la même Compagnie, sur les honneurs que les Chinois rendent à Confucius et aux morts.* Reprinted in 1700, and issued in Italian translation in 1699.
[236] For a summary of its contents see Streit, V, 951–53.
[237] *Conformité des cérémonies chinoises avec l'idolatrie Grecque et Romaine. Pour servir de confirmation à l'apologie des Dominicains missionaires de la Chine* . . . (Cologne). Translated immediately into Italian and Latin. For a summary of its contents and further bibliographical data see Streit, VII, 18–19.
[238] *Lettre d'un docteur de l'ordre de S. Dominique sur les cérémonies de la Chine.* For further detail on these pamphlets see Streit, VII, 29–30.
[239] *Recueil des pièces des differens de messieurs des Missions Etrangères et des religieux de l'Ordre de S. Dominique, touchant le culte qu'on rend à la Chine au philosophe Confucius* (1700).
[240] Charmot edited the collection of materials which made up the case in the *Historia cultus Sinensium* . . . (Cologne, 1700). For a review see *History of the Works of the Learned*, II (1700), pp. 466–72. For its contents in summary see Streit, VII, 23–24. Also see Rosso, *op. cit.* (n. 232), p. 135.
[241] For a fairly complete listing see Streit, VII, 1–44. Some of the more important were the following: Paris, Séminaire des Missions Etrangères, *Lettre* . . . *au Pape, sur les idolatries et les superstitions chinoises* (Brussels, 1700); *Réflexions générales sur la lettre qui paraît sous le nom de messieurs des missions étrangères au pape, touchant les cérémonies chinoises* (Paris, 1700); *Affair de la Chine* (1700), which includes six different pamphlets; L. D. Le Comte, *Lettre à monseigneur le duc de Mayne sur les cérémonies de la Chine* ([Paris], 1700); *Lettre écrite de la province de Fokien, dans la Chine, où l'on rapporte le cruel traitement que les chrétiens des Jesuites ont fait souffrir à Maigrot et au R. P. Croquet* (1700); Bourdaloue and Daniel, *Histoire apologétique de la conduite des Jésuites en Chine adresée a MM. des Missions Etrangères* (n.p., 1700).

crown in commerce with India and China. Many of the French, who had fled Siam in 1688, took refuge at Pondicherry near Madras on the southeast coast of India. In the meantime Louis XIV became involved in the War of the League of Augsburg, which brought France into conflict from 1686 to 1697 with all of the colonial powers. In Asia the major threat came to the French from the Dutch and English who were still hopeful at this period of monopolizing for themselves the trade of the East. In 1690 a French naval squadron was sent to support the outpost at Pondicherry. Its commander, Abraham Duquesne-Guiton, reconnoitered the south coast of India, bombarded a few places, and returned to France in 1691. The following year Claude-Michel Pouchot de Chantassin, who had sailed with Duquesne-Guiton, published at Paris an account of this expedition.[242] Duquesne-Guiton published his own version at Brussels in the same year, and it was translated into English in 1696.[243] Subsequent French naval forays of 1692–93 and 1695–97 were no more successful in combating the Dutch on the seas of the East. The French outposts in India were completely isolated by 1697 and at the mercy of the Dutch.[244]

An account of an earlier French challenge to Dutch positions in south India and Ceylon—the 1670–75 voyage of the royal squadron commanded by Jacob Blanquet de La Haye—appeared in 1697.[245] Its preface asserts that everything in it came from De La Haye and François Caron, the director general of the *Compagnie des Indes Orientales* and that they signed the original journal. Nevertheless the journal is written in the first person and frequently refers to Caron and De La Haye in the third person. It is a detailed account of the activities of the squadron, the negotiations in Surat, the visits to ports on the Malabar Coast and in Ceylon, the battles with the Dutch in Ceylon, the French seizure of San Thomé and the ensuing seige and French surrender to the Dutch. It also contains considerable descriptions of Indian castes and religions, of Goa, Calicut, San Thomé, and other coastal cities. Appended to it is a 1672 letter from Caron to Colbert describing the Dutch and Portuguese positions in India and advising the French to establish their headquarters on Ceylon.

It was the Peace of Ryswick (1697), concluded in Europe, which restored their colonies in India to the French. Pondicherry was returned, as were the

---

[242] *Relation du voyage et retour des Indes orientales, par un garde de la marine, servant à bord du vaisseau de M. Duquesnes.*

[243] *Journal du voyage de Duquesne aux Indes Orientales, par un garde-marine servant sur son escadre.* Translated into English as *New Voyage to the East Indies in 1690 and 1691 . . . By Monsieur Duquesne.* In 1721 Robert Challes published at The Hague a lengthier account of this same expedition. For a discussion of the confusion over the identity of this Norman sailor named Duquesne-Guiton and for his bibliography see A. Jal, *Abraham du Quesne et la marine de son temps* (2 vols.; Paris, 1873), II, 556.

[244] See Jules Sottas, *Histoire de la compagnie royale des Indes Orientales, 1664–1719* (Paris, 1905), pp. 380–88.

[245] *Journal du voyage des grandes Indes . . .* (Orleans, 1697). There appear to have been no subsequent editions.

French commercial outposts at Surat and in Bengal. The Jesuits, who had long been urging and working for a chartered company devoted to development of the China trade, finally managed in 1697–98 to obtain the necessary support and authorization for the foundation of the *Compagnie de la Chine*.[246] Through the Academy of Sciences in Paris and in the periodical press they had kept the public informed of their intellectual and spiritual triumphs in China.[247] They helped to stimulate others to look for alternative routes to China that would circumvent the Dutch and English control of the sea-lanes of Asia. Avril, the proponent of the overland route to China,[248] probably helped to inspire the explorations sent out by Tsar Peter the Great, accounts of which quickly became available in French.[249] The French explorers of North America also continued to look for a waterway that would connect the Atlantic to the Pacific and provide a new water route to China.

Father Bouvet, when he arrived in Europe, urged the directors of the French East India Company to extend their trading activities to China. Once they had explained that they would have to review their own finances and study the risk involved in a new venture so far afield, Bouvet made the acquaintance of Jourdan de Groussy, an important Parisian merchant of glassware who had high hopes for sales in the China market. He enlisted the aid of six of his friends to advance the capital and to obtain the crown's approval for dispatch of a merchant vessel to China. He also envisioned the extension of French activity to the South Seas. The French Jesuits encouraged and promoted these activities in the hope of having a more secure political and financial backing for their missions in China and the Pacific. In connection with these activities a number of books appeared in Paris around the turn of the century that looked toward the entrance of France into what would presumably be a profitable and expanding trade.[250] Throughout the 1690's the reprints of earlier works on the East and translations into French of Dutch and English works on Asian commerce constantly rolled off the printing presses.[251]

★

[246] For its history see Claudius Madrolle, *Les premiers voyages français à la Chine. La Compagnie de la Chine, 1698–1719* (Paris, 1901).

[247] Also see (though this work is cited only by Ternaux-Compans) J. B. Maldonde, *Prodigieux événements de notre temps arrivés à des Portugais dans un voyage extrêmement dangereux du côté de la Chine* (Mons, 1693).

[248] See above, p. 428.

[249] For the land route followed by Galitzin see Foy de La Neuville, *Relation curieuse et nouvelle de Moscovie* (The Hague, 1698), pp. 206–31. Reprinted in 1699. Also see Adam Brand, *Relation du voyage de Mr. Evert Isbrand, envoyé de Sa Majesté Czarienne à l'Empereur de la Chine en 1692, 93, 94* (Amsterdam, 1699).

[250] Giovanni Ghirardini, *Relation du voyage fait à la Chine sur le vaisseau l'Amphitrite en l'année 1698* . . . (Paris, 1700); Charles Le Gobien, *Histoire des isles Marianas nouvellement converties a la religion chrestienne* . . . (Paris, 1700). Also see E. A. Voretzsch (ed.), *François Froger, Relation du premier voyage des François à la Chine, fait en 1698, 1699, et 1700* . . . (Leipzig, 1926).

[251] For example, the atlases and geographical descriptions of Nicolas and Guillaume Sanson in 1690, 1692, and 1700. From English, the works of Robert Knox (1693) and William Dampier

The story of the dissemination in France of knowledge about the East neatly divides into two distinct periods: the first two generations (1600–60) and the remaining two-score years (1660–1700) of the century. In the decades prior to the beginning of Louis XIV's personal rule, France tried vainly to establish a domestic peace, while becoming ever more seriously embroiled in international rivalries and wars. Henry IV's efforts to restore religious and civil peace ended with his assassination in 1610 and was followed by a return under the regency of Marie de' Medici to political and social instability. Richelieu's efforts after 1624 to reestablish the authority of the central government were blunted by France's expanding involvement in the Thirty Years' War (1618–48) and its eventual commitment to full-scale war (1635–59) against the Habsburgs. While the French succeeded in making a separate peace in 1648 with the Austrian Habsburgs, their war against Spain continued until 1659. The regency dominated by Mazarin (1643–61) was meanwhile faced by powerful domestic enemies. The civil wars of the Fronde (1648–53) convinced the young Louis XIV that the crown could never again tolerate a recalcitrant and uncooperative nobility in Paris or in the provinces. The Age of Louis XIV was one in which the crown and its agents sought vigorously to extend the king's authority over many facets of life previously left untouched.

The seventeenth-century French writings about Asia were distinguished by their paucity in the first half of the century and by their abundance and richness in the age of Louis XIV. The central government, which never discouraged overseas relations, became a partner of the missionaries and merchants under Louis XIV. Faced by the enmity of the entrenched Dutch, English, and Iberians in the East, the French first sought to work in Indochina and Siam, regions not subject to other European powers. As their writings show, the French merchants were successful in insinuating themselves individually into the trade with India. Siam, the object of official French interest in the 1680's, was inspected more carefully by Europeans than ever before. China, once it became a chief objective of French missionary activity, stimulated a major controversy and became the nation of the East most admired in France.

While the French concentrated upon the continental countries, certain of their works brought information to Europe about relatively unknown insular places. Early in the century a vocabulary of the language of the Maldive Islands, the first in any European language, appeared in a French

---

(1698) appeared in French. Translations from earlier Dutch works were even more numerous, including Montanus (1696), Pelsaert, (1696), and Bruyn (1700). Special bibliographical works of relevance to Dutch-French relations were also put into print: *Liste de livres nouvellement imprimés en Hollande*. . . . (1693); *Catalogue nouveau de toute sorte de livres françois . . . qui se trouvent à Amsterdam* (1698); A. Moetjens, *Catalogue des livres de Hollande, de France, et des autres pays . . . qui se trouvent à present dans la boutique* (The Hague, 1700). Reprints were also issued of the writings of earlier French travelers: Monconys (1695), Bernier (1699), Dellon (1699), Carré (1699), and Gervaise (1700).

publication. Gervaise published the first separate history of Makassar, on Celebes, to appear in Europe. The French, because of their interest in Madagascar as a foothold, were responsible for highlighting the strategic importance of this and adjacent islands to Asian trade and conquest. The French Jesuits were the first to prepare a systematic work on missionary activities in the Mariana Islands. Nonetheless the French accounts of continental countries were the most important part of their contribution to Europe's knowledge of the East in the seventeenth century. Bernier's voluminous study (1670–71) of India and La Loubère's systematic analysis (1691) of the life and customs of Siam are two of the best books on Asian places produced during the seventeenth century in any European language.

CHAPTER VI

The Netherlandish Literature

The war with Spain (1568–1648) was the great catalyst in the Low Countries. Almost all aspects of Dutch culture seemed to emerge from it in full bloom. The war disrupted normal trade patterns and forced Dutch merchants to make direct contacts with Asia.[1] It provoked experiments in self-government, engendered the establishment of Leyden University, and produced undreamed-of prosperity for Amsterdam and other northern Dutch towns. It attracted—or forced—the migration of many prominent and wealthy Protestants from the south, whose funds and talents contributed greatly to the prosperity of the United Provinces. The war also resulted in the sudden expansion of printing and publishing in Holland's cities both because important printers like Plantin, Blaeu, Elzevier, and Cornelis Claeszoon moved north from Antwerp and Louvain and because of the relative freedom from censorship in Holland. Between 1570 and 1630, sixty-nine printers and book dealers emigrated from the southern Netherlands to Amsterdam and fifty-six to Leyden.[2] The Dutch contribution to Europe's knowledge of Asia also resulted from the coincidence of the new interest in Asian trade and the rapid growth of printing and publishing in Holland. By the end of the seventeenth century, probably more books were being published in the United Provinces than were coming from all the other presses of western Europe put together.

The most important of early Dutch descriptions of Asia were found in the works of Jan Huygen van Linschoten published in 1595 and 1596.

---

[1] See above, pp. 40–42.
[2] See J. G. C. A. Briels, *Zuidnederlandse boekdrukkers en boekverkopers in de Vereenigde Nederlanden omstreeks 1570–1630* (Nieuwkoop 1974), p. 26, table (c).

Linschoten (1563–1611), a native of Enkhuizen in North Holland, knew the Portuguese commercial empire in Asia at first hand. After he returned to Enkhuizen in 1592 he used his personally acquired information and that provided by others to write his *Itinerario*. The second part of the book, called the *Reysgheschrift,* was published first, in 1595. It contained the detailed sailing instructions which Linschoten had culled from the Iberian rutters and was eagerly awaited by the Dutch merchants who were outfitting fleets to trade in Asia. A manuscript copy of it guided De Houtman's fleet which left Amsterdam in April, 1595. Indeed, it guided most Dutch ships to Asia for the rest of the century. Again and again skippers and pilots attested to its accuracy, and it became a standard part of the library carried by East India Company fleets. That the Dutch were ready for the new information is apparent by the book's popularity. Seven Dutch editions were printed between 1596 and 1663; there were also two Latin editions (1599 and 1614), three French editions (1610, 1619, and 1638), and an English edition (1598); German and Latin translations were included in the De Bry collections (1598, 1599, 1601).[3]

While surely the most important, the *Itinerario* was not the only Dutch-language report on Asia to become available during the last decade of the sixteenth century. Varthema's travels had been published in Dutch versions at Antwerp in 1544 and 1563.[4] In 1595, Linschoten's publisher, Cornelis Claeszoon, brought out a Dutch translation of Juan Gonzáles de Mendoza's description of China.[5] Linschoten's description of China was in fact taken almost entirely from Mendoza. Claeszoon also published a translation of Cavendish's and Drake's circumnavigations taken from Hakluyt.[6] Earlier still, Lucas Janszoon Waghenaer had added five treatises dealing with Asian navigation to his *Thresoor der zeevaert* (1592) just before it was published.[7] The first is a brief condensation of the Drake and Cavendish voyages; the second is a report on Portuguese Asian trade based on interviews with Dirck Gerritszoon Pomp, a native of Enkhuizen who had returned home in 1590 after a thirty-five-year stint in Portuguese Asia. The third and fourth treatises taken from Linschoten's letter to his parents of December, 1585, are descriptions of Asian trade and of the sea-routes, and the fifth is a brief account of the routes between India, China, and Japan taken from unidenti-

---

[3] For further discussion of Linschoten's work and its vast importance see *Asia,* I, 198–204, 482–90, *et passim.*

[4] It was published again in 1654. *Die ridd'lycke reyse* . . . (Antwerp, 1544); *Seven boecken Lodowijcx der roomschen raedtsheeren vanden schipvaerden* . . . (Antwerp, 1563); *De uytnemende en seer wonderlicke zee-en land-reyse* . . . (Utrecht, 1654).

[5] *D'historie oft beschryvinghe van het groote rijck van China* (Hoorn). See *Asia,* I, 742–49, for a discussion of Mendoza.

[6] Francis Prettie, *Beschryvinge van de overtreffelijcke ende wijdt-vermaerde zeevaerdt vanden edelen heer end meester Thomas Candish* . . . *Hier noch by ghevoecht de voyagie van Sire Françoys Draeck en Sire Ian Hawkins* . . . (Amsterdam, 1598). For more on Hakluyt's account of the Cavendish and Drake voyages see *Asia,* I, 213–15.

[7] L. J. Waghenaer, *Thresoor der zeevaert* (Leyden).

fied sources.[8] The *Thresoor der zeervaert* went through five more Dutch editions between 1596 and 1608, two French translations (1601 and 1606), and one English translation (1600).[9] All the treatises, except the first, were later reprinted in Isaac Commelin's *Begin ende voortgangh* as appendices to Roelof Roelofszoon's *Journal*.[10]

I

EARLY VOYAGES TO THE EAST INDIES, 1597–1625

Many of the early Dutch reports of voyages, as well as retrospective accounts, were issued originally or reprinted in the great German travel collections of De Bry (*Petits voyages,* Frankfurt, 1598–1628) and Hulsius (Nuremberg, 1598–1640), and in the English collection of Purchas (London, 1625).[11] A series of voyages and maps was published in several languages at Amsterdam from 1596 to 1610 by Claeszoon. Later in the century many early accounts of voyages were issued or reprinted in the Dutch collections of Commelin, Joost Hartgers (1648–52), and Gillis Joosten Saeghman (*ca.* 1663–70).[12]

Firsthand reports of insular Southeast Asia arrived in the Netherlands with Cornelis de Houtman's (d. 1599) fleet in August, 1597. An anonymous *Verhael vande reyse* was published by Barent Langenes of Middelburg in 1597; it went through six editions in that year and the next, including translations into French, German, English, and Latin. The author or, more likely, authors had apparently sailed on the "Hollandia"; one of them was possibly a midshipman named Pieter Stockmans.[13] In 1598 Langenes published another extensively revised edition augmented perhaps by material from still another journal. He also changed the title to *Journael vande reyse*.[14] In 1598

<hr>

[8] Waghenaer, *Thresoor der zeevaert, Leyden, 1592* . . . With an Introduction by R. A. Skelton (Amsterdam, 1965), X, 195–204. For more on Dirck Gerritszoon, including the text of the interview published by Waghenaer, see J. W. Ijzerman, *Dirck Gerritsz. Pomp alias Dirck Gerritz. China, de eerste Nederlander die China en Japan bezocht, 1544–1604* ("Werken uitgegeven door de Linschoten Vereeniging," IX; The Hague, 1915). Works from the Linschoten Vereeniging collection will hereafter be cited as "WLV."

[9] For Waghenaer's works see Thomas I. Arnold, *Bibliographie de l'oeuvre de Lucas Jansz. Waghenaer* (Amsterdam, 1961).

[10] *Begin ende voortgangh van de Vereenighde Nederlantsche Geoctroyeerde Oost-Indische Compagnie* (Amsterdam, 1646), Ib, 32–41. (First edition was published in 1645.) On this compendium see below, pp. 461–73. It will hereafter be cited as *BV*.

[11] On these collections, see below, pp. 515–22, 556–68.

[12] See P. A. Tiele, *Mémoire bibliographique sur les journaux des navigateurs néerlandais* . . . (reprint of 1869 ed., Amsterdam, 1960), pp. 5–20, for bibliographic details.

[13] G. P. Rouffaer and J. W. Ijzerman (eds.), *De eerste schipvaart der Nederlanders naar Oost-Indië onder Cornelis de Houtman* (3 vols.; "WLV," VII, XXV, XXXII; The Hague, 1915–35), II, xxii–xxx.

[14] *Journael vande reyse der Hollandtsche schepen ghedaen* . . . (Middelburg).

[437]

Claeszoon published still another account of De Houtman's voyage, *D'eerste boeck,* written by Willem Lodewyckszoon.[15] It went through seven editions and translations by 1617. Altogether the descriptions of De Houtman's voyage published separately or in collections total at least twenty-four editions.[16]

Following Linschoten's advice, De Houtman's fleet sailed across the Indian Ocean from Madagascar to the Sunda Straits. En route it touched on Sumatra, traded for a time in Bantam, and made several other stops on the north coast of Java and on Bali; on its homeward journey the fleet sailed along the south coast of Java. The published journals of the voyage consequently provided European readers with the most detailed descriptions of Java to date and with the first continuous description of Bali in any language. By sailing around Java, De Houtman's men were able to ascertain its true size and shape. They discovered that it was not nearly as wide from north to south as it appeared on Portuguese maps, and this was reported in the *Verhael vande reyse.*[17] This work also contains a detailed description of Bantam, its harbor, fortifications, buildings, people, and trade, the prices of products, and the foreigners who traded there.

The *Verhael vande reyse* also contains a brief description of Bali.[18] De Houtman's men were enthusiastic about the island's fruitfulness and the friendly reception given them there. They fondly called it "Ionck Hollandt" (New Holland).[19] A slightly expanded description of Bali is included in the *Journael vande reyse.*[20] It also contains many coastline sketches and a vocabulary of Malay, a language useful throughout the East Indies.[21] There are many plates in both the *Verhael* and the *Journael.* Most of them, however, are the engravers' fanciful creations. Some were borrowed from Linschoten's *Itinerario,* but these too are imaginary scenes. Only two, one of Bantam and one of Javan ships, appear to be based on sketches.[22]

The plates in Willem Lodewyckszoon's *D'eerste boeck* (1598) are no improvement, although its abundant coastline sketches must have been helpful to later Dutch voyagers. Lodewyckszoon's book also contains considerably more descriptive material than the other accounts of De Houtman's voyage. It includes the Dutchmen's first eyewitness account of growing pepper and of coconut palms, along with descriptions of the people and other sights on the west coast of Sumatra.[23] Lodewyckszoon's long and detailed description of Java, however, is not an eyewitness account; it is apparently of Portuguese origin. Place names and terms are Portuguese, and it contains information

[15] *D'eerste boeck. Histoire van Indien . . .* (Amsterdam).

[16] For complete bibliographical information see Rouffaer and Ijzerman (eds.), *op. cit.* (n. 13), II, xix–lxxx, and Tiele, *op. cit.* (n. 12), pp. 116–36.

[17] Rouffaer and Ijzerman (eds.), *op. cit.* (n. 13), II, 61–62.

[18] *Ibid.,* pp. 60–61.

[19] *Ibid.,* p. 169.

[20] *Ibid.,* pp. 169–71.

[21] *Ibid.,* pp. 162–68.

[22] *Ibid.,* p. xxx. See our pl. 248.

[23] *Ibid.,* I, 64–69.

about Portuguese trade and forts in the Moluccas where De Houtman's ships did not visit.[24] Perhaps it came from Pedro de Tayde, the Malaccan-born Portuguese pilot who was so helpful to De Houtman's men in Bantam. In any case, it has not been found in any of the printed Portuguese sources.[25]

D'eerste boeck contains the first continuous account of Bali in any European language. Its prosperity is described in even greater detail than in the *Verhael vande reyse* and is effectively illustrated by the observation that on Bali common people ride horses, while the king and great nobles are carried in sedan chairs;[26] on Java, horses are reserved for the wealthy and high-born. Other members of De Houtman's expedition wrote journals, but most were not published.[27]

Despite the loss of many men and one of the ships, troubles with both Javans and Portuguese, and profits barely large enough to cover expenses, the return of De Houtman's fleet set off a flurry of activity among Dutch entrepreneurs. In 1598, the year after its return, no fewer than twenty-five ships were sent out by merchants of the provinces of Holland and Zeeland alone. The fleet sent out from Amsterdam by the successor of the company that financed De Houtman's venture, now called the Old East India Company, was a smashing success. Eight ships commanded by Jacob van Neck and Wybrand van Warwijck left Texel on May 1, 1598. Fifteen months later, on July 17, Van Neck returned from Bantam with four of his ships fully laden with pepper. The rest of the fleet, under Van Warwijck and Jacob van Heemskerck (1567–1607), made other stops on Java and then went to Banda, Amboina, and the Moluccas; here they established the three Dutch factories which became the foundation for later Dutch control of the Moluccan spice trade. Van Heemskerck arrived in Amsterdam with two ships on May 19, 1600; Van Warwijck arrived with the remaining two ships at the end of August, 1600. Profits for the fleet may have run as high as 200 percent.[28]

A brief published account of the voyage by someone on Van Neck's half of the fleet appeared in 1599 and was translated into English in the same year.[29] It contains very little descriptive material, but does report the effect

---

[24] *Ibid.*, pp. 125–28.

[25] *Ibid.*, p. 99n.

[26] *Ibid.*, See our pls. 254, 255.

[27] *Ibid.*, pp. 199–200. Apparently not everything in Pedro de Tayde's description was published in Lodewyckszoon's journal. In 1916 F. C. Wieder found a chart and a descriptive text obviously intended as part of *D'eerste boeck*'s chapter nineteen (Rouffaer and Ijzerman [eds.], *op. cit.* (n. 13), II, 207–29). It apparently had included detailed geographical and commercial information about the Moluccas and had even advised the Dutch how they might monopolize trade with the Moluccas by controlling Bantam and the Straits of Malacca (*ibid.*, p. 218). Obviously, important Amsterdam merchants had been able to suppress such sensitive information.

[28] For details of the voyage see J. Keuning (ed.), *De tweede schipvaart der Nederlanders naar Oost-Indië onder Jacob Corneliszoon van Neck en Wybrant Warwijck, 1598–1600* (5 vols.; "WLV," XLII, XLIV, XLVI, XLVIII, and L; The Hague, 1938–51), I, xvii–xxiii.

[29] There are no extant copies of the *Waarachtige beschryving*. It was apparently published by

of the large Dutch fleet on Bantam pepper prices[30] and the discovery of Mauritius Island.[31] An account of the entire expedition was published in 1600 at Amsterdam after Van Warwijck's return: *Journael ofte dagh-register, inhoudende een waerachtigh verhael ende historische vertellinghe vande reyse.* . . . A second augmented edition called *Het tweede boeck, journael oft dagh-register inhoudende een warachtich verhael* . . . appeared in 1601. With minor variations in text and title this account was translated into English (London, 1601), French (Amsterdam, 1601), German (Arnhem, 1601), and Latin (Frankfurt, 1601). It went through ten editions and translations before 1620. In 1611 an abridged version of the journal was published in Johan Izaakszoon Pontanus, *Rerum et urbis amstelodamensium historia* . . . (Amsterdam). The abridged version augmented by several descriptive inserts was also included in Commelin's *Begin ende voortgangh* (1645). The abridged version appeared in nine editions before the end of the century. At least nineteen editions and translations of the account of Van Neck and Van Warwijck's voyage appeared during the seventeenth century.[32]

The major contributions made by the account of Van Neck and Van Warwijck's voyage were full descriptions of Banda, Amboina, and the Moluccas. If there had been a concern for secrecy regarding the Spiceries in the reports of De Houtman's voyage, it certainly does not show here. *Het tweede boeck* contains all sorts of geographical, hydrographic, navigational, commercial, and political information as well as descriptions of the islanders and the spices. The account of the Javan city of Tuban, for example, includes a discussion of Java-Moluccan trade patterns. Merchants from Java traded pepper for cotton cloth in Bali. Then they traded the cloth for nutmeg, mace, and cloves on Banda and in the Moluccas.[33] *Het tweede boeck* contains a description of Amboina[34] and another of Ternate, which includes details on the cloves and on the enmity between the sultan of Ternate and the Portuguese of the fort on nearby Tidore.[35] The description of cloves was borrowed from Linschoten's *Itinerario*.[36]

Het tweede boeck includes what appears to be the earliest Dutch translation of the dialogue between Abdias and Muhammad. It is an old story, first written in Arabic in 963 A.D., about a Jew named Ahd Allah (Abdias), who met Muhammad, asked him some questions, and was converted. The number of questions grew over the years. Some Persian and Malay editions con-

---

Cornelis Claeszoon in Amsterdam. An English translation of the same year exists: *A True Report of the Gainfull, Prosperous and Speedy Voyage to Java in the East Indies, Performed by a Fleet of Eight Ships of Amsterdam;* . . . (London; W. Aspley, [1599].); this text is also reprinted in Keuning (ed.), *op. cit.* (n. 28), II, 27–41.

[30] Keuning (ed.), *op. cit.* (n. 28), II, 33.

[31] *Ibid.*, pp. 38–39.

[32] For bibliographic information see Tiele, *op. cit.* (n. 12), pp. 136–47. The text of *Het tweede boeck* is reprinted in Keuning (ed.), *op. cit.* (n. 28), III, 1–175.

[33] *Ibid.*, pp. 34–40.   [35] *Ibid.*, pp. 102–22.

[34] *Ibid.*, pp. 55–59.   [36] *Ibid.*, pp. 111–15.

tain a thousand. The version in *Het tweede boeck* contains only thirty-seven questions; it was apparently translated from a Portuguese source.[37] Appended to *Het tweede boeck* is another Malay-Javan-Dutch word list.[38] Both the word list and the dialogue are included in the abridged versions of the journal as well.

Among the many Dutch East Indian ventures of 1598 were two fleets outfitted in Rotterdam for the westward route to Asia through the Straits of Magellan: one fleet of five ships commanded by Jacques Mahu and, after his death, by Simon de Cordes, and another comprising four ships under Olivier van Noort (1558–1627). Mahu's fleet, as intent on raiding Spanish settlements in South America as on Asian trade, was a tragic venture. Only one of the five ships and about 50 of the 507 crewmen returned to the Netherlands. One ship was seized by the Portuguese at Tidore; one, under Dirck Gerritszoon Pomp, was captured by the Spanish at Valparaiso; one disappeared in mid-Pacific near the Hawaiian Islands; one, the "Liefde" commanded by Jacob Janszoon Quaeckernaeck with Will Adams as chief pilot, reached Japan; and one, commanded by Sebald de Weert, turned back to Holland from the Straits of Magellan.[39] The only published account of the voyage was written by Barent Janszoon, the surgeon on De Weert's ship, but it contains nothing about Asia.[40] Some information about the twenty-four surviving crewmen of the "Liefde," with some description of Japan, are found in letters from Will Adams published by Purchas in 1625.[41]

Olivier van Noort's voyage was scarcely more profitable than that of Mahu and De Cordes. Only one of his four ships returned home safely. It was a financial disaster for Van Noort personally and for the company formed to outfit the fleet.[42] Van Noort, however, became the first Dutchman to circumnavigate the globe; in the process he brought the war against Spain not only to the west coast of South America but also to the mouth of Manila Bay. Spanish ships were captured and sunk and Spanish trade disrupted by Van Noort in both areas. Van Noort's achievement captured the imagination of his countrymen, so published accounts of the voyage sold well. The first edition was published by Jan van Waesberge of Rotterdam only eighteen days after Van Noort returned.[43] It was brief and rough, lacked even an en-

---

[37] *Ibid.*, pp. 123–30.

[38] *Ibid.*, pp. 158–75.

[39] For details see F. C. Wieder (ed.), *De reis van Mahu en de Cordes door de Straat van Magalhães naar Zuid-Amerika en Japan;* (3 vols.; "WLV," XXI, XXII, XXIV; The Hague, 1923–25).

[40] *Wijdtloopigh verhael van tgene de vijf schepen* . . . (Amsterdam: Zacharias Heyns, [1600]). For the text see Wieder (ed.), *op. cit.* (n. 39), I, 142–245; also Saeghman (ed.), *Journal van 't geene vijf schepen* (Amsterdam, [1663]).

[41] *PP*, II, 326–46. Text reprinted in Wieder (ed.), *op. cit.* (n. 39), III, 55–76.

[42] J. W. Ijzerman (ed.), *De reis om de wereld door Olivier van Noort 1598–1601* (2 vols.; "WLV," XXVII, XXVIII; The Hague, 1926), I, 92–94.

[43] *Extract oft kort verhael wt het groote journael vande wonderlijcke ende groote reyse ghedaen door de strate Magellana en andere vremde koninkrijcken en landen byden E. Olivier van Noort, admirael en generael vande vier schepen toegerust tot Rotterdam A°. 1598* (1601).

graved title page, but contained the promise that a more complete journal would appear in a few weeks or months.[44] The complete edition was published later in 1601 by both Van Waesberge and Claeszoon of Amsterdam.[45] Two emended editions appeared in 1602,[46] as did a French and a German translation. Another Dutch edition was published in 1618.[47]

The descriptive material in the *Beschryvinghe vande voyagie* is relatively brief and integrated into the narrative. The book is short; the definitive 1602 edition has only ninety-two pages. Nevertheless it contains the earliest first-hand Dutch descriptions of the Ladrones (Marianas), the Philippines, and Borneo. The Dutch describe the Ladrones very much as did the earlier Spanish writers: the people are superb swimmers, incorrigible thieves, live without law, hold women in common, and subsist on bananas, coconuts, sweet potatoes, and sugar cane, which they gladly trade for pieces of old iron. The Dutch writer also reports on the visible damage suffered by many of the islanders from the Spanish pox (syphilis).[48] Like the Spanish before them, the Dutch were impressed and somewhat bewildered by the vast number of Philippine islands. To thread their way from the San Bernardino Straits to Manila they seized both native canoes and a Chinese junk to obtain pilots. They notice the usually naked and tattooed natives, the houses on stilts, and the many boats and ships which bring what is called tribute from the outlying islands to the Spanish at Manila. From a captured Chinese pilot they learned much about Manila's size and fortifications and about its large Chinese settlement. Luzon is thought to be larger than England and Scotland combined.[49] Borneo is described as one of the largest islands in the Indies.[50] From the captain of a captured Japanese ship the Dutch author heard about Japan. In the *Beschryvinghe vande voyagie* he reports that the Japanese are tall, brave, and martial people, who make the best swords in the East Indies. Formerly various "kings" in Japan were continually at war with one another, but now most of the country is subject to one king. The Portuguese carry on a very profitable trade in Japan, bringing in Chinese goods which the Japanese cannot themselves obtain because they are at war with China. The Japanese write with the same characters as the Chinese and so each can read the other's writing even when they cannot understand each other's speech.[51]

All descriptive material was retained in the abridged version of the *Beschryvinghe vande voyagie* included in the *Begin ende voortgangh*.[52] Details

---

[44] Ijzerman (ed.), *op. cit.* (n. 42), II, 85–86.

[45] *Beschryvinghe vande voyagie om de geheelen werelt cloot, ghedaen door Olivier van Noort van Utrecht . . .* (Rotterdam and Amsterdam).

[46] For the differences between the first full edition of 1601 and the definitive edition of 1602 see Ijzerman (ed.), *op. cit.* (n. 42), II, 229–36.

[47] See *ibid.*, pp. 227–55, for complete bibliographical detail.

[48] Ibid., I, 88–90.   [50] *Ibid.*, pp. 121–27.

[49] *Ibid.*, pp. 91–109.   [51] *Ibid.*, pp. 113–15.

[52] "Beschryvinge van de schipvaerd by de Hollanders gedaen onder 't beleydt ende gene-

about courses, winds, weather, and shipboard routine were omitted, but some descriptions not found in the 1602 editions were also included. There are inserts on the Philippines,[53] on Capul,[54] Manila,[55] Borneo,[56] and a sizable "Description of Japan."[57] Some of the matter on Japan appears to have come from Linschoten, although the description also contains considerable information about the wars of unification and about Hideyoshi's government not found in Linschoten. Subsequent editions of Commelin's abridgment appeared in 1648, 1649, 1650, 1652, 1664, and 1684 and in the collections of Hartgers and of Saeghman. German and Latin translations are found in the collections of De Bry (Vol. IX) and Hulsius (Vol. I), and a brief English version is included in Purchas.[58]

Many of the fifteen Dutch voyages to the East between 1598 and the formation of the United East India Company (VOC) in 1602 produced no immediately published account. Jan Harmenszoon Bree's account of the first fleet sent out by the VOC under Van Warwijck and De Weert was not published until 1645.[59] Those that were published at once brought new and more exotic lands to the attention of Dutch readers. Cornelis Janszoon Vennip's account of Joris van Spilbergen's (d. 1620) voyage of 1604 introduced them to Ceylon and the "kingdom" of Acheh on the northern tip of Sumatra.[60]

Financed by Balthasar de Moucheron, Van Spilbergen's three ships left Verre in Zeeland on May 5, 1601.[61] From May 30 to September 2, 1602, the fleet was anchored at Batticaloa on Ceylon while Van Spilbergen and his entourage negotiated a treaty with the king of Kandy. Between September 16, 1602, and March 30, 1603, they were in Acheh negotiating with the sultan and hunting for Portuguese ships. A previous De Moucheron fleet, commanded by De Houtman, had been attacked in Acheh during 1599. Its ships had been saved, but De Houtman and many other Dutchmen had been killed and many others imprisoned. John Davis, the English pilot on one of De Houtman's ships, kept a journal of these events, which was later published by Samuel Purchas.[62] By the time Van Spilbergen arrived in 1602, the prisoners from De Houtman's fleet had been freed, and other Dutch and English ships were trading peacefully in Acheh.[63] In February, 1603, VOC

raelschap van Olivier van Noort door de straet of engte van Magellanes, ende voort de gantsche kloot des aertbodems om," *BV*, Ib.

[53] *Ibid.*, pp. 30–31.

[54] *Ibid.*, p. 34.

[55] *Ibid.*, p. 36.

[56] *Ibid.*, pp. 50–51.

[57] *Ibid.*, pp. 38–44.

[58] For the English excerpt see *PP*, II, 187–206.

[59] *BV*, Ib, 1–88. See Tiele, *op. cit.* (n. 12), p. 167.

[60] *'t Historiael journael van tghene ghepasseert is van weghen dry schepen, den Ram, Schaep, ende 't Lam* . . . ([Delft, 1604]).

[61] See above, p. 44.

[62] "The Voyage of Captain John Davis to Easterne India, Pilot in a Dutch Ship, written by Himself," *PP*, II, 305–26.

[63] For details see below, pp. 1370–71.

ships arrived in Acheh and Van Spilbergen's fleet joined them. After spending most of the summer of 1603 in Bantam, Van Spilbergen returned to Vlissingen on March 24, 1604.

Vennip provides a rather long description of Ceylon. Much of it is devoted to the story of the Portuguese attempt to gain control of Kandy; the Sinhalese commander-in-chief Vimaladharmasuriya's seizure of power there; the Portuguese expedition to put Kusumasana devi, the young daughter of the late king, on the throne; Vimaladharmasuriya's defeat of Pero Lopes de Sousa at Dantur on October 6, 1594; and his subsequent marriage to Kusumasana devi and his consolidation of power. This history was presumably related to Van Spilbergen and Vennip by Vimaladharmasuriya himself. Vennip also describes in detail Van Spilbergen's receptions and negotiations in Ceylon and extolls the fertility and wealth of the island: "certainly the most fruitful of which one may speak or write."[64] Vennip's description of Sinhalese religion is exceptionally uncharitable, and he thought that the conversations between Van Spilbergen and the king offered some hope of the king's conversion.[65] Although the book contains much detail about Van Spilbergen's negotiations and trade in Acheh, there is no separate description of Acheh or Sumatra.

Two editions of Vennip's *'t Historiael journael* appeared in 1605, both by the original publisher. Another was published at Amsterdam in 1617; it was later included in the *Begin ende voortgangh,* in the Hartgers collection, and in the Saeghman collections. Appended to the text of the voyage in the *Begin ende voortgangh* and the Hartgers edition is a description of Java taken from Pontanus, *Beschryvinge van Amsterdam.*[66] An abridgment of Vennip's account was included in both the Latin and the German editions of De Bry's collection.[67] The book contains some beautiful and exotic copper plates done by Floris Balthasar, apparently from Vennip's sketches. One of them shows Van Spilbergen and Vimaladharmasuriya in full regalia shaking hands with each other.[68]

A four-page account of Steven van der Hagen's (1563?–1624) second voyage appeared in 1606.[69] It announces the decisive victories won by the VOC

[64] Wouter Nijhoff, S. P. L'Honoré Naber, F. W. Stapel, and F. C. Wieder (eds.), *De reis van Joris van Spilbergen naar Ceylon, Atjeh en Bantam, 1601–1604* ("WLV," XXXVIII; The Hague, 1933), p. 62; the complete description of Ceylon is found in *ibid.*, pp. 54–65. For an English translation of the matter on Ceylon see D. Ferguson (trans. and ed.), "The Visit of Spilbergen to Ceylon, Translated from Admiral Joris van Spilbergen's 'Relation,'" *JRAS, Ceylon Branch,* XXX (1927), 127–79, 361–409.

[65] See T. Abeyashinge, *Portuguese Rule in Ceylon* (Colombo, 1966), pp. 12–18, for Portuguese relations with Kandy.

[66] *BV,* IB, 58–62.

[67] For bibliographic information see Tiele, *op. cit.* (n. 12), pp. 154–61, and Nijhoff, *et al.* (eds.), *op. cit.* (n. 64), pp. xx–xxii.

[68] Nijhoff, *et al.* (eds.), *op. cit.* (n. 64), pp. liv–lvii. A study of the artistic detail in the portrait may be found in G. P. Rouffaer, *Batik-Kunst in Nederlandsch Indië* (Utrecht, 1914), pp. 151–53. Also see our pls. 178, 180, 181.

[69] *Kort ende warachtich verhael vande heerlicke victorie te weghe gebracht . . .* (Rotterdam).

over the Portuguese in Amboina and the Moluccas during February, 1605, but contains no descriptions of the Moluccas or any other part of Asia. A full account of this voyage in Dutch first appeared in the *Begin ende voort-gangh* (1645), which also contained the first published account of Van der Hagen's first East Indian voyage made in 1600 and 1601. German editions of Van der Hagen's second voyage appeared in the collections of De Bry (1605) and of Hulsius (1606).[70]

The first published reports of Cornelis Matelief's voyage also added little to Europe's knowledge of Asia and its peoples. Two brief editions published soon after the fleet returned in 1608 recount only the voyage out from Holland and the Dutch siege of Malacca in 1606.[71] Matelief's complete journal was not published until its inclusion in the *Begin ende voortgangh* (1645).[72] The account of Matelief's voyage in the Hulsius collection (No. 10, 1613) is a compilation of the two 1608 editions.[73]

Hessel Gerritszoon's (1581?–1632) 1612 description of the Arctic north-eastern and northwestern passages contains, in addition to an account of Henry Hudson's attempts to find a northwest passage, two treatises by Isaac Massa (1587–1635), a Dutchman long resident in Russia. On the basis of reports by Russian travelers, Massa describes Russian travels to the Yenisey River and beyond, perhaps to China's frontiers. He includes brief reports about the peoples whom the Russians encountered.[74] Gerritszoon's compilation also contains a translation of Pedro Fernandez de Quiros' letter to Philip II describing the unknown southern continent which he thought he had discovered in 1606.[75] Both Quiros' letter and Massa's treatises are included in the two Latin editions of Gerritszoon's book (1612 and 1613) and in its 1648 Dutch edition. They were also published in the De Bry and the Hulsius collections and in the *Begin ende voortgangh* (1645). Parts of Massa's treatises appeared in Nicolaas Witsen's *Noord en Oost Tartarye* (1692); an English translation of the treatises appeared in *Purchas His Pilgrimes* (1625).[76]

The best-sellers of the century's second decade were the reports of two more Dutch circumnavigations: Van Spilbergen's voyage of 1614 to 1617 and that made by Jacob Le Maire (1585–1616) and Willem Corneliszoon Schouten (d. 1625) between 1615 and 1617. Van Spilbergen's VOC fleet,

[70] For bibliographic details see Tiele, *op. cit.* (n. 12), pp. 170–74. See below, pp. 465–67.

[71] *Historiale ende ware beschrijvinge* . . . (Rotterdam, 1608) and *Breeder verhael ende klare beschrijvinge* . . . (Rotterdam, 1608). See Tiele, *op. cit.* (n. 12), pp. 208–13 for bibliographic details.

[72] *BV*, IIa, no. 2, pp. 1–139. See below, pp. 467–70.

[73] See Tiele, *op. cit.* (n. 12), p. 213.

[74] Hessel Gerritszoon (ed.), *Beschryvinghe vander Samoyeden landt in Tartarien* . . . (Amsterdam, 1612), pp. 1–22.

[75] *Ibid.*, pp. 23–31. For Quiros' letter see above, pp. 307–8.

[76] For bibliographic details see Tiele, *op. cit.* (n. 12), pp. 179–90. In the *BV*, Massa's treatises follow the voyage of Gerrit de Veer, Ia, 54–67; Quiros' letter follows the account of Jacques L'Hermite's voyage, IIb, 68–74. Massa's treatises are in *PP*, XIII, 180–93. On Massa's treatises see John F. Baddeley, *Russia, Mongolia, China.* (2 vols.; London, 1919), II, 1–15.

which left Texel on August 8, 1614, was as much a military as a commercial venture. After clearing the Straits of Magellan on May 5, 1615, the fleet worked its way up the South American coast, sacking Spanish settlements and preying on Spanish shipping, until it reached Acapulco on October 10. From there it turned west to cross the Pacific. When Van Spilbergen arrived in the Philippines early in February, 1616, he again raided Manila-bound shipping for almost one month before sailing for Ternate. Even then his primary concern was to intercept the Spanish fleet rumored to be moving against the Dutch outposts in the Moluccas.[77] The Spanish fleet, however, withdrew to Manila after the death of its commander, Juan de Silva.[78] Van Spilbergen's fleet meanwhile arrived at Jakatra on September 15, 1616, sailed for home in December, and arrived in Zeeland on July 1, 1617.

While Van Spilbergen was loading pepper at Jakatra one of Le Maire and Schouten's ships, the "Eendracht," arrived there and was immediately seized by Jan Pieterszoon Coen, chief of the VOC establishment in Jakatra. Coen was acting on orders from the directors in Amsterdam, who considered Le Maire and Schouten's independent fleet a serious threat to the VOC monopoly.[79]

The directors had good reasons to suspect Le Maire's and Schouten's motives. Their fleet had been financed and organized by Jacob Le Maire's father, Isaac, perhaps the VOC's ablest and most militant opponent. He had been a member of the first East India Company in Amsterdam and he became one of the directors of the VOC when it was organized in 1602. After an acrimonious quarrel in which he was accused of fraud in the outfitting of Van Warwijck's fleet in 1602, Isaac Le Maire left the VOC in 1605. From that time on he worked tirelessly to infringe upon or to destroy the Company's monopoly. He negotiated with the French to help them establish an East India company—a plan finally frustrated by Henry IV's assassination.[80] He negotiated with Jan van Oldenbarneveldt (1547–1619), a free-trader at heart, to persuade him to rescind the Company's monopoly for not living up to its charter. He formed a secret company to manipulate VOC stocks. Le Maire and his colleagues would sell VOC stocks to each other at low prices to initiate a panic and then would buy up large quantities of stock at the depressed prices. The States General finally countered by making it illegal to sell stocks within one month of their purchase.[81] Finally Le Maire formed the *Australische Compagnie* and received a charter from the States

[77] See J. C. M. Warnsinck (ed.), *De reis om de wereld van Joris van Spilbergen, 1614–1617* (2 vols.; "WLV," XLVII; The Hague, 1943), I, 104–5, and J. A. J. De Villiers (trans.), *The East and West Indian Mirror . . .* ("HS," 2d ser., XVIII; London, 1906), pp. 122–23.

[78] Warnsinck (ed.), *op. cit.* (n. 77), I, 129; De Villiers (trans.), *op. cit.* (n. 77), p. 150.

[79] W. A. Engelbrecht and P. J. Herwerden (eds.), *De ontdekkingsreis van Jacob le Maire en Willem Cornelisz. Schouten in de jaren 1615–1617 . . .* (2 vols.; "WLV," XLIX; The Hague, 1945), II, 65–67.

[80] See above, pp. 93–94.

[81] Engelbrecht and Herwerden, *op. cit.* (n. 79), II, 1–33.

General to discover a new strait south of the Straits of Magellan and to trade in any lands in the South Pacific discovered by the expedition. Le Maire's new company then outfitted two ships which left Texel on June 14, 1615, under the command of his son Jacob and Willem Corneliszoon Schouten.

Le Maire and Schouten indeed discovered a new passage to the Pacific south of the Straits of Magellan. Actually they sailed around Tierra del Fuego, calling the passage between its easternmost promontory and Staten Island the Straits of Le Maire. They named what they thought to be its southernmost point—actually on another island—Cape Horn. They saw no signs of land to the south, however, and on February 12, 1616, convinced that they were now in the Pacific Ocean, they celebrated their successful passage and set out to find the southern continent.[82] After sailing north to about 20° south latitude in order to find favorable winds, they headed west. They found no southern continent. The first islands they discovered were part of the Taumotu archipelago; the Dutch named them Honden, Zonder Grond, Waterland, and Vliegen. Farther west they discovered "Cocos" (Tafahi), "Verraders" (Niuatoputapo), "Goede Hoop" (Niuafo'ou), and the "Hoornsche" Islands, all part of the Tonga group. They also landed at a couple of the Solomon Islands and at several islands along the north coast of New Guinea, finally putting in at Ternate on September 17, 1616. From Ternate they sailed to Jakatra where the ship was seized.[83]

Le Maire and Schouten sailed home with Van Spilbergen's fleet in December, 1616, and Le Maire died enroute.[84] Schouten arrived home on July 1, 1617, and soon thereafter arranged to have Willem Janszoon Blaeu (1571–1638) publish his account of the voyage.[85] Jacob Le Maire's name is not even mentioned in the title and Le Maire's role in the expedition is consciously minimized throughout the narrative. Isaac Le Maire was furious, but could not publish his own version of the voyage because the ship's log book and Jacob's papers had been confiscated along with the "Eendracht." Le Maire sued for damages and after several years of litigation the VOC was ordered to restore the property and to pay damages to Le Maire. An account of the voyage under Jacob Le Maire's name finally appeared in 1622.[86] By that time Schouten's *Journal* had already gone through twelve editions and translations.[87] Le Maire's *Spieghel* denigrates Schouten's contribution to the expedition just as thoroughly as the *Journal* does Le Maire's.

---

[82] *Ibid.*, I, 40, 168–69.

[83] By this time Le Maire and Schouten had only one ship, the "Eendracht." The yacht "Hoorn" was accidently burned at Porto Desire on the Atlantic coast of South America while they were trying to scrape its hull. *Ibid.*, I, 30, 163–64. On the discovery of Tonga, see E. N. Ferdon, *Early Tonga as the Explorers Saw It, 1616–1810* (Tucson, 1987), p. xiii, and map.

[84] Engelbrecht and Herwerden (eds.), *op. cit.* (n. 79), I, 101.

[85] *Journal ofte beschryvinghe van de wonderlicke reyse ghedaen door Willem Corneliszoon Schouten van Hoorn, in de jaren 1615, 1616, en 1617* . . . (Amsterdam, 1618).

[86] *Spieghel der australische navigatie door den wijt vermaerden ende cloeckmoedighen zee-heldt, Jacob le Maire, . . .* (Amsterdam).

[87] Tiele, *op. cit.* (n. 12), pp. 40–47.

Scholars disagree about whether there were two logbooks kept on the "Eendracht" or whether a single logbook served as the basis for both published accounts of the voyage.[88] The plates in the two publications are also similar, although not identical. They were probably made from the same set of sketches.[89] The descriptions of the islands and peoples newly discovered by the expedition—the Taumotu, Tonga, and Solomon islands and those along the New Guinea coast—are nearly identical in the two versions. These descriptions are the major contributions to Europe's knowledge of Asia made by Le Maire and Schouten's publications. Altogether, in one form or the other, thirty-eight editions of Le Maire's and Schouten's voyage were published in Dutch, French, Latin, German, English, and Spanish.[90]

Schouten's account, although under Le Maire's name, was also published with the account of Van Spilbergen's voyage when it appeared in 1619.[91] Van Spilbergen had apparently become impressed with Le Maire and his achievements during the voyage home and was deeply grieved at Le Maire's death.[92] Van Spilbergen's *Spiegel* together with the *Australische Navigatien* went through seven Dutch editions including its appearance in the *Begin ende voortgangh* and the Hartgers collection. It was translated into Latin, French, German, and English, and was included in the collections of De Bry, Hulsius, and Purchas.[93]

The account of Van Spilbergen's voyage contains less descriptive material than that of Le Maire and Schouten. Only the Ladrones and the Philippines are separately treated in the *Spiegel* proper, and these descriptions are brief and add little to what was already known. Appended to the *Spiegel*, however, is a "Discourse" by Appolonius Schotte of Middelburg which contains an extensive description of the Moluccas and of the Dutch and Spanish fortifications there.[94] Another addition to the *Spiegel* briefly describes all the VOC forts and factories in the East Indies.[95] These additions are not included in the *Begin ende voortgangh* edition of Van Spilbergen's voyage but instead are appended to the account of Pieter Willemszoon Verhoeff.[96]

A substantial account of religion and customs on Amboina was published in 1621.[97] Its author, Sebastiaen Danckaerts (b. 1593), had been a minister

---

[88] *Ibid.*, pp. 60–61; Engelbrecht and Herwerden (eds.), *op. cit.* (n. 79), II, 47–49.

[89] Engelbrecht and Herwerden (eds.), *op. cit.* (n. 79), II, 53.

[90] Tiele, *op. cit.* (n. 12), pp. 40–59.

[91] Joris van Spilbergen, *Oost ende West-Indische spiegel der 2 leste navigatien, . . . Met de australische navigatien van Jacob le Maire* (Leyden).

[92] Warnsinck (ed.), *op. cit.* (n. 77), I, 139; De Villiers (trans.), *op. cit.* (n. 7), pp. 162–63.

[93] Warnsinck (ed.), *op. cit.* (n. 77), I, 171–80; Tiele, *op. cit.* (n. 12), pp. 54–63.

[94] Warnsinck (ed.), *op. cit.* (n. 77), I, 114–28; De Villiers (trans.), *op. cit.* (n. 77), pp. 133–49.

[95] "Corte beschryvinghe van het ghetal ende ghelegentheyt vande forten, . . ." Warnsinck (ed.) *op. cit.* (n. 77), I, 132–9; De Villiers (trans.), *op. cit.* (n. 77), pp. 154–62.

[96] *BV*, IIa, 107–30.

[97] Sebastiaen Danckaerts, *Historische ende grondich verhael van de standt des Christendoms int quartier van Amboina. . . .* (The Hague, 1621); reprinted in *BTLV*, n.s., VI (1859), 105–36.

and missionary there since 1617.[98] In addition to Amboinese religious beliefs, which he understood to be demon worship, he describes social customs, marriages, trade, crafts, buildings, and the nature of the people. He
recounts the efforts of the Portuguese to evangelize the Amboinese and reports on the more recent Dutch mission and its prospects for success.[99] An
abridged version of Danckaert's book was included in *Begin ende voortgangh*
as still another appendix to Verhoeff's voyage.[100]

An anonymous pamphlet published in 1622 describes and justifies the
Dutch invasion of the Banda Islands during the previous year to suppress
rebellion and violations of the Dutch clove monopoly. An English translation also appeared in 1622.[101]

The account of another circumnavigation, that headed by Jacques L'Hermite (1582–1624) between 1623 and 1626, was published in 1626.[102] Although L'Hermite's fleet visited the Moluccas and Batavia (formerly Jakatra),
the published journal contains no descriptions of any Asian land except a
brief sketch of the Ladrones (Marianas).[103] Most of the book is devoted to
the fleet's attacks on Spanish shipping and towns along the west coast of
South America and to descriptions of those lands and people. The Amsterdam, 1643, edition and the *Begin ende voortgangh* edition also contain Quiros'
letter describing the unknown southern continent.[104]

Events in Asia were regularly reported in Nicolaes van Wassenaer's
(d. 1631) Amsterdam newssheet during the twenties, usually in connection
with the arrival of a fleet from the East Indies.[105] These reports usually itemize
the cargoes and discuss the activities of the VOC in Asia, but they also
sometimes contain descriptions and other information brought back by the
Dutch ships. The December, 1622, issue, for example, reports war going on
between Siam and Cambodia, a Tartar invasion of China, and the king of

[98] *BTLV*, n.s., VI (1859), 106.
[99] *Ibid.*, pp. 123–36.
[100] *BV*, IIa, 151–62.
[101] *Waerachtich verhael van't geene inde eylanden van Banda, in Oost-Indien, inden jaere sestien-
hondert eenentwintich, ende to vooren is ghepassert* [Amsterdam]. It was also included in the *BV* as
an appendix to l'Hermite's voyage, IIb, 75–9. The English translation is entitled *The Hollanders
Declaration of the Affairs of the East Indies, or a True Relation of that Which Passed in the Islands of
Banda . . .* (Amsterdam, 1622).
[102] *Journael vande Nassausche vloot ofte beschryvingh vande voyagie om den gantschen aerdt-kloot ghedaen met elf schepen: onder't beleydt vanden Admirael Jaques l'Hermite, ende Vice-Admirael Geen
Huygen Schapenham inde jaeren 1623, 1624, 1625, en 1626 . . .* (Amsterdam). Two small pamphlets
based on intercepted Spanish letters describing L'Hermite's attacks on Spain's Peruvian settlements appeared in 1624 and 1625. These should not be confused with the full account of the
voyage published in 1626. See Tiele, *op. cit.* (n. 12), pp. 73–74.
[103] *BV*, IIb, 55–57.
[104] For a complete bibliography of L'Hermite's voyage see Tiele, *op. cit.* (n. 12), pp. 73–81.
See also Willem Voorbeijtel Cannenburg (ed.), *De reis om de wereld van de nassausche vloot
1623–1626* ("WLV," LXV; The Hague, 1964).
[105] Nicolaes à Wassenaer, *Historisch verhael alder ghedenck-weerdichste geschiedenisse . . .* (Amsterdam, 1621–32).

Acheh's determination to rule all of Sumatra and beyond.[106] Cornelis Reijersen's expedition to the Fukien coast (1622–24) and the establishment of Fort Zeelandia on Formosa (1624) are reported in detail.[107] The report of June, 1624, also describes betel, Siamese elephants, and the export of an elephant to the governor of Hirado in Japan.[108] In August, 1624, Wassenaer reported the revolt of the "Great Mogol's" son.[109] In May, 1625, Wassenaer's newssheet contained one of the earliest descriptions of Australia, a brief report of Jan Carstenszoon's exploration along the south coast of New Guinea and the west coast of the Cape York Peninsula.[110] Carstenszoon did not find the Torres Strait, and in fact he asserted that New Guinea was not an island but was attached to the southland.[111]

2

PENETRATIONS BEYOND THE EAST INDIES TO 1645

While the printers of the United Provinces flooded the market with accounts of Dutch voyages and expeditions to the Indies, the press of the Spanish and Catholic Netherlands, primarily at Antwerp, issued Jesuit letters and reports pertaining to the missions in Asia. The Scottish Jesuit John Hay of Kalgetty, for example, translated several Jesuit works into Latin during the first years of the century and had them published at Antwerp: a 1599 letter from Alessandro Valignano in 1603,[112] a large collection of letters from Fróis, Valignano, Gonçalves, and Martinez, among others, in 1605,[113] and parts of Maffei's *Historiarum indicarum* also in 1605.[114] A Dutch translations of Trigault's 1607 Christmas Eve letter was published at Antwerp in 1609.[115] In the same year a Dutch translation of the French edition of Luis de Cerqueira's report on the Japanese martyrs appeared in Antwerp.[116] A Latin translation of João Rodrigues' and Matteo Ricci's Japan and China letters of 1606 and 1607 was published in 1611,[117] and a Latin translation of the 1609 and 1610 Japan letters appeared in 1615.[118] Both had been originally pub-

---

[106] *Ibid.*, IV (Dec., 1622), 87.

[107] *Ibid.*, IV (Oct., 1623), 31–32; VII (June, 1624), 63–70; XI (June, 1626), 94a–96b.

[108] *Ibid.*, VII (June, 1624), 63–70.

[109] *Ibid.*, VII (August, 1624), 147.   [110] *Ibid.*, IX (May, 1625), 68a–69.

[111] *Ibid.*, 69a. For a description of Carstenszoons' voyage see G. Schilder, *Australia Unveiled: The Share of Dutch Navigators in the Discovery of Australia* (Amsterdam, 1976), pp. 80–98.

[112] See Streit, V, 373–74.

[113] *De rebus Iaponicis, Indicis, et Peruanis. . . .* See Streit, V, 28.

[114] See Streit, V, 30–31, for title and contents.

[115] *Ibid.*, p. 50.

[116] *Nieuwe ende waerachtige historie van ses glorieuse martelaers die in Japonien voor't Catholyck geloove ayn in't jaer 1604. . . .*

[117] See Streit, V, 390.

[118] *Ibid.*, p. 406.

lished in Italian. Also a Dutch translation of one of Trigault's China reports was published in Hertogenbosch.[119] Letterbooks of 1618–19 have material on the Philippines and the Jesuit mission there. They were published at Antwerp and Douai. Tursellinus' life of Francis Xavier was translated into Dutch in 1622.[120] A Latin edition of the report on the Japanese martyrs of 1622 was published at Brussels.[121] The Jesuits' Annual Letter from China appeared in Latin at Antwerp in 1625.[122] More news about the Christian martyrs in Japan appeared at Louvain and at Malines during 1628, where letters from Pedro Gomez (d. 1600) and Luis Fróis (d. 1597) were translated into Dutch.[123] The biography of one of the martyrs, Father Carolus Spinola (1564–1622), was translated into Latin and published at Antwerp in 1630.[124]

Two important Latin descriptions of Asia were published by the Elzevier Press of Leyden around 1630 as part of their "Res publicae" series: the *Regni chinensis descriptio* in 1629 and Joannes de Laet's (1582–1649?) *De imperio magni mogolis* in 1631.[125] The first is a description of China taken from various sources, but primarily from Trigault's 1615 *De christiana expeditione apud sinas*.[126] De Laet's description of the Mughul Empire was compiled from a variety of sources. In the preface and in the text he mentions Pedro Teixeira, Richard Hawkins, Thomas Roe, Edward Terry, and other English observers published in Purchas. He also depended very heavily on Francisco Pelsaert's "Remonstrantie," a 1626 report to the VOC directors on the state of Dutch commerce in India.[127] Pelsaert's "Remonstrantie" was perhaps the most detailed and interesting account of Mughul India written by a Dutch observer. His discussion of the trade is extremely candid and thorough. He also describes towns—particularly Agra—landscape, climate, products, people, and religions and customs in the portion of the "Remonstrantie" which De Laet used. He paints a very unflattering picture of Jahangir, of his administration, and of Indian society generally. Since the "Remonstrantie" was never published in Dutch, De Laet's book is the earliest published source for Pelsaert's description of India. In 1663, however, Thévenot published parts of it in his collection.[128]

In the "Remonstrantie" Pelsaert occasionally refers to a history of the Mughul Empire which he had written or was writing. No such history was ever published under his name, but the "Fragmentum historiae indicae" in

---

[119] *Waerachtige verhael van eenige merckelycke saecken des vermaerts coninckrijcx van Syna . . .* (1615).
[120] See Streit, V, 94. Later Dutch editions appeared in Malines (1622), Antwerp, (1646), and Antwerp (1657).
[121] See Streit, V, 477.
[122] *Ibid.*, V, 755.
[123] *Ibid.*, V, 511, 514.
[124] *Ibid.*, V, 528.
[125] *Regni chinensis descriptio ex variis authoribus.* Joannes de Laet (comp.), *De imperio magni mogolis sive India vera commentarius e variis auctoribus congestus.*
[126] For Trigault's book see below, pp. 512–13.
[127] W. H. Moreland and Pieter Geyl (trans. and eds.), *Jahangir's India: The Remonstrantie of Francisco Pelsaert* (Cambridge, 1925), p. xii. For Pelsaert, see below, pp. 475–77.
[128] See above, pp. 410–11.

De imperio magni mogolis appears to have been based on a manuscript history which De Laet ascribed to Pieter van den Broecke but which, for the most part, was prepared by Pelsaert.[129] Van den Broecke (1585–1640), who had headed the VOC operations at Surat, was Pelsaert's superior while Pelsaert was the senior Dutch factor at Agra. In fact, they returned to the Netherlands together in 1627.[130] The "Fragmentum historiae indicae," as published in De Laet's book, provided European readers with what was probably the century's most complete and detailed account of the reigns of Humayun and Akbar and of the early part of Jahangir's reign. Pelsaert apparently consulted several Persian sources, and of course added many observations of his own regarding Jahangir's reign. Recent critics, however, have pointed to many inaccuracies in the piece, some of which they attribute to Pelsaert's inexpert use of the Persian sources and some to the liberties taken by De Laet with Pelsaert's text.[131]

More Dutch-language information about India appeared in 1634 with the publication of Pieter van den Broecke's account of his experiences.[132] After four voyages to Africa, Van den Broecke sailed to the East Indies, where he remained from 1614 to 1630. His was a colorful and busy career. In 1617 he traveled overland from Damão on the Gulf of Cambay to Masulipatam on the Coromandel Coast.[133] He played a major role in the defense of Jakatra against the English and the Javans in 1618–19.[134] From 1620 to 1629 he lived in Surat where he acted as director of all the Dutch factories in Arabia, Persia, and India.[135]

Van den Broecke's journal provides considerable information about the establishment of the Dutch East India Company in India, about Indian cities and their governors, and about commodities and trade. It contains similar, briefer descriptions of the Moluccas and Ceylon.[136] But it includes no large or detailed descriptions of peoples or their customs, beliefs, and daily lives. The *Begin ende voortgangh* (1645), Hartgers (1648), and Saeghman (1663) editions of Van den Broecke's journal, however, contain several inserts, one of

[129] De Laet, *op. cit.* (n. 125), pp. 170–299.

[130] Moreland and Geyl (trans.), *op. cit.* (n. 127), p. xv.

[131] For an English translation of the Dutch text of Pelsaert–Van den Broecke see Brij Narain and Sri Ram Sharma (eds.), *A Contemporary Dutch Chronicle of Mughul India* (Calcutta, 1957), pp. 1–4. The entire *De imperio magni mogolis* was translated from Latin into English in 1928: J. S. Hoyland and S. N. Banerjee (trans. and eds.), *The Empire of the Great Mogol: A Translation of de Laet's "Description of India and Fragment of Indian History"* (Bombay).

[132] *Korte historiael ende journaelsche aenteyckeninghe . . . beneffens de beschrijvingh en af-beeldingh van verscheyden steden, op de custe van Indien, Persien, Arabien, en aen't Roode Meyr; . . .* (Haarlem).

[133] Van den Broecke, "Historische ende journaelsche aenteyckeninghe . . ." in *BV*, IIa, 69–77.

[134] *Ibid.*, 88–95. Van den Broecke's role in Jakatra's defense, however, may not have been as heroic as his book suggests; see J. W. Ijzerman, "Over de belegering van het fort Jacatra (22 Dec. 1618–1 Febr. 1619)," *BTLV*, LXXIII (1917), 558–679. See also W. Ph. Coolhas (ed.), *Pieter van den Broecke in Azië* (2 vols.; "WLV," LXII, LXIV; The Hague, 1962), I, 181.

[135] *BV*, IIa, 97–107.

[136] *Ibid.*, IIa, 27–28.

which is a long description of the kingdom of Golconda on the Coromandel Coast written by someone who had lived there for six years.[137] The *Korte historiael ende journaelsche aenteyckeninghe* was apparently written by Van den Broecke himself, but the published editions are greatly abridged versions of his original manuscript.[138] Altogether seven versions of Van den Broecke's journal were published during the century.[139]

A fairly substantial description of China—the first available in Dutch since those of Mendoza and Linschoten of 1595—was included in the *Journael* of Seyger van Rechteren (1600–1645), published in 1635.[140] Van Rechteren had been a chaplain in the East Indies from 1629 to 1632. He almost certainly never visited China; he probably had not even visited the Dutch settlement on Formosa. His sojourn in the East appears to have been spent entirely on Java and the Banda Islands, where he served for eleven months with but one trip to Makassar (Celebes).[141] While Van Rechteren's description of China cannot have been the result of firsthand observations, it seems nonetheless to be based on descriptions provided by the author's acquaintances or at least by other Dutchmen. The "Brief Account of the Great Kingdom of China" is one of three descriptive passages inserted by Van Rechteren into the narrative; the others are a "Brief Account of Taiwan" and a discussion "Concerning the Commerce of the Dutch in China and Japan." Van Rechteren claimed that all this material was obtained in conversations with certain Dutch officers who had been imprisoned in China for five years. His assertion certainly does not apply to his description of Taiwan or his review of commerce with China and Japan. These were taken from a letter written by the governor of Formosa, Pieter Nuyts (d. 1707), to the VOC directors in 1629.[142] Perhaps Van Rechteren fabricated his source in order to escape the rather severe punishment for the unauthorized publication of official VOC documents.

Van Rechteren's remarks about China were most likely provided by a Dutchman who visited there during the Reijersen expedition (1622–24). They are definitely not based on Mendoza, Linschoten, or Trigault, the usual sources for plagiarized descriptions of China; Van Rechteren's account differs widely from these. For example, Van Rechteren does not discuss Chinese education and learning, or the scholarly attainments of Chinese officials—important topics for Mendoza, Linschoten, and Trigault. He notes that Chinese officials may never rule in the provinces of their birth, a

[137]*Ibid.*, pp. 77–86. Possibly written by Pieter Gierliszoon van Ravesteyn.

[138]See Coolhas, *op. cit.* (n. 134), for the manuscript version.

[139]For bibliography see Tiele, *op. cit.* (n. 12), pp. 236–41.

[140]*Journael gehouden door . . . op zyne gedane voyagie naer Oost-Indien* (Zwolle).

[141]Tiele, *op. cit.* (n. 12), p. 252; Jacob van der Aa, *Biographisch woordenboek der Nederlanden . . .* (21 vols. in 16; Haarlem, 1852), XVI, 127–28.

[142]Tiele, *op. cit.* (n. 12), p. 252. English translations of the letter are included in W. Campbell, *Formosa under the Dutch* (London, 1903), pp. 51–60 and in George Phillips, *Dutch Trade in Formosa in 1629* (Shanghai, 1878), pp. 15–26.

practice much admired by Trigault, Linschoten, and Mendoza but deplored as oppressive by Van Rechteren.[143] Van Rechteren's geographical descriptions alone preclude the possibility of his having borrowed from the standard sources of information. He divides China into thirteen provinces, while Mendoza, Linschoten, and Trigault each list fifteen.[144] He also, mistakenly but understandably, describes the river at Chang-chou, near Amoy, as "the largest and most famous for navigation and commerce in the whole empire of China."[145]

This last observation, and many others made by Van Rechteren, suggests that his description of China originated with a participant in the Reijersen expedition. His account of the imperial government, for example, is extremely superficial, but he describes in tedious detail the elaborate formal reception of a foreigner by a provincial governor and the difficulties encountered by foreigners in dealing with local or provincial Chinese officials. Furthermore, these descriptions are remarkably similar to those found in Reijersen's letters and journals.[146] Van Rechteren's lengthy description of the suspicious and hostile attitude of the Chinese towards foreigners is again quite similar to observations made by Reijersen and his men. Moreover, in the *Begin ende voortgangh* edition of Van Rechteren's *Journael,* the editor inserted a detailed and accurate account of the Reijersen expedition immediately following the description of China.[147]

Van Rechteren's journal also contains the first published Dutch description of Formosa.[148] In the *Begin ende voortgangh* edition of Van Rechteren's journal the "Kort verhael van Tayouang" is followed by George Candidius' "Discours ende cort verhael van't eylant Formosa," perhaps the best-known and most detailed account of Formosa written in the seventeenth century.[149]

Candidius (1595–1647) was the first Dutch missionary to Formosa. He worked there from 1627 to 1631 and again from 1633 to 1637. His description of Formosa was dated December 27, 1628, but does not appear to have been published prior to its inclusion in the *Begin ende voortgangh.* His account forms the basis for almost every subsequent account of the island and its people during the seventeenth century.

Van Rechteren's journal includes what appears to be the first report published in Europe of the Dutch landings on the west coast of Australia.[150] Several Dutch ships had landed on or sighted the Australian coast after 1611

[143] Van Rechteren, "Journael . . ." *BV,* IIb, 43.

[144] *Ibid.,* p. 41.

[145] *Ibid.,* p. 44.

[146] For more information on the Reijersen expedition see W. P. Groenveldt, *De Nederlanders in China,* Vol. XLVIII of *BTLV* (1898).

[147] *BV,* IIb, 45–53.

[148] "Kort verhael van Tayouang," *ibid.,* pp. 53–55.

[149] *Ibid.,* IIb, 55–70. Candidius' account is also printed in François Valentijn, *Oud en nieuw Oost-Indien* (8 vols.; Dordrecht, 1724–26), VI, 33–93. English translations are included in Campbell, *op. cit.* (n. 142), pp. 9–25, and in *CV,* I, 526–33.

[150] *BV,* IIb, 25.

when they began using the southern route from the Cape of Good Hope to Batavia. The first of these was in October, 1616, by Dirk Hartogszoon. Several other sightings were made in the following years. In 1629 Francisco Pelsaert's ship, the "Batavia," was wrecked on the Houtman Rocks along the coast. Pelsaert and some of his men sailed and rowed to Batavia in the ship's boat and came back later to rescue the survivors. On his return Pelsaert found that some members of the crew were terrorizing the rest of the party and had even killed some of them. On its way to Batavia, Van Rechteren's ship also sighted the Australian coast, and at that point in his narrative Van Rechteren briefly describes Pelsaert's shipwreck and the subsequent misadventures of his crew. Van Rechteren refers his readers to Pelsaert's published journal for more details. But Pelsaert's journal was not published until 1647, twele years after Van Rechteren's.[151] This suggests that Van Rechteren saw a manuscript or a Batavia-published edition of Pelsaert's book, but there is no substantial evidence for such a conclusion.[152] Van Rechteren includes no description of the Australian coast. His *Journael* went through only three editions during the seventeenth century: the second appeared in 1639 and the third as part of the *Begin ende voortgangh*.[153]

The publication in 1637 of Reyer Gysbertszoon's book provided Dutch readers with a firsthand report of the persecution of the Christians in Japan between 1622 and 1629.[154] This account corroborates in the words of a Dutch Protestant observer the story then also being told in the Jesuit letters. Gysbertszoon, no less than the Jesuit authors, admired the unswerving devotion of the Japanese Christians. He reports defections and recantations, but always in the context of inhuman tortures in which the victims were denied even the solace of death. While his anti-Catholic bias shows, his attitude towards the martyrs was entirely sympathetic:

> The resolution is all the more to be admired, since they knew so little of God's word, so that one might term it stubbornness rather than steadfastness; because (in so far as the Holy Writ is concerned) they know but little, and can read only a Pater-Noster and an Ave-Maria, besides a few prayers to Saints; the Romish Priests exhorted them not to recant, upon pain of the loss of their salvation, accompanied with many dire threats. It is indeed extraordinary that amongst them are so many who remain steadfast to the end, and endure so many insufferable torments, in despite of their scanty knowledge of the Holy Scriptures.[155]

Some aspects of early Tokugawa society and politics also show through in Gysbertszoon's book, particularly the relationship of the towns to the sho-

[151] Francisco Pelsaert, *Ongeluckige voyagie, van't schip "Batavia"* . . . (Amsterdam, 1647).

[152] See Tiele, *op. cit.* (n. 10), p. 264.

[153] *Ibid.*, pp. 250–53 for bibliographic details.

[154] *De tyrannie ende wreedtheden der Jappanen* . . . (Amsterdam). Translated into English in C. R. Boxer (ed.), *A Description of the Mighty Kingdoms of Japan and Siam by François Caron and Joost Schouten* (London, 1935), pp. 73–88.

[155] Boxer (ed.), *op. cit.* (n. 154), p. 80.

gun and daimyo, and the workings of the five-family system of mutual responsibility. Gysbertszoon's book was reprinted as one of the appendices to Hendrick Hagenaer's voyage in the *Begin ende voortgangh* of 1645,[156] and it was included in all the editions of François Caron's description of Japan (first published in 1645) except for Roger Manley's English translation of 1663.[157]

The first continuous Dutch-language description of Siam, the work of Joost Schouten (d. 1653), appeared in 1638.[158] Schouten first visited Siam in 1628 as a special ambassador bearing a gift from the Prince of Orange, Frederick Henry, to King Prasat Thong of Siam. In 1633 Governor-General Hendrick Brouwer sent him to Ayut'ia to reestablish the Dutch factory first opened by Cornelis Specx in 1604 and then abandoned in 1622. Schouten remained in Siam until 1636, during which time he was favorably accepted by the king and high officials and enabled to place VOC trade in Ayut'ia on a sound footing. He also arranged some not-very-effective Dutch naval help for the Siamese during their campaign against Patani, and the gratified king made him a mandarin. He returned to Siam later in 1636 to present gifts to the king and to negotiate a new trade agreement. He wrote his description of Siam during this visit in response to a list of specific questions put to him by Philips Lucaszoon, the director-general of the VOC. He apparently arranged for its publication when he returned to Holland during the following year. Schouten became a member of the Council of the Indies at Batavia in 1640. He served there and as an ambassador to various Southeast Asian princes until 1644 when he was executed for sodomy, a vice he had acquired during his years in Siam.[159]

Schouten's description of Siam next appeared in 1645–46 as one of the appendices to Hagenaer's voyage included in the *Begin ende voortgangh*.[160] It was included in all subsequent editions of the *Begin ende voortgangh*, in most editions of Caron's description of Japan, and in Adriaen van Nispen's collection of voyages (1652).[161] It also appeared in a French version in Thévenot's collection.[162] Schouten's description is brief, and, while it touches upon geographic, political, social, religious, and economic aspects of Siam, it con-

---

[156] "Historie der martelaeren, die in Iapan om de Roomsche Catolycke Religie schrickelycke, ende onverdraghelycke pynen geleeden hebben, ofte gedoodt zyn," *BV*, IIb, 176–88.

[157] For bibliography see Boxer (ed.), *op. cit.* (n. 154), pp. 73, 169–80, and Tiele, *op. cit.* (n. 12), pp. 253–62.

[158] *Notitie vande situatie, regeeringe, macht, religie, costuymen, trafficquen ende andere remarcquable saecken des coningkrijcks Siam* (The Hague). The English translation of 1663 is included in Boxer (ed.), *op. cit.* (n. 154), pp. 13–91.

[159] For a sketch of Schouten's career see Boxer (ed.), *op. cit.* (n. 154), pp. 139–43.

[160] "Beschrijvinge van de regeeringe, macht, religie, costuymen, traffijcken, ende andere remarquable saecken des coningkrijcks Siam," *BV*, IIb, 203–17.

[161] *Voyagien ende beschryvinge van 't koninckrijck van Siam, Moscovien ofte Russ-landt, Ys-landt ende Groen-landt. Yder vertoonende in 't bysonder de gelegenheyt, religie, macht, regeringe, costumen, koopmanschappen, ende andere aenmerckens-weerdige saken derslever landen* (Dordrecht).

[162] *Relations de divers voyages* . . . (4 vols.; Paris, 1663–96; hereafter cited as TR), I (no. 20), 27–36.

tains somewhat less detail than the works of sixteenth-century writers such as Pires, Barbosa, Barros, and Pinto.[163] Nevertheless, Schouten's became the most widely available and popular Dutch description of Siam produced in the seventeenth century.

The first book on tropical medicine by a Dutch author was published at Leyden in 1642: Jacob de Bondt's (Bontius) *De medicina Indorum.*[164] Bontius (1592–1631), a Leyden-educated physician, went to Batavia in 1627 with the fleet which brought J. P. Coen back to the Indies for his second term as governor-general. Bontius served the VOC as physician, apothecary, and surgical inspector. He died in Batavia in 1631. He apparently sent or had someone else send his unfinished manuscript to Willem Piso, an Amsterdam physician, who had it published by the Elzeviers. The 1642 edition of Bontius' work contains only four books. In 1658 Piso appended it to his own treatise on American natural history and medicine.[165] The Piso edition of Bontius contains six books: two additional books on Asian fauna and flora were added by Piso which also contain Piso's own additions and commentaries. The Piso edition was translated into Dutch in 1694.[166]

Bontius was heavily influenced by Garcia da Orta's work on Indian medicine.[167] He frequently refers to Orta, and Book IV of his treatise is devoted to observations and comments on Orta's work. Following Orta's format, Bontius' Book I is a dialogue between himself and Andraeas Duraeus on how to maintain health in the Indies. Also like Orta, Bontius emphasizes the uselessness of traditional scholastic medicine in the tropics. Book II of Bontius' treatise lists nineteen common Asian diseases, their various names, symptoms, possible causes, and treatment. His prescriptions include both Western and Asian herbs and drugs, but with an emphasis on the Asian pharmacopoeia. Book III describes autopsies performed on people who died from various diseases common in Asia. Bontius gives dates for the dissections and in many cases identifies the corpse. He then describes the disease and the appearance of the involved organs and tissues. He also described Governor-General Coen's death and the appearance of his body, but he apparently did not dissect Coen's corpse.[168] Bontius' description of Asian animals and plants—Books V and VI—is supplemented by a large number of plates, some accurate and some, like that of the orangutan, rather fanciful.[169] Both Book II and Book VI contain descriptions of tea and tea culture.

[163] See *Asia,* I, 519–38.

[164] *Jac. Bontii in indiis archiater de medicina indorum libri IV.* An English translation (London, 1769) is included in *Opuscula selecta Neerlandicorum de arte medica* (Amsterdam, 1931), Vol. X. The text is preceded by an enlightening introduction by M. A. van Andel.

[165] "Historiae naturalis & medicae indiae orientalis, libri sex," in Willem Piso, *De indiae utriusque re naturali et medica libri quatuordecim* (Amsterdam).

[166] *Oost- en West-Indische worande . . .* (Amsterdam).

[167] For Orta, see *Asia,* I, 192–95.

[168] "Historiae naturalis & medicae indiae orientalis," in *op. cit.* (n. 165), pp. 38–49.

[169] *Ibid.,* p. 84. See our pls. 269–77.

Among the several appendices to Hagenaer's journal in the *Begin ende voortgangh,* 1645, the most important is François Caron's (*ca.* 1600–1674) description of Japan, published here for the first time.[170] While Hagenaer's journal was never published apart from the 1645 and 1646 editions of the *Begin ende voortgangh,* the accounts of Caron, Schouten, and Gysbertszoon and the other appendices continued to be published together until the end of the century. They were first published as a separate book by Joost Hartgers in 1648,[171] then again in 1649 and 1652. Hartgers also included them in each of the 1648 editions of his collection of travels.[172] A new and authorized edition, revised by Caron himself, first appeared in 1661.[173] The major difference between this authorized edition and the earlier editions is the omission of Hagenaer's notes to Caron's description. Caron and Hagenaer, who served together in Japan, apparently disliked each other. The 1661 edition includes all of the appendices to Hagenaer's journal except for a Japanese official's letter to the VOC governor-general. The plates and an astonishingly inaccurate map of Japan were added by the publisher, Johannes Tongerloo.[174] Tongerloo republished this edition once in 1661 and twice in 1662.[175]

Caron's and Schouten's treatises along with one of the shorter pieces, that of Coenraet Krammer, were appended to the English translation of Johann Albrecht von Mandelslo's *Travels* in 1662 and 1669; the authors, however, were not identified. Another English translation of Caron and Schouten, by Roger Manley, appeared in 1663 and again in 1671. Manley's translation includes all the shorter treatises except Gysbertszoon's and the Japanese official's letter. All the treatises were included in the 1663 and 1672 German translations of Caron and Schouten's books. A French translation of Caron's account was included in part two of Thévenot's *Relations de divers voyages curieux,* and Bernhard Varen translated it into Latin for the Elzevier "Res publicae" series in 1669. Varen's edition was also republished in Cambridge during 1673. Swedish editions of Caron's account appeared in 1667 and 1674, and an Italian edition in 1693. Altogether Caron's book went through twenty-three editions and translations during the seventeenth century.[176]

Few Europeans in early modern times knew Japan as well as François

---

[170] "Beschrijvinghe van het machtigh coninckrijck Iapan, gestelt door Francoys Caron, directeur des compaignies negotie aldaer, ende met eenige aenteekeningen vermeerdert door Hendrik Hagenaer," *BV,* IIb, 134–75.

[171] François Caron, *Beschrijvinghe van het machtigh coninckrijcke Japan vervattende den aert en eygenschappen van't landt, manieren der volckeren, als mede hare grouwelijcke wreedtheydt teghen de Roomsche Christenen gesteldt,* . . . (Amsterdam).

[172] *Oost-Indische voyagien door dien begin en voortgangh, van de Vereenighde Nederlandtsche Geoctroyeerde Oost-Indische Compagnie* . . . (Amsterdam, 1648). For bibliographic details see Tiele, *op. cit.* (n. 12), pp. 15–18.

[173] *Rechte beschryvinge van het machtigh koninghrijck van Iappan,* . . . (The Hague).

[174] See Boxer (ed.) *op. cit.* (n. 154), pp. 6, 174. On the appendices see below, pp. 460–61.

[175] For bibliographic details of the Dutch editions see *ibid.,* pp. 169–75, and Tiele, *op. cit.* (n. 12), pp. 253–62.

[176] See Boxer (ed.), *op. cit.* (n. 154), pp. 175–80, for bibliographic details on the translations.

Caron.[177] He first went there in 1619 as a nineteen-year-old cook's mate on a VOC ship. He stayed at the Dutch factory in Hirado as a clerk, learned Japanese, and soon became the factory's interpreter. When he finally left Japan in 1641 he was the director of the Dutch factory. Caron lived in Japan for most of the time between 1619 and 1641; during the rest of these years he was advising or negotiating for the VOC on Japanese affairs. These were difficult years for foreigners in Japan, and Caron deserves much of the credit for the VOC's relative success during the period. He was one of the Dutch hostages taken to Japan in 1629, for example, after Governor Pieter Nuyts' high-handed action against Japanese merchants on Formosa resulted in his imprisonment by Japanese seamen in the castle at Fort Zeelandia.[178] Caron was subsequently involved in all the delicate negotiations resulting in Nuyts' being sent prisoner to Japan in 1630 and his eventual release in 1636. He ably guided the Dutch factory through the uncertain and dangerous years of anti-Christian and anti-foreign hysteria in Japan and secured a fairly safe (though strictly limited) place for the VOC on the island of Deshima at Nagasaki before he left. His familiarity with the Japanese language, culture, and behavior was crucial to his success during these years, especially, for example, when he was ordered to demolish the Dutch buildings at Hirado and to move the VOC factory to Deshima in 1640.[179] The Japanese apparently liked and trusted Caron. Even before he became director they frequently insisted on negotiating with him rather than with his superiors.[180] Caron on his side liked the Japanese. He admired and understood Japanese culture to a degree very rare among seventeenth-century Europeans. He had a Japanese wife and he alone among the Europeans in Hirado lived in a Japanese house.[181] Rarer still among Europeans, he may even have developed a taste for Japanese hot baths.[182]

After he left Japan, Caron continued to rise in the VOC administration. He became a member of the Council of the Indies in 1643, he commanded the expedition against the Portuguese in Ceylon in 1643 that lifted the blockade of Galle and recaptured Negombo, and he served as governor of Taiwan and Formosa from 1644 to 1646, and as director-general (second in command) of the VOC from 1646 to 1651. Accused of dishonesty, he was recalled in 1651, and although he was exonerated and compensated, he refused any further Company service. Finally in 1665 he was engaged by Louis XIV's finance minister, Colbert, to organize and direct the new French East India Company. From 1666 until his death in 1673, he and his

[177] For a sketch of Caron's career see *ibid.*, pp. xv–cxxvii.
[178] For the story of Nuyts' troubles with the Japanese see *ibid.*, pp. xvi–xxv; O. Nachod, *Die Beziehungen der Niederlandischen Ostindischen Kompagnie zu Japan im siebzehnten Jahrhundert* (Leipzig, 1897), pp. 188–223; and Campbell, *op. cit.* (n. 142), pp. 38–51.
[179] Cf. Boxer (ed.), *op. cit.* (n. 154), pp. lxi–lxiv.
[180] For example, see *ibid.*, pp. xviii–xxv.
[181] *Ibid.*, p. cxxiv.
[182] *Ibid.*, pp. xcvii–xcviii.

co-director, Jacob Blanquet de La Haye, commanded the fleet that unsuccessfully attempted to establish the French on Ceylon and the Coromandel Coast.[183]

For all his familiarity with Japan, Caron's book is disappointingly small. Like Joost Schouten's treatise on Siam, Caron's description of Japan resulted from a series of specific questions, put to him by Director-General Philips Lucaszoon in 1636. In the 1661 edition the questions became the chapter titles. They are printed in the margins of the *Begin ende voortgangh* and Hartgers editions. He apparently answered the questions as quickly and briefly as possible, with no thought of their possible publication. Indeed the book was first published without his permission.[184] Johannes Tongerloo, the publisher of the 1661 edition, apparently wanted Caron to make extensive revisions. Caron, however, refused, contending that if he wrote all that he really knew about Japan, the volume would become too large and that most of it would not be believed anyway.[185] Despite its brevity, Caron's account became the most popular and influential book about Japan written during the seventeenth century, to be superseded only in 1727–28 by Engelbert Kaempfer's *History*.[186]

The shorter appendices to Caron and Schouten's book presented Dutch readers with other interesting information about Tokugawa Japan and the Dutch presence there. Coenraet Krammer, a VOC envoy, provided a colorful eyewitness account of the pageantry of the dignitaries and the behavior of the crowds in Kyoto on the occasion of the emperor's famous meeting with the shogun Iemitsu and the ex-shogun Hidetada on October 25, 1626.[187] The translation of a 1642 letter from a Nagasaki official, Ebiya Shiroyemon, to the governor-general of the VOC in Batavia provides a revealing glimpse into the new Dutch position on the island of Deshima, into the Japanese paranoia regarding Christianity, and into the VOC's willingness to avoid offending the Japanese for the sake of the trade.[188] It is so revealing, in fact, that Caron omitted it from the 1661 authorized version of his book. Leonard Campen's treatise describes the post-1640 trade from the Dutch point of view, puts it into historical context, and stresses the importance of free access to Chinese products if the VOC is really to exploit its

---

[183] For details see *ibid.*, pp. lxvi–cxxii. On the French East India Company see above, pp. 95–105.

[184] Boxer (ed.), *op. cit.* (n. 154), p. cxxviii.

[185] *Ibid.*, pp. 5–6.

[186] *Ibid.*, p. cxxix.

[187] "Verhael van de groote pracht die daer geschiedt ende ghebruyckt is, op den feest gehouden inde stadt van Meaco, alwaer den Dayro, zijn keyserlijcke mayst. van Jappan quam besoecken, voor gevallen op den 20 October 1626 . . . ," *BV*, IIb, 189–94; English translation in Boxer (ed.), *op. cit.* (n. 154), pp. 65–72.

[188] "Translaet van een Japansche brief, van Siragemondonne, Burgermeester in Nangasacqui, aen den gouverneur-generael etc. door den opperkoopmen Jan van Elzerach overgesonden dato den 28 Oct. 1642," *BV*, IIb, 195–97; Boxer (ed.) *op. cit.* (n. 154), pp. 89–91.

unique position in Japan.[189] Finally an overview of the Japan trade in the commercial picture of the VOC as of 1642 is provided by a brief extract from Governor-General Anthony van Diemen's letter to the directors.[190]

While not as popular as Caron and Schouten's descriptions, Hagenaer's journal also includes valuable information about Japan.[191] Hagenaer served the VOC as a senior merchant for almost seven years, during which time he visited Japan three times, in 1634, from 1635 to 1636, and again in 1637. His journal contains details about Dutch trade in Japan, and especially about the Dutch embassy to Edo in 1635–36. In addition to Japan, Hagenaer also visited Persia, the Malabar Coast of India, Formosa, the Moluccas, and Cambodia. His journal contains a very detailed description of the voyage upriver to the Cambodian court at Phnom Penh in 1637, the reception and negotiations there, including audiences with the kings, and a general description of the kingdom—probably the earliest Dutch description of Cambodia.[192]

3

ISAAC COMMELIN'S "BEGIN ENDE VOORTGANGH" (1645)

Hagenaer's journal first appeared in 1645 as part of the most important Dutch collection of travel literature published during the seventeenth century: Isaac Commelin's (1598–1676) *Begin ende voortgangh van de Vereenighde Nederlantsche Geoctroyeerde Oost-Indische Compagnie* (Amsterdam). The *Begin ende voortgangh* includes a very large number of plates and maps. Almost all of them, however, had been published before either in earlier editions of the journals included in the collection or in other earlier travel accounts. Commelin's introduction to the collection provides a historical sketch of Dutch commerce in the Indies from its beginning until about 1631. It also reproduces the first Dutch East India Company charter of 1602 and the renewed charter of 1622. The book itself contains twenty-one separate voyages in two oblong quarto volumes. Some of the voyages had been published before, but many, like Hagenaer's, appeared here for the first time. P. A. Tiele reports a 1644 edition of the *Begin ende voortgangh* as well as a 1644 collection of seven of the voyages in a volume entitled *Journael van seven voyagien*.[193]

---

[189] "Kort verhael van't profyt, dienst, ende nuttigheyt dat de Oost-Indische Vereen. Nederl. Comp. in Iappan soude genieten, by zoo verre sy de Chineesen handel bequamen," *BV*, IIb, 198–202; Boxer (ed.), *op. cit.* (n. 154), pp. 59–65.

[190] "Extract uyt de missive van den Gouverneur Generael van Indien, aen Heeren Bewinthebbern, gesonden, nopende den handel van Iapan," *BV*, IIb, 196–97; Boxer (ed.), *op. cit.* (n. 154), pp. 58–59.

[191] "Verhael van de reyze gedaen inde meeste deelen van de Oost-Indien" *BV*, IIb, 1–133.

[192] *Ibid.*, pp. 106–22.

[193] Tiele, *op. cit.* (n. 12), pp. 9–11.

C. R. Boxer in his introduction to the recent facsimile edition thinks that both of the 1644 publications should be regarded as prospecti or trial runs, since no copy of the *Seven voyagien* and only one of the 1644 *Begin ende voortgangh* are known to exist.[194] Another edition—perhaps two editions—appeared in 1646, and it was extensively pirated by Joost Hartgers in 1648 and by Gilles Joosten Saeghman between 1663 and 1670.[195] A French translation edited by René Augustin Constantin de Renneville was published in Amsterdam, 1702–6, which was reprinted there and in Rouen in 1725 and again at Amsterdam in 1754.[196] One volume of a projected English edition appeared in London in 1703.[197]

Commelin's collection includes Gerrit de Veer's account of three Dutch voyages in search of a northeast passage (1594–96), De Houtman's voyage to Java, Van Neck and Van Warwijck's voyage, that of Mahu and De Cordes through the Straits of Magellan, Van Noort's circumnavigation, Van Spilbergen's voyage to Ceylon, Van den Broecke's journal, Van Spilbergen's circumnavigation, Schouten and Le Maire's circumnavigation, L'Hermite's circumnavigation, and Van Rechteren's journal—all of which had been published in Dutch before. Commelin inserted additional descriptions or reports into most of these journals. Of those not already discussed above the most interesting piece, inserted in Van Rechteren's journal, is a description of Macao by an Italian named Marcus d'Avalo.[198] D'Avalo provides a rather detailed description of the Portuguese community, its people, institutions, and above all its commerce. He describes the annual Canton fair and the conditions under which the Portuguese are permitted to trade. He especially emphasizes the profits derived from the Japan voyages and appends a list of goods, including quantities and prices, shipped to Japan by the Portuguese in 1637.[199] Commelin occasionally added appendices to the journals and voyages, sometimes, as he put it, merely to fill up empty pages. For example, he added a brief discussion of the circumnavigations previous to Van Noort's voyage,[200] and an account of a famous VOC naval victory over the Portuguese near Goa, September 30, 1639, to Van Rechteren's journal.[201] Like Hagenaer's journal, many of the accounts in the *Begin ende voortgangh* had never been published before, or at least not in Dutch. The first of these, Paulus van Caerden's *Journal,* is very brief—only twenty pages long.[202] It

[194] C. R. Boxer, *Isaac Commelin's "Begin ende voortgangh." Introduction to the Facsimile Edition* (Amsterdam, 1969), pp. 3–4.

[195] For complete bibliographic information see *ibid.*, and Tiele, *op. cit.* (n. 12), pp. 8–10.

[196] *Recueil des voyages qui ont servi à l'etablissement et aux progrez de la Compagnie des Indes Orientale formée dans les Provinces-Unies Païs-Bas . . .* (5 vols.; Amsterdam, 1702–6).

[197] See Boxer, *op. cit.* (n. 194), pp. 5–6.

[198] "Beschryvinge van de stadt *Maccaon,* ofte Maccauw, met haer fortressen, geschut, commercien, ende zeeden der inwoonderen, . . ." *BV,* IIb, 78–86.

[199] *Ibid.*, pp. 84–86.

[200] *BV,* Ib, 54–56.

[201] *Ibid.*, IIb, 90–94.

[202] "Kort verhael, ofte journael, . . . ," *BV,* Ib, 1–18.

describes the voyage of four ships sent out in 1599 under the command of Admiral Pieter Both (d. 1615) and Vice-Admiral van Caerden (d. 1617) by the New Brabant Company. Most of the journal is devoted to Van Caerden's uneasy negotiations in Acheh during the winter of 1600–1601, which resulted in the release of the Dutch prisoners held there since Cornelis de Houtman's unfortunate visit in 1599.[203] It contains no description of any Asian place and it does not seem to have been published again.[204] To fill up some empty pages Commelin appended the text of a treaty between the Dutch and the "Orancays" (Orang Kayas) of Aru Island, off the west coast of New Guinea, negotiated by Jan Carstenszoon on May 26, 1623.[205]

The account of Jacob van Neck's second voyage was included in the De Bry collection (1607) but had not been printed in Dutch before the *Begin ende voortgangh* edition.[206] It was written for the most part by Roelof Roelofszoon, an exhorter or chaplain on one of Van Neck's ships. Van Neck's fleet of six ships left Texel on June 28, 1600, and arrived in Bantam on March 30, 1601. From there the admiral sailed for the Moluccas, two of the ships arriving at Ternate on June 2. The sultan of Ternate visited the Dutch ships and even looked in on a church service which he reportedly found "orderly" in contrast to the services of the Portuguese Catholics.[207] A few days later he accompanied the Dutch ships when they attacked the Portuguese fort on Tidore, a showy and inconclusive engagement that cost Van Neck his right hand.[208] Roelofszoon also describes the banquet given by the sultan for the Dutch before their departure.[209] From Ternate Van Neck went to China, arriving off Macao on September 27, 1601. When a Dutch shore party failed to return to the ship, Van Neck sent a sloop to take soundings closer to the city to see if the ships could move in. The Portuguese attacked the sloop and captured its crew in full view of the Dutch ships which stood by helplessly because of contrary winds.[210] Unable to aid his captured crewmen, and running short of supplies, Van Neck sailed for Patani on October 3.

According to a later unpublished report by Martinus Apius, who led the first Dutch shore party, the twenty Dutch mariners languished in a Macao prison until November, when the incident came to the attention of the Chinese governor at Canton.[211] The governor sent a eunuch to investigate, and

---

[203] For details see W. S. Unger (ed.) *De oudste reizen de Zeeuwen naar Oost-Indië, 1598–1604* ("WLV," LI; The Hague, 1948); and John Davis, *loc. cit.* (n. 62).

[204] See Tiele, *op. cit.* (n. 12), pp. 231–32.

[205] *BV*, Ib, 19–20.

[206] "Kort ende waerachtigh verhael van de tweede schipvaerd by de Hollanders op Oost-Indien gedaen, onder den Heer Admirael Iacob van Neck, . . ." *BV*, Ib, 1–51. For bibliography see Tiele, *op. cit.* (n. 12), pp. 162–66.

[207] *BV*, Ib, 6.   [209] *Ibid.*, pp. 7–8. See our pl. 34.

[208] *Ibid.*, p. 7.   [210] *Ibid.*, pp. 9–10.

[211] For Apius' account see P. A. Tiele (ed.), "Verklaring van Martinus Apius van hetgeen hem en zijne medegevangen van de vloot van Jacob van Neck in 1602 te Macao is overkomen," *Bijdragen en mededeelingen van het Historisch Genootschap gevestigd te Utrecht*, VI (1883), 228–42.

after considerable delay and repeated denials, the Portuguese finally permitted him to question six of the prisoners; the eunuch was told that all the others had died of disease. When, after the eunuch's return to Canton, the governor ordered the Portuguese to send the prisoners to Canton, they decided instead to dispose of the Dutch themselves. Six of the men were publicly hanged; those who were supposed to have died earlier were drowned. Only Apius and two seventeen-year-old cabin boys remained alive and were later permitted to return home by way of India and Portugal. Roelofszoon and Van Neck, of course, did not know about the fate of their captured crewmen, although Commelin inserted a brief report about it in his edition of the journal. No description of China is included, but in another insert Commelin promised to rectify that lack by including one with Matelief's journal.[212]

Van Neck's ships arrived in Patani on November 7 and remained there until August 23, 1602. Despite the fleet's long stay there, Roelofszoon wrote very little about Patani beyond describing the trade and a couple of temples which he visited. Commelin, however, inserted a long and very interesting description of Patani, Siam, and Malacca, taken largely from a 1616 manuscript written by Victor Sprinckel, a merchant sent by Matelief to Patani in 1607, and augmented by details taken from the works of Gotthard Arthus of Danzig, Fernão Mendes Pinto, and Linschoten.[213] Three earlier inserts on the Moluccas and Macao contain little new or detailed information.[214] Following Roelofszoon's journal, Commelin included a brief account of the voyage of the remaining three ships from Van Neck's fleet written by Cornelis Claeszoon. It reports on the fleet's misadventures in Cambodia, where natives killed twenty-three Dutchmen and held Vice-Admiral van Warwijck ransom for two cannons.[215] Commelin also appended several treatises concerning East Indian trade and navigation.[216] The first five of these treatises, except for some minor changes, appear to have been taken from Waghenaer's *Thresoor der zeevaert* (1592).[217] The sixth is a discourse on the five routes to Cathay translated from the third edition of William Bourne's *A Regiment for the Sea, Containing Very Necessary Matters for All Sort of Seamen and Travellers . . . Whereunto is Added a Hidrographicall Discourse to go unto Cattay, Five Severall Wayes* (London, 1580).[218] In addition to the routes over the Cape of Good Hope, the Straits of Magellan, the hoped-for Northwest Passage and Northeast Passage, Bourne also posited a route directly over the North Pole—the shortest route of all—and answered some technical objections to it. The final appendix is a discussion of the variation of the compass as observed on the voyage from Portugal to the East Indies

---

[212] *BV*, Ib, 10.
[213] *Ibid.*, pp. 16–25.
[214] *Ibid.*, pp. 5, 10.
[215] *Ibid.*, pp. 27–31.
[216] *Ibid.*, pp. 32–51.
[217] See above, pp. 436–37.
[218] *BV*, Ib, 41–49. See Tiele *op. cit.* (n. 12), p. 165, for a discussion of the sources of this treatise.

and back again. Commelin took this from Linschoten's *Reysgheschrift*. Subsequent to its appearance in the *Begin ende voortgangh*, Roelofszoon's *Journael* was published by Joost Hartgers in 1648 and in 1650, each time bound with Olivier van Noort's journal. It was also published separately by Gilles Joosten Saeghman, probably in 1663.[219]

Also published for the first time in the *Begin ende voortgangh* was Jan Sas' description of Admiral Steven van der Hagen's first voyage to the East Indies, 1599–1601.[220] Sas' journal describes Van der Hagen's attack on the Portuguese at Amboina and the building of a Dutch fort there—the first Dutch fort in the East Indies. Commelin appended two other journals to Sas' account: one describes the voyage of two ships to Acheh in 1600–1601 and ends abruptly with the capture of the commander and several crewmen by the natives. The other, written by Reyer Corneliszoon, describes Admiral Jacob van Heemskerck's voyage to Sumatra in 1601–2. All of these accounts are very brief; none contains any appreciable descriptions; none appears to have been published elsewhere, although a brief account of Van Heemskerck's voyage is included in Hulsius' collection.[221]

While no descriptions of Asian lands were included in the *Begin ende voortgangh's* account of Wolfert Harmenszoon's fleet, it nevertheless contains a stirring description of Harmenszoon's defeat of Don Andrea Hurtado de Mendoza's armada off Bantam in 1601.[222] Commelin heightened the drama by inserting a historical sketch of European commerce with the Indies which culminated in this battle.[223] Attached to the Harmenszoon voyage is a brief account of the adventures of two ships from Admiral Wybrand van Warwijck's fleet commanded by Cornelis van Veen.[224] Van Veen's ships were sent from Bantam to China on June 6, 1603. When they arrived at Macao on July 30, 1603, they surprised a richly laden unarmed Portuguese carrack about to sail for Nagasaki. Instead of making contact with the Chinese officials as he had been instructed to do, Van Veen seized the carrack, confiscated its cargo of silks, and set it on fire.[225] He then returned to Bantam with the booty. There were no other Dutch editions of either of these journals. The account of Van Veen's voyage is included in De Bry;[226] the recital of Harmenszoon's voyage in Hulsius is not from the same source as the *Begin ende voortgangh* account.[227]

[219] For bibliographical details see Tiele, *op. cit.* (n. 12), pp. 162–66.
[220] "Historisch verhael van de voyagie . . . ," *BV*, Ib, 1–31.
[221] *Cf.* Tiele, *op. cit.* (n. 12), p. 208.
[222] "Journael ofte dach-register vande voyagie, ghedaen onder het beleyt van den Admirael Wolfhart Harmanszn. naer de Oost-Indien, inden jaren 1601, 1602, ende 1603 . . . ," *BV*, Ib, 1–25.
[223] *Ibid.*, pp. 12–15.
[224] "Kort verhaelt van de twee-jaerige voyagie ghedaen door Cornelis van Veen, in de Oost-Indien," *ibid.*, pp. 26–27.
[225] *Ibid.*, p. 26.
[226] Tiele, *op. cit.* (n. 12), pp. 169–70.
[227] *Ibid.*, p. 204.

Considerably more descriptive material is found in the account telling of the first VOC fleet of 1602.[228] Its fifteen ships commanded by Admiral Wybrand van Warwijck and Vice-Admiral Sebald de Weert visited Bantam, Ceylon, Acheh, Johore, Patani, and the Pescadores Islands off the coast of China. Van Warwijck's fleet intensified hostilities with the Portuguese and captured many Portuguese vessels off Ceylon, in the Straits of Malacca, and along the Malay coast. Van Warwijck concluded alliances with the rulers of Johore, Acheh, and Kandy against the Portuguese. He justified his depredations as but proper retaliation for the murder of Van Neck's men at Macao a few years earlier.[229] Apparently because he had released some Portuguese prisoners, Vice-Admiral de Weert and about fifty of his crewmen were massacred by Kandyan soldiers on June 1, 1603.[230]

From August to December of 1604, Van Warwijck negotiated with Chinese officials at P'eng-hu in the Pescadores for permission to trade in China.[231] While the Chinese officials debated about how to deal with the Dutch request, a vigorous illicit trade took place between the Dutch and local Chinese merchants. Finally the Chinese military commander ordered Van Warwijck to leave, offering, if we may believe Van Warwijck's report, to let the Dutch establish themselves on Formosa or some other island outside Chinese jurisdiction.[232] Van Warwijck left convinced that he had laid the foundation for regular trade with China. Some Fukienese silk merchants had also promised to send junks to Patani to trade with the Dutch.[233] Van Warwijck also tried to establish trade with China through Siam. He dispatched Cornelis Specx with letters to accompany a projected Siamese tribute mission to China in 1604. But the Siamese embassy was postponed, and the plan was abandoned entirely when the king of Siam died.[234]

The Pescadores and the negotiations with the Chinese officials are described in considerable detail in Van Warwijck's account. His negotiations in Acheh, Jahore, and Patani, and De Weert's in Ceylon, are painted in rich detail. A rather full description of Acheh is included as well.[235] Commelin inserted into the account several ordinances and instructions for the new factory established by Van Warwijck in Bantam—the first Dutch factory in the Indies.[236] There is also a brief description of Makassar despite the fact that no ships from the fleet went there.[237] No other edition of Van Warwijck's voyage exists; it was not reprinted by Hartgers or Saeghman. With some variations the journal of De Weert's visit to Ceylon, written by Jan Harmenszoon Bree, was included in De Bry.[238]

The second volume of *Begin ende voortgangh* begins with the description of

---

[228] "Historisch verhael vande reyse gedaen inde Oost-Indien, ..." *BV*, Ia, 1–88.
[229] *Ibid.*, p. 35.
[230] *Ibid.*, pp. 21–22.
[231] *Ibid.*, pp. 75–77.
[232] *Ibid.*, p. 76.
[233] *Ibid.*, p. 77.
[234] *Ibid.*, pp. 73–74, 80, 84–85.
[235] *Ibid.*, pp. 14–16.
[236] *Ibid.*, pp. 56–58.
[237] *Ibid.*, p. 35.
[238] For bibliography see Tiele, *op. cit.* (n. 12), pp. 167–69.

Steven van der Hagen's second voyage, also the second VOC voyage.[239] Van der Hagen's fleet of twelve ships left Holland in December, 1603, visited several ports of the Malabar coast and Ceylon, stopped at Acheh and Bantam, and arrived at Amboina in February, 1605. After capturing the Portuguese fort on Amboina, the fleet was divided. The journal is incomplete and contains little of interest apart from the description of the capture of the Portuguese forts on Amboina and on Tidore. Commelin fleshed out the account with lengthy descriptions of Goa, Cochin, and Pegu, all of which were taken from the journal of Gasparo Balbi (Venice, 1590).[240]

Appended to Van der Hagen's voyage is Paulus van Solt's journal of his voyage from Bantam to the Coromandel Coast on one of Van der Hagen's ships, the "Delft."[241] Van Solt's journal contains much detailed information about the trade and the negotiations with rulers and officials on the Coromandel Coast. From it the reader can gain a feel for the growing and successful Dutch establishment in Asia. Van Solt's ship was involved in the inter-Asian carrying trade. It picked up a cargo on the Coromandel Coast and unloaded it in Bantam, where it took on supplies to be delivered in the Moluccas. In every port there seemed to be Dutch ships or Dutch agents. They seized Portuguese ships whenever they could. The Portuguese seemed demoralized and often gave up without a fight. Relations with local rulers appeared to go much more smoothly than they had a few years earlier. There were fewer uncertainties and surprises. And the Dutch appeared far more careful of native shipping than they were at first. Van Solt, for example, was upset with the English whose piracy of Asian ships might be blamed on the Dutch.[242] There are a couple of descriptive inserts in Van Solt's journal: one of Banda and one of Makassar.[243] It is not clear whether they were inserted by Commelin or by Van Solt. Commelin usually placed his inserts in quotation marks, but printed them in the same gothic type as the rest of the text. These are not in quotation marks, and are printed in smaller roman type.

Van der Hagen's voyage had appeared earlier in both the German and the Latin editions of De Bry's collection. In fact, Tiele contends that Commelin translated his account from De Bry's German version and did not use the Dutch original. Even the inserts from Balbi were taken from Arthus' German translation of Balbi in De Bry's seventh volume. The voyage also appeared in the Hulsius collection. Commelin's edition was reprinted by Hartgers in 1648, but without Van Solt's journal, and the entire voyage, including Van Solt's journal, was reprinted by Saeghman around 1663.[244]

Cornelis Matelief's journal was first published in the *Begin ende voort-*

---

[239] "Beschryvinge van de tweede voyagie ghedaen met 12 schepen naer d'Oost-Indien onder den Heer Admirael Steven vander Hagen," *BV*, IIa, 1–91.
[240] *Ibid.*, pp. 4–7, 9–34. For Balbi see *Asia*, I, 474–75.
[241] *BV*, IIa, 40–91.
[242] *Ibid.*, p. 40.   [243] *Ibid.*, pp. 79, 82–83.
[244] For bibliographic details see Tiele, *op. cit.* (n. 12), pp. 170–74.

gangh.[245] The account of Matelief's voyage in the Hulsius collection is a composite of two brief reports first published in Dutch in 1608. These were in fact letters written to the VOC directors; the first by Matelief himself and the second by Jacques L'Hermite the younger, a merchant on one of Matelief's ships.[246]

Matelief's fleet of eleven ships left Texel on May 12, 1605. From April 30 until August 24, 1606, he besieged Malacca in league with the sultan of Johore. He won two impressive naval victories over the Portuguese during this time. After he divided his fleet on January 6, 1607, Matelief visited Bantam, Jakatra, Amboina, and Ternate, where he built a fort, and the China coast, where he attempted to negotiate a trade agreement. He returned to Holland in September, 1608, carrying with him Cornelis Specx and an embassy of five Siamese.[247]

Although he refers to himself in the third person, the journal was apparently written by Matelief himself.[248] It is well written and exceedingly rich in details. There seems no end to the information about receptions, negotiations with princes and officials, banquets and the food served at them, conversations, exchanges of letters, and treaties, all laced with Matelief's salty assessment of the events or the character of the dignitaries he met.

Furthermore, the journal contains several rather interesting inserts: a description of Malacca,[249] Batu,[250] Amboina,[251] and a discourse on the state of Dutch commerce in the Indies.[252] All of these seem to have been written by Matelief himself although the description of Amboina was augmented by Frederick de Houtman, the governor of the Dutch fort there. The discourse on trade is definitely Matelief's own work. It points out the impediments in the way of Dutch trade and power and strongly recommends the establishment of a permanent headquarters. He also stresses the importance of trade with China and contends that the capture of Malacca from the Portuguese is the key to future Dutch power in the Indies. Throughout he assumes that the VOC's goal is to monopolize the trade.[253]

Matelief's voyage is also noteworthy as one of the earliest serious Dutch attempts at direct trade with China. He negotiated with local officials both at Nan-ao, an island off the Kwangtung coast, and at Lan-tao, in the Pearl River estuary, between June and August, 1607.[254] He left only when it became apparent that a large number of Portuguese ships from Macao were preparing to attack him. In all his dealings with the Chinese, Matelief spared

---

[245] "Historische verhael vande treffelijcke reyse gedaen naer de Oost-Indien ende China, met elf schepen," *BV,* IIa, 1–191.

[246] For details see Tiele, *op. cit.* (n. 12), pp. 208–13.

[247] On the Siamese embassy see below, p. 1172.

[248] Tiele, *op. cit.* (n. 12), p. 212.

[249] *BV,* IIa, 41–43.

[250] *Ibid.,* pp. 30–31.

[251] *Ibid.,* pp. 55–61.

[252] *Ibid.,* pp. 72–76.

[253] *Ibid.,* pp. 72, 75.

[254] *Ibid.,* pp. 76–91.

no effort to impress them with his peaceful intentions. He was extremely generous to the officials and their messengers. When one of the Chinese interpreters was caught stealing, Matelief turned him over to the local authorities instead of punishing the culprit himself. Dutch sailors who misbehaved ashore were summarily punished, and the Chinese were doubly recompensed for the damages incurred. Since the officials on Nan-ao and Lan-tao had no power to authorize trade, they promised to take the Dutch request to the governor in Canton. Matelief, nevertheless, was certain that he would have eventually been allowed to trade at Lan-tao if the Portuguese had not chased him away. He thought the Dutch should attempt to trade in the Canton area again, but that they should return there with enough ships to overwhelm the Portuguese.[255]

A considerable amount of firsthand information about the Chinese is included in the relation of Matelief's experiences at Nan-ao and Lan-tao. He accurately describes Chinese restrictions on trade and the difficulties involved in negotiating with officials. He knew, for example, that the Portuguese bridgehead at Macao had not been officially authorized; he was sure that the emperor knew nothing about it.[256] Particularly vivid are his descriptions of a visit to a pagoda on Nan-ao and his reception by a Chinese official on Lan-tao.[257] Matelief's picture of the Chinese corresponds rather closely with that of other early Dutch observers. While not as hostile towards the Chinese as Van Rechteren, he nevertheless describes them as being very clever and greedy. About a particularly devious maneuver by a Chinese official on Nan-ao, for example, he observes: "it was as good as a whole chapter out of Machiavelli."[258] Matelief's journal also contains a rather extensive general description of China.[259] It was apparently inserted by Commelin, who took it from Pierre d'Avity's *Les estats, empires, et principautez du monde*, a one-volume treatise on comparative government first published in 1614.[260] D'Avity's description is in turn a condensation of Mendoza's.

Appended to Matelief's journal are two letters from Jacques L'Hermite to his father. The first was evidently written in January, 1606, on Mauritius, where Matelief's fleet met Steven van der Hagen's fleet, which carried the letter back to Holland.[261] It deals primarily with the earliest parts of the voyage. In addition to a description of Mauritius, it summarizes Van Warwijck's experiences on the China coast and observes that the capture of Malacca, and the establishment of trade in China and in Cambay were the three most important tasks facing the VOC and Matelief's fleet.[262] The second letter was written on January 5, 1607, just before the fleet was divided.[263] It is

[255] *Ibid.*, p. 119.

[256] *Ibid.*, p. 90.

[257] *Ibid.*, pp. 78, 86.

[258] *Ibid.*, p. 88.

[259] *Ibid.*, pp. 91–118.

[260] See above, p. 398.

[261] *BV,* IIa, 140–45; Tiele, *op. cit.* (n. 12), p. 212.

[262] *BV,* IIa, 144–45.

[263] *Ibid.*, pp. 145–87.

much longer than the first and recounts in great detail the siege of Malacca, the battles with the Portuguese armada, and the day-to-day business and counsel meetings on the Dutch ships. Finally, the last pages of Matelief's journal are devoted to a series of questions and answers concerning navigation taken from Linschoten's *Reysgheschrift*.[264] Matelief's journal was reprinted only once, by Joost Hartgers in 1648, but without any of the additions included in the *Begin ende voortgangh*.[265]

Commelin also provided an account of Paulus van Caerden's voyage in 1606–8.[266] Like Matelief's and Van der Hagen's, the fleet of Van Caerden was as much a military as a commercial venture. Following his instructions he first attempted, unsuccessfully, to seize the Portuguese fort at Mozambique, after which he visited Goa, Calicut, the Coromandel Coast, and the Moluccas, capturing Portuguese ships as well as trading. Van Caerden himself was captured by the Spanish during a raid on Morotai on August 27, 1608. After he was released in May, 1610, as part of a prisoner exchange, he became governor of the Moluccas. A month later he was captured again and died a prisoner at Manila in October, 1615.[267] The "Loffelijcke voyagie" does not, of course, describe his capture and subsequent events.

The *Begin ende voortgangh* contains several lengthy descriptive inserts of the places visited by Van Caerden's fleet: Goa,[268] Calicut,[269] and the "Kingdom of Narsinga," or Vijayanagar.[270] The first two of these accounts were taken from Linschoten; the description of Vijayanager was taken from D'Avity.[271]

No other editions of the "Loffelijcke voyagie" were printed. The account of Van Caerden's voyage written by Cornelis Claeszoon in 1651 is entirely different from Commelin's.[272] Claeszoon was a pilot aboard one of Van Caerden's ships and his journal is almost entirely a pilot's log. He describes the winds, weather, currents, courses, depths, and the movements of the fleet, but says nothing about commerce or about the lands and peoples he visited.

Reports about Van Caerden's capture, release, and recapture were included in the journal describing Pieter Willemszoon Verhoeff's voyage of 1607–12, which also appeared for the first time in the *Begin ende voort-*

---

[264] *Ibid.*, pp. 188–91.

[265] *Journael ende historische verhael* . . . (Amsterdam). For bibliography see Tiele, *op. cit.* (n. 12), pp. 208–13.

[266] "Loffelijcke voyagie op Oost-Indien, met 8 schepen uyt Tessel gevaren int jaer 1606 . . . ," *BV*, IIa, 1–48.

[267] Alfred Booy (ed.), *De derde reis van de V.O.C. naar Oost-Indië onder het beleid van Admiraal Paulus van Caerden, uitgezeild in 1606* (2 vols.; "WLV," LXX, LXXI; The Hague, 1968 and 1970), I, 69–82.

[268] *BV*, IIa, 15–29.   [270] *Ibid.*, pp. 35–41.

[269] *Ibid.*, pp. 30–35.   [271] See Tiele, *op. cit.* (n. 12), p. 36.

[272] Cornelis Claeszoon, *Journal, ofte een Oost-Indische-reysbeschrijvinghe, ghedaen door Cornelis Claesz van Purmer-endt* . . . (Amsterdam, 1651).

gangh.[273] If anything, the instructions for Verhoeff's expedition were still more aggressive than those prepared for the earlier VOC fleets. In addition to raiding Iberian shipping its special mission was to drive the enemy out of the Moluccas. That goal was nearly accomplished. By the time Verhoeff's fleet sailed for home, the Dutch had built new forts on Banda and Amboina and had left only the stronghold on Tidore in Spanish hands. While Verhoeff's assault on Mozambique failed, he strengthened the Dutch position on the Coromandel Coast and renewed the alliance with the Zamorin of Calicut. Two of Verhoeff's ships went to Japan, where they were very well received by the shogun, who granted more extensive trading privileges to the Dutch. Verhoeff's fleet did not attempt to take Malacca, nor did it try to establish trade with China, although it was instructed to do both. Part of the fleet under Vice-Admiral François Wittert blockaded Manila for six months. In the end, however, Wittert's squadron was largely destroyed by a Spanish fleet under Juan de Silva. Altogether six ships from Verhoeff's fleet were lost; many men were killed, including all of the original leadership. Verhoeff and most of his ships' council were killed in an ambush by the Bandanese in May, 1609.[274]

The account of Verhoeff's voyage as printed in the *Begin ende voortgangh* is a composite piece. The first sixty-eight pages provide a journal begun by the chief merchant Johan de Moelre and continued by the fleet's treasurer Jacques Le Febvre after De Moelre was killed along with the admiral on Banda. In addition to the activities of the fleet, De Moelre included brief descriptions of Calicut,[275] of Acheh,[276] and of the Moluccas.[277] The next five pages contain extracts from the journal of Reynier Dirckszoon, the pilot aboard one of the ships which sailed to Japan.[278] It contains no descriptive passages.

Much more detail about Japan is included in the journal of the voyage of Jacob Specx and Pieter Segerszoon from Patani to Japan in 1611.[279] It contains a great deal of information about the negotiations at Hirado and at the shogun's court, some description of Japanese towns along the way, and interesting observations about early Tokugawa politics. This piece is followed by a Samuel Bloemaert report about trade and negotiations on Borneo in 1609.[280] Bloemaert describes the products and trade of various places on

[273] "Journael ende verhal van alle het gene dat ghesien ende voor-ghevallen is op de reyse gedaen door . . . ," *BV*, IIa.

[274] For a complete description of the fleet and its accomplishments see M. E. van Opstall (ed.) *De reis van de vloot van Pieter Willemsz. Verhoeff naar Azië 1607–1612.* (2 vols.; "WLV," LXXIII, LXXIV; The Hague, 1974).

[275] *BV*, IIa, 32–33.

[276] *Ibid.*, pp. 37–38.   [277] *Ibid.*, pp. 60–61.

[278] "Aenteecheninghe uyt het *Journael* ghehouden by *Reynier Diecksz.* [sic] *van Nimme-gen* . . . ," *ibid.*, pp. 68–72.

[279] *Ibid.*, pp. 72–98.

[280] "Discours ende ghelegentheyt van het Eylandt Borneo, ende 't gene daer voor ghevallen is int Iaer 1609 . . . ," *ibid.*, pp. 98–107.

Borneo but reports nothing about the people or landscape. He includes the text of a treaty between the VOC and the "King of Sambers" (Sambas) on Borneo.[281]

Two pieces which had been appended to Van Spilbergen's *Spiegel* in earlier editions were added to Commelin's edition of Verhoeff's voyage. They are Appolonius Schotte's "Discourse"[282] and the "Corte beschrijvinghe van het ghetal ende ghelegent vande forten."[283] Sandwiched between them is a letter from Schotte dated July 5, 1613, describing his voyage of that year from Bantam to "Buton" (Butung), Solor, and Timor.[284] He summarizes the treaty negotiated with the king of Butung and describes the capture of the Portuguese fort on Solor. He reports nothing about the people in these places but lists the villages of "New Christians" on Solor. Much of the letter is devoted to the movements of Dutch ships in the Moluccas and to rumors of a new Spanish armada being formed to drive the Dutch out of the Moluccas.

These pieces are followed by a detailed report on the state of the VOC possessions in Amboina and the surrounding islands written by the merchant Gillis Seys in May, 1627.[285] While he says nothing about native customs or life, he provides detailed lists of the villages and the population of each. He lists the Dutch forts, weapons, officials and their wages, and supplies; he describes the schools, the church services and their average attendance, and the difficulties involved in monopolizing the spice trade. Seys' report is followed by Sebastiaen Danckaerts' description of Amboinese religious affairs, first published in 1621.[286] Then, in the next piece, Seys does for the Moluccas in 1627 what he did for Amboina.[287] Finally Commelin included a bundle of reports, letters, official papers, and treaties that bring the story of events in the Moluccas down to 1638.[288] These materials constitute a rich source of information about the expansion of Dutch power in the Spiceries, the negotiations with the islanders, the war with the Spaniards, the details of trade, and the daily life of the Dutch stationed there.

The account of Verhoeff's voyage printed in the *Begin ende voortgangh* was never separately reprinted during the seventeenth century. The account included in De Bry's *Petits voyages* and in the Hulsius collection was written by Johann Verken, a German corporal in the VOC service, and is entirely different from the VOC account.[289]

The most detailed description of any part of India to be found in the *Begin*

---

[281] *Ibid.*, pp. 103–4.
[282] *Ibid.*, pp. 107–16.
[283] *Ibid.*, pp. 125–30. See above, p. 448.
[284] *BV*, IIa, 116–25.
[285] *Ibid.*, pp. 130–51.
[286] *Ibid.*, pp. 151–62. For details see above, pp. 448–49.
[287] *BV*, IIa, 162–87.
[288] *Ibid.*, pp. 187–214.
[289] See below, p. 519. For bibliography see Tiele, *op. cit.* (n. 12), pp. 174–79.

ende voortgangh is by Jonathan Twist (or Johan Van Twist) (d. 1679).[290] It was apparently never printed before, despite the reference in its title to a 1638 edition produced in the "print shop of the goose quill" in Batavia. Perhaps this is merely Van Twist's jocose way of saying that he wrote it when he returned to Batavia in 1638 after having served for some time as director of the Dutch factories in Ahmadabad, Cambay, Baroda, and Broach. In any case, no trace of a 1638 edition remains. Van Twist was a member of the Council of the Indies from 1639 to 1643 and served as governor of Malacca after the Dutch captured it in 1641.

Van Twist's "General Description of India" is primarily a detailed account of Gujarat. He reports on its government, its relationship to the Mughul empire, and the history of how Gujarat came under Mughul control. He describes Gujarat's geography, fauna, flora, cities, food, commerce, religions, and social customs. Much of Van Twist's account comes from previous writers. For example, he quotes Thomas Roe but copies without acknowledgment from Linschoten and Pelsaert.[291] Many other observations appear to be Van Twist's own: the description of the drought in 1630, the floods of 1631 and the consequent famine, and a case of suttee which shows Shah Jahan's relaxation of Jahangir's prohibition of the practice.[292]

Van Twist's description of Gujarat is followed by a brief account of the Deccan, much of which recounts the abortive plot against King "Idelxa" ('Adil Shah of Bijapur) in 1635 and the king's subsequent rule.[293] Finally, Van Twist, or Commelin, includes a rutter providing detailed sailing instructions for most of East and Southeast Asia.[294]

Van Twist's "General Description" was included in all subsequent editions of the *Begin ende voortgangh.* The first part and the rutter were published by Hartgers in 1648. Only the first part, under the title *Beschrijving van Guseratte,* was published by Hendrick Donker in 1647. Donker also published two more editions, one in 1650 and one in 1651, both with the title *Generaele beschrijvinghe van Indien.*[295]

4

NEW HORIZONS AND DIMENSIONS, 1646–71

Dutch reports of the mid-seventeenth century first brought to Europe's serious attention Laos, Australia, the Ainu aborigines of Hokkaido, and the

---

[290]"Generale beschrijvinghe van Indien. Ende in 't besonder van't coninckrijck van Guseratten . . . ," *BV,* IIb, 1–112.

[291]*Ibid.*, pp. 22–25 and 66.

[292]*Ibid.*, pp. 6–9, 32–33.   [293]*Ibid.*, pp. 69–83.

[294]"Aenwysinge van meest alle custen, drooghten ende reden, om door gantsche Indien te seylen," *ibid.*, pp. 84–112.

[295]For bibliographic details see Tiele, *op. cit.* (n. 12), pp. 242–45.

Hermit Kingdom of Korea. Around 1670 Tasmania, New Guinea, New Zealand, and the Fiji Islands make their initial appearance in Dutch literature. New depth was meanwhile added to geographical descriptions by an increased number of ambassadorial reports on the interiors of Java, Japan, and China. Abraham Roger's authoritative book on Hinduism (1651) provided insights into the religious and social life of the Tamil country that had only been touched upon lightly by earlier reporters on south India. It was also in this period that Athanasius Kircher published his encyclopedic *China illustrata* (1667), a compendium of Jesuit materials which remained the most popular western European source on China for the remainder of the century. In the Dutch world, China was read about in the compendia of Johann Nieuhof (1665) and Olfert Dapper (1670).

Perhaps the most popular Dutch travel tale of the century, Willem Ysbrantszoon Bontekoe's (1587–1647?) *Journael* was first published in 1646.[296] It was printed at least thirty times before the end of the century and was translated into almost every European language.[297] The events related in the *Journael* became part of the household vocabulary of seventeenth-century Dutchmen. Bontekoe's adventure was considered an embodiment of Christian courage and fortitude in adversity. Later in the century when Dutchmen selected the books to go into the imaginary sea chest of a young sailor who might be shipwrecked on a deserted island, Bontekoe's *Journael* was usually mentioned along with the New Testament.[298]

The popularity of Bontekoe's book derived primarily from the almost uninterrupted series of crises and catastrophes occurring throughout the story of his East-Indian voyage. The brave skipper left Amsterdam in December, 1618, suffered storms at sea, hostile encounters with islanders, and a threat of mutiny by his crew. His ship was burned in the Indian Ocean and he and the other survivors slowly made their way to Java in an open boat, enduring hunger, thirst, exposure, and attacks by hostile natives, until they were taken aboard Dutch ships in the Sunda Straits and brought to Batavia. In 1622 Bontekoe commanded one of the ships in Cornelis Reijersen's war fleet, and his adventures on the expedition along the China coast were hardly less spectacular than those of the outward voyage. He took part in the attack on Macao, and his ship was one of the fleet which raided the coast of Fukien province. Reijerson himself was a passenger on Bontekoe's ship when he returned to the Netherlands in 1625, and when the commander died at sea Bontekoe presided at his burial.

---

[296] *Journael ofte gedenckwaerdige beschrijvinghe vande Oost-Indische reyse van Willem Ysbrantsz. Bontekoe van Hoorn . . .* (Hoorn).

[297] For bibliography see G. J. Hoogewerff (ed.), *Journalen van de gedenckwaerdige reyse van Willem Iysbrantsz. Bontekoe, 1618–1625* ("WLV," LIV; The Hague, 1952), pp. xlvii–l; and Tiele, *op. cit.* (n. 12), pp. 213–26.

[298] Hoogewerff (ed.), *op. cit.* (n. 297), p. xx. See also G. D. J. Schotel, *Vaderlandsche volksboeken en volksprookjes van den vroegste tijden tot einde der 18ᵉ eeuw* (Haarlem, 1875), p. 149.

All this Bontekoe relates in simple, earthy language. Apart from some description of the Pescadores and the Fukien coast, the book is devoted almost entirely to the adventures of the captain and his crews. He describes in detail, however, the Dutch raids along the China coast and the strange appearance and demeanor of the many Chinese captives taken from the junks he attacked. The image of the Chinese sketched in this immensely popular book is that of a sinister and unscrupulous enemy, totally devoid of Western military virtues and capable of the darkest treachery. And yet the Chinese were not entirely without redeeming qualities. Bontekoe told how he set two prisoners free along the China coast on the condition that they return with provisions for the ship. To his amazement they kept their bargain and returned the next day with food. "In truth a great virtue," said Bontekoe, "putting to shame many Christians, who once they are out of the trap often think little of their promises." [299]

The year 1646 also saw the publication of the journal describing Hendrick Brouwer's expedition around Cape Horn to Chile in 1643. [300] The *Journael* itself contains no mention of Asia, but appended to it is a short description of the island of Yezo (Hokkaido) written by a participant in Martin Gerritszoon Vries' expedition of 1643. [301] Vries' ship coasted the southern and eastern shores of Hokkaido and Sakhalin without realizing that the two were divided from each other and without definitely proving that Hokkaido was an island. His expedition landed on Hokkaido, however, and he established friendly contact with the Ainus. The brief description appended to Brouwer's *Journael,* therefore, is probably the earliest firsthand description by a secular writer of Hokkaido and of the Ainu people. [302] A second edition of Brouwer's book, including the description of Hokkaido, appeared around 1660. Neither the German edition of 1649 nor Thévenot's edition of Brouwer's *Journael* contains the "Kort beschryvinghe." [303] It is, however, included in Witsen's *Noord en Oost Tartarye* (1692). [304]

While brief mention of a Dutch landing on the western coast of Australia had been made by Van Rechteren in 1635, the first independent description of Australia appeared in 1647 with the publication of Francisco Pelsaert's *Ongeluckige voyagie.* [305] Pelsaert's ship, the "Batavia," had become separated

---

[299] Hoogewerff (ed.), *op. cit.* (n. 297), p. 82.

[300] *Journael ende historis verhael van de reyse gedaen by oosten de Straet le Maire naer de custen van Chili . . .* (Amsterdam).

[301] "Kort beschrijvinghe van het eylandt by de Japanders Eso genaemt . . . ," in *ibid.,* pp. 95–104.

[302] On the Vries expedition see P. A. Leupe, *Voyage de M. Gerritsz. Vries vers le nord et l'est du Japon . . .* (Amsterdam, 1858) and Edward Heawood, *A History of Geographical Discovery in the Seventeenth and Eighteenth Centuries* (Cambridge, 1912; reprinted New York, 1969), pp. 86–88. The Jesuits knew by report of the Ainu and Hokkaido in the sixteenth century. See *Asia,* I, 723–25. In 1618 a group of refugee Jesuits fled from Japan to Hokkaido. See above, p. 374.

[303] See Tiele, *op. cit.* (n. 12), pp. 226–28 for bibliography.

[304] See below, pp. 501–2.

[305] *Ongeluckige voyagie, van't schip "Batavia" nae Oost-Indien. Uyt-gevaren onder de E. Francois*

from the rest of the fleet while crossing the Indian Ocean and was wrecked along the Australian coast on the rocks known as Houtman's Abrolhos (28° south latitude) on June 4, 1629.[306] After evacuating the ship's company to a neighboring rocky island, Pelsaert and some of his crew investigated other nearby islands and finally the mainland in search of water and food. Finding only a few natives, who fled at their approach, they went on to Batavia in the ship's boat. When Pelsaert returned to the site of the wreck three months later, he discovered that the supercargo, Jeronymus Corneliszoon, had seized the ship, broken into its cargo, taken the women passengers—ministers' daughters—as mistresses for himself and his cohorts—and killed those who had opposed him. About forty-five others had taken refuge on another island. Pelsaert seized the conspirators and salvaged what he could of the cargo of the "Batavia." Then he tried and executed the mutineers before sailing back to Batavia.[307]

Pelsaert's was not the first Dutch visit to the Australian west coast. Ever since 1616 when Dutch ships began to use the southern route across the Indian Ocean they had made occasional unintentional sightings and landings. The first of these was made by Dirk Hartogszoon on the "Eendracht" in October, 1616. There were many other landings and some wrecks before Pelsaert's tragedy. In the process large parts of the west coast had been charted, as can be seen on the 1627 map compiled by Hessel Gerritszoon, the VOC cartographer.[308] Some deliberate exploration of the north coast of Australia had begun already in 1606. Apparently VOC officials seriously considered Australia as a possible headquarters for the Company, should they not be satisfied with Java, as well as a new area for trade and colonization. They also may have deliberately kept descriptions of the Australian discoveries from being published prior to 1647.

In any case, Pelsaert's description of the western coast was not likely to have touched off a European rush to Australia. It was rocky and barren; in most places it was impossible to land. Once ashore he found a dry barren plain distinguished primarily by numerous, huge anthills. They were continuously pestered by flies. The few people Pelsaert saw were black and completely naked. Pelsaert's description of kangaroos, however—an exceedingly detailed and accurate description of kangaroos—was perhaps the first by a Western observer.[309] Alas, it was not included in any of the printed

---

Pelsaert . . . (Amsterdam). Translated into English in Vol. XI of John Pinkerton, *A General Collection of the Best and Most Interesting Voyages and Travels in all Parts of the World* (17 vols.; London, 1808–14).

[306] Pinkerton, *op. cit.* (n. 305), XI, 428. The wreck, found in 1963, is on the reefs of the Walabi Group, the northernmost of the three groups of islands and reefs which together make up Houtman's Abrolhos. See Schilder, *op. cit.* (n. 111), pp. 111–28.

[307] See H. Drake-Brockman, *Voyage to Disaster* (London, 1964), pp. 73–81.

[308] See J. E. Heeres, *The Part Borne by the Dutch in the Discovery of Australia, 1606–1765* (London, 1899) for the map. For a more recent account see Schilder, *op. cit.* (n. 111), chaps. vii–xiii.

[309] Heeres, *op. cit.* (n. 308), p. 30.

editions. Pelsaert's harrowing adventures proved to be popular. No fewer than nine Dutch editions appeared before the end of the century. Thévenot included an abridged translation of it in his collection of voyages.[310]

Thévenot also translated a large part of an earlier work written by Pelsaert: a report to the VOC directors on the state of Dutch commerce in India prepared in 1626 when Pelsaert had nearly finished his term as chief factor for the Company in Agra.[311] He served in Agra from 1620 to 1627, during which time he reputedly became proficient in the Persian language and knowledgeable about Mughul society and history. No Dutch edition of Pelsaert's report was ever published, but large parts of Joannes de Laet's *De imperio magni mogolis* (Leyden, 1631) appear to have been based on it.[312] The first two editions of Pelsaert's *Ongeluckige voyagie* also contained a report by Jeremias van Vliet describing the VOC's troubles in Siam during 1636. Van Vliet's report was not included in subsequent editions of Pelsaert's book or in Thévenot's translation. In its place some editions include a letter by Gysbert Sebastiaenszoon, a minister on Pelsaert's ship who describes the mutiny and discourses on commerce and navigation.[313]

Another description of Jacob van Heemskerck's 1601 voyage appeared in 1648. It was written by Willem Pieterszoon van West-Zanen and is completely different from that of Reyer Corneliszoon in the *Begin ende voortgangh*.[314] Pieterszoon was skipper of one of the ships in Van Heemskerck's fleet. He had also accompanied De Houtman's voyage and the second Dutch voyage under Van Neck and Van Warwijck. His account of Van Heemskerck's voyage is much larger and more interesting than Corneliszoon's. In addition to Pieterszoon's account of the fleet's activities, Hendrik Jacobszoon Soete-Boom, the editor, inserted many descriptions of the countries visited taken from earlier works, primarily from Linschoten and the accounts of De Houtman's voyage. Among others, there are inserts on the Maldives, Sumatra, the Sunda Straits, Bantam, Java, pepper, Japara, Javan boats, Jortan, Jakatra, cloves, nutmeg, palm trees, and Mauritius. They are all brief, however, and contain no information not found in earlier Dutch publications. Pieterszoon's account also appeared in Amsterdam and in Wormerveer during 1648.[315]

More Jesuit publications emerged from southern presses during the thirties and forties. A Dutch translation of Christoforo Borri's account of the Jesuit mission to Cochin-China appeared at Louvain in 1632.[316] In 1636

[310] For bibliography, see Tiele, *op. cit.* (n. 12), pp. 262–68.

[311] "Tres-humble remonstrance que Francois Pelsaert, ..." TR, II, 10–31.

[312] Moreland and Geyl (trans.), *op. cit.* (n. 127), p. xii. For a discussion of De Laet's book see above, pp. 451–52.

[313] See Tiele, *op. cit.* (n. 12), pp. 262–69.

[314] *Derde voornaemste zee-getocht (der verbondene vrye Nederlanden) na de Oost-Indien . . .* (Amsterdam). For Reyer Corneliszoon's account see above, p. 465.

[315] See Tiele, *op. cit.* (n. 102), pp. 205–8.

[316] See Streit, V, 592, for bibliography. For Borri see above, p. 377.

Joannes van Meurs of Antwerp published a catalog of Jesuit martyrs in Japan in both Latin and Dutch.[317] During the following year he published Marcello Mastrilli's account of his voyage, again in both languages.[318] A Flemish translation of António Cardim's account of the four Portuguese ambassadors who were executed in Nagasaki appeared in 1644.[319]

In 1649 Bernhard Varen (1622–50), an Amsterdam physician and geographer, compiled an Elzevier "Res publicae" series volume on Japan.[320] None of the information in it is new; Varen drew on a wide variety of Jesuit and Dutch published sources, but depended primarily on Caron's account and on the other appendices to Hagenaer's *Begin ende voortgangh* piece. Some of it is translated verbatim. In fact, he even included parts of Joost Schouten's description of Siam.[321] The second part of Varen's book, with separate pagination and a separate title page, treats Japanese religion, the founding and progress of the Jesuit mission in Japan, and the persecutions.[322] Appended to this second part is a treatise on the religions of other Asian peoples, again taken from already published accounts.[323] Varen's version of Siamese religion, for example, derives from Joost Schouten; his account of Chinese religion comes from Trigault. A second edition of Varen's book was published at Cambridge in 1673.[324]

In 1651 a new and apparently independent discussion of south Indian Hinduism appeared, *De open-deure tot het verborgen heydendom* (the open door to occult paganism), prepared by Abraham Roger. Roger was first sent out as a missionary to the Indies by the Dutch Reformed *Classis* of Amsterdam in 1631. The church council in Batavia in turn sent him to Pulicat on the Coromandel Coast where he preached in both Portuguese and Tamil for ten years (1632–42). He returned to Batavia in 1642 and finally to the Netherlands in 1647. He died in 1649, two years before the publication of his book.[325]

De open-deure was the most complete European description of south Indian Hinduism published up to that time—perhaps the most complete before the end of the nineteenth century. It includes a detailed description of the caste system, social life, customs, and religious practices of the Brahmans, as well as a systematic description of their religious and philosophic beliefs. It also contains a translation—more accurately a paraphrase—of

---

[317] See Streit, V, 543–44, for details. First Spanish edition was in 1636.

[318] See *ibid.*, V, 124–25.

[319] See *ibid.*, V, 558.

[320] *Descriptio regni Iaponiae cum quibusdam affinis materiae, ex variis auctoribus collecta* . . . (Amsterdam).

[321] *Ibid.*, pp. 229–67.

[322] *Tractatus in quo agitur de Japoniorum religione.* . . .

[323] *Ibid.*, pp. 216–320.

[324] For bibliography see Streit, V, 563. On Varen see H. Blink, "Bernhard Varenius, de grondlegger der wetenschappelijke geographie," *Tijdschrift van het Nederlandsch Aardrijkskundig Genootschap gevestigd te Amsterdam*, 2d ser., pt. 3 (1887), pp. 182–214.

[325] Leyden, 1651. For biographical sketch see W. Caland (ed.), *De open-deure tot het verborgen heydendom*, ("WLV," X; The Hague, 1915), pp. i–xxvi.

two of the seventh-century poet Bhartrihari's three *śataka*s apparently made for Roger by his close Brahman friend and teacher.[326] Despite its hostile-sounding title, Roger's book is remarkably objective and dispassionate. His Reformed Protestant judgments about Brahman beliefs or practices rarely show.

Roger's work does not seem to have been based on earlier Western-language descriptions of Hinduism. Indeed, they were probably not available to him. He apparently relied solely on his personal observations and on what he learned during many long conversations with his friend "Padmanabha" and with other Brahmans.[327] Because *De open-deure* was therefore a major new contribution to Europe's knowledge of India, it influenced many subsequent seventeenth-century writers. It was translated into German in 1663 and into both French and English in 1670. Some scholars have thought that it was first published in Latin, but no Latin edition has ever been found and the absence of Latin case endings on the Tamil words in the other editions suggests that it was written in Dutch and that the posthumous Dutch edition was the earliest.[328]

A large number of important foreign travel accounts of Asia were translated into Dutch during the fifties. For example, Olearius' account of Mandelslo's journey through Persia to India appeared in 1651 and again in 1658.[329] J. H. Glazemaker translated Pinto's travels into Dutch in 1652[330] and in 1654 he translated Vincent Le Blanc's *Famous Voyages*.[331] Metello Saccano's account of the Jesuit mission in Cochin-China was translated into Dutch in 1654.[332] A Dutch edition of Jean Mocquet's *Voyages* was published in 1656,[333] and a third Dutch edition of Mendoza appeared at Delft in 1656. A Latin Mendoza was published at Antwerp in 1655.[334] Rhodes' French *Relation* appeared in Dutch in 1657,[335] and Dutch editions of the English accounts of Thomas Roe and Thomas Herbert appeared in 1656 and 1658.[336]

Several important Latin works on Asia were published in the Netherlands during the fifties. Willem Piso's *De indiae utriusque re naturali et medica*, which contained the expanded version of Bontius' *De medicina indorum*, appeared in 1658.[337] Johan Blaeu (1598–1673) of Amsterdam published three works

---

[326] Caland (ed.), *op. cit.* (n. 325), p. xxv. For more detail see below, p. 1055.

[327] *Ibid.*, pp. xxi–xxiv.

[328] *Ibid.*, pp. xxvii–xxviii. For a detailed discussion see below, pp. 1029–30.

[329] Olearius, *Persiansche reyse uit Holsteyn . . . met een reyse van daer te lande naer Oost-Indien door Joh. Albr. van Mandelslo . . .* (Amsterdam, 1651); Mandelslo, *Beschryvingh van de gedenkwaerdig zee- en landt-reyze deur Persien naar Oost Indien, . . .* (Amsterdam, 1658).

[330] *De wonderlijke reizen . . .* (Amsterdam).

[331] *De vermaarde reizen . . .* (Amsterdam).

[332] See Streit, V, 599.

[333] *Reysen in Afrique, Asien, Oost-en West-Indien* (Dordrecht).

[334] *Rerum morumque in regno chinensi . . .*

[335] See Streit, V, 565–66.

[336] Thomas Roe, *Journael van de reysen . . .* (Amsterdam); Thomas Herbert, *Zee- en lant-reyse na verscheyde deelen van Asia en Africa* (Amsterdam).

[337] See above, p. 457.

by the Jesuit Martino Martini (1614–61), *De bello tartarico historia* in 1654, *Novus atlas sinensis* in 1655, and the first part of *Sinicae historiae* in 1659. The *De bello tartarico* and the *Sinicae historiae* appear to have been published earlier by German printers.[338] Dutch translations of the *De bello tartarico* appeared both in Delft and Antwerp in 1654.[339] The *Novus atlas sinensis* was first published in 1655 as the sixth volume of Blaeu's *Theatrum orbis terrarum*. It was translated into Dutch, French, and German during the same year.[340]

Martini's *Novus atlas sinensis* was also included in Blaeu's magnificent *Atlas major,* published in 1662.[341] The Blaeu *Atlas,* in eleven superbly printed folio volumes containing six hundred hand-colored maps, was surely the most elegant encyclopedic atlas produced anywhere in Europe during the seventeenth century. It was exceedingly expensive. Only the very rich could possibly afford it. During the last half of the century the Dutch republic and the VOC frequently sent the Blaeu *Atlas* as an official gift to heads of states and other dignitaries whom they wished to honor.[342] A French edition in twelve volumes was published in 1663 and again in 1667. A nine-volume Dutch edition appeared in 1664 and 1665. A Spanish edition was produced between 1662 and 1672. A manuscript edition in Turkish was produced about 1685, as well as a made-to-order German translation.[343] Martini's *Novus atlas sinensis* comprises over half of the large volume on Asia—volume X in the Latin edition—thus giving China a very large place in Blaeu's prestigious publication.

The *Novus atlas sinensis* contains seventeen maps. The first is a map of the entire Chinese empire, followed by a general description of China and its inhabitants. Individual maps of Ming China's fifteen provinces follow, each accompanied by detailed descriptions. Finally there is a map and a brief description of Japan. Martini apparently based his maps and description on the "Mongol Atlas" compiled by Chu Ssu-pen about 1311–12 and later revised by Lo Hung-hsien. Although Martini had traveled widely in China and had apparently surveyed parts of it for the K'ang-hsi emperor, the maps in his *Novus atlas sinensis* were entirely derived from the revised "Mongol Atlas."

---

[338] See below, pp. 525–27.

[339] Streit, V, 797.

[340] *Theatrum orbis terrarum, sive atlas novus;* . . . (Amsterdam, 1635–55). There are many editions of most of the volumes of the *Theatrum orbis terrarum* and its translations. All editions of Volume VI, however, carry the 1655 publication date. See Cornelis Koeman, *Joan Blaeu and His Grand Atlas* (Amsterdam, 1970), pp. 36–39. See also J. J. L. Duyvendak, "Early Chinese Studies in Holland," *T'oung Pao,* XXXII (1936), 305–8.

[341] *Atlas major, sive cosmographia Blauiana, qua solum, salum, coelum, accuratissime describuntur* (Amsterdam).

[342] Koeman, *op. cit.* (n. 340), pp. 41–48.

[343] For bibliography see *ibid.,* pp. 48–51. A facsimile edition of the 1663 French edition was printed by *Theatrum orbis terrarum* of Amsterdam in 1967. In 1981, in connection with an international conference held in Martini's native city of Trent, the original Latin version of the *Novus atlas sinensis* published in 1655 by Blaeu was reissued in an anastatic edition; Martini's informative "To the Reader" was simultaneously published separately in Italian, English, French, and German translations with an introductory essay by Giorgio Melis.

Even so, these were the most accurate maps available during the century, and together with Martini's provincial descriptions, the *Atlas* provided more geographical information about China than became available during the following two centuries.[344]

The general description of China in the *Novus atlas sinensis* resembles the first parts of Trigault's and Semedo's books. Martini discusses the extent of the kingdom and the names by which it was known; he describes its natural resources, climate and trade, and the inhabitants, their government, religions, learning, and customs. Martini's general introduction is considerably shorter than the descriptions of Trigault and Semedo, but he subsequently brings to his readers an abundance of information about the Chinese in the detailed descriptions of the individual provinces. Martini was apparently more impressed by the Chinese than was either Trigault or Semedo. The *Novus atlas sinensis* was published when the rites controversy was becoming increasingly bitter; in fact the controversy was the reason for Martini's presence in Europe. He therefore tends to make even more distinct than the earlier Jesuit writers the difference between the Confucians and the other Chinese religious groups. Martini's enthusiastic admiration for China and his reliance on Chinese writings for much of his information resulted in some idealization and exaggeration of Chinese virtues.

Martini's maps were extremely valuable, however, in presenting Europe with a more accurate geographic picture of the Middle Kingdom. Based as they were on Chinese maps, they rectified much of the erroneous information concerning China's interior geography. One concept the error of which Martini emphasized was the common European belief that beyond China's northern frontier lay the rich kingdom of Cathay, described by Marco Polo in the fourteenth century. This notion apparently persisted despite the earlier identifications of Cathay with China.[345] In fact the *Atlas major* volume which contains the *Novus atlas sinensis* includes a description of the separate "Kingdom of Cathay" based primarily on the writing of Pedro Teixeira, Odoric of Pordenone, and Marco Polo.[346] Martini again points out that beyond the Great Wall there were no rich cities or great kingdoms, only roving bands of Tartars; that Marco Polo's great city of "Cambalu" was none other than Peking; and that Cathay was simply the Saracen name for the Chinese empire.[347]

One of the two appendices to the *Novus atlas sinensis,* that written by the Leyden orientalist Jacob Golius, identifies China and Cathay by still another means.[348] Golius met Martini when the latter was in the Netherlands and

---

[344] Koeman, *op. cit.* (n. 340), pp. 83–88.
[345] See above, pp. 147, 338.
[346] Blaeu, *Le grand atlas . . .* (Amsterdam, 1663; facsimile edition, Amsterdam, 1967), XI, 248–50.
[347] *Ibid.*, p. 4.
[348] Addition du royaume de Catay par Jacques Gool," *ibid.*, separate pagination, i–xvi.

discovered in conversation with him that the chronological and calendar divisions ascribed to the people of Cathay by thirteenth-century Persian writers were identical to those of the Chinese. Golius' "Additamentum" also contains some of the earliest properly written Chinese characters printed in Europe. The other appendix to the *Novus atlas sinensis* is a reprint of Martini's *De bello tartarico*.

The rest of Blaeu's Asia volume contains a general map of Asia done by his father, Willem Blaeu, in 1621, a map of Southeast Asia and the Indian subcontinent, one of the Mughul Empire, one of the Moluccas, and one of Tartary. All of these and the accompanying descriptions were taken from previously printed books, most of them already out of date. Curiously, and perhaps intentionally, Blaeu, who succeeded his father as the official cartographer for the VOC and thus had access to the most recent information about Asian geography, used none of this inside information for the Asia volume of his *Atlas major*.[349]

There were a number of original Dutch contributions to Europe's knowledge of Asia during the fifties. The journals of the indefatigable voyager David Pieterszoon de Vries (1593–1665) appeared in 1655.[350] Between 1618 and 1644 De Vries made seven voyages to all parts of the world, three of them to America. Only the fourth voyage, that of 1627 to 1630, took him to the East Indies. The physician Jacob Bontius traveled to Batavia with him in 1627; Pieter van den Broecke and Jan Pieterszoon Coen's widow returned home with him in 1630. On the outward voyage De Vries' ship, too, sighted the Australian coast.[351] His journal also describes the Javan siege of the Dutch fort at Batavia in 1628 and 1629.[352] Relatively few good descriptive passages appear in the journal and most of these deal with the Coromandel Coast.[353] There seem to be no other seventeenth-century editions of De Vries' journal.

Paul Alofszoon Rotman's *Kort verhael* (brief relation) was also published just once during the century, in 1657. Rotman's ship, bound from Taiwan to Batavia, was wrecked by a typhoon on the China coast near Amoy in 1652. Rotman and the other survivors were held captive for a time by the Ming loyalists who were defending Amoy against the Manchu armies. He was no perceptive observer of things Chinese; he and his shipmates were too worried about their survival to be very curious about their surroundings. The importance of Rotman's account, however, is that it contains eyewitness impressions of the Ming camp during the Manchu's southern campaign. For example, Rotman saw Jesuit priests at the temporary Ming court in Amoy,

---

[349] Koeman, *op. cit.* (n. 340), pp. 23–25, 83–84. See our pls. 2, 4, 9, 11, 286.
[350] *Korte historiael, ende journaels aenteyckeninge van verscheyden voyagiens in de vier deelen des wereldts-ronde, als Europa, Africa, Asia, ende Amerika gedaen* (Hoorn). The modern critical edition of H. T. Colenbrander is in "WLV," III (The Hague, 1911).
[351] Colenbrander (ed.), *op. cit.* (n. 350), p. 102.
[352] *Ibid.*, pp. 116–18.
[353] *Ibid.*, pp. 118–31.

and he saw Portuguese soldiers with the Ming troops.[354] He reported that fear of the Manchus in the outlying villages was mixed with confidence that they would never take the island city of Amoy for lack of war junks.[355]

For the Dutch, the Manchu conquest of China held out the prospect of a regular trade with the Middle Kingdom. Their attempts to establish commerce with Ming China had all failed, and while their attack on the Pescadores and the Fukien coast between 1622 and 1624 resulted in the establishment of a Dutch colony on Formosa, it also gave them a most unsavory reputation among the Chinese and thus made regular, peaceful trade with China even less likely than before. When Martini stopped in Batavia en route to Europe in 1652 (or 1653), however, he told VOC officials that the new Manchu rulers intended to allow all nations to trade freely in Canton. Attempts to test the veracity of Martini's report in Canton convinced the Dutch that regular trade might be obtained if they sent an embassy to Peking. In 1655 their first embassy to the Chinese court left for Peking.

For European readers the Dutch embassy produced in 1665 a major description of China which in a sense combined the two main sources of information about China: the travel relations and the Jesuit missionaries' accounts. Written by the embassy's secretary, Johann Nieuhof (1618–72) it combined the author's firsthand observations with information taken from the works of Trigault, Semedo, and Martini.[356] The first part of the book is a narrative of the travels and experiences of the embassy, introduced by a brief general description of China drawn from Trigault's work and from Martini's *Atlas.* The introduction includes an abridgment of Martini's description of those provinces through which the embassy did not travel. Descriptions of the provinces actually visited by Nieuhof were inserted into the narrative at the appropriate places, but these too were taken from Martini's *Atlas.* The narrative itself contains much descriptive material, most of which was based upon Nieuhof's personal observations.

Part two of Nieuhof's account is a general description of China based primarily on the works of Trigault, Semedo, and Martini. But Nieuhof's general description is longer and more detailed than any of those from which he borrowed. In addition to providing descriptions of Chinese government, religion, learning, customs, etc. Nieuhof also devotes two chapters to Chinese history.[357] Chapter xviii summarizes Chinese history from the mythical emperor Fu Hsi to the Ming dynasty. His discussion of the sage emperors is rather detailed, but beginning with the Hsia dynasty Nieuhof does little more than list the dynasties and their dates. With the Mongol dynasty of the thirteenth century, however, the history becomes more detailed. The chap-

[354] Rotman, *Kort verhael van d'avonteurlicke voyagien en reysen . . .* (Amsterdam 1657), p. 17.
[355] *Ibid.,* p. 29.
[356] *Het gezantschap der Neêrlandtsche Oost-Indische Compagnie aan den grooten tartarischen cham, den tegenwoordigen keizer van China* (2 vols. in 1; Amsterdam, 1665).
[357] *Ibid.,* II, 170–258.

ter ends in about 1640. Martini is the source for all the historical information in the chapter; most of it comes from his *Sinicae historiae* and the rest from his *De bello tartarico*. Chapter xix contains a detailed story of the Manchu conquest in 1644 which follows *De bello tartarico* very closely but is augmented by geographic descriptions taken primarily from Martini's *Atlas*. Nieuhof also devotes many chapters to topics such as temples, flora, minerals and mines, animals, rivers, and mountains. The phenomena are described in these chapters province by province. Most of this information came from Martini's *Atlas*.

Nieuhof's account presented the Dutch reader with the most substantial and detailed description of the Middle Kingdom yet published. It contains information from the most important Jesuit sources and adds to them the observations of one of the first Dutchmen to travel in China's interior and visit the capital. Nieuhof's book is lavishly illustrated. Most of its 150 plates appear to have been based on Nieuhof's own sketches, and while embellishments characteristic of later chinoiserie were added by the engravers or even by Nieuhof himself, they nevertheless provided European readers with more realistic visual images of China's landscape and people than ever before.[358] Despite its expensive format it was enthusiastically received by European readers. Before the end of the century there were six Dutch editions, three German, two English, one Latin, and one French.[359]

In 1663 there appeared a description of Arnold de Vlaming van Oudshoorn's suppression of the 1651 Amboinese revolt against the VOC and its attempts to monopolize the clove trade.[360] No subsequent editions or translations have appeared and it has become very rare.

While many Dutch travelers had described Java's coastal cities and provinces, little had been written about the island's interior. Rijcklof Volckertszoon van Goens' account of his journeys from Batavia to the court of the "Sousouhounan" (Susuhunan) in Mataram helps to fill that lack.[361] Van Goens (1619–82) was certainly one of the VOC's ablest and most diligent officials. He spent almost his entire life in the Indies. His parents took him to Batavia in 1628 when he was but nine years old. By 1630 both his parents had died, leaving him a virtual ward of the Company. Before he died in 1682 he

[358] *Ibid.*, "Opdracht," p. 4. For an analysis of the plates and their relationship to Nieuhof's sketches see Leonard Blussé and R. Falkenburg, *Johan Nieuhofs beelden van een chinareis, 1655–1657* (Middelburg, 1987). Also see many examples from among our pls. 301–81.

[359] Dutch: Amsterdam, 1665, 1669, 1670, 1680, 1693, and Antwerp, 1666 (an expurgated Catholic edition); German: Amsterdam, 1666, 1669, and 1675; English: London, 1669, 1673; French: Leyden, 1665; Latin: Amsterdam, 1668. Another quite different French version, much of it a summary, was published in the Thévenot collection. All but the English editions were published in the Netherlands. For bibliography see P. A. Tiele, *Nederlandsche bibliographie van land- en volkenkunde* (Amsterdam, 1884), pp. 179–80.

[360] Levinus Bor, *Amboinse oorlogen, door Arnold de Vlaming van Oudshoorn als superintendent, over d'oosterse gewesten oorlogaftig ten eind gebracht* (Delft).

[361] *Javaense reijse gedaen van Batavia over Samarangh na de koninckijcke hoofdplaets Mataram, . . .* (Dordrecht, 1666).

had served as assistant, chief merchant, ambassador, member of the Council of the Indies, commander of fleets, governor of Ceylon, and governor-general of the Dutch Indies.[362] Between 1648 and 1654 he made five trips to Mataram as ambassador to the Susuhunan's court.[363]

Van Goens' *Javaense reijse* contains detailed, well-written descriptions of the landscape. Something of the spectacular beauty of the island's streams, mountains, and forests is conveyed by his surprisingly sensitive prose. He seems completely taken by the mountains, the crystal-clear streams, the high valley in which Mataram was located, and in general by the "unbelievably beautiful" landscape. He was far less impressed with the people, whom he describes as haughty, ambitious, greedy, devious, and often dishonest.[364]

Most of Van Goens' book describes the king, his court, his government, banquets, entertainments, and his cruel justice. "Here there is no punishment other than death," he concludes.[365] As Van Goens describes it, the Susuhunan was an autocratic tyrant ruling over obsequious courtiers in a luxurious court. Still, he concludes, no one in all the Indies treated VOC ambassadors with more honor.[366]

In several places Van Goens refers his readers to a description of Java or a history of Java that he had written. A "Brief Description of the Island of Java" by Van Goens exists in manuscript, but it was apparently never published.[367] Nor was the *Javaense reijse* published again during the century.

In 1667 the learned German Jesuit, Athanasius Kircher (1601–80) published his *China illustrata* at Amsterdam.[368] Gathering his material from the works of other members of the Society, Kircher wrote one of the century's most influential treatises on China. His primary purpose was to establish the authenticity of the Nestorian monument discovered in Sian, and to that end he produced in print the original Chinese and Syriac inscriptions on the monument, the Chinese text in romanization, and finally a Latin translation and his explication of the Chinese and Syriac texts. In addition, Kircher included a sizable description of China and other places in Asia. For example, in a section devoted to the various routes to China and the history of Christianity in China, he sketched all the old overland routes, including that

---

[362] See Willem M. Ottow, *Rijckloff Volckertsz, van Goens: de carrière van een diplomaat 1619–1655* (Utrecht, 1954), *passim*.

[363] See H. J. de Graaf (ed.), *De vijf gezantschapsreizen van Ryklof van Goens naar het hoff van Mataram, 1648–1654* ("WLV," LIX; The Hague, 1956).

[364] P. A. Leupe (ed.), "Reijs beschrijving van den weg uit Samarangh nae de konincklijke hoofplaets Mataram . . . ," *BTLV*, IV (1856), 345–47.

[365] *Ibid.*, p. 316.

[366] *Ibid.*, pp. 347–48.   [367] *Ibid.*, pp. 305, 351–67.

[368] *China monumentis qua sacris qua profanis, nec non variis naturae & artis spectaculis, aliarumque rerum memorabilium argumentis illustrata. . . .* Actually two editions of the *China illustrata* were published at Amsterdam in 1667, the first by Jan Janszoon van Waesberge and the widow Eliza Weyerstraet, Kircher's regular publishers; the other a pirated reprint by Jacob van Meurs. On these editions and the relationship between the two publishers see Isabella H. van Eeghen, "Arnoldus Montanus's Book on Japan," *Quaerendo*, II (1972), 252.

of Johann Grueber and Albert d'Orville from Agra to Peking, as well as giving a description of Tibet. He traced the activities of Christians in China from the tradition of St. Thomas to Boym's reports about the conversions at the Ming pretender's court and Adam Schall's experiences at the Ch'ing court during the K'ang-hsi era. Following what he thought to be the spread of idolatry from the Near East to Persia, India, and finally to East Asia, Kircher described the religions of China, Japan, and India. His extensive discussion of Hinduism and of the Mughul Empire derived from the letters of Heinrich Roth, his fellow Jesuit. There are several chapters on government, customs, geography, fauna, flora, and mechanical arts of China, and a very interesting scholarly discussion of the Chinese language, which indicates that Kircher had made considerable progress in it. There is a long Chinese-Latin dictionary, and finally Father Johann Grueber's (1623–80) responses to a long series of questions posed by the duke of Tuscany. Kircher's volume contains several beautiful pictures taken from Chinese and Mughul originals which Grueber had brought back to Europe with him in 1664.[369]

Although the *China illustrata* was not the product of Kircher's own experience in China, it was frequently used or cited as a source of information by later writers. Some of the information contained in it, for example the text of the Nestorian monument,[370] Roth's description of Hindu religion, and Grueber's description of Tibet, had not appeared in print before. Published originally in Latin, the *China illustrata* was translated into Dutch in 1668 and into French in 1670. All three editions were published by Jan Janszoon van Waesberge and Eliza Weyerstraet in Amsterdam.[371]

The publication of Hendrik Hamel's *Journael* in 1668 provided Europeans with their earliest extensive firsthand account of Korea; indeed almost the only glimpse into the Hermit Kingdom before the nineteenth century.[372] Hamel (1630–92) was the secretary aboard the VOC yacht "Sperwer" (Sparrow Hawk) which was caught in a typhoon while en route from Taiwan to Nagasaki in August, 1653. It was wrecked on the island of Cheju do (the Dutch called it Quelpaerts) off the south Korean coast. Thirty-six of the sixty-four-man crew of the "Sperwer" survived the wreck. They were taken into custody by a large number of Koreans who, after salvaging what they could from the wreck, took Hamel and his shipmates to the governor of the island. Here they were kept in comfortable imprisonment for ten months

---

[369] See our pls. 112, 311, 333. Michael Sullivan, *The Meeting of Eastern and Western Art* (Greenwich, Conn., 1973), p. 93. For an evaluation of the *China illustrata* see David Mungello, *Curious Land: Jesuit Accommodation and the Origins of Sinology* (Stuttgart, 1985), pp. 134–73.

[370] Notices of the Nestorian monument began to appear in European works *ca.* 1628. See above, p. 183, and below, pp. 1646–47.

[371] *Tooneel van China, door veel zo geestelijke als werreltlijke, geheugteekenen* . . . , translated by J. H. Glazemaker; *La Chine illustrée de plusieurs monuments tant sacrés que profanes* . . . , translated by F. S. Dalquié.

[372] *Journael van de ongeluckige voyagie van 't jacht de Sperwer* . . . (Amsterdam, 1668).

while the governor awaited instructions from the capital. During that time they met an old Dutchman, Jan Janse Weltevree, who had been captured on the Korean coast in 1627. He lived in Seoul and served the Korean army as a weapons expert. He was not permitted to leave the country. Nor were Hamel and the crew of the "Sperwer" permitted to leave. In June, 1654, they were taken to Seoul, given housing and a stipend in rice, and assigned to the royal guard. After two of the Dutch captives approached the Manchu ambassador on the road to Seoul asking him to help them leave the country, the Dutch were banished from the capital and sent to Pyŏng'-yŏng in Chŏlla province where they did menial labor and were eventually reduced to begging. For seven years the survivors lived in Pyŏng'-yŏng. When they were transferred to three other Chŏlla villages during the famine of 1663, only twenty-two were still alive. Hamel and eleven others were sent to Yosu on the south coast. In September, 1666, eight of the survivors including Hamel escaped to the Goto Islands of Japan in a fishing boat from where they were conveyed to Nagasaki and the Dutch factory at Deshima. Not until October, 1667, were they allowed to leave Japan. The Japanese negotiated for the release of the Dutchmen still held in Korea, and in September, 1668, they too arrived in Nagasaki.[373]

Hamel's book recounts in a simple, straightforward style the adventures of the crew of the "Sperwer" and their eventual escape. It also includes a brief general description of Korea's climate, geography, government, military organization, laws and judicial practices, religion, language, social customs, and relations to China and Japan. Unlike the Jesuit descriptions of China, Hamel's observations about Korea were formed by his personal experiences and his acquaintance with ordinary Koreans; they were not shaped by any overview or ideal notion of Korean society and culture. Nor did Hamel know enough about China or Japan to make comparisons between those lands and Korea. His description of the punishments administered to criminals is graphically detailed while his notions of Korean legal structure are exceedingly vague. He described the life and conduct of some Korean officials in detail, but had no sure grasp of Korean administrative structure. His account of Korean religion, too, emphasizes the people's religious practice, but shows no understanding of Buddhist or Taoist thought. Despite these limitations, however, a great deal of interesting information about Korea was brought to European readers through Hamel's account. Recent scholars have also found it accurate both for its description of the castaway's experiences in Korea—Korean notices about the Dutch visitors support Hamel's story—and for its description of Korea.[374] The picture of elephants

---

[373] For the story of Hamel and his shipmates' adventures see Gari Ledyard, *The Dutch Come to Korea* (Seoul, 1971). Ledyard's book also contains a reprint of the Churchill translation of Hamel's *Journal*.

[374] For an evaluation see *ibid*., pp. 121–34.

and crocodiles and the story about the crocodiles in Korean rivers which have raised questions about Hamel's credibility were apparently added by the editor of the Saeghman editions and later taken up by French and English translators. They are not found in the earlier Dutch editions or in the manuscript of Hamel's journal.[375]

Hamel's journal appeared in three editions by two publishers in 1668. It later became part of the Saeghman collection. It was translated into French in 1670, German in 1672, and English in 1704 (in the Churchill collection). It was included in Arnoldus Montanus' (1625?–83) *Gedenkwaerdige gesantschappen* in 1669, and the account of Korea in Witsen's *Noord en Oost Tartarye* (1692) was based on it.[376]

Some new information along with a lot of old material about Japan became available in 1669 with the publication of Montanus' *Gedenkwaerdige gesantschappen*.[377] Ostensibly a description of several VOC embassies to the shogun's court after 1640, it is in fact an encyclopedia of things Japanese. The narrative of the embassies is interrupted to describe the landscape, Japanese cities, ancient Japanese history, Portuguese trade with Japan, the wars of unification of the late sixteenth century, the Jesuit mission to Japan, the persecutions of Christians, and Japanese religion and customs. When some aspect of Japanese society or history reminded Montanus of similar events or practices in Western history he culled parallel examples from the classics, the Bible, and Western histories, comparing them with the Japanese examples. A paragraph on Japanese creation stories and sun worship, for example, provoked several pages of parallel creation stories and sun worshippers in ancient and modern times.[378] The book begins with a general description of the earth, its geographic parts, the distribution of people on it, the earliest explorations by land and by sea, and finally a sketch of the Portuguese and Dutch navigations generally and of their contact with Japan.[379] Most of the book consists of such digressions; even the digressions have digressions.

The sources for all this information are varied. Much of it comes from previously published descriptions of Japan: Iberian histories, Maffei, and above all the Jesuit letters, as well as the works of earlier Dutch commentators—Linschoten, Caron, Hagenaer, Gysbertszoon, Krammer, Candidius, Hamel, and others. The details of the annual VOC embassies to Edo,

[375] For the original text of Hamel's journal see B. Hoetink (ed.), *Verhaal van het vergaan van het jacht "De Sperwer . . ."* ("WLV," XVIII; The Hague, 1920). See also Hoetink's evaluation, p. xxii, and Ledyard, *op. cit.* (n. 373), pp. 132–33.

[376] For bibliography see Hoetink (ed.), *op. cit.* (n. 375), pp. xix–xxi, 139–47, and Ledyard, *op. cit.* (n. 373), pp. 125–32.

[377] *Gedenkwaerdige gesantschappen der Oost-Indische maatschappy in't Vereenigde Nederland, aen de kaisaren van Japan. . . .* (Amsterdam).

[378] *Ibid.*, pp. 252–60.

[379] *Ibid.*, pp. 1–29.

however, and much of the accompanying descriptive material obviously came from hitherto-unpublished reports from which can be gained interesting glimpses of Japan during the "Closed Country" period.

Despite its repetitiveness, lack of organization, and excessive length, Montanus' book was quite widely distributed. In addition to the Dutch edition of 1669 there was a German edition during the same year, another in 1670, and a French edition in 1680, all published by Jacob van Meurs of Amsterdam. Pirated French editions appeared in Leyden in 1686, and in The Hague in 1693. A second Dutch edition was published around 1680, probably by a company of Amsterdam booksellers, some of whom had been Van Meurs' stiffest competitors.[380] An English translation by John Ogilby appeared at London in 1670.[381]

Also published in 1669 was a small book describing Dutch activities in Cambodia and Laos between 1635 and 1644. Edited or written by Pieter Casteleyn (1618–76), a well-known Haarlem artist and publisher, the first editor of the *Hollandtsche mercurius,* it was apparently based on the journal of Geeraerd van Wusthof, a junior merchant stationed in Cambodia during those years.[382] There seems to have been only one edition of the book, yet it contains interesting information hitherto unavailable to European readers. Casteleyn reports little about the Cambodian countryside or people, but describes in detail the assassination of the Cambodian ruler in 1642 and the subsequent massacre of his family and advisers by the usurper. He contends that twelve hundred people died in the revolution.[383] Casteleyn also describes the trip upriver to the Laotian capital by Van Wusthof and some assistants in 1641, perhaps the first eyewitness report by Europeans.[384] A brief description of Laos is included, which deals primarily with geography, the court, court receptions, and processions.[385] The book ends with an account of the massacre of all the VOC employees in Cambodia by the usurping ruler on November 27, 1643.[386] Van Wusthof had left only a few months before. There are a few curiously irrelevant appendices: one describes St. Thomas' grave on the Coromandel Coast of India and the miracles performed there;[387] another recounts the habits of the "nutmeg bird" (fruit pigeon) on Banda which eats nothing but nutmeg, digesting the meal but passing the nut, thus planting

---

[380] For the publication history of Montanus' book, its sources, plates, and various editions, see Van Eeghen, *loc. cit.* (n. 368), 250–72.

[381] *Atlas Japannensis, Being Remarkable Addresses by Way of Embassy from the East India Company of the United Provinces, to the Emperor of Japan. . . .* This translation was in turn translated into Japanese by Wada Mankichi as *Montanusu Nihon shi* (Tokyo, [1925]).

[382] *Vremde geschiedenissen in de konninckrijcken van Cambodia en Louwen-lant, in Oost-Indien, . . .* (Haarlem). Republished in H. P. N. Muller (ed.), *De Oost-Indische Compagnie in Cambodja en Laos* ("WLV," XIII; The Hague, 1917), pp. 1–54.

[383] Muller (ed.), *op. cit.* (n. 382), pp. 20–25.

[384] *Ibid.,* pp. 28–52.   [386] *Ibid.,* pp. 52–54.

[385] *Ibid.,* pp. 42–45. See below, pp. 1156–59.   [387] *Ibid.,* p. 55.

new trees all over the island.[388] The last appendix reports various encounters with mermaids and mermen around the world.[389]

One of the most comprehensive descriptions of China published in the Netherlands was that contained in the relation of the Dutch admiral Balthasar Bort's expeditions along the Fukien coast of 1663 and 1664 and Pieter van Hoorn's embassy to Peking (1666–68) written by the Amsterdam physician Olfert Dapper (1639–89) and published in 1670.[390] Dapper himself had never visited China. Consequently his book is a conglomeration of reports from members of Bort's expeditions and Hoorn's embassy together with descriptions of China gleaned from other sources. Dapper expended little effort at integrating the material he had collected. Often he reproduced parallel passages from several writers on a single topic without any comment of his own. Unlike Nieuhof, therefore, Dapper did not express a consistent attitude towards the Chinese; like Montanus he was a compiler rather than an author. Probably because of his complete dependence on others, he acknowledged his sources of information more freely than Nieuhof. Although it is chaotically organized, Dapper's book was virtually an encyclopedia of things Chinese for the Dutch reader of the latter part of the century.

The first volume of the work—the two volumes are bound together—deals with the loss of Formosa in 1661, Dutch attempts to regain the island by negotiation with Fukienese officials, and Hoorn's embassy to Peking in 1666. Much more than the relation of these events, however, is included in it. A lengthy description of Formosa, for example, most of which came from Candidius, precedes the story of Bort's voyages along the Fukien coast. The story of the embassies to Foochow and to Peking also contains large quantities of descriptive material: some of it the observations of the ambassadors, some of it taken from other writers. For example, the narrative of Hoorn's embassy is interlaid with descriptions of each of the provinces through which it passed; these provincial descriptions were condensed from Martini's *Atlas.* Following the narrative of the embassy is a rather long general description of China, taken primarily from Trigault, Semedo, Martini, and Kircher.

Volume II is entitled "Description of the Empire of China or Ta Ch'ing" and was composed of material gathered from almost every important seventeenth-century account of China. As might be expected, the Jesuit descriptions of China were the most important sources for this volume, but Dapper also used Mendoza and the works of several Dutch writers, notably Nieuhof. The format of Dapper's second volume is similar to the second part of

---

[388] *Ibid.,* pp. 55–56.

[389] *Ibid.,* pp. 56–57.

[390] O. Dapper, *Gedenkwaerdig bedryf* . . . (2 vols in one; Amsterdam). For a description of Bort's expedition and Hoorn's embassy see above, pp. 60–61, and John E. Wills, Jr., *Pepper, Guns and Parleys, The Dutch East India Company and China, 1627–1681* (Cambridge, Mass., 1974).

Nieuhof's book. It begins with a general description of the land, its location, and the names by which it is called. The problem of the identification of China with Cathay is carefully explored, with quotations taken from every author who had ever dealt with the problem. Following this comes a description of the individual provinces, again condensed from Martini's *Atlas.* The Manchu Conquest, almost exactly as described in Martini's *De bello tartarico,* is included in the section on Chih-li province. Next comes a long section on Chinese religion and philosophy, most of which was taken from Trigault, Semedo, and Martini. A formidable amount of history is also included in this section, based almost exclusively on Martini's *Sinicae historiae.* The remainder of the volume includes relatively short chapters which describe in turn the rivers, lakes, streams, mountains, trees, flowers, beasts, birds, and fishes of the empire. Most of this material comes from the provincial descriptions in Martini's *Atlas,* but the chapters on fauna and flora were extensively augmented by material from Willem Piso and the Polish Jesuit Michael Boym. The volume ends with a chapter on Chinese language and writing compiled from the standard Jesuit accounts.

It is a beautifully printed book, lavishly illustrated with some exceedingly interesting copper plates, among them four foldout pieces of Buddhist iconography obviously of Chinese provenance.[391] In some copies the plates are beautifully colored. In addition to the original Dutch edition of 1670 the publisher, Jacob van Meurs, produced German editions bearing the dates 1673, 1674, 1675, and 1676. John Ogilby's English translation, London, 1671, is entitled *Atlas Chinensis* and was erroneously attributed to Montanus. Perhaps the confusion is understandable. Montanus and Dapper seem to have formed a partnership for the compilation of these large, illustrated volumes on far-away lands. Nor was this the only error regarding the authorship of the volumes. The German translation of Montanus' *Nieuwe en onbekende weereld* was attributed to Dapper.[392] Both the English and the German editions of the *Gedenkwaerdige bedryf* contain the plates found in the original edition.[393]

Dutch attempts to regain a position on Formosa with the aid of the Manchus were poetically described by Mattys Cramer, a participant in the Bort expeditions, in a book published in 1670.[394] Cramer's atrocious verses praise Bort's courage and wisdom, pray for God's aid against Koxinga's armies, and deplore Manchu perfidy. They contain little descriptive material beyond that of burning villages and sinking war junks. Mercifully there were no subsequent editions.

---

[391] Dapper, *op. cit.* (n. 390), II, 106–11. These, too, like those in Kircher's work, seem to be copies of pictures which Grueber acquired in Peking. See Sullivan, *op. cit.* (n. 369), pp. 93–95. *Cf.* our plates 316, 317.

[392] *Cf.* Tiele, *op. cit.* (n. 359), pp. 171–72. See also Van Eeghen, *loc. cit.* (n. 368), 262–63.

[393] Tiele, *op. cit.* (n. 359), p. 73.

[394] *Borts voyagie naer de kuste van China en Formosa* (Amsterdam).

The first published reports of Abel Tasman's Australian discoveries appeared in the Dapper-Montanus compilation on the New World, published in 1671 under Montanus' name.[395] Tasman's two voyages, one in 1642–43 and another in 1644, were part of the VOC's continuing exploration of the Australian coastline. After his second voyage all of the west coast, about two-thirds of the south coast, and almost all of the north coast, including the Gulf of Carpentaria, and the south coast of New Guinea had been charted by Dutch navigators. Tasman discovered Van Dieman's Land—now called Tasmania—and New Zealand. He also landed in the Tonga Islands and in the Fiji group. His navigations rather definitively laid to rest the notion of a large southern continent connected to the polar regions—a notion already seriously questioned by the participants in Schouten and Le Maire's voyage. Despite his voyage along the south coast of New Guinea and the north coast of Australia in 1644, Tasman still thought the two formed a single land mass.[396] The results of these explorations were probably never intended for publication; in fact, there seems to have been some effort to keep them secret. Nevertheless, charts that embodied the results of Tasman's explorations were published as early as 1652 or 1653.[397]

The report on Tasman's 1642–43 voyage in Montanus' *Nieuwe en onbekende weereld* differs greatly from the surviving extract of his original journal.[398] Apparently written by the ship's physician, Hendrik Haelbos, it contains no maps and little precise geographic information, but it includes considerably more description of the peoples than does the extract from the original journal. These descriptions, however, introduced Europeans to no attractive civilizations. The inhabitants of the Southland and the nearby islands are depicted as rude and barbarous tribes, black-skinned, running naked or nearly so, living in primitive round houses of reeds and mud, with no settled governmental or religious institutions.

An English edition of Montanus' *Nieuwe en onbekende weereld,* again by John Ogilby, appeared in 1671, and a German translation appeared in 1673 under Dapper's name. Another version, apparently based on Tasman's original journal, appeared as part of Dirck Rembrantszoon van Nierop's *Eenige oefeningen* in 1674. Finally Nicolaas Witsen included a report on Tasman's voyage in his *Noord en Oost Tartaryen* (1692) based apparently on the original journal or on another, lost extract journal.[399]

[395] *De nieuwe en onbekende weereld; of beschrijving van America en't Zuid-land* (Amsterdam), pp. 577–85.

[396] See R. Posthumus-Meyjes (ed.), *De reizen van Abel Janszoon Tasman en Franchoys Jacobszoon Visscher ter nadere ontdekking van het zuidland in 1642/3 en 1644* ("WLV," XVII; The Hague, 1919).

[397] *Ibid.*, pp. 261–70; and Schilder, *op. cit.* (n. 111), chaps. xiv–xv.

[398] For the extract journal see Posthumus-Meyjes (ed.), *op. cit.* (n. 396), pp. 3–141.

[399] "Een kort verhael uyt het journael van den Kommander Abel Jansen Tasman, in't ontdekken van't onbekende Suit-lant," in Dirck Rembrantszoon van Nierop, *Eenige oefeningen in godlijcke, wis-konstige en natuerlijcke dingen* . . . (2 vols.; Amsterdam); Nicolaas Witsen, *Noord en Oost Tartaryen* . . . (Amsterdam, 1692); for bibliographic details see Posthumus-Meyjes (ed.), *op. cit.* (n. 396), pp. 270–72; and Schilder, *op. cit.* (n. 111), pp. 150–57.

5

FIN DE SIÈCLE: DECLINE

The indefatigable Dapper produced a volume on the Mughul Empire in 1672.[400] Like his earlier works, it is long, encyclopedic, discursive, and lavishly illustrated. To an even greater extent than his China volume, it is dependent on previously published works. While his sources are not always clearly discernible, the list of those actually cited is very long and includes classical as well as numerous contemporary authors. Dapper's *Asia* contains topics on geography, castes, marriage and funeral customs, especially suttee, as well as a Malay-Dutch vocabulary. He also recounts Hindu creation stories, the ten transformations (avatars) of Vishnu, and the epics of Krishna and Rama. He discusses both Hindu and Muslim religious beliefs and practices in considerable detail and includes a rather long section on Mughul history. Finally there are descriptions of the various kingdoms and provinces of the empire. Almost all this information was, of course, available elsewhere. Regarding Hindu religion he depends very heavily on Roger; he copied whole chapters from Roger without bothering to cite him. He did the same with the work of Henry Lord. Dapper's description of the ten transformations of Vishnu and of the Rama and Krishna stories are different from and much more detailed than those found in Roger. These he apparently plagiarized from the manuscript of Philippus Baldaeus' book, which was being printed about the same time and probably fell into Dapper's hands at the engraver's shop.[401] Nevertheless it is possible that Dapper's relation of a Dutch embassy to the King of "Visiapour" (Bijapur) in 1653 was based on VOC letters and journals not previously published.[402] Apart from the details of the embassy and several letters to and from Mughul officials, however, it is of little descriptive value. Dapper's *Asia* was published in English by John Ogilby in 1673 and in German in 1681.[403]

Philippus Baldaeus' (1632–72) *Naauwkeurige beschryvinge,* which came out later in the same year as Dapper's *Asia,* was a much more valuable contribution to Europe's knowledge of India and Ceylon than was Dapper's compilation.[404] Baldaeus had been a missionary in Ceylon from 1656 to 1665 and had also accompanied Rijcklof van Goens' campaigns along the Malabar coast and Ceylon in 1658.[405] His book is divided into three parts: the

---

[400] *Asia, of naukeurige beschrijving van het rijk des Grooten Mogols en de groot gedeelt van Indien . . .* (Amsterdam).

[401] A. J. de Jong (ed.), *Afgoderye der Oost-Indische heydenen door Philippus Baldaeus . . .* (The Hague, 1917), pp. lxxv–lxxxiii. Also see below, pp. 911–17.

[402] Dapper, *op. cit.* (n. 400), pp. 367–79.

[403] For bibliography see Tiele, *op. cit.* (n. 359), pp. 71–72.

[404] *Naauwkeurige beschryvinge van Malabar en Choromandel, der zelver aangrenzende ryken, en het machtige eyland Ceylon . . .* (Amsterdam, 1672).

[405] For biographical details see A. J. de Jong (ed.), *op. cit.* (n. 401), pp. xxxix–lv.

first is a description of coastal India, the second treats Ceylon, and the third is a discussion of Indian religion. Each part has a separate title page and pagination. In the first two parts he describes the towns, their trade, the surrounding countryside, and the people, and he devotes a large amount of space and much detail to the rise of Portuguese power in the various parts of India and to the later Dutch conquest of many of those places. In part 2, for example, he uses about 150 pages to tell the story of the Portuguese conquest of Ceylon, Portuguese relations with the king of Kandy, Dutch negotiations with Kandy beginning with Spilbergen's visit in 1602, the Dutch conquest of Portuguese Ceylon, the VOC's continued difficulties with Kandy, the problems of governing Ceylon, and the attempts to reform the church there, including pictures of each of the churches under his jurisdiction! His history includes letters and reports from the principal people involved. Much of it appears to be based on VOC reports and conversations with participants in the Dutch conquest. Some of it obviously emerges from Baldaeus' personal observations and experiences; he was in Galle as early as 1656, traveled as chaplain with Van Goens in 1658, and was actively involved in Dutch government and in its attempts to reform the churches on Ceylon from 1658 to 1665. His work is therefore an important printed source for the establishment of Dutch power in Ceylon and south India.[406] His history of the Portuguese period in Ceylon and on the Malabar coast obviously derives from Portuguese sources, not all of them previously published. A. J. de Jong, for example, contends that many of Baldaeus' sources came from the captured Jesuit seminary at Jaffnapatam. He thinks that Baldaeus' work and Manuel de Faria y Sousa's *Asia portuguesa* (1666–75) had a common manuscript source because they are in places almost identical and neither one could have been copied from the other.[407] Baldaeus also included a description of the siege of Colombo written by one of the Portuguese survivors, perhaps by Captain General Antonio de Sousa Coutinho.[408]

Baldaeus' description of Hindu religion in part 3 depends heavily on Abraham Roger's work but also contains new information gained from his own observations, from papers he found in the Jesuit seminary at Jaffnapatam, and from conversations he had with a "learned Brahmin" whom he was catechizing. He plagiarized the manuscript of the Jesuit Giacomo Fenicio prepared at Calicut in the early years of the century.[409] Baldaeus is much less understanding of Hinduism than was Roger. He constantly searches out similarities and parallels between Hindu beliefs and those of the ancient pagans, as known from classical and biblical sources, and he laboriously ex-

---

[406] See also *ibid.*, pp. lviii–lix.

[407] *Ibid.*, pp. lxvii–lxxi. See also P. A. Pott, *Naar wijder horizon* (The Hague, 1962), pp. 56–58. On Faria y Sousa see above, pp. 354–55.

[408] Baldaeus, *op. cit.* (n. 404), pp. 205–32.

[409] See J. Charpentier, *The "Livro da seita dos Indios Orientais"* . . . *of Fenicio* (Uppsala, 1933), pp. lxxxii–lxxxv.

poses the errors in the Hindu conceptions. His comparisons and evaluations often take up more space than his descriptions of Hindu religion.

At the end of part 1 are printed six unnumbered foldout pages containing the Tamil alphabet with roman transliterations and the Lord's Prayer and Apostles' Creed in Tamil letters.[410] Following these is a brief description of the Tamil language, an introduction to Tamil grammar—essentially the declension of a noun and the conjugation of a verb—and a roman-alphabet transliteration of the Lord's Prayer and the Creed in Tamil.[411] The declension and conjugation are incomplete and Baldaeus' promised full grammar never appeared, but his effort was probably the first published European attempt at a Tamil grammar.[412] No other Dutch edition of Baldaeus' *Naauwkeurige beschryvinge* was published during the century. A German translation by the original publisher appeared in 1672.

Another Latin account of the Manchu Conquest appeared at Louvain in 1673.[413] Written by François Rougemont (1624–76), a Flemish Jesuit who had worked in China from 1656 to 1676, it describes the conquest, the government and events during the early years of Manchu rule up to 1666, and the effect of these events on the Christian mission. Rougemont's Latin manuscript was also translated into Portuguese and was published in Lisbon even before the Latin edition appeared in Louvain.[414]

A detailed account of the loss of Formosa to Cheng Ch'eng-kung (Koxinga) appeared in 1675 in the form of a pamphlet whose author was mysteriously styled C. E. S.[415] The initials probably stand for "Coyett et socii," since the obvious purpose of the pamphlet was to gain popular support for Frederick Coyett, the last Dutch governor of Formosa, who had been defamed and imprisoned by Batavian officials after the fall of Fort Zeelandia in 1662. The author, or authors, provide a day-to-day account of the defense and loss of Formosa in 1661 and 1662. They also include extensive background material on the Manchu Conquest and the gradual defeat of the Ming supporters on the mainland. They seek to demonstrate that Batavian officials had been derelict in their duty by neglecting to strengthen the fortifications and garrison on Formosa despite the many intimations of trouble they had received. The picture of the Chinese which emerges from this pamphlet, therefore, is somewhat different from that of most Dutch travel

---

[410] Baldaeus, *op. cit.* (n. 404), I, between pages 190 and 191.

[411] *Ibid.*, pp. 191–98. See our pl. 173.

[412] See P. S. van Ronkel, "De eerste europeesche tamilspraakkunst en het eerste malabarsche glossarium," *Mededeelingen van het Nederlandsche Akademie van Wetenschappen, afdeeling letterkunde*, n.s., V (1942), 543–98. Also see below, pp. 994–95.

[413] François Rougement, *Historia Tartaro-Sinica nova.* . . .

[414] *Relaçam do estado politico e espiritual do imperio da China, pellos annos de 1659 até o de 1666* (Lisbon, 1672). See above, p. 358.

[415] C. E. S., *'t Verwaerloosde Formosa* . . . (Amsterdam). See also Inez de Beauclair (ed.), *Neglected Formosa: A Translation of Frederic Coyett's 't Verwaerloosde Formosa* (San Francisco, 1975).

accounts. Cheng's troops and tactics evoke admiration from the authors, an opinion at variance with the Chinese reputation for cowardice in combat built up by many earlier writers. Cheng himself they describe as a clever fox with almost uncanny wisdom. Even his duplicity seems to have won their admiration. The real villains, according to the writers of the pamphlet, were not Cheng Ch'eng-kung and his troops but the Council of the Indies at Batavia. Nevertheless this pamphlet again depicts the Chinese to Dutch readers as their enemy in the Far East, an enemy which perpetrated heinous atrocities against Dutch captives when their compatriots at Fort Zeelandia refused to surrender. Despite the obvious bias of the C. E. S. pamphlet, its description of the loss of Formosa corresponds rather well to that of other Dutch writers on the subject, for example with the accounts of Wouter Schouten, Jan Janszoon Struys, and Albrecht Herport, who himself took part in the defense at Fort Zeelandia.[416]

Shipwreck on a desert island, hunger, and cannibalism are the themes of Franz Janszoon van der Heiden's tale describing the shipwreck of a VOC yacht off the coast of Bengal.[417] According to Van der Heiden the "Schelling" was bound for Bengal from Batavia in October, 1661, when it ran aground during a storm and began to break up. Some of its crew escaped to a desert island where they struggled to stay alive for some time before building a rude raft with which they sailed to the mainland. Once on the mainland they were taken to a Mughul army camp and impressed into service. There is a brief description of the army and of the war they were fighting. Van der Heiden's tale may well be fictitious. The crew of the "Schelling" seems altogether too irresponsible, some of their adventures too unrealistic; the descriptions of the island are so general, it could be anywhere, and there are some serious lapses and illogicalities in the story. Fiction or fact, Van der Heiden's popular book contributed no new information about Asia. There appear to have been two Dutch editions in 1675, one in 1685, and another in 1698; at least five reprintings were issued in the eighteenth century. It was translated into French in 1681, into German in 1676, and into English under the name of Glanius in 1682. The English edition appears to be a translation of the French edition of 1681.[418]

Many of the events of the early sixties were vividly described by Wouter Schouten (1638–1704), another participant in many voyages, whose *Oost-Indische voyagie* was published in 1676.[419] Schouten sailed from Amsterdam as ship's surgeon in April, 1658, and returned there in October, 1665. During his years of service in the East he visited Sumatra, Java, the Moluccas,

---

[416]See below, pp. 532–33.

[417]*Vervarlyke schip-breuk van't Oost-Indische jacht Ter Schelling onder het landt van Bengale; . . .* (Amsterdam, 1675).

[418]See below, p. 586.

[419]*Oost-Indische voyagie, vervattende veel voorname voorvallen en ongeneeme vreemde geschiedenissen, bloedige zee- en landt-gevechten . . .* (Amsterdam).

Amboina, Celebes, Ceylon, Bengal, and Arakan. In Batavia when the survivors from Fort Zeelandia on Formosa arrived, he related what he had
learned from them about the loss of Formosa and reported on Governor
Coyett's trial and banishment.[420] He participated in the Dutch attack on
Makassar in 1660.[421] He visited Colombo in November of 1661 and described the effects of the long siege upon the city.[422] He sailed with Van
Goens' war fleet to the Malabar coast in 1661–62 and observed the capture
of Quilon, Cranganore, and Cochin. He met Baldaeus on that trip. Most of
1664 he spent in Bengal. Schouten was an inquisitive man. On long walks
into the countryside and in villages near every port he visited, he explored
temples and pagodas and observed village life. Sometimes he got into
trouble. In Tegenpatam, for example, he and his friends were chased away
by a group of half-naked village women when they violated a "Gentive"
(Gentile) taboo by touching their lips to the drinking pots at a well.[423]

In addition to recounting his personal adventures, Schouten's book contains a great many descriptions of Asian places and people: he describes both
coasts of India, Java, Sumatra, Arakan, Makassar, the Spice Islands, Malacca, and Ceylon. His account of pearl fishing off Cape Comorin and off
Bengal are particularly good. He also describes places he never visited:
Siam, Japan, Formosa, and Vijayanagar, for example. Obviously much of
this material came from previously published descriptions, but these and his
personal observations are so intertwined that in most cases it is impossible
to be sure where a particular description originated. The plates in Schouten's
book are unusually lively and interesting.[424] No other Dutch editions of
Oost-Indische voyagie were published during the seventeenth century, although there was a German translation also published by Meurs of Amsterdam in 1676. It appears to have been more popular in the eighteenth century,
in which at least five Dutch editions and two French editions appeared.[425]

Even more popular than Schouten's book was the semi-fictional *Reysen* of
Jan Janszoon Struys (d. 1694), also published in 1676.[426] It was translated into
German in 1678, French in 1681, 1682, and 1684, and English in 1683 or
1684. Three more Dutch editions and four French editions appeared during
the eighteenth century. Struys' popularity was no doubt due to the lively
series of adventures he recounts, most of which obviously took place in his
imagination. It is clear from the book itself that he did not keep a diary. He
first went to sea in 1674 as a boy of seventeen, and he traveled continuously
for the next twenty-six years. During that time he endured typhoons, ship-

---

[420] Schouten, *Reys-togten naar en door Oost-Indien* (3d ed.; Amsterdam, 1740), II, 162–70, 321.
[421] *Ibid.*, I, 83–92.
[422] *Ibid.*, II, 183–85.   [423] *Ibid.*, II, 182.
[424] See Pott, *op. cit.* (n. 407), p. 37 for an evaluation. Also see our pls. 132, 261.
[425] Tiele, *op. cit.* (n. 359), pp. 217–18 is incomplete.
[426] *Drie aanmerkelijke en seer rampspoedige reysen* . . . (Amsterdam). For a partial bibliography
see Tiele, *op. cit.* (n. 359), p. 233.

wreck, hunger, and captivity. He was sold as a slave several times and from one of his journeys he returned with a cross carved from the wood of Noah's ark given to him by a hermit who lived on Mount Ararat.[427] All this makes the book difficult to use. It is not always possible to distinguish the author's fabrications from his credulity or confusion. There may even be a substratum of fact beneath some of his most outlandish adventures.[428]

After 1676 the number of new Dutch descriptions of Asia declined strikingly. Travel tales and books about Asia were still being published by Dutch presses, and readers were apparently still eager to buy them, but most of these books were new editions of earlier accounts, foreign works, and translations into Dutch of foreign books, particularly French. None of the new Dutch accounts published during these years became as popular as the mid-century publications, perhaps because they contained little that was new.

Two small books appeared in 1677, neither of which was ever republished. Pieter van der Burg's description of Golconda and Pegu has become so rare that we have not even been able to locate a copy.[429] Gerret Vermeulen's *Gedenkwaerdige voyagie* brought Dutch readers a description of the VOC's war to subjugate Makassar, 1666–69, as well as the text of the treaty which ended the war.[430] It contains a fairly good description of Makassar, including the background to the war with the Dutch, as well as descriptions of Java, Bali, Timor, Ternate, Amboina, and Banda. These are all very brief. The editor fleshed out the account by adding descriptive appendices about every place mentioned by the author, but in spite of his efforts the book contains only ninety-one quarto-sized pages. Vermeulen's account has some interest for today's reader because he was an ordinary soldier and his book provides some firsthand glimpses into the life of VOC soldiers. He also reports amusing tidbits of soldiers' wisdom about Asia. He was very unhappy to be assigned to Makassar, for example, because soldiers in Batavia assured him that only five hundred out of every five thousand Europeans who went there ever returned.[431] There were worse places, however; an island sixty miles from Banda was reported to be so unhealthy that all white men who went there died within six months.[432] His brief descriptions always include comments about the native women who think it a great honor to sleep with

---

[427] Struys, *op. cit.* (n. 426), pp. 229–31.

[428] A thorough examination of Struys' account of Siam reveals that it is derived from earlier works and his fertile imagination. Certainly for Siam, and probably for other Asian places as well, Struys' book should not be used as a reliable source unless its assertions are supported by other independent accounts of established veracity. For an analysis of his account of Siam see G. V. Smith, *The Dutch in Seventeenth-Century Thailand* (De Kalb, Ill., 1977), pp. 128–29.

[429] *Curieuse beschrijving van de gelegentheid, zeden, godsdienst, en ommegang, van verscheyden Oost-Indische gewesten en machtige landschappen. En inzonderheid van Golconda en Pegu. . . .* (Rotterdam, 1677).

[430] Gerret Vermeulen, *De gedenkwaerdige voyagie . . . naar Oost-Indien in't jaer 1668 aangevangen, en in't jaer 1674 voltrokken . . .* (Amsterdam, 1677), pp. 37–73. It is not a firsthand account of the war; he was assigned to Makassar in 1669.

[431] *Ibid.*, p. 60.   [432] *Ibid.*, p. 85.

Europeans.[433] Amboina, he reports, is plagued with the pox, and he describes what appear to be the symptoms of syphilis. He thought, however, that it was spread by a certain kind of fly.[434] The parrots of Amboina evade capture by nesting in high dead trees which no one dares climb because of the voracious red ants which live on their trunks. Birds of paradise die whenever they land on earth.[435]

The first volumes of Baron Hendrik Adriaan van Rheede tot Drakestein's (1637–91) monumental work on Malabar Coast flora were published in 1678.[436] The baron had gone to India in 1671 as a special investigator for the VOC directors. Fascinated with Indian plants, he supported at his own expense a huge cooperative effort to sketch and catalog Malabar trees and plants, which probably involved as many as one hundred European and Indian scholars and workers in Cochin, Negapatam, Batavia, and Leyden before it was completed.[437] Between 1678 and 1703 twelve folio volumes appeared. In them, each of hundreds of trees, shrubs, and plants are meticulously sketched, described, and identified in Latin, Arabic, Sanskrit, Malayalam, and Tamil. Two volumes of the *Hortus indicus malabaricus* were translated into Dutch in 1698.[438]

Translations of foreign travel accounts continued apace during the sixties and seventies. In fact, after 1676 the number of translated travel tales published by Dutch presses were triple the number of new Dutch accounts. During the sixties, for example, Dutch editions of François de La Boullaye Le Gouz's *Voyages,* Niccolo de Conti's *Viaggi,* Marco Polo, Pietro della Valle's *Viaggi,* Vittorio Ricci's letter from Asia, Augustin de Beaulieu's *Voyage,* and Jacques de Bourges' *Relation* all appeared in Dutch translations.[439] Both Beaulieu and Bourges were translated by J. H. Glazemaker, as was the *Oost-Indianische Beschreibung* of Johann Jacob Saar in 1671.[440] Simon de Vries translated François Bernier's travels in India during the following year.[441]

---

[433] *E.g., ibid.,* pp. 79–80.

[434] *Ibid.,* p. 83. He may have been correct. See below, p. 1426.

[435] *Ibid.,* p. 81.

[436] Hendrik Adriaan van Rheede tot Drakestein and Joannes Casearius, *Hortus indicus malabaricus* . . . (12 vols.; Amsterdam, 1678–1703). For further discussion see below, pp. 926–27. Also see our pls. 137, 169–70.

[437] See H. Terpstra, *De Nederlanders in Voor-Indië* (Amsterdam, 1947), pp. 193–98.

[438] *Malabaarse kruidhof, vervattende het raarste slag van allerlei soort van planten die in het koningrijk van Malabaar worden gevonden* . . . (Amsterdam).

[439] François de la Boullaye le Gouz, *De reyse en optekeningh* . . . (Amsterdam, 1660); Niccolo de Conti, *Reysen naar Indien en d'oostersche landen* . . . (Amsterdam, 1664); *Markus Paulus Venetus reisen* . . . (Amsterdam, 1664); Pietro della Valle, *De volkome beschryving der voortreffelijcke reizen* . . . (Amsterdam, 1666); Vittorio Ricci, *Copye van eenen brief* . . . *inden welcken verhaelt wordt het ghene dat in Sina, en Japonien omghegaen is* . . . (Antwerp, 1667); Augustin de Beaulieu, *De ramspoedige scheepvaart der Franschen naar Oost-Indien.* . . . (Amsterdam, 1669); Jacques de Bourges, *Naaukeurig verhael van de reis des Bisschops van Beryte uit Frankrijke te lant en te zee naar China.* . . . (Amsterdam, 1669).

[440] Johann Jacob Saar, *Reisbeschrijving van hem naar Oost-Indien.* . . . (Amsterdam, 1671).

[441] François Bernier, *Verhael van den laetste oproer in den staet des Grooten Mogols* . . . (Amsterdam, 1672). See above, p. 414.

Impressive both in size and content is Johann Nieuhof's *Reizen,* published in 1682.[442] In addition to his trip to Peking in 1655, Nieuhof had served the West India Company in Brazil from 1640 to 1644, and the VOC as director of its affairs on the Malabar coast from 1663 to 1666. After disagreements with the new governor, Rijcklof van Goens, he was sent to Colombo in 1666, where he stayed for one year, and finally to Batavia, where he lived outside VOC service for three years before returning to Amsterdam in 1670. In 1671 he sailed for the Indies a third time but disappeared with a landing party on Madagascar in August, 1672. The *Reizen* was published from his notes and papers edited by his brother Hendrik.[443] Jacob van Meurs published the *Reizen* in a handsomely bound, lavishly illustrated, folio-sized volume, like the earlier account of the Dutch embassy to Peking. The plates were engraved from Nieuhof's own carefully drawn sketches. Unlike the China volume, however, this had no subsequent editions or translations during the century.[444]

The *Reizen* is really two volumes in one: the first is entirely devoted to Brazil, and the second, with separate pagination, treats his voyage to the East Indies. In addition to serving as VOC director on the Malabar coast, Nieuhof had visited Amboina, Formosa on the eve of Koxinga's invasion, Sumatra, the Coromandel Coast, and Ceylon. He had also participated in the expedition led by Van Goens that won the Malabar cities for the Dutch in 1662. The *Reizen* therefore provides firsthand information about these experiences and about Nieuhof's negotiations with several Malabar princes in the years immediately after the Dutch triumph when he was the VOC director there. In addition Nieuhof, as always, was a keen observer of his surroundings, a skillful writer, and judging from the *Reizen*'s plates, a fairly good descriptive artist. The *Reizen* contains descriptions of Amboina, Taiwan and its loss to Koxinga, Malacca, Johore, Patani, Sumatra, the Coromandel Coast, the Malabar coast, the Fishery coast, and Java, especially Batavia. While nicely written, most of the descriptive material would have been familiar to readers of earlier Dutch and Portuguese accounts. The description of Taiwan, for example, adds nothing to Candidius' account, and Nieuhof's relation of its loss to Koxinga agrees perfectly with the C. E. S. pamphlet. The report on Malabar is derived from Barros. Like Vermeulen, he described the symptoms of the "Amboinese pox," but he insisted that it was not identical with the Spanish pox and was not necessarily transmitted by sexual intercourse. He thought it was caused from the unhealthy air on Amboina and from eating too much fish and sago bread.[445] On the other

[442] *Gedenkwaerdige zee- en lant-reizen door de voornaemste landschappen van West en Oostindien* (Amsterdam).

[443] Biographical information culled from the *Reizen* and from J. T. Bodel Nijenhuis, "Johan Nieuhof," *Bijdragen van geschiedenis en oudheidkunde,* n.s., Pt. 2 (1862), pp. 32–51.

[444] See Tiele, *op. cit.* (n. 359), pp. 178–79.

[445] Nieuhof, *op. cit.* (n. 442), pp. 30–31. See below, p. 1426.

hand, his description of Malabar (some of it culled from earlier accounts) and of Batavia are large and packed with information. He sketches virtually every street and building in Batavia, and his description of Javan flora and fauna ranks among the most detailed available in the seventeenth century. He apparently had little to do apart from his writing during the three years he lived independently in Batavia. The many plates in the volume are exceedingly good.

Jeremias van Vliet's *Description of the Kingdom of Siam* appeared in Dutch in 1692, but it was not an up-to-date report.[446] He had arrived at Ayut'ia in 1633 and he was director of the VOC factory from 1636 to 1641. He wrote his description in 1637 or 1638 just before he made a trip to Batavia to present it to his superiors there. In Europe, it had first appeared as a supplement to Abraham de Wicquefort's French translation of Thomas Herbert's *Relation* (Paris, 1663).[447] Van Vliet depended heavily on Joost Schouten, his predecessor at Ayut'ia, whose report he said was so well written "that almost nothing was left for his successors to do."[448] Indeed large parts of Van Vliet's book are condensations of Schouten's, and some passages were directly taken from it. But Van Vliet added appreciably to Europe's knowledge of Siam nonetheless. His book is a fairly good report on developments during the early years of Prasat Thong's reign, both within Siam and in the relations between Siam and Cambodia, Patani, Japan, China, and Acheh. He includes some historical background for these events as well. In fact Van Vliet's account of Siamese government is considerably more complete than Schouten's. So too is his account of the Japanese mercenaries in Siam.[449] There was but one Dutch edition of Van Vliet's book during the seventeenth century. Bound with it were Dutch translations of two contemporary French reports on Siam: Desfarges, *Relation des revolutions de Siam de 1688* (Amsterdam, 1691) and Pierre Joseph d'Orléans, *Histoire de Mons. Constance, premier ministre du roi de Siam* (Paris, 1692).[450]

A very interesting collection of information about northeast Asia appeared at Amsterdam in 1692 as part of Nicolaas Witsen's *Noord en Oost Tartarye*. As a twenty-three-year-old, regent-class young man, just graduated from Leyden University, Witsen (1641–1717) had traveled to Moscow with Dutch ambassador Jacob Borell in 1664–65. Even before he went to Russia he had become interested in the East. He carried with him a series of questions put to him by the Leyden orientalist Jacob Golius and carefully noted answers to them while in Russia. He took copious notes on what he saw and

[446] *Beschryving van het koningryk Siam . . .* (Leyden).

[447] An English translation of the 1663 French version is included in *Selected Articles from the Siam Society Journal*, VII (1959), 31–90. Also see Smith, *op. cit.* (n. 428), pp. 126–27.

[448] Van Vliet, *op. cit.* (n. 446), p. 2.

[449] *Ibid.*, pp. 43–46.

[450] For bibliography see Tiele, *op. cit.* (n. 359), p. 255. Also see above, pp. 425–26, and below, p. 1196.

heard; he talked with and sketched a Tartar, a Samoyed, a Kalmuk, and a Persian.[451] He apparently continued to collect information about Asia in subsequent years, and as a *burgemeester* of Amsterdam, one of Holland's most influential political leaders, and a director of the VOC he was in a good position to do so. He assisted several travelers, and several travel accounts were dedicated to him.[452]

Witsen's *Noord en Oost Tartarye* is therefore a composite work, and none of the material in it on Asia derives from the author's firsthand observations. He talked with people who had traveled with Fedor Baikov's overland journey from Moscow to Peking in 1653. He had Baikov's journal and he translated it into German in 1699. He used Martini as his source for information about the Mongols, Manchus, and north China, and he included an account of the Manchu conquest taken from Martini's *De bello tartarico*. His information about Korea was based on Hamel, and his discussion of Hokkaido came from Martin Gerritszoon Vries' journal. Witsen also included a description of the Australian discoveries, apparently taken from Tasman's unpublished journal. The maps in *Noord en Oost Tartarye*, however, appear to have been done by Witsen himself. A second edition of *Noord en Oost Tartarye* appeared in 1705 which included Baikov's journal. A third edition was published in 1785.

A new, firsthand description of parts of the Coromandel Coast and the "Kingdom of Golconda" appeared in 1693, written by Daniel Havart, a physician who had served VOC establishments there from about 1674 to 1686.[453] Perhaps the greatest value of Havart's book is as source material for VOC personnel and their lives in India during those years. He lists the names, wives, and children, and sketches the careers, of every director, assistant director, special ambassador, and clergyman who served in any Dutch factory on the Coromandel Coast. He describes their weddings if they had been married there and their deaths, where they were buried, and what was inscribed on their tombstones.

But Havart also wrote valuable descriptions of the places he had visited, particularly in Golconda. He reports in detail on the overland routes to its capital city. Havart describes the court and government, and sketches the political history and the lives of its rulers down to 1687 when Aurangzib removed the last sultan from the throne.[454] Havart also comments on products and trade; he provides particularly detailed descriptions of the production of indigo and saltpeter.[455] Interesting too are Havart's accounts of two

---

[451] Th. J. G. Locher and P. de Buck (eds.) *Moscovische reyse, 1664–1665 Journael en aentekeningen* (3 vols.; "WLV," LXVI, LXVII, LXVIII; The Hague, 1966–67), I, xlviii–liii.

[452] For his life see J. F. Gebhard, *Het leven van Mr. Nicolaas Cornelisz. Witsen (1641–1717)* (2 vols.; Utrecht, 1881).

[453] *Op- en ondergang van Cormandel . . .* (3 vols.; Amsterdam).

[454] *Ibid.*, II, 204–41.

[455] *Ibid.*, II, 19–26; III, 51–54.

Dutch embassies to the court of Golconda, that of Pieter Smith in 1671, and of Laurens Pitt in 1686.[456] There appear to have been no other editions of Havart's book.

Jacob Janssen de Roy's book, which probably appeared in 1698 or 1699, is an extended apologia written to the governor-general and council at Batavia by a skipper who had lost his ship on the coast of Borneo in February, 1692, as a result of the mutiny of his largely Chinese and Javan crew.[457] He and his shipmates barely survived hunger, thirst, exposure, hostile natives, and treachery before receiving good treatment and protection from the king of Banjarmasin in return for military assistance. If De Roy's account is accurate, he worked successfully to gain a preferential trading position in Banjarmasin for the VOC, but his letters to Batavia depicting the prospects of such a trade and asking for Dutch ships and gifts to the king were never received or at least never answered.[458] Later he learned that he had been declared an outlaw for absconding with the ship's money, which he indeed had taken ashore and buried in the sand on the day of the mutiny. For the following six years De Roy became a free adventurer and trader in Borneo, Acheh, and Siam, using the ship's money to purchase a sloop and his first cargo. By the end of that time he had amassed a sizable fortune, had been hired by the king of Siam to drive an English pirate out of Siamese waters, and had refused a French offer to serve their cause in Asia as François Caron had done.[459] He finally turned himself in at the VOC factory in Hugli, Bengal, and was conveyed to Batavia.[460] We never learn his fate; the story ends with the submission of his tale to the governor-general.

Obviously De Roy had good reason to distort or embellish his story, and some of his misadventures and heroics indeed strain the reader's credulity. But his descriptions of Borneo and Acheh contain a substratum of truth, even if De Roy too easily found gold in the rivers, diamonds in the hills, and rulers overly anxious to ally with the Dutch. De Roy's book appeared again in 1706 and was translated into German in 1705.[461]

Two accounts of Evert Ysbrandszoon Ides' 1692–95 journey overland from Moscow to Peking appeared around the turn of the century. One was written by Adam Brand, the embassy's secretary, and was published in 1699.[462] It had originally been written in German, however, and a German edition had appeared in 1698. In fact, an English translation also appeared in

---

[456] *Ibid.*, II. 119–64.

[457] *Voyagie gedaan door Jacob Janssen de Roy na Borneo en Atchen, in't jaar 1691 en vorvolgens:* . . . *Gedrukt volgens de copy van Batavia* . . . (n.p., n.d.).

[458] *Ibid.*, pp. 61–66, 68–72, 79.

[459] *Ibid.*, pp. 134–38.

[460] *Ibid.*, pp. 150–53.

[461] See Tiele, *op. cit.* (n. 359), p. 208.

[462] *Seer aenmerklijcke land en water-reys onlanghs gedaen van't gesantschap syn Czaarsche majestijt uyt Muscouw na China* . . . (Utrecht).

1698 and a French in 1699.[463] Ides' own account of the embassy first appeared in 1704.[464] It was translated into English in 1706 and into German in 1707. Another Dutch edition appeared in 1710.

Ides, born in Glückstadt, entered the tsar's service in 1691 and was his ambassador to China from 1692 to 1695. After his return from China he apparently remained in Russia, although he exchanged letters with Nicolaas Witsen and his book was published in Amsterdam. The embassy left Moscow in March, 1692, and arrived in Peking late in October, 1693. Ides' descriptions of the places and people he saw along the way are unusually good, and through them his readers first encountered several tribes in eastern Siberia and Mongolia. He also wrote vivid, detailed descriptions of the Great Wall, of his reception by officials there, of his introduction to Peking, the banquets and entertainments he attended, the imperial palace and the K'ang-hsi emperor himself. Appended to Ides' journal is a brief description of China attributed to a Chinese Christian named Dionysius Kao.[465] Like the Jesuit descriptions it treats each province, including Liaotung, separately before describing in general the people, their customs, their religions, the land, its fruits, neighboring countries, and recent history. Considerable space is devoted to the history of Christianity in China, and the book ends with an adulatory description of the K'ang-hsi emperor and expressions of optimism regarding his and China's conversion to Christianity.[466] Jesuit influence on the writer is quite pronounced.

A report on the last serious attempt by the VOC to explore Australia was published in 1701.[467] The expedition, organized principally by Nicolaas Witsen and commanded by Willem Hesselszoon de Vlamingh (b. 1640), left Amsterdam in 1696. It visited Tristão da Cunha Island in the south Atlantic, and New Amsterdam and St. Paul Islands in the south Indian Ocean, and explored the west coast of Australia from about 34° south to 20° south while the crew charted the coast and made several forays inland to assess the commercial potential of the land. The results were disappointing, apart from the charts, which are very good. De Vlamingh found no trace of gold, precious stones, spices, or fruitful areas for colonization.[468] Even the author's descriptions of the Southland are disappointing. He comments on the abundance of fish, on the unusual flora, and on the black swans, two of which he took

---

[463] For bibliography see Tiele, *op. cit.* (n. 359), p. 47. See below, p. 543, for a discussion of Brand's book.

[464] *Driejaarige reize naar China, te lande gedaan door den Moscovischen afgezant. E. Ysbrants Ides . . . hier is bygevoegt eene beknopte beschryvinge van China, door eenen Chineeschen schryver t'zamengestelt; . . .* (Amsterdam).

[465] Ides, *Three Years Travels from Moscow Overland to China . . .* (London, 1706), pp. 115–210.

[466] *Ibid.*, pp. 205–10.

[467] *Journael wegens een voyagie, gedaan op order der Hollandsche Oost-Indische Maatschappy in de jaaren 1696 en 1697 . . . na het onbekende Zuid-land, en wijders na Batavia* (Amsterdam).

[468] G. G. Schilder (ed.), *De ontdekkingsreis van Willem Hesselsz. de Vlamingh in de jaren 1696–1697* (2 vols.; "WLV," LXXVIII–LXXIX; The Hague, 1976), I, 131–33.

back to Europe,[469] but for the most part he describes an inhospitable, sandy, and rocky coast. They continually saw footprints, fires, and miserable huts, but only once did they spy a few naked black men fleeing from them.[470] Meanwhile their travel ashore was constantly impeded by dense brush, flies, blowing sand, and sore eyes. They left without regret. Witsen was unhappy with the results of the expedition and thought more would have been accomplished if De Vlamingh had not been drunk so frequently and had been willing to make longer trips ashore.[471] The journal attracted little attention. There was apparently but one edition, and it was bound with the second edition of a translation of the *Histoire des Sevarambes,* a totally fictitious description of the Southland.[472]

Much richer in descriptions was Nikolaas de Graaf's *Reisen,* also published in 1701.[473] This durable ship's surgeon enjoyed one of the longest seafaring careers on record. Between 1639 and 1687 he made sixteen voyages to almost every part of the globe. He was apparently a competent surgeon, popular with the other officers, observant and knowledgeable about the world around him. A witty and congenial companion, he was always in on the party, always ready for a new adventure. In forty-eight years of traveling he saw a great deal. He was at the siege of Malacca in 1640;[474] he attended a royal funeral in Acheh in 1644;[475] he visited Japan and in 1684 was on one of the few VOC ships to trade at Canton.[476] He even toured Macao as a guest of the captain-general in return for treating the wife of a high official.[477] In 1670 and '71 he traveled up the Ganges from Hugli to Soepra and back, was imprisoned by Mughul officials in Monghyr for seven weeks, went sightseeing disguised as a Moor, and witnessed a terrible famine in Soepra.[478] He attended a royal wedding feast in Bantam.[479] In 1685 the sixty-four-year-old De Graaf regretfully declined the offer to accompany the Paets and De Keyser embassy to Peking because his skipper was ready to sail for Bengal on the following day. He nevertheless included a brief description of China in his book, taken from Nieuhof.[480]

Somewhat out of character, he added an appendix to his *Reisen* called the *Oost-Indise spiegel,* in which he describes the pampered, luxurious, and offensively haughty life of Dutch women in the Indies, the growing decadence and venality of Dutch society there, and the enormous volume of pri-

[469] *Ibid.,* II, 209–12.
[470] *Ibid.,* p. 215.   [471] *Ibid.,* I, 131.
[472] Denis Vairasse, *Historie der Sevarambes, volkeren die een gedeelte van het derde vast-land bewoonen, gemeenlyk Zuid-land genaamd . . . ,* translated by Gotfried Broekhuyzen (Amsterdam, 1701). See Schilder (ed.), *op. cit.* (n. 111), I, 98–110.
[473] *Reisen van Nicolaus de Graaf na de vier gedeeltens des werelds, als Asia, Africa, America en Europa* (Hoorn).
[474] J. C. M. Warnsinck (ed.), *Reisen van Nicolaus de Graaf, gedaan naar alle gewesten des werelds beginnende 1639 tot 1687 incluis . . .* ("WLV," XXXIII; The Hague, 1930), pp. 9–12.
[475] *Ibid.,* pp. 13–14.   [478] *Ibid.,* pp. 108–30.
[476] *Ibid.,* pp. 174–80.   [479] *Ibid.,* pp. 192–93.
[477] *Ibid.,* pp. 180–81.   [480] *Ibid.,* pp. 185–86.

vate trade carried on by VOC officials on VOC ships.[481] He describes ships so laden with private goods that Company goods are not properly stored and the ships not able to maneuver properly; captains whose main concern is to save their own and their fellows' goods at the expense of the Company; and the regular bribery of VOC officials at Batavia to look the other way while the private goods are unloaded. In 1683, he reported, the "Little Company" as it was called, enjoyed a greater trade than the VOC on the annual Japan voyage. The *Spiegel* provides a revealing picture of the declining state of the Dutch East Indies at the end of the century, reminiscent of Linschoten's description of the decaying Portuguese empire at the end of the sixteenth century. De Graaf's *Reisen* with the *Spiegel* was reissued again in 1704 and translated into French in 1719.

The number of translations from foreign works on Asia compared to new Dutch publications during the last two decades of the century may be another indication of the decadence in the VOC. On the other hand, it also indicates a continuing vigorous interest in Asia on the part of Dutch publishers and readers. Most of the new translations were from French works. For example, J. H. Glazemaker translated Jean Baptiste Tavernier's *Voyages* in 1682.[482] Gottfried van Broekhuysen translated several important French works during the next decade, among them Jean de Thévenot's *Relations,* Guy Tachard's *Voyage de Siam,* Jean Chardin's *Journal,* and Alexandre de Chaumont's *Relation de l'ambassade.*[483] Gabriel Dellon's *Relation d'un voyage* appeared in a Dutch edition, 1687,[484] and a Dutch translation of Philippe Avril's *Voyages* appeared in 1694.[485] At Antwerp, Philippe Couplet's *Histoire d'une dame chrétienne de la Chine* appeared in Dutch in 1694, and Jean-Baptiste de Maldonado's Latin account of João de Britto was published in 1697.[486]

Before the end of the century Louis le Comte's work on China, Joachim Bouvet's biography of the K'ang-hsi emperor, and John Fryer's description of India were also translated into Dutch.[487] As the list of names indicates, France, rather than the United Provinces, was becoming Europe's major entrepôt for information about the East during the last two decades of the century.

★

[481] *Oost-Indise spiegel, behelsende een beschrijving van de stad Batavia, en wijse van leven der hollandse vrouwen in Oost-Indien,* . . . (Hoorn, 1701).

[482] *De sez reizen* . . . (2 vols.; Amsterdam).

[483] Jean de Thévenot, *Gedenkwaerdige en zeer naauwkeurige reizen* . . . (3 vols.; Amsterdam, 1681–88); Guy Tachard, *Reis van Siam* . . . (Utrecht, 1687); Jean Chardin, *Dagverhaal der reis.* . . . (Amsterdam, 1687); Alexandre de Chaumont, *Verhaal van het gezantschap* . . . *aan het hof des konings van Siam* . . . (Amsterdam, 1687).

[484] *Naauwkeurig verhaal van een reyse door Indien gedaen* . . . (Utrecht, 1687).

[485] *Reize door verscheidene staaten van Europa, en Asia* . . . (Utrecht, 1694).

[486] *Historie van een groote Christene Mevrouwe van China* . . . (Antwerp, 1694); *Illustre certamen R. P. Joannis de Britto* . . . (Antwerp, 1697).

[487] Louis le Comte, *Beschryvinge van het machtige keyserryk China* . . . (The Hague, 1698); Joachim Bouvet, *'t Leven en bedrijf van den tegenwoordigen keizer van China* . . . (Utrecht, 1699); John Fryer, *Negenjaarige reyse door Oost-Indien en Persien* (The Hague, 1700).

Fin de siècle: Decline

In the early years of the century, imprints about Dutch activities in the East Indies spilled in a steady stream from the presses of Amsterdam and other northern Netherlandish cities. The Dutch made no secret about their fleets, routes, and Asian markets; in fact, they published newssheets in the 1620's announcing the triumphs and setbacks of their expeditions. Reports of the individual voyages were numerous and very popular. Most of them went through many editions and translations, and many were published in the collections of De Bry, Hulsius, and Purchas. The circumnavigations of Van Noort (1598), Van Spilbergen (1614–17), Le Maire and Schouten (1615–17), and L'Hermite (1623–26) were celebrated in many publications as victories over the Spanish in the Pacific. Translations of these triumphant works were published in the United Provinces and southern Germany for circulation in other parts of western Europe.

Until 1630 the great continental states of Asia were known to the Dutch only at second hand, through earlier foreign publications, or through the Jesuit letters, letterbooks, and histories intermittently published at Antwerp. Around 1630, however, there began to appear eyewitness reports by Dutch merchants about India, Southeast Asia, China, and Japan. Some, such as Joost Schouten's description of Siam (1638) and Caron's account of Japan (1645), became exceedingly important in shaping Europe's image of Asia.

Commelin's *Begin ende voortgangh* (1645–46), the most important Dutch collection to appear in the seventeenth century, contains reports on twenty-one voyages as well as a host of inserts from other published works and from the records of the VOC. Included also are reprints and additional commentary on all the earlier Dutch circumnavigations. It provides a summary coverage of Dutch activities in the East Indies, India, and Japan. It was pillaged and extended for the subsequent collections of Hartgers and Saeghman.

Commelin's collection seemingly opened the floodgates to an outpouring of new publications. For south India and Ceylon, where the Dutch entrenched themselves in the 1650's and 1660's, a rich documentation was published, which included such outstanding publications as Roger's sensitive work on Hinduism and Van Rheede tot Drakestein's magnificent twelve folio volumes on Malabar flora. While Dutch merchants and observers were initially unable to penetrate China, educated Dutch readers had ready access to Martini's fundamental works on the Manchu conquest, and on China's geography and history, all of which were published in Amsterdam during the 1650's. These were followed by the more popular books of Nieuhof (1665) and Dapper (1670), which combined much of the information found in the works of Martini and his Jesuit predecessors with firsthand observations of the Dutch embassies to Peking to form lavishly illustrated compendia on the Middle Kingdom. Kircher's influential *China illustrata* (1667) was also published in Amsterdam. Fresh information about Japan after its closure became available in publications such as Montanus' *Gedenkwaerdige gesantschappen*

(1669). Witsen's *Noord en Oost Tartarye* (1692) contained a similar collection of information provided by those who followed the land route to China via Siberia. Horizons were further broadened during the latter half of the century by firsthand Dutch descriptions of the Ainu of Hokkaido, Mataram and Java's interior, Korea, Cambodia and Laos, Australia, and the insular world of the southwest Pacific. Several of these reports provided European readers with their first glimpses into parts of Asia previously known only by secondhand report, if at all.

Throughout the century, Dutch and Flemish publishers and printers reprinted older works on Asia and quickly translated most of the important contemporary works into various European languages. Many of these publications appeared in editions richly illustrated with maps and engravings of Asian places, peoples, and plants. While some of these depictions were drawn from the imagination, most were based on sketches which ranged from amateurish and impressionistic to professional and scientific. Netherlandish publications were widely circulated in northwestern Europe in both Latin and vernacular versions during the Golden Age of Dutch printing. Indeed, through much of the century the Netherlands served as Europe's primary entrepôt for information about Asia. By century's end, however, Dutch presses were printing more translations of French reports than original Dutch contributions.

CHAPTER VII

The German and Danish Literature

Germany in the latter half of the sixteenth century went through a period of slow recovery and uneasy peace after the wars of the Reformation.[1] Divided internally by religion, its numerous political units tended to cling to old privileges and practices and to resist changes which might produce new civil hostilities. Economically, Germany remained parochial except on its western and northern fringes. While modern national economies were being created in France, the Netherlands, and England, Germany remained the backyard of the emerging Atlantic world and was cut off from eastern European trade by the Ottoman Empire. The Danes were far more involved in nation-building and in colonial ventures than their German neighbors. Germans played no significant role in the colonial enterprises until several decades after the end of the Thirty Years' War in 1648. While the German economy never came to a complete standstill it remained internalized and stagnant. Its market cities and its many administrative centers, except for Nuremberg, Strassburg, and Frankfurt, were heavily and permanently damaged by the Thirty Years' War. During the latter half of the seventeenth century, however, Germany was flooded with foreign products, including books and other luxury goods produced in the Netherlands and France.

Within this economic inland, Frankfurt-on-the-Main remained an ideal distribution center of goods and money for a substantial part of central Europe. After the decline of Antwerp, it was tied economically and financially to Amsterdam. Its spring and autumn trade fairs, especially its book fairs, attracted merchants from all over Europe and gave to Frankfurt its reputation as "the German Athens." The Saxon "territorial city" of Leipzig had

[1] Cf. *Asia*, II, Bk. 2, pp. 59–62, 342–43.

declined as a book mart during the Reformation; by 1600 it had regained strength and in the seventeenth century its book fairs rivaled those of Frankfurt except during the period of disruption produced by the Thirty Years' War.[2] Although many of the books displayed at these fairs were from foreign presses, the printers of the German-speaking lands operated presses of their own in more than two hundred towns and cities in the sixteenth and seventeenth centuries.[3] Many of their products were poorly printed translations and reprints in cheap German editions for sale to a public with little extra cash to spare for books. A few publishers like the De Brys of Frankfurt issued series of works in Latin for the educated public and the international markets.

I

JESUIT LETTERBOOKS AND RELATIONS TO MID-CENTURY

As the century began, the Catholic presses of south Germany ran off numerous Latin and German editions of the Jesuit letters from Asia. Most of these came from the presses of Johann Albin and his widow (to 1621) at Mainz, of Johann Mayer and his widow (to 1619) at Dillingen, and of Adam Berg and his widow (to 1629) at Munich.[4] Chrysostom Dabertzhofer, once an associate of the famous Augsburg publishing house called "Ad insigne Pinus," printed no fewer than seven Jesuit letterbooks when he went into business for himself between 1611 and 1614.[5]

In 1601 Albin published in Latin a collection of Jesuit letters reporting on conditions in China, the Mughul Empire, and Japan.[6] In the same year there appeared Nicolas Pimenta's letter of 1598 and 1599 on Christian activities in the East Indies;[7] his similar letter of 1600 was printed in 1602.[8] A report on conditions in Japan after Hideyoshi's death was translated into Latin from Italian in 1603 and likewise published at Mainz.[9] Another of Pimenta's reportorial letters appeared at Constance in 1603.[10] Francisco Vaez's letter from the Philippines was translated from Italian and published at Mainz in

---

[2] See H. Widmann, "Geschichte des deutschen Buchhandels," in H. Hiller and W. Strauss (eds.), *Der deutsche Buchhandel* (Munich, 1961), pp. 29–32.

[3] See the list in J. Benzing, *Die Buchdrucker des 16. und 17. Jahrhunderts im deutschen Sprachgebiet* (2d rev. ed.; Wiesbaden, 1982).

[4] *Ibid.*, pp. 83, 318, 335.

[5] *Ibid.*, p. 21.

[6] *Recentissimas de amplissimo regno Chinae.* . . . For bibliographical details see Streit, V, 11. For fuller data on the Jesuit letters and letterbooks see list below, beginning on p. 1983.

[7] *Nova relatio historica.* . . . See Streit, V, 373–74.

[8] *Exemplum epistolae . . . de statu rei Christianae in India orientali.* . . . See Streit, V, 15.

[9] *De rebus in Japoniae regno post mortem Taicosamae Japonici monarchae gestis.* . . . See Streit, V, 373–74.

[10] *De felici statu et progressu rei christianae in India orientali.* . . . See Streit, V, 17.

1604.[11] Letters from Jesuit missionaries in China, Japan, and the Moluccas appeared at Mainz in 1607,[12] and an Annual Letter was printed at Dillingen in 1609.[13] None of these Latin letterbooks appears to have been translated into German.

Many other Jesuit letters were translated into German. Francesco Pasio's Latin letter of 1598 appeared in German translation in 1601.[14] A German translation of letters by Alessandro Valignano and Valentim Carvalho written in Italian from Japan appeared at Mainz in 1603.[15] In Munich, Aegidius Albertinus, Duke Maxmilian's librarian and secretary, translated several new Jesuit letters into German. In 1607 he had issued Bishop Luis de Cerqueira's Spanish report on the persecutions in Japan,[16] and in the following year Diego de Pantoja's Italian letter from Peking.[17] Albertinus translated still another collection of letters from the Jesuits in Japan that was printed in 1609.[18]

Francesco Pasio's letters from Japan for 1603–6 were translated into Latin and published at Mainz in 1610.[19] Chrysostom Dabertzhofer in his shop at Augsburg printed in 1611 a translation of Portuguese reports from Pegu, Bengal, and Vijayanagar,[20] a brief report of the baptism of three young Mughul courtiers and news of Spanish successes in the Moluccas,[21] a collection of Jesuit letters from Japan, Mexico, and India,[22] a translation of a new Italian report on Christian martyrs in Japan,[23] and a translation from the

---

[11] *Litterae annuae insularum Philippinarum.* . . . See Streit, V, 247.

[12] *Litterae societatis Iesu, anno MDCII. et MDCIII., e Sinis, Molucis, Iapone datae.* See Streit, V, 40.

[13] Reported in Ternaux-Compans, p. 117.

[14] *Newe historische Relation, und sehr gute fröliche und lustige Bottschaft was sich in vilen gewaltigen Königreichen der Orientalischen Indien wie auch in dem mächtigen Königreich China und bey dem grossen König Mogor* . . . (Dillingen, 1601). Ternaux-Compans reports another edition in 1602, but Streit (V, 10–11) doubts its existence.

[15] *Zwey japponische Sendtschreiben.* . . . See Streit, V, 373.

[16] *Historische Relation von sechs adelichen Christen Mann und Weibspersonnen so in Japon in Königreich Fingo* . . . *anno 1603, theils enthaupt und theils gekreutziget worden* . . . (Dillingen). It was also published at Münster in 1607. See Streit, V, 384.

[17] *Historische und eigentliche Beschreibung erstlich was gestalt* . . . *in dem grossen und gewaltigen Königreich China eingeführt gepflantzt und geprediget wird* . . . (Munich, 1608). See Streit, V, 696–97.

[18] *Historische Relation was sich inn etlichen Jaren hero im Königreich Japan,* . . . (Munich). See Streit, V, 47–48. Ternaux-Compans reports a 1604 Ingolstadt edition, but Streit (V, 48) doubts its existence.

[19] *Relatio historica in Japoniae regno gestarum, anno domini 1603. 1604. 1605. et parte 1606.* . . . See Streit, V, 389. The first Italian edition was published in 1608.

[20] *Indianische Relation was sich in den Königreichen Pegu, Bengala, Bisznaga, und etliche andern Ländern der gegen Auffgang gelegen Indien von 1604,* . . . (1611). Not listed in Streit.

[21] *Drey merkliche Relationes. Erste von der Victori Sigismundi III* . . . *uber der Moscuwiter* . . . *Andere von beförung und Tauff dreyer Junger Herren und Vettern* . . . *Dritte. Wie die Insul und Königreich Ternate in ihr. Mag. Königs in Spanien Namen den Moren und Holländern wiederumb sighafft abgetrungen* (1611). See Streit, V, 62.

[22] *Drey newe Relationes. Erste ausz Japon* . . . *Andere, von Missionibus oder Reisen* . . . *in das Königreich Mexico* . . . *Dritte, von Anbleiben desz mächtigen Königs Mogor* . . . (1611). See Streit, V, 62–63.

[23] *New historischer Bericht wellicher Massen etliche Christen in Japon* . . . (1611). The *Relationi della gloriosa morte* first appeared in Rome, 1611. See Streit, V, 391.

Portuguese of the 1607 China letters from Fernão Guerreiro's compilation.[24] In 1612 Dabertzhofer published Gregorio López' report from the Philippines, first published in Italian in 1611,[25] and in 1614 he published a translation of another letter extracted from Guerreiro.[26]

Pierre Du Jarric's 1608 report on the state of Jesuit missions in Asia was translated into Latin at Cologne in 1615.[27] A German edition of Horatio Tursellinus' life of Francis Xavier was published at Munich in 1615.[28] Nicolas Trigault's collection of Japan letters for the years 1609–12 was published together in Latin at Augsburg in 1615,[29] as were his 1610–11 letters from China.[30] More news about the Christian martyrs in Japan was translated into German at Ingolstadt in 1615.[31] Also in 1615 Andreas Schott produced at Augsburg a Latin translation of João Rodrigues Girão's Italian letters from China and Japan, 1609 and 1610.[32]

Trigault is best known for the *De christiana expeditione apud Sinas,* also first published at Augsburg in 1615.[33] It became the most influential description of China to appear during the first half of the seventeenth century. Trigault, the procurator of the Jesuits' China mission, translated and augmented the pioneer missionary Matteo Ricci's journal, aiming to elicit support for the mission. The *De christiana expeditione,* therefore, is essentially a translation of Ricci's Italian journal. Trigault, however, did not merely translate the journal; he omitted or changed many passages, rearranged its parts, and added material from other China missionaries to complete the story and to depict China and the Jesuit mission in a more favorable light.[34] The resulting

[24] *Historischer Bericht was sich in dem grossen unnd nun je lenger je mehr bekandten Königreich China . . .* (1611). See Streit, V, 704.

[25] *Summarischer Bericht was sich in den Philippinischen Insulen, im Jahr Christi 1608. . . .* See Streit, V, 257.

[26] *Indianische newe Relation, Erster Theil: was sich in der Goanischen Provintz unnd in der Mission Monomatapa Mogor, auch in der Provintz Cochin, Malabaria, China, Pegu, unnd Maluco. . . .* See Streit, V, 70.

[27] *Thesaurus rerum indicarum.* The first French edition was printed at Bordeaux in 1608. See Streit, V, 44, 73.

[28] *Vom tugentreichen Leben und grossen Wunderthaten B. Francisci Xaverii der Societet Iesu, . . . Sechs Bücher,* trans. Martin Hueber Chorherrn. The first Latin edition was in 1594. See Streit, V, 74.

[29] *Rei Christianae apud Japonios commentarius ex litteris annuis Societatis Jesu annorum 1609. 1610. 1611. 1612 collectus. . . .* See Streit, V, 406.

[30] *Litterae Societatis Jesu e regno Sinarum . . . annorum MDCX & XI.* See Streit, V, 716. First Italian edition, Rome, 1615. See Streit, V, 715.

[31] *Frische historische Relation von Mann und Weibspersonen so in Japon . . . den 17. Nov. 1608, den 11. Jan. und 14. Nov. 1609 gemartet worden. . . .* See Streit, V, 407.

[32] *Litterae japonicae et sinicae, annorum 1609 et 1610. . . .* The first Italian edition was published at Rome, 1615. See Streit, V, 401–5.

[33] *De christiana expeditione apud Sinas suscepta ab Societate Jesu. Ex P. Matthaei Ricci . . . commentariis. Libri V . . . in quibus sinensis regni mores, leges, atque instituta & nova illius ecclesiae difficillima primordia . . . describuntur.*

[34] For the original text of Ricci's journal see Pasquale M. d'Elia (ed.), *Storia dell' introduzione del Cristianesimo in Cina,* Vols. I–III of *Fonti Ricciane* (Rome, 1942–49). No unexpurgated version of Ricci's *Storia* appeared during the seventeenth century, and although the preface of the *De christiana expeditione* contains a disclaimer, its authorship was generally credited to Trigault

volume contains a history of the Jesuit mission in China from its inception in 1583 until Ricci's death in 1610, the same year in which Trigault arrived in China. It includes a wealth of information about China in the chapters which recount the history of the mission, prefaced by eleven chapters describing Chinese geography, people, laws, government, religion, learning, commerce, and the like. The *De christiana expeditione,* despite its departures from Ricci's original journal, provided European readers with more, better organized, and more accurate information about China than was ever before available.

Trigault's book appeared in four more Latin editions after 1615. It was translated into German in 1617.[35] The first eleven chapters were published in Leyden as part of the Elzevier "Res publicae" series in 1639. Three French editions as well as a Spanish and an Italian translation appeared during the first half of the century,[36] and excerpts from it appeared in *Purchas, His Pilgrimes* (1625). It was almost universally cited by scholars who mentioned China, and it was regularly pilfered by later authors and publishers.[37]

Also among the mission publications of the century's first decades, the Franciscan Scipione Amati's 1615 report of Oshu in Japan was translated into German at Ingolstadt in 1617.[38] Of the early German missionary publications only Amati's treatise and Trigault's *De christiana expeditione* conveyed new information about Asia not previously published in Europe.

Whether because the Thirty Years' War distracted both publishers and readers from any interest in outside affairs, or for some other less obvious reason, far fewer reports from Asia were published in the German lands between 1620 and 1650 than had been published during the first two decades of the century. Jesuit reports, both in Latin and German, continued to appear, although in declining numbers. Most of these were published during the twenties. A collection of letters reporting on Giacomo Rho, Giovanni Gayati, and Nicolas Trigault's 1618 voyage to India and China and the state of the mission there was translated into German from Italian and French and published at Augsburg in 1620.[39] A separate Latin letter from Trigault describing his return to China and reporting news from the Chinese and Japa-

---

until well into the twentieth century. For a detailed study of the role of the editor, see T. N. Foss, "Nicholas Trigault, S.J.—Amanuensis or Propagandist?" in *International Symposium on Chinese-Western Cultural Interchange . . .* (Taipei, 1983), Supplement, pp. 1–94. Also see J. Spence, "Reflections on Matteo Ricci," in *China and Europe, Sixteenth to Eighteenth Centuries* (International Symposium, Hong Kong, 1987).

[35] *Historie von Einführung der Christlichen Religion in dasz grosze Königreich China . . .* (Augsburg). See Streit, V, 720–21.

[36] See Streit, V, 716–17.

[37] For this volume we have used the modern English translation by Louis J. Gallagher: *China in the Sixteenth Century: The Journals of Matthew Ricci* (New York, 1935). Gallagher's translation is of Trigault's *De christiana expeditione* with all its errors and emendations; it is not a translation of Ricci's original *La storia.*

[38] *Relation und gründtlicher Bericht von desz Königreichs Voxu in japonischen Keyserthumb. . . .* See Streit, V, 417–18.

[39] *Indianische Raisz von dreyen ehrwürdigen Priestern der Societet Jesu; . . .* See Streit, V, 83.

nese church was published at Cologne in 1620, but was not translated into German.[40] Father Wenceslaus Kirwitzer's description of the comets he observed on the way to China in 1618 appeared in 1621.[41] It was published by Balthasar Lipp at Aschaffenburg, where the Jesuits had set up a school the year before.[42]

A report from Jesuit missionaries in Japan and the Philippines was published in German at Augsburg in 1621. It had been translated from the Spanish.[43] In 1622 the same Augsburg publisher, Sara Mang, brought out a German translation of Rho's 1621 letter describing the state of the Asian missions translated from the first Italian edition of 1620.[44]

Trigault's lengthy report on the persecution of Christians in Japan between 1612 and 1620 appeared in Latin at Munich in 1623, but again there seems to have been no German translation.[45] Antonio de Andrade's account of his seven-month journey in 1624 from Agra to Tibet and back, containing descriptions of Tibet and Lamaism, appeared in German translation at Augsburg in 1627.[46] It was translated from the Spanish edition of 1627, which in turn was translated from the original Portuguese edition of 1626.[47] Latin translations of a collection of letters on the persecutions in Japan from Trigault and others appeared in 1627, and a report on Japan from João Rodrigues Girão was published at Mainz in 1628.[48] There appears to be no German edition of Trigault's collection, but Rodrigues' work was translated from the Italian rather than the Latin edition and published in German at Dillingen in 1628.[49] Finally, a German translation of Christoforo Borri's popular description of Cochin-China was published at Vienna in 1633.[50]

---

[40] *Epistola R. P. Nicolai Trigautii e Societate Jesu de felici sua in Indiam navigatione: itemque de statu rei Christianae apud Sinas & Iaponios.* See Streit, V, 82.

[41] *Observationes cometarum anni 1618 factae in India Orientale a quibusdam Soc. Jesu, mathematicis in Sinense regnum navigantibus.* See Streit, V, 736–37. On these comets of 1618 see G. W. Kronk, *Comets, A Descriptive Catalog* (Hillside, N.J., 1984), pp. 9–10.

[42] Benzing, *op. cit.* (n. 3), p. 11.

[43] *Kurtze Relation was inn den Königreich Iapon unnd China, in den Jahren 1618. 1619. und 1620. mit auszbreittung desz Christlichen Glaubens sich begeben . . . Darbey auch etwas Berichts was in den insuln Filippinen sich begeben. . . .* See Streit, V, 456.

[44] *Copia eines Schreibens von P. Jacobo Ro. . . . Ausz den orientalischen Indien, zu Goa, den 27. Februar 1621. datiert. . . . Allerlei Bericht von Japon, China, und India in kurtzem begriffen. . . .* See Streit, V, 94.

[45] Nicolas Trigault, *De christianis apud Iaponios triumphis, sive de gravissima ibidem contra Christi fidem persecutione exorta anno MDC XII usq. ad annum MDCXX. Libri quinq. . . .* See Streit, V, 463–64.

[46] *Beschreibung einer weiten ungefährliche Reisz. . . .* See Streit, V, 109–10. For a description of the journey and of the contents of Andrade's book see below, pp. 1773–83.

[47] See Streit, V, 107, 109.

[48] *De novis christianae religionis progressibus et certaminibus in Iaponia, anno M.DC.XXII. In regno Sinarum, M.DC.XXI. et. M.DC.XXII . . .* (Münster); Giovanni Roiz Giram, *Historia Iaponensis anni MDC.XXIV. continens felicem christianae fidei progressum . . . .* See Streit, V, 497 and 512–13.

[49] *Relation-Schreiben ausz Japon vom M.DC.XXIV Jahr. . . .* See Streit, V, 513.

[50] *Relation von dem newen Königreich Cocincina desz Ehrwürdigen Patris Christophori Borri. . . .* See Streit, V, 592.

The Italian original had been published in Rome just two years before. None of these Jesuit accounts was a German contribution to Europe's knowledge of Asia; they were either written in Latin and merely published at German presses or they were Latin or German translations of works originally written in other languages. Nevertheless, between 1633 and 1658 not even Latin editions or German translations of Jesuit reports appear to have been published in the German lands.

2

TRAVEL COLLECTIONS TO MID-CENTURY

Dutch descriptions of Asia's lands and peoples became available to German and Latin readers through the volumes of the De Bry and the Hulsius collections, both of which had been started during the last years of the sixteenth century.[51] The collection published in Frankfurt by Theodor de Bry (1525–98) and his family comprised two distinct series, called the *Petits voyages* and the *Grand voyages* because of their slightly different formats. The books dealing with Asia were part of the *Petits voyages,* or *India orientalis;* eight volumes of this series had appeared by the end of the first decade of the seventeenth century. Each volume appeared in Latin as well as German. Volume I (1597–98) contains descriptions of the African coast. The first forty-four chapters of Linschoten's *Itinerario* were published as Volume II in 1598 and 1599.[52] Volume III of *India orientalis* (German, 1599; Latin, 1601) contains chapters 92 to 99 of Linschoten's *Itinerario,* Willem Lodewyckszoon's account of Cornelis de Houtman's voyage, and Gerrit de Veer's account of the three Dutch attempts to find a northeastern passage.[53] The middle chapters (45 to 91) of the *Itinerario* appeared in Volume IV of the *India orientalis,* which also includes the last chapters of Lodewyckszoon's journal and a brief summary of the second Dutch East Indian voyage under Van Neck and Van Warwijck. The German version appeared in 1600; the Latin in 1601.[54] The

---

[51] On the collections see *Asia,* I, 216–17. For bibliographical details on the De Bry collection see A. C. Camus, *Mémoire sur la collection des Grands et Petits Voyages . . .* (Paris, 1802), and T. Weigel, *Bibliographische Mittheilungen über die deutschen Ausgaben von de Bry's Sammlungen der Reisen. . .* (Leipzig, 1845). For bibliographical details on the Hulsius collection see Adolph Asher, *Bibliographic Essay on the Collection of Voyages and Travels Edited and Published by Levinus Hulsius and His Successors at Nürnberg and Francfort from Anno 1598 to 1660* (Berlin, 1839). See also P. A. Tiele, *Mémoire bibliographique sur les journeaux des navigateurs néerlandais réimprimés dans les collections de de Bry et de Hulsius, et dans les collections Hollandaises du XVIIᵉ siècle, et sur les anciennes éditions Hollandaises des journeaux de navigateurs étrangers . . .* (Amsterdam, 1867).

[52] A second German edition appeared in 1613. For bibliographical details see Camus, *op. cit.* (n. 51), pp. 189–97.

[53] A second German edition appeared in 1616; additional Latin editions were published in 1601 and 1629. For bibliographical details see *ibid.,* pp. 197–208.

[54] A second German edition appeared at Oppenheim in 1617. For bibliography see *ibid.,* pp. 208–13.

complete account of the Van Neck and Van Warwijck expedition (1598–1600) appeared as Volume V of the De Bry series in both languages in 1601; this was a translation of *Het tweede boeck* (also published in Amsterdam, 1601).[55] Volume VII of the *India orientalis* contains the journal of Joris van Spilbergen's first voyage to the East Indies, especially to Ceylon, and Gasparo Balbi's earlier voyage to Pegu. The German edition was published in 1605, the Latin in 1607.[56] The eighth volume of the *India orientalis* (German, 1606; Latin, 1607) contains two reports of Jacob van Neck's second voyage, Roelof Roelofszoon's journal, and Cornelis Claeszoon's journal; two pieces about the voyage of Wybrand van Warwijck and Sebald de Weert, Jan Harmenszoon Bree's journal, and that of Cornelis van Veen; and the account of Steven van der Hagen's voyage.[57] Although translated from Dutch originals, none of the pieces in Volume VIII had been printed in Dutch prior to its inclusion in the De Bry series. In fact it appears that the earliest Dutch edition of Bree's account, that published in the *Begin ende voortgangh* (1645), may have been translated from the De Bry German edition.[58]

De Bry's *Grands voyages,* most of which treat travels in America, also include accounts of the circumnavigations. Volume IX of this series, published in German in 1601 and in Latin in 1602, includes translations of Sebald de Weert's voyage through the Straits of Magellan (1598) and Olivier van Noort's circumnavigation.[59] Apart from the pieces in the eighth volume of the *Petits voyages,* all the journals published by the De Brys before 1610 were translations of previously published works. The reports of the Dutch voyages found in Volume VIII, however, constitute an important addition to Europe's information about Asia in German despite their originally having been written in Dutch. The Dutch texts were not published until 1645 when they appeared in the *Begin ende voortgangh.*[60]

Generally, the texts of the De Bry volumes leave much to be desired. The translations, many of which were made by Gotthard Arthus of Danzig (1570–1630), are sometimes greatly abridged and frequently inaccurate. Nevertheless, they provided a great store of up-to-date information about Asia for readers of German and Latin. Lavishly illustrated and impressively bound, they no doubt helped excite their readers' imaginations about the exotic world overseas, and they functioned as an encyclopedia of exotic information for other writers. Because they were sold at the Frankfurt book fairs to dealers from abroad, they appreciably widened the impact of the Dutch voyages on the European consciousness.

Much the same can be said for the many volumes published by Levinus

[55] *Ibid.,* pp. 213–17, for bibliography.
[56] For bibliographic details see *ibid.,* pp. 224–35.
[57] For bibliographic details see *ibid.,* pp. 235–45, and Tiele, *op. cit.* (n. 51), pp. 162–74.
[58] Tiele, *op. cit.* (n. 51), p. 169. Also see above, p. 466.
[59] For bibliography see Camus, *op. cit.* (n. 51), pp. 102–27, and Tiele, *op. cit.* (n. 51), pp. 21–37.
[60] See above, pp. 463–66.

Hulsius (d. 1606) during the same years and, after 1602, usually in the same city. If anything, the Hulsius volumes were even more popular. They were published only in German, in a smaller, more convenient, and perhaps somewhat less expensive, size, although they too are lavishly illustrated. The texts of many of the Hulsius volumes are identical to De Bry's texts, although Hulsius and his successors often added notes and maps.[61]

The first volume of the Hulsius collection, published at Nuremberg in 1598, describes the first Dutch voyage to the East Indies under De Houtman. It is a translation of the *Verhael vande reyse* first published at Middelburg in 1597, rather than Willem Lodewyckszoon's journal which was issued by De Bry.[62] Hulsius' Second Voyage (Nuremberg, 1602) is that of Van Neck and Van Warwijck (1598–1600) and is, like Volume V of De Bry's *Petits voyages,* a translation of *Het tweede boeck.* A second edition was published at Frankfurt in 1605 and a third in 1615. Hulsius appears to have at least consulted the original Dutch edition, because some of the errors in the De Bry translation are corrected.[63] Hulsius translated Gerrit de Veer's description of the Dutch northeast passage attempts (1594, 1595, 1596) for his third volume.[64] Hulsius' Sixth Voyage (Nuremberg, 1603) contains translations of the accounts of the first four circumnavigations of Magellan, Drake, Cavendish, and Van Noort.[65] In 1606 two Hulsius volumes appeared: Volume VIII contains a report of Gerard le Roy's capture of a Portuguese carrack near St. Helena, translations of the accounts of Wolfert Harmenszoon's voyage and Jacob van Heemskerck's voyage, and brief notices of Jacob van Neck's second voyage and of Van Warwijck and De Weert's voyage.[66] The original Dutch accounts of the Harmenszoon and the Van Heemskerck voyages were not published until their inclusion in the *Begin ende voortgangh* of 1645.[67] Volume IX (Frankfurt, 1606) is a translation of the journal of Steven van der Hagen's second voyage, 1604–5.[68] It appears to be a different and somewhat better translation than that included in De Bry's *Petits voyages,* Volume VIII. Nor was it published in Dutch before its inclusion in the *Begin ende voortgangh.* In fact, the Dutch editor, Isaac Commelin, may have used one of the German translations for his account.[69] Hulsius' Tenth Voyage, published in

---

[61] For bibliography and evaluation of the Hulsius collection see Asher, *op. cit.* (n. 51).

[62] See Tiele, *op. cit.* (n. 51), pp. 122, 130, and Asher, *op. cit.* (n. 51), pp. 17–18,

[63] See Asher, *op. cit.* (n. 51), pp. 19–21, and Tiele, *op. cit.* (n. 51), pp. 136–44.

[64] It was first published in 1598 by Hulsius, but without reference to the other parts of the collection. A second, abridged, edition appeared at Nuremberg in 1602, a third at Frankfurt in 1612, and a fourth at Frankfurt in 1660. For bibliographic details see Asher, *op. cit.* (n. 51), pp. 22–23, and Tiele, *op. cit.* (n. 51), pp. 103–16.

[65] Second edition, Frankfurt, 1618; third edition, Frankfurt, 1626. For bibliographic details see Asher, *op. cit.* (n. 51), pp. 43–46.

[66] Later editions published at Frankfurt in 1608 and 1640. See Asher, *op. cit.* (n. 51), pp. 52–59, and Tiele, *op. cit.* (n. 51), pp. 162–70, 203–8, for bibliographic details.

[67] See above, p. 465.

[68] See Asher, *op. cit.* (n. 51), p. 60, and Tiele, *op. cit.* (n. 51), pp. 170–74 for details.

[69] See Tiele, *op. cit.* (n. 51), pp. 173.

1608, was compiled from the first two reports of Cornelis Matelief's out-ward voyage and his victories over the Portuguese near Malacca, published also in 1608, together with descriptions of Malacca, Acheh, and Ceylon drawn from other sources. Some news about the return of Matelief's fleet was added at the end of the volume.[70]

Jesuit letterbooks and the De Bry and Hulsius collections were not the only notices about Asia translated into German and Latin around the turn of the century. A separate translation of the *Verhael vande reyse*, the journal of Cornelis de Houtman's voyage of 1595, appeared at Cologne in 1598.[71] A translation of John de Mandeville's travels appeared in 1580 and again in 1600.[72] The tireless translator Hieronymus Megiser produced a German edition of Marco Polo in 1609 and a German Varthema in 1610.[73] Marcus Henning meanwhile translated Mendoza's description of China into Latin for a Frankfurt publisher in 1589 or 1599.[74]

Information about Asia was further spread in the German lands by its in-clusion in historical and chronological compilations by stay-at-home writ-ers; in works like Johannes Mayer's chronological compendium of manners and morals, for example, published in 1598 and again in 1604.[75] Reports of the Portuguese and Spanish discoveries were included in Andreas Schott's four-volume Latin history of Spain published between 1603 and 1608.[76] Much more information was included in Gotthard Arthus' compilation of African and Asian reports, taken primarily from Portuguese and Jesuit sources.[77] Travels to Asia were also included in Jacob Beyrlin's collection published in 1606.[78] While all these translations and compilations produced in German at the beginning of the seventeenth century attest to a brisk mar-ket for German-language travel literature, none can be considered an origi-nal contribution in German to Europe's store of knowledge about Asia. No

---

[70] For bibliographic details see Asher, *op. cit.* (n. 51), pp. 61–62, and Tiele, *op. cit.* (n. 51), pp. 208–13.

[71] *Warhaffter klarer, eigentlicher Bericht von der weiter, wunderbarer und nie bevor gethaner Reiss oder Schiffart, biss in Indien gegen der Sonnenauffgang gelegen.* . . . See Tiele, *op. cit.* (n. 51), p. 122, for bibliographical information.

[72] *Reise und Wanderschaften durch das gelobte Land, Indien, und Persien.* . . .

[73] *Reise in die Tartary und zum grossen Chan von Chatai* . . . (Altenburg); *Hodeporicon Indiae Orientalis; das ist: Warhafftige Beschreibung der ansehlich lobwürdegen Reyss* . . . (Leipzig).

[74] *Nova et succincta, vera tamen historia de amplissimo potentissimoque, nostro quidem orbi hactenus incognito, sed perpaucis abhinc annis explorato regno China.* . . . The *British Museum Catalogue* lists it as 1589. Ternaux-Compans lists editions of 1599 and 1600.

[75] *Compendium chronologicum,* . . . *das ist: Sumarischer Inhalt aller gedenck und glaubwirdigen Sachen* . . . (Münich, 1598). A second, revised, edition appeared in 1604. See *Asia*, Vol. II, Bk. 2, p. 350.

[76] *Hispania illustrata seu rerum urbiumque Hispaniae, Lusitaniae, Aethiopiae et Indiae scriptores varii* (4 vols.; Frankfurt, 1603–8).

[77] *Historia Indiae Orientalis ex variis auctoribus collecta* . . . (Cologne, 1608). For bibliographic details see Streit, V, 43.

[78] *Reyss-Buch; das ist ein gantz schöne Beschreibung und Wegweyser etlicher Reysen durch gantz Teutschlandt, Polen, Siebenbürgen, Dennenmarck, Engeland, Hispanien, Frankreich, Italien, Sicilien, Egyptien, Indien, Ethiopen, und Türkey* (Strassburg).

German travelers to Asia published accounts of their own voyages during the first decade of the century.

But Volume IX of De Bry's *India orientalis,* published in both German and Latin in 1612, is based on a report written by Johann Verken, a German soldier, about Pieter Willemszoon Verhoeff's voyage (1607–9) to the Moluccas.[79] Verken, a native of Meissen in Saxony, joined Verhoeff's fleet in November, 1607, as a "soldier and corporal." Verken took part in, and described in his journal, Verhoeff's attack on Mozambique (July and August, 1608), the negotiations at Calicut and Cochin, the operations in the Straits of Malacca, and the journey to Bantam and to the Banda Islands, where Verhoeff was killed in May, 1609. Verken remained in military service at the new Fort Nassau on Banda Neira until July, 1611, after which he returned to Vlissingen. Verken's diary or journal was extensively edited, perhaps rewritten, by Gotthard Arthus. Arthus interlarded Verken's original account with descriptions culled from other published works on Asia, especially Linschoten's. It is in fact written in the third person. Verken's journal therefore contains relatively little new information about Asia, although his descriptions of the dress and entourage of local dignitaries, for example that of the Zamorin of Calicut, are quite detailed and obviously firsthand observations.[80] Also valuable are Verken's descriptions of the Dutch attack on Mozambique, and especially of Verhoeff's activities in the Banda Islands and his death there. Verken's journal provides an independent and somewhat more detached account of these events than does the account of Verhoeff's voyage published in the *Begin ende voortgangh* or the accounts of William Keeling and David Middleton as published in Purchas.[81] Another edition of Verken's account appeared as the Eleventh Voyage in the Hulsius collection, issued in 1612 and 1613.[82] The Hulsius version was published again in 1623.

Volume X of *India orientalis* is a translation of the pieces describing the Dutch northeast and northwest passage attempts first published by Hessel Gerritszoon in 1612.[83] Both the German and Latin editions of Gotthard Arthus appeared in 1613.[84] It includes reports of Henry Hudson's voyage to the northwest, Linschoten's voyage to the northeast, Isaac Massa's description of Siberia, and Pedro Fernandez de Quiros' letter to King Philip III

---

[79] For bibliography, see Camus, *op. cit.* (n. 51), pp. 246–53, and Tiele, *op. cit.* (n. 51), pp. 174–79.

[80] Reprinted as *Johann Verken, Molukken-Reise, 1607–1612. Neu herausgegeben nach der zu Franckfurt am Main im Verlag Joh. Th. de Bry im Jahre 1612 erschienenen Original-Ausgabe* in S. P. L'Honoré Naber (ed.), *Reisebeschreibungen von deutschen Beamten und Kriegsleuten im Dienst der Niederländischen West- und Ost-Indischen Kompagnien, 1602–1797* (The Hague, 1930–), II, 42–45. Hereafter cited as NR.

[81] See below, pp. 558–59.

[82] See Asher, *op. cit.* (n. 51), pp. 63–64, and Tiele, *op. cit.* (n. 51), pp. 174–79, for bibliographic details.

[83] See above, p. 445.

[84] For bibliography see Camus, *op. cit.* (n. 51), pp. 253–58, and Tiele, *op. cit.* (n. 51), pp. 179–90.

about the southern continent. It contains few descriptions of Asian places. It was republished at Oppenheim (1614) as the Twelfth Voyage in the Hulsius series.[85] Two other German publications reported the northern passage attempts and Quiros' description of the southern continent: a collection by Helisaeus Röslin published at the De Bry firm in Oppenheim, 1611, and a collection by Megiser published in 1613.[86]

A German translation of Robert Coverte's report of his overland journey from Surat to Aleppo appeared in Volume XI of *India orientalis* along with Amerigo Vespucci's third and fourth voyages and Hessel Gerritszoon's description of Spitzbergen. The German edition was published in 1618, the Latin in 1619.[87] The Hulsius edition of Coverte's journal appeared earlier (1617) at Hanau as a separate volume called the Fifteenth Voyage.[88] The journals describing Willem Corneliszoon Schouten and Jacob Le Maire's circumnavigation and Van Spilbergen's circumnavigation were published in 1619 and 1620 as Volume XI of the *Grands voyages*.[89] The two circumnavigations appear as separate volumes in the Hulsius collection: Schouten's as the Sixteenth Voyage in 1619, and Van Spilbergen's as the Seventeenth Voyage in 1620.[90]

Considerable detail about affairs in Portuguese Asia became available with the 1619 publication of Eliud Nicolai's *Newe und warhaffte Relation*.[91] Translated from or extracted from unnamed Spanish and Portuguese sources, Nicolai's book describes the Portuguese discoveries in Asia, the conquests of Goa, of Pegu, and of the Philippines, the intrusion of the Dutch and English into the East Indies, and the conflicts between them and the Iberians. Recent events are treated with more detail than earlier events. One chapter describes Van Spilbergen's voyage, for example,[92] and several chapters are devoted to the exploits of Felipe de Brito and the growth of Portuguese influence in Pegu.[93] Victories over the Dutch are celebrated. It is a collection of pieces rather than a continuous narrative, and most of them recount European activities in Asia. There are a few descriptive passages, however, most notably of Madagascar[94] and Sumatra.[95]

[85] A second edition appeared in 1627. For bibliography see Asher, *op. cit.* (n. 51), pp. 65–67, and Tiele, *op. cit.* (n. 51), pp. 179–90.

[86] Helisaeus Röslin, *Mitternächtige Schiffarth. . . .* ; Hieronymus Megiser (ed.), *Septentrio novantiquus, oder die newe nort Welt. . . .* (Leipzig).

[87] For bibliography see Camus, *op. cit.* (n. 51), pp. 259–71.

[88] A second printing appeared in Frankfurt in 1648. The first English edition of Coverte's journal was published at London in 1612. For bibliography see Asher, *op. cit.* (n. 51), pp. 76–78. For a discussion of Coverte's voyage and journal see below, pp. 552–53.

[89] For bibliographic detail see Camus, *op. cit.* (n. 51), pp. 147–54, and Tiele, *op. cit.* (n. 51), pp. 40–73.

[90] For bibliography see Asher, *op. cit.* (n. 51), pp. 79–85.

[91] *Newe und warhaffte Relation, . . . Alles auss gewissen castiglianischen unnd portugesischen Relationen colligiert . . .* (Munich, 1619).

[92] *Ibid.*, pp. 17–38.   [94] *Ibid.*, pp. 142–45.

[93] *Ibid.*, pp. 39–86.   [95] *Ibid.*, pp. 115–21.

The De Bry and the Hulsius series of voyages were both completed in the years between 1620 and 1650. The last volume of the De Bry *India orientalis* (one volume in Latin, but two volumes in German) appeared at Frankfurt in 1628.[96] The two German volumes contain a large number of short separate pieces describing Asian lands, voyages to Asia including Jacques L'Hermite's circumnavigation, the activities of Europeans in Asia, and the northwest and northeast passage attempts. All were translated from English or Dutch originals written during the seventeenth century. Most of the pieces in the two German volumes appear to have come from Samuel Purchas, *Hakluytus Posthumus,* published in 1625. The Latin edition of *India orientalis,* Volume XII, while it describes the same voyages and places as do the German volumes, has an entirely different format. Its author, Ludovicus Gothofredus (or Louis Godefroi), divided the volume into three books and wrote each as a continuous narrative. Book I contains descriptions of Asian lands and peoples, Book II describes early seventeenth-century expeditions to Asia, and Book III describes the northeast, northwest, and southern voyages.

The fourteenth and last part of De Bry's *Grands voyages* series was published in German at Hanau in 1630. The last (thirteenth) Latin volume appeared at Frankfurt in 1634; it contains the material found in the thirteenth as well as the fourteenth German volume. Each of these volumes includes an account of Jacques L'Hermite's circumnavigation (1623–26), sometimes attributed to Adolph Decker of Strassburg. The Decker edition of L'Hermite's voyage had been published separately in 1629.[97] It is much longer and more detailed than the very brief report contained in Volume XII of *Petits voyages,* and it appears to be primarily a translation from the Dutch original, augmented by Decker, who accompanied the fleet. The first complete Dutch edition appeared in 1626, an expanded version in 1643.[98] Although L'Hermite's fleet visited the Moluccas and Batavia, most of the journal deals with its attacks on Spanish shipping and towns along the west coast of South America and with descriptions of those lands and peoples. He wrote almost nothing about Asian lands and peoples. The Decker edition of L'Hermite's circumnavigation was again published in 1630 as the Twenty-second Voyage of the Hulsius series.[99]

Only two other Hulsius volumes were published between 1630 and 1650 which deal with Asia. Volume XXIV, which appeared in 1648, contains a complete translation of Willem Ysbrantszoon Bontekoe's popular East In-

---

[96] For bibliography see Camus, *op. cit.* (n. 51), pp. 271–78, and Tiele, *op. cit.* (n. 51), pp. 198–202.

[97] *Diurnal der nassawischen Flotta oder Tagregister und historische ordentliche Beschreibung einer gewaltigen mächtigen Schiffarht umb die gantze Erd-Kugel rund umbher. . . .* (Strassburg, 1629).

[98] See above, p. 449. For bibliography see Tiele, *op. cit.* (n. 51), pp. 73–81, and Camus, *op. cit.* (n. 51), pp. 170–78.

[99] For bibliographical information and a description of the contents see Asher, *op. cit.* (n. 51), pp. 96–102.

dian voyage. It is bound with Dirck Albertszoon Raven's voyage to Spitz-bergen.[100] Volume XXV, 1649, mainly devoted to a translation of Hendrick Brouwer's voyage to Chile, apparently also contains translations of George Candidius' description of Formosa and of Martin Gerritszoon Vries' voyage to Hokkaido. Both of these descriptions were published earlier in Dutch.[101]

Between the publication in 1612 of Verken's voyage to the Moluccas and the end of the Thirty Years' War in 1648 only two firsthand German accounts of Asia appeared in print, each in brief editions which were later greatly augmented and expanded. The first of these was Johann Albrecht von Mandelslo's report of his voyage to India, first published in 1645;[102] the other was Johann Sigmund Wurffbain's account of his voyages to India and the Moluccas with the Dutch East India Company, which was first published in 1646.[103]

Mandelslo was a page from the court of the Duke of Holstein who in 1635 accompanied the duke's embassy to Moscow and Persia. Bitten by the travel bug, Mandelslo left the embassy at Ispahan in 1638 to visit India. He arrived at Surat in April, 1638, where he stayed until October, then traveled through Gujarat to Agra and Lahore, Goa, Bijapur, and Malabar, and sailed for England from Surat in January, 1639. He apparently wrote down a rough, disorganized account of his travels. Before he died of smallpox in 1644, he entrusted the publication of his manuscript to Adam Olearius, the duke's librarian and mathematician, who had also been the secretary of the embassy to Russia and Persia.[104]

As it appeared in 1645, Mandelslo's account was bound with Olearius' report on the Duke of Holstein's embassy to Russia and Persia. Both accounts appeared again in 1647.[105] In 1658 a greatly expanded version appeared.[106] German editions were also published in 1656 and in 1668; each time, Mandelslo's account was bound with Olearius' Russian and Persian travelogue. In 1669, Olearius included Mandelslo's travels with his description of the Asian travels of Jürgen Andersen and Volquard Iversen.[107] Finally, in 1696, Olearius published a massive volume which included his Russian and Persian travels, Mandelslo's travels, Andersen and Iversen's travels, a

---

[100] For bibliography see Tiele, *op. cit.* (n. 51), pp. 213–26, and Asher, *op. cit.* (n. 51), pp. 105–8.

[101] See Asher, *op. cit.* (n. 51), pp. 109–10; and Tiele, *op. cit.* (n. 51), pp. 226–28, 250–53.

[102] *Schreiben von seiner ostindischen Reise an Ad. Olearius . . . mit etlichen Anmerkungen Ad. Olearii . . .* (Schleswig, 1645).

[103] *Reisebeschreibung welche er . . . 1632 dahin fürgenommen und 1646 vollendet hat* (Nuremberg).

[104] See M. S. Commissariat, *Mandelslo's Travels in Western India (A.D. 1638–39)* (London, 1931), pp. ix–xiv.

[105] Adam Olearius, *Muskowitische offte begehrte Beschreibung der newen orientalischen Reise . . .* (Schleswig, 1647).

[106] *Des hoch edelgebornen Johan Albrechts von Mandelslo morgenländische Reyse-Beschreibung . . .* (Schleswig, 1658).

[107] Olearius, *Orientalische Reise-Beschreibunge . . .* (Schleswig, 1669). See below, pp. 533–34, for details.

translation of Martini's *De bello tartarico,* and the description of Koxinga's conquest of the Dutch colony on Formosa.[108] The 1647 edition (Mandelslo and Olearius) was translated into Dutch in 1651, and a Dutch translation of the 1658 expanded edition appeared also in 1658. There were many French translations, the first of which appeared in 1656. Subsequent French editions were published in 1659, 1666, 1679, and 1719. John Davis translated it into English in 1662,[109] and a second English edition appeared in 1669.

Even the earliest editions were really written by Olearius, who added voluminous descriptions taken from other popular travel literature, especially from Dutch reports, to Mandelslo's observations about Goa, Surat, and Gujarat. In its later editions, Olearius' account of Mandelslo's travels includes long descriptions of Java, Sumatra, the Moluccas, China, Japan, the history of Portuguese India, and the politics, society, and religions of the various Asian peoples.[110] The French translator, Abraham de Wicquefort, added still more descriptive material, all taken from the available published travel literature. His editions grew to be one-third larger than the largest German edition.[111] And since John Davis used Wicquefort's 1659 edition for his English translation, all the additions made by Olearius and Wicquefort were carried over into the English versions. It is almost impossible to distinguish between Mandelslo's firsthand observations and Olearius' many alterations and additions. In its published form, therefore, Mandelslo's book is a mine of information about Asia; but it is much less a German contribution to Europe's knowledge of Asia than a vehicle for bringing much of the recent and best information about Asia to German readers.

Johann Sigmund Wurffbain (1613–61), the son of a prominent Nuremberg family, had been sent to Amsterdam at age fifteen to learn about commerce and to study Dutch and French. He returned home in 1631 to discover that the war had so limited commercial opportunities in the German lands that his family urged him to seek his fortune with the VOC in Asia. He therefore returned to Amsterdam hoping to go to Asia as a merchant's assistant, but despite his personal connections in Amsterdam he was unable to obtain such a position. Instead, he enlisted for five years with the VOC as a soldier, hoping to improve his lot once in the east.[112]

Wurffbain sailed in April, 1632, spent two months in Batavia, and then went to the Moluccas, where he served in the Amboina garrison, took part

---

[108] Olearius, *Reise Beschreibungen bestehend in der nach Musskau und Persien* . . . (Hamburg, 1696).

[109] Olearius, *The Voyages and Travels of the Ambassadors sent by Frederick Duke of Holstein to the great Duke of Muscovy, and the King of Persia* . . . *Whereto are added the Travels of Johan Albert de Mandelslo* . . . (London, 1662).

[110] Commissariat, *op. cit.* (n. 104), p. x.

[111] *Ibid.,* p. xx.

[112] Johann Sigmund Wurffbain, *Reise nach den Molukken und Vorder-Indien, 1632–1646.* Edited by R. Posthumus Meyjes and reprinted in NR, VIII, ix–x, 30–31.

in a punitive expedition against Ceram in 1633, and spent most of his five-year term at Fort Nassau on Banda Neira. In 1634 he finally became a merchant's assistant, at first on probation and without an appropriate salary increase.[113] When his term expired he decided to stay on with the VOC, in part because the news from home was not very encouraging, but also because the VOC offered him the position of Junior Merchant (*Onder-Koopman*) at the Dutch factory in Surat.[114] Wurffbain worked at the Surat factory until 1645. His responsibilities grew; he made business trips to Bengal, Mocha, Cambay, and Goa, and by January, 1642, he was promoted to Senior Merchant (*Opper-Koopman*). He hoped to become the director of one of the VOC's Asian outposts. But when he learned that Governor-General Johan Maetsuycker and the Council of the Indies had ruled that only native Dutchmen could hold that office, Wurffbain decided to return home.[115] He sailed with the return fleet of December, 1645, and arrived at Nuremberg in September, 1646.

The 1646 edition of Wurffbain's *Reisebeschreibung* was published by his father from Wurffbain's letters as a kind of homecoming present. It reputedly contained many errors and generous injections of his father's ill-informed "wisdom." Wurffbain was not pleased. He bought up and destroyed as many copies as he could find.[116] The edition that has come down to us was published in 1686, long after Wurffbain's death, by his son, and is based on Wurffbain's revised and augmented journals.[117]

The 1686 edition also contains descriptive passages apparently not part of Wurffbain's original journal. Some of these may have been added by his son, but more than likely they were added by Wurffbain himself when he revised and organized his journals. Some of these descriptions seem to be based on the author's own observations, although most of them contain material which was probably taken from other published descriptions of Asia. The book contains some descriptions of places Wurffbain never visited, for example, Borneo,[118] the Australian coast,[119] the Malabar Coast of India,[120] Japan,[121] Siam and Cambodia,[122] and Formosa.[123] He also describes Sumatra,[124] Batavia and Java,[125] Makassar,[126] Buton,[127] Amboina,[128] the Banda Islands,[129]

---

[113] NR, VIII, xv, 129.

[114] *Ibid.*, pp. xv, 175; IX, ix, 1.　　[115] *Ibid.*, IX, ix–xx, 72–73.

[116] J. S. Rouffaer, "Een curieus Duitsch boekje over onze oost uit 1646," *BTLV*, LXIX (1914), 127–29; and NR, VIII, viii–ix.

[117] Joh. *Sigmund Wurffbains vierzehen jährige Ost-Indianische Krieg- und Ober-Kauffmanns-Dienste . . .* (Nuremberg, 1686).

[118] NR, VIII, 122–23.

[119] *Ibid.*, pp. 144–46.

[120] *Ibid.*, IX, 44–46.

[121] *Ibid.*, pp. 85–90.

[122] *Ibid.*, pp. 90–92.

[123] *Ibid.*, pp. 92–94.

[124] *Ibid.*, VIII, 50–52.

[125] *Ibid.*, pp. 51–64.

[126] *Ibid.*, p. 66.

[127] *Ibid.*, pp. 67–70.

[128] *Ibid.*, pp. 71–80.

[129] *Ibid.*, pp. 92–109.

and the Mughul Empire and Surat,[130] places he had visited. These, too, clearly contain information culled from other books. Perhaps more useful than his descriptions is Wurffbain's account of his experiences on Banda, in Surat, or of his other travels and the things he saw along the way. His book is rich in detailed information about the life of VOC soldiers in an island garrison and about VOC trade in India. His long career with the Dutch Company and his extraordinary rise from common soldier to Senior Merchant make him a uniquely interesting observer of Dutch activities in Asia. He described, in detail, as perhaps no one else could, life on a VOC Asian voyage first as a foreign soldier and later as Senior Merchant and president of the ship's council. As published in 1686, Wurffbain's journal is prefaced by a description of the various routes to India[131] and by a short history of the Dutch seaborne empire in Asia.[132] These were probably written by Wurffbain himself. Two years after Wurffbain returned to his native Nuremberg the Peace of Westphalia (1648) was concluded and the prospects for life and commerce looked better than at any time since the twenties. Wurffbain was able to carve out a very successful career for himself in Germany. He invested his capital wisely, and grew prosperous and prominent in Nuremberg, where he remained until his death in 1661.

3

A LIMITED REVIVAL, 1650–1700

The restoration of peace seems to have had some effect on the publishing trade, too, and along with the general increase in book publication some titles dealing with Asia also appeared. The augmented editions of Olearius, for example, belong to the decade of the fifties. Almost all the new works about Asia published in German cities during the fifties were in Latin. Some had been published before or were compilations of earlier descriptions. For example, Theodore Rhay's description of Tibet appears to be in part, at least, a translation of Antonio de Andrade's 1628 description of the Jesuit mission to Tibet of 1625.[133]

The first detailed information about the Manchu conquest of China appeared in Martino Martini's *De bello tartarico,* published in Antwerp, Cologne, and Vienna in 1654.[134] Martini had been sent to Rome by the Jesuits in

---

[130] *Ibid.,* IX, 11–28.

[131] *Ibid.,* VIII, 15–22.   [132] *Ibid.,* pp. 23–29.

[133] *Descriptio regni Thibet* (Paderborn, 1658). See Streit, V, 152, for bibliography. For Andrade's work and the mission of 1625 see above, pp. 338–39, and below, pp. 1773–83.

[134] *De bello tartarico historia: in quâ, quo pacto Tartari hac nostrâ aetate sinicum imperium invaserint, ac ferè totum occuparint, narratur: eorumque mores breviter describuntur.* Also see above, pp. 480–81.

China to defend their cultural accommodation practices against the criticism of Dominican and Franciscan missionaries. As Martini tells it, he staved off seasickness by writing during the long ocean voyage.[135] He appears to have been successful, for upon his arrival in Europe in August, 1653, he immediately arranged for the publication of several important volumes, the first of which was the *De bello tartarico;* it became the best-known description of the Manchu Conquest available to Europeans during the seventeenth century. The Latin text was republished seven times, and it was translated into nine other European languages. Altogether at least twenty-five editions and translations appeared before the end of the century.[136] A German translation was published at Amsterdam by Blaeu in 1654.[137]

Two brief German notices of the Manchu Conquest had appeared earlier in Augsburg. The Polish Jesuit Michael Boym's account of the conversion of several members of the Ming pretender's court appeared in German translation in 1653.[138] It contained a brief history of the conquest. The conquest was also briefly described in an Augsburg newssheet called *Zeitung auss der newen Welt,* published earlier in 1654, which reported Martini's arrival in Europe, the state of the Jesuit mission in China, and the length of Martini's beard.[139] Streit claims the *Zeitung* is a translation of Martini's *Brevis relatio* (Rome, 1654), but its author says the *Zeitung* was based on letters sent by Martini from Holland to friends in Ingolstadt.[140]

Before he returned to China in 1656, Boym also published a scholarly account of Chinese flora and fauna. It became one of the most important and influential sources for Europe's knowledge of Chinese natural history during the seventeenth century.[141] It influenced many subsequent publications and was translated into French for a volume in Thévenot's collection published in 1696.

In addition to his *Atlas* and his account of the Manchu Conquest, Martini also produced a Latin work on ancient Chinese history before he left for China in 1657. Published at Munich in 1658, his *Sinicae historiae decas prima*

---

[135] *Ibid.,* p. 2.

[136] For a bibliography of most of the editions see H. Cordier, *Bibliotheca sinica* (2d ed., 6 vols.; New York, 1968), I, 623–27, and Streit, V, 797–800.

[137] *Histori von dem Tartarischen Kriege in welcher erzehlt wird wie die Tartaren zu unserer Zeit in das grosse Reich Sina eingefallen sind und dasselbe fast gantz unter sich gebracht haben. . . .*

[138] *Sehr wehrte und angenehme newe Zeitung von der Bekehrung zum Catholischen Glauben desz jungen Königs in China und anderer fürstlichen Personen.* Another German edition appeared in Munich in 1653, and a French edition appeared at Liège in 1653. The original Italian edition was published at Rome in 1652. See Streit, V, 793–95, for bibliography.

[139] *Zeitung auss der newen Welt oder chinesischen Königreichen. . . .*

[140] *Brevis relatio de numero, & qualitate christianorum apud Sinas. . . ;* another edition was published at Cologne, 1655. See Streit, V, 800.

[141] Michael Boym, *Flora sinensis, id est fructuum florum & nonullorum animalium sinensium historia insignii imagium apparatu exornatae* (Vienna, 1656). For Boym's career see Robert Chabrié, *Michel Boym. Jésuite Polonais et la fin des Ming en Chine (1646–1662)* (Paris, 1933). For bibliography see Boleslaw Szczesniak, "The Writings of Michael Boym," *Monumenta serica,* XIV (1949–55), 481–538, and Streit, V, 793–94.

was the first serious attempt by a European to write Chinese history.[142] It traces Chinese history from earliest times to the birth of Christ, or the middle of the Han Dynasty. Basically a court chronicle, Martini's *Decas prima* contains a chapter on each emperor from Fu Hsi, the first legendary sage emperor, whose reign Martini calculated began in 2952 B.C., to the end of the Former Han Dynasty. It contains a wealth of detail not only about the emperors and high officials, but also about Chinese religious and intellectual life, internal conflicts, and foreign relations. It provoked a rather heated controversy among European scholars, because according to Martini's calculations seven Chinese emperors had reigned before the generally accepted date for the biblical flood (2349 B.C.) in which all people on earth except Noah and his family were supposed to have drowned. Martini was aware of the problem but offered no solutions. European theologians and historians, however, busied themselves with it for a century or more after Martini returned to China.[143] A second Latin edition of the first part of *Sinicae historiae* appeared in Amsterdam in 1659; a French translation of what might be its second part was published by Thévenot.[144]

Jesuit publications in both Latin and German continued to appear in German publishing centers during the sixties. A collection of extracts from the China letters appeared in German translation at Munich in 1662.[145] Excerpts from a letter by the German Jesuit Heinrich Roth (1620–68) appeared in Latin at Aschaffenburg in 1665.[146] This publication contains a description of the Mughul Empire as well as reports of events in India; it appears to have been taken from an original unpublished German letter of 1664.[147] Roth had returned to Europe after about ten years in Agra when he wrote the letter. According to Athanasius Kircher, he was proficient in Persian, Hindi, and Sanskrit.[148] Kircher in fact used Roth as one of his main sources for the descriptions of the Mughul Empire and of Hindu religion found in his *China illustrata* (Amsterdam, 1667).[149] Roth's contributions to Kircher's work include a description of the ten transformations (avatars) of Vishnu and several illustrations of Indian provenance, as well as a discussion of the Sanskrit language which is illustrated with five plates presenting examples of Sanskrit writing (see pl. 129).

---

[142] *Sinicae historiae decas prima res à gentis origine ad Christum natum in extremâ Asia, sive magno Sinarum imperio gestas complexa.*

[143] For a discussion of the controversies generated by the *Sinicae historiae* and its effects on Europe's view of ancient history see E. Van Kley, "Europe's 'Discovery' of China and the Writing of World History," *The American Historical Review*, LXXVI (1971), 358–85.

[144] See Streit, V, 812–13; and below, pp. 1682–83.

[145] *Extract Schriebens ausz dem weitberühmten gegen Aufgang gelegenem Königreich China . . . 6 Febr. 1659, in Europa 1662 angelangt.* For bibliography see Streit, V, 821.

[146] *Relatio rerum notabilium regni Mogor in Asia. . . .* For full title see Streit, V, 163.

[147] See Streit, V, 160–61, for the title and for a sketch of Roth's career. See also E. MacLagan, *The Jesuits and the Great Mogul* (London, 1932), pp. 109–11.

[148] *La Chine illustrée* (Amsterdam, 1670), pp. ii, 7.

[149] *Ibid.*, pp. 104–15, 215–22.

Roth returned to Europe in 1662 accompanied by Johann Grueber, another German Jesuit, who with Father Albert d'Orville had journeyed overland from Peking to Agra by way of Lhasa. In the busy years after his return to Europe, Grueber evidently tried to write a description of Tibet and of his journey across the Himalayas. Apparently he never finished it. He may have sent parts of it to Kircher, however; he wrote several letters to Kircher and apparently sent him some of his sketches, all of which formed the basis for a description of Tibet and of Grueber and D'Orville's journey in Kircher's *China illustrata*—probably Europe's earliest account of the Tibetan capital. Kircher's account also contains eleven very interesting plates made from Grueber's sketches, including one of the Dalai Lama and one of the Potala Palace in Lhasa which was frequently reproduced and served as Europe's only glimpse of Lhasa for the following 250 years.[150] A description of Grueber's Tibetan travels also appeared in the Thévenot collection printed in 1666.[151]

In 1665 at Vienna there appeared a Latin description of the Jesuit mission in China based on the letters of Johann Adam Schall von Bell (1592–1666).[152] Schall, who went to China in 1618, became the most prominent and influential member of the Jesuit mission. He headed the Calendrical Bureau in Peking from 1630 to 1644 and its successor, the Imperial Board of Astronomy, under the Manchus from 1645 to 1665. He was the confidante of more than one Chinese emperor, received many honors and titles, including that of *Chin-shih,* the highest Chinese civil service degree, and published more than twenty-five books in Chinese on Christian theology, mathematics, and astronomy.[153] His *Historica narratio* describes the Jesuit mission in China through the years of its highest achievements. Schall's account of the Manchu Conquest is particularly interesting, because it describes his personal experiences in Peking during Li Tzu-ch'eng's capture of the city in 1644, during the sack and burning of the capital when Li's armies fled, and during the first days of the new dynasty. A second, expanded, Latin edition appeared in 1672 which brought the story of the mission down to 1669 and which contained more descriptive material.[154]

[150] *Ibid.,* pp. 88–104. For details of Grueber's career and on the sources for his journey to Tibet see Bruno Zimmel, "Der erste Bericht über Tibets Hauptstadt Lhasa aus dem Jahr 1661," *Biblos,* II (1953), 127–45. See also C. Wessels, *Early Jesuit Travellers in Central Asia, 1603–1721* (The Hague, 1924). See pls. 384, 385.

[151] TR, Vol. IV.

[152] *Historica narratio de initio et progressu missionis Societatis Jesu apud Chinenses, praesertim in regia Pequinensi. . . .* Also see Streit, V, 827.

[153] See Streit, V, 718–20, for his bibliography. For Schall's life see Alfons Väth, *Johann Adam Schall von Bell, S. J. Missionar in China, kaiserlicher Astronom und Ratgeber am Hofe von Peking, 1592–1666* (Cologne, 1933).

[154] *Historica relatio de ortu et progressu fidei orthodoxae in regno chinensi per missionarios Societatis Jesu ab anno 1581. usque ad annum 1669. . . .* (Ratisbon, 1672). It also contains a description of the persecution of the early 1660s. See Streit, V, 851. Also among 1665 publications Ternaux-Compans lists Neichart, *Zwaanzigjahrige Wanderschaff und Reisen in alle vier Theile der Welt* (Onolzbach). We have found no other reference to either the book or its author.

Another translation of Jesuit letters appeared in 1668, that of Joseph Zanzini's report of the mission in Cochin-China and especially of the thirty-seven Christians martyred there in 1664.[155] Several Dutch descriptions of Asia were translated into German during the sixties. The Nuremberg professor Christoph Arnold translated two of them in 1663: Abraham Roger's description of Hindu religion[156] and the descriptions of Japan and Siam by François Caron and Joost Schouten.[157] A description of Dutch victories on the Malabar Coast in 1663 was appended to a German translation of Jan Somer's Levant voyages in 1664.[158]

The most unusual aspect of German publications about Asia during the sixties is the large number of firsthand accounts written in German by German travelers. Most of these travelers were young men who enlisted as soldiers in the Dutch East India Company. In many cases their reports added little to Europe's stock of information about the East. What they report is usually better described in Dutch publications. Indeed, their narratives are frequently fattened by descriptions from the standard Dutch sources. Nevertheless, these German travelers helped bring the Asian world closer to German readers, and their more detached and sometimes critical view of Dutch activities in Asia frequently provides insights that make their reports valuable.

Johann Jacob Saar (1625–ca. 1672) was such a traveler. Born in Nuremberg in 1625, Saar served fifteen years, from 1644 to 1659, as a soldier with the VOC. He apparently kept a diary during these years, but lost it on the homeward voyage. His published account, therefore, was written from memory with the aid of Daniel Wülfer, the pastor of St. Lorentz church in Nuremberg and a boyhood friend of Saar. It was first published in 1662.[159] Wülfer apparently used other published descriptions to aid Saar's memory and flesh out his descriptions. In the second edition, published in 1672, Wülfer inserted more descriptions in the text and added many voluminous notes, citing as authorities a great many of the published descriptions of Asia available at the time.[160] A Dutch translation of the first edition was published at Amsterdam in 1671.

Saar served with the VOC military forces in Batavia for three months, in

---

[155] *Relation von der Verfolgung so in dem Reich Cocincinna* . . . (Munich). See Streit, V, 616.

[156] *Offne Thür zu dem verborgenen Heydenthum.* . . . (Nuremberg, 1663). The first Dutch edition was published in 1651. See above, pp. 478–79.

[157] *Fr. Caron und Jod. Schouten wahrhaftige Beschreibungen zweyer mächtigen Königreiche Jappan und Siam* . . . (Nuremberg). See above, pp. 456–60.

[158] *Johann Sommers See- und Land Reysz nach der Levante,* . . . (Frankfurt). Somer's voyage was first published by Joost Hartgers at Amsterdam in 1649. Another German translation was published in Amsterdam in 1664.

[159] *Johann Jacob Saars Ost-Indianische fünfzehen-jährige Kriegs-Dienste, und wahrhafftige Beschreibung* . . . (Nuremberg).

[160] *Johann Jacob Saars Ost-indianische fünfzehen-jährige Kriegs-Dienste und wahrhafftige Beschreibung* . . . *zum anderen Mahl heraus gegeben* . . . (Nuremberg). This edition is reprinted in NR, Vol. VI.

the Banda Islands for nineteen months, and on several short expeditions, including one to Surat and Persia in 1649. Most of his years, however, were spent in Ceylon. His account is very useful for its description of the daily life of a VOC soldier, and it is particularly valuable for its detailed portrayal of the Dutch conquest of Colombo and Jaffnapatam from the Portuguese in the 1655–58 campaigns, in which Saar participated.[161] Saar describes Java,[162] Batavia,[163] Amboina,[164] and Banda,[165] but the most interesting and that containing the largest amount of firsthand information is his description of Ceylon.[166] Saar was always the soldier. He was much more interested in exotic plants and food, in snakes, crocodiles, elephants, and strange birds, or in weapons and military tactics than in Sinhalese religion, government, or social structure.

Johann Jacob Merklein, who met Saar in Ceylon, was a more sophisticated observer. The son of a physician from Winsheim, he went to sea as a barber and surgeon's mate on a VOC ship in December, 1644. His was a fortunate voyage. His ship arrived at Batavia late in May, 1645, just five months after leaving Texel, and he reported that no one died along the way.[167] Saar had reported fourteen deaths on his ship and fifty-four on the admiral's ship despite their having taken regular doses of lemon juice.[168] After brief voyages to Sumatra and Banda, Merklein was assigned to the fort at Batavia in January, 1646, where he remained until June, 1648, when he was promoted to Senior Barber and surgeon (*Ober-Barbirer*) and assigned to a ship. Before he returned to Europe in 1653, Merklein had visited both Indian coasts, Ceylon, Gambroon in Persia, and Nagasaki in Japan.

Merklein's journal was first published in 1663 when Christoph Arnold added it to his translation of Caron and Schouten.[169] Arnold published a new and revised edition in 1672 which included the translation of Caron and Schouten as well as a translation of Hendrick Hamel's Korean adventure.[170] Apparently Merklein's journal was never published separately.

Merklein describes Java and Batavia in considerable detail, including a historical sketch of events since the Dutch first arrived there and a rather interesting appraisal of city government in Batavia.[171] His journal also contains brief descriptions of most of the places he visited and several which he

[161] NR, VI, 128–66.

[162] *Ibid.*, pp. 24–30.

[163] *Ibid.*, pp. 31–43.

[164] *Ibid.*, pp. 45–47.

[165] *Ibid.*, pp. 48–54.

[166] *Ibid.*, pp. 65–110.

[167] See Johann Jacob Merklein, *Reise nach Java, Vorder- und Hinter-Indien, China und Japan, 1644–1653*, in NR, III, 10.

[168] NR, VI, 30.

[169] *Journal, oder Beschreibung alles dess jenigen was sich auf währender unserer neunjährigen Reise im Dienst der Vereinigten Geoctroyrten Niederländischen Ost-Indischen Compagnie, besonders in denselbigen Ländern täglich begeben und zugetragen* . . . (Nuremberg). This is actually the title page of Merklein's voyage only, and not of the entire volume. See above, p. 458.

[170] Christoph Arnold (ed.), *Wahrhaftige Beschreibungen dreyer mächtigen Königreiche, Japan, Siam und Corea* . . . (2 vols.; Nuremberg). For Hamel see above, pp. 486–88.

[171] NR, III, 11–19.

did not. The 1672 edition contains many comments and notes written by Arnold and taken from current travel literature. Arnold cites Andersen, Iversen, Baldaeus, Bontius, Candidius, Roger, Dapper, Linschoten, Montanus, and many others. We have not seen the 1663 edition and therefore do not know if Arnold's notes were included in it.

More interesting than Merklein's descriptions are his reports of events in Asia and the glimpses of life in the Dutch overseas world that his account provides. He notes, for example, the failure of a Dutch expedition against Manila,[172] an attack on a Dutch fort by the king of Kandy,[173] the Dutch massacre of three to four thousand Chinese migrants to Formosa,[174] and the amusing embassy of Petrus Blokovius and Andreas Frisius to Japan.[175] Merklein also describes the ruthless enslavement of the natives of Engano in the Sunda Straits, who regularly killed shipwrecked seamen. The Dutch carried them off to Batavia, where most of them died.[176] He tells of the high mortality rate on some of the East Asian voyages and of the brutal punishments inflicted on sailors guilty of sodomy.[177] He observed the loading of opium onto Dutch ships in Bengal,[178] and he describes the Dutch treatment of a Venetian ship forced into Batavia. Since they were not at war with Venice, VOC officials merely removed all seamen of Dutch origin from the ship. When the Venetian masters realized they could no longer sail it, they sold the ship and turned over the non-Dutch members of the crew to the VOC.[179]

Johann von der Behr (d. *ca.* 1692) sailed to the East on a VOC ship about one year before Merklein. His voyage out was also very fast—about four and one-half months. Indeed, the captain received a reward for the speedy voyage. There had been some scurvy on board, but the captain and the ship's council nevertheless decided against stopping at the Cape of Good Hope. Fifteen men died before they reached Batavia.[180] Behr had enlisted in the VOC as a soldier, and he served until October, 1649, in Batavia, along the Malabar Coast with Johan Maetsuycker's fleet, on a voyage to Persia, and for almost four of his six years on Ceylon. His journal was not published until 1668, eighteen years after he had returned home.[181]

Behr's account of Java and Batavia includes nothing not found in earlier descriptions. In fact, some sections of it closely resemble the descriptions written by Saar and Merklein.[182] Daniel Wülfer, in the 1672 edition of Saar's voyage, frequently accused Behr of plagiarizing Saar. The only other major

---

[172] *Ibid.*, pp. 31–34.
[173] *Ibid.*, p. 29.   [174] *Ibid.*, pp. 35–36.
[175] *Ibid.*, pp. 59–61. See below, pp. 1876, 1882–83.
[176] NR, III, 23–25.   [178] *Ibid.*, p. 47.
[177] *Ibid.*, pp. 40–41.   [179] *Ibid.*, pp. 58–59.
[180] Johann von der Behr, *Reise nach Java, Vorder-Indien, Persien und Ceylon, 1641–1650* . . . in NR, IV, 27–28.
[181] *Diarium; oder Tage-Büch, über desjenige, so sich zeit einer neunjährigen Reise zu Wasser und Lande, meistentheils in Dienst der Vereinigten Geoctroyrten Niederländischen Ost-Indischen Compagnie* . . . (Jena).
[182] NR, IV, 28–45.

descriptive passage in Behr's volume is about Ceylon.[183] This, too, is rather familiar material.[184] Behr seems to have anticipated the charge of plagiarism; in the preface of his book he unapologetically advises his readers:

If you find something therein, most esteemed reader, that you indeed did not know, be grateful that you chose to be informed through me, your servant. If you find nothing, even so do not consider the time wasted, but think, you have by yourself administered a recitation and examination, and have briefly repeated and recapitulated what you knew before and have read scattered in other books.[185]

Even in reporting events, Behr was not as close an observer as Merklein or Saar. The events he chose to report are less important, sometimes trivial—clearly the sorts of things most interesting to a not-very-well-informed soldier. But therein lies the major contribution of Behr's account; it provides, like Saar's, insights into the daily life of a VOC soldier and a view of the Dutch overseas empire from the bottom up.

Behr served the VOC in Asia during fairly tranquil years, from 1644 to 1650. Albrecht Herport (1641–1730) from Bern, who soldiered with the VOC between 1659 and 1668, found the experience much more difficult and dangerous. After six months in Batavia he sailed to Macao and Formosa with Johann van der Laan's fleet. When Van der Laan returned to Batavia, Herport was among the soldiers assigned to reinforce the garrison at Fort Zeelandia on Formosa. He consequently took part in the tragic and unsuccessful defense of the fort against Cheng Ch'eng-kung's (Koxinga's) armies from May, 1661, to February, 1662, and returned to Batavia after the Dutch surrender.[186] After an inland expedition on Java in May, 1662,[187] he was sent to the Malabar Coast to join Rijcklof van Goens' expedition against the Portuguese. He took part in the siege and capture of Cochin (October 25, 1662, to January 9, 1663),[188] and the seizure of Cannanore in February, 1663.[189] In March, 1663, he was assigned to the Ceylon garrison, where he remained until October of 1666, when he left for Batavia and home. During the years on Ceylon he participated in elephant hunts, the annual pearl fishing near Mannar, and in several Malabar Coast expeditions.

Herport's journal was first published in Bern in 1669.[190] It was translated into Dutch along with Saar's and Volquard Iversen's accounts by J. H. Glazemaker in 1671. It contains relatively brief descriptions of Java,[191] For-

[183] *Ibid.*, pp. 54–67.
[184] Rowland Raven-Hart contends, as did Wülfer, that it is largely plagiarized from Saar; Raven-Hart (trans. and ed.), *Germans in Dutch Ceylon* (Colombo [1953]), p. 1.
[185] *Ibid.*, p. 6.
[186] Albrecht Herport, *Reise nach Java, Formosa, Vorder-Indien und Ceylon, 1659–1668.* . . . in NR, Vol. V.
[187] *Ibid.*, pp. 89–94.
[188] *Ibid.*, pp. 95–108.   [189] *Ibid.*, pp. 108–11.
[190] *Eine kurtze ost-indianische Reiss-Beschreibung.* . . .
[191] NR, V, 27–31.

mosa,[192] the Malabar Coast,[193] and Ceylon.[194] Of what they contain little would have been new to European readers, but they have the freshness of firsthand observations. None seems to be dependent on other published works. The real merit of Herport's account, however, lies in his vivid description of the military campaigns in which he took part. His account of the loss of Formosa, for example, is obviously independent of other accounts and yet, in the main, corroborates the C. E. S. account of those events.[195] It is thus an important source for the fall of Dutch Formosa. His account of Van Goens' Malabar Coast campaigns likewise remains an important independent source for that phase of Dutch expansion on the subcontinent. Herport's description of these campaigns is detailed, colorful, and realistic: complete with insufferable heat, monsoonal rains, mosquitoes, leeches, tigers, hunger, thirst, disease, fatigue, and overbearing Dutch officers. Soldiering with the VOC was a hard calling. His account of the elephant roundup on Ceylon and of the Mannar pearl fishery are also detailed, accurate, and interesting. In addition to his literary descriptions, Herport frequently made sketches of the places he visited. He appears to have been a fairly good artist, or at least a meticulous draftsman. Nine plates made from his sketches are included in the volume.

Accounts of two more German travelers, Jürgen Andersen and Volquard Iversen, were published together in 1669 as edited by Adam Olearius.[196] They are difficult accounts to assess. Each soldiered with the VOC and apparently each returned with a journal. But the published accounts of their travels are so heavily edited and augmented by Olearius that the original journals, and even the facts of the voyages, have been almost completely obscured. Olearius apparently used their journals simply as the outline for a voluminous description of Asian lands and peoples based on other published works. In fact, he appears to have added to the outline to allow for the description of more countries.

Andersen, for example, sailed from Texel on April 24, 1644, and returned to his home in Holstein in November, 1650. According to Olearius he accompanied an embassy to Mataram shortly after arriving in Batavia. Soon after that he went on a general inspection tour of Dutch establishments in Asia: Surat, Broach, Ahmadabad, Agra, Mocha, Gambroon, Ceylon, the Malabar Coast, Malacca, Formosa, and Nagasaki. VOC records, however, contain no reports of an embassy to Mataram until eighteen months after Andersen was supposed to have gone there, and the general inspection tour also is not supported by VOC records. With such a beginning it is even more difficult to accept Olearius' account of Andersen's shipwreck off the China coast as he was returning from Japan to Batavia, and his overland

---

[192] *Ibid.*, pp. 38–44, 81–86. [193] *Ibid.*, pp. 116–26. [194] *Ibid.*, pp. 129–37.
[195] *Ibid.*, pp. 51–58. For the C. E. S. pamphlet see above, pp. 495–96.
[196] *Orientalische Reise-Beschreibungen* . . . (Schleswig).

journey home by way of Canton, Samarkand, Ispahan, Ormuz, Baghdad, Aleppo, and Jerusalem. Olearius appears to have fabricated the journey in order to include descriptions of these places.

Olearius' version of Iversen's account likewise suffers from the editor's heavy hand. Iversen sailed from Texel in April, 1655, stopped at Table Bay in southern Africa, and was assigned to the fort on Ceram soon after he arrived in Batavia. He served five years there. All of that seems credible enough, as does the description of some of his activities during those years. He appears, for example, to have had some conscience trouble when assigned to uproot nutmeg trees as part of the VOC attempt to control the supply and price of the spices. But on his homeward voyage, December, 1661, to April, 1663, Olearius had him sail on the "Arnhem," which was shipwrecked. For the story of the shipwreck and the subsequent voyage to Mauritius in an open boat Olearius followed Andries Stokram's published account of the voyage of the "Arnhem." [197] But instead of returning to Holland with a Dutch freebooter flying French colors, as Stokram describes it, Olearius put Iversen on an English ship which took him back to Surat, where he reenlisted in the VOC military and did not return home until 1667. This apparently permitted Olearius to write several more descriptive chapters. [198]

In short, therefore, Olearius' account of Andersen's and Iversen's voyages appears to have contributed little to Europe's knowledge of Asia, and it is almost impossible to determine just what it did contribute. Like Olearius' earlier publications, however, this one helped spread the published descriptions of Asia to German readers. Curiously, J. H. Glazemaker translated both accounts into Dutch (Amsterdam, 1670 and 1671).

In addition to expanded and improved editions of Schall, Saar, and Merklein, firsthand accounts by German travelers continued to appear during the seventies. The travels of Heinrich von Poser und Gross Nedlitz (1599–1661), a Silesian nobleman, were published by Poser's son in 1675. [199] In 1620, Poser traveled overland to Constantinople and in January, 1621, he left for Persia, arriving in Ispahan on June 14, 1621. A month later he began his trek to India, arriving at Agra, by way of Lahore, late in December, 1621. In Agra he availed himself of Dutch and English hospitality, rode on an elephant, and watched the Mughul emperor through the window at one of his daily public appearances. [200] Late in January, 1622, he returned to Lahore, but

---

[197] Andries Stokram, *Korte beschryvinge van de ongeluckige weer-om-reys, van het schip Aernhem, . . .* (Amsterdam, 1663). There were several other accounts of this popular shipwreck story.

[198] The above analysis is based on L'Honoré Naber's introduction in NR, III, viii–xii.

[199] . . . *Lebens und Todes Geschichte, worinnen das Tage Buch seiner Reise von Constantinople aus durch die Bulgarey, Armenien, Persien, und Indien aus Liecht gestellet . . .* (Jena). Poser's book contains no page numbers. Numbers cited in brackets below refer to unnumbered pages within chapter cited.

[200] *Ibid.,* chap. ii, pp. [57–65].

in May he was back in Agra. In July, 1622, Poser moved south, meandering through the Deccan states until he reached Masulipatam just in time to celebrate Christmas at the Dutch factory there. In January, 1623, he embarked on a Dutch ship which sailed up the Malabar Coast to Tegenpatam, where Poser disembarked and returned overland to Masulipatam by way of Negapatam and Tranquebar. From there he traveled through Golconda to Surat, where he arrived early in June, 1623. In September and October of 1623 he visited Cambay and Ahmadabad, and on November 15, 1623, he sailed from Surat for Ormuz and the long journey back to Silesia. He arrived home in December, 1625.

After his death in 1661, his son had Poser's Latin journal translated and published together with brief accounts of Poser's family and early life and of his life after his return from India. Despite his fascinating itinerary, however, the published account of Poser's travels is somewhat disappointing. After readers are apprised of so many "beautiful" and "pleasant" gardens, "splendid" and "secure" castles, "powerful" and "wealthy" nobles, "pure" and "refreshing" springs of water, they are not likely to be able to distinguish one such instance from another. Poser's descriptions, in short, are brief and superficial. His descriptions of Agra,[201] Masulipatam,[202] and Cambay[203] are probably the best in his account. Poser was most interested in politically powerful persons. The account of his Deccan travels, for example, is filled with descriptions of political leaders, their relations with each other, and their roles during the Deccan wars. No complete translations or subsequent editions of Poser's journal appear to have been published.[204]

Another interesting VOC soldier's account appeared in 1678, written in Danish by Frederick Bolling, who served with the VOC from 1669 until 1673.[205] Bolling had been the tutor for a Norwegian major general's family before going to the East, and he became a language teacher in Copenhagen after he returned. His description of life among the troops on VOC ships, therefore, shows a sense of detachment. He comments on the fights between sailors and soldiers and between soldiers of different nationalities.[206] Language and nationality problems were epitomized by two Polish soldiers who were accused of stabbing someone and were unable to explain what had happened because no one on board could speak Polish.[207] Bolling was also very Lutheran and very Danish. Perhaps this explains why he argued

---

[201] *Ibid.*, pp. [57–60].

[202] *Ibid.*, pp. [95–96].   [203] *Ibid.*, pp. [114–19].

[204] For an English translation of his Deccan journey see Ghita Dharampal (trans.), "Heinrich von Poser's Travelogue of the Deccan (1622)," *Quarterly Journal of the Mythic Society*, LXXIII (1982), 103–14.

[205] *Oost-Indiske Reise-Bog hvor udi befattis hans Reise til Oost-Indien saa vel og eendeel Platzers Beskrifvelse med en Andtall hedningers Ceremonier* . . . (Copenhagen).

[206] See "Friderici Bollingii, Oost-Indische reisboek . . . 1678, uit het Deensch vertaald door Mej. Joh. Visscher; met voorbericht en slotnoot van G. P. Rouffaer," *BTLV*, LXVIII (1913), 298.

[207] *Ibid.*, p. 303.

against Copernicus with the ship's pilot, citing Tycho Brahe to support his position.[208] Still, most of Bolling's descriptions are rather ordinary, some may have been fabricated, and some are ill-informed. Even his remarks about Java and Batavia, which contain a great deal of firsthand observation, also contain some oft-repeated stories and stereotypes.[209] The descriptions of places he never visited were apparently intended to fill out his catalog of VOC commercial outposts in Asia. His visits to Tierra del Fuego[210] and to the west coast of Australia[211] may have been fabricated so that he could claim to have been in all five parts of the globe. He also reports some nonsensical things which he apparently misunderstood or uncritically accepted from others: for example, that each Batavian Chinese had at least twenty concubines,[212] that the inhabitants of the Malabar coast spoke Malay,[213] and that people with elephantiasis were a distinct race.[214]

Bolling's descriptions of Batavia during the seventies, and of its churches, preachers, and prominent officials, are quite detailed. Interesting too is his description of the private but illegal trade with the Chinese in the small islands off the coast near Macao. Bolling went there as a bookkeeper for a private merchant in 1672, and he describes his experiences as well as the profits made from the voyage.[215] Apparently his book was not translated or republished during the seventeenth century.

Johann Schreyer's *Neue ost-indianische Reise-Beschreibung,* first published in 1679, contains descriptions of the VOC possessions in Asia.[216] They were apparently all culled from other published accounts. Schreyer, a surgeon who served as a soldier with the VOC from 1669 to 1677, spent his entire enlistment at the Cape of Good Hope and never traveled to Asia.[217] His description of the Hottentots is one of the most important of the century, the result of careful, scientific observation; his remarks about Asia, however, are secondhand.

Translations of foreign works continued to attest to the popularity of Asian travel literature with German readers during the seventies. Most of these were translations from the Dutch. In 1672 Christoph Arnold of Nuremberg brought out, in two volumes, a translation of Caron's Japan, Joost Schouten's Siam, and Hamel's Korea, to which he also added a new

---

[208] *Ibid.,* p. 305.
[209] For Java see *ibid.,* pp. 326–63.   [211] *Ibid.,* p. 324.
[210] *Ibid.,* pp. 307–8.   [212] *Ibid.,* p. 343.
[213] *Ibid.,* p. 358. Perhaps he confused Malay with Malayalam.
[214] *Ibid.,* p. 340.
[215] *Ibid.,* pp. 368–71.
[216] *Neue ost-indianische Reise-Beschreibung, von Anno 1669 biss 1677. Handelnde von unterschiedenen africanischen und barbarischen Völckern, sonderlich derer an dem vor Gebürge Caput Bonae Spei . . .* (Salfeld, 1679; 2d ed., Leipzig, 1681).
[217] Johann Schreyer, *Reise nach dem Kaplande und Beschreibung der Hottentotten, 1669–1677 . . .* in NR, Vol. VII, Pt. 2, p. xii.

edition of Merklein's voyage.[218] Philip Baldaeus' *Naauwkeurige beschryvinge van Malabar en Choromandel* was translated into German by its original Amsterdam publisher in 1672.[219] Also in Amsterdam, the publisher of Olfert Dapper's account of the second Dutch embassy to China translated it into German in 1674.[220] Van Meurs of Amsterdam published a German translation of Jan Janszoon Struys' voyages in 1678.[221] An abridged translation of Struys' third voyage appeared at Zurich during the following year.[222]

Jacques de Bourges' account of the Bishop of Beryte's (Beirut) voyage to Siam and China was translated from the French in 1671.[223] Also in 1671, Philippe de Sainte-Trinité's travels in India appeared in German at Frankfurt.[224] Two more German editions appeared at Frankfurt during the century, one in 1673 and one in 1696.[225] A German translation of Pietro della Valle's *Viaggi* was printed in 1674.[226]

Very few Jesuit publications appeared in the German lands during the seventies, and those which did were not firsthand reports from missionaries. For example, Karl Libertinus (b. 1638) wrote a life of Francis Xavier in 1673,[227] and Mathias Tanner (1630–92) wrote a global history of Jesuit missions and martyrs in 1675.[228] Tanner's work was translated into German and published in 1683 by the Jesuit press in Prague.[229]

Translations of foreign books, scholarly works about Asia, and novels with Asian themes or settings comprise a large share of the Asia-related publications during the eighties, as well. Several of the translations were from French originals: Jean Baptiste Tavernier's travels were published in German translation both at Nuremberg and at Geneva in 1681.[230] According to Ternaux-Compans, the account of the Chevalier de Chaumont's embassy

---

[218] Christoph Arnold (ed.), *Wahrhaftige Beschreibungen dreyer mächtigen Königreiche* . . . (2 vols.; Nuremberg).

[219] *Wahrhaftige ausführliche Beschreibung der berühmten ost-indischen Küsten Malabar und Coromandel, als auch der Insel Zeylon.* . . . The first Dutch edition was also in 1672.

[220] *Gedenkwürdige Verrichtung der Niederländischen Ost-Indischen Gesellschaft in dem Käiserreich Taising oder Sina.* . . . The original Dutch edition was published by Van Meurs in 1670. See above, pp. 490–91.

[221] *Joh. Jansz. Strauszens sehr schwere wiederwertige, und denckwürdige Reysen, durch Italien, Griechenland, Lifland, Moscau, Tartarey, Meden, Persien, Türckey, Ost-Indien, Japan, und unterschiedliche andere Länder.* . . . First Dutch edition, 1676. See above, pp. 497–98.

[222] Struys, *Unglückliche Schiffs-leute; oder merkwirdige Reise zwenzig Holländeren.* . . .

[223] Published in Leipzig. The first French edition was published in Paris, 1661. See Streit, V, 612–13.

[224] The first Latin edition appeared at Lyon in 1649. See Streit, V, 140 and 171, for details.

[225] See Streit, V, 174 and 204, for titles.

[226] *Reiss-Beschreibung in unterschiedliche Theile der Welt, nemlich in Türkey, Aegypten, Palestina, Persien, Ost-Indien, und andere weit entlegene Landschaften* . . . (4 vols. in 2; Geneva). First Italian edition, Rome, 1650–53.

[227] *Divus Franciscus Xavierus indiarum apostolus elogiis illustratus* (Prague).

[228] *Societas Jesu usque ad sanguinis et vitae profusionem militans* . . . (Prague).

[229] *Die Gesellschafft Jesu biss zur Vergiessung ihres Blutes.* . . .

[230] *Vierzig-jährige Reise-Beschreibung* . . . and *Beschreibung der sechs Reisen.* . . . First French edition, 1675.

to Siam appeared in 1687 at Frankfurt.[231] A German translation of Jean Mocquet's *Voyages* appeared in 1688.[232] From the English, Jean Chardin's *Travels*
were translated in 1687,[233] and Robert Knox's important description of
Ceylon in 1689.[234] Olfert Dapper's description of the Mughul Empire was
translated from the Dutch in 1681.[235] In 1687 and 1688 Johann Christoph
Wagner of Nuremberg published two rambling compilations from the available travel literature: one on India and Southeast Asia and one on China and
the Asian steppe lands.[236]

Several firsthand reports from or about Asia appeared in German towns
during the eighties as well, some in Latin, written by Jesuits, and some in
German. Johann Christian Hoffman (*ca.* 1650–82), for example, served as
chaplain with the VOC from 1671 to 1676, dividing his time between the
Cape of Good Hope, Mauritius, and Batavia. The account of his experiences was published in 1680.[237] It is a relatively brief journal, and his description of Batavia adds nothing to what was commonly in print when he
wrote. His description of Mauritius is more useful simply because there are
so few such descriptions.[238] Hoffman's account of a Dutch slaving expedition
to Madagascar and Mozambique is much more interesting, but has to do
with Asia only insofar as the slaves were taken to VOC Asian settlements.[239]
Hoffman incidentally reports the disappearance and presumed death of
Johann Nieuhof on this expedition.[240] He also translated a vividly detailed
Dutch account of the major earthquake which struck Amboina on February
17, 1674.[241]

Before he left China, Michael Boym had prepared for publication several
treatises on Chinese medicine, including a Latin translation of Wang Shu-
hua's work on the pulse and its use in the diagnosis of disease. These fell into
the hands of the Dutch botanist Andreas Cleyer, who published them at
Frankfurt in 1682.[242] A few years later Cleyer apparently received more of

---

[231] *Gesandschaft nach Siam.* First French edition, 1686.

[232] *Wunderbare jedoch gründlich- und warhaffte Geschichte und Reise Begebnisse in Africa, Asia, Ost-
und West Indien . . .* (Lüneburg). First French edition, 1617.

[233] *Curieuse persian- und ost-indische Reisebeschreibung bestehend in einem ordentlichen Journal oder
täglichen Verzeichnüss seiner in Persien und Ost-Indien . . .* (Leipzig). Chardin's journal was written in French but first published in English translation at London in 1686. The first French
edition (Amsterdam, 1686) is a translation of the London edition.

[234] *Ceylonische Reise-Beschreibung; oder historische Erzehlung von der in Ost-Indien gelegenen Insul
Ceylon . . .* (Leipzig). Ternaux-Compans lists a Leipzig, 1680, edition, but this is very likely an
error, since the first English edition was not published until 1681.

[235] *Asia; oder ausführliche Beschreibung des Reichs des Grossen Mogols, und eines grossen Theils von
Indien . . .* (Nuremberg). Another edition by the same publisher appeared in 1688–89.

[236] *Interiora orientis detecta, oder grundrichtige und eigentliche Beschreibung aller heut zu Tag bekandten grossen und herrlichen Reiche des Orients; . . .* (Augsburg, 1687); *Das mächtige Kayser-
Reich Sina und die asiatische Tartarey vor Augen gestellet* (Augsburg, 1688).

[237] *Oost-indianische Voyage; oder eigentliches Verzeichnüs worin nicht nur einige merckwürdige
Vorfälle . . .* (Cassel). Reprinted in part in NR, VII, 55–67.

[238] *Ibid.,* pp. 42, 46–52.   [240] *Ibid.,* pp. 41–44.

[239] *Ibid.,* pp. 32–43.   [241] *Ibid.,* pp. 67–71.

[242] *Specimen medicinae sinicae, sive opuscula medica ad mentem sinensium . . . editit Andreas Cleyer.*

Boym's manuscripts, including the prefaces which help make the *Specimen mediciae* understandable; these he published in 1686.[243]

Another important Jesuit publication appeared at Dillingen in 1687—Ferdinand Verbiest's account of the troubles which plagued the official Jesuit astronomers in Peking during the late sixties and of their rehabilitation under the K'ang-hsi emperor.[244] Included with Verbiest's report is Father Philippe Couplet's catalog of the Jesuit missionaries who served in China from 1581 to 1681.[245]

A very interesting account by Elias Hesse (b. 1630) of Dresden first appeared in 1687.[246] Hesse had been recruited in 1680 along with a group of Saxon miners by Benjamin Olitz, the VOC commissioner of mines. Olitz' assignment was to exploit the gold mines at Sillida, south of Padang on the west coast of Sumatra: mines that some Dutch enthusiasts thought might rival Spain's Peruvian lode. Malayans had worked these mines earlier, and extravagant rumors about their richness circulated among European travelers in Asia. Since few seventeenth-century Dutchmen knew anything about mining, the VOC directors entrusted the operation to Olitz and his fellow Saxons. Hesse was the secretary or clerk of the expedition.

Hesse was a perceptive, although not always unbiased, observer, a clever writer with a delightfully sour sense of humor. Few travelers so vividly conveyed the feel of life in Dutch Asia. For Olitz, Hesse, and their compatriots, it was not a good trip. The sea was an alien place to them. They all became desperately seasick, and it comforted Hesse little to observe that none of the Dutch sailors became ill.[247] The harsh life at sea, the unappetizing food, and the severe punishments for small crimes led Hesse to describe it as "slavery" under the "tyranny" of a skipper.[248] It was also a dangerous life. If the poor German soldier or miner survived the terrifying storms, the scurvy and dysentery, rancid rations, hostile natives at watering stops, and harsh shipboard justice, he might still be done in by a sailor. Hesse contended that the animosity between Germans and Poles, Danes and Swedes, English and Scots, French and Spanish, Persians and Turks, and Chinese and Japanese all paled in comparison to that between sailors and soldiers on

---

[243] *Clavis medica ad chinarum doctrinam de pulsibus*. . . . published as Appendix 1 in *Miscellanea curiosa* (Nuremberg). For a convincing discussion of Boym's authorship of these treatises as well as of the *Les secrets de la médecine des Chinois* (Grenoble, 1671) and of the migration of Boym's manuscripts to Europe see Edward Kajdanski, "Michael Boym's *Medicus sinicus*," *T'oung Pao*, LXXIII (1987), 161–89. Cleyer, a corresponding fellow of the Nuremberg academy, also sent descriptions and drawings of Asian plants to the academy for publication in the *Miscellanea* (see pls. 356–58).

[244] *Astronomia europaea sub imperatore tartaro sinico Cám Hý appellato ex umbra in lucem revocata*. . . .

[245] "Catalogus Patrem Societatis Jesu qui post obitum S. Francisci Xavieri ab anno 1581. usque ad annum 1681. in imperio sinarum Jesu Christi fidem propagarunt," in *ibid.*, pp. 100–126.

[246] The second, revised, edition is entitled *Ost-Indische Reise-Beschreibung oder Diarium*, . . . (Leipzig, 1690).

[247] Elias Hesse, *Gold-Bergwerke in Sumatra, 1680–1683* . . . in NR, X, 19.

[248] *Ibid.*, pp. 22–23.

VOC East Indiamen.[249] Nor did things improve when they reached Sumatra's west coast—the pest coast Hesse called it. As he describes it, the work was frustrating and difficult, the heat and insects unbearable; most of the Germans were sick, and the Sumatrans and Javans could not be trusted. He yearned for home. For Olitz, things were worse. He was almost continuously ill since putting out from Amsterdam, his wife died at sea, one of his sons died at Batavia, and Olitz himself died at Sillida in May, 1682. The whole operation was a failure. Olitz's report, which Hesse delivered to Batavia, paints a very gloomy outlook. He found no rich veins, and the cost of extracting the gold was much too high for the venture to be profitable.[250] The VOC closed down the enterprise entirely in 1694.[251] Hesse returned to his beloved Saxony in 1683 with Olitz' remaining son and personal effects. Before he left Batavia he composed two long poems to bid a happy farewell to Asia.[252] He might have been less jubilant had he known how rough the homeward passage would be.

In addition to descriptions of Sumatra and the mines, Hesse describes Java, Batavia, and the Malabar coast of India. Some of his descriptions were borrowed from other works—especially the material on India—but much of it was, if not new, at least based on his own observations. His word pictures of the hustle and bustle of life in Batavia, the pompous processions, and the coming and going of native princes and their entourages are particularly vivid. He describes the celebrations in Batavia and in Bantam in 1683 after the Dutch victory in the war with Bantam.[253] He also sailed close enough to Krakatoa in the Sunda Straits to see and describe the effects of the 1680 eruption.[254] A second, revised, edition of Hesse's book came out in 1690; a third in 1735. Simon de Vries translated it into Dutch in 1694.[255] De Vries' translation of Hesse's account also contains the accounts of two other German travelers to the Dutch Asian empire: Christoph Schweitzer's and Christoph Frick's.

The Württemberger Schweitzer's journal was first published at Tübingen in 1688.[256] He too had enlisted as a soldier with the VOC and sailed from Holland in January, 1676. After a brief stay on Java, Schweitzer was assigned to Ceylon, where he spent the remainder of his five-year enlistment. Schweitzer was literate and apparently rather bright. He claimed to have quickly learned both Sinhalese and Portuguese after his arrival in Ceylon.[257] This may account for his fairly rapid advancement. He became the storekeeper and paymaster for the small Dutch fort at Sitavaka and a secretary to

[249] *Ibid.,* p. 52.
[250] *Ibid.,* pp. 61–72.
[251] *Ibid.,* p. ix.
[252] *Ibid.,* pp. 117–26.
[253] *Ibid.,* pp. 109–10, 128–34.
[254] *Ibid.,* p. 54.
[255] *Drie seer aenmercklijcke reysen nae en door veelerley gewesten in Oost-Indien . . .* (Utrecht, 1694).
[256] *Journal- und Tage-Buch seiner sechs-jährigen Ost-Indianischen Reise. . . .* The materials on Ceylon are translated into English in Raven-Hart (trans.), *op. cit.* (n. 184), pp. 37–82.
[257] See *Reise nach Java und Ceylon, 1675–1682 . . .* in NR, XI, 45.

the Dutch commander at Colombo; he served with the temporary rank of captain on a mission to Kandy, commanded the troops in a small squadron which tried to suppress infringers in the pepper trade along the Malabar coast, and finally was made the supervisor of clerks at the VOC factory in Colombo.

Schweitzer's journal displays more literary skill and a broader view of his activities than did most of the other soldiers' accounts. He was a perceptive observer and he conveyed what he saw in an entertaining, sometimes witty, style. As with most of the soldiers' accounts, his description of his daily life and duties is more useful and interesting than his attempts to describe Java or Ceylon systematically. Much can be learned from Schweitzer's journal about the daily life of VOC soldiers and the society they created in the Dutch outposts. He writes about the soldiers' food and drink, the prices they paid, the wages they earned, their leisure-time activities, and the discipline and punishments with which they lived. Schweitzer's sketch of the racially mixed society of German or Dutch soldiers, their Sinhalese wives, and their half-breed children is particularly perceptive. His description of Ceylon is also better than most such soldiers' descriptions.[258] He seems to have borrowed little from other accounts and to have based his own primarily on what he saw himself. He was sometimes gullible, however, and repeated some of the superstitious and outlandish stories that apparently circulated among the VOC soldiery. He was also capable of stretching the truth on occasion. For example, he reported the arrival at Sitavaka, where he was stationed, of the Englishmen Robert Knox and Stephen Nuttall in June, 1680.[259] In fact, Knox and Nuttall escaped from their nineteen-year imprisonment in Kandy to Areppa, another Dutch fort, in October, 1679.[260] Nevertheless, Schweitzer's account of Ceylon remains a fairly accurate, independent description of the island and its inhabitants.

Christoph Frick's *Ost-Indianische Räysen* was first published at Ulm in 1692.[261] A surgeon from a medical family in that city, Frick served the VOC as a surgeon from May, 1680, until late in 1685. The urge to travel in strange countries drove him to join the VOC,[262] and even shipwreck during a snowstorm at False Cape on the outward voyage failed to dull his taste for the changing scene. He survived the wreck, walked to Table Bay, and continued to Batavia in another VOC ship.[263] Once there, he served in the 1682 war

---

[258] *Ibid.*, pp. 46–80.

[259] *Ibid.*, p. 116.

[260] Robert Knox, *An Historical Relation of Ceylon*, ed. S. D. Saparamadu, in *Ceylon Historical Journal*, Vol. VI, Nos. 1–4 (July, 1956, to April, 1957), p. 271.

[261] *Ost-Indianische Räysen und Krieges-Dienste, . . . Da den insonderheit der Bantamische Krieg auf Gross-Java von Anfang bis zu Ende wahrhafftig vorgestellt und entworffen. . . .*

[262] See C. E. Fayle (ed.), *Voyages to the East Indies: Christopher Fryke and Christopher Schweitzer . . .* (London, [1929]), p. 1.

[263] *Ibid.*, p. ix.

with Bantam, after which he was put in charge of the hospital at Batavia. But Frick still had the wanderlust, and he continually used his skill and influence to obtain shipboard assignments. Before he left for home in February of 1685 he had visited the north coast of Java, Bali, Banda, Amboina, the Moluccas, Formosa, Japan, Malacca, Ceylon, the Malabar Coast, Surat, the Coromandel Coast, Bengal, Pegu, Arakan, Siam, and Makassar. He saw, in short, a great deal more than either Hesse or Schweitzer.[264]

Frick was an intelligent and open-minded observer. His descriptions of Java, Batavia, and the Batavian Chinese, for example, contain much that was commonly available in other travel books, but they also contain new information resulting from his own observations.[265] What he reports is generally accurate; his account of the war with Bantam in 1682, the largest section in his book, is a good example.[266] He seems to have taken some pains to get the story straight. So, too, when describing people with elephantiasis, he reports that the tissue in the swollen leg is soft and spongy to the touch and that the victims seem able to run unimpeded by the malady.[267] The general accuracy of his account makes it difficult to dismiss his matter-of-fact observation that there were three or four English and French ships in Nagasaki harbor when he visited there.[268] Like most European writers, he thought very poorly of the Javans.[269] That, however, did not prevent him from describing the community of holy men living at the Blue Pepper Mountain near Batavia dispassionately and with some understanding.[270]

There appears to have been no other German editions of Frick's account. It was included in Simon de Vries' 1694 *Drie seer aenmercklijcke reysen*.[271] De Vries' Dutch translation of both Frick and Schweitzer's accounts—but not Hesse's—was in turn translated into English in 1700.[272]

Another account of the VOC mining operation on Sumatra appeared in 1690 at Nuremberg, written by Johann Wilhelm Vogel (1637–1723), who became director of mines for the VOC when Olitz died.[273] It was republished in 1704 and again in 1716.

In 1692 George Meister's *Der orientalisch-indianische Kunst- und Lust-Gärtner* appeared, a large, lavishly illustrated description of the flora of Java, Japan, and Malacca.[274] Meister, another Saxon, went to Java as a VOC soldier in 1677. After a brief period of military service, he became an assistant to the botanist Andreas Cleyer in Batavia, with whom he also made journeys to

[264] For a brief sketch of Frick's voyages see *ibid.*, pp. ix–xii.
[265] *Ibid.*, pp. 26–30.
[266] *Ibid.*, pp. 38–69.   [269] *Ibid.*, p. 53.
[267] *Ibid.*, pp. 106–7.   [270] *Ibid.*, pp. 152–53.
[268] *Ibid.*, p. 98.   [271] See above, p. 540.
[272] *A Relation of Two Several Voyages Made into the East-Indies, by C. F. and C. Schewitzer* [*sic*] . . . , trans. S. L. (London, 1700).
[273] *Diarium oder Journal seiner gethanen Reise aus Teutschland nach Holland und Ost-Indien.*
[274] Published in Dresden; further editions of 1710, 1713, 1730, and 1731.

Japan and Malacca before returning to Saxony in 1689. Meister's book contains not only descriptions of Asian plants, but also much good information about Japan and about VOC affairs in Asia during the eighties. He also brought back to Europe specimens of trees, plants, and seeds at the behest of Cleyer. Packets of the seed samples were forwarded to Christian Mentzel in Berlin, to Jacobus Breynius in Danzig, and to Pieter van Dam in Amsterdam. The story of the return voyage of 1688 is told by Vogel, who was a shipboard companion to Meister, in his *Diarium oder Journal.*[275]

In 1690 there appeared an account of journeys into Russia and Siberia by Georg Adam Schleusing of Bautzen.[276] Besides writing about various parts of the Russian empire, Schleusing gives a useful description of the overland route to China.[277] He apparently did not visit China himself, although he included a brief notice of the Manchu Conquest taken from Martini.[278]

Another description of the overland journey to China appeared in 1698 with the publication of Adam Brand's *Beschreibung der chinesischen Besandschaft.*[279] Brand was the secretary to Evert Ysbrandszoon Ides' embassy from the Russian Czar to Peking of 1693–95. His *Beschreibung* is valuable not only for its description of the route and the Siberian tribes he encountered along the way, but especially for his vivid account of the embassy's experiences in China, his description of the Great Wall and Chinese frontier settlements, and his report of the embassy's reception in Peking. Brand includes a brief general description of China, which appears to have been taken from standard published works.[280] His eyewitness reports of the temples he visited, the dust on Peking streets, the negotiations with Chinese officials, the official banquets he attended, and so forth, are his most important contributions to Europe's knowledge of Asia. Brand's *Beschreibung* reappeared several times during the eighteenth century. The philosopher Leibniz had already translated it into Latin and included it in his *Novissima sinica* in 1697.[281] It was translated into English in 1698, French in 1699, and Dutch in 1699.

In 1697 Daniel Parthey of Frankenberg had an account of his travels published at Nuremberg.[282] Parthey appears to have been another German vic-

---

[275] See below, p. 1884–86. In 1693 a book by Christian Burckhard, *Ost-Indianische Reisebeschreibung* (Halle and Leipzig) was also published. There is a copy at the University of Minnesota, bound with Dellon, *Neue Reisebeschreibungen nach Ost-Indien.*

[276] *Neu-entdecktes Sibyrien oder Siewerien, . . . gräntzen so wohl bisz an Kara Kathaya und Chinesische Mauer . . .* (Jena).

[277] *Ibid.*, pp. 61–71.

[278] *Ibid.*, p. 65.

[279] *Beschreibung der chinesischen Reise, welche vermittelst einer zaaris. Besandschaf[t] durch dero Ambassadeur, Herrn Isbrand . . .* (Hamburg).

[280] Brand, *A Journal of an Embassy from their Majesties John and Peter Alexowits, Emperors of Muscovy . . . into China . . .* (London, 1698), pp. 100–106.

[281] See D. Lach, *The Preface to Leibniz' "Novissima sinica"* (Honolulu, 1957), pp. 53–54.

[282] *. . . ost-indische und persianische neun-jährige Kriegs-Dienste und warhafftige Beschreibung. A*

tim of the wanderlust. After traveling around the continent for several years, he and three companions arrived at Amsterdam in March, 1677, hoping to find a ship for London. He writes that the war between the Dutch Republic and France prevented them from going to England, and subsequently they signed on as soldiers with the VOC.[283] He sailed from Texel on May 28 and arrived at Colombo on December 23, 1677. Except for an antibandit expedition to the Persian Gulf in 1679–80 and a voyage to Batavia to participate in the attack on Bantam in January, 1683, Parthey remained on Ceylon until January, 1686, when he embarked for Europe. The account of his travels and experiences is brief—only 113 duodecimo pages. Little of Ceylon's landscape and people shows through it. His description of the cities he visited—Colombo, Galle, Batavia, and Bantam—are mostly confined to the buildings, streets, and fortifications. His best eyewitness descriptions are of an elephant roundup in February, 1684,[284] and a hike up Adam's Peak in May, 1684.[285] The last part of the book contains descriptions of Ceylon, Bengal, Banda, St. Jago, Amboina, Bantam, and Persia. Most of these places Parthey never visited, and even the descriptions of Ceylon and Bantam seem to have come largely from the books of his predecessors.

In 1704 an account of David Tappen's VOC service appeared at Hannover and Wolfenbüttel.[286] Tappen served in the Dutch Asian empire from 1667 to 1682, first as a soldier and later as a tutor to the children of a Dutch official. As a soldier he visited Batavia, Malacca, and Surat; as a tutor he accompanied the Dutch commercial expedition to Foochow from 1677 to 1679.[287] He apparently had sufficient leisure to do considerable sightseeing, and his account contains some interesting, if unsophisticated, descriptions of the Chinese he observed, of Foochow and its environs, and of the Dutch activities there.

Several foreign descriptions of Asia were translated into German during the last decade of the century. Jacob Spon and George Wheeler's travels were translated from French and appeared in 1690.[288] A German edition of Jean de Thévenot's travels was published at Frankfurt in 1693;[289] also from the French, Father Louis Le Comte's description of China became available to

---

copy of this very rare account is in the University of Minnesota library. Ternaux-Compans lists a Nuremberg, 1687, edition, but we can find no other reference to it. The last two pages of Parthey's book contain his VOC passport in Dutch and German bearing the date 30 April 1687. This is a reissued passport, however; Parthey lost the original to the bandits who robbed him while enroute from Hamburg to his family home in Frankenberg in September, 1686.

[283] *Ibid.*, pp. 6–7.
[284] *Ibid.*, pp. 68–74.   [285] *Ibid.*, pp. 75–78.
[286] *Fünffzehen-jährige curiöse und denkwürdige auch sehr gefährliche ost-indianische Reise-Beschreibung* . . .
[287] See John E. Wills, *Pepper, Guns, and Parleys* . . . (Cambridge, Mass., 1974), pp. 160–79.
[288] *Italienische, dalmatische griechische und orientalische Reise-Beschreibung* . . . (Nuremberg).
[289] *Dess Herrn Thevenots Reysen in Europa, Asia, und Africa, worinnen gehandelt wird von der morgenlandischen Reise.* . . .

German readers in 1699.[290] Gabriel Dellon's account of the Inquisition at Goa was translated into German in 1698,[291] and the account of his voyage to India was translated in 1700.[292]

Finally, German scholars like the philosopher Leibniz and Christian Mentzel, the long-time personal physician and sinological adviser to the Great Elector, also published works during the century's last decade which made information about China available to more readers in the German lands. Mentzel's translation of Philippe Couplet's earlier work on Chinese chronology appeared in 1696.[293] It also included a brief account of Ides' overland trip to China. The first edition of Leibniz' *Novissima sinica* appeared in the following year. Still more information about China appeared in the major Rites Controversy publications of 1700: the Jesuit *Historia cultus sinensium* and *Continuatio historiae sinensium*[294] as well as the *De ritibus sinensium*, a response to the Jesuit publications.

The first two decades of the seventeenth century saw a large volume of publications pertaining to Asia roll from German presses. Almost all these books were either Jesuit works translated from other languages into Latin or German or translations of Dutch travel reports. While they do not constitute a German contribution to Europe's knowledge of Asia, they attest to a strong demand for information about Asia in the German lands. The most impressive of these publications were the large and lavish collections of travel relations compiled by Theodor de Bry and by Levinus Hulsius.

Whether because of the Thirty Years' War or for other reasons, far fewer books about Asia were printed in the German lands between 1620 and 1650; almost none during the 1630's. After the war the volume of publications increased again, giving evidence of a still vigorous demand for news from Asia among readers in central Europe. Most of the reports about Asia published during the latter half of the century were still translated from foreign works, and many were still in Latin. Throughout the century, Germans were primarily consumers rather than producers of information about the overseas world. Nevertheless, some of the many Germans who traveled to Asia as servants of the Dutch East India Company produced a fairly impressive number of eyewitness accounts of what they had seen and done. These reports, while not major contributions to Europe's knowledge of

---

[290] *Das heutige China* . . . (Frankfurt and Leipzig). Two parts were published in 1699; a third part appeared in 1700.

[291] *Die niemals erhörte Tyranney und Grausamkeit der portugiesischen Inquisition, oder des geistlichen Richter-Stuels, in der ost-indianischen Haupt-Statt Goa;* . . . (Frankfurt).

[292] *Neue Reisebeschreibung nach Ost-Indien* . . . (Dresden, 1700). This citation comes from Ternaux-Compans. We have found no other reference to it.

[293] Christian Mentzel, *Kurtze chinesische Chronologia oder Zeit-Register aller chinesischen Käyser* . . . (Berlin).

[294] Both published at Cologne.

Asia, were nevertheless useful bits of corroboration or detached commentary on what was reported in far greater volume and detail by the Dutch. Finally, German publishers produced some of the major Jesuit works on China written during the seventeenth century: Trigault's landmark description of China, Martini's account of the Manchu Conquest, his ancient Chinese history, Schall's relation, and Boym's study of Chinese flora.

CHAPTER VIII

The English Literature

In England the last decades of the sixteenth century saw a flurry of activity in the publication of travel literature, much of it resulting from the efforts of Richard Eden, Richard Willes, and Richard Hakluyt. They coupled their collections of travelogues and translations of foreign travel literature with pleas to the royalty and merchants of England to claim a share in the exploration, commerce, and colonization of the overseas world.[1] There was much to report. During these years Gilbert, Frobisher, Davis, and Hudson searched for a northeast passage to Asia and Englishmen cheered the daring exploits of Drake, Hawkins, Cavendish, and Raleigh and, of course, the defeat of the Armada. Ralph Fitch returned in 1591 from his travels in India and Southeast Asia with up-to-date reports on trade and political conditions there and with sound advice about English commercial opportunities in Asia. In the nineties, too, the first English fleets under James Lancaster and Benjamin Wood had sailed around the Cape of Good Hope to India, and while these were not successful voyages in themselves, they demonstrated Iberian weakness by the many Portuguese prizes they took. Meanwhile numerous Dutch fleets were profiting from the Asian trade because of the inability of the Portuguese to retain their control over it. English observers at first admired the Dutch successes, but soon feared they would be more effectively excluded by the Dutch than by the Portuguese. The culmination of all this activity was the establishment of the royally chartered East India Company in 1600.[2]

[1] For details see *Asia,* I, 208–15; and J. Parker, *Books to Build an Empire* (Amsterdam, 1965), pp. 1–172.

[2] See for general background W. Foster, *England's Quest of Eastern Trade* (London, 1933); B. Penrose, *Tudor and Early Stuart Voyages* (Washington, 1962); G. D. Ramsay, *English Overseas*

Most of these English achievements as well as the accomplishments of earlier English mariners had been reported by Eden and Willes, and by Hakluyt in his *Divers Voyages Touching the Discovery of America* (1582) and in the first edition of his *Principall Navigations* (1589). In 1580 there had appeared the third edition of William Bourne's *A Regiment for the Sea* (London). This was the first English book on navigation, and this edition was the first to contain a discourse on navigation to Cathay; it was republished seven more times before 1631. More important for the English readers' knowledge of Asia, however, were the translations of Mendoza's *History of China* (1588), Cesare Fedrici's *Voyages* (1588), Linschoten's *Itinerario* (1598), and the reports of the first two Dutch voyages to the East Indies (1598 and 1599).[3] Apparently most of the translations resulted from Hakluyt's influence and urging.[4] The capstone of all this literary activity, and a fitting parallel to the establishment of the East India Company, was the publication of the second edition of Hakluyt's *Principall Navigations* between 1598 and 1600.[5] Together with the translations from Mendoza, Fedrici, and Linschoten, Hakluyt's collection provided English readers with the most important and recent information about Asia resulting from the sixteenth-century discoveries and travels overseas.

The second edition of the *Principall Navigations* was much more than a republication of the original; it was an entirely new work. It is much larger and differs from the first edition in both scope and emphasis. Voyages to Asia occupy a much larger place than they did in the first edition, and, unlike the first edition, the second includes accounts of foreign voyages as well as English. Still Hakluyt published only those accounts written by observers who had actually made journeys on their own. All of the many translated materials had appeared in print before; only Fedrici's *Voyage* had earlier been translated into English. Despite the inclusion of foreign voyages, Hakluyt's primary concern, as the title indicates, was still the English voyages. The second edition includes Queen Elizabeth's letters to the "Great

Trade during the Centuries of Emergence (London, 1957); and C. Tragen, *Elizabethan Venture* (London, 1953).

³Juan Gonzales de Mondoza, *The History of the Great and Mighty Kingdom of China, and the Situation thereof. . . ,* trans. R. Parke (London, 1588); Cesare Fedrici, *The Voyage and Travaile of M. C. Federici, Merchant of Venys into the Easte India and Indys and Beyond the Indys. . . ,* trans. T. Hickok (London, 1588); John Huyghen van Linschoten, *His Discours of Voyages into ye East and West Indies* (London, 1598); *The Description of a Voyage Made by Certain Ships of Holland into the East Indies, with their Adventures and Successe . . . who Set forth on the Second of Aprill, 1595, and Returned on the 14 of August, 1597,* trans. W. P. (London, 1598); *A True Report of the Gainfull, Prosperous, and Speedy Voyage to Java in the East Indies, Performed by a Fleete of Eight Ships of Amsterdam: Which set forth from Texell in Holland, the First of Maie, 1598. Stilo Novo. Whereof Foure Returned Again the 19 of July 1599, in Less than 15. Moneths, the Other Foure Went Forward from Java for the Moluccas* (London, [1599]). On Eden, Willes, and Hakluyt see *Asia*, I, 209–15.

⁴See G. B. Parks, *Richard Hakluyt and the English Voyages* (New York, 1928), and J. A. Williamson, "Richard Hakluyt," in *Richard Hakluyt and His Successors* (London, 1946), pp. 20–40.

⁵Richard Hakluyt, *The Principall Navigations, Voiages and Discoveries of the English Nation, Made by Sea and Overland* (3 vols., London).

Mogul" and to the emperor of China (II.i, 245, and III, 842–54), John New-berry's letters (II.i, 245–50), Ralph Fitch's letter and account of his travels (II.i, 250–65), Thomas Stevens' letter from Goa (1579) (II.i, 99–101), an account of Lancaster's voyage of 1591 (II.ii, 102–10), and an account of Drake and Cavendish's circumnavigations (III, 730–825).[6]

Hakluyt was an avid collector and a competent editor. He occasionally trimmed the lengthy introductions or prefaces to the accounts—thus irritat-ing modern researchers—but he did not tinker with the narrations them-selves, probably because he not only hoped the descriptions of the overseas world would challenge his countrymen to undertake overseas trade and travel, but he also wanted *The Principall Navigations* to serve as a reliable guide to those who accepted the challenge.

I

THE FIRST GENERATION, 1600–1626

Hakluyt's work surely helped encourage English overseas enterprises. But despite the impressive foundation he had laid, English printed contributions to Europe's knowledge of Asia during the first two decades of the seven-teenth century were limited in number and thin on information. The *Prin-cipall Navigations* was never republished. It was an expensive set of volumes, to be sure, but it also seems that there was insufficient demand for travel literature in England to make its republication profitable. Rather, English printers of the century's earlier half concentrated on publishing controversial religious and political tracts in cheap and shoddy editions.[7] A comparison with Dutch publications during the same decades proves to be astonishing. For example, Linschoten's *Itinerario* went through fifteen editions and trans-lations during the seventeenth century; twenty-four publications, editions, and translations resulted from the first Dutch voyage to the East Indies under De Houtman, and nineteen from the second fleet, commanded by Van Neck and Van Warwijck.[8] About the first English East India Company voyage under Sir James Lancaster, 1601–3, only two brief accounts were issued, neither of which was republished during the seventeenth century.

The first of the 1603 publications was apparently written by someone from the "Ascension," the ship which did not accompany Lancaster to Ban-tam but returned to England after the fleet left Sumatra.[9] It traces the voyage

---

[6] See D. F. Lach, "The Far East," and M. F. Strachen, "India," in D. B. Quinn (ed.), *The Hakluyt Handbook* (2 vols., London, 1974), I, 208–22.

[7] See C. Clair, *A History of European Printing* (London, 1976), p. 273.

[8] *Cf.* above, pp. 435–41.

[9] *A True and Large Discourse of the Voyage of the Whole Fleete of Ships Set Forth the 20. of Aprill 1601. by the Gouvernours and Assistants of the East-Indian Merchants in London, to the East In-dies . . .* (London, 1603).

out, the landing in the Nicobar Islands, the reception and trade at Acheh, and the voyage home. The descriptions of Acheh and of Lancaster's reception by its sultan are detailed and interesting.[10] The account also contains a list of Malay words and a list of "certain words of the Pegu language," most of which are recognizably from the Mon language.[11]

The other 1603 account, *A Letter Written to the Right Worshipfull the Governours and Assistants of the East Indian Merchants in London,* was also composed by someone aboard the "Ascension." It is much briefer than *A True and Large Discourse* and contains almost no description of Asian people or places. The version of this voyage later published by Purchas (1625) was apparently based on the 1603 publications and on reports from someone else who accompanied Lancaster. It tells of the negotiations and trade at Bantam and Acheh, but it contains only a slight description of Bantam. The description of Acheh in Purchas is slightly more detailed than that in *A True and Large Discourse;* both describe a strange tree found in the Nicobar Islands that seemed to grow from a large worm. All three accounts relate in detail the capture of a Portuguese carrack off Sumatra. Purchas also tells how Lancaster greatly reduced deaths from survy on his ship by dosing his crew with lemon juice.[12] Losses from scurvy on the other ships ran very high, as indeed they did on subsequent voyages; apparently the Company did not follow Lancaster's effective prescription.

Lancaster's voyage was a qualified financial success; despite the high mortality rate, all four ships returned with an ample cargo of pepper. The Dutch, however, had been flooding the market with pepper, and the price was down. The English company, therefore, paid out dividends in pepper rather than in cash, and competition among the investor-sellers further depressed the price. Lancaster had also left factors at Bantam to buy pepper for the next fleet, thus founding the first English factory in Asia, and thereby committing the Company to a second voyage.[13]

Lancaster returned to London on September 11, 1603. Not until April, 1604, were the ships readied and sufficient capital raised for a second voyage. The four ships of the first voyage were employed and they were commanded by Henry Middleton, who had been second in command on the first voyage. Having arrived at Bantam on December 23, 1604, two of the ships were quickly sent home loaded with the pepper Lancaster's factors had purchased. Middleton took the other two ships to the Moluccas where he found Steven van der Hagen's huge fleet busily reducing Portuguese strongholds and consolidating Dutch control over the Spiceries. Despite Dutch

[10] *Ibid.*, unnumbered pages 13–23.

[11] W. Foster (ed.), *The Voyages of Sir James Lancaster to Brazil and the East Indies, 1591–1603* ("HS," 2d ser., LXXXV; London, 1940), pp. 133, 141.

[12] *Ibid.*, p. 79. On Purchas' collection see below, pp. 556–68.

[13] Foster (ed.), *op. cit.* (n. 11), pp. xxx–xxxii.

hostility Middleton was able to buy some cloves at Tidore and some mace and nutmeg in the Bandas. He returned to the Downs with three ships on May 6, 1606.[14]

An anonymous report of Middleton's voyage was published in 1606.[15] It is particularly rich in details about the negotiations, politics, trade, and battles in the Spiceries during the eventful year of 1605. Middleton treated with all parties: the Portuguese on Amboina and Tidore, the "kings" of Tidore and Ternate, and the Dutch. The Portuguese were cordial and willing to let the English trade, apparently in the hope that Middleton would help them against the Dutch. The Dutch feared—indeed suspected—such an alliance and therefore treated the English warily; the Dutch obviously had no intension of permitting Middleton to poach on a commercial preserve which they planned to monopolize. Middleton meanwhile watched Van der Hagen capture the Portuguese forts on Amboina and Tidore, and conclude or tighten treaties with native princes to close out the English. The writer of *The Last East-Indian Voyage* observed that the Moluccans disliked the Dutch as much as they did the Portuguese, and included copies of friendly letters from the rulers of Ternate, Tidore, and Bantam; but he saw little cause for optimism about the future of English trade in the Spiceries.

Much more interesting as a description was Edmund Scott's account of his nearly three years' residence in Bantam, also published in 1606.[16] Scott was one of the factors left in Bantam by Lancaster in 1603. He became chief of the English factory after the two senior merchants died. His report is a rather pathetic tale of how the small group of Englishmen struggled to survive, trade, and preserve their goods until the next English fleet arrived. They were constantly threatened by fire and theft. Scott reported that at least seven fires were set during his residence in Bantam, several of which destroyed large sections of the city. "Villains," he reported, would brazenly examine the locks on the factory doors in broad daylight while the English were watching.[17] One group of Chinese tried to enter the warehouse by tunneling from a neighboring compound.[18] The English had to keep a continuous sharp watch and were so frequently awakened to fight intruders or fire that they could scarcely sleep at night.[19] Because about one-half of the English died during the three years—victims of Bantam's unhealthy climate, Scott thought—the watching and fire-fighting had to be done by fewer and fewer men. One can at least sympathize with him when he soberly avers

---

[14] For details see W. Foster (ed.), *The Voyage of Sir Henry Middleton to Moluccas, 1604–1606* ("HS," 2d ser., LXXXVIII; London, 1943), pp. ix–xxx.

[15] *The Last East-Indian Voyage. Containing Much Varietie of the State of the Severall Kingdomes where they have traded; . . .* (London).

[16] *An Exact Discourse of the Subtilties, Fashishions, Pollicies, Religion, and Ceremonies of the East Indians, as well Chyneses as Javans . . .* (London).

[17] *Ibid.*, unnumbered p. 3.

[18] *Ibid.*, unnumbered pp. 29–44.   [19] *Ibid.*, unnumbered pp. 14–15.

that "the *Javans* and *Chyneses,* from the highest to the lowest, are all villains, and have not one sparke of grace in them." [20]

The trade also presented problems: duties and customs appeared to be arbitrary and had to be negotiated, presents had to be given to local officials, Chinese middlemen were frequently dishonest and often adulterated the pepper by adding dirt and water to the sacks; the Dutch drove up the prices or bribed officials to interfere with English purchases. While the Dutch were, here as elsewhere, tough competitors in commerce, Scott reports that in matters relating to the preservation of lives, property, or general well-being, the Dutch and English unstintingly helped each other. [21] Nevertheless Scott dressed his men in royal colors and held a coronation day parade each November 17 in an effort to distinguish the English from the Dutch who, he said, were developing a bad reputation for drunkenness and rowdyness in Bantam. [22]

In telling his story Scott naturally includes a great deal of information about life in Bantam. Readers could learn about its insecure government during the reign of an underaged king, about Bantam's relationship to other Javan rulers, and about a major rebellion. They could read about a great many Javan social or religious customs and about the importance of the Chinese community in Bantam. Scott witnessed and described a royal progress [23] and the month-long celebration attending the young king's circumcision. [24] Finally he includes a ten-page description of Bantam and Java at the end of his account—the best English description of any Asian place since those printed in Hakluyt. [25] Neither of the two 1606 publications saw subsequent editions, although an abbreviated version of Scott's *Discourse* appeared in Purchas' collection in 1625.

While the literary results of the first two English seventeenth-century voyages were disappointing, they were certainly better than what followed. Most of the voyages made by English East India Company ships during the next two decades produced only manuscripts which went unpublished until their appearance in Purchas' collection. In fact, after Scott's the next English firsthand account of Asia published was that of Robert Coverte in 1612. [26]

Coverte had sailed with the unfortunate fourth East India Company voyage in 1607. It was poorly financed, comprising only two ships, both of which were lost. One was wrecked on the coast of Brittany, losing all but nine men. Coverte's ship, the "Ascension," foundered off Surat in September, 1609. Most of the crew survived, but the ship and cargo were lost. Because they were not permitted to remain in Surat, the crew scattered, each finding his own way home. Some, including Coverte and Commander Alexander Sharpey, set out for the Mughul court at Agra. On the way Sharpey

[20] *Ibid.,* unnumbered p. 43.
[21] *Ibid.,* unnumbered p. 57.
[22] *Ibid.,* unnumbered pp. 16–17, 65–66.
[23] *Ibid.,* unnumbered pp. 55–65.
[24] *Ibid.,* unnumbered pp. 75–84.
[25] *Ibid.,* unnumbered pp. 89–99.
[26] *A True and Almost Incredible Report of an Englishman* . . . (London).

fell ill and could travel no farther. Coverte and a few others went on to Agra and eventually returned to England by way of Persia and Aleppo. Sharpey's party too eventually got to Agra but then returned to Surat in 1611 to sail home with the sixth English fleet. Others of the crew of the "Ascension" walked across India to Masulipatam from where the Dutch took them to Bantam.[27] Reports written by other survivors of this wreck were later published by Purchas.

Coverte describes the entire journey from the time his ship left England in March, 1607, until his return in 1611. Most of it treats his overland journey from Surat to Aleppo with brief but fairly good descriptions of the towns and countryside along the route. His merchant's eye notes the products of each town, their prices, and whether or not English textiles could be vended there. He describes the religion of the "Banyans" and is intrigued by their worship of cows, their belief in the transmigration of souls, and the custom of suttee.[28] Elephants fascinate him, and he relates several stories about their musket-proof hides, their sensitivity to insults, their wisdom, and their sexual modesty.[29] He also describes the imperial court and seems particularly impressed with the emperor's religious tolerance and his respect for Christianity.[30] The book is very brief, only sixty-eight pages in its first edition. There were two subsequent English editions, one in 1614 and another in 1631, and two German editions of 1617 and 1648.

Samuel Purchas, the English clergyman and collector of travel tales (1575?–1626) first published his *Pilgrimage* in 1613. It is not, however, a collection of firsthand reports and does not contain much new material on Asia.[31] It is rather a natural history of the world's religions. Nevertheless it contains a substantial amount of geographical, cultural, and historical information, and demonstrates the author's deep familiarity with most of the materials about Asia available to Europeans in his day. While he usually cites his sources, Purchas here uses only materials already in print. *Purchas His Pilgrimage* was more popular than any of the firsthand Asian travel literature of the early decades of the century. A second edition was published in 1614, a third in 1617, and a greatly enlarged edition in 1626. Other comprehensive publications of the first quarter of the century were similarly popular. Edward Brerewood's *Enquiries* on languages and religions went through five editions and translations between 1614 and 1674.[32] Robert Stafforde's *A Geo-*

---

[27] For details see B. Penrose (ed.), *The Travels of Captain Robert Coverte* (Philadelphia, 1931), pp. 4–10.

[28] *Ibid.*, pp. 47, 53, 56–59.

[29] *Ibid.*, pp. 48–49, 60–62.   [30] *Ibid.*, pp. 57–59, 62–65.

[31] *Purchas His Pilgrimage. Or, Relations of the World and of Religions Observed in all Ages and Places Discovered, from the Creation unto this Present* (London). This publication should not be confused with Purchas' *Hakluytus Posthumus, or Purchas His Pilgrimes* (4 vols.; London, 1625) for which see below, pp. 556–68.

[32] *Enquiries touching the Diversity of Languages and Religions through the Chiefe Parts of the World* (London, 1614).

graphicall and Anthropologicall Description of Empires and Kingdoms saw four editions between 1607 and 1634. Pierre d'Avity's natural history of governments was translated into English in 1615.[33] Many English translations of earlier foreign descriptions of Asia were also published during the early seventeenth century.[34] That of Henri de Feynes appeared in English translation (1615) before it was published in French (1630).

The next firsthand reports from Asia were the letters of Thomas Coryate (1577?–1617) published in 1616 and in 1618.[35] Coryate was jester to James I's London. His ludicrous appearance and clever wit apparently made him an almost indispensable part of court entertainments. As resident buffoon he associated intimately with courtiers and with London's leading literary figures. His strange role also got him a pension from the Prince of Wales. But he loved to travel. Between 1608 and 1611 he made a walking tour of Europe as far as Venice and upon his return published *His Crudities* (1611), "the Baedeker of the seventeenth century."[36] In 1612 he set out for India in order, as he told his friends, "to ride upon an elephant and to deliver an oration to the Great Mogol."[37] He moved slowly, spending time in Constantinople, Damascus, Aleppo, and Ispahan along the way. In India he visited Lahore, Delhi, and Agra, before arriving at the court at Ajmer in July, 1615. He attached himself to the Englishmen there. Sir Thomas Roe arrived later that year and appears to have kept Coryate around as his own court fool. While in Ajmer, Coryate took his elephant ride, and became sufficiently competent in Persian to deliver an oration to Jahangir from the street below a palace window during one of the emperor's public appearances. The emperor threw him a much-appreciated purse containing silver. The Reverend Edward Terry, who was also at the Mughul court during these years, reports that Coryate possessed a vocabulary of Persian invectives sufficient to silence a particularly shrewish laundress at the English house. He also climbed a minaret one morning to contradict the muezzin by shouting that there was

[33] *The Estates, Empires, and Principalities of the World . . .* trans. Edward Grimstone (London).

[34] For example, Jacob Corneliszoon van Neck, *The Journall, or Dayly Register . . .* (London, 1601); Antonio Galvão, *The Discoveries of the World from their First Origine unto the Year of Our Lord 1555 . . .* (London, 1601); Abraham Ortelius, *Abraham Ortelius his Epitome of the Theater of the World* (London, 1603); Cornelis Matelief, *An Historical and True Discourse of a Voyage Made . . . into the East Indies* (London, 1608); Henri de Feynes, *An Exact and Curious Survey of all the East Indies, Even to Canton, the Chiefe Cittie of China* (London, 1615); Pedro Fernandes de Queiros, *Terra Australis Incognita, or a New Southerne Discoverie, containing a Fifth Part of the World* (London, 1617); Willem Corneliszoon Schouten, *The Relation of a Wonderfull Voiage . . . Shewing How South from the Straights of Magelan . . . he found and Discovered a Newe Passage through the Great South Sea* (London, 1619); [Pedro Morejon], *A Briefe Relation of the Persecution Lately Made Against the Catholike Christians in the Kingdome of Iaponia* (trans. W. W., [St. Omer, 1619]).

[35] *Thomas Coriate, Traveller for the English Wits: Greetings from the Court of the Great Mogul, Resident at the Towne of Asmere in Eastern India* (London, 1616); *Mr. Thomas Coriat to his Friends in England Sendeth Greetings* (London, 1618).

[36] Quoted from B. Penrose, *Urbaine Travelers, 1591–1635* (Philadelphia, 1942), p. 63.

[37] *Ibid.,* p. 97.

"no God but one God and Christ the Sonne of God, and . . . Mohamet . . . an Imposter." [38]

From Ajmer, Coryate wrote four letters to England which were published at London in 1616. They describe his travels and the places he visited. He writes about the Mughul emperor's appearance and his court: the ceremonial weighing of the emperor on his fifty-third birthday, his three public appearances each day, the royal elephants, and an extraordinary gift of thirty-one elephants dressed in chains of pure gold. [39] He also describes Lahore and Agra, and relates the custom of a mountain tribe between Lahore and Agra to take but one wife for all the brothers in the family. [40] Perhaps most significant for those who knew him, this book contains a woodcut of Coryate riding an elephant. [41]

Coryate left Ajmer in September, 1616, spent a couple of months in Agra, traveled to Hardwar on the Ganges, went back to Agra, and finally, because he was becoming quite ill, returned to Surat in November, 1618, where he died within a month. [42] While in Agra he wrote the fifth letter home which was published in 1618. It contains Coryate's oration and some other observations about the character of Jahangir and Akbar. He also reports on Jahangir's distaste for people who change religion and tells how the emperor tried to convert a Christian with bribes and threats, and of his pleasure when he failed.

For all his buffoonery Coryate was apparently a perceptive observer and obviously an engaging storyteller. If he had lived to return to England he might have produced a description of India as rich and useful as *His Crudities* was for Europe. His published letters from India, however, are brief; they contain more wit than description and add virtually nothing to what was already known. They were not published again during the seventeenth century except for their abridgment in Purchas' collection. [43]

In 1622 two pamphlets appeared in London, one a translation from the Dutch and the other an English answer to it, pertaining to Dutch-English hostilities in Banda. [44] Two years later the first group of pamphlets treating the troubles of the two nations in Amboina—the "Amboyna Massacre" of February, 1622—were published. [45] In each case the VOC published a justi-

[38] Terry in *PP*, IX, 37.
[39] Coryate, *Traveller, op. cit.* (n. 35), pp. 20–26, 31–32.
[40] *Ibid.*, pp. 13–18.
[41] Coryate, *Traveller, op. cit.* (n. 35), p. 27.
[42] For details on Coryate's life see Penrose, *op. cit.* (n. 36), pp. 58–108, and Michael Strachan, *The Life and Adventures of Thomas Coryate* (London, 1962).
[43] *PP*, IV, 469–95.
[44] *The Hollanders Declaration of the Affairs of the East Indies, or a True Relation of that which Passed in the Islands of Banda* . . . (Amsterdam, 1622); *An Answer to the Hollanders Declaration Concerning the Occurrents in the East India* (London, 1622).
[45] *A True Relation of the Unjust, Cruell, and Barbarous Proceedings against the English at Amboyna* . . . (London, 1624); *A True Declaration of the News that came out of the East Indies with the*

fication of its action which was translated into English and published with an English East India Company refutation of the Dutch position. The controversy continued through the remainder of the century. Purchas included the 1622 pamphlet and a condensation of the 1624 pamphlets in his collection.[46] Another Dutch apologia appeared in English in 1628[47] which was reprinted with refutations in 1632.[48] More English pamphlets describing the "massacre" came out in 1651, 1653, and 1665.[49] Sermons were preached on it.[50] John Dryden wrote a play about it in 1673 that was republished in 1691,[51] and Elkanah Settle, another playwright, was still passionately condemning the Dutch for the massacre in 1688.[52]

Without doubt the most impressive English contribution to Europe's store of information about Asia during the first generation of the seventeenth century—perhaps for the entire century—was Samuel Purchas' *Hakluytus Posthumus or Purchas His Pilgrimes,* published at London in 1625. This collection is difficult to use. Purchas was not always a reliable editor. Some of the accounts are drastically condensed or summarized; in some cases they are synopses of primary accounts, written by Purchas. On the other hand, he sometimes reproduced the original manuscripts faithfully. And while comparisons with the manuscripts show that Purchas occasionally mutilated an interesting account, they also sometimes prove him to have been accurate and responsible in his summaries. In many cases the original manuscripts no longer exist; for all his faults, Purchas preserved a large number of firsthand travel accounts that otherwise would have been lost. For most of the early seventeenth-century English voyages Purchas provided the only published edition.[53]

The *Hakluytus Posthumus* is an exceedingly large work: four volumes and

Pinnace called the Hare . . . (London, 1624); *The Answer unto the Dutch Pamphlet made in Defense of the Unjust and Barbarous Proceedings against the English at Amboyna* . . . (London, 1624).

[46] *PP*, V, 137–74, and X, 507–22.

[47] *A True Declaration of the News Concerning a Conspiracy Discovered in the Island of Amboyna and the Punishment that followed thereof* (London).

[48] *A Remonstrance of the Directors of the Netherlands East-India Company . . . and the Reply of the English East India Company to the Said Remonstrance and Defence* (London, 1632).

[49] *Bloody News of the East-Indies, being a Relation and Perfect Abstract of the Barbarous Proceedings of the Dutch against the English at Amboyna* (London, 1651); *A Memento for Holland, or a True and Exact History of the Cruelties used on the English Merchants Residing in Amboyna* (London, 1653); John Quarles, *The Tyranny of the Dutch against the English* (London, 1653); *The Second Part of Amboyna* . . . (London, 1665).

[50] For example, Robert Wilkinson, *The Stripping of Joseph, or the Crueltie to a Brother* (London, 1625).

[51] John Dryden, *Amboyna: A Tragedy As it is Acted by their Majesties Servants* (London, 1691).

[52] *Insigniae Batavia: or the Dutch Trophies Displayed; being exact relations of the Unjust, Horrid, and most Barbarous Proceedings of the Dutch against the English in the East Indies* . . . (London).

[53] For a brief evaluation see William Foster, "Samuel Purchas," in Edward Lynam (ed.), *Richard Hakluyt and His Successors* (London: The Hakluyt Society, 1946), and L. E. Pennington, *Hakluytus Posthumus: Samuel Purchas and the Promotion of English Overseas Expansion* ("Emporia State Research Studies," XIV, no. 3; Emporia, Kansas, 1966). See also Pennington (ed.), *The Purchas Handbook* (forthcoming).

4,262 densely packed folio-sized pages; the 1905 (Glasgow) reprint comprises twenty volumes. In 1625 it was the largest work thus far printed in English.[54] The title suggests that Purchas intended his collection to complete or to supersede Hakluyt's. Somehow he had obtained possession of the unpublished material Hakluyt had been collecting since the second edition of the *Principall Navigations* (1600). Purchas included this material as well as many of the accounts already printed in the *Principall Navigations* or published after its appearance. For example, he included all the circumnavigations—Magellan, Drake, Hawkins, Cavendish, Van Noort, Van Spilbergen, and Schouten and Le Maire—all the Northeast and Northwest Passage attempts, and all the reports on the voyages to America. He also reprinted most of the medieval accounts already found in Hakluyt. He reprinted the journals of Fitch, Fedrici, Lancaster, Scott, and Linschoten, Coryate's letters, the Banda and Amboina pamphlets, and Thomas Mun's *A Discourse of Trade from England into the East Indies* (1621), all of which had appeared in English before.[55] Purchas included many other foreign accounts. He wrote a chapter, based on primary accounts, about the early Dutch voyages to the East Indies,[56] and he included abridgments, excerpts, or summaries of Varthema, Duarte de Meneses, Pyrard, Galvão, Balbi, Pimenta, Conti, Da Cruz, and Pinto, of Trigault's description of China, and of a number of the Jesuit letters from Japan and China, notably those of Ricci, Longobardo, and Pantoja.

Purchas, like Hakluyt, was an ardent advocate of English imperial expansion. The *Hakluytus Posthumus* begins with an account of Solomon's voyage to Ophir and goes on to describe the travels of Hebrew patriarchs, Greek philosophers, and the twelve Apostles, apparently in an attempt to show that God approved of travel and exploration. He then defended the East India Company against its critics. He was concerned in his selection of material for the collection to include reports that would whip up enthusiasm and support for English overseas ventures and hatred for their major antagonists and competitors, the Dutch. In the process he brought out a wealth of first-hand English reports about Asia that otherwise might never have been published.

Purchas provides the only printed materials on several of the English voyages to Asia during the first quarter of the seventeenth century. He includes, for example, the only report of the disastrous voyage of Benjamin Wood, 1595–1601, from which there was but one survivor,[57] and the only account of John Mildenhall's travels in Persia and the Mughul Empire.[58] Neither of these contains much description, although Mildenhall affords the first English glimpse of Mughul court intrigue and the role of the Jesuits there.

---

[54]Foster, *loc. cit.* (n. 53), p. 58.
[55]On Mun see above, p. 77.
[56]*PP*, V, 193–241.

[57]*Ibid.*, II, 288–97.
[58]*Ibid.*, pp. 297–305.

Some description of Sumatra appears in John Davis' report of his voyage with Cornelis de Houtman's fleet in 1598.[59] Davis also describes the Achinese attack on the Dutch ships in which De Houtman was killed and many of his crew killed or captured. Purchas printed two letters from Will Adams (1575?–1620), who had sailed as a pilot on one of Mahu and De Cordes' Dutch ships through the Straits of Magellan to Japan. Adams spent the rest of his life in Japan as a trusted advisor to Tokugawa Ieyasu.[60] His letters, one to the English East India Company and one to his wife, are primarily concerned with the voyage across the Pacific and his first months in Japan. They contain disappointingly little about Japan and the Japanese. Purchas also reported a second voyage by John Davis in 1604, this time on an English ship commanded by Edward Michelbourne. This account relates his experiences in Sumatra and Bantam and concludes abruptly with Davis' death in a battle with Japanese pirates while en route from Bantam to Patani.[61]

The accounts of the first and second Company voyages included in Purchas had been published earlier, except for Thomas Claybourne's. But there had been no previous publication of the third Company voyage under William Keeling. Purchas printed an abridgment of Keeling's journal.[62] Keeling's fleet of three ships left England in April, 1607, and returned in May, 1610. They traded at Priaman on Sumatra, at Bantam, and at Banda where they met with hostility from the Dutch. Keeling was at Banda in 1609 when the Dutch Admiral Verhoeff was murdered.[63]

One of Keeling's captains, William Hawkins, went to Surat in August 1608, and traded there until the Portuguese seized his ship and cargo. Hawkins appeared at the Mughul court in Agra in February, 1609. Jahangir allowed him daily attendance at court, provided him with lodgings and maintenance, and even found him a wife, the daughter of an Armenian Christian. Hawkins, meanwhile, pressed the emperor for a trade agreement and for permission to build a factory in Surat, while the Jesuits at court and their ally "Bocreb Chan" (Muqarrib Khan) in Surat continued to plot against him. At one point, the emperor granted him permission to build a factory, only to withdraw it the following day. Hawkins fell from favor with the emperor and lost his living at court late in 1611. He and his wife left India with Middleton's fleet in January, 1612, and from there sailed to Sumatra and Bantam before leaving for England in 1613. Hawkins died on the homeward voyage.

Hawkins' journal as published in Purchas' collection includes all these adventures.[64] In addition it contains "A Briefe Discourse of the Strength, Wealth, and Government, with Some Customs of the Great Mogul," which provides interesting eyewitness information on Mughul government, court routines, wealth, and entertainments—the earliest English report on most

[59] *Ibid.*, pp. 305–26.
[60] *Ibid.*, pp. 326–47.
[61] *Ibid.*, pp. 347–66.

[62] *Ibid.*, pp. 502–49.
[63] See above, pp. 470–71.
[64] *PP*, III, 1–51.

of these matters.[65] For example, he gives a long list of the emperor's precious possessions and reports that the emperor surveys a part of his wealth each day. He describes the annual birthday weighing and the distribution to the poor of the gold and jewels put into the balance by the imperial nobles. He describes the tent camps that accompanied the emperor when he traveled; as large as the city of London, he thought. He notes the *mansabdari* system of ranks and stipends given in return for imperial service, and observes that the emperor always confiscates the wealth of deceased nobles and gives only what he wishes to their children. More important, Hawkins' description as well as his journal affords some fascinating glimpses into Jahangir's personality: his cupidity and sadistic cruelty as well as his generosity, tolerance, and urbanity.

The brief account of David Middleton's voyage to the Moluccas, 1606–8, as printed by Purchas, contains no description beyond that of his reception by native princes.[66] Nor is much information about Asia to be found in the four accounts written by survivors of the "Ascension," wrecked off Surat on the fourth voyage in 1609. Thomas Jones describes the voyage out and the shipwreck, and he includes a very brief description of "Gandeuee" (Gandevi, a town south of Surat) and of suttee. He returned to Europe in a Portuguese ship.[67] William Nicols traveled overland from Burhampur to Masulipatam dressed like a Turk in the company of three Jews who he feared might cut his throat at any moment; in fact, he had overheard them plotting to do so. From Masulipatam he sailed to Bantam in a Dutch ship. His brief report describes only his personal adventures and fears.[68] Joseph Salbranche, who accompanied Robert Coverte overland to Agra, Persia, and Aleppo, describes some of the towns along the way and their products.[69] Coverte's descriptions of the same places are better, but Purchas did not reprint Coverte's account.

The story of the fifth Company voyage to Java and the Banda Islands in 1609–11 appears in *Hakluytus Posthumus* as a letter from David Middleton to the Company.[70] It contains considerable detail on the trade and on the affairs of the Dutch in the Moluccas and Banda. According to Middleton, the Bandanese all hated the Dutch, and he reports with some satisfaction the news received in Bantam of Admiral Paulus van Caerden's capture and Admiral François Wittert's death. Two accounts of the sixth voyage, 1611–13, are found in Purchas: one by the commander, Sir Henry Middleton, and the other by Captain Nicholas Downton.[71] Both journals recount the long, stormy, and unsuccessful negotiations with "Mocerif Khan" (Muqarrib Khan) at Surat which finally ended after Hawkins returned from Agra to take passage on Middleton's fleet. Downton's account is in most places fuller

[65] *Ibid.*, pp. 29–51.
[66] *Ibid.*, pp. 51–61.
[67] *Ibid.*, pp. 61–72.
[68] *Ibid.*, pp. 72–73.
[69] *Ibid.*, pp. 82–89.
[70] *Ibid.*, pp. 90–115.
[71] *Ibid.*, pp. 115–303.

than Middleton's; it also describes the voyage to Sumatra and the trade there.

The seventh Company voyage was the first to trade in the Bay of Bengal and the Gulf of Siam. It was directed and partially financed by two Dutchmen known as Pieter Floris and Lucas Antheunis, each of whom had had several years' service with the VOC as factors on the Coromandel Coast. Their knowledge of local markets and politics proved indispensible to the success of the voyage. Their single ship, the "Globe," traded along the Coromandel Coast, to Bengal, Pegu, Siam, Johore, and Patani, and returned to England in August, 1615, after an absence of four and a half years, with a cargo that produced profits of 218 percent on the Company's investment.[72] Purchas included two journals from the voyage: the first, written by Nathaniel Martin, a master's mate on the "Globe," is very brief and contains only nautical information.[73] The other is a condensation of Floris' journal and contains a great deal of intelligence about the trade and the negotiations with local officials as well as some good descriptions of people and places.[74] He notes, for example, the death of the "king" of Masulipatam, describes a reception by the queen of Patani, a fire and riot in Patani, and sketches the recent history of Siam and of its relations with Pegu, Patani, and other neighboring kingdoms. A comparison with the extant manuscript of Floris' journal shows that while Purchas condensed it considerably, he did so without distorting or seriously impoverishing the original.[75]

The journal of Captain John Saris, commander of the eighth Company voyage, contains extensive descriptions of the Red Sea ports, the Moluccas, and especially of Japan; it too was published only in the Purchas collection.[76] Saris' fleet of three ships left England on April 8, 1611, and traded and raided in the Red Sea, anchoring at Bantam on October 24, 1611. On January 15, 1613, they left for Japan, sailing first, however, to Banda and the Moluccas. Saris sketches the development of European trade in the Moluccas from the earliest Portuguese visits to the consolidation of Dutch control in the Spiceries down to 1613. He was received civilly by the Dutch and visited several of their forts and factories, but the Dutch effectively prevented the natives from trading with the English. Saris also comments on the widespread destruction in the Moluccas resulting from the constant wars, and on the growing hostility of the Moluccans to the Dutch.[77] Saris arrived in Japan on June 10, 1613, where he was graciously received by local officials and by the shogun. He was quickly granted permission to trade and

---

[72] For details of the voyage see W. H. Moreland (ed.), *Pieter Floris, his Voyage to the East Indies in the Globe, 1611–1615; the Contemporary Translation of his Journal. . .* ("HS," 2d ser., LXXIV; London, 1934).

[73] *PP*, III, 304–19.

[74] *Ibid.*, pp. 319–43.

[75] See Moreland (ed.), *op. cit.* (n. 72), pp. lxv–lxviii.

[76] *PP*, III, 357–490.

[77] *Ibid.*, pp. 408–34.

to establish a permanent factory. Will Adams' influence was obviously effective, although Saris grumbles that Adams seemed more Japanese than English and seemed to prefer the Dutch and Spanish to his own countrymen.
Saris and Adams simply did not get along, and their antipathy probably
hurt the English position in Japan. For example, Adams advised Saris to set
up the English factory in Uraga, nearer to Edo. Saris obstinately insisted on
Hirado, where the Dutch were already established and would continue
to overshadow the English.[78] Nevertheless Saris' journal contains many
perceptive observations about Japan, as well as what Purchas calls a letter
from the shogun granting trading rights to the English.[79] He left Japan on
December 5, 1613, stopped at Bantam to load pepper, and anchored at
Plymouth on September 27, 1614.

Saris had been to the East Indies before, with the second voyage, under
Henry Middleton; he had been left in charge of the English factory at Bantam from October, 1605, to October, 1609. Purchas also printed extracts of
the journal Saris kept during these years to serve, so he put it, as a continuation of Edmund Scott's *Discourse*.[80] From Saris' journal it appears that life
for the English at Bantam had improved somewhat since Scott's experience;
he reports far fewer fires and attempted robberies. He also records the activities of the Dutch in Bantam and Jakatra, and offers advice on the pepper
and spice trade as well as on the sorts of goods which might be sold in Japan.
Finally he describes the trade, currency, weights, and measures in several
Javan ports and in Makassar, Bali, Timor, Banda, the Moluccas, Borneo,
and Siam.

When Saris departed from Japan in December, 1613, he left behind a merchant, Richard Cocks, to manage the newly established factory at Hirado.
Cocks kept a journal covering the years 1615–22, and Purchas published
extracts from it.[81] It is full of the minutiae of daily life at the English and
Dutch factories and of Cocks' jealousies and complaints. But it also contains
some richly detailed, firsthand descriptions of Japan and the Japanese: the
effects of a typhoon, local customs, feasts, and receptions. Purchas published but a small part of Cocks' original journal and only a few of his many
letters.[82]

Some excellent firsthand observations about Mughul India are found
in Purchas' extracts from William Finch's journal.[83] Finch arrived in India in
1608 with William Hawkins; and during the following years he lived in

[78] For details see Ernest M. Satow (ed.), *The Voyage of Captain John Saris to Japan, 1613* ("HS,"
2d ser., V; London, 1900), pp. li–lv.
[79] *PP*, III, 422–77, 488–89. See also pl. 432 for a discussion of the letter.
[80] *Ibid.*, pp. 490–515. On Scott's book see above, pp. 551–52.
[81] *Ibid.*, pp. 519–70.
[82] For the original journal see Edward Maunde Thompson (ed.), *Diary of Richard Cocks, Cape
Merchant in the English Factory in Japan, 1615–1622* . . . ("HS," 2d ser., LXVI–LXVII; London,
1883).
[83] *PP*, IV, 1–77.

Surat and Agra and traveled in northwest India. He did not confine his observations to the capital and the court, but describes many towns and villages and the countryside through which he traveled, as well as the people, products, buildings, plants, animals, and customs which he encountered. He wrote particularly vivid and detailed descriptions of Surat, Agra, and Lahore. Finch was one of the earliest English travelers to comment on Mughul paintings and architecture. He notes a stone elephant in Burhanpur so lifelike that live elephants charge it and break their tusks against it.[84] He describes a terrible fire in Agra during late May and early June, 1610. He marvels at the emperor's unique hunting methods: his soldiers encircle an area and gradually constrict the perimeter, claiming everything within it for the emperor. The surplus game is given to the emperor's hunting companions; the unfortunate people found within the perimeter are enslaved.[85] Finch's description of indigo is one of the earliest in English.[86] He also repeated the popular stories about Prince Khusru's rebellion against his father and how Jahangir blinded his son as punishment.[87] Finally Finch describes, briefly and superficially, the Deccan wars and the lands east of the Mughul territories: Bengal, Arakan, Pegu, and Golconda. His account contains some vivid and delightful passages in language liberally sprinkled with Indian words.

The ninth Company voyage (1611–15) was reported in Purchas' collection through the journal of John Davys of Limehouse, the master of one of the ships.[88] Davys' journal covers the entire voyage and the return to England, but it contains only navigational details. Purchas also printed Davys' rutter for the East Indies, a very detailed navigational guide based on his five voyages to the east.[89]

Purchas included parts of four journals from the tenth Company voyage of 1612–14. He printed about one-third of Commander Thomas Best's journal,[90] and parts of journals written by Master Copeland, a minister, Robert Bonner, a shipmaster, and Nicholas Withington, a merchant.[91] Best's fleet sailed first to Surat, where he finally obtained from the local authorities a trade agreement and permission to build a factory. He was probably successful because Surat officials feared that if refused Best would pillage shipping as Middleton had done on a preceding voyage.[92] His successful defense against a Portuguese attack at Surat on March 28, 1612, probably raised the English still higher in local esteem. From Surat, Best sailed down the coast, captured a Portuguese ship, and then sailed to Acheh where he was well re-

---

[84] *Ibid.*, p. 32.
[85] *Ibid.*
[86] *Ibid.*, pp. 45–46.
[87] *Ibid.*, pp. 50–56. Also see below, pp. 633–34.
[88] *Ibid.*, pp. 77–87.
[90] *Ibid.*, pp. 119–47.
[89] *Ibid.*, pp. 88–119.
[91] *Ibid.*, pp. 147–75.
[92] William Foster (ed.), *The Voyage of Thomas Best to the East Indies, 1612–1614* ("HS," 2d ser., LXXV; London, 1934), p. xxvii.

ceived. His journal includes considerable detail on the reception at Acheh, the banquets and negotiations, and the elephant fights he watched.[93] From Acheh he sailed to Bantam before returning to England. Copeland, too, wrote a good description of Best's reception at Acheh, including some interesting details on the sultan's court.[94] Bonner's journal is exclusively concerned with nautical details, while Withington's, despite its truncation by Purchas, contains some rather good description of his overland journeys in the Mughul Empire.[95] His account of Sind, for example, where he was robbed several times and captured by bandits, is the earliest in English and reveals how ineffective Mughul rule was in that area.

The account of the eleventh Company voyage (1611–13) in Purchas was written by Ralph Wilson, one of the mates. It is very brief and contains only nautical details.[96] Walter Payton's account of the twelfth voyage, 1612–14, is much more descriptive, but most of it deals with Persia. It contains, however, a fairly detailed account of the trade at Diu.[97] The twelfth voyage was the last of the so-called separate voyages, each of which had been financed and equipped as a separate enterprise with a distinct list of investors who divided the profits if any. Sometime during 1613 the East India Company was reorganized as a joint-stock company with a common capital. All subsequent fleets were part of a common enterprise and financially part of the Company's common accounts.

Among the earliest enterprises of the newly reorganized Company was the fleet of four ships under Nicholas Downton dispatched on February 28, 1614, to Surat as a follow-up to Best's successes there. When Downton arrived in Surat on October 15, he found the English factors exceedingly uneasy about recent Portuguese attempts to force the Mughuls to drive out the English. They had seized a Surat ship and demanded that the English be expelled before they would return it or its crew and cargo. In retaliation Jahangir closed all Jesuit churches and attacked several Portuguese strongholds. Downton's fleet strengthened the English position. He refused to use his ships to attack the Portuguese, despite Muqarrib Khan's urging, but when the Portuguese attacked his fleet in Surat harbor he repelled them with very heavy losses. When he left Surat on March 3, 1615, the English still had their factory and their trade agreement. Downton himself sailed to Bantam while one of his ships went to Acheh and another returned home. Another was sunk at Jakatra, and Downton died at Bantam on August 6, 1615. His ship left Bantam on December 22, 1615, under the command of Thomas Elkington and returned to England on June 25, 1616. Elkington, however, died at the Cape of Good Hope in January, 1616.[98]

[93] *PP*, IV, 138–42.
[94] *Ibid.*, pp. 147–54.
[95] *Ibid.*, pp. 162–75.
[96] *Ibid.*, pp. 175–80.
[97] *Ibid.*, pp. 200–209.
[98] For details of the voyage see William Foster (ed.), *The Voyage of Nicholas Downton to the East Indies, 1614–1615* ("HS," 2d. ser., LXXXII; London, 1939), pp. xi–xxxiv.

The English Literature

Purchas included four relations of Downton's voyage: first he made extensive extracts from Downton's own journal, which brought the story of the voyage down to March, 1615, when the fleet was en route to Bantam.[99] For the second part of the voyage he excerpted the journals of Elkington and of Edward Dodsworth, a merchant.[100] Finally he traced the homeward voyage through Martin Pring's journal.[101] Downton's account deals almost entirely with the negotiations with Muqarrib Khan and with the battle against the Portuguese at Surat. Elkington's journal is very brief and contains even less description. Dodsworth's again is primarily concerned with the negotiations and decision-making at Surat, while Pring's very brief journal contains only navigational details.

Many more descriptions of Asian peoples and places can be found in Purchas' account of Richard Steele's and John Crawther's journey from Ajmer to Ispahan in 1615–16, but most of it deals with Persia rather than India.[102] John Milward's brief account of a voyage to Sumatra in 1614 contains some description of Acheh, but nothing beyond what could be found in earlier reports.[103] The relation of Walter Payton's second voyage contains a description of Acheh and a list of the Portuguese forts in India.[104] Sir Thomas Roe (1581?–1644), James I's special ambassador to the Mughul emperor, sailed to Surat aboard one of Payton's ships.

Roe's journal, as excerpted by Purchas, was a major contribution to Europe's knowledge of Asia.[105] He was sent by James I to obtain a "firman" (*farman*) from the emperor which would guarantee free trade for the English at Surat and thus end the constant harassment, arbitrary tariffs, and occasional confiscations which the English suffered at the hands of local officials. Roe disembarked in Surat on September 26, 1615, and arrived at the court of Ajmer on December 23. For nearly three years he stayed at the court. He moved with it and he attended the emperor at one of his public appearances almost every day. But he never got his "firman"! Finally he asked the emperor for permission to leave and for a reply to the letter from King James which he had delivered when he first arrived. These requests Jahangir granted. In exasperation Roe wrote: "my toyle with barbarous and unjust people is beyond patience."[106]

Roe mostly discusses his negotiations and his daily life at court, and in doing so provides his readers with fascinating insights into Jahangir's character, that of his sons and chief ministers, and of the court generally. He reports conversations with the emperor and others at court, and he tells many good stories. Jahangir appears in these pages as capricious, sometimes viciously cruel, sometimes magnanimous and gentle, often drunk, and childishly fascinated with presents from far-away places. He continually ca-

[99] *PP*, IV, 214–51.
[100] *Ibid.*, pp. 251–66.
[101] *Ibid.*, pp. 567–71.
[102] *Ibid.*, pp. 266–80.

[103] *Ibid.*, pp. 280–89.
[104] *Ibid.*, pp. 289–310.
[105] *Ibid.*, pp. 310–468.
[106] *Ibid.*, p. 406.

joled Roe to have a horse sent to him from England. When Roe objected that a horse could not survive the sea voyage, Jahangir insisted that if six were sent, one would surely survive.[107] Roe was first and always an Englishman, a representative of his king. He felt continually constrained to maintain his dignity as ambassador against real or imagined slights or discourtesies. He always dressed in English clothes and ate in English fashion. He would never kneel, but rendered respect to the emperor and other dignitaries in the English manner. He usually found the lodgings provided for him on journeys inadequate and would sleep in his own tents instead. He found Jahangir's throne room, for example, opulent rather than tasteful; rather like the room of a lady who, in an attempt to display her finery, places a pair of embroidered slippers on the cupboard along with her silver and porcelain.[108] Roe also gave his readers detailed descriptions of the emperor's daily routine, of his birthday celebration, of his sons' rivalries, of the empress Nur Mahal's baleful influence over him, and of the imperial camp on march or hunt. The emperor's tent camp on such occasions, he reported, was as large as any European city.[109]

Purchas did not print Roe's journal in its entirety. In fact he reduced what was available to him to about one-third its original size.[110] Nor was it all available to him. He complained that the last part of the journal was missing, and used printed excerpts from Roe's letters to fill the gap.[111] Still Purchas' edition contains much new, firsthand information about the Mughul court and emperor. No other English editions were published during the seventeenth century. A Dutch translation appeared in 1656,[112] and Thévenot translated it into French for his *Relation de divers voyages curieux* in 1663.[113]

Small bits of description may be found in the numerous short excerpts that follow Roe's journal in the *Hakluytus Posthumus,* but most were already available in English. Roger Hawes, for example, reported that the Zamorin of Calicut proposed an agreement with the British in March, 1615, if they would protect him from the Portuguese. He also volunteered to cooperate with the English in an attempt to take over Cranganore and Cochin, his traditional rivals. The offer came to naught.[114] Thomas Spurway's letter of November 20, 1617, reports the expropriation of the English forts on Pulau Run and Pulau Ai in Banda by the Dutch and includes a brief description of Pulau Run.[115] Purchas' brief excerpts from John Hatch's report of his voyage

[107] *Ibid.,* p. 364.

[108] *Ibid.,* pp. 332–33.   [109] *Ibid.,* p. 385.

[110] William Foster (ed.), *The Embassy of Sir Thomas Roe to India, 1615–1619* (rev. ed.; London, 1926), p. lxxiv.

[111] *PP,* IV, 429.

[112] *Journael van de reysen ghedaen door . . . Sr. Th. Roe, ambassadeur van S. Con. Maej. van Groot Brittanje, afgevaerdicht naer Oost-Indien aan den Grooten Mogul . . .* (Amsterdam).

[113] For complete bibliography see William Foster (ed.), *op. cit.* (n. 110), pp. lxx–lxxvii.

[114] *PP,* IV, 495–502.

[115] *Ibid.,* pp. 508–35.

to Java, 1616–21, contains little description beyond that of engagements with Dutch ships.[116]

Martin Pring's second voyage, 1616–21, took him to both coasts of India, Java, Patani, and Japan; as printed by Purchas, his journal provides an English version of the troubles with the Dutch, including the siege of Jakatra in 1618.[117] Beyond that, however, it includes only nautical and housekeeping details. Pring's description of the voyage from Bantam to Patani and Japan is in fact a very detailed rutter.[118] William Hore's journal, too, is primarily concerned about hostilities with the Dutch during his voyage from Surat to Sumatra and Bantam in 1618–20.[119] Among other offenses, he reports, the Dutch seized four English ships at Tiku on Sumatra in 1619.[120] He also describes a trial by ordeal there: a native accused of killing an Englishman was required to retrieve a small ball from a pot of boiling oil. He did so without being burned and was therefore exonerated. Hore thought the devil had helped him.[121] Reports of hostilities with the Dutch completely dominate Nathaniel Courthop's journal of a voyage to the Banda Islands.[122] It is followed in Purchas by a series of short pieces devoted entirely to the troubles with the Dutch, some of which had been published before.[123] Even Humphrey Fitzherbert's "A Pithy Description of the Chiefe Ilands of Banda and Moluccas" is primarily a description of Dutch forts and Dutch insolences.[124]

Firsthand observations of Mughul India are plentiful in the Rev. Edward Terry's relation as printed by Purchas.[125] Terry (1590–1660) was chaplain to Thomas Roe's embassy, and his account nicely complements Roe's. While Roe was primarily concerned with affairs at court and with his negotiations, Terry describes the land and the people. He was, of course, particularly interested in religious beliefs and practices and in social customs, but he also describes towns, buildings, plants, animals, dress, food, and products. While he records what he saw quite correctly, he is not very critical of the stories told him. For example, he reports that Ganges water weighs less than other water,[126] that Hindu women have easier deliveries than others, that elephants wear their testicles on their foreheads and their breasts between their forelegs.[127] To illustrate the elephant's amazing wisdom and memory he tells how a mad elephant charging through a busy village market stops to save the child of a woman who used to feed him.[128] Even his remarks about Indian religion, while generally true, are quite superficial. Much of what he describes had been printed in Europe before; still, many of his observations were fresh even if somewhat superficial and not always accurate.

Purchas printed only an abridgment of Terry's original narrative. The en-

[116] *Ibid.*, pp. 535–47.
[117] *Ibid.*, V, 1–63.
[118] *Ibid.*, pp. 33–63.
[119] *Ibid.*, pp. 64–86.
[120] *Ibid.*, pp. 80–81.
[121] *Ibid.*, pp. 78–79.
[122] *Ibid.*, pp. 86–126.
[123] *Ibid.*, pp. 126–93.
[124] *Ibid.*, pp. 174–81.
[125] *Ibid.*, IX, 1–55.
[126] *Ibid.*, p. 20.
[127] *Ibid.*, pp. 28–29.
[128] *Ibid.*, pp. 26–27.

tire work—in fact, the original work revised and greatly expanded by the author—was published in 1655.[129] It is much wordier than the Purchas edition and contains a great many digressions, preachments, and quotations from Scripture, the classics, and the poets. It probably deserved to be condensed. Of course the 1655 edition also contains a considerable amount of material not found in the Purchas condensation, and, curiously, it lacks some of the anecdotes found there. Terry's absurd report about the location of an elephant's genitalia, for example, is not found in the 1655 edition. Terry's journal appeared again, in 1665, appended to a translation of Pietro della Valle's travels.[130] The text of this edition is essentially the same as that of 1655, but the inserts and quotations, as well as some of the more obviously irrelevant digressions, were omitted. Thévenot translated the Purchas version into French for his collection published in 1663.

Among the translated and reprinted accounts in the *Hakluytus Posthumus* is a letter describing Japan, written to Purchas by Arthur Hatch on November 26, 1623.[131] It is brief and general, but quite accurate. Hatch describes the shogun's court and government and observes that while most Japanese nobles keep many women, the shogun had but one wife. He accurately describes the shogun's policy of impoverishing the vassal daimyos. He comments on Japanese laws, manners, festivals, and language. Curiously, he reports that the Japanese could not pronounce H, B, or T. Finally, also among the translated and reprinted accounts, Purchas included extracts from Arnold Brown's journal of his five years' travels to Bantam, Patani, Japan, the Philippines, and the China coast from 1617 to 1623.[132] Brown reports on the unsuccessful Dutch attack on Macao in 1622.

No descriptions of Asia were published in Russian during the seventeenth century, but Purchas included several accounts of eastern Siberia and the frontiers of the Chinese empire which had been based on Russian accounts or on interviews with Russians who had traveled to the east. For example, Purchas included a translation of Isaac Massa's account first published in 1612 with Hessel Gerritszoon's volume on the northeast passage attempts.[133] Using Russian reports, Massa had described Russian travels to the Yenisey River and beyond, including descriptions of the Tungusic tribes which lived along its banks. Similar information can be found in the reports written or translated by John Mericke, Josias Logan, and William Pursglove, first published in Purchas' *Pilgrimes*.[134] These reports, like Massa's, are admittedly vague and scanty, but they all at least mention the Tungus peoples, the

[129] *A Voyage to East India. Wherein Some Things Are Taken Notice of in Our Passage Thither, but Many More in Our Abode There, Within that Rich and Spacious Empire of the Great Mogul . . .* (London).

[130] *The Travels of Sig. Pietro della Valle, a Noble Roman, into East India and Arabia Deserta . . . Whereunto is Added a Relation of Sir Thomas Roe's Voyage into the East Indies* (London), pp. 325–480.

[131] *PP*, X, 83–88.

[132] *Ibid.*, pp. 499–507.

[133] *Ibid.*, XIII, 180–93.

[134] *Ibid.*, pp. 193–94, 236–38, 249–55.

Yenisey River, "Pisida" (?), the Altan (or Altine) Khan, and the borders of Cathay. Much more informative was Purchas' account of Ivan Petlin and Andrei Mundoff's 1618 Russian embassy to the Chinese court, the first Russian eyewitness account of China to be published.[135] Petlin and Mundoff's group stayed in Peking for four days until the Chinese determined that it was not a proper tribute mission and sent the Russians away. On their return they carried with them a letter inviting the tsar to join the Chinese tributary system, but they complained that "there is none in Tobolsko to translate it." According to Purchas the Russians thought the letter was from "Tambur, King of Cathay," apparently referring to Tamerlane, who had ruled the Mongol empire centuries before.[136] Such was Russian knowledge of China in 1618. In addition to providing some fairly good glimpses of China and of the Great Wall, Petlin also described what he called "Mongal Land," apparently the area between Turfan and the wall and from Eastern Turkestan to the sea, commenting on its divisions, products, and religion.

The *Hakluytus Posthumus* was not republished before the twentieth century. Perhaps it was simply too large and too expensive; perhaps Purchas' enthusiasm simply was not shared by enough of his countrymen. In fact, apart from the journals of Roe and Terry, none of the seventeenth-century English reports about Asia included in the *Hakluytus Posthumus* reappeared during the following two centuries. Many of them, however, were translated into French for Thévenot's collection in 1663, and in the early eighteenth century Pieter van der Aa of Leyden began to translate them into Dutch, a project never completed.

Purchas was responsible for the publication of another major English description of India, William Methwold's relation of Golconda.[137] Methwold wrote his relation at Purchas' request for inclusion in the *Hakluytus Posthumus,* but the manuscript arrived too late. Purchas consequently printed it at the end of the enlarged and revised fourth edition of his *Pilgrimage* that appeared in 1626. No other English edition was published during the seventeenth century. Thévenot translated it into French for his collection in 1663, and Pieter van der Aa produced a Dutch edition in 1707.[138]

Methwold sailed for the Indies in 1616 on the same ship that brought Edward Terry to Surat. After visiting Surat, several Malabar ports, Sumatra, and Bantam, he became the principal English factor at Masulipatam in May, 1618. He served there until October, 1622, when he was accused of private trading and recalled. The accusation apparently did not damage his subsequent career with the Company. He became president of the English factory

---

[135] *Ibid.,* XIV, 272–84.

[136] *Ibid.,* pp. 272–73.

[137] William Methwold, "Relations of the Kingdom of Golconda, and Other Neighboring Nations within the Gulf of Bengala . . ." in *Purchas His Pilgrimage* (4th ed., revised; London, 1626), pp. 993–1007.

[138] For bibliographical details see W. H. Moreland (ed.), *Relations of Golconda in the Early Seventeenth Century* ("HS," 2d. ser., LXVI; London, 1931), pp. xxv, xxvii.

at Surat from 1633 to 1639, a director of the East India Company in 1640, and its deputy governor from 1643 until his death in 1653.[139]

Methwold's description is unusually balanced, perceptive, and accurate. He first describes the Coromandel Coast generally and the Portuguese, Dutch, and English trade and settlements there. Then in more detail he discusses Masulipatam, its climate, the surrounding countryside, and finally the capital city of Golconda. His description includes details about government, the common people, religion, social customs, products, and trade.

2

THE TURBULENT MIDDLE YEARS, 1630–80

The most important contributions to Europe's knowledge of Asia made by English observers during the first generation of the seventeenth century pertained to western India and, more precisely, to the Mughul Empire and Gujarat. Another work on northwestern India appeared in 1630, Henry Lord's description of the religion of the Banyans (Hinduism) and of the Parsis (Zoroastrianism).[140] Actually the volume contains two books bound together, each with a separate title page and pagination.[141]

Lord served as chaplain to the East India Company's factory in Surat for about five years and while there acquired some knowledge of Hindustani and Persian. He claims to have drawn his picture of the Banyans' religion from the Hindu scriptures which he calls "the *Shaster*." Which *shastra*s he used is not clear. The Banyans with whom he consulted were themselves probably confused or uninformed about the teachings of the Vedas, Brahmanas, and Puranas.[142] His accounts of Hindu cosmology, the three ages of the earth, the origin of the four major castes and other Hindu beliefs, laws, and ceremonies are therefore confused and inaccurate in places. Some parts of Lord's account are consistent with traditional Hindu beliefs and practices, and others may accurately reflect the understanding of the Banyans of Surat about their religion.

Lord's account of Surat's Parsi community and its beliefs is still more superficial. He claims to have found his information in the Zend-Avesta, but more likely he depended on a Parsi interpreter who may not himself have adequately understood the Zend-Avesta.[143] Lord's sketch of early Parsi his-

---

[139] *Ibid.*, pp. xxviii–xxxvii.

[140] *A Display of Two Forraigne Sects in the East Indies* . . . (London). "Banians" or "Banyans" was a term commonly applied by Europeans to the Hindu traders or money-lenders of Gujarat or to the Hindus of western India generally. The word derives from *vāṇiya* or merchant.

[141] *A Discovery of the Sect of the Banyans. . . ;* and *The Religion of the Persies. . . .*

[142] Suggestions of Ram Chandra Prasad, *Early English Travellers in India:* . . . (Delhi, Patna, and Varanasi, 1965), pp. 327–28, 331.

[143] *Ibid.*, p. 344.

tory is accurate and he retells familiar stories about Zoroaster's birth and life; he erroneously thought fire worship was central to Zoroastrianism. He also stresses, as did most Western observers, the Parsi custom of exposing their dead in towers rather than burying or burning them. But, again, Zoroastrianism in Surat seems to have degenerated into a sect of fire worshippers, and their burial practices surely were among their most conspicuous ceremonies.[144]

For all his superficiality and inaccuracy, Lord was one of the earliest Westerners to dig beneath observable Hindu and Parsi religious practices in an attempt to study these beliefs more systematically. As such his book was an important contribution to Europe's meager understanding of Indian thought and religion. The effort, however, seems to have produced in him little appreciation or sympathy for the Indian religions. He dedicated his book to the Archbishop of Canterbury as an indictment of the false religions for the prelate's judgment. Lord's review was often quoted or inserted into other accounts, but it was not republished in English during the seventeenth century. There was, however, a French translation in 1667.[145]

A brief—twelve pages—anonymous description of Mughul India appeared in 1632 under the title, *A True Relation.*[146] It contains a few anecdotes about the Mughul emperor and the court, and some superficial description of the empire, all of which appear to have been taken from the reports of Roe and Terry. The last two pages of *A True Relation* contain sketchy comments about Ceylon, Sumatra, Patani, and Japan, which apparently also derive from other reports.

In 1633, nearly twenty years after the expedition, another report by a member of Downton's fleet of 1614 was published.[147] The author, Christopher Farewell, was a merchant who spent some time at the English factories and lodgings in Surat, Ahmadabad, and other places in Gujarat. He apparently had some difficulties with his colleagues and superiors in Ahmadabad and was sent home in September, 1616.[148] Farewell's book is short, only sixty-five pages, but it is written in a delightfully witty style and contains considerably more good description than any of the other journals from Downton's voyage. He describes Surat and its Banyan residents—he was not much interested in the Muslims—and the daily life of the English residents there. He also describes other towns and villages he visited on his travels through Gujarat. Farewell was fascinated with the monkeys of Surat and apparently spent a great deal of time watching them leap from roof to

[144] *Ibid.,* p. 355.

[145] *Histoire de la religion de Banian, avec un traité de la religion des anciens Persans* (Paris).

[146] *A True Relation Without All Exceptions of Strange and Admirable Accidents which Lately Happened in the kingdom of the Great Magor or Mugul, Who is the Greatest Monarch in the East Indies, as also with a True Report of the Manners of the Country* . . . (London).

[147] C.[hristopher] F.[arewell], *An East-India Colation, or a Discourse of Travels;* . . . (London).

[148] See Foster (ed.), *op. cit.* (n. 98), pp. 153–54.

roof, pull up loose tiles, and drop things on people's heads.[149] This account was never republished.

More news from India was contained in Thomas Herbert's account of his travels first published in 1634.[150] Through the influence of his relative, the Earl of Pembroke, Herbert (1606–82) was appointed to accompany Sir Dodmore Cotton, the newly appointed English ambassador to Persia in 1627. Cotton's appointment resulted from Robert Sherely's embassy from Persia to England in 1623, an embassy that produced two rival ambassadors, Sherely and Nadg Ali Beg, each of whom denounced the other as an imposter. Charles I sent Cotton to Persia to clarify matters, and both Sherely and Nagd Ali Beg sailed with him.[151] They arrived in Surat on November 27, 1627, where Nagd Ali Beg deliberately took an overdose of opium and died, thus revealing which Persian ambassador was an imposter. He was buried, Herbert reported, close to Tom Coryate's grave near Surat.[152] Herbert also notes that Shah Jahan had just been crowned emperor in 1628 when the English fleet arrived in Surat. Jahangir had died in the previous October (there were rumors that he had been poisoned), and after a series of intrigues among the rival claimants to the throne, Shah Jahan was finally crowned.[153] Herbert also gives a description of Surat, of its people, their religion, castes, social customs, and morals.[154] Some of this is based on Herbert's personal observations, but much of it obviously was taken from earlier printed sources. Herbert remained in Surat for only about three weeks on this first visit. On December 18, 1627, he sailed with the ambassador for Persia, where they remained for about one year. Both Cotton and Sherely died of dysentery during that time. Herbert himself was very ill. He returned to Surat in December, 1628, and in April, 1629, embarked on the homeward voyage. After a few stops along the Malabar Coast, he arrived at Plymouth on December 18, 1629.

Most of Herbert's *Relation* deals with Persia and his experiences there. His return to India on the way home apparently induced him to include descriptions of the Malabar Coast, Ceylon, the Coromandel Coast, Pegu, Siam, Patani, Sumatra, Java, and China.[155] Apart from a few firsthand observations about the Malabar Coast, all this information was borrowed from other printed sources. Herbert's descriptions tend to be simple and uncritical. He is mostly interested in bizarre religious or sexual practices and seems to have readily believed almost any outlandish story told him. He correctly reports that Peguan men wore bells in their genitals and that young girls were deflowered on idols;[156] less accurately, he claims that the dark skin of the Mala-

[149] Farewell, *op. cit.* (n. 147), pp. 58–60.
[150] *A Relation of Some Yeares Travaile, Begunne Anno 1626* . . . (London).
[151] For details on Herbert's career see Penrose, *op. cit.* (n. 36), pp. 174–214.
[152] Herbert, *op. cit.* (n. 150), pp. 27–29.
[153] *Ibid.*, pp. 29–35.
[154] *Ibid.*, pp. 35–43.
[155] *Ibid.*, pp. 182–206.
[156] *Ibid.*, p. 41.

bars is the result of the scorching sun, and that their priests usually spend the first night with a new bride. He writes that the people of Calicut exchange wives,[157] that young girls on the Coromandel Coast prostitute themselves in the pagodas, and that worshippers there often die after throwing themselves in front of the Juggernaut's chariot (or Jagannath, from Sanskrit *Jagannātha*).[158] He claims that the former queen of Siam took measures to reduce sodomy in her lands,[159] and reported that the men of Patani gladly lend their daughters and nieces to travelers.[160] In Makassar they "drink" a lot of tobacco and sometimes kill strangers by sharing a poisoned pipe with them.[161] Reportedly the crocodiles in Sumatra shed bloody tears after eating a man. Sumatran women are very courageous but unchaste.[162] On Java a condemned man might try to fight his way free with a kris.[163] Herbert made little effort to understand what he read or saw; for example, he seems to identify all Hindu or Buddhist deities and saints with the devil.

Herbert continued to revise and augment his *Relation* and to publish it in new editions. That of 1638 is about 150 pages longer than the original edition and contains many more copper plates.[164] It also includes a history of the "Great Mogul," a description of Mughul cities, a survey of Japan and the Moluccas, and a greatly expanded word portrait of China. All of this appears to have come from other printed sources. A third edition was issued in 1639. During the Civil War in England, Herbert was busy with other affairs. He served on some committees for Parliament and as a commissioner for Lord Fairfax's parliamentary army. He was appointed to the king's retinue by Parliament in 1644 and remained with Charles I until his execution. After Charles' funeral, which Herbert arranged, he returned to his home in Yorkshire. He was made a baronet by Charles II in 1660. Whatever else he did during these years, he surely continued to revise his *Relation*. Greatly enlarged editions came out in 1665 and in 1677. The last one was fully three and one-half times as large as the 1634 edition and seems more a general secondary account of Asia than a personal relation. Herbert died in March, 1682. His *Relation* was translated into Dutch in 1658 and into French in 1663.[165]

William Bruton's *Newes from the East Indies,* published in 1638, brought information from the other side of the Indian subcontinent, from Bengal and the Coromandel Coast.[166] Bruton went to Masulipatam as a quartermaster and spent seven years there and in Bengal between 1630 and 1638. Most of his written account describes an embassy to the nabob or viceroy of

[157] *Ibid.*, pp. 187–89.
[158] *Ibid.*, p. 192.
[159] *Ibid.*, p. 195.
[160] *Ibid.*, p. 198.
[161] *Ibid.*, pp. 198–99.
[162] *Ibid.*, pp. 199–200.
[163] *Ibid.*, pp. 200–201.
[164] *Some Yeares Travels into Divers Parts of Asia and Afrique* . . . (London).
[165] *Zee en lant reyse na verscheyde deelen van Asia en Africa;* . . . (Dordrecht); *Relation de voyage de Perse et des Indes Orientales* (Paris).
[166] *Newes from the East Indies; or a Voyage to Bengalla* . . . (London).

Bengal's court in 1633. In addition to observations about the countryside and towns along the way, it contains a richly detailed description of the nabob's palace, his retinue, and the embassy's reception and negotiations. Bruton reports that the nabob still sleeps in a tent because no Mughul would sleep in a palace built for another. He was currently building an even grander palace for himself.[167] Bruton also reported that at their first meeting the nabob presented his foot for Ambassador Cartwright to kiss. Cartwright refused, twice, but finally acquiesced. Bruton describes the pagoda, the image of Jagannath, and the annual festival in which the image is pulled through the streets on a huge chariot with sixteen wheels on each side.[168] Bruton's *Newes* was not reprinted during the seventeenth century.

Very few firsthand accounts of Asia were published in England during the Civil War and the Protectorate (1640–60). The interests and energies of the English—or at least of the people who published books—were apparently too absorbed with troubles at home to be concerned with distant peoples and events. Charles I seriously hurt the East India Company; he licensed William Courteen's rival company in violation of the Company's charter and indeed without even warning it. Then in 1640 the king bilked the Company out of £63,000 in an effort to raise money for his campaign against the Scotch.[169] Cromwell at least wished the Company well, but he too was busy with other matters. The Dutch Wars (1652–74), while popular and successful at home, also made things very difficult for the Company in Asia.[170]

A report in English of Robert Junius' missionary successes on Formosa was published in 1650.[171] The author describes the mass conversion of Formosans to Dutch Reformed Christianity by Junius, but he includes no descriptions of Formosa and its people. This account was originally written in Latin, but had never been published before. Apparently the only English report from these middle years that had anything to do with Asia was the pamphlet dealing with the Courteen expedition which appeared in 1652.[172] Its author defends Courteen's adventure and his competition with the East India Company generally, on the grounds that the old Company was sadly neglecting its opportunities and falling hopelessly behind the Dutch. He then recounts the injuries done to Courteen's ships and factories by the Company and demands compensation for Courteen's heirs and the reorganization of the Company. The controversy continued for many years, and

---

[167] Bruton, "News from the East Indies . . ." in *Hakluyt's Collection of Early Voyages, Travels, and Discoveries. . .* , A New Edition, with Additions (5 vols.; London, 1807–12), V, 54.

[168] *Ibid.,* pp. 56–57.

[169] See H. Rawlinson, *British Beginnings in Western India, 1579–1657* (Oxford, 1920), pp. 100–111.

[170] *Ibid.,* p. 114.

[171] Caspar Sibelius, *Of the Conversion of Five Thousand and Nine Hundred East Indians, in the Isle Formosa, Neere China, to the Profession of the True God in Jesus Christ, by Means of M. Ro. Junius, a Minister Lately of Delph in Holland . . .* (London).

[172] J. D.[arrell], *Strange News from the Indies; or East India Passages Further Discovered . . .* (London).

claims for damages by Courteen's heirs were finally presented to Parliament. More pamphlets on the Courteen affair appeared in 1679 and 1680.[173]

A few important foreign works about Asia were translated into English during these turbulent years. An account of the persecution in Japan translated from Jesuit letters appeared in 1630.[174] In 1653 Robert Ashley published translated extracts from Cristoforo Borri's 1633 account of Cochin-China.[175] An English translation of Pinto's *Peregrinaçam* appeared in the same year.[176] John Crook published an English translation of Martino Martini's history of the Manchu Conquest in 1654.[177] It appeared again in 1655, appended to Crook's English edition of Semedo's book on China.[178]

After the Restoration, too, the most obvious activity in the writing and publishing of literature about Asia was the translation of foreign accounts into English. Adam Olearius' account of Mandelslo's journey from Persia to India was translated by John Davies; it appeared in 1662 and again in 1669. Sir Roger Manley translated Caron's description of Japan and Joost Schouten's account of Siam; they appeared in a single volume in 1663. Another edition of Caron and Schouten appeared in 1671. In 1664 Sir Peter Wycke translated Jacinot Freyre de Andrade's *The Life of Dom John de Castro*, the Portuguese viceroy. An English edition of Pietro della Valle's *Travels* appeared in 1665. Johann Nieuhof's account of the VOC embassy to China in 1655 was translated from the Dutch and published by John Ogilby in 1669 and reissued four years later. In 1670 Ogilby published Montanus' account of the VOC embassies to Japan, and in 1671 a translation of Dapper's account of the second and third VOC embassies to China which he erroneously attributed to Montanus. Also in 1671 appeared François Bernier's account of the Mughul succession struggle of 1657–59 which brought Aurangzib to the throne and

[173] Edward Graves, *et al., A Brief Narrative and Deduction of the Several Remarkable Cases of Sir William Courten, and Sir Paul Pyndar. . . , and William Courten, . . .* (London, 1679); John Brown, *A Brief Remonstrance of the Grand Grievances and Opressions Suffered by Sir William Courten, and Sir Paul Pyndar, Knts. Deceased . . .* (London, 1680).

Peter Mundy was in India and other parts of Asia in 1628–34, 1635–38, and 1655–56. Between 1620 and 1667 he wrote and revised a voluminous, detailed record of his travels including excellent descriptions of the places he visited. It is obviously the work of an intelligent observer, who carefully distinguished between what he saw and knew to be true from what was related to him by others. But it was not published until the twentieth century. See Richard Carnac Temple (ed.), *The Travels of Peter Mundy in Europe and Asia, 1608–1667* (5 vols.; "HS," 2d ser., XVII, XXXV, XLV, XLVI, LV, LXXVIII; Cambridge, 1907–36).

[174] *The Palme of Christian Fortitude or the Glorious Combats of Christians in Iaponia. Taken out of the Letters of the Society of Iesus from thence, Anno 1624* (St. Omer, 1630).

[175] *Cochinchina, Containing Many Admirable Rarities and Singularities of that Country, Extracted out of an Italian Relation . . .* (London).

[176] Fernão Mendez Pinto, *The Voyages and Adventures in Ethiopia, China, Tartary, etc. . . . ,* trans. H. Cogan (London). Reprinted in 1663 and 1692.

[177] *Bellum Tartaricum, or the Conquest of the Great and Most Renouwned Empire of China, by the Invasion of the Tartars . . .* (London).

[178] Alvaro Semmedo, *The History of that Great and Renouwned Monarchy of China . . .* (London, 1655).

a translation of Juan de Palafox y Mendoza's history of the Manchu Conquest of China. English versions of Domingo Fernández Navarrete's description of China and Johann Grueber's reports from China appeared in 1675 and 1676 respectively.[179]

The steady publication of all these translated works surely demonstrates a growing interest in Asia among English readers. English observers of the Asian scene, however, contributed almost nothing to satisfy that interest. During the entire two decades from 1660 to 1680 only two pieces that could be called firsthand reports appeared in English. Both of these were pamphlets that revived memories of the Amboina Massacre and subsequent Dutch hostilities with the English.[180] Neither of these pamphlets contains any description of Asia. Nor did the recently available information about Asia show impressively in the secondary literature of the Restoration Period. For example, Thomas Powell's history of humanity's progress in the manual arts (1661) contains a few brief references to Chinese sailing chariots, writing, printing, sericulture, and use of the compass, but none to the skills and crafts of any other Asian people.[181] The Chinese are also the only Asian people treated in G. Hussey's world history (1670), but the account is very brief and appears to have been based entirely on Mendoza.[182] Only John Webb's treatise on the probability that Chinese was the original language of all mankind shows much familiarity with the recent literature about China available in Europe.[183]

[179] Adam Olearius, *The Voyages and Travels of the Ambassadors Sent by Frederick Duke of Holstein, to the Great Duke of Muscovy, and the King of Persia . . . Whereto are added the Travels of John Albert de Mandelslo. . . ,* trans. John Davies (London, 1662); François Caron and Joost Schouten, *A True Description of the Mighty Kingdoms of Japan and Siam. . . ,* trans. Roger Manley (London, 1663), reprinted in 1671; Pietro della Valle, *The Travels . . .* (London, 1665); Nieuhof, *An Embassy from the East-India Company of the United Provinces, to the Great Tartar Cham, Empereur of China. . . ,* trans. John Ogilby (London, 1669); *Atlas Japannensis,* trans. John Ogilby (London, 1671); François Bernier, *The History of the Late Revolution of the Empire of the Great Mogul. . .* (3 vols. in one; London, 1671); Juan Palafox y Mendoza, *History of the Conquest of China by the Tartars . . .* (London, 1671); Domingo Fernandez Navarrete, *An Account of the Empire of China . . .* (London, 1675); Johann Grueber, *China and France, or Two Treatises. The One of the Present State of China, . . .* (London, 1676).

[180] J.[ohn] D.[arrell], *A True and Compendious Narration; or (Second Part of Amboyna) of Sundry Notorious or Remarkable Injuries, Insolencies, and Acts of Hostility . . .* (London, 1665); *The Emblem of Ingratitude: or the Hollanders Insolencies & Cruelties Detected . . .* (London, 1672).

[181] *Humane Industry; or a History of Most Manual Arts, Deducing their Original, Progress, and Improvement of Them . . .* (London, 1661), pp. 29–31, 47, 67, 89, 161.

[182] G. Hussey, *Memorabilia Mundi; or Choice Memoirs of the History and Description of the World* (London).

[183] *An Historical Essay Endeavoring a Probability that the Language of the Empire of China is the Primitive Language* (London, 1669). A second edition appeared in 1678.

What might have been the best English contribution to Europe's knowledge of Asia during these years was not published until the twentieth century. John Marshall served as a factor in the English establishment on the Coromandel Coast and in Bengal from 1668 until 1672. He apparently learned Sanskrit, studied Indian antiquities, collected Indian books, and made a translation of the Bhagavata-Purana. He also kept notes and a diary of all these activities. His modern editor thinks Marshall's observations and translations were better than anything pub-

The English Literature

3

A LATE HARVEST, 1680–1700

The last two decades of the century saw the appearance of some really significant English contributions to Europe's store of knowledge about Asia, beginning with Robert Knox's account of Ceylon.[184] Knox (1640–1720) sailed from England with his father's ship in January, 1657. On November 19, 1659, en route home after trading for over one year in Bengal, Fort St. George (Madras), and Acheh, their ship was crippled in a storm off the coast of Ceylon. They put in at Katthia Bay and traded there while they repaired the ship. About twenty days after their arrival a royal official from the Sinhalese court of Kandy came down to the coast to investigate. After he had lured the captain, Knox's father, and many others ashore, his soldiers surprised and captured the Englishmen and also tried to seize the ship. The ship escaped, but Knox, his father, and fourteen other crewmen remained in Sinhalese hands.

After a few days they were taken into the hills and distributed among several villages. They were given food and housing, were permitted to move about freely within their villages—later even between villages—and were generally treated civilly. Knox and his father both suffered from a long bout of malaria. The son eventually recovered, but the father died of the disease. Despite the free food they continued to receive, the captives were forced to find ways to earn money to replace their worn-out clothing. Many of them knitted caps and sold them until the market was saturated. Most arranged with the village authorities to receive their rations uncooked so that they could sell the surplus. Knox eventually also lent seed rice for interest and did some peddling. He became moderately prosperous, bought some land, and built a house. Peddling allowed him to travel about the country looking for ways to escape. Most of the men married and built homes. Some became farmers, and others took service with the king.[185]

Knox thought they had been captured because they had not reported their arrival to the king or sent him a present.[186] That seems unlikely. Many envoys to the court of Kandy, those from Jacob de La Haye's French fleet in 1672, for example, were held captive despite their letters and presents.[187] The ambassador sent by the Dutch governor of Ceylon to negotiate the release of captives was also detained.[188] Collecting Europeans seems to have been a hobby of Raja Sinha II (r. 1635–87) in the later years of his reign.

---

lished before 1800. Unfortunately they found no seventeenth-century publisher. See Sharfaat Ahmed Khan (ed.), *John Marshall in India. Notes and Observations in Bengal, 1668–1672* (London, 1927).

[184] *An Historical Relation . . .* (London, 1681).
[185] For details on their life in Kandy see *ibid.,* pp. 117–74.
[186] *Ibid.,* p. 120.
[187] *Ibid.,* pp. 183–86.   [188] *Ibid.,* pp. 180–82.

Apparently there were between five hundred and one thousand captives living in Kandyan villages during these years. They were not mistreated. In fact they were a privileged group enjoying special royal protection.[189] At the end of his book Knox describes their privileged position and speculates that the king kept Europeans simply because he liked to receive them at court, liked to talk to them, and liked to have them in his army and retinue.[190]

Following long preparation, Knox and one of his fellow English captives set out to escape in September, 1679, while on a peddling trip. After a harrowing journey they made their way to the Dutch fort at Areppa on October 18, 1679. From there they were taken to Colombo and finally to Batavia and Bantam, where they boarded a ship for England.[191] Knox had been in Ceylon for almost twenty years. He apparently began writing down some of his reminiscences while he was at Batavia and later on shipboard. Upon his return to England his cousin, the Reverend John Strype, helped him organize his notes. Robert Hooke, secretary of the Royal Society, interviewed Knox and encouraged him to publish an account of his experiences. He may have helped Knox with the writing. The book was published by Richard Chiswell, the Royal Society's printer, and Hooke wrote a preface for it.[192]

Knox's *Relation* was the most comprehensive and accurate description of the kingdom of Kandy written during the seventeenth century. Even the Dutch writers had not enjoyed the opportunities for observing the kingdom that Knox had. After having lived in Kandyan villages for nearly twenty years and having become fluent in Sinhalese, his was very much a view from the inside. It is a fascinating account and in the judgment of his modern editor still "the best available source book for the social and economic history of Ceylon in the seventeenth century."[193]

Knox's *Relation* was republished in 1705 as part of the Harris collection.[194] During the seventeenth century it was translated into Dutch (1692), French (1693), and German (1689).[195] John Locke read it, and in his *Two Treatises of Civil Government* used Kandy as an example of the evils of despotism.[196] Daniel De Foe apparently drew on it heavily for his *Robinson Crusoe*.[197]

Several pamphlets relating to the civil war in Bantam during 1681 and 1682 were published in England during the eighties. None of them contains a description of Bantam or Java, but they report progressively the events relating to the "Young King's" (Prince Hadji's) rebellion against his father,

[189] See S. D. Saparamadu (ed.), *An Historical Relation of Ceylon*, in *Ceylon Historical Journal*, VI (1956–57), pp. xii–xxi.
[190] Knox, *op. cit.* (n. 184), p. 186.
[191] *Ibid.*, pp. 156–74.
[192] See Saparamadu (ed.), *op. cit.* (n. 189), xxx–xxxi.
[193] *Ibid.*, p. xxxv.
[194] John Harris, *Navigantium atque itinerantium bibliotheca* (London).
[195] For details see Saparamadu (ed.), *op. cit.* (n. 189), p. vii.
[196] *Ibid.*, p. xxxvi.   [197] *Ibid.*, pp. xxxix–xl.

Sultan Abulfatah, the help he received from the Dutch, the burning of the city, and the closure of the English factory after Prince Hadji's victory. The main emphasis in all these pamphlets is on the responsibility of the Dutch for all these troubles. The first was a single-sheet letter written by a resident of the English factory in Bantam describing the outbreak of the rebellion and Sultan Abulfatah's burning of the city.[198] In 1683 another such letter describes the Dutch role in more detail and reports Abulfatah's surrender.[199] A more comprehensive account of the rebellion was provided in 1683 in a collection of letters from Bantam which also reported the closing of the English factories and their negotiations with the Dutch governor-general in Batavia.[200] It was published with the VOC's answer to official English protests against Dutch activities during the rebellion.[201] Finally, in 1688 another Dutch *Justification* of the VOC's activities, not only in Bantam but in other parts of Asia, was published together with a large collection of letters and depositions refuting the Dutch position.[202]

One of the popular small books published by Nathaniel Crouch of London under the pseudonym of R. B. (Robert Burton) contained information about Asia. His *A View of the English Acquisitions in Guiana and the East Indies* (1685) describes each English factory in India and Southeast Asia, the government of the Mughul Empire, the career of the Mahratta leader Sivaji, and the Manchu Conquest. It contains no new information or firsthand reports; all of it was taken from previously published works. Later editions appeared in 1686, 1726, and 1728.

A five-page letter from an English factor in Siam published in 1687 recounts an unsuccessful revolt of a large group of men from Makassar against the king of Siam.[203] News of the 1688 *coup d'état* in Siam and the subsequent expulsion of the French first arrived in England in 1690 with the publication of a small pamphlet containing letters and a brief journal translated from French.[204] According to its anonymous editor, none of the pieces had been previously published in any language. They briefly sketch the main events:

[198] *A True Account of the Burning and Sad Condition of Bantam, in the East Indies* . . . (London, 1682).

[199] *A Short Account of the Siege of Bantam: and his Surrender to the Rebels, who were Assisted by the Dutch, and their Fleet in the East Indies* (London, 1683).

[200] E. G., *The Civil Wars of Bantam:* . . . (London, 1683).

[201] *An Answer to the Committee of Seventeen;* . . . (London, n.d.).

[202] *An Impartial Vindication of the English East India Company, from the Unjust and Slanderous Imputations Cast upon them in a Treatise Intituled, a Justification of the Directors of the Netherlands East India Company* . . . (London, 1688).

[203] Samuel White, *A Letter from Mr. Samuel White to his Brother in London* . . . *Giving a Full Account of the Late Rebellion Made by the People of Macassar, Inhabiting in that Country, Which Ended in the Death of all the Rebells, Who Were Totally Destroyed by the King's Forces, Assisted by Some Europeans, of Several Nations, Amongst Whom Capt. Henry Udall, and Some Others of our Countrymen Most Unhappily Lost their Lives* (London, 1687). On White's career in the East see M. Collis, *Siamese White* (rev. ed.; London, 1951).

[204] *A Full and True Relation of the Great and Wonderful Revolution that Happened Lately in the Kingdom of Siam in the East Indies* . . . (London, 1690).

the illness and death of the king, "Opra Pitrachard's" (Phra Phetracha, r. 1688–1703) seizure of power, the murder of the dead king's natural and adopted sons, the torture and execution of Constantine Phaulkon, the Francophile minister of the king, and the expulsion of the French from the country.

John Ovington's *A Voyage to Surat,* published in 1696, presented new, firsthand observations about Surat and western India.[205] Ovington (1653–1731) sailed for India in 1689 as a chaplain on an East India Company ship. He stayed at Bombay for about three and one-half months after his arrival and declined an invitation to become the English factory's chaplain there. He accepted the chaplaincy at Surat, however, and remained there for another two and one-half years.

Ovington arrived at Bombay in late May, reputedly the unhealthiest time of the year. What is more, he came to Bombay when its fortunes seemed particularly low. Sir Josiah Child, the governor of the East India Company, favored the development of Surat rather than Bombay, and after the death of Gerald Aungier in 1677 there was apparently no effective spokesman for Bombay's interests. Furthermore, there had been a revolt of the garrison at Bombay in 1683, and in 1686 the island was attacked by a Mughul fleet.[206] All of this shows up in Ovington's description of Bombay. The climate he thought was particularly unhealthy for Europeans: they were sickly, plagued with vermin, and had wounds that would not heal. He thought it unwise that English women were permitted to live there; few of their children survived, and those who did appeared sickly.[207] He found morale low, the population declining and given to all sorts of vice, all of which he attributed to the climate.[208] Nevertheless he did a little sightseeing. In addition to the island of Bombay and the English factory he describes the island of Elephanta with its stone carvings and caves and the famous pagoda that so many other European travelers had described.[209]

Ovington was favorably impressed with Surat, and he devotes the largest part of his book to it. He describes the city, its various inhabitants—Moors, Banyans, Fakirs, and Parsis—its trade, and its daily life.[210] His account is interesting and detailed, probably the most comprehensive account of Surat to this date. As might be expected of a cleric, he was particularly perceptive regarding religious practices and customs. Much less valuable are Ovington's descriptions of the "Great Mogul" and his court,[211] and of the lands on the Arabian Sea and Persian Gulf.[212] These were not based on firsthand observations.

---

[205] *A Voyage to Suratt in the Year, 1689* . . . (London).
[206] For details see the introduction to H. G. Rawlinson (ed.), *A Voyage to Surat* (London, 1929).
[207] Ovington, *op. cit.* (n. 205), pp. 145–46.
[208] *Ibid.,* pp. 143–44.
[209] *Ibid.,* pp. 158–62.
[211] *Ibid.,* pp. 165–213.
[210] *Ibid.,* pp. 214–383.
[212] *Ibid.,* pp. 420–78.

Appended to Ovington's account are four treatises taken from other sources: a history of the succession crisis in Golconda, a description of Arakan and Pegu, a list of Indian coins, and a treatise on the nature of silkworms.[213] The history of Golconda contains some interesting insights about "Abdulla Hoosan's" (Abu'l-Hasan, r. 1672–87) rise to power and succession to the throne, events not recounted in English before.[214] The description of Arakan and Pegu is very general and appears to have been taken from earlier Portuguese accounts, perhaps that of Manrique.[215] Ovington's account was not republished in English until the twentieth century. It was translated into French in 1725.[216]

An even longer account of India, that of John Fryer (*ca.* 1650–1733), appeared two years after Ovington's.[217] It was based on experiences which had occurred much earlier. Fryer, an East India Company surgeon, left England in December, 1672, and arrived at Masulipatam in June, 1673. He spent some time there and at Madras (Fort St. George) on the Coromandel Coast, and at Bombay and Surat on the West Coast. During his stay in India he also traveled to Gokarna, Karwar, Goa, and inland to Junnar. He was in Persia from 1677 to 1679, after which he returned to India, where he remained until 1681. He arrived back in England in August, 1682, seven years before Ovington sailed for India.[218]

Fryer's book for the most part describes the places he actually visited: Golconda (especially Masulipatam), Madras, Bombay, Surat, Junnar, and the way over the Ghats from Bombay to Karwar and Goa. What he writes about the Deccan generally and about the Mughul Empire is based on oral reports or earlier descriptions. Fryer was a good storyteller with a fine sense of humor, and his descriptions are graphic and clear. He was much less interested in religion and caste than was Ovington, and his discussions of such topics are general and brief. He was also considerably less sympathetic and more prejudiced against Indian religion and customs than Ovington and readier to dismiss Indians as "superstitious heathens." Ovington, for example, seemed genuinely impressed with the Hindu respect for life. Fryer, on the other hand, cynically observed that the Gentiles who so scrupulously avoided killing insects and animals nevertheless worked their pack animals to death without feeding them adequately. Worse still, he once discovered a sick dancing girl who had been abandoned among the tombs to die.[219] As he watched the vermin-infested Banyans near Surat he thought of the Banyans themselves as so many vermin swarming around him at Swally Hole

[213] *Ibid.,* pp. 523–606.
[214] *Ibid.,* pp. 525–52. See pls. 204, 205.　　[215] See above, pp. 349–50.
[216] *Ses voyages fait à Surate, et en d'autres lieux de l'Asie et de l'Afrique* . . . (Paris).
[217] John Fryer, *A New Account of East India and Persia, in Eight Letters, Being Nine Years Travels, Begun 1672. and Finished 1681* . . . (London, 1698).
[218] For bibliographical details see John Fryer, *A New Account of East India and Persia,* . . . ed. W. Crooke (3 vols.; "HS," 2d ser., XIX, XX, XXXIX; London, 1909–15), I, xi–xxvii.
[219] Fryer, *op. cit.* (n. 217), p. 143.

(Suwali).[220] On the other hand, Fryer thought the meatless Hindu diet might be healthy in a climate where meat spoiled so quickly.[221] On several occasions he denounces the Fakirs, Muslim ascetics who in Fryer's eyes were nothing but thieves who robbed travelers and terrorized towns.

Fryer was on surer ground in his description of natural phenomena. He provides good scientific descriptions of the weather, plants, animals, and diseases. In fact he describes several dissections of animals, including his dissection of a giant sea-turtle to test the popular fable about its three hearts, which allegedly represent its tripartite nature of fish, flesh, and fowl.[222] Fryer found only a single heart. "To me," he reports, "it seems (though the flesh be highly extolled for the taste and colour of veal) neither fish, nor flesh, nor good Red Herring."[223] Perhaps it was his medical and scientific training that made him generally a shrewd and cautious rather than gullible observer.

Fryer's account also includes information about the events of the seventies in India. He arrived on the Coromandel Coast soon after De La Haye's French fleet attacked the Dutch in Ceylon and seized San Thomé. He describes this conflict and the eventual expulsion of the French. He also reports on Deccan politics and the Mughul wars with Sivaji. He shrewdly concludes that the Mughuls were unable to defeat Sivaji or complete the conquest of Golconda and the Deccan because the Mughul generals had much to gain from prolonging the wars.[224] Fryer's political information was mainly at second hand, but his depiction of the scars left in Surat by Sivaji's raids and the fear of its inhabitants for the Mahratta armies adds eyewitness color to the political reports. Interesting too is his description of Goa in decline with carracks rotting in the harbor for want of cargo.[225] Despite his apparent disdain for Indians, Fryer on several occasions sympathetically describes the sufferings of the poor people caught in the interminable wars. Sivaji's subjects in his eyes were harshly governed and oppressively taxed.[226] Others in the Deccan were continually plundered by Sivaji's troops and were always fearful that their crops would be harvested by the Mahrattas.[227]

Among Fryer's most fascinating experiences, and one that produced one of his more humorous descriptions, was his trip inland to the Mughul fort at Junnar near Poona in 1675 to treat one of the governor's wives.[228] After waiting for a propitious day he was taken into the harem to feel the sick woman's pulse, but not until attendants had tested his skill by giving him the hand of a healthy servant girl. On a subsequent visit a curtain fell down exposing the harem to Fryer's view. The women did not run away, he reports, but hid their faces in their hands and peered at him between their

---

[220] *Ibid.*, p. 82.
[221] *Ibid.*, p. 182.
[222] *Ibid.*, pp. 122–23.
[223] *Ibid.*, p. 123.
[224] *Ibid.*, p. 167.

[225] *Ibid.*, pp. 149–57.
[226] *Ibid.*, pp. 146–48.
[227] *Ibid.*, p. 142.
[228] *Ibid.*, pp. 123–44.

fingers. Fryer, too, kept cool, even to the point of observing half-peeled mangoes and needlework lying about, suggesting that the women did some honest work.[229]

Fryer became a member of the Royal Society after he returned to England. Although he never contributed to the *Philosophical Transactions,* his account was published by the Royal Society's printer. It was not republished in England until the twentieth century. A Dutch translation appeared in 1700.[230]

For sober, scientific accuracy and rich detail, no seventeenth-century descriptions of Asia surpass those of William Dampier (1652–1715), whose first volume, *A New Voyage Round the World,* was published at London in 1697. Dampier's circumnavigation was unintentional. After a decade of seafaring, including a voyage to the East Indies, Dampier left England for Jamaica in 1679 intending to cut logs in the Bay of Campeachy. He remained in Jamaica all year, and when the crew of his homeward-bound ship mutinied, Dampier joined them. He traveled with the buccaneers for almost six years, raiding Spanish towns, seizing ships, and twice crossing the Isthmus of Panama on foot. In 1686 he joined a group who had decided to cross the Pacific in a pirated ship to continue the spoilation of the Spaniards on its western shores. Altogether Dampier's voyage around the world took twelve and one-half years, involved probably a dozen ships, as well as native canoes and boats, and included substantial periods ashore in Central America, Mindanao, Sumatra, and Tongking. He returned to England in 1691.

Dampier's relationship to the buccaneers is not very clear. In his book he seems detached and aloof, and nowhere can his readers learn what sort of position he held. While relating the exciting adventures which surely account for the popularity of his book, Dampier provides almost no clues to indicate whether he took part in raids, participated in decisions, commanded men, or followed orders. Personal references usually have to do with his observations and writing. It is obvious that he possessed all the knowledge and skill of an expert navigator, but it is not at all clear that he had any responsibility for navigating the ships. He occasionally deplores the drunkenness, bickering, and crudeness of his shipmates. Nevertheless he stayed with them until 1688 before he persuaded Captain Read to set him ashore on one of the Nicobar Islands.[231] It is unlikely that the buccaneers carried him along as a privileged passenger for all those years.[232]

Whatever Dampier's role among the buccaneers, the reader of *A New Voyage Round the World* is quickly convinced that his motive in joining them was not to acquire wealth but to gather information. He returned to En-

[229] *Ibid.,* pp. 130–33.

[230] *Negenjaarige reyse door Oost-Indien en Persien, . . .* (The Hague).

[231] Dampier, *A New Voyage Round the World,* pp. 482–84.

[232] For bibliographical details see Joseph Shipman, *William Dampier, Seaman Scientist* (Lawrence, Kansas, 1962); John Masefield (ed.), *Dampier's Voyages . . .* (2 vols.; London, 1906), I, 1–13; C. C. Lloyd, *William Dampier* (London, 1966).

gland with no wealth beyond a tattooed Filipino slave he had acquired in Sumatra; also he still had his notes and journal, the preservation of which had always been his first concern during storms, shipwrecks, and other troubles. The notes and journal proved far more valuable to him than the tattooed slave, whom he was soon forced to sell. After his book was published, members of the Royal Society sought him out, introduced him to important people, and even obtained a position for him in the customs office.

A New Voyage Round the World contains first of all a great deal of navigational information. Wherever he traveled, Dampier meticulously noted winds, currents, shoals, shoreline characteristics, and weather. But he was more scientist than pilot. He was more concerned to understand global systems than to provide discrete navigational data. He made generalizations from his particular observations. He concluded, for example, that the Pacific Ocean was greater from east to west by twenty-five degrees than was commonly reckoned, and that the Indian Ocean must consequently be smaller than was usually understood, which, he thought, might explain why Dutch ships so frequently raised the Australian coast before they expected it.[233] He also observed the loss of a day by mariners sailing across the Pacific from east to west.[234] He provides several superb descriptions of typhoons and hurricanes, which he concluded were identical kinds of storms.[235] From a great many examples he concluded that deep seas are found alongside steep coasts while shallow anchorages are usually found along lower shores.[236]

Dampier described shorelines, soil, plants, animals, fish, and the weather of the places where he landed or along which he coasted. He frequently made sketches, and his notations can best be described as careful, disciplined—scientific—observations. No wonder that Royal Society members recognized him as a kindred spirit. His descriptions of natives and their societies are balanced and scholarly. For each new group of people he notes stature, shape of heads and limbs, lips, teeth, eyes, noses, hair, and skin. He discusses diet, houses, crafts, social customs, political forms, religion, and general disposition. His explications are unusually detailed, frequently including things not found in the accounts of others who visited the same places: for example, the construction of outrigger canoes on Guam,[237] the cylindrical bellows used by blacksmiths on Mindanao,[238] the differences between Mindanao and Manila tobacco,[239] the watertight compartments of a Chinese junk,[240] and the fact that natives on Mindanao measured visiting ships in imitation of the Chinese, although they seemed not to know why they were doing it.[241] He was not gullible, nor did he include more in his

[233] Dampier, *op. cit.* (n. 231), pp. 285–90.
[234] *Ibid.*, p. 376.
[235] *Ibid.*, pp. 321–23, 414–15, 451–53.
[236] *Ibid.*, pp. 422–25.
[237] *Ibid.*, pp. 298–99.
[238] *Ibid.*, p. 332.
[239] *Ibid.*, p. 333.
[240] *Ibid.*, pp. 412–13.
[241] *Ibid.*, p. 354.

depictions than he actually saw without telling his readers where he obtained the additional information. Frequently he admitted that he could not learn how far a ruler's territory extended, what the inland parts of an island looked like, or what sort of religion a people had, even for places that had been repeatedly described in previous travel literature. He did not accept commonly told stories about Asian peoples unless he personally found them to be true. He doubted the existence of cannibals, for example, because each time he had been able to test such stories he found them to be false. The prospect of being put ashore alone on the Nicobar Islands was not at all frightening to him:

I am of the opinion, that there are no people in the world so barbarous, as to kill a simple Man that falls accidentally into their hands, or comes to live among them; except they have before been injured, by some outrage, or violence committed against them. Yet even then, or afterwards, if a Man could but preserve his Life from their first Rage, and come to treat with them (which is the hardest thing, because their way is usually to abscond, and rushing suddenly upon their Enemy to kill him unawares) one might by some slight insinuate ones self into their favours again. Especially by showing some toy or knack, that they did never see before: which any *European,* that has seen the world, might soon contrive to amuse them withal: as might be done generally, even with a Little Fire struck from a Flint and Steel.[242]

Dampier exercises his impressive observational and narrative skills on descriptions of Guam, Mindanao, Pulau Condore, St. John's Island (Shang-ch'uan) near Macao, the Pescadores, the Australian coast, the Nicobar Islands, and numerous other South Pacific and Southeast Asian islands.

A "Supplement" to *A New Voyage Round the World* was published in 1699 as Part I of a volume entitled *Voyages and Descriptions* (London). It contains a lengthy description of Tongking, where Dampier spent much of 1688, as well as surveys of Cambodia, Acheh, the Moluccas, and Benkulen on the west coast of Sumatra. All of these were done with the same precision and elegance of style as those in his earlier volume. The *Voyages and Descriptions* also includes accounts of Dampier's two voyages to Campeachy and "A Discourse of Trade Winds, Breezes, Storms, Seasons of the Year, Tides and Currents of the Torrid Zone throughout the World," a treatise which established his reputation as a hydrographer.

His books made Dampier famous, and as a consequence he was given command of an exploratory voyage to Australia in 1699. It was not a very successful expedition. Dampier's ship was old and in poor repair. His crew was not much better than the buccaneer crews he had sailed with before, and Dampier's leadership abilities do not seem to have equalled his scholarly and literary skills. Sailing by way of the Cape Route he coasted western and northwestern Australia, but left for Timor without testing his hunch that

[242] *Ibid.,* p. 484.

there was some sort of passage between Australia and New Guinea.[243] After refitting on Timor he and his crew visited many of the smaller islands in the southern Moluccas and others to the north of New Guinea, sailed around New Britain, back along the north coast of New Guinea, and then turned toward home with stopovers at Timor and Batavia. The tired old ship finally gave out and sank in shallow water off Ascension Island.[244] All of the crew and most of the goods were saved, and Dampier's expedition returned to England in May, 1702, on other English ships which had stopped at Ascension. Dampier's voyage to Australia was unusual in that it was undertaken solely for the sake of exploration and discovery; it was also the first English intrusion into what had hitherto been an exclusive Dutch preserve. It is a pity that the ship and crew were not adequate to carry out Dampier's planned investigation of eastern Australia and New Guinea's southern coast. As it turned out, the only significant geographic or cartographic result of the voyage was Dampier's discovery of New Britain and the passage between it and New Guinea.

The literary results of the voyage were more impressive. They were published in two parts, the first of which appeared in 1703, the second in 1709.[245] Again this work is characterized by careful, accurate descriptions of natural phenomena along Australia's west coast, on Timor, New Guinea, New Britain, and many other islands. Dampier provides sketches of many of the plants and animals as well as maps and coastal outlines. Regarding Australia he adds little to what had been published by the Dutch except for the fact that his descriptions of plants and animals are generally superior to those of his Dutch predecessors.

Subsequent editions of Dampier's *A New Voyage Round the World* appeared in 1697, 1698, 1699, 1703, 1717, and 1729. His *Voyages and Discoveries* was republished in 1700, 1703, and 1729. The second edition of *A Voyage to New Holland* appeared in 1709, and a third came out in 1729. John Knapton's 1729 edition, usually called "Dampier's Works in Four Volumes," also contains William Funnell's account of Dampier's voyage of 1703. *A New Voyage Round the World* was translated into German in 1701–14, into Dutch in 1704 and 1715, and into French in 1723.[246]

Captain Ambrose Cowley, one of Dampier's associates during part of his first voyage around the world, also wrote an account of the circumnavigation, which was printed in William Hacke's collection of voyages in 1699.[247] It contains brief descriptions of Guam, Borneo, and Batavia, but none of

[243] Dampier, *A Voyage to New Holland, &c. in the Year, 1699* (London, 1703), p. 135.

[244] *Ibid.*, pp. 191–96.

[245] Dampier, *op. cit.* (n. 243), *A Continuation of a Voyage to New Holland &c. in the Year 1699* . . . (London).

[246] For bibliography see Albert Gray (ed.), *A New Voyage Round the World* (London, 1937), pp. v–vi.

[247] *A Collection of Original Voyages* . . . (London).

them adds anything to what had been reported by earlier English travelers. Cowley's was the only account in Hacke's collection which treats of Asia.

In the eighties and nineties too, despite the fine contributions of Knox, Ovington, Fryer, and Dampier, the foreign works translated into English remain more impressive in both number and quality than the English first-hand accounts. In 1682, for example, a translation of Jan Janszoon Struys' first voyage appeared under the name of Glanius, which must have been the pseudonym of the translator or translator-pirate.[248] It is not a very reliable translation, and it is augmented by long descriptions apparently pilfered from other works. In the same year, also under Glanius' name, a translation appeared of Franz Janszoon van der Heiden's relation of his shipwreck off the coast of Bengal.[249] A totally different translation of all Struys' voyages, this one by John Morrison, was printed in 1683.[250] A second edition of this translation, in 1684, appears to have been made from the same sheets, adding only a new title page, preface, and the first two pages of the text.

A great many French works were translated into English during the last decades of the century. Jean Chardin's *Travels,* however, was published in English before it appeared in French.[251] The French edition, published at Amsterdam in 1686, is a translation of the English edition. It contains al-most nothing about Asia. Reports about Louis XIV's embassy to Siam ap-peared in English translation during the eighties; that of the ambassador Alexandre de Chaumont appeared in 1687, the Jesuit Guy Tachard's in 1688.[252] Jean de Thévenot's *Travels* was translated in 1687.[253] In 1688 transla-tions from the French of both Gabriel de Magalhães' history of China and Charles Dellon's history of the inquisition at Goa appeared.[254] Confucius be-came available to English readers in 1691, in an abridged translation of In-torcetta and Couplet's Latin translation of the *Four Books.*[255] Two years later both La Loubère's account of Siam and Avril's overland travels to China were translated from the French.[256]

[248] Glanius, *A New Voyage to the East Indies; Containing an Account of Several of those Rich Coun-tries, and more particularly of the Kingdom of Bantam* (London).

[249] Glanius, *A Relation of an Unfortunate Voyage to the Kingdom of Bengala . . .* (London, 1682).

[250] John Struys, *The Perilous and Most Unhappy Voyages of John Struys through Italy, Greece, Lifeland, Moscovia, Tartary, Media, Persia, East-India, Japan, and other Places in Europe, Africa, and Asia. . . ,* trans. John Morrison (London).

[251] *The Travels of Sir John Chardin into Persia and the East Indies, the First Volume . . .* (London, 1686).

[252] Alexandre de Chaumont, *A Relation of the Late Embassy of Moncr. de Chaumont, Knt. to the Court of the King of Siam . . .* (London, 1687); Guy Tachard, *A Relation of the Voyage to Siam Performed by Six Jesuits, Sent by the French King to the Indies and China, in the Year, 1684 . . .* (London, 1688).

[253] Jean Thévenot, *The Travels of Monsieur de Thevenot into the Levant. In Three Parts . . .* (London).

[254] Gabriel Magaillans, *A New History of China, Containing a Description of the Most Consider-able Particulars of that Vast Empire . . .* (London, 1688); [Charles] Dellon, *The History of the In-quisition, as it is Exercised at Goa . . .* (London, 1688).

[255] *The Morals of Confucius, a Chinese Philosopher* (London, 1691).

[256] Simon de La Loubère, *A New Historical Relation of the Kingdom of Siam* (London, 1693);

Michael Geddes' *History of the Church of Malabar* is not merely a translation.[257] The first part of it—the historical sketch—was culled from Portuguese sources but written by Geddes.[258] The second part, an account of
the Synod of Diamper, was translated from Dom Frey Aleixo de Meneses'
history. Finally, the book contains Geddes' observations about some similarities between the Malabar church and the Church of England.

Translated from the Spanish in 1695 was a partial version of Faria y
Sousa's history of Portuguese Asia.[259] Translations of French works continued to dominate the publication of travelogues during the last years of
the century. Abraham Duquesne-Guiton's account of the French expedition
to Ceylon and India in 1690 was translated in 1696, as was Jean Moquet's
travels.[260] Louis le Comte's relation of China saw three English editions of
1697, 1698, and 1699.[261] Dellon's voyage to India was translated in 1698, and
in 1699 an English translation of Bouvet's life of the K'ang-hsi emperor appeared.[262] Finally, in the last three years of the century English translations
of two German books appeared: Adam Brand's account of the Russian
embassy to China in 1693–95, and the voyages of Christoph Frick and
Christoph Schweitzer with the Dutch East India Company.[263]

A more concerted effort was made at century's end to provide an account
of the progress of navigation and to publish hitherto unprinted voyages and
English translations of foreign relations. The London bookseller Awnsham
Churchill (d. 1728), encouraged to some degree by John Locke, the philosopher, published four folio volumes in 1704 called *A Collection of Voyages and
Travels*. It brings together in English versions many of the best seventeenth-
century writings on Asia. Volume I includes as its first item the English
translation of Domingo Navarrete's work on China, the anti-Jesuit tract that
was probably more widely read in Protestant England during the eighteenth
century than anywhere else in Europe.[264] Volume II contains the English

Philippe Avril, *Travels into Divers Parts of Europe and Asia undertaken by the French King's order to
Discover a New Way by Land into China; . . .* (London, 1693).

[257] *The History of the Church of Malabar, from the Time of its being First Discovered by the Portuguese in the Year 1501 . . . Together with the Synod of Diamper . . . 1599. With Some Remarks
upon the Faith and Doctrine of the Christians of St. Thomas of the Indies, Agreeing with the Church of
England, in Opposition to that of Rome . . .* (London, 1694).

[258] See above, pp. 320–21.

[259] Manuel de Faria y Sousa, *The Portuguese Asia, or the History of the Discovery and Conquest of
India by the Portuguese . . .* trans. Capt. J. Stevens (3 vols.; London, 1695).

[260] *New Voyage to the East Indies in 1690 and 1691 . . . by Monsieur Duquesne* (London, 1696);
John Moquet, *Travels and Voyages. . . ,* trans. Nathaniel Pullen (London, 1696). See ch. 5,
n. 243, above, on confusion of Duquesne-Guiton and an earlier Abraham Duquesne.

[261] Louis Le Comte, *Memoirs and Observations of China . . .* (London).

[262] Charles Dellon, *A Voyage to the East Indies . . .* (London, 1698); Joachim Bouvet, *The History of Cang-hy, the Present Emperor of China, . . .* (London, 1699).

[263] Adam Brand, *A Journal of an Embassy from their Majesties John and Peter Alexowitz, Emperors
of Muscovy etc. into China, . . . Performed by Everard Isbrand, . . .* (London, 1698); *A Relation of
Two Voyages Made into the East Indies by C. F. and C. Schweitzer . . .* (London, 1700).

[264] See J. S. Cummins (ed. and trans.), *The Travels and Controversies of Friar Domingo Navarrete, 1618–1686* (2 vols.; "HS," 2d ser., CXVIII; Cambridge, 1962), I, ci.

version of Johann Nieuhof's travels along with reproductions of his engravings. This is followed by a brief relation of the Muscovite embassy of 1645 to China and by Borri's important account of Cochin-China.[265] Volume III includes an English version of Baldaeus' work on south India and Ceylon.[266] The final volume contains Careri's around-the-world voyage and Hamel's account of Korea.[267] Churchill's original four volumes were reissued in 1732 followed by two additional volumes. Volume V contains no accounts of Asia; Volume VI, however, first prints Samuel Baron's account of Tongking and reprints Henry Lord's 1630 book on the two chief religions of the "Banians."[268]

The English writings, compared to those of the Dutch, were fewer and more derivative, particularly those of the first half of the century. The reports on the early voyages concentrate on the maritime routes, overland connections, hostilities with the Dutch and the Portuguese, and trading conditions at Surat, Bantam, the Spiceries, and other eastern ports. It is only with the appearance of Purchas' *Hakluytus Posthumus* (1625) that substantial new information appears in English on India, particularly in the reports of Roe and Terry. Henry Lord's 1630 publication on Hinduism and on the religion of the Parsis of Surat was the first English report which endeavored to probe below the surface manifestations of Indian beliefs. In the Jesuit letters, translated in Purchas from continental books, firsthand references could also be found to other Asian religious and social practices. In Protestant England the Jesuit writings of all kinds were available only in translation, if at all.

Translations of continental publications continued to appear sporadically throughout the century. A hiatus in the publication of works on Asia, except for a few translations, occurred from the outbreak of the Civil War in 1640 to the Restoration of 1660. Translations again became more numerous after 1660, but in the last two decades there suddenly appeared a number of original and important accounts of Asia. Robert Knox's relation (1681) of Ceylon was unquestionably the most comprehensive and accurate work on the Sinhalese kingdom of Kandy issued over the century. Several pamphlets of the 1680's reported on the civil war in Bantam at the beginning of that decade. The cleric John Ovington's *A Voyage to Surat* (1696) described Bombay and Surat and the English role in western India from 1689 to 1692. Appended to Ovington's book was an anonymous but important relation of the crisis of the 1680's in Golconda. John Fryer, a surgeon, published in 1698 his extended account of the India he had known in the 1670's. It is particularly notable for its descriptions of interior places and of natural phenomena

---

[265] On Borri see below, pp. 1253–54, 1257–66.
[266] On Baldaeus see above, pp. 493–95, and below, pp. 911–18, 954–96.
[267] On Careri see above, pp. 386–87; on Hamel, pp. 486–88, 1785–97.
[268] Baron's work was written in response to Tavernier's book on Tongking. See below pp. 1267–68. On Henry Lord see above, pp. 569–70.

in western India, the Deccan, and Coromandel. The century ended with the publication of William Dampier's books on his circumnavigation. Aside from his accurate descriptions of coastal features, he provided significant new descriptions of Guam, Mindanao, Tongking, and the Nicobar Islands. Churchill's *Voyages* (1704) brought together in one collection many of the seventeenth-century's leading foreign and English works on Asia.

Iberian works predominated throughout the first generation of the century, especially Jesuit publications. Jesuit letters and letterbooks were quickly translated from the Iberian languages into Italian and Latin versions for more general diffusion throughout the rest of Catholic Europe. The Jesuits themselves produced French and Flemish versions of many letterbooks, and others were issued in pirated editions by commercial printers. Guerreiro's great Portuguese *Relaçao* of the Jesuit missions from 1600 to 1609 became the model for Du Jarric's similar French collection published between 1608 and 1614. The books of Ribadeneira (1601), Chirino (1604), and San Antonio (1604) centered on the Philippines and Southeast Asia and emphasized the importance of the missions to the spread of Spanish civilization in the East. The secular writers Morga and Argensola in their books of 1609 described the strategic place of the Philippines to Spanish expansion in the southwest Pacific region. While Morga advised building up the Philippines first, Argensola celebrated the Spanish conquest of the Moluccas in 1606, probably to the delight of the expansionists. These substantial books were accompanied and followed by a spate of memorials advising the crown to carry out further conquest, by the first-time publication of the Portuguese rutters, by tracts and books inspired by the canonization of Xavier (1622), and by the printing of popular books relating to the overseas world. Both the Spanish and the Dutch were attracted by reports of circumnavigations.

While Iberia remained the main publication center for books on Asia, the Dutch and the English began to issue pamphlets and books on their own voyages. The Dutch printed many more of these than the English, but Purchas in his *Hakluytus Posthumus* (1625) put together a great collection of travel literature that was the largest work published in English to that time. In Germany meanwhile there were being printed the travel collections of De Bry and Hulsius, which included many Latin and German versions of the early Dutch voyages. German presses also printed numerous Jesuit letterbooks. In 1615 Nicolas Trigault's *De expeditione apud Sinas* was published at Augsburg; it was probably the most influential book about China of the first half of the century. In France, where both the nation and the Jesuits were slow to enter the race to Asia, Pyrard in 1619 published a major book about his experiences in the Maldive Islands, Ceylon, and India. In Iberia itself leadership passed after 1612 to the Portuguese. Proud of their national achievements, the Portuguese issued biographies of their great leaders and writers of the previous century and sought to continue Barros' *Decadas,* the epic in prose of their sixteenth-century expansion into Asia. In 1616 both the Italians and Portuguese learned about the Jesuit penetration of Tibet. Throughout Catholic Europe the persecution of the Christians in Japan inspired the publication of martyrologies from 1620 to 1640. Very little new was added in the first generation to Europe's knowledge of Mughul India except for the English reports of Roe and Terry included in the Purchas collection.

The Dutch replaced the Iberians after 1630 as the predominant publishers of Asian materials. Despite their renewed war (1621–48) with Spain, the Dutch continued to expand their empire in the East and to write about it. Dutch merchant reports on the Mughul Empire began to appear in Latin and Dutch around 1630, the year when Henry Lord published his English books on the religion of the Hindus and Parsis of northwestern India. As the Iberians were forced out of Siam and Japan, the Dutch merchant reports became the main European sources on both of these countries. Especially important were the reports of Schouten (1638) on Siam and of Caron (1645) on Japan. Meanwhile Aduarte's Spanish history of the Dominicans in the Philippines was published (1640). Commelin's *Begin ende voortgangh* (1645–46), the most comprehensive Dutch collection of travel accounts compiled in the seventeenth century, included most of the Dutch reports on the East Indies and India as well as those on the earlier Dutch circumnavigations.

Several important books were published around mid-century in Rome. Manrique's work (1649) in Spanish added new dimensions to what was known about north India, Arakan, and places further east. Della Valle's *Viaggi* (1650) in western India opened south Kanara to European inspection, and Rhodes' book (1650) on Tongking raised Europe's consciousness about the importance of evangelizing in Indochina. Roger's *De open-deure* (1651) examined Hinduism in depth, especially as it was practiced in the Tamil region of south India. The Jesuit Martini added substantially to the available knowledge of China with the publication in 1654 of his account of the Manchu conquest and in 1655 of his *Novus atlas sinensis.* The decade concluded on another upbeat note with the publication in Latin of the first part of Martini's history (1658) of China based on native sources. In the early sixties Magistris published his account (1661) of the Madura mission and Marini his survey (1663) of Jesuit activities in Laos. Colin, another Jesuit, published in 1663 his detailed Spanish survey of the Philippines and Hamel, a shipwrecked Dutch sailor, his pioneering account of Korea, in 1668.

French publications became constantly more significant along with the foundation in 1664 of the Paris Society of Missions and the French East India Company. Ecclesiastical and lay writers produced a wealth of books in French on the continental countries of Asia, many of which remain basic to our understanding of those countries. Melchisédech Thévenot, the great collector, began in 1663 to publish his *Relations,* travel accounts which would be reissued for the remainder of the century in revised and augmented editions. Greslon, from his post in China, had published at Paris in 1671 his experiences during a period (1651–69) of dynastic change. Bernier's four volumes on his travels and the history of Mughul India at mid-century were published in 1670–71. The documentation on the Mughul Empire, Goa, and Golconda was significantly amplified by the publication in 1676–77 of Tavernier's *Les six voyages,* one of the most popular and controversial travel books of the century.

Contemporaneously, significant new books also appeared outside France. Combés' description (1667) of the southern Philippines was the last of the excellent histories of the islands published in this century by the Spanish Jesuits. In 1667 Kircher published his *China illustrata,* one of the best works produced in Europe from Jesuit mission accounts. Nieuhof (1665) and Dapper (1670) published large, lavishly illustrated encyclopedic volumes on China which combined the best Jesuit descriptions with fresh observations made during the Dutch embassies to China. Montanus in 1669 produced a similar volume on Japan. Castelyn in 1669 published a series of Dutch merchant reports on Cambodia and Laos. In 1672 the Dutch pastor Baldaeus published his large work on the east and west coasts of south India, on Ceylon, and on the Dutch victories in these regions. Four years later the Dominican Navarrete published the *Tratados,* an influential series of tracts about China which elevated the rites controversy in Europe to an impassioned religious and political brawl. In England Knox quietly published his memoir (1681) on Ceylon, probably the single most important book ever to be printed about that island.

The 1680's was a decade in which major publications on Asia appeared in a steady stream from the printing presses of France. In anticipation of closer relations with Siam, the French geographer De L'Isle compiled an introduction (1684) to Siam for the court and the literate public. The travels in India of Jean de Thévenot during 1666 were published at Paris in 1684. This was followed by Dellon's description of Portuguese India (1685) and by the same author's bitter attack (1688) on the Goa inquisition. In 1686–87 there appeared three accounts of the first French embassy to Siam by De Chaumont, the ambassador, by the Abbé de Choisy, his second-in-command, and by Tachard, their Jesuit interpreter and guide. The Jesuit Couplet, who was in Europe from 1682 to 1692, guided through the press the *Confucius Sinarum philosophus* (1687), a Latin translation of and commentary on certain of the classical Chinese writings. Gervaise, a French secular priest, published two books in 1688. One was the first separate book to appear on Makassar and the great island of Celebes, and the other was a natural and political history of Siam based exclusively on his own four years of experience there. French study of Siam received its crowning glory with the publication in 1691 of La Loubère's two volumes.

In the century's closing decade, and after the French debacle in Siam, Europe's attention focused more sharply upon China, always the final goal and great hope of European merchants and missionaries. Joseph d'Orleans and Charles Le Gobien, the French Jesuit publicists, began to compile in Paris materials on China and other parts of Asia. They celebrated the successes of the French Jesuits in Peking, particularly the Edict of Toleration granted in 1692 by the K'ang-hsi emperor. Louis Le Comte, a leading spokesman for the Jesuits in the rites controversy, published in 1696 his *Nouveaux mémoires de la Chine,* which brought to a fever pitch the multi-sided debate over control of the mission and its Chinese converts. Bouvet, the Jesuit who compared K'ang-hsi to Louis XIV in his *Portrait historique* (1697), urged French businessmen to organize themselves for direct participation in the China trade. Both the Jesuits and the Dutch began early in the 1690's to write about the possibility of establishing a land route to China across Russia with the concurrence of Tsar Peter the Great. Several fine descriptions of eastern Siberia and the lands on China's frontier resulted. Even the philosopher Leibniz was attracted by the idea that commercial, religious, and intellectual ties with China might be realized through the development of the overland route.

Although China supplanted India as the major target, publications continued to appear in Dutch and English relating to the subcontinent. Havart, a Dutch physician and student of Persian, published in 1693 his excellent book on Coromandel and the demise of the independent Muslim kingdom of Golconda. The English pastor Ovington wrote on Surat (1696) and western India. His work was followed by the retrospective memoir (1698) of Dr. Fryer which deals with western India and its relations to the Deccan in the time of Sivaji. William Dampier's *Voyages* (1699) brought to England fresh news of Mindanao, Tongking, and Cambodia. In France a jubilant Le Gobien published a history (1700) of the Jesuit-Spanish conquest of the Mariana Islands. Finally the Neapolitan lawyer and world traveler Careri published his volumes (1700), which threw light on contemporary conditions in Goa, Malacca, China, the Philippines, and the Marianas and rounded out in fine style the European publications about Asia.

Seventeenth-century European publications treated almost all parts of Asia much more extensively and intensively than had been done in the sixteenth century. By the end of the century China was probably the best known part of Asia to European readers. In addition to scores of letterbooks, to the compilations of Guerreiro and Du Jarric, in which China figured prominently, and to numerous shorter or derivative descriptions, there were over fifty major independent accounts of China and its periphery published during the century. Many of these are large volumes and many can be numbered among the most popular publications of the century. The coverage of other parts of Asia, however, did not lag far behind. There were sixteen major separate accounts of the Mughul Empire and perhaps another ten which reported extensively on it along with other parts of Asia. For the various parts of southern India, including Ceylon, there were about a dozen major independent accounts, out of more than twenty-five extensive descriptions. Furthermore, India was penetrated by a wider variety of observers than China, the Jesuits being by far the main commentators on China. Merchants, physicians, and Protestant pastors as well as Catholic priests highlighted from their own viewpoints the diversity of India. The French physician Bernier, for example, spent a lengthy time at the Mughul court and traveled with the emperor into Kashmir and other places. Out of sixty or more sizable descriptions of mainland Southeast Asia at least fifteen were major independent accounts devoted exclusively to the area. More of these described Siam than Cambodia, Laos, Vietnam, or Malaya. Perhaps half of the twenty or more descriptions of the Philippines can be called major separate accounts. And for all these areas there is a plethora of Jesuit letterbooks, other missionaries' reports, and short notices by travelers. They are all also treated in the Jesuit compilations of Guerreiro and Du Jarric. For insular Southeast Asia, however, there are very few reports from missionaries, although shorter notices by travelers abound. At least sixty fairly extensive descriptions of Insulindia were published during the century, of which eighteen to twenty could be considered major contributions.

Only Japan seems to have been less well known to European readers at the end of the century than at its beginning. Dozens of letterbooks and martyrologies and five large but repetitive ecclesiastical histories contain reports about the political events of the late sixteenth and early seventeenth centuries and their effects on the Christian mission. Most of these were published during the early decades of the century. Apart from these, about twelve English and Dutch descriptions appeared, a few of which could be considered major contributions to Europe's knowledge of Japan: those of Caron, Montanus, and Meister, and the description of the Ainu appended to Brouwer's *Journael*.

In size, seventeenth-century publications on Asia ranged from pamphlets to lavishly illustrated folio volumes. Jesuit letterbooks predominated in the Catholic lands at the century's start. Until about mid-century these were systematically translated, pirated, and circularized in relatively cheap editions for the faithful. While they were regularly read in Jesuit schools, the letterbooks were suppressed in Protestant countries or circulated only in expurgated editions. The content of the letters also reappeared in large compilations such as Guerreiro's or Du Jarric's and in the histories of Jesuit missions such as Trigault's or Semedo's history of the China mission or Guzman's or Solier's history of the Japan mission. The Jesuit histories circulated in Protestant as well as in Catholic lands.

Information pilfered from the Jesuit letterbooks and histories was frequently larded into the Dutch and English travel tales which began to appear in large numbers after the return of the first Dutch fleets. The two streams of information about Asia available to seventeenth-century readers, therefore, did not run entirely separate courses; the usually less sophisticated travel reports were often enriched by the more perceptive observations of the missionaries, either by the secular writers themselves or by their publishers. The huge encyclopedic works of Nieuhof, Dapper, and Montanus, which blended Jesuit and lay sources, are the finest examples.

Following the example of Ramusio and Hakluyt in the sixteenth century, enterprising seventeenth-century editors published multivolume collections of travel tales. The most important collections were those of De Bry and Hulsius in Latin and German, Purchas in English, Commelin in Dutch, and Thévenot in French. All of them were published in northern Europe. While many of the pieces included in the travel collections had been published previously, each collection also contains important accounts not available anywhere else. The account of Petlin's embassy from the tsar to the emperor of China, for example, is found only in Purchas, as are several of the early English voyages; some versions of the early Dutch voyages were never published apart from the De Bry and Hulsius editions; several important Dutch descriptions were published only in Commelin's *Begin ende voortgangh;* Beaulieu's description of Acheh and what appears to be Martini's *Decas secunda* appear only in Thévenot's collection.

In addition to Jesuit letterbooks and histories, travel accounts, and composite encyclopedic descriptions, the last half of the century saw published several important scholarly studies pertaining to Asia. For example, Bontius (1642) introduced European readers to tropical medicine, Boym to south China's flora (1656) and to Chinese medicine (1682). Roger (1651) presented a scholarly analysis of Hindu religion and a description of some Hindu texts. A team of Jesuits provided translations of three of the Confucian Four Books in their *Confucius Sinarum philosophus* (1687), Martini introduced European readers to ancient Chinese history, and Van Rheede tot Drakestein with a group of scholars from India and the Netherlands produced a magnificent twelve-volume study of south Indian plants (1678–1703).

Several of the scientific studies are beautifully illustrated, none better than Van Rheede tot Drakestein's *Hortus malabaricus.* Its plates were unmatched during the century for their scientific accuracy and fine printing. In general, Dutch publications were the best illustrated of the century. The published accounts of the earliest Dutch voyages were already generously illustrated, although some of the illustrations better reflected the engravers' imagination than any Asian scene. Most of these illustrations were taken up by Commelin in his *Begin ende voortgangh,* which, with Commelin's additions, became a profusely illustrated collection. Perhaps the most lavishly illustrated volumes of the century were those of Nieuhof, Dapper, and Montanus, all published by Jacob van Meurs of Amsterdam, which together formed a collection of five impressive folio-sized coffee-table volumes on India, insular Southeast Asia, China, and Japan. Many of the plates for these volumes were made from the travelers' own sketches. In some exemplars the illustrations are colored. Kircher's *China illustrata* (Amsterdam, 1667), one Latin edition of which was also published by Van Meurs, is similarly illustrated. Both Kircher's and Dapper's books contain beautiful Buddhist prints obviously made from Chinese originals. Kircher's contains the picture of the Potala palace in Lhasa, apparently sketched by someone in Grueber's party, which served as Europe's sole image of the Dalai Lama's residence until the twentieth century. Less accurate, perhaps, but surely lively and entertaining are the illustrations which grace Wouter Schouten's and Havart's volumes.

Although the French and German printers were not as liberal with illustrations as the Dutch, many French publications and some German publications are amply illustrated. The De Bry and Hulsius collections, for example, contain many illustrations, some identical with or similar to those used by Dutch printers, many of which must have been done by German engravers. Thévenot's collection, too, contains many impressive, folio-sized illustrations, and the travel accounts of Bernier and Tachard contain many fine prints. Even Purchas printed some illustrations, some examples of Asian languages, and some interesting maps. Among the century's more influential maps were De Angelis' map of Yezo (1624), Ginnaro's (1641) and Cardim's (1646) maps of Japan, and Della Valle's (1650) map of India. But with maps as with illustrations, Dutch printers were preeminent. The *Begin ende voortgangh* (1645–46), for example, contains no fewer than thirty-two maps, five of which are large foldouts. And surely the single most impressive collection of Asian maps printed during the seventeenth century was the Asia volume of Blaeu's *Atlas major* (1662), of which Martini's *Novus atlas sinensis* (1655) was a major part.

Books on Asia were printed over the course of the century at Lisbon, Madrid, Rome, Amsterdam, Paris, Frankfurt, Augsburg, Vienna, and London, but also at a host of smaller centers such as Middelburg, Hoorn, Rotterdam, The Hague, Leyden, Antwerp, Brussels, Lyons, Venice, Cologne, Leipzig, Coimbra, Seville, and at Jesuit presses in places like Dillingen and Ingolstadt. Printing runs probably ranged between 250 and 1,000 copies. Presumably for titles which were regularly reissued, press runs would be closer to the maximum than to the minimum. The travel accounts, but many other books as well, were frequently reprinted. Five to ten editions is not at all uncommon, and some of the more popular accounts must be regarded as best-sellers. Among the century's most popular were Le Maire and Schouten's circumnavigation (1617), which saw thirty-eight editions and translations during the century; Bontekoe's *Journael,* thirty editions and translations after its publication in 1646; Caron's description of Japan and Joost Schouten's description of Siam, twenty-three editions and translations after 1646; and Martini's history of the Manchu Conquest, twenty-five editions and translations after 1654. Of those published during the last few decades of the century, Bernier's travels (1670–71) went through at least seven editions and translations before the end of the century; Tavernier's (1676–77) saw twelve before 1712; Tachard's voyage appeared in five editions and translations between 1686 and 1700; Le Comte's controversial book on China appeared seven times between its publication in 1696 and 1739; and eight editions and translations of Brand and Ides' overland journey appeared between 1699 and 1710. Some very expensive books were widely diffused: Nieuhof's lavishly published book on China was reissued or translated thirteen times between 1665 and 1700, Dapper's and Martini's *Atlas* six times each. For most of the century, Dutch books were the most widely diffused, further attesting to the dominance of Dutch printers. During the last quarter of the century, however, French titles seem more popular. Iberian and English accounts were the least widely diffused, although Pinto (nineteen editions in six languages from 1614 to 1700) and Andrade (ten editions and translations after 1626) deserve to be mentioned among the more popular writers.

Most texts were published in the vernaculars except for the more ambitious Latin volumes produced by the Jesuits and some of their letterbooks. Translations were published everywhere; a determined enthusiast for travel literature could probably have read most of the literature in his own language. Many of the Latin works were translated into the vernaculars, but some of the secular vernacular accounts were also translated into Latin, a transformation that may have lent them some scholarly respectability. Furthermore, authors and editors regularly plagiarized earlier books to fill out their own, and printers borrowed or stole maps and engravings from one another, all of which increased the availability of information about Asia. Trigault's *De christiana expeditione apud Sinas* (1615), for example, saw relatively few editions and translations. Its descriptive parts, however, were so frequently plagiarized by later writers that it enjoyed a far larger readership and much greater influence than could be guessed by counting editions.

Further attesting to the diffusion and popularity of the literature about Asia, references to Asia or to the literature also appeared in the periodical literature of the day. The new scientific journals—the *Philosophical Transactions,* the *Journal des Sçavants,* the *Miscellanea Curiosa,* and the *Acta Eruditorum*—occasionally carried articles on Asian topics or reviewed books about Asia. The broadsheets and other prototypes of modern newspapers also contained notices of events in Asia, and some contained considerable descriptions of Asian places. Wassenaer's *Historisch verhael,* for example, contained detailed descriptions of every incoming Dutch fleet's cargo. On such occasions it also printed the news brought back from Asia with the fleet. Carstenszoon's discoveries in Australia, earthquakes in Japan, volcanic eruptions, the fire in Edo, and the progress of the Manchu conquest of China were among the items reported. In conclusion, the number of books about Asia printed in Europe, the wide diffusion of these books in all European languages, and the references in both popular and scholarly writings to these books and to information about Asia, all enabled seventeenth-century European readers to obtain a better-informed idea than previously of the reality of Asia and a clearer image of its dimensions, its peoples, and its various languages, religions, and cultures.

Index

Index

Amsterdam (*continued*)
  printing in, 302–3, 382, 394, 399, 401, 409n, 411n, 413–14, 419, 425n, 426, 435–36n, 437, 439–40, 442, 444, 449, 479, 485–86, 489, 497, 500, 504, 507, 516, 526–27, 529, 537; and VOC, 44–45, 116. *See also* United Provinces; VOC
Anabaptists, 270
Anaukpetlun of Burma (r. 1605–1628), 329
Andersen, Jürgen, 522, 533–34
Andrada, Luis de, 138–39
Andrade, Antonio de, 147, 338–39, 404, 514; and Tibet, 375–76, 525
Andrade, Francisco de, 324
Angelis, Girolamo de, 175n, 374
Angkor, 309
Ango, Jean, 391
Ankamali, 162–63
Anlung, 194
Antheunis, Lucas, 75, 560
António da Encarnação, 343–44
Antunes, Diogo, 372
Antwerp, 40, 302; printing in, 301, 307, 356, 369, 392, 395n, 402, 436, 450–51, 478–80, 506–7, 525
Apius, Martinus, 463
Arakan, 497, 580; Augustinians in, 143, 349; and the Portuguese, 142
Aranda, Gabriel de, 357n
Arcamone, Ignacio, 135n, 356
Areppa (in Ceylon), 541
Arevalo, 204
Argensola, Bartolomé Leonardo de, 589; *Conquista de las islas Malucas (1609)*, 311–12; and Morga, 326
Armenians, 111, 114; in Europe, 379
Arnauld, Antoine, 362, 423
Arnault de la Borie, François, 392n
Arnedo, Juan Antonio, 260
Arnhem: printing in, 440
Arnold, Christoph, 529–31, 536
Arras: printing in, 395n
Arthus, Gotthard, 516, 518–19
Aru Islands, 463
Ascension Island, 585
Aschaffenburg: printing in, 514, 527
Ashley, Robert, 574
Asia: Catholic missions in, 201, 231–32, 244, 291–92; comparisons, 328; European reports on, 515, 518–20; Europeans in, 10, 106, 520–21, 525, 533, 536; fauna, 421, 457, 581; flora, 368, 421, 457, 499,

501, 504, 526, 542, 594; interregional trade, 22, 27, 30, 109, 467, 479; medicine, 457, 594; naval powers, 30; novels about, 537; overland routes, 73, 108, 194, 225, 230, 232, 244, 264, 338, 349, 354, 360, 366, 380, 385, 408–9, 411–12, 416, 428, 432, 485, 502–4, 515, 517, 519–20, 528, 533–34, 543, 547, 553–54, 557, 559, 592; Portuguese empire in, 22, 66, 297; printing in, 304, 351; and the Propaganda, 228–29; sea routes to, 26–27, 34, 133, 464, 476; ten-year (1641–51) Luso-Dutch truce in, 22; in worldwide commerce, 108–9. *See also* Buddhism; Cannibalism; Cartography; Christianity; Elephants; Gold; Islam; Silver; Slavery; Tobacco
Atáide, António de, 313–14
Ataide, Luis de, 329–30, 340
Atallah, 164
Augsburg: Peace of (1555), 270; printing in, 400, 510–12, 514, 526; War of the League of (1688–97), 86, 92
Augustin de la Magdalena, 356
Augustinian Recollects, 202; in the Philippines, 203, 207
Augustinians, 141, 144, 380, 405; in Arakan, 143, 349; in Bengal, 142–43, 234, 259, 349, 395; in Ceylon, 167; in China, 262, 266; conversion policy, 141, 143–44; in Goa, 140–41, 320, 347, 349, 395; in Japan, 174, 208–10, 213, 341, 364; at Macao, 208; at Malacca, 141; and the Muslims, 395n; in the Persian Gulf, 140–41; in the Philippines, 201, 203–4, 207–8, 344, 364–65; in the Spiceries, 216
Aungier, Gerald, 287, 579
Australia, 48, 450, 473, 482, 536; and Dampier, 584–85; descriptions, 454–55, 475–77, 502, 504–5; discovery of, 328; and the Dutch, 53, 492; flora, 504; map, 476
Ava, 16
Avril, Philippe, 428, 432, 506
Ayala, Hernando, 213
Ayut'ia, 101, 232–33, 252, 292, 412, 420. *See also* Siam

Bachan Island, 216
Baeza, Pedro de, 15, 312
Bagot, Louis, 230
Bahrein, 20
Baikov, Fedor, 411, 502
Balbi, Gasparo, 467, 516

Index

Index

Index

Index

Index

Index

Le Maire, Jacob, 308, 445, 447, 520; circumnavigation of, 330, 446; *Spieghel*, 447–48
Lencastre, Maria Guadalupe de, 221
Leo X, pope: *Jus patronatus*, 130
Leonardo da Graça, 142
Leon Pinelo, A. R.: *Epitome*, 335
Leria, Giovanni Maria, 383
Lerma, duke of, 337
Lesser Sundas, 3, 14, 22, 216; civil wars, 139; Jesuits in, 139; Portuguese-Dominican enterprise, 138–39, 218, 295; sandalwood of, 14
L'Estra, François, 418
Le Tellier, Jean, 404
Le Tellier, Michel, 362, 423
Letona, Bartolomé de, 353
Leyden, 568; libraries, 410; printing in, 435–36n, 451, 489, 513; university, 272, 435
Leyte, 354
Lhasa: Potala Palace, 528
L'Hermite, Jacques, 468–69, 521; circumnavigation, 449
Liaotung, 374, 504; Manchu occupation of, 193, 375
Libertinus, Karl, 537
Li Chih-tsao, 178, 180
Liège: printing in, 526n
Lille: printing in, 400, 405, 426
Linhares. *See* Noronha
Linschoten, Jan Huygen van, 311, 435, 443, 453; *Itinerario* (1596), 6, 42, 313, 394, 436, 515, 549; *Reysgeschrift* (1595), 42
Lionne, Abbé de, 255
Lipp, Balthasar, 514
Lisbon, 5, 336–37, 347; Armazem da India (dockyards and warehouses), 26; Carreira da India, 26–27, 31, 34, 133; Casa da India, 33; diamond-cutting, 114; Inquisition of, 156; printing in, 324, 334, 338, 343, 347–48, 350–51, 358, 360, 363, 365, 495; trade, 3, 11, 21, 31. *See also* Portugal
L'Isle, Claude de: *Relation historique*, 420
Li Tzu-ch'eng, 192, 528
Liu-ch'iu Islands, 323
Livorno (Leghorn), 62, 109, 379, 388
Locke, John, 577
Lodewyckszoon, Willem, 515, 517; *D'eerste boeck*, 438–39
Logan, Josias, 567
Lo Hung-hsien, 480
Lombard, Nicolas. *See* Longobardo, Niccolò

Lombard, Peter, 156
London, 116; auctions, 112; Blackwell Yard, 78; coffee houses, 113; commerce with Asia, 74, 79, 109; merchants, 73, 75; population, 74, 116; printing in, 407n, 411n, 426, 440, 520n, 555–56, 578, 585–86; weaver riots, 87. *See also* England
Longobardo, Niccolò, 177, 184, 186, 189, 191, 196, 320, 371–72, 392; and Ricci's methods, 184–85; superior of China mission, 178
Lopes (or Lopez, or Lo), Gregorio (or Gregory), Chinese Dominican, 251, 266
Lopes (or Lopez), Gregory (or Gregorio), Jesuit provincial in Philippines, 373, 400, 512
Lord, Henry, 493, 588; on Hinduism, 569; on the Parsis, 569–70
Lorient, 97, 109
Louis XIII, king of France, 95, 229, 402, 405
Louis XIV, king of France, 93, 95, 98, 422, 424; and the Asian missions, 244, 263, 413n, 429; and the K'ang-hsi emperor, 428; and Narai, 421; and overseas expansion, 408–9; and Siam, 244, 425; and Tavernier, 416
Louvain: printing in, 392, 451, 477, 495
Loyola, Ignatius, 224, 333
Lualdi, Michele Angelo, 381
Lucaszoon, Philips, 456, 460
Lucena, João de, 333
Ludovisi, Ludovico, 223–24
Luís, Gaspar, 374
Lull, Ramón, 223
Lutheranism: and the missions, 269–70, 289–90
Luzon, 328, 442; map of, 336; as mission center, 204. *See also* Philippines
Lyons: printing in, 392, 394–95n, 399–400, 407, 409, 412, 415, 419, 427

Mabre-Cramoisy, Sebastien, 410n
Macao, 3, 8, 19, 22, 29, 169, 241, 358, 505; bishopric of, 130, 134, 168, 174, 199, 201, 229, 266; and the Ch'ing, 241; descriptions, 462, 536; Dominicans in, 137; and the Dutch, 52, 172, 187, 463, 465, 474, 567; Franciscans in, 215; and Japan, 18–19, 29, 173; and the Jesuits, 131, 169, 176, 187, 216, 334, 348, 372; and Manila, 19, 35; as mission center, 236, 259; and munitions, 187; population of, 13, 24, 30, 169; and the Portuguese, 13; trade, 13, 18, 169,

Index

Index

Index

Portugal (*continued*)
160–61; and Pegu, 328; policy of secrecy, 303, 313; population of, 25; precious metals, 27; printing in, 303–4, 589–90; Restoration era, 22, 26; *roteiros* (rutters), 5, 313–14, 348; Sebastianism, 26; and Siam, 16, 235; and Spain, 22, 336–37; spice imports, 17, 26, 29, 34; and St. Thomas Christians, 162; trade missions to Peking, 22; treaty of 1598 with Calicut, 131, 146; treaty of 1661 with the Dutch, 140; "tridimensional empire," 8; truce with the Dutch (1642), 139; wars with Kandy, 166. *See also* Estado da India; Lisbon; *Padroado*

Portuguese, 8; in Ceylon, 12, 21; in India, 20, 28; in Macao, 13; in Malacca, 12; as middlemen, 29, 35; in Solor, 14; in the Spanish empire, 9

Portuguese India Company, 26, 32–33, 110–11, 292, 338

Poser und Gross Nedlitz, Heinrich von: travels of, 534

Powell, Thomas, 575

Praet, J. du, 273

Prague: printing in, 537

Prasat Thong of Siam (r. 1630–56), 235, 456, 501

Prévost, Abbé, 387

Priaman (in Sumatra), 558

Prideaux, Humphrey, 289

Priezac, Salomon de, 407n

Pring, Martin, 564, 566

Printing: in Asia, 304, 351; broadsheets, 596; of Chinese characters in Europe, 482; circumnavigations, 549, 557, 582, 585, 589, 592, 595; the Dutch predominance, 508; editions, 301, 595–96; encyclopedic works, 591, 594; in Europe, 301–9; illustrations, 594–95; maps, 595; plagiarism, 531–32, 594, 596; runs, 595; scholarly studies, 594, 596; and the Thirty Years' War, 513, 525, 545; translations, 301, 523, 536–37, 544–45, 548, 554, 574–75, 586–88; travel collections, 515–18, 557, 594; in the vernaculars, 596. *See also under individual cities and countries*

Proenza, Antão, 159

Propaganda fide (or Congregation for the Propagation of the Faith), 4, 132–33, 198, 222–29, 384; "apostolic congregation," 244; and book publication, 227, 261; and Burma, 234–35; and Ceylon, 282; and the China mission, 262–63, 266; and cultural adaptation, 226–27; East Indies Commission, 250–51, 256; finances, 224–25, 230; and the French, 228–29, 254, 292; and Goa, 252; and India, 163–64, 224, 228, 234, 257; and Japan mission, 226; and the Jesuits, 134, 242–45, 251–52, 429; and missionary orders, 225–26, 252; and native clergy, 225–26, 231–32; and the *padroado*, 230; and the Paris Society, 263; personnel, 224, 230; and the Portuguese, 245; reports to, 225; and Rhodes, 229; secretaries of, 224n; Urban College, 224; vicars apostolic, 228, 231–32, 256, 262, 429; and Vietnam, 240, 259. *See also* Papacy; Rome

Protestantism, 289, 296–97. *See also* Calvinism; Lutheranism

Puente, José Martinez de la, 361

Puget de la Serre, Jean, 405n

Pulau Condore, 584

Pulau Run, 565

Pulicat, 478

Purchas, Samuel, 303, 437, 443, 448, 520, 550; as editor, 556–57; *Hakluytus Posthumus or Purchas His Pilgrimes* (1625), 552, 555–68, 589; and the Jesuits, 513; *Pilgrimage* (1613–26), 553

Pursglove, William, 567

Pyong'-yong (in Korea), 487

Pyrard de Laval, François, 93, 589; *Discours*, 396–97; vocabulary of Maldive words, 397

Quaeckernaeck, Jacob Janszoon, 15, 441

Quelpaerts (also Cheju) Island, 486

Queyroz, Fernão, 361

"Quietism," 414n

Quilon, 20, 28, 58; and the Dutch, 497

Quiroga, Pedro de, 38

Quiroga de San Antonio, Gabriel, 326; on Cambodia, 309

Quiros, Pedro Fernandez de, 6, 8, 48, 218–19, 308, 399, 445, 449, 519–20

Racine, Jean, 414

Raghunatha Setupati (of Marava), 160

Ragusa (Dubrovnik), 111

Rama Ragio, 259

Ramayana, 493

Ramnad, 160–61

Rangel, Miguel, 138–39, 298, 344

Ratisbon, 291; printing in, 528n

Raven, Dirck Albertszoon, 522

Index

Reballosa, Jaime, 323
Rebello (or Rebelo), Gabriel, 311, 315n
Rechteren, Seyger van: *Journael*, 453–55
Régale, 250n
Regensburg. *See* Ratisbon
Régimont, Gilles de, 95, 404
Reijersen, Cornelis, 450, 474; his expedition, 453–54
Reimão, Gaspar Ferreira, 313–14
Remon, Alonso, 326
Rennefort, Urbain Souchu de: *Mémoires*, 422
Rennes: printing in, 395n, 405
Renneville, Rene Augustin Constantin de, 462
Resende, Pedro Barreto, 345
Retana, W. E., 326
Reynst, Gerald, 50
Rhay, Theodore: on Tibet, 525
Rheede (also Reede) tot Drakestein, Hendrik Adriaan van: and Ceylon, 283; *Hortus indicus malabaricus*, 499
Rho, Giacomo, 189, 513
Rhodes, Alexandre de, 230, 241; and the Annamese language, 380–81, 408; *Divers voyages*, 408; in Europe, 239, 381; and Macao, 238; *Relazione . . . di Tunchino* (1650), 380–81; in Vietnam, 229, 236–38
Rhodes, Raphael, 242
Ribadeneira, Marcelo de, 589; *Historia* (1601), 321–22
Ribeiro, Pedro, 185
Ribera, Juan de, 372
Ribeyro de Souza, Salvador, 16, 329
Ricci, Matteo, 131, 292, 320, 371–72, 400; journals, 512; life of, 427; mission methods, 176–77
Ricci, Vittorio, 499; biography, 352
Richard de St. Anne, 416
Richelieu, cardinal, 94–95, 401, 404, 433
Rios Coronel, Hernando de los, 18; *Memorial*, 336
Riquebourg-Trigault, D. F. de, 400
Rites Controversy, 264, 269, 358; in China, 134, 269; in Europe, 195, 260, 267–69, 385–86, 423–24, 427–30, 592; and the Jansenists, 423; and Martini, 481; "term question," 179, 183–86, 204
Roc, Thomas, 451
Rocca, Carlo della, 239–40, 384
Rodrigues, João ("the Interpreter"), 169–73, 181, 185, 370–71n, 378
Rodrigues, Nuño, 146
Rodrigues, Vincente, 313–14

Rodrigues Girão, João, 370–71n, 376, 512, 514
Rodriguez, Francisco, 341
Roe, Thomas, Sir, 76, 554, 564–65
Roelofszoon, Roelof, 463–64, 516
Roger (also Rogerius), Abraham, 474, 493, 529; *De open-deure*, 478–79
Rome, 4, 190; and Asian missions, 131–32, 195, 218, 223, 385; and Carmelites of India, 164; and China missions, 178–79; and Goa Inquisition, 245; *Index of Forbidden Books*, 133; missionary methods in Asia, 134, 154, 198, 292; and Nobili, 153–54, 156–57; and the *padroado*, 132–34; Palazzo Ferrantini, 224; and Portugal, 195, 256; printing in, 350, 368–70, 372, 374–78, 382–84, 408, 526n, 590; and the St. Thomas Christians, 164, 320; Urban College, 224. *See also* Papacy; *Propaganda fide*
Ros (also Roz), Francisco, 151, 153–55, 162–63
Rosenkranz, Herman, 89
Röslin, Helisaeus, 520
Rosnel, Pierre de, 413n
Rosso, Francisco Maria del, 350
Rota (in the Marianas), 222
Roteiros (rutters, navigational manuals), 5, 313–14, 348
Roth, Heinrich, 385, 486, 528; on India, 527
Roti (in Timor), 14
Rotman, Paul Alofszoon, 482
Rotterdam, 441; printing in, 441
Rouen, 94, 397; printing in, 392, 395n, 398, 400, 402n
Rougemont, François de, 358, 495
Roy, Jacob Janssen de, 503
Rougemont, Antonio, 214, 238, 381n, 383
Rubino, Antonio, 214, 238, 381n, 383
Rubruquis, William de, 405
Ruggiero (also Ruggieri), Michele, 176, 335
Russia, 4, 411, 428; and China, 264, 504; and the Dutch, 445, 501; embassies to China, 543, 568; and Tavernier, 418; treaties with China, 264

Sá, Constantino de, 21
Sá, Cristovão de, 135, 154–56, 298
Saar, Johann Jacob, 529–30; *Ost-Indianische Beschreibung*, 499
Saccano, Metello, 239, 408, 479
Sacred Congregation for the Propagation of the Faith. *See Propaganda fide*

[lxix]

Index

REF.
D
20
S52

Sharp, Harold S.

Footnotes to world
history